A TREASURY OF
Great Poems

A TREASURY OF
Great Poems

AN INSPIRING COLLECTION OF THE BEST-LOVED, MOST

MOVING VERSE IN THE ENGLISH LANGUAGE

COMPILED AND SELECTED

BY

LOUIS UNTERMEYER

GALAHAD BOOKS
NEW YORK

First Galahad Books edition published in 1993.

Galahad Books
A division of BBS Publishing Corporation
386 Park Avenue South
New York, NY 10016

Galahad Books is a registered trademark of BBS Publishing Corporation.

This edition was reprinted with expressed permission by
Laurence S. Untermeyer.

Library of Congress Catalog Card Number: 92-72499

ISBN: 0-88365-796-1

Printed in the United States of America.

ACKNOWLEDGMENTS

Many recent and practically all contemporary poems are copyright, and may not be reprinted or reproduced without the consent of the owners or their agents. A full listing of such poems, as well as a record of indebtedness to authors, publishers, colleagues, and researchers, will be found at the back of the book on pages 1236 through 1239.

IN PRAISE OF POETRY

Poetry is the music of the soul; and, above all, of great and feeling souls. —VOLTAIRE

Now therein of all sciences is our poet the monarch. For he doth not only show the way, but giveth so sweet a prospect into the way as will entice any man to enter into it. Nay, he doth, as if your journey should lie through a fair vineyard, at the very first give you a cluster of grapes, that full of that taste you may long to pass further. He cometh to you with words set in delightful proportion . . . and with a tale which holdeth children from play and old men from the chimney-corner. —SIR PHILIP SIDNEY

Poetry is the art of uniting pleasure with truth by calling imagination to the help of reason. . . . The essence of poetry is invention, such invention as, by producing something unexpected, surprises and delights. —SAMUEL JOHNSON

The poet is the rock of defence for human nature; an upholder and preserver, carrying everywhere with him relationship and love. In spite of differences of soil and climate, of language and manners, of laws and customs; in spite of things silently gone out of mind, and things violently destroyed, *the poet binds together by passion and knowledge the vast empire of human society, as it is spread over the whole earth, and over all time.* —WILLIAM WORDSWORTH

The poet brings the whole soul of man into activity. . . . He diffuses a tone and spirit of unity that blends, and (as it were) fuses, each faculty into each other by that synthetic and magical power to which we have exclusively appropriated the name of Imagination. —SAMUEL TAYLOR COLERIDGE

Poetry is the universal language which the heart holds with nature and itself. He who has a contempt for poetry cannot have much respect for himself or anything else. . . . Poetry is that fine particle within us that expands, rarefies, refines, raises our whole being. —WILLIAM HAZLITT

Poetry is the record of the best and happiest moments of the best minds. . . . A poem is the very image of life expressed in its eternal truth. —PERCY BYSSHE SHELLEY

The poetic character lives in gusto, be it foul or fair, high or low, rich or poor, mean or elevated—it has as much delight in conceiving an Iago as an Imogen. . . . Poetry must work out its own salvation in a man; it cannot be matured by laws and precepts, but by sensations and watchfulness. . . . Poetry should strike the reader as a wording of his own highest thoughts, and appear almost a remembrance.   —JOHN KEATS

If I read a book and it makes my whole body so cold no fire can warm me, I know that is poetry. If I feel physically as if the top of my head were taken off, I know that is poetry. These are the only ways I know it. Is there any other way? —EMILY DICKINSON

It is absurd to think that the only way to tell if a poem is lasting is to wait and see if it lasts. The right reader of a good poem can tell the moment it strikes him that he has taken an immortal wound—that he will never get over it. That is to say, permanence in poetry as in love is perceived instantly. It hasn't to await the test of time.   —ROBERT FROST

Poetry is the synthesis of hyacinths and biscuits.   —CARL SANDBURG

Poetry is not greatly concerned with what a man thinks, but with what is so embedded in his nature that it never occurs to him to question it; not a matter of which idea he holds, but of the depth at which he holds it.   —EZRA POUND

Poetry is not the assertion that something is true, but the making of that truth more fully real to us.   —T. S. ELIOT

The poet, with the adjustment of a phrase, with the contrast of an image, with the rhythm of a line, has fixed a focus which all the talk and all the staring of the world has been unable to fix before him. His is a labor which is at all times necessary, for without it that sense of human reality which is the poet's greatest accomplishment is lost.   —ARCHIBALD MACLEISH

The charm of poetry is its unpredictability. Its element is surprise: the surprise of finding something strange in the familiar, something familiar in the strange. . . . The power of poetry is the ability to express the inexpressible—and to express it in terms of the unforgettable.   —MICHAEL LEWIS

There is a light upon them (the poets), especially upon the Elizabethans and Keats, Wordsworth, Coleridge, Shelley. . . . *Those are the people with whom I want to live, those are the men I feel are our brothers.*   —KATHERINE MANSFIELD

CONTENTS

I

The Bible

II

Foundations of the English Spirit

III

The Popular Ballad

IV

Early Songs of Unknown Authorship

V

Toward the Golden Age

VI

Elizabethan Songs of Unknown Authorship

VII

The Mirror of Mankind

VIII

Anatomy of the World

IX

Gallants, Puritans, and Divines

X

The Rise and Fall of Elegance

XI

Pure Vision, Pure Song

XII

The Spirit of Revolution and Romance

XIII

Faith, Doubt, and Democracy

XIV

Challenge to Tradition

XV

The World of the Twentieth Century

PREFACE

Aｌｔｈｏｕｇｈ nearly one thousand poems are contained in these pages, this volume is not another effort to outdo the many existing anthologies in length, breadth, and thickness. Differing from other collections in kind as well as degree, this is an attempt to combine the lives of the poets and the work they produced, to trace the record of shifting taste, and to present the poetry as living documents of renewed experience. It is primarily a work of integration rather than of assembly.

Nevertheless, it is as an assembly that the book must justify itself. And it is here that every editor, unhappily but inevitably assuming the defensive, must explain in what way his selections differ from—and are obviously better than—any other. Struggling to overcome his modesty, the half-apologetic, half-defiant compiler usually indicates that time has revised many of his predecessors' judgments and that he has been chosen to re-estimate the past in terms of the more critical present. He goes on to imply that his function is not only to revalue but to correct; that, much though he admires his famous forerunners, he deplores the errors in the work of P and Q and has therefore restored certain poems to their original purity—in short, that his ear is a little more sensitive, his eye a little sharper, and his mind a little livelier than his dead confreres' and living competitors'.

The editor of this compilation is not less immodest than his fellows, but his claims upon the reader are somewhat different. His book, ranging over six centuries, presumes to be comprehensive enough to include utterances of mind-shaking sublimity without neglecting inspired and equally unforgettable nonsense. But—to stress its chief difference—this is not only a book of poetry, but a book about poets and their poems. The prose paragraphs are not designed to interrupt the reader's progress but to increase his pleasure: to act as living backgrounds for the verse. Sometimes the prose is in the nature of a condensed biography or a fragment of forgotten history; sometimes it is a journey to the source of the poem or a speculation concerning its origin; sometimes it attempts to explain the seeming obscurities which prevent the reader from obtaining complete en-

joyment. In short, the running commentary presumes to show in
what way one poet differs from every other poet and in what way
poetry remains a constant, a permanent paradox: a solace and an
excitement, an escape and an adventure, the highest and most varied
expression of mankind.

II

Perhaps this is too presumptuous a claim, and it may well be
asked: to whom are you talking? For whom is this book intended?
The editor cannot guess the answer to the first query, but he knows
what audience he does *not* plan to reach. His book is not for the
advanced scholar; it is neither an analytical survey nor an appraisal
of movements, controversial tendencies and techniques. It is de-
signed primarily for immediate pleasure, but it hopes to indicate
the deeper enjoyment which comes from appreciation. The gap
between the casual reading of a poem and an understanding of the
rich implication is great but not difficult; once the gap is bridged,
the close communication between the writer and the reader is es-
tablished.

This book purposes to aid the establishment of that communica-
tion. A poem is, first of all, an act of pure creation. In the throes of
an emotional or intellectual excitement, the poet has achieved a
magic: he has brought order out of chaos. This excitement must be
shared before the enchantment can exert its spell. But, besides being
an act of creation, poetry is a piece of concentrated power; every
lyric is a miracle of condensation.

It is this combination of rapt creativeness and firm craftsmanship,
of intensity and industry, which gives poetry its everlasting appeal.
Although a few souls in hermetically sealed ivory towers still clamor
for a poetry of abstract beauty divorced from powerful emotions and
provoking ideas, poetry continues to delight in its contradictory in-
fluence: it inspires and instructs in the same breath. It awakes the
imagination while it excites the intellect; it stirs the mind with its
curious blend of fact and fancy. Possibly poetry's chief magic is that,
with the twist of a word, or the shift of a picture, or the abruptness
of a comparison, it can simultaneously enlighten and enrich.

III

If poetry is the most potent of human communications, it should
also be the simplest and the most logical expression. It should,
some say, require no particular cogitation, no afterthoughts, no

exercise of the speculative mind. But poetry, being the product of intuition as well as experience, transcends plain statements; it surpasses fact and leaps ahead of logic. Simple arithmetic to the contrary, a poem is not the sum of its parts. A poem is greater than its parts; it is even something beyond its parts. It is prompted by an idea, enhanced by rhyme, pointed by meter, colored by metaphor. This fusion, this enrichment and intensification, has created a new thing: the poem itself, which is beyond analysis—even, at times, beyond logic.

If a poem may be said to have an aim, it must be to make the reader see with a new acuteness and feel with a new awareness. To do this the poet may use statement or suggestion; he may try to persuade by careful reason or hypnotize the reader by a frenzied energy of words. He may intoxicate himself and his readers with rhythmical orgies like Swinburne; he may plunge into a flood of free associations and erupting images like Gerard Manley Hopkins and Hart Crane; he may build a world directly from his backgrounds, like Robert Burns and Robert Frost, or, like Edgar Allan Poe, turn hallucination into an unforgettable otherworld, a misty mid-region of ghoul-haunted palaces, pendulous shadows, and desperate seas.

Not only the landscape and atmosphere of the poet's world, but the very nuances of his character are implicit in his language. We learn about the music-makers, "the movers and shakers, world-losers and world-forsakers," not only from their official biographers and the gossip of their less worshipful contemporaries, but from their idiom. Milton's personality is felt in his characteristic choice of words; his love of the majestic, of the profound and almost overpowering, is reflected in his fondness for such sonorous epithets as "celestial," "barbaric," "immortal," "infernal," "fierce," "royal," "bottomless perdition," "dubious battle," "transcendent brightness," "innumerable force." Keats, on the other hand, wanted no such rebounding syllables and rousing action; he delighted to drug himself with the sweet and heady luxuriance of "full-ripened," "purple-stained," "mellow fruitfulness," "fume of poppies," "soft incense," "murmurous haunt," "fast-fading violets," "verdurous glooms," "drowsy numbness," "magic casements," "faery lands forlorn." Herrick's is a brisker tune from quite another world; a witty and lightly wanton realm is immediately disclosed in the poet's preoccupation with a "careless" shoestring, "erring" laces and a general "sweet disorder," with the silky "liquefaction" of his mistress' clothes and "brave vibrations," with coy but ultimately complaisant virgins, brief prayers, "dainty delights," "cleanly-wantonness"—the very words reveal Herrick as the singer of frail virtue and harmless vice, a laureate crowned with "a little garland" and "some small stock of innocence." Shelley reveals himself in words that aspire dreamily toward some superb vagueness: "the gloom of thought," "blithe spirit," "nursling of the sky," "all-sufficing Nature," "Life, like a dome of many-colored glass," "joy that is almost pain," "aereal kisses," "wrecks of a dissolving dream," "the white radiance of eternity," "O world! O life! O time!"

IV

To suggest the vastness of the poets' imaginations and the variety of their multiple worlds is one of the functions of an anthology, and this collection ranges somewhat more widely than most. Its extensiveness may be challenged, but the editor would defeat his purpose by limiting the contents to a rigid alignment. The departures from conventionality are such as to permit the inclusion of many kinds of poetry—and, though the aim is to show the best of each kind, it is the incredible diversity of human experience which speaks more powerfully than the rare pieces of superhuman perfection.

This collection, therefore, presents a combination of the imperative and the persuasive, of the little-known and the familiar. It includes poems which are part of the great tradition and poems which are isolated examples of individuality; poems which are as ready to hand as today's almanac and poems which are as relatively inaccessible as a medieval pomander. That a poem has been countlessly reprinted is nothing against it; repeated quotation, on the other hand, is no proof of its excellence. A great poem is equally beyond popularity and neglect; it will not fail to find its reader.

And what is "great"? The answer might well be another question: what is "red"? Greatness, like redness (or a perfume or a beautiful face), is as unmistakable as it is undefinable. But a collection of poetry must not boast of being indefinite. In this collection greatness is determined, if not defined, by two things: time and taste. The first is, of course, the undebatable standard. Time, which triumphs over every controversy, is the perfect anthologist; time has an authority which no contemporary enthusiasm can hope to attain. But must we, then, always withhold judgment; must we wait for permanence before we can approve the work of our own time? Robert Frost says with reassuring conviction, "It is absurd to think that the only way to tell if a poem is lasting is to wait and see if it lasts. The right reader of a good poem can tell the moment it strikes him that he has taken an immortal wound—that he will never get over it."

This is the reply to the test of time. It is the power of immediate cognition, full awareness, compulsion, heightened sensibility, love—in short, personal taste. Every reader is an instinctive though usually unpublished editor; and the editor, as Constant Reader, must fall back upon the complex of reason and intuition, immediate experience and remote association, the mixture of preferences and prejudices which makes his taste somehow his own.

A TREASURY OF GREAT POEMS: ENGLISH AND AMERICAN thereby confesses its limitations as well as its range. It endeavors to include the best of tradition and experiment. But, since it represents a compromise between the authority of time and the hazard of personal taste, it cannot include everything calculated to please everybody. It omits Longfellow's PSALM OF LIFE because it is a soggy pudding of rhymes stuffed with questionable moral maxims; and it includes Longfellow's PAUL REVERE'S RIDE because it is a fine narrative which still starts the pulse galloping. It omits Joyce Kilmer's TREES, not because it is popular and sentimental, but because it is a mélange of silly metaphors; and it includes Kipling's equally popular and sentimental MANDALAY because it is an unpretentious but fully realized picture, a straightforward expression of nostalgia, a modern ballad with the honest ring of folk stuff—in short, a good poem.

Although this is not an anthology of light verse, it is not neglectful of the part that humor has played in poetry. It is a part which is not always recognized and, when recognized, not always approved. But the wit of Pope, an eminence of its own, is not so sky-consuming that it need crowd out the smaller peaks attained by Edward Lear and W. S. Gilbert. The lyrics of Lear and the BAB BALLADS are not only as worthy of a place in literary history as THE RAPE OF THE LOCK, they are, with ALICE IN WONDERLAND, as much a part of English culture as the gravest meditations of Wordsworth and the most ecstatic rhapsodies of Shelley.

V

But, the reader may persist, what is "great"? Contemporary estimates are scarcely trustworthy. Who today can read Jean Ingelow, Michael Wigglesworth, Fitz-Greene Halleck? How many poetry lovers of our time have even heard of Richard Monckton Milnes, Martin Farquhar Tupper, the Reverend John Keble, Letitia Landon, Lydia Sigourney, Maria G. Brooks, and Frances Sargent Osgood? Yet these poets were considered "great" in their day. POEMS of Jean Ingelow (1820–1897), published less than eighty years ago, ran rapidly through twenty-two editions in England and sold more than 200,000 copies in America. Michael Wigglesworth's THE DAY OF DOOM (1662), one of the most ferocious poems ever written, horrible in conception, ugly in execution, was the best seller of the century; "it was the solace," wrote James Russell Lowell with grim facetiousness, "of every fireside, the flicker of the pine-knots by which it was conned perhaps adding a livelier relish to its premonitions of eternal combustion." Fitz-Greene Halleck (1790–1867), author of MARCO BOZZARIS and one of the first of the Knickerbocker School, was the idol of the elocutionists; Rufus Griswold, perhaps the most influential critic of his day, refused to include Whitman in his American anthology, but considered Fitz-Greene Halleck "not only one of the chief ornaments of a new literature, but one of the great masters in a language classical and immortal." Richard Monckton Milnes (1809–1885) is a name that suggests nothing to the modern reader but a few curious syllables; yet Walter Savage Landor, poet and critic—writing during the era of Browning and Tennyson—threw off all critical restraint and declared that "Milnes is the greatest poet now living." PROVERBIAL PHILOSOPHY by Martin Farquhar Tupper (1810–1889) was quoted by tens of thousands; it shared the place and popularity of the Bible on the parlor tables of the eighteen fifties. A few hymns still carry the accents of the Reverend John Keble (1792–1866), but in the years between 1827 and 1870 one hundred and fifty-eight editions of Keble's THE CHRISTIAN YEAR were printed, and in 1870 a college was founded in his memory. Letitia Landon (1802–1838) was continually hailed by nineteenth-century admirers as the Tenth Muse. Lydia Sigourney (1791–1865) published fifty-three assorted volumes of prolific morals and profitable sentimentality. Maria G. Brooks (1795–1845), wife of a Boston merchant, was renowned for her "refined sensuousness"; Southey, the English poet laureate, christened her "Maria del Occidente" and declared that she was "the most impassioned and most imaginative of all poetesses." Frances Sargent Osgood (1811–1850) was a pretty and buoyant lady remembered today only as the author of LITTLE DROPS OF WATER, LITTLE GRAINS OF SAND and the lyric beginning "Call me pet names, dearest! call me a bird!" Yet Edgar Allan Poe, whose

indiscreet fondness for Mrs. Osgood may have influenced his judg-
ment, concluded that, "In that vague and anomalous something
which we call grace Mrs. Osgood has assuredly no superior in Amer-
ica, if indeed she has any equal under the sun."

Faced with time's cruelly revised verdicts, the reputations faded,
the names difficult to recall, the anthologist may well hesitate. Yet
one may hesitate too long. And the editor, emboldened by the
proverb, looking even as he leaps, must conclude that he might
better be lost through adventurousness than through timidity. He
decides to mingle old and new, the well-known with the neglected,
and present the best—subject to the limitations of his taste and
temperament—wherever he finds it, irrespective of its unpopularity
or, contrariwise, its approval by time.

VI

"Poetry should surprise by a fine excess and not by singularity,"
John Keats wrote to John Taylor in 1818. "Its touches of beauty
should never be half-way. . . . If poetry comes not as naturally as
the leaves to a tree, it had better not come at all."

The notion that poetry is something alien to the average man is
a belief which, though prevalent, is wholly false. The very man who
belittles poetry in public practices it in private; it comes as naturally
to him "as the leaves of the tree." His dreams are poetry, although
of an illogical and distorted kind; his simplest sentences rely on
the power of imagery. "There is no gap," says the English critic
I. A. Richards, "between our everyday emotional life and the mate-
rial of poetry. . . . If we do not live in consonance with good
poetry, we must live in consonance with bad poetry." Emerson in-
sisted that men were not only stirred spiritually by poetry, but
moved to action through its agency. "See the power of national em-
blems," Emerson wrote. "Some stars, lilies, leopards, a crescent, a
lion, an eagle or other figure which came into credit God knows
how, an old rag of bunting blowing in the wind . . . shall make the
blood tingle under the rudest or most conventional exterior. The
people fancy they hate poetry—and they are all poets and mystics!"

The average man, intent upon his daily work, considers himself
bound to a factual existence; he would scorn to be indebted to
anything as fanciful as poetry. Yet he never ceases to use poetry; he
employs it to make his life more vivid, to transfix an emotion or
dramatize an event. Were the average man as prosy as he imagines

himself to be, he would merely state that his motorcar runs well
and rapidly. But this is too dull a statement for vigor, and so the
power of metaphor is employed to say endearingly "the old boat
purred along" or (a domesticated mechanical dragon) "ate up the
road at sixty." The sailor does not regard his ship as a mechanical
assembly of inanimate parts; to him, who never heard of the figure
of speech known as "metonymy," it is a personal "she"—a sentiment
crystallized by Kipling when he wrote:

> The liner, she's a lady.

We cannot escape from poetry. We need its power of quick com-
munication in every casual activity. The stereotypes of conversation
are enriched by poetic comparisons; the original daring has gone
out of the phrase, but we still delight to intensify a hard drizzle by
saying "it's raining cats and dogs." We are not merely hungry but
"hungry as a bear," a good servant is not merely rare but "scarce as
hen's teeth," a delay is not merely long but "longer than a month
of Sundays." Country expressions are rich in picturesque com-
parisons. A farmer will not tell you that his hired man is slow; he
must use a simile to say that the man is slow "as molasses in Janu-
ary." His colt is fantastically fast "as greased lightning." His wife is
plain "as a turnip" with a tongue "sharp as vinegar," but she is "a
diamond in the rough" and she has "a heart of gold." The adver-
tiser understands better than most the "pulling power" of poetic
imagery. The fruit grower appreciates that oranges are warmed,
and ripened, and even nourished by sunlight; but he capitalizes the
power of poetry by saying that they are *Sunkist,* a conceit worthy
of the Elizabethan singers. A favorite melon is sold on the strength
of its romantic syllables; its supersweetness is conveyed in the name
Honeydew—and the word not only carries the overtones of poetry
but brings us directly to Coleridge's voluptuous phrase:

> For he on honey-dew hath fed
> And drunk the milk of Paradise.

The annals of American commerce yield countless examples of
poetic compression and exuberance. The paint manufacturer labels
his product "barreled sunlight." The automobile designer evokes
the irresistible course of water by giving his model a "streamline";
the architect daringly suggests the tower of Babel with the "sky-

scraper"; the man in the street intensifies his speech by tightening it into slang, the shorthand of the people, by "crashing" a party, "muscling" in, "hitting" the high spots. Language is continually being made swift and powerful through the medium of the poetic phrase.

Perhaps the poetic instinct is best illustrated by the difference between the botanist and the countryman. In every instance the common country name for a flower is not only more charming but more exact than that of the botanist's. The *Physostegia* becomes the "obedient plant" because its buds can be pushed about the stem. The *Arisaema triphyllum* becomes a "jack-in-the-pulpit," and we see the flower more clearly because we see it through the eye of the imagination. *Nigella* has little meaning to most, but "love-in-a-mist" completely describes the bashful blue flower in its aura of green. We know the look as well as the characteristic of the common flower from such playful, and precise, sometimes humorous, but always poetic appellations as Jacob's-ladder, bleeding heart, deadly nightshade, snow-in-summer, Indian pipes, wandering Jew, Johnny-jump-up, foxglove and monkshood (rather than the forbidding medicinal *Digitalis* and *Aconite*), creeping Jennie, forget-me-not, Queen Anne's lace, lady's-slipper, bachelor's-buttons, Aaron's-rod, bear's-foot, barber's-brush, frostweed, foamflower, heal-all, Turk's-cap lily, thimbleweed, bouncing Bet, buttered haycocks, jill-over-the-ground, Solomon's-seal, jewelweed, butter-and-eggs, bee balm, wormwood, snake's-head, snapdragon, black-eyed Susan, devil's-paintbrush, daisy (originally "the day's eye"), buttercup, pennyroyal, love-lies-bleeding, meet-me-in-the-entry, kiss-her-in-the-buttery.

VII

Every effort has been made to ensure textual accuracy for this volume. The standard "authorities" have been consulted, and, for the most part, the traditional form of each poem has been maintained. A uniformity of spelling has been aimed at, even where such uniformity may sometimes violate the original text. It seems unnecessarily pedantic to retain spelling which has been discarded or altered by time and geography; but, although "labor" has been preferred to "labour" and "center" to "centre," there has been no absolute rigidity of form. In this volume the spelling has been kept as nearly uniform as possible, and consistent within the poem.

One or two exceptions to this rule of consistency must be noted. In the case of Blake, for example, the first line of one of his most famous poems is printed:

> Tyger! Tyger! burning bright

instead of:

> Tiger, tiger, burning bright

The editor prefers the first instead of the second not only because Blake originally spelled it that way, but because "Tyger!" suggests a much handsomer and far more arresting creature than a mere "tiger."

In the case of the old ballads, too, archaic spellings and phrases have been preserved. Although the texts are as authoritative as can be determined, certain disputed versions may lead to controversy. In spite of the labors of scholars and researchers, there is practically no anonymous ballad which has a perfect finality. The story-poems may be said to have evolved, to have been remade as much as made. The poetry which frames the tales struggled to the surface through many adaptations. No version of any ancient ballad can therefore claim to be the "original," but the editor's choice has in all cases been directed toward maintaining the tempo, the vivacity, and the strong feeling of the old rhymed narratives.

When we come to Chaucer a special problem arises. Many a reader has been kept from tasting the full vintage of Chaucer's bubbling spirit because he has not the leisure to learn a new (or rather, an old) language, or because he has been frightened off by the batteries of bristling footnotes which usually accompany Chaucer's texts. Yet when a tale is told by such a poet as Chaucer a liberty with his words is a debatable matter. In this volume the editor attempts a compromise. The most accurate obtainable text of Chaucer's Middle English therefore appears facing the most recent, and the most readable, modern version.

With few exceptions the poems are complete. It would be unthinkable to "condense" such a lengthy masterpiece as Coleridge's THE RIME OF THE ANCIENT MARINER. It is obvious that the import, as well as the full impact, of such a poem can be felt only by its cumulative power; only the foolhardy would attempt to save space at the expense of the rich content. Yet, here again, an exception or two must be made to the generality. Although most of Christopher Smart's magnificent rhapsody, A SONG TO DAVID, is printed in this collection—far more than is usually quoted—several stanzas have been omitted for the sake of unity. Wherever occasional excerpts appear, the source is either indicated in the subtitle of the poem or in the title of the selection.

The subtitle of this collection indicates that it is not a compendium of the world's great poetry, but is confined to the poetry of the English-speaking countries. There may be those who will quibble at the inclusion of the RUBÁIYÁT of Omar Khayyám and certain sections of the Old Testament. But the RUBÁIYÁT, as we know it, owes as much to the nineteenth-century FitzGerald as it does to the eleventh-century Omar, and the King James Version of the Bible is one of the chief glories of English literature.[1]

VIII

"The poet," said Wordsworth in his memorable preface to the second edition of LYRICAL BALLADS, "is a man speaking to men: a man, it is true, imbued with more lively sensibility, more enthusiasm and tenderness, who has a greater knowledge of human nature and a more comprehensive soul than are supposed to be common among mankind; a man pleased with his own passions and volitions and who rejoices more than other men in the spirit of life that is in him, delighting to contemplate similar volitions and passions as manifested in the goings-on of the Universe, and habitually impelled to create them where he does not find them."

The poet, therefore, is not only a visionary but a recorder, not only a creative spirit but a creature of joy—"a man pleased with his own passions and volitions . . . delighting to contemplate similar volitions and passions as manifested in the goings-on of the Universe." He is so intent a seeker after the truth and establishment of the "spirit of life that is in him" that he is determined to share his sense of discovery—from strict observation to headlong ecstasy— with everyone; he even dares to make his truths come true, "to create them where he does not find them." And this, perhaps, is his highest function. Greater than the recorder is the communicator, the indefatigable, yea-saying ambassador. Poetry is the highest level of communication, a simple but transcendent communion; and the

---

[1] *Although a strict chronological arrangement might place the Authorized English translation of the Bible in the seventeenth century, the Biblical literature is the oldest in terms of original composition. It seems proper, therefore, that the* TREASURY *should begin with the poetry of the Bible.*

poet is compelled by his very nature to share the glory of the world with all—"a man speaking to men."

Today the poet's function has increased in scope and responsibility. What the poet has to say to his fellows is particularly needed in these toppling times. More than ever, the "defense" of Wordsworth is true today: "In spite of things silently gone out of mind, and things violently destroyed, the poet binds together by passion and knowledge the vast empire of human society, as it is spread over the whole earth and over all time."

Thus the poet is not only a communicator, a creator and stimulator, but a preserver of "things silently gone out of mind and things violently destroyed," an upholder of everything which humanity loves, works for, and hopes to maintain.

L. U.

I

The Bible

THE SONG OF SONGS

N o poem has had a more curious or confused history than the
song of songs. There it is, a divine irrelevance, a passionately
living, frankly sexual love poem in the midst of Holy Writ. The
surcharged images and burning apostrophes follow the grim cyni-
cisms of ecclesiastes and precede the rapt prophecies of isaiah.
Never has there been a more magnificently inappropriate setting
for a collection of amorous lyric poems.

Whether or not the all-too-brief set of eight chapters can be called
a collection of lyrics has always been a matter of acrid dispute. The
unpretentious little book has been a source of endless debates.
Only a work so human and so supernal, so simple and so timeless,
so curiously local and so deeply universal, could survive the war of
scholarly dialectics, the embattled exegeses, the fiercely opposed
interpretations.

The common form of the title plunges us into mystery. The
song of songs, which is solomon's. Why Solomon's? Was Solomon
the author of the work? If he was not its author, was he its hero,
the kingly suitor, the traditional great lover? Impartial scholars
were quick to point out that the songs are Solomon's only by asso-
ciation; that the allusions to the monarch are few and vague; and
that the verbal mixtures indicate a much later period in history
than that of the idealized ruler and builder.

It is generally agreed that the name of Solomon was added to give
authority to this lyrical outpouring. But there never has been una-
nimity of opinion as to the full meaning of the work. There are

three interpretations: (1) THE SONG OF SONGS is an allegory; (2) it is a drama; (3) it is an anthology.

The allegorical interpretation is the oldest. It is also the most ingenious and implausible. It seems fairly certain that the lines were originally enjoyed purely as erotic songs. But, even though the stamp of holiness had been placed upon the verses, how were the pious to stand up in the hushed synagogue and unblushingly recite:

> Let him kiss me with the kisses of his mouth:
> For thy love is better than wine.
>
> A bundle of myrrh is my wellbeloved unto me;
> He shall lie all night betwixt my breasts.
>
> Until the day break, and the shadows flee away,
> Turn, my beloved, and be thou like a roe
> Or a young hart upon the mountains of Bether.
>
> Thy lips, O my spouse, drop as the honeycomb:
> Honey and milk are under thy tongue;
> And the smell of thy garments is like the smell of Lebanon.

Taking their cue from the mystical East where the poems of Hafiz were sung by the dervishes, the zealous rabbis hid the simple and forthright design under a fantastic structure of elaborations. They drew out the rich lifeblood and substituted an injection of thinly sugared parable. Thus even the youngest child could be told that the lover was God and that the beloved was Israel.

The churchmen followed suit. Origen in the third century, Jerome in the fourth, Augustine in the fifth, and the Venerable Bede in the seventh and eighth centuries reinterpreted the lines. They established the allegory that the lover was Christ, and the beloved was (according to the fancy of the interpreter) either the Church or the adoring Christian. Later commentators read in the passion of the leading characters the union of a human tradition and a divine abstraction: to them it was nothing less than an impersonal Solomon and his pure love of Wisdom.

The dramatic interpretation is somewhat more plausible. Proceeding on the theory that this was a secular work, various commentators sought to give the book a dramatic unity. Since the arrangement of segments in the accepted version showed no definite continuity. these commentators broke up the chapters, furnished dramatis personae, and reassembled the material into the shape of a play. Obviously influenced by the Greek dramas, the dramatizers went to work; the lines were distributed among a set of characters headed by the lover and the beloved, aided by choruses of maidens, watchmen, and king's henchmen. Some of the commentators conceived the work as a cantata; they maintained it was an unquestioned oratorio in which the music had been lost and only parts of the libretto had survived. Others rearranged the verses into plays of three and five acts. The work itself was so formless in outline and so vague in narrative that every other reference served as a cue to another plot.

There was, for example, the rearrangement (favored by the English scholars) which made Solomon the hero of the play, and in which the chief incident was his nuptials with a dusky Egyptian princess, sometimes identified as the Queen of Sheba. She introduced herself with the words, "I am black, but comely, O ye daughters of Jerusalem, as the tents of Kedar, as the curtains of Solomon." But Solomon already had a Jewish bride, Sulamith, or the Shulamite. Impassioned entreaties, love scenes, and quarrels ensued. In this version the play ran the gamut from joy to jealousy, from ecstatic pageantry to inglorious domestic comedy.

An even more popular treatment changes the emphasis and reverses the plot. The structure of the triangle is maintained; but, instead of the tragicomic situation of the man with two wives, there is presented the more idyllic theme of the girl between two lovers. In this version Sulamith becomes the center of the play. Here the heroine is courted by the king and even carried into his palace. But, though dazzled by her impetuous royal suitor and captivated by promised magnificence, she yearns for the shepherd to whom she is unalterably attached. In the end virtue is rewarded; Sulamith resists the monarch and is reunited with her bucolic lover.

There are many objections to the dramatic rearrangement. For one thing THE SONG OF SONGS is, except for arbitrary juxtapositions, almost wholly undramatic. There is practically no action; several 'scenes" consist of only one line. Moreover, the Jews had no drama, and there is no parallel to the play form in Semitic literature. Finally, the essential motivations—the capture of the heroine, the shifting attitudes of the king, the reunion of the heroine and her lover—are all imagined rather than supplied by the text.

The anthological interpretation is the most reasonable. It was Origen who first tentatively suggested that the material was "in the

nature of" an epithalamium, a wedding song, possibly composed by
Solomon. Other commentators hinted at something of the sort, but
it was not until the nineteenth century that the suggestion was con-
firmed and enlarged. The Prussian consul at Damascus, one J. G.
Wetstein, had been studying the wedding ritual of Syrian peasants,
and certain songs and ceremonies recalled passages in THE SONG OF
SONGS. He connected the phenomena, published his data; and within
twenty years his conclusions were accepted by many Biblical scholars.
In 1899 Cheyne summarized it: "The book is an anthology of songs
used at marriage festivals in or near Jerusalem, revised and loosely
connected by an editor without regard to temporal sequence."

The new interpretation gained favor. Repetition and "responsive"
phrases revealed kinship to older nuptial songs and pointed to an
origin beyond the accepted date of the work, about 300 B.C. Literary
evidence stressed the anthological nature of the work. Passages of
intense imagination in the midst of passages on a colloquial level
made researchers suspect that the work was a combination of in-
spired individual authorship and uncertain folklore.

Some day a compiler will trace all the analogies between THE
SONG OF SONGS and the ancient Egyptian, the later Arabian, and the
modern Palestinian love songs. The relationship between all these
fragmentary lyrics may lead to further discovery and wider implica-
tions. Meanwhile our own literature has been enriched for cen-
turies with a mosaic-poem or a broken collection of poems candid
and concise, realistic and rhapsodic, unaffected and unforgettable.

The remote backgrounds, the dim history, must remain forever
hidden. Sources may be challenged; scholarship may be distrusted.
But not the work itself, not the final authority of phrase which sup-
ports the spirit. We may doubt that the Bible as a whole is a word-
for-word inspiration; but who can doubt that these songs were in-
spired? They are unquestionably the word of God, of God to man.
The tireless Creator, the cosmic Author, was never happier, never
more delightfully naïve and lyrically exalted, never more in love
with life than when he dictated THE SONG OF SONGS.

The Song of Songs

1

Let him kiss me with the kisses of his mouth:
For thy love is better than wine.
Because of the savor of thy good ointments
Thy name is as ointment poured forth;
Therefore do the virgins love thee.

Draw me. We will run after thee.

The king hath brought me into his chambers.
(We will be glad and rejoice in thee,
We will remember thy love more than wine:
The upright love thee.)

I am black, but comely,
O ye daughters of Jerusalem,
As the tents of Kedar,
As the curtains of Solomon.

Look not upon me, because I am black,
Because the sun hath looked upon me:
My mother's children were angry with me;
They made me the keeper of the vineyards;
But mine own vineyard have I not kept.

Tell me, O thou whom my soul loveth,
Where thou feedest,
Where thou makest thy flock to rest at noon:
For why should I be as one that turneth aside
By the flocks of thy companions?

"If thou know not, O thou fairest among women,
Go thy way forth by the footsteps of the flock,
And feed thy kids beside the shepherds' tents."

I have compared thee, O my love,
To a company of horses in Pharaoh's chariots.
Thy cheeks are comely with rows of jewels,
Thy neck with chains of gold.

(We will make thee borders of gold
With studs of silver.)

While the king sitteth at his table,
My spikenard sendeth forth the smell thereof.

A bundle of myrrh is my wellbeloved unto me;
He shall lie all night betwixt my breasts.
My beloved is unto me as a cluster of camphire
In the vineyards of En-gedi.

"Behold, thou art fair, my love;
Behold, thou art fair;
Thou hast doves' eyes.
Behold, thou art fair, my beloved, yea pleasant;
Also our bed is green.
The beams of our house are cedar,
And our rafters are fir."

2

I am the rose of Sharon,
And the lily of the valleys.
As the lily among thorns,
So is my love among the daughters.
As the apple tree among the trees of the wood,
So is my beloved among the sons.

I sat down under his shadow with great delight,
And his fruit was sweet to my taste.
He brought me to the banqueting house,
And his banner over me was love.

Stay me with flagons, comfort me with apples
For I am sick of love.
His left hand is under my head,
And his right hand doth embrace me.

I charge you, O ye daughters of Jerusalem,
By the roes, and by the hinds of the field,
That ye stir not up, nor awake my love,
Till he please.

The voice of my beloved!
Behold, he cometh leaping upon the mountains,
Skipping upon the hills.
My beloved is like a roe or a young hart.
Behold, he standeth behind our wall,
He looketh forth at the windows,
Showing himself through the lattice.
My beloved spake, and said unto me,
"Rise up, my love, my fair one, and come away.
For, lo, the winter is past,
The rain is over and gone;
The flowers appear on the earth;
The time of the singing of birds is come,
And the voice of the turtle is heard in our land;
The fig tree putteth forth her green figs,
And the vines with the tender grape give a good smell.
Arise, my love, my fair one, and come away.

"O my dove, that art in the clefts of the rock,
In the secret places of the stairs,
Let me see thy countenance,
Let me hear thy voice;
For sweet is thy voice,
And thy countenance is comely."

Take us the foxes,
The little foxes, that spoil the vines:
For our vines have tender grapes.

My beloved is mine, and I am his:
He feedeth among the lilies.
Until the day break, and the shadows flee away,
Turn, my beloved, and be thou like a roe
Or a young hart upon the mountains of Bether.

3

By night on my bed I sought him whom my soul loveth:
I sought him, but I found him not.

I will rise now,
And go about the city in the streets,
And in the broad ways I will seek him whom my soul loveth:
I sought him, but I found him not.

The watchmen that go about the city found me:
To whom I said, "Saw ye him whom my soul loveth?"

It was but a little that I passed from them,
But I found him whom my soul loveth:
I held him, and would not let him go,
Until I had brought him into my mother's house,
And into the chamber of her that conceived me.

I charge you, O ye daughters of Jerusalem,
By the roes, and by the hinds of the field,
That ye stir not up, nor awake my love,
Till he please.

Who is this that cometh out of the wilderness
Like pillars of smoke, perfumed with myrrh and frankincense,
With all powders of the merchant?
Behold his bed, which is Solomon's;
Threescore valiant men are about it, of the valiant of Israel.
They all hold swords, being expert in war:
Every man hath his sword upon his thigh
Because of fear in the night.

King Solomon made himself a chariot
Of the wood of Lebanon.
He made the pillars thereof of silver,
The bottom thereof gold,
The covering of it of purple,
The midst thereof being paved with love,
For the daughters of Jerusalem.

Go forth, O ye daughters of Zion,
And behold king Solomon
With the crown wherewith his mother crowned him in the day of
    his espousals,
And in the day of the gladness of his heart.

4

Behold, thou art fair, my love;
Behold, thou art fair;
Thou hast doves' eyes within thy locks:
Thy hair is as a flock of goats that appear from mount Gilead.

Thy teeth are like a flock of sheep that are even shorn,
Which came up from the washing;

Whereof every one bear twins,
And none is barren among them.
Thy lips are like a thread of scarlet,
And thy speech is comely;
Thy temples are like a piece of a pomegranate
Within thy locks;
Thy neck is like the tower of David
Builded for an armory,
Whereon there hang a thousand bucklers,
All shields of mighty men.
Thy two breasts are like two young roes that are twins,
Which feed among the lilies.

Until the day break, and the shadows flee away,
I will get me to the mountain of myrrh,
And to the hill of frankincense.

Thou art all fair, my love;
There is no spot in thee.
Come with me from Lebanon, my spouse,
With me from Lebanon:
Look from the top of Amana,
From the top of Shenir and Hermon,
From the lions' dens,
From the mountains of the leopards.
Thou hast ravished my heart, my sister, my spouse;
Thou hast ravished my heart with one of thine eyes,
With one chain of thy neck.

How fair is thy love, my sister, my spouse!
How much better is thy love than wine!
And the smell of thine ointments than all spices!
Thy lips, O my spouse, drop as the honeycomb:
Honey and milk are under thy tongue;
And the smell of thy garments is like the smell of Lebanon.

A garden inclosed is my sister, my spouse;
A spring shut up, a fountain sealed.
Thy plants are an orchard of pomegranates,
With pleasant fruits; camphire, with spikenard,
Spikenard and saffron;
Calamus and cinnamon,
With all trees of frankincense;
Myrrh and aloes,

With all the chief spices:
A fountain of gardens,
A well of living waters,
And streams from Lebanon.

Awake, O north wind; and come, thou south;
Blow upon my garden,
That the spices thereof may flow out.
Let my beloved come into his garden,
And eat his pleasant fruits.

5

"I am come into my garden, my sister, my spouse:
I have gathered my myrrh with my spice;
I have eaten my honeycomb with my honey;
I have drunk my wine with my milk:
Eat, O friends;
Drink, yea, drink abundantly, O beloved."

I sleep, but my heart waketh:
It is the voice of my beloved that knocketh, saying,
"Open to me, my sister, my love, my dove, my undefiled:
For my head is filled with dew,
And my locks with the drops of the night."

I have put off my coat; how shall I put it on?
I have washed my feet; how shall I defile them?

My beloved put in his hand by the hole of the door,
And my bowels were moved for him.
I rose up to open to my beloved;
And my hands dropped with myrrh,
And my fingers with sweet-smelling myrrh,
Upon the handles of the lock.

I opened to my beloved;
But my beloved had withdrawn himself, and was gone;
My soul failed when he spake:
I sought him, but I could not find him;
I called him, but he gave me no answer.

The watchmen that went about the city found me,
They smote me, they wounded me;
The keepers of the walls took away my veil from me.

I charge you, O daughters of Jerusalem,
If ye find my beloved, that ye tell him,
That I am sick of love.

"What is thy beloved more than another beloved,
O thou fairest among women?
What is thy beloved more than another beloved,
That thou dost so charge us?"

My beloved is white and ruddy,
The chiefest among ten thousand.
His head is as the most fine gold;
His locks are bushy, and black as a raven;
His eyes are as the eyes of doves by the rivers of waters,
Washed with milk, and fitly set;
His cheeks are as a bed of spices,
As sweet flowers;
His lips like lilies, dropping sweet-smelling myrrh;
His hands are as gold rings set with the beryl;
His belly is as bright ivory overlaid with sapphires;
His legs are as pillars of marble,
Set upon sockets of fine gold;
His countenance is as Lebanon,
Excellent as the cedars;
His mouth is most sweet:
Yea, he is altogether lovely.
This is my beloved,
And this is my friend,
O daughters of Jerusalem.

6

"Whither is thy beloved gone,
O thou fairest among women?
Whither is thy beloved turned aside?
That we may seek him with thee."

My beloved is gone down into his garden,
To the beds of spices,
To feed in the gardens, and to gather lilies.
I am my beloved's, and my beloved is mine:
He feedeth among the lilies.

Thou art beautiful, O my love, as Tirzah,
Comely as Jerusalem,
Terrible as an army with banners.

Turn away thine eyes from me,
For they have overcome me:
Thy hair is as a flock of goats
That appear from Gilead.
Thy teeth are as a flock of sheep
Which go up from the washing,
Whereof every one beareth twins,
And there is not one barren among them.
As a piece of a pomegranate are thy temples
Within thy locks.

"There are threescore queens, and fourscore concubines,
And virgins without number.
My dove, my undefiled is but one;
She is the only one of her mother,
She is the choice one of her that bare her.
The daughters saw her, and blessed her;
Yea, the queens and the concubines, and they praised her."

"Who is she that looketh forth as the morning,
Fair as the moon, clear as the sun,
And terrible as an army with banners?"

I went down into the garden of nuts
To see the fruits of the valley,
And to see whether the vine flourished,
And the pomegranates budded.
Or ever I was aware,
My soul made me
Like the chariots of Ammi-nadib.

"Return, return, O Shulamite;
Return, return, that we may look upon thee."

What will ye see in the Shulamite?

"As it were the company of two armies."

7

How beautiful are thy feet with shoes,
O prince's daughter!
The joints of thy thighs are like jewels,
The work of the hands of a cunning workman.

Thy navel is like a round goblet,
Which wanteth not liquor;
Thy belly is like an heap of wheat
Set about with lilies;
Thy two breasts are like two young roes that are twins;
Thy neck is as a tower of ivory;
Thine eyes like the fishpools in Heshbon,
By the gate of Bath-rabbim;
Thy nose is as the tower of Lebanon
Which looketh toward Damascus;
Thine head upon thee is like Carmel,
And the hair of thine head like purple—
The king is held in the galleries.
How fair and how pleasant art thou,
O love, for delights!

This thy stature is like to a palm tree,
And thy breasts to clusters of grapes.

I said "I will go up to the palm tree,
I will take hold of the boughs thereof."
Now also thy breasts shall be as clusters of the vine;
And the smell of thy nose like apples;
And the roof of thy mouth like the best wine for my beloved,
That goeth down sweetly,
Causing the lips of those that are asleep to speak.

I am my beloved's,
And his desire is toward me.

Come, my beloved,
Let us go forth into the field;
Let us lodge in the villages:
Let us get up early to the vineyards;
Let us see if the vine flourish,
Whether the tender grape appear,
And the pomegranates bud forth.
There will I give thee my loves.

The mandrakes give a smell,
And at our gates are all manner of pleasant fruits,
New and old, which I have laid up for thee,
O my beloved.

8

O that thou wert as my brother,
That sucked the breasts of my mother!
When I should find thee without, I would kiss thee;
Yea, I should not be despised.

I would lead thee, and bring thee into my mother's house,
Who would instruct me:
I would cause thee to drink of spiced wine,
Of the juice of my pomegranate.

His left hand should be under my head,
And his right hand should embrace me.

I charge you, O daughters of Jerusalem,
That ye stir not up, nor awake my love,
Until he please.

"Who is this that cometh up from the wilderness,
Leaning upon her beloved?"

I raised thee up under the apple tree:
There thy mother brought thee forth:
There she brought thee forth that bare thee.

Set me as a seal upon thine heart,
As a seal upon thine arm:
For love is strong as death;
Jealousy is cruel as the grave:
The coals thereof are coals of fire,
Which hath a most vehement flame.

Many waters cannot quench love,
Neither can the floods drown it:
If a man would give all the substance of his house for love,
It would utterly be contemned.

"We have a little sister,
And she hath no breasts:
What shall we do for our sister
In the day when she shall be spoken for?

"If she be a wall,
We will build upon her a palace of silver:

And if she be a door,
We will inclose her with boards of cedar."

I am a wall,
And my breasts like towers:
Then was I in his eyes as one that found favor.

Solomon had a vineyard at Baal-hamon;
He let out the vineyard unto keepers;
Every one for the fruit thereof
Was to bring a thousand pieces of silver.

My vineyard, which is mine, is before me:
Thou, O Solomon, must have a thousand,
And those that keep the fruit thereof two hundred.

Thou that dwellest in the gardens,
The companions hearken to thy voice:
Cause me to hear it.

Make haste, my beloved,
And be thou like to a roe or to a young hart
Upon the mountains of spices.

FROM

THE BOOK OF JOB

THE BOOK OF JOB, like THE SONG OF SONGS, has been the subject of endless controversy. It began as a riddle for the philosophers; it remains a puzzle for scholars. The "plot" of JOB centers about a devout spirit shaken by personal suffering and universal distress; a patient man, tortured by misfortune and his friends, who breaks out into perplexed lamentations, even accusations against God's justice, and who is finally answered if not comforted by God Himself. But the form of the work has caused critics to go far toward making a problem of its date and authorship, its purpose and relationship to other writings. Some commentators have found a resemblance between THE BOOK OF JOB and the Greek philosophical dialogue; others claim that it resembles a Greek tragedy; still others have contended that there are striking analogies in a Babylonian monologue of a devout ruler who is afflicted with unbearable hardships but is finally rescued by his god. But the problems are, on the whole, academic. To enjoy the work it is not necessary to know how much of it was written in the fourth century B.C. and how much was added in the third, whether or not the theme was influenced by Greek thought or whether it is peculiarly Hebraic in its application of practical wisdom. What is important to the general reader is the blend of philosophy and poetry, a fusion never surpassed in literature.

One of the most beautiful of the supposed "interpolations" is the twenty-eighth chapter. Many commentators have insisted that it is "out of place," that it weakens the grim dogmatism of Job's friends and the vehemence of Job's anguish. But no one has questioned the perfection of the passage—the revelation of simple wisdom and the confident assurance of natural things.

The Price of Wisdom

Surely there is a vein for the silver,
And a place for gold where they fine it.
Iron is taken out of the earth,
And brass is molten out of the stone.
He setteth an end to darkness,
And searcheth out all perfection:
The stones of darkness, and the shadow of death.
The flood breaketh out from the inhabitant;
Even the waters forgotten of the foot:
They are dried up, they are gone away from men.
As for the earth, out of it cometh bread:
And under it is turned up as it were fire.
The stones of it are the place of sapphires:
And it hath dust of gold.
There is a path which no fowl knoweth,
And which the vulture's eye hath not seen:
The lion's whelps have not trodden it,
Nor the fierce lion passed by it.
He putteth forth his hand upon the rock;
He overturneth the mountains by the roots.
He cutteth out rivers among the rocks;
And his eye seeth every precious thing.

He bindeth the floods from overflowing;
And the thing that is hid bringeth he forth to light.

But where shall wisdom be found?
And where is the place of understanding?
Man knoweth not the price thereof;
Neither is it found in the land of the living.
The depth saith, It is not in me:
And the sea saith, It is not with me.
It cannot be gotten for gold,
Neither shall silver be weighed for the price thereof.
It cannot be valued with the gold of Ophir,
With the precious onyx, or the sapphire.
The gold and the crystal cannot equal it:
And the exchange of it shall not be for jewels of fine gold,
No mention shall be made of coral, or of pearls:
For the price of wisdom is above rubies.
The topaz of Ethiopia shall not equal it,
Neither shall it be valued with pure gold.

Whence then cometh wisdom?
And where is the place of understanding?
Seeing it is hid from the eyes of all living,
And kept close from the fowls of the air.
Destruction and death say,
We have heard the fame thereof with our ears.
God understandeth the way thereof,
And he knoweth the place thereof.
For he looketh to the ends of the earth,
And seeth under the whole heaven;
To make the weight for the winds;
And he weigheth the waters by measure.
When he made a decree for the rain,
And a way for the lightning of the thunder:
Then did he see it, and declare it;
He prepared it, yea, and searched it out.
And unto man he said,
Behold, the fear of the Lord, that is wisdom;
And to depart from evil is understanding.

Chapter 28

One of the greatest, as well as one of the darkest, outbursts of passion occurs near the beginning of the book. God has permitted Satan to afflict Job and test his devotion to the Lord, and God's

Adversary has smitten Job with a heavy hand. Job's comforters
have visited him "and they saw that his grief was very great." After
a long silence, Job loses his patience, rends his mantle, and lifts his
voice in protest.

Job Complains

Let the day perish wherein I was born,
And the night in which it was said, There is a man child conceived.
Let that day be darkness;
Let not God regard it from above,
Neither let the light shine upon it.
Let darkness and the shadow of death stain it;
Let a cloud dwell upon it;
Let the blackness of the day terrify it.
As for that night, let darkness seize upon it;
Let it not be joined unto the days of the year,
Let it not come into the number of the months.
Lo, let that night be solitary,
Let no joyful voice come therein.
Let them curse it that curse the day,
Who are ready to raise up their mourning.
Let the stars of the twilight thereof be dark;
Let it look for light, but have none;
Neither let it see the dawning of the day:
Because it shut not up the doors of my mother's womb,
Nor hid sorrow from mine eyes.
Why died I not from the womb?
Why did I not give up the ghost when I came out of the belly?
Why did the knees prevent me?
Or why the breast that I should suck?
For now should I have lain still and been quiet,
I should have slept: then had I been at rest,
With kings and counselors of the earth,
Which built desolate places for themselves;
Or with princes that had gold,
Who filled their houses with silver:
Or as an hidden untimely birth I had not been;
As infants which never saw light.
There the wicked cease from troubling;
And there the weary be at rest.
There the prisoners rest together;
They hear not the voice of the oppressor.

The small and great are there;
And the servant is free from his master.
Wherefore is light given to him that is in misery,
And life unto the bitter in soul;
Which long for death, but it cometh not;
And dig for it more than for hid treasures;
Which rejoice exceedingly,
And are glad, when they can find the grave?
Why is light given to a man whose way is hid,
And whom God hath hedged in?
For my sighing cometh before I eat,
And my roarings are poured out like the waters.
For the thing which I greatly feared is come upon me,
And that which I was afraid of is come unto me.
I was not in safety, neither had I rest, neither was I quiet;
Yet trouble came.

Chapter 3

The climax of the poem is anticipated by the question of God's relation to man. What is God if He is not good? Job knows he cannot contend with deity, but he pleads with Him for understanding, for comfort, even for the ease of death. Once again he cries out in a speech of accusation and bitter self-justification.

Job Cries Out

Man that is born of a woman
Is of few days, and full of trouble.
He cometh forth like a flower, and is cut down:
He fleeth also as a shadow, and continueth not.
And dost thou open thine eyes upon such an one,
And bringest me into judgment with thee?
Who can bring a clean thing out of an unclean? not one.
Seeing his days are determined, the number of his months are with
    thee,
Thou hast appointed his bounds that he cannot pass;
Turn from him, that he may rest,
Till he shall accomplish, as an hireling, his day.
For there is hope of a tree, if it be cut down, that it will sprout again,
And that the tender branch thereof will not cease.
Though the root thereof wax old in the earth,
And the stock thereof die in the ground;

Yet through the scent of water it will bud,
And bring forth boughs like a plant.
But man dieth, and wasteth away:
Yea, man giveth up the ghost, and where is he?
As the waters fail from the sea,
And the flood decayeth and drieth up:
So man lieth down, and riseth not:
Till the heavens be no more, they shall not awake,
Nor be raised out of their sleep.
O that thou wouldest hide me in the grave,
That thou wouldest keep me secret, until thy wrath be past,
That thou wouldest appoint me a set time, and remember me!
If a man die, shall he live again?
All the days of my appointed time will I wait,
Till my change come.
Thou shalt call, and I will answer thee:
Thou wilt have a desire to the work of thine hands.
For now thou numberest my steps:
Dost thou not watch over my sin?
My transgression is sealed up in a bag,
And thou sewest up mine iniquity.
And surely the mountain falling cometh to nought,
And the rock is removed out of his place.
The waters wear the stones:
Thou washest away the things which grow out the dust of the earth;
And thou destroyest the hope of man.
Thou prevailest forever against him, and he passeth:
Thou changest his countenance, and sendest him away.
His sons come to honor, and he knoweth it not;
And they are brought low, but he perceiveth it not of them.
But his flesh upon him shall have pain,
And his soul within him shall mourn.

Chapter 14

The full climax comes at the end of the poem when the voice of
God answers out of the whirlwind. God enters not to answer Job,
but to question him; instead of comforting Job with easy solutions,
He propounds universal and overwhelming riddles. G. K. Chester-
ton, expert in paradox, has written of this paradoxical situation:

A more trivial poet would have made God enter in some sense
or other in order to answer the questions. By a touch truly to be
called inspired, when God enters, it is to ask a number of more
questions on His own account. In this drama of skepticism God
Himself takes up the role of skeptic. He does what all the great

voices defending religion have always done. He does, for instance, what Socrates did. He turns rationalism against itself. He seems to say that if it comes to asking questions, He can ask some questions which will fling down and flatten out all conceivable human questioners. The poet by an exquisite intuition has made God ironically accept a kind of controversial equality with His accusers. He is willing to regard it as if it were a fair intellectual duel: "Gird up now thy loins like a man; for I will demand of thee, and answer thou me." The Everlasting adopts an enormous and sardonic humility. He is quite willing to be prosecuted. He only asks for the right which every prosecuted person possesses; He asks to be allowed to cross-examine the witness for the prosecution. And He carries yet further the correctness of the legal parallel. For the first question, essentially speaking, which He asks of Job is the question that any criminal accused by Job would be most entitled to ask. He asks Job who he is. And Job, being a man of candid intellect, takes a little time to consider, and comes to the conclusion that he does not know.

Thus, as Chesterton implies, human doubt is rebuked by a cosmic skepticism, and the doubter is confronted with enigmas beyond his penetration. "He has been told nothing, but he feels the terrible and tingling atmosphere of something too good to be told. The riddles of God," concludes Chesterton, "are more satisfying than the solutions of man."

God Replies

Who is this that darkeneth counsel
By words without knowledge?
Gird up now thy loins like a man;
For I will demand of thee, and answer thou me.
Where wast thou when I laid the foundations of the earth?
Declare, if thou hast understanding.
Who hath laid the measures thereof, if thou knowest?
Or who hath stretched the line upon it?
Whereupon are the foundations thereof fastened?
Or who laid the cornerstone thereof;
When the morning stars sang together,
And all the sons of God shouted for joy?
Or who shut up the sea with doors,
When it brake forth, as if it had issued out of the womb?
When I made the cloud the garment thereof,
And thick darkness a swaddling band for it,

And brake up for it my decreed place,
And set bars and doors,
And said, Hitherto shalt thou come, but no further:
And here shall thy proud waves be stayed?
Hast thou commanded the morning since thy days;
And caused the dayspring to know his place;
That it might take hold of the ends of the earth,
That the wicked might be shaken out of it?
It is turned as clay to the seal;
And they stand as a garment.
And from the wicked their light is withholden,
And the high arm shall be broken.
Hast thou entered into the springs of the sea?
Or hast thou walked in the search of the depth?
Have the gates of death been opened unto thee?
Or hast thou seen the doors of the shadow of death?
Hast thou perceived the breadth of the earth?
Declare if thou knowest it all.
Where is the way where light dwelleth?
And as for darkness, where is the place thereof,
That thou shouldest take it to the bound thereof,
And that thou shouldest know the paths to the house thereof?
Knowest thou it, because thou wast then born?
Or because the number of thy days is great?
Hast thou entered into the treasures of the snow?
Or hast thou seen the treasures of the hail,
Which I have reserved against the time of trouble,
Against the day of battle and war?
By what way is the light parted,
Which scattereth the east wind upon the earth?
Who hath divided a watercourse for the overflowing of waters,
Or a way for the lightning of thunder;
To cause it to rain on the earth, where no man is;
On the wilderness, wherein there is no man;
To satisfy the desolate and waste ground;
And to cause the bud of the tender herb to spring forth?
Hath the rain a father?
Or who hath begotten the drops of dew?
Out of whose womb came the ice?
And the hoary frost of heaven, who hath gendered it?
The waters are hid as with a stone,
And the face of the deep is frozen.
Canst thou bind the sweet influences of Pleiades,
Or loose the bands of Orion?
Canst thou bring forth Mazzaroth in his season?

Or canst thou guide Arcturus with his sons?
Knowest thou the ordinances of heaven?
Canst thou set the dominion thereof in the earth?
Canst thou lift up thy voice to the clouds,
That abundance of waters may cover thee?
Canst thou send lightnings, that they may go,
And say unto thee, Here we are?
Who hath put wisdom in the inward parts?
Or who hath given understanding to the heart?
Who can number the clouds in wisdom?
Or who can stay the bottles of heaven,
When the dust groweth into hardness,
And the clods cleave fast together?
Wilt thou hunt the prey for the lion?
Or fill the appetite of the young lions,
When they couch in their dens,
And abide in the covert to lie in wait?
Who provideth for the raven his food?
When his young ones cry unto God,
They wander for lack of meat.

Chapter 38

In the midst of God's relentless questioning, there are moments of the most exquisite description. Still challenging man's desire to know the reason for everything, and insisting on a final inexplicability—"Hath the rain a father? Who hath begotten the drops of dew?"—God pauses to emphasize the mystery of creation and the wonder of living things: the wild goats bearing their young in the inhospitable rocks, the proud peacock warming her eggs in the humble dust, the unicorn refusing to be tamed, the ravens miraculously fed, the eagle high and lonely, the hippopotamus with his tail "like a cedar." Perhaps the most winning tribute to His own creation is the half-realistic, half-rhapsodic picture of the horse.

The Horse

Hast thou given the horse strength?
Hast thou clothed his neck with thunder?
Canst thou make him afraid as a grasshopper?
The glory of his nostrils is terrible.
He paweth in the valley, and rejoiceth in his strength:
He goeth on to meet the armed men,

He mocketh at fear, and is not affrighted;
Neither turneth he back from the sword.
The quiver rattleth against him,
The glittering spear and the shield,
He swalloweth the ground with fierceness and rage:
Neither believeth he that it is the sound of the trumpet.
He saith among the trumpets, Ha! ha!
And he smelleth the battle afar off,
The thunder of the captains, and the shouting.

Chapter 39

Even more terrifying than God's splendor is His sarcasm. After inquiring where Job was when God first laid the foundations of the earth, the Almighty continues His devastating ironies in a mounting and never-to-be-forgotten interrogation. The portrait of leviathan, that monstrous crocodile turned dragon, is convincing not because of its cumulative array of facts, but because of its forceful poetry, its sense of breath-taking power.

Leviathan

Canst thou draw out leviathan with an hook?
Or his tongue with a cord which thou lettest down?
Canst thou put an hook into his nose?
Or bore his jaw through with a thorn?
Will he make many supplications unto thee?
Will he speak soft words unto thee?
Will he make a covenant with thee?
Wilt thou take him for a servant forever?
Wilt thou play with him as with a bird?
Or wilt thou bind him for thy maidens?
Shall the companions make a banquet of him?
Shall they part him among the merchants?
Canst thou fill his skin with barbed irons?
Or his head with fish spears?
Lay thine hand upon him,
Remember the battle, do no more.
Behold, the hope of him is in vain:
Shall not one be cast down even at the sight of him?
None is so fierce that dare stir him up:
Who then is able to stand before me?
Who hath prevented me, that I should repay him?

Whatsoever is under the whole heaven is mine.
I will not conceal his parts,
Nor his power, nor his comely proportion.
Who can discover the face of his garment?
Or who can come to him with his double bridle?
Who can open the doors of his face?
His teeth are terrible round about.
His scales are his pride,
Shut up together as with a close seal.
One is so near to another,
That no air can come between them.
They are joined one to another,
They stick together, that they cannot be sundered.
By his sneezings a light doth shine,
And his eyes are like the eyelids of the morning.
Out of his mouth go burning lamps,
And sparks of fire leap out.
Out of his nostrils goeth smoke,
As out of a seething pot or caldron.
His breath kindleth coals,
And a flame goeth out of his mouth.

Chapter 41

FROM

THE BOOK OF PSALMS

For most readers the heart of the Bible is THE BOOK OF PSALMS. The PSALMS are the peak of sacred poetry, a vast anthology of hymns which form "a divine poem." Three and a half centuries ago, Sir Philip Sidney, in THE DEFENSE OF POETRY, wrote that the author of the PSALMS made the reader see "God coming in His majesty, his telling of the beasts' joyfulness and the hills' leaping—a heavenly poesy wherein he showeth himself a passionate lover of that unspeakable and everlasting beauty to be seen by the eyes of the mind, only cleared by faith."

Three centuries later, R. E. Prothero extended Sidney's implication that the PSALMS were not limited to any age, country, or faith. In the PSALMS, wrote Prothero, are gathered a translation of man's victories and defeats, his proud passions, and his most beseeching prayers; "in the PSALMS the vast hosts of suffering humanity have found the deepest expression of their hopes and fears."

The Hebrew name for the PSALMS is *tehillim,* literally "praise-songs," and, although the PSALMS include meditations and laments, petitions and exhortations, most of the poems are songs of praise and thanksgiving. One of the most beautiful of the poems in which God's glory is magnified and man humbled is one of the earliest.

What Is Man?

O Lord our Lord,
How excellent is thy name in all the earth!
Who hast set thy glory above the heavens.
Out of the mouth of babes and sucklings hast thou ordained strength
Because of thine enemies,
That thou mightest still the enemy and the avenger.
When I consider thy heavens, the work of thy fingers,
The moon and the stars, which thou hast ordained;
What is man, that thou art mindful of him?
And the son of man, that thou visitest him?
For thou hast made him a little lower than the angels,
And hast crowned him with glory and honor.
Thou madest him to have dominion over the works of thy hands;
Thou hast put all things under his feet:
All sheep and oxen,
Yea, and the beasts of the field;
The fowl of the air, and the fish of the sea,
And whatsoever passeth through the paths of the seas.
O Lord our Lord,
How excellent is thy name in all the earth!

Psalm 8

The Hebrew poets rarely used rhyme. Instead of rhyming syllables, they employed the equally effective devices of balance and repetition to achieve sonority. The sustained music was carried over into English by the more than fifty scholars who, led by Lancelot Andrewes in the first part of the seventeenth century, prepared the Authorized Version for King James I. The Bible had been made into English as early as 1382; Tyndale's translation of 1526 was revised by many hands during the succeeding century. But it was not until 1611 that the work achieved a splendor of language which

English has never surpassed. The PSALMS were not only the most beautifully rendered but the most beloved. They won their place not only by their intrinsic splendor of language, but, as Henry Wheeler Robinson wrote in THE ENCYCLOPAEDIA BRITANNICA, by their power of reinterpretation "in order to meet the ever-changing needs of the unchanging human heart."

The "ever-changing needs of the unchanging human heart" are immediately apparent in the following three Psalms, the last of which is a masterpiece of simplicity and one of the deepest expres, sions of confidence ever uttered by man.

God's Glory

The heavens declare the glory of God;
And the firmament showeth his handiwork.
Day unto day uttereth speech,
And night unto night showeth knowledge.
There is no speech nor language
Where their voice is not heard.
Their line is gone out through all the earth,
And their words to the end of the world.
In them hath he set a tabernacle for the sun,
Which is as a bridegroom coming out of his chamber,
And rejoiceth as a strong man to run a race.
His going forth is from the end of the heaven,
And his circuit unto the ends of it:
And there is nothing hid from the heat thereof.
The law of the Lord is perfect, converting the soul:
The testimony of the Lord is sure, making wise the simple.
The statutes of the Lord are right, rejoicing the heart:
The commandment of the Lord is pure, enlightening the eyes.
The fear of the Lord is clean, enduring forever:
The judgments of the Lord are true and righteous altogether.
More to be desired are they than gold, yea, than much fine gold;
Sweeter also than honey and the honeycomb.
Moreover by them is thy servant warned;
In keeping of them there is great reward.
Who can understand his errors?
Cleanse thou me from secret faults.
Keep back thy servant also from presumptuous sins;
Let them not have dominion over me: then shall I be upright,

And I shall be innocent from the great transgression.
Let the words of my mouth, and the meditation of my heart, be
    acceptable in thy sight,
O Lord, my strength, and my redeemer.

Psalm 19

A Cry in Distress

My God, my God, why hast thou forsaken me?
Why art thou so far from helping me, and from the words of my
    roaring?
O my God, I cry in the daytime, but thou hearest not;
And in the night season, and am not silent.
But thou art holy,
O thou that inhabitest the praises of Israel.
Our fathers trusted in thee;
They trusted, and thou didst deliver them.
They cried unto thee, and were delivered;
They trusted in thee, and were not confounded.
But I am a worm, and no man;
A reproach of men, and despised of the people.
All they that see me laugh me to scorn;
They shoot out the lip, they shake the head, saying,
"He trusted on the Lord that he would deliver him:
Let him deliver him, seeing he delighted in him."
But thou art he that took me out of the womb:
Thou didst make me hope when I was upon my mother's breasts.
I was cast upon thee from the womb:
Thou art my God from my mother's belly.
Be not far from me; for trouble is near;
For there is none to help.
Many bulls have compassed me;
Strong bulls of Bashan have beset me round.
They gaped upon me with their mouths,
As a ravening and a roaring lion.
I am poured out like water,
And all my bones are out of joint:
My heart is like wax;
It is melted in the midst of my bowels.
My strength is dried up like a potsherd;
And my tongue cleaveth to my jaws;
And thou hast brought me into the dust of death.

Psalm 22

The Twenty-third Psalm

The Lord is my shepherd; I shall not want.
He maketh me to lie down in green pastures;
He leadeth me beside the still waters.
He restoreth my soul;
He leadeth me in the paths of righteousness for his name's sake.
Yea, though I walk through the valley of the shadow of death,
I will fear no evil: for thou art with me;
Thy rod and thy staff they comfort me.
Thou preparest a table before me in the presence of mine enemies:
Thou anointest my head with oil; my cup runneth over.
Surely goodness and mercy shall follow me all the days of my life,
And I will dwell in the house of the Lord forever.

Psalm 23

Many modern commentators have pointed out the resemblance between the loose meters of the ancient Hebrews and the broad rhythms of free verse. But, though recurrent cadences and parallel phrases form the basis of Biblical poetry, the movement of the PSALMS is more regular. In the surge of deep emotion, in the rise and fall of impassioned utterance, the blend of meaning and music, the PSALMS approximate a fluctuating blank verse. Only in Shakespeare can one find a movement so rich, a language so resonant.

Lift up Your Heads

The earth is the Lord's, and the fullness thereof;
The world, and they that dwell therein.
For he hath founded it upon the seas,
And established it upon the floods.
Who shall ascend into the hill of the Lord?
Or who shall stand in his holy place?
He that hath clean hands, and a pure heart;
Who hath not lifted up his soul unto vanity, nor sworn deceitfully.
He shall receive the blessing from the Lord,
And righteousness from the God of his salvation.
This is the generation of them that seek him,
That seek thy face, O Jacob.

Lift up your heads, O ye gates;
And be ye lift up, ye everlasting doors;
And the King of glory shall come in.
Who is this King of glory?
The Lord strong and mighty,
The Lord mighty in battle.
Lift up your heads, O ye gates;
Even lift them up, ye everlasting doors;
And the King of glory shall come in.
Who is this King of glory?
The Lord of hosts,
He is the King of glory.

Psalm 24

My Soul Thirsteth for God

As the hart panteth after the water brooks,
So panteth my soul after thee, O God.
My soul thirsteth for God, for the living God:
When shall I come and appear before God?
My tears have been my meat day and night,
While they continually say unto me, Where is thy God?
When I remember these things, I pour out my soul in me:
For I had gone with the multitude, I went with them to the house
    of God,
With the voice of joy and praise, with a multitude that kept holy-
    day.
Why art thou cast down, O my soul?
And why art thou disquieted in me?
Hope thou in God: for I shall yet praise him
For the help of his countenance.
O my God, my soul is cast down within me:
Therefore will I remember thee from the land of Jordan,
And of the Hermonites, from the hill Mizar.
Deep calleth unto deep at the noise of thy waterspouts;
All thy waves and thy billows are gone over me.
Yet the Lord will command his lovingkindness in the daytime,
And in the night his song shall be with me,
And my prayer unto the God of my life.
I will say unto God my rock, "Why hast thou forgotten me?
Why go I mourning because of the oppression of the enemy?"
As with a sword in my bones, mine enemies reproach me,
While they say daily unto me, "Where is thy God?"

Why art thou cast down, O my soul?
And why art thou disquieted within me?
Hope thou in God: for I shall yet praise him,
Who is the health of my countenance, and my God.

Psalm 42

Though the Earth Be Removed

God is our refuge and strength,
A very present help in trouble.
Therefore will not we fear, though the earth be removed,
And though the mountains be carried into the midst of the sea;
Though the waters thereof roar and be troubled,
Though the mountains shake with the swelling thereof.
There is a river, the streams whereof shall make glad the city of God,
The holy place of the tabernacles of the most High.
God is in the midst of her; she shall not be moved:
God shall help her, and that right early.
The heathen raged, the kingdoms were moved;
He uttered his voice, the earth melted.
The Lord of hosts is with us;
The God of Jacob is our refuge.
Come, behold the works of the Lord,
What desolations he hath made in the earth.
He maketh wars to cease unto the end of the earth;
He breaketh the bow, and cutteth the spear in sunder;
He burneth the chariot in the fire.
"Be still, and know that I am God:
I will be exalted among the heathen,
I will be exalted in the earth."
The Lord of hosts is with us;
The God of Jacob is our refuge.

Psalm 46

A Mighty Fortress

He that dwelleth in the secret place of the most High
Shall abide under the shadow of the Almighty.
I will say of the Lord, "He is my refuge and my fortress;
My God, in him will I trust."
Surely he shall deliver thee from the snare of the fowler.

And from the noisome pestilence.
He shall cover thee with his feathers,
And under his wings shalt thou trust;
His truth shall be thy shield and buckler.
Thou shalt not be afraid for the terror by night;
Nor for the arrow that flieth by day;
Nor for the pestilence that walketh in darkness;
Nor for the destruction that wasteth at noonday.
A thousand shall fall at thy side,
And ten thousand at thy right hand;
But it shall not come nigh thee.
Only with thine eyes shalt thou behold
And see the reward of the wicked.
Because thou hast made the Lord, which is my refuge,
Even the most High, thy habitation;
There shall no evil befall thee,
Neither shall any plague come nigh thy dwelling.
For he shall give his angels charge over thee,
To keep thee in all thy ways.
They shall bear thee up in their hands,
Lest thou dash thy foot against a stone.
Thou shalt tread upon the lion and adder;
The young lion and the dragon shalt thou trample under feet.
Because he hath set his love upon me, therefore will I deliver him:
I will set him on high, because he hath known my name.
He shall call upon me, and I will answer him;
I will be with him in trouble;
I will deliver him, and honor him.
With long life will I satisfy him,
And show him my salvation.

Psalm 91

The Floods Clap Their Hands

O sing unto the Lord a new song,
For he hath done marvelous things:
His right hand, and his holy arm, hath gotten him the victory.
The Lord hath made known his salvation;
His righteousness hath he openly showed in the sight of the heathen.
He hath remembered his mercy and his truth toward the house of
    Israel:
All the ends of the earth have seen the salvation of our God.
Make a joyful noise unto the Lord, all the earth:

Make a loud noise and rejoice, and sing praise.
Sing unto the Lord with the harp,
With the harp, and the voice of a psalm.
With trumpets and sound of cornet
Make a joyful noise before the Lord, the King.
Let the sea roar, and the fullness thereof;
The world, and they that dwell therein.
Let the floods clap their hands;
Let the hills be joyful together before the Lord;
For he cometh to judge the earth;
With righteousness shall he judge the world,
And the people with equity.

Psalm 98

A Song of Trust

I will lift up mine eyes unto the hills,
From whence cometh my help.
My help cometh from the Lord,
Which made heaven and earth.
He will not suffer thy foot to be moved;
He that keepeth thee will not slumber.
Behold, he that keepeth Israel
Shall neither slumber nor sleep.
The Lord is thy keeper;
The Lord is thy shade upon thy right hand.
The sun shall not smite thee by day,
Nor the moon by night.
The Lord shall preserve thee from all evil;
He shall preserve thy soul.
The Lord shall preserve thy going out and thy coming in
From this time forth, and even for evermore.

Psalm 121

A Song of Supplication

Out of the depths have I cried unto thee, O Lord.
Lord, hear my voice:
Let thine ears be attentive to the voice of my supplications.
If thou, Lord, shouldest mark iniquities,
O Lord, who shall stand?

But there is forgiveness with thee,
That thou mayest be feared.
I wait for the Lord, my soul doth wait,
And in his word do I hope.
My soul waiteth for the Lord
More than they that watch for the morning,
I say, more than they that watch for the morning.
Let Israel hope in the Lord,
For with the Lord there is mercy,
And with him is plenteous redemption.
And he shall redeem Israel
From all his iniquities.

Psalm 130

A Song of Exile

By the rivers of Babylon,
There we sat down, yea, we wept,
When we remembered Zion.
We hanged our harps
Upon the willows in the midst thereof.
For there they that carried us away captive required of us a song,
And they that wasted us required of us mirth, saying,
"Sing us one of the songs of Zion."
How shall we sing the Lord's song
In a strange land?
If I forget thee, O Jerusalem,
Let my right hand forget her cunning.
If I do not remember thee,
Let my tongue cleave to the roof of my mouth;
If I prefer not Jerusalem above my chief joy.

Psalm 137

A Song of Praise

Praise ye the Lord.
Praise ye the Lord from the heavens:
Praise him in the heights.
Praise ye him, all his angels:
Praise ye him, all his hosts.
Praise ye him, sun and moon:

Praise him, all ye stars of light.
Praise him, ye heavens of heavens,
And ye waters that be above the heavens.
Let them praise the name of the Lord:
For he commanded, and they were created.
He hath also stablished them for ever and ever;
He hath made a decree which shall not pass.
Praise the Lord from the earth,
Ye dragons, and all deeps,
Fire and hail, snow and vapors,
Stormy wind fulfilling his word,
Mountains and all hills,
Fruitful trees and all cedars,
Beasts and all cattle,
Creeping things and flying fowl,
Kings of the earth and all people,
Princes and all judges of the earth:
Both young men and maidens,
Old men and children—
Let them praise the name of the Lord;
For his name alone is excellent;
His glory is above the earth and heaven.
He also exalteth the horn of his people,
The praise of all his saints;
Even of the children of Israel, a people near unto him.
Praise ye the Lord.

Psalm 148

FROM

THE PROVERBS

SCHOLARS agree that the Bible is not a unified work, but a vast assembly of actual history and fantastic legend; of eternal law, indisputable logic, and rolling lamentations; of exalted hymns and erotic songs; of tales that turn into parables, and parables that have become the world's great stories; of prophetic prose and exalted poetry—in short, an entire literature in itself. Heinrich Heine said that the Book embodied "the whole drama of humanity"; to James George Frazer, author of THE GOLDEN BOUGH, the Bible "is the epic of the world." Arthur Quiller-Couch wrote that the scope of the

Bible could only be indicated by imagining a volume including
the great books of our literature all bound together in magnificent
confusion.

The Bible's lack of orderly sequence applies particularly to THE
PROVERBS. This collection of adages and gnomic poetry comes im-
mediately after the last exhortation of the PSALMS and precedes the
stubborn cynicism of ECCLESIASTES. The proverbs themselves are of
many sorts. Some are questionable conclusions, others are eternally
applicable; some are prudent social maxims, others are daringly
imaginative flights. In the best of them wisdom is packed in an epi-
gram, and a calm reasonableness rises into poetry.

A Reproof

Go to the ant, thou sluggard;
Consider her ways, and be wise:
Which having no guide,
Overseer, or ruler,
Provideth her meat in the summer,
And gathereth her food in the harvest.

How long wilt thou sleep, O sluggard?
When wilt thou arise out of thy sleep?
Yet a little sleep, a little slumber,
A little folding of the hands to sleep:
So shall thy poverty come as one that traveleth,
And thy want as an armed man.

Chapter 6

Seven Evils

These six things doth the Lord hate;
Yea, seven are an abomination unto him:
A proud look, a lying tongue,
And hands that shed innocent blood;
An heart that deviseth wicked imaginations,
Feet that be swift in running to mischief;
A false witness that speaketh lies,
And he that soweth discord among brethren.

Chapter 6

The House of Wisdom

Wisdom hath builded her house,
She hath hewn out her seven pillars:
She hath killed her beasts; she hath mingled her wine;
She hath also furnished her table.
She hath sent forth her maidens, she crieth
Upon the highest places of the city,
"Whoso is simple, let him turn in hither":
As for him that wanteth understanding, she saith to him,
"Come, eat ye of my bread,
And drink of the wine which I have mingled.
Forsake the foolish, and live;
And go in the way of understanding."

Chapter 9

The Lips of the Wise

A soft answer turneth away wrath:
But grievous words stir up anger.
The tongue of the wise useth knowledge aright:
But the mouth of fools poureth out foolishness.

The eyes of the Lord are in every place,
Beholding the evil and the good.

A wholesome tongue is a tree of life:
But perverseness therein is a breach in the spirit.

A fool despiseth his father's instruction:
But he that regardeth reproof is prudent.

.   .   .   .   .   .

The lips of the wise disperse knowledge:
But the heart of the foolish doeth not so.

The sacrifice of the wicked is an abomination to the Lord:
But the prayer of the upright is his delight.

.   .   .   .   .   .

All the days of the afflicted are evil:
But he that is of a merry heart hath a continual feast.

Better is little with the fear of the Lord
Than great treasure and trouble therewith.

Better is a dinner of herbs where love is,
Than a stalled ox and hatred therewith.

Chapter 15

The Bible is full of parallelisms in thought and phrase, and THE
PROVERBS make particular use of this device. Balance and contrast
are employed with vigorous effect in the comparison of the foolish
woman and the good wife.

A Foolish Woman

A foolish woman is clamorous;
She is simple, and knoweth nothing.
For she sitteth at the door of her house,
On a seat in the high places of the city,
To call passengers
Who go right on their ways.
Whoso is simple, let him turn in hither:
And as for him that wanteth understanding, she saith to him,
"Stolen waters are sweet,
And bread eaten in secret is pleasant."
But he knoweth not that the dead are there;
That her guests are in the depths of hell.

Chapter 9

The Good Wife

Who can find a virtuous woman?
For her price is far above rubies.

The heart of her husband doth safely trust in her,
So that he shall have no need of spoil.

She will do him good and not evil
All the days of her life.

She seeketh wool and flax,
And worketh willingly with her hands.

She is like the merchants' ships;
She bringeth her food from afar.

She riseth also while it is yet night,
And giveth meat to her household, and a portion to her maidens.
She considereth a field, and buyeth it:
With the fruit of her hands she planteth a vineyard.

She girdeth her loins with strength,
And strengtheneth her arms.
She perceiveth that her merchandise is good:
Her candle goeth not out by night.

She layeth her hands to the spindle,
And her hands hold the distaff.
She stretcheth out her hand to the poor;
Yea, she reacheth forth her hands to the needy.

She is not afraid of the snow for her household:
For all her household are clothed with scarlet.
She maketh herself coverings of tapestry;
Her clothing is silk and purple.

Her husband is known in the gates,
When he sitteth among the elders of the land.

She maketh fine linen, and selleth it;
And delivereth girdles unto the merchant.

Strength and honor are her clothing;
And she shall rejoice in time to come.
She openeth her mouth with wisdom;
And in her tongue is the law of kindness.

She looketh well to the ways of her household,
And eateth not the bread of idleness.
Her children arise up, and call her blessed;
Her husband also, and he praiseth her:
"Many daughters have done virtuously,
But thou excellest them all."

Favor is deceitful, and beauty is vain:
But a woman that feareth the Lord,
She shall be praised.

Give her of the fruit of her hands;
And let her own works praise her in the gates.

Chapter 31

Stress has often been laid upon the "international" character of
THE PROVERBS. The various contributors to this anthology of
thoughts—and Solomon was only one of the more famous—implied
that their words came from the Lord and that Jehovah was the
unique source of all wisdom. But the virtues of truthfulness, thrift,
industry, and honesty were universally accepted, if not always prac-
ticed, before Solomon's sponsorship, about one thousand years B.C.
Many of the gnomic sayings were common throughout the Orient
in pre-Solomonic days; one section of THE PROVERBS bears startling
resemblances to a recently deciphered Egyptian text, THE TEACHING
OF AMENOPHIS.

The "words" of Agur are among the most inspirational and the
most puzzling in the collection. We know little of Agur except that
he was the son of Jakeh, of whom we know nothing. He seems to
have been a foreign prophet, but his aphorisms were so suggestive
that the Hebrew sages gladly incorporated them into their doc-
trine. Agur was a mystic who anticipated the disciples in their belief
in the limitations of the intellect and in their faith in things unseen.
His cryptic questions, illumined with imaginative daring, echo the
penetrating inquiries of the Voice that challenged Job out of the
whirlwind.

The Words of Agur

Who hath gathered the wind in his fists?
Who hath bound the waters in a garment?
Who hath established all the ends of the earth?
What is his name, and what is his son's name,
If thou canst tell?

    .   .   .   .   .

There are three things that are never satisfied,
Yea, four things say not, "It is enough":

The grave; and the barren womb;
The earth that is not filled with water;
And the fire that saith not, "It is enough."

    .   .   .   .

There be three things which are too wonderful for me,
Yea, four which I know not:

The way of an eagle in the air;
The way of a serpent upon a rock;
The way of a ship in the midst of the sea;
And the way of a man with a maid.
. . . .
There be four things which are little upon the earth,
But they are exceeding wise:

The ants are a people not strong,
Yet they prepare their meat in the summer;

The conies are but a feeble folk,
Yet they make their houses in the rocks;

The locusts have no king,
Yet they go forth all of them by bands;

The spider taketh hold with her hands,
And is in kings' palaces.

Chapter 30

FROM

EXODUS

THE children of Israel had escaped one of the earliest and harsh-
est of their oppressors. They had found a path in the midst of
the sea; the water had made way for the Chosen People and then,
returning to its place, had engulfed the pursuing enemy. The
Egyptians were overthrown "and the people feared the Lord and
His servant Moses." They said it over and over again in their song
of triumph.

It was not a formal song, although the scribes later gave it a
form. It was a half-religious, half-savage outburst, punctuated with
the clapping of hands and the beating of drums, a song of a vast
community. One must imagine a single voice announcing the
theme. and choruses of many voices repeating the responses. Women

added a mixed harmony, but the men predominated. It is likely that the chant was danced as well as sung, each of the twelve tribes echoing the refrain. All night they sang and danced around huge campfires piled high with driftwood and the Egyptians' chariot wheels.

Triumphal Chant

I will sing unto the Lord, for he hath triumphed gloriously:
The horse and his rider hath he thrown into the sea.

The Lord is my strength and song,
And he is become my salvation:
He is my God, and I will prepare him an habitation;
My father's God, and I will exalt him.

The Lord is a man of war:
The Lord is his name.
Pharaoh's chariots and his host hath he cast into the sea:
His chosen captains also are drowned in the Red Sea.
The depths have covered them:
They sank into the bottom as a stone.

Thy right hand, O Lord, is become glorious in power:
Thy right hand, O Lord, hath dashed in pieces the enemy.
And in the greatness of thine excellency thou hast overthrown them
    that rose up against thee:
Thou sentest forth thy wrath, which consumed them as stubble.
And with the blast of thy nostrils the waters were gathered together,
The floods stood upright as a heap,
And the depths were congealed in the heart of the sea.

The enemy said, "I will pursue, I will overtake, I will divide the
    spoil;
My lust shall be satisfied upon them;
I will draw my sword, my hand shall destroy them."
Thou didst blow with thy wind, the sea covered them:
They sank as lead in the mighty waters.

Who is like unto thee, O Lord, among the gods?
Who is like thee, glorious in holiness,
Fearful in praises, doing wonders?

Thou stretchedst out thy right hand,
The earth swallowed them.

Thou in thy mercy hast led forth the people
Which thou hast redeemed:
Thou hast guided them in thy strength
Unto thy holy habitation.

.   .   .   .

The Lord shall reign
For ever and ever.

Chapter 15

FROM

NUMBERS

THE Old Testament luxuriates in contrasts, and no contrast to the triumphal chant of Moses could be greater than the benediction which occurs in NUMBERS. In the very midst of codes, legal regulations, petty injunctions, dry computations, and census taking, there suddenly appears a form of blessing which is elemental in its grace, eternal in its comfort.

Benediction

The Lord bless thee and keep thee:
The Lord make his face shine upon thee,
And be gracious unto thee:
The Lord lift up his countenance upon thee,
And give thee peace.

Chapter 6

NUMBERS is distinguished by one of the most dramatic narratives in the Old Testament. It centers about Balaam, King of Pethor, a seer and a man divided against himself. Bound in a treaty to the kings of Moab, he opposed the Israelites, yet his prophetic nature could not deny their God. Balaam went out to denounce the Hebrews and to destroy them; but "the spirit of God came upon him," and the necromancer was lost in the visionary. Instead of cursing the Israelites, he found himself blessing them.

Balaam's Blessing

How goodly are thy tents, O Jacob,
And thy tabernacles, O Israel!
As the valleys are they spread forth,
As gardens by the river's side,
As the trees of lign aloes which the Lord hath planted,
And as cedar trees beside the waters.
He shall pour the water out of his buckets,
And his seed shall be in many waters,
And his king shall be higher than Agag,
And his kingdom shall be exalted.

God brought him forth out of Egypt;
He hath as it were the strength of a unicorn:
He shall eat up the nations his enemies,
And shall break their bones,
And pierce them through with his arrows.
He couched, he lay down as a lion,
And as a great lion: who shall stir him up?
Blessed is he that blesseth thee,
And cursed is he that curseth thee.

Chapter 24

FROM

THE BOOK OF RUTH

THE BOOK OF RUTH originated as a piece of history; it is remem-
bered as a work of fiction. Presumably written in the fourth
century B.C. as a protest against Nehemiah's and Ezra's restrictions
on racial intermarriage, the work has been relished for centuries
because of the appeal of its characters and the sheer telling of a
tale. It echoes through the ages. We hear its overtones in a nine-
teenth-century poet's evocation of heartache when Keats, in the
ODE TO A NIGHTINGALE (page 768), follows the bird's song back
through the centuries—

Through the sad heart of Ruth, when, sick for home,
She stood in tears amid the alien corn.

This pastoral of Boaz, "a mighty man of wealth," an ancestor of King David, and Ruth, a poor Moabite girl, has retained its popu·larity, not because of its message of racial tolerance, but because of the simple legend told in simple language. It is almost the first, as it is the loveliest, of the long line of Cinderella myths.

Perhaps the most famous passage is Ruth's moving address to Naomi, her mother-in-law. The short speech is a model of dignity and unshakable devotion.

Ruth to Naomi

Entreat me not to leave thee,
Or to return from following after thee:
For whither thou goest,
I will go;
And where thou lodgest,
I will lodge.
Thy people shall be my people,
And thy God my God.
Where thou diest, will I die,
And there will I be buried.

The Lord do so to me, and more also,
If ought but death part thee and me.
Chapter 1

FROM

THE SECOND BOOK OF SAMUEL

DAVID had been a shepherd, a harpist, the "sweet singer of Israel," an outlaw, and a man of war. He had been the right hand of King Saul and had fought against him; he had sworn blood brotherhood with Saul's son, Jonathan—"the soul of Jonathan was knit with the soul of David." Now David was ruler, but the price of his crown was the slaughter of his king and the death of his beloved friend.

David's triumph is signaled by an outburst of grief. His lament
is noble and eloquent, a dirge which is one of the world's most
moving poems.

David's Lament

The beauty of Israel is slain upon thy high places:
How are the mighty fallen!
Tell it not in Gath,
Publish it not in the streets of Askelon;
Lest the daughters of the Philistines rejoice,
Lest the daughters of the uncircumcised triumph.

Ye mountains of Gilboa,
Let there be no dew, neither let there be rain, upon you, nor fields
    of offerings:
For there the shield of the mighty is vilely cast away,
The shield of Saul, as though he had not been anointed with oil.
From the blood of the slain, from the fat of the mighty,
The bow of Jonathan turned not back,
And the sword of Saul returned not empty.

Saul and Jonathan were lovely and pleasant in their lives,
And in their death they were not divided:
They were swifter than eagles,
They were stronger than lions.
Ye daughters of Israel, weep over Saul,
Who clothed you in scarlet, with other delights,
Who put on ornaments of gold upon your apparel.
How are the mighty fallen in the midst of the battle!

O Jonathan, thou wast slain in thine high places.
I am distressed for thee, my brother Jonathan:
Very pleasant hast thou been unto me:
Thy love to me was wonderful,
Passing the love of women.

How are the mighty fallen,
And the weapons of war perished!

Chapter 1

FROM

ECCLESIASTES

H IS name in Hebrew was Koheleth; the Greek translators turned it into Ecclesiastes, one who takes part in the debates of an assembly, or *ecclesia*. At the beginning the sage was identified with King Solomon, but his name gave him away. The root of Koheleth is *kahal*, an assembly. Yet, instead of indicating that the author was a member of an august body, it meant merely that his book was a collection of thoughts, an assembling of observations and speculations.

Koheleth's book begins and ends with "Vanity of vanities; all is vanity." But, though this is the keynote of his philosophy, it is a wry commentary rather than a serious criticism of life. The author takes life lightly, and he rather expects his reader to take him without undue solemnity. Later editors made the book solemn enough. Many hands interpolated extrareligious conclusions and twisted the gentle cynicism to fit a work of sacred character. Morris Jastrow, Jr., one of the keenest modern Biblical scholars, published an entire volume to show how the text of the original Koheleth was converted from an unorthodox production into an unobjectionable one. Pointing out the contradictions and inconsistencies, Jastrow wrote: "If we can imagine Homer or Virgil published with the scholia of later commentators put into the body of the text, or the quatrains of Omar Khayyám with the comments and pious reflections of orthodox Mohammedans added, as though forming part of the original, in order to counteract unorthodox sentiments about 'wine, woman, and song,' one will be able to form an impression of the text as finally fixed and as it now stands in our Bible."

One of Koheleth's most famous utterances is neither misanthropic nor skeptical. It is a short essay in which he speaks as an observer, an observer who recognizes order in the universe and in the very antitheses of things.

A Time for Everything

To everything there is a season,
And a time to every purpose under the heaven:
A time to be born, and a time to die;
A time to plant, and a time to pluck up that which is planted;
A time to kill, and a time to heal;
A time to break down, and a time to build up;
A time to weep, and a time to laugh;
A time to mourn, and a time to dance;
A time to cast away stones, and a time to gather stones together;
A time to embrace, and a time to refrain from embracing;
A time to get, and a time to lose;
A time to keep, and a time to cast away;
A time to rend, and a time to sew;
A time to keep silence, and a time to speak;
A time to love, and a time to hate;
A time of war, and a time of peace.

Chapter 3

Human life, Koheleth concludes, is brief and unsatisfying. Man thinks too little and talks too much. Even in the third century B.C. there was an overproduction of literature: "of the making of many books there is no end." Men plan great works and amuse themselves with follies, collect treasures, pass laws, and beget children. But to what purpose? "All is vanity, absolute vanity," Koheleth tells us with casual but grim reiteration.

If there is nothing sacred, or even dignified in human existence, there are at least some compensating pleasures to be wrung from life. Seize the present, gather ye rosebuds while ye may, says this unorthodox preacher, anticipating the hedonists and the reckless Elizabethans; take joy in youth, exult in strength, for old age comes fast with crippling infirmities. Soon, Koheleth insists in a half-realistic, half-allegorical climax, the legs grow weak ("the strong men shall bow themselves"), the teeth decay ("the grinders cease because they are few"), the eyes fail ("those that look out of the windows be darkened"), familiar sounds begin to blur ("the sound of the grinding is low"), walking on the highway is dangerous, sleep becomes difficult, and desire dies. Therefore, before the machine

breaks down and the evil days draw near, take hold of happiness—
and, Koheleth adds in a pious afterthought, "remember thy Cre-
ator."

Youth and Age

Remember now thy Creator in the days of thy youth,
While the evil days come not,
Nor the years draw nigh, when thou shalt say,
"I have no pleasure in them";
While the sun, or the light,
Or the moon, or the stars, be not darkened,
Nor the clouds return after the rain:
In the day when the keepers of the house shall tremble,
And the strong men shall bow themselves,
And the grinders cease because they are few,
And those that look out of the windows be darkened,
And the doors shall be shut in the streets;
When the sound of the grinding is low,
And he shall rise up at the voice of the bird,
And all the daughters of music shall be brought low;
Also when they shall be afraid of that which is high,
And fears shall be in the way;
And the almond tree shall flourish,
And the grasshopper shall be a burden,
And desire shall fail:
Because man goeth to his long home,
And the mourners go about the streets:
Or ever the silver cord be loosed,
Or the golden bowl be broken,
Or the pitcher be broken at the fountain,
Or the wheel broken at the cistern;

Then shall the dust return to the earth as it was,
And the spirit shall return unto God who gave it.

Vanity of vanities, saith the preacher;
All is vanity.

Chapter 12

FROM

ISAIAH

THE plain heresies of ECCLESIASTES, like the sensual ecstasies of THE SONG OF SONGS, are incongruities in the Bible; they were incorporated in the Scriptures not only because they were relished by unbelievers, but because they were popular with the average tolerant man. The words of Isaiah appealed to a wholly different audience. Isaiah spoke as a patrician; although he was sympathetic with the "proletarian" prophets, his idiom was intellectually, even spiritually, aristocratic. A shrewd statesman, he helped guide the Jews of the eighth century B.C. through alliances and invasions, appeasement and perilous wars. In the end he lost. When the pagan influence conquered, Isaiah was martyred; it is said that he was sawn in two.

As prophet Isaiah was the first fully to express the Messianic ideal. His visionary power extended beyond contemporary conflict to reconstruction and peace. "And there shall come forth a rod out of the stem of Jesse, and a branch shall grow out of his roots: and the spirit of the Lord shall rest upon him." In that time, Isaiah foresaw, "the wolf shall dwell with the lamb and the leopard shall lie down with the kid . . . and a little child shall lead them." Tyrants shall be humbled, the wicked city brought low, Israel shall be restored, and the Golden Age dawn on a world transformed.

Downfall of the Tyrant

How hath the oppressor ceased!
The golden city ceased!
The Lord hath broken the staff of the wicked,
And the scepter of the rulers.
He who smote the people in wrath with a continual stroke,
He that ruled the nations in anger,
Is persecuted, and none hindereth.
The whole earth is at rest, and is quiet:
They break forth into singing.
Yea, the fir trees rejoice at thee,

And the cedars of Lebanon, saying,
"Since thou art laid down,
No feller is come up against us."
Hell from beneath is moved for thee
To meet thee at thy coming:
It stirreth up the dead for thee,
Even all the chief ones of the earth;
It hath raised up from their thrones all the kings of the nations.
All they shall speak and say unto thee,
"Art thou also become weak as we?
Art thou become like unto us?"
Thy pomp is brought down to the grave,
And the noise of thy viols:
The worm is spread under thee,
And the worms cover thee.
How art thou fallen from heaven,
O Lucifer, son of the morning!
How art thou cut down to the ground,
Which didst weaken the nations!
For thou hast said in thine heart, "I will ascend into heaven,
I will exalt my throne above the stars of God:
I will sit also upon the mount of the congregation,
In the sides of the north:
I will ascend above the heights of the clouds;
I will be like the most High."
Yet thou shalt be brought down to hell,
To the sides of the pit.
They that see thee shall narrowly look upon thee.
And consider thee, saying,
"Is this the man that made the earth to tremble,
That did shake kingdoms;
That made the world as a wilderness, and destroyed the cities
    thereof;
That opened not the house of his prisoners?"
All the kings of the nations, even all of them, lie in glory,
Every one in his own house.
But thou art cast out of thy grave
Like an abominable branch,
And as the raiment of those that are slain,
Thrust through with a sword,
That go down to the stones of the pit;
As a carcass trodden under feet.

Chapter 14

FROM

FROM
THE GOSPEL ACCORDING TO SAINT MATTHEW

ALTHOUGH the dates of the four Gospels are still disputed, the order of the Gospels is generally accepted. The first is the basis for the others; Mark is the authority for the narrative which incorporates the events in the life of Jesus. Matthew was less concerned with the tale than with the teaching. Matthew had a sense that was both literary and visionary; it is to Matthew that we owe the beauty of the Sermon on the Mount with the perfection of the Beatitudes and the Lord's Prayer. Luke, the physician, drew upon Mark's biographical narrative, made some corrections, and added a new gentleness. John was the mystic; it was John who insisted that Jesus, instead of being the human Messiah awaited by the Jews, was actually a divine spirit, the very Son of God.

There is no more exalted moment in the New Testament than the beginning of the fifth chapter in MATTHEW. Here Jesus, seeing the multitudes before him, delivers "the new Law of the Kingdom of Heaven" which has been immortalized as the Sermon on the Mount.

The Beatitudes

Blessed are the poor in spirit:
For theirs is the kingdom of heaven.

Blessed are they that mourn:
For they shall be comforted.

Blessed are the meek:
For they shall inherit the earth.

Blessed are they which do hunger and thirst after righteousness:
For they shall be filled.

Blessed are the merciful:
For they shall obtain mercy.

Blessed are the pure in heart:
For they shall see God.

Blessed are the peacemakers:
For they shall be called the children of God.

Blessed are they which are persecuted for righteousness' sake:
For theirs is the kingdom of heaven.
                              Chapter 5: Sermon on the Mount

The Lord's Prayer

Our Father which art in heaven,
Hallowed be thy name.
Thy kingdom come.
Thy will be done
In earth, as it is in heaven.

Give us this day
Our daily bread.
And forgive us our debts,
As we forgive our debtors.
And lead us not into temptation,
But deliver us from evil

For thine is the kingdom,
And the power,
And the glory,
Forever. Amen.
                    Chapter 6: Sermon on the Mount

Treasures

Lay not up for yourselves treasures upon earth,
Where moth and rust doth corrupt,
And where thieves break through and steal:

But lay up for yourselves treasures in heaven,
Where neither moth nor rust doth corrupt,
And where thieves do not break through nor steal.
For where your treasure is, there will your heart be also.
                         Chapter 6: Sermon on the Mount

FROM

THE GOSPEL ACCORDING TO SAINT JOHN

JOHN, the latest of the Gospel writers, is a link between his predecessors and Paul. John's central message is love: the love of man for God and the love of God for man. John the mystic does not scorn the world of action, but he stresses faith rather than works. The very prologue to his book radiates mystical affirmation.

The Word

In the beginning was the Word,
And the Word was with God,
And the Word was God.

The same was in the beginning with God.

All things were made by Him;
And without Him was not anything made that was made.

In Him was life;
And the life was the light of men.

And the light shineth in darkness;
And the darkness comprehended it not.

Chapter 1

FROM

THE FIRST EPISTLE TO THE CORINTHIANS

PAUL OF TARSUS, born an orthodox Jew and trained as a rabbi, was the first great Christian missionary. His travels, his broad culture, and his fervid spirit changed Christianity from a sect of Judaism to a world religion. His many letters written between A.D. 50 and A.D. 70 prove him to be the most forceful of converts and the fiercest of theologians.

THE FIRST EPISTLE TO THE CORINTHIANS shows Paul at his most eloquent. The preacher becomes the poet, and (except for Paul's low estimate of women) argument is transcended by nobility.

The Greatest of These

Though I speak with the tongues of men and of angels,
And have not charity,
I am become as sounding brass,
Or a tinkling cymbal.

And though I have the gift of prophecy,
And understand all mysteries, and all knowledge;
And though I have all faith,
So that I could remove mountains,
And have not charity,
I am nothing.

And though I bestow all my goods to feed the poor,
And though I give my body to be burned,
And have not charity,
It profiteth me nothing.

Charity suffereth long, and is kind;
Charity envieth not;
Charity vaunteth not itself, is not puffed up,

Doth not behave itself unseemly,
Seeketh not her own.

Is not easily provoked,
Thinketh no evil;
Rejoiceth not in iniquity, but rejoiceth in the truth;
Beareth all things,
Believeth all things,
Hopeth all things,
Endureth all things.

Charity never faileth:
But whether there be prophecies, they shall fail;
Whether there be tongues, they shall cease;
Whether there be knowledge, it shall vanish away.

    .   .   .   .

When I was a child,
I spake as a child,
I understood as a child,
I thought as a child.
But when I became a man,
I put away childish things.

For now we see through a glass, darkly;
But then face to face:
Now I know in part;
But then shall I know even as also I am known.

And now abideth faith, hope, charity,
These three;
But the greatest of these is charity.

Chapter 13

FROM

THE REVELATION OF SAINT JOHN THE DIVINE

THE Bible comes to a tumultuous close with an apocalyptical
vision, supposed to be the revelation of Jesus to John on Pat-
mos. The work is one of great tension and urgency, for it presumes
to show "the things which must come to pass shortly."
The book does not lend itself to ready comprehension; it is pos-

sible that during a time of persecution and suppression—the time of the early Christian martyrs—the writing was purposely obscure, a set of elaborate double meanings. "Dominated by conceptions of war and revenge," Ernest Sutherland Bates concluded, "the work is ethically on a lower plane than the rest of the New Testament, but from the strictly literary point of view it is the most magnificent of the later books of the Bible . . . the drama is enacted in an unearthly metallic atmosphere, at times grimly lurid and then again blinding in its splendor; and always to the accompaniment of piercing choruses of despair or victory."

The Apocalypse has as its background the downfall of tyranny, as symbolized by Rome, the kingdom of Antichrist. But its fierce imagery, its pictorial power and sonority, create an intensity beyond explanation.

The New Jerusalem

And I saw a new heaven and a new earth:
For the first heaven and the first earth were passed away;
And there was no more sea.

And I, John, saw the holy city,
The new Jerusalem,
Coming down from God out of heaven,
Prepared as a bride adorned for her husband.

And I heard a great voice out of heaven saying,
"Behold, the tabernacle of God is with men,
And he will dwell with them,
And they shall be his people,
And God himself shall be with them,
And be their God.

"And God shall wipe away all tears from their eyes;
And there shall be no more death,
Neither sorrow, nor crying,
Neither shall there be any more pain:
For the former things are passed away."

And he that sat upon the throne said,
"Behold, I make all things new."
And he said unto me,
"Write: for these words are true and faithful."

And he said unto me,
"It is done.
I am Alpha and Omega,
The beginning and the end.
I will give unto him that is athirst
Of the fountain of the water of life freely."

    .   .   .   .

And he carried me away in the spirit
To a great and high mountain,
And showed me that great city,
The holy Jerusalem,
Descending out of heaven from God,

Having the glory of God:
And her light was like unto a stone most precious,
Even like a jasper stone,
Clear as crystal;

And had a wall great and high,
And had twelve gates,
And at the gates twelve angels,
And names written thereon,
Which are the names of the twelve tribes
Of the children of Israel.

    .   .   .   .   .   .

And the twelve gates were twelve pearls;
Every several gate was of one pearl:
And the street of the city was pure gold,
As it were transparent glass.

    .   .   .   .   .   .

And the city had no need of the sun,
Neither of the moon, to shine in it:
For the glory of God did lighten it,
And the Lamb is the light thereof.

And the nations of them which are saved
Shall walk in the light of it:
And the kings of the earth
Do bring their glory and honor into it.

And the gates of it shall not be shut at all by day:
For there shall be no night there.

Chapter 21

There Shall Be No Night

And he showed me a pure river of water of life,
Clear as crystal,
Proceeding out of the throne of God and of the Lamb.

In the midst of the street of it,
And on either side of the river,
Was there the tree of life,
Which bare twelve manner of fruits,
And yielded her fruit every month:
And the leaves of the tree were for the healing of the nations.

And there shall be no more curse:
But the throne of God and of the Lamb shall be in it;
And his servants shall serve him:

And they shall see his face;
And his name shall be in their foreheads.

And there shall be no night there;
And they need no candle, neither light of the sun;
For the Lord God giveth them light:
And they shall reign for ever and ever.

Chapter 22

II

Foundations of the English Spirit

THE first great work of English literature is a throwback to the heroic age of the Anglo-Saxons, yet no Anglo-Saxon character is celebrated in the poem. The epic of unknown authorship, BEOWULF, dates from a manuscript of the tenth century and concerns itself with Swedes and Danes and an uncertain but warlike tribe called the Geats. It is thought that the Viking Danes may have brought the outlines of the poem to England as early as the seventh century, but researchers are still busy tracing its remote origins. The work itself is partly historical, partly mythical. It revolves about Beowulf, King of the Geats, his companion, his exploits—particularly his combats with a treasure-guarding dragon and a pair of monsters, Grendel and Grendel's mother—and his death.

Written in Old English, a language incomprehensible to all but the scholars, with a vocabulary practically obsolete, BEOWULF lends itself poorly to translation. It is not only the language hazards but the very devices of Anglo-Saxon poetry which make the poem difficult to follow. The rules were strict. Each line of BEOWULF contains four accented syllables plus several unaccented ones, and the rule insisted that there should be a marked pause between the second and third accents. To make the verse more resonant, and more difficult, the first three accented syllables in each line were forced to begin with the same sound. Besides the strict alliteration, the

Anglo-Saxons were also fond of a primitive kind of metaphor known as a *kenning*. A kenning was something between a puzzle and a packed phrase, often a compound noun, which described a thing in terms of its use. Thus the sea was "the sail road" or "the gannet's bath" or the "devils' mere" or the "whale path"; a ship was the "sea wood" or a "seahorse"; a sword was the "light of bat-tle" or "warriors' friend"; a spear was the "shaft of laughter"; the sun was the "rapture of heaven" or the "sky candle"; a wife was the "weaver of peace."

Heroic deeds were celebrated by the Anglo-Saxon bards, the *scops,* or "shapers," who unlocked their "word-hoard." But the epic-forming tradition gave way to a more personal expression, and the bards alternated between legends and lyrics. One of the oldest of these lyrical pieces is DEOR'S LAMENT. Deor pictures himself as a discarded poet, a victim of unhappy times. But he comforts himself by recalling the misfortunes of past heroes and the wrongs of oppressed people. "Their troubles passed; so can mine," Deor re-peats in a self-consoling refrain at the end of each stanza, or, as Margaret Williams translates it in her gathering of Old English literature, WORD-HOARD, "That went by; so can this." It is a stoical cry whose echoes have lasted over a thousand years.

The fever for the sea, glorified in our own day by Masefield and Conrad, was first expressed by the monkish poets who, hearing tales of old mariners, wove pious comments into the narrative. Shorn of the didactic additions, THE WANDERER and THE SEAFARER (about 850) alternate between the irresistible call of "the whale road" over the wastes of ocean and the weary longing for a life that is done with voyaging.

Two battle pieces by unknown poets contain a similar personal utterance, although one commemorates a defeat and the other celebrates a victory. THE BATTLE OF MALDON is a fragmentary poem which breathes the spirit of undying loyalty, but it is truncated and suffers badly in translation. THE BATTLE OF BRUNANBURH is a vivid rendering of a heroic episode in the tenth century. Translated by Alfred, Lord Tennyson, the modern English version captures the atmosphere, the muscular language, and much of the alliteration of the original text. Tennyson introduced the poem with this note: "Constantinus, King of the Scots, after having sworn allegiance to Æthelstan, allied himself with the Danes of Ireland under Anlaí, and, invading England, was defeated by Æthelstan and his brother Edmund with great slaughter at Brunanburh in year 937."

The Battle of Brunanburh

I

Æthelstan King,
Lord among Earls,
Bracelet-bestower and
Baron of Barons,
He with his brother,
Edmund Atheling,
Gaining a lifelong
Glory in battle,
Slew with the sword-edge
There by Brunanburh,
Brake the shield-wall,
Hewed the linden-wood,
Hacked the battle-shield,
Sons of Edward with hammered brands.

II

Theirs was a greatness
Got from their grandsires—
Theirs that so often in
Strife with their enemies
Struck for their hoards and their hearths and their homes.

III

Bowed the spoiler,
Bent the Scotsman,
Fell the ship-crews
Doomed to the death.
All the field with blood of the fighters
Flowed, from when first the great
Sun-star of morning-tide,
Lamp of the Lord God,
Lord everlasting,
Glowed over earth till the glorious creature
Sank to his setting.

IV

There lay many a man
Marred by the javelin,
Men of the Northland
Shot over shield.
There was the Scotsman
Weary of war.

V

We the West-Saxons
Long as the daylight
Lasted, in companies
Troubled the track of the host that we hated.
Grimly with swords that were sharp from the grind-stone,
Fiercely we hacked at the flyers before us.

VI

Mighty the Mercian,
Hard was his hand-play,
Sparing not any of
Those that with Anlaf,
Warriors over the
Weltering waters
Borne in the bark's-bosom,
Drew to this island—
Doomed to the death.

VII

Five young kings put asleep by the sword-stroke,
Seven strong Earls of the army of Anlaf
Fell on the war-field, numberless numbers,
Shipmen and Scotsmen.

VIII

Then the Norse leader,
Dire was his need of it,
Few were his following,
Fled to his war-ship;
Fleeted his vessel to sea with the king **in it,**
Saving his life on the fallow flood.

IX

Also the crafty one,
Constantinus,
Crept to his North again,
Hoar-headed hero!

X

Slender warrant had
He to be proud of
The welcome of war-knives—
He that was reft of his
Folk and his friends that had
Fallen in conflict,
Leaving his son too
Lost in the carnage,
Mangled to morsels.
A youngster in war!

XI

Slender reason had
He to be glad of
The clash of the war-glaive—
Traitor and trickster
And spurner of treaties—
He nor had Anlaf
With armies so broken
A reason for bragging
That they had the better
In perils of battle
On places of slaughter—
The struggle of standards,
The rush of the javelins,
The crash of the charges,
The wielding of weapons—
The play that they played with
The children of Edward.

XII

Then with their nailed prows
Parted the Norsemen, a
Blood-reddened relic of
Javelins over
The jarring breaker, the deep-sea billow,
Shaping their way toward Dyflen [1] again,
Shamed in their souls.

XIII

Also the Brethren,
King and Atheling,
Each in his glory,
Went to his own in his own West-Saxonland,
Glad of the war.

XIV

Many a carcase they left to be carrion,
Many a livid one, many a sallow-skin—
Left for the white-tailed eagle to tear it, and
Left for the horny-nibbed raven to rend it, and
Gave to the garbagin [2] war-hawk to gorge it, and
That gray beast, the wolf of the weald. [3]

XV

Never had huger
Slaughter of heroes
Slain by the sword-edge—
Such as old writers
Have writ of in histories—
Hapt in this isle, since
Up from the East hither
Saxon and Angle from
Over the broad billow

[1] *Dublin.*   [2] *Ravenous.*   [3] *A wooded region*

Broke into Britain with
Haughty war-workers who
Harried the Welshman, when
Earls that were lured by the
Hunger of glory gat
Hold of the land.

Although the smoke of battle hangs over Anglo-Saxon poetry, the note of peace grows as the Scandinavian sea rovers vanish and leave their cultural mark in the verse of their followers. The foundation of the English spirit is felt in the masculine beat of Anglo-Saxon poetry: the strong rhythm of steady oars, hoarse chants, and heavy marching feet. Uninterrupted invasion gives way to intermittent war; the bloody heath brings the soldier-singer back to the quiet hearth.

A poem in the Exeter Book, a large collection of Old English poetry presented to Exeter Cathedral in 1071 by its first bishop, Leofric, contains a small but significant set of verses. The lines entitled WULF AND EADWACER are strangely personal, a dramatic monologue tightened into a lyric. Some translators have given the poem an enigmatic character, interpreting it as a riddle or charade; others have considered it a segment of a long legend. But, even in the modernized version, the words and the bitterly brief refrain tell all there is to tell of a married woman's grief for her lover, a lover lost in battle and held by the enemy.

Wulf and Eadwacer

Men proffer presents   here to my people.
Who feeds him there   when he is famished?
                    Alas for us.

Wulf is war-weary,   held on some highland;
He on one island,   I on another.
                    Alas for us.

Far is that island,   filthy with fens.
Who feeds him there   when he is famished?

I wait for Wulf   wasting with longing;
My tears and torrents   of rain fall together . . .

When Wulf the warrior   wound arms about me
Fierce was the mingling;   pleasure and pain . . .

Sick am I now,   hapless, heart-hungry;
Sick with not-seeing,   craving his coming . . .

Hear me, Eadwacer: the brat that I bore thee,
Wulf will deliver   the whelp to the wildwood . . .

Now it is broken   which never was blended:
The song and the strength   of the trial together.

The Legend of the Eaten Heart has many folklore versions; its
origins are lost in ancient sacrifices and family taboos. It attained
particular significance in an age of dark chance and cruel customs,
for it is one of the darkest and cruelest of tales. Stripped of its
embellishments, the story concerns an unfaithful wife, a slain lover,
and a vengeful husband who tricks his wife into eating her lover's
heart.

The barbaric tale is known in many countries and in almost all
literatures. It occurs in the ancient Indian tale of Raja Rasalu, in
a Provençal version that Boccaccio used twice in THE DECAMERON,
and in a South American legend in which the lover is a captured
slave. The Middle English poem, however, was borrowed from the
French and consisted of more than five hundred lines. The part of
it which follows was rendered into modern English by Pearl London.

The Eaten Heart

"Make it sweet and delicate to eat;
Serve it to my lady bright.
Should she suspect this meat
Her heart would not be light."

And soon the lord sat down to dine,
His lady at his side;
The heart was served in red, red wine,
But there was grief inside.

"Madame, eat of this," he said.
"It is both dainty and pleasant,"

The lady ate and was not dismayed,
For of spice there was no want.

When she had feasted well
Her lord said to her there,
"Let the heart that you have eaten knell
For him who toyed with your yellow hair.

"As you can see, your knight is dead;
I tell you, lady, do not cry.
It was his heart on which you fed;
Madame, at last we all must die."

Up she rose with heart full woe
And straight into her chamber went;
And there confessed devoutly so
That shortly she received the sacrament.

And mourning lay in her last bed;
God knows right woeful was her moan.
"Alas, my own dear love," she said,
"Since you are dead my joy is gone.

"With me thy eaten heart shall die;
I have received the sacrament;
All earthly food I shall deny.
With woe and pain my life is spent."

from THE KNIGHT OF CURTESY

JOHN BARBOUR
[1316?–1395]

ONE of the first poems by a known author is typical of the foun-
dations of the English spirit. A quarter of a century before
Chaucer wrote his ballade on truth (page 118) John Barbour, a Scot-
tish archdeacon, composed his lines in praise of liberty.

Part of an epic, THE BRUCE, written about 1375, the fragment sur-
vives its grandiose setting. Barbour's other work has become little
more than a historian's curiosity, but FREEDOM remains vibrantly

alive. It is not only a living poem but a motto, a slogan, a war cry, and a prayer for peace.

Freedom

Ah! Fredome is a noble thing!
Fredome mayse man to haif liking; [1]
Fredome all solace to man giffis,
He livis at ese [2] that freely livis!
A noble hart may haif nane ese,
Na ellys nocht [3] that may him plese,
Gif fredome fail'th; for free liking
Is yharnit [4] ouer all othir thing.
Na he that ay has livit free
May nocht knaw well the property,
The anger, na the wretchit doom
That is couplit to foul thraldome.
But gif he had assayit it,
Then all perquer he suld it wit; [5]
And suld think fredome mar to prise
Than all the gold in warld that is.

GEOFFREY CHAUCER

[1340?–1400]

BORN about 1340, Geoffrey Chaucer, son of a London brewer and wine merchant, brought continual excitement into his life and exuberance into his work. Writing almost six hundred years ago in a dialect which became the national language, Chaucer expressed his time—and escaped it. He is as vibrantly alive today as he was in the fourteenth century.

Chaucer's quick spirit, his vivid appreciation, his generously appraising eye, and his unflagging gusto distinguished him even in the most glittering of golden ages. His was a richly varied and vigorous

---

[1] *Liberty.*   [2] *Ease.*   [3] *Nor aught else.*   [4] *To be desired.*   [5] *Learn it thoroughly*

world, a world of Froissart and Petrarch, of the battle of Crécy and the Black Death, of Rienzi and Sir John Mandeville, of Wyclif and Wat Tyler's rebellion, of the three great pestilences and THE VISION OF PIERS PLOWMAN. The poet was anything but the languid and incompetent figure of unpopular tradition. Chaucer did not withdraw from the world of reality; he lived in action. Before he was twenty he had entered military service, had served in France, and had been taken prisoner in Brittany when it was invaded by Edward III. At twenty-seven he was appointed "valet of the king's chamber." At thirty he became a highly valued servant of the state, being something between an ambassador and a commercial traveler. He helped conduct negotiations for peace with France and concluded a business treaty in Genoa. At thirty-three he was sent on a mission to Florence, where he seems to have met Boccaccio and learned from Petrarch the tale of the patient Griselda, which was retold by the Clerk in THE CANTERBURY TALES. At thirty-four, he was appointed comptroller of customs in the port of London, a position he held for almost ten years. As a result of secret services in Flanders, he was attached to various embassies, and at forty-six he sat in Parliament as a knight of Kent. At fifty he was appointed clerk of the king's works; he supervised repairs of Westminster Abbey, where, after receiving pensions from four monarchs and suffering from the vagaries of politics, he was buried. In his late fifties he was reduced to continual borrowing; nearing sixty, "letters of protection" were issued to save him from being arrested for debt. A new pension was forthcoming, but Chaucer did not live long to enjoy it. He died on October 25, 1400, in his sixty-first year. A monument was erected to him in Westminster Abbey in 1555.

It was in April, 1388, when Chaucer in his late forties made the Canterbury pilgrimage. He went, along with other pilgrims, to visit the shrine of Thomas Becket. He was not looking for material; he scarcely envisioned the work which was to earn him the title of "the father of English poetry and perhaps the prince of it." But he was struck by the mixed company assembled at the Tabard Inn at Southwark, and he remembered them when he designed the cavalcade of fourteenth-century English life in THE CANTERBURY TALES. The happy PROLOGUE sets the background and establishes the mood. The very opening lines reflect the poet's liveliness of vision—the flower's new strength, the west wind's sweet breath, the small birds' sleeping all night with open eyes; they create an eternal April.

Prologue

Whan that Aprille with his shoures sote
The droghte of Marche hath perced to the rote,
And bathed every veyne in swich licour
Of which vertu engendred is the flour;
Whan Zephirus eek with his swete breeth
Inspired hath in every holt and heeth
The tendre croppes, and the yonge sonne
Hath in the Ram his halfe cours y-ronne,
And smale fowles maken melodye
That slepen al the night with open yë
(So priketh hem nature in hir corages):
Than longen folk to goon on pilgrimages,
And palmers for to seken straunge strondes,
To ferne halwes couthe in sondry londes;
And specially, from every shires ende
Of Engelond, to Caunterbury they wende
The holy blisful martir for to seke
That hem hath holpen, whan that they were seke.

from THE CANTERBURY TALES

Chaucer lives most vividly in his dramatis personae. They are all sharply individualized; their identities are exact and unmistakable —the large, rough host of the Tabard Inn, a seemly man, fit "to han been a marshal in an halle"; the Knight, meek in manner as a maid, "a verray parfit gentil knight"; the youthful Squire, "a lovyere, and a lusty bacheler," with his locks curled as though "they were leyd in presse"; the Monk who preferred hunting to studying and who loved a fat roasted swan best of all; the coy Prioress whose "gretteste ooth was but by sëynt Loy" and whose table manners were so dainty that she never dropped a morsel of food and "ne wette hir fingres in hir sauce depe"; the Reeve, that "sclendre colerik man"; the Wife of Bath who, although deaf, seems to have heard everything

Prologue

When the sweet showers of April follow March,
Piercing the dryness to the roots that parch,
Bathing each vein in such a flow of power
That a new strength's engendered in the flower—
When, with a gentle warmth, the west-wind's breath
Awakes in every wood and barren heath
The tender foliage, when the vernal sun
Has half his course within the Ram to run—
When the small birds are making melodies,
Sleeping all night (they say) with open eyes
(For Nature so within their bosom rages)—
Then people long to go on pilgrimages,
And palmers wander to the strangest strands
For famous shrines, however far the lands.
Especially from every shire's end
Of England's length to Canterbury they wend,
Seeking the martyr, holiest and blest
Who helped them, healed their ills, and gave them rest.

Modern version by L. U.

and who had had five church-door husbands, not including "other companye in youthe"; the thickset, short-shouldered Miller with his beard as red as any fox, who excelled at wrestling and playing the bagpipe, roaring out his lewd jokes from a mouth as broad "as a greet forneys" . . . All is mirrored in the poet's loving scrutiny. Here are the little tricks of gesture and the large generalities, the homely accents and the very shades of complexion, the rare virtues and the human vices—not a whisper, not a wart, is omitted. Chaucer towers above the writers of his times not by transcribing, but by transmuting the looks and lives of his people, by uplifting characteristics into character.

Seven Pilgrims

A KNIGHT

A Knight ther was, and that a worthy man
That from the tyme that he first bigan
To ryden out, he loved chivalrye,
Trouthe and honour, fredom and curteisye.
Ful worthy was he in his lordes werre,
And therto hadde he riden (no man ferre)
As wel in Cristendom as hethenesse,
And ever honoured for his worthinesse . .
At mortal batailles hadde he been fiftene,
And foughten for our feith at Tramissene
In listes thryes, and ay slayn his fo.
This ilke worthy knight had been also
Somtyme with the lord of Palatye,
Ageyn another hethen in Turkye:
And evermore he hadde a sovereyn prys.
And though that he were worthy, he was wys,
And of his port as meke as is a mayde.
He never yet no vileinye ne sayde
In al his lyf, un-to no maner wight.
He was a verray parfit gentil knight.

A SQUYER

With him ther was his sone, a yong Squyer,
A lovyere, and a lusty bacheler,
With lokkes crulle, as they were leyd in presse
Of twenty yeer of age he was, I gesse.
Of his stature he was of evene lengthe,
And wonderly deliver, and greet of strengthe.
And he had been somtyme in chivachye,
In Flaundres, in Artoys, and Picardye.
And born him wel, as of so litel space,
In hope to stonden in his lady grace.
Embrouded was he, as it were a mede
Al ful of fresshe floures, whyte and rede.
Singinge he was, or floytinge, all the day;
He was as fresh as is the month of May.
Short was his goune, with sleves longe and wyde.

Seven Pilgrims

A KNIGHT

A Knight there was, and that a worthy man,
Who, from the moment when he first began
To ride forth, loved the code of chivalry:
Honor and truth, freedom and courtesy.
His lord's war had established him in worth;
He rode—and no man further—ends of earth
In heathen parts as well as Christendom,
Honored wherever he might go or come . . .
Of mortal battles he had seen fifteen,
And fought hard for our faith at Tramassene
Thrice in the lists, and always slain his foe.
This noble knight was even led to go
To Turkey where he fought most valiantly
Against the heathen hordes for Palaty.
Renowned he was; and, worthy, he was wise—
Prudence, with him, was more than mere disguise;
He was as meek in manner as a maid.
Vileness he shunned, rudeness he never said
In all his life, respecting each man's right.
He was a truly perfect, noble knight.

A SQUIRE

With him there was his son, a youthful Squire,
A merry blade, a lover full of fire;
With locks as curled as though laid in a press—
Scarce twenty years of age was he, I guess.
In stature he was of an average length,
Wondrously active, bright, and great in strength.
He proved himself a soldier handsomely
In Flanders, in Artois and Picardy,
Bearing himself so well, in so short space,
Hoping to stand high in his lady's grace.
Embroidered was his clothing, like a mead
Full of fresh flowers, shining white and red.
Singing he was, or fluting, all the day—
He was as fresh as is the month of May.
Short was his gown; his sleeves were long and wide;

Wel coude he sitte on hors, and faire ryde.
He coude songes make and wel endyte,
Juste and eek daunce, and wel purtreye and wryte.
So hote he lovede, that by nightertale
He sleep namore than dooth a nightingale.
Curteys he was, lowly, and servisable,
And carf biforn his fader at the table.

A PRIORESSE

Ther was also a Nonne, a Prioresse,
That of hir smyling was ful simple and coy:
Hir gretteste ooth was but by sëynt Loy;
And she was cleped madame Eglentyne.
Ful wel she song the service divyne,
Entuned in hir nose ful semely;
And Frensh she spak ful faire and fetisly,
After the scole of Stratford atte Bowe,
For Frensh of Paris was to hir unknowe.
At mete wel y-taught was she with-alle;
She leet no morsel from hir lippes falle,
Ne wette hir fingres in hir sauce depe.
Wel coude she carie a morsel, and wel kepe,
That no drope ne fille up-on hir brest.
In curteisye was set ful muche hir lest.
Hir over lippe wyped she so clene,
That in hir coppe was no ferthing sene
Of grece, whan she dronken hadde hir draughte.
Ful semely after hir mete she raughte,
And sikerly she was of greet disport,
And ful pleasaunt, and amiable of port,
And peyned hir to countrefete chere
Of court, and been estatlich of manere,
And to ben holden digne of reverence.
But, for to speken of hir conscience,
She was so charitable and so pitous,
She wolde wepe, if that she sawe a mous
Caught in a trappe, if it were deed or bledde.
Of smale houndes had she, that she fedde
With rosted flesh, or milk and wastel-breed,
But sore weep she if oon of hem were deed,
Or if men smoot it with a yerde smerte:
And al was conscience and tendre herte.
Ful semely hir wimpel pinched was;

Well did he sit his horse, and nimbly ride,
He could make songs, intune them or indite,
Joust, play and dance, and also draw and write.
So well could he repeat love's endless tale,
He slept no more than does the nightingale.
Yet he was humble, courteous and able,
And carved before his father when at table.

A PRIORESS

There also was a nun, a Prioress
Whose smile was simple. Quiet, even coy,
The worst oath that she swore was, "By Saint Loy!"
And she was known as Sister Eglantine.
Sweetly she sang the services divine,
Intoning through her nose the melody.
Fairly she spoke her French, and skillfully,
After the school of Stratford-at-the-Bow—
Parisian French was not for her to know.
Precise at table and well-bred withal
Her lips would never let a morsel fall;
She never wet her fingers in her sauce,
But carried every tidbit without loss
Of even the smallest drop upon her breast.
Manners and good behavior pleased her best.
She always wiped her upper lip so clean
That not a speck of grease was ever seen
Upon the cup from which she drank. Her food
Was reached for neatly; she was never rude.
Though her demeanor was the very best,
Her mood was amiable, she loved a jest;
She always tried to copy each report
Of how the latest fashion ran at court,
And yet to hold herself with dignity.
But, speaking of her inner nature, she
Was so devout, so full of sympathy,
She would lament if she would have to see
A mouse caught in a trap, or it had bled.
A few small dogs she had, and these she fed
With roasted meat, or milk and sweetened bread,
And wept aloud if one of them were dead,
Or if a person struck and made them smart—
She was all goodness and a tender heart.
Her wimple draped itself a modest way;

Hir nose tretys; hir eyen greye as glas;
Hir mouth ful smal, and ther-to softe and reed;
But sikerly she hadde a fair forheed;
It was almost a spanne brood, I trowe;
For, hardily, she was nat undergrowe.
Ful fetis was hir cloke, as I was war.
Of smal coral aboute hir arm she bar
A peire of bedes, gauded al with grene;
And ther-on heng a broche of gold ful shene,
On which ther was first writ a crowned A,
And after, *Amor vincit omnia.*

A MONK

A Monk ther was, a fair for the maistrye,
An out-rydere, that lovede venerye;
A manly man, to been an abbot able.
Ful many a deyntee hors hadde he in stable:
And, whan he rood, men mighte his brydel here
Ginglen in a whistling wind as clere,
And eek as loude as dooth the chapel-belle
Ther as this lord was keper of the celle.
The reule of seint Maure or of seint Beneit,
By-cause that it was old and som-del streit,
This ilke monk leet olde thinges pace,
And held after the newe world the space.
He yaf nat of that text a pulled hen,
That seith, that hunters been nat holy men;
Ne that a monk, whan he is cloisterlees,
Is lykned til a fish that is waterlees;
This is to seyn, a monk out of his cloistre.
But thilke text held he nat worth an oistre;
And I seyde, his opinioun was good.
What sholde he studie, and make himselven wood,
Upon a book in cloistre alwey to poure,
Or swinken with his handes, and laboure? . . .
Therefore he was a pricasour aright;
Grehoundes he hadde, as swifte as fowel in flight
Of priking and of hunting for the hare
Was al his lust, for no cost wolde he spare.
I seigh his sleves purfiled at the hond
With grys, and that the fyneste of a lond;
And, for to festne his hood under his chin,
He hadde of gold y-wroght a curious pin:

Her nose was straight, her eyes transparent grey,
Her mouth was small, but very soft and red,
Hers was a noble and a fair forehead,
Almost a span in breadth, one realized;
For she was small but scarcely undersized.
Her cloak was well designed, I was aware;
Her arm was graced with corals, and she bare
A string in which the green glass beads were bold,
And from it hung a brilliant brooch of gold
On which there was engraved a large, crowned *A,*
Followed by *Amor vincit omnia.*

A MONK

A Monk there was, a monk of mastery;
Hunting he loved—and that exceedingly.
A manly man, to be an abbot able.
Many a worthy horse was in his stable;
And, when he rode, his bridle all might hear
Jing-jingling in a whistling wind as clear
And lingering-loud as rings the chapel-bell
Where he himself was keeper of the cell.
The rules of Saint Maurice or Benedict,
Because they were both old and somewhat strict,
This monk passed by, let what was outworn go;
New times demand new customs here below.
He scorned that text not worth a poor, plucked hen
Which says that hunters are not holy men.
Or that a monk, of walls and cloister free,
Is like a fish that's out of water. He—
That is to say a monk out of his cloister—
Considered such a text not worth an oyster.
A good opinion, thought I, and it fits.
What! Should he study till he lose his wits
Poring on books he scarcely understands,
Always at work or laboring with his hands? . . .
Therefore he rode and hunted as he might.
Greyhounds he had, swift as a finch in flight;
Rousing the game and hunting for the hare
Was his delight and no cost would he spare.
His sleeves, I saw, were fitted near the hand
With the gray squirrel's fur, best in the land;
And, to attach the hood beneath his chin,
He had, all wrought in gold, a curious pin:

A love-knotte in the gretter end ther was.
His heed was balled, that shoon as any glas,
And eek his face, as he had been anoint.
He was a lord ful fat and in good point;
His eyen stepe, and rollinge in his heed,
That stemed as a forneys of a leed;
His botes souple, his hors in gret estate.
Now certeinly he was a fair prelate;
He was nat pale as a for-pynèd ghost.
A fat swan loved he best of eny roost.

A CLERK

A Clerk ther was of Oxenford also,
That un-to logik hadde longe y-go.
As lene was his hors as is a rake,
And he nas nat right fat, I undertake;
But loked holwe, and ther-to soberly.
Ful thredbar was his overest courtepy;
For he had geten him yet no benefyce,
Ne was so worldly for to have offyce.
For him was lever have at his beddes heed
Twenty bokes, clad in blak or reed,
Of Aristotle and his philosophye,
Than robes riche, or fithele, or gay sautrye.
But al be that he was a philosophre,
Yet hadde he but litel gold in cofre;
But al that he mighte of his freendes hente,
On bokes and on lerninge he it spente,
And bisily gan for the soules preye
Of hem that yaf him wher-with to scoleye.
Of studie took he most cure and most hede.
Noght o word spak he more than was nede,
And that was seyd in forme and reverence,
And short and quik, and ful of hy sentence.
Souninge in moral vertu was his speche,
And gladly wolde he lerne, and gladly teche.

A WYF OF BATHE

A good Wyf was ther of bisyde Bathe,
But she was som-del deef, and that was scathe.
Of clooth-making she hadde swiche an haunr,

A love-knot at the larger end there was.
His head was bald and shed the sun like glass,
Likewise his face, as though anointed, shone—
A fine, stout monk, if ever there was one.
His glittering eyes that never seemed to tire
But blazed like copper caldrons in a fire—
His supple boots, his well-appointed horse—
Here was a prelate! fairness linked with force!
He was not pale or hollow, like a ghost;
He loved a fat swan best of any roast.

A STUDENT

A Student came from Oxford town also,
Wedded to lore and logic long ago.
The horse he rode was lean as any rake;
Himself was scarcely fat, I'll undertake,
But hollow in his sad sobriety.
His overcoat was threadbare, too; for he
Was yet to win a single benefice,
And worldly thoughts of office were not his.
For he would rather have at his bed's head
Twenty great books, all bound in black or red,
Of Aristotle and his philosophy
Than rich robes, fiddle, or gay psaltery.
Though a philosopher, he could not proffer
A treasury of gold from his scant coffer;
Anything he could borrow from a friend
On books and learning he would quickly spend,
And constantly he prayed for those who'd give
Help for the means by which his soul might live.
He gave most care to study and most heed;
Never a word he spoke beyond his need.
His speech was framed in form and reverence,
Pointed and quick and always packed with sense.
Moral his mind, and virtuous his speech;
And gladly would he learn, and gladly teach.

A WIFE OF BATH

There was a Wife from Bath, a well-appearing
Woman who was (alas!) quite hard of hearing.
She had such skill in making cloth that all

She passed hem of Ypres and of Gaunt.
In al the parisshe wyf ne was ther noon
That to th' offring bifore hir sholde goon;
And if ther dide, certeyn, so wrooth was she,
That she was out of alle charitee.
Hir coverchiefs ful fyne were of ground;
I dorste swere they weyeden ten pound
That on a Sonday were upon hir heed.
Hir hosen weren of fyn scarlet reed,
Ful streite y-teyd, and shoos ful moiste and newe.
Bold was hir face, and fair, and reed of hewe.
She was a worthy womman al hir lyve,
Housbondes at chirche-dore she hadde fyve,
Withouten other companye in youthe;
But therof nedeth nat to speke as nouthe.
And thryes hadde she been at Jerusalem;
She hadde passed many a straunge streem;
At Rome she hadde been, and at Boloigne,
In Galice at seint Jame, and at Coloigne.
She coude muche of wandring by the weye:
Gat-tothed was she, soothly for to seye.
Up-on an amblere easily she sat,
Y-wimpled wel, and on hir heed **an hat**
As brood as is a bokeler or a targe;
A foot-mantel aboute hir hipes large,
And on hir feet a paire of spores sharpe.
In felawschip wel coude she laughe and **carpe**.
Of remedyes of love she knew perchaunce,
For she coude of that art the olde daunce.

A MILLER

The Miller was a stout carl, for the nones,
Ful big he was of braun, and eek of bones;
That proved wel, for over-al ther he cam,
At wrastling he wolde have alwey the ram.
He was short-sholdred, brood, a thikke knarre,
Ther nas no dore that he nolde heve of harre,
Or breke it, at a renning, with his heed.
His berd as any sowe or fox was reed,
And ther-to brood, as though it were a spade.
Up-on the cop right of his nose he hade
A werte, and ther-on stood a tuft of heres,
Reed as the bristles of a sowes eres;

The weaver's guilds of Ypres and Ghent looked small.
In all the parish, not a soul dared offer
A thing to her, or, if they did, they'd suffer—
So loud she railed, so full of wrath was she
That she would lose all sense of charity.
The kerchiefs that she used were finely wound—
I'd take an oath they weighed above ten pound—
Which, of a Sunday, were upon her head.
Her stockings were the finest scarlet-red,
Tightly held up; her shoes were soft and new.
Bold was her face, and fair, and red of hue.
She was a worthy woman all her life;
She'd had five church-door husbands as a wife,
And others in her youth she would allow—
But there's no need to mention such things now.
Thrice had she visited Jerusalem
And she had crossed o'er many a foreign stream.
She'd been at Rome, she'd journeyed to Boulogne,
To Saint James' in Galicia, to Cologne.
She'd gathered much from wandering by the way:
She was gap-toothed and loose-tongued, truth to say.
Upon an ambling mare she easily sat,
Her face half-veiled, and on her head a hat
Broad as a buckler, broader than a shield.
A mantle fell about her, but revealed
Large hips and feet equipped with sharpened spurs.
In company the laugh was always hers.
The remedies for love she knew, perchance—
She knew the art of dancing that old dance!

A MILLER

The Miller, stout and sturdy as the stones,
Delighted in his muscles, big of bones;
They served him well; at fair and tournament
He took the wrestling prize where'er he went.
He was short-shouldered, broad, knotty and tough;
He'd tear a door down easily enough
Or break it, charging thickly with his head.
His beard, like any sow or fox, was red,
And broadly built, as though it were a spade.
Upon the tiptop of his nose he had
A wart, and thereon stood a tuft of hairs,
Bright as the bristles of a red sow's ears.

His nose-thirles blake were and wyde.
A swerd and bokeler bar he by his syde;
His mouth as greet was as a greet forneys.
He was a janglere and a goliardeys,
And that was most of sinne and harlotryes.
Wel coude he stelen corn, and tollen thryes;
And yet he hadde a thombe of gold, pardee.
A whyt cote and a blew hood wered he.
A baggepype wel coude he blowe and sowne,
And ther-with-al he broghte us out of towne.

from THE CANTERBURY TALES

THE CANTERBURY TALES, a work of some seventeen thousand lines, is built upon a framework which has served from Boccaccio's DECAMERON to Longfellow's TALES OF A WAYSIDE INN: a set of unconnected stories held together by some unifying device. In THE CANTERBURY TALES the device is the simplest: the host proposes that each of the twenty-nine pilgrims tell a story, adding that the teller of the best tale shall be rewarded with a dinner on his return. The proposition is accepted and, though Chaucer never completed his plan—there being only twenty-four tales—practically every type of medieval narrative is represented. Although Chaucer made his own contributions as a writer of rhymed fiction, most of the tales did not originate with him; he nonchalantly took his fictions wherever he found them. THE KNIGHT'S TALE is a condensed version of Boccaccio's LA TESEIDE; THE MONK'S TALE was inspired by the same author's DE CASIBUS VIRORUM ET FEMINARUM ILLUSTRIUM. THE REEVE'S TALE is a treatment of an old French fabliau. THE MAN OF LAW'S TALE is taken from Gower, who did not invent it. Livy is quoted as the source of THE DOCTOR'S TALE. THE MANCIPLE'S TALE was first related as a fable by Ovid.

His nostrils matched the miller, black and wide.
He bore a sword and buckler by his side.
His mouth was broad as a great furnace door.
He loved to tell a joke, and boast, and roar
About his many sins and harlotries.
He stole, and multiplied his thefts by threes.
And yet he had a thumb of gold, 'tis true.
He wore a white coat and a hood of blue,
And he could blow the bagpipe up and down—
And with a tune he brought us out of town.

Modern English version by L. U.

Some critics have seen a "moral purpose" in the tales; some have even attempted to find parables in the most scurrilous passages. But the tales carry their own argument and fulfill their own purpose. Here the easygoing but hearty Chaucer moves in the midst of his creations. He comes among us with a broad appetite and unbounded vitality. Like Whitman, he seizes "the descending man and raises him with resistless will"; he sings of "life, immense in passion, pulse and power."

THE NUN'S PRIEST'S TALE is one of the examples of Chaucer's skillful borrowings. It contains reminders of the French story of Reynard the Fox, in which the villain is beaten after his victim has been beguiled; but in the telling Chaucer has made the tale completely his own. Delicately but straightforwardly the story becomes more than a popular beast fable—a fable which has its modern counterpart in the adventures of Br'er Fox and Br'er Rabbit—it combines allegorical satire and social comedy. The tale, which has been a favorite for centuries, has obviously been chiefly enjoyed because of its lightly communicated learning, easy grace, and never-aging charm.

The Nonne Preestes Tale

A povre widwe, somdel stape in age,
Was whylom dwelling in a narwe cotage,
Bisyde a grove, stonding in a dale.
This widwe, of which I telle yow my tale,
Sin thilke day that she was last a wyf,
In pacience ladde a ful simple lyf,
For liter was hir catel and hir rente;
By housbondrye, of such as God hir sente,
She fond hir-self, and eek hir doghtren two.
Three large sowes hadde she, and namo,
Three kyn, and eek a sheep that highte Malle,
Ful sooty was hir bour, and eek hir halle,
In which she eet ful many a sclendre meel.
Of poynaunt sauce hir neded never a deel.
No deyntee morsel passed thurgh hir throte;
Hir dyete was accordant to hir cote.
Repleccioun ne made hir never syk;
Attempree dyete was al hir phisyk,
And exercyse, and hertes suffisaunce.
The goute lette hir no-thing for to daunce,
N'apoplexye shente nat hir heed;
No wyn ne drank she, neither whyt ne reed;
Hir bord was served most with whyt and blak,
Milk and broun breed, in which she fond no lak,
Seynd bacoun, and somtyme an ey or tweye,
For she was as it were a maner deye.
  A yerd she hadde, enclosed al aboute
With stikkes, and a drye dich with-oute,
In which she hadde a cok, hight Chauntecleer,
In al the land of crowing nas his peer.
His vois was merier than the mery orgon
On messe-dayes that in the chirche gon;
Wel sikerer was his crowing in his logge,
Than is a clokke, or an abbey orlogge.
By nature knew he ech ascencioun
Of equinoxial in thilke toun;
For whan degrees fiftene were ascended,
Thanne crew he, that it mighte nat ben amended.
His comb was redder than the fyn coral,
And batailed, as it were a castel-wal.

The Nuns' Priest's Tale

Once, long ago, set close beside a wood,
Meager of look, a little cottage stood
Where dwelt a poor old widow in a dale.
This widow, she of whom I tell my tale,
Even since the day when she was last a wife
All patiently had led a simple life;
Small were her earnings and her property,
But what God sent she used with husbandry,
And kept two daughters and herself. Of sows
Three and no more she had about the house,
Also a sheep called Molly, and three kine.
Her sooty hall and bower were nothing fine,
And there full many a slender meal she ate.
No poignant sauce was needed for her plate;
No dainty morsel passed her throat; her fare
Accorded with the clothes she had to wear.
With surfeit she was never sick, but in
A temperate diet was her medicine,
And busy labor, and a heart's content.
Gout never kept her from a dance; nor bent
With stroke of apoplexy was her head.
Of wine none drank she, neither white nor red;
Her board was mostly served with white and black.
Milk and brown bread; of these she found no lack,
And bacon, or an egg, was not uncommon,
For in her way she was a dairywoman.

   She had a yard, that was enclosed about
By sticks, and a dry ditch that ran without,
And there she kept a cock named Chanticleer;
None in the land at crowing was his peer.
His voice was merrier than the organ's tone
That loud on mass-days in the church is blown,
And surer from his lodge his crowing fell
Than stroke of any clock or abbey bell.
He knew by nature each ascension of
The equinoxial circle arched above,
For when fifteen degrees had been ascended,
He crowed, so that it could not be amended.
Redder than coral was his comb, and all
Crested with notches, like a castle wall;

His bile was blak, and as the jeet it shoon;
Lyk asur were his legges, and his toon;
His nayles whytter than the lilie flour,
And lyk the burned gold was his colour.
This gentil cok hadde in his governaunce
Sevene hennes, for to doon al his plesaunce,
Whiche were his sustres and his paramours,
And wonder lyk to him, as of colours.
Of whiche the faireste hewed on hir throte
Was cleped faire damoysele Pertelote.
Curteys she was, discreet, and debonaire,
And compaignable, and bar hir-self so faire,
Sin thilke day that she was seven night old,
That trewely she hath the herte in hold
Of Chauntecleer loken in every lith;
He loved hir so, that wel was him therwith.
But such a joye was it to here hem singe,
Whan that the brighte sonne gan to springe,
In swete accord, 'my lief is faren in londe.'
For thilke tyme, as I have understonde,
Bestes and briddes coude speke and singe.
　　And so bifel, that in a daweninge,
As Chauntecleer among his wyves alle
Sat on his perche, that was in the halle,
And next him sat this faire Pertelote,
This Chauntecleer gan gronen in his throte,
As man that in his dreem is drecched sore.
And whan that Pertelote thus herde him rore,
She was agast, and seyde, 'O herte dere,
What eyleth yow, to grone in this manere?
Ye been a verray sleper, fy for shame!'
And he answerde and seyde thus, 'madame,
I pray yow, that ye take it nat a-grief:
By god, me mette I was in swich meschief
Right now, that yet myn herte is sore afright.
Now god,' quod he, 'my swevene recche aright,
And keep my body out of foul prisoun!
Me mette, how that I romed up and doun
Withinne our yerde, wher-as I saugh a beste,
Was lyk an hound, and wolde han maad areste
Upon my body, and wolde han had me deed.
His colour was bitwixe yelwe and reed;
And tipped was his tail, and bothe his eres,
With blak, unlyk the remenant of his heres;
His snowte smal, with glowinge eyen tweve.

His bill was black—like jet it seemed to glow—
Like azure shone each leg and every toe,
His nails were white—the lily flower is duller;
And gold all burnished was his body's color.
This noble cock had under governance
Seven hens, to do all wholly his pleasance;
Which were his paramours and sisters dear
And in their colors matched him wondrous near;
Of whom she that was fairest hued of throat
Fairly was called, Damoselle Pertelote.
Courteous she was, discreet and debonaire,
Companionable, and bore herself so fair
Even since the day that she was seven nights old,
She hath the heart of Chanticleer in hold—
Locked in each motion, in each graceful limb;
He loved her so, that this was well with him.
But what a joy it was to hear them sing
In sweet accord: "My Love's Gone Journeying"
While the bright sun uprose from out the land,
For this was in the time, I understand,
When all the birds and beasts could sing and speak.
    So once it fell, as day began to break,
And Chanticleer with his wives one and all
Was sitting on his perch within the hall,
And next him sat this fair Dame Pertelote,
That Chanticleer groaned deeply in his throat,
Like one that in his dream sore troubled is.
And when she heard this roaring groan of his,
Pertelote was aghast, and cried: "Dear heart,
What aileth you, that thus ye groan and start?
What a fine sleeper! Fie now, fie for shame!"
But Chanticleer replied: "I pray you, Dame,
Take it not so amiss; by God, I seemed
Just now in such a danger as I dreamed
That still my heart is strangely terrified.
God bring my dream to something good!" he cried
"And out of prison foul my body keep!
Now I was roaming (so i dreamed in sleep)
Within our yard, and there I saw a beast
Was like a dog, and would have made arrest
Upon my body, and would have had me dead.
His color was between a yellow and red,
And tipped his tail was, likewise both his ears,
With black, quite different from his other hairs
His snout was small between two glowing eyes;

Yet of his look for fere almost I deye;
This caused me my groning, doutelees.'
  'Avoy!' quod she, 'fy on yow, hertelees!
Allas!' quod she, 'for, by that god above,
Now han ye lost myn herte and al my love;
I can nat love a coward, by my feith.
For certes, what so any womman seith,
We alle desyren, if it mighte be,
To han housbondes hardy, wyse, and free,
And secree, and no nigard, ne no fool,
Ne him that is agast of every tool,
Ne noon avauntour, by that god above!
How dorste ye seyn for shame unto your love,
That any thing mighte make yow aferd?
Have ye no mannes herte, and han a berd?
Allas! and conne ye been agast of swevenis?
No-thing, god wot, but vanitee, in sweven is.
Swevenes engendren of replecciouns,
And ofte of fume, and of complecciouns,
Whan humours been to habundant in a wight.
Certes this dreem, which ye han met to-night,
Cometh of the grete superfluitee
Of youre rede *colera*, pardee,
Which causeth folk to dreden in here dremes
Of arwes, and of fyr with rede lemes,
Of grete bestes, that they wol hem byte,
Of contek, and of whelpes grete and lyte;
Right as the humour of malencolye
Causeth ful many a man, in sleep, to crye,
For fere of blake beres, or boles blake,
Or elles, blake develes wole hem take.
Of othere humours coude I telle also,
That werken many a man in sleep ful wo;
But I wol passe as lightly as I can.
  Lo Catoun, which that was so wys a man,
Seyde he nat thus, ne do no fors of dremes?
Now, sire,' quod she, 'whan we flee fro the bemes,
For Goddes love, as tak som laxatyf;
Up peril of my soule, and of my lyf,
I counseille yow the beste, I wol nat lye,
That bothe of colere and of malencolye
Ye purge yow; and for ye shul nat tarie,
Though in this toun is noon apotecarie,
I shal my-self to herbes techen yow,
That shul ben for your hele, and for your prow;

Even now my heart with terror almost dies;
And doubtless it was this which made me start."
    "For shame!" quoth she. "Fie on you, small of heart!
Alas!" she cried, "for, by the God above,
Now have ye lost my heart and all my love:
I cannot love a coward, by my faith.
For truly, what so any woman saith,
We all desire, if such a thing can be,
Husbands that shall be sturdy, wise, and free,
Trusty, and not a fool, nor one to hoard,
Nor such as stands aghast to see a sword,
Nor yet a boaster, by the God above:
How durst ye say for shame unto your love
That there was anything on earth ye feared?
Have ye no man's heart, though ye have a beard?
And was it dreams that brought this melancholy?
God knows that nothing is in dreams but folly.
Dreams are engendered out of gluttony,
And drink, and from complexions, it may be,
That show of humors more than should be right.
Surely this vision which ye dreamed last night
Comes of the too great superfluity
Ye have of your red *colera*, pardee,
Which makes folk in their dreams to have great dread
Of arrows, or of fire with tongues of red,
Of great beasts, that will bite them, and of all
Struggle and strife, and dogs both great and small--
Just as the humor of melancholy will make
Full many a man within his sleep to break
Out crying with fear of black bears or black bulls
Or else of some black devil that at him pulls.
Of other humors I could tell you still
That work on many a sleeping man much ill,
But I will pass as quickly as I can.
    "Lo, Cato, he that was so wise a man,
Said he not thus: Take no account of dreams?
Now, sire," she said, "when we fly from the beams
For God's love take a little laxative;
Upon my soul, and as I hope to live,
My counsel is the best, and it is wholly
The truth: for choler and for melancholy
Purge yourself now and, since ye must not tarry,
And in this town is no apothecary,
I will myself to certain herbs direct you
That shall be profit to you, and correct you;

And in our yerd tho herbes shal I finde,
The wiche han of hir propretee, by kinde,
To purgen yow binethe, and eek above.
Forget not this, for Goddes owene love!
Ye been ful colerik of compleccioun.
Ware the sonne in his ascencioun
Ne fynde yow nat repleet of humours hote;
And if it do, I dar wel leye a grote,
That ye shul have a fevere terciane,
Or an agu, that may be youre bane.
A day or two ye shul have digestyves
Of wormes, er ye take your laxatyves,
Of lauriol, centaure, and fumetere,
Or elles of ellebor, that groweth there,
Of catapuce, or of gaytres beryis,
Of erbe yve, growing in our yerd, that mery is;
Pekke hem up right as they growe, and ete hem in.
Be mery, housbond, for your fader kin!
Dredeth no dreem; I can say yow na-more.'
　　'Madame,' quod he, '*graunt mercy* of your lore.
But nathelees, as touching daun Catoun,
That hath of wisdom such a greet renoun,
Though that he bad no dremes for to drede,
By god, men may in olde bokes rede
Of many a man, more of auctoritee
Than ever Catoun was, so mote I thee,
That al the revers seyn of his sentence,
And han wel founden by experience,
That dremes ben significaciouns,
As wel of joye as tribulaciouns
That folk enduren in this lyf present.
Ther nedeth make of this noon argument;
The verray preve sheweth it in dede.
　　Oon of the gretteste auctours that men rede
Seith thus, that whylom two felawes wente
On pilgrimage, in a ful good entente;
And happed so, thay come into a toun,
Wher-as ther was swich congregacioun
Of peple, and eek so streit of herbergage
That they ne founde as muche as o cotage
In which they bothe mighte y-logged be.
Wherfor thay mosten, of necessitee,
As for that night, departen compaignye;
And ech of hem goth to his hostelrye,
And took his logging as it wolde falle.

And in our very yard such herbs should be
Which of their nature have the property
To purge you wholly, under and above.
Forget this not, I say, for God's own love!
Ye are too choleric of complexion;
Then take good heed lest the ascending sun
Shall find you all replete with humors hot;
For if it do, I dare to lay a groat
That ye shall straightway have a tertian fever
Or ague, that may be your bane forever.
A day or two ye shall your diet make
On worms, and then your laxatives shall take:
Spurge-laurel, for example, and centaury
And fumitory, or hellebore, may be,
With caper-spurge, too, or the gay-tree berry,
And herb-ive, with the taste that makes you merry.
Just peck them where they grow, and eat. But make
Good cheer now, husband, for your fathers' sake.
Fear ye no dream; now can I say no more."
    "Madam," quoth he, "*grand merci* for your lore
Yet touching this Lord Cato who, I own,
Hath for his wisdom such a great renown,
Though he adviseth us to take no heed
Of dreams—by God, in old books can ye read
Of many a man, more in authority
Than ever Cato was, God prosper me,
That say just the reverse of what he says,
And by experience in many ways
Find that our dreams may be prophetic things
Alike for joys and woeful happenings
That in this present life all folk endure.
This needs no argument to make it sure,
For the full proof is shown in many a deed.
    "One of the greatest authors that men read
Says thus: that on a time two friends set out
On pilgrimage, and they were both devout;
And it befell they came unto a town
Where were such crowds of people up and down
And in the hostelries so little space
There was not even a cottage in the place
Wherein the both of them might harbored be.
So they were forced, of sheer necessity,
For that night's sleeping to part company,
And each of them goes to his hostelry
To take his lodging as it might befall.

That oon of hem was logged in a stalle,
Fer in a yerd, with oxen of the plough;
That other man was logged wel y-nough,
As was his aventure, or his fortune,
That us governeth alle as in commune.
     And so bifel, that, longe er it were day,
This man mette in his bed, ther-as he lay,
How that his felawe gan up-on him calle,
And seyde, "allas! for in an oxes stalle
This night I shal be mordred ther I lye.
Now help me, dere brother, ere I dye;
In alle haste com to me," he sayde.
This man out of his sleep for fere abrayde;
But whan that he was wakned of his sleep,
He turned him, and took of this no keep;
Him thoughte his dreem nas but a vanitee.
Thus twyës in his sleping dremed he.
And atte thridde tyme yet his felawe
Cam, as him thoughte, and seide, "I am now slawe;
Bihold my blody woundes, depe and wyde!
Arys up erly in the morwe-tyde,
And at the west gate of the toun," quod he,
"A carte ful of dong ther shaltow see,
In which my body is hid ful prively;
Do thilke carte aresten boldely.
My gold caused my mordre, sooth to sayn";
And tolde him every poynt how he was slayn,
With a ful pitous face, pale of hewe.
And truste wel, his dreem he fond ful trewe;
For on the morwe, as sone as it was day,
To his felawes in he took the way;
And whan that he cam to this oxes stalle,
After his felawe he bigan to calle.
     The hostiler answered him anon,
And seyde, "sire, your felawe is agon,
As sone as day he wente out of the toun."
This man gan fallen in suspecioun,
Remembring on his dremes that he mette,
And forth he goth, no lenger wolde he lette,
Unto the west gate of the toun, and fond
A dong-carte, as it were to donge lond,
That was arrayed in the same wyse
As ye han herd the dede man devyse;
And with an hardy herte he gan to crye
Vengeaunce and justice of this felonye:—

The one of them was bedded in a stall
Out in a yard with oxen of the plow;
The other got a proper place somehow,
As was his chance, or fortune, it may be,
That governs all lives universally.
   "And it befell that, long before the day,
This man, as dreaming in his bed he lay,
Thought that he heard his friend begin him call,
Crying: 'Alas! for in an ox's stall
This night shall I be murdered as I lie.
Now help me, dear my brother, ere I die.
Arise! in all haste come to me!' he said.
His comrade started from his sleep in dread,
But when he was awakened from his dreaming
He turned, and gave no notice to it, deeming
That all his dream was but a vanity!
And twice as he was sleeping thus dreamed he.
And then he thought he saw his friend again
A third time, and he said, 'Now am I slain.
Behold my wounds, bloody and deep and wide!
Arise up early on the morrow-tide
And at the west gate of the town,' quoth he,
'A cart with dung full laden shalt thou see.
In which my body is hidden secretly;
Then boldly stop that dung-cart instantly.
My gold did cause my murder, to say truly.'
Then all the slaying did he tell him duly,
With a full piteous face and pale of hue.
And ye may trust, his dream he found full true.
For on the morrow, with the break of day,
Unto his comrade's inn he took his way,
And when he came upon the ox's stall
To his companion he began to call.
   "The landlord spoke and answered him anon
After this fashion: 'Sir, your friend is gone;
He went from out the town when day first broke.'
Then straightway in this man suspicion woke,
For he remembered what he dreamed, and he
Would stay no more, but went forth instantly
Unto the west gate of the town, and found
A dung-cart, set as if to dung the ground,
That was arrayed exactly in the way
As in his dream he heard the dead man say.
Then with a bold heart he began to cry
Justice and vengeance on this villainy:

"My felawe mordred is this same night,
And in this carte he lyth gapinge upright.
I crye out on the ministres," quod he,
"That sholden kepe and reulen this citee;
Harrow! allas! her lyth my felawe slayn!"
What sholde I more un-to this tale sayn?
The peple out-sterte, and caste the cart to grounde,
And in the middel of the dong they founde
The dede man, that mordred was al newe.

O blisful god, that art so just and trewe!
Lo, how that thou biwreyest mordre alway!
Mordre wol out, that see we day by day.
Mordre is so wlatsom and abhominable
To god, that is so just and resonable,
That he ne wol nat suffre it heled be;
Though it abyde a yeer, or two, or three,
Mordre wol out, this my conclusioun.
And right anoon, ministres of that toun
Han hent the carter, and so sore him pyned,
And eek the hostiler so sore engyned,
That they biknewe hir wikkednesse anoon,
And were an-hanged by the nekke-boon.

Here may men seen that dremes been to drede.
And certes, in the same book I rede,
Right in the nexte chapitre after this,
(I gabbe nat, so have I joye or blis,)
Two men that wolde han passed over see,
For certeyn cause, in-to a fer contree,
If that the wind ne hadde been contrarie,
That made hem in a citee for to tarie,
That stood ful mery upon an haven-syde.
But on a day, agayn the even-tyde,
The wind gan chaunge, and blew right as hem leste.
Jolif and glad they wente un-to hir reste,
And casten hem ful erly for to saille;
But to that oo man fil a greet mervaille.
That oon of hem, in sleping as he lay,
Him mette a wonder dreem, agayn the day;
Him thoughte a man stood by his beddes syde,
And him comaunded, that he sholde abyde,
And seyde him thus, "if thou to-morwe wende,
Thou shalt be dreynt; my tale is at an ende."
He wook, and tolde his felawe what he mette,
And preyde him his viage for to lette;
As for that day, he preyde him to abyde.

'My friend was slain last night, and in this cart
Lies staring with a wound above his heart!
I cry upon the officers,' quoth he,
'That should keep rule here, and security!
Help! Help! Alas, here lies my comrade slain!'
What should I add to make the tale more plain?
The folk rushed out and cast the cart to ground,
And in the middle of the dung they found
The body of the man, murdered all new.
　　"O blissful God, that art so just and true!
Lo! always thus murder dost thou betray!
Murder will out, we see it day by day.
So loathsome is it, and such cursèd treason
To God, the soul of justice and of reason,
That never will He let it hidden be;
Though it should stay a year or two or three,
Murder will out—this is my whole opinion.
Straightway the officers that had dominion
Over the city seized and tortured so
The carter, and the landlord with him, too,
That soon they both confessed their villainy
And by the neck were hanged. So men may see
From such examples, dreams are to be feared.
And truly, in the same book there appeared,
Right in the chapter following on this
(I lie not, as I hope for joy or bliss)
A tale of two that would have left the strand
To cross the sea and reach a far-off land
If the wind's motion had not been contrary,
But in a city this had made them tarry
That stood full pleasant by a harbor-side.
But finally, one day, toward eventide,
The wind made change; right as they wished it blew.
Then happy to their slumber went the two
With hope full early to be voyaging.
But unto one befell a marvellous thing,
For, in his sleep, almost at break of day,
He had a wondrous vision as he lay.
It seemed to him a man stood at his side
Warning him in that city to abide,
Saying: 'If thou tomorrow go thy way
Thou shalt be drowned; I have no more to say.'
He woke, and told his vision to his friend,
And prayed him, lest the dream some ill portend,
To put the voyage off beyond that morn.

His felawe, that lay by his beddes syde,
Gan for to laughe, and scorned him ful faste.
"No dreem," quod he, "may so myn herte agaste,
That I wol lette for to do my thinges.
I sette not a straw by thy dreminges,
For swevenes been but vanitees and japes.
Men dreme al-day of owles or of apes,
And eke of many a mase therwithal;
Men dreme of thing that never was ne shal.
But sith I see that thou wolt heer abyde,
And thus for-sleuthen wilfully thy tyde,
God wot it reweth me; and have good day."
And thus he took his leve, and wente his way.
But er that he hadde halfe his cours y-seyled,
Noot I nat why, ne what mischaunce it eyled,
But casuelly the shippes botme rente,
And ship and man under the water wente
In sighte of othere shippes it byside,
That with hem seyled at the same tyde.
And therfor, faire Pertelote so dere,
By swiche ensamples olde maistow lere,
That no man sholde been to recchelees
Of dremes, for I sey thee, doutelees,
That many a dreem ful sore is for to drede.
    Lo, in the lyf of seint Kenelm, I rede,
That was Kenulphus sone, the noble king
Of mercenrike, how Kenelm mette a thing;
A lyte er he was mordred, on a day,
His mordre in his avisioun he say.
His norice him expouned every del
His sweven, and bad him for to kepe him wel
For traisoun; but he nas but seven yeer old,
And therfore litel tale hath he told
Of any dreem, so holy was his herte.
By god, I hadde lever than my sherte
That ye had rad his legende, as have I.
Dam Pertelote, I sey yow trewely,
Macrobeus, that writ th'avisioun
In Affrike of the worthy Cipioun,
Affermeth dremes, and seith that they been
Warning of thinges that men after seen.
    And forther-more, I pray yow loketh wel
In th'olde testament, of Daniel,
If he held dremes any vanitee.
Reed eek of Joseph, and ther shul ye see

At that his friend began to laugh in scorn
Lying the while near by within his bed,
'No dream shall ruin my affairs,' he said,
'Stirring my fears with fancies wild and teeming.
I wouldn't give a straw for all thy dreaming.
Vain tricks are dreams wherethrough the mind escapes
To fashion fantasies of owls or apes,
And many a maze. By God, for certainty,
Men dream what never was and cannot be.
But since I see that thou art bent on staying,
Wasting thy time with visions and delaying,
God knows I am sorry for it—so good day.'
And thus he took his leave and went his way.
But it befell ere half his course was sailed,
I know not why, nor what it was that failed,
By accident his vessel's hull was rent,
And ship and man beneath the water went
In sight of other ships not far away
That at the same time sailed with them that day.
Therefore, my fair, belovèd Pertelote,
From such old stories mayst thou clearly note
That no man should too greatly scoff about
His dreams; indeed, I tell thee, out of doubt
Full many a dream deserveth well our dread.
    "Lo, lately in Saint Kenelm's life I read—
That was Kenulphus' son, the noble king
Of Mercia, how young Kenelm dreamed a thing.
One night, a little time ere he was slain,
His murder in a dream was shown him plain.
His nurse explained this vision well unto him,
And warned him of the treason men might do him
And bade him be on guard; yet having but seven
Years only, and a heart all fixed on heaven,
To any vision little heed gave he.
By God, but it were worth my shirt to me
If thou hadst read this, Madam, as have I.
Dame Pertelote, this truth I certify:
Macrobeus, that wrote down long ago
In Africa the dream of Scipio,
Commendeth dreams, and says they often be
Warnings of things that afterwards men see.
    "And furthermore, I pray you notice well
In the Old Testament, if Daniël
Believed that dreams were any vanity,
And read of Joseph too, and ye shall see

Wher dremes ben somtyme (I sey nat alle)
Warning of thinges that shul after falle.
Loke of Egipt the king, daun Pharao,
His bakere and his boteler also,
Wher they ne felte noon effect in dremes.
Who-so wol seken actes of sondry remes,
May rede of dremes many a wonder thing.
    Lo Cresus, which that was of Lyde king,
Mette he nat that he sat upon a tree,
Which signified he sholde anhanged be?
Lo heer Andromacha, Ectores wyf,
That day that Ector sholde lese his lyf,
She dremed on the same night biforn,
How that the lyf of Ector sholde be lorn,
If thilke day he wente in-to bataille;
She warned him, but it mighte nat availle;
He wente for to fighte nathelees,
But he was slayn anoon of Achilles.
But thilke tale is al to long to telle,
And eek it is ny day, I may nat dwelle.
Shortly I seye, as for conclusioun,
That I shal han of this avisioun
Adversitee; and I seye forther-more,
That I ne telle of laxatyves no store,
For they ben venimous, I woot it wel;
I hem defye, I love hem never a del.
    Now let us speke of mirthe, and stinte al this;
Madame Pertelote, so have I blis,
Of o thing god hath sent me large grace;
For whan I see the beautee of your face,
Ye ben so scarlet-reed about your yën,
It maketh al my drede for to dyen;
For, also siker as *In principio*,
Mulier est hominis confusio;
Madame, the sentence of this Latin is—
Womman is mannes joye and al his blis.
For whan I fele a-night your softe syde,
Al-be-it that I may nat on you ryde,
For that our perche is maad, so narwe, alas!
I am so ful of joye and of solas
That I defye bothe sweven and dreem.'
And with that word he fley doun fro the beem,
For it was day, and eek his hennes alle;
And with a chuk he gan hem for to calle,
For he had founde a corn, lay in the yerd.
Royal he was, he was namore aferd;

Whether some dreams may be (I say not all)
Warnings of things that afterwards befall.
Consider Egypt's King, Dan Pharao,
And let his baker and his butler show
Whether of dreams they felt not the result.
Whoso will divers histories consult
May read of dreams full many a wondrous thing.
  "Lo, Crœsus, that in Lydia was king—
Did he not dream he sat upon a tree,
Which signified his hanging that should be?
And lo, Andromache, Dan Hector's wife—
Before the day that Hector lost his life
Dreams gave her warning that should Hector go
With day to join the fight against the foe,
The life of Hector would be lost, and she
Warned him of this, but unsuccessfully.
He went to fight, holding her vision vain,
And so was shortly by Achilles slain.
But this tale is too long to tell, and dawn
Draws near already; I may not go on.
In brief, and for conclusion, I assert
That of this vision I shall have some hurt.
And, Madam, I will tell you furthermore
That on these laxatives I set no store,
For they are venomous, I'll never try them;
I love them never a jot, and I defy them!
  "Now let us speak of mirth, and stop all this;
Dame Pertelote, as I have hope of bliss,
In one thing God hath richly sent me grace,
For when I see the beauty of your face
Ye be so scarlet red about the eyes
That as I gaze all dread within me dies,
For sure as gospel I would have you know,
Mulier est hominis confusio;
Madam, the meaning of this Latin is—
Woman's the joy of man and all his bliss.
For when at night I feel your fluffy side,
Although I may not then upon you ride,
Because our perch, alas, is made so narrow,
Such joy and solace pierce me to the marrow
That then do I defy both vision and dream."
And with that word he flew down from the beam—
For it was day—and his hens one and all;
And with a chucking he commenced to call,
For in the yard he had found a grain of corn.
His fear he scorned now with a royal scorn;

He fethered Pertelote twenty tyme,
And trad as ofte, er that it was pryme.
He loketh as it were a grim leoun;
And on his toos he rometh up and doun,
Him deyned not to sette his foot to grounde.
He chukketh, whan he hath a corn y-founde,
And to him rennen thanne his wyves alle.
Thus royal, as a prince is in his halle,
Leve I this Chauntecleer in his pasture;
And after wol I telle his aventure.

  Whan that the month in which the world bigan,
That highte March, whan god first maked man,
Was complet, and [y]-passed were also,
Sin March bigan, thritty dayes and two,
Bifel that Chauntecleer, in al his pryde,
His seven wyves walking by his syde,
Caste up his eyen to the brighte sonne,
That in the signe of Taurus hadde y-roone
Twenty degrees and oon, and somwhat more;
And knew by kynde, and by noon other lore,
That it was pryme, and crew with blisful stevene.
'The sonne,' he sayde, 'is clomben up on hevene
Fourty degrees and oon, and more, y-wis.
Madame Pertelote, my worldes blis,
Herkneth thise blisful briddes how they singe,
And see the fresshe floures how they springe;
Ful is myn herte of revel and solas.'
But sodeinly him fil a sorweful cas;
For ever the latter ende of joye is wo.
God woot that worldly joye is sone ago;
And if a rethor coude faire endyte,
He in a cronique saufly mighte it wryte,
As for a sovereyn notabilitee.
Now every wys man, lat him herkne me;
This storie is al-so trewe, I undertake,
As is the book of Launcelot de Lake,
That wommen holde in ful gret reverence.
Now wol I torne agayn to my sentence.

  A col-fox, ful of sly iniquitee,
That in the grove hadde woned yeres three,
By heigh imaginacioun forn-cast,
The same night thurgh-out the hegges brast
Into the yerd, ther Chauntecleer the faire
Was wont, and eek his wyves, to repaire;
And in a bed of wortes stille he lay,

He feathered Pertelote full twenty time,
And trod as often, ere that it was prime.
All like unto a lion grim he goes,
And strutteth up and down upon his toes.
Scarcely he deigned with foot to touch the ground,
And chucked all proudly when a corn he found,
And then his wives ran to him, one and all.
Thus royal, like a prince within his hall,
Here of this Chanticleer I take farewell,
And after of his danger will I tell.
Now when the month in which the world began,
That March is called, when God first fashioned man,
Was ended; yea, and in addition too
(Since March began) thirty more days and two,
It fell that Chanticleer, in all his pride,
His wives all seven walking by his side,
Cast his eye upward to the shining sun
That in the sign of Taurus now had run
Twenty and one degrees and somewhat more,
And knew by nature (and no other lore)
That it was prime, and crew out lustily.
And, "Now the sun has climbed the heaven," said he,
"Forty degrees and one, and more for sure;
Dame Pertelote, my bliss and paramour,
Hearken these birds how joyfully they sing,
And see the flowers, how fresh and bright they spring;
Full is my heart of joy and revelling."
But suddenly befell a grievous thing,
For ever the farther end of joy is woe.
God know'th that joys of earth are soon to go,
And if an orator could write this well,
He might embed it in a chronicle
As a fact of sovereign notability.
Let every wise man listen unto me;
This story is just as true, I undertake,
As is the book of Launcelot of the Lake,
Whereof are ladies reverent and fain;
Now to my theme will I return again.
A black-marked fox, wicked and very sly,
Had lurked for three years in the wood near by,
And by a fine, premeditated plot
That same night, breaking through the hedge, had got
Into the yard where Chanticleer the fair
Was with his wives accustomed to repair;
And in a bed of herbs stone-still he lay

Til it was passed undern of the day,
Wayting his tyme on Chauntecleer to falle,
As gladly doon thise homicydes alle,
That in awayt liggen to mordre men.
O false mordrer, lurking in thy den!
O newe Scariot, newe Genilon!
False dissimilour, O Greek Sinon,
That broghtest Troye al outrely to sorwe!
O Chauntecleer, acursed be that morwe,
That thou into that yerd flough fro the bemes,
Thou were ful wel y-warned by thy dremes,
That thilke day was perilous to thee.
But what that god forwoot mot nedes be,
After the opinioun of certeyn clerkis.
Witnesse on him, that any perfit clerk is,
That in scole is gret altercacioun
In this matere, and greet disputisoun,
And hath ben of an hundred thousand men.
But I ne can not bulte it to the bren,
As can the holy doctour Augustyn,
Or Boëce, or the bishop Bradwardyn,
Whether that goddes worthy forwiting
Streyneth me nedely for to doon a thing,
(Nedely clepe I simple necessitee);
Or elles, if free choys be graunted me
To do that same thing, or do it noght,
Though god forwoot it, er that it was wroght;
Or if his witing streyneth nevere a del
But by necessitee condicionel.
I wol not han to do of swich matere;
My tale is of a cok, as ye may here,
That took his counseil of his wyf, with sorwe,
To walken in the yerd upon that morwe
That he had met the dreem, that I yow tolde.
Wommennes counseils been ful ofte colde;
Wommannes counseil broghte us first to wo,
And made Adam fro paradys to go,
Ther-as he was ful mery, and wel at ese.—
But for I noot, to whom it mighte displese,
If I counseil of wommen wolde blame,
Passe over, for I seyde it in my game.
Rede auctours, wher they trete of swich matere,
And what thay seyn of wommen ye may here.
Thise been the cokkes wordes, and nat myne;
I can noon harm of no womman divyne.—

Till onward to eleven went the day,
Waiting his time on Chanticleer to fall
As do the murderers gladly—one and all—
That low in ambush crouch to murder men.
O treacherous murderer, lurking in thy den!
O new Iscariot! O new Ganilon!
O false dissembler, O thou Greek Sinon
That broughtest Troy all utterly to sorrow!
O Chanticleer, accursèd be that morrow
That thou into the yard flew from the beams.
Thou hadst been well admonished in thy dreams
That this same day was perilous to thee.
But that which God foreknows must surely be
As certain scholars make the matter work.
This ye will learn from any well-trained clerk:
Upon that point has been great altercation
Within the schools, and lengthy disputation
Among a hundred thousand if a man!
But I could never sift it to the bran
As could the holy doctor Augustine,
Or Boëthius, or Bishop Bradwardine
To say if God's divine forewitnessing
Compelleth me of need to do a thing
(By need I mean simple necessity)
Or whether a free choice be granted me
To do that same thing or to do it not,
Though God foreknew it ere that it was wrought;
Or if his knowing binds me not a whit,
Save on condition, to accomplish it!
In no such matters will I interfere;
My tale is of a cock, as ye may hear,
That from his wife took counsel, to his sorrow,
To walk within the yard upon that morrow
That he had dreamed the dream I have related.
Women's advice is oftentimes ill-fated!
Counsel of woman brought us first to woe
And out of Paradise made Adam go
Though he was merry there, and well at ease.
But since I know not whom it might displease
Should I the advice of women hold to blame—
Forget it, for I said it but in game.
Read authors where they treat of such affairs
And hear of women in these books of theirs;
These are the cock's words only, none of mine,
For in no woman can I harm divine!

Faire in the sond, to bathe hir merily,
Lyth Pertelote, and alle hir sustres by,
Agayn the sonne; and Chauntecleer so free
Song merier than the mermayde in the see;
For Phisiologus seith sikerly,
How that they singen wel and merily
And so bifel that, as he caste his yë,
Among the wortes, on a boterflye,
He was war of this fox that lay ful lowe.
No-thing ne liste him thanne for to crowe,
But cryde anon, 'cok, cok,' and up he sterte,
As man that was affrayed in his herte.
For naturelly a beest desyreth flee
Fro his contrarie, if he may it see,
Though he never erst had seyn it with his yë.
   This Chauntecleer, when he gan him espye,
He wolde han fled, but that the fox anon
Seyde, 'Gentil sire, allas! wher wol ye gon?
Be ye affrayed of me that am your freend?
Now certes, I were worse than a feend,
If I to yow wolde harm or vileinye.
I am nat come your counseil for t'espye;
But trewely, the cause of my cominge
Was only for to herkne how that ye singe.
For trewely ye have as mery a stevene
As eny aungel hath, that is in hevene;
Therwith ye han in musik more felinge
Than hadde Boëce, or any that can singe.
My lord your fader (god his soule blesse!)
And eek your moder, of hir gentilesse,
Han in myn hous y-been, to my gret ese;
And certes, sire, ful fayn wolde I yow plese.
But for men speke of singing, I wol saye,
So mote I brouke wel myn eyen tweye,
Save yow, I herde never man so singe
As dide your fader in the morweninge;
Certes, it was of herte, al that he song.
And for to make his voys the more strong,
He wolde so peyne him, that with bothe his yën
He most winke, so loude he wolde cryen,
And stonden on his tiptoon ther-with-al,
And strecche forth his nekke long and smal.
And eek he was of swich discrecioun,
That ther nas no man in no regioun
That him in song or wisdom mighte passe.

Fair in the sand, to bathe her merrily
Lieth Pertelote, with all her sisters nigh
In the warm sun, and Chanticleer so free,
Sung merrier than the mermaid in the sea;
(*Physiologus* says for certainty
That they sing very well and merrily).
And so it fell that, as he cast his eye
Among the worts, upon a butterfly,
He saw this fox before him, crouching low.
Nowise it pleased him then to strut or crow,
But quick "Cok, Cok," he cried, and up he started
Like one fear striketh suddenly weak-hearted.
For any creature will desire to flee
If suddenly his enemy he see,
Though never before he saw it with his eye.
    This Chanticleer, when he the fox did spy,
He would have fled, but that the fox anon
Said, "Noble sire, alas! will ye be gone?
Be ye afraid of me that am your friend?
Now truly, I were worse than any fiend
If I should plan you hurt or villainy.
I came not to disturb your privacy;
Surely, the one and only reason bringing
Me here—it was to listen to your singing.
For certainly ye have as merry a steven
As any angel hath that sings in heaven;
There is more feeling in your music than
Boëthius had, or any singing man.
My lord your father (God him sanctify)
Likewise your mother (in her great courtesy)
Have been within my house, to my great ease,
And truly, sire, full fain I would you please.
But with respect to singing, in this wise
I say: that as I hope to keep my eyes
I never heard such singing from a man
As from your father when the day began—
Truly, it was full lusty, all his song;
And that his voice might ring more clear and strong
He used to strain until his eyes would close,
So loudly would he cry; and he uprose
Upon his toe tips as he crowed withal,
And stretched his neck out very long and small,
He was of such discretion, too, that there
Was none in any country anywhere
That him in song or wisdom might surpass.

I have wel rad in daun Burnel the Asse,
Among his vers, how that ther was a cok,
For that a preestes sone yaf him a knok
Upon his leg, whyl he was yong and nyce,
He made him for to lese his benefyce.
But certeyn, ther nis no comparisoun
Bitwix the wisdom and discrecioun
Of youre fader, and of his subtiltee.
Now singeth, sire, for seinte Charitee,
Let see, conne ye your fader countrefete?'
This Chauntecleer his winges gan to bete,
As man that coude his tresoun nat espye,
So was he ravisshed with his flaterye.

    Allas! ye lordes, many a fals flatour
Is in your courtes, and many a losengeour,
That plesen yow wel more, by my feith,
Than he that soothfastnesse unto yow seith.
Redeth Ecclesiaste of flaterye;
Beth war, ye lordes, of hir trecherye.

    This Chauntecleer stood hye up-on his toos,
Strecching his nekke, and heeld his eyen cloos,
And gan to crowe loude for the nones;
And daun Russel the fox sterte up at ones,
And by the gargat hente Chauntecleer,
And on his bak toward the wode him beer,
For yet ne was ther no man that him sewed.
O destinee, that mayst nat been eschewed!
Allas, that Chauntecleer fleigh fro the bemes!
Allas, his wyf ne roghte nat of dremes!
And on a Friday fil al this meschaunce.
O Venus, that art goddesse of plesaunce,
Sin that thy servant was this Chauntecleer,
And in thy service dide al his poweer,
More for delyt, than world to multiplye,
Why woldestow suffre him on thy day to dye?
O Gaufred, dere mayster soverayn,
That, whan thy worthy king Richard was slayn
With shot, compleynedest his deth so sore,
Why ne hadde I now thy sentence and thy lore
The Friday for to chyde, as diden ye?
(For on a Friday soothly slayn was he.)
Than wolde I shewe yow how that I coude pleyne
For Chauntecleres drede, and for his peyne.

    Certes, swich cry ne lamentacioun
Was never of ladies maad, whan Ilioun

True, I have read in *Sir Burnell the Ass,*
Among his verse, how that there was a cock
Who, all because a priest's son gave a knock
Unto his leg when he was young—for this
Schemed that he later lost his benefice;
But certainly, no man can well compare
The high discretion and the wisdom rare
Your father had, with that cock's trickery.
But sing, sire, sing for holy charity;
Try now, can ye your father counterfeit?"
This Chanticleer his wings began to beat
As one that could no treachery descry—
So was he ravished by this flattery.

    Alas! ye lords, how many a rogue resides
Within your courts, and flatterers besides,
That are in faith more popular with you,
Than he who tells you plainly what is true.
Go read Ecclesiasticus, and see;
Beware, ye lordings, of their treachery!

    This Chanticleer stood high upon his toes,
He stretched his neck, he made his eyes to close,
And thus began to make a mighty cry.
Sir Russell Fox up-bounded instantly
And by the throat he seized this Chanticleer,
And flung him on his back, and sped from there
Off toward the wood, and no man saw him run.
O Destiny, that none of us may shun!
Alas! that Chanticleer flew from the beams!
Alas! that Pertelote recked not of dreams!
And on a Friday fell all this mischance!
O Venus, that art goddess of pleasance,
Since Chanticleer was servant unto thee
And spent himself to serve thee faithfully,
More for delight than the world to multiply,
Why wouldst thou suffer him on thy day to die?
O Geoffrey, master dear, supreme, and skilled,
That when King Richard was with arrow killed
Made for thy noble lord complaint so sore,
Why do I lack thy meaning and thy lore,
Friday to chide with singing, as did ye?
(For truly, on a Friday slain was he.)
Then would I raise my sorrowful refrain
For Chanticleer's affright, and for his pain.

    Not such a lamentation and great crying
Did Trojan ladies make for Ilium dying,

Was wonne, and Pirrus with his streite swerd,
Whan he hadde hent king Priam by the berd,
And slayn him (as saith us *Eneydos*),
As maden alle the hennes in the clos,
Whan they had seyn of Chauntecleer the sighte.
But sovereynly dame Pertelote shrighte,
Ful louder than dide Hasdrubales wyf,
Whan that hir housbond hadde lost his lyf,
And that the Romayns hadde brend Cartage;
She was so ful of torment and of rage,
That wilfully into the fyr she sterte,
And brende hir-selven with a stedfast herte.
O woful hennes, right so cryden ye,
As, whan that Nero brende the citee
Of Rome, cryden senatoures wyves,
For that hir housbondes losten alle hir lyves;
Withouten gilt this Nero hath hem slayn.
Now wol I torne to my tale agayn:—
This sely widwe, and eek hir doghtres two,
Herden thise hennes crye and maken wo,
And out at dores sterten they anoon,
And seyen the fox toward the grove goon,
And bar upon his bak the cok away;
And cryden, 'Out! harrow! and weylaway!
Ha, ha, the fox!' and after him they ran,
And eek with staves many another man;
Ran Colle our dogge, and Talbot, and Gerland,
And Malkin, with a distaf in hir hand;
Ran cow and calf, and eek the verray hogges
So were they fered for berking of the dogges
And shouting of the men and wimmen eke,
They ronne so, hem thoughte hir herte breke.
They yelleden as feendes doon in helle;
The dokes cryden as men wolde hem quelle;
The gees for fere flowen over the trees;
Out of the hyve cam the swarm of bees;
So hidous was the noyse, a! *benedicite!*
Certes, he Jakke Straw, and his meynee,
Ne made never shoutes half so shrille,
Whan that they wolden any Fleming kille,
As thilke day was maad upon the fox.
Of bras thay broghten bemes, and of box,
Of horn, of boon, in whiche they blewe and pouped,
And therwithal thay shryked and they houped;
It semed as that heven sholde falle.

When fire and Pyrrhus' naked sword they feared,
Who seized the aged Priam by the beard
And slew him (so the *Æneid* tells the tale)
As did these hens that in the yard made wail
To see their Chanticleer in fearsome plight.
But Pertelote shrieked with surpassing might;
Louder she cried than did Hasdrubal's wife
What time she saw Hasdrubal lose his life
And Carthage burned by Roman torches. She
Was filled with grief and torment utterly,
And in the fire she flung herself, and so
Steadfast of heart in flames to death did go.
O woeful hens, your cry was like the cry
When Nero sent Rome City to the sky
And there was fearful wailing from the wives
Of Roman senators that lost their lives;
All guiltless, wicked Nero had them slain!
Now to my tale will I return again.
    This simple widow and her daughters two
Heard all these hens lament with great to-do,
And rushing out of doors at once, they see
The fox make toward the forest hastily
Bearing the cock away upon his back.
They cried: "Out!" "Harrow!" "Welladay!" "Alack!"
"Ha! Ha! the fox!" and after him they ran,
And with them waving sticks came many a man;
And Collie our dog and Talbot and Gerland,
And Malkin, with a distaff in her hand;
The cows and calves ran, and the very hogs,
Crazed as they were with the barking of the dogs
And men and women making great halloo;
Their hearts with running all but burst in two.
They yelled like fiends in hell—who could have stilled them?
And the ducks cried as someone would have killed them.
The geese for fear went flying over trees,
Out of the hive there poured a swarm of bees;
Ah! *Benedicite!* such wild noise rang
In truth, that Jack Straw ramping with his gang
In search of some poor Fleming they could kill
Never made shouting that was half so shrill
As on that day was made about this fox.
They came with trumpets made of brass and box,
Of horn and bone on which they blew and tooted,
And therewithal they shrieked and whooped and hooted
Until it seemed that heaven itself would fall.

Now, gode men, I pray yow herkneth alle!
  Lo, how fortune turneth sodeinly
The hope and pryde eek of hir enemy!
This cok, that lay upon the foxes bak,
In al his drede, un-to the fox he spak,
And seyde, 'sire, if that I were as ye,
Yet sholde I seyn (as wis god helpe me),
Turneth agayn, ye proude cherles alle!
A verray pestilence up-on yow falle!
Now am I come un-to this wodes syde,
Maugree your heed, the cok shal heer abyde;
I wol him ete in feith, and that anon.'—
The fox answerde, 'in feith, it shal be don.'—
And as he spak that word, al sodeinly
This cok brak from his mouth deliverly,
And heighe up-on a tree he fleigh anon.
And whan the fox saugh that he was y-gon,
'Allas!' quod he, 'O Chauntecleer, allas!
I have to yow,' quod he, 'y-doon trespas,
In-as-muche as I maked yow aferd,
Whan I yow hente, and broghte out of the yerd;
But, sire, I dide it in no wikke entente;
Com doun, and I shal telle yow what I mente.
I shal seye sooth to yow, god help me so.'
'Nay than,' quod he, 'I shrewe us bothe two,
And first I shrewe my-self, bothe blood and bones,
If thou bigyle me ofter than ones.
Thou shalt na-more, thurgh thy flaterye,
Do me to singe and winke with myn yë.
For he that winketh, whan he sholde see,
Al wilfully, god lat him never thee!'
'Nay,' quod the fox, 'but god yeve him meschaunce,
That is so undiscreet of governaunce,
That jangleth whan he sholde holde his pees.'
  Lo, swich it is for to be recchelees,
And necligent, and truste on flaterye.
But ye that holden this tale a folye,
As of a fox, or of a cok and hen,
Taketh the moralitee, good men.
For seint Paul seith, that al that writen is,
To our doctryne it is y-write, y-wis.
Taketh the fruyt, and lat the chaf be stille.
  Now, gode God, if that it be thy wille,
As seith my lord, so make us alle good men;
And bringe us to his heighe blisse. Amen.

                from THE CANTERBURY TALES

And now, good men, I pray you hearken all!
　Look now how Fortune turneth suddenly
The hope and triumph of their enemy.
This cock, upon the fox's back that lay,
Despite his fear, still found a voice to say
Thus to the fox: "Now, sire, were I as ye,
God help me, I would shout defiantly:
'Turn once again, proud churls, turn one and all!
A very pestilence upon you fall!
Look ye, at last I stand within the wood!
Now do your worst, the cock is mine for good,
For I will eat him up, and quickly, too.' "
The fox replied: "In faith, that will I do!"—
But as he spoke the word, the cock broke free
Out of his open mouth full dextrously
And flew high up and perched upon a limb.
And the fox saw him there and called to him:
"Alas! O Chanticleer, alas!" quoth he,
"I fear that I have done you injury!
I frightened you by seizing you so hard
And rushing with you hither from your yard;
But, sire, I did it with no ill intent—
Come down, and I will tell you what I meant.
God help me, I will speak you fair and true."
"Nay, then," quoth he, "my curse upon us two,
And first I'll curse myself, both blood and bones,
If thou shalt fool me oftener than once!
Thou shalt no more with crafty flatteries
Make me to sing for thee and close my eyes.
For he who shuts his eyes when he should see—
God give no good to any such as he!"
"Nay," quoth the fox, "but God give him mischance
That is so indiscreet of governance
That jabbers when he ought to hold his tongue!"
　So of the negligent my tale is sung,
That reckless are, and trust in flattery.
But if ye deem this naught but vanity,
As of a fox, or of a cock and hen,
Take ye the moral that it hath, good men.
For Saint Paul, saith he not that all things writ
Can point our doctrine and embellish it?
Then take the grain and let the chaff lie still.
And now, good God, if it shall be Thy will
As saith my lord, so make us all good men
And bring us into holy bliss. *Amen.*
　　　　　Modern English version by Frank Ernest Hill

One of Chaucer's most ingratiating though not one of his greatest poems, THE PARLEMENT OF FOULES (or THE PARLIAMENT OF BIRDS), opens with what is perhaps his most famous line, a line which has been consciously or unconsciously echoed by every maker in every medium:

The lyf so short, the craft so long to lerne—

THE PARLEMENT OF FOULES exhibits Chaucer in many unsuspected ways. It shows that Chaucer's genius was not limited to narrative poetry, that he could compose lyrics as well as legends, and that he

Foules Rondel

Now welcom somer, with thy sonne softe
That hast this wintres weders over-shake,
And driven awey the longe nightes blake!

Seynt Valentyn, that art ful hy on-lofte;—
Thus singen smale foules for thy sake—
   Now welcom somer, with thy sonne softe
   That hast this wintres weders over-shake.

Wel han they cause for to gladen ofte,
Sith ech of hem recovered hath his make
Ful blisful may they singen whan they wake;
   Now welcom somer, with thy sonne softe,
   That hast this wintres weders over-shake,
   And driven awey the longe nightes blake!
   from THE PARLEMENT OF FOULES

A Rondel of Merciles Beautè

Your eyen two wol slee me sodenly,
I may the beautè of hem not sustene,
So woundeth hit through-out my herte kene.

could translate so ingeniously that the paraphrases became pure Chaucer. In the midst of THE PARLEMENT OF FOULES, for example, there is a rondel, one of the strictest and most delicate of the old French forms; yet Chaucer has turned the tune so dexterously that it becomes a perfect English song.

The reference to "Seynt Valentyn" reminds us that the day of the saint's martyrdom is coincidental with the beginning of spring in southern climes. Moreover, there is a tradition that birds choose their mates on February 14. Thus a celibate Roman priest becomes the patron saint of lovers.

The Birds' Rondel

Now welcome, summer, with thy sunshine soft,
This wintry weather thou wilt overtake,
And drive away the night so long and black!

Saint Valentine, thou who art crowned aloft,
The little birds are singing for thy sake:
  Now welcome, summer, with thy sunshine soft,
  This wintry weather thou wilt overtake.

They have good reason to be glad, and oft,
Since each has found his mate in bush and brake.
O blissfully they sing when they awake:
  Now welcome, summer, with thy sunshine soft,
  This wintry weather thou wilt overtake,
  And drive away the nights so long and black!
    Modern English version by L. U.

Another rondel, a tribute to merciless beauty, strikes a deeper note. Always adhering to the demands of the form, Chaucer takes the pattern and, infusing it with passion, lifts it above artifice.

A Rondel of Merciless Beauty

Your two great eyes will slay me suddenly;
Their beauty shakes me who was once serene;
Straight through my heart the wound is quick and keen.

And bu. your word wol helen hastily
My hertes wounde, whyl that hit is grene,
Your eyen two wol slee me sodenly,
I may the beautè of hem not sustene.

Upon my trouthe I sey yow feithfully,
That ye ben of my lyf and deeth the quene;
For with my deeth the trouthe shal be sene.
Your eyen two wol slee me sodenly,
I may the beautè of hem not sustene,
So woundeth hit through-out my herte kene.

Though not one of his most important poems, Chaucer's COM-
PLAINT TO HIS EMPTY PURSE is suggestive because it conveys real
necessity beneath a surface lightness, and because it is supposed to
be one of the last pieces, if not the very last poem, he wrote. The
date of the composition (1399) is determined by an envoy—or mes-
sage—added to the verses. This envoy departs from the rest of the
poem, which begins as a true ballade, both in rhyme and form; the

The Compleinte of Chaucer to His Empty Purs

To you, my purs, and to non other wight
Compleyne I, for ye be my lady dere!
I am so sory, now that ye be light;
For certes, but ye make me hevy chere,
Me were as leef be leyd up-on my bere;
For whiche un-to you mercy thus I crye:
Beth hevy ageyn, or elles mot I dye!

Now voucheth sauf this day, or hit be night,
That I of you the blisful soun may here,
Or see your colour lyk the sonne bright,
That of yelownesse hadde never pere.
Ye be my lyf, ye be myn hertes stere,
Quene of comfort and of good companye:
Beth hevy ageyn, or elles mot I dye!

Now purs, that be to me my lyves light,
And saveour, as doun in this worlde here,
Out of this toune help me through your might,

Only your word will heal the injury
To my hurt heart, while yet the wound is clean—
Your two great eyes will slay me suddenly;
Their beauty shakes me who was once serene.

Upon my word, I tell you faithfully
Through life and after death you are my queen;
For with my death the whole truth shall be seen.
Your two great eyes will slay me suddenly;
Their beauty shakes me who was once serene;
Straight through my heart the wound is quick and keen.
Modern English version by L. U.

chief interest lies in its appeal to the new king, Henry IV, to remedy Chaucer's financial embarrassment.

It is pleasant to record that the monarch turned from the affairs of state to become a patron of poetry. One of the first acts of Henry IV after his accession was the granting of a new pension to the sixty-year-old poet, who, unfortunately, lived to enjoy it for only a few months.

Chaucer's Complaint to His Empty Purse

To you, my purse, and to no other wight [1]
Complain I, for you are my lady dear!
I am unhappy, now that you are light,
For certainly you give so little cheer
I would as lief be laid upon my bier.
Therefore unto your mercy thus I cry:
"Once more be heavy; otherwise I die."

Vouchsafe this day (or it will be as night)
That I the blissful sound of you may hear,
Or see your color, like the sunlight bright,
That for pure yellow never had a peer.
You are my life; my wandering heart you steer;
Queen of my comfort and good company:
Once more be heavy; otherwise I die.

Now purse, who are to me my life's own light,
My saviour, the way the world runs here,
Out of this trouble help me with your might,

[1] *Human being.*

Sin that ye wole nat been my tresorere;
For I am shave as nye as any frere.
But yit I pray un-to your curtesye:
Beth hevy ageyn, or elles mot I dye!

John Denham, a minor seventeenth-century poet, was the first to speak of Chaucer as "the morning star," and one likes to believe that the epithet entitled Denham to the tomb so close to Chaucer's in Westminster Abbey. Wordsworth and Tennyson echoed the phrase; the former enlarged the tribute to Chaucer when he wrote:

O great Precursor, genuine morning star.

Although Chaucer's scope and energy are revealed in the long narratives, his strength is indicated in the very compactness of his shorter poems. Even his use of the French forms establishes his genius. The BALADE OF BON COUNSEILL is particularly illuminating; it expresses a full philosophy in a medium usually employed for courtly affectation, technical ingenuity, and elaborate badinage.

Balade of Bon Counseill

Flee fro the prees, and dwelle with soth-fastnesse,
Suffyce unto thy good, though hit be smal;
For hord hath hate, and climbing tikelnesse,
Prees hath envye, and wele blent overal;
Savour no more than thee bihove shal;
Werk wel thy-self, that other folk canst rede;
And trouthe shal delivere, hit is no drede.

Tempest thee noght al croked to redresse,
In trust of hir that turneth as a bal:
Gret reste stant in litel besinesse;
And eek be war to sporne ageyn an al;
Stryve noght, as doth the crokke with the wal.
Daunte thy-self, that dauntest otheres dede;
And trouthe shal delivere, hit is no drede.

That thee is sent, receyve in buxumnesse,
The wrastling for this worlde axeth a fal.

Since you refuse to be my treasurer;
Never was friar clipped so close, I fear.
But yet I pray unto your courtesy:
Once more be heavy; otherwise I die.
Modern English version by L. U.

The translation by Henry van Dyke was originally prepared for his essay in THE MAN BEHIND THE BOOK and was one of the "proofs" that "old Dan Chaucer, like practically all the great authors, ended up as a preacher." Van Dyke's original paraphrase failed to include the disputed envoy—"disputed" because it is found in only one Chaucer manuscript—but the poet and essayist was persuaded to supply the stanza. It was written for the editor shortly before van Dyke's death.

The word "vache" (literally "beast") in the envoy is a proof that Chaucer was not above punning. The poem itself was addressed to one of Chaucer's intimates, Sir Philip la Vache. Thus the opening line of the envoy is both a record of his friend's name and a teasing comment upon it.

Ballade of Good Counsel

Flee from the crowd and dwell with truthfulness:
    Suffice thee with thy goods, though they be small:
To hoard brings hate, to climb brings giddiness;
    The crowd has envy, and success blinds all;
    Desire no more than to thy lot may fall;
Work well thyself to counsel others clear,
And Truth shall make thee free, there is no fear!

Torment thee not all crooked to redress,
    Nor put thy trust in fortune's turning ball;
Great peace is found in little busy-ness;
    And war but kicks against a sharpened awl;
    Strive not, thou earthen pot, to break the wall;
Subdue thyself, and others thee shall hear;
And Truth shall make thee free, there is no fear!

What God doth send, receive in gladsomeness;
    To wrestle for this world foretells a fall.

Her nis non hoom, her nis but wildernesse:
Forth, pilgrim, forth! Forth, beste, out of thy stal!
Know thy contree, look up, thank God of al;
Hold the hye wey, and lat thy gost thee lede:
And trouthe shal delivere, hit is no drede.

L'ENVOYE

Therefore, thou vache, leve thyn old wrecchednesse
Unto the worlde; leve now to be thral;
Crye him mercy that of his hy goodnesse
Made thee of noght, and in especial
Draw unto him, and pray in general
For thee, and eek for other, hevenlich mede;
And trouthe shal delivere, hit is no drede.

Here is no home, here is but wilderness:
  Forth, pilgrim, forth! Up, beast, and leave thy stall!
  Know thy country, look up, thank God for all:
Hold the high way, thy soul the pioneer;
And Truth shall make thee free, there is no fear!

ENVOY

Therefore, poor beast, forsake thy wretchedness;
  No longer let the vain world be thy stall.
His mercy seek who in his mightiness
  Made thee of naught, but not to be a thrall.
  Pray freely for thyself and pray for all
Who long for larger life and heavenly cheer;
And Truth shall make thee free, there is no fear!
                Modern version by Henry van Dyke

III

The Popular Ballad

THE old ballads are called "popular" in a double sense. Their appeal was immediate and permanent; their origin was among the people instead of among princes or prelates. The ancient story-poems were sung for the delight of the populace in market places and fairs, in taverns and on street corners, rather than for the delectation of lords and ladies in great mansions and the courts of kings. It might even be said that the people made their own songs. The ballads may have been conceived by a "professional" poet, but, since they were transmitted orally instead of written down, variations grew rapidly. Improvisations were added, lines interpolated—and what began as a product of an individual author became the expression of a community.

Toward the end of the nineteenth century Francis James Child, who performed one of the finest pieces of extended scholarship ever achieved by an American, collected more than three hundred extant English and Scottish ballads, many of which had been brought to America and were leading lives of their own in the New World. They adopted not only the transformed scene but the local accents wherever they found themselves, from the mountain songs of Maine to the "lonesome tunes" of Kentucky. Thus the ballads spanned the centuries; they reached from the events of antiquity to tomorrow's radio program. Bishop Percy first printed his pioneering RELIQUES OF ANCIENT ENGLISH POETRY in 1765, but he had little idea of the antiquity of the sources. Many of Percy's "finds" had their origins in the Middle Ages. In THE CANTERBURY TALES Chaucer imitated rhymed romances which were old in 1380; PIERS PLOWMAN, written some years earlier than Chaucer's masterpiece, casually mentions the versified tales of Robin Hood which had a great vogue in the early fourteenth century.

But the roots of the ballad penetrate soil which is still older and more remote. They can be found in Teutonic towns and Scandinavian forests; their beginnings are in the medieval words of the scalds and gleemen, the "smoothers and polishers of speech."

It was in the Cheviot Hills along the Scottish border that the English ballad attained its greatest power; the harpers were, almost always, "of the North Country." They employed their medium for current events as well as old legends; their tales were usually highly colored but, more often than not, they recorded the history of the period and the news of the day. Refrains, or "burdens," crept in; these refrains were sung as "responses" by the hearers. Words and music were often accompanied by choral dancing. The ballad was truly a communal affair, for it united the whole group. The soloist merged with the audience, and the audience roared approval of its own performance.

Since the ballad is essentially a story—a story for the crowd—it demands immediate comprehension. There is no time to be lost in preliminaries; the first line plunges the hearer into the heart of a situation. There are no digressions. Everything is swift, direct, and decisive. Before the first stanza has been completed, the characters leap into life.

One of the oldest of the ballads is also one of the most terrifying. In EDWARD the note of horror is struck in the first line. The ominous question about the blood-dripping sword summons the primitive violence of the times. The evasive answers add to the tension; it is not until the last line that the weak-willed son reveals the full extent of the tragedy.

Edward

"Why dois your brand sae drap wi bluid,
Edward, Edward,
Why dois your brand sae drap wi bluid,
  And why sae sad gang yee O?"
"O I hae killed my hauke sae guid,
Mither, mither,
O I hae killed my hauke sae guid,
  And I had nae mair but hee O."

"Your haukis bluid was nevir sae reid,[1]
>Edward, Edward,
Your haukis bluid was nevir sae reid,
>My deir son I tell thee O."
"O I hae killed my reid roan steid,
>>Mither, mither,
O I hae killed my reid roan steid,
>That erst [2] was sae fair and free O."

"Your steid was auld, and ye hae gat mair,
>Edward, Edward,
Your steid was auld, and ye hae gat mair,
>Sum other dule ye drie [3] O."
"O I hae killed my fadir deir,
>>Mither, mither,
O I hae killed my fadir deir,
>Alas, and wae is mee O!"

"And whatten penance wul ye drie for that,
>Edward, Edward?
And whatten penance wul ye drie for that?
>My deir son, now tell me O."
"Ile set my feet in yonder boat,
>>Mither, mither,
Ile set my feet in yonder boat,
>And Ile fare ovir the sea O."

"And what wul ye doe wi your towirs and your ha,[4]
>Edward, Edward?
And what wul ye doe wi your towirs and your ha,
>That were sae fair to see O?"
"Ile let thame stand tul they doun fa,[5]
>>Mither, mither,
Ile let thame stand tul they doun fa,
>For here nevir mair maun [6] I bee O."

"And what wul ye leive to your bairns and your wife,
>Edward, Edward?
And what wul ye leive to your bairns and your wife,
>Whan ye gang ovir the sea O?"
"The warldis [7] room, let them beg thrae life,
>>Mither, mither,
The warldis room, let them beg thrae life,
>For thame nevir mair wul I see O."

---

[1] *Red.*   [2] *Once.*   [3] *Grief you suffer.*   [4] *Hall.*   [5] *Fall.*   [6] *Must.*   [7] *World's.*

"And what wul ye leive to your ain mither deir?
                                    Edward, Edward?
And what wul ye leive to your ain mither deir?
    My deir son, now tell me O."
"The curse of hell frae me sall ye beir,[8]
                                    Mither, mither,
The curse of hell frae me sall ye beir,
    Sic [9] counseils ye gave to me O."

In EDWARD a son has murdered his father at the instigation of his
mother. In LORD RANDAL, a companion piece, a son has been subtly
done to death by his sweetheart. Here again the tragedy is antici-
pated in the first anxious question. And here, also, another char-
acteristic of the ballad emerges. The tale is not only swift but
simple. The tone is forthright; the language is the language of the
people. The very dialect has the ring of authentic speech. More-
over, the attitude is impersonal. The ballad maker is a true story-
teller, the more so since he is outside of the story. He rarely philoso-
phizes; he scarcely comments; his voice is never raised in outrage.
If his tale is bloody (and it usually is), the teller makes no effort to
soften the crude outlines. He is speaking to ordinary people who
relish extraordinary gossip and a bloody deed. Their enjoyment
would be spoiled by moralizing, and the ballad maker never permits
himself to be shocked. He is a narrator not a judge; he is not sur-
prised by illicit love, agitated by murder, or agonized by betrayal.

Lord Randal

"O where hae ye been, Lord Randal, my son?
O where hae ye been, my handsome young man?"
"I hae been to the wild wood; mother, make my bed soon,
For I'm weary wi' hunting, and fain wald lie down."

"Where gat ye your dinner, Lord Randal, my son?
Where gat ye your dinner, my handsome young man?"
"I dined wi' my true-love; mother, make my bed soon,
For I'm weary wi' hunting, and fain wald lie down."

"What gat ye to your dinner, Lord Randal, my son?
What gat ye to your dinner, my handsome young man?"

---

[8] *Bear.*   [9] *Such.*

"I gat eels boil'd in broo ª; mother, make my bed soon,
For I'm weary wi' hunting, and fain wald lie down."

"What became of your bloodhounds, Lord Randal, my son?
What became of your bloodhounds, my handsome young man?"
"O they swell'd and they died; mother, make my bed soon,
For I'm weary wi' hunting, and fain wald lie down."

"O I fear ye are poison'd, Lord Randal, my son!
O I fear ye are poison'd, my handsome young man!"
"O yes! I am poison'd; mother, make my bed soon,
For I'm sick at the heart, and I fain wald lie down."

The ballad maker's detached attitude is strikingly exemplified in
SIR PATRICK SPENS, one of the indisputably historical ballads. The
hero was a warrior-mariner of the thirteenth century, beloved by all
except a small faction. Yet the ballad maker utters no criticism of
the malevolence which influenced the king to send Spens and the
Scots nobles to their death at sea. The ballad maker is content to
give the facts, to paint the picture, to indicate the cabal, and let the
reader regard the adventure as a terrible betrayal or a matter of
course.

Sir Patrick Spens

The king sits in Dunfermline town
  Drinking the blude-red wine;
"O whare will I get a skeely ¹ skipper
  To sail this new ship o' mine?"

O up and spak an eldern knight,
  Sat at the king's right knee:
"Sir Patrick Spens is the best sailor
  That ever sail'd the sea."

Our king has written a braid letter,²
  And seal'd it with his hand,
And sent it to Sir Patrick Spens,
  Was walking on the strand.

ª *Broth.* ¹ *Skillful.* ² *A broad-sheeted official document.*

"To Noroway, to Noroway,
 To Noroway o'er the faem;
The king's daughter o' Noroway,
 'Tis thou must bring her hame."

The first word that Sir Patrick read
 A loud, loud laugh'd he;
The next word that Sir Patrick read
 The tear blinded his e'e.

"O wha is this has done this deed
 This ill deed unto me,
To send us out, at this time o' year,
 To sail upon the sea?

"Be it wind, be it weet, be it hail, be it sleet,
 Our ship must sail the faem;
The king's daughter o' Noroway,
 'Tis we must fetch her hame.

"Mak ready, mak ready, my merry men a'!
 Our gude ship sails the morn."—
"Now ever alack, my master dear,
 I fear a deadly storm.

"I saw the new moon late yestreen
 Wi' the auld moon in her arm;
And if we gang to sea, master,
 I fear we'll come to harm."

They hadna sail'd a league, a league,
 A league but barely three,
When the lift ³ grew dark, and the wind blew loud,
 And gurly ⁴ grew the sea.

The ankers brak, the topmast split,
 It was sic a deadly storm:
And the waves cam owre the broken ship
 Till a' her sides were torn.

O laith, laith ⁵ were our gude Scots lords
 To wet their cork-heel'd shoon;
But lang or a' the play was plav'd
 Their hats they swam aboon.⁶

---

3 *Sky.*   4 *Angry.*   5 *Loath.*   6 *Their hats swam above their heads.*

O lang, lang may the ladies sit,
  Wi' their fans into their hand,
Before they see Sir Patrick Spens
  Come sailing to the strand.

And lang, lang may the maidens sit
  Wi' their gold kames in their hair,
A-waiting for their ain dear loves,
  For them they'll see nae mair.

Half-owre, half-owre to Aberdour,
  'Tis fifty fathoms deep;
And there lies gude Sir Patrick Spens,
  Wi' the Scots lords at his feet.

In SIR PATRICK SPENS and EDWARD the Scots dialect captures the savage color of the clan wars. It is the brusque and powerful language which gives strength and speed to the narrative; there are no literary evasions and elaborate images. The ballad maker discards the devices of learning; he knows his hearers must take in the full import of his story without a background of knowledge or benefit of culture. He never employs a kenning; he would not speak of a "sea tree" or a "sea horse" when he means a ship.

THE DOUGLAS TRAGEDY and CHILDE MAURICE are somewhat less dependent on the quaintness of dialect and more on the terror of their tales. In the former, the desperate Lady Margret is torn between loyalty to her father and passion for her lover. The story has gone through many versions, but all the variants are associated by popular tradition with a particular family and a particular spot in Selkirkshire. Seven large stones on the heights of Blackhouse are said to mark the spot where the "seven brethren" were slain, and the Douglas rivulet is supposed to be the very stream at which the lovers alighted to drink from "the spring that ran sae clear" and which soon ran red with Lord William's "gude heart's blood."

CHILDE MAURICE is one of the ballads which deal with absolute romance rather than quasi history. Here a magnificent theme takes a surprising turn and ascends inevitably to a terrifying but wholly unexpected climax.

The Douglas Tragedy

"Rise up, rise up, now, Lord Douglas," she says,
    "And put on your armor so bright;
Let it never be said that a daughter of thine
    Was married to a lord under night.

"Rise up, rise up, my seven bold sons,
    And put on your armor so bright,
And take better care of your youngest sister,
    For your eldest's awa' last night."

Lady Margret was on a milk-white steed,
    Lord William was on a grey,
With a bugelet horn hung down by his side,
    And lightly they rode away.

Lord William lookit o'er his left shoulder,
    To see what he could see,
And there he spy'd her seven brethren bold,
    Come riding o'er the lee.

"Light down, light down, Lady Margret," he said,
    "And hold my steed in your hand,
Until that against your seven brethren bold,
    And your father, I make a stand."

She held his steed in her milk-white hand,
    And never shed one tear,
Until that she saw her seven brethren fa',
    And her father hard fighting, who loved her so dear.

"O hold your hand, Lord William!" she said,
    "For your strokes they are wondrous sair;
True lovers I can get many a ane,
    But a father I can never get mair."

O she's ta'en out her handkerchief,
    It was o' the holland sae fine,
And aye she dighted [1] her father's bloody wounds,
    That were redder than the wine.

"O chuse, O chuse, Lady Margret," he said,
    "O whether will ye gang or bide?" [2]

[1] *Dressed.*   [2] *Go or stay.*

"I'll gang, I'll gang, Lord William," she said,
   "For you have left me no other guide."

He's lifted her on a milk-white steed,
   And himself on a dapple grey,
With a bugelet horn hung down by his side,
   And slowly they baith rade away.

O they rade on, and on they rade,
   And a' by the light of the moon,
Until they came to yon wan water,
   And there they lighted down.

They lighted down to take a drink
   Of the spring that ran sae clear,
And down the stream ran his gude heart's blood,
   And sair she 'gan to fear.

"Hold up, hold up, Lord William," she says,
   "For I fear that you are slain!"
"'Tis naething but the shadow of my scarlet cloak,
   That shines in the water sae plain."

O they rade on, and on they rade,
   And a' by the light of the moon,
Until they cam to his mother's ha' door,
   And there they lighted down.

"Get up, get up, lady mother," he says,
   "Get up, and let me in!
Get up, get up, lady mother," he says,
   "For this night my fair lady I've win.

"O make my bed, lady mother," he says,
   "O make it braid and deep!
And lay Lady Margret close at my back,
   And the sounder I will sleep."

Lord William was dead lang ere midnight,
   Lady Margret lang ere day,
And all true lovers that go thegither,
   May they have mair luck than they!

Lord William was buried in St. Marie's kirk,
   Lady Margret in Marie's quire:

Out o' the lady's grave grew a bonny red rose,
    And out o' the knight's a brier.

And they twa met, and they twa plat,[3]
    And fain they wad be near;
And a' the warld might ken right weel
    They were twa lovers dear.

Childe Maurice

Childe Maurice hunted the Silver Wood,
    He whistled and he sang:
"I think I see the woman yonder
    That I have lovèd lang."

He called to his little man John,
    "You do not see what I see;
For yonder I see the very first woman
    That ever lovèd me."

"Here is a glove, a glove," he says,
    "Lined all with fur it is;
Bid her to come to Silver Wood
    To speak with Childe Maurice."

"And here is a ring, a ring," he says,
    "A ring of the precious stone:
He prays her come to Silver Wood
    And ask the leave of none."

"Well do I love your errand, master,
    But better I love my life.
Would you have me go to John Steward's castle,
    To tryst away his wife?"

"Do not I give you meat?" he says,
    "Do not I give you fee?
How dare you stop my errand
    When that I bid you flee?"

When the lad came to John Steward's castle,
    He ran right through the gate
Until he came to the high, high hall
    Where the company sat at meat.

3 *Grew about each other.*

"Here is a glove, my lady," said he,
  "Lined all with fur it is;
It bids you to come to Silver Wood
  And speak with Childe Maurice.

"And here is a ring, a ring of gold,
  Set with the precious stone:
It prays you to come to Silver Wood
  And ask the leave of none."

Out then spake the wily nurse,
  With the bairn upon her knee:
"If this be come from Childe Maurice
  It's dearly welcome to me."

"Thou liest, thou liest, thou wily nurse,
  So loud as I hear thee lie!
I brought it to John Steward's lady,
  And I trow thou be not she."

Then up and rose him John Steward.
  And an angry man was he:
"Did I think there was a lord in the world
  My lady loved but me!"

He dressed himself in his lady's gown,
  Her mantle and her hood;
But a little brown sword hung down by his knee,
  And he rode to Silver Wood.

   .   .   .   .

Childe Maurice sat in Silver Wood,
  He whistled and he sang,
"I think I see the woman coming
  That I have loved so lang."

But then stood up Childe Maurice
  His mother to help from horse:
"O alas, alas!" says Childe Maurice,
  "My mother was never so gross!"

"No wonder, no wonder," John Steward he said,
  "My lady loved thee well,
For the fairest part of my body
  Is blacker than thy heel."

John Steward took the little brown sword
   That hung low down by his knee;
He has cut the head off Childe Maurice
   And the body put on a tree.

And when he came to his lady—
   Looked over the castle-wall—
He threw the head into her lap,
   Saying, "Lady, take the ball!"

Says, "Dost thou know Childe Maurice' head,
   When that thou dost it see?
Now lap it soft, and kiss it oft,
   For thou loved'st him better than me."

But when she looked on Childe Maurice' head
   She ne'er spake words but three:
"I never bare no child but one,
   And you have slain him, trulye."

"I got him in my mother's bower
   With mickle [1] sin and shame;
I brought him up in the good greenwood
   Under the shower and rain."

And she has taken her Childe Maurice
   And kissed him, mouth and chin:
"O better I loved my Childe Maurice
   Than all my royal kin!"

"Woe be to thee!" John Steward he said,
   And a woe, woe man was he;
"For if you had told me he was your son
   He had never been slain by me."

Says, "Wicked be my merry men all,
   I gave meat, drink and cloth!
But could they not have holden me
   When I was in all that wrath?"

It is futile to speak of a "pure" ballad. The ballads have no cer-
tain chronology, and the originals have been lost in shifting forms
and changing times. Quiller-Couch, in THE OXFORD BOOK OF BALLADS,

[1] *Great.*

reminds the reader that the ballads have been continually reshaped
and that no one arrangement can claim to be the "authorized" ver-
sion; "it may easily happen—in fact happens not seldom—that a
really old ballad 'of the best period' has reached us late and in a
corrupted form, its original gold overlaid with silver and bronze."

It may not be a bad thing that there are no originals to act as
standards of comparison. The multiform nature of the ballads is
part of their charm; "the ballads," wrote William Allingham in his
selection of the choicest British examples, "owe no little of their
merit to the countless riddlings, siftings, shiftings, omissions, and
additions of innumerable reciters." In the ballads we must, there-
fore, accept the story-poems with all their defects, their sometimes
annoying gaps, their unaccountable leaps, their sudden descents
from high poetry to flat statement. But, in the very haphazard man-
ner, the strong feeling comes through; the spirit is as spontaneous
today as when the rhymed narratives were composed three to five
centuries ago.

Johnie Armstrong

There dwelt a man in faire Westmerland,
    Johnie Armstrong men did him call,
He had neither lands nor rents coming in,
    Yet he kept eight score men in his hall.

He had horse and harness for them all,
    Goodly steeds were all milke-white;
O the golden bands about their necks,
    And their weapons, they were alike.

Newes then was brought unto the king,
    That there was sicke a won [1] as he,
That lived lyke a bold out-law,
    And robbed all the north country.

The king he writ a letter then,
    A letter large and long;
He signed it with his owne hand,
    And he promised to doe him no wrong.

[1] *Such a one.*

When this letter came Johnie untill,[2]
  His heart it was as blythe as birds on the tree;
"Never was I sent for before any king,
  My father, my grandfather, nor none but me.

"And if we goe the king before,
  I would we went most orderly;
Every man of you shall have his scarlet cloak,
  Laced with silver laces three.

"Every one of you shall have his velvet coat,
  Laced with silver lace so white;
O the gold bands about your necks,
  Black hats, white feathers, alyke."

By the morrow morninge at ten of the clock,
  Towards Eddenburrough gon was he,
And with him all his eight score men;
  Good lord, it was a goodly sight for to see!

When Johnie came befower the king,
  He fell downe on his knee;
"O pardon, my soveraine leige," he said,
  "O pardon my eight score men and me!"

"Thou shalt have no pardon, thou traitor strong,
  For thy eight score men nor thee;
For tomorrow morning by ten of the clock,
  Thou shalt all hang on the gallow-tree."

But Johnie looked over his left shoulder,
  Good Lord, what a grevious look looked he!
Saying, "Asking grace of a graceles face—
  Why there is none for you nor me."

But Johnie had a bright sword by his side,
  And it was made of the mettle so free,
That had not the king stept his foot aside,
  He had smitten his head from his faire bodie.

Saying, "Fight on, my merry men all,
  And see that none of you be taine[3];
For rather than men shall say we were hanged,
  Let them report how we were slaine."

2 *Unto.*   3 *Captured alive.*

Then like a mad man Johnie laide about,
And like a mad man then fought he,
Untill a falce Scot came Johnie behinde,
And run him through the faire bodie.

Saying, "Fight on, my merry men all,
And see that none of you be taine;
For I will lie down but to bleed awhile,
And then will I rise and fight againe."

JOHNIE ARMSTRONG is a story of treachery, but the tale is one of
heroism rather than horror. The Armstrongs were independent
lairds who lived on the border and refused to be allied either with
the English or the Scots, and the death of their leader was proudly
recorded in their annals.

ROBIN HOOD'S DEATH also deals with treachery, but here the hero
is betrayed not by his king but by his cousin. No motive is given
for the treachery—the ballad maker is content to show the crime—
but, as usual, the sympathy is obviously with the outlaw who robbed
the rich and helped the poor.

The Robin Hood saga is so great, so many story-poems have clus-
tered about it, that the accumulated series comes close to being an
epic. Completely unhistorical, Robin Hood and his followers, the
ever-sportive Friar Tuck and the ever-faithful Little John, are not
only heroic but epic figures. Efforts have been made to link Robin
Hood with old Germanic myths—he has sometimes been identified
with a humanized Woden—but, as Francis James Child has con-
cluded, "Robin Hood is absolutely a creation of the ballad muse."

When the poem is sung, the refrain (the second and sixth lines of
the opening stanza) is repeated throughout the poem, indicating
that this ballad was relished not only for group singing but—incon-
gruously enough—for choral dancing.

Robin Hood's Death

When Robin Hood and Little John
Down a down a down a down
Went o'er yon bank of broom,
Said Robin Hood to Little John,
We have shot for many a pound.
Hey down a down a down a down!

But I am not able to shoot one shot more,
   My broad arrows will not flee;
But I have a cousin lives down below,
   Please God, she will bleed me.

Now Robin he is to fair Kirkly gone,
   As fast as he can win;
But before he came there, as we do hear,
   He was taken very ill.

And when he came to fair Kirkly-hall,
   He knock'd all at the ring,
But none was so ready as his cousin herself
   For to let bold Robin in.

"Will you please to sit down, cousin Robin," she said,
   "And drink some beer with me?"
"No, I will neither eat nor drink,
   Till I am blooded by thee."

"Well, I have a room, cousin Robin," she said,
   "Which you did never see,
And if you please to walk therein,
   You blooded by me shall be."

She took him by the lily-white hand,
   And led him to a private room,
And there she blooded bold Robin Hood,
   While one drop of blood would run down.

She blooded him in a vein of the arm,
   And locked him up in the room;
There did he bleed the live-long day,
   Until the next day at noon.

He then bethought him of a casement there,
   Thinking for to get down;
But was so weak he could not leap,
   He could not get him down.

He then bethought him of his bugle-horn,
   Which hung low down to his knee;
He set his horn unto his mouth,
   And blew out weak blasts three.

Then Little John, when hearing him,
    As he sat under a tree,
"I fear my master is now near dead,
    He blows so wearily."

Then Little John to fair Kirkly is gone,
    As fast as he can dri'e [1]
But when he came to Kirkly-hall,
    He broke locks two or three;

Until he came bold Robin to see,
    Then he fell on his knee;
"A boon, a boon," cries Little John,
    "Master, I beg of thee."

"What is that boon," said Robin Hood,
    "Little John, thou begs of me?"
"It is to burn fair Kirkly-hall,
    And all their nunnery."

"Now nay, now nay," quoth Robin Hood,
    "That boon I'll not grant thee;
I never hurt woman in all my life,
    Nor men in woman's company.

"I never hurt fair maid in all my time,
    Nor at mine end shall it be;
But give me my bent bow in my hand,
    And a broad arrow I'll let flee;
And where this arrow is taken up,
    There shall my grave digged be.

"Lay me a green sod under my head,
    And another at my feet;
And lay my bent bow by my side,
    Which was my music sweet;
And make my grave of gravel and green,
    Which is most right and meet.

"Let me have length and breadth enough,
    With a green sod under my head;
Then they may say, when I am dead,
    'Here lies bold Robin Hood.' "

[1] *Drive.*

These words they readily granted him,
Which did bold Robin please;
And there they buried bold Robin Hood,
Within the fair Kirkleys.

No ballad has suffered so many sea changes and has adapted itself
so readily as BONNY BARBARA ALLAN. It has borne a dozen different
titles and has acquired countless local accents. In his TRADITIONAL
BALLADS OF VIRGINIA Arthur Kyle Davis, Jr., relates that he found
ninety-two versions within a single state, many of them presenting
entirely different texts. "BARBARA ALLAN's ninety-two progeny are
something of a record achievement," writes Professor Davis, "cer-
tainly for a lady who, according to the ballad, scorned her lover.
One is thankful that she did not encourage him!" Wherever it may
be found, there is remarkable vitality in this ballad of a rejected
lover and his sweetheart who, touched by his death, dies in sym-
pathy.

Bonny Barbara Allan

In Scarlet town, where I was born,
    There was a fair maid dwelling,
Made every youth cry *Well-a-way!*
    Her name was Barbara Allan.

All in the merry month of May,
    When green buds they were swelling,
Young Jemmy Grove on his death-bed lay,
    For love of Barbara Allan.

O slowly, slowly rose she up,
    To the place where he was lying,
And when she drew the curtain by,
    "Young man, I think you're dying."

"O 'tis I'm sick, and very, very sick,
    And 'tis a' for Barbara Allan";
"O the better for me ye's never be,
    Tho your heart's blood were spilling.

"O dinna ye mind, young man," said she,
    "When ye was in the tavern drinking,
That ye made the healths go round and round,
    And slighted Barbara Allan?"

He turned his face unto the wall,
  And death was with him dealing:
"Adieu, adieu, my dear friends all,
  And be kind to Barbara Allan."

And slowly, slowly rose she up,
  And slowly, slowly left him,
And sighing said she could not stay,
  Since death of life had reft him.

She had not gane a mile but twa,
  When she heard the dead-bell knelling,
And every jow [1] that the dead-bell gave
  Cried, "Woe to Barbara Allan!"

"O mother, mother, make my bed!
  O make it saft and narrow!
Since my love died for me today,
  I'll die for him tomorrow."

Perhaps the most treasured ballads are those which deal with the supernatural. In such ballads as BINNORIE: OR, THE TWO SISTERS, THE WIFE OF USHER'S WELL, and TRUE THOMAS, the balladist ceases to tell facts and sings about unearthly fancies. He moves about easily enough in the world of reality, but he roams the borderland of faery with even greater confidence. Magic takes hold of him when he whispers of dead girls risen from the grave, love-driven spirits, revengeful ghosts, and rhymers bewitched by faery queens.

BINNORIE: OR, THE TWO SISTERS is known by a variety of names and has been used for many purposes from the chill of pure sensation to a child's tune with a happy ending.

Binnorie: or, The Two Sisters

There were twa sisters sat in a bower;
  Binnorie, O Binnorie!
There cam a knight to be their wooer,
  By the bonnie milldams o' Binnorie.

He courted the eldest with glove and ring,
But he lo'ed the youngest abune a' thing.

[1] *Beat, toll.*

The eldest she was vexed sair,
And sair envied her sister fair.

Upon a morning fair and clear,
She cried upon her sister dear:

"O sister, sister, tak my hand,
And let's go down to the river-strand."

She's ta'en her by the lily hand,
And led her down to the river-strand.

The youngest stood upon a stane,
The eldest cam and push'd her in.

"O sister, sister, reach your hand!
And ye sall be heir o' half my land:

"O sister, reach me but your glove!
And sweet William sall be your love."

"Foul fa' the hand that I should take;
It twin'd [1] me o' my worldis make. [2]

"Your cherry lips and your yellow hair
Gar'd me gang maiden evermair."

Sometimes she sank, sometimes she swam,
Until she cam to the miller's dam.

Out then cam the miller's son,
And saw the fair maid soummin' [3] in.

"O father, father, draw your dam!
There's either a mermaid or a swan."

The miller hasted and drew his dam,
And there he found a drown'd woman.

You couldna see her middle sma',
Her gowden girdle was sae braw.

You couldna see her lily feet,
Her gowden fringes were sae deep.

[1] *Robbed.*   [2] *Earthly mate.*   [3] *Swimming.*

All amang her yellow hair
A string o' pearl was twisted rare.

You couldna see her fingers sma',
Wi' diamond rings they were cover'd a'.

And by there cam a harper fine,
That harped to nobles when they dine.

And when he look'd that lady on,
He sigh'd and made a heavy moan.

He's made a harp of her breast-bane,
Whose sound wad melt a heart of stane.

He's ta'en three locks o' her yellow hair,
And wi' them strung his harp sae rare.

He went into her father's hall,
And there was the court assembled all.

He laid his harp upon a stane,
And straight it began to play by lane.[4]

"O yonder sits my father, the King,
And yonder sits my mother, the Queen;

"And yonder stands my brother, Hugh,
And by him my William, sweet and true."

And then as plain as plain could be,
        Binnorie, O Binnorie!
"There sits my sister wha drowned me!"
        By the bonnie milldams o' Binnorie.

THE WIFE OF USHER'S WELL is one of the most effective of the ghost tales in which a widow's sons, drowned at sea, return to visit her. The story has never lost its hold on the imagination. As late as 1900 the English author, W. W. Jacobs, wrote one of the most intensive horror stories, THE MONKEY'S PAW, on the same theme.

"And their hats were o the birk" is a line which has puzzled many. It is explained by an ancient tradition that one returning

[4] *By itself.*

from the dead is protected from the power of mortality if he wears some leaf or flower from the other world—and

> . . . at the gates o Paradise,
>   That birk grew fair eneugh.

The Wife of Usher's Well

There lived a wife at Usher's Well,
  And a wealthy wife was she;
She had three stout and stalwart sons,
  And sent them oer the sea.

They hadna been a week from her,
  A week but barely ane,
Whan word came to the carline [1] wife
  That her three sons were gane.

They hadna been a week from her,
  A week but barely three,
Whan word came to the carline wife
  That her sons she'd never see.

"I wish the wind may never cease,
  Nor fashes [2] in the flood,
Till my three sons come hame to me,
  In earthly flesh and blood."

It fell about the Martinmass,
  When nights are lang and mirk,
The carline wife's three sons came hame,
  And their hats were o the birk. [3]

It neither grew in syke [4] nor ditch,
  Nor yet in ony sheugh; [5]
But at the gates o Paradise,
  That birk grew fair eneugh.

"Blow up the fire, my maidens,
  Bring water from the well;
For a' my house shall feast this night,
  Since my three sons are well."

[1] *Old.*   [2] *Storms.*   [3] *Birch.*   [4] *Marsh.*   [5] *Trench.*

And she has made to them a bed,
She's made it large and wide,
And she's taen her mantle her about,
Sat down at the bed-side.

Up then crew the red, red cock,
And up and crew the gray;
The eldest to the youngest said,
" 'Tis time we were away."

The cock he hadna crawd but once,
And clappd his wings at a',
When the youngest to the eldest said,
"Brother, we must awa.

"The cock doth craw, the day doth daw,
The channerin [6] worm doth chide;
Gin we be mist out o our place,
A sair pain we maun bide.

"Fare ye weel, my mother dear!
Fareweel to barn and byre!
And fare ye weel, the bonny lass
That kindles my mother's fire!"

"Few personages," says Sir Walter Scott, "are so renowned in tra-
dition as Thomas of Erceldoune, known by the appellation of *The
Rhymer*. Uniting, or supposed to unite, in his person, the powers
of poetical composition and of vaticination, his memory, even after
the lapse of five hundred years, is regarded with veneration by his
countrymen." It is supposed that Thomas of Erceldoune lived dur-
ing the thirteenth century and that he could be found sitting under
the Eildon Tree, where he delivered his prophecies. He was also the
reputed author of SIR TRISTREM, the earliest specimen of Scottish
poetry and a remarkable version of the old romance.

TRUE THOMAS has an additional appeal because it echoes the tale
of Tannhäuser, the story of a mortal singer seduced by an immortal
queen. Even the Venusberg is suggested by the seven years during
which the prophet-poet lived in dalliance and "on earth was never
seen." Five hundred years after Thomas's fabled seduction, John
Keats added his particular enchantment. Keats broadened the theme
and gave it the whispered eeriness of LA BELLE DAME SANS MERCI, on
page 755.

[6] *Fretting.*

True Thomas

True Thomas lay on Huntlie bank;
   A ferlie [1] he spied wi' his e'e;
And there he saw a ladye bright
   Come riding down by the Eildon Tree.

Her skirt was of the grass-green silk,
   Her mantle of the velvet fine,
At ilka tett [2] of her horse's mane
   Hung fifty silver bells and nine.

True Thomas he took off his hat,
   And bowed him low down till his knee:
"Hail to thee, Mary, Queen of Heaven!
   For thy peer on earth I never did see."

"O no, O no, True Thomas," she says,
   "That name does not belong to me;
I am but the queen of fair Elfland,
   That am hither come to visit thee.

"Harp and carp, [3] Thomas," she said;
   "Harp and carp along wi' me;
And if ye dare to kiss my lips,
   Sure of your body I will be."

"Betide me weal, betide me woe,
   That doom shall never daunten me."
Syne he has kiss'd her rosy lips,
   All underneath the Eildon Tree,

"Now ye maun [4] go wi' me," she said,
   "True Thomas, ye maun go wi' me;
And ye maun serve me seven years,
   Thro' weal or woe as may chance to be."

She's mounted on her milk-white steed,
   She's ta'en True Thomas up behind;
And aye, whene'er her bridle rang,
   The steed gaed swifter than the wind.

[1] *Marvel.*   [2] *Every tuft.*   [3] *Play and talk lightly.*   [4] *Must.*

O they rade on, and farther on,
 The steed gaed swifter than the wind;
Until they reach'd a desert wide,
 And living land was left behind.

"Light down, light down now, True Thomas,
 And lean your head upon my knee;
Abide ye there a little space,
 And I will show you ferlies three.

"O see ye not yon narrow road,
 So thick beset wi' thorns and briers?
That is the Path of Righteousness,
 Though after it but few inquires.

"And see ye not yon braid, braid road
 That lies across the lily leven? [5]
That is the Path of Wickedness,
 Though some call it the Road to **Heaven**.

"And see ye not yon bonny road
 That winds about the fernie brae? [6]
That is the Road to fair Elfland,
 Where thou and I this night maun gae.

"But, Thomas, ye sall haud your tongue,
 Whatever ye may hear or see;
For speak ye word in Elfin-land,
 Ye'll ne'er win back to your ain countrie."

O they rade on, and farther on,
 And they waded rivers abune the knee;
And they saw neither sun nor moon,
 But they heard the roaring of the sea.

It was mirk, mirk night, there was nae starlight,
 They waded thro' red blude to the knee;
For a' the blude that's shed on the earth
 Rins through the springs o' that countrie.

Syne they came to a garden green,
 And she pu'd an apple frae a tree:
"Take this for thy wages, True Thomas;
 It will give thee the tongue that can never **lee.**"

[5] *Lovely lawn.*   [6] *Ferny hill.*

"My tongue is my ain," True Thomas he said;
   "A gudely gift ye wad gie to me!
I neither dought [7] to buy or sell
   At fair or tryst where I might be.

"I dought neither speak to prince or peer,
   Nor ask of grace from fair ladye!"—
"Now haud thy peace, Thomas," she said,
   "For as I say, so must it be."

He has gotten a coat of the even [8] cloth,
   And a pair o' shoon of the velvet green;
And till seven years were gane and past,
   True Thomas on earth was never seen.

MAY COLVIN is often known as THE WESTERN TRAGEDY, but the conclusion is anything but tragic. MAY COLVIN begins on a note of high adventure, comes to the very edge of tragedy, makes an ironic turnabout, and ends with grim humor. This ballad is full of happy touches: the heroine's modest ruse, the wry retort to the discomfited lover, the wholly unexpected introduction and bribery of the talkative parrot. It is no wonder that MAY COLVIN has never ceased to be a favorite, particularly along the wild coast of Ayrshire where the ballad is looked upon as a record of unquestionable fact.

May Colvin

False Sir John a-wooing came
   To a maid of beauty fair;
May Colvin was this lady's name,
   Her father's only heir.

He woo'd her but, he woo'd her ben,[1]
   He woo'd her in the ha';
Until he got the lady's consent
   To mount and ride awa'.

"Go fetch me some of your father's gold,
   And some of your mother's fee,
And I'll carry thee into the north land,
   And there I'll marry thee."

[7] *Would be able.*   [8] *Smooth.*
[1] *Both in the outer and inner rooms.*

She's gane to her father's coffers
  Where all his money lay,
And she's taken the red, and she's left the white,
  And so lightly she's tripp'd away.

She's gane to her father's stable
  Where all the steeds did stand,
And she's taken the best, and she's left the warst
  That was in her father's land.

She's mounted on a milk-white steed,
  And he on a dapple-grey,
And on they rade to a lonesome part,
  A rock beside the sea.

"Leap off the steed," says false Sir John,
  "Your bridal bed you see;
Seven ladies I have drowned here,
  And the eighth one you shall be.

"Cast off, cast off your silks so fine
  And lay them on a stone,
For they are too fine and costly
  To rot in the salt sea foam.

"Cast off, cast off your silken stays,
  For and your broider'd shoon,
For they are too fine and costly
  To rot in the salt sea foam.

"Cast off, cast off your Holland smock
  That's border'd with the lawn,
For it is too fine and costly
  To rot in the salt sea foam."

"O turn about, thou false Sir John,
  And look to the leaf o' the tree;
For it never became a gentleman
  A naked woman to see."

He turn'd himself straight round about
  To look to the leaf o' the tree;
She's twined her arms about his waist
  And thrown him into the sea.

"O hold a grip o' me, May Colvin,
   For fear that I should drown;
I'll take you home to your father's bower
   And safe I'll set you down."

"No help, no help, thou false Sir John,
   No help, no pity for thee!
For you lie not in a caulder bed
   Than you thought to lay me."

She mounted on her milk-white steed,
   And led the dapple-grey,
And she rode till she reach'd her father's gate,
   At the breakin' o' the day.

Up then spake the pretty parrot,
   "May Colvin, where have you been?
What has become o' false Sir John
   That went with you yestreen?"

"O hold your tongue, my pretty parrot!
   Nor tell no tales o' me;
Your cage shall be made o' the beaten gold
   And the spokes o' ivorie."

Up then spake her father dear,
   In the bed-chamber where he lay:
"What ails the pretty parrot,
   That prattles so long ere day?"

"There came a cat to my cage, master,
   I thought 't would have worried me,
And I was calling to May Colvin
   To take the cat from me."

The broadly humorous ballads have sometimes been considered to mark the decline of the story-poems. But Shakespeare was not above employing as well as enjoying them. The richly human dialogue of THE OLD CLOAK—a domestic colloquy in which the language is ever fresh and the argument never failing—is quoted in OTHELLO. After Iago has made the cannikin clink, he trolls out the stanza beginning "King Stephen was a worthy peer." The quietly comic situation implied in the ballad's debate sets off the oncoming domestic tragedy around which OTHELLO centers. But it is doubtful whether the Shakespearean audiences paused to consider the aesthetic contrast; it is more likely that they appreciated the comic interlude and joined in the rollicking chorus of a ballad they immediately and joyfully recognized.

The Old Cloak

This winter's weather it waxeth cold,
    And frost it freezeth on every hill,
And Boreas blows his blast so bold
    That all our cattle are like to spill.[1]
Bell, my wife, she loves no strife;
    She said unto me quietly,
"Rise up, and save cow Crumbock's life!
    Man, put thine old cloak about thee!"

HE

O Bell my wife, why dost thou flyte?[2]
    Thou kens my cloak is very thin:
It is so bare and over worn,
    A cricket cannot creep therein.
Then I'll no longer borrow nor lend;
    For once I'll new apparell'd be;
To-morrow I'll to town and spend;
    For I'll have a new cloak about me.

SHE

Cow Crumbock is a very good cow:
    She has been always true to the pail;
She has help'd us to butter and cheese, I trow,
    And other things she will not fail.
I would be loth to see her pine.
    Good husband, counsel take of me:
It is not for us to go so fine—
    Man, take thine old cloak about thee!

HE

My cloak it was a very good cloak,
    It hath been always true to the wear;
But now it is not worth a groat:
    I have had it four and forty year.

[1] *Spoil, die.* [2] *Scold, quarrel.*

Sometime it was of cloth in grain: [3]
'Tis now but a sieve, as you may see:
It will neither hold out wind nor rain;
And I'll have a new cloak about me.

SHE

It is four and forty years ago
    Since the one of us the other did ken;
And we have had, betwixt us two,
    Of children either nine or ten:
We have brought them up to women and men:
    In the fear of God I trow they be:
And why wilt thou thyself misken? [4]
    Man, take thine old cloak about thee!

HE

O Bell my wife, why dost thou flyte?
    Now is now, and then was then:
Seek now all the world throughout,
    Thou kens not clowns from gentlemen:
They are clad in black, green, yellow and blue,
    So far above their own degree.
Once in my life I'll take a view;
    For I'll have a new cloak about me.

SHE

King Stephen was a worthy peer;
    His breeches cost him but a crown;
He held them sixpence all too dear,
    Therefore he called the tailor 'lown.'
He was a king and wore the crown,
    And thou'se but of a low degree:
It's pride that puts this country down:
    Man, take thine old cloak about thee!

HE

Bell my wife, she loves not strife,
    Yet she will lead me, if she can:
And to maintain an easy life
    I oft must yield, though I'm good-man.

[3] *Fine scarlet cloth.*   [4] *Mistake.*

It's not for a man with a woman to threap,[5]
  Unless he first give o'er the plea:
As we began, so will we keep,
  And I'll take my old cloak about me.

Another domestic scene is humorously exposed in GET UP AND BAR THE DOOR. The interior is depicted with all the exactitude of a Flemish genre painter. Only a Breughel or a Teniers could have reproduced the homely world with such choice details: the puddings simmering on the stove, the goodwife with her hand in her "hussyfskap," or household work, stolidly challenging her husband, who is equally stubborn but more easily disturbed.

Get Up and Bar the Door

It fell about the Martinmas time,
  And a gay time it was then,
When our goodwife got puddings to make,
  And she's boild them in the pan.

The wind sae cauld blew south and north,
  And blew into the floor;
Quoth our goodman to our goodwife,
  "Gae out and bar the door."

"My hand is in my hussyfskap,
  Goodman, as ye may see;
It shoud nae be barrd this hundred year,
  If it's to be barrd by me!"

They made a paction tween them twa,
  They made it firm and sure,
That the first word whae'er shoud speak,
  Shoud rise and bar the door.

Then by there came two gentlemen,
  At twelve oclock at night,
And they could neither see house nor hall,
  Nor coal nor candle-light.

[5] *Argue, contend.*

"Now whether is this a rich man's house,
　　Or whether is it a poor?"
But neer a word would ane o them speak,
　　For barring of the door.

And first they [1] ate the white puddings,
　　And then they ate the black;
Tho muckle thought the goodwife to hersel,
　　Yet neer a word she spake.

Then said the one unto the other,
　　"Here, man, tak ye my knife;
Do ye tak off the auld man's beard,
　　And I'll kiss the goodwife."

"But there's nae water in the house,
　　And what shall we do than?"
"What ails ye at the pudding-broo,
　　That boils into the pan?"

O up then started our goodman,
　　An angry man was he:
"Will ye kiss my wife before my een,
　　And scald me wi pudding-bree?" [2]

Then up and started our goodwife,
　　Gied three skips on the floor:
"Goodman, you've spoken the foremost word,
　　Get up and bar the door!"

In his RELIQUES OF ANCIENT ENGLISH POETRY, Thomas Percy,
eighteenth-century bishop and pioneer in ballad research, assured
the reader that "the common popular ballad of KING JOHN AND THE
ABBOT seems to have been abridged and modernized about the time
of James I from one much older." But there is reason to believe
that Percy himself took a few liberties with the stanzas; in fact, the
ballad as we know it is a successful piece of rewriting, and the im-
provements are largely due to the good bishop's good use of the
original. Percy was not always so careful. He gathered his material
from many sources, but his chief prize was a manuscript dating from
the middle of the seventeenth century which he rescued from house-
maids who were tearing pages from it to light the evening fires.

[1] *"They" refers to the two strangers.*
[2] *The broth in which the pudding was boiled.*

Since the folio was long and narrow, the maids frequently tore out half-pages, and the portions that remained were not only tantalizing but tempting to the researcher. Percy confessed that he himself tore out several pages "to save the trouble of transcribing" when he was preparing his collection for publication. However, Frank Sidgwick wrote in his LEGENDARY BALLADS, "our consolation must be that the greater part of the manuscript survived both the housemaids and the bishop; after further adventures it is now safe in the British Museum."

Some commentators have seen in KING JOHN AND THE ABBOT OF CANTERBURY echoes of an attack against the clergy, and it is hinted that the author may well have been a Puritan haranguing the luxury-loving prelates and princes of the Church. But it needs no moral to adorn this particular tale; its essence is the combination of lighthearted shrewdness and wholehearted laughter.

King John and the Abbot of Canterbury

An ancient story I'll tell you anon,
Of a notable prince, that was called King John;
He ruled over England with main and might,
But he did great wrong, and maintained little right.

And I'll tell you a story, a story so merry,
Concerning the Abbot of Canterbury;
How for his housekeeping and high renown,
They rode post to bring him to London town.

A hundred men, as the King heard say,
The Abbot kept in his house every day;
And fifty gold chains, without any doubt,
In velvet coats waited the Abbot about.

"How now, Father Abbot? I hear it of thee,
Thou keepest a far better house than me;
And for thy housekeeping and high renown,
I fear thou work'st treason against my crown."

"My liege," quoth the Abbot, "I would it were known,
I am spending nothing but what is my own;
And I trust your Grace will not put me in fear,
For spending my own true-gotten gear."

"Yes, yes, Father Abbot, thy fault is high,
And now for the same thou needest must die;
And except thou canst answer me questions three,
Thy head struck off from thy body shall be.

"Now first," quo' the King, "as I sit here,
With my crown of gold on my head so fair,
Among all my liegemen of noble birth,
Thou must tell to one penny what I am worth.

"Secondly, tell me, beyond all doubt,
How quickly I may ride the whole world about;
And at the third question thou must not shrink,
But tell me here truly, what do I think?"

"O, these are deep questions for my shallow wit,
And I cannot answer your Grace as yet;
But if you will give me a fortnight's space,
I'll do my endeavor to answer your Grace."

"Now a fortnight's space to thee will I give,
And that is the longest thou hast to live;
For unless thou answer my questions three,
Thy life and thy lands are forfeit to me."

Away rode the Abbot all sad at this word;
He rode to Cambridge and Oxenford;
But never a doctor there was so wise,
That could by his learning an answer devise.

Then home rode the Abbot, with comfort so cold,
And he met his shepherd, a-going to fold:
"Now, good Lord Abbot, you are welcome home;
What news do you bring us from great King John?"

"Sad news, sad news, Shepherd, I must give;
That I have but three days more to live.
I must answer the King his questions three,
Or my head struck off from my body shall be.

"The first is to tell him, as he sits there,
With his crown of gold on his head so fair
Among all his liegemen of noble birth,
To within one penny, what he is worth.

"The second, to tell him, beyond all doubt,
How quickly he may ride this whole world about;
And at question the third, I must not shrink,
But tell him there truly, what does he think?"

"O, cheer up, my lord; did you never hear yet
That a fool may teach a wise man wit?
Lend me your serving-men, horse, and apparel,
And I'll ride to London to answer your quarrel.

"With your pardon, it oft has been told to me
That I'm like your lordship as ever can be:
And if you will but lend me your gown,
There is none shall know us at London town."

"Now horses and serving-men thou shalt have,
With sumptuous raiment gallant and brave;
With crosier and mitre, and rochet, and cope,
Fit to draw near to our father, the pope."

"Now welcome, Sir Abbot," the King he did say,
" 'Tis well thou'rt come back to keep thy day;
For if thou canst answer my questions three,
Thy life and thy living both saved shall be.

"And first, as thou seest me sitting here,
With my crown of gold on my head so fair,
Among my liegemen of noble birth,
Tell to one penny what I am worth."

"For thirty pence our Saviour was sold
Among the false Jews as I have been told;
And twenty-nine is the worth of thee;
For I think thou art one penny worse than he."

The King, he laughed, and swore by St. Bittle.[1]
"I did not think I was worth so little!
Now secondly tell me, beyond all doubt,
How quickly I may ride this world about."

"You must rise with the sun, and ride with the same,
Until the next morning he riseth again;
And then your Grace need never doubt
But in twenty-four hours you'll ride it about."

[1] *Probably Saint Botolph.*

The King he laughed, and swore by St. Jone,
"I did not think I could do it so soon!
Now from question the third thou must not shrink,
But tell me truly, what do I think?"

"Yea, that I shall do, and make your Grace merry:
You think I'm the Abbot of Canterbury.
But I'm his poor shepherd, as plain you may see,
That am come to beg pardon for him and for me."

The King he laughed, and swore by the mass,
"I'll make thee Lord Abbot this day in his place!"
"Now nay, my Liege, be not in such speed;
For alas! I can neither write nor read."

"Four nobles a week, then I'll give to thee,
For this merry jest thou has shown to me;
And tell the old Abbot, when thou gettest home,
Thou has brought a free pardon from good King John."

It is difficult to draw the line between some of the early carols and
ballads of Holy Writ. THE CHERRY-TREE CAROL is one of those poems
which are as lyrical as they are dramatic; its antiquity has been
questioned, but not its vitality.

SAINT STEPHEN AND KING HEROD, on the other hand, is indisputably
one of the oldest of the religious ballads. Fragments of it have been
found in the Middle Ages; the climax, when the roast cock crows its
defiant answer, was used with great effect by the ancient ballad
singers in Denmark. Both THE CHERRY-TREE CAROL and SAINT STEPHEN
AND KING HEROD accomplish their effect by announcing the super-
natural in the simplest setting and the calmest tone of voice.

Saint Stephen and King Herod

Saint Stephen was a clerk
    In King Herod's hall,
And served him of bread and cloth
    As every king befall.

Stephen out of kitchen came
    With boar's head on hand,
He saw a star was fair and bright
    Over Bethlehem stand.

He cast adown the boar's head
 And went into the hall;
"I forsake thee, Herod,
 And thy workes all.

"I forsake thee, King Herod,
 And thy workes all,
There is a child in Bethlehem born
 Is better than we all."

"What aileth thee, Stephen?
 What is thee befall?
Lacketh thee either meat or drink
 In King Herod's hall?"

"Lacketh me neither meat ne drink
 In King Herod's hall;
There is a child in Bethlehem born
 Is better than we all."

"What aileth thee, Stephen?
 Art wode or 'ginnest to brede? [1]
Lacketh thee either gold or fee,
 Or any rich weed?" [2]

"Lacketh me neither gold ne fee
 Ne none rich weed;
There is a child in Bethlehem born
 Shall helpen us at our need."

"That is all so sooth, Stephen,
 All so sooth, I-wys, [3]
As this capon crowe shall
 That lieth here in my dish."

That word was not so soon said,
 That word in that hall,
The capon crew *Christus natus est*
 Among the lordes all.

"Risit up, my tormentors,
 By two and all by one,
And leadit Stephen out of this town,
 And stonit him with stone."

[1] *Art thou insane or going mad?* [2] *Clothing.* [3] *I know.*

Tooken they Stephen
And stoned him in the way;
And therefore is his even
On Christe's own day.

The Cherry-Tree Carol

Joseph was an old man,
    and an old man was he,
When he wedded Mary,
    in the land of Galilee.

Joseph and Mary walked
    through an orchard good,
Where was cherries and berries,
    so red as any blood.

O then bespoke Mary,
    so meek and so mild:
"Pluck me one cherry, Joseph,
    for I am with child."

O then bespoke Joseph,
    with words most unkind:
"Let him pluck thee a cherry
    that brought thee with child."

O then bespoke the babe,
    within his mother's womb:
"Bow down then the tallest tree,
    for my mother to have some."

Then bowed down the highest tree
    unto his mother's hand;
Then she cried, "See, Joseph,
    I have cherries at command."

Then Mary plucked a cherry,
    as red as the blood,
Then Mary went home
    with her heavy load.

THE THREE RAVENS has had many local variants, the best Scottish
version being THE TWA CORBIES. A few of the balladists distrusted

the innocent symbolism of the end; in their versions the "fallow doe" became a "lady full of woe." But the graphic pathos persists in every version; it is intensified because the sad picture is presented not by a sympathetic onlooker but by three ravens intent on nothing more than their breakfast.

The Three Ravens

There were three Ravens sat on a tree,
Down-a-down, hey down, hey down!
There were three Ravens sat on a tree,
With a down!
There were three Ravens sat on a tree:
They were as black as they might be,
With a down, derry derry derry down down!

The one of them said to his make: [1]
Where shall we our breakfast take?

Down in yonder greene field
There lies a knight slain under nis shield.

His hounds they lie down at his feet;
So well they their master keep.

His hawks, they fly so eagerly,
There's no fowl dare him come nigh.

Down there comes a fallow doe,
Great with young as she might go.

She lifted up his bloody head,
And kiss'd his wounds that were so red.

She gat him upon her back,
And carried him to earthen lake. [2]

She buried him before the prime,
She was dead ere even-time.

God send every gentleman
Such hounds, such hawks, and such leman!
With a down, derry—

[1] *Mate.*   [2] *I.e., the grave.*

IV

Early Songs
of Unknown Authorship

ANGLO-SAXON poetry is predominantly rugged, heroic, and some-
times epical, but, although a refrain or a lyric outcry occa-
sionally breaks through, it is not lyrical. After the Norman Con-
quest a fresh impulse is apparent; under French influence echoes of
the troubadours and jongleurs are heard in English poetry. A new
mood as well as a new music stirs in the amatory and courtly songs.
It is heard even in the religious lyrics, in which the spirit of as-
ceticism is strangely crossed with a sensuous movement and a fervor
which is too direct to be wholly devout. Even the unforgettable
early poem to Mary (I SING OF A MAIDEN THAT IS MAKELES) is as much
a tribute to the grace of woman as it is to the mother of God.

Gallantry appears for the first time in Middle English poetry; na-
ture itself becomes romantic as the stern northern spirit is softened
by the South. THE KINGIS QUAIR (literally "The King's Book"), writ-
ten about 1423 by James I of Scotland, while he was a prisoner in
England, is significant of the change in manner:

> Worshipe, ye that lovers been, this May,
> For of your bliss the kalends are begun;
> And sing with us, "Away, Winter, away!
> Come, Summer, come, the sweet season and sun!"
> Awake, for shame! that have your heavens won,
> And amorously lift up your heades all;
> Thank Love, that list you to his mercy call.

But there had already been in circulation a romantic and happy nature song which had been enjoyed for more than a century. Some authorities believe that the CUCCU SONG, which opens THE OXFORD BOOK OF ENGLISH VERSE, was composed as early as 1250.

Cuccu Song

Sumer is icumen in;
    Lhude [1] sing cuccu!
Groweth sed, and bloweth med,[2]
    And springeth the wude nu.
      Sing cuccu!

Ewe bleteth after lomb,
    Lhouth [3] after calve cu;
Bulluc sterteth,[4] bucke verteth,[5]
    Murie sing cuccu!

Cuccu, cuccu, well singest thu, cuccu:
    Ne swike [6] thu naver nu;
Sing cuccu, nu, sing cuccu,
    Sing cuccu, sing cuccu, nu!

Contrasts in tone and feeling are manifest in the early Tudor religious lyrics. The following three (one of which is printed in a condensed version) were all written somewhat earlier than 1500. The first, which is from GUDE AND GODLY BALLETS, is a compromise between a ballad and a song, a dialogue between God and a mortal spirit.

Who Is At My Window?

Who is at my window? Who? Who?
Go from my window! Go! Go!
Who callis thair, lyke a strangeir?
Go from my window! Go!

"Lord, I am hair,[7] a wretchit mortall,
That for thy mercy dois cry and call
Unto thee, my lord celestiall,
See who is at thy window, who?"

[1] *Loud.*   [2] *Meadow.*   [3] *Loweth.*   [4] *Leapeth.*   [5] *Hides in the forest.*   [6] *Cease.*
[7] *Here.*

Remember thy sin, and also thy smart,
And also for thee what was my part,
Remember the speir that pierced my hart,
And in at my dure thou sall go.

I ask na thing of thee thairfor,
But love for love, to lay in store.
Gif me thy hart, I ask no more,
And in at my dure thou sall go.

Who is at my window? Who?
Go from my window! Go!
Cry na mair thair, lyke a strangeir,
But in at my dure thou go!

A Christmas Carol

Thys ender nyght [1]
I saw a syght,
    A star as bright as day;
And ever among
A maydyn sung:
    "By-by, baby, lullay."

Thys vyrgyn clere
Wythowtyn pere
    Unto hur son gane say:
"My son, my lorde,
My fathere dere,
    Why lyest thow in hay?"

.   .   .   .   .   .

"Now ye shall see
That kynges three
    Shall cum on the twelfe day.
For thys behest
Geffe me thy brest
    And syng, 'By-by, lullay!' "

"My son, my lorde,
My fader dere,
    Syth all ys at thy wyll.

---

[1] *The other night.*

I pray the, son,
Graunte me a boone,
    Yff hyt be ryght and skylle;

"That chylde or man,
Whoever can
    Be mery on thys day,
To blys them bryng
And I shall syng:
    'By-by, baby, lullay!' "

I Sing of a Maiden

I sing of a maiden
    That is makeles: [1]
King of all kings
    To her son she ches.[2]

He came al so stille
    There his moder was,
As dew in Aprille
    That falleth on the grass.

He came al so stille
    To his moder's bour,
As dew in Aprille
    That falleth on the flour.

He came al so stille
    There his moder lay,
As dew in Aprille
    That falleth on the spray.

Moder and maiden
    Was never none but she:
Well may such a lady
    Goddes moder be.

Although the impulse of the poet was anything but sacred, the
tone in the love poems of the period is not dissimilar to the warmth
of the religious lyrics. This tone was to undergo rapid changes; it
was to become formalized, and the clear speech was doomed to

[1] *Mateless*, i.e., *matchless*.   [2] *Chose.*

degenerate into a convention. But, until the minor Elizabethans fixed the mood into a formula and turned happy phrases to hyperbole, the song was spontaneous and without affectation.

The first of the secular lyrics still carries a sacred overtone; it recalls the scene in Wagner's adaptation of the Parzival legend in which Amfortas, surrounded by knights of the Grail, lies bleeding from a never-healing wound. The other lyrics free themselves lightly of religious implications.

The Bereaved Maid

Lully lullay, lully lullay!
The falcon hath borne my mate away.

He bare him up, he bare him down,
He bare him into an orchard brown.

In that orchard there was a hall
That was hangèd with purple and pall;

And in that hall there was a bed,
It was hangèd with gold so red;

And in that bed there lieth a knight,
His woundes bleeding day and night;

By that bedside kneeleth a may,[1]
And she weepeth both night and day;

And by that bedside there standeth a stone,
Corpus Christi written thereon.

Lully lullay, lully lullay!
The falcon hath borne my mate away.

That Ever I Saw

She is gentil and al so wise;
Of all other she beareth the prize,
That ever I saw.

[1] *Maid.*

To heare her sing, to see her dance!
She will the best herself advance,
   That ever I saw.

To see her fingers that be so small!
In my conceit she passeth all
   That ever I saw.

Nature in her hath wonderly wrought.
Christ never such another bought,
   That ever I saw.

I have seen many that have beauty,
Yet is there none like to my lady
   That ever I saw.

Therefore I dare this boldly say,
I shall have the best and fairest may
   That ever I saw.

The Nightingale

The little pretty nightingale
   Among the leaves grene:
I would I were with her all night—
   But yet ye wot not whom I mene.

The nightingale sat on a brere [1]
   Among the thornes sharpe and keene.
And comfort me with merry chere—
   But yet ye wot not whom I mene.

She did appear all on her kind
   A lady right well to be seene.
With words of love told me her mind—
   But yet ye wot not whom I mene.

It did me good upon her to look,
   Her corse was clothèd all in grene;
Away fro me her heart she took—
   But yet ye wot not whom I mene.

[1] Brier

"Lady," I cry'd with rufull mone,
"Have mind of me that true hath bene:
For I love none but you alone."—
But yet ye wot not whom I mene.

As I Lay Sleeping

As I lay sleeping,
In dremes fleeting,
Ever my sweeting
  Is in my mind:
She is so goodly,
With locks so lovely,
Like to her surely
  Such none can find.

Her beauty so pure,
It doth under lure
My poor heart full sure
  In governaunce:
Therefore will I
Unto her apply
And ever will cry
  For remembraunce.

Alas, will not she
Now shew her pitye,
But thus will take me
  In such disdain.
Methinketh, iwis,
Unkind she is
That bindeth me thus
  In such hard pain.

Though she me bind,
Yet shall she not find
My poor heart unkind,
  Do what she can:
For I will her pray,
Whiles I leve a day,
Me to take for aye
  For her owne man.

In the early sixteenth century the lyric grew in intensity; the form was limited, but not the feeling. In two of the briefest snatches of melody there ring two of the clearest extremities of emotion: the voice of passion and the voice of innocence. The plaint of the lonely lover contrasts poignantly with the shy whisper of the girl too young for love and marriage.

O Western Wind

O Western wind, when wilt thou blow
    That the small rain down can rain?
Christ, that my love were in my arms,
    And I in my bed again!

Young Girl's Song

The maidens came
When I was in my mother's bower:
I had all that I would.
The bailey [1] beareth the bell away:
The lily, the rose, the rose I lay.

The silver is white, red is the gold:
The robes they lay in fold.
The bailey beareth the bell away:
The lily, the rose, the rose I lay.

And through the glass window shines the sun.
How should I love, and I so young?
The bailey beareth the bell away:
The lily, the lily, the rose I lay.

The note of pity blends with self-pity in many of the poems of unknown authorship. The lullaby which follows is a strange cradle-song, but the music promises to comfort the mother even as it soothes the child.

In this poem, as well as those which immediately precede it and those which come after, the spelling has been modernized. No effort

[1] *The bailiff, a deputy who serves warrants and issues licenses.*

has been made to "correct" the original versions or rob them of their quaintness; but many of the lyrics are already familiar in their modern spelling, and to restore the antique orthography would give them nothing more than the effect of oddity. If anything is lost, much is gained by revealing the poetic content in its purity and dateless power.

By-Low, My Babe

By-low, my babe, lie still and sleep;
It grieves me sore to see thee weep.
If thou wert quiet I'd be glad;
Thy mourning makes my sorrow sad.
By-low, my boy, thy mother's joy,
Thy father breeds me great annoy—
    By-low, lie low.

When he began to court my love,
And me with sugared words to move,
His feignings false and flattering cheer
To me that time did not appear.
But now I see most cruelly
He cares not for my babe nor me—
    By-low, lie low.

Lie still, my darling, sleep awhile,
And when thou wak'st thou'llt sweetly **smile;**
But smile not as thy father did,
To cozen maids—nay, God forbid!
But yet I fear thou wilt grow near
Thy father's heart and face to bear—
    By-low, lie low.

I cannot choose, but ever will
Be loving to thy father still;
Where'er he stay, where'er he ride
My love with him doth still abide.
In weal or woe, where'er he go,
My heart shall not forsake him; so
    By-low, lie low.

Probably the first and certainly the greatest of all "mad songs," the violent poem known as TOM O' BEDLAM'S SONG has never ceased

to work its magic "out of space, out of time." Its author is un-
known; its origins are obscure. We know that Bedlam is a corrup-
tion of Bethlehem, and that it was not applied to the birthplace of
Jesus, but to St. Mary's of Bethlehem, founded as a priory in Lon-
don in 1246. In 1330 the establishment was turned into a general
hospital; in 1402 it became crowded with lunatics; in 1547 it was
incorporated as a royal foundation for the insane. Since there was
insufficient room for all the patients, many of the inmates were
allowed to travel about the country. When the religious institutions
were dissolved, there was no longer provision for the demented
poor, and they roamed singly and in bands, begging, dancing, and
singing for pennies. The pursuit was so profitable that many of the
beggars, quick to learn the tricks of the trade, pretended to be mad.
There are many late sixteenth- and early seventeenth-century refer-
ences to these "Bedlam beggars." In KING LEAR Edgar disguises him-
self in grimy nakedness to "outface the winds and persecutions of
the sky"; he follows the precedent

> Of Bedlam beggars, who, with roaring voices,
> Strike in their numb'd and mortified bare arms
> Pins, wooden pricks, nails, sprigs of rosemary;
> And with this horrible object, from low farms,
> Poor pelting villages, sheep-cotes, and mills,
> Sometime with lunatic bans, sometime with prayers,
> Enforce their charity.

It is said that the Bedlamites invented many mad songs; it is safe
to assume that they made countless variations on their favorite
theme. But, though many variants exist, none has the excitement,
the crazy force, of the original, which is here reprinted. Its imagery
is so daring, its language so wild and yet so eloquent, that it could
only have been written by a greatly gifted poet. It has been sug-
gested that the author may even have been Shakespeare himself.

Tom o' Bedlam's Song

> From the hag and hungry goblin
> That into rags would rend ye,
>   All the spirits that stand
>   By the naked man
> In the book of moons, defend ye,

That of your five sound senses
You never be forsaken,
  Nor wander from
  Yourselves with Tom
Abroad to beg your bacon.

With a thought I took for Maudlin,
And a cruse of cockle pottage,
  With a thing thus tall,
  Sky bless you all,
I befell into this dotage.

I slept not since the Conquest,
Till then I never wakèd,
  Till the roguish boy
  Of love where I lay
Me found and stript me naked.

The moon's my constant mistress,
And the lonely owl my marrow;
  The flaming drake
  And the night-crow make
Me music to my sorrow.

I know more than Apollo,
For oft, when he lies sleeping,
  I see the stars
  At mortal wars
In the wounded welkin weeping,

The moon embrace her shepherd,
And the queen of love her warrior,
  While the first doth horn
  The star of morn,
And the next the heavenly farrier.

With an host of furious fancies,
Whereof I am commander,
  With a burning spear
  And a horse of air
To the wilderness I wander;

By a knight of ghosts and shadows
I summoned am to tourney
  Ten leagues beyond
  The wide world's end—
Methinks it is no journey.

V

Toward the Golden Age

Between the twelfth and fifteenth centuries English literature was as diffused as it was diverse; it was composed for no one type of audience and no special class. The ballads were written primarily for the entertainment of the common people, but even in so "courtly" a writer as Chaucer there is much that is forthright, racy, and vulgar—in the sense of *vulgus*, pertaining to "the people."

As we approach the sixteenth century, literature grows more patrician; with Wyatt, Howard, Raleigh, and Spenser poetry becomes the expression of an aristocracy. The aristocratic spirit remained dominant for almost two centuries, when it gave way to a literature written with organized society as its background, a literature concerned with the middle class and written chiefly by the middle class. Another century brought another change. Society itself was challenged by the industrial revolution of the nineteenth century; the "romantic" period of Wordsworth and Shelley was devoted to the idea of individualism. But, as the "new learning" began to lure the fifteenth- and sixteenth-century man of culture, civilization was reflected in an increasing "elevation" of manner. The social sense, as V. de Sola Pinto wrote in THE ENGLISH RENAISSANCE, "was established by the Tudors, and exploited by the Stuarts, till it came to an end at the Revolution of 1688," when James II fled to France.

JOHN SKELTON
[1460?–1529]

THE lively and erratic work of John Skelton acted as a "bridge" between medieval solemnity and Tudor sprightliness. Skelton was born about 1460, was applauded and attacked during his time, was forgotten shortly after, and had to wait four hundred years to be rediscovered. His life was a series of contradictions. He had an impudent brain and a loose tongue; yet he received the official laurel from Louvain, Cambridge, and Oxford, and the universities created him "poet laureate." He was outspoken to the point of lese majesty; yet he was tutor to Prince Henry, and became court poet when the Prince ascended the throne as Henry VIII. He was admitted to holy orders in 1498, and occupied a parsonage in Norfolk; yet he attacked the powerful Cardinal Wolsey and as a result was forced to take sanctuary in Westminster Abbey, where he died in 1529.

The same contradictions continued to pursue Skelton after his death. Erasmus referred to "Skelton, the only light and glory of English letters." William Lily, from his high eminence as author of a short Latin syntax, dismissed Skelton as "neither learned, nor a poet," and Pope extended the condemnation by speaking of "beastly" Skelton, adding that his poems "are all low and bad, there is nothing in them that is worth reading." In THE COURT OF HENRY VIII Mrs. Thomson claimed that "the instruction bestowed upon Prince Henry by his preceptor Skelton was calculated to render him a scholar and a churchman"; but Agnes Strickland, in her LIVES OF THE QUEENS OF ENGLAND, contemptuously concluded, "How probable is it that the corruption imparted by this ribald and ill-living wretch laid the foundation for his royal pupil's grossest crimes!"

Whether or not Skelton influenced the monarch, the poet and his royal pupil had more than ribaldry in common. There were a mutual power of language, a gusty humor, and an intensity of serious feeling beneath the boisterousness. But, as Richard Hughes, the twentieth-century poet and novelist, pointed out, "The learned admired him for his learning, and the people admired him as one of the most amusing writers of any century: Skelton, knowing himself to be not only a scholar and a jocular but a poet, looked to Posterity for nice appreciation . . . and Posterity has played the jade with him: never quite giving him his *congé*, she has kept him dangling. . . . For four centuries he has lain in his grave, food for the grammarians."

It is not hard to find reasons for this neglect. Skelton wrote at a time when the pronunciation of English was changing; as a consequence the scansion of his lines was misunderstood, and his rhythms became unintelligible. He also suffered, as his modern "disciple" Robert Graves maintained, "an undeserved reputation as an obscene writer." This reputation was largely due to THE TUNNING [or BREWING] OF ELINOUR RUMMING, in which the rowdy laureate gave all his faculties a swinging carouse. Yet even here the carefully observing eye of the poet controls the high spirits with critical detachment; beneath the blowzy episodes, the catch-as-catch-can rhymes, and the breathless speed there are portraits which recall the best of Chaucer and anticipate the coarse and brilliant portraits of Hogarth and Rowlandson.

FROM

The Tunning of Elinour Rumming

Tell you I chyll,[1]
If that ye will
A while be still,
Of a comely Gill [2]
That dwelt on a hill:

But she is somewhat sage
And well worne in age;
For her viságe
It would assuage [3]
A man's couráge,
Droupy and drowsy,
Scurvy and lowsy;
Her face all bowsy,
Comely crinkled,
Wondrously wrinkled
Like a roast pig's ear
Bristled with hair.

[1] *Shall.*
[2] *A pun is indicated here, for Gill (or Jill) not only means "girl" but also one who brews beer (from the French* guiller), *which was Elinour's trade.*
[3] *Dampen.*

Her lewd lippes twayne,
They slaver, men sayne,
Like a ropy rain . . .
Her nose somdele [4] hooked
And camously [5] crooked,
Never stopping
But ever dropping;
Her skin loose and slack
Grained [6] like a sack
With a crooked back.

A man would have pity
To see how she is gummed,
Fingered and thumbed
Gently jointed,
Greased and anointed
Up to the knuckles;
The bones of her huckles [7]
Like as they were with buckles
Together made fast.
Her youth is far past.

Her cloak of Lincoln green
It had been hers, I ween,
More than forty year;
And so doth it appear,
For the green bare threads
Look like sere weeds
Withered like hay,
The wool worn away.
And yet, I dare say,
She thinketh herself gay
Upon the holy day,
When she doth her array
And girdeth in her geyts [8]
Stitched and pranked with pleats;
Her kirtle, Bristol-red,
With clothes upon her head
That weigh a sow of lead,
Writhen [9] in wondrous wise
After the Saracen's guise;
With a whim-wham [10]
Knit with a trim-tram [11]

4 *Somewhat.*   5 *Distortedly.*   6 *Wrinkled.*   7 *Hips.*   8 *Clothes.*   9 *Twisted.*
10 *Silly decoration.*   11*Trifle.*

Upon her brain-pan,
Like an Egyptián [12]
Cappéd about.

When she goeth out
Herself for to show
She driveth down the dew
With a pair of heels
As broad as two wheels.
She hobbles as a goose
With her blanket hose,
Greased with dirt
That soileth her skirt.

. . . .

And this comely dame,
I understand her name
Is Elinour Rumming,
At home in her wonning [13] . . .
But to make up my tale,
She breweth nappy ale
To travellers, to tinkers,
To sweaters, to swinkers,[14]
And all good ale-drinkers,
That will nothing spare
But drink till they stare
And bring themselves bare,
With "Now aware the mare! [15]
And let us slay Care!"

Another example of Skelton's rough-and-tumble manner is the long COLIN CLOUT, a lively attack upon the rich ecclesiastics by an ordinary country person. Although Skelton declared that he wrote in defense of the church and attacked only the sinful clergy, the poem is the most scathing indictment of the period couched in the most nimble couplets. The opening gives Skelton's purpose as well as his own estimate of his verse.

[12] *Gypsy.* [13] *Dwelling.* [14] *Toilers.* [15] *"Away with trouble!"*

The Prelates

My name is Colin Clout.
I purpose to shake out
All my cunning bag
Like a clerkly hag:
For, though my rhyme be ragged,
Tattered and jagged,
Rudely rain-beaten,
Rusty and moth-eaten,
If ye take well therewith
It hath in it some pith.
For, as far as I can see,
It is wrong with each degree.
The temporal
Accuseth the spiritual;
The spiritual again
Doth grudge and complain
Upon the temporal men.
Thus each raiseth a pother,
One against the other.
Alas, they make me shudder!
For (do not say it loud!)
The prelates are so proud,
They say, and look so high
As though they would fly
Above the starry sky.

Laymen say indeed
How they take no heed
Their silly sheep to feed,
But pluck away and pull
The fleeces of their wool;
Scarcely they leave a lock
Of wool among their flock.
And as for their cunning,
A-humming and mumming,
They make of it a jape.
They gasp and they gape
All to have promotion—
That is their whole devotion!

from COLIN CLOUT

Yet Skelton is not always impudent and helter-skelter, a sort of
Anglicized Villon. In the midst of rudeness, rapidly accumulating
epithets, and uneven but breathlessly recurring rhymes, he is often
unashamedly tender. Such poems as THE BOOK OF PHILIP SPARROW
and his tributes to Margery Wentworth, Isabel Pennell, and Mar-
garet Hussey were popular with readers of all classes. His rough
warmth, as well as his love of practical jokes, endeared him to the
populace; and his hold on the public imagination was not lessened
by the suspicion that, though a priest, he was secretly married to
the woman who kept house for him and was the mother of his chil-
dren. Skelton appears, slightly disguised, in two sixteenth-century
plays; in one of them he is happily cast as Friar Tuck.

THE BOOK OF PHILIP SPARROW is a poem of more than a thousand
lines in which Skelton, remembering Catullus' sympathy with Les-
bia's grief for her lost sparrow, expands the lament of Jane Scroop,
a schoolgirl, for her dead bird. Too long to reprint and too in-
tegrated to cut, its qualities—Skelton's characteristic humor and
pathos, gracefulness half-concealed in levity—are suggested in the
delightful verses which follow. In the first there is a typical Skel-
tonian wordplay: the flower of goodlihood, the aromatic herb "mar-
joram" is employed not only for its floral association as a symbol
of virtue, but because it is a punning tribute to "Margery," to whom
the poem is dedicated.

To Mistress Margery Wentworth

With marjoram gentle,
  The flower of goodlihood,
Embroidered the mantle
  Is of your maidenhood.

Plainly, I cannot glose; [1]
  Ye be, as I divine,
The pretty primrose,
  The goodly columbine.

With marjoram gentle,
  The flower of goodlihood,
Embroidered the mantle
  Is of your maidenhood.

[1] *Flatter.*

Benign, courteous, and meek,
  With wordes well devised,
In you, who list to seek,
  Be virtues well comprised.

With marjoram gentle,
  The flower of goodlihood,
Embroidered the mantle
  Is of your maidenhood.

To Mistress Margaret Hussey

Merry Margaret,
As midsummer flower,
Gentle as falcon
Or hawk of the tower;
With solace and gladness,
Much mirth and no madness,
All good and no badness;
So joyously,
So maidenly,
So womanly,
Her demeaning;
In every thing
Far far passing
That I can indite
Or suffice to write
Of merry Margaret,
As midsummer flower,
Gentle as falcon
Or hawk of the tower.

As patient and as still,
And as full of good will,
As the fair Isyphill,[1]
Coriander,
Sweet pomander,[2]
Good Cassander; [3]
Steadfast of thought,

[1] *Hypsipyle, who saved her father, the king of Lemnos, when all the other men were killed.*

[2] *A ball of perfume, often worn as a charm.*

[3] *Cassandra, deified for her beauty and prophetic power.*

Well made, well wrought.
Far may be sought
Ere than ye can find
So courteous, so kind,
As merry Margaret,
This midsummer flower,
Gentle as falcon
Or hawk of the tower.

To Mistress Isabel Pennell

By Saint Mary, my lady,
Your mammy and your daddy
Brought forth a goodly baby.

My maiden Isabel,
Reflaring rosabel,[1]
The fragrant camomel,

The ruddy rosary,[2]
The sovran rosemary,
The pretty strawberry,

The columbine, the nept,[3]
The gillyflower well set,
The proper violet.

Ennewed [4] your colóur
Is like the daisy flower
After the April shower.

Star of the morrow gray,
The blossom on the spray,
The freshest flower of May,

Maidenly demure,
Of womanhood the lure;
Wherefore I you assure,

It were a heavenly health,
It were an endless wealth,
A life for God himself,

[1] *Highly perfumed rose.* [2] *Rose tree.* [3] *Nepeta, a kind of mint.* [4] *Vivid.*

To hear this nightingale
Among the birdes smale
Warbling in the vale,

"Dug, dug,
Jug, jug!
Good year and good luck!"
With "Chuck, chuck, chuck, chuck!"

STEPHEN HAWES

[1474–1523]

PRACTICALLY nothing has been learned about Stephen Hawes. The critics describe him vaguely as "a poet of the school of Chaucer," and the encyclopedias recite that he was groom of the chamber to Henry VII. Two of his longer works were printed by the great Wynkyn de Worde in 1509 and 1512, but Hawes persists as a poet by virtue of two short and pointed lyrics.

True Knighthood

For knighthood is not in the feats of warre,
    As for to fight in quarrel right or wrong,
But in a cause which truth can not defarre: [1]
    He ought himself for to make sure and strong,
    Justice to keep mixt with mercý among:
        And no quarrel a knight ought to take
        But for a truth, or for a woman's sake.

Epitaph

O mortal folk, you may behold and see
How I lie here, sometime a mighty knight.
The end of joy and all prosperity

---

[1] *Defeat.*

Is death at last—thorough his course and might.
After the daye there cometh the dark night:
For though the daye be never so long,
At last the bell ringeth to even-song.

HENRY VIII

[1491–1547]

POPULAR imagination delights to think of Henry VIII as a merry
monarch who spent his time carelessly carousing and flitting
from one wife to another. But Henry VIII was also a Machiavellian
strategist, a "Defender of the Faith" who challenged the Pope and
joined a company of Protestant princes, a monarch who began his
career with a book written against heresy, a musician, and a poet.
As a poet he had been instructed by Skelton (see page 176), who
boasted that he had taught "the honor of England" how to spell
and that he gave Henry VIII

> drink of the sugared well
> Of Helicon's waters crystalline,
> Acquainting him with the Muses nine.

Henry VIII surrounded himself with men of culture who stimu-
lated him to compose lively measures as well as reverent anthems;
one of his hymns, O LORD, THE MAKER OF ALL THINGS, is still sung.
His two most characteristic poems present a pretty contrast. The
first protests his never-changing fidelity, a fidelity to which history
has written an ironic footnote; the second, which celebrates pleas-
ure—"pastime with good company"—is a truer reflection of the
king's lusty spirit.

Green Groweth the Holly

Green groweth the holly, so doth the ivy.
Though winter blasts blow never so high,
Green groweth the holly.

As the holly groweth green
  And never changeth hue,
So I am, and ever hath been,
  Unto my lady true.
  Green groweth the holly . . .

As the holly groweth green,
  With ivy all alone,
When flowers cannot be seen
  And green-wood leaves be gone,
  Green groweth the holly . . .

Now unto my lady
  Promise to her I make:
From all other only
  To her I me betake.
  Green groweth the holly . . .

Adieu, mine own lady,
  Adieu, my speciál,
Who hath my heart truly,
  Be sure, and ever shall.
  Green groweth the holly . . .

Green groweth the holly, so doth the ivy.
Though winter blasts blow never so high,
Green groweth the holly.

Good Company

Pastime with good company
I love, and shall until I die.
Grouch who list, but none deny,
So God be pleased, thus live will I.
For my pastànce,[1]
Hunt, sing, and dance,
My heart is set;
All goodly sport
For my comfòrt,
Who shall me let?

1 *Pastime.*

Youth must have some dalliance,
Of good or ill some pastànce;
Company, methinks, then best
All thoughts and fancies to digest.
For idleness is chief mistress
Of vices all; then who can say
But mirth and play
Is best of all?

Company with honesty
Is virtue, vice to flee;
Company is good and ill,
But every man hath his free will.
The best ensue,
The worst eschew;
My mind shall be—
Virtue to use,
Vice to refuse,
Thus shall I use me.

Anthologists might well turn to 1557 with veneration, for in that year Richard Tottel issued a collection of SONGS AND SONNETS, which was reprinted numerous times. Popularly known as Tottel's MISCELLANY, it flattered, if it did not enrich, its publisher by occasioning a flood of imitations; and, though the subsequent collections embodied a wider range and a fuller music, Tottel's assembly was a pioneering expression, a reaching toward the golden age. Shakespeare referred to Tottel's book as a classic; the gravedigger in HAMLET accompanies his work with one of the songs, and Slender in THE MERRY WIVES OF WINDSOR, seeing the lovely Anne Page, says wistfully, "I had rather than forty shillings, I had my book of SONGS AND SONNETS here."

Although the collections which followed were more varied, Tottel's is a landmark, not only because it is the first, but because it contained the best work of Sir Thomas Wyatt and Henry Howard, Earl of Surrey.

SIR THOMAS WYATT
[1503?–1542]

THE reputation of Thomas Wyatt rests, rather heavily, on the fact that he was the first to employ the Italian sonnet form in English poetry. This characterization presents Wyatt in the role of a research student and a cold formalist. It is anything but a true picture. Born about 1503, dead before he was forty, Wyatt was a hot-blooded courtier. Married at eighteen to Lord Cobham's daughter, he was Anne Boleyn's lover before she was married to Henry VIII, and he was imprisoned in the Tower of London after Anne's later infidelities were discovered. In his mid-thirties he was again imprisoned on suspicion of treason, and it required a strong personal following to procure his release.

As a poet, Wyatt was precocious. He entered St. John's College, Cambridge, when he was thirteen, in 1516, the year of its opening. His undergraduate verses were being quoted when he received his M.A. at seventeen. At twenty-five he was sent as an ambassador to Italy, and it was there that he came under the influence of the Italian love poets, especially Petrarch, whom he translated.

But Wyatt was more than a translator and transplanter; he was an innovator. His experiments were as bold as they were accomplished; his sonnets gave a new stimulus to English poetry. The first of the following sonnets, although adapted from Petrarch, is presumed to refer to Anne Boleyn, and the thirteenth line—

"Noli me tangere, for Caesar's I am"—

indicates that Anne Boleyn was either married to the king or was considered his exclusive property.

The Hind

Whoso list to hunt, I know where is an **hind**,
But as for me, *helas!* I may no more.
The vain travail hath wearied me so sore,
I am of them that furthest come behind.

> Yet may I, by no means, my wearied mind
>   Draw from the deer; but as she fleeth afore
>   Fainting I follow. I leave off therefore,
> Since in a net I seek to hold the wind.
> Who list her hunt, I put him out of doubt,
>   As well as I, may spend his time in vain;
>   And graven with diamonds in letters plain
> There is written, her fair neck round about,
>   "*Noli me tangere*,[a] for Caesar's I am,
>   And wild for to hold, though I seem tame."

The Lover Renounceth Love

Farewell, Love, and all thy laws for ever!
Thy baited hooks shall tangle me no more:
Senec[1] and Plato call me from thy lore
To perfect wealth my wit for to endeavor.
In blindest error when I did perséver,
Thy sharp repulse, that pricketh aye so sore,
Hath taught me to set in trifles no store;
And 'scape forth, since liberty is lever.[2]
Therefore, farewell! go trouble younger hearts,
And in me claim no more authority.
With idle youth go use thy property,
And thereon spend thy many brittle darts;
  For hitherto though I have lost my time,
  Me list[3] no longer rotten boughs to climb.

Description of the Contrarious Passions

I find no peace, and all my war is done;
I fear and hope, I burn and freeze like ice;
I fly aloft yet can I not arise;
And nought I have, and all the world I seize on,
That locks nor looseth, holdeth me in prison,
And holds me not, yet can I 'scape no wise:
Nor letteth me live, nor die at my devise,
And yet of death it giveth me occasion.
Without eye I see; without tongue I plain:
I wish to perish yet I ask for health;

[a] *Touch me not!* [1] *Seneca.* [2] *Preferable.* [3] *I care.*

> I love another, and I hate myself;
> I feed me in sorrow, and laugh in all my pain.
>   Lo, thus displeaseth me both death and life;
>   And my delight is causer of this strife.

Although Wyatt is continually classed as a sonneteer, he was a lyric poet of the first order. His passionate measures—at their best in the lines beginning:

> They flee from me, that sometimes did me seek—

strongly influenced his young friend, Henry Howard, Earl of Surrey, and the lyricists who followed him. Wyatt's verse had its beginnings in the work of foreign poets, but its energetic fulfillment is his own. The quality may be undefinable, but it springs from a fresh awareness, an alertness which is immediately recognizable and finally unmistakable.

The Lover Showeth How He Is Forsaken

> They flee from me, that sometime did me seek,
> With naked foot stalking within my chamber:
> Once have I seen them gentle, tame, and meek,
> That now are wild, and do not once remember,
> That sometime they have put themselves in danger
> To take bread at my hand; and now they range
> Busily seeking with a continual change.
>
> Thankèd be Fortune, it hath been otherwise
> Twenty times better; but once in special,
> In thin array, after a pleasant guise,
> When her loose gown did from her shoulders fall,
> And she me caught in her arms long and small,
> And therewithal so sweetly did me kiss,
> And softly said, "Dear heart, how like you this?"
>
> It was no dream; for I lay broad awaking:
> But all is turned now through my gentleness
> Into a bitter fashion of forsaking,
> And I have leave to go of her goodness,
> And she also to use new-fangledness.
> But since that I unkindly so am servèd,
> "How like you this?"—What hath *she* now deservèd?

The Lover Complaineth

My lute awake! Perform the last
Labor that thou and I shall waste,
  The end that I have now begun:
For when this song is sung and past,
  My lute be still, for I have done.

As to be heard where ear is none,
As lead to grave in marble stone,
  My song may pierce her heart as soon.
Should we then sigh, or sing, or moan?
  No, no, my lute, for I have done.

The rocks do not so cruelly
Repulse the waves continually,
  As she my suit and affectión;
So that I am past remedy,
  Whereby my lute and I have done.

Vengeance shall fall on thy disdain
That mak'st but game on earnest pain.
  Think not alone under the sun
Unquit to cause thy lovers plain,
  Although my lute and I have done.

Perchance thee lie withered and old
In winter nights that are so cold,
  Plaining in vain unto the moon:
Thy wishes then dare not be told.
  Care then who list, for I have done.

And then may chance thee to repent
The time that thou hast lost and spent
  To cause thy lovers sigh and swoon:
Then shalt thou know beauty but lent,
  And wish and want as I have done.

Now cease, my lute: this is the last
Labor that thou and I shall waste,
  And ended is that we begun.
Now is this song both sung and past:
  My lute be still, for I have done.

The Lover Rejoiceth

Tangled was I in Love's snare,
Oppressed with pain, torment with care;
Of grief right sure, of joy quite bare,
Clean in despair by cruelty.
But ha! ha! ha! full well is me,
For I am now at liberty.

The woeful days so full of pain,
The weary nights all spent in vain,
The labor lost for so small gain,
To write them all it will not be.
But ha! ha! ha! full well is me,
For I am now at liberty.

With feignéd words which were but wind
To long delays was I assign'd;
Her wily looks my wits did blind;
Whate'er she would I would agree.
But ha! ha! ha! full well is me,
For I am now at liberty.

Was never bird tangled in lime
That broke away in better time,
Than I, that rotten boughs did climb
And had no hurt but 'scapéd free.
Now ha! ha! ha! full well is me,
For I am now at liberty.

Patience

Patience, though I have not
   The thing that I require,
I must, of force, God wot,
   Forbear my most desire;
      For no ways can I find
      To sail against the wind.

Patience, do what they will
  To work me woe or spite,
I shall content me still
  To think both day and night;
    To think and hold my peace,
    Since there is no redress.

Patience, withouten blame,
  For I offended nought;
I know they know the same,
  Though they have changed their thought.
    Was ever thought so moved
    To hate that it hath loved?

Patience of all my harm,
  For fortune is my foe;
Patience must be the charm
  To heal me of my woe.
    Patience without offence
    Is a painful patience.

Disdain

If in the world there be more woe
Than I have in my heart,
Whereso it is, it doth come fro,
And in my breast there doth it grow
For to increase my smart.
Alas, I am receipt of every care,
And of my life each sorrow claims his part.
Who list to live in quietness
By me let him beware:
For I by high disdain
Am made without redress;
And unkindness, alas, hath slain
My poor true heart all comfortless.

HENRY HOWARD, EARL OF SURREY

[1517?–1547]

WYATT's most eminent disciple, Henry Howard, Earl of Surrey, was about fourteen years younger than his master. The date of Surrey's birth is uncertainly given as 1517, but there seems no doubt of his royal blood; his father was descended from Edward the Confessor, and his mother from Edward III. Brought up at court, he was companioned by princes; his most intimate comrade was the Duke of Richmond, the illegitimate son of Henry VIII. The two boys went to France when Surrey was fifteen; a year later they were recalled to England, where Richmond married Surrey's sister, Mary Howard.

During the next dozen years Surrey was considered one of the most active, as well as one of the most fascinating, members of the court. He helped suppress a rebellion; he took command of a naval campaign against France; he jousted, quarreled continually, and wrote intermittently. His temper was easily roused—a record of 1539, when Surrey was twenty-two, describes him as "the most foolish and proud boy that is in England." His pride was his undoing. A foolish joining of the heraldic emblem of Edward the Confessor with his own was interpreted as a claim to succeed Henry VIII. The charge seemed frivolous, but Surrey's impulsiveness had made many enemies. Jealously at first, savagely at last, they testified against him, and he was convicted. On January 21, 1547, he was beheaded on Tower Hill. He was still in his thirtieth year.

Although Surrey lacked the strength of his master, he surpassed him in range and refinement. As an innovator he was the first to use blank verse consistently; he translated two books of the AENEID. But, although, like Wyatt, he learned much from the Italians, the forty poems Tottel printed in the MISCELLANY proved that he could play new—and native—tunes upon old and imported instruments.

Complaint of a Lover Rebuked

Love, that doth reign and live within my thought,
And build his seat within my captive breast,
Clad in the arms wherein with me he fought,
Oft in my face he doth his banner rest.
But she that taught me love, and suffer pain,
My doubtful hope and eke my hot desire
With shamefast look to shadow and refrain,
Her smiling grace converteth straight to ire.
And coward Love then to the heart apace
Taketh his flight, where he doth lurk and plain [1]
His purpose lost, and dare not show his face.
For my lord's guilt thus faultless bide I pain.
Yet from my lord shall not my foot remove—
Sweet is his death that takes his end by love.

Vow to Love Faithfully

Set me whereas the sun doth parch the green,
Or where his beams do not dissolve the ice,
In temperate heat where he is felt and seen;
In presence 'prest of people, mad or wise;
Set me in high or yet in low degree,
In longest night or in the shortest day,
In clearest sky or where clouds thickest be,
In lusty youth or when my hairs are gray.
Set me in heaven, in earth, or else in hell;
In hill, or dale, or in the foaming flood;
Thrall or at large, alive, whereso I dwell,
Sick or in health, in evil fame or good;
Hers will I be, and only with this thought
Content myself although my chance be nought.

[1] *Complain.*

Brittle Beauty

Brittle beauty that nature made so frail,
Whereof the gift is small, and short the season,
Flow'ring today, tomorrow apt to fail,
Tickle treasure, abhorrèd of reason,
Dangerous to deal with, vain, of none avail,
Costly in keeping, passed not worth two peason,[1]
Slippery in sliding as an eelès tail,
Hard to attain, once gotten not geason,[2]
Jewel of jeopardy that peril doth assail,
False and untrue, enticèd oft to treason,
Enemy to youth (that most may I bewail!),
Ah, bitter sweet! infecting as the poison,
Thou farest as fruit that with the frost is taken:
Today ready ripe, tomorrow all too shaken.

One of the poems with which Surrey's name is most closely associated did not appear with his others in Tottel's MISCELLANY but in William Baldwin's TREATIES OF MORAL PHILOSOPHY. Strictly speaking, it is not Surrey's, for the original is in Latin, an expanded "epigram" by Martial. But, though the concept was not the English poet's, and though the sentiment was not new even in Martial's day, Surrey's translation has become a classic of English literature.

The Things That Cause a Quiet Life

My friend, the things that do attain
The happy life be these, I find:
The riches left, not got with pain;
The fruitful ground, the quiet mind;

The equal friend; no grudge, no strife;
No charge of rule, nor governance;
Without disease the healthful life;
The household of continuance;[3]

The mean diet, no dainty fare;
True wisdom joined with simpleness;

---

[1] *Not worth two peas.* [2] *No longer wonderful.* [3] *Security.*

> The night dischargéd of all care,
>   Where wine the wit may not oppress;
>
> The faithful wife, without debate;
>   Such sleeps as may beguile the night:
> Content thyself with thine estate,
>   Ne wish for death ne fear his might.

GEORGE GASCOIGNE
[1542?–1577]

IN COMMON with many of his more famous contemporaries, George Gascoigne led a colorful and even scandalous life. It is assumed that his life was as brief as it was adventurous, but this has been questioned; some authorities deduce that Gascoigne was born as early as 1525, while others fix the date as late as 1542. It is a matter of record, however, that after a checkered career, Gascoigne married Elizabeth Breton, a widow, who was said to be involved with another gentleman. Gascoigne's marriage resulted in a street brawl, a lawsuit, and a strange paternity, for Gascoigne became the stepfather of the poet Nicholas Breton (see page 202). Further trouble followed the publication of A HUNDRETH SUNDRY FLOWERS (1573), to which Gascoigne was only one contributor, and which, two years later, was enlarged into THE POSIES OF GEORGE GASCOIGNE, with an introduction which made it appear that Gascoigne was the author of all the poems. This led to other imbroglios; he was disinherited by his father and prevented from taking a seat in Parliament. The charges against him included not only slander, forgery, and atheism, but manslaughter. His last work, presented to Queen Elizabeth as a New Year's gift in 1577, was a series of elegies completed, appropriately enough, a month or so before his death.

Like Wyatt and Surrey, Gascoigne was influenced by Italian literature and, like them, he was something of a pioneer. His SUPPOSES, adapted from Ariosto, is the first comedy in English prose. CERTAIN NOTES OF INSTRUCTION CONCERNING THE MAKING OF VERSE is the earliest critical essay on English prosody. THE SPOIL OF ANTWERP is one of the first pieces of English reporting. THE STEELE GLAS is nearly the first, if not the very first, satire in blank verse, the "steele glas" being a mirror in which the author sees the duplicated faults of humanity. When he was not politically exercised, Gascoigne was both charming and direct. In his best verse genuine emotion lies beneath a flickering surface of wit.

In his half-analytical, half-speculative study of the Elizabethan poet, Charles Prouty suggests that Gascoigne was a self-doomed failure. He was a lawyer, and could find no practice. He was a courtier, and was unhappy at court. He was a soldier, and hated army life. He was one of the most promising of the poets surrounding the young Elizabeth, but he gained neither popularity nor preferment.

That Gascoigne was aware of his own futility is evident enough. In a frank couplet he wrote:

The fatal Sisters three, which spun my slender twine,
Knew well how rotten was the yarn, from which they drew their
line.

Rarely has there been a more deprecating and more revealing self-estimate.

Gascoigne's Lullaby

Sing lullaby, as women do,
Wherewith they bring their babes to rest,
And lullaby can I sing too
As womanly as can the best.
With lullaby they still the child,
And if I be not much beguiled,
Full many wanton babes have I
Which must be stilled with lullaby.

First, lullaby, my youthful years,
It is now time to go to bed,
For crooked age and hoary hairs
Have won the haven within my head;
With lullaby, then, youth be still,
With lullaby, content thy will,
Since courage quails and comes behind,
Go sleep, and so beguile thy mind.

Next, lullaby, my gazing eyes,
Which wonted were to glance apace.
For every glass may now suffice
To show the furrows in my face;
With lullaby, then, wink awhile,
With lullaby, your looks beguile,
Let no fair face nor beauty bright
Entice you eft [1] with vain delight.

And lullaby, my wanton will,
Let reason's rule now reign thy thought,
Since all too late I find by skill
How dear I have thy fancies bought;
With lullaby, now take thine ease,
With lullaby, thy doubts appease;
For trust to this, if thou be still,
My body shall obey thy will.

And lullaby, my loving boy,
My little Robin, take thy rest;
Since age is old and nothing coy,
Keep close thy coin, for so is best;
With lullaby, be thou content,
With lullaby, thy lusts relent,
Let others pay which have more pence,
Thou art too poor for such expense.

Thus lullaby, my youth, mine eyes,
My will, my ware, and all that was!
I can no more delays devise,
But welcome pain, let pleasure pass;
With lullaby, now take your leave,
With lullaby, your dreams deceive,
And when you rise with waking eye,
Remember Gascoigne's lullaby.

Inscription in a Garden

If any flower that here is grown,
  Or any herb, may ease your pain,
Take and account it as your own,
  But recompense the like again;
    For some and some is honest play,
    And so my wife taught me to say.

[1] *Again.*

If here to walk you take delight,
　　Why, come and welcome, when you will;
If I bid you sup here this night,
　　Bid me another time, and still
　　　　Think some and some is honest play,
　　　　For so my wife taught me to say.

Thus if you sup or dine with me,
　　If you walk here or sit at ease,
If you desire the thing you see,
　　And have the same your mind to please,
　　　　Think some and some is honest play,
　　　　And so my wife taught me to say.

JOHN STILL
[1543?–1608]

IN HIS sixty-five years John Still managed to accumulate a set of
imposing titles. He was bishop of Bath and Wells, fellow of
Christ's College, and master of St. John's. He is also a candidate
for the authorship of GAMMER GURTON'S NEEDLE, the second English
comedy in verse, the first being RALPH ROISTER DOISTER.

GAMMER GURTON'S NEEDLE includes a drinking song whose re-
frain was older than the comedy. Whether the good churchman
wrote all the other verses or amplified certain stanzas of an old
rhyme has never been conclusively established. But it is pleasant to
think that a bishop of Bath and Wells and a master of St. John's is
remembered not for his scholarship or his piety, but for his lusty
appreciation of "jolly good ale and old."

In Praise of Ale

I cannot eat but little meat,
　　My stomach is not good;
But sure I think that I can drink
　　With him that wears a hood.
Though I go bare, take ye no care,
　　I nothing am a-cold;

I stuff my skin so full within
  Of jolly good ale and old.
    Back and side go bare, go bare;
    Both foot and hand go cold;
    But, belly, God send thee good ale enough,
    Whether it be new or old.

I love no roast but a nut-brown toast,
  And a crab laid in the fire;
A little bread shall do me stead;
  Much bread I not desire.
No frost nor snow, no wind, I trow,
  Can hurt me if I wold;
I am so wrapped and thoroughly lapped
  With jolly good ale and old.
    Back and side go bare, go bare . . .

And Tib, my wife, that as her life
  Loveth well good ale to seek,
Full oft drinks she till ye may see
  The tears run down her cheek:
Then doth she troll to me the bowl
  Even as a maltworm should,
And saith, "Sweetheart, I took my part
  Of this jolly good ale and old."
    Back and side go bare, go bare . . .

Now let them drink till they nod and wink,
  Even as good fellows do;
They shall not miss to have the bliss
  Good ale doth bring men to;
And all poor souls that have scoured bowls
  Or have them lustily trolled,
God save the lives of them and their wives,
  Whether they be young or old.
    Back and side go bare, go bare;
    Both foot and hand go cold;
    But, belly, God send thee good ale enough,
    Whether it be new or old.

NICHOLAS BRETON
[1545–1626]

PERHAPS the best of the collections which followed Tottel's MISCELLANY is ENGLAND'S HELICON, published in 1600. This anthology is a perfect treasury of Elizabethan verse; lyrics by the greatest of Elizabethans predominate, particularly lyrics which sound the pastoral note.

The pastorals give a remarkable, if untrustworthy, picture of the period. To judge from their ardor, as well as their prevalence, England was chiefly populated by hotly pursuing, rhyme-twisting nobles disguised as peasants, and virtuous but eventually yielding milkmaids. Corydon, a shepherd emerging from the ECLOGUES of Virgil, was elevated to national prominence, and the affairs of state were, seemingly, less vital than the affairs of Corydon and his Phyllis.

Nicholas Breton, stepson of George Gascoigne (see page 197), turned the pastoral notes on a particularly deft flute. He was among the most popular as well as one of the most prolific of Elizabethan authors. It is said that his mother's marriage to Gascoigne had an unhappy effect on Breton's boyhood; and he may well have turned to poetry not only as an escape, but in an effort to surpass his stepfather. It is, however, to this poetry of escape that Breton owes his popularity. His many moral pamphlets are forgotten, but his skillful songs have been repeated and put to music countless times. No one knew better than Breton how to mingle art and artificiality with an effect of simple spontaneity.

A Pastoral

In the merry month of May,
In a morn by break of day
Forth I walked by the wood-side,
When as May was in his pride.
There I spiéd, all alone,
Phyllida and Corydon.
Much ado there was, God wot,
He would love and she would not.

She said, "Never man was true."
He said, "None was false to you."
He said he had loved her long.
She said, "Love should have no wrong."
Corydon would kiss her then.
She said maids must kiss no men
Till they did for good and all.
Then she made the shepherd call
All the heavens to witness truth,
Never loved a truer youth.
Thus, with many a pretty oath,
Yea and nay, and faith and troth,
Such as silly shepherds use
When they will not love abuse,
Love which had been long deluded
Was with kisses sweet concluded.
And Phyllida with garlands gay
Was made the lady of the May.

Phyllida aṅd Corydon

On a hill there grows a flower,
    Fair befall the dainty sweet!
By that flower there is a bower
    Where the heavenly Muses meet.

In that bower there is a chair
    Fringèd all about with gold,
Where doth sit the fairest fair
    That did ever eye behold.

It is Phyllis fair and bright,
    She that is the shepherds' joy,
She that Venus did despite
    And did blind her little boy.

This is she, the wise, the rich,
    All the world desires to see;
This is *ipsa quæ* [1] the which
    There is none but only she.

[1] *She herself.*

Who would not this face admire?
  Who would not this saint adore?
Who would not this sight desire,
  Though he thought to see no more?

O fair eyes, yet let me see!
  One good look, and I am gone,
Look on me, for I am he—
  Thy poor silly Corydon.

Thou that art the shepherds' queen,
  Look upon thy silly swain;
By thy comfort have been seen
  Dead men brought to life again.

Phyllis

Sweet birds that sit and sing amid the shady valleys,
And see how sweetly Phyllis walks amid her garden alleys,
Go round about her bower, and sing as ye are bidden:
To her is only known his faith that from the world is hidden.
And she among you all that hath the sweetest voice,
Go chirp of him that never told, yet never changed, his choice;

And not forget his faith that lived for ever lovéd,
Yet never made his fancy known, nor ever favor movéd;
And ever let the ground of all your grace be this:
"To you, to you, to you the due of love and honor is,
On you, on you, on you our music all attendeth,
For as on you our Muse begun, in you all music endeth!"

Country Song

Shall we go dance the hay, the hay?
Never pipe could ever play
Better shepherd's roundelay.

Shall we go sing the song, the song?
Never Love did ever wrong.
Fair maids, hold hands all along.

Shall we go learn to woo, to woo?
Never thought came ever to,
Better deed could better do.

Shall we go learn to kiss, to kiss?
Never heart could ever miss
Comfort, where true meaning is.

Thus at base they run, they run,
When the sport was scarce begun.
But I waked—and all was done.

SIR EDWARD DYER
[1550?–1607]

THE name of Sir Edward Dyer persists because he was closely
associated with Sir Philip Sidney and because of his one fa-
mous poem, MY MIND TO ME A KINGDOM IS, which reflects the quiet
seclusion of his later life. Contemporary reports suggest his per-
sonal detachment; they credit him with having translated much of
Theocritus and being "famous for elegy." Few of Dyer's poems re-
main; one of his "minor verses" here reprinted carries out the
modest implications of his more familiar lines.

Love Is Love

The lowest trees have tops, the ant her gall,
    The fly her spleen, the little sparks their heat;
The slender hairs cast shadows, though but small,
    And bees have stings, although they be not great;
Seas have their source, and so have shallow springs;
And love is love, in beggars as in kings.

Where rivers smoothest run, deep are the fords;
    The dial stirs, yet none perceives it move;
The firmest faith is in the fewest words;
    The turtles cannot sing, and yet they love:
True hearts have eyes and ears, no tongues to speak;
They hear and see, and sigh, and then they break.

My Mind to Me a Kingdom Is

My mind to me a kingdom is;
   Such present joys therein I find
That it excels all other bliss
   That earth affords or grows by kind.
Though much I want which most would have,
Yet still my mind forbids to crave.

No princely pomp, no wealthy store,
   No force to win the victory,
No wily wit to salve a sore,
   No shape to feed a loving eye;
To none of these I yield as thrall—
For why? My mind doth serve for all.

I see how plenty surfeits oft,
   And hasty climbers soon do fall;
I see that those which are aloft
   Mishap doth threaten most of all;
They get with toil, they keep with fear—
Such cares my mind could never bear.

Content to live, this is my stay;
   I seek no more than may suffice;
I press to bear no haughty sway;
   Look, what I lack my mind supplies.
Lo, thus I triumph like a king,
Content with that my mind doth bring.

Some have too much, yet still do crave;
   I little have, and seek no more.
They are but poor, though much they have,
   And I am rich with little store.
They poor, I rich; they beg, I give;
They lack, I leave; they pine, I live.

I laugh not at another's loss;
   I grudge not at another's pain;
No worldly waves my mind can toss;
   My state at one doth still remain.
I fear no foe, I fawn no friend;
I loathe not life, nor dread my end.

Some weigh their pleasure by their lust,
  Their wisdom by their rage of will;
Their treasure is their only trust;
  A cloakèd craft their store of skill.
But all the pleasure that I find
Is to maintain a quiet mind.

My wealth is health and perfect ease;
  My conscience clear my chief defense;
I neither seek by bribes to please,
  Nor by deceit to breed offense.
Thus do I live; thus will I die;
Would all did so as well as I!

SIR WALTER RALEIGH
[1552?–1618]

THE careful Muse of history allows herself a romantic aside as she reminds us that when Queen Elizabeth stepped across Raleigh's cloak, Sir Walter himself stepped into immortality. But, though this gallant if doubtful episode may be the only one that most readers remember, Raleigh was much more than a handsome courtier. He was the typical man of the English Renaissance: a soldier, a sailor, a statesman, an explorer, and a poet. The great navigator, Sir Humphrey Gilbert, was his half brother, and Raleigh was in command of one of the vessels when Gilbert made his first voyage to America in 1578. After Gilbert went down on the *Golden Hind,* Raleigh, setting out "to discover and conquer unknown lands and take possession of them in the Queen's name," founded the colony which, in honor of the Virgin Queen, was named Virginia.

In his forties Raleigh joined Essex and fought in Spain and Ireland. His favor at court dwindled; Elizabeth was jealous or, at least, disapproved of his relations with one of her maids of honor, whom he subsequently married. After James I ascended the throne Raleigh was suspected of plotting against the new monarch, and the judges, after an unfair trial, played cat and mouse with his career. He was committed to the Tower and sentenced to death; he was then reprieved and sentenced to prison for fourteen years. Past sixty when he was released, he had the hardihood to undertake an expedition to the Orinoco in search of gold. Tragedy accompanied the voyage. The expedition failed, and upon his return Raleigh was arrested; the Spanish ambassador insisted that Raleigh was responsible for the burning of a Spanish settlement. The old charge of conspiracy against the King was revived, and Raleigh was once more put in custody. He was tried, found guilty, and executed on October 29, 1618, one of the noblest spirits of his day.

Raleigh's character is manifest even in his prose, in his accounts of journeys and his voluminous THE HISTORY OF THE WORLD, written during his long imprisonment for the instruction of the young Prince of Wales. But his nobility lives in his poems. Although Raleigh's reputation as a poet has been engulfed by his fame as courtier and explorer, his verse is richer and more varied than that of most of his contemporaries. Raleigh turns persiflage into sudden realism, as in his most quoted poem, THE NYMPH'S REPLY TO THE SHEPHERD, written in answer to the poem by Christopher Marlowe, on page 322. Raleigh braves the opinion of the worldly in THE LIE; mixes grimness and humor in THE WOOD, THE WEED, THE WAG, a poem which has been far too little appreciated; and lifts bitterness into resignation in THE PASSIONATE MAN'S PILGRIMAGE, which bore the subtitle "Supposed to be written by one at the point of death," and which may well serve as Raleigh's own elegy.

The Nymph's Reply to the Shepherd

If all the world and love were young,
And truth in every shepherd's tongue,
These pretty pleasures might me move,
To live with thee and be thy love.

Time drives the flocks from field to fold,
When rivers rage, and rocks grow cold;
And Philomel becometh dumb;
The rest complain of cares to come.

The flowers do fade, and wanton fields
To wayward winter reckoning yields;
A honey tongue, a heart of gall,
Is fancy's spring, but sorrow's fall.

Thy gowns, thy shoes, thy beds of roses,
Thy cap, thy kirtle, and thy posies,
Soon break, soon wither, soon forgotten;
In folly ripe, in reason rotten.

Thy belt of straw and ivy buds,
Thy coral clasps and amber studs,
All these in me no means can move,
To come to thee and be thy love.

But could youth last, and love still breed,
Had joys no date, nor age no need,
Then these delights my mind might move
To live with thee and be thy love.

The Lie

Go, soul, the body's guest,
  Upon a thankless arrant.[1]
Fear not to touch the best;
  The truth shall be thy warrant.
  Go, since I needs must die,
  And give the world the lie.

Say to the court, it glows
  And shines like rotten wood;
Say to the church, it shows
  What's good, and doth no good.
  If church and court reply,
  Then give them both the lie.

Tell potentates, they live
  Acting by others' action;
Not loved unless they give;
  Not strong but by affection.
  If potentates reply,
  Give potentates the lie.

Tell men of high condition
  That manage the estate,
Their purpose is ambition,
  Their practice only hate;
  And if they once reply,
  Then give them all the lie.

[1] *Errand.*

Tell them that brave it most,
  They beg for more by spending,
Who, in their greatest cost,
  Like nothing but commending;
  And if they make reply,
  Then give them all the lie.

Tell zeal it wants devotion;
  Tell love it is but lust;
Tell time it meets but motion;
  Tell flesh it is but dust;
  And wish them not reply,
  For thou must give the lie.

Tell age it daily wasteth;
  Tell honor how it alters;
Tell beauty how she blasteth;
  Tell favor how it falters;
  And as they shall reply,
  Give every one the lie.

Tell wit how much it wrangles
  In tickle-points of niceness;
Tell wisdom she entangles
  Herself in over-wiseness;
  And when they do reply,
  Straight give them both the lie.

Tell physic of her boldness;
  Tell skill it is prevention;
Tell charity of coldness;
  Tell law it is contention;
  And as they do reply,
  So give them still the lie.

Tell fortune of her blindness;
  Tell nature of decay;
Tell friendship of unkindness;
  Tell justice of delay;
  And if they will reply,
  Then give them all the lie.

Tell arts they have no soundness,
  But vary by esteeming;

Tell schools they want profoundness,
  And stand too much on seeming;
  If arts and schools reply,
  Give arts and schools the lie.

Tell faith it's fled the city;
  Tell how the country erreth;
Tell, manhood shakes off pity,
  Tell, virtue least preferreth;
  And if they do reply,
  Spare not to give the lie.

So when thou hast, as I
  Commanded thee, done blabbing;
Because to give the lie
  Deserves no less than stabbing.
  Stab at thee he that will—
  No stab thy soul can kill.

The Wood, the Weed, the Wag

TO HIS SON

Three things there be that prosper all apace
And flourish while they grow asunder far;
But on a day, they meet all in a place,
And when they meet, they one another mar.

And they be these: the wood, the weed, the wag.
The wood is that which makes the gallows tree;
The weed is that which strings the hangman's bag;
The wag, my pretty knave, betokens thee.

Now mark, dear boy, while these assemble not,
Green springs the tree, hemp grows, the wag is wild;
But when they meet, it makes the timber rot,
It frets the halter, and it chokes the child.

Then bless thee, and beware, and let us pray
We part not with thee at this meeting day.

The Passionate Man's Pilgrimage

SUPPOSED TO BE WRITTEN BY ONE AT THE POINT OF DEATH

Give me my scallop-shell [1] of quiet,
My staff of faith to walk upon,
My scrip of joy, immortal diet,
My bottle of salvation,
My gown of glory, hope's true gage,
And thus I'll take my pilgrimage.

Blood must be my body's balmer,[2]
No other balm will there be given,
Whilst my soul, like a white palmer,
Travels to the land of heaven,
Over the silver mountains,
Where spring the nectar fountains;
And there I'll kiss
The bowl of bliss,
And drink my eternal fill
On every milken hill.
My soul will be a-dry before,
But, after, it will ne'er thirst more.

And by the happy blissful way
More peaceful pilgrims I shall see,
That have shook off their gowns of clay
And go appareled fresh like me.
I'll bring them first
To slake their thirst,
And then to taste those nectar suckets,[3]
At the clear wells
Where sweetness dwells,
Drawn up by saints in crystal buckets.

And when our bottles and all we
Are filled with immortality,
Then the holy paths we'll travel,
Strewed with rubies thick as gravel,
Ceilings of diamonds, sapphire floors,
High walls of coral, and pearl bowers.
From thence to heaven's bribeless hall

[1] *Worn as an emblem by pilgrims.*   [2] *Embalmer.*   [3] *Fruits and sweetmeats.*

Where no corrupted voices brawl,
No conscience molten into gold,
Nor forged accusers bought and sold,
No cause deferred, nor vain-spent journey,
For there Christ is the king's attorney,
Who pleads for all without degrees,
And he hath angels,⁴ but no fees.

When the grand twelve million jury
Of our sins and sinful fury,
'Gainst our souls black verdicts give,
Christ pleads his death, and then we live.
Be thou my speaker, taintless pleader,
Unblotted lawyer, true proceeder,
Thou movest salvation even for alms,
Not with a bribèd lawyer's palms.

And this is my eternal plea
To him that made heaven, earth, and sea,
Seeing my flesh must die so soon,
And want a head to dine next noon,
Just at the stroke when my veins start and spread
Set on my soul an everlasting head.
Then am I ready, like a palmer fit,
To tread those blest paths which before I writ.

Proof that popular ballads were relished not only by the common people but by the great poets as well is found in the recurrence of imitations as well as outright quotations. As YOU CAME FROM THE HOLY LAND is a poem which has had many echoes. Its first form must date back considerably before Raleigh's birth, even before 1538, when the wonder-working shrine at Walsingham was destroyed. Shakespeare knew Raleigh's poem, but he may have been paraphrasing the vanished original when, like a curious distortion of Raleigh's second verse, the love-mad Ophelia sings:

> How should I your true love know
>   From another one?
> By his cockle hat and staff,
>   And his sandal shoon.

Some commentators have classed AS YOU CAME FROM THE HOLY LAND among the "doubtful" poems. But, although Raleigh seldom

⁴ *An unexpected pun; "angels" were also gold coins.*

used the ballad motif, there is little doubt about the authenticity
of the poem; it moves with his characteristic pace and is colored
by his gravity and restrained sadness.

As You Came from the Holy Land

"As you came from the holy land
    Of Walsinghame,
Met you not with my true love
    By the way as you came?"

"How shall I know your true love,
    That have met many one
As I went to the holy land,
    That have come, that have gone?"

"She is neither white nor brown,
    But as the heavens fair,
There is none hath a form so divine
    In the earth or the air."

"Such an one did I meet, good Sir,
    Such an angelic face,
Who like a queen, like a nymph, did appear
    By her gait, by her grace."

"She hath left me all alone,
    All alone as unknown,
Who sometimes did me lead with herself,
    And me loved as her own."

"What's the cause that she leaves you alone
    And a new way doth take,
Who loved you once as her own
    And her joy did you make?"

"I have loved her all my youth,
    But now old as you see,
Love likes not the falling fruit
    From the withered tree.

"Know that Love is a careless child,
    And forgets promise past;
He is blind, he is deaf, when he list
    And in faith never fast.

"His desire is a dureless [1] content
   And a trustless joy;
He is won with a world of despair
   And is lost with a toy.

"Of womenkind such indeed is the love
   Or the word love abused,
Under which many childish desires
   And conceits are excused.

"But love is a durable fire
   In the mind ever burning;
Never sick, never old, never dead,
   From itself never turning."

"It is difficult to believe in Sir Walter Raleigh," writes Agnes
M. C. Latham in the introduction to her careful collection of
Raleigh's POEMS. "There is and always has been something legend-
ary, something fantastic and not quite credible about him. Even
to his contemporaries he seemed a man of more than normal stat-
ure: so monstrously proud, so dangerously subtle, and in the end
so horribly wronged. They never viewed him calmly as a fellow
creature, with flaws and talents like their own and a like fate. They
must either execrate or laud him, as though, whatever he was, he
was in excess of the common. He might have walked out of an
Elizabethan play, a figment of the Renaissance imagination, com-
pact of inordinate vices and virtues and destined to strange ends
. . . a lonely and an enigmatic figure."

Perhaps because Raleigh lived more fully than most men of his
period, life treated him more cruelly than most. Tricked by his
king and betrayed by his friends, Raleigh went to his death with
a wry pun: "When I come to the sad parting you shall see me
grave enough." He was too proud to cry out with bitterness. The
few lines which were supposed to have been written the night
before he died may have been composed at an earlier time, but
they are undoubtedly his personal epitaph. They were found in
his Bible after his death.

[1] *Not enduring, fading.*

His Epitaph

Even such is Time, which takes in trust
Our youth, our joys, and all we have,
And pays us but with age and dust,
Who, in the dark and silent grave,
When we have wandered all our ways,
Shuts up the story of our days.
    Yet from this earth, and grave, and dust,
    The Lord shall raise me up I trust.

EDMUND SPENSER

[1552?–1599]

UNLIKE many of his contemporary fellow poets, Edmund Spenser was not born to the purple. He was not brought up at court; his family could boast no heraldic devices. Spenser's father was a clothmaker, and the son of the middle-class journeyman was educated at the Merchant Tailors' School. Good fortune, however, enabled the father to send the boy to Cambridge, where he took his M.A. in 1576 and graduated into a circle of influential friends. Spenser became secretary to the Earl of Leicester, one of Queen Elizabeth's favorites, and this position brought him in close association with Leicester's nephew, Sir Philip Sidney. The two young men became the nucleus of a small literary group, but Spenser's poetry failed to win him advancement.

In 1580 Spenser became secretary to the ruthless Lord Deputy of Ireland. And in Ireland he stayed, except for two visits to London, until shortly before his death. He never ceased to long for England and hoped for preferment there. He grew to look upon Ireland as a place of exile; he shared the cruel theories of his chief to such an extent that he defended the Lord Deputy in a long piece of prose and idealized him as the Knight-errant of Justice in THE FAERIE QUEENE. In his mid-thirties Spenser, profiting by the Lord Deputy's methods, acquired an Irish estate and moved into Kilcolman Castle. For the next fifteen years he seemed to be fortune's favorite child. Raleigh visited him in Ireland, heard the first part of Spenser's major work, and was so impressed that he made Spenser return to London to supervise its publication. In 1590 the first three books of THE FAERIE QUEENE were published and dedicated to "the most Mightie and Magnificent Empresse Elizabeth." The fame which followed was accompanied by a pension. In 1594 Spenser married the wealthy Elizabeth Boyle, commemorated in his AMO-RETTI. A few years later, while he was planning an extension of his chief poem, the Irish rebellion of 1598 broke out. Kilcolman Castle was burned; manuscripts were lost; Spenser, his wife, and four children saved themselves by fleeing to Cork. Shortly after the catastrophe Spenser came to London, a broken and destitute man. He died January 16, 1599, in a cheap lodginghouse. The funeral expenses were born by the Earl of Essex, and Spenser was buried in Westminster Abbey near the tomb of Chaucer to whom so often he had been compared.

The comparison to Chaucer is a tribute to Spenser's literary style, but there is little other likeness. Spenser has none of Chaucer's quick-blooded warmth and round heartiness; Spenser was all for cool tranquillity, for a fastidious beauty, for a decorous and even overdecorated loveliness. In Spenser everything is precise to the point of preciousness. Moreover, Spenser was the last of the medieval poets who trained themselves to strict subjectivity. Unlike Chaucer, who reveled in homely emotions, Spenser reflected his world with a skilled impersonality. The impersonal tone preserved so little of the actual world that Spenser's language was archaic even in his own day.

The result, too often, is a kind of cold imagery, a beauty which is brilliant but remote. THE CANTERBURY TALES are as alive today as when they were written three and a half centuries ago. Chaucer's people have never lost their reality; they are, as Siegfried Sassoon wrote, "our comfortable, though distant, kith and kin." But THE FAERIE QUEENE is peopled with ghosts; it is a fantasy which has no relation to any time, a bloodless and confused allegory which fails to come off even as an allegory.

Yet if Spenser's most famous poem is also his dullest, it contains passages of great charm. Some of its pictures are done in pure enamel. There is no better example of Spenser's delicacy and conscious refinement than the description of a dance which occurs in the sixth book of THE FAERIE QUEENE.

The Dance

It was an hill placed in an open plain,
   That round about was bordered with a wood
Of matchless height, that seemed th'earth to disdain,
   In which all trees of honor stately stood,
   And did all winter as in summer bud,
Spreading pavilions for the birds to bower,
   Which in their lower branches sung aloud;
And in their tops the soaring hawk did tower,
Sitting like king of fowls in majesty and power.

And at the foot thereof, a gentle flood
   His silver waves did softly tumble down,
Unmarred with ragged moss or filthy mud,
   Ne mote [1] wild beasts, ne mote the ruder clown
   Thereto approach, ne filth mote therein drown:
But nymphs and fairies by the banks did sit,
   In the wood's shade, which did the waters crown,
Keeping all noisome things away from it,
And to the water's fall tuning their accents fit.

And on the top thereof a spacious plain
   Did spread itself, to serve to all delight,
Either to dance, when they to dance would fain,
   Or else to course about their bases [2] light;
   Ne aught there wanted, which for pleasure might
Desired be, or thence to banish bale:
   So pleasantly the hill with equal height
Did seem to overlook the lowly vale;
Therefore it rightly cleped [3] was mount Acidale.

They say that Venus, when she did dispose
   Herself to pleasance, used to resort
Unto this place, and therein to repose
   And rest herself, as in a gladsome port,
   Or with the Graces there to play and sport;
That even her own Citheron, though in it
   She used most to keep her royal court,

[1] *Might.* [2] *Lines in a game.* [3] *Named.*

And in her sovereign majesty to sit,
She in regard hereof refused and thought unfit.

Unto this place when as the Elfin Knight
    Approached, him seemed that the merry sound
Of a shrill pipe he playing heard on height,
    And many feet fast thumping th' hollow ground,
    That through the woods their echo did rebound.
He nigher drew, to wit what mote it be;
    There he a troop of ladies dancing found
Full merrily, and making gladful glee,
And in the midst a shepherd piping he did see.

He durst not enter into th'open green,
    For dread of them unwares to be descried,
For breaking of their dance, if he were seen;
    But in the covert of the wood did bide,
    Beholding all, yet of them unespied.
There he did see, that pleased much his sight,
    That even he himself his eyes envied,
An hundred naked maidens lily white,
All ranged in a ring, and dancing in delight.

from THE FAERIE QUEENE

Spenser's greatness has become vague with time. But if his power seems antiquated and his diction archaic, he comes to us with a poetical purity that few poets have surpassed. His crystalline quality is revealed in the limpid if overlengthy EPITHALAMION, written for his own marriage, and PROTHALAMION, another espousal poem, with its placid and perfect refrain:

Sweet Thames, run softly, till I end my song.

It is in his sonnets that Spenser triumphs over affectations and fleshlessness. The language of the AMORETTI, a sequence of eighty-eight sonnets celebrating the poet's love for Elizabeth Boyle, is rich and flexible. Although much of it is given to lofty allusions and conventional tributes, many of the separate sonnets display not only Spenser's high seriousness but, beneath the flood of images, his essential serenity.

FROM

Amoretti

What guile is this, that those her golden tresses
She doth attire under a net of gold;
And with sly skill so cunningly them dresses,
That which is gold or hair, may scarce be told?
Is it that men's frail eyes, which gaze too bold,
She may entangle in that golden snare;
And being caught may craftily enfold
Their weaker hearts, which are not well aware?
Take heed therefore, mine eyes, how ye do stare
Henceforth too rashly on that guileful net,
In which if ever ye entrapped are,
Out of her bands ye by no means shall get.
  Folly it were for any being free,
    To covet fetters, though they golden be.

*

My Love is like to ice, and I to fire:
How comes it then that this her cold so great
Is not dissolved through my so hot desire,
But harder grows the more I her entreat?
Or how comes it that my exceeding heat
Is not allayed by her heart-frozen cold,
But that I burn much more in boiling sweat,
And feel my flames augmented manifold?
What more miraculous thing may be told,
That fire, which all things melts, should harden ice,
And ice, which is congeal'd with senseless cold,
Should kindle fire by wonderful device?
  Such is the power of love in gentle mind,
    That it can alter all the course of kind.

*

Ye tradeful merchants that, with weary toil,
Do seek most precious things to make your gain,
And both the Indias of their treasure spoil,
What needeth you to seek so far in vain?

For lo! my Love doth in herself contain
All this world's riches that may far be found:
If sapphires, lo! her eyes be sapphires plain;
If rubies, lo! her lips be rubies sound;
If pearls, her teeth be pearls, both pure and round;
If ivory, her forehead ivory ween;
If gold, her locks are finest gold on ground;
If silver, her fair hands are silver sheen:
  But that which fairest is but few behold:
  Her mind, adorn'd with virtues manifold.

*

So oft as I her beauty do behold,
And therewith do her cruelty compare,
I marvel of what substance was the mould
The which her made at once so cruel-fair.
Not earth; for her high thoughts more heavenly are:
Not water; for her love doth burn like fire:
Not air; for she is not so light or rare:
Not fire; for she doth freeze with faint desire.
Then needs another element inquire
Whereof she might be made; that is, the sky.
For to the heaven her haughty looks aspire,
And eke her love is pure immortal high.
  Then since to heaven ye likened are the best,
  Be like in mercy as in all the rest.

*

Like as a huntsman after weary chase,
Seeing the game from him escaped away,
Sits down to rest him in some shady place,
With panting hounds, beguiléd of their prey:
So, after long pursuit and vain assay,
When I all weary had the chase forsook,
The gentle deer return'd the self-same way,
Thinking to quench her thirst at the next brook.
There she, beholding me with milder look,
Sought not to fly, but fearless still did bide,
Till I in hand her yet half trembling took,
And with her own good-will her firmly tied.
  Strange thing, me seemed, to see a beast so wild
  So goodly won, with her own will beguiled.

*

More than most fair, full of the living fire
Kindled above unto the Maker near:
No eyes, but joys, in which all powers conspire,
That to the world naught else be counted dear:
Through your bright beams doth not the blinded guest
Shoot out his darts to base affection's wound;
But angels come, to lead frail minds to rest
In chaste desires, on heavenly beauty bound.
You frame my thoughts, and fashion me within,
You stop my tongue, and teach my heart to speak,
You calm the storm that passion did begin,
Strong through your cause, but by your virtue weak.
  Dark is the world where your light shinéd never;
  Well is he born that may behold you ever.

*

Trust not the treason of those smiling looks,
Until ye have their guileful trains well tried!
For they are like but unto golden hooks,
That from the foolish fish their baits do hide:
So she with flatt'ring smiles weak hearts doth guide
Unto her love, and tempt to their decay;
Whom, being caught, she kills with cruel pride,
And feeds at pleasure on the wretched prey.
Yet even whilst her bloody hands them slay,
Her eyes look lovely, and upon them smile,
That they take pleasure in their cruel play,
And, dying, do themselves of pain beguile.
  O mighty charm! which makes men love their bane,
  And think they die with pleasure, live with pain.

JOHN LYLY

[1554?–1606]

JOHN LYLY was known in his time chiefly as a playwright; literary historians credit him with having written the first high social comedies in prose, comedies of intellectual laughter rather than common humor. Dictionaries preserve his name because he contributed a new word to the language. The word is *euphuism*, defined as "excessive elegance and refinement of language." Euphues was the chief character in Lyly's prose romance, a work of such high-flown diction and careful complexity that the style became a model for elaborate affectation.

In his more restrained moments, Lyly was a poet. In his verse he did not aim at excessiveness, and the songs which enlivened his plays still hold their light wit and easy charm. At least one (the third in this group) is the anthologists' standby. Inconsequential though the first song appears, this salutation to spring has had lasting echoes. "The lark at heaven's gate" is heard in Shakespeare's CYMBELINE, and "the ravish'd nightingale" sings "Jug, Jug" to dirty ears in T. S. Eliot's THE WASTE LAND, written more than three hundred years after Lyly's death.

Trico's Song

What bird so sings, yet so does wail?
O! 'tis the ravished nightingale.
"Jug, Jug, Jug, Jug, Tereu," [1] she cries,
And still her woes at midnight rise.
Brave prick-song! [2] who is't now we hear?
None but the lark so shrill and clear;
Now at heaven's gates she claps her wings,
The morn not waking till she sings.
Hark, hark, with what a pretty throat
Poor robin redbreast tunes his note;
Hark how the jolly cuckoos sing
"Cuckoo," to welcome in the spring,
"Cuckoo," to welcome in the spring.

Fools in Love's College

O Cupid! monarch over kings,
Wherefore hast thou feet and wings?
It is to show how swift thou art,
When thou wound'st a tender heart!
Thy wings being clipped, and feet held still,
Thy bow so many could not kill.

[1] *Tereus dishonored Philomela, deprived her of her tongue, and later attempted to kill her. The gods transformed her into a nightingale, and the bird's plaintive cry still reveals the name of her betrayer as she sings, "Tereu! Tereu!"*
[2] *A song with written notes in counterpoint.*

It is all one in Venus' wanton school,
Who highest sits, the wise man or the fool.
  Fools in love's college
  Have far more knowledge
  To read a woman over,
  Than a neat prating lover:
  Nay, 'tis confessed
  That fools please women best.

from MOTHER BOMBIE

Apelles' Song

Cupid and my Campaspe played
At cards for kisses; Cupid paid:
He stakes his quiver, bow and arrows,
His mother's doves, and team of sparrows;
Loses them too: then down he throws
The coral of his lip, the rose
Growing on's cheek (but none knows how);
With these, the crystal of his brow,
And then the dimple of his chin.
All these did my Campaspe win.
At last he set her both his eyes.
She won, and Cupid blind did rise.
  O Love! has she done this to thee?
  What shall, alas! become of me?

from CAMPASPE

SIR PHILIP SIDNEY
[1554–1586]

WITH the possible exception of Sir Walter Raleigh, Sir Philip
Sidney is the finest example of the man of the English Renais-
sance—and he was Raleigh's opposite. Raleigh's life was an accumu-
lation of failures; Sidney's was a series of increasing triumphs.
Raleigh moved in a circle of enemies; Sidney was surrounded by
worshipful friends. Born on November 30, 1554, the scion of a dis-
tinguished family, Sidney was brought up on his father's luxurious

country place in Kent and, in order to get the best of both leading universities, was educated at Oxford and Cambridge. At eighteen he went to the Continent and studied with the humanist Languet, with whom he traveled through Europe. Upon his return to England Sidney became a favorite at court. In youth, according to his friend and fellow poet, Fulke Greville, Sidney "carried grace and reverence above greater years. His very play tended to enrich his mind, so that even his teachers found something in him to observe and learn." At twenty-one he was, in Chaucer's phrase, "a verray parfit gentil knight," and Shakespeare must have had Sidney in mind when Ophelia described Hamlet, the courtier, the soldier, the scholar—

> The expectancy and use of the fair state,
> The glass of fashion and the mold of form,
> The observed of all observers.

Sidney was at Kenilworth during the famous reception of Queen Elizabeth by his uncle, the Earl of Leicester. He followed the Queen and her court to the home of Lord Essex, where he met Essex's daughter, Penelope Devereux. It is an open question whether Sidney became engaged to Penelope; but there is little doubt that ASTROPHEL AND STELLA was addressed to her, and there is still less dispute that this sequence of 108 sonnets was so popular that it was largely responsible for the flood of sonnet cycles which dominated English poetry toward the end of the sixteenth century.

History gives no reason why the union was not consummated, but Penelope became the unhappy wife of Lord Rich, and Sidney married Frances Walsingham. He sat in Parliament, and Elizabeth knighted him. It is said that he refused the crown of Poland. In his thirtieth year he was appointed governor of Flushing, and in 1586 he was wounded at the battle of Zutphen. Blessed by a glorious beginning, crowned by a brilliant career, Sidney was immortalized by a noble end. Fatally wounded in the thigh, dying of pain and thirst, he was putting an almost empty bottle to his lips when he saw a common soldier looking longingly at him. Sidney, according to Greville, passed the bottle and said, "Thy necessity is greater than mine."

After lingering for some days, Sidney died on October 7, 1586. In another month he would have been thirty-two years old.

As a poet Sidney has first claim upon his fellows for his APOLOGY FOR POETRY, a defense which is as enthusiastic as it is scholarly. It marks the beginning of English literary criticism and is an eloquent forerunner of similar essays by Dryden, Pope, Hazlitt, and Shelley. As a sonneteer Sidney does not wholly free himself from the elaborate conventions of the period, yet his poems are not only less artificial but far more personal than most. It will never be known how fully Sidney revealed himself in ASTROPHEL AND STELLA—none of his work was printed during his lifetime, and his famous sonnet sequence was not published until five years after his death. But a quick spirit keeps the sonnets ever fresh; the occasional verbal ornaments bring his frankness into greater relief. If Sidney insists too much on moral restrictions, it is with the insistence of a romancer. And his lines, together with his life, lift romance to the pitch of passion.

The last line of the first sonnet in ASTROPHEL AND STELLA expresses it in all sincerity:

"Fool!" said my Muse to me, "look in thy heart and write."

It is a line which might well serve as a motto for any writer.

FROM

Astrophel and Stella[1]

Loving in truth, and fain in verse my love to show,
That she, dear she, might take some pleasure of my pain,
Pleasure might cause her read, reading might make her know,
Knowledge might pity win, and pity grace obtain,
I sought fit words to paint the blackest face of woe,
Studying inventions fine, her wits to entertain,
Oft turning others' leaves, to see if thence would flow
Some fresh and fruitful showers upon my sunburnt brain.
But words came halting forth, wanting Invention's stay;
Invention, Nature's child, fled step-dame Study's blows;
And others' feet still seemed but strangers in my way.
Thus great with child to speak, and helpless in my throes,
Biting my truant pen, beating myself for spite:
"Fool!" said my Muse to me, "look in thy heart and write."

*

[1] *In its original form the title was spelled* ASTROPHIL AND STELLA, *indicating the intention—"star-lover and star"—and half concealing the first name of the author.*

With how sad steps, O Moon, thou climb'st the skies,
How silently, and with how wan a face!
What, may it be that even in heav'nly place
That busy archer his sharp arrows tries?
Sure, if that long-with-love-acquainted eyes
Can judge of love, thou feel'st a lover's case;
I read it in thy looks: thy languisht grace,
To me, that feel the like, thy state descries.
Then, ev'n of fellowship, O Moon, tell me,
Is constant love deem'd there but want of wit?
Are beauties there as proud as here they be?
Do they above love to be lov'd, and yet
Those lovers scorn whom that love doth possess?
Do they call virtue there ungratefulness?

*

Come, Sleep! O Sleep, the certain knot of peace,
The baiting-place of wit, the balm of woe,
The poor man's wealth, the prisoner's release,
Th' indifferent judge between the high and low;
With shield of proof shield me from out the prease [2]
Of those fierce darts Despair at me doth throw:
O, make in me those civil wars to cease;
I will good tribute pay if thou do so.
Take thou of me smooth pillows, sweetest bed,
A chamber deaf to noise and blind to light,
A rosy garland and a weary head:
And if these things, as being thine in right,
Move not thy heavy grace, thou shalt in me
Livelier than elsewhere, Stella's image see.

*

Because I breathe not love to everyone,
Nor do not use set colors for to wear,
Nor nourish special locks of vowèd hair,
Nor give each speech a full point of a groan,
The Courtly nymphs, acquainted with the moan
Of them who on their lips Love's standard bear,
"What, he!" say they of me. "Now I dare swear
He cannot love; no, no, let him alone."
And think so still, so Stella know my mind;
Profess indeed I do not Cupid's art;

2 *Press, multitude.*

But you, fair maids, at length this true shall find,
That his right badge is but worn in the heart;
Dumb swans, not chattering pies, do lovers prove:
They love indeed who quake to say they love.

*

O joy too high for my low style to show!
O bliss fit for a nobler state than me!
Envy, put out thine eyes, lest thou do see
What oceans of delight in me do flow!
My friend, that oft saw through all masks my woe,
Come, come, and let me pour myself on thee.
Gone is the winter of my misery!
My spring appears, O, see what here doth grow:
For Stella hath, with words where faith doth shine,
Of her high heart giv'n me the monarchy;
I, I, oh I, may say that she is mine!
And though she give but thus conditionly
This realm of bliss, while virtuous course I take,
No kings be crown'd but they some covenants make.

That Shakespeare appreciated Sidney is scarcely to be doubted;
he echoed him in the most unexpected places. Shakespeare seems
to have been particularly indebted to the forty-seventh sonnet in
ASTROPHEL AND STELLA, in which the tortured lover cries out against
the cruel coquetry of his lady. The first quatrain finds its echo in
Hamlet's soliloquy beginning:

O, what a rogue and peasant slave am I!

And the end of the sonnet, with its abrupt change of mood, is heard
again in Hamlet's very phrases in his rejection of Ophelia: "Soft
you now! The fair Ophelia! . . . I loved you not . . . Go to, I'll no
more on't." Only in a few of the sonnets of Shakespeare has despera-
tion, caused by love's doubt and self-division, gone farther.

The Yoke of Tyranny

What! Have I thus betrayed my liberty?
Can those black beams such burning marks engrave
In my free side? Or am I born a slave,
Whose neck becomes such yoke of tyranny?
Or want I sense to feel my misery?

Or sprite,[1] disdain of such disdain to have?
Who for long faith, though daily help I crave,
May get no alms but scorn of beggary.
Virtue [2] awake! Beauty but beauty is.
I may, I must, I can, I will, I do
Leave following that, which it is gain to miss.
Let her go! . . . Soft, but here she comes. Go to,
Unkind, I love you not! . . . O me, that eye
Doth make my heart give to my tongue the lie.

Another sonnet, not to be found in the famous series, is an even harsher dissonance in the midst of dulcet harmonies. It is all the more revealing because of its bitterness. Here, after the most courtly praise and tenderest vows, is a sudden revulsion, a fierce outcry against the relentlessness of passion. "Thou blind man's mark," "fool's self-chosen snare," "fond fancy's scum," "dregs of scattered thought," "cradle of causeless care"—Shakespeare alone excelled Sidney in his epithets and the final renunciation in which the lover's one desire is to kill desire.

Desire

Thou blind man's mark, thou fool's self-chosen snare,
Fond fancy's scum, and dregs of scattered thought;
Band of all evils, cradle of causeless care;
Thou web of will, whose end is never wrought;
Desire, desire! I have too dearly bought,
With price of mangled mind, thy worthless ware;
Too long, too long, asleep thou hast me brought,
Who should my mind to higher things prepare.
But yet in vain thou hast my ruin sought;
In vain thou madest me to vain things aspire;
In vain thou kindlest all thy smoky fire;
For virtue hath this better lesson taught—
Within myself to seek my only hire,
Desiring nought but how to kill desire.

Perhaps the greatest contrast to DESIRE is MY TRUE-LOVE HATH MY HEART. One of Sidney's briefest poems, it is also one of his loveliest. It is as simple as a folk song, reminiscent of the Old German:

Du bist mein, ich bin dein.

[1] *The faculty of thought.* [2] *Inherent strength.*

Sidney used the poem as a basis for a sonnet in his ARCADIA, but it is more appealing in the original, which follows the impulse of swift and artless song.

My True-Love Hath My Heart

My true-love hath my heart, and I have his,
By just exchange one for another given:
I hold his dear, and mine he cannot miss,
There never was a better bargain driven:
    My true-love hath my heart, and I have his.

His heart in me keeps him and me in one,
My heart in him his thoughts and senses guides:
He loves my heart, for once it was his own,
I cherish his because in me it bides:
    My true-love hath my heart, and I have his.

THOMAS LODGE
[1558?–1625]

THOMAS LODGE never made up his mind what career to follow. Son of a lord mayor of London, he was trained to be a lawyer, abandoned law for literature, became a soldier, joined an expedition to South America in 1591, and, in his mid-forties, took the degree of M.D. at Oxford. Thereafter he practiced in London and for almost twenty-five years was famous as a physician. His skill was not proof against pestilence, and he died of the plague in 1625.

Lodge was as versatile as most writers of the period, but his plays were unsuccessful and his pamphlets were read without excitement. One piece of prose, however, has outlived most of his other work. It is ROSALYNDE: EUPHUES' GOLDEN LEGACIE and it is, as the subtitle indicates, an imitation. But, though the artificial style is borrowed from Lyly (see page 222), Lodge brought so fresh and pastoral a quality to his romance that Shakespeare used it as the basis of AS YOU LIKE IT.

The lyrics which Lodge used for "interpolations" are spiced with humor. Though their rusticity smacks of the town, they are never stilted and are always tuneful.

Rosalynde

Like to the clear in highest sphere
Where all imperial glory shines,
Of selfsame color is her hair
Whether unfolded, or in twines:
    Heigh ho, fair Rosalynde!
Her eyes are sapphires set in snow
Resembling heaven by every wink;
The Gods do fear whenas they glow,
And I do tremble when I think
    Heigh ho, would she were mine!

Her cheeks are like the blushing cloud
That beautifies Aurora's face,
Or like the silver crimson shroud
That Phoebus' smiling looks doth grace:
    Heigh ho, fair Rosalynde!
Her lips are like two budded roses
Whom ranks of lilies neighbor nigh,
Within which bounds she balm encloses
Apt to entice a deity:
    Heigh ho, would she were mine!

Her neck is like a stately tower
Where Love himself imprison'd lies,
To watch for glances every hour
From her divine and sacred eyes:
    Heigh ho, fair Rosalynde!
Her paps are centres of delight,
Her breasts are orbs of heavenly frame,
Where Nature moulds the dew of light
To feed perfection with the same:
    Heigh ho, would she were mine!

With orient pearl, with ruby red,
With marble white, with sapphire blue
Her body every way is fed,
Yet soft in touch and sweet in view:
    Heigh ho, fair Rosalynde!

Nature herself her shape admires;
The Gods are wounded in her sight;
And Love forsakes his heavenly fires
And at her eyes his brand doth light:
  Heigh ho, would she were mine!

Then muse not, Nymphs, though I bemoan
The absence of fair Rosalynde,
Since for a fair there's fairer none,
Nor for her virtues so divine:
  Heigh ho, fair Rosalynde!
Heigh ho, my heart! would God that she were mine!

Rosalynde's Madrigal

Love in my bosom like a bee
  Doth suck his sweet;
Now with his wings he plays with me,
  Now with his feet.
Within mine eyes he makes his nest,
His bed amidst my tender breast;
My kisses are his daily feast,
And yet he robs me of my rest.
  Ah, wanton, will ye?

And if I sleep, then percheth he
  With pretty flight,
And makes his pillow of my knee
  The livelong night.
Strike I my lute, he tunes the string;
He music plays if so I sing;
He lends me every lovely thing;
Yet cruel he my heart doth sting.
  Whist, wanton, still ye!

Else I with roses every day
  Will whip you hence
And bind you, when you long to play,
  For your offence.
I'll shut mine eyes to keep you in,
I'll make you fast it for your sin,
I'll count your power not worth a pin.
Alas, what hereby shall I win,
  If he gainsay me?

What if I beat the wanton boy
  With many a rod?
He will repay me with annoy,
  Because a god.
Then sit thou safely on my knee.
Then let thy bower my bosom be;
Lurk in mine eyes, I like of thee.
O Cupid, so thou pity me,
  Spare not, but play thee.

My Mistress

My mistress when she goes
To pull the pink and rose
Along the river bounds,
And trippeth on the grounds,
And runs from rocks to rocks
With lovely scattered locks,
Whilst amorous wind doth play
With hairs so golden gay—
The water waxeth clear,
The fishes draw her near,
The sirens sing her praise,
Sweet flowers perfume her ways,
And Neptune, glad and fain,
Yields up to her his reign.

GEORGE PEELE

[1558?–1597?]

THE poets of the Elizabethan era represented the two extremes of society. At one extreme were the aristocrats, the courtiers and diplomats; at the other there were the roistering blades and braggarts, frequenters of brothels, companions to criminals. Among the latter were many of the more eminent dramatists, such as Christopher Marlowe, Ben Jonson, Thomas Nashe, Robert Greene, and George Peele.

Peele was the son of a London salter, a clerk who wrote two treatises on bookkeeping. Turned out of his father's house, Peele went from one dissipation to another. Literary hack-work during a reckless life brought him to the theater, for which he wrote works of all sorts. One of his plays, THE OLD WIVES' TALE, is the main source of Milton's COMUS. As a playwright, Peele is interesting only to the literary historians. He brought a new smoothness to theatrical diction, and a few of his lyrics have achieved permanence.

The Old Knight

His golden locks time hath to silver turned;
    O time too swift, O swiftness never ceasing!
His youth 'gainst time and age hath ever spurned,
    But spurned in vain; youth waneth by increasing:
Beauty, strength, youth, are flowers but fading seen;
Duty, faith, love, are roots, and ever green.

His helmet now shall make a hive for bees,
    And, lovers' sonnets turn'd to holy psalms,
A man-at-arms must now serve on his knees,
    And feed on prayers, which are age his alms:
But though from court to cottage he depart,
His saint is sure of his unspotted heart.

And when he saddest sits in homely cell,
    He'll teach his swains this carol for a song:
"Blest be the hearts that wish my sovereign well,
    Curst be the souls that think her any wrong."
Goddess, allow this aged man his right,
To be your beadsman [1] now that was your knight.

Harvester's Song

All ye that lovely lovers be,
Pray you for me:
Lo, here we come a-sowing, a-sowing,
And sow sweet fruits of love;
In your sweet hearts well may it prove!

[1] *One who prays for another and counts his beads.*

Lo, here we come a-reaping, a-reaping, a-reaping,
To reap our harvest-fruit!
And thus we pass the year so long,
And never be we mute.

Bethsabe Bathing

Hot sun, cool fire, tempered with sweet air,
Black shade, fair nurse, shadow my white hair:
Shine, sun; burn, fire; breathe, air, and ease me;
Black shade, fair nurse, shroud me, and please me:
Shadow, my sweet nurse, keep me from burning,
Make not my glad cause cause of mourning,
    Let not my beauty's fire
    Inflame unstaid desire,
    Nor pierce any bright eye
    That wandereth lightly.

ROBERT GREENE
[1558?–1592]

O F ALL the rogues and swashbucklers, Robert Greene was the
most irresponsible poet of his day. Born of a good family
and educated at Cambridge, he graduated to the gutter. He grew
a long red beard which was described as "a beacon and a terror
to all good citizens"; by his own confession he "delighted in wicked-
ness as sundry have in godliness, and I took as much felicity in
villainy as others have in honesty." Flourishing among purse
snatchers and other companions "as lewd as myself," he picked up
a livelihood of sorts. When he was out of funds he wrote love
pamphlets; his pen was always for hire. In spite of his carousing,
he was friendless "except in a few alehouses." His two intimates
were a leatherworker, who sold shoes when he was not drinking,
and a sister of a notorious thief, the mother of his illegitimate son,
whom Greene, with grim humor, called Fortunatus.

Greene's end was miserable. At supper with Nashe he consumed
so many pickled herrings and drank such a quantity of Rhenish

wine that he contracted a mortal illness. He lingered on for a month, but finally died in agony. The funeral cost four shillings, and the expenses were paid by the leatherworker. As a last pathetic irony the leatherworker's wife placed upon the cheap casket a few sprigs of bay, the poet's traditional garland.

It is supposed that Greene had some share in the historical plays of Shakespeare, probably KING HENRY THE SIXTH, but most of his own publications have little merit. The best of Greene's work is in the autobiographical sketches in which he reveals the life of London's underworld, and in his occasional lyrics, which are lightly phrased and curiously innocent in tone.

Sephestia's Song to Her Child

Weep not, my wanton, smile upon my knee;
When thou art old there's grief enough for thee.
        Mother's wag, pretty boy,
        Father's sorrow, father's joy;
        When thy father first did see
        Such a boy by him and me,
        He was glad, I was woe;
        Fortune changéd made him so,
        When he left his pretty boy
        Last his sorrow, first his joy.

Weep not, my wanton, smile upon my knee;
When thou art old, there's grief enough for thee.
        Streaming tears that never stint,
        Like pearl-drops from a flint,
        Fell by course from his eyes,
        That one another's place supplies;
        Thus he grieved in every part,
        Tears of blood fell from his heart,
        When he left his pretty boy,
        Father's sorrow, father's joy.

Weep not, my wanton, smile upon my knee;
When thou art old there's grief enough for thee.
        The wanton smiled, father wept,
        Mother cried, baby leapt;
        More he crowed, more he cried,
        Nature could not sorrow hide.

He must go, he must kiss
Child and mother, baby bless,
For he left his pretty boy,
Father's sorrow, father's joy.

Weep not, my wanton, smile upon my knee,
When thou art old, there's grief enough for thee.

Ah Were She Pitiful

Ah were she pitiful as she is fair,
Or but as mild as she is seeming so,
Then were my hopes greater than my despair,
Then all the world were heaven, nothing woe.
Ah were her heart relenting as her hand,
That seems to melt even with the mildest touch,
Then knew I where to seat me in a land
Under wide heavens, but yet there is none such.
So, as she shows, she seems the budding rose,
Yet sweeter far than is an earthly flower;
Sovran of beauty! like the spray she grows,
Compassed she is with thorns and cankered bower.
Yet were she willing to be plucked and worn,
She would be gathered, though she grew on thorn.

A song from Greene's FAREWELL TO FOLLY is more self-revealing than most of his verse. The last line is obviously an echo of the first line of Dyer's MY MIND TO ME A KINGDOM IS (see page 206), but in the praise of beggary and irresponsibility, the very content in carelessness, we hear Greene's own voice.

The Poor Estate

Sweet are the thoughts that savor of content;
The quiet mind is richer than a crown;
Sweet are the nights in careless slumber spent;
The poor estate scorns Fortune's angry frown:
Such sweet content, such minds, such sleep, such bliss,
Beggars enjoy, when princes oft do miss.

The homely house that harbors quiet rest,
The cottage that affords nor pride nor care,
The mean that 'grees with country music best,
The sweet consort of mirth and modest fare,
Obscuréd life sets down a type of bliss:
A mind content both crown and kingdom is.

"A. W."

WE KNOW nothing whatsoever about the author of a few of the most charming Elizabethan verses. He emerges from A POETICAL RHAPSODY (1602)—the last of the Elizabethan miscellanies—as a pair of tantalizing initials; and as "A. W." he remains. He may have been some such minor figure as Andrew Willet, Arthur Warren, or Ambrose Willoughby; but it is just as likely that the initials stand for nothing more identifiable than Anonymous Writer.

It is improbable that "A. W." refused to sign his name because he loved mystery or even because he was unusually reticent. Anonymity was a fashion among author-aristocrats; it was almost a compulsion. Raleigh, Sidney, and other patricians never published their verses. It was taken for granted that a gentleman of the court wrote poetry, but he was not supposed to profit by it. During his lifetime his poems were circulated in manuscript; a courtier could not bring his passion to market. A cultivated creator remained an "amateur"; publication had the taint of professionalism. As Agnes M. C. Latham wrote in her introduction to THE POEMS OF SIR WALTER RALEIGH, "A brilliant man then liked to be known as a good poet, much as his modern fellow might like to be known as a good conversationalist, and would as little have thought of taking money for his poetry as a raconteur today would think of hiring himself out as a public entertainer."

The editor of A POETICAL RHAPSODY hinted that "A. W." was "his dear friend" and that the poems were written at least twenty years before the publication of his anthology. This would indicate that the unknown poet was writing in about 1580, and thus it is unlikely that he was born before 1560. But no further clues have been found, and "A. W." lives for us only in his happily recovered lines.

Dispraise of Love

If love be life, I long to die,
  Live they that list for me;
And he that gains the most thereby
  A fool at least shall be:
But he that feels the sorest fits
'Scapes with no less than loss of wits.
    Unhappy life they gain
    Which love do entertain.

In day by feignéd looks they live;
  By lying dreams in night.
Each frown a deadly wound doth give,
  Each smile a false delight.
If't hap their lady pleasant seem,
It is for other's love they deem;
    If void she seem of joy,
    Disdain doth make her coy.

Such is the peace that lovers find,
  Such is the life they lead,
Blown here and there with every wind,
  Like flowers in the mead.
Now war, now peace, then war again,
Desire, despair, delight, disdain.
    Though dead, in midst of life;
    In peace, and yet at strife.

Give Me Leave

When will the fountain of my tears be dry?
  When will my sighs be spent?
When will desire agree to let me die?
  When will thy heart relent?
It is not for my life I plead,
Since death the way to rest doth lead;
    But stay for thy consent,
    Lest thou be discontent.

For if myself without thy leave I kill,
　My ghost will never rest;
So hath it sworn to work thine only will,
　And holds that ever best;
For since it only lives by thee,
Good reason thou the ruler be.
　　Then give me leave to die,
　　And show thy power thereby.

IN PRAISE OF A BEGGAR'S LIFE stands out strongly in the midst of
the courtly verse with which the miscellanies of the period are
crowded. It is futile to speculate, but it is just possible that "A. W."
may have been the irresponsible Robert Greene; here, at least,
Greene may have used the cloak of anonymity to glorify squalor
and celebrate his way of life in Villonesque rhymes.

In Praise of a Beggar's Life

Bright shines the sun; play, beggars, play!
　Here's scraps enough to serve today.
What noise of viols is so sweet,
　As when our merry clappers ring?
What mirth doth want where beggars meet?
　A beggar's life is for a king.
Eat, drink, and play; sleep when we list;
Go where we will, so stocks be missed.
　　Bright shines the sun; play, beggars, play!
　　Here's scraps enough to serve today.

The world is ours, and ours alone,
　For we alone have world at will;
We purchase not, all is our own;
　Both fields and streets we beggars fill.
Nor care to get nor fear to keep
Did ever break a beggar's sleep.
　　Bright shines the sun; play, beggars, play!
　　Here's scraps enough to serve today.

A hundred head of black and white
　Upon our gowns securely feed;
If any dare his master bite,
　He dies therefore, as sure as creed.

Thus beggars lord it as they please;
And none but beggars live at ease.
Bright shines the sun; play, beggars, play!
Here's scraps enough to serve today.

CHIDIOCK TICHBORNE
[1558?–1586]

CHIDIOCK TICHBORNE is a name as obscure as it is odd. The antiquarian syllables, remembered only by a few, are difficult to place, harder to locate. Tichborne does not appear in either THE GOLDEN TREASURY or THE OXFORD BOOK OF ENGLISH VERSE; he cannot be found even in THE ENCYCLOPÆDIA BRITANNICA. Yet he wrote one of the most moving poems of his century.

Tichborne was not pre-eminently a poet but a conspirator. History is not sure of the part he played in the attempt to do away with Queen Elizabeth; it is not even certain of the date of his birth. Conjecture has it that he was born about 1558 somewhere in Southampton, and it is said that his father, Peter Tichborne, traced his descent from Roger de Ticheburne, a knight in the reign of Henry II. His family was ardently Catholic; both Chidiock and his father were zealous champions of the Church of Rome; they did not scruple to abet the king of Spain in "holy" attacks upon the English government. In 1583 Chidiock and his father were questioned concerning the possession and use of certain "popish relics"; somewhat later they were further implicated as to their "sacrilegious and subversive practices." In April, 1586, Chidiock joined a group of conspirators at the instance of the persuasive John Ballard. From this point on the record seems to be fairly clear. In June, 1586, at a meeting held in St. Giles-in-the-Fields he agreed to be one of six who were pledged to murder the Queen and restore the kingdom to Rome. The conspiracy was discovered in time; most of the conspirators fled. But Tichborne, who had remained in London because of an injured leg, was captured on August 14 and taken to the Tower. On September 14, 1586, he was tried and pled guilty. He was executed on September 20. In a grim finale, history relates, he was "disemboweled before life was extinct" and the news of the barbarity "reached the ears of Elizabeth, who forbade the recurrence."

On September 19, 1586, the night before he was executed, Chidiock wrote to his wife Agnes. The letter enclosed three stanzas beginning: "My prime of youth is but a frost of cares." This elegy is so restrained yet so eloquent, so spontaneous, and so skillfully made that it must be ranked among the little masterpieces of literature. The grave but not depressing music of the lines is emphasized by the repetition of the rhymed refrain, as though the poet were anticipating the slow tolling of the bell announcing his death. He was twenty-eight years old.

On the Eve of His Execution

My prime of youth is but a frost of cares,
    My feast of joy is but a dish of pain,
My crop of corn is but a field of tares,
        And all my good is but vain hope of gain;
            The day is past, and yet I saw no sun,
            And now I live, and now my life is done.

My tale was heard and yet it was not told,
    My fruit is fallen, yet my leaves are green,
My youth is spent and yet I am not old,
        I saw the world and yet I was not seen;
            My thread is cut and yet it is not spun,
            And now I live, and now my life is done.

I sought my death and found it in my womb,
    I looked for life and saw it was a shade,
I trod the earth and knew it was my tomb,
        And now I die, and now I was but made;
            My glass is full, and now my glass is run,
            And now I live, and now my life is done.

BARTHOLOMEW GRIFFIN
[?–1602]

B ARTHOLOMEW GRIFFIN is another mysterious Elizabethan figure. Only two dates are certain: 1596, the year in which his one volume was published, and 1602, the year of his death.

Griffin's single volume, FIDESSA, MORE CHASTE THAN KIND, is a series of sixty-two sonnets. Only three copies are in existence. There are clues—chiefly in the dedication—which suggest that Griffin was a gentleman and a lawyer. But nothing more. Griffin's verse is charming rather than remarkable. Historians remember him because the third sonnet of his sequence ("Venus and young Adonis sitting by her") was printed in the miscellany entitled THE PASSION-ATE PILGRIM and credited (falsely) to Shakespeare. Two other sonnets are more interesting: the first for its varying repetition of the word "heart," a curious example of identity of sound as a substitute for rhyme; the second for its strange mixture of sexual symbolism (borrowed from THE SONG OF SONGS) with the polite artifice of the Elizabethan sonneteers.

Her Heart

Fly to her heart, hover about her heart,
With dainty kisses mollify her heart,
Pierce with thy arrows her obdurate heart,
With sweet allurements ever move her heart,
At mid-day and at midnight touch her heart,
Be lurking closely, nestle about her heart,
With power (thou art a god) command her heart,
Kindle thy coals of love about her heart,
Yea, even into thyself transform her heart.
Ah, she must love! Be sure thou have her heart,
And I must die if thou have not her heart,
Thy bed, if thou rest well, must be her heart,
He hath the best part sure that hath the heart.
What have I not, if I have but her heart!

My Love

Fair is my love that feeds among the lilies,
The lilies growing in the pleasant garden
Where Cupid's mount that well-belovèd hill is,
And where that little god himself is warden.
See where my love sits in the bed of spices,
Beset all round with camphor, myrrh, and roses,
And interlaced with curious devices
Which her from all the world apart encloses.
There doth she tune her lute for her delight
And with sweet music makes the ground to move,
Whilst I, poor I, do sit in heavy plight,
Wailing alone my unrespected love;
Not daring rush into so rare a place
That gives to her, and she to it, a grace.

ROBERT SOUTHWELL
[1561?–1595]

AMONG the groups of courtiers and the rabble of rowdies, Robert
Southwell stands out strangely, a fanatic spirit, like a portrait
of a gaunt zealot painted by El Greco. Prefect of studies in the Eng-
lish College at Rome, ordained in his early twenties, Southwell re-
turned to his native country at a time when it was dangerous for a
Catholic priest to remain in England. He changed his name and
tried to conceal his profession, but he was arrested in 1592 while
celebrating Mass. Tortured mentally and physically for three years,
he was executed by hanging.

Southwell hoped to be known by a long narrative, SAINT PETER'S
COMPLAINT, in which the final days of Christ are pictured by the
contrite disciple; but he is read only for his short verses. Most of
these poems were written while he was in prison, and Southwell
dedicated himself to spiritual passion rather than to "unworthy
affections." Ben Jonson said that he would have been content to
destroy many of his famous lines had he been able to compose
Southwell's brief allegory, THE BURNING BABE.

The Burning Babe

As I in hoary winter's night stood shivering in the snow,
Surprised I was with sudden heat which made my heart to glow;
And lifting up a fearful eye to view what fire was near,
A pretty babe all burning bright did in the air appear;
Who, scorchéd with excessive heat, such floods of tears did shed
As though his floods should quench his flames which with his tears
    were fed.
"Alas," quoth he, "but newly born in fiery heats I fry,
Yet none approach to warm their hearts or feel my fire but I!
My faultless breast the furnace is; the fuel, wounding thorns;
Love is the fire, and sighs the smoke; the ashes, shame and scorns;
The fuel justice layeth on, and mercy blows the coals;
The metal in this furnace wrought are men's defiléd souls,
For which, as now on fire I am to work them to their good;
So will I melt into a bath to wash them in my blood."
With this he vanished out of sight and swiftly shrunk away—
And straight I calléd unto mind that it was Christmas Day.

SAMUEL DANIEL
[1562–1619]

THE sonnet, literally "a little song," originated in Italy—there is a theory that the precise fourteen-line form resulted from the mingling of Arabian mathematicians and Italian poets at the court of Frederick II in Sicily. Brought to England in the early sixteenth century, the "courtly" medium with its formal melodiousness, its combination of delicacy and dignity, won instant approval. It was not long before the English poets, following the examples of Petrarch and Tasso, began to fashion sequences and chains of interlocking sonnets. Sidney's ASTROPHEL AND STELLA set the fashion of dedicating whole cycles to some real or disguised or imaginary mistress. There was a convention to which almost all the poets adhered: the mistress was always superhumanly beautiful and inhumanly cruel; the lover was always burning with passion or freezing with despair. Even the images of comparison were conventionalized—*cheeks:* lilies and roses; *brows:* alabaster; *mouth:* coral; *teeth:* pearls; *hair:* gold—so that women were not pictured as living persons but as lifeless metaphors.

   Nevertheless, many of the sonnet sequences rose to surprising levels of emotion, even to heights of passion. Samuel Daniel, in his sonnet sequence DELIA, was one of those content to rely on grace of language and the charm of the picturesque. Born in 1562, tutor to William Herbert, Earl of Pembroke, hailed by Spenser as the "new shepherd late upsprung," Daniel was praised not only by his contemporaries (though criticized by Ben Jonson), but by nineteenth-century commentators as well. Coleridge, seeing in Daniel a forerunner, applauded his style—"a style which, as the neutral ground of prose and verse, is common to both"—and wrote that his language was "such as any pure and manly writer of the present day—Wordsworth, for example—would use."

FROM

Delia

Fair is my love, and cruel as she's fair:
Her brow shades frowns, although her eyes are sunny,
Her smiles are lightning, though her pride despair,
And her disdains are gall, her favors honey.
A modest maid, decked with a blush of honor,
Whose feet do tread green paths of youth and love;
The wonder of all eyes that look upon her,
Sacred on earth, designed a saint above!

Chastity and beauty, which were deadly foes,
Live reconcilèd friends within her brow;
And had she pity to conjoin with those,
Then who had heard the plaints I utter now?
For had she not been fair and thus unkind,
My Muse had slept, and none had known my mind.

*

If this be love, to draw a weary breath,
To paint on floods till the shore cry to th'air;
With downward looks, still reading on the earth
The sad memorials of my love's despair:

If this be love, to war against my soul,
Lie down to wail, rise up to sigh and grieve,
The never-resting stone of care to roll,
Still to complain my griefs whilst none relieve:

If this be love, to clothe me with dark thoughts,
Haunting untrodden paths to wail apart;
My pleasures horror, music tragic notes,
Tears in mine eyes and sorrow at my heart.
If this be love, to live a living death,
Then do I love and draw this weary breath.

*

Care-charmer Sleep, son of the sable Night,
Brother to Death, in silent darkness born,
Relieve my languish, and restore the light;
With dark forgetting of my care return.
And let the day be time enough to mourn
The shipwreck of my ill-adventured youth:
Let waking eyes suffice to wail their scorn,
Without the torment of the night's untruth.

Cease, dreams, the images of day-desires,
To model forth the passions of the morrow;
Never let rising sun approve you liars,
To add more grief to aggravate my sorrow:
Still let me sleep, embracing clouds in vain,
And never wake to feel the day's disdain.

*

When men shall find thy flower, thy glory, pass,
And thou, with careful brow sitting alone,
Receivèd hast this message from thy glass,
That tells the truth and says that all is gone;
Fresh shalt thou see in me the wounds thou madest,
Though spent thy flame, in me the heat remaining;
I that have loved thee thus before thou fadest,
My faith shall wax when thou art in thy waning.

The world shall find this miracle in me,
That fire can burn when all the matter's spent;

Then what my faith hath been, thyself shall see,
And that thou wast unkind, thou mayst repent.
Thou mayst repent that thou hast scorned my tears,
When winter snows upon thy sable hairs.

MICHAEL DRAYTON
[1563–1631]

PRACTICALLY nothing is known of Michael Drayton beyond his
work. It is presumed that he was a tutor, and it is supposed that
Ann, the younger daughter of Sir Henry Goodere, was the "Idea"
who prompted his cycle of sonnets. But this is conjecture. We know
for a certainty only that Drayton's output was great and varied.
The poet seemed equally at home in odes and sonnets, in legends
and plays, in historical narratives and in a dutiful, if overlengthy,
compliment to the topographical charms of England, the wearying
POLY-OLBION. His patriotic ballad of AGINCOURT and TO THE VIRGINIAN
VOYAGE, a tribute to the explorers who went with Raleigh, are
proofs of his patriotism.

Drayton's power, so often submerged, struggles to a peak in the
sonnet sequence IDEA. Here he transcends the conventions of the
day and frees himself from the demands of the form. Passion smol-
ders throughout the cycle; it breaks through the precision of such
little-known lines as those beginning "To nothing fitter can I thee
compare," threshes desperately in the sonnet "You're not alone
when you are still alone," and spans the centuries in the almost
overpowering "Since there's no help, come, let us kiss and part."
Such utterances continue to vibrate in the heart of every hurt lover.

FROM
Idea

To nothing fitter can I thee compare
Than to the son of some rich penny-father,
Who having now brought on his end with care,
Leaves to his son all he had heaped together;

This new-rich novice, lavish of his chest,
To one man gives, doth on another spend,
Then here he riots; yet amongst the rest
Haps to lend some to one true honest friend.

Thy gifts thou in obscurity dost waste,
False friends thy kindness, born but to deceive thee;
Thy love, that is on the unworthy placed;
Time hath thy beauty, which with age will leave thee;
  Only that little which to me was lent,
  I give thee back, when all the rest is spent.

                            *

I hear some say, "This man is not in love!"
"Who! can he love? a likely thing!" they say.
"Read but his verse, and it will easily prove!"
O judge not rashly, gentle sir, I pray!
Because I loosely trifle in this sort,
As one that fain his sorrows would beguile,
You now suppose me, all this time, in sport,
And please yourself with this conceit the while

Ye shallow Censures! sometimes, see ye not,
In greatest perils some men pleasant be?
Where Fame by death is only to be got,
They resolute! So stands the case with me.
  Where other men in depth of passion cry,
  I laugh at Fortune, as in jest to die!

                            *

When first I ended, then I first began;
Then more I travelled further from my rest.
Where most I lost, there most of all I won;
Pinéd with hunger, rising from a feast.
Methinks I fly, yet want I legs to go;
Wise in conceit, in act a very sot;
Ravished with joy amidst a hell of woe;
What most I seem that surest am I not.

I build my hopes a world above the sky,
Yet with the mole I creep into the earth;

In plenty, I am starved with penury,
And yet I surfeit in the greatest dearth.
  I have, I want; despair, and yet desire;
  Burned in a sea of ice, and drowned amidst a fire.

*

You're not alone when you are still alone;
O God! from you that I could private be!
Since you one were, I never since was one,
Since you in me, myself since out of me,
Transported from myself into your being,
Though either distant, present yet to either;
Senseless with too much joy, each other seeing
And only absent when we are together.

Give me my self, and take your self again!
Devise some means by how I may forsake you!
So much is mine that doth with you remain,
That taking what is mine, with me I take you.
  You do bewitch me! O that I could fly
  From my self you, or from your own self I!

It is assumed that there is a great discrepancy between Drayton's
other sonnets and the one sonnet from IDEA which is continually
quoted. Actually there is no such difference; tone and substance are
close-knit throughout. But if IDEA is unified by an intensity and
directness of utterance, it reaches a fierce climax in the masterpiece
(often called THE PARTING) by which Drayton has won immortality.

Since There's No Help

Since there's no help, come, let us kiss and part;
Nay, I have done, you get no more of me;
And I am glad, yea, glad with all my heart
That thus so cleanly I myself can free.
Shake hands for ever, cancel all our vows,
And, when we meet at any time again,
Be it not seen in either of our brows
That we one jot of former love retain.

Now at the last gasp of Love's latest breath,
When, his pulse failing, Passion speechless lies,
When Faith is kneeling by his bed of death,
And Innocence is closing up his eyes—
   Now if thou wouldst, when all have given him over,
   From death to life thou might'st him yet recover.

VI

Elizabethan Songs of Unknown Authorship

Nowhere in English poetry is there a greater sense of joyful artlessness, of happy spontaneity, than in the Elizabethan songs. The mood is youthfully elated, light rather than headlong; the emotion is arrested and refined; the manner is seemingly careless. But if the melody is slight it is perfect. Intellectual subtlety, which has no place in song, gives way to lyric fluency; meaning is suggested, not underscored, by an idealized music.

The limitations of sixteenth- and seventeenth-century lyrics are obvious. Stressing the music instead of the meaning, the poets sometimes fell into a pattern of refinement, a diction which Sir Walter Raleigh declared was "appareled, or rather disguised, in a courtisanlike painted affectation." In a world of conventional amour, of pretty languors and no apparent labor, the poet's lady—whether a court nymph or a country Nell—was herself a convention, a literary stock in trade. Yet, in spite of a restraint that was frequently a pretense, frank and intimate emotions broke through. The best of the Elizabethan songs retain their personality even when the persons who wrote them are unknown.

The two main sources of Elizabethan lyrics are the miscellanies or anthologies modeled on Tottel's SONGS AND SONNETS, and the music sheets and songbooks in which the words were not merely "set" but written to be sung. Part songs were a passion in the late sixteenth century; publication of songs for three, four, and five voices be-

gan in 1571, attained a peak a quarter of a century later with the
vogue of unaccompanied songs known as "madrigals," and lasted
until 1640. The Elizabethans were natural singers; if a man could
not invent a three-voiced melody, at least he was expected to lend
his voice to one. Thomas Deloney, a silk weaver as well as a ballad
writer of the sixteenth century, wrote that every craftsman was also
a musician; even the shoemaker had to learn to "sound the trumpet,
or play upon the flute, and bear his part in a three-man's song."

The songbooks advertised their contents with severe titles; the
miscellanies, on the other hand, flourished in elaborations. Follow-
ing Tottel's lead, but rejecting his simplicity, the editors of the mis-
cellanies called their collections THE PARADISE OF DAINTY DEVICES
(1576), FLOWERS OF EPIGRAMS (1577), A GORGEOUS GALLERY OF GAL-
LANT INVENTIONS (1578)—a title chosen after A HANDFUL OF HIDDEN
SECRETS and DELICATE DAINTIES TO SWEETEN LOVERS' LIPS WITHAL had
been, somehow, rejected—THE FOREST OF FANCY (1579), A HANDFUL
OF PLEASANT DELIGHTS (1584), BRETON'S BOWER OF DELIGHT (1592),
THE PHOENIX NEST (1593), THE PASSIONATE PILGRIM (1599), ENGLAND'S
HELICON (1600), actually a selected anthology of other anthologies,
and A POETICAL RHAPSODY (1602), in many ways the richest of them
all.

Many of the contributors to the songbooks and miscellanies were
known; the identities of others have been discovered. But the author-
ship of some of the most exquisite lyrics remains a mystery. The
following three songs, which appear in different songbooks and mis-
cellanies, were evidently written by different poets. But they have
this in common: besides their anonymity, they were set to haunting
music by Robert Jones.

A Woman's Looks

A woman's looks
Are barbed hooks,
That catch by art
The strongest heart,
When yet they spend no breath.
But let them speak,
And sighing break
Forth into tears,
Their words are spears
That wound our souls to death.

The rarest wit
Is made forget,
And like a child
Is oft beguiled
With Love's sweet-seeming bait.
Love with his rod
So like a god
Commands the mind
We cannot find,
Fair shows hide foul deceit.

Time, that all things
In order brings,
Hath taught me now
To be more slow
In giving faith to speech:
Since women's words
No truth affords,
And when they kiss
They think by this
Us men to overreach.

Love Winged My Hopes

Love winged my hopes and taught me how to fly
Far from base earth, but not to mount too high.
    For true pleasure
    Lives in measure,
   Which, if men forsake,
Blinded they into folly run, and grief for pleasure take.

But my vain hopes, proud of their new-taught flight,
Enamored, sought to woo the sun's fair light,
    Whose rich brightness
    Moved their lightness
   To aspire so high,
That, all scorched and consumed with fire, now drowned in woe
   they lie.

And none but Love their woeful hap did rue;
For Love did know that their desires were true.
    Though Fate frowned,
    And now drowned
   They in sorrow dwell,
It was the purest light of heaven for whose fair love they fell.

Pride Is the Canker

Do not, O do not prize thy beauty at too high a rate;
Love to be loved whilst thou art lovely, lest thou love too late.
    Frowns print wrinkles in thy brows,
      At which spiteful age doth smile,
    Women in their froward vows
      Glorying to beguile.

Wert thou the only world's-admired, thou canst love but one;
And many have before been loved, thou art not loved alone.
    Couldst thou speak with heavenly grace,
      Sappho might with thee compare;
    Blush the roses in thy face,
      Rosamund was as fair.

Pride is the canker that consumeth beauty in her prime.
They that delight in long debating feel the curse of time.
    All things with the time do change,
      That will not the time obey.
    Some e'en to themselves seem strange
      Thorough their own delay

Three of the simplest madrigals of the period have outlived their original melodies. The first two were set by Thomas Morley; the third, perhaps the loveliest of its kind, has firmly lodged itself in anthologies ever since its first publication in 1602.

All Seasons in One

April is in my mistress' face,
And July in her eyes hath place,
Within her bosom is September,
But in her heart a cold December.

To Live in Pleasure

Sing we and chant it,
While love doth grant it.
Not long youth lasteth,
And old age hasteth.
Now is best leisure
To take our pleasure.

All things invite us
Now to delight us.
Hence, care, be packing,
No mirth be lacking.
Let spare no treasure
To live in pleasure.

Beauty's Self

My love in her attire doth show her wit,
    It doth so well become her:
For every season she hath dressings fit,
    For winter, spring, and summer.
No beauty she doth miss
    When all her robes are on;
But Beauty's self she is
    When all her robes are gone.

It became the convention to picture the country girl as unrealistically as possible; her skin was Dresden china, her clothes were spotless, and her coyness became a tradition. PHILLADA FLOUTS ME, sometimes called THE DISDAINFUL SHEPHERDESS, says it all, and says it more charmingly than most. The frank note of acceptance—"I never meant to live and die a maid"—was rarely uttered, but its candid expression in O STAY, SWEET LOVE is a cheerful contrast.

Phillada Flouts Me

O what a plague is love!
    How shall I bear it?
She will inconstant prove,
    I greatly fear it.
She so torments my mind
    That my strength faileth,
And wavers with the wind
    As a ship saileth.
Please her the best I may,
She loves still to gainsay;
Alack and well-a-day!
    Phillada flouts me.

At the fair yesterday
    She did pass by me;
She looked another way
    And would not spy me:
I wooed her for to dine,
    But could not get her;
Will had her to the wine—
    He might entreat her.
With Daniel she did dance,
On me she looked askance:
O thrice unhappy chance!
    Phillada flouts me.

Fair maid, be not so coy,
    Do not disdain me!
I am my mother's joy:
    Sweet, entertain me!
She'll give me, when she dies,
    All that is fitting:
Her poultry and her bees,
    And her goose sitting,
A pair of mattress beds,
And a bag full of shreds;
And yet, for all these goods,
    Phillada flouts me.

            .   .   .

In the last month of May
    I made her posies;

I heard her often say
    That she loved roses.
Cowslips and gillyflowers
    And the white lily
I brought to deck the bowers
    For my sweet Philly.
But she did all disdain,
And threw them back again;
Therefore 'tis flat and plain
    Phillada flouts me.

Fair maiden, have a care,
    And in time take me;
I can have those as fair
    If you forsake me:
For Doll the dairy-maid
    Laugh'd at me lately,
And wanton Winifred
    Favors me greatly.
One throws milk on my clothes,
T'other plays with my nose;
What wanting signs are those?
    Phillada flouts me.

I cannot work nor sleep
    At all in season:
Love wounds my heart so deep,
    Without all reason.
I fade and pine away,
    With grief and sorrow;
I fall quite to decay
    Like any shadow.
I shall be dead, I fear,
Within a thousand year;
And all for that my dear
    Phillada flouts me.

O Stay, Sweet Love

O stay, sweet love; see here the place of sporting;
    These gentle flowers smile sweetly to invite us,
And chirping birds are hitherward resorting,
    Warbling sweet notes only to delight us:
Then stay, dear love, for, tho' thou run from me
Run ne'er so fast, yet I will follow thee.

I thought, my love, that I should overtake you;
    Sweet heart, sit down under this shadowed tree,
And I will promise never to forsake you,
    So you will grant to me a lover's fee.
Whereat she smiled, and kindly to me said,
"I never meant to live and die a maid."

A sudden arresting note is struck in O DEATH, ROCK ME ASLEEP. This somber poem has often been ascribed to Anne Boleyn; it has even been conjectured that it was written a few hours before her execution, Anne having protested her innocence to the last. Some critics suppose that Anne's brother George, Viscount Rochford, may have written the poem as a tribute to his sister's "weary guiltless ghost" in disproof of the charges of adultery and incest. But this, too, is conjecture. The brief and dignified elegy appears in several contemporary manuscripts, always unsigned.

O Death, Rock Me Asleep

O death, rock me asleep,
    Bring me to quiet rest,
Let pass my weary guiltless ghost
    Out of my careful breast.
Toll on, thou passing bell;
Ring out my doleful knell;
Let thy sound my death tell.
    Death doth draw nigh;
    There is no remedy.

My pains who can express?
    Alas, they are so strong;
My dolor will not suffer strength
    My life to prolong.
Toll on, thou passing bell;
Ring out my doleful knell;
Let thy sound my death tell.
    Death doth draw nigh;
    There is no remedy.

Alone in prison strong
    I wait my destiny.
Woe worth this cruel hap that I
    Should taste this misery!

Toll on, thou passing bell;
Ring out my doleful knell;
Let thy sound my death tell.
    Death doth draw nigh;
    There is no remedy.

Farewell, my pleasures past,
    Welcome, my present pain!
I feel my torments so increase
    That life cannot remain.
Cease now, thou passing bell;
Rung is my doleful knell;
For the sound my death doth tell.
    Death doth draw nigh;
    There is no remedy.

In 1597 John Dowland published his FIRST BOOK OF SONGS OR AIRS, establishing the difference between the air and the madrigal. The madrigal was a polyphonic song for three to six voice parts; moreover, it was unaccompanied. The air was a song written for a solo voice accompanied by an instrument. Dowland, one of the most celebrated lute players of his day, was quick to supply the demand for the simpler and more melodic settings. It is possible that he wrote several of the lyrics printed in his songbooks; one would like to believe that he was the author as well as the composer of the exquisite WEEP YOU NO MORE and BEHOLD A WONDER HERE!, both of which appeared in Dowland's THIRD AND LAST BOOK OF SONGS OR AIRS. But there is little likelihood of certain knowledge; the poems are their own authenticity.

Weep You No More

Weep you no more, sad fountains;
    What need you flow so fast?
Look how the snowy mountains
    Heaven's sun doth gently waste!
But my sun's heavenly eyes,
    View not your weeping,
    That now lies sleeping
Softly, now softly lies
    Sleeping.

Sleep is a reconciling,
　A rest that peace begets;
Doth not the sun rise smiling
　When fair at even he sets?
Rest you then, rest, sad eyes!
　Melt not in weeping,
　While she lies sleeping,
Softly, now softly lies
　Sleeping.

Behold a Wonder Here!

Behold a wonder here!
Love hath received his sight!
Which many hundred years
Hath not beheld the light.

Such beams infusèd be
By Cynthia in his eyes,
As first have made him see
And then have made him wise.

Love now no more will weep
For them that laugh the while!
Nor wake for them that sleep,
Nor sigh for them that smile!

So powerful is the Beauty
That Love doth now behold,
As Love is turned to Duty
That's neither blind nor bold.

Thus Beauty shows her might
To be of double kind;
In giving Love his sight
And striking Folly blind.

The scholar and researcher A. H. Bullen discovered a startling collection of music books preserved in the library of Christ Church, Oxford. All were in manuscript. Two of the unfamiliar texts are among the finest lyrics of the period. The brief oddity, HEY NONNY NO!, is a charming snatch of song, and the verses beginning "Yet if

His Majesty, our sovereign lord" are unique in their fusion of eloquence and satire. Since the Christ Church manuscript contains other lyrics known to be by Henry Vaughan (see page 487), Bullen surmises that this hitherto unknown poem is also by Vaughan. It is definitely in Vaughan's manner, particularly the ironic contrast between the arrangements made for an earthly king and the reception provided for the King of Heaven. "The detailed description of the preparations made by a loyal subject for the entertainment of his 'earthly king' is singularly impressive," Bullen writes. "Few could have dealt with common household objects—tables and chairs and candles and the rest—in so dignified a spirit."

Hey Nonny No!

Hey nonny no!
Men are fools that wish to die!
Is't not fine to dance and sing
When the bells of death do ring?
Is't not fine to swim in wine,
And turn upon the toe
And sing hey nonny no,
When the winds blow and the seas flow?
Hey nonny no!

The Coming of the King

Yet if His Majesty, our sovereign lord,
Should of his own accord
Friendly himself invite,
And say, "I'll be your guest tomorrow night,"
How should we stir ourselves, call and command
All hands to work! "Let no man idle stand!

"Set me fine Spanish tables in the hall;
See they be fitted all;
Let there be room to eat
And order taken that there want no meat.
See every sconce and candlestick made bright,
That without tapers they may give a light.

"Look to the presence. Are the carpets spread?
The dais o'er the head?
The cushions in the chairs,
And all the candles lighted on the stairs?
Perfume the chambers, and in any case
Let each man give attendance in his place!"

Thus, if a king were coming, would we do;
And 'twere good reason, too.
For 'tis a duteous thing
To show all honor to an earthly king,
And after all our travail and our cost
So he be pleased, to think no labor lost.

But, at the coming of the King of Heaven
All's set at six and seven;
We wallow in our sin.
Christ cannot find a chamber in the inn.
We entertain Him always like a stranger,
And, as at first, still lodge Him in the manger.

Artful artlessness is the chief characteristic of most of the anon-
ymous Elizabethan poems. The mood, as well as the manner, was an
inevitable expression of a time in which the senses dominated men's
lives. Frederick Ives Carpenter, an American scholar, concludes that
"the Elizabethan song lyric is a holiday lyric, the sweetener and
solace of life in hall and bower, in court and city. It responds to the
superabundant play instinct of the age—the instinct of men seeking
free expression after the long ascetic repression of the Middle Ages.
. . . It is still a half century before the relapse into the black re-
morse of Puritanism. And so, meanwhile, the romantic comedy of
life is played out to the sound of the lyre and of song."

Here, then, are a few of the holiday songs which sweetened and
solaced the Elizabethans, which put happy words on the tongue and
blithe music in the heart.

Love's Unreason

Love me not for comely grace,
For my pleasing eye or face,
Nor for any outward part:
No, nor for a constant heart!

For these may fail or turn to ill:
 So thou and I shall sever.
Keep therefore a true woman's eye,
And love me still, but know not why!
So hast thou the same reason still
 To doat upon me ever.

I Saw My Lady Weep

I saw my lady weep,
 And Sorrow proud to be advancéd so
In those fair eyes where all perfections keep.
 Her face was full of woe;
But such a woe, believe me, as wins more hearts,
Than Mirth can do with her enticing parts.

Sorrow was there made fair,
 And Passion wise, tears a delightful thing;
Silence beyond all speech a wisdom rare.
 She made her sighs to sing,
And all things with so sweet a sadness move,
As made my heart at once both grieve and love.

O fairer than aught else
 The world can show, leave off in time to grieve.
Enough, enough your joyful looks excels;
 Tears kills the heart, believe.
O! strive not to be excellent in woe,
Which only breeds your beauty's overthrow.

Your Beauty and My Reason

Like two proud armies marching in the field,
Joining a thundering fight, each scorns to yield;
So in my heart your Beauty and my Reason,
The one claims the crown, the other says 'tis treason.
But O! your Beauty shineth as the sun,
And dazzled Reason yields as quite undone.

So Fast Entangled

Her hair the net of golden wire,
Wherein my heart, led by my wandering eyes,
So fast entangled is that in no wise
It can, nor will, again retire;
But rather will in that sweet bondage die
Than break one hair to gain her liberty.

Sweet, Let Me Go

Sweet, let me go! sweet, let me go!
What do you mean to vex me so?
Cease your pleading force!
Do you think thus to extort remorse?
Now, now! no more! alas, you overbear me,
And I would cry—but some, I fear, might hear me.

No Other Choice

Fain would I change that note
To which fond Love hath charmed me
Long long to sing by rote,
Fancying that that harmed me.
Yet when this thought doth come,
"Love is the perfect sum
Of all delight,"
I have no other choice
Either for pen or voice
To sing or write.

O Love, they wrong thee much
That say thy sweet is bitter,
When thy rich fruit is such
As no thing can be sweeter.
Fair house of joy and bliss
Where truest pleasure is,
I do adore thee;

I know thee what thou art,
I serve thee with my heart,
And fall before thee.

So Sleeps My Love

Sleep, wayward thoughts, and rest you with my love;
    Let not my love be with my love displeased;
Touch not, proud hands, lest you her anger move,
    But pine you with my longings long diseased.
Thus, while she sleeps, I sorrow for her sake;
So sleeps my love—and yet my love doth wake.

But O the fury of my restless fear,
    The hidden anguish of my chaste desires;
The glories and the beauties that appear
    Between her brows, near Cupid's closèd fires!
Sleep, dainty love, while I sigh for thy sake;
So sleeps my love—and yet my love doth wake.

Sic Transit . . .

Ay me, ay me, I sigh to see the scythe afield:
Down goeth the grass, soon wrought to withered hay.
Ay me, alas, ay me, alas, that beauty needs must yield,
And princes pass, as grass doth fade away!

Ay me, ay me, that life cannot have lasting leave,
Nor gold take hold of everlasting joy.
Ay me, alas, ay me, alas, that time hath talents to receive,
And yet no time can make a surer stay.

Ay me, ay me, that no sure staff is given to age,
Nor age can give sure wit that youth will take.
Ay me, alas, ay me, alas, that no counsel wise and sage
Will shun the show that all doth mar and make.

Ay me, ay me, come Time, shear on, and shake the hay!
It is no boot to balk thy bitter blows.
Ay me, alas, ay me, alas, come Time, take everything away!
For all is thine, be it good or bad, that grows.

Love's Limit

Ye bubbling springs that gentle music makes
To lovers' plaints with heart-sore throbs immixt,
Whenas my dear this way her pleasure takes,
Tell her with tears how firm my love is fixt;
And, Philomel, report my timorous fears,
And, Echo, sound my heigh-ho's in her ears.
But if she asks if I for love will die,
Tell her, Good faith, good faith, good faith—not I!

There Is a Lady Sweet and Kind

There is a lady sweet and kind,
Was never face so pleased my mind.
I did but see her passing by,
And yet I love her till I die.

Her gesture, motion, and her smiles,
Her wit, her voice my heart beguiles,
Beguiles my heart, I know not why,
And yet I love her till I die.

Cupid is wingèd and doth range,
Her country so my love doth change;
But change she earth, or change she sky,
Yet will I love her till I die.

Against Fulfillment of Desire

There is not half so warm a fire
In the fruition as desire.
When I have got the fruit of pain
Possession makes me poor again:
Expected forms and shapes unknown
Whet and make sharp temptatión.
Sense is too niggardly for bliss,

And pays me dully with what is;
But fancy's liberal and gives all
That can within her vastness fall.
Veil therefore still, while I divine
The treasure of this hidden mine,
And make imagination tell
What wonder doth in beauty dwell.

VII

The Mirror of Mankind

WILLIAM SHAKESPEARE
[1564–1616]

THE books, articles, dissertations, and theses written about Shakespeare constitute an entire literature; the Folger Shakespeare Library in Washington, D. C., includes more than 100,000 "items." Never has a poet received so much critical scrutiny, and never has there been so little known about the person.

The authentic history of Shakespeare the man can be quickly summarized; all the accounts consist of a few undisputed facts and many fanciful legends. The factual evidence is this: William Shakespeare was born in Stratford-on-Avon in April, 1564; the exact date of his birth remains uncertain. He was the third of eight children. His father was a glover, dealer in hides, and perhaps a butcher; his mother was a farmer's daughter. His boyhood was over early, for he became a father at nineteen. At eighteen he had married a woman eight years older than himself, some think at the compulsion of Ann Hathaway's brothers; he left her a few years later to go up to London. In the metropolis he became an actor-manager, adapting other men's plays besides creating dramas for his own theatrical company. His poetry was so popular that it was often pirated, and his name was attached to productions he never undertook. He made friends with the great and secured a much-desired coat of arms for his father. Before he was fifty, and at the very height of his powers, he retired to his native town. There he died, in his fifty-second year, on April 23, 1616, and was buried in the chancel of the Stratford church. The rest is speculation and controversy.

Controversy has raged about all of Shakespeare's work—there have been cults which refused to admit that Shakespeare was the author of Shakespeare's plays. But the most acrid arguments have centered about his SONNETS. No part of his writing has been more carefully examined and furiously debated than these 154 poems. The "plot" of the sequence is not spectacular or even unusual. The first 126 are addressed to a young man. The youth is advised to marry—not for passion but for posterity, to perpetuate his beauty. A rival poet enters, but the real villain of the piece is the poet's own mistress. A married woman, she is black-haired, raven-eyed, and skilled in infidelity both to her lover and to her husband. This "dark lady" threatens to wreck the intimacy between the poet and his young patron. But the poet loves his friend more than his mistress, and there is a promised reconciliation.

The "plot" as such is none too clear, and, since the first printing in 1609 was a pirated volume which Shakespeare never supervised, it is doubtful that the sonnets are arranged in proper sequence.

It is the dedication which has caused most of the controversy:

> TO THE ONLIE BEGETTER OF
> THESE INSUING SONNETS
> Mr. W. H. ALL HAPPINESSE
> AND THAT ETERNITIE
> PROMISED BY
> OUR EVER-LIVING POET
> WISHETH
> THE WELL-WISHING
> ADVENTURER IN
> SETTING FORTH.
> T. T.

T. T. was the piratical publisher, Thomas Thorpe, and the dedication may be nothing more than his gesture of thanks to one "Mr. W. H." for having collected, or stolen, or otherwise obtained copies of the sonnets which had been privately circulated. His gratitude to "Mr. W. H." as the "begetter" (in the sense of being the actual "getter") would have been genuine enough, for anything by Shakespeare was sure to sell. But since "begetter" usually meant "inspirer," the scholars, believing that Shakespeare had furnished the dedication, looked elsewhere for the identity of "Mr. W. H." Many candidates have been suggested. Perhaps the most fantastic is Oscar

Wilde's special pleading for the boy actor Willie Hughes as "the master-mistris" in Wilde's self-revealing THE PORTRAIT OF MR. W. H. But the chief claimants are two: (1) William Herbert, afterwards Earl of Pembroke, whose beauty, reluctance to marry, and extreme youth suggest the "hero" of the sonnets; and (2) Henry Wriothesley, Earl of Southampton, who was Shakespeare's patron, to whom Shakespeare had already dedicated VENUS AND ADONIS and LUCRECE and whose high position was possibly being disguised by the transposed initials.

It cannot be proved that the sonnets are autobiographical. Many critics and most poets believe they are. Wordsworth confidently wrote:

> . . . with this key Shakespeare unlocked his heart.

But Browning protested:

> Did Shakespeare? If so, the less Shakespeare he!

Some commentators agree with Browning. They argue that Shakespeare was merely exercising his ingenuity in a form popular in his day, and that the subject matter—the devotion of an older for a younger man—was a platonic ideal and a Renaissance fashion. But if the sonnets do not tell a straightforward narrative, they are unquestionably the most personal poems Shakespeare ever wrote. If some of them are conventional, even artificial, most of them sound the limits of emotion, the depth of grief, and the height of sublimity. Here, free of the necessity of speaking through the characters in his plays, the poet is himself. He gives his passions their way with him, from scornful bitterness to blind idolatry. The secure peace of love is pitted against the warring agony of lust; thoughtful tenderness alternates with rapt exultation. There can be little doubt that Shakespeare's deepest experiences find utterance in some of the richest lines ever written. "Here, and here alone," says Georg Brandes, "we see Shakespeare himself, as distinct from his poetical creations, loving, admiring, longing, yearning, adoring, disappointed, humiliated, tortured. Here alone does he enter the confessional."

FROM

Sonnets

1

From fairest creatures we desire increase,
That thereby beauty's rose might never die,
But as the riper should by time decease,
His tender heir might bear his memory:
But thou, contracted to thine own bright eyes,
Feed'st thy light's flame with self-substantial fuel,
Making a famine where abundance lies,
Thyself thy foe, to thy sweet self too cruel.
Thou that art now the world's fresh ornament
And only herald to the gaudy spring,
Within thine own bud buriest thy content
And, tender churl, mak'st waste in niggarding.
    Pity the world, or else this glutton be,
      To eat the world's due, by the grave and thee.

15

When I consider every thing that grows
Holds in perfection but a little moment,
That this huge stage presenteth nought but shows
Whereon the stars in secret influence comment;
When I perceive that men as plants increase,
Cheered and checked even by the self-same sky,
Vaunt in their youthful sap, at height decrease,
And wear their brave state out of memory;
Then the conceit of this inconstant stay
Sets you most rich in youth before my sight,
Where wasteful Time debateth with Decay,
To change your day of youth to sullied night;
    And all in war with Time for love of you,
      As he takes from you, I engraft you new.

18

Shall I compare thee to a summer's day?
Thou art more lovely and more temperate.
Rough winds do shake the darling buds of May,

And summer's lease hath all too short a date:
Sometimes too hot the eye of heaven shines,
And often is his gold complexion dimmed:
And every fair from fair sometime declines,
By chance, or nature's changing course, untrimmed:
But thy eternal summer shall not fade
Nor lose possession of that fair thou owest;
Nor shall Death brag thou wanderest in his shade
When in eternal lines to time thou growest.
    So long as men can breathe or eyes can see
    So long lives this, and this gives life to thee.

19

Devouring Time, blunt thou the lion's paws,
And make the earth devour her own sweet brood;
Pluck the keen teeth from the fierce tiger's jaws,
And burn the long-lived phœnix in her blood;
Make glad and sorry seasons as thou fleet'st,
And do whate'er thou wilt, swift-footed Time,
To the wide world and all her fading sweets;
But I forbid thee one most heinous crime:
O, carve not with thy hours my love's fair brow,
Nor draw no lines there with thine antique pen;
Him in thy course untainted do allow
For beauty's pattern to succeeding men.
    Yet do thy worst, old Time: despite thy wrong,
    My love shall in my verse ever live young.

29

When in disgrace with fortune and men's eyes
I all alone beweep my outcast state,
And trouble deaf heaven with my bootless cries,
And look upon myself and curse my fate,
Wishing me like to one more rich in hope,
Featured like him, like him with friends possessed,
Desiring this man's art, and that man's scope,
With what I most enjoy contented least;
Yet in these thoughts myself almost despising,
Haply I think on thee—and then my state,
Like to the lark at break of day arising
From sullen earth, sings hymns at heaven's gate;
    For thy sweet love remembered, such wealth brings
    That then I scorn to change my state with kings.

30

When to the sessions of sweet silent thought
I summon up remembrance of things past,
I sigh the lack of many a thing I sought,
And with old woes new wail my dear time's waste.
Then can I drown an eye, unused to flow,
For precious friends hid in death's dateless night,
And weep afresh love's long-since cancelled woe,
And moan the expense of many a vanished sight.
Then can I grieve at grievances foregone,
And heavily from woe to woe tell o'er
The sad account of fore-bemoaned moan,
Which I new pay as if not paid before.
    But if the while I think on thee, dear friend,
    All losses are restored, and sorrows end.

33

Full many a glorious morning have I seen
Flatter the mountain-tops with sovereign eye,
Kissing with golden face the meadows green,
Gilding pale streams with heavenly alchemy;
Anon permit the basest clouds to ride
With ugly rack on his celestial face,
And from the forlorn world his visage hide,
Stealing unseen to west with this disgrace.
Even so my sun one early morn did shine
With all-triumphant splendor on my brow;
But out, alack! he was but one hour mine,
The region cloud hath masked him from me now.
    Yet him for this my love no whit disdaineth;
    Suns of the world may stain when heaven's sun staineth.

55

Not marble, nor the gilded monuments
Of princes, shall outlive this powerful rhyme;
But you shall shine more bright in these contents
Than unswept stone, besmeared with sluttish time.
When wasteful war shall statues overturn,
And broils root out the work of masonry,
Nor Mars his sword nor war's quick fire shall burn
The living record of your memory.

'Gainst death and all-oblivious enmity
Shall you pace forth; your praise shall still find room
Even in the eyes of all posterity
That wear this world out to the ending doom.
    So, till the judgment that yourself arise,
    You live in this, and dwell in lovers' eyes.

66

Tired with all these, for restful death I cry—
As, to behold desert a beggar born,
And needy nothing trimmed in jollity,
And purest faith unhappily forsworn,
And gilded honor shamefully misplaced,
And maiden virtue rudely strumpeted,
And right perfection wrongfully disgraced,
And strength by limping sway disabled,
And art made tongue-tied by authority,
And folly, doctor-like, controlling skill,
And simple truth miscalled simplicity,
And captive good attending captain ill:—
    —Tired with all these, from these would I be gone,
    Save that, to die, I leave my love alone.

71

No longer mourn for me when I am dead
Than you shall hear the surly sullen bell
Give warning to the world that I am fled
From this vile world, with vilest worms to dwell;
Nay, if you read this line, remember not
The hand that writ it, for I love you so
That I in your sweet thoughts would be forgot,
If thinking on me then should make you woe.
Oh, if, I say, you look upon this verse
When I perhaps compounded am with clay,
Do not so much as my poor name rehearse,
But let your love even with my life decay;
    Lest the wise world should look into your moan,
    And mock you with me after I am gone.

73

That time of year thou may'st in me behold
When yellow leaves, or none, or few, do hang
Upon those boughs which shake against the cold,

Bare ruined choirs, where late the sweet birds sang.
In me thou seest the twilight of such day
As after sunset fadeth in the west,
Which by and by black night doth take away,
Death's second self, that seals up all in rest:
In me thou seest the glowing of such fire
That on the ashes of his youth doth lie,
As the death-bed whereon it must expire,
Consumed with that which it was nourished by.
　　This thou perceiv'st, which makes thy love more strong,
　　To love that well which thou must leave ere long.

87

Farewell! thou art too dear for my possessing,
And like enough thou know'st thy estimate:
The charter of thy worth gives thee releasing;
My bonds in thee are all determinate.
For how do I hold thee but by thy granting?
And for that riches where is my deserving?
The cause of this fair gift in me is wanting,
And so my patent back again is swerving.
Thyself thou gav'st, thy own worth then not knowing,
Or me, to whom thou gav'st it, else mistaking;
So thy great gift, upon misprision growing,
Comes home again, on better judgment making.
　　Thus have I had thee, as a dream doth flatter,
　　In sleep, a king; but waking, no such matter.

94

They that have power to hurt, and will do none,
That do not do the thing they most do show,
Who, moving others, are themselves as stone,
Unmoved, cold, and to temptation slow—
They rightly do inherit heaven's graces,
And husband nature's riches from expense;
They are the lords and owners of their faces,
Others, but stewards of their excellence.
The summer's flower is to the summer sweet
Though to itself it only live and die,
But if that flower with base infection meet,
The basest weed outbraves his dignity:
　　For sweetest things turn sourest by their deeds;
　　Lilies that fester smell far worse than weeds.

95

How sweet and lovely dost thou make the shame
Which, like a canker in the fragrant rose,
Doth spot the beauty of thy budding name!
O, in what sweets dost thou thy sins inclose!
That tongue that tells the story of thy days,
Making lascivious comments on thy sport,
Cannot dispraise but in a kind of praise;
Naming thy name blesses an ill report.
O, what a mansion have those vices got
Which for their habitation chose out thee,
Where beauty's veil doth cover every blot
And all things turn to fair that eyes can see!
    Take heed, dear heart, of this large privilege;
    The hardest knife ill used doth lose his edge.

97

How like a winter hath my absence been
From thee, the pleasure of the fleeting year!
What freezings have I felt, what dark days seen!
What old December's bareness everywhere!
And yet this time removed was summer's time;
The teeming autumn, big with rich increase,
Bearing the wanton burthen of the prime,
Like widowed wombs after their lords' decease:
Yet this abundant issue seemed to me
But hope of orphans and unfathered fruit;
For summer and his pleasures wait on thee,
And, thou away, the very birds are mute;
    Or, if they sing, 'tis with so dull a cheer
    That leaves look pale, dreading the winter's **near.**

106

When in the chronicle of wasted time
I see descriptions of the fairest wights,
And beauty making beautiful old rhyme
In praise of ladies dead, and lovely knights,
Then, in the blazon of sweet beauty's best,
Of hand, of foot, of lip, of eye, of brow,
I see their antique pen would have expressed
Even such a beauty as you master now.

So all their praises are but prophecies
Of this our time, all you prefiguring;
And, for they looked but with divining eyes,
They had not skill enough your worth to sing!
  For we, which now behold these present days,
  Have eyes to wonder, but lack tongues to praise.

116

Let me not to the marriage of true minds
Admit impediments. Love is not love
Which alters when it alteration finds,
Or bends with the remover to remove.
O no! it is an ever-fixed mark
That looks on tempests, and is never shaken;
It is the star to every wandering bark,
Whose worth's unknown, although his height be taken.
Love's not Time's fool, though rosy lips and cheeks
Within his bending sickle's compass come;
Love alters not with his brief hours and weeks,
But bears it out even to the edge of doom.
  If this be error and upon me proved,
  I never writ, nor no man ever loved.

123

No, Time, thou shalt not boast that I do change!
Thy pyramids built up with newer might,
To me are nothing novel, nothing strange;
They are but dressings of a former sight.
Our dates are brief, and therefore we admire
What thou dost foist upon us that is old,
And rather make them born to our desire
Than think that we before have heard them told.
Thy registers and thee I both defy,
Not wondering at the present nor the past;
For thy records and what we see doth lie,
Made more or less by thy continual haste.
  This I do vow, and this shall ever be:
  I will be true, despite thy scythe and thee.

129

The expense of spirit in a waste of shame
Is lust in action; and till action, lust
Is perjured, murderous, bloody, full of blame,

Savage, extreme, rude, cruel, not to trust;
Enjoyed no sooner but despisèd straight;
Past reason hunted; and no sooner had,
Past reason hated, as a swallowed bait
On purpose laid to make the taker mad:
Mad in pursuit, and in possession so;
Had, having, and in quest to have, extreme;
A bliss in proof, and proved, a very woe;
Before, a joy proposed; behind, a dream.
    All this the world well knows; yet none knows well
    To shun the heaven that leads men to this hell.

138

When my love swears that she is made of truth,
I do believe her, though I know she lies,
That she might think me some untutored youth,
Unlearnèd in the world's false subtleties.
Thus vainly thinking that she thinks me young,
Although she knows my days are past the best,
Simply I credit her false-speaking tongue:
On both sides thus is simple truth suppressed.
But wherefore says she not she is unjust?
And wherefore say not I that I am old?
O, love's best habit is in seeming trust,
And age in love loves not to have years told.
    Therefore I lie with her and she with me,
    And in our faults by lies we flattered be.

141

In faith, I do not love thee with mine eyes,
For they in thee a thousand errors note;
But 'tis my heart that loves what they despise,
Who, in despite of view, is pleased to dote;
Nor are mine ears with thy tongue's tune delighted,
Nor tender feeling, to base touches prone,
Nor taste, nor smell, desire to be invited
To any sensual feast with thee alone:
But my five wits nor my five senses can
Dissuade one foolish heart from serving thee,
Who leaves unswayed the likeness of a man,
Thy proud heart's slave and vassal wretch to be.
    Only my plague thus far I count my gain,
    That she that makes me sin awards me pain.

146

Poor soul, the center of my sinful earth,
Pressed by those rebel powers that thee array,
Why dost thou pine within and suffer dearth,
Painting thy outward walls so costly gay?
Why so large cost, having so short a lease,
Dost thou upon thy fading mansion spend?
Shall worms, inheritors of this excess,
Eat up thy charge? is this thy body's end?
Then, soul, live thou upon thy servant's loss,
And let that pine to aggravate thy store;
Buy terms divine in selling hours of dross;
Within be fed, without be rich no more:—
So shalt thou feed on Death, that feeds on men,
And Death once dead, there's no more dying then.

PASSAGES FROM THE PLAYS

IT WAS Georg Brandes who pointed out that Michelangelo died the year in which Shakespeare was born and that death overtook Shakespeare and Cervantes on the same date; whereupon Brandes concluded that "Shakespeare stands co-equal with Michelangelo in pathos and with Cervantes in humor."

If this estimate seems extravagant, reaching across the world and all the arts for an appraisal, it must be remembered that Shakespearean criticism has always been self-defeating. Shakespeare created a crowded universe of many worlds. Such a universe cannot be suggested, much less revealed, by the most sweeping analysis or the most minute examination. We do not encompass a play by Shakespeare; it contains us.

Mark Van Doren, in his remarkable study, SHAKESPEARE (1939), has put it subtly and convincingly: "It is literally true that while we read a play of Shakespeare's we are in it. . . . He conditions us to a particular world before we are aware that it exists; then he absorbs us in its particulars. . . . With each new line a play of Shakespeare's lights its own recesses, deepens its original hue, echoes, supports, and authenticates itself. The world is not there, but this part of it is so entirely there that we miss nothing. It is as if existence had decided to measure itself by a new standard."

It does not require an evening in the theater to transport us into Shakespeare's universe. A few lines from ANTONY AND CLEOPATRA and we are in an Egypt that never was. A vaster Nile, a richer pageantry, a more voluptuous and yet more noble queen are immediately created by a few lines spoken by the dazzled Enobarbus and the dying Cleopatra.

Cleopatra's Barge

The barge she sat in, like a burnished throne,
Burned on the water: the poop was beaten gold;
Purple the sails, and so perfumed that
The winds were love-sick with them; the oars were silver,
Which to the tune of flutes kept stroke, and made
The water which they beat to follow faster,
As amorous of their strokes. For her own person,
It beggared all description: she did lie
In her pavilion—cloth-of-gold of tissue—
O'er-picturing that Venus where we see
The fancy outwork nature: on each side her
Stood pretty dimpled boys, like smiling Cupids,
With divers-colored fans, whose wind did seem
To glow the delicate cheeks which they did cool,
And what they undid did.

from ANTONY AND CLEOPATRA

Cleopatra's Death

Give me my robe, put on my crown; I have
Immortal longings in me: now no more
The juice of Egypt's grape shall moist this lip:—
Yare, yare,[1] good Iras; quick. Methinks I hear
Antony call; I see him rouse himself
To praise my noble act; I hear him mock
The luck of Caesar, which the gods give men
To excuse their after wrath:—husband, I come:
Now to that name my courage prove my title!

[1] *Hurry! Hurry!*

I am fire and air; my other elements
I give to baser life.—So—have you done?
Come then, and take the last warmth of my lips.
Farewell, kind Charmian. Iras, long farewell.
Have I the aspic in my lips? Dost fall?
If thou and nature can so gently part,
The stroke of death is as a lover's pinch,
Which hurts, and is desired. Dost thou lie still?
If thus thou vanishest, thou tell'st the world
It is not worth leave-taking.

from ANTONY AND CLEOPATRA

"Shakespeare was the only lonely and perfectly happy creature whom God ever formed," wrote Keats in an attempt to explain Shakespeare's inconsistencies. Keats completed the paradox by adding, "He could never have a mate—being most unmatchable."

In nothing was Shakespeare so unmatchable as in his power of speech. He used language not only to convey meaning and create character but to compose the most splendid verbal music ever heard. His images were not only visual but heavy with the impact of the other senses. Shakespeare seems, said Logan Pearsall Smith, "to have been especially fond of images of reverberating sound, trumpets and horns and the baying of hounds from afar. Motor images, as they are called, sensations of effort, strain, movement, of rushing winds or horses, are frequent in his poetry, and also of the sea ('surge' is a favorite word with Shakespeare) and of the flow of rivers, as in one of his most splendid images, of the Pontic sea."

The surge of the senses is carried by the flow of sounds; they rush equally through the outcry of Lear and the resignation of Richard the Second.

Blow, Winds

Blow, winds, and crack your cheeks! rage! blow!
You cataracts and hurricanoes, spout
Till you have drenched our steeples, drowned the cocks!
You sulphurous and thought-executing fires,
Vaunt-couriers to oak-cleaving thunderbolts,
Singe my white head! And thou, all-shaking thunder,
Smite flat the thick rotundity o' the world!
Crack nature's molds, all germins spill at once

That make ingrateful man! . . .
Rumble thy bellyful! Spit, fire! spout, rain!
Nor rain, wind, thunder, fire, are my daughters:
I tax not you, you elements, with unkindness;
I never gave you kingdom, called you children,
You owe me no subscription: then let fall
Your horrible pleasure; here I stand, your slave,
A poor, infirm, weak and despised old man:
But yet I call you servile ministers,
That have with two pernicious daughters joined
Your high-engendered battles 'gainst a head
So old and white as this. O! O! 'tis foul!

from KING LEAR

Take Physic, Pomp

Poor naked wretches, wheresoe'er you are,
That bide the pelting of this pitiless storm,
How shall your houseless heads and unfed sides,
Your loopt and windowed raggedness, defend you
From seasons such as these? O, I have ta'en
Too little care of this! Take physic, pomp;
Expose thyself to feel what wretches feel,
That thou mayst shake the superflux to them,
And show the heavens more just.

from KING LEAR

The Death of Kings

Let's talk of graves, of worms, and epitaphs.
Make dust our paper, and with rainy eyes
Write sorrow on the bosom of the earth . . .
For God's sake, let us sit upon the ground,
And tell sad stories of the death of kings:
How some have been deposed; some slain in war;
Some haunted by the ghosts they have deposed;
Some poisoned by their wives; some sleeping killed;
All murdered:—for within the hollow crown
That rounds the mortal temples of a king
Keeps Death his court; and there the antick sits,
Scoffing his state, and grinning at his pomp;

Allowing him a breath, a little scene,
To monarchize, be feared, and kill with looks;
Infusing him with self and vain conceit—
As if this flesh, which walls about our life,
Were brass impregnable; and humored thus,
Comes at the last, and with a little pin
Bores through his castle-wall, and—farewell king!
                    from KING RICHARD THE SECOND

Never have observation and imagination been so perfectly fused.
Shakespeare lived in all his people. He was the mad man who saw
"more devils than vast hell can hold." He was the frantic lover
who beheld "Helen's beauty in a brow of Egypt." But, first of all,
he was a poet. He confessed it in A MIDSUMMER NIGHT'S DREAM:

The poet's eye, in a fine frenzy rolling,
Doth glance from heaven to earth, from earth to heaven,
And, as imagination bodies forth
The forms of things unknown, the poet's pen
Turns them to shapes, and gives to airy nothing
A local habitation and a name.

The power to give "airy nothing a local habitation and a name"
reaches its height in Shakespeare. The known as well as "the forms
of things unknown" are fixed forever, turned into weight and sub-
stance, transfused through a miracle of portraiture and rhetoric.

Portrait of Cressida

                              Fie, fie upon her!
There's language in her eye, her cheek, her lip,
Nay, her foot speaks; her wanton spirits look out
At every joint and motive of her body.
O, these encounterers, so glib of tongue,
That give accosting welcome ere it comes,
And wide unclasp the tables of their thoughts
To every ticklish reader! set them down
For sluttish spoils of opportunity
And daughters of the game.
                    from TROILUS AND CRESSIDA

Portrait of Helen

He brought a Grecian queen, whose youth and freshness
Wrinkles Apollo's, and makes stale the morning:
Is she worth keeping? why, she is a pearl,
Whose price hath launched above a thousand ships,
And turned crowned kings to merchants.

    .   .   .   .

She's bitter to her country: hear me, Paris:—
For every false drop in her bawdy veins
A Grecian's life hath sunk; for every scruple
Of her contaminated carrion weight
A Trojan hath been slain; since she could speak,
She hath not given so many good words breath
As for her Greeks and Trojans suffered death.

from TROILUS AND CRESSIDA

Portrait of Brutus

This was the noblest Roman of them all:
All the conspirators, save only he,
Did that they did in envy of great Cæsar;
He only, in a general honest thought
And common good to all, made one of them.
His life was gentle, and the elements
So mixed in him that Nature might stand up
And say to all the world "This was a man!"

from JULIUS CAESAR

Portrait of Caesar

Why, man, he doth bestride the narrow world
Like a Colossus, and we petty men
Walk under his huge legs and peep about
To find ourselves dishonorable graves.
Men at some time are masters of their fates:
The fault, dear Brutus, is not in our stars,
But in ourselves, that we are underlings.
Brutus, and Cæsar: what should be in that Cæsar?

Why should that name be sounded more than yours?
Write them together, yours is as fair a name;
Sound them, it doth become the mouth as well;
Weigh them, it is as heavy; conjure with 'em,
Brutus will start a spirit as soon as Cæsar.
Now, in the names of all the gods at once,
Upon what meat doth this our Cæsar feed,
That he is grown so great? Age, thou art shamed!
Rome, thou hast lost the breed of noble bloods!
When went there by an age, since the great flood,
But it was famed with more than with one man?
When could they say till now that talked of Rome
That her wide walls encompassed but one man?
Now is it Rome indeed, and room enough,
When there is in it but one only man.

from JULIUS CAESAR

That Men Should Fear

Cowards die many times before their death;
The valiant never taste of death but once.
Of all the wonders that I yet have heard,
It seems to me most strange that men should fear;
Seeing that death, a necessary end,
Will come when it will come.

from JULIUS CAESAR

Antony's Oration

Friends, Romans, countrymen, lend me your ears;
I come to bury Cæsar, not to praise him.
The evil that men do lives after them;
The good is oft interred with their bones;
So let it be with Cæsar. The noble Brutus
Hath told you Cæsar was ambitious:
If it were so, it was a grievous fault,
And grievously hath Cæsar answered it.
Here, under leave of Brutus and the rest—
For Brutus is an honorable man;
So are they all, all honorable men—
Come I to speak in Cæsar's funeral.

He was my friend, faithful and just to me:
But Brutus says he was ambitious;
And Brutus is an honorable man.
He hath brought many captives home to Rome,
Whose ransoms did the general coffers fill:
Did this in Cæsar seem ambitious?
When that the poor have cried, Cæsar hath wept:
Ambition should be made of sterner stuff:
Yet Brutus says he was ambitious;
And Brutus is an honorable man.
You all did see that on the Lupercal
I thrice presented him a kingly crown,
Which he did thrice refuse: was this ambition?
Yet Brutus says he was ambitious;
And, sure, he is an honorable man.
I speak not to disprove what Brutus spoke,
But here I am to speak what I do know.
You all did love him once, not without cause:
What cause withholds you then to mourn for him?
O judgment! thou art fled to brutish beasts,
And men have lost their reason. Bear with me;
My heart is in the coffin there with Cæsar,
And I must pause till it come back to me.

. . . .

If you have tears, prepare to shed them now.
You all do know this mantle: I remember
The first time ever Cæsar put it on;
'Twas on a summer's evening, in his tent,
That day he overcame the Nervii:
Look, in this place ran Cassius' dagger through:
See what a rent the envious Casca made:
Through this the well-beloved Brutus stabbed;
And as he plucked his cursed steel away,
Mark how the blood of Cæsar followed it,
As rushing out of doors, to be resolved
If Brutus so unkindly knocked, or no:
For Brutus, as you know, was Cæsar's angel:
Judge, O you gods, how dearly Cæsar loved him!
This was the most unkindest cut of all;
For when the noble Cæsar saw him stab,
Ingratitude, more strong than traitors' arms,
Quite vanquished him: then burst his mighty heart;
And, in his mantle muffling up his face,
Even at the base of Pompey's statue,

Which all the while ran blood, great Cæsar fell.
O, what a fall was there, my countrymen!
Then I, and you, and all of us fell down,
Whilst bloody treason flourished over us.

from JULIUS CAESAR

Much of Shakespeare's power is achieved not only by the flexi-
bility of his language but by the suppleness of the form in which
it was cast. There is something odd, almost magical, about the form
of blank verse. Those weighted unrhymed lines have an extraordi-
nary carrying power. The gravely moving ten syllables seem to
carry a thought through the ages with particular authority, an au-
thority never quite achieved by a more rapid line of eight syllables
or a more ponderously burdened line of twelve. It is the form as
well as his spirit which makes Shakespeare the most English of
poets, the ageless spokesman of a people to all the peoples of the
earth.

This England

This royal throne of kings, this sceptered isle,
This earth of majesty, this seat of Mars,
This other Eden, demi-Paradise;
This fortress built by Nature for herself
Against infection and the hand of war;
This happy breed of men, this little world;
This precious stone set in the silver sea,
Which serves it in the office of a wall,
Or as a moat defensive to a house,
Against the envy of less happier lands;
This blessed plot, this earth, this realm, this England,
This nurse, this teeming womb of royal kings,
Feared by their breed, and famous by their birth,
Renowned for their deeds as far from home,
For Christian service and true chivalry,
As is the sepulchre, in stubborn Jewry,
Of the world's ransom, blessed Mary's Son;
This land of such dear souls, this dear dear land,
Dear for her reputation through the world,
Is now leased out—I die pronouncing it—
Like to a tenement or pelting farm:
England, bound in with the triumphant sea,
Whose rocky shore beats back the envious siege

Of watery Neptune, is now bound in with shame,
With inky blots, and rotten parchment bonds:
That England, that was wont to conquer others,
Hath made a shameful conquest of itself.

from KING RICHARD THE SECOND

The Blast of War

Once more unto the breach, dear friends, once more;
Or close the wall up with our English dead!
In peace there's nothing so becomes a man
As modest stillness and humility:
But when the blast of war blows in our ears,
Then imitate the action of the tiger;
Stiffen the sinews, summon up the blood,
Disguise fair nature with hard-favored rage:
Then lend the eye a terrible aspect;
Let it pry through the portage of the head
Like the brass cannon; let the brow o'erwhelm it
As fearfully as doth a galled rock
O'erhang and jutty his confounded base,
Swilled with the wild and wasteful ocean.
Now set the teeth, and stretch the nostril wide;
Hold hard the breath, and bend up every spirit
To his full height!—On, on, you noble English,
Whose blood is fet [1] from fathers of war-proof!—
Fathers that, like so many Alexanders,
Have in these parts from morn till even fought,
And sheathed their swords for lack of argument.
Dishonor not your mothers; now attest
That those whom you called fathers did beget you!
Be copy now to men of grosser blood,
And teach them how to war!—And you, good yeomen,
Whose limbs were made in England, show us here
The mettle of your pasture; let us swear
That you are worth your breeding: which I doubt not;
For there is none of you so mean and base,
That hath not noble lustre in your eyes.
I see you stand like greyhounds in the slips,
Straining upon the start. The game's afoot:
Follow your spirit; and, upon this charge,
Cry "God for Harry, England, and Saint George!"

from KING HENRY THE FIFTH

[1] Fetched, inherited.

Hate the Idle Pleasures

Now is the winter of our discontent
Made glorious summer by this sun of York;
And all the clouds that loured upon our house
In the deep bosom of the ocean buried.
Now are our brows bound with victorious wreaths;
Our bruised arms hung up for monuments;
Our stern alarums changed to merry meetings,
Our dreadful marches to delightful measures.
Grim-visaged war hath smoothed his wrinkled front;
And now—instead of mounting barbed steeds
To fright the souls of fearful adversaries—
He capers nimbly in a lady's chamber
To the lascivious pleasing of a lute.
But I, that am not shaped for sportive tricks,
Nor made to court an amorous looking-glass;
I, that am rudely stamped, and want love's majesty
To strut before a wanton ambling nymph;
I, that am curtailed of this fair proportion,
Cheated of feature by dissembling nature,
Deformed, unfinished, sent before my time
Into this breathing world, scarce half made up,
And that so lamely and unfashionable
That dogs bark at me as I halt by them;—
Why, I, in this weak piping time of peace,
Have no delight to pass away the time,
Unless to spy my shadow in the sun,
And descant on mine own deformity:
And therefore, since I cannot prove a lover,
To entertain these fair well-spoken days,
I am determined to prove a villain,
And hate the idle pleasures of these days.

from KING RICHARD THE THIRD

Farewell to Greatness

Farewell, a long farewell, to all my greatness!
This is the state of man: today he puts forth
The tender leaves of hope; tomorrow blossoms,
And bears his blushing honors thick upon him;

The third day comes a frost, a killing frost,
And—when he thinks, good easy man, full surely
His greatness is a-ripening—nips his root,
And then he falls, as I do. I have ventured,
Like little wanton boys that swim on bladders,
This many summers in a sea of glory;
But far beyond my depth: my high-blown pride
At length broke under me; and now has left me,
Weary and old with service, to the mercy
Of a rude stream, that must for ever hide me.
Vain pomp and glory of this world, I hate ye:
I feel my heart new opened. O, how wretched
Is that poor man that hangs on princes' favors!
There is, betwixt that smile we would aspire to,
That sweet aspect of princes, and their ruin,
More pangs and fears than wars or women have;
And when he falls, he falls like Lucifer,
Never to hope again.

from KING HENRY THE EIGHTH

Ambition

Cromwell, I charge thee, fling away ambition:
By that sin fell the angels; how can man, then,
The image of his Maker, hope to win by it?
Love thyself last; cherish those hearts that hate thee;
Corruption wins not more than honesty.
Still in thy right hand carry gentle peace,
To silence envious tongues. Be just, and fear not:
Let all the ends thou aim'st at be thy country's,
Thy God's, and truth's; then if thou fall'st, O Cromwell,
Thou fall'st a blessed martyr! . . .
        O Cromwell, Cromwell!
Had I but served my God with half the zeal
I served my king, He would not in mine age
Have left me naked to mine enemies.

from KING HENRY THE EIGHTH

Shakespeare's far-reaching wisdom and seemingly limitless humor
stretched incalculably beyond his native England. He influenced
French thought through Voltaire and Victor Hugo; he changed
German thinking through Lessing and Goethe. Modern Europe is

unthinkable without him. If his purpose was the portrayal of humanity, it was not hard for him to hold a mirror up to nature; he himself was the mirror of mankind.

The Uses of Adversity

Now, my co-mates and brothers in exile,
Hath not old custom made this life more sweet
Than that of painted pomp? Are not these woods
More free from peril than the envious court?
Here feel we not the penalty of Adam,
The seasons' difference, as the icy fang
And churlish chiding of the winter's wind,
Which, when it bites and blows upon my body,
Even till I shrink with cold, I smile and say,
"This is no flattery: these are counsellors
That feelingly persuade me what I am."
Sweet are the uses of adversity,
Which, like the toad, ugly and venomous,
Wears yet a precious jewel in his head.
And this our life, exempt from public haunt,
Finds tongues in trees, books in the running brooks,
Sermons in stones, and good in everything.

from AS YOU LIKE IT

All the World's a Stage

All the world's a stage
And all the men and women merely players:
They have their exits and their entrances;
And one man in his time plays many parts,
His acts being seven ages. At first the infant,
Mewling and puking in the nurse's arms.
Then the whining school-boy, with his satchel
And shining morning face, creeping like snail
Unwillingly to school. And then the lover,
Sighing like furnace, with a woeful ballad
Made to his mistress' eyebrow. Then a soldier,
Full of strange oaths, and bearded like the pard,[1]
Jealous in honor, sudden and quick in quarrel,

[1] *Leopard.*

Seeking the bubble reputation
Even in the cannon's mouth. And then the justice,
In fair round belly with good capon lined,
With eyes severe and beard of formal cut,
Full of wise saws and modern instances;
And so he plays his part. The sixth age shifts
Into the lean and slippered pantaloon,
With spectacles on nose and pouch on side,
His youthful hose, well saved, a world too wide
For his shrunk shank; and his big manly voice,
Turning again toward childish treble, pipes
And whistles in his sound. Last scene of all,
That ends this strange eventful history,
Is second childishness and mere oblivion,
Sans teeth, sans eyes, sans taste, sans every thing.

from AS YOU LIKE IT

Motley's the Only Wear

A fool, a fool! I met a fool i' the forest,
A motley fool; a miserable world!
As I do live by food, I met a fool;
Who laid him down and basked him in the sun
And railed on Lady Fortune in good terms,
In good set terms, and yet a motley fool.
"Good morrow, fool," quoth I. "No sir," quoth he,
"Call me not fool till heaven hath sent me fortune":
And then he drew a dial from his poke,
And, looking on it with lack-luster eye,
Says very wisely, "It is ten o'clock:
Thus we may see," quoth he, "how the world wags:
'Tis but an hour ago since it was nine;
And after one hour more 'twill be eleven;
And so, from hour to hour, we ripe and ripe,
And then, from hour to hour, we rot and rot;
And thereby hangs a tale." When I did hear
The motley fool thus moral on the time,
My lungs began to crow like chanticleer,
That fools should be so deep-contemplative;
And I did laugh sans intermission
An hour by his dial. O noble fool!
A worthy fool! Motley's the only wear.

from AS YOU LIKE IT

Let Me Play the Fool

Let me play the fool:
With mirth and laughter let old wrinkles come;
And let my liver rather heat with wine
Than my heart cool with mortifying groans.
Why should a man, whose blood is warm within,
Sit like his grandsire cut in alabaster?
Sleep when he wakes, and creep into the jaundice
By being peevish? I tell thee what, Antonio—
I love thee, and it is my love that speaks—
There are a sort of men, whose visages
Do cream and mantle like a standing pond;
And do a willful stillness entertain,
With purpose to be dressed in an opinion
Of wisdom, gravity, profound conceit;
As who should say, "I am Sir Oracle,
And, when I ope my lips, let no dog bark!"
O my Antonio, I do know of these,
That therefore only are reputed wise
For saying nothing; when, I am very sure,
If they should speak, would almost damn those ears,
Which, hearing them, would call their brothers fools.

from THE MERCHANT OF VENICE

Mercy

The quality of mercy is not strained,
It droppeth as the gentle rain from heaven
Upon the place beneath: it is twice blest;
It blesseth him that gives, and him that takes:
'Tis mightiest in the mightiest: it becomes
The throned monarch better than his crown;
His scepter shows the force of temporal power,
The attribute to awe and majesty,
Wherein doth sit the dread and fear of kings;
But mercy is above this sceptered sway;
It is enthroned in the hearts of kings,
It is an attribute to God himself;
And earthly power doth then show likest God's
When mercy seasons justice. Therefore, Jew,

Though justice be thy plea, consider this,
That, in the course of justice, none of us
Should see salvation; we do pray for mercy;
And that same prayer doth teach us all to render
The deeds of mercy.

from THE MERCHANT OF VENICE

How Sweet the Moonlight Sleeps

How sweet the moonlight sleeps upon this bank!
Here will we sit, and let the sounds of music
Creep in our ears: soft stillness and the night
Become the touches of sweet harmony.
Sit, Jessica. Look how the floor of heaven
Is thick inlaid with patines of bright gold:
There's not the smallest orb which thou behold'st
But in his motion like an angel sings,
Still quiring to the young-eyed cherubins;
Such harmony is in immortal souls;
But whilst this muddy vesture of decay
Doth grossly close it in, we cannot hear it.
Come, ho, and wake Diana with a hymn!
With sweetest touches pierce your mistress' ear,
And draw her home with music.

from THE MERCHANT OF VENICE

Love-in-Idleness

That very time I saw, but thou couldst not,
Flying between the cold moon and the earth,
Cupid all armed: a certain aim he took
At a fair vestal throned by the west,
And loosed his love-shaft smartly from his bow,
As it should pierce a hundred thousand hearts:
But I might see young Cupid's fiery shaft
Quenched in the chaste beams of the watery moon,
And the imperial votaress passed on,
In maiden meditation, fancy-free.
Yet marked I where the bolt of Cupid fell:
It fell upon a little western flower,
Before milk-white, now purple with love's wound,

And maidens call it love-in-idleness.
Fetch me that flower; the herb I showed thee once:
The juice of it on sleeping eye-lids laid
Will make or man or woman madly dote
Upon the next live creature that it sees.
Fetch me this herb; and be thou here again
Ere the leviathan can swim a league.

from A MIDSUMMER NIGHT'S DREAM

Where the Wild Thyme Blows

I know a bank where the wild thyme blows,
Where oxlips and the nodding violet grows;
Quite over-canopied with luscious woodbine,
With sweet musk-roses, and with eglantine:
There sleeps Titania sometime of the night,
Lulled in these flowers with dances and delight;
And there the snake throws her enamelled skin,
Weed wide enough to wrap a fairy in:
And with the juice of this I'll streak her eyes,
And make her full of hateful fantasies.

from A MIDSUMMER NIGHT'S DREAM

The Living Juliet

He jests at scars that never felt a wound . . .
But, soft! what light through yonder window breaks?
It is the east, and Juliet is the sun!
Arise, fair sun, and kill the envious moon,
Who is already sick and pale with grief,
That thou her maid are far more fair than she.
Be not her maid, since she is envious;
Her vestal livery is but sick and green,
And none but fools do wear it; cast it off.
It is my lady; O, it is my love!
O, that she knew she were!
She speaks, yet she says nothing. What of that?
Her eye discourses, I will answer it.
I am too bold, 'tis not to me she speaks:
Two of the fairest stars in all the heaven,
Having some business, do intreat her eyes
To twinkle in their spheres till they return.
What if her eyes were there, **they** in her head?

The brightness of her cheek would shame those stars,
As daylight doth a lamp; her eyes in heaven
Would through the airy region stream so bright
That birds would sing and think it were not night.

from ROMEO AND JULIET

Mercutio Describes Queen Mab

She is the fairies' midwife, and she comes
In shape no bigger than an agate-stone
On the fore-finger of an alderman,
Drawn with a team of little atomies
Over men's noses as they lie asleep;
Her waggon-spokes made of long spinners' legs.
The cover of the wings of grasshoppers,
Her traces of the smallest spider web,
Her collars of the moonshine's watery beams,
Her whip of cricket's bone, the lash of film,
Her waggoner a small grey-coated gnat,
Not half so big as a round little worm
Prick'd from the lazy finger of a maid;
Her chariot is an empty hazel-nut
Made by the joiner squirrel, or old grub,
Time out o' mind the fairies' coachmakers.
And in this state she gallops night by night
Through lovers' brains, and then they dream of love;
On courtiers' knees, that dream on curtsies straight;
O'er lawyers' fingers, who straight dream on fees;
O'er ladies' lips, who straight on kisses dream,
Which oft the angry Mab with blisters plagues,
Because their breath with sweetmeats tainted are.
Sometimes she gallops o'er a courtier's nose,
And then dreams he of smelling out a suit;
And sometime comes she with a tithe-pig's tail
Tickling a parson's nose as 'a lies asleep,
Then dreams he of another benefice.
Sometime she driveth o'er a soldier's neck,
And then dreams he of cutting foreign throats,
Of breaches, ambuscadoes, Spanish blades,
Of healths five fathom deep: and then anon
Drums in his ear, at which he starts and wakes,
And being thus frighted, swears a prayer or two
And sleeps again.

from ROMEO AND JULIET

Thus With a Kiss I Die

For here lies Juliet, and her beauty makes
This vault a feasting presence full of light.
Death, lie thou there, by a dead man interred.
How oft when men are at the point of death
Have they been merry! which their keepers call
A lightning before death: O, how may I
Call this a lightning? O my love! my wife!
Death, that hath sucked the honey of thy breath,
Hath had no power yet upon thy beauty:
Thou art not conquered; beauty's ensign yet
Is crimson in thy lips and in thy cheeks,
And death's pale flag is not advanced there.
Tybalt, liest thou there in thy bloody sheet?
O, what more favor can I do to thee
Than with that hand that cut thy youth in twain
To sunder his that was thine enemy?
Forgive me, cousin! Ah, dear Juliet,
Why art thou yet so fair? shall I believe
That unsubstantial death is amorous,
And that the lean abhorred monster keeps
Thee here in dark to be his paramour?
For fear of that, I still will stay with thee,
And never from this palace of dim night
Depart again: here, here will I remain
With worms that are thy chamber-maids; O, here
Will I set up my everlasting rest,
And shake the yoke of inauspicious stars
From this world-wearied flesh. Eyes, look your last!
Arms, take your last embrace! and, lips, O you
The doors of breath, seal with a righteous kiss
A dateless bargain to engrossing death!
Come, bitter conduct, come, unsavory guide!
Thou desperate pilot, now at once run on
The dashing rocks thy sea-sick weary bark.
Here's to my love! [*Drinks*] O true apothecary!
Thy drugs are quick. Thus with a kiss I die.

from ROMEO AND JULIET

The Food of Love

If music be the food of love, play on;
Give me excess of it, that, surfeiting,
The appetite may sicken, and so die.
That strain again! it had a dying fall:
O, it came o'er my ear like the sweet sound,
That breathes upon a bank of violets,
Stealing and giving odor! Enough; no more:
'Tis not so sweet now as it was before.
O spirit of love, how quick and fresh art thou!
That, notwithstanding thy capacity
Receiveth as the sea, nought enters there,
Of what validity and pitch soe'er,
But falls into abatement and low price,
Even in a minute! so full of shapes is fancy,
That it alone is high fantastical.

from TWELFTH NIGHT

Patience on a Monument

                    . . . She never told her love,
But let concealment, like a worm i' the bud,
Feed on her damask cheek; she pined in thought
And with a green and yellow melancholy
She sat like patience on a monument,
Smiling at grief. Was not this love indeed?
We men may say more, swear more: but indeed
Our shows are more than will; for still we prove
Much in our vows, but little in our love.

from TWELFTH NIGHT

Beauty Is a Witch

Friendship is constant in all other things
Save in the office and affairs of love:
Therefore all hearts in love use their own tongues;
Let every eye negotiate for itself,
And trust no agent; for beauty is a witch

Against whose charms faith melteth into blood.
This is an accident of hourly proof,
Which I mistrusted not.

                          from MUCH ADO ABOUT NOTHING

I Have Lived Long Enough

I have lived long enough: my way of life
Is fallen into the sere, the yellow leaf,
And that which should accompany old age,
As honor, love, obedience, troops of friends,
I must not look to have; but, in their stead,
Curses, not loud but deep, mouth-honor, breath,
Which the poor heart would fain deny, and dare not.

.   .   .   .

Canst thou not minister to a mind diseased,
Pluck from the memory a rooted sorrow,
Raze out the written troubles of the brain,
And with some sweet oblivious antidote
Cleanse the stuffed bosom of that perilous stuff
Which weighs upon the heart?

                                       from MACBETH

Tomorrow, and Tomorrow, and Tomorrow

Tomorrow, and tomorrow, and tomorrow,
Creeps in this petty pace from day to day,
To the last syllable of recorded time;
And all our yesterdays have lighted fools
The way to dusty death. Out, out, brief candle!
Life's but a walking shadow, a poor player
That struts and frets his hour upon the stage
And then is heard no more: it is a tale
Told by an idiot, full of sound and fury,
Signifying nothing.

                              from MACBETH

This Above All

And these few precepts in thy memory
See thou character. Give thy thoughts no tongue,
Nor any unproportioned thought his act.
Be thou familiar, but by no means vulgar.
Those friends thou hast, and their adoption tried,
Grapple them to thy soul with hoops of steel,
But do not dull thy palm with entertainment
Of each new-hatched unfledged comrade. Beware
Of entrance to a quarrel; but being in,
Bear't, that the opposed may beware of thee.
Give every man thy ear, but few thy voice:
Take each man's censure, but reserve thy judgment.
Costly thy habit as thy purse can buy,
But not expressed in fancy; rich, not gaudy:
For the apparel oft proclaims the man;
And they in France of the best rank and station
Are of a most select and generous chief in that.
Neither a borrower nor a lender be:
For loan oft loses both itself and friend,
And borrowing dulls the edge of husbandry.
This above all: to thine own self be true,
And it must follow, as the night the day,
Thou canst not then be false to any man.

from HAMLET

Frailty, Thy Name Is Woman

O, that this too too solid flesh would melt,
Thaw and resolve itself into a dew!
Or that the Everlasting had not fix'd
His canon 'gainst self-slaughter! O God! O God!
How weary, stale, flat and unprofitable
Seem to me all the uses of this world!
Fie on't! oh fie! 'tis an unweeded garden,
That grows to seed; things rank and gross in nature
Possess it merely. That it should come to this!
But two months dead! nay, not so much, not two:
So excellent a king; that was, to this,
Hyperion to a satyr: so loving to my mother,

That he might not beteem the winds of heaven
Visit her face too roughly. Heaven and earth!
Must I remember? why, she would hang on him,
As if increase of appetite had grown
By what it fed on: and yet, within a month—
Let me not think on't—Frailty, thy name is woman!—
A little month, or ere those shoes were old
With which she follow'd my poor father's body,
Like Niobe, all tears:—why she, even she—
O God! a beast that wants discourse of reason
Would have mourned longer—married with my uncle,
My father's brother, but no more like my father
Than I to Hercules: within a month;
Ere yet the salt of most unrighteous tears
Had left the flushing in her galled eyes,
She married. O, most wicked speed, to post
With such dexterity to incestuous sheets!
It is not, nor it cannot come to good:
But break, my heart, for I must hold my tongue!

from HAMLET

To Be, or Not to Be

To be, or not to be: that is the question:
Whether 'tis nobler in the mind to suffer
The slings and arrows of outrageous fortune,
Or to take arms against a sea of troubles,
And by opposing end them. To die: to sleep;
No more; and by a sleep to say we end
The heart-ache, and the thousand natural shocks
That flesh is heir to. 'Tis a consummation
Devoutly to be wish'd. To die, to sleep;
To sleep? Perchance to dream! aye, there's the rub;
For in that sleep of death what dreams may come,
When we have shuffled off this mortal coil,
Must give us pause: there's the respect
That makes calamity of so long life;
For who would bear the whips and scorns of time,
The oppressor's wrong, the proud man's contumely,
The pangs of despised love, the law's delay,
The insolence of office, and the spurns
That patient merit of the unworthy takes,
When he himself might his quietus make

With a bare bodkin? who would fardels [1] bear,
To grunt and sweat under a weary life,
But that the dread of something after death,
The undiscovered country from whose bourn
No traveler returns, puzzles the will,
And makes us rather bear those ills we have
Than fly to others that we know not of?
Thus conscience does make cowards of us all,
And thus the native hue of resolution
Is sicklied o'er with the pale cast of thought,
And enterprises of great pitch and moment
With this regard their currents turn awry
And lose the name of action.

from HAMLET

Farewell Content

. . . O, now, for ever
Farewell the tranquil mind! farewell content!
Farewell the plumed troop, and the big wars,
That make ambition virtue! O, farewell!
Farewell the neighing steed, and the shrill trump,
The spirit-stirring drum, th'ear-piercing fife,
The royal banner, and all quality,
Pride, pomp, and circumstance of glorious war!
And, O you mortal engines, whose rude throats
Th'immortal Jove's dread clamors counterfeit,
Farewell! Othello's occupation's gone!

from OTHELLO

THE TEMPEST is one of Shakespeare's least dramatic but one of his noblest plays. In what is supposedly his last great work, Shakespeare conjured up the dreams of humanity: in Caliban the primitive man, in Prospero the seer and superman, in Miranda the embodiment of innocent beauty, in Ariel the spirit of unfettered imagination. Here, and especially in the valedictory—"We are such stuff as dreams are made on, and our little life is rounded with a sleep"—Shakespeare summoned the world, and bade farewell to it.

[1] *Burdens.*

To Dream Again

Be not afeared; the isle is full of noises,
Sounds and sweet airs, that give delight, and hurt not.
Sometimes a thousand twangling instruments
Will hum about mine ears; and sometime voices,
That, if I then had waked after long sleep,
Will make me sleep again: and then, in dreaming,
The clouds methought would open, and show riches
Ready to drop upon me; that, when I waked,
I cried to dream again.

from THE TEMPEST

Brave New World

O, wonder!
How many goodly creatures are there here!
How beauteous mankind is! O brave new world,
That has such people in't.

from THE TEMPEST

Such Stuff as Dreams Are Made On

Our revels now are ended. These our actors,
As I foretold you, were all spirits, and
Are melted into air, into thin air:
And, like the baseless fabric of this vision,
The cloud-capped towers, the gorgeous palaces,
The solemn temples, the great globe itself,
Yea, all which it inherit, shall dissolve,
And, like this insubstantial pageant faded,
Leave not a rack behind. We are such stuff
As dreams are made on, and our little life
Is rounded with a sleep.

from THE TEMPEST

SONGS FROM THE PLAYS

Some of the purest lyrics in the English language were originally written as theatrical expedients. They were not composed as poetry *per se,* but designed to punctuate a scene, to help clear the stage of actors, as excuses for incidental music, as commentaries and epilogues.

Primarily Shakespeare wrote his lyrics to be sung. The printed page scarcely does them justice; isolation robs them of their author's masterly stagecraft. It is not enough to see the words; we must hear O MISTRESS MINE and WHO IS SILVIA? and HARK! HARK! THE LARK —three of the musicians' favorites—in the contemporary settings by Morley or the later arrangements by Schubert. Shakespeare lived in the golden age of English music; his plays are full of tributes to its power: "Music with her silver sound" and "If music be the food of love, play on" and

> The man that hath no music in himself,
> Nor is not moved with concord of sweet sounds
> Is fit for treasons, stratagems, and spoils . . .

Never have words been crystallized in purer sound.

O Mistress Mine

> O Mistress mine, where are you roaming?
> O, stay and hear—your true love's coming,
>   That can sing both high and low.
> Trip no further, pretty sweeting;
> Journeys end in lovers' meeting,
>   Every wise man's son doth know.
>
> What is love? 'tis not hereafter;
> Present mirth hath present laughter;
>   What's to come is still unsure:
> In delay there lies no plenty—
> Then come kiss me, sweet-and-twenty,
>   Youth's a stuff will not endure.
>   *from* TWELFTH NIGHT

Who Is Silvia?

Who is Silvia? What is she,
    That all our swains commend her?
Holy, fair, and wise is she;
    The heaven such grace did lend her,
That she might admired be.

Is she kind as she is fair?
    For beauty lives with kindness.
Love doth to her eyes repair,
    To help him of his blindness;
And, being helped, inhabits there.

Then to Silvia let us sing,
    That Silvia is excelling;
She excels each mortal thing,
    Upon the dull earth dwelling:
To her let us garlands bring.
        from TWO GENTLEMEN OF VERONA

Hark! Hark! The Lark

Hark! hark! the lark at heaven's gate sings,
    And Phoebus 'gins arise,
His steeds to water at those springs
    On chaliced flowers that lies;
And winking Mary-buds [1] begin
    To ope their golden eyes.
With every thing that pretty is,
    My lady sweet, arise;
        Arise, arise!
        from CYMBELINE

LOVE'S LABOR'S LOST concludes with a pair of matching songs which are not only delightful but extraordinarily graphic. The first is sung by Ver (or Spring) dressed in the costume of a cuckoo, the vernal bird; the second is sung by Hiems (or Winter), appareled

[1] *Sleeping marigolds.*

like a snowy owl. The bird refrains are thus not only comic but characteristic—the sound of the cuckoo was obviously "unpleasing to a married ear" because the name as well as the notes of his song suggested "cuckold."

All of April is summoned with the striped or "pied" daisies and the gold buttercups or "cuckoo-buds"; the larks, which punctually wake the plowman; the querulous turtledoves strutting in the loft; the girls getting their dresses ready for the summer. And all of winter is evoked by the shivering Dick trying to warm his fingers with his breath; Tom breathing hard as he brings in the heavy logs under the icicles; the contrast between the milkmaid with her frozen milk and Joan stirring her pot in the overheated kitchen; the chill of the outdoors and the hot comfort of the wine bowl with roasted crab apples put in for spice.

But these songs are more than songs. By the secret device of words, says Walter de la Mare (see page 1071), "the several scenes become at last a unity, and we have the complete old English farmhouse, with its barns and its cowsheds, its stacks and its acres under the winter sky, and not only in three but in four dimensions. As for precise observation combined with atmosphere what could surpass the effect of the 'all aloud' in the second stanza, and the 'sit brooding' of the next line—so vividly evoking the birds themselves, dazzled and bewildered in the strange unheavenly glare of the snow, as almost to amount to an hallucination!"

Spring

When daisies pied and violets blue,
    And lady-smocks all silver-white,
And cuckoo-buds of yellow hue
    Do paint the meadows with delight,
The cuckoo then, on every tree,
Mocks married men, for thus sings he:
"Cuckoo! cuckoo!" O word of fear,
Unpleasing to a married ear.

When shepherds pipe on oaten straws,
    And merry larks are ploughmen's clocks,
When turtles tread, and rooks, and daws,
    And maidens bleach their summer smocks,
The cuckoo then, on every tree,

Mocks married men, for thus sings he:
"Cuckoo! cuckoo!" O word of fear,
Unpleasing to a married ear.
from LOVE'S LABOR'S LOST

Winter

When icicles hang by the wall
    And Dick the shepherd blows his nail,
And Tom bears logs into the hall,
    And milk comes frozen home in pail;
When blood is nipped, and ways be foul,
Then nightly sings the staring owl
"To-whit! Tu-whoo!" A merry note,
While greasy Joan doth keel the pot.

When all aloud the wind doth blow,
    And coughing drowns the parson's saw,
And birds sit brooding in the snow,
    And Marian's nose looks red and raw;
When roasted crabs hiss in the bowl—
Then nightly sings the staring owl
"To-whit! Tu-whoo!" A merry note,
While greasy Joan doth keel the pot.
from LOVE'S LABOR'S LOST

It is thought that A MIDSUMMER NIGHT'S DREAM was written as a masque, a festival play in celebration of the marriage of Essex and the widow of Sir Philip Sidney. It is certain that the play is a captivating mixture of clowns and elves, of laughing grace and light parody, of innocent love and irrepressible youth. Human beings and fairies move about with equal ease in a wood near Athens; it is sometimes hard to distinguish the bewildered mortals from the immortal mischief-makers.

The world of A MIDSUMMER NIGHT'S DREAM is a world of melody. It is an opera rather than a drama; the very characters breathe the air of music. Nowhere is this so true as in the fairy songs which occur with such regularity that the whole piece seems a dramatized lyric rather than a drama, a prolonged and fantastic song.

Fairy Songs

1

Over hill, over dale,
  Thorough bush, thorough brier,
Over park, over pale,
  Thorough flood, thorough fire,
I do wander everywhere,
Swifter than the moonès sphere;
And I serve the fairy queen,
To dew her orbs upon the green.
The cowslips tall her pensioners be;
In their gold coats spots you see,
Those be rubies, fairy favors,
In those freckles live their savors:
I must go seek some dewdrops here,
And hang a pearl in every cowslip's ear.

2

You spotted snakes with double tongue,
  Thorny hedge-hogs, be not seen;
Newts, and blind-worms, do no wrong;
  Come not near our fairy queen.
  Philomel, with melody,
  Sing in our sweet lullaby;
Lulla, lulla, lullaby, lulla, lulla, lullaby.
  Never harm, nor spell, nor charm,
  Come our lovely lady nigh;
  So, good night, with lullaby.

Weaving spiders, come not here:
  Hence, you long-legged spinners, hence!
Beetles black, approach not near;
  Worm, nor snail, do no offence.
  Philomel, with melody,
  Sing in our sweet lullaby;
Lulla, lulla, lullaby, lulla, lulla, lullaby.
  Never harm, nor spell, nor charm,
  Come our lovely lady nigh;
  So, good night, with lullaby.

3

Now the hungry lion roars,
    And the wolf behowls the moon;
Whilst the heavy ploughman snores,
    All with weary task fordone.
Now the wasted brands do glow,
    Whilst the screech-owl, screeching loud,
Puts the wretch that lies in woe
    In remembrance of a shroud.
Now it is the time of night
    That the graves, all gaping wide,
Everyone lets forth his sprite,
    In the churchway paths to glide.
And we fairies, that do run
    By the triple Hecate's team,
From the presence of the sun,
    Following darkness like a dream,
Now are frolic; not a mouse
Shall disturb this hallowed house:
I am sent with broom before,
To sweep the dust behind the door.

4

Now, until the break of day,
Through this house each fairy stray.
To the best bride-bed will we,
Which by us shall blessed be;
And the issue there create
Ever shall be fortunate.
So shall all the couples three
Ever true in loving be;
And the blots of Nature's hand
Shall not in their issue stand:
Never mole, hare-lip, nor scar,
Nor mark prodigious, such as are
Despised in nativity,
Shall upon their children be.
With this field-dew consecrate,
Every fairy take his gait,
And each several chamber bless,
Through this palace with sweet peace.
Ever shall in safety rest,

> And the owner of it blest.
> Trip away!
> Make no stay;
> Meet me all by break of day.
>   *from* A MIDSUMMER NIGHT'S DREAM

If Shakespeare had written nothing but his interludes and occasional songs his greatness would still be unquestionable. It is inherent in the bucolic ditties in AS YOU LIKE IT as well as in the somber elegy about golden lads and girls sung at the grave of the supposedly dead Imogen in CYMBELINE. Even when the harmonies are missing and the composer's tunes are forgotten, the songs continue to be a succession of triumphs. They make their own melodies. Shakespeare's incomparable union of sounds is in the least of his work. His mastery of phrase turns a speaking word into a flight of singing syllables.

Songs of the Greenwood

1

> Under the greenwood tree
> Who loves to lie with me,
> And turn his merry note
> Unto the sweet bird's throat—
> Come hither, come hither, come hither!
>   Here shall he see
>   No enemy
> But winter and rough weather.
>
> Who doth ambition shun
> And loves to live i' the sun,
> Seeking the food he eats
> And pleased with what he gets—
> Come hither, come hither, come hither!
>   Here shall he see
>   No enemy
> But winter and rough weather.

2

> Blow, blow, thou winter wind!
> Thou art not so unkind
> As man's ingratitude;

Thy tooth is not so keen
Because thou art not seen,
    Although thy breath be rude.
Heigh ho! sing heigh ho! unto the green holly:
Most friendship is feigning, most loving mere folly:
        Then, heigh ho! the holly!
        This life is most jolly.

Freeze, freeze, thou bitter sky,
Thou dost not bite so nigh
    As benefits forgot:
Though thou the waters warp,
Thy sting is not so sharp
    As friend remembered not.
Heigh ho! sing heigh ho! unto the green holly:
Most friendship is feigning, most loving mere folly:
        Then, heigh ho! the holly!
        This life is most jolly.

from AS YOU LIKE IT

Country Song

It was a lover and his lass,
    With a hey, and a ho, and a hey nonino,
That o'er the green corn-field did pass
    In the spring-time, the only pretty ring-time,
When birds do sing, hey ding a ding, ding!
    Sweet lovers love the spring.

Between the acres of the rye,
    With a hey, and a ho, and a hey nonino,
These pretty country folks would lie,
    In spring-time, the only pretty ring-time,
When birds do sing, hey ding a ding, ding!
    Sweet lovers love the spring.

This carol they began that hour,
    With a hey, and a ho, and a hey nonino,
How that a life was but a flower
    In spring-time, the only pretty ring-time,
When birds do sing, hey ding a ding, ding!
    Sweet lovers love the spring.

And therefore take the present time,
  With a hey, and a ho, and a hey nonino,
For love is crowned with the prime
  In spring-time, the only pretty ring-time,
When birds do sing, hey ding a ding, ding!
  Sweet lovers love the spring.

from AS YOU LIKE IT

Sigh No More

Sigh no more, ladies, sigh no more;
  Men were deceivers ever;
One foot in sea, and one on shore,
  To one thing constant never:
Then sigh not so, but let them go,
  And be you blithe and bonny,
Converting all your sounds of woe
  Into "Hey nonny, nonny!"

Sing no more ditties, sing no moe,
  Of dumps so dull and heavy;
The fraud of men was ever so,
  Since summer first was leavy:
Then sigh not so, but let them go,
  And be you blithe and bonny,
Converting all your sounds of woe
  Into "Hey nonny, nonny!"

from MUCH ADO ABOUT NOTHING

A Sea Dirge

Full fathom five thy father lies:
  Of his bones are coral made;
Those are pearls that were his eyes;
  Nothing of him that doth fade
But doth suffer a sea-change
Into something rich and strange.
Sea-nymphs hourly ring his knell:
  Hark! now I hear them—
    Ding, dong, bell.

from THE TEMPEST

Fancy

Tell me where is Fancy bred,
Or in the heart, or in the head?
How begot, how nourishèd?
    Reply, reply.

It is engendered in the eyes;
With gazing fed; and Fancy dies
In the cradle where it lies.
Let us all ring Fancy's knell.
I'll begin it:—Ding, dong, bell.
    —Ding, dong, bell.
from THE MERCHANT OF VENICE

Seals of Love

Take, O take those lips away
That so sweetly were forsworn,
And those eyes, the break of day,
Lights that do mislead the morn.
But my kisses bring again,
    Bring again—
Seals of love, but sealed in vain,
    Sealed in vain!
from MEASURE FOR MEASURE

Love's Despair

Come away, come away, death,
And in sad cypress let me be laid;
Fly away, fly away, breath;
I am slain by a fair cruel maid.
My shroud of white, stuck all with yew,
    O prepare it!
My part of death no one so true
    Did share it.

Not a flower, not a flower sweet
On my black coffin let there be strown;
Not a friend, not a friend greet
My poor corpse, where my bones shall be thrown;
A thousand thousand sighs to save,
Lay me, O where
Sad true lover never find my grave,
To weep there!

from TWELFTH NIGHT

A Merry Heart

Jog on, jog on, the footpath way,
And merrily hent [1] the stile-a;
A merry heart goes all the day,
Your sad tires in a mile-a.

from A WINTER'S TALE

Ophelia's Songs

1

How should I your true love know
From another one?
By his cockle hat and staff,
And his sandal shoon.

He is dead and gone, lady,
He is dead and gone;
At his head a grass-green turf,
At his heels a stone.

White his shroud as the mountain snow,
Larded with sweet flowers,
Which bewept to the grave did go
With true-love showers.

2

And will he not come again?
And will he not come again?
No, no, he is dead:
Go to thy death-bed:
He never will come again.

[1] *Grasp, surmount.*

His beard was as white as snow,
All flaxen was his poll:
  He is gone, he is gone,
  And we cast away moan;
God ha' mercy on his soul!
                    from HAMLET

Fear No More

Fear no more the heat o' the sun
  Nor the furious winter's rages;
Thou thy worldly task hast done,
  Home art gone and ta'en thy wages:
Golden lads and girls all must,
As chimney-sweepers, come to dust.

Fear no more the frown o' the great,
  Thou art past the tyrant's stroke;
Care no more to clothe and eat;
  To thee the reed is as the oak:
The sceptre, learning, physic, must
All follow this, and come to dust.

Fear no more the lightning-flash
  Nor the all-dreaded thunder-stone;
Fear not slander, censure rash;
  Thou hast finished joy and moan:
All lovers young, all lovers must
Consign to thee, and come to dust.

No exorciser harm thee!
Nor no witchcraft charm thee!
Ghost unlaid forbear thee!
Nothing ill come near thee!
Quiet consummation have;
And renowned be thy grave!
                    from CYMBELINE

VIII

Anatomy of the World

T HE Elizabethan era lifted itself above political struggles and religious wars. It took on amplitude and attained unprecedented vitality; it became a Golden Age of art and adventure because of its healthy passion for experiment, its lust for exploration, and its inherent flexibility. England adapted itself to rapid cultural changes; the country grew equally upon the strength of the southern Renaissance and the northern Reformation.

The English spirit was thus liberated for new concepts in literature and science as well as for a revival in statecraft and religion. Freedom and spontaneity were the characteristics of a period which, within a quarter century, produced such immortals as Drake, Raleigh, Shakespeare, Marlowe, Campion, Jonson, and Donne. Shakespeare was the central sun, but the Elizabethan heavens were crowded with brilliant lesser luminaries. John Addington Symonds wrote in his introduction to THE MERMAID SERIES:

In order to comprehend the English Renaissance, we must not be satisfied with studying only Shakespeare. We must learn to know his predecessors, contemporaries, and successors; that multitude of men inferior to him in stature, but of the same lineage; each of whom in greater or less degree was inspired with the like genius; each of whom possessed a clairvoyance into human nature and a power of presenting it vividly to the imagination which can be claimed by no similar group of fellow workers in the history of any literature known to us. What made the playwrights of that epoch so great as to deserve the phrase which Dryden found for them—"Theirs was the giant race before the flood"—

was that they lived and wrote in fullest sympathy with the whole people. The public to which they appealed was the English nation, from Elizabeth upon the throne down to the lowest ragamuffin of the streets.

The spirit of the times was unconsciously summed up by Donne in a long anniversary poem entitled AN ANATOMY OF THE WORLD:

> Well died the world, that we might live to see
> This world of wit, in his anatomy . . .

Donne used the word "wit" in its prime sense of understanding, of a superior degree of probing intelligence. The new influences, the new forms and philosophies, were simultaneously accepted and analyzed; that they were enthusiastically received did not prevent them from being endlessly dissected. Never had the world been so vigorously alive, and never had it been so scrupulously anatomized.

CHRISTOPHER MARLOWE
[1564–1593]

IT SEEMS impossible to write about Marlowe except in dramatic accents and headlong superlatives. Marlowe compels such treatment, for his life, setting a model for his style, was a burst of eloquence, a drama swiftly conceived and violently ended. Almost three hundred years after his death at the age of twenty-nine, he was hailed by Swinburne in terms that were extreme even for Swinburne:

> Crowned, girdled, garbed and shod with light and fire,
> Son first-born of the morning, sovereign star!

Marlowe's contemporaries were almost as enthusiastic. Shakespeare praised him unreservedly. Jonson spoke of his "mighty line." Drayton, in a phrase which any poet might envy having written or received in tribute, said that Marlowe had in him "brave translunary things."

Although Marlowe was a friend of some of the most cultured men of the times, he was anything but an aristocrat. His father was a shoemaker, his grandfather a tanner. Marlowe himself was born in Canterbury, February 6, 1564. At twenty he was graduated B.A. from Corpus Christi College, Cambridge, where he came under the influence of the mystic Francis Kett, later burnt for heresy. Whispers against Marlowe were heard even in his youth. Before he was twenty-three he went to London, where he thought himself free to express his unorthodox opinions. It is a pretty irony that, among Marlowe's companions, the lawless Robert Greene (see page 235) was loudest in his objections to the young poet's "atheism."

Marlowe's career has never been fully recorded or satisfactorily explicated. His unusual familiarity with military terms has led some commentators to believe that he may have followed Sidney as a soldier in the Low Countries. It has been conjectured, on even less evidence, that he was an actor. It is possible that he was secretly employed in devious and obscure political affairs. It is fairly certain that he was connected with at least two theatrical companies, and it is known that his four great plays—TAMBURLAINE THE GREAT, THE TRAGICAL HISTORY OF DOCTOR FAUSTUS, THE JEW OF MALTA, and EDWARD THE SECOND—were written within six years. He was arrested in 1588 on some mysterious charge. In 1593 he was again arrested, and the Privy Council were about to investigate the new and more serious charges when Marlowe was killed. Legends multiplied about the death. It was repeatedly maintained that Marlowe was slain in a brawl over a tavern wench. However, in an uncanny piece of research, THE DEATH OF CHRISTOPHER MARLOWE, Leslie Hotson recently established the fact that Marlowe fought with a drinking companion, one Ingram Frizer, about paying the bill. The quarrel grew ugly, and Frizer, having been attacked, stabbed Marlowe, who died instantly.

Although Marlowe was pre-eminently a dramatist, his name would have persisted had he never written a play. A reputation could rest on THE PASSIONATE SHEPHERD TO HIS LOVE, a flawless lyric and one of the most melodic love songs ever written. The poem established itself as a favorite even in its own day. It was so popular that it elicited many sequels and "replies." The best as well as the most reasonable rejoinder was Sir Walter Raleigh's THE NYMPH'S REPLY TO THE SHEPHERD, which appears on page 208.

The Passionate Shepherd to His Love

Come live with me and be my love,
And we will all the pleasures prove
That hills and valleys, dales and fields,
And all the craggy mountains yields.

And we will sit upon the rocks
Seeing the shepherds feed their flocks,
By shallow rivers, to whose falls
Melodious birds sing madrigals.

And I will make thee beds of roses
And a thousand fragrant posies,
A cap of flowers, and a kirtle
Embroidered all with leaves of myrtle;

A gown made of the finest wool,
Which from our pretty lambs we pull;
Fair linéd slippers for the cold,
With buckles of the purest gold;

A belt of straw and ivy buds
With coral clasps and amber studs:
And if these pleasures may thee move,
Come live with me and be my love.

The shepherd swains shall dance and sing
For thy delight each May morning:
If these delights thy mind may move,
Then live with me and be my love.

Marlowe's HERO AND LEANDER helped make a fashion of erotic poems founded on mythological themes. Like its successor, Shakespeare's VENUS AND ADONIS, Marlowe's long poem is a mixture of uninhibited sentiment and calculated set pieces. But a few of its lines have become household quotations, in particular Marlowe's characterization of first love.

FROM

Hero and Leander

It lies not in our power to love or hate,
For will in us is over-ruled by fate.
When two are stripped, long ere the course begin
We wish that one should lose, the other win;
And one especially do we affect
Of two gold ingots, like in each respect.
The reason no man knows; let it suffice,
What we behold is censured by our eyes.
Where both deliberate, the love is slight;
Who ever loved, that loved not at first sight?

Marlowe's powers of cumulative sonority and almost savage rhetoric are indicated in a line from TAMBURLAINE THE GREAT. The Persian captain Meander has just informed Tamburlaine:

> Your majesty shall shortly have your wish,
> And ride in triumph through Persepolis.

Whereupon the conquering invader, once a Scythian shepherd, is so struck with coming glory that he cannot relinquish either the thought or its expression. The phrase—pure Marlowe—is too rich to let go; he rolls the stately syllables over and over:

> "And ride in triumph through Persepolis!"
> Is it not brave to be a king, Techelles?
> Is it not passing brave to be a king
> "And ride in triumph through Persepolis?"

Marlowe lacks Shakespeare's humor, but he sometimes rivals the greater dramatist in intensity; his scenes, never as far-reaching or as integrated as Shakespeare's, are sustained by sheer exuberance and energy. When Marlowe rants, he surpasses mortal bombast; he uses Olympian thunder. He was the first to use English speech as though it were a great instrument. Havelock Ellis claims that Marlowe's "mighty line" is the chief creation of English literary art: "Shakespeare absorbed it and gave it out again with many broad

and lovely modifications. It has become the lifeblood of our litera-
ture; Marlowe's place is at the heart of English poetry, and his
pulses still thrill in our verse."

Nature That Framed Us of Four Elements

Nature that framed us of four elements,
Warring within our breasts for regiment,
Doth teach us all to have aspiring minds:
Our souls, whose faculties can comprehend
The wondrous architecture of the world,
And measure every wandering planet's course,
Still climbing after knowledge infinite,
And always moving as the restless spheres,
Will us to wear ourselves, and never rest,
Until we reach the ripest fruit of all,
That perfect bliss and sole felicity,
The sweet fruition of an earthly crown.
                    from TAMBURLAINE THE GREAT, Part I

Now Clear the Triple Region of the Air

Now clear the triple region of the air,
And let the majesty of Heaven behold
Their scourge and terror tread on emperors.
Smile stars, that reigned at my nativity,
And dim the brightness of your neighbor lamps!
Disdain to borrow light of Cynthia! [1]
For I, the chiefest lamp of all the earth,
First rising in the East with mild aspéct,
But fixéd now in the meridian line,
Will send up fire to your turning spheres,
And cause the sun to borrow light of you.
My sword struck fire from his coat of steel,
Even in Bithynia, when I took this Turk;
As when a fiery exhalation,
Wrapt in the bowels of a freezing cloud
Fighting for passage, makes the welkin crack,
And casts a flash of lightning to the earth:
But ere I march to wealthy Persia,
Or leave Damascus and the Egyptian fields.

[1] *The moon.*

As was the fame of Clymene's brain-sick son,
That almost brent [2] the axle-tree of Heaven,
So shall our swords, our lances, and our shot
Fill all the air with fiery meteors:
Then when the sky shall wax as red as blood
It shall be said I made it red myself,
To make me think of nought but blood and war.

from TAMBURLAINE THE GREAT, Part I

Emperor of the Threefold World

Now crouch, ye kings of greatest Asia,
And tremble when ye hear this scourge will come
That whips down cities and controlleth crowns,
Adding their wealth and treasure to my store.
The Euxine sea, north to Natolia;
The Terrene, west; the Caspian, north-north-east;
And on the south, Sinus Arabicus;
Shall all be loaden with the martial spoils
We will convey with us to Persia.
Then shall my native city, Samarcanda,
And crystal waters of fresh Jaertis' stream,
The pride and beauty of her princely seat,
Be famous through the furthest continents,
For there my palace-royal shall be placed,
Whose shining turrets shall dismay the heavens
And cast the fame of Ilion's tower to hell.
Thorough the streets with troops of conquered kings,
I'll ride in golden armor like the sun;
And in my helm a triple plume shall spring,
Spangled with diamonds, dancing in the air,
To note me emperor of the threefold world;
Like to an almond tree y-mounted high
Upon the lofty and celestial mount
Of ever green Selinus quaintly decked
With blooms more white than Erycina's brows,
Whose tender blossoms tremble every one,
At every little breath through heaven is blown.
Then in my coach, like Saturn's royal son
Mounted, his shining chariot gilt with fire
And drawn with princely eagles through the path
Paved with bright crystal and enchased with stars,

[2] *Burnt.*

When all the gods stand gazing at his pomp,
So will I ride through Samarcanda streets,
Until my soul, dissevered from this flesh,
Shall mount the milk-white way, and meet him there.
To Babylon, my lords; to Babylon!
                    from TAMBURLAINE THE GREAT, Part II

If Marlowe's plays sometimes fail to rise in action and fall into
a series of monologues, many of the soliloquies are among the most
eloquent in the language. TAMBURLAINE THE GREAT in a succession
of surprises halts its bluster to make one of the finest declarations
ever written in praise of beauty. Swinburne wrote of this passage:

> In the most glorious verses ever fashioned by a poet to express
> the supreme aim and the supreme limit of his art, Marlowe has
> summed up all that can be said or thought on the office and the
> object, the means and the end, of this highest form of spiritual
> ambition.

Beauty

If all the pens that ever poets held
Had fed the feeling of their masters' thoughts,
And every sweetness that inspired their hearts,
Their minds, and muses on admiréd themes;
If all the heavenly quintessence they still
From their immortal flowers of poesy,
Wherein, as in a mirror, we perceive
The highest reaches of a human wit;
If these had made one poem's period,
And all combined in beauty's worthiness,
Yet should there hover in their restless heads
One thought, one grace, one wonder, at the least,
Which into words no virtue can digest.
But how unseemly is it for my sex,
My discipline of arms and chivalry,
My nature and the terror of my name,
To harbor thoughts effeminate and faint!
Save only that in beauty's just applause,
With whose instinct the soul of man is touched;
And every warrior that is wrapt with love
Of fame, of valor, and of victory,
Must needs have beauty beat on his conceits:

> I thus conceiving and subduing both
> That which hath stooped the chiefest of the gods,
> Even from the fiery-spangled veil of Heaven,
> To feel the lowly warmth of shepherds' flames,
> And mask in cottages of strowéd reeds,
> Shall give the world to note for all my birth,
> That virtue solely is the sum of glory,
> And fashions men with true nobility.
>
> *from* TAMBURLAINE THE GREAT, Part I

The legend of the mortal who sells his soul to the devil antedates Marlowe by almost a thousand years. A crude version appeared in the sixth century; by 1500 the story had a well-defined shape, and its central figure a name, Faustus. Marlowe seems to have been the first to put the tale into dramatic form. His version became the accepted interpretation—so much so that Goethe followed Marlowe's lead and made the traditional doctor of magic a power-hungry, thought-ridden human being, obsessed by beauty and tortured with too much knowledge.

Two of the most famous passages from Marlowe's DOCTOR FAUSTUS are ageless in their contrasts of grandeur. In the first monologue ("Was this the face that launched a thousand ships") the vision of Helen is intensified in words and associations that create magic in the mind. In the second ("Ah, Faustus, Now hast thou but one bare hour to live") the note of doom is heightened by the tension of the staccato phrases, the breath of frantic agony, the sense of final horror. No passage in English surpasses it for sheer force.

Was This the Face

> Was this the face that launched a thousand ships,
> And burnt the topless towers of Ilium?
> Sweet Helen, make me immortal with a kiss
>   [*Kisses her.*
> Her lips suck forth my soul: see, where it flies!
> Come, Helen, come, give me my soul again!
> Here will I dwell, for heaven is in these lips,
> And all is dross that is not Helena.
> I will be Paris, and for love of thee,
> Instead of Troy, shall Wertenberg be sacked;
> And I will combat with weak Menelaus,

And wear thy colors on my pluméd crest;
Yea, I will wound Achilles in the heel,
And then return to Helen for a kiss.
O, thou art fairer than the evening air
Clad in the beauty of a thousand stars;
Brighter art thou than flaming Jupiter
When he appeared to hapless Semele;
More lovely than the monarch of the sky
In wanton Arethusa's azured arms;
And none but thou shalt be my paramour.
from THE TRAGICAL HISTORY OF DOCTOR FAUSTUS

The End of Faustus

Faustus.   Ah, Faustus,
Now hast thou but one bare hour to live,
And then thou must be damned perpetually!
Stand still, you ever-moving spheres of heaven,
That time may cease, and midnight never come;
Fair Nature's eye, rise, rise again, and make
Perpetual day; or let this hour be but
A year, a month, a week, a natural day,
That Faustus may repent and save his soul!
O lente, lente currite, noctis equi! [1]
The stars move still, time runs, the clock will strike,
The devil will come, and Faustus must be damned.
O, I'll leap up to my God! Who pulls me down?—
See, see, where Christ's blood streams in the firmament!
One drop would save my soul—half a drop: ah, my Christ!—
Ah, rend not my heart for naming of my Christ!
Yet will I call on him: O, spare me, Lucifer!—
Where is it now? 'Tis gone: and see, where God
Stretcheth out his arm, and bends his ireful brows!
Mountains and hills, come, come, and fall on me,
And hide me from the heavy wrath of God!
No! No!
Then will I headlong run into the earth:
Earth, gape! O, no, it will not harbor me!
You stars that reigned at my nativity,
Whose influence hath allotted death and hell,
Now draw up Faustus, like a foggy mist,
Into the entrails of yon laboring clouds,

[1] *"Oh, run slowly, slowly, horses of the night"—misquoted from Ovid.*

That, when they vomit forth into the air,
My limbs may issue from their smoky mouths,
So that my soul may but ascend to heaven!
                    [*The clock strikes the half-hour.*
Ah, half the hour is past! 'twill all be past anon.
O God,
If thou wilt not have mercy on my soul,
Yet for Christ's sake, whose blood hath ransomed me,
Impose some end to my incessant pain;
Let Faustus live in hell a thousand years—
A hundred thousand, and at last be saved!
O, no end is limited to damnéd souls!
Why wert thou not a creature wanting soul?
Or why is this immortal that thou hast?
Ah, Pythagoras' metempsychosis! were that true,
This soul should fly from me, and I be changed
Unto some brutish beast! All beasts are happy,
For, when they die,
Their souls are soon dissolved in elements;
But mine must live still to be plagued in hell.
Cursed be the parents that engendered me!—
No, Faustus, curse thyself, curse Lucifer
That hath deprived thee of the joys of heaven.
                    [*The clock strikes twelve.*
O, it strikes, it strikes! Now, body, turn to air,
Or Lucifer will bear thee quick to hell!
O soul, be changed into little water-drops,
And fall into the ocean, ne'er be found!

Enter DEVILS.

My God! my God! look not so fierce on me!
Adders and serpents, let me breathe a while!
Ugly hell, gape not! come not, Lucifer!
I'll burn my books!—Ah, Mephistophilis!
                    [*Exeunt* DEVILS *with* FAUSTUS.

Enter CHORUS.

Chorus. Cut is the branch that might have grown full
    straight,
And burnéd is Apollo's laurel bough,
That sometime grew within this learned man.
Faustus is gone: regard his hellish fall,
Whose fiendful fortune may exhort the wise,

Only to wonder at unlawful things,
Whose deepness doth entice such forward wits
To practice more than heavenly power permits.
Terminat hora diem; terminat auctor opus.[1]
from THE TRAGICAL HISTORY OF DOCTOR FAUSTUS

THOMAS NASHE
[1567–1601]

IT MAY seem strange that the sheltered son of a curate became a
blunt satirist, a writer of frank burlesques and racy adventures
which have made many readers think of Rabelais. But Nashe was
one of the anatomists of his day, a critical spirit in revolt against
the conventions of his predecessors. He attended St. John's College,
Cambridge, as a sizar, a student of limited means whose expenses
are partly defrayed by the college, and he learned to distrust the
patricians as well as the Puritans. It was inevitable that he should
turn against the "sugared romances" of Lodge and Lyly; as soon as
he was graduated he came to London and joined the warring pam-
phleteers.

Using the material of everyday life, Nashe alternately wrote pam-
phlets and picaresque tales; THE LIFE OF JACK WILTON is said to have
anticipated Defoe's MOLL FLANDERS in its sharply realistic manner.
Nashe's poetry is seldom as racy as his prose, but it does not fail to
take account of the contemporary scene. Even his idyls reflect the
London of hasty pleasures against a background of plague and
pestilence. That background is intensified by lines of pure en-
chantment:

> Beauty is but a flower
> Which wrinkles will devour;
> Brightness falls from the air;
> Queens have died young and fair;
> Dust hath closed Helen's eye.

No poet has ever expressed the mutations of time and the eternal
fragility of beauty with such simple finality.

[1] *The hour ends the day; the author ends his work.*

In a Time of Pestilence

Adieu, farewell earth's bliss.
This world uncertain is;
Fond are life's lustful joys,
Death proves them all but toys.
None from his darts can fly;
I am sick, I must die.
      Lord, have mercy on us!

Rich men, trust not in wealth,
Gold cannot buy your health;
Physic himself must fade;
All things to end are made;
The plague full swift goes by.
I am sick, I must die.
      Lord, have mercy on us!

Beauty is but a flower
Which wrinkles will devour;
Brightness falls from the air;
Queens have died young and fair;
Dust hath closed Helen's eye.
I am sick, I must die.
      Lord, have mercy on us!

Strength stoops unto the grave,
Worms feed on Hector brave;
Swords may not fight with fate;
Earth still holds ope her gate;
Come, come! the bells do cry.
I am sick, I must die.
      Lord, have mercy on us!

Wit with his wantonness
Tasteth death's bitterness;
Hell's executioner
Hath no ears for to hear
What vain art can reply.
I am sick, I must die.
      Lord, have mercy on us!

Haste therefore each degree
To welcome destiny;
Heaven is our heritage,
Earth but a player's stage.
Mount we unto the sky.
I am sick, I must die.
          Lord, have mercy on us!

Autumn

Autumn hath all the summer's fruitful treasure;
Gone is our sport, fled is our Croydon's pleasure.
Short days, sharp days, long nights come on apace;
Ah, who shall hide us from the winter's face?
Cold doth increase, the sickness will not cease,
And here we lie, God knows, with little ease.
    From winter, plague, and pestilence, good Lord, deliver us!

London doth mourn, Lambeth is quite forlorn.
Trades cry, woe worth that ever they were born!
The want of term is town and city's harm;
Close chambers we do want to keep us warm.
Long banished must we live from all our friends;
This low-built house will bring us to our ends.
    From winter, plague, and pestilence, good Lord, deliver us!

Spring

Spring, the sweet Spring, is the year's pleasant king;
Then blooms each thing, then maids dance in a ring,
Cold doth not sting, the pretty birds do sing,
    Cuckoo, jug-jug, pu-we, to-witta-woo!

The palm and may make country houses gay,
Lambs frisk and play, the shepherds pipe all day,
And we hear aye birds tune this merry lay,
    Cuckoo, jug-jug, pu-we, to-witta-woo!

The fields breathe sweet, the daisies kiss our feet,
Young lovers meet, old wives a-sunning sit,
In every street these tunes our ears do greet,
    Cuckoo, jug-jug, pu-we, to-witta-woo!
          Spring! the sweet Spring!

THOMAS CAMPION
[1567?–1619]

ALTHOUGH Thomas Campion was one of the most prolific of Elizabethan song writers, surprisingly little is known of him. He apparently studied law but was not called to the bar. He also seems to have taken a degree in medicine, for he is referred to as a "doctor in phisicke."

But it was as a poet-musician that Campion began and ended the career by which he is known. In his early thirties he collaborated with a fellow musician, Philip Rosseter, in the publication of A BOOK OF AIRS; Campion wrote all the lyrics and the musical settings for the first half. He was immediately successful, liberally praised by his fellows, and widely patronized by the public. Yet Campion continued to devote himself to medicine, never yielding himself completely to the Muse. Even in his FOURTH BOOK OF AIRS Campion wrote modestly, "The apothecaries have Books of Gold, whose leaves, being opened, are so light that they are subject to be shaken with the least breath; yet, rightly handled, they serve both for ornament and use." Campion's airs were as "useful" as they were ornamental; many of the favorite songs of the day were his, and no one can say how many of the anonymous lyrics in the anthologies are from his pen.

A vogue in his day, Campion was strangely forgotten until the end of the nineteenth century when A. H. Bullen, that sensitive and scholarly researcher, established Campion's extraordinary variety. It is now apparent that Campion was not only one of the lightest but one of the most dexterous of Elizabethan lyrists. A trained musician's knowledge of music made his lines unusually flexible and delicate, and a true poet's sensibility gave them substance. His changing rhythms, his nimble rhymes, and his unrhymed lyrics (such as ROSE-CHEEKED LAURA) are rewarding studies for the technician and a set of increasing pleasures for readers who have not the slightest interest in technique.

My Life's Delight

Come, O come, my life's delight,
  Let me not in languor pine!
Love loves no delay; thy sight,
  The more enjoyed, the more divine:
O come, and take from me
The pain of being deprived of thee!

Thou all sweetness dost enclose,
  Like a little world of bliss.
Beauty guards thy looks: the rose
  In them pure and eternal is.
Come, then, and make thy flight
As swift to me, as heavenly light.

Kind Are Her Answers

Kind are her answers,
But her performance keeps no day;
Breaks time, as dancers
From their own music when they stray:
All her free favors
And smooth words wing my hopes in vain.
O did ever voice so sweet but only feign?
Can true love yield such delay,
Converting joy to pain?

Lost is our freedom,
When we submit to women so:
Why do we need 'em,
When in their best they work our woe?
There is no wisdom
Can alter ends, by Fate prefixed.
O why is the good of man with evil mixed?
Never were days yet called two,
But one night went betwixt.

There Is a Garden in Her Face

There is a garden in her face,
Where roses and white lilies grow;
  A heav'nly paradise is that place,
Wherein all pleasant fruits do flow.
    There cherries grow which none may buy
    Till "cherry-ripe" [1] themselves do cry.

Those cherries fairly do enclose
Of orient pearls a double row,
  Which when her lovely laughter shows,
They look like rosebuds filled with snow.
    Yet them nor peer nor prince can buy,
    Till "cherry-ripe" themselves do cry.

Her eyes like angels watch them still;
Her brows like bended bows do stand,
  Threat'ning with piercing frowns to kill
All that attempt with eye or hand
    Those sacred cherries to come nigh,
    Till "cherry-ripe" themselves do cry.

Rose-Cheeked Laura

Rose-cheeked Laura, come,
Sing thou smoothly with thy beauty's
Silent music, either other
    Sweetly gracing.

Lovely forms do flow
From concent [2] divinely framèd;
Heaven is music, and thy beauty's
    Birth is heavenly.

These dull notes we sing
Discords need for helps to grace them;
Only beauty purely loving
    Knows no discord,

[1] *A street-cry of the London vendors.*   [2] *Harmony; concord of sounds.*

But still moves delight,
Like clear springs renewed by flowing,
Ever perfect, ever in them-
    Selves eternal.

Corinna

When to her lute Corinna sings,
Her voice revives the leaden strings
And doth in highest notes appear
As any challenged echo clear;
But when she doth of mourning speak,
Even with her sighs the strings do break.

And as her lute doth live or die,
Led by her passion, so must I.
For when of pleasure she doth sing,
My thoughts enjoy a sudden spring;
But if she doth of sorrow speak,
Even from my heart the strings do break.

Beauty Is Not Bound

Give beauty all her right!
She's not to one form tied;
Each shape yields fair delight
Where her perfections bide:
Helen, I grant, might pleasing be,
And Rosamond was as sweet as she.

Some the quick eye commends,
Some swelling lips and red;
Pale looks have many friends,
Through sacred sweetness bred:
Meadows have flowers that pleasures move,
Though roses are the flowers of love.

Free beauty is not bound
To one unmovèd clime;
She visits every ground
And favors every time.
Let the old loves with mine compare;
My sovereign is as sweet and fair.

Follow Your Saint

Follow your saint, follow with accents sweet!
Haste you, sad notes, fall at her flying feet!
There, wrapped in clouds of sorrow, pity move,
And tell the ravisher of my soul I perish for her love.
But, if she scorns my never-ceasing pain,
Then burst with sighing in her sight, and ne'er return again.

All that I sang still to her praise did tend,
Still she was first, still she my songs did end;
Yet she my love and music both doth fly,
The music that her echo is and beauty's sympathy.
Then let my notes pursue her scornful flight!
It shall suffice that they were breathed, and died for her delight.

Never Love Unless

Never love unless you can
Bear with all the faults of man:
Men sometimes will jealous be
Though but little cause they see;
And hang the head, as discontent,
And speak what straight they will repent.

Men that but one saint adore
Make a show of love to more.
Beauty must be scorned in none,
Though but truly served in one:
For what is courtship but disguise?
True hearts may have dissembling eyes.

Men, when their affairs require,
Must awhile themselves retire;
Sometimes hunt, and sometimes hawk,
And not ever sit and talk.
If these and such-like you can bear,
Then like, and love, and never fear!

Sleep, Angry Beauty

Sleep, angry beauty, sleep, and fear not me.
For who a sleeping lion dares provoke?
It shall suffice me here to sit and see
Those lips shut up, that never kindly spoke.
What sight can more content a lover's mind
Than beauty seeming harmless, if not kind?

My words have charmed her, for secure she sleeps;
Though guilty much of wrong done to my love;
And in her slumber, see! she, close-eyed, weeps!
Dreams often more than waking passions move.
Plead, Sleep, my cause, and make her soft like thee,
That she in peace may wake and pity me.

Tell, O Tell

When thou must home to shades of underground,
And there arrived, a new admired guest,
The beauteous spirits do engirt thee round,
White Iope, blithe Helen and the rest,
To hear the stories of thy finished love
From that smooth tongue whose music hell can move;
Then wilt thou speak of banqueting delights,
Of masques and revels which sweet youth did make,
Of tourneys and great challenges of knights,
And all these triumphs for thy beauty's sake.
When thou hast told these honors done to thee,
Then tell, O tell, how thou didst murder me.

Campion's subtle cadences are not always complex. Frequently
they are as direct and simple as the lines beginning "My sweetest
Lesbia, let us live and love," which is a free paraphrase of Catullus'
"*Vivamus, mea Lesbia, atque amemus,*" and which, in Campion's
musical rendering, has become an English classic.

My Sweetest Lesbia

My sweetest Lesbia, let us live and love;
And though the sager sort our deeds reprove,
Let us not weigh them. Heaven's great lamps do dive
Into their west, and straight again revive;
But, soon as once set is our little light,
Then must we sleep one ever-during night.

If all would lead their lives in love like me,
Then bloody swords and armor should not be;
No drum nor trumpet peaceful sleeps should move,
Unless alarm came from the camp of love.
But fools do live and waste their little light,
And seek with pain their ever-during night.

When timely death my life and fortunes ends,
Let not my hearse be vexed with mourning friends;
But let all lovers rich in triumph come,
And with sweet pastime grace my happy tomb.
And, Lesbia, close up thou my little light,
And crown with love my ever-during night.

SIR HENRY WOTTON
[1568–1639]

Born in Kent in 1568 and educated at Oxford, Henry Wotton came from a family of diplomats. He followed the family tradition; at twenty-one he went abroad to prepare himself for a career of travel and intrigue. Before he was thirty he had become secretary to some of the mightiest men in England; he was equally successful as secret agent and unofficial ambassador. He warned James VI of Scotland of a plot to poison him, was knighted, and was offered various embassies. One of Wotton's indiscreet epigrams was quoted against him: "An ambassador is an honest man sent to lie abroad for the good of his country." But Wotton survived attacks. He had not tied himself "unto the world with care of public fame";

he understood the difference between "rules of state" and "rules of good." He said it all in his famous epigrammatic CHARACTER OF A HAPPY LIFE.

Character of a Happy Life

How happy is he born and taught
    That serveth not another's will;
Whose armor is his honest thought,
    And simple truth his utmost skill!

Whose passions not his masters are,
    Whose soul is still prepared for death,
Not tied unto the world with care
    Of public fame or private breath;

Who envies none that chance doth raise,
    Or vice; who never understood
How deepest wounds are given by praise;
    Nor rules of state, but rules of good;

Who hath his life from rumors freed,
    Whose conscience is his strong retreat;
Whose state can neither flatterers feed,
    Nor ruin make oppressors great;

Who God doth late and early pray
    More of his grace than gifts to lend;
And entertains the harmless day
    With a well-chosen book or friend;

This man is freed from servile bands
    Of hope to rise, or fear to fall;
Lord of himself, though not of lands;
    And having nothing, yet hath all.

As an author Wotton was extremely reserved and self-critical. RELIQUIÆ WOTTONIANÆ, which appeared twelve years after his death, contains only twenty-five poems, and it is doubtful whether more than fifteen of these are actually Wotton's. Of the undisputed authentic verses, none is more touching than the lines ON HIS MISTRESS, THE QUEEN OF BOHEMIA. Wotton had been sent to Vienna to intercede for James' daughter Elizabeth and her husband Frederick, Elector Palatine. He could do little for Frederick, who was driven out of his newly acquired kingdom of Bohemia; but he was of great service to Elizabeth, who won not only his admiration but his devotion. Wotton's poem in praise of her—"th' eclipse and glory of her kind"—was continually quoted, paraphrased, and imitated.

On His Mistress, the Queen of Bohemia

You meaner beauties of the night,
    That poorly satisfy our eyes
More by your number than your light,
    You common people of the skies—
    What are you when the sun shall rise?

You curious chanters of the wood
    That warble forth dame nature's lays,
Thinking your voices understood
    By your weak accents, what's your praise
    When Philomel her voice shall raise?

You violets that first appear,
    By your pure purple mantles known
Like the proud virgins of the year,
    As if the spring were all your own—
    What are you when the rose is blown?

So, when my mistress shall be seen
    In form and beauty of her mind,
By virtue first, then choice, a queen,
    Tell me if she were not designed
    Th' eclipse and glory of her kind?

Wotton's shortest poem is perhaps his most moving. His nephew Sir Albert Morton, a poet and Wotton's secretary at Venice, died after having been married less than a year; his wife died shortly after. Wotton's two obituary lines have outlived thousands of longer elegies.

On the Death of Sir Albert Morton's Wife

He first deceased—she, for a little, tried
To live without him, liked it not, and died.

JOHN DAVIES
[1569–1626]

JOHN DAVIES was eminent in several roles and just missed great-
ness in whatever he undertook. Educated at Oxford, a lawyer in
his twenties, disbarred in his thirties, he turned to writing poetry.
Restored to the bar and thence to the King's Bench, he upheld the
legality of the "loans" forced by Charles I. For this he was well
rewarded. After years of shrewd manipulation, he was appointed
Lord Chief Justice. He celebrated the appointment too lavishly at
a large dinner party and, before he could assume office, was stricken
with apoplexy and died.

As a poet Davies has suffered from the whims of fashion. His
"major" works have become a minor interest of literary historians.
NOSCE TEIPSUM, a long philosophical poem on the nature of man
and the immortality of the soul, was praised by Coleridge; it is
barely readable today. ORCHESTRA, an inflated imitation of Spenser,
is an extended apostrophe to dancing; the best that this almost
eight-hundred-line poem deserves has been said by Hoyt Hudson
and J. William Hebel in POETRY OF THE ENGLISH RENAISSANCE: "It
is not wholly lacking in grace and music consonant with its sub-
ject."

But there is another side to Davies, a side that is both tender and
teasing. This aspect is observed in his "gulling sonnets," in which
Davies parodies the sonneteers' artificial conventions, and in HYMNS
TO ASTRÆA. Astræa was Queen Elizabeth, and the "hymns" were—of
all forms—a set of acrostics. In these ingenious verses Davies lifted
himself above cleverness and turned a rhymer's trick into a lasting
tribute.

To the Nightingale

E very night from eve till morn,
L ove's chorister amid the thorn
I s now so sweet a singer;
S o sweet, as for her song I scorn
A pollo's voice and finger.

B ut nightingale, since you delight
E ver to watch the starry night,
T ell all the stars of heaven,
H eaven never had a star so bright,
A s now to earth is given.

R oyal Astræa makes our day
E ternal with her beams, nor may
G ross darkness overcome her.
I now perceive why some do write,
N o country hath so short a night,
A s England hath in summer.

Of Astræa

E arly before the day doth spring
L et us awake, my Muse, and sing,
I t is no time to slumber;
S o many joys this time doth bring
A s time will fail to number.

B ut whereto shall we bend our lays?
E ven up to heaven, again to raise
T he maid which, thence descended,
H ath brought again the golden days
A nd all the world amended.

R udeness itself she doth refine,
E 'en like an alchemist divine,
G ross times of iron turning
I nto the purest form of gold,
N ot to corrupt till heaven wax old,
A nd be refined with burning.

THOMAS DEKKER
[1570?–1632]

NOTHING could crush the happy spirit of Thomas Dekker, born in want, reared in poverty. He spent much of his time in prison without becoming morose, self-pitying, or bitter. On the contrary, his surroundings filled him with an understanding of the poor, and a sympathy with the oppressed—even with dumb animals —shines out of his work. Instead of attempting to escape the difficult world of reality, Dekker turned to it with love, even with liveliness, as in THE SHOEMAKER'S HOLIDAY. He knew London as intimately as Dickens, and with the same combination of humor and sentiment. His affability made him a born collaborator; he wrote plays with Drayton, Jonson, Ford, Middleton, and Massinger. His pamphlets were deservedly famous; one of them, THE WONDERFUL YEAR 1603, is a remarkably graphic description of London during the plague.

The first two frolicsome songs are from THE SHOEMAKER'S HOLIDAY; they synthesize the spirit of that buoyant comedy. The other three poems are from the tenderer PATIENT GRISSILL and are as gravely haunting in phrase as they are persuasive in melody.

Drinking Song

Cold's the wind, and wet's the rain,
    Saint Hugh be our good speed!
Ill is the weather that bringeth no gain,
    Nor helps good hearts in need.

Troll the bowl, the jolly nut-brown bowl,
    And here, kind mate, to thee!
Let's sing a dirge for Saint Hugh's soul,
    And down it merrily.

Down-a-down, hey, down-a-down,
    Hey derry derry down-a-down!
Ho! well done, to me let come,
    Ring compass,[1] gentle joy!

1 *Complete the circle, i.e., pass the bowl around.*

Maytime

O! the month of May, the merry month of May,
  So frolic, so gay, and so green, so green, so green!
O! and then did I unto my true love say,
  Sweet Peg, thou shalt be my summer's queen.

Now the nightingale, the pretty nightingale,
  The sweetest singer in all the forest's choir,
Entreats thee, sweet Peggy, to hear thy true love's tale:
  Lo! yonder she sitteth, her breast against a briar.

But O! I spy the cuckoo, the cuckoo, the cuckoo;
  See where she sitteth; come away, my joy.
Come away, I prithee, I do not like the cuckoo
  Should sing where my Peggy and I kiss and toy.

O! the month of May, the merry month of May,
  So frolic, so gay, and so green, so green, so green!
And then did I unto my true love say,
  Sweet Peg, thou shalt be my summer's queen.

Bridal Song

Beauty, arise, show forth thy glorious shining!
Thine eyes feed love, for them he standeth pining;
Honor and youth attend to do their duty
To thee, their only sovereign, Beauty.
Beauty, arise, whilst we, thy servants, sing
Io to Hymen, wedlock's jocund king.
  Io to Hymen, Io, Io, sing,
  Of wedlock, love, and youth is Hymen king.

Basket Maker's Song

Art thou poor, yet hast thou golden slumbers?
      O sweet content!
Art thou rich, yet is thy mind perplexed?
      O punishment!
Dost thou laugh to see how fools are vexed
To add to golden numbers, golden numbers?

O sweet content! O sweet, O sweet content!
  Work apace, apace, apace, apace;
  Honest labor bears a lovely face;
Then hey nonny nonny, hey nonny nonny!

Canst drink the waters of the crisped spring?
            O sweet content!
Swimm'st thou in wealth, yet sink'st in thine own tears?
            O punishment!
Then he that patiently want's burden bears
No burden bears, but is a king, a king!
O sweet content! O sweet, O sweet content!
  Work apace, apace, apace, apace;
  Honest labor bears a lovely face;
Then hey nonny nonny, hey nonny nonny!

Cradle Song

Golden slumbers kiss your eyes;
Smiles awake you when you rise.
Sleep, pretty wantons, do not cry,
And I will sing a lullaby:
Rock them, rock them, lullaby.

Care is heavy, therefore sleep you;
You are care, and care must keep you.
Sleep, pretty wantons, do not cry,
And I will sing a lullaby:
Rock them, rock them, lullaby.

BEN JONSON
[1573–1637]

BEN JONSON's accomplishments were so varied and paradoxical that
he seems to have been a congregation of authors, a school of
playwrights, rather than one man. His father, at one time a minister,
had suffered many reverses, and the boy, born a month after his
father's death, was brought up by his stepfather, a master brick-

layer. Following his stepfather's trade after a common-school education, Jonson became the model of the self-taught scholar; it is said that he went to Cambridge, but there is no record of his attendance at any university. In his early twenties he served as a soldier in the Netherlands; upon his return to England he joined a theatrical company as an actor, then as a director, then as a playwright. Before Jonson was thirty the critic Meres had referred to him as "one of the best for tragedy."

The early reference to Jonson's excellence as a writer of tragedies is strange, for Jonson began his dramatic career with a comedy, EVERY MAN IN HIS HUMOR. It is fairly well established that Shakespeare acted in the play; it is even conjectured that the portrait of Shakespeare in the 1623 folio displays him in the part of Old Knowell. A close intimacy sprang up between the two men; the son of the country glover and the bricklayer's stepchild formed a companionship which rose above every difference, above Jonson's outspoken criticism and a more or less constant rivalry. (One of the best, though wholly speculative, accounts of the relation between the two dramatists is detailed in Edwin Arlington Robinson's poem BEN JONSON ENTERTAINS A MAN FROM STRATFORD.) Shakespeare and Jonson drew a great company of friends about them; the circle usually met at the Mermaid Tavern, which boasted of entertaining "the tribe of Ben." Beaumont, in his contemporary tribute to Jonson, celebrated the place:

> . . . What things have we seen
> Done at the Mermaid! Heard words that have been
> So nimble, and so full of subtle flame,
> As if that every one from whence they came
> Had meant to put his whole life in a jest.

More than two centuries later Keats apostrophized the convivial gathering:

> Souls of poets dead and gone,
> What Elysium have ye known,
> Happy field or mossy cavern,
> Choicer than the Mermaid Tavern?

Jonson's great vitality won him extremes of praise and censure. Those who admired him claimed he was nobly impulsive; his detractors declared he was merely wayward and wholly undependable.

Jonson married before he was twenty, but left his wife for long periods. He fought with an actor, killed him, was sentenced to prison, and escaped the gallows only by pleading self-defense. In his twenty-sixth year he was converted to the Church of Rome; later in life he returned to the Church of England.

He lived expansively and wrote voluminously. He was patronized by three monarchs: Elizabeth enjoyed his comedies; James I encouraged him to leave tragedy for the popular and more profitable masques; Charles I made him poet laureate—an office founded upon letters patent, with a gratifying salary and (probably in deference to Jonson's tastes) an annual cask of wine. In spite of his industry and the royal pensions, Jonson was never affluent nor at ease. It is likely that he did not care about security; he preferred to rollick through life. He was lusty even in his sixties; when death came to him on April 6, 1637, he was furiously engaged on a work of unusual power and beauty. He was buried in Westminster Abbey, and his grave is marked with that terse but illuminating epitaph: "O rare Ben Jonson."

Two of Jonson's finest tributes are to widely differing personalities. The first is to Shakespeare, "sweet swan of Avon . . . The applause, delight, the wonder of our stage!"—a particularly generous gesture when it is recalled that Shakespeare's plays were competing with Jonson's and notably outshining them. The second was written upon the death of a thirteen-year-old child, a boy-musician of Queen Elizabeth's chapel and an actor in Jonson's company.

To the Memory of My Beloved Master William Shakespeare

To draw no envy, Shakespeare, on thy name,
Am I thus ample to thy book and fame;
While I confess thy writings to be such
As neither man nor Muse can praise too much.
'Tis true, and all men's suffrage. But these ways
Were not the paths I meant unto thy praise;
For silliest ignorance on these may light,
Which, when it sounds at best, but echoes right;
Or blind affection, which doth ne'er advance
The truth, but gropes, and urgeth all by chance;
Or crafty malice might pretend this praise,

And think to ruin, where it seemed to raise.
These are, as some infamous bawd or whore
Should praise a matron. What could hurt her more?
But thou art proof against them, and, indeed,
Above the ill fortune of them, or the need.
I therefore will begin. Soul of the age!
The applause, delight, the wonder of our stage!
My Shakespeare, rise! I will not lodge thee by
Chaucer, or Spenser, or bid Beaumont lie
A little further, to make thee a room;
Thou art a monument without a tomb,
And art alive still while thy book doth live
And we have wits to read and praise to give.
That I not mix thee so, my brain excuses,
I mean with great, but disproportioned Muses;
For if I thought my judgment were of years,
I should commit thee surely with thy peers,
And tell how far thou didst our Lyly outshine,
Or sporting Kyd, or Marlowe's mighty line.
And though thou hadst small Latin and less Greek,
From thence to honor thee, I would not seek
For names; but call forth thundering Aeschylus,
Euripides, and Sophocles to us;
Pacuvius, Accius, him of Cordova dead,
To life again, to hear thy buskin tread,
And shake a stage; or, when thy socks were on,
Leave thee alone for the comparison
Of all that insolent Greece or haughty Rome
Sent forth, or since did from their ashes come.
Triumph, my Britain, thou hast one to show
To whom all scenes of Europe homage owe.
He was not of an age, but for all time!
And all the Muses still were in their prime,
When, like Apollo, he came forth to warm
Our ears, or like a Mercury to charm!
Nature herself was proud of his designs
And joyed to wear the dressing of his lines!
Which were so richly spun, and woven so fit,
As, since, she will vouchsafe no other wit.
The merry Greek, tart Aristophanes,
Neat Terence, witty Plautus, now not please,
But antiquated and deserted lie,
As they were not of Nature's family.
Yet must I not give Nature all; thy art,
My gentle Shakespeare, must enjoy a part.

For though the poet's matter Nature be,
His art doth give the fashion; and, that he
Who casts to write a living line, must sweat
(Such as thine are) and strike the second heat
Upon the Muses' anvil; turn the same
(And himself with it) that he thinks to frame,
Or, for the laurel, he may gain a scorn;
For a good poet's made, as well as born.
And such wert thou! Look how the father's face
Lives in his issue; even so the race
Of Shakespeare's mind and manners brightly shines
In his well turned, and true filed lines;
In each of which he seems to shake a lance,
As brandished at the eyes of ignorance.
Sweet Swan of Avon! what a sight it were
To see thee in our waters yet appear,
And make those flights upon the banks of Thames,
That so did take Eliza, and our James!
But stay, I see thee in the hemisphere
Advanced, and made a constellation there!
Shine forth, thou star of poets, and with rage
Or influence, chide or cheer the drooping stage,
Which, since thy flight from hence, hath mourned like night
And despairs day, but for thy volume's light.

An Epitaph on Salathiel Pavy

Weep with me, all you that read
    This little story:
And know, for whom a tear you shed
    Death's self is sorry.
'Twas a child that so did thrive
    In grace and feature,
As Heaven and Nature seem'd to strive
    Which own'd the creature.
Years he number'd scarce thirteen
    When Fates turn'd cruel,
Yet three fill'd zodiacs had he been
    The stage's jewel;
And did act, what now we moan,
    Old men so duly,
As, sooth, the Parcae thought him one,
    He play'd so truly.

So, by error, to his fate
       They all consented;
But viewing him since, alas, too late!
       They have repented;
And have sought, to give new birth,
       In baths to steep him;
But being so much too good for Earth,
       Heaven vows to keep him.

No poem of Jonson's is as famous as the lines TO CELIA; the tune comes to mind with the unforgettable opening phrase: "Drink to me only with thine eyes." But many of the less-known lyrics are equally exquisite. Readers are continually discovering the limpid grace and quiet pathos of the songs in Jonson's masques and plays. In a letter to a friend, dated November 15, 1913, "somewhere near Fiji," Rupert Brooke wrote: "Kindly turn up Jonson's NEW INN (which is sheer Meredith) and read Lovel's Song in Act IV. The second verse will dispel the impression of the first, that it is by Robert Browning. The whole thing is pure beauty."

Lovel's Song

It was a beauty that I saw
       So pure, so perfect, as the frame
       Of all the universe was lame,
To that one figure, could I draw,
Or give least line of it a law!

A skein of silk without a knot.
       A fair march made without a halt.
       A curious form without a fault.
A printed book without a blot.
All beauty, and without a spot!
                    from THE NEW INN

To Celia

Drink to me only with thine eyes,
       And I will pledge with mine;
Or leave a kiss but in the cup
       And I'll not look for wine.

The thirst that from the soul doth rise
   Doth ask a drink divine;
But might I of Jove's nectar sup,
   I would not change for thine.

I sent thee late a rosy wreath,
   Not so much honoring thee
As giving it a hope that there
   It could not withered be;
But thou thereon didst only breathe
   And sent'st it back to me;
Since when it grows, and smells, I swear,
   Not of itself but thee!

Echo's Song

Slow, slow, fresh fount, keep time with my salt tears;
   Yet slower, yet; O faintly, gentle springs;
List to the heavy part the music bears,
   Woe weeps out her division when she sings.
      Droop, herbs and flowers;
      Fall, grief, in showers,
      Our beauties are not ours;
         O, I could still,
Like melting snow upon some craggy hill,
   Drop, drop, drop, drop,
Since nature's pride is now a withered daffodil.
                              from CYNTHIA'S REVELS

Hymn to Diana

Queen and huntress, chaste and fair,
   Now the sun is laid to sleep,
Seated in thy silver chair
   State in wonted manner keep:
      Hesperus entreats thy light,
      Goddess excellently bright.

Earth, let not thy envious shade
   Dare itself to interpose;
Cynthia's shining orb was made
   Heaven to clear when day did close:
      Bless us then with wished sight,
      Goddess excellently bright.

Lay thy bow of pearl apart
  And thy crystal-shining quiver;
Give unto the flying hart
  Space to breathe, how short soever:
    Thou that makest a day of night,
    Goddess excellently bright.
      from CYNTHIA'S REVELS

Clerimont's Song

Still to be neat, still to be drest
As you were going to a feast:
Still to be powdered, still perfumed:
Lady, it is to be presumed,
Though art's hid causes are not found,
All is not sweet, all is not sound.

Give me a look, give me a face
That makes simplicity a grace;
Robes loosely flowing, hair as free:
Such sweet neglect more taketh me,
Than all the adulteries of art,
That strike mine eyes, but not my heart.
    from THE SILENT WOMAN

Nano's Song

Fools, they are the only nation
Worth men's envy or admiration;
Free from care or sorrow-taking,
Selves and others merry making:
All they speak or do is sterling.
Your fool, he is your great man's darling,
And your ladies' sport and pleasure;
Tongue and bauble are his treasure.
Ev'n his face begetteth laughter,
And he speaks truth free from slaughter.
He's the grace of every feast,
And sometimes the chiefest guest;
Hath his trencher and his stool,
When wit waits upon the fool.
  O, who would not be
    He, he, he?
      from VOLPONE

Oak and Lily

It is not growing like a tree
In bulk, doth make man better be;
Or standing long an oak, three hundred year,
To fall a log at last, dry, bald, and sere:
    A lily of a day
    Is fairer far in May,
Although it fall and die that night;
It was the plant and flower of light.
In small proportions we just beauties see;
And in short measures life may perfect be.
from UNDERWOODS

So White, So Soft, So Sweet

Have you seen but a bright lily grow
    Before rude hands have touched it?
Have you marked but the fall of the snow
    Before the soil hath smutched it?
Have you felt the wool of the beaver,
    Or swan's down ever?
Or have smelt o' the bud of the brier,
    Or the nard [1] in the fire?
Or have tasted the bag of the bee?
O so white, O so soft, O so sweet is she!
from THE DEVIL IS AN ASS

Jonson's large nature matched his robust frame. His was a spirit
which has been variously characterized, but its quality seems to rest
in a quick but sensitive manliness. This is Jonson's very accent. It
is heard in all his work, even in his rendering of Catullus' *"Vi-
vamus, mea Lesbia, atque amemus,"* so different from Campion's
version on page 339, as well as from Herrick's and Marvell's treat-
ments of the same theme.

[1] *Spikenard, an aromatic oil used as incense.*

Come, My Celia

Come, my Celia, let us prove,
While we can, the sports of love.
Time will not be ours for ever;
He, at length, our good will sever.
Spend not then his gifts in vain:
Suns that set may rise again.
But if once we lose this light,
'Tis with us perpetual night.
Why should we defer our joys?
Fame and rumor are but toys.
Cannot we delude the eyes
Of a few poor household spies?
Or his easier ears beguile,
Thus removéd by our wile?
'Tis no sin love's fruits to steal,
But the sweet thefts to reveal;
To be taken, to be seen,
These have crimes accounted been.

JOHN DONNE
[1573–1631]

Extravagantly admired in his own day, angrily belittled in the eighteenth century, and enthusiastically rediscovered in the twentieth, Donne is a prime example of the mutations of taste. Donne's conflicts between flesh and spirit, his battles between individual faith and general disillusionment, are as characteristic of our age as of Donne's. It is significant that, more than three hundred years after Donne's death, one of the most powerful and controversial books of our time, Ernest Hemingway's FOR WHOM THE BELL TOLLS, owes its title to Donne and its "motto"—so deep in its present implications—to one of his DEVOTIONS:

No man is an Iland, intire of it selfe; every man is a peece of the Continent, a part of the maine; if a Clod bee washed away by the

Sea, Europe is the lesse, as well as if a Promontorie were, as well
as if a Mannor of thy friends or of thine own were. Any mans
death diminishes me, because I am involved in Mankinde. And
therefore never send to know for whom the bell tolls. It tolls for
thee.

The unresolved discords in Donne have roused dissonant echoes;
the critics' verdicts have been far from unanimous. In every gen-
eration Donne has been a storm center, and the winds of opinion
have beat wildly about the value of his work. In a recent reappraisal
of Donne's contribution, Hugh I'Anson Fausset declares: "He
teaches us, not how to worship God, but how to relate ourselves to
God, and he shows that religious experience is the prize of that
battle between life and death which is the agony and exultation of
the creature in us striving after the divine." But the 1940 edition
of THE ENCYCLOPÆDIA BRITANNICA still carries Edmund Gosse's esti-
mate, which insists: "The influence of Donne upon the literature
of England was singularly wide and deep, *although almost wholly
malign.*" (Italics mine.—L. U.)

Such striking differences of opinion can be traced to Donne's own
problems and the paradox of his career. Son of a well-to-do London
ironmonger, Donne was brought up as a Catholic, attended both
Cambridge and Oxford, and studied law. When he came of age he
discarded the Catholic doctrine, turned to satirical writing, enlisted
for foreign service, and accompanied Essex on the famous expedi-
tions to Cadiz and the Azores. Upon his return in his mid-twenties,
Donne became private secretary to Sir Thomas Egerton, Lord
Keeper of the Great Seal. Thereupon another metamorphosis oc-
curred. The soldier-student became the man about town, "a great
visitor of ladies, a great frequenter of plays, a great writer of con-
ceited verses." In his twenty-seventh year he suddenly, and secretly,
married Egerton's niece, Anne More, whereupon his employer
promptly dismissed him.

Worried by debts, hounded by poverty, and faced with a rapidly
increasing family, Donne turned to any expedient. He wrote pam-
phlets against the papists; he composed pious epistles; he even con-
sidered migrating to Virginia. When he was most in need, shabby
and lacking food, his father-in-law forgave him and set aside an
allowance for his household. The wealthy Sir Robert Drury offered
Donne's family part of his home, and took the poet with him on
various journeys. When Donne left London for Paris, his wife, who

was expecting her eighth child, was loath to let him go. The poem that Donne wrote to cheer her upon his departure is one of his simplest and tenderest.

Sweetest Love, I Do Not Go

Sweetest love, I do not go,
  For weariness of thee,
Nor in hope the world can show
  A fitter love for me;
    But since that I
At the last must part, 'tis best,
Thus to use myself in jest
  By feigned deaths to die.

Yesternight the Sun went hence,
  And yet is here to-day;
He hath no desire nor sense,
  Nor half so short a way;
    Then fear not me,
But believe that I shall make
Speedier journeys, since I take
  More wings and spurs than he.

O how feeble is man's power,
  That if good fortune fall,
Cannot add another hour,
  Nor a lost hour recall;
    But come bad chance,
And we join it to our strength,
And we teach it art and length,
  Itself o'er us to advance.

When thou sigh'st, thou sigh'st not wind,
  But sigh'st my soul away;
When thou weep'st, unkindly kind,
  My life's blood doth decay.
    It cannot be
That thou lov'st me as thou say'st,
If in thine my life thou waste,
  That art the best of me.

            Let not thy divining heart
            Forethink me any ill;
            Destiny may take thy part,
            And may thy fears fulfil.
            But think that we
            Are but turned aside to sleep;
            They who one another keep
            Alive, ne'er parted be.

Donne's poems had been widely circulated and applauded, but in his late thirties he put most of his energy into tracts and treatises attempting to convert Roman Catholics to the Church of England. In his early forties James I persuaded Donne to enter into sacred orders; in 1615 he was ordained, first deacon, then priest. Presently he was appointed royal chaplain; it is said that his first sermon before the king and his nobles carried everyone "to heaven in holy raptures." In 1621 he was made Dean of St. Paul's.

Donne's popularity as a preacher increased under Charles I. But his health, never the best, was treacherous; he collapsed in his fifty-seventh year, the very year in which he was to have been made a bishop. He knew he was dying. He posed for the funereal statue in St. Paul's which shows him in his winding sheet, his eyes tightly closed and his limbs stiff, as though in rigor mortis. He died March 31, 1631, and was survived by six of his twelve children.

The man who became Dean of St. Paul's was a deeply, even darkly, religious soul; but this did not prevent him from writing some of the most impassioned and least inhibited love poems in the English language. Donne revolted against the prim tradition and ornate prettiness of his contemporaries. He abandoned all the stereotypes, wrote in a speech as intimate as conversation, and created a language of his own. As though impatient of subterfuge and elaborate innuendoes, THE CANONIZATION begins "For God's sake hold your tongue, and let me love," while in THE SUN RISING the poet breaks out with "Busy old fool, unruly Sun." Such poems differ from the work of his predecessors and from Donne's supposedly "obscure" verse by being both fervid and colloquial, as forthright as they are intense. Here the erotic and the mystical are joined.

The Canonization

For God's sake hold your tongue, and let me love,
　　Or chide my palsy, or my gout,
　　My five grey hairs, or ruined fortune flout;
With wealth your state, your mind with arts improve,
　　Take you a course, get you a place,
　　Observe his Honor, or his Grace;
Or the king's real, or his stamped face
Contemplate; what you will, approve,
　　So you will let me love.

Alas, alas, who's injured by my love?
　　What merchant's ships have my sighs drowned?
　　Who says my tears have overflowed his ground?
When did my colds a forward spring remove?
　　When did the heats which my veins fill
　　Add one more to the plaguy bill?
Soldiers find wars, and lawyers find out still
Litigious men, which quarrels move,
　　Though she and I do love.

Call us what you will, we are made such by love;
　　Call her one, me another fly,
　　We're tapers too, and at our own cost die,
And we in us find the eagle and the dove
　　The phœnix riddle hath more wit
　　By us; we two being one are it.
So to one neutral thing both sexes fit,
　　We die and rise the same, and prove
　　Mysterious by this love.

We can die by it, if not live by love,
　　And if unfit for tomb or hearse
　　Our legend be, it will be fit for verse;
And if no piece of chronicle we prove,
　　We'll build in sonnets pretty rooms;
　　As well a well-wrought urn becomes
The greatest ashes, as half-acre tombs,
　　And by these hymns all shall approve
　　Us canonized for love:

And thus invoke us, "You, whom reverend love
  Made one another's hermitage;
  You, to whom love was peace, that now is rage;
Who did the whole world's soul contract, and drove
    Into the glasses of your eyes
    (So made such mirrors, and such spies,
That they did all to you epitomize);
  Countries, towns, courts beg from above
  A pattern of your love."

The Sun Rising

    Busy old fool, unruly Sun,
      Why dost thou thus,
Through windows, and through curtains, call on us?
Must to thy motions lovers' seasons run?
    Saucy pedantic wretch, go chide
    Late school-boys and sour prentices,
  Go tell court-huntsmen that the king will ride,
  Call country ants to harvest offices;
Love, all alike, no season knows nor clime,
Nor hours, days, months, which are the rags of time.

    Thy beams so reverend and strong
      Why shouldst thou think?
I could eclipse and cloud them with a wink,
But that I would not lose her sight so long.
    If her eyes have not blinded thine,
    Look, and tomorrow late tell me,
  Whether both th' Indias of spice and mine
  Be where thou left'st them, or lie here with me.
Ask for those kings whom thou saw'st yesterday,
And thou shalt hear, "All here in one bed lay."

    She's all states, and all princes I;
      Nothing else is.
Princes do but play us; compared to this,
All honor's mimic, all wealth alchemy.
    Thou, Sun, art half as happy as we,
    In that the world's contracted thus;
  Thine age asks ease, and since thy duties be
  To warm the world, that's done in warming us.
Shine here to us, and thou art everywhere;
This bed thy centre is, these walls thy sphere.

The Good Morrow

I wonder, by my troth, what thou and I
Did, till we loved? were we not weaned till then?
But sucked on country pleasures, childishly?
Or snorted we in the Seven Sleepers' den?
'Twas so; but this, all pleasures fancies be;
If ever any beauty I did see,
Which I desired, and got, 'twas but a dream of thee.

And now good morrow to our waking souls,
Which watch not one another out of fear;
For love all love of other sights controls,
And makes one little room an everywhere.
Let sea-discoverers to new worlds have gone;
Let maps to other, worlds on worlds have shown;
Let us possess one world; each hath one, and is one.

My face in thine eye, thine in mine appears,
And true plain hearts do in the faces rest;
Where can we find two better hemispheres
Without sharp north, without declining west?
Whatever dies, was not mix'd equally;
If our two loves be one, or thou and I
Love so alike that none can slacken, none can die.

The Legacy

When last I died, and, dear, I die
   As often as from thee I go,
   Though it be but an hour ago,
—And lovers' hours be full eternity—
I can remember yet, that I
   Something did say, and something did bestow;
Though I be dead, which sent me, I might be
Mine own executor, and legacy.

I heard me say, "Tell her anon,
   That myself," that is you, not I,
   "Did kill me," and when I felt me die,
I bid me send my heart, when I was gone;

But I alas! could there find none;
  When I had ripp'd, and search'd where **hearts should lie,**
It kill'd me again, that I who still was true
In life, in my last will should cozen you.

Yet I found something like a heart,
  But colors it and corners had;
  It was not good, it was not bad,
It was entire to none, and few had part;
As good as could be made by art
  It seemed, and therefore for our loss be sad.
I meant to send that heart instead of mine,
But O! no man could hold it, for 'twas thine.

Break of Day

Stay, O sweet, and do not rise;
The light that shines comes from thine eyes;
The day breaks not, it is my heart,
Because that you and I must part.
  Stay, or else my joys will die
  And perish in their infancy.

The characterizing adjective "metaphysical" helped commentators to confuse the readers of Donne's poetry. As a description of his style, it is worthless. It was Dryden who first said that "Donne affects the metaphysics not only in his satires, but in his amorous verses. . . . He perplexes the minds of the fair sex with nice speculations of philosophy when he should engage their hearts and entertain them with the softnesses of love." And it was Dr. Johnson who took an unaffiliated group of seventeenth-century poets and called it "the Metaphysical School." Dryden and Johnson were referring less to the philosophical and "ethereal" connotations than to a combination of wit and subtlety, of profundity and fantasy, which marks Donne's knotted verse. As late as the nineteenth century, critics kept speaking of Donne's "far-fetched allusiveness," "misspent learning and excessive ingenuity," of his "wearying cleverness" which elicits "amazement rather than pleasure." Ward's scholarly, if rather stolid, collection of THE ENGLISH POETS permits itself this smirking epigram: "One may almost invert Jonson's famous panegyric on Shakespeare, and say that Donne was not for all time but for an age."

The paradox, new in Donne's day, has not grown old: Donne combined intricacy of idea with verbal straightforwardness, and the more complex was his thought, the simpler grew his language. It was a paradox without humor, but not without point. THE FLEA, for example, dramatizes a stock situation of the Elizabethan gallants: the ardent lover repulsed, or, at least, temporarily held off by the virtuous lady. But the tone has altered violently; the image is monstrous; the polite metaphors have changed to brusque mockery. The flood of imitation rubies is actual blood; the amorous couch set in a rosy bower has become the black body of a flea, the "living walls of jet."

The Flea

Mark but this flea, and mark in this,
How little that which thou deniest me is;
It sucked me first, and now sucks thee,
And in this flea our two bloods mingled be.
Thou know'st that this cannot be said
A sin, nor shame, nor loss of maidenhead;
   Yet this enjoys before it woo,
   And pampered swells with one blood made of two;
   And this, alas! is more than we would do.

Oh stay, three lives in one flea spare,
Where we almost, yea, more than married are.
This flea is you and I, and this
Our marriage bed, and marriage temple is.
Though parents grudge, and you, we're met,
And cloistered in these living walls of jet.
   Though use make you apt to kill me,
   Let not to that self-murder added be,
   And sacrilege, three sins in killing three.

Cruel and sudden, hast thou since
Purpled thy nail in blood of innocence?
Wherein could this flea guilty be,
Except in that drop which it sucked from thee?
Yet thou triumph'st, and sayest that thou
Find'st not thyself nor me the weaker now.
   'Tis true; then learn how false fears be;
   Just so much honor, when thou yieldest to me,
   Will waste, as this flea's death took life from thee.

If the poet sometimes roughly united passion and intellect, Donne was aware of what he was doing. He announced, "I sing not sirenlike to tempt, for I am harsh." Yet several of Donne's lyrics are among the purest of contemplative songs. There is nothing crabbed in the swift if cynical "Go and catch a falling star" and in that poem of transfiguration, THE ECSTASY, where wit is lifted above its own conceits, and mysticism speaks through intellect.

Song

Go and catch a falling star,
   Get with child a mandrake root,
Tell me where all past years are,
   Or who cleft the devil's foot;
Teach me to hear mermaids singing,
Or to keep off envy's stinging,
     And find
     What wind
Serves to advance an honest mind.

If thou be'st born to strange sights,
   Things invisible to see,
Ride ten thousand days and nights
   Till Age snow white hairs on thee;
Thou, when thou return'st, wilt tell me
All strange wonders that befell thee,
     And swear
     No where
Lives a woman true and fair.

If thou find'st one, let me know;
   Such a pilgrimage were sweet.
Yet do not; I would not go,
   Though at next door we might meet.
Though she were true when you met her,
And last, till you write your letter,
     Yet she
     Will be
False, ere I come, to two or three.

The Ecstasy

Where, like a pillow on a bed,
    A pregnant bank swelled up, to rest
The violet's reclining head,
    Sat we two, one another's best.

Our hands were firmly cémented
    By a fast balm, which thence did spring;
Our eye-beams twisted, and did thread
    Our eyes upon one double string.

So to engraft our hands, as yet
    Was all the means to make us one;
And pictures in our eyes to get
    Was all our propagation.

As, 'twixt two equal armies, Fate
    Suspends uncertain victory,
Our souls—which to advance their state,
    Were gone out—hung 'twixt her and me.

And whilst our souls negotiate there,
    We like sepulchral statues lay;
All day the same our postures were,
    And we said nothing all the day.

If any, so by love refined,
    That he soul's language understood,
And by good love were grown all mind,
    Within convenient distance stood,

He—though he knew not which soul spake,
    Because both meant, both spoke the same—
Might thence a new concoction take,
    And part far purer than he came.

This ecstasy doth unperplex
    (We said) and tell us what we love;
We see by this, it was not sex;
    We see, we saw not, what did move:

But as all several souls contain
  Mixture of things they know not what,
Love these mixed souls doth mix again,
  And makes both one, each this and that.

A single violet transplant,
  The strength, the color, and the size—
All which before was poor and scant—
  Redoubles still, and multiplies.

When love with one another so
  Interinanimates two souls,
That abler soul, which thence doth flow,
  Defects of loneliness controls.

We then, who are this new soul, know,
  Of what we are composed and made,
For th' atomies of which we grow
  Are souls, whom no change can invade.

But, O alas! so long, so far,
  Our bodies why do we forbear?
They are ours, though they're not we; we are
  Th' intelligences, they the spheres.

We owe them thanks, because they thus
  Did us, to us, at first convey,
Yielded their senses' force to us,
  Nor are dross to us, but allay.

On man heaven's influence works not so,
  But that it first imprints the air;
So soul into the soul may flow,
  Though it to body first repair.

As our blood labors to beget
  Spirits, as like souls as it can,
Because such fingers need to knit
  That subtle knot, which makes us man:

So must pure lovers' souls descend
  To affections, and to faculties,
Which sense may reach and apprehend,
  Else a great prince in prison lies.

To our bodies turn we then, that so
　Weak men on love reveal'd may look;
Love's mysteries in souls do grow,
　But yet the body is his book.

And if some lover, such as we,
　Have heard this dialogue of one,
Let him still mark us, he shall see
　Small change when we're to bodies gone.

Donne's DIVINE POEMS are not free of tension; here, in fact, the figures of speech are most violent, the sensation most agonized. In one of the strangest religious poems, Donne confesses his need of God. But, in a prolonged and almost incredible metaphor, he compares himself to a walled city that longs to open its gates to the invader, and to a virgin who longs to give herself but cannot make the complete surrender. Here, again, is the Elizabethan theme of the impatient lover and his reticent beloved. But, by a curious set of double meanings, it is the poet who has now become the half-willing, half-resisting woman. The town, the virgin body, the eager spirit must be taken by force—and the reader looks on with a kind of terror as the word is made flesh, and the poet cries out his appeal.

Batter My Heart

Batter my heart, three-personed God; for you
As yet but knock, breathe, shine, and seek to mend.
That I may rise and stand, o'erthrow me and bend
Your force to break, blow, burn, and make me new.
I, like an usurped town, to another due,
Labor to admit you, but, oh, to no end;
Reason, your viceroy in me, me should defend,
But is captived and proves weak or untrue.

Yet dearly I love you and would be loved fain,
But am betrothed unto your enemy:
Divorce me, untie or break that knot again,
Take me to you, imprison me, for I,
Except you enthrall me, never shall be free,
Nor ever chaste, except you ravish me.

With Donne poetry takes an entirely new turn. A new sensibility creates a more nervous utterance; a sense of sin cuts through and gives the lyric an astringent power, almost an austerity. A HYMN TO GOD THE FATHER and the tenth of the HOLY SONNETS are enriched with mature experience and controlled emotion. "Those two poems," Robert Hillyer wrote, "are Donne's biography, his double epitaph."

Death, Be Not Proud

Death, be not proud, though some have called thee
Mighty and dreadful, for thou are not so;
For those whom thou think'st thou dost overthrow
Die not, poor Death; nor yet canst thou kill me.
From rest and sleep, which but thy picture be,
Much pleasure; then from thee much more must flow;
And soonest our best men with thee do go—
Rest of their bones and souls' delivery!
Thou'rt slave to fate, chance, kings, and desperate men,
And dost with poison, war, and sickness dwell;
And poppy or charms can make us sleep as well
And better than thy stroke. Why swell'st thou then?
One short sleep past, we wake eternally,
And Death shall be no more: Death, thou shalt die.

A Hymn to God the Father

Wilt Thou forgive that sin where I begun,
    Which was my sin, though it were done before?
Wilt Thou forgive that sin, through which I run,
    And do run still, though still I do deplore?
        When Thou hast done, Thou hast not done,
            For I have more.

Wilt Thou forgive that sin which I have won
    Others to sin, and made my sin their door?
Wilt Thou forgive that sin which I did shun
    A year or two, but wallowed in a score?
        When Thou hast done, Thou hast not done,
            For I have more.

I have a sin of fear, that when I have spun
My last thread, I shall perish on the shore;
But swear by Thyself, that at my death Thy Son
Shall shine as he shines now, and heretofore;
And, having done that, Thou hast done;
I fear no more.

The three-hundredth anniversary of Donne's death was the occasion for fresh tributes and reappraisals. Perhaps the most marked exhibit of Donne's influence in our time was A GARLAND FOR JOHN DONNE: 1631–1931 edited by Theodore Spencer. T. S. Eliot ended the first essay in the volume: "At any time Donne ought always to be recognized as one of the few great reformers and preservers of the English tongue." But there is another explanation for Donne's hold upon this generation. We respond to Donne's contradiction of sensibility and skepticism, of faith and faithlessness, because we too yearn for a life of reason, and alternately hope and despair of finding it.

JOHN FLETCHER

[1579–1625]

JOHN FLETCHER seems to have been the most industrious playwright of his day. Born in the coastal village of Rye, he was educated at Cambridge and came to London in his early twenties. There he consorted with the metropolitan poets and dramatists who, recognizing his value as well as his charm, became his good friends and ready partners. It is estimated that Fletcher wrote not less than sixteen plays by himself; about the same number with Francis Beaumont; two or three with Shakespeare—THE WOMAN'S PRIZE, OR THE TAMER TAMED (probably by Fletcher alone) depicts the domestication of Shakespeare's Petruchio—and more than a dozen comedies and tragedies with other collaborators. He was planning more work in his favorite genre, tragicomedy, when he succumbed to the plague and died in his forty-sixth year.

Fletcher's closest friend and best collaborator was the precocious Beaumont (see page 381); theirs has been called "a perfect union of genius and friendship." They lived together for several years;

it is said that they shared the same clothes and the same mistress. Beaumont's was the more dramatic power, Fletcher's the lyric talent. Fletcher's songs, gracefully moving and seemingly spontaneous in their ease, are as light in texture as they are sure in tone. Short though they are, they had their influence. THE FAITHFUL SHEPHERDESS was the forerunner of Milton's COMUS. Fletcher's fluent couplets of THE RIVER GOD anticipated L'ALLEGRO, and the lines beginning "Hence, all you vain delights" were amplified in IL PENSEROSO. "Milton himself," said A. C. Bradley, "though he put a greater volume of imagination and sound into the measure, never gave it such an airy lightness, and we must look on to Shelley for an echo to these lyrics."

After a period of long neglect, Fletcher's poetry is beginning to attract a new audience and a fresh appreciation. It deserves more than it has received.

O Sweetest Melancholy

Hence, all you vain delights,
As short as are the nights
   Wherein you spend your folly!
There's nought in this life sweet,
If man were wise to see't,
   But only melancholy;
   O sweetest melancholy!

Welcome, folded arms and fixed eyes,
A sigh that piercing mortifies,
A look that's fastened to the ground,
A tongue chained up without a sound!
Fountain-heads and pathless groves,
Places which pale passion loves!
Moonlight walks, when all the fowls
Are warmly housed save bats and owls!
A midnight bell, a parting groan,
These are the sounds we feed upon;
Then stretch our bones in a still gloomy valley;
Nothing's so dainty sweet as lovely melancholy.
from THE NICE VALOR

The River God

I am this fountain's god. Below
My waters to a river grow,
And 'twixt two banks with osiers set,
That only prosper in the wet,
Through the meadows do they glide,
Wheeling still on every side,
Sometimes winding round about
To find the evenest channel out.
And if thou wilt go with me,
Leaving mortal company,
In the cool streams shalt thou lie,
Free from harm as well as I;
I will give thee for thy food
No fish that useth [1] in the mud,
But trout and pike, that love to swim
Where the gravel from the brim
Through the pure streams may be seen;
Orient pearl fit for a queen
Will I give, thy love to win,
And a shell to keep them in;
Not a fish in all my brook
That shall disobey thy look,
But, when thou wilt, come gliding by
And from thy white hand take a fly:
And to make thee understand
How I can my waves command,
They shall bubble whilst I sing,
Sweeter than the silver string.

from THE FAITHFUL SHEPHERDESS

To Pan

All ye woods, and trees, and bowers,
All ye virtues and ye powers
That inhabit in the lakes,
In the pleasant springs or brakes,

[1] *Lives.*

Move your feet
To our sound
Whilst we greet
All this ground
With his honor and his name
That defends our flocks from blame.

He is great, and he is just,
He is ever good, and must
Thus be honored. Daffadillies,
Roses, pinks, and loved lilies,
Let us fling,
Whilst we sing,
Ever holy,
Ever holy,
Ever honored, ever young!
Thus great Pan is ever sung.
from THE FAITHFUL SHEPHERDESS

Mourn No More

Weep no more, nor sigh, nor groan,
Sorrow calls no time that's gone:
Violets plucked the sweetest rain
Makes not fresh nor grow again.
Trim thy locks, look cheerfully;
Fate's hid ends eyes cannot see.
Joys as wingèd dreams fly fast;
Why should sadness longer last?
Grief is but a wound to woe:
Gentlest fair, mourn, mourn no moe!
from THE QUEEN OF CORINTH

Mighty Love

Hear, ye ladies that despise
What the mighty love has done;
Fear examples and be wise:
Fair Callisto was a nun;
Leda, sailing on the stream
To deceive the hopes of man,

Love accounting but a dream,
Doted on a silver swan;
Danaë, in a brazen tower,
Where no love was, loved a shower.

Hear, ye ladies that are coy,
What the mighty Love can do;
Fear the fierceness of the boy:
The chaste Moon he makes to woo;
Vesta, kindling holy fires,
Circled round about with spies,
Never dreaming loose desires,
Doting at the altar dies;
Ilion, in a short hour, higher
He can build, and once more fire.

from VALENTINIAN

Care-Charming Sleep

Care-charming Sleep, thou easer of all woes,
Brother to Death, sweetly thyself dispose
On this afflicted prince. Fall like a cloud
In gentle showers. Give nothing that is loud,
Or painful to his slumbers; easy, light,
And as a purling stream, thou son of Night,
Pass by his troubled senses. Sing his pain,
Like hollow murmuring wind or silver rain.
Into this prince gently, oh, gently slide,
And kiss him into slumbers like a bride.

from VALENTINIAN

Bridal Song

Hold back thy hours, dark Night, till we have done;
    The Day will come too soon.
Young maids will curse thee, if thou steal'st away
And leav'st their losses open to the day.
    Stay, stay, and hide
    The blushes of the bride.

Stay, gentle Night, and with thy darkness cover
   The kisses of her lover.
Stay, and confound her tears and her shrill cryings,
Her weak denials, vows, and often-dyings;
   Stay, and hide all:
   But help not, though she call.
                              from THE MAID'S TRAGEDY

Aspatia's Song

Lay a garland on my hearse
   Of the dismal yew:
Maidens, willow branches bear;
   Say, I died true.

My love was false, but I was firm
   From my hour of birth.
Upon my buried body lie
   Lightly, gentle earth!
            from THE MAID'S TRAGEDY

Shakespeare and Fletcher collaborated on KING HENRY THE EIGHTH
and, though it is impossible to say what parts were written by
whom, many scholars have attributed ORPHEUS WITH HIS LUTE to
Shakespeare, perhaps because of the great name, perhaps because
it seems another proof of Shakespeare's preoccupation with the
power of music. Recent critics, basing their conclusions on style
and accent, believe the poem to be by Fletcher.

Orpheus With His Lute

Orpheus with his lute made trees,
And the mountaintops that freeze,
   Bow themselves when he did sing:
To his music plants and flowers
Ever sprung; as sun and showers
   There had made a lasting spring.

Everything that heard him play,
Even the billows of the sea,
   Hung their heads, and then lay by.

In sweet music is such art:
Killing care and grief of heart
Fall asleep, or, hearing, die.
from KING HENRY THE EIGHTH

Fletcher's most "modern" poem is his least known set of verses.
THE DEAD HOST'S WELCOME occurs in a play written solely by
Fletcher and produced a year or two before the author's death. The
couplets have the easy colloquial tone heard almost three centuries
later in the work of A. E. Housman (see page 1023). It is not only
Fletcher's idiom which anticipates the twentieth-century poet, it is
the wry philosophy, the very turn of the phrase:

I could wish you wenches, too,
But I am dead and cannot do.
. . . Drink apace, while breath you have;
You'll find but cold drink in the grave.

It appears again in a song from Beaumont and Fletcher's THE
KNIGHT OF THE BURNING PESTLE, and especially in the opening lines:

'Tis mirth that fills the veins with blood,
More than wine, or sleep, or food;
Let each man keep his heart at ease;
No man dies of that disease!

Every reader of modern poetry will recognize that grimly care-
less inflection. There, but for the grace of Time, goes the Shrop-
shire lad.

The Dead Host's Welcome

'Tis late and cold; stir up the fire;
Sit close, and draw the table nigher.
Be merry, and drink wine that's old,
A hearty medicine 'gainst a cold.
Your beds of wanton down the best,
Where you shall tumble to your rest;
I could wish you wenches, too,
But I am dead, and cannot do.
Call for the best the house may ring,
Sack, white, and claret, let them bring,

And drink apace, while breath you have;
You'll find but cold drink in the grave.
Plover, partridge, for your dinner,
And a capon for the sinner,
You shall find ready when you're up,
And your horse shall have his sup.
"Welcome! welcome!" shall fly round,
And I shall smile, though underground.

from THE LOVER'S PROGRESS

Laugh and Sing

'Tis mirth that fills the veins with blood,
More than wine, or sleep, or food;
Let each man keep his heart at ease;
No man dies of that disease!
He that would his body keep
From diseases, must not weep;
But whoever laughs and sings,
Never he his body brings
Into fevers, gouts, or rheums,
Or lingeringly his lungs consumes;
Or meets with ague in his bone,
Or catarrhs, or griping stone:
But contented lives for aye;
The more he laughs, the more he may!

from THE KNIGHT OF THE BURNING PESTLE

JOHN WEBSTER
[1580?–1625?]

SON of a London tailor, and himself a member of the tailors' guild,
Webster was no immured scholar. He was intimately con-
nected with the brawling affairs of the city, with hot life and sud-
den death. Death in most of the Elizabethan dramas was the tri-
umphant solution if not the central theme. Death was no mere exit,
a shuffling end, but a climax in a world of quick thought and

passionate action, a kaleidoscope of wonder and terror. Webster himself affirmed it in THE DUCHESS OF MALFI:

> I know death hath ten thousand several doors
> For men to take their exits; and 'tis found
> They go on such strange geometrical hinges
> You may open them both ways; any way for heaven sake
> So I were out of your whispering. Tell my brothers
> That I perceive death now I am well awake
> Best gift that they can give or I can take.

More than most of his contemporaries, Webster mirrored his tempestuous times. Only Shakespeare and Marlowe surpassed him in intensity. His lyrics are few but fine. The one beginning "All the flowers of the spring" has an added interest for the reader of contemporary verse; the last part of the last line became the title of Elinor Wylie's first book, NETS TO CATCH THE WIND.

Cornelia's Song

> Call for the robin redbreast and the wren,
> Since o'er shady groves they hover,
> And with leaves and flowers do cover
> The friendless bodies of unburied men.
> Call unto his funeral dole
> The ant, the field-mouse, and the mole,
> To rear him hillocks that shall keep him warm,
> And (when gay tombs are robbed) sustain no harm;
> But keep the wolf far thence, that's foe to men,
> For with his nails he'll dig them up again.
>
> *from* THE WHITE DEVIL

Nets to Catch the Wind

> All the flowers of the spring
> Meet to perfume our burying;
> These have but their growing prime,
> And man does flourish but his time.
> Survey our progress from our birth—
> We are set, we grow, we turn to earth.

Courts adieu, and all delights,
All bewitching appetites.
Sweetest breath and clearest eye
Like perfumes go out and die;
Vain the ambition of kings
Who seek by trophies and dead things
To leave a living name behind,
And weave but nets to catch the wind.

from THE DEVIL'S LAW CASE

RICHARD CORBET
[1582–1635]

RICHARD CORBET was a multiple personality. An intimate of Ben
Jonson, he caroused at the Mermaid Tavern with the best of
them; his readily improvised verses were always met with roaring
approval. But his delight in persiflage and practical jokes did
not prevent him—an Oxford graduate—from becoming Bishop of
Oxford and Norwich. He was an ardent churchman but loved
play acting in life as well as in the theater. Once when he saw a
ballad singer who was having a hard time selling his songs, Corbet
exchanged his dignified gown for the street singer's worn leather
jacket, "and being a handsome man, and a rare full voice, he
presently vended a great many, and had a great audience." It is
not hard to believe the report that when Corbet was appointed
Dean of Christ Church in his thirty-ninth year "the schoolboys
stopped bowling their hoops in amazement at seeing a Dean so
like themselves."

Like John Still (see page 200), who was also a poetizing bishop,
Corbet disliked lugubrious verse. His taste was for jovial rhymes—
he put a tramping expedition into vagabond measures—and happy
fancies. A set of little-known lines to his young son displays his
characteristic combination of teasing and tenderness.

To His Son, Vincent

What I shall leave thee none can tell,
But all shall say I wish thee well:
I wish thee, Vin, before all wealth,
Both bodily and ghostly health;
Nor too much wealth, nor wit, come to thee,
So much of either may undo thee.
I wish thee learning, not for show,
Enough for to instruct and know,
Not such as gentlemen require
To prate at table or at fire.
I wish thee all thy mother's graces,
Thy father's fortunes, and his places.
I wish thee friends, and one at court,
Not to build on, but support,
To keep thee, not in doing many
Oppressions, but from suffering any.
I wish thee peace in all thy ways
Nor lazy nor contentious days;
And when thy soul and body part,
As innocent as now thou art.

Still more typical of Corbet's spirit is the lightly mocking ballad
entitled THE FAIRIES' FAREWELL, OR GOD A MERCY WILL. It appeared
in CERTAIN ELEGANT POEMS in 1647. Two and a half centuries later,
Rudyard Kipling borrowed the first line for the title of one of his
best books for children, REWARDS AND FAIRIES.

The Fairies' Farewell

Farewell, rewards and fairies,
  Good housewives now may say,
For now foul sluts in dairies
  Do fare as well as they.
And though they sweep their hearths no less
  Than maids were wont to do,
Yet who of late, for cleanliness,
  Finds sixpence in her shoe?

Lament, lament, old Abbeys,
　　The fairies' lost command;
They did but change priests' babies,
　　But some have changed your land!
And all your children sprung from thence
　　Are now grown Puritans,
Who live as changelings ever since,
　　For love of your domains.

At morning and at evening both
　　You merry were and glad;
So little care of sleep or sloth
　　These pretty ladies had;
When Tom came home from labor,
　　Or Ciss to milking rose,
Then merrily went their tabor
　　And nimbly went their toes.

Witness those rings and roundelays
　　Of theirs, which yet remain,
Were footed in Queen Mary's days
　　On many a grassy plain;
But since of late, Elizabeth
　　And, later, James came in,
They never danced on any heath
　　As when the time hath been.

By which we note the fairies
　　Were of the old profession;
Their songs were *Ave-Maries*,
　　Their dances were procession.
But now, alas! they all are dead,
　　Or gone beyond the seas;
Or farther for religion fled;
　　Or else they take their ease.

A tell-tale in their company
　　They never could endure;
And whoso kept not secretly
　　Their mirth, was punished sure;
It was a most just Christian deed
　　To pinch such black and blue:
Oh, how the Commonwealth doth need
　　Such justices as you!

FRANCIS BEAUMONT
[1584–1616]

FRANCIS BEAUMONT was an infant prodigy. Born of a noble and distinguished family, he entered Oxford at twelve, and it is said that he had already written two tragedies in imitation of Marlowe's TAMBURLAINE and Shakespeare's TITUS ANDRONICUS. Although he left college without having taken his degree, his brothers stood sponsor for him when he became a member of the Middle Temple at the age of fifteen. But law could not hold one already pledged to literature, and in his youth Beaumont entered the inner circle of London playwrights. In his early twenties he joined fortunes with John Fletcher (see page 369), a few years his senior, and their collaboration became legendary. In order to be near the theater, they lived together not far from the Globe. They shared everything in common, clothing and money, even bed and bawd. Together they wrote not less than sixteen plays and probably more. A precocious creator, Beaumont was also a critical intelligence. A warm friend of Ben Jonson's, he was by no means the great man's satellite; Jonson submitted his work to Beaumont and, according to Dryden, "used Beaumont's judgment in correcting, if not contriving, all his plots." There is no telling what Beaumont might finally have accomplished; he died a few months after his thirty-first birthday.

If Fletcher accentuated their joint productions by his lyrical gift, Beaumont heightened them by his feeling for cumulative dramatic effects. Yet Beaumont's instinct for verse, though not as buoyant as Fletcher's, was natural and animated. His LETTER TO BEN JONSON vividly recreates the scene and surroundings at the Mermaid Tavern, and his occasional songs are both supple and grave. Doubt has been cast upon Beaumont's authorship of ON THE TOMBS IN WESTMINSTER ABBEY—a longer version appeared anonymously a few years after his death—but most scholars still list the lines as the most famous of Beaumont's poems and as a particular example of his concentrated vigor.

On the Tombs in Westminster Abbey

Mortality, behold and fear
What a change of flesh is here!
Think how many royal bones
Sleep within this heap of stones;
Here they lie, had realms and lands,
Who now want strength to stir their hands,
Where from their pulpits seal'd with dust
They preach, "In greatness is no trust."
Here's an acre sown indeed
With the richest royallest seed
That the earth did e'er suck in
Since the first man died for sin:
Here the bones of birth have cried
"Though gods they were, as men they died!"
Here are sands, ignoble things,
Dropt from the ruin'd sides of kings:
Here's a world of pomp and state
Buried in dust, once dead by fate.

Songs from a Masque

Shake off your heavy trance!
   And leap into a dance
Such as no mortals use to tread:
   Fit only for Apollo
To play to, for the moon to lead,
   And all the stars to follow!

*

Ye should stay longer if we durst:
Away! Alas that he that first
Gave Time wild wings to fly away
Hath now no power to make him stay!
And though these games must needs be played,
I would this pair, when they are laid,
   And not a creature nigh 'em,
Could catch his scythe, as he doth pass,
And clip his wings, and break his glass,
   And keep him ever by 'em.
        from THE MASQUE OF THE INNER TEMPLE

WILLIAM DRUMMOND
[1585–1649]

IN MOST collections his name appears imposingly as "William Drummond of Hawthornden," reminding the reader that he was laird of that celebrated manor near Edinburgh. Like many of his fellow poets, Drummond was educated to be a lawyer, and promptly deserted law for letters. Although a friend of Drayton and Jonson, he never entered into the swaggering life of the town. His fiancée, Mary Cunningham, died on the eve of their wedding, and Drummond withdrew into himself. Surrounded by a huge library of Latin, Italian, and Hebrew, he became a recluse, wrote religious pamphlets, and roused himself only to support the Royalist cause. It is said that the execution of Charles I hastened his own death.

Most of Drummond's work is graceful rather than great. A much-quoted song beginning

> Phœbus, arise,
> And paint the sable skies
> With azure, white, and red

foreshadows a kind of pleasure in nature expressed by Milton in his earlier and lighter vein. Drummond's deeper emotions are in FLOWERS OF ZION, which earned him the title of "the Scottish Petrarch." But, though Drummond scarcely merits the appellation, a few of his smaller poems have insured him a modest immortality.

Tell Me No More

No more with candied words infect mine ears,
Tell me no more how that you pine in anguish,
When sound you sleep no more say that you languish,
No more in sweet despite say you spend tears.
Who hath such hollow eyes as not to see
How those that are hare-brained boast of Apollo,
And bold give out the Muses do them follow,
Though in love's library yet no lovers be.

If we poor souls least favor do them show,
That straight in wanton lines abroad is blazed;
Their names doth soar on our fame's overthrow,
Marked is our lightness whilst their wits are praised.
In silent thought who can no secret cover,
He may, say we, but not well, be a lover.

This Life

This life, which seems so fair,
Is like a bubble blown up in the air
By sporting children's breath,
Who chase it everywhere,
And strive who can most motion it bequeath:
And though it sometime seem of its own might,
Like to an eye of gold, to be fixed there,
And firm to hover in that empty height,
That only is because it is so light.
But in that pomp it doth not long appear;
For even when most admired, it in a thought,
As swelled from nothing, doth dissolve in nought.

The Baptist

The last and greatest herald of heaven's king,
Girt with rough skins, hies to the deserts wild,
Among that savage brood the woods forth bring,
Which he than man more harmless found and mild;
His food was locusts and what there doth spring.
With honey that from virgin hives distilled;
Parched body, hollow eyes, some uncouth thing
Made him appear, long since from earth exiled.
There burst he forth: "All ye whose hopes rely
On God, with me amidst these deserts mourn,
Repent! Repent! and from old errors turn."
Who listened to his voice? obeyed his cry?
Only the echoes which he made relent,
Rung from their flinty caves, "Repent! Repent!"

GEORGE WITHER
[1588–1667]

A T FIFTEEN, a precocious undergraduate of Magdalen College, Oxford, George Wither determined to be a satirist. At twenty-five his skill in satire lodged him in prison. Admirers of his ABUSES STRIPT AND WHIPT pleaded in vain; Wither's release was effected only by the intercession of the Princess Elizabeth and a poem pledging uncritical allegiance to the king. But Wither could not check his fluent irony: "I cannot dam it though it damn me." In his early thirties he was again in trouble. Thirty thousand copies of WITHER'S MOTTO: NEC HABEO, NEC CAREO, NEC CURO were sold within a few months. It was considered libelous; Wither was again imprisoned and, after more legal threats, again released.

With suspicious complaisance, Wither turned to religious verse. But, although a large collection entitled HALLELUIAH: OR BRITAIN'S SECOND REMEMBRANCER was printed in his fifty-third year, Wither's spirit was not strict or devotional. Witty as a spontaneous poet, he was prosy as a rhyming preacher. He struggled against self-division and, even in action, failed to resolve his conflict. He joined Charles I against the Covenanters but a few years later supported the rebellious Parliament. He was granted a large sum for property which had been plundered, but he received only a small part of it. He ingratiated himself with the new regime and then lost favor by telling Cromwell "those truths which he was not willing to hear."

Although several of Wither's hymns are still sung, and a few of his songs are lightly sentimental, Wither lives by his rhymed satires. The punning couplet placed beneath his portrait is typical:

> I grow and wither
> Both together.

A sonnet or two and the mocking lyric, beginning "Shall I, wasting in despair," written in his late twenties, have outlasted all the emblematic verses, sacred melodies, and metrical psalms that he wrote with such desperate industry.

What Care I

Shall I, wasting in despair,
Die because a woman's fair?
Or my cheeks make pale with care
'Cause another's rosy are?
Be she fairer than the day
Or the flowery meads in May—
    If she be not so to me,
      What care I how fair she be?

Shall my foolish heart be pined
'Cause I see a woman kind?
Or a well disposéd nature
Joinéd with a lovely feature?
Be she meeker, kinder, than
Turtle-dove or pelican,
    If she be not so to me,
      What care I how kind she be?

Shall a woman's virtues move
Me to perish for her love?
Or her merits' value known
Make me quite forget mine own?
Be she with that goodness blest
Which may gain her name of Best;
    If she seem not such to me,
      What care I how good she be?

'Cause her fortune seems too high,
Shall I play the fool and die?
Those that bear a noble mind
Where they want of riches find,
Think what with them they would do
Who without them dare to woo;
    And unless that mind I see,
      What care I how great she be?

Great or good, or kind or fair.
I will ne'er the more despair:
If she love me, this believe,
I will die ere she shall grieve;

If she slight me when I woo,
I can scorn and let her go.
  For if she be not for me,
  What care I for whom she be?

The Divided Heart

I wandered out awhile agone,
  And went I knew not whither.
But there do beauties many a one
  Resort and meet together.
And Cupid's power will there be shown,
  If ever you come thither.

For, like two suns, two beauties bright
  I shining saw together,
And, tempted by their double light,
  My eyes I fixed on either:
Till both at once so thralled my sight,
  I loved, and knew not whether.

A lover of the curioused eye,
  Might have been pleased in either:
And so, I must confess, might I,
  Had they not been together.
Now both must love, or both deny;
  In one enjoy I neither.

But yet at last I 'scaped the smart
  I feared at coming hither:
For, seeing my divided heart,
  I choosing knew not whether,
Love angry grew, and did depart—
  And now I care for neither.

IX

Gallants, Puritans, and Divines

ROBERT HERRICK

[1591–1674]

ROBERT HERRICK was born into a family of jewelers—both his father and his uncle were goldsmiths—and it is not too far-fetched to find the family influence in the poet's delicately engraved, jewel-encrusted work. After serving as his uncle's apprentice and originating his own patterns in rings and brooches, Herrick was sent to St. John's College, but took his degree from Trinity Hall.

Little is known of the next ten years in Herrick's life. It has been conjectured that he spent most of the time preparing for the ministry. A completely contrary rumor placed Herrick in the metropolis, where he is said to have spent his days wildly and most of his nights in doing nothing seriously. This is not too plausible; Herrick's verse rarely pictures the author as a thoroughgoing roisterer. Never rowdy, it is often lascivious, but seldom rudely lecherous. Even when Herrick boasts of being wanton, he does so with a deprecation which is almost a denial. A couplet entitled POETS reassures us:

> Wantons we are; and though our words be such,
> Our lives do differ from our lines by much.

It is more than likely, however, that Herrick joined the company at the Sun, the Triple Tun, and other taverns shortly after, if not during, his career as jeweler and scholar. Cherished by the individ-

uals at "those lyric feasts" and sponsored by the group, he became
a poet. He was known as one of the "sons of Ben"; Jonson
"adopted" him as his poetic stepchild. Herrick acknowledged the
literary paternity not only by surpassing his master in charm and
craftsmanship but by poems of praise and homage.

His Prayer to Ben Jonson

When I a verse shall make,
Know I have prayed thee,
For old religion's sake,
Saint Ben, to aid me.

Make the way smooth for me,
When I, thy Herrick,
Honoring thee, on my knee,
Offer my lyric.

Candles I'll give to thee,
And a new altar;
And thou, Saint Ben, shalt be
Writ in my psalter.

An Ode for Ben Jonson

Ah, Ben!
Say how or when
Shall we, thy guests,
Meet at those lyric feasts
Made at the Sun,
The Dog, the Triple Tun?
Where we such clusters had
As made us nobly wild, not mad;
And yet each verse of thine
Outdid the meat, outdid the frolic wine.

My Ben,
Or come again,
Or send to us
Thy wit's great overplus;

But teach us yet
Wisely to husband it,
Lest we that talent spend;
And having once brought to an end
That precious stock, the store
Of such a wit, the world should have no more.

In his thirty-eighth year Herrick was made vicar at Dean Prior in Devonshire. He went there almost against his will. The village seemed dull, the countryfolk resentful; even his parishioners were suspicious of the stranger. He felt isolated from culture, bitterly alone. It is related that, on a particularly depressing Sunday, Herrick, seeing that half his congregation were gossiping, and the other half asleep, flung his sermon at the pewholders and cursed them from the pulpit. But there was no hate in him. Gradually Herrick was drawn into the life of the countryside. The innocent and half-pagan customs of the mummers and morris dancers, the winter revels and the spring Maypole festivities, delighted him more than he admitted to his London friends. It was not the town Muse but the country Muse he invoked in his celebration of rude wassails and gay wakes, of farm wagons in holiday colors and carts piled high with the harvest. In a spirit of "cleanly-wantonness," he made his quiet surroundings the "plot," or "argument," of his work.

The Argument of His Book

I sing of Brooks, of Blossoms, Birds, and Bowers:
Of April, May, of June, and July-Flowers.
I sing of May-poles, Hock-carts, Wassails, Wakes,
Of Bride-grooms, Brides, and of their Bridal-cakes.
I write of Youth, of Love, and have access
By these, to sing of cleanly-wantonness.
I sing of Dews, of Rains, and piece by piece
Of Balm, of Oil, of Spice, and Amber-Greece.
I sing of Times trans-shifting; and I write
How Roses first came red, and Lilies white.
I write of Groves, of Twilights, and I sing
The Court of Mab, and of the Fairie-King.
I write of Hell; I sing (and ever shall)
Of Heaven, and hope to have it after all.

When Herrick published his HESPERIDES in his late fifties, his friends must have been surprised to find that the collection included all of twelve hundred poems. Almost all were written in Devonshire. Never has a poet so dexterously mingled rural fact and rootless fancy. Here are honest milkmaids and mischievous elves, sober meditations and lightly voluptuous thoughts.

Corinna's Going A-Maying

Get up, get up for shame! The blooming morn
Upon her wings presents the god unshorn.
   See how Aurora throws her fair,
   Fresh-quilted colors through the air.
   Get up, sweet slug-a-bed, and see
   The dew bespangling herb and tree!
Each flower has wept and bowed toward the east
Above an hour since, yet you not drest;
   Nay! not so much as out of bed?
   When all the birds have matins said
   And sung their thankful hymns, 'tis sin,
   Nay, profanation, to keep in,
Whenas a thousand virgins on this day
Spring sooner than the lark, to fetch in May.

Rise and put on your foliage, and be seen
To come forth, like the springtime, fresh and green,
   And sweet as Flora. Take no care
   For jewels for your gown or hair.
   Fear not; the leaves will strew
   Gems in abundance upon you.
Besides, the childhood of the day has kept
Against you come, some orient pearls unwept.
   Come, and receive them while the light
   Hangs on the dew-locks of the night;
   And Titan on the eastern hill
   Retires himself, or else stands still
Till you come forth! Wash, dress, be brief in praying;
Few beads are best when once we go a-Maying.

Come, my Corinna, come; and coming, mark
How each field turns a street, each street a park,
   Made green and trimmed with trees! see how
   Devotion gives each house a bough

Or branch! each porch, each door, ere this,
An ark, a tabernacle is,
Made up of white-thorn neatly interwove,
As if here were those cooler shades of love.
    Can such delights be in the street
    And open fields, and we not see't?
    Come, we'll abroad; and let's obey
    The proclamation made for May,
And sin no more, as we have done, by staying;
But, my Corinna, come, let's go a-Maying.

There's not a budding boy or girl this day
But is got up and gone to bring in May.
    A deal of youth ere this is come
    Back, and with white-thorn laden home.
    Some have dispatched their cakes and cream,
    Before that we have left to dream;
And some have wept and wooed, and plighted troth,
And chose their priest, ere we can cast off sloth.
    Many a green-gown has been given,
    Many a kiss, both odd and even;
    Many a glance, too, has been sent
    From out the eye, love's firmament;
Many a jest told of the keys betraying
This night, and locks picked; yet we're not a-Maying!

Come, let us go, while we are in our prime,
And take the harmless folly of the time!
    We shall grow old apace, and die
    Before we know our liberty.
    Our life is short, and our days run
    As fast away as does the sun.
And, as a vapor or a drop of rain,
Once lost, can ne'er be found again,
    So when or you or I are made
    A fable, song, or fleeting shade,
    All love, all liking, all delight
    Lies drowned with us in endless night.
Then, while time serves, and we are but decaying,
Come, my Corinna, come, let's go a-Maying.

Oberon's Feast

Shapcot! to thee the Fairy State
I with discretion, dedicate.
Because thou prizest things that are
Curious, and unfamiliar.
Take first the feast; these dishes gone;
We'll see the Fairy-Court anon.

A little mushroom-table spread,
After short prayers, they set on bread;
A moon-parcht grain of purest wheat,
With some small glitt'ring grit, to eat
His choice bits with; then in a trice
They make a feast less great than nice.
But all this while his eye is served,
We must not think his ear was starved:
But that there was in place to stir
His spleen, the chirring grasshopper;
The merry cricket, puling fly,
The piping gnat for minstrelsy.
And now, we must imagine first,
The elves present to quench his thirst
A pure seed-pearl of infant dew,
Brought and besweetened in a blue
And pregnant violet; which done,
His kitling [1] eyes begin to run
Quite through the table, where he spies
The horns of papery butterflies:
Of which he eats, and tastes a little
Of that we call the cuckoo's spittle.
A little fuzz-ball pudding stands
By, yet not blessed by his hands,
That was too coarse. But then, forthwith,
He ventures boldly on the pith
Of sugared rush, and eats the sag
And well bestrutted [2] bee's sweet bag,
Gladding his palate with some store
Of emmets' [3] eggs. What would he more?
But beards of mice, a newt's stewed thigh,
A bloated earwig, and a fly,

[1] *Kittenish.*   [2] *With legs far apart.*   [3] *Ants'.*

With the red-capped worm that's shut
Within the concave of a nut,
Brown as his tooth. A little moth,
Late fattened in a piece of cloth:
With withered cherries; mandrake's ears;
Moles' eyes; to these, the slain stag's tears:
The unctuous dewlaps of a snail;
The broke' heart of a nightingale
O'er-come in music; with a wine,
Ne'er ravished from the flattering vine,
But gently pressed from the soft side
Of the most sweet and dainty bride,
Brought in a dainty daisy, which
He fully quaffs up to bewitch
His blood to height. This done, commended
Grace by his priest. *The feast is ended.*

The Mad Maid's Song

Good morrow to the day so fair;
   Good morning, sir, to you:
Good morrow to mine own torn hair
   Bedabbled with the dew.

Good morning to this primrose, too;
   Good morrow to each maid
That will with flowers the tomb bestrew,
   Wherein my love is laid.

Ah! woe is me; woe, woe is me!
   Alack and welladay!
For pity, sir, find out that bee,
   Which bore my love away.

I'll seek him in your bonnet brave;
   I'll seek him in your eyes;
Nay, now I think they've made his grave
   I' the bed of strawberries.

I'll seek him there; I know, ere this,
   The cold, cold earth doth shake him;
But I will go, or send a kiss
   By you, sir, to awake him.

Pray hurt him not; though he be dead,
 He knows well who do love him,
And who with green-turfs rear his head,
 And who do rudely move him.

He's soft and tender (pray take heed),
 With bands of cowslips bind him;
And bring him home; but 'tis decreed,
 That I shall never find him.

Perhaps Herrick's most famous poems are those to his real or imaginary mistresses. They are dexterous variations on the old conflict between love and lover, chastity and possession, and, in particular, the cruel swiftness of time. In Donne the theme was twisted in agony; in Marvell it was teased into deceptive badinage; in Herrick it was prettily, and at times indelicately, delicate.

To the Virgins to Make Much of Time

Gather ye rose-buds while ye may,
 Old Time is still a-flying:
And this same flower that smiles today,
 Tomorrow will be dying.

The glorious lamp of heaven, the Sun,
 The higher he's a-getting
The sooner will his race be run,
 And nearer he's to setting.

That age is best which is the first,
 When youth and blood are warmer;
But being spent, the worse, and worst
 Times, still succeed the former.

Then be not coy, but use your time;
 And while ye may, go marry:
For having lost but once your prime,
 You may for ever tarry.

To Daisies, Not to Shut So Soon

Shut not so soon; the dull-eyed night
   Has not as yet begun
To make a seizure on the light,
   Or to seal up the sun.

No marigolds yet closéd are:
   No shadows great appear;
Nor doth the early shepherd's star
   Shine like a spangle here.

Stay but till my Julia close
   Her life-begetting eye;
And let the whole world then dispose
   Itself to live or die.

To Daffodils

Fair daffodils, we weep to see
   You haste away so soon:
As yet the early-rising sun
   Has not attained his noon.
     Stay, stay,
   Until the hasting day
     Has run
   But to the even-song;
And, having prayed together, we
   Will go with you along.

We have short time to stay, as you,
   We have as short a Spring!
As quick a growth to meet decay
   As you, or any thing.
     We die,
   As your hours do, and dry
     Away
   Like to the Summer's rain;
Or as the pearls of morning's dew
   Ne'er to be found again.

To Violets

Welcome, maids of honor,
  You do bring
  In the spring,
And wait upon her.

She has virgins many,
  Fresh and fair;
  Yet you are
More sweet than any.

You're the maiden posies,
  And so graced
  To be placed
'Fore damask roses.

Yet though thus respected,
  By and by
  Ye do lie,
Poor girls, neglected.

Delight in Disorder

A sweet disorder in the dress
Kindles in clothes a wantonness:
A lawn about the shoulders thrown
Into a fine distraction,
An erring lace, which here and there
Enthralls the crimson stomacher,
A cuff neglectful, and thereby
Ribbands to flow confusedly,
A winning wave (deserving note)
In the tempestuous petticoat,
A careless shoe-string, in whose tie
I see a wild civility,
Do more bewitch me, than when art
Is too precise in every part.

To Dianeme

Sweet, be not proud of those two eyes,
Which, star-like, sparkle in their skies;
Nor be you proud that you can see
All hearts your captives, yours yet free;
Be you not proud of that rich hair,
Which wantons with the love-sick air:
Whenas that ruby which you wear,
Sunk from the tip of your soft ear,
Will last to be a precious stone,
When all your world of beauty's gone.

To Anthea, Who May Command Him Anything

Bid me to live, and I will live
   Thy protestant to be:
Or bid me love, and I will give
   A loving heart to thee.

A heart as soft, a heart as kind,
   A heart as sound and free
As in the whole world thou canst find,
   That heart I'll give to thee.

Bid that heart stay, and it will stay,
   To honor thy decree:
Or bid it languish quite away,
   And 't shall do so for thee.

Bid me to weep, and I will weep
   While I have eyes to see:
And having none, yet I will keep
   A heart to weep for thee.

Bid me despair, and I'll despair,
   Under that cypress tree:
Or bid me die, and I will dare
   E'en Death. to die for thee.

Thou art my life, my love, my heart,
 The very eyes of me,
And hast command of every part,
 To live and die for thee.

The Bracelet to Julia

Why I tie about thy wrist,
Julia, this my silken twist;
For what other reason is't,
But to show thee how in part
Thou my pretty captive art?
But thy bond-slave is my heart.
'Tis but silk that bindeth thee,
Snap the thread and thou art free:
But 'tis otherwise with me;
I am bound, and fast bound so
That from thee I cannot go;
If I could, I would not so.

Upon Julia's Clothes

Whenas in silks my Julia goes
Then, then (methinks) how sweetly flows
That liquefaction of her clothes.

Next, when I cast mine eyes and see
That brave vibration each way free;
O how that glittering taketh me!

Herrick's love poems range from the elaborately courteous to the deliberately frank—there are even a few surprisingly brusque attacks. His art was more consistent than his aim. It is, for example, hard to know whether the following poem is a piece of boastfulness or a defeated wish, or a combination of the two.

What Kind of Mistress He Would Have

Be the mistress of my choice
Clean in manners, clear in voice;
Be she witty, more than wise,
Pure enough, though not precise;
Be she showing in her dress
Like a civil wilderness,
That the curious may detect
Order in a sweet neglect;
Be she rolling in her eye,
Tempting all the passers-by,
And each ringlet of her hair
An enchantment or a snare
For to catch the lookers-on;
But herself held fast by none.
Let her Lucrece all day be,
Thais in the night, to me.
Be she such as neither will
Famish me nor over-fill.

Always in danger as a bachelor, Herrick flirted with his sweet-hearts, but escaped them for a houseful of pets. Attempting to live up to a philosophy of indulgence, he wooed with fervor and all the expected warm protestations. But, somehow, he kept himself from being deeply involved. It is doubtful that, for all his love lyrics, he really wanted the passionate fulfillment of love. That he dreaded its demands is revealed in a curious and little-known dream poem in which the light measures are weighted with fear and the very grace becomes macabre.

Upon Love

Love brought me to a silent grove,
  And showed me there a tree,
Where some had hanged themselves for love,
  And gave a twist to me.

The halter was of silk and gold,
  That he reached forth unto me:
No otherwise, than if he would
  By dainty things undo me.

He bade me then that necklace use;
And told me too, he maketh
A glorious end by such a noose,
His death for love that taketh.

'Twas but a dream; but had I been
There really alone,
My desperate fears, in love, had seen
Mine execution.

As in nis verse, so in his life, Herrick avoided excess. He tippled
and trifled—but cautiously. He said, rather ruefully, he could never
"thrive in frenzy." It must be remembered that, besides being a
poet, Herrick was a preacher. As a divine he composed many "pious
pieces," most of which he offered in a collection called, somewhat
vaingloriously, NOBLE NUMBERS. The best of these are not the more
solemn but the more childlike, particularly the little verses to and
about children. Herrick also delighted in whimsical verses about
birds, beasts, and flowers. His lines to the robin redbreast form one
of the most delightful of all punning epitaphs.

Grace for a Child

Here a little child I stand,
Heaving up my either hand;
Cold as paddocks though they be,
Here I lift them up to Thee,
For a benison to fall
On our meat and on us all.

Upon a Child

Here a pretty baby lies
Sung asleep with lullabies;
Pray be silent, and not stir
Th' easy earth that covers her.

To Robin Redbreast

Laid out for dead, let thy last kindness be
With leaves and moss-work for to cover me.
And while the wood-nymphs my cold corpse inter,
Sing thou my dirge, sweet-warbling chorister.
For epitaph, in foliage, next write this:
Here, here the tomb of Robin Herrick is.

For more than a century after his death Herrick was completely forgotten. It was not until John Nichols "revived" him in 1796 that Herrick was again read with fresh delight. Today he is appreciated not only for his picturesqueness but for his purity. Perhaps he is too naïve; perhaps there never were such exquisite creatures and such Arcadian countrysides. But, if they are unreal, they are as haunting, as tantalizingly dear, as a happy dream. Certainly Herrick is not one of the major poets, but he is a craftsman in the great tradition. His work is a chain of carved gems, nonessential luxuries, semiprecious but perfect.

FRANCIS QUARLES
[1592–1644]

FRANCIS QUARLES was one of the fortunate. He did not have to pursue success; it followed him. Careers were thrust upon him as soon as he graduated from Christ's College, Cambridge. He was cupbearer to the Princess Elizabeth and went abroad in her suite when she married the Elector Palatine. After twelve years of luxurious living, he returned to become secretary to the famous Ussher, Primate of Ireland. Back in England in his forties, he succeeded Ben Jonson as city chronologer. Although Quarles favored the Royalists and wrote pamphlets in support of the King's cause, the Civil War affected him only temporarily. He was fortune's confident child. There was no stint to the fullness of his domestic life; his wife bore him eighteen children.

Quarles was, as might be expected, a prolific poet. He labored lightly and won immediate fame with his "emblematic" verse. His chief book, EMBLEMS, is one of the curiosities of literature. Many of the poems are whimsically shaped; others are so patterned as to read two ways. Each "emblem" consists of an elaborate paraphrase from the Scriptures, followed by a more or less relevant passage from the Fathers of the Church, and rounded off with an epigram. Critics condemned the dubious artistry; clergymen questioned the taste of the juxtapositions. But the poems were singularly popular.

A Good Night

Close now thine eyes and rest secure;
Thy soul is safe enough, thy body sure;
        He that loves thee, he that keeps
And guards thee, never slumbers, never sleeps.
The smiling Conscience in a sleeping breast
        Has only peace, has only rest;
        The music and the mirth of kings
Are all but very discords, when she sings;
        Then close thine eyes and rest secure;
No sleep so sweet as thine, no rest so sure.

On the Needle of a Sundial

Behold this needle when the arctic stone
Has touched it, how it trembles up and down;
Hunts for the Pole, and cannot be possessed
Of peace until it find that point, and rest:

Such is the heart of man, which when it hath
Attained the virtue of a lively faith,
It finds no rest on earth, makes no abode,
In any object but his heaven, his God.

"*My Beloved Is Mine, and I Am His*"

THE SONG OF SONGS ii, 16

Even like two little bank-dividing brooks
  That wash the pebbles with their wanton streams,
And having ranged and searched a thousand nooks,
  Meet both at length in silver-breasted Thames,
    Where in a greater current they conjoin,
So I my best beloved's am; so he is mine.

Even so we met, and after long pursuit,
  Even so we joined; we both became entire.
No need for either to renew a suit,
  For I was flax, and he was flames of fire,
    Our firm-united souls did more than twine;
So I my best beloved's am; so he is mine.

Nor time, nor place, nor chance, nor death can bow
  My least desires unto the least remove;
He's firmly mine by oath, I his by vow;
  He's mine by faith, and I am his by love;
    He's mine by water, I am his by wine;
Thus I my best beloved's am; thus he is mine.

He is my altar; I, his holy place;
  I am his guest, and he my living food;
I'm his by penitence, he mine by grace;
  I'm his by purchase, he is mine by blood!
    He's my supporting elm, and I his vine;
Thus I my best beloved's am; thus he is mine

He gives me wealth, I give him all my vows;
  I give him songs, he gives me length of days;
With wreaths of grace he crowns my conquering brows,
  And I his temples with a crown of praise,
    Which he accepts as an everlasting sign
That I my best beloved's am, that he is mine.

HENRY KING

[1592–1669]

HENRY KING fished with Izaak Walton, drank with Ben Jonson, and argued with John Donne; but he followed the calling of his father, a celebrated churchman. A prebend of St. Paul's in his thirties, he became Bishop of Chichester in his fiftieth year. He did not enjoy his eminence long. A few months later the Puritans expelled him from his see, and the bishopric was not restored to him until after Charles II regained the throne. King lived on until his late seventies, beloved by all. He was Donne's executor, and it was King who arranged to have Donne's cadaverous monument put in St. Paul's.

Critical opinion has always been divided between appreciation of King's sacred and profane poems. The religious verse shows traces of Donne; the secular stanzas are influenced by Jonson, to whom King's book was dedicated. Lacking Donne's intensity and Jonson's nimbleness, King's touch is more tentative, his music is thinner. But the best of his verses are memorably, though unpretentiously, his own.

That Distant Bliss

Tell me no more how fair she is,
    I have no mind to hear
The story of that distant bliss
    I never shall come near;
By sad experience I have found
That her perfection is my wound.

And tell me not how fond I am
    To tempt a daring fate,
From whence no triumph ever came,
    But to repent too late;
There is some hope ere long I may
In silence dote myself away.

        I ask no pity, Love, from thee,
          Nor will thy justice blame,
        So that thou wilt not envy me
          The glory of my flame;
        Which crowns my heart whene'er it dies,
        In that it falls her sacrifice.

The Surrender

My once dear love, hapless that I no more
Must call thee so: the rich affections' store
That fed our hopes, lies now exhaust and spent,
Like sums of treasure unto bankrupts lent.

We that did nothing study but the way
To love each other, with which thoughts the day
Rose with delight to us, and with them set,
Must learn the hateful art, how to forget.

We that did nothing wish that heaven could give
Beyond ourselves, nor did desire to live
Beyond that wish, all these now cancel must
As if not writ in faith, but words and dust.

Yet witness those clear vows which lovers make;
Witness the chaste desires that never break
Into unruly heats; witness that breast
Which in thy bosom anchored his whole rest.
'Tis no default in us, I dare acquite
Thy maiden faith, thy purpose fair and white
As thy pure self. Cross planets did envý
Us to each other, and heaven did untie
Faster than vows could bind. O that the stars,
When lovers meet, should stand opposed in wars!

Since then some higher destinies command,
Let us not strive, nor labor to withstand
What is past help. The longest date of grief
Can never yield a hope of our relief;
And though we waste ourselves in moist laments,
Tears may drown us, but not our discontents.

Fold back our arms, take home our fruitless loves,
That must new fortunes try, like turtle doves
Dislodgéd from their haunts. We must in tears
Unwind a love knit up in many years.
In this last kiss I here surrender thee
Back to thyself, so thou again art free;
Thou in another, sad as that, resend
The truest heart that lover e'er did lend.

Now turn from each. So fare our severed hearts
As the divorced soul from her body parts.

A Contemplation Upon Flowers

Brave flowers—that I could gallant it like you,
  And be so little vain!
You come abroad, and make a harmless show,
  And to your beds of earth again.
You are not proud: you know your birth:
For your embroider'd garments are from earth.

You do obey your months and times, but I
  Would have it ever Spring:
My fate would know no Winter, never die,
  Nor think of such a thing.
O that I could my bed of earth but view
And smile, and look as cheerfully as you!

O teach me to see Death and not to fear,
  But rather to take truce!
How often have I seen you at a bier,
  And there look fresh and spruce!
You fragrant flowers, then teach me, that my breath
Like yours may sweeten and perfume my death.

Of Human Life

  Like to the falling of a star,
  Or as the flights of eagles are,
  Or like the fresh spring's gaudy hue,
  Or silver drops of morning dew,

Or like a wind that chafes the flood,
Or bubbles which on water stood:
Even such is man, whose borrowed light
Is straight called in, and paid to night.
The wind blows out, the bubble dies;
The spring entombed in autumn lies;
The dew dries up, the star is shot;
The flight is past—and man forgot.

Although a minor poet, King has been admired by the great. The dark genius of Poe responded to the spirit of the seventeenth-century prelate. Poe prefaced his story THE ASSIGNATION with a quotation from King's THE EXEQUY (a poem written in memory of King's first wife, who died young), and the climax of Poe's Gothic tale is pointed by two lines from King, a couplet which is curiously Poesque:

Stay for me there! I will not fail
To meet thee in that hollow vale.

FROM

The Exequy

Sleep on, my love, in thy cold bed,
Never to be disquieted!
My last good-night! Thou wilt not wake
Till I thy fate shall overtake;
Till age, or grief, or sickness must
Marry my body to that dust
It so much loves, and fill the room
My heart keeps empty in thy tomb.
Stay for me there! I will not fail
To meet thee in that hollow vale.
And think not much of my delay;
I am already on the way,
And follow thee with all the speed
Desire can make, or sorrows breed.
Each minute is a short degree,
And every hour a step towards thee.
At night when I betake to rest,
Next morn I rise nearer my west
Of life, almost by eight hours' sail,
Than when sleep breathed his drowsy gale.

GEORGE HERBERT
[1593–1633]

I**T IS** little wonder that he was known as "holy George Herbert," for all the commentators stress his kindness, sweetness, and even saintliness. These usually cloying characteristics affected neither Herbert nor his work with sentimentality. On the contrary, his poetry is distinguished by quaintness, inventiveness, and continual oddity. Never has there been a poetry at once so pious and so playful.

Born of a noble family, educated at Westminster and Trinity College, Cambridge, Herbert went to court in his early twenties and seemed destined for a political career. But he was strongly influenced by his mother's great friend, John Donne, and turned to religious verse with a fixed intention of devoting himself only to the "Divine Muse"; it is said that Donne "converted" Herbert not only to poetry but to the church. Seeking the further stability of marriage, at thirty-six he was fortunate enough to find Jane Danvers, who was young, beautiful, and wealthy, if not too intelligent. They were married three days after he met her. A few months later Herbert "changed his sword and silk clothes into a canonical habit" and was made rector of Bemerton, where he lived out his few remaining years. The poet's life at Bemerton has been tenderly described by Izaak Walton, who pictures Herbert walking miles to the cathedral at Salisbury, singing and playing his part at musical gatherings, so beloved by his parishioners that even the farmers "let their plows rest when Mr. Herbert's saint's bell rung to prayers, that they might also offer their devotions to God with him."

It is not known when Herbert contracted the consumption which killed him in his fortieth year, but he must have been aware of it for some time. He made many preparations for the end. Like Donne he regarded dying as a ritual; like Campion, musician as well as poet, Herbert sang his own songs and accompanied himself on the lute. On his deathbed he composed "such hymns and anthems as the angels and he now sing in heaven."

Although Herbert's first love was music, his deepest passion was for the church. The church is not only Herbert's symbol of Christianity, it is the source of his metaphors. His poetry is built about it. The church floor becomes the foundation of faith; the trodden stones represent patience and humility; the plaster that holds all together is love; even the key of the church door suggests the sin that locks the poet's hands. Yet Herbert is rarely sanctimonious. Wit saves him from pomposity, and when Herbert is most devout he is most fanciful. He has a way of treating the most solemn things in the most startling manner; of the 169 poems in THE TEMPLE, more than one hundred are written in differing meters, meters which are never repeated. Moreover, Herbert delights in peculiar forms, odd patterns, and anagrams. He can keep serious emotions and whimsical ideas in the air like a juggler's balls; he can compose a poem the point of which is the pun "Jesu: I-Ease-U." A poem entitled EASTER WINGS is so spaced that the two verses become a pair of long, pointed wings. THE ALTAR is so written and arranged that the first four lines represent the top of the altar, the middle eight lines are the column, and the concluding four lines are the stone base.

The Altar

A   broken   altar,   Lord,   thy   servant   rears,
Made   of   a   heart   and   cémented   with   tears;
  Whose   parts   are   as   thy   hand   did   frame;
  No   workman's   tool   hath   touched   the   same.
     A   heart   alone
     Is   such   a   stone
     As   nothing   but
     Thy power doth cut.
     Wherefore each part
     Of   my   hard   heart
     Meets   in   this   frame
     To   praise   thy   name;
  That   if   I   chance   to   hold   my   peace,
  These   stones   to   praise   thee   may   not   cease.
Oh,   let   thy   blesséd   sacrifice   be   mine,
And   sanctify   this   altar   to   be   thine.

Another poem, appropriately entitled OUR LIFE IS HID, is orthodox enough on the surface, but the key words are concealed in an elaborate acrostic. Even more diverting and equally devout are the stanzas entitled PARADISE. Here Herbert's ingenuity and imagination are perfectly fused. The rhymes are attained in an unexpected manner: the first letter of each rhyming word is successively dropped ("grow," "row," "ow") and what begins as an artful technique ends in quiet dignity.

Paradise

I bless Thee, Lord, because I GROW
Among Thy trees, which in a ROW
To Thee both fruit and order OW(E).

What open force, or hidden CHARM
Can blast my fruit, or bring me HARM,
While the inclosure is Thine ARM:

Inclose me still for fear I START;
Be to me rather sharp and TART,
Than let me want Thy hand and ART.

When Thou dost greater judgments SPARE,
And with Thy knife but prune and PARE,
Even fruitful trees more fruitful ARE:

Such sharpness shows the sweetest FR(I)END,
Such cuttings rather heal than REND,
And such beginnings touch their END.

Herbert is never without the gift of surprise. Other versifiers have used "echo rhymes" for purely humorous effects, such as John G. Saxe in the facetious ECHO. But Herbert adds earnestness to the pattern and makes a poem which is not merely facile, but personal and poignant

Heaven

O, who will show me those delights on high?
                  ECHO: *I.*
Thou Echo, thou art mortal, all men know.
                  ECHO: *No.*
Wert thou not born among the trees and leaves?
                  ECHO: *Leaves.*

And are there any leaves that still abide?
> ECHO: *Bide.*

What leaves are they? impart the matter wholly.
> ECHO: *Holy.*

Are holy leaves the Echo, then, of bliss?
> ECHO: *Yes.*

Then tell me, what is that supreme delight?
> ECHO: *Light.*

Light to the mind; what shall the will enjoy?
> ECHO: *Joy.*

But are there cares and business with the pleasure?
> ECHO: *Leisure.*

Light, joy, and leisure; but shall they perséver?
> ECHO: *Ever.*

The linking of nobility with trickery is found not only in Herbert's verses which are novel but in the most straightforward of his poems. THE PULLEY is a prime example of Herbert's peculiar symbolism. The central figure is arresting, the lines stretch the metaphor almost beyond its bounds, the play upon the word "Rest" and "the rest" is amusing, but the poem itself transcends entertainment.

The Pulley

When God at first made man,
Having a glass of blessings standing by—
"Let us," said he, "pour on him all we can;
Let the world's riches, which disperséd lie,
   Contract into a span."

So strength first made a way,
Then beauty flowed, then wisdom, honor, pleasure
When almost all was out, God made a stay,
Perceiving that, alone of all his treasure,
   Rest in the bottom lay.

"For if I should," said he,
"Bestow this jewel also on my creature,
He would adore my gifts instead of me,
And rest in nature, not the God of nature:
   So both should losers be.

> "Yet let him keep the rest,
> But keep them with repining restlessness;
> Let him be rich and weary, that at least,
> If goodness lead him not, yet weariness
> May toss him to my breast."

Herbert usually shields his troubled emotion behind an ingenuity so dazzling that it is sometimes distracting, but there are moments when his passion breaks through ambiguity. THE COLLAR is a magnificent instance. In TEXTS AND PRETEXTS Aldous Huxley says flatly that THE COLLAR is "among the most moving poems in all our literature."

The Collar

> I struck the board and cried, No more!
>   I will abroad.
> What! Shall I ever sigh and pine?
> My lines and life are free, free as the road,
>   Loose as the wind, as large as store.
>   Shall I be still in suit?
>   Have I no harvest but a thorn
>   To let me blood, and not restore
> What I have lost with cordial fruit?
>   Sure there was wine
> Before my sighs did dry it; there was corn
>   Before my tears did drown it.
>   Is the year only lost to me?
>   Have I no bays to crown it?
> No flowers, no garlands gay? All blasted?
>   All wasted?
>   Not so, my heart! But there is fruit,
>   And thou hast hands.
>   Recover all thy sigh-blown age
> On double pleasures. Leave thy cold dispute
> Of what is fit and not. Forsake thy cage,
>   Thy rope of sands,
> Which petty thoughts have made, and made to thee
>   Good cable, to enforce and draw,
>   And be thy law,
> While thou didst wink and wouldst not see.
>   Away! Take heed!
>   I will abroad.

Call in thy death's head there. Tie up thy fears.
He that forbears
To suit and serve his need
Deserves his load.
But as I raved and grew more fierce and wild
At every word,
Methought I heard one calling, "Child!"
And I replied, "My Lord."

One of Herbert's noblest poems has occasioned a scholars' un-settled dispute. Most editors print the eighth line of MAN as

And more: He is a tree, yet bears no fruit.

Such a reading contradicts the sense and is at complete variance with Herbert's intention. It is likely that a copyist mistook the obsolete word "mo" or "moe" for "no" and thus perpetuated the error. That it is a serious error can scarcely be doubted. Herbert is declaring that man "is everything," the peak of creation—"and more!" He is a tree, not because he bears *no* fruit (which would be a false fact as well as a poetic anticlimax), but because he bears more various, more splendid, and ever-renewing fruit.

Man

My God, I heard this day
That none doth build a stately habitation,
But he that means to dwell therein.
What house more stately hath there been,
Or can be, than is man? to whose creation
All things are in decay.

For man is everything,
And more: He is a tree, yet bears more fruit;
A beast, yet is, or should be, more:
Reason and speech we only bring;
Parrots may thank us, if they are not mute,
They go upon the score.[1]

Man is all symmetry,
Full of proportions, one limb to another,
And all to all the world besides;
Each part may call the furthest, brother,
For head with foot hath private amity,
And both with moons and tides.

[1] *That is, by what they learn from man.*

Nothing hath got so far,
But man hath caught and kept it as his prey;
  His eyes dismount [2] the highest star;
  He is in little all the sphere;
Herbs gladly cure our flesh, because that they
    Find their acquaintance there.

For us the winds do blow;
The earth doth rest, heaven move, and fountains flow;
  Nothing we see but means our good,
  As our delight or as our treasure.
The whole is either our cupboard of food,
    Or cabinet of pleasure.

The stars have us to bed;
Night draws the curtain, which the sun withdraws;
  Music and light attend our head.
  All things unto our flesh are kind
In their descent and being; to our mind
    In their ascent and cause.

Each thing is full of duty:
Waters united are our navigation;
  Distinguishéd, our habitation.
  Below, our drink; above, our meat;
Both are our cleanliness. Hath one such beauty?
    Then how are all things neat!

More servants wait on man
Than he'll take notice of: in every path
  He treads down that which doth befriend him
  When sickness makes him pale and wan.
O mighty love! Man is one world, and hath
    Another to attend him.

Since then, my God, thou hast
So brave a palace built, O dwell in it,
  That it may dwell with thee at last!
  Till then afford us so much wit,
That, as the world serves us, we may serve thee,
    And both thy servants be.

Never commonplace, Herbert's poetry strikes a continual balance
between solemn spirit and buoyant intellect. His poetry is a para-

2 *Bring near the earth.*

dox uniting the homely and the bizarre, a controlled effusiveness. It can celebrate the idea of worship and service—"Who sweeps a room as for thy laws Makes that and the action fine"—as roundly as Browning. Its strength is so secure that it can dispense with conceits and images. It can be as clipped as in DISCIPLINE, as direct as in VIRTUE, as melodious as in EASTER, and as radiantly simple as in LOVE.

Easter

I got me flowers to straw thy way,
  I got me boughs off many a tree,
But thou wast up by break of day,
  And brought'st thy sweets along with thee.

The sun arising in the east,
  Though he give light, and the east perfume,
If they should offer to contest
  With thy arising, they presume.

Can there be any day but this,
  Though many suns to shine endeavor?
We count three hundred, but we miss;
  There is but one, and that one ever.

Discipline

Throw away thy rod,
Throw away thy wrath;
  O my God,
Take the gentle path.

For my heart's desire
Unto thine is bent;
  I aspire
To a full consent.

Not a word or look
I affect to own,
  But by book,
And thy Book alone.

Though I fail, I weep;
Though I halt in pace,
    Yet I creep
To the throne of grace.

Then let wrath remove;
Love will do the deed;
    For with love
Stony hearts will bleed.

Love is swift of foot;
Love's a man of war,
    And can shoot,
And can hit from far.

Who can 'scape his bow?
That which wrought on thee,
    Brought thee low,
Needs must work on me.

Throw away thy rod:
Though man frailties hath,
    Thou art God;
Throw away thy wrath.

The Elixir[1]

Teach me, my God and King,
    In all things thee to see,
And what I do in anything
    To do it as for thee.

Not rudely, as a beast,
    To run into an action;
But still to make thee prepossest,
    And give it his perfection.

A man that looks on glass,
    On it may stay his eye;
Or, if he pleaseth, through it pass,
    And then the heaven espy.

[1] *Sometimes entitled, and with equal appropriateness,* PERFECTION.

All may of thee partake:
  Nothing can be so mean
Which with his tincture (for thy sake)
  Will not grow bright and clean.

A servant with this clause
  Makes drudgery divine;
Who sweeps a room as for thy laws
  Makes that and the action fine.

This is the famous stone
  That turneth all to gold;
For that which God doth touch and own
  Cannot for less be told.

Virtue

Sweet day, so cool, so calm, so bright,
The bridal of the earth and sky;
The dew shall weep thy fall tonight,
        For thou must die.

Sweet rose, whose hue, angry and brave,
Bids the rash gazer wipe his eye;
Thy root is ever in its grave,
        And thou must die.

Sweet spring, full of sweet days and roses,
A box where sweets compacted lie;
My music shows ye have your closes,
        And all must die.

Only a sweet and virtuous soul,
Like seasoned timber, never gives;
But though the whole world turn to coal,
        Then chiefly lives.

Love

Love bade me welcome; yet my soul drew back
        Guilty of dust and sin.
But quick-eyed Love, observing me grow slack
        From my first entrance in,
Drew nearer to me, sweetly questioning
        If I lacked anything.

"A guest," I answered, "worthy to be here."
   Love said, "You shall be he."
"I, the unkind, ungrateful? Ah, my dear,
   I cannot look on Thee."
Love took my hand, and smiling, did reply,
   "Who made the eyes but I?"

"Truth, Lord, but I have marred them: let my shame
   Go where it doth deserve."
"And know you not," says Love, "who bore the blame?"
   "My dear, then I will serve."
"You must sit down," says Love, "and taste my meat."
   So I did sit and eat.

THOMAS CAREW

[1595?–1639?]

CAREW enjoyed life and the King's favor more than most of his
contemporaries. An aristocrat by birth, he entered Merton
College, Oxford, at thirteen and took his B.A. in his seventeenth
year. Before he was twenty he was sent to Italy in the ambassador's
retinue, and he remained in Europe in diplomatic service until he
was made gentleman of the privy chamber. He was then thirty-three,
an intimate of Ben Jonson and Sir John Suckling, and "server" or
"taster" to Charles I. He arranged masques and entertainments for
the royal household, charmed the court with his "pleasant and
facetious wit," and allowed himself more than the usual amount
of excesses. He is supposed to have died in 1639, at forty-four, after
a life begun in luxury, "spent with less severity and exactness than
it ought to have been," and ending with a deathbed repentance.

His contemporaries admired the sharpness of Carew's fancies,
although Suckling hinted that Carew's Muse was "hard-bound"
and his verse "was seldom brought forth but with trouble and
pain." It is true that many of Carew's lines are artfully contrived
and even "sleeked." But a dozen or more of his terser poems are
so neatly manipulated and yet so apparently natural that they are
among the best of their kind.

A Song

Ask me no more where Jove bestows,
When June is past, the fading rose;
For in your beauty's orient deep
These flowers, as in their causes, sleep.

Ask me no more whither do stray
The golden atoms of the day;
For in pure love heaven did prepare
Those powders to enrich your hair.

Ask me no more whither doth haste
The nightingale, when May is past;
For in your sweet dividing throat
She winters, and keeps warm her note.

Ask me no more where those stars light,
That downwards fall in dead of night;
For in your eyes they sit, and there
Fixed become, as in their sphere.

Ask me no more if east or west
The phœnix builds her spicy nest;
For unto you at last she flies,
And in your fragrant bosom dies.

More Love or More Disdain

Give me more love or more disdain;
    The torrid or the frozen zone
Bring equal ease unto my pain,
    The temperate affords me none:
Either extreme of love or hate,
Is sweeter than a calm estate.

Give me a storm; if it be love,
    Like Danaë in that golden shower,
I swim in pleasure; if it prove
    Disdain, that torrent will devour
My vulture-hopes; and he's possess'd
Of heaven, that's but from hell released.

Then crown my joys or cure my pain:
Give me more love or more disdain.

Spring

Now that the winter's gone, the earth hath lost
Her snow-white robes; and now no more the frost
Candies the grass, or casts an icy cream
Upon the silver lake or crystal stream:
But the warm sun thaws the benumbed earth,
And makes it tender; gives a sacred birth
To the dead swallow; wakes in hollow tree
The drowsy cuckoo and the humble-bee.
Now do a choir of chirping minstrels bring,
In triumph to the world, the youthful spring:
The valleys, hills, and woods in rich array
Welcome the coming of the longed-for May.

Now all things smile: only my love doth lower,
Nor hath the scalding noon-day sun the power
To melt that marble ice, which still doth hold
Her heart congealed, and makes her pity cold.
The ox, which lately did for shelter fly
Into the stall, doth now securely lie
In open fields; and love no more is made
By the fire-side, but in the cooler shade
Amyntas now doth with his Chloris sleep
Under a sycamore, and all things keep
Time with the season: only she doth carry
June in her eyes, in her heart January.

Carew's reputation for profligacy is not sustained by most of his verses, although A RAPTURE and THE SECOND RAPTURE are frankly licentious. Yet many of Carew's songs break through the period's conventions and their own prettiness. TO MY INCONSTANT MISTRESS is an example of Carew's ability to put a shrug to music. And the last, and usually omitted, verse of the famous "He that loves a rosy cheek" returns scorn for disdain.

To My Inconstant Mistress

When thou, poor excommunicate
  From all the joys of love, shalt see
The full reward and glorious fate
  Which my strong faith shall purchase me,
  Then curse thine own inconstancy.

A fairer hand than thine shall cure
  That heart, which thy false oaths did wound;
And to my soul a soul more pure
  Than thine shall by Love's hand be bound,
  And both with equal glory crown'd.

Then shalt thou weep, entreat, complain
  To Love, as I did once to thee;
When all thy tears shall be as vain
  As mine were then, for thou shalt be
  Damned for thy false apostasy.

The Lover Consults With Reason

Lover

Weep not, nor backward turn your beams,
  Fond eyes! Sad sighs, lock in your breath,
Lest on this wind, or in those streams,
  My grieved soul fly or sail to death.
Fortune destroys me if I stay,
Love kills me if I go away:
Since Love and Fortune both are blind,
Come, Reason, and resolve my doubtful mind.

Reason

Fly! and blind Fortune be thy guide,
  And 'gainst the blinder god rebel.
Thy love-sick heart shall not reside
  Where scorn and self-willed error dwell;
Where entrance unto Truth is barred,
Where Love and Faith find no reward:
For my just hand may sometimes move
The wheel of Fortune, not the sphere of Love.

Disdain Returned

He that loves a rosy cheek,
   Or a coral lip admires,
Or from star-like eyes doth seek
   Fuel to maintain his fires;
As old Time makes these decay,
So his flames must waste away.

But a smooth and steadfast mind,
   Gentle thoughts and calm desires,
Hearts with equal love combined,
   Kindle never-dying fires.
Where these are not, I despise
Lovely cheeks, or lips, or eyes.

No tears, Celia, now shall win
   My resolved heart to return;
I have searched thy soul within,
   And find nought but pride and scorn:
I have learned thy arts, and now
Can disdain as much as thou.
   Some power in my revenge convey
   That love to her I cast away.

JAMES SHIRLEY
[1596–1666]

UNTIL he found success as a dramatist, Shirley suffered a series
of broken careers. He planned to be a scholar, chose to be a
clergyman and held a living near St. Albans, was converted to
Catholicism, became master of a grammar school, and finally set-
tled in London. He began to write plays in his late twenties, and
he had produced more than thirty tragedies and comedies when the
Puritan edict of 1642 put a stop to it. Thereafter he supported him-
self by teaching and occasional pamphleteering. He lived in relative
security until after his seventieth birthday, when he was driven
from his home by the Great Fire of London. He and his wife died
of shock and exposure.

As a dramatist, Shirley was effective without being original. He had the ability to take stock situations and ring new changes upon them; Edmund Gosse speaks of THE CARDINAL as "perhaps the last great play produced by the giants of the Elizabethan age." Most of Shirley's poems are forgotten, not undeservedly; but THE GLORIES OF OUR BLOOD AND STATE is so restrained and yet so eloquent that it is sure of its place in English poetry, a place not far from Shakespeare's dirge:

> Golden lads and girls all must,
> As chimney sweepers, come to dust.

It is said that the implications of the song, which used to be sung to King Charles, terrified Cromwell.

The Glories of Our Blood and State

The glories of our blood and state
    Are shadows, not substantial things;
There is no armor against fate;
    Death lays his icy hand on kings:
        Sceptre and Crown
        Must tumble down,
And in the dust be equal made
With the poor crooked scythe and spade.

Some men with swords may reap the field,
    And plant fresh laurels where they kill:
But their strong nerves at last must yield;
    They tame but one another still:
        Early or late
        They stoop to fate,
And must give up their murmuring breath
When they, pale captives, creep to death.

The garlands wither on your brow;
    Then boast no more your mighty deeds;
Upon Death's purple altar now
    See where the victor-victim bleeds:
        Your heads must come
        To the cold tomb.
Only the actions of the just
Smell sweet, and blossom in their dust.

from AJAX AND ULYSSES

Victorious Men of Earth

Victorious men of earth, no more
   Proclaim how wide your empires are;
Though you bind in every shore
   And your triumphs reach as far
      As night or day,
Yet you, proud monarchs, must obey
And mingle with forgotten ashes, when
Death calls ye to the crowd of common men.

Devouring Famine, Plague, and War,
   Each able to undo mankind,
Death's servile emissaries are;
   Nor to these alone confined,
      He hath at will
More quaint and subtle ways to kill;
A smile or kiss, as he will use the art,
Shall have the cunning skill to break a heart.
          from CUPID AND DEATH

WILLIAM DAVENANT
[1606–1668]

Two things have given Davenant's work extra glamour: he was England's second poet laureate, and legend credited him with being the illegitimate son of Shakespeare. His mother was the attractive wife of the proprietor of the Crown Inn at Oxford; and Shakespeare, it is said, found it agreeable if not imperative to visit Oxford more than his business warranted. Since Shakespeare never concealed his regard for the innkeeper's wife, gossip fastened Davenant's paternity on him; and Davenant, later in life, took care to abet the rumor.

His star was swift in its ascendancy. After attending Lincoln College, Oxford, but not waiting to graduate, Davenant became a page to the Duchess of Richmond, supported King Charles during the Civil War, was knighted at the siege of Gloucester, joined the exiled royal family in France, and went back and forth on diplomatic missions. Before the flight, Davenant had achieved success with plays and masques; the court voted him its favorite poet; in his thirty-second year he followed Jonson as laureate. After the victories of Cromwell, Davenant, in his forty-fourth year, organized an expedition to sail to Virginia, but his ship was stopped in the Channel. He was seized, charged with treason, sent to prison, and released (according to one story) on the personal plea of Milton. One likes to believe the pleasant, but unverified, report that Davenant, in turn, interceded for Milton when Charles II was restored to the throne.

Davenant was one of the first, if not the very first, to "modernize" the stage by employing elaborate changes of scenery and by training women instead of boys to play the female roles. He adapted many of his predecessors' plays, especially Shakespeare's, and "refined" them to conform to the bad taste of his day. His liberties were seldom condemned; on the contrary, Davenant was applauded for having "promoted those rational pleasures that are fittest for the entertainment of a civilized people." His popularity was so great that, in spite of inconsiderable achievements, he was ceremoniously laid to rest in Westminster Abbey. A few years later Milton was buried in the ordinary graveyard of a small church.

Davenant's reputation as a poet grew on GONDIBERT, a long "heroic" poem. A sprawling, theatrical narrative, it continued to fascinate readers in spite of its faults of proportion, its laborious idealizations, its stilted philosophy. Yet Scott admired it, and Isaac Disraeli acclaimed the author as a great poet and predicted that his work was "imperishable." Alas for prophecy! GONDIBERT has permanently perished, buried beyond hope of resurrection. Only a few lyrics persist, the best of them being the little MORNING SONG which Davenant wrote for no particular play and for no other purpose than a moment's pleasure.

Morning Song

The lark now leaves his watery nest,
    And, climbing, shakes his dewy wings.
He takes this window for the East,
    And to implore your light he sings—
Awake! awake! The morn will never rise
Till she can dress her beauty at your eyes.

The merchant bows unto the seaman's star,
   The ploughman from the sun his season takes;
But still the lover wonders what they are
   Who look for day before his mistress wakes.
Awake! awake! Break through your veils of lawn!
Then draw your curtains, and begin the dawn!

What Is Past

Weep no more for what is past,
For Time in motion makes such haste
He hath no leisure to descry
Those errors which he passeth by.
If we consider accident,
   And how repugnant unto sense
It pays desert with bad event,
   We shall disparage Providence.

from THE CRUEL BROTHER

EDMUND WALLER
[1606–1687]

EXCELLENTLY educated, handsomely provided for, the inheritor
of Beaconsfield in Buckinghamshire, Edmund Waller (the say-
ing went) was "nursed in parliaments." So zealous was he of remain-
ing in office that he shifted causes and changed sides with consistent
inconsistency. His allegiances were so quickly formed and so readily
broken, his self-seeking so adroit, that he seems to have had every
political sense except a sense of loyalty. A trained sycophant, he was
equally at home in King Charles' court and the recalcitrant House
of Commons. He headed a Royalist intrigue, known as "Waller's
Plot," was arrested and sent to the Tower, paid a fine of ten thou-
sand pounds, recanted, and, in one of the shabbiest confessions ever
recorded, betrayed all his friends.

As a professional poet Waller was scarcely more honorable. In
his fiftieth year, he wrote A PANEGYRIC TO MY LORD PROTECTOR and a
few years later a fulsome tribute TO THE KING, UPON HIS MAJESTY'S

HAPPY RETURN. The second piece was obviously inferior to the first, and when Charles II demanded to know the reason for this, Waller glibly replied, "Sir, we poets never succeed so well in writing truth as in fiction." Waller's smaller verses were more esteemed and often reprinted. Many of them, particularly the graceful ON A GIRDLE and GO, LOVELY ROSE, which is an extension of Herrick's favorite theme, owed much of their popularity to the exquisite settings by Henry Lawes. Dryden commended Waller's "polished simplicity," and Waller's closely organized rhymes led to the stricter couplets' of Pope. But it is by the least pretentious of his verse that Waller is best known.

Go, Lovely Rose!

Go, lovely rose!
Tell her, that wastes her time and me,
    That now she knows,
When I resemble her to thee,
How sweet and fair she seems to be.

Tell her that's young
And shuns to have her graces spied,
    That hadst thou sprung
In deserts, where no men abide,
Thou must have uncommended died.

Small is the worth
Of beauty from the light retired:
    Bid her come forth,
Suffer herself to be desired,
And not blush so to be admired.

Then die! that she
The common fate of all things rare
    May read in thee:
How small a part of time they share
That are so wondrous sweet and fair!

On a Girdle

That which her slender waist confined
Shall now my joyful temples bind;
No monarch but would give his crown
His arms might do what this has done.

It was my heaven's extremest sphere,
The pale which held that lovely deer;
My joy, my grief, my hope, my love
Did all within this circle move.

A narrow compass! and yet there
Dwelt all that's good, and all that's fair.
Give me but what this ribband bound,
Take all the rest the sun goes round.

The Dancer

Behold the brand of beauty tossed!
See how the motion does dilate the flame!
Delighted love his spoils does boast,
And triumph in this game.
Fire, to no place confined,
Is both our wonder and our fear;
Moving the mind,
As lightning hurled through air.

High heaven the glory does increase
Of all her shining lamps, this artful way;
The sun in figures, such as these,
Joys with the moon to play.
To the sweet strains they all advance,
Which do result from their own spheres,
As this nymph's dance
Moves with the numbers which she hears.

To a Very Young Lady

Why came I so untimely forth
Into a world which wanting thee
Could entertain us with no worth,
Or shadow of felicity?
    That time should me so far remove
    From that which I was born to love!

Yet, fairest blossom, do not slight
That eye which you may know so soon.
The rosy morn resigns her light
And milder splendors to the noon:
    If such thy dawning beauty's power,
    Who shall abide its noon-tide hour?

Hope waits upon the flowery prime,
And summer though it be less gay,
Yet is not looked on as a time
Of declination and decay.
    For with a full hand that does bring
    All that was promised by the spring.

An unusually interesting and little-known poem expresses a note not often heard in Waller's day, when fidelity was not only the accepted moral code, but the poet's stock in trade. Yet TO PHYLLIS is a plea for promiscuity.

    Let not you and I inquire
    What has been our past desire . . .
    Leave it to the planets, too,
    What we shall hereafter do.

Three centuries later one of the most popular poets of her day expressed it even more pertly. Edna St. Vincent Millay sang insouciantly:

    And why you come complaining
    Is more than I can see.
    I loved you Wednesday—yes—but what
    Is that to me?

To Phyllis

Phyllis! why should we delay
Pleasures shorter than the day?
Could we (which we never can!)
Stretch our lives beyond their span,
Beauty like a shadow flies,
And our youth before us dies.
Or, would youth and beauty stay,
Love hath wings, and will away.
Love hath swifter wings than Time:
Change in love to Heaven does climb.
Gods, that never change their state,
Vary oft their love and hate.

Phyllis! to this truth we owe
All the love betwixt us two:
Let not you and I inquire
What has been our past desire;
On what shepherd you have smiled,
Or what nymphs I have beguiled.
Leave it to the planets, too,
What we shall hereafter do.
For the joys we now may prove,
Take advice of present love.

JOHN MILTON
[1608–1674]

THE adventurous Edward John Trelawny, friend of Shelley and
Byron, was often quoted to the effect that if Milton was not
the greatest poet who ever lived, he was the greatest man. The schol-
arly Denis Saurat went further. Saurat contended that Milton was
not only the greatest of English poets but also one of the greatest
of thinkers.

There have been dissenting opinions. In our own time the pendu-
lum of taste has swung violently back and forth. As late as 1941

Logan Pearsall Smith wrote MILTON AND HIS MODERN CRITICS in de-
fense against those critics (chiefly Ezra Pound and T. S. Eliot) who
undertake "to scale the skies and topple Milton from his place."
An examination of Milton's life reveals the complicated issues be-
tween the politician and the poet, the harassed public servant and
the unhappy private individual, the man who sacrificed more than
his eyesight to a cause.

Milton was born December 9, 1608, at the Sign of the Spread
Eagle, in Cheapside, London. His grandfather was a Catholic, his
father a Protestant. Both were intractable, and the boy inherited
the family's obstinate pride. Milton's father, by preference a musi-
cian and "by profession a scrivener," hoped that his son would
enter the Church. But when young Milton produced a set of poems
at the age of ten, his father foresaw a greater career, and the boy
was thereupon "brought up deliberately to be a man of genius."
Genius undoubtedly Milton was from the beginning, and he was
never one to deny it. At Cambridge, which Milton entered at six-
teen, he was unpopular. The boys resented his obvious superiority;
he quarreled with his tutor. Some of his comrades, mocking his
handsome appearance as well as his boasted virtue, nicknamed him
"the lady of Christ's." Yet it was at Cambridge that Milton wrote
some of his best early poetry: SONG ON MAY MORNING, ON HIS HAVING
ARRIVED AT THE AGE OF TWENTY-THREE, and ON SHAKESPEARE. Al-
though the last-named poem was Milton's first appearance in print,
the short eulogy received the distinction of being prefixed to the
second folio edition of Shakespeare. It was published when Milton
was twenty-three.

On His Having Arrived at the Age of Twenty-three

How soon hath Time, the subtle thief of youth,
Stolen on his wing my three and twentieth year!
My hasting days fly on with full career,
But my late spring no bud or blossom shew'th.
Perhaps my semblance might deceive the truth
That I to manhood am arrived so near;
And inward ripeness doth much less appear,
That some more timely-happy spirits endu'th.

Yet be it less or more, or soon or slow,
It shall be still in strictest measure even
To that same lot, however mean or high,
Toward which Time leads me, and the will of **Heaven**;
All is, if I have grace to use it so,
As ever in my great Task-Master's eye.

Song on May Morning

Now the bright morning-star, Day's harbinger,
Comes dancing from the East, and leads with her
The flowery May, who from her green lap throws
The yellow cowslip and the pale primrose.
    Hail, bounteous May, that dost inspire
    Mirth, and youth, and warm desire!
    Woods and groves are of thy dressing;
    Hill and dale doth boast thy blessing.
Thus we salute thee with our early song,
And welcome thee, and wish thee long.

On Shakespeare

What needs my Shakespeare for his honored bones,
The labor of an age in piléd stones?
Or that his hallowed reliques should be hid
Under a star-ypointing pyramid?
Dear son of memory, great heir of fame,
What need'st thou such weak witness of thy name?
Thou in our wonder and astonishment
Hast built thyself a livelong monument.
For whilst, to the shame of slow-endeavoring **art**,
Thy easy numbers flow, and that each heart
Hath from the leaves of thy unvalued book
Those Delphic lines with deep impression took;
Then thou, our fancy of itself bereaving,
Dost make us marble with too much conceiving,
And so sepulchred in such pomp dost lie
That kings for such a tomb would wish to die.

Although Milton schooled himself to remain at Cambridge seven
years, he was glad to return to his father's home in Horton, Buck·

inghamshire. At the age of twenty-four he "retired," devoted himself to the study of the classics, comparative literatures, and "by the help of Heaven, an immortality of fame." He occasionally allowed himself a "gaudy day" in London, even though he repented of it afterward. Poems came easily to him at Horton, poems written in conflicting moods of gaiety and gravity. L'ALLEGRO and IL PENSEROSO, the most famous of all paired poems, were written in Milton's mid-twenties. In their alternating pictures of the poet they symbolize two opposed states of man's spirit. The music shifts with the mood. The light syllables of L'ALLEGRO express the happy man; they dance, slide, and trip without weight or effort. But, although the number of syllables in each line of IL PENSEROSO is the same as of those in its companion piece, the words are heavily charged, the pace is retarded, and the beat is accentuated to suggest slow thought and the pursuit of steadfast contemplation.

L'Allegro

Hence, loathed Melancholy,
  Of Cerberus and blackest Midnight born,
In Stygian cave forlorn
  'Mongst horrid shapes, and shrieks, and sights unholy!
Find out some uncouth cell
  Where brooding Darkness spreads his jealous wings
And the night-raven sings;
  There under ebon shades, and low-browed rocks
As ragged as thy locks,
  In dark Cimmerian desert ever dwell.
But come, thou goddess fair and free,
In heaven yclept Euphrosyne,
And by men, heart-easing Mirth,
Whom lovely Venus at a birth
With two sister Graces more
To ivy-crownéd Bacchus bore;
Or whether (as some sager sing)
The frolic wind that breathes the spring,
Zephyr, with Aurora playing,
As he met her once a-Maying—
There on beds of violets blue
And fresh-blown roses washed in dew
Filled her with thee, a daughter fair,

So buxom, blithe, and debonair.
　Haste thee, Nymph, and bring with thee
Jest and youthful Jollity,
Quips and Cranks and wanton Wiles,
Nods and Becks and wreathéd Smiles,
Such as hang on Hebe's cheek
And love to live in dimple sleek;
Sport that wrinkled Care derides,
And Laughter holding both his sides.
Come, and trip it as you go
On the light fantastic toe;
And in thy right hand lead with thee
The mountain-nymph, sweet Liberty;
And if I give thee honor due
Mirth, admit me of thy crew,
To live with her, and live with thee
In unreprovéd pleasures free;
To hear the lark begin his flight
And singing startle the dull night
From his watch-tower in the skies,
Till the dappled dawn doth rise;
Then to come, in spite of sorrow,
And at my window bid good-morrow
Through the sweetbriar, or the vine,
Or the twisted eglantine:
While the cock with lively din
Scatters the rear of darkness thin,
And to the stack, or the barn-door,
Stoutly struts his dames before:
Oft listening how the hounds and horn
Cheerly rouse the slumbering morn,
From the side of some hoar hill,
Through the high wood echoing shrill;
Sometime walking, not unseen,
By hedge-row elms, on hillocks green,
Right against the eastern gate
Where the great Sun begins his state,
Robed in flames and amber light,
The clouds in thousand liveries dight;
While the ploughman, near at hand,
Whistles o'er the furrowed land,
And the milkmaid singeth blithe,
And the mower whets his scythe,
And every shepherd tells his tale

Under the hawthorn in the dale.
  Straight mine eye hath caught new pleasures
Whilst the landscape round it measures:
Russet lawns, and fallows gray,
Where the nibbling flocks do stray;
Mountains, on whose barren breast
The laboring clouds do often rest;
Meadows trim with daisies pied,
Shallow brooks, and rivers wide.
Towers and battlements it sees
Bosomed high in tufted trees,
Where perhaps some beauty lies,
The cynosure of neighboring eyes.
Hard by, a cottage chimney smokes
From betwixt two aged oaks,
Where Corydon and Thyrsis met
Are at their savory dinner set
Of herbs, and other country messes
Which the neat-handed Phillis dresses;
And then in haste her bower she leaves,
With Thestylis to bind the sheaves;
Or, if the earlier season lead,
To the tanned haycock in the mead.
  Sometimes with secure delight
The upland hamlets will invite,
When the merry bells ring round,
And the jocund rebecks [1] sound
To many a youth and many a maid,
Dancing in the chequered shade;
And young and old come forth to play
On a sunshine holy-day,
Till the livelong daylight fail:
Then to the spicy nut-brown ale,
With stories told of many a feat,
How faery Mab the junkets eat:—
She was pinched, and pulled, she said;
And he, by friar's lantern [2] led,
Tells how the drudging Goblin sweat
To earn his cream-bowl duly set,
When in one night, ere glimpse of morn,
His shadowy flail hath threshed the corn
That ten day-laborers could not end;
Then lies him down the lubber [3] fiend,

---

[1] *Fiddles.*   [2] *The will-o'-the wisp.*   [3] *Clumsy.*

And, stretched out all the chimney's length,
Basks at the fire his hairy strength;
And crop-full out of doors he flings,
Ere the first cock his matin rings.
Thus done the tales, to bed they creep,
By whispering winds soon lulled asleep.
Towered cities please us then
And the busy hum of men,
Where throngs of knights and barons bold,
In weeds of peace, high triumphs hold,
With store of ladies, whose bright eyes
Rain influence, and judge the prize
Of wit or arms, while both contend
To win her grace, whom all commend.
There let Hymen oft appear
In saffron robe, with taper clear,
And pomp, and feast, and revelry,
With mask, and antique pageantry;
Such sights as youthful poets dream
On summer eves by haunted stream.
Then to the well-trod stage anon,
If Jonson's learnéd sock [4] be on,
Or sweetest Shakespeare, Fancy's child,
Warble his native wood-notes wild.
    And ever against eating cares
Lap me in soft Lydian airs,
Married to immortal verse,
Such as the meeting soul may pierce,
In notes with many a winding bout
Of linkéd sweetness long drawn out,
With wanton heed and giddy cunning,
The melting voice through mazes running,
Untwisting all the chains that tie
The hidden soul of harmony;
That Orpheus' self may heave his head
From golden slumber, on a bed
Of heaped Elysian flowers, and hear
Such strains as would have won the ear
Of Pluto, to have quite set free
His half-regained Eurydice.
    These delights if thou canst give,
Mirth, with thee I mean to live.

[4] *The traditional soft shoe once worn by actors in comedy.*

Il Penseroso

Hence, vain deluding Joys,
   The brood of Folly without father bred!
How little you bestead
   Or fill the fixéd mind with all your toys!
Dwell in some idle brain,
   And fancies fond with gaudy shapes possess
As thick and numberless
   As the gay motes that people the sunbeams,
Or likest hovering dreams,
   The fickle pensioners of Morpheus' train.
But hail, thou goddess sage and holy,
Hail, divinest Melancholy!
Whose saintly visage is too bright
To hit the sense of human sight,
And therefore to our weaker view
O'erlaid with black, staid Wisdom's hue;
Black, but such as in esteem
Prince Memnon's sister might beseem,
Or that starred Ethiop queen that strove
To set her beauty's praise above
The sea-nymphs, and their powers offended.
Yet thou art higher far descended:
Thee bright-haired Vesta long of yore
To solitary Saturn bore;
His daughter she; in Saturn's reign
Such mixture was not held a stain:
Oft in glimmering bowers and glades
He met her, and in secret shades
Of woody Ida's inmost grove,
While yet there was no fear of Jove.
   Come, pensive Nun, devout and pure,
Sober, steadfast, and demure,
All in a robe of darkest grain
Flowing with majestic train,
And sable stole of cypress lawn
Over thy decent shoulders drawn.
Come, but keep thy wonted state,
With even step, and musing gait,
And looks commercing with the skies,
Thy rapt soul sitting in thine eyes:

There, held in holy passion still,
Forget thyself to marble, till
With a sad leaden downward cast
Thou fix them on the earth as fast.
And join with thee calm Peace, and Quiet,
Spare Fast, that oft with gods doth diet,
And hears the Muses in a ring
Aye round about Jove's altar sing:
And add to these retired Leisure
That in trim gardens takes his pleasure:—
But first and chiefest, with thee bring
Him that yon soars on golden wing
Guiding the fiery-wheelèd throne,
The cherub Contemplatión;
And the mute Silence hist along,
'Less Philomel will deign a song
In her sweetest saddest plight,
Smoothing the rugged brow of Night,
While Cynthia [1] checks her dragon yoke
Gently o'er the accustomed oak.
Sweet bird, that shunn'st the noise of folly,
Most musical, most melancholy!
Thee, chauntress, oft the woods among
I woo, to hear thy even-song;
And missing thee, I walk unseen
On the dry smooth-shaven green,
To behold the wandering Moon
Riding near her highest noon,
Like one that had been led astray
Through the heaven's wide pathless way,
And oft, as if her head she bowed,
Stooping through a fleecy cloud.
    Oft, on a plat of rising ground
I hear the far-off curfew sound
Over some wide-water'd shore,
Swinging slow with sullen roar;
Or, if the air will not permit,
Some still removed place will fit,
Where glowing embers through the room
Teach light to counterfeit a gloom;
Far from all resort of mirth,
Save the cricket on the hearth,
Or the bellman's drowsy charm

---

[1] *The moon.*

To bless the doors from nightly harm.
Or let my lamp at midnight hour
Be seen in some high lonely tower,
Where I may oft out-watch the Bear
With thrice-great Hermes, or unsphere [2]
The spirit of Plato, to unfold
What worlds or what vast regions hold
The immortal mind that hath forsook
Her mansion in this fleshly nook;
And of those Daemons that are found
In fire, air, flood, or underground,
Whose power hath a true consent
With planet, or with element.
Sometime let gorgeous Tragedy
In sceptered pall come sweeping by,
Presenting Thebes, or Pelops' line,
Or the tale of Troy divine;
Or what (though rare) of later age
Ennobled hath the buskined [3] stage.
But, O sad Virgin, that thy power
Might raise Musaeus from his bower,
Or bid the soul of Orpheus sing
Such notes as, warbled to the string,
Drew iron tears down Pluto's cheek
And made Hell grant what Love did seek!
Or call up him [4] that left half-told
The story of Cambuscan bold,
Of Camball, and of Algarsife,
And who had Canace to wife,
That owned the virtuous ring and glass,
And of the wondrous horse of brass,
On which the Tartar king did ride;
And if aught else great bards beside
In sage and solemn tunes have sung,
Of tourneys, and of trophies hung,
Of forests, and enchantments drear,
Where more is meant than meets the ear.
Thus, Night, oft see me in thy pale career,
Till civil-suited Morn appear,
Not tricked and frounced as she was wont
With the Attic boy to hunt,

---

[2] *Summon.*
[3] *The buskin was the heavy shoe once worn by actors in tragedy.*
[4] *Chaucer. The reference is to the unfinished tale by the Squire in* THE
CANTERBURY TALES.

But kerchiefed in a comely cloud
While rocking winds are piping loud,
Or ushered with a shower still,
When the gust hath blown his fill,
Ending on the rustling leaves
With minute-drops from off the eaves.
And when the sun begins to fling
His flaring beams, me, goddess, bring
To arched walks of twilight groves,
And shadows brown, that Sylvan loves,
Of pine, or monumental oak,
Where the rude axe, with heavéd stroke,
Was never heard the nymphs to daunt
Or fright them from their hallowed haunt.
There in close covert by some brook
Where no profaner eye may look,
Hide me from day's garish eye,
While the bee with honeyed thigh,
That at her flowery work doth sing,
And the waters murmuring,
With such consort as they keep,
Entice the dewy-feathered Sleep;
And let some strange mysterious dream
Wave at his wings in airy stream
Of lively portraiture displayed,
Softly on my eyelids laid:
And, as I wake, sweet music breathe
Above, about, or underneath,
Sent by some spirit to mortals good,
Or the unseen Genius of the wood.
   But let my due feet never fail
To walk the studious cloister's pale
And love the high-embowéd roof,
With antique pillars massy proof
And storied windows richly dight,[5]
Casting a dim religious light:
There let the pealing organ blow
To the full-voiced quire below
In service high and anthems clear,
As may with sweetness, through mine ear,
Dissolve me into ecstasies,
And bring all Heaven before mine eyes.
   And may at last my weary age

[5] *"Dressed" or decorated with stained glass.*

Find out the peaceful hermitage,
The hairy gown and mossy cell
Where I may sit and rightly spell
Of every star that heaven doth shew,
And every herb that sips the dew;
Till old experience do attain
To something like prophetic strain.
   These pleasures, Melancholy, give,
And I with thee will choose to live.

It was at Horton that Milton began the masque entitled ARCADES, performed by the young people of the neighborhood, and it was there that he completed COMUS, the best-known of his minor poems. COMUS, half drama, half opera, was written, like ARCADES, at the request of Henry Lawes, who furnished the music. It is a beautiful and curious composition, a tract which turns against itself. Its theme is temperance, chastity, the self-restraint of the Puritan, but the manner is pagan. Milton invents a son of Bacchus and Circe, makes him (Comus) a tempter of virtuous mortals, and finally has his heady enchantment broken by Sabrina, pure spirit of the river Severn. The plot demands that water should triumph over wine, and reason over sensuality, but Milton uses every sensuous device to proclaim that victory.

Song

O'er the smooth enameled green,
Where no print of step hath been,
  Follow me, as I sing
  And touch the warbled string;
Under the shady roof
Of branching elm star-proof
    Follow me.
I will bring you where she sits,
Clad in splendor as befits
    Her deity.
Such a rural Queen
All Arcadia hath not seen.

from ARCADES

Comus' Invocation to His Revelers

The star that bids the shepherd fold
Now the top of heaven doth hold;
And the gilded car of day
His glowing axle doth allay
In the steep Atlantic stream;
And the slope sun his upward beam
Shoots against the dusky pole,
Pacing toward the other goal
Of his chamber in the east.
Meanwhile, welcome joy and feast,
Midnight shout and revelry,
Tipsy dance and jollity.
Braid your locks with rosy twine,
Dropping odors, dropping wine.
Rigor now is gone to bed;
And Advice with scrupulous head,
Strict Age, and sour Severity,
With their grave saws, in slumber lie.
We, that are of purer fire,
Imitate the starry quire,
Who, in their nightly watchful spheres,
Lead in swift round the months and years.
The sounds and seas, with all their finny drove,
Now to the moon in wavering morrice move;
And on the tawny sands and shelves
Trip the pert fairies and the dapper elves.
By dimpled brook and fountain-brim,
The wood-nymphs, decked with daisies trim,
Their merry wakes and pastimes keep:
What hath night to do with sleep?
Night hath better sweets to prove;
Venus now wakes, and wakens Love.
Come, let us our rites begin;
'Tis only daylight that makes sin. . . .
Come, knit hands, and beat the ground
In a light fantastic round.

from COMUS

Lady's Song

Sweet Echo, sweetest nymph, that liv'st unseen
    Within thy airy shell
By slow Meander's margent green,
And in the violet-embroidered vale
    Where the love-lorn nightingale
Nightly to thee her sad song mourneth well:
Canst thou not tell me of a gentle pair
    That likest thy Narcissus are?
      O, if thou have
    Hid them in some flowery cave,
     Tell me but where,
Sweet Queen of Parley, Daughter of the Sphere!
So may'st thou be translated to the skies,
And give resounding grace to all Heaven's harmonies!

from COMUS

Farewell of the Attendant Spirit

To the ocean now I fly,
And those happy climes that lie
Where day never shuts his eye,
Up in the broad fields of the sky.
There I suck the liquid air,
All amidst the gardens fair
Of Hesperus, and his daughters three
That sing about the golden tree.
Along the crispéd shades and bowers
Revels the spruce and jocund Spring;
The Graces and the rosy-bosomed Hours
Thither all their bounties bring.
There eternal Summer dwells,
And west winds with musky wing
About the cedarn alleys fling
Nard and cassia's balmy smells.
Iris there with humid bow
Waters the odorous banks, that blow
Flowers of more mingled hue
Than her purfled [1] scarf can shew,

[1] *Embroidered.*

And drenches with Elysian dew
(List, mortals, if your ears be true)
Beds of hyacinth and roses,
Where young Adonis oft reposes,
Waxing well of his deep wound,
In slumber soft, and on the ground
Sadly sits the Assyrian queen.
But far above, in spangled sheen,
Celestial Cupid, her famed son, advanced,
Holds his dear Psyche, sweet entranced
After her wandering labors long,
Till free consent the gods among
Make her his eternal bride,
And from her fair unspotted side
Two blissful twins are to be born,
Youth and Joy; so Jove hath sworn.

But now my task is smoothly done:
I can fly, or I can run
Quickly to the green earth's end,
Where the bowed welkin slow doth bend,
And from thence can soar as soon
To the corners of the Moon.
Mortals, that would follow me,
Love Virtue; she alone is free.
She can teach ye how to climb
Higher than the sphery chime;
Or, if Virtue feeble were,
Heaven itself would stoop to her.

from COMUS

Milton had few intimates at college, and he lost touch with most
of these after he left Cambridge. But there was one whose short
life he remembered and whose death he immortalized. Edward
King sailed from Chester to visit his family in Ireland; his ship
struck a rock, and King was one of the passengers who went down.
King's friends issued a set of obituary verses, concluding with a
"monody" entitled LYCIDAS, signed "J.M." Milton chose the antique
form of a pastoral for his elegy: an invocation, a statement of loss
in which the poet and his dead friend appear as shepherds, an
appeal to the Muses ("Sisters of the sacred well"), and an assurance
that the ideals of the dead man will be acknowledged by the hosts
of heaven ("Look homeward, Angel") and revered by men. But

the twenty-nine-year-old Puritan poet could not write an elegy without making the moral plain and pointing it at the evils of his day. The subtitle of LYCIDAS reads: "In this monody the author bewails a learned friend, unfortunately drowned in his passage from Chester on the Irish Seas, 1637; and, by occasion, foretells the ruin of our corrupted clergy, then in their height."

The difficulties of LYCIDAS decrease, if they do not vanish, when Milton's contrary aims are understood. To carry out his program the poet mingles pagan mythology and Christian theology, "heathen fictions" and "sacred truths." In "a dreamy passionate flux"—the phrase is Robert Bridges'—Milton assembles the blind Furies and Saint Peter ("the Pilot of the Galilean Lake"), "smooth-sliding Mincius" (the river near Mantua, birthplace of Virgil) and "Camus, reverend sire" (god of the river Cam, which flows past Cambridge), Neptune and the Archangel Michael. But it is not necessary to know that Mona in line 54 is the old Roman name for the Isle of Man or that the Nereid Panope probably symbolizes the boundlessness of ocean. The names, the remote allusions, are the properties which build the poem, not the poem itself. The poem is in the paradox of expression: in the calm tone and the impassioned feeling, the personal grief and the universal sublimation.

Lycidas

Yet once more, O ye laurels, and once more,
Ye myrtles brown, with ivy never sere,
I come to pluck your berries harsh and crude,
And with forced fingers rude
Shatter your leaves before the mellowing year.
Bitter constraint and sad occasion dear
Compels me to disturb your season due:
For Lycidas is dead, dead ere his prime,
Young Lycidas, and hath not left his peer.
Who would not sing for Lycidas? he knew
Himself to sing, and build the lofty rhyme.
He must not float upon his watery bier
Unwept, and welter to the parching wind,
Without the meed of some melodious tear.

Begin then, Sisters of the sacred well
That from beneath the seat of Jove doth spring;

Begin, and somewhat loudly sweep the string;
Hence with denial vain and coy excuse:
So may some gentle Muse
With lucky words favor *my* destined urn;
And as he passes, turn
And bid fair peace be to my sable shroud.

For we were nursed upon the self-same hill,
Fed the same flock by fountain, shade, and rill.
Together both, ere the high lawns appeared
Under the opening eye-lids of the Morn,
We drove a-field, and both together heard
What time the gray-fly winds her sultry horn,
Battening our flocks with the fresh dews of night;
Oft till the star, that rose at evening bright,
Toward heaven's descent had sloped his westering wheel.
Meanwhile the rural ditties were not mute;
Tempered to the oaten flute,
Rough Satyrs danced, and Fauns with cloven heel
From the glad sound would not be absent long;
And old Damoetas loved to hear our song.

But, O! the heavy change, now thou art gone,
Now thou art gone, and never must return!
Thee, Shepherd, thee the woods and desert caves,
With wild thyme and the gadding vine o'ergrown,
And all their echoes, mourn:
The willows and the hazel copses green
Shall now no more be seen
Fanning their joyous leaves to thy soft lays.
As killing as the canker to the rose,
Or taint-worm to the weanling herds that graze,
Or frost to flowers, that their gay wardrobe wear
When first the white-thorn blows;
Such, Lycidas, thy loss to shepherd's ear.

Where were ye, Nymphs, when the remorseless deep
Closed o'er the head of your loved Lycidas?
For neither were ye playing on the steep
Where your old bards, the famous Druids, lie,
Nor on the shaggy top of Mona high,
Nor yet where Deva spreads her wizard stream.
Ay me! I fondly dream
"Had ye been there," . . . for what could that have done?
What could the Muse herself that Orpheus bore,

The Muse herself, for her enchanting son,
Whom universal nature did lament,
When by the rout that made the hideous roar
His gory visage down the stream was sent,
Down the swift Hebrus to the Lesbian shore?

Alas! what boots it with uncessant care
To tend the homely, slighted, shepherd's trade
And strictly meditate the thankless Muse?
Were it not better done, as others use,
To sport with Amaryllis in the shade,
Or withe [1] the tangles of Neaera's hair?
Fame is the spur that the clear spirit doth raise
(That last infirmity of noble mind)
To scorn delights, and live laborious days;
But the fair guerdon when we hope to find,
And think to burst out into sudden blaze,
Comes the blind Fury with the abhorréd shears
And slits the thin-spun life. "But not the praise,"
Phoebus replied, and touched my trembling ears:
"Fame is no plant that grows on mortal soil,
Nor in the glistering foil
Set off to the world, nor in broad rumor lies:
But lives and spreads aloft by those pure eyes
And perfect witness of all-judging Jove;
As he pronounces lastly on each deed,
Of so much fame in heaven expect thy meed."

O fountain Arethusa, and thou honored flood,
Smooth-sliding Mincius, crowned with vocal reeds,
That strain I heard was of a higher mood.
But now my oat proceeds,
And listens to the herald of the sea
That came in Neptune's plea;
He asked the waves, and asked the felon winds,
What hard mishap hath doomed this gentle swain?
And questioned every gust of rugged wings
That blows from off each beaked promontory:
They knew not of his story;
And sage Hippotades their answer brings,
That not a blast was from his dungeon strayed;
The air was calm, and on the level brine

---

[1] *In most editions the word is "with," making the line awkward, weak, and wholly uncharacteristic of the poet. The word "withe" (meaning to wreathe or bind) not only gives the line more sense but a more Miltonic balance.*

Sleek Panope with all her sisters played.
It was that fatal and perfidious bark
Built in the eclipse, and rigged with curses dark,
That sunk so low that sacred head of thine.

Next Camus, reverend sire, went footing slow,
His mantle hairy, and his bonnet sedge,
Inwrought with figures dim, and on the edge
Like to that sanguine flower inscribed with woe.
"Ah! who hath reft," quoth he, "my dearest pledge?"
Last came, and last did go
The Pilot of the Galilean lake;
Two massy keys he bore of metals twain
(The golden opes, the iron shuts amain);
He shook his mitred locks, and stern bespake:
"How well could I have spared for thee, young swain,
Enow of such, as for their bellies' sake
Creep and intrude and climb into the fold!
Of other care they little reckoning make
Than how to scramble at the shearers' feast,
And shove away the worthy bidden guest.
Blind mouths! that scarce themselves know how to hold
A sheep-hook, or have learned aught else the least
That to the faithful herdman's art belongs!
What recks it them? What need they? They are sped;
And when they list, their lean and flashy songs
Grate on their scrannel pipes of wretched straw;
The hungry sheep look up, and are not fed,
But swol'n with wind and the rank mist they draw
Rot inwardly, and foul contagion spread:
Besides what the grim wolf with privy paw
Daily devours apace, and nothing said.
But that two-handed engine at the door
Stands ready to smite once, and smite no more."

Return, Alpheus; the dread voice is past
That shrunk thy streams; return, Sicilian Muse,
And call the vales, and bid them hither cast
Their bells and flowerets of a thousand hues.
Ye valleys low, where the mild whispers use
Of shades, and wanton winds, and gushing brooks
On whose fresh lap the swart star sparely looks;
Throw hither all your quaint enameled eyes
That on the green turf suck the honeyed showers,
And purple all the ground with vernal flowers.

Bring the rathe [2] primrose that forsaken dies,
The tufted crow-toe, and pale jessamine,
The white pink, and the pansy freaked [3] with jet,
The glowing violet,
The musk-rose, and the well-attired woodbine,
With cowslips wan that hang the pensive head,
And every flower that sad embroidery wears:
Bid amaranthus all his beauty shed,
And daffadillies fill their cups with tears
To strew the laureate hearse where Lycid lies.
For, so to interpose a little ease,
Let our frail thoughts dally with false surmise.
Ay me! whilst thee the shores and sounding seas
Wash far away—where'er thy bones are hurled;
Whether beyond the stormy Hebrides
Where thou, perhaps, under the whelming tide,
Visit'st the bottom of the monstrous world;
Or whether thou, to our moist vows denied,
Sleep'st by the fable of Bellerus old,
Where the great Vision of the guarded mount
Looks toward Namancos and Bayona's hold—
Look homeward, Angel, now, and melt with ruth:
And, O ye dolphins, waft the hapless youth!

Weep no more, woeful shepherds, weep no more,
For Lycidas, your sorrow, is not dead,
Sunk though he be beneath the watery floor;
So sinks the day-star in the ocean bed,
And yet anon repairs his drooping head,
And tricks his beams, and with new-spangled ore
Flames in the forehead of the morning sky:
So Lycidas sunk low, but mounted high
Through the dear might of Him that walked the waves;
Where, other groves and other streams along,
With nectar pure his oozy locks he laves,
And hears the unexpressive [4] nuptial song
In the blest kingdoms meek of joy and love.
There entertain him all the saints above
In solemn troops, and sweet societies,
That sing, and singing in their glory move,
And wipe the tears for ever from his eyes.
Now, Lycidas, the shepherds weep no more;
Henceforth thou art the Genius of the shore

---

[2] *Early.* [3] *Marked.* [4] *Inexpressible.*

In thy large recompense, and shalt be good
To all that wander in that perilous flood.

Thus sang the uncouth swain to the oaks and rills,
While the still morn went out with sandals gray;
He touched the tender stops of various quills,
With eager thought warbling his Doric lay:
And now the sun had stretched out all the hills,
And now was dropt into the western bay.
As last he rose, and twitched his mantle blue:
Tomorrow to fresh woods, and pastures new.

In his thirtieth year Milton went abroad. His goal was the antique world; the God-fearing Puritan yielded to the poet enchanted by the elder gods. He luxuriated in the charms of Tuscany, argued with scholars, and visited with noblemen. In a villa near Florence he listened to Galileo, seventy-four years old and blind, surrounded by disciples and still watched for new heresies by the Inquisitors. He traveled south to Rome and Naples, intending eventually to journey to Greece. But the news of civil war in England made him cancel all plans. "I thought it base that I should be traveling for intellectual diversion while friends at home were fighting for liberty." The Reformation, with its denial of the divinity of kings and its insistence on the rights of the common man, found its militant leader in Cromwell and its inspired champion in Milton. Fired with an ideal of service in a great cause, Milton flung all his energy into the conflict. He turned from poetry to prose; he issued one controversial pamphlet after another, saying proudly, "When God commands to take the trumpet and blow a dolorous or a jarring blast, it lies not in man's will what he shall say or what he shall conceal." He attacked vigorously, even grossly, in his ardor for freedom. He charged at pedantic opponents with the full weight of his erudition, and buried churchly antagonists beneath a flood of his religious zeal. He planned a great epic but put it aside for necessary polemics. He translated an epigram by Seneca with enthusiasm:

There can be slain
No sacrifice to God more acceptable
Than an unrighteous and a wicked King.

Suddenly, to everyone's surprise, the determined bachelor of thirty-five married a seventeen-year-old girl. Mary Powell, the child of a

Royalist family, was uninterested in Milton's work and opposed to the few ideas she could comprehend. The marriage was doomed before it was consummated. It was evident to Milton that he "hasted too eagerly to light the nuptial torch" and that he felt guilty of the "brutish congress" with "two carcasses chained unnaturally together." There was a fierce conflict between the demanding flesh and the harshly denying spirit. It is little wonder that his frightened wife left him within a month. The Cavalier Powells sided with their daughter, but Milton's violent pamphlets favoring divorce—a divorce to be obtained upon the husband's petition—together with Cromwell's victories persuaded them it would be convenient to have a son-in-law who was prominent in the ranks of the ruling group. But although Mary was forced to return to Milton, and meekly bore his children, she died, a few days after the birth of her fourth child, at the age of twenty-six.

Milton's work increased; he was appointed Latin secretary to the Council of State. His eyesight, always impaired, troubled him continually; he was helped in his duties by another poet, Andrew Marvell. He married again, Catharine Woodcock, of whom nothing is known except that she and her child died fifteen months later. Meanwhile, Milton had become totally blind.

Scholars as well as ophthalmological experts have failed to agree upon the cause of Milton's blindness. The contemporary clergy held that it was a judgment from God, a divine punishment for Milton's heresy, and particularly for his iconoclastic pamphlets on divorce. Lay commentators believed that the constant strain put upon his eyes, complicated by Milton's poor health, weakened and finally ruined his vision. Saurat deduced that Milton suffered from congenital syphilis inherited from his mother, a condition which (Saurat implied) caused the deaths of two of his wives and several children. On the other hand, Dr. Eleanor Gertrude Brown disputes Saurat's theory in a remarkable recent study, MILTON'S BLINDNESS. Dr. Brown proves that, in spite of many domestic fatalities, Milton had many survivors, and she suggests that the blindness was caused by glaucoma or paralysis of the optic nerve. Milton himself was unable to analyze his affliction, although his work is full of references to it. Perhaps the most appealing as well as the most popular of Milton's poems is the autobiographical sonnet beginning "When I consider how my light is spent." The poem is a triumph of resignation, a fusion of great art and tragic experience.

On His Blindness

When I consider how my light is spent
Ere half my days in this dark world and wide,
And that one talent which is death to hide
Lodged with me useless, though my soul more bent
To serve therewith my Maker, and present
My true account, lest He returning chide;
"Doth God exact day-labor, light denied?"
I fondly ask. But Patience, to prevent
That murmur, soon replies, "God doth not need
Either man's work or his own gifts. Who best
Bear his mild yoke, they serve him best. His state
Is kingly: thousands at his bidding speed,
And post o'er land and ocean without rest;
They also serve who only stand and wait."

The sonnet to his pupil Cyriack Skinner is less popular but no less revealing. It, too, is an acceptance of the inevitable, but it is a poem which tells less of what Milton thought about his affliction and more of what he wanted others to think. It is for a cause that Milton has suffered; and if Milton acknowledges that all Europe talks about his sacrifice in defense of liberty, he says so with pride, even self-approval, but not with self-pity.

To Cyriack Skinner

Cyriack, this three years' day these eyes, though clear
To outward view, of blemish or of spot,
Bereft of light, their seeing have forgot;
Nor to their idle orbs doth sight appear
Of sun or moon or star throughout the year,
Or man or woman. Yet I argue not
Against Heaven's hand or will, nor bate a jot
Of heart or hope, but still bear up and steer
Right onward. What supports me, dost thou ask?
The conscience, friend, to have lost them overplied
In liberty's defense, my noble task,
Of which all Europe talks from side to side.
This thought might lead me through the world's vain mask
Content, though blind, had I no better guide.

Another sonnet, written at the height of Milton's heroic struggle, shows the man's fervor as well as his stony patience. Milton's books and Cromwell's battles were winning respect for the new government; but Milton, praising the Protector, reminded him that much was still to be done, that "free conscience" must be protected even from the clergy, and, in one immortal phrase, that "peace hath her victories no less renowned than war."

To the Lord General Cromwell

Cromwell, our chief of men, who through a cloud
Not of war only, but detractions rude,
Guided by faith and matchless fortitude
To peace and truth thy glorious way hast ploughed,
And on the neck of crownéd Fortune proud
Hast reared God's trophies, and His work pursued,
While Darwen stream with blood of Scots imbrued
And Dunbar field resounds thy praises loud,
And Worcester's laureate wreath. Yet much remains
To conquer still; peace hath her victories
No less renowned than war; new foes arise
Threatening to bind our souls with secular chains.
Help us to save free conscience from the paw
Of hireling wolves whose gospel is their maw.

After the death of Cromwell, Milton fought hard for the tottering Protectorate. But the people were tired of factions and the difficulties of self-government. They longed for a return to monarchy. The House of Lords was revived, and when Charles II landed at Dover he was greeted with delirium. The right-about-face was celebrated by the poets, notably Dryden and Cowley, with promptness and enthusiasm. Milton alone refused to recant; he risked the scaffold and, somehow, escaped it. He was arrested and released through the influence either of Davenant or Marvell, but his books were burned by the public hangman. Finally he was spirited away from the wrath of the Restoration avengers.

But Milton's troubles were by no means over. His private life became increasingly lonely and complicated. He desperately needed pupils and amanuenses. He depended on his three almost illiterate daughters, who had been taught to pronounce the six languages in which they read to their father but not to understand a single one of them. The older daughters, Anne and Mary, rebelled against the drudgery of reading aloud, cheated their father, and disposed of many of his books. When Milton, at fifty-four, married his third wife, Elizabeth Minshull, twenty-four, Mary remarked that a wedding was no news, but "if she could hear of his death that would be something."

Milton had already begun the epic of man's destiny, PARADISE LOST, a gigantic wrestling of hope and disillusion, confidence battling with despair. He had seen England free herself from slavery, and he had seen the people return to unashamed slavishness. As Denis Saurat wrote, "The greatness of PARADISE LOST, like that of the DIVINA COMMEDIA, lies in this, that neither of the two European epics was written by mere literary men, but by men who had fought and suffered in the great enterprises of their time. . . . That is why PARADISE LOST is a universal and human poem and not merely a work of rhetoric." Yet rhetoric is one of the chief glories of PARADISE LOST. Never has language been used with greater effect; never has it flowed more musically or more majestically, with organlike solemnity and Oriental sensuality. Even when the allusions are half comprehended or wholly lost, the magnificence has a sonority that is heard only in the prophetic books of the Old Testament.

Satan

> . . . His pride
> Had cast him out from Heaven, with all his host
> Of rebel Angels, by whose aid, aspiring
> To set himself in glory above his peers,
> He trusted to have equalled the Most High,
> If he opposed, and, with ambitious aim
> Against the throne and monarchy of God,
> Raised impious war in Heaven and battle proud,
> With vain attempt. Him the Almighty Power
> Hurled headlong flaming from the ethereal sky,
> With hideous ruin and combustion, down
> To bottomless perdition, there to dwell
> In adamantine chains and penal fire,
> Who durst defy the Omnipotent to arms.
>   Nine times the space that measures day and night
> To mortal men, he, with his horrid crew,
> Lay vanquished, rolling in the fiery gulf,

Confounded, though immortal. But his doom
Reserved him to more wrath; for now the thought
Both of lost happiness and lasting pain
Torments him: round he throws his baleful eyes,
That witnessed huge affliction and dismay,
Mixed with obdurate pride and steadfast hate.
At once, as far as Angels ken, he views
The dismal situation waste and wild.
A dungeon horrible, on all sides round,
As one great furnace flamed; yet from those flames
No light; but rather darkness visible
Served only to discover sights of woe,
Regions of sorrow, doleful shades, where peace
And rest can never dwell, hope never comes
That comes to all, but torture without end
Still urges, and a fiery deluge, fed
With ever-burning sulphur unconsumed.
Such place Eternal Justice had prepared
For those rebellious; here their prison ordained
In utter darkness, and their portion set,
As far removed from God and light of Heaven
As from the centre thrice to the utmost pole.
Oh, how unlike the place from whence they fell!

.   .   .   .   .   .

Forthwith upright he rears from off the pool
His mighty stature; on each hand the flames
Driven backward slope their pointing spires, and, rolled
In billows, leave i' the midst a horrid vale.
Then with expanded wings he steers his flight
Aloft, incumbent on the dusky air,
That felt unusual weight; till on dry land
He lights—if it were land that ever burned
With solid, as the lake with liquid fire;
And such appeared in hue as when the force
Of subterranean wind transports a hill
Torn from Pelorus, or the shattered side
Of thundering Ætna, whose combustible
And fuelled entrails, thence conceiving fire,
Sublimed with mineral fury, aid the winds,
And leave a singèd bottom all involved
With stench and smoke.

.   .   .   .   .

All these and more came flocking; but with looks
Downcast and damp; yet such wherein appeared
Obscure some glimpse of joy to have found their Chief
Not in despair, to have found themselves not lost
In loss itself; which on his countenance cast
Like doubtful hue. But he, his wonted pride
Soon recollecting, with high words, that bore
Semblance of worth, not substance, gently raised
Their fainting courage, and dispelled their fears:
Then straight commands that, at the warlike sound
Of trumpets loud and clarions, be upreared
His mighty standard. That proud honor claimed
Azazel as his right, a Cherub tall:
Who forthwith from the glittering staff unfurled
The imperial ensign; which, full high advanced,
Shone like a meteor streaming to the wind,
With gems and golden lustre rich emblazed,
Seraphic arms and trophies; all the while
Sonorous metal blowing martial sounds:
At which the universal host up-sent
A shout that tore Hell's concave, and beyond
Frighted the reign of Chaos and old Night.

from PARADISE LOST, Book I

PARADISE LOST is a dual attempt to "justify the ways of God to man" and to explain the prevalence of evil—the indefatigable power of self-interest and the continual triumphs of corruption. Yet there are passages of simple beauty to be found in the titanic work. The scene in which Adam and Eve approach their bower with night coming on in Eden is almost lyrical, a momentary idyl in the midst of universal passions and cosmic wars.

Eve to Adam

With thee conversing, I forget all time,
All seasons, and their change, all please alike.
Sweet is the breath of morn, her rising sweet,
With charm of earliest birds; pleasant the sun,
When first on this delightful land he spreads
His orient beams, on herb, tree, fruit, and flower,
Glistering with dew; fragrant the fertile earth
After soft showers; and sweet the coming-on

Of grateful evening mild; then silent night,
With this her solemn bird, and this fair moon,
And these the gems of heaven, her starry train.
But neither breath of morn, when she ascends
With charm of earliest birds; nor rising sun
On this delightful land; nor herb, fruit, flower,
Glistering with dew; nor fragrance after showers;
Nor grateful evening mild; nor silent night,
With this her solemn bird; nor walk by moon,
Or glittering starlight, without thee is sweet.
But wherefore all night long shine these? for whom
This glorious sight, when sleep hath shut all eyes?
                    from PARADISE LOST, Book IV

Misfortune continued to plague the blind poet who, in Words-worth's tribute,

> Stood almost single, uttering odious truth,
> Darkness before and danger's voice behind.

Milton was forced to prepare a Latin grammar, a textbook on logic, a history, a compendium of theology. He sold the copyright of PARADISE LOST for ten pounds. After his death his widow settled all claims upon the publisher for an additional eight pounds. The world was always too much with Milton.

The struggle between man's spirit and the inimical world is intensified in PARADISE REGAINED and SAMSON AGONISTES. Milton obviously identified himself with Samson, the hero of his last great work. His were the struggles of that other blind iconoclast. He, too, was condemned to servitude—"Eyeless in Gaza, at the mill with slaves"—and "dark, dark, dark . . . irrecoverably dark, without all hope of day," he cried out with the enslaved Israelite:

>   I, dark in light, exposed
> To daily fraud, contempt, abuse, and wrong,
> Within doors, or without, still as a fool,
> In power of others, never in my own;
> Scarce half I seem to live, dead more than half.

In his old age the disappointed poet, "on evil days fallen and evil tongues," made a kind of peace with the world and himself. He refused to argue; he declined to attend church and permitted no religious observances in his home. He sent his daughters out to learn embroidery or some "sorts of manufacture that are proper for women." At sixty-six he died "in a fit of the gout, long troubled with the disease." Since Milton's death was scarcely caused by high living and overindulgence in rich food, it is reasonable to suppose that the ailment which finally killed him was arthritis. The contemporary critics had little to say about his passing; one of them spoke of him as "a blind old man who wrote Latin documents."

Modern criticism has busied itself too much with Milton's philosophy and too little with the power of his imagination. It is maintained that he overawes the reader without winning him, that his Sinaic utterances are eloquent, even enduring, but not endearing. Yet Milton's thunder is a portent, and liberty-loving spirits may well cry with Wordsworth:

> Milton! thou shouldst be living at this hour!

"The reader of Milton must always be on his duty," wrote Coleridge in his LECTURES ON SHAKESPEARE. "There are no lazy intervals; all has been considered, and demands observation. If this be called obscurity, let it be remembered that it is such obscurity as is a compliment to the reader, not that vicious obscurity which proceeds from a muddled head." Milton did not merely use language: he carved it, shaped it with the vigor of a baroque architect, and piled it up until it became a monument of words in marble.

SIR JOHN SUCKLING
[1609–1642]

S IR JOHN SUCKLING's claim upon posterity is less special than the charm of his lyrics. Society was indebted to him for more than two hundred years, and, although his name is unknown to the players, cards are still counted in his memory. He invented the game of cribbage.

The greatest gamester of his day, Suckling was also (according to Davenant) the greatest gallant. Born February 1, 1609, in the parish of Twickenham, Middlesex, he was sent to Trinity College in his fifteenth year. His father, who had been knighted by James I, died two years later and bequeathed his son a fortune which, even in those times, was enormous. Suckling immediately left college, rushed off to the Continent, and returned to dazzle England with one extravagance after another. It is not hard to believe that he was popular at court, that he made friends and influenced people with little effort, and was praised equally for his generosity and his "ready, sparkling wit." When his play AGLAURA was produced in his twenty-eighth year, he refused to let the actors wear the usual costumes and tinsel; the property lace collars were real lace, the embroideries were "pure gold and silver." A year later, when Suckling decided to accompany Charles on the Scottish expedition of 1639, he raised a troop of one hundred horse at a cost of twelve thousand pounds and furnished the horsemen with fine white doublets, soft leather breeches, and luxurious scarlet coats. In a life of easy triumphs Suckling made one serious mistake. He conspired to rescue the loyal Strafford after the Earl had been abandoned by the irresolute Charles; he failed, was discovered, and fled to France. There, at the age of thirty-three he died. One account has it that he committed suicide; a more sordid report claims that he was stabbed to death by a disgruntled servant.

Though Suckling was not the greatest of dramatists, he was one of the most astute. Determined to win the favor of the public, he gave AGLAURA two different productions in the same year; one version had a tragic finale and the other a happy ending. The lyrics were particularly appreciated. They still retain their lightheartedness and seeming spontaneity.

The Constant Lover

Out upon it, I have loved
　　Three whole days together!
And am like to love three more,
　　If it prove fair weather.

Time shall moult away his wings
　　Ere he shall discover
In the whole wide world again
　　Such a constant lover.

But the spite on't is, no praise
　　Is due at all to me:
Love with me had made no stays,
　　Had it been but she.

Had it any been but she,
    And that very face,
There had been at least ere this
    A dozen in her place.

The Bride

Her feet beneath her petticoat,
Like little mice, stole in and out,
    As if they fear'd the light:
But O she dances such a way!
    No sun upon an Easter-day
    Is half so fine a sight.

Her finger was so small, the ring
Would not stay on, which they did bring,
    It was too wide a peck:
And to say truth (for out it must)
It looked like the great collar, just,
    About our young colt's neck.

Her cheeks so rare a white was on,
No daisy makes comparison;
    Who sees them is undone;
For streaks of red were mingled there,
Such as are on a Catherine pear,
    The side that's next the sun.

Her lips were red, and one was thin,
Compar'd to that was next her chin
    (Some bee had stung it newly);
But, Dick, her eyes so guard her face;
I durst no more upon them gaze
    Than on the sun in July.

Her mouth so small, when she does speak,
Thou'dst swear her teeth her words did break,
    That they might passage get;
But she so handled still the matter,
They came as good as ours, or better,
    And are not spent a whit. . . .

from A BALLAD UPON A WEDDING

The Besieged Heart

'Tis now, since I sat down before
    That foolish fort, a heart,
(Time strangely spent) a year and more,
    And still I did my part.

Made my approaches; from her hand
    Unto her lip did rise,
And did already understand
    The language of her eyes;

Proceeded on with no less art,
    My tongue was engineer;
I thought to undermine the heart
    By whispering in the ear.

When this did nothing, I brought down
    Great cannon-oaths, and shot
A thousand thousand to the town;
    And still it yielded not.

I then resolved to starve the place
    By cutting off all kisses,
Praising and gazing on her face,
    And all such little blisses.

To draw her out and from her strength,
    I drew all batteries in,
And brought myself to lie at length
    As if no siege had been.

When I had done what man could do,
    And thought the place mine own,
The enemy lay quiet too,
    And smiled at all was done.

I sent to know from whence and where
    These hopes and this relief;
A spy informed, Honor was there,
    And did command in chief.

March, march, quoth I, the word straight give,
    Let's lose no time, but leave her;
That giant upon air will live,
    And hold it out forever.

To such a place our camp remove,
    As will no siege abide.
I hate a fool that starves her love,
    Only to feed her pride.

Why So Pale and Wan

Why so pale and wan, fond lover?
    Prithee, why so pale?
Will, when looking well can't move her,
    Looking ill prevail?
    Prithee, why so pale?

Why so dull and mute, young sinner?
    Prithee, why so mute?
Will, when speaking well can't win her,
    Saying nothing do 't?
    Prithee, why so mute?

Quit, quit for shame! This will not move;
    This cannot take her.
If of herself she will not love,
    Nothing can make her.
    The devil take her!

In his colloquial ease Suckling recalls Ben Jonson, by whom he was obviously influenced. That Suckling realized the debt is apparent not only from his style but from a particular poem, "Hast thou seen the down i' th' air." This is not only an imitation of Jonson, but a "reply" to the latter's SO WHITE, SO SOFT, SO SWEET, which appears on page 354.

Song to a Lute

Hast thou seen the down i' th' air
  When wanton blasts have tossed it,
Or the ship upon the sea
  When ruder waves have crossed it?
Hast thou marked the crocodile's weeping,
  Or the fox's sleeping?
Or hast viewed the peacock in his pride,
  Or the dove by his bride
When he courts for lechery?
O so fickle, O so vain, O so false, so false is she!

JOHN CLEVELAND
[1613–1658]

FORGOTTEN except for a few amiable but undistinguished lyrics,
John Cleveland should be remembered for his short impassioned
tribute to the Earl of Strafford. His contemporaries praised his
loyalty more than his verse—he forced the conceit to go even beyond
its far-fetched exaggerations—and he was known as "a disputant
rather than a poet." He pledged himself to the Royalist cause not
only with his pen but his sword. When Strafford, the weak King's
most devoted adviser, was sacrificed to the Puritans, Cleveland
protested against the impeachment. When Strafford was executed on
May 12, 1641, Cleveland was still in his headstrong twenties; he
risked displeasure, and possibly his life, not only by writing the
Earl's epitaph, but by circulating it.

Epitaph on the Earl of Strafford

Here lies wise and valiant dust
Huddled up 'twixt fit and just,
Strafford, who was hurried hence
'Twixt treason and convenience.

He spent his time here in a mist,
A Papist, yet a Calvinist;
His Prince's nearest joy and grief,
He had, yet wanted all relief;
The prop and ruin of the state;
The people's violent love and hate;
One in extremes loved and abhorred.
Riddles lie here, or in a word—
Here lies blood; and let it lie
Speechless still, and never cry.

Almost two hundred years later Robert Browning wrote his most ambitious tragedy on the noble spirit

. . . who was hurried hence
'Twixt treason and convenience.

Browning's STRAFFORD was produced in 1837 at Covent Garden with every indication of success. But the settings were shabby, the acting was poor, and the play closed after a few nights.

RICHARD CRASHAW
[1613?–1649]

RICHARD CRASHAW, sometimes styled "the divine," inherited his passion both for theology and poetry from his father, the Reverend William Crashaw. Son of a fierce antipapist, Crashaw spent his youth among a religious set, became an intimate associate of Abraham Cowley (see page 475) at college, escaped to France at the time of the Civil War in England, and turned Roman Catholic. His most famous book, STEPS TO THE TEMPLE, was published during his exile. In his early thirties Crashaw left Paris for Italy, entered the service of a cardinal, and, though described as "a man of angelical life," became progressively involved in political and personal intrigues. He died suddenly at Loretto in his thirty-sixth year. It was given out that he had succumbed to fever, but it is quite possible that he was poisoned.

Crashaw's verse is so ornate, so overrichly embellished, that it is sometimes hard to see the poetry because of the words. His images are alternately gorgeous and grotesque. Some of his finest sacred poems are so inflated that what begins to be grandiose becomes ludicrous. Thus THE WEEPER, which contains a moving portrait of Mary Magdalen, also contains one of the worst conceits in all literature when Crashaw speaks of the Magdalen's tears as:

> Two walking baths, two weeping motions,
> Portable and compendious oceans.

Even the much-quoted WISHES TO HIS (SUPPOSED) MISTRESS is marred by farfetched and incongruous metaphors. The poem begins with debonair grace:

> Whoe'er she be,
> That not impossible She
> That shall command my heart and me;
>
> Where'er she lie,
> Locked up from mortal eye,
> In shady leaves of destiny . . .

But Crashaw's ingenuity runs away with him. He employs elaborate methods to tell the reader that his supposed mistress' color is not artificial, and it takes him no less than forty-two verses to establish the simple fact that her beauty is natural and equally her own.

In most of the religious poems, however, the ardor is less induced. If Crashaw's sensuousness is not always simple, his spirit is clear. The exaggerations of the poet who was a "fantastic" are refined through the ineffable mind.

Shepherds' Hymn

> We saw Thee in Thy balmy nest,
> Young dawn of our eternal day!
> We saw Thine eyes break from their east,
> And chase the trembling shades away.
> We saw Thee, and we blest the sight;
> We saw Thee by Thine Own sweet light.

Poor world (said I), what wilt thou do
To entertain this starry Stranger?
  Is this the best thou canst bestow?
A cold, and not too cleanly, manger?
    Contend, the powers of heaven and earth,
    To fit a bed for this huge birth?

  Proud world, said I, cease your contést,
And let the mighty Babe alone.
  The phoenix builds the phoenix' nest,
Love's architecture is his own.
    The Babe whose birth embraves this morn,
    Made His own bed ere He was born.
          from IN THE HOLY NATIVITY OF OUR LORD

FROM

Upon the Bleeding Crucifix

Jesu, no more! It is full tide;
  From Thy head and from Thy feet,
From Thy hands, and from Thy side,
  All the purple rivers meet.

What need Thy fair head bear a part
  In showers, as if Thine eyes had none?
What need they help to drown Thy heart,
  That strives in torrents of its own?

Thy restless feet now cannot go
  For us and our eternal good,
As they were ever wont. What though?
  They swim, alas! in their own flood.

Thy hands to give Thou canst not lift;
  Yet will Thy hand still giving be.
It gives, but O itself's the gift:
  It gives though bound; though bound 'tis free.

Samson to His Delilah

Could not once blinding me, cruel, suffice?
When first I looked on thee I lost mine eyes.

An Epitaph Upon Husband and Wife, Which Died, and Were Buried Together

To these, whom death again did wed,
This grave's the second marriage-bed.
For though the hand of fate could force
'Twixt soul and body a divorce,
It could not sunder man and wife,
Because they both lived but one life.
Peace, good reader. Do not weep.
Peace, the lovers are asleep.
They, sweet turtles, folded lie
In the last knot love could tie.
And though they lie as they were dead,
Their pillow stone, their sheets of lead
(Pillow hard, and sheets not warm),
Love made the bed; they'll take no harm.
Let them sleep: let them sleep on,
Till this stormy night be gone,
Till the eternal morrow dawn.
Then the curtains will be drawn
And they wake into a light
Whose day shall never die in night.

Crashaw's greatest poems are undoubtedly those in praise of
Saint Teresa. Of the climax of one of them, THE FLAMING HEART,
Helen C. White has written in THE METAPHYSICAL POETS: "There is
no mistaking the central aspiration of a passage like this, the great
yearning, the basic passion, that gives volume and meaning to the
ecstasy of the verse . . . Teresa is one of the greatest mystics of the
century preceding Crashaw's. This woman has found her way to
Divine Love. Her fire kindles Crashaw, and, looking at her picture,
Crashaw feels himself closer to her goal."

FROM

The Flaming Heart

UPON THE BOOK AND PICTURE OF THE SERAPHICAL SAINT TERESA

O Heart! the equal poise of love's both parts,
Big alike with wound and darts,
Live in these conquering leaves; live all the same;
And walk through all tongues one triumphant flame.
Live here, great Heart, and love and die and kill,
And bleed and wound, and yield and conquer still.
Let this immortal life, where e'er it comes,
Walk in a crowd of loves and martyrdoms.
Let mystic deaths wait on 't, and wise souls be
The love-slain witnesses of this life of thee.
O sweet incendiary! show here thy art
Upon this carcass of a hard cold heart!
Let all thy scattered shafts of light, that play
Among the leaves of thy large books of day,
Combined against this breast, at once break in
And take away from me my self and sin!
This gracious robbery shall thy bounty be,
And my best fortunes such fair spoils of me.

O thou undaunted daughter of desires,
By all thy dower of lights and fires,
By all the eagle in thee, all the dove,
By all thy lives and deaths of love,
By thy large draughts of intellectual day,
And by thy thirsts of love more large than they,
By all thy brim-filled bowls of fierce desire,
By thy last morning's draught of liquid fire;
By the full kingdom of that final kiss
That seized thy parting soul and sealed thee His,
By all the heaven thou hast in Him—
Fair sister of the Seraphim!—
By all of Him we have in thee,
Leave nothing of my self in me.
Let me so read thy life that I
Unto all life of mine may die.

RICHARD LOVELACE
[1618–1658]

THE names of Suckling and Lovelace are commonly paired as Cavalier poets, and the similarity extends to part of their lives. Like Suckling, Lovelace was also the son of a gentleman who had received his knighthood from James I; he was a child of wealth and romance, a handsome youth, a court favorite. Unlike Suckling, Lovelace was always in trouble, spent much of his time in prison, and died in want.

Educated at Oxford, heir to four great estates in Kent, Lovelace chose the wrong political faction and, in his twenty-fourth year, was committed to the Gatehouse jail, where he wrote his most celebrated poem, TO ALTHEA FROM PRISON. Liberated on bail—the amount is variously given as four and forty thousand pounds—he raised men for the Royalist army, although still a prisoner on parole. He followed Charles I to France, was wounded at the siege of Dunkirk, and returned to England in his thirtieth year. Once again he was imprisoned, and, while he was confined, collected a volume entitled LUCASTA. Gossip had it that the name "Lucasta" (a contraction of *Lux Casta,* the Pure Light) was a disguise for Lucy Sacheverell, who, having heard that Lovelace had died of his wounds at Dunkirk, had married another.

An outcast when he was released from prison, the last ten years of Lovelace's life were spent in utter poverty. The courtier who had glittered in cloth of silver became a ragged object of charity, "poor in body and purse, befitting the worst of beggars and the poorest of servants." Afraid of his friends, ashamed of himself, he haunted alleys for scraps of food. His quarters may be imagined when it is learned that they were in Gunpowder Alley, near Shoe Lane. He contracted consumption and died in a cellar.

It is not the impoverished creature but the dandy that persists in Lovelace's lines. Fastidious as a person, he was a scrupulous craftsman; his manuscripts show the most minute revisions. Lovelace's lines move lightly, but it is an intricate art which balances and measures the words, words which were eagerly set to music by Henry Lawes, John Wilson, and other composers.

To Althea from Prison

When Love with unconfinèd wings
   Hovers within my gates,
And my divine Althea brings
   To whisper at the grates;
When I lie tangled in her hair
   And fetter'd to her eye,
The birds that wanton in the air
   Know no such liberty.

When flowing cups run swiftly round
   With no allaying Thames,
Our careless heads with roses crown'd,
   Our hearts with loyal flames;
When thirsty grief in wine we steep,
   When healths and draughts go free,
Fishes that tipple in the deep
   Know no such liberty.

When, like committed linnets, I
   With shriller voice shall sing
The sweetness, mercy, majesty
   And glories of my King;
When I shall voice aloud, how good
   He is, how great should be,
Enlargéd winds that curl the flood
   Know no such liberty.

Stone walls do not a prison make,
   Nor iron bars a cage;
Minds innocent and quiet take
   That for an hermitage;
If I have freedom in my love
   And in my soul am free,
Angels alone, that soar above,
   Enjoy such liberty.

To Lucasta, on Going to the Wars

Tell me not, Sweet, I am unkind
   That from the nunnery
Of thy chaste breast and quiet mind,
   To war and arms I fly.

True, a new mistress now I chase,
   The first foe in the field;
And with a stronger faith embrace
   A sword, a horse, a shield.

Yet this inconstancy is such
   As you too shall adore;
I could not love thee, dear, so much,
   Loved I not honor more.

Lovelace and Suckling combine true gallantry with facile badinage. They treat love with a lightness which would have offended Donne, they consider life and its few years with a levity which would have outraged Milton. Even when the subjects are serious, they are not taken seriously, neither the sensuality nor the cynicism. THE SCRUTINY is an example of Lovelace's compromise between banter and audacity, a praise of inconstancy which echoes Suckling's THE CONSTANT LOVER in its mockery.

To Amarantha

THAT SHE WOULD DISHEVEL HER HAIR

Amarantha, sweet and fair,
Ah, braid no more that shining hair!
As my curious hand or eye
Hovering round thee, let it fly!

Let it fly as unconfined
As its calm ravisher the wind,
Who hath left his darling East
To wanton o'er that spicy nest.

Every tress must be confest,
But neatly tangled at the best;
Like a clue of golden thread
Most excellently ravelléd.

Do not, then, wind up that light
In ribbands, and o'ercloud in night,
Like the Sun in's early ray;
But shake your head, and scatter day!

The Scrutiny

Why shouldst thou swear I am forsworn,
    Since thine I vowed to be?
Lady, it is already Morn,
    And 'twas last night I swore to thee
    That fond impossibility.

Have I not loved thee much and long,
    A tedious twelve hours' space?
I should all other beauties wrong,
    And rob thee of a new embrace
    Should I still dote upon thy face.

Not but all joy in thy brown hair
    In others may be found;
But I must search the black and fair,
    Like skilful minerallists that sound
    For treasure in un-plowed-up ground.

Then if, when I have loved my round,
    Thou prov'st the pleasant she,
With spoils of meaner beauties crowned
    I laden will return to thee,
    Even sated with variety.

ABRAHAM COWLEY
[1618–1667]

S ON of a wealthy London stationer, Abraham Cowley was almost unbelievably precocious. At ten he wrote an epical romance, PYRAMUS AND THISBE; at eleven he composed a more "mature" epic, CONSTANTIA AND PHILETUS; his first volume, POETICAL BLOSSOMS, was published at the age of fifteen. From that time on Cowley's industry was as prodigious as it was varied. He wrote a pastoral drama at eighteen, a Latin comedy six months later, and, as an ardent Royalist of twenty-three, a dramatic satire directed against the Puritans.

At Cambridge Cowley delighted and astounded his teachers, but he was forced to leave college because of his political opinions. Devoted to the Stuarts, he joined Henrietta Maria in France and became her secretary. During twelve years of exile he acted as decoder of messages between the Queen and Charles, and was sent on dubious diplomatic missions, probably as a secret agent. He was imprisoned as a spy in England, was released, studied medicine at Oxford after the Restoration, and was given a small estate in Chertsey, where he spent his last years "in beloved obscurity, and possessed that solitude which from his very childhood he had always passionately desired." That solitude and "beloved obscurity" were only an intermittent passion, but the growing desire for a small house and a large garden is genuinely and memorably expressed in THE WISH.

The Wish

Well then! I now do plainly see
This busy world and I shall ne'er agree.
The very honey of all earthly joy
Does of all meats the soonest cloy;
   And they, methinks, deserve my pity
Who for it can endure the stings,
The crowd and buzz and murmurings
   Of this great hive, the city.

Ah, yet, ere I descend to th' grave
May I a small house and large garden have;
And a few friends, and many books, both true,
Both wise, and both delightful too!
    And since love ne'er will from me flee,
A mistress moderately fair,
And good as guardian angels are,
    Only beloved and loving me.

O fountains! when in you shall I
Myself eased of unpeaceful thoughts espy?
O fields! O woods! when, when shall I be made
The happy tenant of your shade?
    Here's the spring-head of pleasure's flood:
Here's wealthy nature's treasury,
Where all the riches lie that she
    Has coin'd and stamped for good.

Pride and ambition here
Only in far-fetch'd metaphors appear;
Here nought but winds can hurtful murmurs scatter,
And nought but echo flatter.
    The gods, when they descended, hither
From heaven did always choose their way:
And therefore we may boldly say
    That 'tis the way, too, thither.

How happy here should I
And one dear She live, and embracing die!
She who is all the world, and can exclude
In deserts solitude.
    I should have then this only fear:
Lest men, when they my pleasure see,
Should hither throng to live like me,
    And make a city here.

Cowley's reputation as a poet rose and fell with the flash of a skyrocket. A love cycle entitled THE MISTRESS was one of the most popular books of the period; today it is read only as a curiosity of exaggerated expression. THE DAVIDEIS was relished for its embroideries on the Biblical history of David; its metaphysical conceits spun out in lengthy couplets are an almost insurmountable barrier to enjoyment. His PINDARIQUE ODES set a fashion in English verse and represented the pure classical spirit to his contemporaries. But

Cowley failed to comprehend the purpose of Pindar's arrangement; his English ode was "a blunder founded upon a misconception"; and his loosely patterned structure attained dignity only when it was employed and heightened by Dryden.

It is in the smaller pieces that Cowley is most winning. If he lacks the wit and passion of Donne, to whom he was indebted, he has an ingenuity of his own. Even when he is emotional, the emotion is directed, if not wholly disciplined, by the mind.

The Prophet

Teach me to love? Go teach thy self more wit:
    I chief professor am of it.
    Teach craft to Scots, and thrift to Jews,
    Teach boldness to the stews;
In tyrant's courts teach supple flattery,
Teach Jesuits, that have travelled far, to lie.
    Teach fire to burn, and winds to blow,
    Teach restless fountains how to flow,
    Teach the dull earth, fixt, to abide,
Teach woman-kind inconstancy and pride.
See if your diligence here will useful prove;
    But, pr'ithee, teach me not to love.

The god of love, if such a thing there be,
    May learn to love from me;
    He who does boast that he has been
    In every heart since Adam's sin;
I'll lay my life, nay, mistress on't, that's more,
I'll teach him things he never knew before;
    I'll teach him a receipt to make
    Words that weep, and tears that speak,
    I'll teach him sighs, like those in death,
At which the souls go out too with the breath:
Still the soul stays, yet still does from me run;
    As light and heat does with the sun.

'Tis I who love's Columbus am; 'tis I,
    Who must new worlds in it descry:
    Rich worlds, that yield of treasure more
    Than all that has been known before.
And yet like his (I fear) my fate must be,
To find them out for others; not for me.

Me, times to come (I know it) shall
Love's last and greatest prophet call.
But, ah, what's that, if she refuse
To hear the wholesome doctrines of my Muse?
If to my share the prophet's fate must come,
    Hereafter fame, here martyrdom.

Beauty

Beauty, thou wild fantastic ape,
Who dost in ev'ry country change thy shape!
Here black, there brown, here tawny, and there white;
Thou flatterer which compli'st with every sight!
    Thou Babel which confound'st the eye
    With unintelligible variety!
    Who hast no certain What, nor Where,
But vari'st still, and dost thy self declare
Inconstant, as thy she-possessors are.

Beauty, love's scene and masquerade,
So gay by well-placed lights, and distance made!
False coin, with which th' impostor cheats us still;
The stamp and color good, but metal ill!
    Which light, or base we find, when we
    Weigh by enjoyment, and examine thee!
    For though thy being be but show,
'Tis chiefly night which men to thee allow:
And choose t' enjoy thee, when thou least art thou.

Beauty, thou active, passive ill!
Which diest thy self as fast as thou dost kill!
Thou tulip, who thy stock in paint dost waste,
Neither for physic good, nor smell, nor taste.
    Beauty, whose flames but meteors are,
    Short-liv'd and low, though thou wouldst seem a star,
    Who dar'st not thine own home descry,
Pretending to dwell richly in the eye,
When thou, alas, dost in the fancy lie.

Dryden explained Cowley's declining reputation by saying that
he could not relinquish a single simile, no matter how farfetched,
and "could never forgive any conceit which came in his way." But
this scarcely applies to Cowley's lighter verses, and in particular his

paraphrases from Anacreon, the Greek forerunner of Omar Khay-
yám. Cowley, the Cavalier, could appreciate the fact that Anacreon
lived gaily and died with poetic appropriateness; the Attic cele-
brant of wine choked to death on a grape pit.

Today Is Ours

Fill the bowl with rosy wine,
Around our temples roses twine;
And let us cheerfully awhile
Like the wine and roses smile.
Crowned with roses we contemn
Gyges' wealthy diadem.
Today is ours. What do we fear!
Today is ours. We have it here!
Let's treat it kindly, that it may
Wish, at least, with us to stay.
Banish business, banish sorrow.
To the gods belongs tomorrow.

Drinking

The thirsty earth soaks up the rain,
And drinks and gapes for drink again;
The plants suck in the earth, and are
With constant drinking fresh and fair;
The sea itself (which one would think
Should have but little need of drink)
Drinks twice ten thousand rivers up,
So filled that they o'erflow the cup.
The busy sun (and one would guess
By's drunken fiery face no less)
Drinks up the sea, and when he's done,
The moon and stars drink up the sun:
They drink and dance by their own light,
They drink and revel all the night.
Nothing in nature's sober found,
But an eternal health goes round.
Fill up the bowl, then, fill it high!
Fill all the glasses there—for why
Should every creature drink but I?
Why, man of morals. tell me why?

ANDREW MARVELL
[1621–1678]

ANDREW MARVELL'S career towered on a shifting base. Other careers were wrecked on a wrong choice of parties or an injudicious word, but Marvell's life was solidly built upon a set of contradictions. One of the leading Puritan poets, he preferred Cavaliers as his intimates. He strongly sympathized with Charles I; yet he was Milton's assistant when Milton became Latin secretary under Cromwell and, upon Cromwell's return from Ireland, Marvell wrote an ode in which the Protector was hailed as a Caesar. Upon Cromwell's death Marvell went into deep mourning and assisted at the pompous burial in the Abbey; two years later he was a member of the Restoration parliament when that parliament voted to dishonor Cromwell by digging up his body and beheading it. An apparently timid man, Marvell often expressed himself in a manner that was not only bellicose but abusive. He remained friends with men as opposed in character as Lovelace and Milton. It has been suggested that Marvell never meant to be a partisan, that he clung to people rather than to causes, and that he loved order with such passion that he was willing to sacrifice anything for it. Either an extraordinarily adroit opportunist or a supremely lucky man, he was able to fasten upon many points of view without impaling himself on any of them.

Marvell received his early education from a father who was both a minister and a master of a grammar school. Securing a scholarship at Trinity College, he took his B.A. at eighteen and immediately started out on his paradoxical course. A relative of Cyriack Skinner financed him, introduced him to Milton, and bequeathed him an estate. He had already become tutor to Lord Fairfax's daughter Mary, afterwards Duchess of Buckingham, and lived contentedly in the spacious Fairfax country home, Appleton House. It was there that he wrote the "garden poetry" for which he became immediately famous. THE GARDEN, one of the most expressive of nature poems, justifies the enthusiasts; it is seemingly traditional but actually unique. Marvell exhibits the nature images of his predecessors but turns them toward a new consciousness, the scientific perceptions of the age.

The Garden

How vainly men themselves amaze
To win the palm, the oak, or bays;
And their incessant labors see
Crowned from some single herb, or tree,
Whose short and narrow-vergéd shade
Does prudently their toils upbraid;
While all flowers and all trees do close
To weave the garlands of repose.

Fair Quiet, have I found thee here,
And Innocence, thy sister dear?
Mistaken long, I sought you then
In busy companies of men.
Your sacred plants, if here below,
Only among the plants will grow;
Society is all but rude
To this delicious solitude.

No white nor red was ever seen
So amorous as this lovely green.
Fond lovers, cruel as their flame,
Cut in these trees their mistress' name:
Little, alas! they know or heed
How far these beauties hers exceed!
Fair trees! wheres'e'er your barks I wound
No name shall but your own be found.

When we have run our passion's heat,
Love hither makes his best retreat.
The gods, that mortal beauty chase,
Still in a tree did end their race;
Apollo hunted Daphne so,
Only that she might laurel grow;
And Pan did after Syrinx speed,
Not as a nymph, but for a reed.

What wondrous life is this I lead!
Ripe apples drop about my head;
The luscious clusters of the vine
Upon my mouth do crush their wine;

The nectarine, and curious peach,
Into my hands themselves do reach;
Stumbling on melons, as I pass,
Insnared with flowers, I fall on grass.

Meanwhile, the mind, from pleasure less,
Withdraws into its happiness:
The mind, that ocean where each kind
Does straight its own resemblance find;
Yet it creates, transcending these,
Far other worlds, and other seas;
Annihilating all that's made
To a green thought in a green shade.

Here at the fountain's sliding foot,
Or at some fruit-tree's mossy root,
Casting the body's vest aside,
My soul into the boughs does glide:
There like a bird it sits, and sings,
Then whets and claps its silver wings;
And, till prepared for longer flight,
Waves in its plumes the various light.

Such was that happy garden-state,
While man there walked without a mate:
After a place so pure and sweet,
What other help could yet be meet!
But 'twas beyond a mortal's share
To wander solitary there:
Two paradises 'twere in one,
To live in Paradise alone.

How well the skilful gardener drew
Of flowers, and herbs, this dial new;
Where, from above, the milder sun
Does through a fragrant zodiac run;
And, as it works, the industrious bee
Computes its time as well as we.
How could such sweet and wholesome hours
Be reckoned but with herbs and flowers!

FROM

Upon Appleton House

See how the flowers, as at parade,
Under their colors stand displayed;
Each regiment in order grows,
That of the tulip, pink, and rose.
But when the vigilant patrol
Of stars walks round about the pole,
Their leaves that to the stalks are curled
Seem to their staves the ensigns furled.
Then in some flower's belovéd hut,
Each bee, as sentinel, is shut,
And sleeps so too, but, if once stirred,
She runs you through, nor asks the word.

Oh thou, that dear and happy isle,
The garden of the world erewhile,
Thou Paradise of the four seas,
Which Heaven planted us to please,
But, to exclude the world, did guard
With watery, if not flaming sword—
What luckless apple did we taste,
To make us mortal, and thee waste?
Unhappy! shall we never more
That sweet militia restore,
When gardens only had their towers
And all the garrisons were flowers;
When roses only arms might bear,
And men did rosy garlands wear?

Paradox is the outstanding quality of Marvell's poetry. It is both
worldly and detached from the world, elaborate and yet colloquial,
rhetorical yet essentially reasonable. This combination is perhaps
best illustrated by Marvell's most famous poem, TO HIS COY MISTRESS.
Here the poet employs the conventionally elegant manner and arti-
ficial tone to convey meanings beyond what he seems to be saying.
The poem is by no means as straightforward as it appears. It argues
the difficult case of platonic versus sexual love sharply, with heat
and irony. But beneath the sense of haste and compulsion, of eager
love and immediate need, is the suggestion that the deepest passion

rises from frustration and finally accustoms itself to an incomplete acceptance. Marvell's wit solves the paradox; it opposes and, somehow, combines resentment and resignation.

To His Coy Mistress

Had we but world enough, and time,
This coyness, lady, were no crime.
We would sit down, and think which way
To walk, and pass our long love's day.
Thou by the Indian Ganges' side
Should'st rubies find: I by the tide
Of Humber would complain. I would
Love you ten years before the Flood,
And you should, if you please, refuse
Till the conversion of the Jews.
My vegetable love should grow
Vaster than empires, and more slow.
An hundred years should go to praise
Thine eyes, and on thy forehead gaze:
Two hundred to adore each breast:
But thirty thousand to the rest;
An age at least to every part,
And the last age should show your heart.
For, lady, you deserve this state,
Nor would I love at lower rate.
    But at my back I always hear
Time's wingéd chariot hurrying near:
And yonder all before us lie
Deserts of vast eternity.
Thy beauty shall no more be found;
Nor, in thy marble vault, shall sound
My echoing song: then worms shall try
That long-preserved virginity,
And your quaint honor turn to dust,
And into ashes all my lust.
The grave's a fine and private place,
But none, I think, do there embrace.
    Now, therefore, while the youthful hue
Sits on thy skin like morning dew,
And while thy willing soul transpires
At every pore with instant fires,
Now let us sport us while we may;

And now, like amorous birds of prey,
Rather at once our Time devour,
Than languish in his slow-chapt [1] power.
Let us roll all our strength and all
Our sweetness up into one ball,
And tear our pleasures with rough strife
Thorough the iron gates of life.
Thus, though we cannot make our Sun
Stand still, yet we will make him run.

To HIS COY MISTRESS is one of the smaller monuments of the century, but it is perfect. Later in life Marvell turned to satires in verse, diatribes, political lampoons, even to a parody of the style of Charles II, a burlesque of a King's speech to both houses of parliament in which Charles supposedly went into scandalous detail concerning his domestic affairs. (Charles was so amused that he forgave the audacious lese majesty.) Today Marvell's satires are forgotten, but his lyrics are still read with increasing appreciation and analyzed to an extent that would not only have surprised but shocked the poet and parliamentarian. Literary historians stress Marvell's function as a "reviver"; the metaphysical conceit had been elaborately thinning itself out, and Marvell restored it to vigor. But the lay reader will be drawn to Marvell for his combination of earnestness and cynicism, of delicacy and downrightness, and for an originality as unpredictable as it is unmistakable.

The Definition of Love

My Love is of a birth as rare
As 'tis, for object, strange and high:
It was begotten by despair
Upon impossibility.

Magnanimous despair alone
Could show me so divine a thing,
Where feeble hope could ne'er have flown
But vainly flapped its tinsel wing.

And yet I quickly might arrive
Where my extended soul is fixed,
But Fate does iron wedges drive,
And always crowds itself betwixt.

[1] *Slow-devouring. "Chaps" are jaws.*

For Fate with jealous eye does see
Two perfect loves; nor lets them close:
Their union would her ruin be,
And her tyrannic power depose.

And therefore her decrees of steel
Us as the distant poles have placed,
(Though love's whole world on us doth wheel)
Not by themselves to be embraced.

Unless the giddy heaven fall,
And earth some new convulsion tear;
And. us to join, the world should all
Be cramped into a planisphere.

As lines, so love's oblique may well
Themselves in every angle greet:
But ours, so truly parallel,
Though infinite, can never meet.

Therefore the love which us doth bind,
But Fate so enviously debars,
Is the conjunction of the mind,
And opposition of the stars.

The Mower to the Glow-worms

Ye living lamps, by whose dear light
The nightingale does sit so late,
And studying all the summer night,
Her matchless songs does meditate;

Ye country comets, that portend
No war nor prince's funeral,
Shining unto no higher end
Than to presage the grass's fall;

Ye glow-worms, whose officious flame
To wandering mowers shows the way,
That in the night have lost their aim,
And after foolish fires do stray;

Your courteous lights in vain you waste,
Since Juliana here is come,
For she my mind hath so displaced
That I shall never find my home.

HENRY VAUGHAN
[1622–1695]

A COUNTRY doctor, who called himself the "Silurist" (from "Siluria," the Latin name for his native district in South Wales), Henry Vaughan came of an ancient Welsh family. He and his twin brother Thomas were privately educated in Wales. Thomas became an alchemist and expert in magic; Henry went to London to study law, turned instead to medicine, and settled in his native Newton by Usk as a practicing physician. The Civil War interrupted his work; he became one of the Welsh bodyguard of horsemen that gathered about the King on the field of Rowton Heath. Two years later he retired to devote himself to his patients and his poetry.

Vaughan has often been compared to Herbert, and Vaughan confessed himself Herbert's disciple. In a dedication to a book published in his late thirties, Vaughan insisted that the first who had diverted the stream of profane poetry into pure channels was "the blessed man, Mr. George Herbert, whose holy life and verse gained many pious converts, of whom I am the least." But there is actually little similarity in the work of these two religious poets. Herbert's images were inspired by the church, whereas Vaughan's inspirations came from ordinary experience, from a close observation heightened by imaginative intensity.

The Revival

Unfold, unfold! take in his light,
Who makes thy cares more short than night,
The joys which with his day-star rise
He deals to all but drowsy eyes;
And (what the men of this world miss)
Some drops and dews of future bliss.

Hark, how his winds have changed their note,
And with warm whispers call thee out.
The frosts are past, the storms are gone,
And backward life at last comes on.

The lofty groves in express joys
Reply unto the turtle's voice;
And here in dust and dirt, O here
The lilies of his love appear!

Vaughan's intimacy with God is startling. It remains unmatched until, two hundred years later, it is sharpened almost to impertinence by Emily Dickinson. Like Emily Dickinson, also, Vaughan has a way of animating the inanimate. He cries, "My dew! my dew! my early love!" and "I saw Eternity the other night." He wrote not only as men spoke, but as men would like to talk. Poets who followed him appreciated his freshness and ease. THE RETREAT is a poem which has borne many children; Wordsworth borrowed the central idea for his ODE: INTIMATIONS OF IMMORTALITY, and Traherne (see page 496) based a whole philosophy upon it.

The Retreat

Happy those early days, when I
Shined in my Angel-infancy!
Before I understood this place
Appointed for my second race,
Or taught my soul to fancy aught
But a white, celestial thought;
When yet I had not walked above
A mile or two from my first Love,
And looking back, at that short space
Could see a glimpse of His bright face;
When on some gilded cloud or flower
My gazing soul would dwell an hour,
And in those weaker glories spy
Some shadows of eternity;
Before I taught my tongue to wound
My conscience with a sinful sound,
Or had the black art to dispense
A several sin to every sense,
But felt through all this fleshly dress
Bright shoots of everlastingness.

O how I long to travel back,
And tread again that ancient track!
That I might once more reach that plain

Where first I felt my glorious train;
From whence th' enlightened spirit sees
That shady City of palm trees!
But ah! my soul with too much stay
Is drunk, and staggers in the way.
Some men a forward motion love,
But I by backward steps would move;
And when this dust falls to the urn,
In that state I came, return.

The World

I saw Eternity the other night,
Like a great Ring of pure and endless light,
    All calm, as it was bright;
And round beneath it, Time in hours, days, years,
    Driven by the spheres
Like a vast shadow moved; in which the world
    And all her train were hurled.

The doting lover in his quaintest strain
    Did there complain;
Near him, his lute, his fancy, and his flights,
    Wit's sour delights,
With gloves, and knots, the silly snares of pleasure,
    Yet his dear treasure,
All scattered lay, while he his eyes did pour
    Upon a flower.

The darksome statesman, hung with weights and woe,
Like a thick midnight-fog, moved there so slow,
    He did not stay, nor go;
Condemning thoughts—like sad eclipses—scowl
    Upon his soul,
And clouds of crying witnesses without
    Pursued him with one shout.
Yet digged the mole, and lest his ways be found,
    Worked under ground,
Where he did clutch his prey (But one did see
    That policy);
Churches and altars fed him; perjuries
    Were gnats and flies;
It rained about him blood and tears; but he
    Drank them as free.

The fearful miser on a heap of rust
Sat pining all his life there, did scarce trust
   His own hands with the dust,
Yet would not place one piece above, but lives
   In fear of thieves.
Thousands there were as frantic as himself
   And hugged each one his pelf,
The downright epicure placed heaven in sense
   And scorned pretence,
While others, slipped into a wide excess,
   Said little less;
The weaker sort slight, trivial wares enslave,
   Who think them brave;
And poor, despiséd Truth sat counting by
   Their victory.

Yet some, who all this while did weep and sing,
And sing, and weep, soared up into the Ring;
   But most would use no wing.
O fools (said I) thus to prefer dark night
   Before true light!
To live in grots and caves, and hate the day
   Because it shows the way,
The way, which from this dead and dark abode
   Leads up to God,
A way where you might tread the sun, and be
   More bright than he.
But as I did their madness so discuss,
   One whispered thus:
"This Ring the Bridegroom did for none provide,
   But for his bride."

If his devotion was too deep and his passion too austere for popularity, Vaughan's poetry is richer than that of most of his generation. His landscapes suddenly open into flashes from another world, beautiful but seldom glimpsed. Vaughan is among those poets who, by a just paradox, says Francis Meynell, "are famous for being unknown, and cherished because of their neglect."

The Night

Dear Night! this world's defeat,
The stop to busy fools, care's check and curb,
The day of spirits, my soul's calm retreat
    Which none disturb;
  Christ's progress, and his prayer time;
  The hours to which high Heaven doth chime.

God's silent, searching flight,
When my Lord's head is filled with dew, and all
His locks are wet with the clear drops of night;
    His still, soft call;
  His knocking time; the soul's dumb watch
  When spirits their fair kindred catch:

Were all my loud, evil days
Calm and unhaunted as is thy dark tent,
Whose peace but by some angel's wing or voice,
    Is seldom rent;
  Then I in heaven all the long year
  Would keep, and never wander here . . .

There is in God, some say,
A deep but dazzling darkness: as men here
Say it is late and dusky, because they
    See not all clear.
  O for that Night! where I in him
  Might live invisible and dim!

JOHN COLLOP
[1625–1662?]

LITTLE known in his day and unremembered in our own, the
name of John Collop has almost vanished from the annals of
history. It is not in the encyclopedias; it cannot be found in the
general collections of poetry; it is not even in the more specialized

anthology devoted to his century, the excellent and voluminous
OXFORD BOOK OF SEVENTEENTH CENTURY VERSE.

Yet Collop was the typical metaphysical poet of the period; not
one of the great ones of his time, but better than many. Like
Vaughan, he was a doctor by profession; unlike Vaughan, Collop
was a liberal with the stubborn habit of questioning. He wrote a
plea for religious tolerance, which was commended, condemned,
and reprinted. His POESIS REDIVIVA appeared in 1656; it was patron-
izingly applauded and promptly forgotten. But some of the verses,
preserved in odd volumes, have survived the almost universal neg-
lect. Of THE LEPER CLEANSED, John Drinkwater, who drew attention
to the unknown poem, wrote: "It is a great religious lyric, with a
close which is as wonderful as anything in seventeenth-century
poetry. It is interesting to note the variation in design midway
through the poem, so unexpected and so successful."

The fierceness of metaphor recalls his predecessor John Donne,
and the breathlessness of phrase anticipates Gerard Manley Hop-
kins (see page 977). But Collop has a spiritual vigor and a singular
expressiveness which are quite his own.

The Leper Cleansed

Hear, Lord, hear
The rhetoric of a tear.
Hear, hear my breast;
While I knock there, Lord, take no rest.

Open! ah, open wide!
Thou art the door, Lord! Open! hide
My sin; a spear once entered at thy side.

See! ah, see
A Naaman's leprosy!
Yet here appears
A cleansing Jordan in my tears.

Lord, let the faithless see
Miracles ceased, revive in me.
The leper cleansed, blind healed, dead raised by thee.

Whither? ah, whither shall I fly?
To heaven? my sins, ah, sins there cry!
Yet mercy, Lord, O mercy! hear
Th'atoning incense of my prayer.
A broken heart thou'lt not despise.
See! see a contrite's sacrifice!

Keep, keep, vials of wrath, keep still!
I'll vials, Lord, of odors fill:
Of prayers, sighs, groans, and tears a shower;
I'll 'noint, wash, wipe, kiss, wash, wipe, weep.
My tears, Lord, in thy bottle keep,
Lest flames of lust, and fond desire,
Kindle fresh fuel for thine ire,
Which tears must quench; like Magdalene
I'll wash thee, Lord, till I be clean.

To the Soul

Dull soul aspire;
Thou art not earth. Mount higher!
Heaven gave the spark; to it return the fire.

Let sin ne'er quench
Thy high-flamed spirit hence;
To earth the heat, to heaven the flame dispense!

Rejoice! Rejoice!
Turn, turn, each part a voice;
While to the heart-strings' tune ye all rejoice.

The house is swept
Which sin so long foul kept;
The penny's found for which the loser wept.

And, purged with tears,
God's image reappears.
The penny truly shows whose stamp it bears.

The sheep long lost,
Sin's wilderness oft crossed,
Is found, regained, returned. Spare, spare no cost!

'Tis heaven's own suit;
Hark how it woos you to't.
When angels needs must speak, shall man be mute?

CHARLES COTTON
[1630–1687]

CHARLES COTTON is best known as the friend of that piscatorial
genius, Izaak Walton; the initials of the two were intertwined
above the door of Walton's fishing cottage, and Cotton added "In-
structions how to Angle for Trout in a Clear Stream" to THE COM-
PLEAT ANGLER. In his time Cotton was known as a translator of
Montaigne, a traveler, and a writer of rough parodies. This by no
means ends the list of his accomplishments. His VOYAGE TO IRELAND
IN BURLESQUE discloses that Cotton held a captain's commission;
his SCARRONIDES, which went through fifteen editions, shows how
boldly he could travesty Virgil; THE COMPLEAT GAMESTER revealed
him in the role of a rake; THE PLANTER'S MANUAL proved him a
good gardener.

As a poet Cotton's gift was limited but not to be despised. His
lyrics are brightly spontaneous; his sonnets, as lyrical as many songs,
are spiced with smiling indelicacies. Coleridge praised their "purity
and unaffectedness," but one does not have to agree with the author
of BIOGRAPHIA LITERARIA to relish Cotton. There is certainly no
question about his unaffectedness.

Alice

Alice is tall and upright as a pine,
White as blanched almonds or the falling snow,
Sweet as are damask roses when they blow,
And doubtless fruitful as the swelling vine.

Ripe to be cut and ready to be pressed,
Her full-cheeked beauties very well appear;
And a year's fruit she loses every year,
Wanting a man to improve her to the best.

Full fain she would be husbanded; and yet,
Alas, she cannot a fit laborer get
To cultivate her to his own content.

Fain would she be (God wot) about her task,
And yet (forsooth) she is too proud to ask,
And (which is worse) too modest to consent.

Margaret

Margaret of humbler stature by the head
Is (as it oft falls out with yellow hair)
Than her fair sister, yet so much more fair
As her pure white is better mixed with red.

This, hotter than the other ten to one,
Longs to be put unto her mother's trade,
And loud proclaims she lives too long a maid,
Wishing for one to untie her virgin zone.

She finds virginity a kind of ware
That's very, very troublesome to bear,
And being gone she thinks will ne'er be missed:

And yet withal the girl has so much grace,
To call for help I know she wants the face,
Though, asked, I know not how she would resist.

ALICE and MARGARET are part of a group of sonnets which combine naughtiness with canniness. Scarcely less delightful are the homely details of the "summer quatrains" in which Cotton made a background for lively pictures, dedicating them to a morning, noon, evening, and night of a particularly happy June.

Summer Evening

The day's grown old, the fainting sun
Has but a little way to run;
And yet his steeds, with all his skill,
Scarce lug the chariot down the hill.

The shadows now so long do grow
That brambles like tall cedars show;
Mole-hills seem mountains, and the ant
Appears a monstrous elephant.

A very little little flock
Shades thrice the ground that it would stock;
Whilst the small stripling following them
Appears a mighty Polypheme.

These being brought into the fold,
And by the thrifty master told,
He thinks his wages are well paid
Since none are either lost or strayed.

The hedge is stripped, the clothes brought in;
Naught's left without that should be in.
The bees are hived and hum their charm,
Whilst every house does seem a swarm.

The cock now to the roost is pressed:
For he must call up all the rest.
The sow's fast pegged within the sty
To still her squeaking progeny.

Each one has had his supping mess;
The cheese is put into the press;
The pans and bowls, clean scalded all,
Reared up against the milk-house wall.

And now on benches all are sat
In the cool air to sit and chat
Till Phoebus, dipping in the west,
Shall lead the world the way to rest.

THOMAS TRAHERNE

[1633?–1674]

THOMAS TRAHERNE, a Hereford shoemaker's son, attended Brase-
nose College, Oxford, took holy orders, and was appointed
rector near the place of his birth. His life was simple to the extreme
of austerity; his unworldliness is proved by a will in which he left

trivial possessions to his friends, including an old hat to his brother, but made no mention of a profitable row of houses which, later, enriched the parish of Hereford.

Not one of Traherne's poems appeared in print during his lifetime. His writings, preserved by his brother, neglected by his descendants, were rejected by libraries, disdained by publishers, and passed from one uninterested bookseller to another. More than two hundred years after Traherne's death, the pages of two anonymous manuscripts were tossed on the shelf of an outdoor bookstall. There they were picked up for a few shillings by a scholar, Alexander Balloch Grosart, who thought they were unknown poems of Vaughan. Research revealed Dr. Grosart's error and established the real author. Even then the poems, edited by Bertram Dobell, were not printed until 1903.

Although Traherne was a minister of the Church of England, his was the faith and humility of an early Christian. His style was strange: plain speaking intensified by prophecy, an exalted primitivism. He regarded the small happenings of everyday with simple wonder; his nostalgia for childhood and his idealization of that state of "Angel-infancy" is an echo of Vaughan's THE RETREAT, which appears on page 488. That Traherne realized his backward yearning is evident not only from his study of "common untutored things," but from the subtitle of his collection: "Divine Reflections on the Native Objects of an Infant-Eye." It was as a child that Traherne observed the world, and it was as a child that he aimed to reflect his observations with unsophisticated directness. In this he succeeded. If Traherne is sometimes awkward, he has both the awkwardness and the grace of an unspoiled child.

Wonder

How like an angel came I down!
How bright are all things here!
When first among His works I did appear,
O how their glory me did crown!
The world resembled His eternity,
In which my soul did walk;
And everything that I did see
Did with me talk.

The skies in their magnificence,
        The lively, lovely air,
Oh, how divine, how soft, how sweet, how fair!
        The stars did entertain my sense;
And all the works of God so bright and pure,
        So rich and great did seem
        As if they ever must endure
            In my esteem.

A native health and innocence
        Within my bones did grow;
And while my God did all his glories show,
        I felt a vigor in my sense
That was all spirit: I within did flow
        With seas of life like wine;
        I nothing in the world did know
            But 'twas divine.

Harsh, ragged objects were concealed:
        Oppressions, tears, and cries,
Sins, griefs, complaints, dissensions, weeping eyes
        Were hid, and only things revealed
Which heavenly spirits and the angels prize.
        The state of innocence
        And bliss, not trades and poverties,
            Did fill my sense.

The streets were paved with golden stones;
        The boys and girls were mine:
Oh, how did all their lovely faces shine!
        The sons of men were holy ones;
In joy and beauty they appeared to me;
        And everything which here I found,
        While like an angel I did see,
            Adorned the ground.

Rich diamond and pearl and gold
        In every place was seen;
Rare splendors, yellow, blue, red, white, and green,
        Mine eyes did everywhere behold.
Great wonders clothed with glory did appear;
        Amazement was my bliss;
        That and my wealth was everywhere;
            No joy to this!

Cursed and devised proprieties,
    With envy, avarice,
And fraud (those fiends that spoil even Paradise)
    Flew from the splendor of mine eyes;
And so did hedges, ditches, limits, bounds:
    I dreamed not aught of those,
    But in surveying all men's grounds
        I found repose.

For property itself was mine,
    And hedges, ornaments:
Walls, houses, coffers, and their rich contents
    To make me rich combine.
Clothes, ribbons, jewels, laces I esteemed
    My wealth by others worn;
    For me they all to wear them seemed
        When I was born.

If WONDER bears overtones of the mystical Vaughan, it carries the vision further. The best of Traherne is on a high plane of innocence. Sometimes imperfectly formed, sometimes unequal to the demands of his structure, Traherne's lines are charmingly undistracted. Shyly curious, quietly absorbed, this meditative poet impresses by his complete naturalness; he is unaffected and yet completely individual. For him the common street was glorious, truly "paved with golden stones." His singular verses are, to use his own title, poems of felicity.

Eden

A learned and a happy ignorance
        Divided me
        From all the vanity,
From all the sloth, care, sorrow, that advance
    The madness and the misery
Of men. No error, no distraction, I
Saw cloud the earth, or overcast the sky.

I knew not that there was a serpent's sting,
        Whose poison, shed
        On men, did overspread
The world; nor did I dream of such a thing

As sin, in which mankind lay dead.
They all were brisk and living things to me,
Yea, pure, and full of immortality. . . .

Only what Adam in his first estate
      Did I behold;
    Hard silver and dry gold
As yet lay underground: my happy fate
  Was more acquainted with the old
And innocent delights which he did see
In his original simplicity.

Those things which first his Eden did adorn,
      My infancy
    Did crown: simplicity
Was my protection when I first was born.
  Mine eyes those treasures first did see
Which God first made: the first effects of love
My first enjoyments upon earth did prove,

And were so great and so divine, so pure,
      So fair and sweet,
    So true; when I did meet
Them here at first, they did my soul allure,
  And drew away mine infant feet
Quite from the works of men, that I might see
The glorious wonders of the Deity.

Walking

To walk abroad is, not with eyes,
But thoughts, the fields to see and prize;
  Else may the silent feet,
    Like logs of wood,
Move up and down, and see no good,
  Nor joy nor glory meet.

Ev'n carts and wheels their place do change,
But cannot see; though very strange
  The glory that is by:
    Dead puppets may
Move in the bright and glorious day,
  Yet not behold the sky.

And are not men than they more blind,
Who having eyes yet never find
   The bliss in which they move:
      Like statues dead
They up and down are carrièd,
   Yet neither see nor love. . . .

Observe those rich and glorious things;
The rivers, meadows, woods, and springs,
   The fructifying sun;
      To note from far
The rising of each twinkling star
   For us his race to run.

A little child these well perceives,
Who, tumbling in green grass and leaves,
   May rich as kings be thought.
      But there's a sight
Which perfect manhood may delight,
   To which we shall be brought.

While in those pleasant paths we talk
'Tis that towards which at last we walk;
   For we may by degrees
      Wisely proceed
Pleasures of love and praise to heed,
   From viewing herbs and trees.

Childhood

         My childhood is a sphere
Wherein ten thousand heavenly joys appear.
      Those thoughts it doth include
   And those affections, which reviewed,
         Again present to me
In better sort the things that I did see.
         Imaginations real are
         Unto my mind again appear:
Which makes my life a circle of delights,
A hidden sphere of obvious benefits:
An earnest that the actions of the just
Shall still revive and flourish in the dust.[1]

[1] *The last two lines are an intentional echo, almost a direct quotation, of the concluding lines of Shirley's poem on page 425.*

X

The Rise and Fall of Elegance

THE eighteenth century, that controversial era, is distinguished by many tendencies, but it may safely be said to have marked the rise and fall of elegance. Much ink has been spilled in the attempt to characterize the age as "a revival of classicism" and in the vainer effort to define the undefinable differences between 'classicism" and "romanticism." But when the formal manner began to dominate at the end of the seventeenth century, poetry took a turn toward pedantry, imitated the principles supposedly embodied by the great Greeks and Latins, and made a fetish of dignity and precision.

The initial result was a sharpening of technique and a clarification of ideas. But the performance fell short of the program, and what began as high principles ended in mere patternmaking. The dignity degenerated into dullness, the precision tightened into rigidity. The formal manner was allied with artificiality, and erudition could not separate itself from intellectual snobbery. "Man had ceased to live from the depths of his nature," wrote A. E. Housman in THE NAME AND NATURE OF POETRY. "He occupied himself by choice with thoughts which do not range beyond the sphere of his understanding." Lucidity became the prime virtue, rationalism was almost deified. The "bridge" between the seventeenth-century devotion to the passions and the eighteenth century's so-called scientific detachment was a long and hazardous one, but it was finally spanned by John Dryden, who combined energy and precision.

JOHN DRYDEN
[1631–1700]

RYDEN has been called "both the glory and the shame of our
literature." Even his admirers, conceding his great gift of
satire, his mastery of a sinewy prose, and the power of his reason-
ing, have bewailed his failure to reach the peaks. But Dryden's life
"proves that it was clearly by his own choice that he missed the
highest." He sacrificed values for versatility, and, though he de-
spised the taste of his day, he did his best to please it.

Born at Aldwinkle, in Northamptonshire, son of a Puritan,
Dryden took his degree at Trinity College in 1654. Accepting the
antimonarchial principles of his family, he admired Cromwell and
wrote a series of HEROIC STANZAS in eulogy of the Protector. When
the monarchy was restored, Dryden hailed the coronation of Charles
II with the fulsome ASTRÆA REDUX, which he followed with a lavish
tribute to the "modern Augustus" entitled A PANEGYRIC ON THE
RESTORATION. A few years later he was appointed poet laureate.

In his early thirties Dryden married Lady Elizabeth Howard,
who was somewhat his senior. The marriage was uncongenial and,
although there is no evidence of a separation, Dryden scarcely ever
mentioned marriage without attacking it. Even before his wife's
death he wrote an epitaph that is beautifully concise and unfor-
gettably savage.

Epitaph on His Wife

Here lies my wife: here let her lie!
Now she's at rest. And so am I.

When Dryden turned to the stage he hoped to write tragedies,
but the public demanded comedies and, although Dryden disliked
them, he did what the age demanded. Samuel Pepys spoke of THE
RIVAL LADIES as "a very innocent and most pretty witty play," but
most of the other plays were extravagant in tone and indecent in
humor. The form was presumably "classical," but Dryden was far

too busy to learn the discipline of the ancients. With gathering speed and with little insight into character, Dryden turned out fifth-rate imitations of Shakespeare—ALL FOR LOVE, OR THE WORLD WELL LOST is a curious rewriting of ANTONY AND CLEOPATRA— operas for which Purcell furnished the music, essays, swiftly intemperate satires, translations of Greek and Latin poets, modernizations of Chaucer, and an astonishing work called THE STATE OF INNOCENCE AND FALL OF MAN, which is an attempt to enliven PARADISE LOST by the addition of rhymes.

Dryden's characteristic vacillation failed him at the end. When James II ascended the throne, Dryden, a determined timeserver, became a Roman Catholic. He was then in his mid-fifties. He prepared THE HIND AND THE PANTHER as an argument for Roman Catholicism, but the public was tired of him and exasperated with the Stuarts. James fled to France; Dryden was deposed from the laureateship, and Thomas Shadwell, the very poet Dryden had attacked in his satire MACFLECKNOE, was appointed laureate. A hundred years later Southey said that of all his predecessors Nahum Tate would rank the lowest of the laureates if he had not succeeded Shadwell.

FROM

MacFlecknoe

SHADWELL, OR THE TRIUMPH OF DULLNESS

All human things are subject to decay
And, when Fate summons, monarchs must obey.
This Flecknoe found, who, like Augustus, young
Was called to empire and had governed long,
In prose and verse was owned without dispute
Through all the realms of Nonsense absolute.
This aged prince, now flourishing in peace
And blest with issue of a large increase,
Worn out with business, did at length debate
To settle the succession of the state;
And pondering which of all his sons was fit
To reign and wage immortal war with wit,
Cried, " 'Tis resolved, for Nature pleads that he
Should only rule who most resembles me.
Shadwell alone my perfect image bears,

Mature in dullness from his tender years;
Shadwell alone of all my sons is he
Who stands confirmed in full stupidity.
The rest to some faint meaning make pretence,
But Shadwell never deviates into sense.
Some beams of wit on other souls may fall,
Strike through, and make a lucid interval;
But Shadwell's genuine night admits no ray,
His rising fogs prevail upon the day.
Besides, his goodly fabric fills the eye
And seems designed for thoughtless majesty,
Thoughtless as monarch oaks that shade the plain
And, spread in solemn state, supinely reign . . .
All arguments, but most his plays, persuade
That for anointed dullness was he made."

His office lost, his plays no longer in demand, Dryden suffered twelve years of hack-work. Upon his death, the poverty of his situation was emphasized by the pomp with which he was buried in Westminster Abbey.

More than most, Dryden has suffered from the changes in temper of the reading public, from the excessive praise of his adulators and the violence of his detractors. As late as the nineteenth century Leslie Stephen conceded that Dryden was a master "within his own sphere. But there is something depressing about his atmosphere. He ought to be on our shelves, but he will rarely be found in our hearts." Yet Dryden was not only a superb craftsman but an innovator. If his Latinized style is too literary for any but a select audience, he rediscovered the rich humanity of Chaucer. He perfected the heroic couplet which was to be used with such effect by his great disciple, Alexander Pope. The last twelve years of his life produced the finest verse. A SONG FOR SAINT CECILIA'S DAY and ALEXANDER'S FEAST, written under the pressure of poverty, are brilliant in their changes of tone, evoking the very timbres of the instruments. No poems ever written have expressed the power of music more sonorously.

Alexander's Feast; or, The Power of Music

AN ODE IN HONOR OF SAINT CECILIA'S DAY

1

'Twas at the royal feast, for Persia won
   By Philip's warlike son:
   Aloft in awful state
   The godlike hero sate
   On his imperial throne:
His valiant peers were placed around;
Their brows with roses and with myrtles bound
(So should desert in arms be crowned).
The lovely Thaïs, by his side,
Sate like a blooming Eastern bride
In flower of youth and beauty's pride.
   Happy, happy, happy pair!
    None but the brave,
    None but the brave,
None but the brave deserves the fair.

CHORUS

Happy, happy, happy pair!
   None but the brave,
   None but the brave,
None but the brave deserves the fair.

2

Timotheus, placed on high
   Amid the tuneful choir,
With flying fingers touched the lyre:
The trembling notes ascend the sky,
   And heavenly joys inspire.
The song began from Jove,
Who left his blissful seats above
(Such is the power of mighty love).
A dragon's fiery form belied the god:
Sublime on radiant spires he rode,
When he to fair Olympia pressed;
And while he sought her snowy breast:

Then, round her slender waist he curled,
And stamped an image of himself, a sovereign of the world.
The listening crowd admire the lofty sound;
"A present deity," they shout around;
"A present deity," the vaulted roofs rebound:
    With ravished ears
    The monarch hears,
    Assumes the god,
    Affects to nod,
And seems to shake the spheres.

CHORUS

    With ravished ears
    The monarch hears,
    Assumes the god,
    Affects to nod,
And seems to shake the spheres.

3

The praise of Bacchus then the sweet musician sung,
    Of Bacchus ever fair and ever young:
    The jolly god in triumph comes;
    Sound the trumpets; beat the drums;
      Flushed with a purple grace
      He shows his honest face:
Now give the hautboys breath; he comes, he comes.
    Bacchus, ever fair and young,
      Drinking joys did first ordain;
    Bacchus' blessings are a treasure,
    Drinking is the soldier's pleasure:
      Rich the treasure,
      Sweet the pleasure,
    Sweet is pleasure after pain.

CHORUS

    Bacchus' blessings are a treasure,
    Drinking is the soldier's pleasure;
      Rich the treasure,
      Sweet the pleasure,
    Sweet is pleasure after pain.

4

Soothed with the sound, the king grew vain;
    Fought all his battles o'er again;
And thrice he routed all his foes; and thrice he slew the slain.
  The master saw the madness rise;
  His glowing cheeks, his ardent eyes;
  And, while he heaven and earth defied,
  Changed his hand, and checked his pride
    He chose a mournful Muse,
    Soft pity to infuse:
  He sung Darius great and good,
    By too severe a fate,
Fallen, fallen, fallen, fallen,
    Fallen from his high estate,
And weltering in his blood;
Deserted, at his utmost need,
By those his former bounty fed;
On the bare earth exposed he lies,
With not a friend to close his eyes.
With downcast looks the joyless victor sate,
    Revolving in his altered soul
      The various turns of chance below;
    And, now and then, a sigh he stole;
    And tears began to flow.

CHORUS

    Revolving in his altered soul
      The various turns of chance below;
    And, now and then, a sigh he stole;
    And tears began to flow.

5

The mighty master smiled to see
That love was in the next degree:
'Twas but a kindred sound to move,
For pity melts the mind to love.
  Softly sweet, in Lydian measures,
  Soon he soothed his soul to pleasures.
"War," he sung, "is toil and trouble;
Honor, but an empty bubble;
  Never ending, still beginning,
Fighting still, and still destroying:

If the world be worth thy winning,
Think, O think it worth enjoying;
Lovely Thaïs sits beside thee,
Take the good the gods provide thee."
The many rend the skies with loud applause;
So Love was crowned, but Music won the cause.
The prince, unable to conceal his pain,
Gazed on the fair
Who caused his care,
And sighed and looked, sighed and looked,
Sighed and looked, and sighed again:
At length, with love and wine at once oppressed,
The vanquished victor sunk upon her breast.

CHORUS

The prince, unable to conceal his pain,
Gazed on the fair
Who caused his care,
And sighed and looked, sighed and looked,
Sighed and looked, and sighed again:
At length, with love and wine at once oppressed,
The vanquished victor sunk upon her breast.

6

Now strike the golden lyre again:
A louder yet, and yet a louder strain.
Break his bands of sleep asunder,
And rouse him, like a rattling peal of thunder.
Hark, hark, the horrid sound
Has raised up his head:
As awaked from the dead,
And amazed, he stares around.
"Revenge, revenge!" Timotheus cries,
"See the Furies arise!
See the snakes that they rear,
How they hiss in their hair,
And the sparkles that flash from their eyes!
Behold a ghastly band,
Each a torch in his hand!
Those are Grecian ghosts, that in battle were slain,
And unburied remain
Inglorious on the plain:
Give the vengeance due
To the valiant crew.

Behold how they toss their torches on high,
How they point to the Persian abodes,
And glittering temples of their hostile gods!"
The princes applaud, with a furious joy;
And the king seized a flambeau with zeal to destroy;
Thaïs led the way,
To light him to his prey,
And, like another Helen, fired another Troy.

CHORUS

And the king seized a flambeau with zeal to destroy;
Thaïs led the way,
To light him to his prey,
And, like another Helen, fired another Troy.

7

Thus, long ago,
Ere heaving bellows learned to blow,
While organs yet were mute;
Timotheus, to his breathing flute,
And sounding lyre,
Could swell the soul to rage, or kindle soft desire.
At last, divine Cecilia came,
Inventress of the vocal frame; [1]
The sweet enthusiast, from her sacred store,
Enlarged the former narrow bounds,
And added length to solemn sounds,
With nature's mother wit, and arts unknown before.
Let old Timotheus yield the prize,
Or both divide the crown;
He raised a mortal to the skies;
She drew an angel down.

GRAND CHORUS

At last, divine Cecilia came,
Inventress of the vocal frame;
The sweet enthusiast, from her sacred store,
Enlarged the former narrow bounds,
And added length to solemn sounds,
With nature's mother wit, and arts unknown before.

[1] *The organ, which Cecilia is supposed to have invented.*

> Let old Timotheus yield the prize,
>   Or both divide the crown;
> He raised a mortal to the skies;
>   She drew an angel down.

Saint Cecilia, a Christian martyr who died at Rome in 230, was revered as the patroness of church music. Chaucer told her story in THE SECOND NUN'S TALE in THE CANTERBURY TALES.

A Song for Saint Cecilia's Day, November 22, 1687

> From harmony, from heavenly harmony
>   This universal frame began;
> When Nature underneath a heap
>   Of jarring atoms lay,
> And could not heave her head,
> The tuneful voice was heard from high,
>   Arise, ye more than dead.
> Then cold and hot and moist and dry [1]
>   In order to their stations leap,
>   And Music's power obey.
> From harmony, from heavenly harmony
>   This universal frame began;
>   From harmony to harmony
> Through all the compass of the notes it ran,
> The diapason closing full in Man.
>
> What passion cannot Music raise and quell?
>   When Jubal [2] struck the corded shell,
>   His listening brethren stood around,
>   And, wondering, on their faces fell
>   To worship that celestial sound.
> Less than a god they thought there could not dwell
>   Within the hollow of that shell,
>   That spoke so sweetly, and so well.
> What passion cannot Music raise and quell?
>
>   The trumpet's loud clangor
>   Excites us to arms
>   With shrill notes of anger
>   And mortal alarms.

[1] *Air, Fire, Water, and Earth: the four elements supposed to form the universe.*
[2] *Jubal "was the father of all such as handle the harp and pipe."*

The double, double, double beat
    Of the thundering drum
    Cries, "Hark! the foes come;
Charge, charge, 'tis too late to retreat!"

    The soft complaining flute
    In dying notes discovers
    The woes of hopeless lovers,
Whose dirge is whispered by the warbling lute.

    Sharp violins proclaim
Their jealous pangs and desperation,
Fury, frantic indignation,
Depth of pains and height of passion,
    For the fair, disdainful dame.

    But, oh! what art can teach,
    What human voice can reach
        The sacred organ's praise?
    Notes inspiring holy love,
    Notes that wing their heavenly ways
        To mend the choirs above.

Orpheus could lead the savage race,
And trees unrooted left their place,
    Sequacious of the lyre;
But bright Cecilia raised the wonder higher;
When to her organ vocal breath was given,
An angel heard, and straight appeared,
    Mistaking earth for heaven.

As from the power of sacred lays
    The spheres began to move,
And sung the great Creator's praise
    To all the blest above;
So when the last and dreadful hour
This crumbling pageant shall devour,
The trumpet shall be heard on high,
The dead shall live, the living die,
And Music shall untune [3] the sky.

---

[3] *Destroy. Therefore Music will mark the beginning and end of creation.*

Epigram on Milton

Three poets,[1] in three distant ages born,
Greece, Italy, and England did adorn.
The first in loftiness of thought surpassed;
The next in majesty; in both the last.
The force of Nature could no farther go;
To make a third she joined the former two.

In his HOMAGE TO JOHN DRYDEN, T. S. Eliot admits Dryden's lack of insight and profundity. He acknowledges the nineteenth-century condemnation of Dryden's falsely patrician manner. But, Eliot adds, "in the next revolution of taste it is possible that poets may turn to the study of Dryden. He remains one of those who have set standards for English verse which it is desperate to ignore."

APHRA BEHN
[1640–1689]

O NE is likely to think of woman in the late seventeenth century as a composite of cream, honey, and roses; a creature extolled by the poets as perennially desirable and unobtainable, and always far removed from reality. But Aphra (also known as Afra, Aphara, and Ayfara) Behn was a military spy.

One of the most exotic figures of her time, she was born Aphra Johnson, in Kent. Her father was a barber, her mother a domestic. As a child she was taken to Surinam, then an English possession, where she married a merchant of Dutch extraction. Returning to England in her nineteenth year, she became the "toast of London"; she was known as "the Incomparable"; her wit was enjoyed at court for its combination of light humor and startling coarseness. After her husband's death in her twenty-sixth year, Charles II sent her to the Netherlands during the Dutch war. The enemy succumbed to her. She had no difficulty extracting secret information, and

---

1 *The poets are Homer, Virgil, and Milton.*

some of the plans she communicated were of utmost importance. But there were enemies at court; jealousy was accompanied by intrigue; suddenly she fell into disfavor and poverty.

It was during the period of poverty that Aphra Behn determined to be a writer. Within two years she established herself as the first Englishwoman to earn her living as an author. Between her early thirties and late forties she wrote and produced fifteen plays, vivacious, keen, coarse, and extraordinarily versatile. In between the plays she wrote poems and novels. OROONOKO, founded upon childhood memories, is a tale of a philosophic slave in Surinam, a story which influenced the development of the novel and announced a theme which was to become the favorite of an entire movement: the theme of the Noble Savage.

As she grew older, she became more popular, sought after as a playwright and pursued as a person. In spite of being the center of scandal at the time of her death, she was buried in Westminster Abbey.

Song

Love in fantastic triumph sate
　Whilst bleeding hearts around him flowed
For whom fresh pains he did create
　And strange tyrannic power showed.
From thy bright eyes he took his fires,
　Which round about in sport he hurled;
But 'twas from mine he took desires
　Enough to undo the amorous world.

From me he took his sighs and tears,
　From thee his pride and cruelty;
From me his languishments and fears,
　And every killing dart from thee.
Thus thou and I the god have armed
　And set him up a deity;
But my poor heart alone is harmed
　Whilst thine the victor is, and free.

The Coquette

Melinda, who had never been
Esteemed a beauty at fifteen,
Always amorous was and kind.
    To every swain she lent an ear,
Free as air but false as wind;
    Yet none complained she was severe.
She eased more than she made complain,
Was always singing, pert, and vain.

Where'er the throng was, she was seen,
And swept the youths along the green.
With equal grace she flattered all;
    And fondly proud of all address,
Her smiles invite, her eyes do call,
    And her vain heart her looks confess.
She rallies this, to that she bowed,
Was talking ever, laughing loud.

On every side she makes advance,
And everywhere a confidence;
She tells for secrets all she knows,
    And all to know she does pretend.
Beauty in maids she treats as foes,
    But every handsome youth as friend.
Scandal still passes off for truth,
And noise and nonsense, wit and youth.

Coquette all o'er and every part,
Yet wanting beauty even of art,
Herds with the ugly and the old,
    And plays the critic on the rest;
Of men the bashful and the bold
    Either and all by turns likes best;
Ev'n now, though youth be languished, she
Sets up for love and gallantry.

JOHN WILMOT, EARL OF ROCHESTER
[1647–1680]

THE life of John Wilmot was brief, but it was profligate. More-
over, he was as fearless as he was wanton; he made friends and
enemies with equal nonchalance. Born at Ditchley in Oxfordshire,
April 1, 1647, he succeeded his father as second Earl of Rochester
in his twelfth year. In 1661 he received his M.A. at Wadham Col-
lege, Oxford, although he was only fourteen years old. After travel-
ing in Europe with a tutor, he was welcomed at the dissolute court
of Charles II, where at seventeen he became the scandal and ad-
miration of all because of his youth, his position, and his breath-
taking impertinences. He pledged himself to the "only important
businesses of the age: Women, Politics, and Drinking," and he more
than fulfilled his pledges. His intimates were the most corrupt
young men and court ladies. The notorious George Villiers, Charles
Sackville, and Charles Sedley envied his inexhaustible talent for
fresh follies; the King himself was his companion in wantonness.
On the night that the Dutch sailed up the Thames and burnt the
English fleet, the King was dallying with Lady Castelmaine, and
Rochester was reveling with Mrs. Malet, the heiress, whom, failing
to seduce, he married.

Rochester's marriage did not make him monogamous. On the
contrary, he indiscriminately enjoyed country wives, common sluts,
and the King's mistresses. Like his royal master, he "was soon
cloyed with the enjoyment of any one woman, though the fairest
in the world, and soon forsook her." He delighted to plan dis-
reputable adventures for himself and the King, and then write
bawdy satires upon Charles II, satires which were circulated for
the entertainment of the licentious court. When his rhymes went
too far—and they usually did—Rochester was banished; he seems to
have spent part of each year "in banishment" at his or his wife's
estate. Appropriately enough, he was gentleman of the bedchamber
to Charles II, for whom he furnished an epitaph long before that
monarch's decease.

Epitaph on Charles II

Here lies our Sovereign Lord the King,
  Whose word no man relies on,
Who never said a foolish thing,
  Nor ever did a wise one.

At thirty-one, Rochester's health suddenly gave way. A "fever"
he had contracted prematurely wasted his body and depressed his
spirit. But his mind was as keen as ever. During the year Rochester
lay dying he wrote the savage FAREWELL TO THE COURT, which has
been variously considered his most moving or his most hypocritical
poem.

FROM

Farewell to the Court

Tired with the noisome follies of the age,
And weary of my part, I quit the stage;
For who in Life's dull farce a part would bear
Where rogues, whores, bawds, all the head actors are?
Long I with charitable malice strove,
Lashing the Court those vermin to remove.
Yet though my life has unsuccessful been
(For who can this Augæan stable clean),
My generous end I will pursue in death
And at mankind rail with my parting breath.

When Rochester died at thirty-three he left a confused reputa-
tion. Bishop Burnet assured the family that Rochester died repent-
ant, and Aphra Behn wrote an elegy upon him. Before this, Dry-
den had dedicated his MARRIAGE À LA MODE to Rochester, although,
with typical double-dealing, the laureate, two years later, dedicated
AURENG-ZEBE to Rochester's chief enemy—a gesture for which Roches-
ter had Dryden beaten up by a gang of roughs. The eighteenth
century relished Rochester's obscene verses, but the rest of his
poems were forgotten. Time scattered impartially the products of
his wit and the rhymes of his debauches. His poems were all post-
humously published, many remained in manuscript, and it was not
until 1926 that a large collection was prepared by John Hayward.

printed by the Nonesuch Press in England—and forbidden entry to the United States.

Upon Leaving His Mistress

'Tis not that I am weary grown
Of being yours, and yours alone;
But with what face can I incline
To damn you to be only mine—
You, whom some kinder power did fashion,
By merit, and by inclination,
The joy at least of a whole nation?

Let meaner spirits of your sex
With humble aims their thoughts perplex,
And boast if by their arts they can
Contrive to make one happy man;
While, moved by an impartial sense,
Favors, like Nature, you dispense
With universal influence.
See, the kind seed-receiving earth
To every grain affords a birth:
On her no showers unwelcome fall;
Her willing womb retains them all.
And shall my Celia be confined?
No, live up to thy mighty mind,
And be the mistress of mankind!

Love and Life

All my past life is mine no more;
   The flying hours are gone,
Like transitory dreams given o'er,
Whose images are kept in store
   By memory alone.

The time that is to come is not;
   How can it then be mine?
The present moment's all my lot;
And that, as fast as it is got,
   Phillis, is only thine.

Then talk not of inconstancy,
    False hearts, and broken vows;
If I by miracle can be
This live-long minute true to thee,
    'Tis all that Heaven allows.

Upon Nothing

Nothing! thou elder brother even to Shade,
Thou hadst a being ere the world was made,
And (well fixt) art alone of ending not afraid.

Ere time and place were, time and place were not,
When primitive Nothing something straight begot,
Then all proceeded from the great united—What.

Something the general attribute of all,
Sever'd from thee, its sole original,
Into thy boundless self must undistinguish'd fall.

Yet something did thy mighty pow'r command,
And from thy fruitful emptiness's hand,
Snatched men, beasts, birds, fire, air and land.

Matter, the wickedest off-spring of thy race,
By Form assisted, flew from thy embrace,
And rebel Light obscured thy reverend dusky face.

With Form, and Matter, Time and Place did join,
Body, thy foe, with thee did leagues combine,
To spoil thy peaceful realm, and ruin all thy line.

But turn-coat Time assists the foe in vain,
And, bribed by thee, assists thy short-lived reign,
And to thy hungry womb drives back thy slaves again.

                 .   .   .   .   .

Great Negative, how vainly would the wise
Inquire, define, distinguish, teach, devise,
Didst thou not stand to point their dull philosophies?

The great man's gratitude to his best friend,
Kings' promises, whores' vows, towards thee they bend,
Flow swiftly into thee, and in thee never end.

Although only sixteen years elapsed between the death of Donne and the birth of Rochester, the two poets are separated by an age. The spirit of the times had completely changed. Newton brought light into the theological darkness; Satan became a splendid literary figure instead of the fearful lord of hell-fire. The religious horrors were failing to horrify; they belonged, says John Hayward, "to a class of almost medieval superstition which was soon to be engulfed by a wave of fresh and vital thought. The end of the seventeenth century is the beginning of a new, the so-called modern world."

There were others besides Dryden who spanned the gulf between the two centuries, between an era of poetry and passion and—Matthew Arnold's phrase for the eighteenth century—"an age of prose and reason." Among those who immediately preceded the age dominated by an excess of sanity and social elegance were Anne Finch, Countess of Winchilsea, Matthew Prior, and George Berkeley, Bishop of Cloyne. Of these "transition" poets, none is more typical than Lady Winchilsea, and none is so little known.

ANNE FINCH, COUNTESS OF WINCHILSEA
[1661–1720]

DAUGHTER of Sir William Kingsmill of Sidmonton, near Southampton, Anne became one of the maids of honor to the Duchess of York at twenty-one and, at twenty-three, wife of Colonel Finch, later fourth Earl of Winchilsea. Devoted to verse since her childhood, she read Dryden in youth, and "discovered" Pope in her late thirties. Like him she avoided anything ecstatic or headlong; she, too, sharpened with wit the orderly "contemplations of the mind." Unlike Pope, Lady Winchilsea sought "absolute retreat" in her garden and the composure of the rural landscape. Against Pope's barbed literature of the town she proffered the more rounded if less reasoned grace of the countryside.

If Lady Winchilsea cannot shake the reader with passion, she can charm him—especially with small felicities.

Nor will in fading silks compose
Faintly the inimitable rose.

Hugh I'Anson Fausset calls attention to her "exquisite gift for evoking the indefinite out of the definite, for distilling a faint fragrance and drawing a silvery music out of things distinctly seen, heard, or felt . . . The quality in her lines owes nothing, as the magic of a Coleridge or a Poe does, to fever in the blood. It is the music, not of the dreaming or the drugged senses, but of a mind which floats above the sensible world with a soft awareness."

FROM

Petition for Absolute Retreat

Give me, O indulgent fate!
Give me yet, before I die,
A sweet, but absolute retreat,
'Mongst paths so lost, and trees so high,
That the world may ne'er invade
Through such windings and such shade
My unshaken liberty.

No intruders thither come,
Who visit but to be from home!
None who their vain moments pass
Only studious of their glass;
News, that charm to listening ears,
That false alarm to hopes and fears,
That common theme of every fop,
From the statesmen to the shop,
In those coverts ne'er be spread
Of who's deceased, or who's to wed;
Be no tidings thither brought
But silent as a midnight thought:
Where the world may ne'er invade
Be those windings and that shade . . .

Let me then, indulgent fate!
Let me still in my retreat
From all roving thoughts be freed,
Or aims that may contention breed:
Nor be my endeavors led

By goods that perish with the dead!
Fitly might the life of man
Be indeed esteemed a span,
If the present moment were
Of delight his only share:
If no other joys he knew
Than what round about him grew.
But as those who stars would trace
From a subterranean place,
Through some engine lift their eyes
To the outward, glorious skies:
So th' immortal spirit may,
When descended to our clay,
From a rightly govern'd frame
View the height from whence she came:
To her paradise be caught,
And things unutterable taught.
Give me then, in that retreat,
Give me, O indulgent fate!
For all pleasures left behind
Contemplations of the mind.
Let the fair, the gay, the vain
Courtship and applause obtain;
Let th' ambitious rule the earth;
Let the giddy fool have mirth;
Give the epicure his dish,
Every one their several wish,
Whilst my transports I employ
On that more extensive joy:
When all heaven shall be surveyed
From those windings and that shade.

The Greater Trial

Wretched Amintor with a flame
    Too strong to be subdued,
A nymph above his rank and name
    Still eagerly pursued.

To gain her every art he tried,
    But no return procured,
Mistook her prudence for her pride,
    Nor guessed what she endured.

Till prostrate at her feet one day
Urging in deep despair,
Thus softly was she heard to say,
Or sighed it to the air:

Witness ye secret cares I prove,
Which is the greater trial,
To sue for unrewarded love,
Or die by self-denial.

On Myself

Good heaven, I thank thee since it was designed
I should be framed but of the weaker kind,
That yet my soul is rescued from the love
Of all those trifles which their passions move.
Pleasures, and praise, and plenty have with me
But their just value. If allowed they be,
Freely and thankfully as much I taste
As will not reason or religion waste.
If they're denied, I on myself can live,
And slight those aids unequal chance does give:
When in the sun, my wings can be displayed,
And in retirement, I can bless the shade.

MATTHEW PRIOR

[1664–1721]

LITTLE known today except for a few epigrams and neatly turned
stanzas, Matthew Prior was one of the most skillful depicters
of the frivolous society of his day. Having lost his father—a Dorset-
shire joiner—in childhood, Prior was educated under the patronage
of Lord Dorset. At thirteen he translated Horace and Ovid into
English verse. After being graduated from St. John's College, Cam-
bridge, he was appointed secretary to the ambassador in Holland
and went to Paris as a secret agent during important negotiations.
The Treaty of Utrecht in 1713 was known as "Matt's Peace."

Unattractive physically—he was dour-looking and deaf—by his good nature Prior won friends in every circle. He was equally popular with common soldiers and Louis XIV, but his easy humor could turn to rankling wit. Even as a diplomat he did not withhold the quick thrust; when asked if the English monarch could boast of any monument as beautiful as Versailles, Prior answered, "The monuments of my master's actions are to be seen everywhere but in his own house." His career touched the extremes of affluence and poverty; after he had lost everything, his admirers subscribed four thousand pounds to an edition of his poems, and a nobleman gave him another four thousand pounds for an estate in Essex. Although he was at home among the nobility, he consorted chiefly with women of the lowest class. A wench whom he kept in his house stole his silverware; he was on the point of marrying a woman who kept an alehouse, and it was to her that he left most of his estate.

A Reasonable Affliction

On his death-bed poor Lubin lies:
  His spouse is in despair;
With frequent cries, and mutual sighs,
  They both express their care.

"A different cause," says Parson Sly,
  "The same effect may give:
Poor Lubin fears that he may die;
  His wife, that he may live."

Song

The merchant, to secure his treasure,
  Conveys it in a borrowed name:
Euphelia serves to grace my measure,
  But Cloe is my real flame.

My softest verse, my darling lyre
  Upon Euphelia's toilet lay—
When Cloe noted her desire
  That I should sing, that I should play.

My lyre I tune, my voice I raise,
  But with my numbers mix my sighs;
And whilst I sing Euphelia's praise,
  I fix my soul on Cloe's eyes.

Fair Cloe blushed; Euphelia frowned:
  I sung, and gazed; I played, and trembled:
And Venus to the Loves around
  Remarked how ill we all dissembled.

The Remedy Worse Than the Disease

I sent for Radcliffe; was so ill,
  The other doctors gave me over:
He felt my pulse, prescribed his pill,
  And I was likely to recover.

But when the wit began to wheeze,
  And wine had warmed the politician,
Cured yesterday of my disease,
  I died last night of my physician.

Prior prepared his own estimate in a set of memorial verses entitled FOR MY OWN MONUMENT; but his casual epitaph is both more modest and more memorable.

Prior's Epitaph

Nobles and heralds, by your leave,
  Here lies what once was Matthew Prior,
The son of Adam and of Eve.
  Can Bourbon or Nassau claim higher?

GEORGE BERKELEY, BISHOP OF CLOYNE
[1685–1753]

BY THE philosophers George Berkeley is credited with the theory that matter is merely a set of perceptions and, since our knowledge of anything is derived from our sensations of it, no object can exist apart from mind. But orators and politicians, who seldom give credit, are indebted to Berkeley for a continually quoted phrase: "Westward the course of empire takes its way."

The phrase occurs in a poem entitled ON THE PROSPECT OF PLANTING ARTS AND LEARNING IN AMERICA. The prospect was not too promising in the early eighteenth century, and many of Berkeley's countrymen considered him overoptimistic when he hailed America as "Time's noblest offspring" and predicted that "in distant lands now waits a better time" where "shall be sung another golden age."

Son of an Irish customs official, George Berkeley was born March 12, 1685, in Kilkenny County, and educated at Trinity College, Dublin. He came to England in his late twenties, and it was evident that he was to be a dialectician of the first order. Attacking the concept of material "reality," he united theology and utility. In his thirty-eighth year he was appointed Dean of Derry and began planning extensions of his work abroad. In 1728 he came to America and spent three years in Rhode Island. Two years after his return to Ireland, he was raised to the bishopric of Cloyne. Admired for his lucid prose, revered for his dignified spirit, he died suddenly in his sixty-eighth year.

On the Prospect of Planting Arts and Learning in America

The Muse, disgusted at an age and clime
　Barren of every glorious theme,
In distant lands now waits a better time,
　Producing subjects worthy fame:

In happy climes the seat of innocence,
  Where nature guides and virtue rules,
Where men shall not impose for truth and sense,
  The pedantry of courts and schools:

There shall be sung another golden age,
  The rise of empire and of arts,
The good and great inspiring epic rage,
  The wisest heads and noblest hearts.

Not such as Europe breeds in her decay;
  Such as she bred when fresh and young,
When heavenly flame did animate her clay,
  By future poets shall be sung.

Westward the course of empire takes its way;
  The four first acts already past,
A fifth shall close the drama with the day;
  Time's noblest offspring is the last.

ALEXANDER POPE
[1688–1744]

THE man who perfected the shapeliest verse of his day was a malignant little hunchback, "a gargoyle of a man," as James Branch Cabell calls him in the short story A BROWN WOMAN, not so much a human being as "a book in breeches." To his few friends he was an amazing but unhappy wit; to the ever-increasing army of enemies he was a hateful though clever deformity.

A crippled dwarf from birth, Alexander Pope was born in London, May 21, 1688, the son of a linen draper. In the cruelest of times for a creative artist, he came into the world with every disadvantage. He was handicapped not only by being "a crazy little carcass" and a Roman Catholic when Catholics could neither attend universities nor hold public office, but by being the son of a commoner at a time when titles smoothed the way to privilege. Realizing even in childhood that his life was to be "one long disease," he developed a precocity so intense as to be ferocious. At ten he translated Greek and Latin and plotted a lifetime course of study. Mozart created his first sonata at six, and Mendelssohn composed a symphony for strings at fourteen, but these compositions are rarely heard. Pope, on the other hand, wrote one of his most celebrated poems, SOLITUDE, at the age of twelve. If the middle-age sentiment seems strange for a twelve-year-old boy, it should be remembered that, although the treatment is Pope's, the idea was suggested to the precocious child by one of Horace's epodes.

Solitude

Happy the man, whose wish and care
A few paternal acres bound,
Content to breathe his native air
    In his own ground.

Whose herds with milk, whose fields with bread,
Whose flocks supply him with attire;
Whose trees in summer yield him shade,
    In winter, fire.

Blest, who can unconcernedly find
Hours, days, and years slide soft away
In health of body, peace of mind;
    Quiet by day.

Sound sleep by night; study and ease
Together mixed, sweet recreation,
And innocence, which most does please
    With meditation.

Thus let me live, unseen, unknown;
Thus unlamented let me die,
Steal from the world, and not a stone
    Tell where I lie.

By the time he was seventeen Pope was recognized as a prodigy, and the literary dictators of the day were forced to admit him to their company. His will to live was strengthened by a lust for power; his offensive tactics were a defense which needs no psychoanalysis. Men and women slighted Pope at their peril; they would be lampooned and pilloried, castigated for characteristics they never possessed and for crimes they had never committed. He dared to make love to Lady Mary Montagu, and she, with even greater daring, repulsed him in "an immoderate fit of laughter." Pope retaliated by vilifying the lady and all her associates. He accepted a huge bribe from the Duchess of Marlborough to suppress a libelous passage in one of his EPISTLES—and then printed the stanzas unchanged. He sought publicity and literary fame by every form of intrigue—it was said that Pope could not sit down to tea without a stratagem—and then lashed out at the whole literary world in an epic of resentment, THE DUNCIAD. Satire was his element, his luxury, and his livelihood.

On a Certain Lady at Court

I know the thing that's most uncommon
(Envy, be silent, and attend!);
I know a reasonable woman,
Handsome and witty, yet a friend.
Not warped by passion, awed by rumor,
Not grave through pride, or gay through folly,
An equal mixture of good humor,
And sensible soft melancholy.
"Has she no faults then (Envy says), Sir?"
Yes, she has one, I must aver:
When all the world conspires to praise her,
The woman's deaf, and does not hear.

In his twenty-third year Pope published his rhymed ESSAY ON CRITICISM. It was a celebration of the chief virtues of the day—Elegance, Wit, and Decorum—and its precision was so glittering that it dazzled all readers. Twenty years later Pope prepared the more sententious ESSAY ON MAN; but, although the "sequel" was the work of Pope's maturity, its bundled epigrams barely matched the critical dexterity of the earlier poem.

FROM

An Essay on Criticism

A little learning is a dangerous thing;
Drink deep, or taste not the Pierian spring:
There shallow draughts intoxicate the brain,
And drinking largely sobers us again.

Fired at first sight with what the Muse imparts,
In fearless youth we tempt the heights of Arts,
While from the bounded level of our mind
Short views we take, nor see the lengths behind;
But more advanced, behold with strange surprise
New distant scenes of endless science rise!
So pleased at first the towering Alps we try,
Mount o'er the vales, and seem to tread the sky,
The eternal snows appear already past,
And the first clouds and mountains seem the last;
But, those attained, we tremble to survey
The growing labors of the lengthened way,
The increasing prospects tire our wandering eyes,
Hills peep o'er hills, and Alps on Alps arise!

*

True ease in writing comes from art, not chance,
As those move easiest who have learned to dance.
'Tis not enough no harshness gives offence;
The sound must seem an Echo to the sense:
Soft is the strain when Zephyr gently blows,
And the smooth stream in smoother numbers flows;
But when loud surges lash the sounding shore,
The hoarse, rough verse should like the torrent roar:
When Ajax strives some rock's vast weight to throw,
The line too labors, and the words move slow;
Not so, when swift Camilla scours the plain,
Flies o'er the unbending corn, and skims along the
    main.
Hear how Timotheus'[1] varied lays surprise,
And bid alternate passions fall and rise!
While, at each change, the son of Libyan Jove
Now burns with glory, and then melts with love,
Now his fierce eyes with sparkling fury glow,
Now sighs steal out, and tears begin to flow:
Persians and Greeks like turns of nature found,
And the world's victor stood subdued by Sound!
The power of Music all our hearts allow,
And what Timotheus was, is DRYDEN now.

[1] *A celebrated Greek poet and musician. See Dryden's* ALEXANDER'S FEAST *on page 507.*

FROM

An Essay on Man

Hope humbly then; with trembling pinions soar;
Wait the great teacher, Death, and God adore.
What future bliss, he gives not thee to know,
But gives that hope to be thy blessing now;
Hope springs eternal in the human breast—
Man never is, but always to be blessed.
The soul, uneasy and confined from home,
Rests and expatiates in a life to come.
Lo, the poor Indian! whose untutored mind
Sees God in clouds, or hears him in the wind;
His soul proud science never taught to stray
Far as the solar walk, or milky way,
Yet simple nature to his hope has given,
Behind the cloud-topped hill, an humbler heaven.

*

Know then thyself, presume not God to scan,
The proper study of mankind is man.
Placed on this isthmus of a middle state,
A being darkly wise, and rudely great:
With too much knowledge for the sceptic side,
With too much weakness for the stoic's pride,
He hangs between; in doubt to act, or rest;
In doubt to deem himself a god, or beast;
In doubt his mind or body to prefer;
Born but to die, and reasoning but to err;
Alike in ignorance, his reason such,
Whether he thinks too little or too much!
Chaos of thought and passion, all confused;
Still by himself abused or disabused;
Created half to rise and half to fall;
Great lord of all things, yet a prey to all;
Sole judge of truth, in endless error hurled:
The glory, jest, and riddle of the world!

*

Whate'er the passion—knowledge, fame, or pelf,
Not one will change his neighbor with himself.

The learned is happy nature to explore,
The fool is happy that he knows no more;
The rich is happy in the plenty given,
The poor contents him with the care of Heaven.
See the blind beggar dance, the cripple sing,
The sot a hero, lunatic a king;
The starving chemist in his golden views
Supremely blest, the poet in his muse.
See some strange comfort every state attend,
And pride bestowed on all, a common friend;
See some fit passion every age supply,
Hope travels through nor quits us when we die.
Behold the child, by nature's kindly law,
Pleased with a rattle, tickled with a straw:
Some livelier plaything gives his youth delight,
A little louder, but as empty quite:
Scarfs, garters, gold, amuse his riper stage,
And beads and prayer-books are the toys of age:
Pleased with this bauble still, as that before;
Till tired he sleeps, and life's poor play is o'er.

*

Honor and shame from no condition rise;
Act well your part, there all the honor lies.
Fortune in men has some small difference made,
One flaunts in rags, one flutters in brocade;
The cobbler aproned, and the parson gowned,
The friar hooded, and the monarch crowned.
"What differ more (you cry) than crown and cowl!"
I'll tell you, friend! a wise man and a fool.
You'll find, if once the monarch acts the monk,
Or, cobbler-like, the parson will be drunk,
Worth makes the man, and want of it the fellow;
The rest is all but leather or prunella.[1]

If Pope conformed to the spirit of his times by steering a middle
course between the flagellating negations of the Puritans and the
profligacy of the Restoration, he glorified the compromise. If he
could not master ecstasy in a day when even enthusiasm was sus-
pect, he subjected his material to a compactness and clarity which
have never been equaled. As Louis Kronenberger writes in AN

[1] *The material of which the parson's gown is made, in distinction to the cob-
bler's leather apron. An ironic paraphrase of "Clothes make the man."*

EIGHTEENTH CENTURY MISCELLANY: "Through a supreme manipulation of the heroic couplet he was able to terrify his own generation, to enslave the poets of the generations which followed, and to delight and disgust posterity. Ranging literature where we will, we cannot find another man so purely venomous; and his brilliant couplets wring all the changes of a morbid hate." Thus Pope, as Kronenberger goes on to show, made art out of the failure of his life; and, in an epoch devoted to a spuriously "aristocratic" literature, the poet was the victim of his age. "He was at bottom a man of sentiment, and the age was hard; of vanity, and the age was cruel; of sensibility, and the age was coarse. Hence the deformed, disabled poet with his biting tongue fell in with the practices of the day, and in settling private scores became the most formidable of satirists."

Though most of Pope's satire was bitter and malign, it could be turned to light and even likable malice. Through his quick eye and quicker wit, one of the foibles of the day was enlarged into a masterpiece of acid verse. A certain Lord Petre had surreptitiously cut a lock of hair from the head of a Miss Arabella Fermor. The liberty was resented and grew into a scandal, a social tempest in fine china teacups. Hearing of it, Pope expanded the subject and treated it in a mock-heroic style which became a parody of an epic. When THE RAPE OF THE LOCK was completed, Pope sent it to Miss Fermor with a letter of dedication. The dedication was necessary not only because Pope had to placate Miss Fermor for exposing the inane elegances and affectations of her circle, but because—since the lady was not too intelligent—he had to explain the poem. He knew that the "machinery" would cause trouble, and so he added, with waspish airiness:

> The Machinery, Madam, is a term invented by the Critics to signify that part which the Deities, Angels, or Daemons are made to act in a Poem; For the ancient Poets are in one respect like modern Ladies: Let an action be never so trivial in itself, they always make it appear of the utmost importance. . . . The Gnomes or Daemons of Earth delight in mischief; but the Sylphs, whose habitation is in the Air, are the best-conditioned creatures imaginable. For they say, any mortals may enjoy the most intimate familiarities with these gentle Spirits, upon a condition very easy to all true Adepts, an inviolate preservation of Chastity.

The Rape of the Lock

CANTO I

What dire offence from amorous causes springs,
What mighty contests rise from trivial things,
I sing—This verse to CARYL,[1] Muse! is due:
This, even Belinda may vouchsafe to view:
Slight is the subject, but not so the praise,
If She inspire, and He approve my lays.
   Say what strange motive, Goddess! could compel
A well-bred Lord to assault a gentle Belle?
O say what stranger cause, yet unexplored,
Could make a gentle Belle reject a Lord?
In tasks so bold, can little men engage,
And in soft bosoms dwells such mighty Rage?
   Sol through white curtains shot a timorous ray,
And oped those eyes that must eclipse the day:
Now lap-dogs give themselves the rousing shake,
And sleepless lovers, just at twelve, awake:
Thrice rung the bell, the slipper knocked the ground,[2]
And the pressed watch returned a silver sound.
Belinda still her downy pillow prest,
Her guardian SYLPH prolonged the balmy rest:
'Twas He had summoned to her silent bed
The morning-dream that hovered o'er her head;
A Youth more glittering than a Birth-night Beau
(That even in slumber caused her cheek to glow),
Seemed to her ear his winning lips to lay,
And thus in whispers said, or seemed to say:
   "Fairest of mortals, thou distinguished care
Of thousand bright Inhabitants of Air!
If e'er one vision touched thy infant thought,
Of all the Nurse and all the Priest have taught;
Of airy Elves by moonlight shadows seen,
The silver token, and the circled green,
Or virgins visited by Angel-powers,
With golden crowns and wreaths of heavenly flowers;
Hear and believe! thy own importance know,
Nor bound thy narrow views to things below.

[1] *John Caryl, common friend of Pope, Petre (the "Baron"), and Miss Fermor ("Belinda").* [2] *Called the maid.*

Some secret truths, from learned pride concealed,
To Maids alone and Children are revealed:
What though no credit doubting Wits may give?
The Fair and Innocent shall still believe.
Know, then, unnumbered Spirits round thee fly,
The light Militia of the lower sky:
These, though unseen, are ever on the wing,
Hang o'er the Box, and hover round the Ring.[8]
Think what an equipage thou hast in Air,
And view with scorn two Pages and a Chair.
As now your own, our beings were of old,
And once inclosed in Woman's beauteous mould;
Thence, by a soft transition, we repair
From earthly Vehicles to these of air.
Think not, when Woman's transient breath is fled,
That all her vanities at once are dead.
For when the Fair in all their pride expire,
To their first Elements their Souls retire:
The Sprites of fiery Termagants in Flame
Mount up, and take a Salamander's name.
Soft yielding minds to Water glide away,
And sip, with Nymphs, their elemental Tea.
The graver Prude sinks downward to a Gnome,
In search of mischief still on Earth to roam.
The light Coquettes in Sylphs aloft repair,
And sport and flutter in the fields of Air.

Know further yet: whoever fair and chaste
Rejects mankind, is by some Sylph embraced:
For Spirits, freed from mortal laws, with ease
Assume what sexes and what shapes they please.
What guards the purity of melting Maids,
In courtly balls, and midnight masquerades,
Safe from the treacherous friend, the daring spark,
The glance by day, the whisper in the dark,
When kind occasion prompts their warm desires,
When music softens, and when dancing fires?
'Tis but their Sylph, the wise Celestials know,
Though Honor is the word with Men below.

Some nymphs there are, too conscious of their face,
For life predestined to the Gnomes' embrace.
These swell their prospects and exalt their pride,
When offers are disdained, and love denied:
Then gay Ideas crowd the vacant brain,
While Peers, and Dukes, and all their sweeping train,

[8] *The riding ring in Hyde Park.*

And Garters, Stars, and Coronets appear,
And in soft sounds, Your Grace salutes their ear.
'Tis these that early taint the female soul,
Instruct the eyes of young Coquettes to roll,
Teach Infant-cheeks a bidden blush to know,
And little hearts to flutter at a Beau.
  Oft, when the world imagine women stray,
The Sylphs through mystic mazes guide their way;
Through all the giddy circle they pursue,
And old impertinence expel by new.
What tender maid but must a victim fall
To one man's treat, but for another's ball?
When Florio speaks what virgin could withstand,
If gentle Damon did not squeeze her hand?
With varying vanities, from every part,
They shift the moving Toyshop of their heart;
Where wigs with wigs, with sword-knots sword-knots strive,
Beaux banish beaux, and coaches coaches drive.
This erring mortals Levity may call;
Oh blind to truth! the Sylphs contrive it all.
  Of these am I, who thy protection claim,
A watchful sprite, and Ariel is my name.
Late, as I ranged the crystal wilds of air,
In the clear Mirror of thy ruling Star
I saw, alas! some dread event impend,
Ere to the main this morning sun descend,
But heaven reveals not what, or how, or where:
Warned by the Sylph, oh pious maid, beware!
This to disclose is all thy guardian can:
Beware of all, but most beware of man!"
  He said; when Shock,[4] who thought she slept too
      long,
Leaped up, and waked his mistress with his tongue.
'Twas then, Belinda, if report say true,
Thy eyes first opened on a Billet-doux;
Wounds, Charms, and Ardors were no sooner read,
But all the vision vanished from thy head.
  And now, unveiled, the Toilet stands displayed,
Each silver Vase in mystic order laid.
First, robed in white, the Nymph intent adores,
With head uncovered, the Cosmetic powers,
A heavenly image in the glass appears,
To that she bends, to that her eyes she rears;
Th' inferior Priestess,[5] at her altar's side,

---

[4] *Shock was Belinda's dog.*   [5] *The maid.*

Trembling begins the sacred rites of **Pride**.
Unnumbered treasures ope at once, and here
The various offerings of the world appear;
From each she nicely culls with curious toil,
And decks the Goddess with the glittering spoil.
This casket India's glowing gems unlocks,
And all Arabia breathes from yonder box.
The Tortoise here and Elephant unite,
Transformed to combs, the speckled and the white.
Here files of pins extend their shining rows,
Puffs, Powders, Patches, Bibles, Billet-doux.
Now awful Beauty puts on all its arms;
The Fair each moment rises in her charms,
Repairs her smiles, awakens every grace,
And calls forth all the wonders of her face;
Sees by degrees a purer blush arise,
And keener lightnings quicken in her eyes.
The busy Sylphs surround their darling care,
These set the head, and those divide the hair,
Some fold the sleeve, whilst others plait the gown;
And Betty's praised for labors not her own.

CANTO II

Not with more glories, in the ethereal plain,
The Sun first rises o'er the purpled main,
Than, issuing forth, the rival of his beams
Launched on the bosom of the silver Thames.
Fair Nymphs and well-drest Youths around her
    shone,
But every eye was fixed on her alone.
On her white breast a sparkling Cross she wore.
Which Jews might kiss, and Infidels adore.
Her lively looks a sprightly mind disclose,
Quick as her eyes, and as unfixed as those:
Favors to none, to all she smiles extends;
Oft she rejects, but never once offends.
Bright as the sun, her eyes the gazers strike,
And, like the sun, they shine on all alike.
Yet graceful ease, and sweetness void of pride,
Might hide her faults, if Belles had faults to hide:
If to her share some female errors fall,
Look on her face, and you'll forget 'em all.
    This Nymph, to the destruction of mankind,
Nourished two Locks, which graceful hung behind

In equal curls, and well conspired to deck
With shining ringlets the smooth ivory neck.
Love in these labyrinths his slaves detains,
And mighty hearts are held in slender chains.
With hairy springes [6] we the birds betray,
Slight lines of hair surprise the finny prey,
Fair tresses man's imperial race ensnare,
And beauty draws us with a single hair.
  The adventurous Baron the bright locks admired;
He saw, he wished, and to the prize aspired.
Resolved to win, he meditates the way,
By force to ravish, or by fraud betray;
For when success a Lover's toil attends,
Few ask, if fraud or force attained his ends.
  For this, ere Phoebus rose, he had implored
Propitious heaven, and every power adored,
But chiefly Love—to Love an Altar built,
Of twelve vast French Romances, neatly gilt.
There lay three garters, half a pair of gloves;
And all the trophies of his former loves;
With tender Billet-doux he lights the pyre,
And breathes three amorous sighs to raise the fire.
Then prostrate falls, and begs with ardent eyes
Soon to obtain, and long possess the prize;
The powers gave ear, and granted half his prayer,
The rest, the winds dispersed in empty air.
  But now secure the painted vessel glides,
The sun-beams trembling on the floating tides:
While melting music steals upon the sky,
And softened sounds along the waters die;
Smooth flow the waves, the Zephyrs gently play,
Belinda smiled, and all the world was gay.
All but the Sylph—with careful thoughts opprest,
The impending woe sat heavy on his breast.
He summons straight his Denizens of air;
The lucid squadrons around the sails repair;
Soft o'er the shrouds aërial whispers breathe,
That seemed but Zephyrs to the train beneath.
Some to the sun their insect-wings unfold,
Waft on the breeze, or sink in clouds of gold;
Transparent forms, too fine for mortal sight,
Their fluid bodies half dissolved in light,
Loose to the wind their airy garments flew,
Thin glittering textures of the filmy dew,

[6] *Snares made of horsehair.*

Dipt in the richest tincture of the skies,
Where light disports in ever-mingling dyes,
While every beam new transient colors flings,
Colors that change whene'er they wave their wings.
Amid the circle, on the gilded mast,
Superior by the head, was Ariel placed;
His purple pinions opening to the sun,
He raised his azure wand, and thus begun:

"Ye Sylphs and Sylphids, to your chief give ear!
Fays, Fairies, Genii, Elves, and Daemons, hear!
Ye know the spheres and various tasks assigned
By laws eternal to the aërial kind.
Some in the fields of purest Aether play,
And bask and whiten in the blaze of day.
Some guide the course of wandering orbs on high,
Or roll the planets through the boundless sky.
Some less refined, beneath the moon's pale light
Pursue the stars that shoot athwart the night,
Or suck the mists in grosser air below,
Or dip their pinions in the painted bow,
Or brew fierce tempests on the wintry main,
Or o'er the glebe distil the kindly rain.
Others on earth o'er human race preside,
Watch all their ways, and all their actions guide:
Of these the chief the care of Nations own,
And guard with Arms divine the British throne.
    Our humbler province is to tend the Fair,
Not a less pleasing, though less glorious care;
To save the powder from too rude a gale,
Nor let the imprisoned essences exhale;
To draw fresh colors from the vernal flowers;
To steal from rainbows ere they drop in showers
A brighter wash; to curl their waving hairs,
Assist their blushes, and inspire their airs;
Nay oft, in dreams, invention we bestow,
To change a Flounce, or add a Furbelow.
    This day, black Omens threat the brightest Fair
That e'er deserved a watchful spirit's care;
Some dire disaster, or by force, or slight;
But what, or where, the fates have wrapt in night.
Whether the nymph shall break Diana's law,
Or some frail China jar receive a flaw;
Or stain her honor or her new brocade;
Forget her prayers, or miss a masquerade;

Or lose her heart, or necklace, at a ball;
Or whether Heaven has doomed that Shock must fall.
Haste, then, ye spirits! to your charge repair:
The fluttering fan be Zephyretta's care;
The drops to thee, Brillante, we consign;
And, Momentilla, let the watch be thine;
Do thou, Crispissa, tend her favorite Lock;
Ariel himself shall be the guard of Shock.
    To fifty chosen Sylphs, of special note,
We trust the important charge, the Petticoat:
Oft have we known that seven-fold fence to fail,
Though stiff with hoops, and armed with ribs of whale;
Form a strong line about the silver bound,
And guard the wide circumference around."

He spoke; the spirits from the sails descend;
Some, orb in orb, around the nymph extend;
Some thrid the mazy ringlets of her hair;
Some hang upon the pendants of her ear;
With beating hearts the dire event they wait,
Anxious, and trembling for the birth of Fate.

CANTO III

    Close by those meads, for ever crowned with
      flowers,
Where Thames with pride surveys his rising towers,
There stands a structure of majestic frame,
Which from the neighboring Hampton takes its name.
Here Britain's statesmen oft the fall foredoom
Of foreign tyrants and of nymphs at home;
Here thou, great ANNA! whom three realms obey,
Dost sometimes counsel take—and sometimes Tea.
    Hither the heroes and the nymphs resort,
To taste awhile the pleasures of a Court;
In various talk the instructive hours they past,
Who gave the ball, or paid the visit last;
One speaks the glory of the British Queen,
And one describes a charming Indian screen;
A third interprets motions, looks, and eyes;
At every word a reputation dies.
Snuff, or the fan, supply each pause of chat,
With singing, laughing, ogling, and all that.
    Meanwhile, declining from the noon of day,

The sun obliquely shoots his burning ray;
The hungry Judges soon the Sentence sign,
And wretches hang that jurymen may dine;
The merchant from the Exchange returns in peace,
And the long labors of the Toilet cease. . . .
     For lo! the board with cups and spoons is crowned,
The berries crackle, and the mill turns round; [7]
On shining Altars of Japan they raise
The silver lamp; the fiery spirits blaze:
From silver spouts the grateful liquors glide,
While China's earth receives the smoking tide:
At once they gratify their scent and taste,
And frequent cups prolong the rich repast.
Straight hover round the Fair her airy band;
Some, as she sipped, the fuming liquor fanned,
Some o'er her lap their careful plumes displayed,
Trembling, and conscious of the rich brocade.
Coffee (which makes the politician wise,
And see through all things with his half-shut eyes),
Sent up in vapors to the Baron's brain
New Stratagems, the radiant Lock to gain. . . .
     But when to mischief mortals bend their will,
How soon they find fit instruments of ill!
Just then, Clarissa drew with tempting grace
A two-edged weapon from her shining case:
So Ladies in Romance assist their Knight,
Present the spear, and arm him for the fight.
He takes the gift with reverence, and extends
The little engine on his fingers' ends;
This just behind Belinda's neck he spread,
As o'er the fragrant steams she bends her head.
Swift, to the Lock a thousand Sprites repair,
A thousand wings, by turns, blow back the hair;
And thrice they twitched the diamond in her ear;
Thrice she looked back, and thrice the foe drew near.
Just in that instant, anxious Ariel sought
The close recesses of the Virgin's thought;
As on the nosegay in her breast reclined,
He watched the Ideas rising in her mind,
Sudden he viewed, in spite of all her art,
An earthly Lover lurking at her heart,
Amazed, confused, he found his power expired,
Resigned to fate, and with a sigh retired.

[7] *The berries (coffee beans) were ground on a sideboard by the ladies.*

The Peer now spreads the glittering Forfex [8] wide,
To inclose the Lock; now joins it, to divide.
Even then, before the fatal engine closed,
A wretched Sylph too fondly interposed;
Fate urged the shears, and cut the Sylph in twain
(But airy substance soon unites again):
The meeting points the sacred hair dissever
From the fair head, for ever, and for ever!
  Then flashed the living lightning from her eyes,
And screams of horror rend the affrighted skies.
Not louder shrieks to pitying Heaven are cast,
When husbands or when lap-dogs breathe their last;
Or when rich China vessels fallen from high,
In glittering dust and painted fragments lie!
  "Let wreaths of triumph now my temples twine
(The victor cried); the glorious Prize is mine!
While fish in streams, or birds delight in air,
Or in a coach and six the British Fair,
As long as *Atalantis* [9] shall be read,
Or the small pillow grace a Lady's bed,
While visits shall be paid on solemn days,
When numerous wax-lights in bright order blaze,
While nymphs take treats, or assignations give,
So long my honor, name, and praise shall live!
What Time would spare, from Steel receives its date,
And monuments, like men, submit to fate!
Steel could the labor of the Gods destroy,
And strike to dust the imperial towers of Troy;
Steel could the works of mortal pride confound,
And hew triumphal arches to the ground.
What wonder then, fair nymph! thy hairs should feel
The conquering force of unresisted steel?"

CANTO IV

But anxious cares the pensive nymph oppressed,
And secret passions labored in her breast.
Not youthful kings in battle seized alive,
Not scornful virgins who their charms survive,
Not ardent lovers robbed of all their bliss,
Not ancient ladies when refused a kiss,
Not tyrants fierce that unrepenting die,
Not Cynthia when her manteau's pinned awry,

[8] *Scissors.*   [9] *A popular book of scandal.*

E'er felt such rage, resentment, and despair,
As thou, sad Virgin! for thy ravished Hair.
    For, that sad moment, when the Sylphs withdrew
And Ariel weeping from Belinda flew,
Umbriel, a dusky, melancholy sprite,
As ever sullied the fair face of light,
Down to the central earth, his proper scene,
Repaired to search the gloomy Cave of Spleen.
    Swift on his sooty pinions flits the Gnome,
And in a vapor reached the dismal dome.
No cheerful breeze this sullen region knows,
The dreaded East is all the wind that blows.
Here in a grotto, sheltered close from air,
And screened in shades from day's detested glare,
She sighs for ever on her pensive bed,
Pain at her side, and Megrim [10] at her head.
    Two handmaids wait the throne: alike in place,
But diff'ring far in figure and in face.
Here stood Ill-nature like an ancient maid,
Her wrinkled form in black and white arrayed;
With store of prayers, for mornings, nights, and noons,
Her hand is filled; her bosom with lampoons.
    There Affectation, with a sickly mien,
Shows in her cheek the roses of eighteen,
Practised to lisp, and hang the head aside,
Faints into airs, and languishes with pride,
On the rich quilt sinks with becoming woe,
Wrapt in a gown, for sickness, and for show.
The fair ones feel such maladies as these,
When each new night-dress gives a new disease.
    A constant Vapor o'er the palace flies;
Strange phantoms rising as the mists arise;
Dreadful, as hermit's dreams in haunted shades,
Or bright, as visions of expiring maids.
Now glaring fiends, and snakes on rolling spires,
Pale spectres, gaping tombs, and purple fires:
Now lakes of liquid gold, Elysian scenes,
And crystal domes, and angels in machines.
    Unnumbered throngs on every side are seen,
Of bodies changed to various forms by Spleen.
Here living Tea-pots stand, one arm held out,
One bent; the handle this, and that the spout:
A Pipkin there, like Homer's Tripod walks;
Here sighs a Jar, and there a Goose-pie talks;

[10] *Headache.*

Men prove with child, as powerful fancy works,
And maids turned bottles, call aloud for corks.
  Safe passed the Gnome through this fantastic band,
A branch of healing Spleenwort in his hand.
Then thus addressed the power: "Hail, wayward Queen!
Who rule the sex to fifty from fifteen:
Parent of vapors and of female wit,
Who give the hysteric or poetic fit,
On various tempers act by various ways,
Make some take physic, others scribble plays;
Who cause the proud their visits to delay,
And send the godly in a pet to pray.
A nymph there is, that all thy power disdains,
And thousands more in equal mirth maintains.
But oh! if e'er thy Gnome could spoil a grace,
Or raise a pimple on a beauteous face,
Like Citron-waters matrons' cheeks inflame,
Or change complexions at a losing game;
If e'er with airy horns I planted heads,
Or rumpled petticoats, or tumbled beds,
Or caused suspicion when no soul was rude,
Or discomposed the head-dress of a Prude,
Or e'er to costive lap-dog gave disease,
Which not the tears of brightest eyes could ease:
Hear me, and touch Belinda with chagrin,
That single act gives half the world the spleen."
  The Goddess with a discontened air
Seems to reject him, though she grants his prayer.
A wondrous Bag with both her hands she binds,
Like that where once Ulysses held the winds;
There she collects the force of female lungs,
Sighs, sobs, and passions, and the war of tongues.
A Vial next she fills with fainting fears,
Soft sorrows, melting griefs, and flowing tears.
The Gnome rejoicing bears her gifts away,
Spreads his black wings, and slowly mounts to day.
  Sunk in Thalestris' arms the nymph he found,
Her eyes dejected and her hair unbound.
Full o'er their heads the swelling bag he rent,
And all the Furies issued at the vent.
Belinda burns with more than mortal ire,
And fierce Thalestris fans the rising fire.
"O wretched maid!" she spread her hands, and cried
(While Hampton's echoes, "Wretched maid!" replied),
"Was it for this you took such constant care

The bodkin, comb, and essence to prepare?
For this your locks in paper durance bound,
For this with torturing irons wreathed around?
For this with fillets strained your tender head,
And bravely bore the double loads of lead?
Gods! shall the ravisher display your hair,
While the Fops envy, and the Ladies stare!
Honor forbid! at whose unrivalled shrine
Ease, pleasure, virtue, all our sex resign.
Methinks already I your tears survey,
Already hear the horrid things they say,
Already see you a degraded toast,
And all your honor in a whisper lost!
How shall I, then, your helpless fame defend?
'Twill then be infamy to seem your friend!
And shall this prize, the inestimable prize,
Exposed through crystal to the gazing eyes,
And heightened by the diamond's circling rays,
On that rapacious hand for ever blaze?
Sooner shall grass in Hyde-park Circus grow,
And wits take lodgings in the sound of Bow; [11]
Sooner let earth, air, sea, to Chaos fall,
Men, monkeys, lap-dogs, parrots, perish all!"

CANTO V

She said: the pitying audience melt in tears;
But Fate and Jove had stopped the Baron's ears.
In vain Thalestris with reproach assails,
For who can move when fair Belinda fails?
Not half so fixed the Trojan [12] could remain,
While Anna begged and Dido raged in vain.
Then grave Clarissa graceful waved her fan;
Silence ensued, and thus the nymph began:
   "Say why are Beauties praised and honored most,
The wise man's passion, and the vain man's toast?
Why decked with all that land and sea afford,
Why Angels called, and Angel-like adored?
Why round our coaches crowd the white-gloved Beaux,
Why bows the side-box from its inmost rows;
How vain are all these glories, all our pains,
Unless good sense preserve what beauty gains:
That men may say, when we the front-box grace:

11 *The church bells of St. Mary-le-Bow, in a vulgar part of London.*
12 *Aeneas, the Trojan wanderer.*

'Behold the first in virtue as in face!'
Oh! if to dance all night, and dress all day,
Charmed the small-pox, or chased old-age away;
Who would not scorn what housewife's cares produce,
Or who would learn one earthly thing of use?
To patch, nay ogle, might become a saint,
Nor could it sure be such a sin to paint.
But since, alas! frail beauty must decay,
Curled or uncurled, since locks will turn to grey;
Since painted, or not painted, all shall fade,
And she who scorns a man, must die a maid;
What then remains but well our power to use,
And keep good-humor still whate'er we lose?
And trust me, dear! good-humor can prevail,
When airs, and flights, and screams, and scolding fail.
Beauties in vain their pretty eyes may roll;
Charms strike the sight, but merit wins the soul."

So spoke the Dame, but no applause ensued;
Belinda frowned, Thalestris called her Prude.
"To arms, to arms!" the fierce Virago cries,
And swift as lightning to the combat flies.
All side in parties, and begin the attack;
Fans clap, silks rustle, and tough whalebones crack;
Heroes' and Heroines' shouts confusedly rise,
And bass, and treble voices strike the skies.
No common weapons in their hands are found,
Like Gods they fight, nor dread a mortal wound.

So when bold Homer makes the Gods engage,
And heavenly breasts with human passions rage;
'Gainst Pallas, Mars; Latona, Hermes arms;
And all Olympus rings with loud alarms:
Jove's thunder roars, heaven trembles all around,
Blue Neptune storms, the bellowing deeps resound,
Earth shakes her nodding towers, the ground gives way,
And the pale ghosts start at the flash of day!

Triumphant Umbriel on a sconce's height
Clapped his glad wings, and sate to view the fight:
Propped on their bodkin spears, the Sprites survey
The growing combat, or assist the fray.

While through the press enraged Thalestris flies,
And scatters death around from both her eyes,
A Beau and Witling perished in the throng,
One died in metaphor, and one in song.
"O cruel nymph! a living death I bear,"
Cried Dapperwit, and sunk beside his chair.

A mournful glance Sir Fopling upwards cast,
"Those eyes are made so killing"—was his last.
Thus on Maeander's flowery margin lies
The expiring Swan, and as he sings he dies.
    When bold Sir Plume had drawn Clarissa down,
Chloe stepped in, and killed him with a frown;
She smiled to see the doughty hero slain.
But, at her smile, the Beau revived again.
    Now Jove suspends his golden scales in air,
Weighs the Men's wits against the Lady's hair;
The doubtful beam long nods from side to side;
At length the wits mount up, the hairs subside.
    See, fierce Belinda on the Baron flies,
With more than usual lightning in her eyes:
Nor feared the Chief the unequal fight to try,
Who sought no more than on his foe to die.
But this bold Lord with manly strength endued,
She with one finger and a thumb subdued:
Just where the breath of life his nostrils drew,
A charge of snuff the wily virgin threw;
The Gnomes direct, to every atom just,
The pungent grains of titillating dust.
Sudden, with starting tears each eye o'erflows,
And the high dome re-echoes to his nose.
    "Now meet thy fate," incensed Belinda cried,
And drew a deadly bodkin from her side.
(The same, his ancient personage to deck,
Her great great grandsire wore about his neck,
In three seal-rings; which after, melted down,
Formed a vast buckle for his widow's gown:
Her infant grandame's whistle next it grew,
The bells she jingled, and the whistle blew;
Then in a bodkin graced her mother's hairs,
Which long she wore, and now Belinda wears.)
    "Boast not my fall" (he cried), "insulting foe!
Thou by some other shalt be laid as low,
Nor think, to die dejects my lofty mind:
All that I dread is leaving you behind!
Rather than so, ah let me still survive,
And burn in Cupid's flames—but burn alive."
    "Restore the Lock!" she cries; and all around
"Restore the Lock!" the vaulted roofs rebound.[13]
Not fierce Othello in so loud a strain

13 *An echo of lines 71-32 in Dryden's* ALEXANDER'S FEAST.

Roared for the handkerchief that caused his pain.
But see how oft ambitious aims are crossed,
And chiefs contend 'till all the prize is lost!
The Lock, obtained with guilt, and kept with pain,
In every place is sought, but sought in vain:
With such a prize no mortal must be blest,
So heaven decrees! with heaven who can contest?
    Some thought it mounted to the Lunar sphere,
Since all things lost on earth are treasured there.
There heroes' wits are kept in ponderous vases,
And beaux' in snuff-boxes and tweezer-cases.
There broken vows and death-bed alms are found,
And lovers' hearts with ends of riband bound,
The courtier's promises, and sick man's prayers,
The smiles of harlots, and the tears of heirs,
Cages for gnats, and chains to yoke a flea,
Dried butterflies, and tomes of casuistry.
    But trust the Muse—she saw it upward rise,
Though marked by none but quick, poetic eyes
(So Rome's great founder to the heavens withdrew,
To Proculus alone confessed in view):
A sudden Star, it shot through liquid air,
And drew behind a radiant trail of hair,
Not Berenice's Locks [14] first rose so bright,
The heavens bespangling with dishevelled light.
The Sylphs behold it kindling as it flies,
And pleased pursue its progress through the skies.
    This the Beau monde shall from the Mall survey,
And hail with music its propitious ray.
This the blest Lover shall for Venus take,
And send up vows from Rosamonda's lake.[15]
This Partridge [16] soon shall view in cloudless skies,
When next he looks through Galileo's eyes; [17]
And hence the egregious wizard shall foredoom
The fate of Louis, and the fall of Rome.
    Then cease, bright Nymph! to mourn thy ravished hair,
Which adds new glory to the shining sphere!
Not all the tresses that fair head can boast,
Shall draw such envy as the Lock you lost.
For, after all the murders of your eye,

[14] *The constellation of seven stars.*
[15] *Pond in St. James's Park "consecrated to disastrous love and elegiac poetry."*
[16] *A popular London astrologer and soothsayer.*
[17] *The telescope.*

When, after millions slain, yourself shall die:
When those fair suns shall set, as set they must,
And all those tresses shall be laid in dust,
This Lock, the Muse shall consecrate to fame,
And 'midst the stars inscribe Belinda's name.

Although THE RAPE OF THE LOCK is completely cynical, it was immediately popular; the disdain with which Pope treated his characters, and especially the women, added to the popularity. He attached himself to the Tory party; he was praised by Steele, welcomed by Congreve, encouraged by Swift. His alliance with the savage Dean was a queer one—an alliance of mutual envy and distrust—but, though the relations were often strained, they remained unbroken. Pope was now in a position of authority. He could afford to undertake work of a more serious character, and for twelve years he labored at a translation of Homer. Although much of the task was farmed out to hack writers, Pope took all the credit; he was indignant when the critic Bentley put his finger on the mincing artificialities and said, "A fine poem, Mr. Pope, but you must not call it Homer." Nevertheless, Pope made a fortune from his translation. The success of his flashy but inaccurate edition of Shakespeare added to the sum, and he was able to purchase two estates in the country, while his publisher retired from business and bought himself the office of High Sheriff of Sussex.

Pope's unscrupulous passion for fame was still unsatisfied. He published his correspondence and manipulated the letters so as to give a falsely flattering picture of his relations with the great ones of his day. He claimed that copies of his work were pirated; after the sales had mounted and the hubbub was over, it was discovered that the source of the "piracy" was Pope himself. Success made him more brilliant but no less bitter. He died snarling at society at the beginning of his fifty-seventh year. His property was left to Martha Blount, a childhood friend who had become something of a platonic companion and something of a caretaker.

Pope's reputation has suffered from the vagaries of changing taste. Scorned by the romantic writers of the nineteenth century, he has been rediscovered by the precisionists of our own time. And the unlettered of both centuries, unaware of the source, continue to quote him in phrases that have become English proverbs: "To err is human; to forgive divine." "A little learning is a dangerous thing." "Hope springs eternal in the human breast." "The proper study of mankind is man." "Fools rush in where angels fear to tread." "Order is Heaven's first law." "The feast of reason and the flow of soul." "An honest man's the noblest work of God."

WILLIAM OLDYS
[1696–1761]

BORN into a literary London family, the illegitimate son of the chancellor to the Bishop of Lincoln, William Oldys made books his career. He became a noted bibliographer and antiquary, and sold his collection of rare volumes to the Earl of Oxford, who appointed him his secretary. After a lifetime spent chiefly in annotations, Oldys died in his sixty-fifth year.

Librarians are indebted to Oldys for his bibliographical articles and miscellanies. The ordinary reader remembers him for a few modest lyrics, particularly one naïve poem ON A FLY DRINKING FROM HIS CUP, which Blake echoed, perhaps unconsciously, in THE FLY, on page 603.

On a Fly Drinking from His Cup

Busy, curious, thirsty fly!
Drink with me, and drink as I;
Freely welcome to my cup,
Couldst thou sip, and sip it up;
Make the most of life you may,
Life is short and wears away.

Just alike, both mine and thine,
Hasten quick to their decline.
Thine's a summer, mine no more,
Though repeated to three-score.
Three-score summers, when they're gone,
Will appear as short as one.

JOHN DYER
[1699–1758]

JOHN DYER was born in Carmathanshire, Wales. Son of a solicitor,
he studied law, turned to painting, and finally was ordained a
priest in his fortieth year. Fascinated by the so-called Pindaric odes
of Cowley, Dyer attempted to create in the grandiose manner. He
disdained smaller work (such as his picturesque GRONGAR HILL) for
didactic length. THE FLEECE, a blank-verse epic of the wool trade, is
devoted to the care and feeding of sheep, the shearing, cleaning
and weaving of the fleece, and, in a fine commercial climax, the
marketing of the product. Yet it is the less ambitious GRONGAR HILL
which survives.

FROM

Grongar Hill

O may I with myself agree,
And never covet what I see:
Content me with an humble shade,
My passions tamed, my wishes laid;
For while our wishes wildly roll,
We banish quiet from the soul:
'Tis thus the busy beat the air,
And misers gather wealth and care.
      Now, even now, my joy runs high,
As on the mountain-turf I lie;
While the wanton Zephyr sings,
And in the vale perfumes his wings;
While the waters murmur deep;
While the shepherd charms his sheep;
While the birds unbounded fly,
And with music fill the sky,
Now, even now, my joy runs high.
      Be full, ye courts, be great who will;
Search for Peace with all your skill:
Open wide the lofty door,
Seek her on the marble floor,

In vain ye search, she is not there;
In vain ye search the domes of Care!
Grass and flowers Quiet treads,
On the meads and mountain-heads,
Along with Pleasure, close allied,
Ever by each other's side:
And often, by the murmuring rill,
Hears the thrush, while all is still,
Within the groves of Grongar Hill.

Dyer looked with admiring innocence on the industriousness of nature and the nature of industry. Nevertheless, his is one of the first attempts to grapple with such realistic material as the rise of industrialism. And his description of the London fog might be recorded today—although the same expressions might not be used concerning the "trifling Gaul, effeminate" and the general enervating effect of the European scene!

The English Fog

How erring oft the judgment in its hate
Or fond desire! Those slow-descending showers,
Those hovering fogs, that bathe our growing vales
In deep November (loathed by trifling Gaul,
Effeminate), are gifts the Pleiads shed,
Britannia's handmaids. As the beverage falls,
Her hills rejoice, her valleys laugh and sing.

Hail noble Albion! where no golden mines,
No soft perfumes, nor oils, nor myrtle bowers,
The vigorous frame and lofty heart of man
Enervate: round whose stern cerulean brows
White-winged snow, and cloud, and pearly rain,
Frequent attend, with solemn majesty:
Rich queen of mists and vapors!

from THE FLEECE

It is an error to think of eighteenth-century literature as a unified expression, a smooth record of sophistication and artificiality. The generation of Pope was dominated by his clipped disposals, but there was another tendency. A contrary current to the mainstream was soon apparent. Opposed to Pope's treacherous rapids, this was a smaller current, slow, almost turgid; instead of dashing toward the metropolis, it meandered through the little villages and "retreats." New ground was watered, new soil nourished. Urban brilliance was met, if not matched, by what has been called "suburbanity," and the town's double-dealing was answered by rural sincerity. The straightforward sentiment which was to be fully orchestrated by Burns and Wordsworth was already sounded by James Thomson, whose indolence unfortunately inflated itself in stilted and circumlocutory verbiage, and by William Collins and Thomas Gray.

THOMAS GRAY
[1716–1771]

I T IS a wonder that Thomas Gray lived beyond infancy; his mother bore twelve children, of whom Thomas was the fifth and sole surviving child. As a baby he suffered from convulsions, and it is related that his mother once opened a vein to relieve the pressure on his brain. Gray's father, who was brutal and probably mad, contributed nothing except misery to the home. His mother finally separated herself from her husband, kept a shop, and took care of all the child's expenses alone.

At Eton Gray was closely attached to Horace Walpole and Richard West, and it was West's premature death which inspired Gray's first fine poem, a sonnet written in his twenty-fifth year.

On the Death of Mr. Richard West

In vain to me the smiling mornings shine,
    And reddening Phoebus lifts his golden fire:
The birds in vain their amorous descant join,
    Or cheerful fields resume their green attire.
These ears, alas! for other notes repine,
    A different object do these eyes require.
My lonely anguish melts no heart but mine;
    And in my breast the imperfect joys expire.
Yet morning smiles the busy race to cheer,
    And new-born pleasure brings to happier men:

The fields to all their wonted tribute bear:
To warm their little loves the birds complain:
I fruitless mourn to him, that cannot hear,
And weep the more because I weep in vain.

Gray traveled in Europe with Walpole, quarreled with him, and returned to the village of Stoke Poges, where his mother had retired from business. It was from Stoke Poges that Gray, after a reconciliation with Walpole, sent his friend "a thing to which he had at last put an end." The "thing" was the ELEGY WRITTEN IN A COUNTRY CHURCHYARD. The ELEGY had been begun shortly after the death of West, and the spirit of the elegiac sonnet to his young friend still moved in Gray. But Gray, who was never an energetic worker, put aside the poem and did not complete it until seven years later. The finished manuscript came into the hands of a piratical editor, and it took all of Walpole's skill to get the publisher Dodsley to rush through an edition in a few days. Gray refused to accept any payment for the ELEGY, but Dodsley made more than a thousand pounds out of it.

Although it is apparent from the concluding stanzas that the ELEGY was written with Richard West in mind, its content is a collection of generalities. The effect is attained not so much from the reflection of emotion but from the presentation: a succession of thoughtful pictures and a chain of epigrams skillfully arranged.

Elegy Written in a Country Churchyard

The curfew tolls the knell of parting day,
The lowing herd wind slowly o'er the lea,
The ploughman homeward plods his weary way,
And leaves the world to darkness and to me.

Now fades the glimmering landscape on the sight,
And all the air a solemn stillness holds,
Save where the beetle wheels his droning flight,
And drowsy tinklings lull the distant folds:

Save where from yonder ivy-mantled tower
The moping owl does to the moon complain
Of such as, wandering near her secret bower,
Molest her ancient solitary reign.

Beneath those rugged elms, that yew-tree's shade
Where heaves the turf in many a moldering heap,
Each in his narrow cell for ever laid,
The rude forefathers of the hamlet sleep.

The breezy call of incense-breathing morn,
The swallow twittering from the straw-built shed,
The cock's shrill clarion, or the echoing horn,
No more shall rouse them from their lowly bed.

For them no more the blazing hearth shall burn,
Or busy housewife ply her evening care:
No children run to lisp their sire's return,
Or climb his knees the envied kiss to share.

Oft did the harvest to their sickle yield,
Their furrow oft the stubborn glebe has broke;
How jocund did they drive their team afield!
How bowed the woods beneath their sturdy stroke!

Let not ambition mock their useful toil,
Their homely joys, and destiny obscure;
Nor grandeur hear with a disdainful smile
The short and simple annals of the poor.

The boast of heraldry, the pomp of power,
And all that beauty, all that wealth e'er gave
Awaits alike th' inevitable hour:—
The paths of glory lead but to the grave.

Nor you, ye proud, impute to these the fault,
If memory o'er their tomb no trophies raise,
Where through the long-drawn aisle and fretted vault
The pealing anthem swells the note of praise.

Can storied urn or animated bust
Back to its mansion call the fleeting breath?
Can honor's voice provoke the silent dust,
Or flattery soothe the dull, cold ear of death?

Perhaps in this neglected spot is laid
Some heart once pregnant with celestial fire;
Hands, that the rod of empire might have swayed,
Or waked to ecstasy the living lyre.

But knowledge to their eyes her ample page,
Rich with the spoils of time, did ne'er unroll;
Chill penury repressed their noble rage,[1]
And froze the genial current of the soul.

Full many a gem of purest ray serene
The dark unfathomed caves of ocean bear:
Full many a flower is born to blush unseen,
And waste its sweetness on the desert air.

Some village-Hampden,[2] that with dauntless breast
The little tyrant of his fields withstood;
Some mute inglorious Milton here may rest,
Some Cromwell, guiltless of his country's blood.

Th' applause of listening senates to command,
The threats of pain and ruin to despise,
To scatter plenty o'er a smiling land,
And read their history in a nation's eyes,

Their lot forbade: nor circumscribed alone
Their growing virtues, but their crimes confined;
Forbade to wade through slaughter to a throne,
And shut the gates of mercy on mankind;

The struggling pangs of conscious truth to hide,
To quench the blushes of ingenuous shame,
Or heap the shrine of luxury and pride
With incense kindled at the Muse's flame.

Far from the madding crowd's ignoble strife,
Their sober wishes never learned to stray;
Along the cool sequestered vale of life
They kept the noiseless tenor of their way.

Yet e'en these bones from insult to protect
Some frail memorial still erected nigh,
With uncouth rhymes and shapeless sculpture decked
Implores the passing tribute of a sigh.

Their name, their years, spelt by th' unlettered Muse,
The place of fame and elegy supply:

---

[1] *Enthusiasm.*

[2] *John Hampden, a soldier-patriot whose courage during the Civil War was surpassed only by his statesmanship.*

And many a holy text around she strews,
That teach the rustic moralist to die.

For who, to dumb forgetfulness a prey,
This pleasing anxious being e'er resigned,
Left the warm precincts of the cheerful day,
Nor cast one longing, lingering look behind?

On some fond breast the parting soul relies,
Some pious drops the closing eye requires;
E'en from the tomb the voice of Nature cries,
E'en in our ashes live their wonted fires.

For thee,[3] who, mindful of th' unhonored dead,
Dost in these lines their artless tale relate;
If chance, by lonely contemplation led,
Some kindred spirit shall enquire thy fate

Haply some hoary-headed swain may say,
"Oft have we seen him at the peep of dawn
Brushing with hasty steps the dews away,
To meet the sun upon the upland lawn;

"There at the foot of yonder nodding beech
That wreathes its old fantastic roots so high,
His listless length at noon-tide would he stretch,
And pore upon the brook that babbles by.

"Hard by yon wood, now smiling as in scorn,
Muttering his wayward fancies he would rove;
Now drooping, woeful-wan, like one forlorn,
Or crazed with care, or crossed in hopeless love.

"One morn I missed him on the customed hill,
Along the heath, and near his favorite tree;
Another came; nor yet beside the rill,
Nor up the lawn, nor at the wood was he;

"The next, with dirges due in sad array
Slow through the church-way path we saw him borne—
Approach and read (for thou canst read) the lay
Graved on the stone beneath yon aged thorn."

[3] *The reference here and in the rest of the poem is to Gray's friend, Richard West.*

THE EPITAPH

Here rests his head upon the lap of earth
A youth, to fortune and to fame unknown;
Fair science frowned not on his humble birth
And melancholy marked him for her own.

Large was his bounty, and his soul sincere;
Heaven did a recompense as largely send:
He gave to misery all he had, a tear;
He gained from heaven ('twas all he wished) a friend.

No farther seek his merits to disclose,
Or draw his frailties from their dread abode
(There they alike in trembling hope repose),
The bosom of his Father and his God.

After reaching thirty Gray lived more and more quietly in the country, something of a recluse and something of a hypochondriac. Apathetic to women, he buried himself in his books and experimented with Pindaric odes which were intricate and all but consistently uninteresting. At forty-one he refused the laureateship which previously had been conferred upon such nonentities as Thomas Shadwell, Nahum Tate, Nicholas Rowe, Lawrence Eusden, and Colley Cibber. Even when promised that no "occasional" or "official" poems would be expected of him, Gray remained firm, and the honor went to the unknown William Whitehead. In his fifty-second year Gray was appointed professor of history and modern languages at Cambridge. At fifty-four he became strongly attached to Charles Victor de Bonstetten, a Swiss youth who was attending Cambridge—"My life now is but a conversation with your shadow," Gray wrote to his "dearest friend." A year later, when Gray was planning to visit Bonstetten in Switzerland, the poet suffered a violent attack of gout and died July 30, 1771. On the seventh anniversary of his funeral, a monument was erected to his memory in Westminster Abbey.

The eighteenth century was the time of Pope, the period—tradition as well as alliteration demands it—of polish and pedantry. Yet the vaunted "Age of Reason" was also the age of unfettered imagination. Pope's reliance on the life of London parlors was countered by Gray's celebration of a country churchyard; the century, seemingly so disciplined, responded to the acute sensibility of Collins, shook with the wild experiments of Chatterton and the rapt ecstasies of Smart, and ended with the fiery vision of Blake. Sanity itself was transcended; such poets as Collins, Cowper, and Smart spent some of their years in madhouses.

WILLIAM COLLINS
[1721–1759]

THE short life of William Collins was a tragedy of vacillation and maladjustment. Born in the cathedral town of Chichester, son of a well-to-do hatter, Collins wrote poems as a schoolboy; a pamphlet of his verse was published when he was thirteen. Still an undergraduate, he produced a set of PERSIAN ECLOGUES, and it seemed that the young poet was at the beginning of an auspicious career. But Collins was both intemperate and irresolute. He wavered between the church and the army, and joined neither. He plunged into excesses and, though his uncle left him a fortune, showed himself irresponsible.

At twenty-five Collins published his best work, a set of twelve ODES. The publication was a flat failure, and he fell into extreme despondency. He tried to dissipate the gathering melancholia by travel, but before he was thirty it was evident that his reason was affected. The last nine years of his life were spent in mental anguish and physical agony. He was confined for a while in an asylum near Oxford; he could not meet his friends, some of whom thought he was dead. When he actually died in his thirty-eighth year, no newspaper carried a notice of his death.

Few poets have left so small a body of work, but almost all of it is exquisitely made. Collins' odes, compared to Cowley's and Gray's, are slight; but if the texture is thin, it is strong, fine-spun but not fragile. The odes lack fire, but "in charm and precision of diction," wrote Edmund Gosse, "they stand unrivaled." In his best poems, according to Hugh I'Anson Fausset, "he transmuted a style which he derived from classical models into something which was more than individual, which was impalpable."

Ode: Written in 1746

How sleep the brave, who sink to rest,
By all their country's wishes blest!
When Spring, with dewy fingers cold,
Returns to deck their hallowed mold,
She there shall dress a sweeter sod,
Than Fancy's feet have ever trod.

By fairy hands their knell is rung,
By forms unseen their dirge is sung;
There Honor comes, a pilgrim grey,
To bless the turf that wraps their clay,
And Freedom shall awhile repair,
To dwell a weeping hermit there!

Ode to Evening

If aught of oaten stop, or pastoral song,
May hope, chaste Eve, to soothe thy modest ear,
    Like thine own solemn springs,
    Thy springs and dying gales;

O nymph reserved—while now the bright-haired sun
Sits in yon western tent, whose cloudy skirts,
    With brede ethereal wove,[1]
    O'erhang his wavy bed;

Now air is hushed, save where the weak-eyed bat
With short shrill shriek flits by on leathern wing,
    Or where the beetle winds
    His small but sullen horn,

As oft he rises, 'midst the twilight path
Against the pilgrim borne in heedless hum—
    Now teach me, maid composed,
    To breathe some softened strain,

Whose numbers, stealing through thy darkening vale,
May not unseemly with its stillness suit,
    As, musing slow, I hail
    Thy genial loved return!

[1] *Airily woven braids.*

For when thy folding-star arising shows
His paly circlet, at his warming lamp
    The fragrant Hours, and elves
    Who slept in buds the day,

And many a nymph who wreathes her brows with sedge,
And sheds the freshening dew, and, lovelier still,
    The pensive Pleasures sweet,
    Prepare thy shadowy car.

Then lead, calm votaress, where some sheety lake
Cheers the lone heath, or some time-hallowed pile,
    Or upland fallows grey
    Reflect its last cool gleam.

But when chill blustering winds, or driving rain,
Prevent my willing feet, be mine the hut
    That from the mountain's side
    Views wilds and swelling floods,

And hamlets brown, and dim-discovered spires,
And hears their simple bell, and marks o'er all
    Thy dewy fingers draw
    The gradual dusky veil.

While Spring shall pour his show'rs, as oft he wont,
And bathe thy breathing tresses, meekest Eve!
    While Summer loves to sport
    Beneath thy lingering light;

While sallow Autumn fills thy lap with leaves,
Or Winter, yelling through the troublous air,
    Affrights thy shrinking train,
    And rudely rends thy robes;

So long, regardful of thy quiet rule,
Shall fancy, friendship, science, rose-lipped health,
    Thy gentlest influence own,
    And love thy favorite name!

It is hazardous to read autobiography into a man's poetry. But there seems little doubt that Collins was revealing his own disordered mind and his anxious premonitions in his ODE TO FEAR, with its evocation of the "mad nymph" and her "ghastly train" of frantic monsters.

Ode to Fear

Thou, to whom the world unknown
With all its shadowy shapes is shown;
Who see'st appalled th' unreal scene,
While Fancy lifts the veil between:
   Ah Fear! Ah frantic Fear!
   I see, I see thee near.
I know thy hurried step, thy haggard eye!
Like thee I start, like thee disordered fly,
For lo what Monsters in thy train appear!
Danger, whose limbs of giant mold
What mortal eye can fixed behold?
Who stalks his round, an hideous form,
Howling amidst the midnight storm,
Or throws him on the ridgy steep
Of some loose hanging rock to sleep:
And with him thousand phantoms joined,
Who prompt to deeds accursed the mind:
And those, the fiends, who near allied,
O'er Nature's wounds, and wrecks preside;
Whilst Vengeance, in the lurid air,
Lifts her red arm, exposed and bare:
On whom that ravening brood of fate,
Who lap the blood of sorrow, wait;
Who, Fear, this ghastly train can see,
And look not madly wild, like thee?

       *

Thou who such weary lengths hast past,
Where wilt thou rest, mad nymph, at last?
Say, wilt thou shroud in haunted cell,
Where gloomy Rape and Murder dwell?
Or, in some hollowed seat,
'Gainst which the big waves beat,
Hear drowning sea-men's cries in tempests brought!
Dark power, with shuddering meek submitted thought
Be mine, to read the visions old,
Which thy awakening bards have told:
And lest thou meet my blasted view,
Hold each strange tale devoutly true;

Ne'er be I found, by thee o'erawed,
In that thrice-hallowed eve abroad,
When ghosts, as cottage-maids believe,
Their pebbled beds permitted leave,
And Goblins haunt from fire, or fen,
Or mine, or flood, the walks of men!
        O thou whose spirit most possest
The sacred seat of Shakespeare's breast!
By all that from thy prophet broke,
In thy divine emotions spoke:
Hither again thy fury deal,
Teach me but once like him to feel:
His cypress wreath my meed decree,
And I, O Fear, will dwell with thee!

CHRISTOPHER SMART

[1722–1771]

CHRISTOPHER SMART would have been a fantastic figure at any time in the world's history; in the eighteenth century he was incredible. A mad enigma, he was summarized by Odell Shepard as "a university wit and scholar, a translator of Horace and a Grub Street hack, a drunkard, a Bedlamite, and a radiantly happy Christian who died in debtor's prison."

Smart's beginnings were propitious enough. His father was the steward of large estates in Kent; young Christopher spent much time at Raby Castle; the Duchess of Cleveland was his patron. But as soon as he entered Pembroke College, Cambridge, he gave himself over to every form of wildness. He wrote and produced a queer play and cast himself in five of the roles. He slept in class and seemed to be awake only when he was drinking in taverns. In his twenty-fifth year Smart was so heavily in debt that he could not leave his room for fear of creditors. Nevertheless, in spite of dissipations, he became fellow of his college and lectured on philosophy. At thirty he suddenly left Cambridge, went to London, and determined to earn a living by journalism. He wrote under various pseudonyms, two of them being Pentweazle and Mary Midnight. He translated

the classics and amused himself with a burlesque entitled THE
HILLIAD, a Homeric satire directed against John Hill, a quack
doctor.

Before he left Cambridge, Smart had already shown signs of
mental disorder. The aberrations, chiefly of a religious character,
became so pronounced that he was committed to an asylum from
his thirty-fourth to his thirty-sixth year. There he was visited by
Samuel Johnson, who believed him sane. Smart's infirmities, John-
son concluded, "were not noxious to society. He insisted on people
praying with him—also falling on his knees and saying his prayers
in the street—but I'd as lief pray with Kit Smart as anyone else."

It was in the asylum that Smart wrote his one great poem. He
was denied the use of pen and paper, and it is said that most of the
lengthy SONG TO DAVID was minutely scratched with a key upon the
wainscot of his room. After his release, Smart was supported by
small contributions from his friends. But he drifted always further
into recklessness. Unwilling to stop drinking, unable to work, Smart
was thrown into debtor's prison. There he died in his forty-ninth
year.

Smart's lesser poems were assembled, but his one exceptional
masterpiece was ignored. When the POEMS OF THE LATE CHRISTOPHER
SMART were published twenty years after his death, the rapt SONG TO
DAVID was excluded because it bore "melancholy proofs of the re-
cent estrangement of his mind." For more than a century the re-
verberating lines remained unknown until Robert Browning wrote
his PARLEYINGS WITH CERTAIN PEOPLE OF IMPORTANCE IN THEIR DAY.
In one of the "parleyings," entitled WITH CHRISTOPHER SMART,
Browning reconstructed the poet's erratic life and the source of his
ecstatic imagery.

> Was it because you judged (I know full well
> You never had the fancy)—judged—as some—
> That who makes poetry must reproduce
> Thus ever and thus only, as they come,
> Each strength, each beauty, everywhere diffuse
> Throughout creation, so that eye and ear,
> Seeing and hearing, straight shall recognize,
> At touch of just a trait, the strength appear,—
> Suggested by a line's lapse see arise
> All evident the beauty,—fresh surprise
> Startling at fresh achievement?

Smart's vision is both childlike and startling, full of "fresh surprise." The imaginative leaps which characterize his extended poem distinguish the headlong prose of the recently discovered REJOICE IN THE LAMB, a book published as late as 1940. But REJOICE IN THE LAMB is an uncontrolled mixture; A SONG TO DAVID is sheer magnificence. It is distracting in its speed, in its very strain of rapture; prayer and praise are fused in a fire of concentrated creation. Revealing new meanings and far-reaching glories with each rereading, it towers above the careful ever-so-reasonable writing of the day—a monument of nobility among memorials of wit.

Although A SONG TO DAVID is not reprinted in full, more of its eighty-six stanzas than are usually printed are given here. One common error has been corrected in this version. Practically all the collections bring the majestic poem to a close with the lines:

> Thou that stupendous truth believed,
> And now the matchless deed's achieved,
>   Determined, dared, and done.

But a rare edition printed in 1763 shows the line to be:

> Thou *at* stupendous truth believed.

Smart used the word "at" to indicate a "reaching toward" revelation, the struggle of the determined and aspiring soul.

A Song to David

> O thou, that sit'st upon a throne,
> With harp of high majestic tone,
>   To praise the King of kings:
> And voice of heaven-ascending swell,
> Which, while its deeper notes excel,
>   Clear, as a clarion, rings:
>
> To bless each valley, grove and coast,
> And charm the cherubs to the post
>   Of gratitude in throngs;
> To keep the days on Zion's mount,
> And send the year to his account,
>   With dances and with songs:

O Servant of God's holiest charge,
The minister of praise at large,
    Which thou may'st now receive;
From thy blest mansion hail and hear,
From topmost eminence appear
    To this the wreath I weave.

Great, valiant, pious, good, and clean,
Sublime, contemplative, serene,
    Strong, constant, pleasant, wise!
Bright effluence of exceeding grace,
Best man—the witness and the race,
    The peril and the prize!

Great—from the luster of his crown,
From Samuel's horn and God's renown,
    Which is the people's voice;
For all the host, from rear to van,
Applauded and embraced the man—
    The man of God's own choice . . .

He sang of God—the mighty source
Of all things—the stupendous force
    On which all strength depends;
From whose right arm, beneath whose eyes,
All period, power, and enterprise
    Commences, reigns, and ends.

Angels—their ministry and meed,
Which to and fro with blessings speed,
    Or with their citterns [1] wait;
Where Michael with his millions bows,
Where dwells the seraph and his spouse,
    The cherub and her mate.

Of man—the semblance and effect
Of God and Love—the Saint elect
    For infinite applause—
To rule the land, and briny broad,
To be laborious in his laud,
    And heroes in his cause.

[1] *Citherns, stringed instruments.*

The world—the clustering spheres he made,
The glorious light, the soothing shade,
          Dale, champaign, grove, and hill;
The multitudinous abyss,
Where secrecy remains in bliss.
          And wisdom hides her skill.

Trees, plants, and flowers—of virtuous [2] root;
Gem yielding blossom, yielding fruit,
          Choice gums and precious balm;
Bless ye the nosegay in the vale,
And with the sweetness of the gale
          Enrich the thankful psalm;

Of fowl—e'en every beak and wing
Which cheer the winter, hail the spring,
          That live in peace or prey;
They that make music, or that mock,
The quail, the brave domestic cock,
          The raven, swan, and jay.

Of fishes—every size and shape,
Which nature frames of light escape,
          Devouring man to shun:
The shells are in the wealthy deep,
The shoals upon the surface leap,
          And love the glancing sun.

Of beasts—the beaver plods his task;
While the sleek tigers roll and bask,
          Nor yet the shades arouse:
Her cave the mining coney [3] scoops;
Where o'er the mead the mountain stoops,
          The kids exult and browse:

Of gems—their virtue and their price,
Which hid in earth from man's device,
          Their darts of luster sheathe;
The jasper of the master's stamp,
The topaz blazing like a lamp
          Among the mines beneath. . . .

[2] *Having healing virtues or powers.*   [3] *Rabbit.*

O David, highest in the list
Of worthies, on God's ways insist,
⠀⠀⠀The genuine word repeat.
Vain are the documents of men,
And vain the flourish of the pen
⠀⠀⠀That keeps the fool's conceit.

PRAISE above all—for praise prevails;
Heap up the measure, load the scales,
⠀⠀⠀And good to goodness add
The generous soul her Saviour aids,
But peevish obloquy degrades;
⠀⠀⠀The Lord is great and glad.

For ADORATION all the ranks
Of angels yield eternal thanks,
⠀⠀⠀And David in the midst;
With God's good poor, which, last and least
In man's esteem, thou to thy feast,
⠀⠀⠀O blessed bridegroom, bidst.

For ADORATION seasons change,
And order, truth, and beauty range,
⠀⠀⠀Adjust, attract, and fill:
The grass the polyanthus cheques; [4]
And polished porphyry reflects
⠀⠀⠀By the descending rill.

Rich almonds color to the prime
For ADORATION; tendrils climb,
⠀⠀⠀And fruit-trees pledge their gems;
And Ivis [5] with her gorgeous vest
Builds for her eggs her cunning nest,
⠀⠀⠀And bell-flowers bow their stems.

With vinous syrups cedars spout;
From rocks pure honey, gushing out,
⠀⠀⠀For ADORATION springs:
All scenes of painting crowd the map
Of nature; to the mermaid's pap
⠀⠀⠀The scaled infant clings.

[4] *The grass and the primroses make a checkered pattern.*
[5] *The hummingbird.*

The spotted ounce [6] and playsome cubs
Run rustling 'mongst the flowering shrubs,
   And lizards feed the moss;
For ADORATION beasts embark,
While waves upholding halycon's ark
   No longer roar and toss.

While Israel sits beneath his fig,
With coral root and amber sprig
   The weaned adventurer sports;
Where to the palm the jasmine cleaves,
For ADORATION 'mongst the leaves
   The gale his peace reports. . . .

The laurels with the winter strive;
The crocus burnishes alive
   Upon the snow-clad earth.
For ADORATION myrtles stay
To keep the garden from dismay,
   And bless the sight from dearth.

The pheasant shows his pompous neck;
And ermine, jealous of a speck,
   With fear eludes offence:
The sable, with his glossy pride,
For ADORATION is descried,
   Where frosts the wave condense.

The cheerful holly, pensive yew,
And holy thorn, their trim renew;
   The squirrel hoards his nuts:
All creatures batten o'er their stores,
And careful nature all her doors
   For ADORATION shuts.

For ADORATION, David's Psalms
Lift up the heart to deeds of alms;
   And he who kneels and chants,
Prevails his passions to control,
Finds meat and medicine to the soul,
   Which for translation [7] pants.

6 *Panther.* 7 *Transport to heaven.*

For ADORATION, beyond match,
The scholar bullfinch [8] aims to catch
　　　The soft flute's ivory touch;
And, careless on the hazel spray,
The daring redbreast keeps at bay
　　　The damsel's greedy clutch.

For ADORATION, in the skies,
The Lord's philosopher espies
　　　The Dog, the Ram, and Rose;
The Planet's ring, Orion's sword;
Nor is his greatness less adored
　　　In the vile worm that glows.

For ADORATION on the strings
The western breezes work their wings,
　　　The captive ear to soothe.
Hark! 'tis a voice—how still, and small—
That makes the cataracts to fall,
　　　Or bids the sea be smooth. . . .

For ADORATION, all the paths
Of grace are open, all the baths
　　　Of purity refresh;
And all the rays of glory beam
To deck the man of God's esteem,
　　　Who triumphs o'er the flesh.

For ADORATION, in the dome
Of Christ the sparrows find an home;
　　　And on his olives perch:
The swallow also dwells with thee,
O man of God's humility,
　　　Within his Saviour's Church.

Sweet is the dew that falls betimes,
And drops upon the leafy limes;
　　　Sweet Hermon's fragrant air:
Sweet is the lily's silver bell,
And sweet the wakeful tapers smell
　　　That watch for early prayer.

8 *The bullfinch is a "scholar" because he can learn to carry tunes.*

Sweet the young nurse with love intense,
Which smiles o'er sleeping innocence;
      Sweet when the lost arrive:
Sweet the musician's ardor beats,
While his vague mind's in quest of sweets,
      The choicest flowers to hive.

Sweeter in all the strains of love,
The language of thy turtle dove,
      Paired to thy swelling chord;
Sweeter with every grace endued,
The glory of thy gratitude,
      Respired unto the Lord.

Strong is the horse upon his speed;
Strong in pursuit the rapid glede,[9]
      Which makes at once his game;
Strong the tall ostrich on the ground;
Strong through the turbulent profound
      Shoots xiphias [10] to his aim.

Strong is the lion—like a coal
His eyeball—like a bastion's mole
      His chest against the foes:
Strong the gier-eagle [11] on his sail,
Strong against tide, the enormous whale
      Emerges, as he goes.

But stronger still, in earth and air,
And in the sea, the man of prayer;
      And far beneath the tide;
And in the seat to faith assigned,
Where ask is have, where seek is find,
      Where knock is open wide.

Beauteous the fleet before the gale;
Beauteous the multitudes in mail,
      Ranked arms and crested heads:
Beauteous the garden's umbrage mild,
Walk, water, meditated wild,
      And all the bloomy beds.

[9] *The hawk.* [10] *The swordfish.* [11] *The vulture.*

Beauteous the moon full on the lawn;
And beauteous, when the veil's withdrawn,
    The virgin to her spouse:
Beauteous the temple decked and filled,
When to the heaven of heavens they build
    Their heart-directed vows.

Beauteous, yea beauteous more than these,
The shepherd king upon his knees,
    For his momentous trust;
With wish of infinite conceit,[12]
For man, beast, mute, the small and great,
    And prostrate dust to dust.

Precious the bounteous widow's mite;
And precious, for extreme delight,
    The largess from the churl:
Precious the ruby's blushing blaze,
And alba's blest imperial rays,
    And pure cerulean pearl,

Precious the penitential tear;
And precious is the sigh sincere,
    Acceptable to God:
And precious are the winning flowers,
In gladsome Israel's feast of bowers,
    Bound on the hallowed sod.

More precious that diviner part
Of David, ev'n the Lord's own heart,
    Great, beautiful, and new:
In all things where it was intent,
In all extremes, in each event,
    Proof—answering true to true.

Glorious the sun in mid career;
Glorious the assembled fires appear;
    Glorious the comet's train:
Glorious the trumpet and alarm;
Glorious the almighty stretched-out arm;
    Glorious the enraptured main:

[12] *Comprehension.*

Glorious the northern lights astream;
Glorious the song, when God's the theme;
      Glorious the thunder's roar:
Glorious hosanna from the den;
Glorious the catholic amen;
      Glorious the martyr's gore:

Glorious—more glorious is the crown
Of Him that brought salvation down
      By meekness, called thy Son;
Thou at stupendous truth believed,
And now the matchless deed's achieved,
      DETERMINED, DARED, and DONE.

OLIVER GOLDSMITH
[1728–1774]

For a moralist, son of an Irish clergyman, Oliver Goldsmith led a singularly irregular life. The date and place of his birth are uncertain, but it is known that he had difficulty with the world even in childhood. He was a dull and badly behaved boy, and his harsh features, which even the painter Reynolds could not flatter, were not improved by being deeply pitted with smallpox. The butt of his companions, Goldsmith was considered the village blockhead. Charitable friends of his father found a place for him at Trinity College, Dublin, but Goldsmith paid no attention to his studies, played the clown in class, and ran away when he was chastised for giving a dance for the gayer boys and girls of the town. He was finally persuaded to return to college, and took his degree at about twenty-one, the lowest on the list.

A small inheritance left to him on the death of his father was soon squandered. Macaulay wrote that Goldsmith lived for a while "between squalid distress and squalid dissipation." He applied for holy orders and was rejected. He became tutor in a rich family, but lost the position because of an angry dispute. He taught school and quit because of the routine. His uncle gave him fifty pounds to study law, but Goldsmith promptly gambled the money away. After attempting two or three other professions unsuccessfully, he decided to leave England. He started for America, changed his mind, and went off to the Continent, ostensibly to become a doctor. It is said that he set out "with one shirt to his back, a guinea in his pocket, and a flute in his hand." He seems to have spent most of his time furnishing music for country dances and often earned board and lodging by playing in streets and taverns.

In his late twenties Goldsmith returned to England, where, according to his own not too reliable account, he lived among the beggars of London. He became an usher, a bookseller's hack, a reviewer, and, finally, a professional writer. He was an unwilling author. Although his style was fluent and his manner popular, he regarded writing as drudgery. Always in debt, he was forever being pursued by sheriffs.

In his mid-thirties Goldsmith was introduced to Samuel Johnson, who helped him out of more than one difficulty. On one occasion Johnson learned that Goldsmith was about to be dispossessed because of failure to pay rent, and sent the poet a guinea. A few hours later Johnson discovered that Goldsmith had spent most of the money on a bottle of Madeira. Johnson, according to Macaulay, "put the cork into the bottle and entreated his friend to consider calmly how money was to be procured." Goldsmith replied that he had a novel practically ready for the press. Johnson pocketed the manuscript, took it to a publisher, sold it for sixty pounds, and paid Goldsmith's rent. The manuscript was THE VICAR OF WAKEFIELD.

Song

When lovely woman stoops to folly,
  And finds too late that men betray,
What charm can soothe her melancholy?
  What art can wash her guilt away?

The only art her guilt to cover,
  To hide her shame from every eye,
To give repentance to her lover,
  And wring his bosom, is—to die.
    from THE VICAR OF WAKEFIELD

Shortly before his fortieth year Goldsmith's fortunes took a sudden turn for the better. His long poem, THE TRAVELER, was commended by the critics and purchased in quantity by the public.

THE DESERTED VILLAGE added both to his fame and popularity; its
charmingly drawn details and its highly quotable lines compen-
sated for certain basic blemishes. The incongruous mixture of
idealized description and faulty observation was criticized by a few;
the vivacious portraits, easy manner, the very didacticisms were
relished by the many.

The Village

Sweet Auburn! loveliest village of the plain;
Where health and plenty cheered the laboring swain,
Where smiling spring its earliest visit paid,
And parting summer's lingering blooms delayed:
Dear lovely bowers of innocence and ease,
Seats of my youth, when every sport could please,
How often have I loitered o'er thy green,
Where humble happiness endeared each scene!
How often have I paused on every charm,
The sheltered cot, the cultivated farm,
The never-failing brook, the busy mill,
The decent church that topped the neighboring hill,
The hawthorn bush, with seats beneath the shade,
For talking age and whispering lovers made!
How often have I blest the coming day,
When toil remitting lent its turn to play,
And all the village train, from labor free,
Led up their sports beneath the spreading tree,
While many a pastime circled in the shade,
The young contending as the old surveyed;
And many a gambol frolicked o'er the ground,
And sleights of art and feats of strength went round.
And still, as each repeated pleasure tired,
Succeeding sports the mirthful band inspired;
The dancing pair that simply sought renown,
By holding out to tire each other down;
The swain mistrustless of his smutted face,
While secret laughter tittered round the place;
The bashful virgin's side-long looks of love,
The matron's glance that would those looks reprove:
These were thy charms, sweet village! sports like these,
With sweet succession, taught even toil to please:
These round thy bowers their cheerful influence shed:
These were thy charms—but all these charms are fled.
                                    from THE DESERTED VILLAGE

The Village Schoolmaster

Beside yon straggling fence that skirts the way,
With blossomed furze unprofitably gay,
There, in his noisy mansion, skilled to rule,
The village master taught his little school;
A man severe he was, and stern to view;
I knew him well, and every truant knew:
Well had the boding tremblers learned to trace
The day's disasters in his morning face;
Full well they laughed, with counterfeited glee,
At all his jokes, for many a joke had he;
Full well the busy whisper, circling round,
Conveyed the dismal tidings when he frowned;
Yet he was kind, or, if severe in aught,
The love he bore to learning was in fault.
The village all declared how much he knew—
'Twas certain he could write, and cipher too;
Lands he could measure, terms and tides presage,
And e'en the story ran that he could gauge;
In arguing, too, the parson owned his skill,
For, e'en though vanquished, he could argue still,
While words of learnéd length and thundering sound
Amazed the gazing rustics ranged around;
And still they gazed, and still the wonder grew
That one small head could carry all he knew.

from THE DESERTED VILLAGE

The Village Preacher

Beside the bed where parting life was laid,
And sorrow, guilt, and pain by turns dismayed,
The reverend champion stood. At his control
Despair and anguish fled the struggling soul;
Comfort came down the trembling wretch to raise,
And his last faltering accents whispered praise.
At church, with meek and unaffected grace,
His looks adorned the venerable place;
Truth from his lips prevailed with double sway,
And fools, who came to scoff, remained to pray.
The service past, around the pious man,
With steady zeal, each honest rustic ran;
Even children followed with endearing wile,
And plucked his gown to share the good man's smile.

His ready smile a parent's warmth expressed—
Their welfare pleased him, and their cares distressed.
To them his heart, his love, his griefs were given,
But all his serious thoughts had rest in heaven.
As some tall cliff that lifts its awful form,
Swells from the vale, and midway leaves the storm,
Though round its breast the rolling clouds are spread,
Eternal sunshine settles on its head.

from THE DESERTED VILLAGE

In his forties Goldsmith turned from poetry to playwriting. THE GOOD-NATURED MAN was not well received, although Goldsmith benefited to the extent of five hundred pounds, but SHE STOOPS TO CONQUER became one of the most successful farces of the times. At forty-five Goldsmith was prosperous. But dissipation ruined him; he continued to gamble and lose. His health gave way. He doctored himself and, although he did not get well, attempted to procure a medical practice. When patients would not come, he excused himself by saying "I prescribe only for my friends," and was thereupon advised to prescribe only for his enemies. He grew worse under his own treatment. Finally, he called in professional assistance. One of the doctors asked him, "Is your mind at ease?" "No, it is not," replied Goldsmith, and died. He was scarcely forty-six on the day of his death, April 4, 1774.

WILLIAM COWPER

[1731–1800]

THE genealogy of William Cowper is no orderly array of progenitors. An ancestor, John Cooper, was an alderman of London in the sixteenth century. His mother, Anne Donne, belonged to the same family as the poet, John Donne. Cowper's father was rector of the parish of Great Berkhampstead, Hertfordshire, and chaplain to George II. But Cowper's grandfather, a judge of the Court of Common Pleas, was tried for murder and narrowly escaped the gallows.

Cowper seems to have inherited an unhappy mixture of sensitivity and insecurity; as he grew older he was oppressed with an increasing sense of guilt. He was bullied at school, attained a brief happiness at Westminster, and became a solicitor in his twenty-first year. At twenty-two he began to suffer from the depression which fastened upon him for the rest of his life. The feeling that he was hopelessly damned drove him insane, and when, in his thirty-second year, he was offered a clerkship to the House of Lords, he attempted suicide. He was thereupon sent to an asylum and remained there for eighteen months. From that time on he was cared for by various friends, chiefly by the Unwins. After Morley Unwin was thrown from his horse and killed, Cowper retired with Unwin's widow, Mary, to the village of Olney. Here he lived serenely for a while, nursed by the faithful Mary.

To Mary Unwin

Mary! I want a lyre with other strings,
Such aid from Heaven as some have feigned they drew,
An eloquence scarce given to mortals, new
And undebased by praise of meaner things;
That ere through age or woe I shed my wings,
I may record thy worth with honor due,
In verse as musical as thou art true,
And that immortalizes whom it sings:
But thou hast little need. There is a Book
By seraphs writ with beams of heavenly light,
On which the eyes of God not rarely look,
A chronicle of actions just and bright—
    There all thy deeds, my faithful Mary, shine;
    And since thou own'st that praise, I spare thee mine.

In his early forties Cowper became secretly engaged to Mary Unwin, but the contemplated marriage was interrupted by another breakdown. The derangement was serious, and there were several other attacks of mania. But Cowper survived them all until his seventieth year, when he died of dropsy.

In a beautifully written biography, which won the Hawthornden Prize in 1929, Lord David Cecil traced the course of Cowper's melancholy, the paradox of domesticity and insanity. Cecil entitled his biography THE STRICKEN DEER, and the appropriateness of the

title is marked by a "motto" taken from Cowper's long poem,
THE TASK:

> I was a stricken deer that left the herd
> Long since; with many an arrow deep infixt
> My panting side was charged, when I withdrew
> To seek a tranquil death in distant shades.

Curiously enough, Cowper's poetry is not disordered or even fanciful. Unlike Smart, who carried his spiritual excitement into his work, Cowper's verse is quiet and kindly, even sedate. Formal in pattern, it conveys an unobstrusive love for humanity, a sentiment which came to full flower in the nineteenth-century romantic poets. His one burst of high spirits, THE DIVERTING HISTORY OF JOHN GILPIN, is still to be found in collections of humor and light verse; but the subdued and natural lyrics are less popular. They are none the less notable for their simple, forthright tenderness.

The Poplar Field

> The poplars are felled, farewell to the shade
> And the whispering sound of the cool colonnade,
> The winds play no longer, and sing in the leaves,
> Nor Ouse on his bosom their image receives.
>
> Twelve years have elapsed since I first took a view
> Of my favorite field and the bank where they grew,
> And now in the grass behold they are laid,
> And the tree is my seat that once lent me a shade.
>
> The blackbird has fled to another retreat
> Where the hazels afford him a screen from the heat,
> And the scene where his melody charmed me before,
> Resounds with his sweet-flowing ditty no more.
>
> My fugitive years are all hasting away,
> And I must ere long lie as lowly as they,
> With a turf on my breast, and a stone at my head,
> Ere another such grove shall arise in its stead.
>
> 'Tis a sight to engage me, if any thing can,
> To muse on the perishing pleasures of man;
> Though his life be a dream, his enjoyments, I see,
> Have a being less durable even than he.

On the Loss of the Royal George

Toll for the brave!
  The brave that are no more!
All sunk beneath the wave,
  Fast by their native shore!

Eight hundred of the brave,
  Whose courage well was tried,
Had made the vessel heel,
  And laid her on her side.

A land-breeze shook the shrouds,
  And she was overset;
Down went the Royal George,
  With all her crew complete.

Toll for the brave!
  Brave Kempenfelt is gone;
His last sea-fight is fought;
  His work of glory done.

It was not in the battle;
  No tempest gave the shock;
She sprang no fatal leak;
  She ran upon no rock.

His sword was in its sheath;
  His fingers held the pen,
When Kempenfelt went down
  With twice four hundred men.

Weigh the vessel up,
  Once dreaded by our foes!
And mingle with our cup
  The tears that England owes.

Her timbers yet are sound,
  And she may float again
Full charged with England's thunder,
  And plough the distant main.

> But Kempenfelt is gone,
>   His victories are o'er;
> And he and his eight hundred
>   Shall plough the wave no more.

Busy as a country spinster with his pets, his greenhouse, and his garden, Cowper lived a gradual diminuendo. The writing was inevitably softened, pleasant rather than profound. Escaping from delusions of unfitness and manias of persecution, at Olney he lived a life that was an unreal idyl interrupted by real nightmares. It was here that Cowper wrote the devotional verses which appeared as the OLNEY HYMNS. Several of them still are Sunday familiars.

Light Shining Out of Darkness

> God moves in a mysterious way
>   His wonders to perform;
> He plants his footsteps in the sea,
>   And rides upon the storm.
>
> Deep in unfathomable mines,
>   With never-failing skill,
> He treasures up his bright designs,
>   And works his sovereign will.
>
> Ye fearful saints, fresh courage take;
>   The clouds ye so much dread
> Are big with mercy, and shall break
>   In blessings on your head.
>
> Judge not the Lord by feeble sense,
>   But trust him for his grace;
> Behind a frowning providence
>   He hides a smiling face.
>
> His purposes will ripen fast,
>   Unfolding every hour;
> The bud may have a bitter taste,
>   But sweet will be the flower.
>
> Blind unbelief is sure to err,
>   And scan his work in vain;
> God is his own interpreter,
>   And he will make it plain.

THOMAS CHATTERTON
[1752–1770]

Posthumous son of a dissipated schoolmaster, Thomas Chatterton was born at Bristol, November 20, 1752. His mother, little more than a child at the time of her husband's death, had hoped to be a singer; instead she became a dressmaker. At school Chatterton was considered a dull pupil; but, secretly and steadily, he began writing poems in his tenth year. He had access to a room of deeds and records in the church of St. Mary Redcliff, Bristol, and the boy familiarized himself with the old handwriting and archaic spelling. At the age of fourteen he prepared a pedigree for a Bristol pewterer, a Mr. Burgum, tracing the merchant's family back to the Norman Conquest. Chatterton accompanied the document with a poem entitled THE ROMAUNTE OF THE CNYGHTE, which he declared was written by John de Burgham, one of Burgum's ancestors. Both documents were forgeries.

At fifteen Chatterton seems to have fallen in love with a Miss Rumsey, but he was also intimate with a few Bristol girls who were less respectable. He wrote several poems to a Miss Hoyland at the request of one of his companions, but he was faithful only to the imaginary heroines of the fifteenth-century world in which he wanted to live. He was already bound apprentice to a Bristol attorney, but he paid little attention to office work. The church of St. Mary Redcliff, of which Chatterton's uncle had been sexton, contained many papers by and referring to Thomas Rowley, a priest. Shortly after his sixteenth birthday Chatterton wrote to Dodsley, the London publisher, offering to send him copies of certain valuable ancient manuscripts, "and an interlude, perhaps the oldest dramatic piece extant, wrote by one Rowley." He enclosed a "fragment" from the tragedy of ÆLLA and described the work: "the language spirited; the songs (interspersed in it) are flowing and elegantly simple; the similes judiciously applied, and, though wrote in the reign of Henry the VI not inferior to many of the present age." Dodsley was not interested. Chatterton next applied to Horace Walpole for help, but Walpole, after a little encouragement, was even more evasive than Dodsley.

Chatterton thereupon determined to go up to London and earn his living by the pen. He was not yet seventeen, but he wrote pieces imitating Smollett, Pope, and Gray; he composed eclogues and satires, political letters and librettos for operas, lyrics and elegies— a feverish industry of prose and verse. Overworked and under- nourished, he still managed to make more "transcriptions" of the Rowley "manuscripts," including the lengthy EXCELENTE BALADE OF CHARITIE.

Chatterton was often cold and always hungry, but he continued to write cheerfully to his mother; he went days without food in order to buy presents for her. He was living in a garret, and his landlady offered to return part of his rent. But he was too proud to accept the money, and said, pointing to his forehead, "I have that here which will get me more." His pride was profitless. Realiz- ing he could not live on poetry and recognizing his failure as a journalist, he tried to obtain a position on a ship trading to Africa. The appeal was not successful.

On August 24, 1770, his landlady, shocked at his haggard appear- ance and knowing he had been living all week on a stale loaf of bread, invited him to eat with her. He refused, saying he was not hungry. That night he went to the baker and asked for a fresh loaf on credit. When this was refused, he wheedled some arsenic from a friendly apothecary with the excuse that he wanted to rid his quarters of rats. Two days later, after no sounds had been heard in his room, the door was broken in, and his body was found. He was seventeen years and nine months old when he was interred as a pauper in the burying ground of Shoe Lane workhouse.

Nothing is known of Chatterton's method of composition. It is thought that he wrote his poems in ordinary English and then put them into archaic language with the help of glossaries and his imagination. Nor can the boy's character be traced from his work; his poetry is almost wholly objective. As objective poetry it bears the stamp of genius. The lyrics are haunting, the choruses excitingly inventive. The unfinished so-called ODE TO LIBERTY, with which GODDWYN concludes, has been ranked among the finest martial lyrics in the language.

Minstrel's Song

Oh! sing unto my roundelay;
   Oh! drop the briny tear with me;
Dance no more at holiday;
   Like a running river be.
     My love is dead,
     Gone to his death-bed,
     All under the willow-tree.

Black his hair as the winter night,
   White his skin as the summer snow,
Red his face as the morning light;
   Cold he lies in the grave below.
     My love is dead,
     Gone to his death-bed,
     All under the willow-tree.

Sweet his tongue as the throstle's note,
   Quick in dance as thought can be,
Deft his tabor, cudgel stout;
   Oh! he lies by the willow-tree.
     My love is dead,
     Gone to his death-bed,
     All under the willow-tree.

See! the white moon shines on high,
   Whiter is my true love's shroud,
Whiter than the morning sky,
   Whiter than the evening cloud.
     My love is dead,
     Gone to his death-bed,
     All under the willow-tree.

Come, with acorn-cup and thorn,
   Drain my own heart's blood away;
Life and all its good I scorn,
   Dance by night, or feast by day.
     My love is dead,
     Gone to his death-bed,
     All under the willow-tree.
          from ÆLLA

Song of the Three Minstrels

First Minstrel

The budding floweret blushes at the light,
The meads are sprinkled with the yellow hue;
In daisied mantles is the mountain dight,
The nesh [1] young cowslip bendeth with the dew;
The trees enleaféd, unto heaven straught,[2]
When gentle winds do blow, to whistling din are brought.

The evening comes, and brings the dew along;
The ruddy welkin shineth to the eyne;
Around the ale-stake minstrels sing the song,
Young ivy round the doorpost doth entwine;
I lay me on the grass; yet, to my will,
Albeit all is fair, there lacketh something still.

Second Minstrel

So Adam thought when once, in Paradise,
All heaven and earth did homage to his mind;
In woman only mannes pleasure lies,
As instruments of joy are those of kind.
Go, take a wife unto thine arms, and see
Winter, and barren hills, will have a charm for thee.

Third Minstrel

When Autumn bleak and sunburnt doth appear,
With his gold hand gilding the falling leaf,
Bringing up Winter to fulfil the year,
Bearing upon his back the ripened sheaf,
When all the hills with woody seed are white,
When lightning-fires and lemes [3] do meet from far the sight;

When the fair apples, red as evening sky,
Do bend the tree unto the fruitful ground,
When juicy pears, and berries of black dye,
Do dance in air and call the eyes around,
Then, be the evening foul or be it fair,
Methinks my hartys joy is steyncéd [4] with some care.

[1] *Tender.*   [2] *Stretched.*   [3] *Gleams.*   [4] *Mingled.*

Second Minstrel

Angels are wrought to be of neither kind,
Angels alone from hot desire are free;
There is a somewhat ever in the mind
That, without woman, cannot stilléd be.
No saint in cell but, having blood and tere,[5]
Do find the sprite [6] to joy in sight of woman fair.

from ÆLLA

Ode to Liberty

When Freedom, dressed in bloodstained vest,
To every knight her war-song sung,
Upon her head wild weeds were spread
A gory sword-blade by her hung.
She dancéd on the heath,
She heard the voice of death.

Pale-eyed Affright, his heart of silver hue,
In vain assailed her bosom to acale.[1]
She heard, unmoved, the shrieking voice of woe,
And sadness in the owlet shake the dale,
She shook the arméd spear,
On high she raised her shield;
Her foemen all appear,
And fly along the field.

Power, with heasod straught [2] into the skies,
His spear a sunbeam and his shield a star;
Alike two flaming meteors rolls his eyes,
Stamps with his iron feet, and sounds to war.
She sits upon a rock,
She bends before his spear,
She rises from the shock,
Wielding her own in air.

Hard as the thunder doth she drive it on;
Wit, closely mantled, guides it to his crown;
His long sharp spear, his spreading shield is gone.
He falls, and, falling, rolleth thousands down.

[5] *Muscle.*   [6] *Spirit.*   [1] *Chill.*   [2] *Head stretched.*

War, gore-faced War, by Envy armed, arist,[3]
His fiery helmet nodding to the air,
Ten bloody arrows in his straining fist!
                              from GODDWYN

A monument was erected to his memory by Bristol citizens in Redcliff churchyard. It carries a few lines from Chatterton's "Will": "Reader, judge not. If thou art a Christian, believe that he shall be judged by a Superior Power. To that Power only is he now answerable." But Chatterton had already paid his "respects" to the abhorred city of his birth in his LAST VERSES, written the night he committed suicide.

Last Verses

Farewell, Bristolia's dingy piles of brick,
Lovers of mammon, worshippers of trick!
Ye spurned the boy who gave you antique lays,
And paid for learning with your empty praise.
Farewell, ye guzzling aldermanic fools,
By nature fitted for corruption's tools!
I go to where celestial anthems swell;
But you, when you depart, will sink to hell.
Farewell, my mother!—cease, my anguished soul,
Nor let distraction's billows o'er me roll!
Have mercy, Heaven! when here I cease to live,
And this last act of wretchedness forgive.

*

The first American poet of any consequence was a woman, Anne Bradstreet. Daughter of one governor and wife of another, Anne Dudley was born in England in 1612. Her father had soldiered in the Thirty Years' War, had joined a party of refugees who sailed for Massachusetts, and had brought with him his eighteen-year-old daughter who was already married to Simon Bradstreet. She bore her husband eight children, attended to the details of a large farmhouse, and filled her sixty years with energetic creation. When her first collection of poetry was published in 1650, a year after Charles I had been beheaded, she was hailed as "The Tenth Muse, Lately Sprung up in America." Cotton Mather went further. He made

3 *Arisen.*

comparisons (in Mrs. Bradstreet's favor) to all the learned women of antiquity from Hypatia to the Empress Eudocia, and concluded that room must now be given "unto Madam Anne Bradstreet, the daughter of our Governor Dudley and the consort of our Governor Bradstreet, whose poems have afforded a grateful entertainment unto the ingenious and a monument for her memory beyond the stateliest marbles." But, although Mrs. Bradstreet was a serious poet, her importance is only historical. Her verse was painstakingly unoriginal, written under the influence of Quarles, Lyly, and other Euphuists. Her outer self was adjusted to the life of New England, but her spirit yearned for the quiet English library, where she could read, absorb, and imitate pedantic verses devoted chiefly to metrical theology.

The Colonial period passed with small literary distinction, and it was not until the Revolution that there emerged the first genuinely American poet, Philip Freneau.

PHILIP FRENEAU
[1752–1832]

BORN January 2, 1752, of French Huguenot stock, his grandfather having come to America in 1707, Philip Freneau attended Princeton. Upon graduation he engaged in activities that were as impulsive as they were short-lived. He taught in Long Island, but abandoned teaching within two weeks. He became a pamphleteer in New York, emigrated to the West Indies, and was captured in 1780, at which time he was confined on a British prison ship.

After the Revolutionary War, Freneau edited THE FREEMAN'S JOURNAL and flourished in controversy. Washington referred to him as "that rascal, Freneau." In his late forties he became master of a merchant ship, lost his money, and retired to a small farm in New Jersey. Drink seems to have been his one consolation. His constitution remained tough, although his tippling increased. One night in his eightieth year Freneau left his favorite tavern during a snowstorm, insisting that he wanted to walk home alone. Next morning he was found dying of exposure a few feet from his door.

Freneau was the first American poet to express the philosophy of his day. Most of his poetry has perished, but a few of the lyrics still hold the reader by their felicity of phrase. THE INDIAN STUDENT, unfortunately too long to quote, is typical of Freneau's verse in which the wild woods and wild spirits have come to terms. And THE WILD HONEYSUCKLE is one of the first as well as one of the finest nature lyrics produced in the New World.

The Wild Honeysuckle

Fair flower, that dost so comely grow,
Hid in this silent, dull retreat,
Untouched thy honied blossoms blow,
Unseen thy little branches greet:
   No roving foot shall crush thee here,
   No busy hand provoke a tear.

By Nature's self in white arrayed,
She bade thee shun the vulgar eye;
And planted here the guardian shade,
And sent soft waters murmuring by;
   Thus quietly thy summer goes,
   Thy days declining to repose.

Smit with those charms, that must decay,
I grieve to see your future doom;
They died—nor were those flowers more gay,
The flowers that did in Eden bloom;
   Unpitying frosts, and Autumn's power
   Shall leave no vestige of this flower.

From morning suns and evening dews
At first thy little being came:
If nothing once, you nothing lose,
For when you die you are the same;
   The space between is but an hour,
   The frail duration of a flower.

GEORGE CRABBE
[1754–1832]

THE story of Crabbe's life is a history of victorious struggle, and an account of his work is a tangle of contradictions. Son of a customs officer at Aldeburgh, Suffolk, the boy spent his early life in a warehouse. Hoping to be a doctor, Crabbe became a druggist's apprentice, then a surgeon's assistant, then a midwife. While he was studying, he worked as a day laborer at Aldeburgh. At twenty-six he became an object of charity. A local philanthropist gave him five pounds so that he might make his way in London.

Crabbe took many manuscripts with him to the metropolis; after reading them, Edmund Burke advised Crabbe to enter the church. Nothing loath, Crabbe was ordained at twenty-seven and returned to Aldeburgh as a curate. But the villagers, if not openly hostile, scarcely respected the man who had lately been doing day labor, and Crabbe was unhappy in his own home. At Burke's solicitation the Duke of Rutland rescued him and established him in Dorsetshire. Here Crabbe wrote THE VILLAGE, which, with its unflattering pictures, was a realistic rebuke to the romanticism of Goldsmith's THE DESERTED VILLAGE. Scott was so impressed with it that he recited the whole poem from memory ten years after he first read it. Befriended and admired, Crabbe ended his days in comfort and died in his seventy-ninth year.

Commended by the critics, Crabbe was almost unread by the public. His realism seems to have been too harsh, too relentless, for the general reader. Neglected by most anthologists, Crabbe, by his persistent honesty, has somehow survived. Thomas Hardy confessed that he could not have written his novels had it not been for THE VILLAGE. More than a hundred years after the publication of that work, the American poet Edwin Arlington Robinson praised the author's "plain excellence and stubborn skill." Conceding Crabbe's unpopularity—"Give him the darkest inch your shelf allows; Hide him in lonely garrets, if you will"—Robinson concluded:

> Whether or not we read him, we can feel
> From time to time the vigor of his name
> Against us like a finger for the shame

And emptiness of what our souls reveal
In books that are as altars where we kneel
To consecrate the flicker, not the flame.

Crabbe's utterance is low, but it is not dull. It still throbs with
unashamed truth and the "hard human pulse."

Late Wisdom

We've trod the maze of error round,
    Long wandering in the winding glade;
And now the torch of truth is found,
    It only shows us where we strayed:

By long experience taught, we now
    Can rightly judge of friends and foes;
Can all the worth of these allow,
    And all their faults discern in those.

Relentless hatred, erring love,
    We can for sacred truth forgo;
We can the warmest friend reprove,
    And bear to praise the fiercest foe:

To what effect? Our friends are gone
    Beyond reproof, regard or care;
And of our foes remains there one
    The mild relenting thoughts to share?

Now 'tis our boast that we can quell
    The wildest passions in their rage;
Can their destructive force repel,
    And their impetuous wrath assuage.

Ah! Virtue, dost thou arm, when now
    This bold rebellious race are fled;
When all these tyrants rest, and thou
    Art warring with the mighty dead?

The Whistling Boy

The whistling boy that holds the plough
  Lured by the tale that soldiers tell,
Resolves to part, yet knows not how
  To leave the land he loves so well.
He now rejects the thought, and now
  Looks o'er the lea, and sighs "Farewell!"

"Farewell!" the pensive maiden cries.
  Who dreams of London, dreams awake—
But when her favorite lad she spies,
  With whom she loved her way to take,
Then doubts within her soul arise,
  And equal hopes her bosom shake.

Thus, like the boy, and like the maid,
  I wish to go, yet tarry here,
And now resolved, and now afraid:
  To minds disturbed old views appear
In melancholy charms arrayed,
  And once, indifferent, now are dear.
How shall I go, my fate to learn—
And, oh! how taught shall I return?

XI

Pure Vision, Pure Song

WILLIAM BLAKE
[1757–1827]

WHEN William Blake was four years old he screamed because
he saw God put his forehead against the window. At eight,
when he was walking in the fields, he beheld "a tree filled with
angels, bright angelic wings bespangling every bough with stars."
Even the year of his birth was prophetic. Swedenborg, whose mysti-
cal philosophy was an answer to eighteenth-century rationalism,
had predicted that the old world would end and a new one begin
in the year 1757.

Blake's gift of vision may have seemed strange in the London
hosiery shop which was his home; but his father was of Irish de-
scent, and the family were Swedenborgians. Blake was never sent
to school. Apprenticed as a child to an engraver, he found his own
way into art and literature. Between his twelfth and twentieth year
he wrote a series of poems as amazing as anything in English litera-
ture. Seemingly imitative of his predecessors, and in particular of
the Elizabethan and Jacobean song writers, he surpassed all but
the very greatest in his youthful POETICAL SKETCHES. Such poems as
the SONG: "How sweet I roamed from field to field," reputedly writ-
ten before Blake was fourteen, the SONG: "My silks and fine array,"
TO THE EVENING STAR, and TO THE MUSES carry on the tradition of
English lyrics. But they add a new purity; they enrich the language
with unexplainable perfection. These early poems may be re-exam-
ined as a "bridge" between the Elizabethan Renaissance and the

Romantic Revival of Wordsworth, Shelley, and Keats; but their glory is their own, a miraculous mingling of quiet beauty and breathless ecstasy.

Song: How Sweet I Roamed

How sweet I roamed from field to field
    And tasted all the summer's pride,
Till I the prince of love beheld
    Who in the sunny beams did glide!

He showed me lilies for my hair,
    And blushing roses for my brow;
He led me through his gardens fair
    Where all his golden pleasures grow.

With sweet May dews my wings were wet,
    And Phoebus fired my vocal rage;
He caught me in his silken net,
    And shut me in his golden cage.

He loves to sit and hear me sing,
    Then, laughing, sports and plays with me;
Then stretches out my golden wing,
    And mocks my loss of liberty.

Song: My Silks and Fine Array

My silks and fine array,
    My smiles and languished air,
By love are driven away;
    And mournful lean Despair
Brings me yew to deck my grave;
Such end true lovers have.

His face is fair as heaven
    When springing buds unfold;
Oh, why to him was't given,
    Whose heart is wintry cold?
His breast is love's all-worshiped tomb
Where all love's pilgrims come.

Bring me an axe and spade,
  Bring me a winding-sheet;
When I my grave have made,
  Let winds and tempests beat:
Then down I'll lie, as cold as clay.
True love doth pass away!

Mad Song

The wild winds weep,
And the night is a-cold;
Come hither, Sleep,
And my griefs unfold:
But lo! the morning peeps
Over the eastern steeps,
And the rustling birds of dawn
The earth do scorn.

Lo! to the vault
Of pavéd heaven,
With sorrow fraught
My notes are driven:
They strike the ear of night,
Make weep the eyes of day;
They make mad the roaring winds,
And with tempests play.

Like a fiend in a cloud,
With howling woe
After night I do crowd,
And with night will go;
I turn my back to the east
From whence comforts have increased;
For light doth seize my brain
With frantic pain.

To the Evening Star

Thou fair-haired angel of the evening,
Now, whilst the sun rests on the mountains, light
Thy bright torch of love; thy radiant crown
Put on, and smile upon our evening bed!

Smile on our loves, and, while thou drawest the
Blue curtains of the sky, scatter thy silver dew
On every flower that shuts its sweet eyes
In timely sleep. Let thy west wind sleep on
The lake; speak silence with thy glimmering eyes,
And wash the dusk with silver. Soon, full soon,
Dost thou withdraw; then the wolf rages wide,
And the lion glares through the dun forest:
The fleeces of our flocks are covered with
Thy sacred dew: protect them with thine influence.

To the Muses

Whether on Ida's shady brow,
  Or in the chambers of the East,
The chambers of the sun that now
  From ancient melody have ceased;

Whether in Heaven ye wander fair,
  Or the green corners of the earth,
Or the blue regions of the air,
  Where the melodious winds have birth;

Whether on crystal rocks ye rove,
  Beneath the bosom of the sea
Wandering in many a coral grove,
  Fair Nine, forsaking Poetry;

How have you left the ancient love
  That bards of old enjoyed in you!
The languid strings do scarcely move;
  The sound is forced, the notes are few!

In his twenty-sixth year Blake married Catherine Boucher, daugh-
ter of a market gardener, a beautiful girl with a natural talent for
drawing but with no education. Unable to read or write, she signed
her mark in the marriage register when, at twenty-one, she became
Blake's wife. Nevertheless, theirs was a true marriage, even though
she once complained, "I have very little of Mr. Blake's company.
He is always in Paradise."

At thirty-two Blake issued his SONGS OF INNOCENCE. These lyrics
had been written in his twenties; Blake, with the help of his wife,

issued them in a form unique in the history of printing. The poems were not printed, but drawn in varnish with marginal designs upon metal plates. The plates were plunged in acid baths, the parts not covered by the varnish were eaten away, and the letters and designs stood out like engravings. Blake and his wife then colored them variously, sometimes embellishing them with gold. With one exception, all of Blake's books were so prepared, and his industry becomes the more remarkable when it is remembered that, in order to appear correctly to the reader, all the words had to be written backward.

With the SONGS OF INNOCENCE Blake leaves the tradition and makes a tradition of his own. He exchanges charm for divination, discards dependable stereotypes for burning symbols. Though he appears to speak as an artless child—hence his title—his poetry approaches a central subject. It becomes his ever-growing theme: the destiny of the human spirit. The objects of the visible world are still seen with the eye of the imagination; experience has not yet disturbed the naïveté. Wonder, independent of maturity, has its own wisdom.

Introduction

Piping down the valleys wild,
Piping songs of pleasant glee,
On a cloud I saw a child,
And he laughing said to me:

"Pipe a song about a Lamb!"
So I piped with merry cheer.
"Piper, pipe that song again";
So I piped: he wept to hear.

"Drop thy pipe, thy happy pipe;
Sing thy songs of happy cheer":
So I sang the same again,
While he wept with joy to hear.

"Piper, sit thee down and write
In a book, that all may read."
So he vanished from my sight,
And I plucked a hollow reed,

And I made a rural pen,
And I stained the water clear,
And I wrote my happy songs
Every child may joy to hear.

The Lamb

Little Lamb, who made thee?
Dost thou know who made thee;
Gave thee life and bid thee feed
By the stream and o'er the mead;
Gave thee clothing of delight,
Softest clothing, woolly, bright;
Gave thee such a tender voice
Making all the vales rejoice?
Little Lamb, who made thee?
Dost thou know who made thee?

Little Lamb, I'll tell thee,
Little Lamb, I'll tell thee:
He is called by thy name,
For He calls Himself a Lamb.
He is meek and He is mild;
He became a little child.
I a child and thou a lamb,
We are called by His name.
Little Lamb, God bless thee.
Little Lamb, God bless thee.

The Little Black Boy

My mother bore me in the southern wild,
And I am black, but O! my soul is white;
White as an angel is the English child,
But I am black, as if bereaved of light.

My mother taught me underneath a tree,
And, sitting down before the heat of day,
She took me on her lap and kisséd me,
And, pointing to the east, began to say:

"Look on the rising sun—there God does live,
And gives his light, and gives his heat away;
And flowers and trees and beasts and men receive
Comfort in morning, joy in the noon day.

"And we are put on earth a little space,
That we may learn to bear the beams of love;
And these black bodies and this sunburnt face
Is but a cloud, and like a shady grove.

"For when our souls have learned the heat to bear,
The cloud will vanish, we shall hear his voice,
Saying: 'Come out from the grove, my love and care,
And round my golden tent like lambs rejoice.' "

Thus did my mother say, and kisséd me;
And thus I say to little English boy.
When I from black, and he from white cloud free,
And round the tent of God like lambs we joy,

I'll shade him from the heat, till he can bear
To lean in joy upon our father's knee;
And then I'll stand and stroke his silver hair,
And be like him, and he will then love me.

Blake worked in a fury of creation. He wrote, engraved, and illuminated a series of prophetic books in prose and verse—THE BOOK OF THEL, TIRIEL, the MARRIAGE OF HEAVEN AND HELL, and THE FRENCH REVOLUTION all appeared before Blake was thirty-three. He supported himself by the sale of engravings and his own books; the handmade SONGS OF INNOCENCE and SONGS OF EXPERIENCE were bound together and offered for one pound. He illustrated volumes by other writers, painted in various mediums with an exactitude and exaltation reminiscent of Michelangelo's, and expressed himself so lavishly that much of his work is still being unearthed. Twenty-eight illustrations for THE PILGRIM'S PROGRESS, stowed away for more than a century, were published by The Limited Editions Club as late as 1941. It has never been decided whether Blake was primarily a painter who wrote poetry or a poet who translated his metaphors into pigments.

Five years after the SONGS OF INNOCENCE, Blake issued his SONGS OF EXPERIENCE. This collection is more than a sequel; it is a fully orchestrated statement of what, in the earlier volume, was an emerg-

ing theme. In SONGS OF INNOCENCE Blake, like Vaughan and Tra-
herne, was content to hymn the happiness of a child's world. But a
growing consciousness recognizes that the child must leave its Eden
and struggle with a world that has lost its Paradise. Evil must be
recognized and understood. To deny it is futile, to fight it is vain;
it must be joined to goodness and merged with it. This is Blake's
philosophy, a continual union of opposites: the fusion of innocence
and experience, good and evil, flesh and spirit, the marriage of
heaven and hell. Blake balances one demand against another. In
THE CLOD AND THE PEBBLE, he symbolizes impartially the surrender
of the self-sacrificing and the rights of the frankly selfish.

The Clod and the Pebble

"Love seeketh not itself to please,
  Nor for itself hath any care,
But for another gives its ease,
  And builds a heaven in hell's despair."

So sung a little clod of clay,
  Trodden with the cattle's feet;
But a pebble of the brook
  Warbled out these meters meet:

"Love seeketh only Self to please,
  To bind another to its delight,
Joys in another's loss of ease,
  And builds a hell in heaven's despite."

In the SONGS OF EXPERIENCE Blake wrote with an enthusiasm
which is almost fanatic; he was, says Arthur Symons, "drunk with
intellectual vision." Blake trusted that vision with complete con-
sistency. "Imagination," he wrote, "is the divine vision, not of the
world, nor of man, nor from man as he is a natural man, but only
as he is a spiritual man. Imagination has nothing to do with mem-
ory." It is the sheer daring of the imagination that can pit the
tiger ("experience") against the lamb ("innocence") and find both
equally beautiful, equally framed by the "immortal hand and eye."

The Tyger

Tyger! Tyger! burning bright
In the forests of the night,
What immortal hand or eye
Could frame thy fearful symmetry?

In what distant deeps or skies
Burnt the fire of thine eyes?
On what wings dare he aspire?
What the hand dare seize the fire?

And what shoulder, and what art,
Could twist the sinews of thy heart?
And when thy heart began to beat,
What dread hand? and what dread feet?

What the hammer? what the chain?
In what furnace was thy brain?
What the anvil? what dread grasp
Dare its deadly terrors clasp?

When the stars threw down their spears
And watered heaven with their tears,
Did he smile his work to see?
Did he who made the Lamb make thee?

Tyger! Tyger! burning bright
In the forests of the night,
What immortal hand or eye
Dare frame thy fearful symmetry?

The Fly

Little Fly,
Thy summer's play
My thoughtless hand
Has brushed away.

Am not I
A fly like thee?
Or art not thou
A man like me?

For I dance
And drink and sing,
Till some blind hand
Shall brush my wing.

If thought is life
And strength and breath,
And the want
Of thought is death,

Then am I
A happy fly
If I live
Or if I die.

The Sunflower

Ah, Sunflower! weary of time,
Who countest the steps of the Sun,
Seeking after that sweet golden clime
Where the traveler's journey is done:

Where the Youth pined away with desire,
And the pale Virgin shrouded in snow,
Arise from their graves, and aspire
Where my Sunflower wishes to go.

The Sick Rose

O rose, thou art sick:
The invisible worm
That flies in the night,
In the howling storm,

Has found out thy bed
Of crimson joy,
And his dark secret love
Does thy life destroy.

A Poison Tree

I was angry with my friend:
I told my wrath, my wrath did end.
I was angry with my foe:
I told it not, my wrath did grow.

And I watered it in fears
Night and morning with my tears,
And I sunnéd it with smiles
And with soft deceitful wiles.

And it grew both day and night,
Till it bore an apple bright,
And my foe beheld it shine,
And he knew that it was mine—

And into my garden stole
When the night had veiled the pole;
In the morning, glad, I see
My foe outstretched beneath the tree.

Love's Secret

Never seek to tell thy love,
   Love that never told can be;
For the gentle wind does move
   Silently, invisibly.

I told my love, I told my love,
   I told her all my heart;
Trembling, cold, in ghastly fears,
   Ah! she did depart!

Soon as she was gone from me,
   A traveler came by,
Silently, invisibly:
   He took her with a sigh.

   Although Blake was pre-eminently a mystic whose poems exist on more than one plane of meaning, his thinking was not blurred. His mind was as sharp as it was independent; he challenged dictates in art with the same fierceness that he questioned religious doctrines.

Physically courageous—he beat a huge drayman who was discourteous to women, and drove a Royal Dragoon out of his garden—he was intellectually brave enough to attack every fashionable idol of the period. Joshua Reynolds was the chief English painter of his day, founder of the Society of British Artists and, later, president of the Royal Academy. This did not deter Blake from writing, "His [Reynolds'] softness and candor [are] the hidden trap and the poisoned feast. He praises Michelangelo for qualities which Michelangelo abhorred, and blames Raphael for the only qualities which Raphael valued."

Blake's bitter and sarcastic side is usually glossed over, but many of his gnomic verses and epigrams serious and satirical are as Blakelike as his transcendental lyrics.

Gnomic Verses

Great things are done when men and mountains meet;
This is not done by jostling in the street.

*

They said this mystery shall never cease:
The priest promotes war, and the soldier peace.

*

He has observed the golden rule
Till he's become the golden fool.

*

Abstinence sows sand all over
The ruddy limbs and flaming hair;
But Desire gratified
Plants fruits of life and beauty there.

*

The sword sang on the barren heath,
   The sickle in the fruitful field:
The sword he sang a song of death,
   But could not make the sickle yield.

*

The Angel that presided o'er my birth
Said, "Little creature, formed of joy and mirth,
Go, love without the help of anything on earth."

Riches

The countless gold of a merry heart,
The rubies and pearls of a loving eye,
The indolent never can bring to the mart,
Nor the secret hoard up in his treasury.

To Hayley

Thy friendship oft has made my heart to ache:
Do be my enemy—for friendship's sake.

Mockery

Mock on, mock on, Voltaire, Rousseau;
Mock on, mock on; 'tis all in vain.
You throw the sand against the wind,
And the wind blows it back again.

And every sand becomes a gem
Reflected in the beams divine;
Blown back they blind the mocking eye,
But still in Israel's path they shine.

Eternity

He who binds [1] to himself a Joy
Doth the wingéd life destroy;
But he who kisses the Joy as it flies
Lives in Eternity's sunrise.

Perhaps Blake's most famous as well as most far-reaching lines
are the opening quatrain of AUGURIES OF INNOCENCE. The poem
itself is a long set of proverbs, a series of jottings rather than an

[1] *Almost all collections perpetuate the error of printing "binds" as "bends,"
which is neither what Blake wrote nor meant.*

ordered sequence. Various editors have rearranged the couplets so that the poem may be read as a continuing whole, and the condensed version here printed is another such rearrangement. Some of the statements are obscure, some are immediately compelling; in their cumulative effect they extend the epigrams into a glory of revelation.

Auguries of Innocence

To see a world in a grain of sand
And a Heaven in a wild flower,
Hold Infinity in the palm of your hand
And Eternity in an hour.

A robin redbreast in a cage
Puts all Heaven in a rage.
A dove-house filled with doves and pigeons
Shudders Hell through all its regions.
A dog starved at his master's gate
Predicts the ruin of the state.
A horse misused upon the road
Calls to Heaven for human blood.
Each outcry of the hunted hare
A fibre from the brain does tear.
A skylark wounded in the wing,
A cherubim does cease to sing.
The game cock clipped and armed for fight
Does the rising sun affright.
Every wolf's and lion's howl
Raises from Hell a human soul.
The wild deer wandering here and there
Keeps the human soul from care.
The lamb misused breeds public strife
And yet forgives the butcher's knife.
The bat that flits at close of eve
Has left the brain that won't believe.
The owl that calls upon the night
Speaks the unbeliever's fright.

He who shall hurt the little wren
Shall never be beloved by men.
He who the ox to wrath had moved
Shall never be by woman loved.

The wanton boy that kills the fly
Shall feel the spider's enmity.
He who torments the chafer's sprite
Weaves a bower in endless night.

The caterpillar on the leaf
Repeats to thee thy mother's grief.
Kill not the moth nor butterfly
For the Last Judgment draweth nigh.

He who mocks the infant's faith
Shall be mocked in Age and Death.
He who shall teach the child to doubt
The rotting grave shall ne'er get out.
He who respects the infant's faith
Triumphs over Hell and Death.

The child's toys and the old man's reasons
Are the fruits of the two seasons.
The questioner who sits so sly
Shall never know how to reply.

He who doubts from what he sees
Will ne'er believe, do what you please.
If the sun and moon should doubt,
They'd immediately go out.

To be in a passion you good may do,
But no good if a passion is in you.

The whore and gambler, by the state
Licenced, build that nation's fate.
The harlot's cry from street to street
Shall weave Old England's winding sheet.
The winner's shout, the loser's curse,
Dance before dead England's hearse.

Every night and every morn
Some to misery are born.
Every morn and every night
Some are born to sweet delight.
Some are born to sweet delight,
Some are born to endless night.

We are led to believe a lie
When we see *with,* not *through,* the eye,
Which was born in a night, to perish in a night,
When the soul slept in beams of light.

God appears, and God is Light
To those poor souls who dwell in night,
But does a human form display
To those who dwell in realms of day.

Subsisting on a level a little above poverty, unrecognized by his contemporaries, Blake filled his seventy years with relentless creation. One purpose impelled his energy: the regeneration of man. The intensity of his belief animated every piece of prose and verse, every drawing, engraving, and water color; he invented a whole mythology to expound it. Some of Blake's work is charged with clear meaning; some of it is too clairvoyant for immediate comprehension. But his poetry is so often unadulterated that, as A. E. Housman wrote, "Nothing except poetic emotion is perceived and matters." One editor after another has attempted to explore Blake's mind and explain the man. But the depths are always just beyond in this "most poetical of all poets," and Blake remains unfathomable, as pure as he is inexplicable.

To the Accuser Who Is the God of This World

Truly, my Satan, thou art but a dunce,
And dost not know the garment from the man;
Every harlot was a virgin once,
Nor canst thou ever change Kate into Nan.

Tho' thou art worshiped by the names divine
Of Jesus and Jehovah, thou art still
The Son of Morn in weary Night's decline,
The lost traveller's dream under the hill.
Epilogue to THE GATES OF PARADISE

A New Jerusalem

And did those feet in ancient time
Walk upon England's mountains green?
And was the Holy Lamb of God
On England's pleasant pastures seen?

And did the countenance divine
Shine forth upon our clouded hills?
And was Jerusalem builded here
Among these dark satanic mills?

Bring me my bow of burning gold!
Bring me my arrows of desire!
Bring me my spear! O clouds, unfold!
Bring me my chariot of fire!

I will not cease from mental fight,
Nor shall my sword sleep in my hand,
Till we have built Jerusalem
In England's green and pleasant land.

from MILTON

ROBERT BURNS

[1759-1796]

A PLOWMAN and the son of a plowman, Robert Burns was born at Alloway, in Ayrshire, Scotland, January 25, 1759. With his own hands, his father had built the clay cottage which was the poet's early home—two small rooms, with a concealed bed in the kitchen—and young Burns spent his youth on the farm. He managed to get some schooling; he discovered Shakespeare and Pope, but all he knew of Latin, as he gallantly confessed to a lady, was *Omnia vincit amor.* "At the plow, scythe, or reap hook, I feared no competitor," he wrote, "but I spent the evenings after my own heart. . . . To the sons and daughters of labor and poverty, the ardent hope, the stolen interview, the tender farewell, are the greatest and most delicious enjoyments."

It was with "the sons and daughters of labor and poverty" that Burns spent his youth, and his straightforward melodies speak not only to them but for them. He was, first and last, a people's poet because he was most at home with the common folk, with farmers in the field, companions at an inn, complaisant girls, rowdy countrymen, beggars, and bawdy fellows. Burns fell in love at fourteen, and, seemingly, never fell out of it; consistently a lover, he was inconstant only to the objects of his affection. When he was in his twenty-sixth year Jean Armour confessed that she was with child by Burns, and he promised to marry her by Scottish law. But her family would have none of the young farmer; and, though Jean gave birth to twins and Burns acknowledged the paternity, he became engaged to Mary Campbell ("Highland Mary"), who died in childbirth a month after Jean Armour's twins were born. After Jean had borne him two more children, he married her in his twenty-ninth year.

The poems Burns wrote to Jean Armour are among his loveliest, but he celebrated his other amours with equal fervor. He welcomed his illegitimate children in verse that was much deeper than bravado, but he never ceased to exult in the triumphs of the flesh. Few love songs present a greater contrast than the expression of constancy in the famous poems to Jean and Mary, and the joy of incontinence in the poem to the barmaid Anne Parker, whose child Jean brought up with her own. Burns spoke of the latter poem as "the best love song I ever composed in my life, though it is not quite a lady's song."

Jean

Of a' the airts the wind can blaw,
    I dearly like the west,
For there the bonie lassie lives,
    The lassie I lo'e best:
There's wild woods grow, and rivers row,
    And mony a hill between;
But day and night my fancy's flight
    Is ever wi' my Jean.

I see her in the dewy flowers,
   I see her sweet and fair:
I hear her in the tunefu' birds,
   I hear her charm the air:
There's not a bonie flower that springs
   By fountain, shaw, or green,
There's not a bonie bird that sings,
   But minds me o' my Jean.

Highland Mary

Ye banks and braes and streams around
   The castle o' Montgomery,
Green be your woods, and fair your flowers,
   Your waters never drumlie! [1]
There simmer first unfauld her robes,
   And there the langest tarry;
For there I took the last fareweel
   O' my sweet Highland Mary.

How sweetly bloomed the gay green birk,
   How rich the hawthorn's blossom,
As underneath their fragrant shade
   I clasped her to my bosom!
The golden hours on angel wings
   Flew o'er me and my dearie;
For dear to me as light and life
   Was my sweet Highland Mary.

Wi' monie a vow and locked embrace
   Our parting was fu' tender;
And, pledging aft to meet again,
   We tore ourselves asunder;
But oh! fell Death's untimely frost,
   That nipped my flower sae early!
Now green's the sod, and cauld's the clay,
   That wraps my Highland Mary!

O pale, pale now, those rosy lips
   I aft hae kissed sae fondly!
And closed for aye the sparkling glance
   That dwelt on me sae kindly!

[1] *Muddy.*

And mold'ring now in silent dust,
That heart that lo'ed me dearly!
But still within my bosom's core
Shall live my Highland Mary.

Anna

Yestreen I had a pint o' wine,
A place where body saw na;
Yestreen lay on this breast o' mine
The gowden locks of Anna.

The hungry Jew in wilderness,
Rejoicing o'er his manna,
Was naething to my hinnie [1] bliss
Upon the lips of Anna.

Ye monarchs, take the East and West
Frae Indus to Savannah;
Gie me, within my straining grasp,
The melting form of Anna.

There I'll despise imperial charms,
An empress or sultana,
While dying raptures in her arms
I give and take wi' Anna!

Awa, thou flaunting God of Day!
Awa, thou pale Diana!
Ilk star, gae hide thy twinkling ray,
When I'm to meet my Anna!

Come, in thy raven plumage, night
(Sun, moon, and stars, withdrawn a');
And bring an angel-pen to write
My transports wi' my Anna!

The Kirk an' State may join, an' tell
To do sic things I maunna: [2]
The Kirk an' State may gae to hell,
And I'll gae to my Anna.

Burns's many loves produced many lyrics, some of them among
the most spontaneous in the language. They range from the lightly

[1] *Honey.*   [2] *Should not.*

erotic to the deeply poignant, yet all are distinguished by an inno-
cent candor, an inspired simplicity. Some of Burns's lines had their
origins in folk tunes; but, as James Douglas wrote, "It is not easy
to tell where the vernacular ends and the personal magic begins.
Burns ennobled his larcenies and glorified his thefts."

My Luve

O my luve is like a red, red rose,
    That's newly sprung in June:
O my luve is like the melodie,
    That's sweetly played in tune.

As fair art thou, my bonie lass,
    So deep in luve am I;
And I will luve thee still, my dear,
    Till a' the seas gang dry.

Till a' the seas gang dry, my dear,
    And the rocks melt wi' the sun:
And I will luve thee still, my dear,
    While the sands o' life shall run.

And fare thee weel, my only luve!
    And fare thee weel a while!
And I will come again, my luve,
    Tho' it were ten thousand mile.

O Wert Thou in the Cauld Blast

O wert thou in the cauld blast,
    On yonder lea, on yonder lea,
My plaidie to the angry airt,
    I'd shelter thee, I'd shelter thee.
Or did misfortune's bitter storms
    Around thee blaw, around thee blaw,
Thy bield [1] should be my bosom,
    To share it a', to share it a'.

Or were I in the wildest waste,
    Sae black and bare, sae black and bare,

[1] *Shelter, protection.*

The desert were a Paradise,
    If thou wert there, if thou wert there;
Or were I monarch o' the globe,
    Wi' thee to reign, wi' thee to reign,
The brightest jewel in my crown
    Wad be my queen, wad be my queen!

The Banks o' Doon

Ye flowery banks o' bonnie Doon,
    How can ye blume sae fair!
How can ye chant, ye little birds,
    And I sae fu' o' care!

Thou'll break my heart, thou bonnie bird
    That sings upon the bough;
Thou minds me o' the happy days
    When my fause Luve was true.

Thou'll break my heart, thou bonnie bird
    That sings beside thy mate;
For sae I sat, and sae I sang,
    And wist na o' my fate.

Aft hae I roved by bonnie Doon
    To see the woodbine twine,
And ilka [1] bird sang o' its love;
    And sae did I o' mine.

Wi' lightsome heart I pu'd a rose,
    Frae aff its thorny tree;
And my fause luver staw [2] the rose,
    But left the thorn wi' me.

Mary Morison

Oh, Mary, at thy window be,
    It is the wished, the trysted hour!
Those smiles and glances let me see,
    That make the miser's treasure poor:
How blithely wad I bide the stour,[3]

[1] *Every.*   [2] *Stole.*   [3] *Struggle.*

A weary slave frae sun to sun,
   Could I the rich reward secure,
The lovely Mary Morison.

Yestreen, when to the trembling string
   The dance gaed thro' the lighted ha',
To thee my fancy took its wing,
   I sat, but neither heard nor saw:
Tho' this was fair, and that was braw,
And yon the toast of a' the town,
   I sighed, and said amang them a',
"Ye are na Mary Morison."

Oh, Mary, canst thou wreck his peace,
   Wha for thy sake wad gladly die?
Or canst thou break that heart of his,
   Whose only faut is loving thee?
If love for love thou wilt na gie,
   At least be pity to me shown;
A thought ungentle canna be
The thought o' Mary Morison.

Sweet Afton

Flow gently, sweet Afton! among thy green braes,
Flow gently, I'll sing thee a song in thy praise;
My Mary's asleep by thy murmuring stream,
Flow gently, sweet Afton, disturb not her dream.

Thou stock-dove whose echo resounds through the glen,
Ye wild whistling blackbirds in yon thorny den,
Thou green-crested lapwing, thy screaming forbear,
I charge you, disturb not my slumbering fair.

How lofty, sweet Afton, thy neighboring hills,
Far marked with the courses of clear, winding rills;
There daily I wander as noon rises high,
My flocks and my Mary's sweet cot in my eye.

How pleasant thy banks and green valleys below,
Where, wild in the woodlands, the primroses blow;
There oft, as mild ev'ning weeps over the lea,
The sweet-scented birk shades my Mary and me.

Thy crystal stream, Afton, how lovely it glides,
And winds by the cot where my Mary resides;
How wanton thy waters her snowy feet lave,
As, gathering sweet flowerets, she stems thy clear wave.

Flow gently, sweet Afton, among thy green braes,
Flow gently, sweet river, the theme of my lays;
My Mary's asleep by thy murmuring stream,
Flow gently, sweet Afton, disturb not her dream.

In 1786 Burns printed a collection of poems on a small provincial press at Kilmarnock. A few copies found their way to Edinburgh, and the farmer-poet was invited to the capital. Nothing could have been worse for Burns, for he became the fashion of the moment. He was fulsomely praised by the intelligentsia and courted by nonentities, sought after by the metropolitan society not because he was a true pastoral poet, but because he was a rustic novelty. He learned to swagger with the town idlers; soon he outdid them in dissipation and arrogance. He returned to buy a farm for Jean and himself, but the mischief of a few months could not be undone.

After his visit to Edinburgh, Burns lived in two worlds and was unhappy in both. He grew restless and unsettled; he abandoned the farm and obtained an appointment as an assessor. He began to drink more heavily. An early digestive ailment was aggravated by rheumatic fever, and he was warned that he would have to be more temperate. But Burns could not restrain himself. During a prolonged drinking bout he contracted a severe cold, developed a fever, and never recovered. He died in delirium in his thirty-seventh year. Ten thousand people of all classes followed his coffin to the grave.

The core of Burns's tragedy was his jealous hatred of the social circle to which he did not belong and his failure to enjoy the society in which he was at home. Burns recognized the dichotomy; he called himself "a poor, damned, incautious, duped, unfortunate fool; the sport, the miserable victim of rebellious pride and bedlam passions." But this self-characterization omits the love of humanity which rose above distrust and jealousy. Burns's sensibility was quick and keen; his love went out to old friends and the dignity of "honest poverty" and a mouse beneath the plowshare.

John Anderson, My Jo

John Anderson, my jo, John,
  When we were first acquent;
Your locks were like the raven,
  Your bonie brow was brent; [1]
But now your brow is bald, John,
  Your locks are like the snow;
But blessings on your frosty pow, [2]
  John Anderson, my jo.

John Anderson, my jo, John,
  We clamb the hill thegither;
And mony a cantie [3] day, John,
  We've had wi' ane anither:
Now we maun totter down, John,
  And hand in hand we'll go,
And sleep thegither at the foot,
  John Anderson, my jo.

To a Mouse

ON TURNING HER UP IN HER NEST WITH THE PLOW

Wee, sleekit, cowrin, tim'rous beastie,
O, what a panic's in thy breastie!
Thou need na start awa sae hasty,
  Wi' bickering brattle!
I wad be laith to rin an' chase thee,
  Wi' murd'ring pattle! [4]

I'm truly sorry man's dominion,
Has broken nature's social union,
An' justifies that ill opinion,
  Which makes thee startle
At me, thy poor, earth-born companion,
  An' fellow-mortal!

[1] *Bright.*   [2] *Head.*   [3] *Merry.*   [4] *Plow-stick.*

I doubt na, whiles, but thou may thieve;
What then? poor beastie, thou maun live!
A daimen icker in a thrave [5]
        'S a sma' request;
I'll get a blessin wi' the lave,[6]
        An' never miss't!

Thy wee bit housie, too, in ruin!
It's silly wa's the winds are strewin!
An' naething, now, to build a new ane,
        O' foggage [7] green!
An' bleak December's winds ensuin,
        Baith snell [8] an' keen!

Thou saw the fields laid bare an' waste,
An' weary winter comin' fast,
An' cozie here, beneath the blast,
        Thou thought to dwell—
Till crash! the cruel coulter past
        Out thro' thy cell.

That wee bit heap o' leaves an' stibble,
Has cost thee mony a weary nibble!
Now thou's turned out, for a' thy trouble,
        But house or hald,
To thole [9] the winter's sleety dribble,
        An' cranreuch cauld! [10]

But, Mousie, thou art no thy lane,[11]
In proving foresight may be vain;
The best-laid schemes o' mice an' men
        Gang aft agley,[12]
An' lea'e us nought but grief an' pain
        For promised joy!

Still thou art blest, compared wi' me;
The present only toucheth thee:
But och! I backward cast my e'e,
        On prospects drear!
An' forward, tho' I canna see,
        I guess an' fear!

---

[5] *An odd ear of corn in two shocks of grain.* [6] *Remainder.*
[7] *Coarse grass.* [8] *Bitter.* [9] *Endure.* [10] *Sharp hoarfrost.*
[11] *Not alone.* [12] *Often go wrong.*

A Man's a Man for A' That

Is there, for honest poverty,
   That hangs his head, an' a' that?
The coward slave, we pass him by,
   We dare be poor for a' that!
     For a' that, an' a' that,
     Our toils obscure, an' a' that;
     The rank is but the guinea's stamp;
     The man's the gowd [13] for a' that.

What though on hamely fare we dine,
   Wear hodden-gray, an' a' that;
Gie fools their silks, and knaves their wine,
   A man's a man for a' that.
     For a' that, an' a' that,
     Their tinsel show, an' a' that;
     The honest man, though e'er sae poor,
     Is king o' men for a' that.

Ye see yon birkie,[14] ca'd a lord,
   Wha struts, an' stares, an' a' that;
Though hundreds worship at his word,
   He's but a coof [15] for a' that.
     For a' that, an' a' that,
     His riband, star, an' a' that,
     The man o' independent mind,
     He looks and laughs at a' that.

A prince can mak a belted knight,
   A marquis, duke, an' a' that;
But an honest man's aboon [16] his might,
   Guid faith he mauna fa' [17] that!
     For a' that, an' a' that,
     Their dignities, an' a' that,
     The pith o' sense, an' pride o' worth,
     Are higher rank than a' that.

Then let us pray that come it may,
   As come it will for a' that,

[13] *Pure gold.*   [14] *Fellow.*   [15] *Fool.*   [16] *Above.*   [17] *Attempt.*

That sense and worth, o'er a' the earth,
May bear the gree,[18] an' a' that.
For a' that, an' a' that,
    It's coming yet, for a' that,
That man to man, the warld o'er,
    Shall brothers be for a' that.

Bruce's March to Bannockburn

Scots, wha hae wi' Wallace bled,
Scots, wham Bruce has aften led,
Welcome to your gory bed,
        Or to victorie!

Now's the day, and now's the hour;
See the front o' battle lour;
See approach proud Edward's power—
        Chains and slaverie!

Wha will be a traitor knave?
Wha can fill a coward's grave?
Wha sae base as be a slave?
        Let him turn and flee!

Wha, for Scotland's king and law,
Freedom's sword will strongly draw,
Free-man stand, or free-man fa',
        Let him follow me!

By oppression's woes and pains,
By your sons in servile chains,
We will drain our dearest veins,
        But they shall be free!

Lay the proud usurpers low!
Tyrants fall in every foe!
Liberty's in every blow!—
        Let us do or die!

The convivial poet was at his worst when he envied the famous
ones of his day and attempted to be "literary"; imitating the fash-
ion, Burns often fell into a style that was stilted and commonplace.

[18] *Victory.*

He was a true poet only when he was completely true to himself. And he was himself in more ways than is commonly supposed, not only in the popular love songs but in the country scenes and satires. His love of irresponsibility and his native understanding and audacity are clinched with humor. The ADDRESS TO THE UNCO GUID is, as the subtitle tells us, a mockery of the rigidly righteous. It laughs out loud even while it attacks the pretensions of all creeds and philosophies. In THE JOLLY BEGGARS no one, from the country parson to the prime minister, is safe.

> Poor Andrew that tumbles for sport,
>   Let naebody name wi' a jeer:
> There's even, I'm tauld, i' the Court
>   A tumbler that's ca' d the Premier.

The DRINKING SONG from THE JOLLY BEGGARS is Burns's final gesture of annihilating humor. Here, with happy abandon, he treats the whole world of morality as though its existence were mythical.

Drinking Song

A fig for those by law protected!
    Liberty's a glorious feast!
Courts for cowards were erected,
    Churches built to please the priest.

What is title, what is treasure,
    What is reputation's care?
If we lead a life of pleasure,
    'Tis no matter how or where!
        A fig for, *etc.*

With the ready trick and fable,
    Round we wander all the day;
And at night in barn or stable,
    Hug our doxies on the hay.
        A fig for, *etc.*

Does the train-attended carriage
    Thro' the country lighter rove?
Does the sober bed of marriage
    Witness brighter scenes of love?
        A fig for, *etc.*

Life is all a variorum,
    We regard not how it goes;
Let them cant about decorum,
    Who have character to lose.
        A fig for, *etc.*

Here's to budgets, bags and wallets!
Here's to all the wandering train.
Here's our ragged brats and callets,[1]
One and all cry out: Amen!

Chorus
A fig for those by law protected!
Liberty's a glorious feast!
Courts for cowards were erected,
    Churches built to please the priest.
                from THE JOLLY BEGGARS

Address to the Unco Guid, or the Rigidly Righteous

O ye wha are sae guid yoursel,
    Sae pious and sae holy,
Ye've nought to do but mark and tell
    Your neibor's fauts and folly!
Whase life is like a weel-gaun mill,
    Supplied wi' store o' water;
The heapet happer's[2] ebbing still,
    And still the clap plays clatter.

Hear me, ye venerable core,[3]
    As counsel for poor mortals,
That frequent pass douce[4] Wisdom's door,
    For glaikit[5] Folly's portals;
I, for their thoughtless, careless sakes,
    Would here propone defenses—
Their donsie[6] tricks, their black mistakes,
    Their failings and mischances.

---

[1] *Wenches.* [2] *Heaped hopper.* [3] *Company.* [4] *Somber.* [5] *Giddy.*
[6] *Mischievous.*

Ye see your state wi' theirs compared,
  And shudder at the niffer; [7]
But cast a moment's fair regard—
  What maks the mighty differ?
Discount what scant occasion gave,
  That purity ye pride in,
And (what's aft mair than a' the lave) [8]
  Your better art o' hidin'.

Think, when your castigated pulse
  Gies now and then a wallop,
What ragings must his veins convulse,
  That still eternal gallop!
Wi' wind and tide fair i' your tail,
  Right on ye scud your seaway;
But in the teeth o' baith to sail,
  It makes an unco leeway.

See Social life and Glee sit down,
  All joyous and unthinking,
Till, quite transmogrified they're grown
  Debauchery and Drinking.
O would they stay to calculate
  Th' eternal consequences;
Or your more dreaded hell to state,
  Damnation of expenses!

Ye high, exalted, virtuous Dames,
  Tied up in godly laces,
Before ye gie poor Frailty names,
  Suppose a change o' cases;
A dear loved lad, convenience snug,
  A treacherous inclination—
But, let me whisper i' your lug, [9]
  Ye're aiblins [10] nae temptation.

Then gently scan your brother man,
  Still gentler sister woman;
Though they may gang a kennin [11] wrang,
  To step aside is human.
One point must still be greatly dark,
  The moving Why they do it;
And just as lamely can ye mark
  How far perhaps they rue it.

[7] *Exchange.*   [8] *Rest.*   [9] *Ear.*   [10] *Most likely.*   [11] *Trifle.*

Who made the heart, 'tis He alone
    Decidedly can try us;
He knows each chord, its various tone,
    Each spring, its various bias.
Then at the balance let's be mute,
    We never can adjust it;
What's done we partly may compute,
    But know not what's resisted.

Burns's Rabelaisian humor is at its richest in TAM O' SHANTER.
In this most characteristic work, his human sympathy encompasses
an idyl of witches and warlocks. Burns remembered the tales told
in his childhood, legends of ghosts and goblins, brownies and
bogeys; in TAM O' SHANTER he turned them into a headlong frolic.
What might have been a piece of antiquarianism, a saga of Scot-
tish folklore, has become a galloping adventure of universal de-
light.

Tam o' Shanter

When chapman billies[1] leave the street,
And drouthy neibors neibors meet;
As market days are wearing late,
And folk begin to tak the gate,
While we sit bousing at the nappy,[2]
An' getting fou and unco happy,
We think na on the lang Scots miles,
The mosses, waters, slaps[3] and stiles,
That lie between us and our hame,
Where sits our sulky, sullen dame,
Gathering her brows like gathering storm,
Nursing her wrath to keep it warm.

This truth fand honest Tam o' Shanter,
As he frae Ayr ae night did canter
(Auld Ayr, wham ne'er a town surpasses,
For honest men and bonie lasses).

O Tam! had'st thou but been sae wise,
As taen thy ain wife Kate's advice!
She tauld thee weel thou was a skellum,[4]
A blethering, blustering, drunken blellum;[5]

[1] *Peddlers.*   [2] *Drinking ale.*   [3] *Hedge gaps.*   [4] *Rascal.*   [5] *Babbler.*

That frae November till October,
Ae market-day thou was no sober;
That ilka melder [6] wi' the Miller,
Thou sat as lang as thou had siller; [7]
That ev'ry nag was ca'd a shoe on [8]
The Smith and thee gat roarin fou on;
That at the Lord's house, ev'n on Sunday,
Thou drank wi' Kirkton Jean till Monday;
She prophesied that late or soon,
Thou wad be found, deep drowned in **Doon,**
Or catched wi' warlocks in the mirk,
By Alloway's auld, haunted kirk.

Ah, gentle dames! it gars me greet,[9]
To think how mony counsels sweet,
How mony lengthened, sage advices,
The husband frae the wife despises!

But to our tale:—Ae market night,
Tam had got planted unco right,
Fast by an ingle, bleezing finely,
Wi' reaming swats [10] that drank divinely;
And at his elbow, Souter [11] Johnie,
His ancient, trusty, drouthy crony:
Tam lo'ed him like a very brither;
They had been fou for weeks thegither.
The night drave on wi' sangs an' clatter;
And aye the ale was growing better:
The Landlady and Tam grew gracious,
Wi' favors secret, sweet and precious:
The Souter tauld his queerest stories;
The Landlord's laugh was ready chorus:
The storm without might rair and rustle,
Tam did na mind the storm a whistle.

Care, mad to see a man sae happy,
E'en drowned himsel amang the nappy.
As bees flee hame wi' lades [12] o' treasure,
The minutes winged their way wi' pleasure:
Kings may be blest, but Tam was glorious,
O'er a' the ills o' life victorious!

---

6 *Every corn-grinding.*   **7** *Silver, i.e. money.*   **8** *Called for another drink.*
9 *Makes me weep.*   **10** *Tankards of foaming ale.*   **11** *Cobbler.*   **12** *Loads.*

But pleasures are like poppies spread,
You seize the flow'r, its bloom is shed;
Or like the snow falls in the river,
A moment white—then melts for ever;
Or like the borealis race,
That flit ere you can point their place;
Or like the rainbow's lovely form
Evanishing amid the storm.
Nae man can tether time or tide;—
The hour approaches Tam maun ride;
That hour, o' night's black arch the key-stane,
That dreary hour he mounts his beast in;
And sic a night he taks the road in,
As ne'er poor sinner was abroad in.

The wind blew as 'twad blawn its last;
The rattling showers rose on the blast;
The speedy gleams the darkness swallowed;
Loud, deep, and lang, the thunder bellowed:
That night, a child might understand,
The Deil had business on his hand.

Weel mounted on his gray mare, Meg,
A better never lifted leg,
Tam skelpit [13] on through dub [14] and mire,
Despising wind, and rain, and fire;
Whiles holding fast his guid blue bonnet;
Whiles crooning o'er some auld Scots sonnet;
Whiles glowering round wi' prudent cares,
Lest bogles [15] catch him unawares;
Kirk Alloway was drawing nigh,
Whare ghaists and houlets [16] nightly cry.

By this time he was cross the ford,
Whare in the snaw the chapman smoored,[17]
And past the birks and meikle stane,[18]
Whare drunken Charlie brak's neckbane;
And through the whins,[19] and by the cairn,[20]
Whare hunters fand the murdered bairn:
And near the thorn, aboon the well,
Whare Mungo's mither hanged hersel.
Before him Doon pours all his floods;
The doubling storm roars through the woods;

[13] *Splashed.*   [14] *Puddle.*   [15] *Goblins.*   [16] *Owls.*   [17] *Smothered.*   [18] *Huge stone.*
[19] *Bushes.*   [20] *Stone pile.*

The lightnings flash from pole to pole;
Near and more near the thunders roll:
When, glimmering through the groaning trees,
Kirk Alloway seemed in a bleeze;
Through ilka bore [21] the beams were glancing;
And loud resounded mirth and dancing.

Inspiring bold John Barleycorn!
What dangers thou canst make us scorn!
Wi' tippenny,[22] we fear nae evil;
Wi' usquebae,[23] we'll face the Devil!
The swats sae reamed in Tammie's noddle,
Fair play, he cared na deils a boddle.[24]
But Maggie stood right sair astonished,
Till, by the heel and hand admonished,
She ventured forward on the light;
And, wow! Tam saw an unco sight!

Warlocks and witches in a dance;
Nae cotillion brent-new frae France,
But hornpipes, jigs, strathspeys, and reels,
Put life and mettle in their heels.
At winnock-bunker [25] in the east,
There sat auld Nick, in shape o' beast;
A towzie tyke,[26] black, grim, and large,
To gie them music was his charge:
He screwed the pipes and gart them skirl,[27]
Till roof and rafters a' did dirl.— [28]
Coffins stood round, like open presses,
That shawed the dead in their last dresses;
And by some devilish cantrip sleight,[29]
Each in its cauld hand held a light—
By which heroic Tam was able
To note upon the holy table
A murderer's banes in gibbet-airns; [30]
Two span-lang, wee, unchristened bairns;
A thief, new-cutted frae a rape,
Wi' his last gasp his gab did gape;
Five tomahawks wi' blude red-rusted;
Five scimitars wi' murder crusted;
A garter which a babe had strangled;
A knife a father's throat had mangled,

[21] *Chink.* [22] *Twopenny ale.* [23] *Whisky.* [24] *Didn't care a farthing.*
[25] *Window seat.* [26] *Shaggy cur.* [27] *Made them squeal.* [28] *Rattle.*
[29] *Magic trick.* [30] *Gallows irons.*

Whom his ain son of life bereft,
The gray hairs sticking to the heft;
Wi' mair of horrible and awfu',
Which even to name wad be unlawfu'.

As Tammie glowered, amazed and curious,
The mirth and fun grew fast and furious;
The Piper loud and louder blew,
The dancers quick and quicker flew,
They reeled, they set, they crossed, they cleekit,[31]
Till ilka carlin swat and reekit,[32]
And coost her duddies to the wark,[33]
And linkit at it in her sark! [34]

    .   .   .   .

But Tam kent what was what fu' brawlie:
There was ae winsome wench and waulie [35]
That night enlisted in the core
(Lang after kenned on Carrick shore
For mony a beast to dead she shot,
And perished mony a bonie boat,
And shook baith meikle corn and bear,[36]
And kept the country-side in fear);
Her cutty-sark,[37] o' Paisley harn,
That while a lassie she had worn,
In longitude though sorely scanty,
It was her best, and she was vauntie.[38]
Ah! little kenned thy reverend grannie,
That sark she coft [39] for her wee Nannie,
Wi' twa pund Scots ('twas a' her riches),
Wad ever graced a dance of witches!

But here my Muse her wing maun cower,
Sic flights are far beyond her power;
To sing how Nannie lap and flang
(A souple jade she was and strang),
And how Tam stood, like ane bewitched,
And thought his very een enriched:
Even Satan glowered, and fidged fu' fain,
And hotched [40] and blew wi' might and main:

[31] *Joined hands.*   [32] *Every hag sweat and smoked.*
[33] *Cast off her clothes for the work.*   [34] *Danced in her shirt.*   [35] *Jolly.*
[36] *Barley.*   [37] *Short shirt.*   [38] *Proud.*   [39] *Bought.*   [40] *Squirmed.*

Till first ae caper, syne anither,
Tam tint [41] his reason a' thegither,
And roars out, "Weel done, Cutty-sark!"
And in an instant all was dark:
And scarcely had he Maggie rallied,
When out the hellish legion sallied.

As bees bizz out wi' angry fyke,[42]
When plundering herds assail their byke; [43]
As open pussie's [44] mortal foes,
When, pop! she starts before their nose;
As eager runs the market-crowd,
When "Catch the thief!" resounds aloud;
So Maggie runs, the witches follow,
Wi' mony an eldritch [45] skreich and hollo.

Ah, Tam! Ah, Tam! thou'll get thy fairin! [46]
In hell they'll roast thee like a herrin!
In vain thy Kate awaits thy comin!
Kate soon will be a woefu' woman!
Now, do thy speedy utmost, Meg,
And win the key-stane o' the brig; [47]
There, at them thou thy tail may toss,
A running stream they dare na cross;
But ere the key-stane she could make,
The fiend a tail she had to shake!
For Nannie, far before the rest,
Hard upon noble Maggie prest,
And flew at Tam wi' furious ettle; [48]
But little wist she Maggie's mettle!
Ae spring brought off her master hale,
But left behind her ain gray tail:
The carlin claught her by the rump,
And left poor Maggie scarce a stump.

Now wha this tale o' truth shall read,
Ilk' man and mother's son, take heed:
Whene'er to drink you are inclined,
Or cutty-sarks run in your mind,
Think, ye may buy the joys o'er dear,
Remember Tam o' Shanter's mare!

[41] *Lost.* [42] *Fuss.* [43] *Hive.* [44] *The hare's.* [45] *Unearthly.* [46] *Reward.*
[47] *Bridge.* [48] *Intent.*

Although Burns was Blake's contemporary and, like him, a lyric poet, he is Blake's opposite. There is little ecstasy and no mysticism in Burns; thought seldom ranges beyond immediate sensation and experience. But, if Burns's intellect is bound, his melodies rise freely. If he lacks pure vision, he lives in pure song.

XII

The Spirit of
Revolution and Romance

ROMANTICISM has been so variously defined that it has come to mean anything the critic wants it to mean, from Heinrich Heine's "the reawakening of the Middle Ages" to Walter Pater's "the addition of strangeness to beauty." But as the term is commonly used today, romanticism primarily implies a reaction from rationalism. Stressing emotion rather than reason, instinct rather than experience, the romantic writers of the nineteenth century emphasized self and sensibility. Echoing Rousseau, who maintained that man was corrupted by civilized society, they turned the common man into a Noble Savage, glorified Nature as Divine Healer, and struggled to establish liberty in the ever-sharpening conflict between materialism and idealism.

The destruction of the Bastille in 1789 spread the spirit of revolution and romance. Insurgence leaped the Channel, and its challenge was answered by such ardent young men as Coleridge, Southey, Landor, and Hazlitt. Wordsworth, leading them all in enthusiasm, envisioned the rescue of mankind and declared in his FRENCH REVOLUTION:

> Bliss was it in that dawn to be alive,
> But to be young was very heaven!

Poems became battle cries; the inert were aroused; a new dream, gathering strength and swiftness, took on fierce reality. But the reality soon grew too terrible for its disciples; the revolutionary dream became a nightmare of indiscriminate fury and violent excess. Four years after the beginning of the French Revolution, England went to war with France; the dawn of the nineteenth century brought the threat of Napoleon. It was no longer possible to believe in revolt as a liberation, or war as a great catharsis, and the intransigent youths became middle-aged conservatives. Southey lived to be the "turncoat" poet laureate, and Wordsworth, renegade rebel and Tory, was characterized by Browning as "the lost leader."

Nevertheless, it was the flame of revolt that burned out the cynical social doctrines of the eighteenth century and kindled in the younger men a hot hatred of injustice and an even more fiery love of humanity.

WILLIAM WORDSWORTH
[1770–1850]

CHAMPION of the "humble and rustic life" in which "the essential passions of the heart find a better soil," William Wordsworth was born April 7, 1770, at Cockermouth, Cumberland, near the river Derwent in the Lake District. His father was an attorney; his mother, who died when Wordsworth was eight years old, was the daughter of a dry-goods merchant. Five years after his mother's death his father died, and the five children were scattered among schools and guardians. At seventeen Wordsworth was sent to St. John's College, Cambridge, and it was here that he began to connect the images of the countryside with his own thoughts, to celebrate the simple but romantic aspects of nature, and feel:

A motion and a spirit that impels
All thinking things, all objects of all thoughts,
And rolls through all things.

Wordsworth's guardians intended him for the Church, but the young poet put them off with various excuses. After graduating, he convinced them that he needed a year of French, and at twenty-two crossed the Channel, became intimate with members of the French revolutionary party, and lived a year in Blois and Orléans. At Orléans Wordsworth fell in love with Marie-Anne ("Annette") Vallon, four years his senior, who bore him a daughter, Carolyn. It is possible that Wordsworth hoped to marry Annette and settle in France, but the Continental disorders and the war between France and England in 1793 upset any plans which Wordsworth may have made toward this end. Whether or not Wordsworth's double passion for Annette and France had cooled, it is apparent that marriage was no longer considered, although, as G. M. Harper wrote in his remarkable piece of research, WORDSWORTH'S FRENCH DAUGHTER, "Whatever, from a legal point of view, may have been the nature of the connection between Wordsworth and Marie-Anne Vallon, it was openly acknowledged and its consequences were honorably endured." In 1802, when Wordsworth was thirty-two, he returned to France for four weeks and walked by the seashore almost every evening with Annette and Carolyn. One result of these walks on the beach near Calais was the sonnet beginning "It is a beauteous evening, calm and free." Written to his ten-year-old daughter, it is a poem as tranquil in tone as it is moving in spirit.

On the Beach at Calais

It is a beauteous evening, calm and free;
The holy time is quiet as a nun
Breathless with adoration; the broad sun
Is sinking down in its tranquillity;
The gentleness of heaven broods o'er the sea:
Listen! the mighty Being is awake,
And doth with his eternal motion make
A sound like thunder—everlastingly.
Dear child! dear girl! that walkest with me here,
If thou appear untouched by solemn thought,
Thy nature is not therefore less divine:
Thou liest in Abraham's bosom all the year,
And worship'st at the Temple's inner shrine,
God being with thee when we know it not.

The love affair and its consequences, together with his disillusionment in the revolutionary cause, unsettled Wordsworth for years. Unable to live in a fading dream, he found it difficult to adjust himself to the hard world of reality. Even with the coming of April, when "every flower enjoys the air it breathes," he mused unhappily in LINES WRITTEN IN EARLY SPRING:

> To her fair works did Nature link
> The human soul that through me ran;
> And much it grieved my heart to think
> What man has made of man.

"What man has made of man" continued to trouble Wordsworth. The French Revolution brought hope to millions, particularly to the Negroes in Haiti. But the National Assembly was not ready to extend the "rights of man" to slaves. The Haitian blacks revolted, led by Pierre Dominique Breda, who adopted the sobriquet of Toussaint L'Ouverture. After a struggle of twenty years, the Haitians won their freedom; but, long before independence had been achieved, Toussaint L'Ouverture had been seized and transported to France. When Toussaint was imprisoned, Wordsworth, deeply shaken, addressed one of his most nobly affecting sonnets to the captured liberator.

To Toussaint L'Ouverture

> Toussaint, the most unhappy man of men!
> Whether the whistling rustic tend his plough
> Within thy hearing, or thy head be now
> Pillowed in some deep dungeon's earless den—
> O miserable Chieftain! where and when
> Wilt thou find patience! Yet die not; do thou
> Wear rather in thy bonds a cheerful brow:
> Though fallen thyself, never to rise again,
> Live, and take comfort. Thou hast left behind
> Powers that will work for thee; air, earth, and skies.
> There's not a breathing of the common wind
> That will forget thee; thou hast great allies;
> Thy friends are exultations, agonies,
> And love, and man's unconquerable mind.

Wordsworth wandered about England with his sister Dorothy, whose "exquisite regard for common things" intensified his observation and preserved the poet in him.

She gave me eyes, she gave me ears;
And humble cares, and delicate fears;
A heart, the fountain of sweet tears;
And love, and thought, and joy.

An influence second only to Dorothy's came into Wordsworth's life in his twenty-sixth year, when he first met Samuel Taylor Coleridge. A few months later William, who had come into a small inheritance, moved with Dorothy to Somerset in order to be near Coleridge. There, visiting daily, collaborating, and continually encouraged by Dorothy, the poets flourished, and the trio became "three persons with one soul."

In September, 1798, Wordsworth and Coleridge published a volume unpretentiously entitled LYRICAL BALLADS, a book which the otherwise restrained ENCYCLOPAEDIA BRITANNICA unreservedly calls "the most important event in the history of English poetry after Milton." Both poets were pledged to the romantic position, but their approach was essentially different. It was agreed that Coleridge was to make incredible romances seem real, while Wordsworth was to reveal the romance of the commonplace. Wordsworth's object was to give "the charm of novelty to things of every day . . . by awakening the mind's attention and directing it to the loveliness and the wonders of the world before us." Thus the LYRICAL BALLADS mingled the "natural" and "supernatural," and revealed them as contrasting marvels of observation and imagination.

The reception accorded to the LYRICAL BALLADS was such as might have discouraged spirits less ardent than Wordsworth's and Coleridge's. Coleridge's major poem, THE RIME OF THE ANCIENT MARINER, one of the chief glories of English poetry, was contemptuously derided, and Wordsworth's magnificent soliloquy, LINES COMPOSED A FEW MILES ABOVE TINTERN ABBEY, was wholly ignored. TINTERN ABBEY justifies Wordsworth's conception of the romantic nature of poetry as "the spontaneous overflow of powerful feelings," a kind of poetry which "takes its origin from emotion recollected in tranquillity." More than most, this is a poem which recollects and confirms, which recalls beloved sights and sensations, and reaffirms their unity. In a beautiful cadence addressed to Dorothy, Wordsworth summons "the still, sad music of humanity" and repeats his faith in Nature, which "never did betray the heart that loved her."

Lines

COMPOSED A FEW MILES ABOVE TINTERN ABBEY, ON REVISITING
THE BANKS OF THE WYE DURING A TOUR, JULY 13, 1798

Five years have passed; five summers, with the length
Of five long winters! and again I hear
These waters, rolling from their mountain springs
With a soft inland murmur.—Once again
Do I behold these steep and lofty cliffs,
That on a wild, secluded scene impress
Thoughts of more deep seclusion; and connect
The landscape with the quiet of the sky.
The day is come when I again repose
Here, under this dark sycamore, and view
These plots of cottage-ground, these orchard-tufts,
Which at this season, with their unripe fruits,
Are clad in one green hue, and lose themselves
'Mid groves and copses. Once again I see
These hedge-rows, hardly hedge-rows, little lines
Of sportive wood run wild; these pastoral farms,
Green to the very door; and wreaths of smoke
Sent up, in silence, from among the trees!
With some uncertain notice, as might seem
Of vagrant dwellers in the houseless woods,
Or of some hermit's cave, where by his fire
The hermit sits alone.
                            These beauteous forms,
Through a long absence, have not been to me
As is a landscape to a blind man's eye;
But oft, in lonely rooms, and 'mid the din
Of towns and cities, I have owed to them
In hours of weariness, sensations sweet,
Felt in the blood, and felt along the heart;
And passing even into my purer mind,
With tranquil restoration:—feelings, too,
Or unremembered pleasure; such, perhaps,
As have no slight or trivial influence
On that best portion of a good man's life,
His little, nameless, unremembered acts
Of kindness and of love. Nor less, I trust,
To them I may have owed another gift,
Of aspect more sublime; that blessed mood,

In which the burthen of the mystery,
In which the heavy and the weary weight
Of all this unintelligible world,
Is lightened—that serene and blessed mood
In which the affections gently lead us on—
Until, the breath of this corporeal frame
And even the motion of our human blood
Almost suspended, we are laid asleep
In body, and become a living soul;
While with an eye made quiet by the power
Of harmony, and the deep power of joy,
We see into the life of things.
                    If this
Be but a vain belief, yet, oh! how oft—
In darkness and amid the many shapes
Of joyless daylight; when the fretful stir
Unprofitable, and the fever of the world,
Have hung upon the beatings of my heart—
How oft, in spirit, have I turned to thee,
O sylvan Wye! thou wanderer through the woods,
How often has my spirit turned to thee!
    And now, with gleams of half-extinguished thought,
With many recognitions dim and faint,
And somewhat of a sad perplexity,
The picture of the mind revives again;
While here I stand, not only with the sense
Of present pleasure, but with pleasing thoughts
That in this moment there is life and food
For future years. And so I dare to hope,
Though changed, no doubt, from what I was when first
I came among these hills; when like a roe
I bounded o'er the mountains, by the sides
Of the deep rivers, and the lonely streams,
Wherever Nature led; more like a man
Flying from something that he dreads, than one
Who sought the thing he loved. For Nature then
(The coarser pleasures of my boyish days,
And their glad animal movements all gone by)
To me was all in all.—I cannot paint
What then I was. The sounding cataract
Haunted me like a passion; the tall rock,
The mountain, and the deep and gloomy wood,
Their colors and their forms, were then to me
An appetite; a feeling and a love,
That had no need of a remoter charm,

By thought supplied, nor any interest
Unborrowed from the eye.—That time is past,
And all its aching joys are now no more,
And all its dizzy raptures. Not for this
Faint I, nor mourn, nor murmur; other gifts
Have followed; for such loss, I would believe,
Abundant recompense. For I have learned
To look on Nature, not as in the hour
Of thoughtless youth; but hearing oftentimes
The still, sad music of humanity,
Nor harsh nor grating, though of ample power
To chasten and subdue. And I have felt
A presence that disturbs me with the joy
Of elevated thoughts; a sense sublime
Of something far more deeply interfused,
Whose dwelling is the light of setting suns,
And the round ocean and the living air,
And the blue sky, and in the mind of man;
A motion and a spirit, that impels
All thinking things, all objects of all thought,
And rolls through all things. Therefore am I still
A lover of the meadows and the woods,
And mountains; and of all that we behold
From this green earth; of all the mighty world
Of eye, and ear—both what they half create,
And what perceive; well pleased to recognize
In Nature and the language of the sense,
The anchor of my purest thoughts, the nurse,
The guide, the guardian of my heart, and soul
Of all my moral being.
                                  Nor perchance,
If I were not thus taught, should I the more
Suffer my genial spirits to decay;
For thou art with me here upon the banks
Of this fair river; thou my dearest Friend,
My dear, dear Friend; and in thy voice I catch
The language of my former heart, and read
My former pleasures in the shooting lights
Of thy wild eyes. Oh! yet a little while
May I behold in thee what I was once,
My dear, dear sister! and this prayer I make,
Knowing that Nature never did betray
The heart that loved her; 'tis her privilege,
Through all the years of this our life, to lead
From joy to joy; for she can so inform

The mind that is within us, so impress
With quietness and beauty, and so feed
With lofty thoughts, that neither evil tongues,
Rash judgments, nor the sneers of selfish men,
Nor greetings where no kindness is, nor all
The dreary intercourse of daily life,
Shall e'er prevail against us, or disturb
Our cheerful faith that all which we behold
Is full of blessings. Therefore let the moon
Shine on thee in thy solitary walk;
And let the misty mountain-winds be free
To blow against thee; and in after years,
When these wild ecstasies shall be matured
Into a sober pleasure; when thy mind
Shall be a mansion for all lovely forms,
Thy memory be as a dwelling-place
For all sweet sounds and harmonies; oh! then,
If solitude, or fear, or pain, or grief,
Should be thy portion, with what healing thoughts
Of tender joy wilt thou remember me,
And these my exhortations! Nor, perchance—
If I should be where I no more can hear
Thy voice, nor catch from thy wild eyes these gleams
Of past existence—wilt thou then forget
That on the banks of this delightful stream
We stood together; and that I, so long
A worshiper of Nature, hither came
Unwearied in that service; rather say
With warmer love—oh! with far deeper zeal
Of holier love. Nor wilt thou then forget
That after many wanderings, many years
Of absence, these steep woods and lofty cliffs,
And this green pastoral landscape, were to me
More dear, both for themselves and for thy sake!

After a trip to Germany with Coleridge, the Wordsworths settled in Grasmere, and there, except for occasional jaunts, they remained the rest of their lives. In his thirty-third year Wordsworth married Mary Hutchinson, a friend of Dorothy's, and the two women devoted themselves to the poet, sharing the housekeeping and the ever-increasing secretarial labors. Three editions of LYRICAL BALLADS were printed before 1805; the second was enriched by a preface which served as the manifesto of the romantic movement. The "advertisement" said that the BALLADS were an experiment to ascertain "how far the language of conversation is adapted for the purposes of poetic pleasure"; and, though many of the poems were flat failures—being as dull and colorless as conversation is likely to be—a new diction had been created. This talk-flavored speech tightened many of Wordsworth's lyrics, and Wordsworth's kinship with natural things gave his domesticated blank verse a quality as different from the sonorous blank verse of Milton as from the pedestrian blank verse of Cowper.

It is in the lyrics that Wordsworth most freely used the "language actually spoken" in contrast to the traditional poetic speech He achieved a frank and often noble simplicity, a plain but penetrating power, by avoiding the artificial elegance of Pope, by shunning inversions, and intensifying "the unassuming commonplace of nature" with "thoughts too deep for tears."

The Solitary Reaper

Behold her, single in the field,
Yon solitary highland lass!
Reaping and singing by herself;
Stop here, or gently pass!
Alone she cuts and binds the grain,
And sings a melancholy strain;
O listen! for the vale profound
Is overflowing with the sound.

No nightingale did ever chaunt
More welcome notes to weary bands
Of travelers in some shady haunt,
Among Arabian sands:
A voice so thrilling ne'er was heard
In spring-time from the cuckoo-bird,
Breaking the silence of the seas
Among the farthest Hebrides.

Will no one tell me what she sings?—
Perhaps the plaintive numbers flow
For old, unhappy, far-off things,
And battles long ago:
Or is it some more humble lay,
Familiar matter of today?

Some natural sorrow, loss, or pain,
That has been, and may be again?

Whate'er the theme, the maiden sang
As if her song could have no ending;
I saw her singing at her work,
And o'er the sickle bending;—
I listened, motionless and still;
And, as I mounted up the hill
The music in my heart I bore,
Long after it was heard no more.

The Daffodils

I wandered lonely as a cloud
That floats on high o'er vales and hills,
When all at once I saw a crowd,
A host of golden daffodils,
Beside the lake, beneath the trees
Fluttering and dancing in the breeze.

Continuous as the stars that shine
And twinkle on the milky way,
They stretched in never-ending line
Along the margin of a bay:
Ten thousand saw I at a glance
Tossing their heads in sprightly dance.

The waves beside them danced, but they
Out-did the sparkling waves in glee:
A poet could not but be gay
In such a jocund company!
I gazed—and gazed—but little thought
What wealth the show to me had brought:

For oft, when on my couch I lie
In vacant or in pensive mood,
They flash upon that inward eye
Which is the bliss of solitude;
And then my heart with pleasure fills,
And dances with the daffodils.

To the Cuckoo

O blithe new-comer! I have heard,
I hear thee and rejoice:
O cuckoo! shall I call thee Bird,
Or but a wandering Voice?

While I am lying on the grass
Thy twofold shout I hear;
From hill to hill it seems to pass,
At once far off and near.

Though babbling only to the vale
Of sunshine and of flowers,
Thou bringest unto me a tale
Of visionary hours.

Thrice welcome, darling of the Spring!
Even yet thou art to me
No bird, but an invisible thing,
A voice, a mystery;

The same whom in my school-boy days
I listened to; that cry
Which made me look a thousand ways
In bush, and tree, and sky.

To seek thee did I often rove
Through woods and on the green;
And thou wert still a hope, a love;
Still longed for, never seen!

And I can listen to thee yet;
Can lie upon the plain
And listen, till I do beget
That golden time again.

O blessèd bird! the earth we pace
Again appears to be
An unsubstantial, faery place,
That is fit home for thee!

To a Skylark

Ethereal minstrel! pilgrim of the sky!
Dost thou despise the earth where cares abound?
Or, while the wings aspire, are heart and eye
Both with thy nest upon the dewy ground?
Thy nest which thou canst drop into at will,
Those quivering wings composed, that music still!

Leave to the nightingale her shady wood;
A privacy of glorious light is thine;
Whence thou dost pour upon the world a flood
Of harmony, with instinct more divine;
Type of the wise who soar, but never roam;
True to the kindred points of Heaven and home!

She Was a Phantom of Delight

She was a phantom of delight
When first she gleamed upon my sight;
A lovely apparition, sent
To be a moment's ornament;
Her eyes as stars of twilight fair;
Like twilight's, too, her dusky hair;
But all things else about her drawn
From May-time and the cheerful dawn;
A dancing shape, an image gay,
To haunt, to startle, and way-lay.

I saw her upon nearer view,
A spirit, yet a woman too!
Her household motions light and free,
And steps of virgin-liberty;
A countenance in which did meet
Sweet records, promises as sweet;
A creature not too bright or good
For human nature's daily food;
For transient sorrows, simple wiles,
Praise, blame, love, kisses, tears, and smiles.

And now I see with eye serene
The very pulse of the machine;
A being breathing thoughtful breath,
A traveller between life and death;
The reason firm, the temperate will,
Endurance, foresight strength, and skill;
A perfect woman, nobly planned,
To warn, to comfort, and command;
And yet a spirit still, and bright
With something of angelic light.

My Heart Leaps Up When I Behold

My heart leaps up when I behold
    A rainbow in the sky:
So was it when my life began;
So is it now I am a man;
So be it when I shall grow old,
    Or let me die!
The Child is father of the Man;
And I could wish my days to be
Bound each to each by natural piety.

Perhaps the most famous of Wordsworth's simple lyrics are the so-called "Lucy Poems." Written during the poet's sojourn in Germany about an English girl known and lost in boyhood, the sequence is nostalgic in theme and mournful in tone. The plaintive note, however, changes at the end to an uplifted resignation, as Wordsworth reaffirms the unity of all life—and even death—with nature.

Lucy

STRANGE FITS OF PASSION HAVE I KNOWN

Strange fits of passion have I known:
    And I will dare to tell,
But in the Lover's ear alone,
    What once to me befell.

When she I loved looked every day,
  Fresh as a rose in June,
I to her cottage bent my way,
  Beneath an evening moon.

Upon the moon I fixed my eye,
  All over the wide lea;
With quickening pace my horse drew nigh
  Those paths so dear to me.

And now we reached the orchard plot;
  And as we climbed the hill,
The sinking moon to Lucy's cot
  Came near and nearer still.

In one of those sweet dreams I slept,
  Kind Nature's gentlest boon!
And all the while my eyes I kept
  On the descending moon.

My horse moved on; hoof after hoof
  He raised, and never stopped:
When down behind the cottage roof,
  At once, the bright moon dropped.

What fond and wayward thought will slide
  Into a lover's head!—
"Oh, mercy!" to myself I cried,
  "If Lucy should be dead!"

I TRAVELED AMONG UNKNOWN MEN

I traveled among unknown men,
  In lands beyond the sea;
Nor, England! did I know till then
  What love I bore to thee.

'Tis past, that melancholy dream!
  Nor will I quit thy shore
A second time; for still I seem
  To love thee more and more.

Among thy mountains did I feel
  The joy of my desire;
And she I cherished turned her wheel
  Beside an English fire.

Thy mornings showed, thy nights concealed
The bowers where Lucy played;
And thine too is the last green field
That Lucy's eyes surveyed.

THREE YEARS SHE GREW IN SUN AND SHOWER

Three years she grew in sun and shower,
Then Nature said, "A lovelier flower
On earth was never sown;
This child I to myself will take;
She shall be mine, and I will make
A lady of my own.

"Myself will to my darling be
Both law and impulse: and with me
The girl, in rock and plain,
In earth and heaven, in glade and bower,
Shall feel an overseeing power
To kindle or restrain.

"She shall be sportive as the fawn
That wild with glee across the lawn,
Or up the mountain springs;
And hers shall be the breathing balm,
And hers the silence and the calm
Of mute insensate things.

"The floating clouds their state shall lend
To her; for her the willow bend;
Nor shall she fail to see
Even in the motions of the storm
Grace that shall mold the maiden's form
By silent sympathy.

"The stars of midnight shall be dear
To her; and she shall lean her ear
In many a secret place
Where rivulets dance their wayward round,
And beauty born of murmuring sound
Shall pass into her face.

"And vital feelings of delight
Shall rear her form to stately height,
Her virgin bosom swell;

Such thoughts to Lucy I will give
While she and I together live
Here in this happy dell."

Thus Nature spake—The work was done—
How soon my Lucy's race was run!
She died, and left to me
This heath, this calm, and quiet scene;
The memory of what has been,
And never more will be.

SHE DWELT AMONG THE UNTRODDEN WAYS

She dwelt among the untrodden ways
    Beside the springs of Dove,
A maid whom there were none to praise
    And very few to love:

A violet by a mossy stone
    Half hidden from the eye.
—Fair as a star, when only one
    Is shining in the sky.

She lived unknown, and few could know
    When Lucy ceased to be;
But she is in her grave, and, oh,
    The difference to me!

A SLUMBER DID MY SPIRIT SEAL

A slumber did my spirit seal;
    I had no human fears:
She seemed a thing that could not feel
    The touch of earthly years.

No motion has she now, no force;
    She neither hears nor sees;
Rolled round in earth's diurnal course,
    With rocks, and stones, and trees.

Approaching forty, Wordsworth published his POEMS IN TWO
VOLUMES, which marked him not only as an innovator but as an
influence. In an overenthusiastic tribute De Quincey wrote that up
to 1820 Wordsworth's name was trampled under foot, from 1820 to
1830 it was militant, and from 1830 to 1835 it was triumphant.

Although this is something of an exaggeration, it is true that Wordsworth made readers reappraise themselves; he taught them to re-estimate their concepts of poetry and regard life itself with new eyes. The sonnets are particularly worthy of the praise showered upon them; they lift to the heights what Wordsworth considered the three great subjects of poetry: "On man, on nature, and on human life." In the sonnets the significance of ordinary experience is enriched and enlarged; they are the autobiography of the spirit as well as a reflection of the times.

Sonnets

THE WORLD IS TOO MUCH WITH US

The world is too much with us; late and soon,
Getting and spending, we lay waste our powers:
Little we see in Nature that is ours;
We have given our hearts away, a sordid boon!
The sea that bares her bosom to the moon;
The winds that will be howling at all hours,
And are up-gathered now like sleeping flowers;
For this, for everything, we are out of tune;
It moves us not.—Great God! I'd rather be
A pagan suckled in a creed outworn.
So might I, standing on this pleasant lea,
Have glimpses that would make me less forlorn;
Have sight of Proteus rising from the sea;
Or hear old Triton blow his wreathed horn.

COMPOSED UPON WESTMINSTER BRIDGE
SEPTEMBER 3, 1802

Earth has not anything to show more fair:
Dull would he be of soul who could pass by
A sight so touching in its majesty:
This city now doth, like a garment, wear
The beauty of the morning; silent, bare,
Ships, towers, domes, theaters, and temples lie
Open unto the fields, and to the sky;
All bright and glittering in the smokeless air.
Never did sun more beautifully steep
In his first splendor, valley, rock, or hill;

Ne'er saw I, never felt, a calm so deep!
The river glideth at his own sweet will:
Dear God! the very houses seem asleep;
And all that mighty heart is lying still!

TO MILTON

Milton! thou shouldst be living at this hour:
England hath need of thee: she is a fen
Of stagnant waters: altar, sword, and pen,
Fireside, the heroic wealth of hall and bower,
Have forfeited their ancient English dower
Of inward happiness. We are selfish men;
Oh! raise us up, return to us again;
And give us manners, virtue, freedom, power.
Thy soul was like a star, and dwelt apart:
Thou hadst a voice whose sound was like the sea:
Pure as the naked heavens, majestic, free,
So didst thou travel on life's common way,
In cheerful godliness; and yet thy heart
The lowliest duties on herself did lay.

WRITTEN IN LONDON, SEPTEMBER, 1802

O Friend! [1] I know not which way I must look
For comfort, being, as I am, opprest,
To think that now our life is only drest
For show; mean handy-work of craftsman, cook,
Or groom!—We must run glittering like a brook
In the open sunshine, or we are unblest:
The wealthiest man among us is the best:
No grandeur now in nature or in book
Delights us. Rapine, avarice, expense,
This is idolatry; and these we adore:
Plain living and high thinking are no more:
The homely beauty of the good old cause
Is gone; our peace, our fearful innocence,
And pure religion breathing household laws.

ON THE EXTINCTION OF THE VENETIAN REPUBLIC

Once did she hold the gorgeous east in fee;
And was the safeguard of the west: the worth
Of Venice did not fall below her birth,

[1] *Coleridge.*

Venice, the eldest child of liberty.
She was a maiden city, bright and free;
No guile seduced, no force could violate;
And, when she took unto herself a mate,
She must espouse the everlasting sea.
And what if she had seen those glories fade,
Those titles vanish, and that strength decay;
Yet shall some tribute of regret be paid
When her long life hath reached its final day:
Men are we, and must grieve when even the shade
Of that which once was great, is passed away.

TO SLEEP

A flock of sheep that leisurely pass by,
One after one; the sound of rain, and bees
Murmuring; the fall of rivers, winds and seas,
Smooth fields, white sheets of water, and pure sky;
I have thought of all by turns, and yet do lie
Sleepless! and soon the small birds' melodies
Must hear, first uttered from my orchard trees;
And the first cuckoo's melancholy cry.
Even thus last night, and two nights more, I lay,
And could not win thee, Sleep! by any stealth:
So do not let me wear tonight away:
Without Thee what is all the morning's wealth?
Come, blessed barrier between day and day,
Dear mother of fresh thoughts and joyous health!

THE SONNET

Scorn not the Sonnet; critic, you have frowned,
Mindless of its just honors; with this key
Shakespeare unlocked his heart; the melody
Of this small lute gave ease to Petrarch's wound;
A thousand times this pipe did Tasso sound;
With it Camöens soothed an exile's grief;
The Sonnet glittered a gay myrtle leaf
Amid the cypress with which Dante crowned
His visionary brow: a glow-worm lamp,
It cheered mild Spenser, called from faëryland
To struggle through dark ways; and, when a damp
Fell round the path of Milton, in his hand
The thing became a trumpet; whence he blew
Soul-animating strains—alas, too few!

After his forties Wordsworth's power declined. Influenced by Coleridge, he ceased to be a radical. Although he asserted his continued faith in freedom and the aspirations of youth, he became increasingly conservative. He opposed a free press, and placed "security" above liberty. In 1813 the government gave him a sinecure as distributor of stamps for Westmoreland. In 1818 he helped his patron, Lord Lonsdale, to procure votes by subterfuge; the same year the party of the aristocrats appointed him a justice of the peace. By 1821 he had repudiated all liberalism and had grown into a stubborn Tory. In 1843, when Wordsworth was seventy-three, he succeeded Southey (see page 687) as poet laureate.

Before this, however, his poetry had suffered from attrition. With the loss of convictions, his verse lost strength; it fell into barren platitudes and the inflation of trivialities. Even when it occasionally ascended into emotion, it was emotion too carefully hoarded, the emotion of a pragmatic recluse. Wordsworth died April 23, 1850, shortly after his eightieth birthday.

Wordsworth has often been accused of being both too consciously childlike and too determinedly didactic. Yet in the ODE: INTIMATIONS OF IMMORTALITY, begun in his thirty-third and finished in his thirty-fifth year, Wordsworth combines childlike perceptiveness and didacticism and lifts the combination to one of the peaks of poetry. The poem is a deliberate harking back to "that dreamlike vividness and splendor which invest the objects of sight in childhood." The spirit is that of Vaughan and Traherne. Vaughan's opening lines in THE RETREAT (see page 488):

> Happy those early days when I
> Shined in my Angel-infancy

are echoed in Wordsworth's first lines and in:

> Heaven lies about us in our infancy.

But Wordsworth carries the idea further than Vaughan's idealization of innocence. To the thoughtless acceptance of youth and the impulse to forget, maturity adds a more passionate awareness. Memory is thus neither an escape nor an unhappy disillusion, but to the philosophic mind, a preparation for wisdom.

Ode

INTIMATIONS OF IMMORTALITY FROM RECOLLECTIONS
OF EARLY CHILDHOOD

The Child is Father of the Man;
And I could wish my days to be
Bound each to each by natural piety.

There was a time when meadow, grove, and stream,
    The earth, and every common sight,
            To me did seem
        Appareled in celestial light,
The glory and the freshness of a dream.
It is not now as it hath been of yore;—
            Turn whereso'er I may,
                By night or day,
The things which I have seen I now can see no more.

        The rainbow comes and goes,
        And lovely is the rose,
        The moon doth with delight
Look round her when the heavens are bare,
        Waters on a starry night
        Are beautiful and fair;
    The sunshine is a glorious birth;
    But yet I know, where'er I go,
That there hath passed away a glory from the earth.

Now, while the birds thus sing a joyous song,
    And while the young lambs bound
        As to the tabor's sound,
To me alone there came a thought of grief;
A timely utterance gave that thought relief,
        And I again am strong:
The cataracts blow their trumpets from the steep;
No more shall grief of mine the season wrong;
I hear the echoes through the mountains throng;
The winds come to me from the fields of sleep,
        And all the earth is gay;
            Land and sea
    Give themselves up to jollity,
        And with the heart of May
    Doth every beast keep holiday;—
        Thou child of joy,

Shout round me, let me hear thy shouts, thou happy
shepherd-boy.

Ye blessed Creatures, I have heard the call
    Ye to each other make; I see
The heavens laugh with you in your jubilee;
    My heart is at your festival,
    My head hath its coronal,
The fullness of your bliss, I feel—I feel it all.
    Oh evil day! if I were sullen
    While Earth herself is adorning,
        This sweet May-morning,
    And the children are culling
        On every side,
    In a thousand valleys far and wide,
    Fresh flowers; while the sun shines warm,
And the babe leaps up on his mother's arm:—
    I hear, I hear, with joy I hear!
    —But there's a tree, of many, one,
A single field which I have looked upon,
Both of them speak of something that is gone:
    The pansy at my feet
    Doth the same tale repeat:
Whither is fled the visionary gleam?
Where is it now, the glory of the dream?

Our birth is but a sleep and a forgetting:
The soul that rises with us, our life's star,
    Hath had elsewhere its setting,
        And cometh from afar;
    Not in entire forgetfulness,
    And not in utter nakedness,
But trailing clouds of glory do we come
        From God, who is our home.
Heaven lies about us in our infancy;
Shades of the prison-house begin to close
        Upon the growing boy,
But he beholds the light, and whence it flows.
        He sees it in his joy;
The youth, who daily farther from the east
    Must travel, still is Nature's priest,
        And by the vision splendid
        Is on his way attended;
At length the man perceives it die away,
And fade into the light of common day.

Earth fills her lap with pleasures of her own;
Yearnings she hath in her own natural kind,
And, even with something of a mother's mind,
  And no unworthy aim,
 The homely nurse doth all she can
To make her foster-child, her inmate man,
 Forget the glories he hath known,
And that imperial palace whence he came.

Behold the child among his newborn blisses,
 A six years' darling of a pygmy size!
See, where 'mid work of his own hand he lies,
Fretted by sallies of his mother's kisses,
With light upon him from his father's eyes!
See, at his feet, some little plan or chart,
Some fragment from his dream of human life,
Shaped by himself with newly learned art;
 A wedding or a festival,
 A mourning or a funeral;
  And this hath now his heart,
 And unto this he frames his song:
  Then will he fit his tongue
To dialogues of business, love, or strife;
 But it will not be long
 Ere this be thrown aside,
 And with new joy and pride
The little actor cons another part;
Filling from time to time his "humorous stage"
With all the persons, down to palsied age,
That life brings with her in her equipage;
 As if his whole vocation
 Were endless imitation.

Thou, whose exterior semblance doth belie
 Thy soul's immensity;
Thou best philosopher, who yet dost keep
Thy heritage, thou eye among the blind,
That, deaf and silent, read'st the eternal deep,
Haunted forever by the eternal mind—
 Mighty prophet! seer blest!
 On whom those truths do rest,
Which we are toiling all our lives to find,
In darkness lost, the darkness of the grave;
Thou, over whom thy immortality
Broods like the day, a master o'er a slave,

A presence which is not to be put by;
Thou little Child, yet glorious in the might
Of heaven-born freedom on thy being's height,
Why with such earnest pains dost thou provoke
The years to bring the inevitable yoke,
Thus blindly with thy blessedness at strife?
Full soon thy Soul shall have her earthly freight,
And custom lie upon thee with a weight,
Heavy as frost, and deep almost as life!

O joy! that in our embers
Is something that doth live,
That nature yet remembers
What was so fugitive!

The thought of our past years in me doth breed
Perpetual benediction: not indeed
For that which is most worthy to be blest—
Delight and liberty, the simple creed
Of childhood, whether busy or at rest,
With new-fledged hope still fluttering in his breast:—
Not for these I raise
The song of thanks and praise;
But for those obstinate questionings
Of sense and outward things,
Falling from us, vanishings;
Blank misgivings of a creature
Moving about in worlds not realized,
High instincts before which our mortal nature
Did tremble like a guilty thing surprised:
But for those first affections,
Those shadowy recollections,
Which, be they what they may,
Are yet the fountain-light of all our day,
Are yet a master-light of all our seeing;
Uphold us, cherish, and have power to make
Our noisy years seem moments in the being
Of the eternal silence: truths that wake,
To perish never;
Which neither listlessness, nor mad endeavor,
Nor man nor boy,
Nor all that is at enmity with joy,
Can utterly abolish or destroy!
Hence in a season of calm weather,
Though inland far we be,

Our souls have sight of that immortal sea
  Which brought us hither,
  Can in a moment travel thither,
And see the children sport upon the shore,
And hear the mighty waters rolling evermore.

Then sing, ye birds! sing, sing a joyous song!
    And let the young lambs bound
    As to the tabor's sound!
We in thought will join your throng,
    Ye that pipe and ye that play,
    Ye that through your hearts today
    Feel the gladness of the May!
What though the radiance which was once so bright
Be now forever taken from my sight,
    Though nothing can bring back the hour
Of splendor in the grass, or glory in the flower;
    We will grieve not, rather find
    Strength in what remains behind;
    In the primal sympathy
    Which having been must ever be;
    In the soothing thoughts that spring
    Out of human suffering;
    In the faith that looks through death,
In years that bring the philosophic mind.

And oh, ye fountains, meadows, hills, and groves,
Forebode not any severing of our loves!
Yet in my heart of hearts I feel your might;
I only have relinquished one delight
To live beneath your more habitual sway.
I love the brooks which down their channels fret,
Even more than when I tripped lightly as they;
The innocent brightness of a new-born day
          Is lovely yet;
The clouds that gather round the setting sun
Do take a sober coloring from an eye
That hath kept watch o'er man's mortality;
Another race hath been, and other palms are won.
Thanks to the human heart by which we live,
Thanks to its tenderness, its joys, and fears,
To me the meanest flower that blows can give
Thoughts that do often lie too deep for tears.

The fluctuations of Wordsworth's character have been violently condemned and hotly defended. Few appraisers have taken a middle ground, although Wordsworth himself represented the golden mean. Tennyson said that Wordsworth gave us "a sense of the permanent amid the transitory." But it was Shelley who, half proudly, half sadly, weighed the once revolutionary poet of nature in the delicate balance of a sonnet which ends:

> In honored poverty thy voice did weave
> Songs consecrate to truth and liberty—
> Deserting these, thou leavest me to grieve,
> Thus having been, that thou shouldst cease to be.

SIR WALTER SCOTT
[1771–1832]

NO WRITER ever bore a more appropriate surname, for Scott came of an old Border family and was born at Edinburgh, Scotland, August 15, 1771. Author of some of the world's most famous romances, Scott was already acquainted in boyhood with the romantic literature of France and Italy. When he was fifteen, young Walter attended a reception given to honor the poet Burns, and he was the only one of the company who could translate and explain some lines appended to a picture which had attracted Burns's attention. An attack of fever in infancy had crippled him, but, in spite of his lameness, Scott was as robust as he was high-spirited.

Admitted to the bar in his twenty-first year, Scott gradually advanced to the upper circles of his profession; he was clerk of session for twenty-five years. But determined to make a reputation in literature rather than in law, he began with poetry. Inspired by the German ballads he had translated, and stimulated by a study of Percy's RELIQUES OF ANCIENT ENGLISH POETRY, he prepared his own autochthonous collection: MINSTRELSY OF THE SCOTTISH BORDER. The first installment of this compilation was published just after Scott had turned thirty, and the success of the subsequent LAY OF THE LAST MINSTREL, his first important original work, decided Scott's future

for him. The subsequent MARMION (1808) and THE LADY OF THE
LAKE (1810) were immensely popular. Readers immediately re-
sponded to Scott's patriotism, his sense of abounding life, and his
glorification of the heroic.

Native Land

Breathes there the man, with soul so dead,
Who never to himself hath said,
This is my own, my native land?
Whose heart hath ne'er within him burned,
As home his footsteps he hath turned
From wandering on a foreign strand?
If such there breathe, go, mark him well;
For him no minstrel raptures swell;
High though his titles, proud his name,
Boundless his wealth as wish can claim—
Despite those titles, power, and pelf,
The wretch, concentred all in self,
Living, shall forfeit fair renown,
And, doubly dying, shall go down
To the vile dust from whence he sprung,
Unwept, unhonored, and unsung.
from THE LAY OF THE LAST MINSTREL

Hunting Song

Waken, lords and ladies gay,
On the mountain dawns the day,
All the jolly chase is here,
With hawk and horse and hunting-spear!
Hounds are in their couples yelling,
Hawks are whistling, horns are knelling,
Merrily, merrily, mingle they,
"Waken, lords and ladies gay."

Waken, lords and ladies gay,
The mist has left the mountain gray,
Springlets in the dawn are steaming,
Diamonds on the brake are gleaming:

And foresters have busy been
To track the buck in thicket green;
Now we come to chant our lay,
"Waken, lords and ladies gay."

Waken, lords and ladies gay,
To the green-wood haste away;
We can show you where he lies,
Fleet of foot and tall of size;
We can show the marks he made,
When 'gainst the oak his antlers frayed;
You shall see him brought to bay,
"Waken, lords and ladies gay."

Louder, louder chant the lay,
Waken, lords and ladies gay!
Tell them youth and mirth and glee
Run a course as well as we;
Time, stern huntsman, who can balk,
Stanch as hound and fleet as hawk?
Think of this and rise with day,
Gentle lords and ladies gay.

from THE LAY OF THE LAST MINSTREL

One Crowded Hour [1]

Sound, sound the clarion, fill the fife!
To all the sensual world proclaim,
One crowded hour of glorious life
Is worth an age without a name.

from OLD MORTALITY

THE LADY OF THE LAKE is liberally interspersed with lyrics of which the world, in spite of changes in poetic taste, has never grown weary. SOLDIER, REST! is a dirge which expresses the spirit of the Highlands but which is universal in its application. CORONACH is a lament in which the images are more "in character." "It is," wrote Scott, "a wild expression of lamentation, poured forth by the mourners over the body of a departed friend."

[1] *This poem has sometimes been attributed to Major Thomas Osbert Mordaunt.*

Soldier, Rest!

Soldier, rest! thy warfare o'er,
  Sleep the sleep that knows not breaking;
Dream of battled fields no more,
  Days of danger, nights of waking.
In our isle's enchanted hall,
  Hands unseen thy couch are strewing,
Fairy strains of music fall,
  Every sense in slumber dewing.
Soldier, rest! thy warfare o'er,
Dream of fighting fields no more;
Sleep the sleep that knows not breaking,
Morn of toil, nor night of waking.

No rude sound shall reach thine ear,
  Armor's clang of war-steed champing,
Trump nor pibroch summon here
  Mustering clan or squadron tramping.
Yet the lark's shrill fife may come
  At the daybreak from the fallow,
And the bittern sound his drum,
  Booming from the sedgy shallow.
Ruder sounds shall none be near,
Guards nor warders challenge here,
Here's no war-steed's neigh and champing,
Shouting clans or squadrons stamping. . . .

Huntsman, rest! thy chase is done;
  While our slumbrous spells assail ye,
Dream not, with the rising sun,
  Bugles here shall sound reveillé.
Sleep! the deer is in his den;
  Sleep! thy hounds are by thee lying:
Sleep! nor dream in yonder glen
  How thy gallant steed lay dying.
Huntsman, rest! thy chase is done;
Think not of the rising sun,
For at dawning to assail ye
Here no bugles sound reveillé.

                    from THE LADY OF THE LAKE

Coronach

He is gone on the mountain,
    He is lost to the forest,
Like a summer-dried fountain,
    When our need was the sorest.
The fount, reappearing,
    From the rain-drops shall borrow,
But to us comes no cheering,
    To Duncan no morrow!

The hand of the reaper
    Takes the ears that are hoary,
But the voice of the weeper
    Wails manhood in glory.
The autumn winds rushing
    Waft the leaves that are searest,
But our flower was in flushing,
    When blighting was nearest.

Fleet foot on the correi,[1]
    Sage counsel in cumber,[2]
Red hand in the foray,
    How sound is thy slumber!
Like the dew on the mountain,
    Like the foam on the river,
Like the bubble on the fountain,
    Thou art gone, and forever.
        from THE LADY OF THE LAKE

Scott was no less a romantic than Wordsworth. But Wordsworth was intent upon the daily wonder of contemporary life, while Scott devoted himself to the romance of the past. There is no doubt that Scott overloaded his dramatic incidents and overcolored the glamours of history, but there is also no question about the vitality of his characters and situations. He was the father of the modern historical novel. Before he was sixty he had written more than thirty books of fiction, to say nothing of many essays, plays, biographies, and various antiquarian works.

Scott's novels are adorned with verse. THE HEART OF MIDLOTHIAN

[1] *A hollow in the hills.* [2] *Trouble.*

contains one of his most quoted poems; PROUD MAISIE, sung by the demented Madge Wildfire upon her deathbed, is a lyric which is also an extraordinarily condensed ballad.

Proud Maisie

Proud Maisie is in the wood,
 Walking so early;
Sweet Robin sits on the bush,
 Singing so rarely.

"Tell me, thou bonny bird,
 When shall I marry me?"—
"When six braw gentlemen
 Kirkward shall carry ye."

"Who makes the bridal bed,
 Birdie, say truly?"—
"The gray-headed sexton
 That delves the grave duly.

"The glow-worm o'er grave and stone
 Shall light thee steady.
The owl from the steeple sing,
 'Welcome, proud lady.' "

So successful were his efforts that in 1809 Scott entered into partnership with the publisher John Ballantyne and built the magnificent estate of Abbotsford. When the firm failed, Scott refused to take advantage of the bankruptcy laws; although fifty-six years old and ill, he worked harder than ever and turned over his earnings to the creditors. Thus, without ostentation, he proved as heroic as any of his characters.

Excessive work hastened the end. Scott's health gave way under the strain, and his doctors compelled him to take a long sea voyage. When he realized that he was dying, Scott insisted that he meet death at home. Carried across Europe, he died at Abbotsford, September 21, 1832.

SAMUEL TAYLOR COLERIDGE

[1772–1834]

COLERIDGE's life was a long ambivalence, an alternate acceptance of and struggle with irresolution. Born at his father's vicarage of Ottery St. Mary in Devonshire, the boy was fretful and precocious, morbidly lost in fancies. When his father died, Coleridge at the age of nine was sent to London to live with his uncle; he entered the charity school of Christ's Hospital, and took refuge in books.

Before he was nineteen Coleridge's vacillations had begun. After reading a medical dictionary he planned to be a surgeon. A few months later, he discovered Voltaire and decided to become a philosopher. Means were found so that he could attend Jesus College at Cambridge, but he tired of university life in less than two years. He enlisted in a regiment of dragoons under the grotesque name of Silas Tomkyn Comberback, but a few weeks of discipline convinced him that he was not fitted for military life. He met Southey, who was aflame with the promise of the French Revolution, and immediately became converted to the hope of a government of all by all, a scheme which went by the high-sounding title of Pantisocracy. The two young men determined to migrate to the Promised Land of America, found a utopian colony on the banks of the Susquehanna, and establish an ideal community of brotherly love. Since the young pantisocrats needed wives as well as companions, Southey married Edith Fricker, the daughter of a draper, and Coleridge married her sister Sara. None of them ever reached America. Southey settled in Lisbon, and Coleridge, failing to adjust himself to an unfortunate marriage, immured himself in the English countryside.

Three things reconciled Coleridge to a fitful existence: the use of drugs, a reliance on fantasy, and his friendship with the Wordsworths. An admirer made it possible for Coleridge to write in comparative comfort in a cottage in Somersetshire, and Wordsworth joined him there. Harsh experiences brought the poets closer to each other; Wordsworth's sister Dorothy surrounded them with ministering protectiveness; revolutionary ardors were translated into poetry. A joint volume was discussed, and LYRICAL BALLADS resulted.

The scheme of LYRICAL BALLADS was no mere gathering of scattered poems. The book was to establish the two cardinal points of poetry: "the power of exciting the sympathy of the reader by a faithful adherence to the truth of nature, and the power of giving the interest of novelty to the modifying colors of imagination." Wordsworth, so Coleridge tells us in his BIOGRAPHIA LITERARIA, was to take subjects from ordinary life: "The characters and incidents were to be such as will be found in every village and its vicinity." Coleridge's endeavors were to be directed "to persons and characters supernatural, or at least romantic; yet so as to procure for these shadows of imagination that willing suspension of disbelief for the moment, which constitutes poetic faith."

With this view Coleridge wrote THE RIME OF THE ANCIENT MARINER, a cumulatively exciting poem in the style of an ancient ballad. John Livingston Lowes has traced the sources of this remarkable creation, in THE ROAD TO XANADU, a commentary which is also a masterpiece of deduction. Lowes reveals the intricate web of vision and meditation, of accurate research and unfettered romanticism, spun throughout the work. But the central persuasiveness of this rhymed narrative remains unanalyzable. The employment of archaic words and plain rhythms helps re-create the atmosphere of the old ballads, but the extraordinary power of the poem goes far beyond its rich language and varying movement. Its power is incalculable magic, the magic (as William Hazlitt wrote) "of wild, irregular, overwhelming imagination."

The Rime of the Ancient Mariner

PART I

An ancient Mariner meeteth three Gallants bidden to a wedding-feast, and detaineth one.

It is an ancient Mariner,
And he stoppeth one of three.
"By thy long gray beard and glittering eye,
Now wherefore stopp'st thou me?

The Bridegroom's doors are opened wide,
And I am next of kin;
The guests are met, the feast is set:
May'st hear the merry din."

He holds him with his skinny hand,
"There was a ship," quoth he.
"Hold off! unhand me, gray-beard loon!"
Eftsoons his hand dropt he.

The Wedding-Guest is spellbound by the eye of the old seafaring man, and constrained to hear his tale.

He holds him with his glittering eye—
The Wedding-Guest stood still,
And listens like a three years' child:
The Mariner hath his will.

The Wedding-Guest sat on a stone:
He cannot choose but hear;
And thus spake on that ancient man,
The bright-eyed Mariner.

"The ship was cheered, the harbor cleared,
Merrily did we drop
Below the kirk, below the hill,
Below the lighthouse top.

The Mariner tells how the ship sailed southward with a good wind and fair weather, till it reached the Line.

The sun came up upon the left,
Out of the sea came he!
And he shone bright, and on the right
Went down into the sea.

Higher and higher every day,
Till over the mast at noon—"
The Wedding-Guest here beat his breast,
For he heard the loud bassoon.

The Wedding-Guest heareth the bridal music; but the Mariner continueth his tale.

The bride hath paced into the hall,
Red as a rose is she;
Nodding their heads before her goes
The merry minstrelsy.

The Wedding-Guest he beat his breast,
Yet he cannot choose but hear;
And thus spake on that ancient man,
The bright-eyed Mariner.

The ship driven by a storm toward the south pole.

"And now the storm-blast came, and he
Was tyrannous and strong:
He struck with his o'ertaking wings,
And chased us south along.

With sloping masts and dipping prow,
As who pursued with yell and blow
Still treads the shadow of his foe,
And forward bends his head,
The ship drove fast, loud roared the blast,
And southward aye we fled.

And now there came both mist and snow,
And it grew wondrous cold:
And ice, mast-high, came floating by,
As green as emerald.

*The land of
ice, and of
fearful
sounds where
no living
thing was to
be seen.*

And through the drifts the snowy clifts
Did send a dismal sheen:
Nor shapes of men nor beasts we ken—
The ice was all between.

The ice was here, the ice was there,
The ice was all around:
It cracked and growled, and roared and howled,
Like noises in a swound!

*Till a great
sea-bird,
called the
Albatross,
came
through the
snow-fog,
and was re-
ceived with
great joy and
hospitality.*

At length did cross an Albatross,
Thorough the fog it came;
As if it had been a Christian soul,
We hailed it in God's name.

It ate the food it ne'er had eat,
And round and round it flew.
The ice did split with a thunder-fit;
The helmsman steered us through!

*And lo! the
Albatross
proveth a
bird of good
omen, and
followeth the
ship as it re-
turned north-
ward through
fog and
floating ice.*

And a good south wind sprung up behind;
The Albatross did follow,
And every day, for food or play,
Came to the mariners' hollo!

In mist or cloud, on mast or shroud,
It perched for vespers nine;
Whiles all the night, through fog-smoke white,
Glimmered the white moon-shine."

*The ancient
Mariner in-
hospitably
killeth the
pious bird of
good omen.*

"God save thee, ancient Mariner!
From the fiends, that plague thee thus!—
Why look'st thou so?"—"With my cross-bow
I shot the Albatross.

PART II

"The Sun now rose upon the right:
Out of the sea came he,
Still hid in mist, and on the left
Went down into the sea.

And the good south wind still blew behind,
But no sweet bird did follow,
Nor any day for food or play
Came to the mariners' hollo!

And I had done a hellish thing,
And it would work 'em woe:
For all averred, I had killed the bird
That made the breeze to blow.
'Ah wretch!' said they, 'the bird to slay,
That made the breeze to blow!'

Nor dim nor red, like God's own head,
The glorious Sun uprist:
Then all averred, I had killed the bird
That brought the fog and mist.
' 'Twas right,' said they, 'such birds to slay,
That bring the fog and mist.'

The fair breeze blew, the white foam flew,
The furrow followed free;
We were the first that ever burst
Into that silent sea.

Down dropt the breeze, the sails dropt down,
'Twas sad as sad could be;
And we did speak only to break
The silence of the sea!

All in a hot and copper sky,
The bloody Sun, at noon,
Right up above the mast did stand,
No bigger than the Moon.

Day after day, day after day,
We stuck, nor breath nor motion;
As idle as a painted ship
Upon a painted ocean.

Water, water, everywhere,
And all the boards did shrink;
Water, water, everywhere
Nor any drop to drink.

The very deep did rot: O Christ!
That ever this should be!
Yea, slimy things did crawl with legs
Upon the slimy sea.

About, about, in reel and rout
The death-fires danced at night;
The water, like a witch's oils,
Burnt green, and blue, and white.

A Spirit had followed them; one of the invisible inhabitants of this planet, neither departed souls nor angels; concerning whom the learned Jew, Josephus, and the Platonic Constantinopolitan, Michael Psellus, may be consulted. They are very numerous, and there is no climate or element without one or more.

And some in dreams assured were
Of the Spirit that plagued us so:
Nine fathom deep he had followed us
From the land of mist and snow.

And every tongue, through utter drought,
Was withered at the root;
We could not speak, no more than if
We had been choked with soot.

The ship-mates, in their sore distress, would fain throw the whole guilt on the ancient Mariner: in sign whereof they hang the dead sea-bird round his neck.

Ah! well a-day! what evil looks
Had I from old and young!
Instead of the cross, the Albatross
About my neck was hung.

PART III

The ancient Mariner beholdeth a sign in the element afar off.

"There passed a weary time. Each throat
Was parched, and glazed each eye.
A weary time! a weary time!
How glazed each weary eye,
When looking westward, I beheld
A something in the sky.

At first it seemed a little speck,
And then it seemed a mist;
It moved and moved, and took at last
A certain shape, I wist.

A speck, a mist, a shape, I wist!
And still it neared and neared:
As if it dodged a water-sprite,
It plunged and tacked and veered.

At its nearer approach, it seemeth him to be a ship; and at a dear ransom he freeth his speech from the bonds of thirst.

With throats unslaked, with black lips baked,
We could nor laugh nor wail;
Through utter drought all dumb we stood!
I bit my arm, I sucked the blood,
And cried, 'A sail! a sail!'

A flash of joy;

With throats unslaked, with black lips baked,
Agape they heard me call;
Gramercy! they for joy did grin,
And all at once their breath drew in,
As they were drinking all.

And horror follows. For can it be a ship that comes onward without wind or tide?

'See! see! (I cried) she tacks no more!
Hither to work us weal;
Without a breeze, without a tide,
She steadies with upright keel!'

The western wave was all a-flame;
The day was well nigh done!
Almost upon the western wave
Rested the broad bright Sun;
When that strange shape drove suddenly
Betwixt us and the Sun.

It seemeth him but the skeleton of a ship.

And straight the Sun was flecked with bars
(Heaven's Mother send us grace!)
As if through a dungeon-grate he peered
With broad and burning face.

Alas! (thought I, and my heart beat loud)
How fast she nears and nears!
Are those her sails that glance in the Sun,
Like restless gossameres?

And its ribs are seen as bars on the face of the setting Sun. The Spectre-Woman and her Death-mate, and no other on board the skeleton-ship. Like vessel, like crew!

Are those her ribs through which the Sun
Did peer, as through a grate?
And is that Woman all her crew?
Is that a Death? and are there two?
Is Death that woman's mate?

Her lips were red, her looks were free,
Her locks were yellow as gold:
Her skin was as white as leprosy,
The nightmare Life-in-Death was she,
Who thicks man's blood with cold.

The naked hulk alongside came,
And the twain were casting dice;
'The game is done! I've won! I've won!'
Quoth she, and whistles thrice.

The Sun's rim dips; the stars rush out:
At one stride comes the dark;
With far-heard whisper, o'er the sea,
Off shot the spectre-bark.

We listened and looked sideways up!
Fear at my heart, as at a cup,
My life-blood seemed to sip!
The stars were dim, and thick the night,
The steersman's face by his lamp gleamed white
From the sails the dew did drip—
Till clomb above the eastern bar
The horned Moon, with one bright star
Within the nether tip.

One after one, by the star-dogged Moon,
Too quick for groan or sigh,
Each turned his face with a ghastly pang,
And cursed me with his eye.

Four times fifty living men
(And I heard nor sigh nor groan)
With heavy thump, a lifeless lump,
They dropped down one by one.

The souls did from their bodies fly—
They fled to bliss or woe!
And every soul, it passed me by,
Like the whizz of my cross-bow!"

PART IV

"I fear thee, ancient Mariner!
I fear thy skinny hand!
And thou art long, and lank, and brown,
As is the ribbed sea-sand.

I fear thee and thy glittering eye,
And thy skinny hand, so brown."—
"Fear not, fear not, thou Wedding-Guest!
This body dropt not down.

ceedeth to
relate his
horrible pen-
ance.

Alone, alone, all, all alone,
Alone on a wide, wide sea!
And never a saint took pity on
My soul in agony.

He despiseth
the creatures
of the calm.

The many men, so beautiful!
And they all dead did lie:
And a thousand thousand slimy things
Lived on; and so did I.

And envieth
that they
should live,
and so many
lie dead.

I looked upon the rotting sea,
And drew my eyes away;
I looked upon the rotting deck,
And there the dead men lay.

I looked to heaven, and tried to pray;
But or ever a prayer had gusht,
A wicked whisper came, and made
My heart as dry as dust.

I closed my lids, and kept them close,
And the balls like pulses beat;
For the sky and the sea, and the sea and the sky
Lay like a load on my weary eye,
And the dead were at my feet.

But the curse liveth for
him in the eye of the
dead men.

The cold sweat melted from their limbs,
Nor rot nor reek did they:
The look with which they looked on me
Had never passed away.

An orphan's curse would drag to hell
A spirit from on high;
But oh! more horrible than that
Is the curse in a dead man's eye!
Seven days, seven nights, I saw that curse,
And yet I could not die.

in his loneliness and
fixedness he yearneth
toward the journeying
Moon, and the stars that
still sojourn, yet still
move onward; and every-

The moving Moon went up the sky,
And nowhere did abide:
Softly she was going up,
And a star or two beside—

where the blue sky belongs to them, and is their appointed rest, and their native country and their own natural homes, which they enter unannounced, as lords that are certainly expected and yet there is a silent joy at their arrival.

Her beams bemocked the sultry main,
Like April hoar-frost spread;
But where the ship's huge shadow lay,
The charmed water burnt alway
A still and awful red.

By the light of the Moon he beholdeth God's creatures of the great calm.

Beyond the shadow of the ship,
I watched the water-snakes:
They moved in tracks of shining white,
And when they reared, the elfish light
Fell off in hoary flakes.

Within the shadow of the ship
I watched their rich attire:
Blue, glossy green, and velvet black,
They coiled and swam; and every track
Was a flash of golden fire.

Their beauty and their happiness.

O happy living things! no tongue
Their beauty might declare:
A spring of love gushed from my heart,
And I blessed them unaware:

He blesseth them in his heart.

Sure my kind saint took pity on me,
And I blessed them unaware.

The spell begins to break.

The selfsame moment I could pray;
And from my neck so free
The Albatross fell off, and sank
Like lead into the sea.

PART V

"Oh sleep! it is a gentle thing,
Beloved from pole to pole!
To Mary Queen the praise be given!
She sent the gentle sleep from Heaven,
That slid into my soul.

By grace of the holy Mother, the ancient Mariner is refreshed with rain.

The silly buckets on the deck,
That had so long remained,
I dreamt that they were filled with dew;
And when I awoke, it rained.

My lips were wet, my throat was cold,
My garments all were dank;
Sure I had drunken in my dreams,
And still my body drank.

I moved, and could not feel my limbs;
I was so light—almost
I thought that I had died in sleep,
And was a blessed ghost.

He heareth
sounds and
seeth strange
sights and
commotions
in the sky
and the
element.
And soon I heard a roaring wind:
It did not come anear;
But with its sound it shook the sails,
That were so thin and sere.

The upper air burst into life!
And a hundred fire-flags sheen,
To and fro they were hurried about!
And to and fro, and in and out,
The wan stars danced between.

And the coming wind did roar more loud,
And the sails did sigh like sedge;
And the rain poured down from one black cloud;
The Moon was at its edge.

The thick black cloud was cleft, and still
The Moon was at its side:
Like waters shot from some high crag,
The lightning fell with never a jag,
A river steep and wide.

The loud wind never reached the ship,
Yet now the ship moved on!
Beneath the lightning and the Moon
The dead men gave a groan.

The bodies
of the ship's
crew are in-
spired, and
the ship
moves on:
They groaned, they stirred, they all uprose,
Nor spake, nor moved their eyes;
It had been strange, even in a dream,
To have seen those dead men rise.

The helmsman steered, the ship moved on;
Yet never a breeze up blew;
The mariners all 'gan work the ropes,
Where they were wont to do;
They raised their limbs like lifeless tools—
We were a ghastly crew.

The body of my brother's son
Stood by me, knee to knee:
The body and I pulled at one rope

But not by
the souls of
the men,· nor
by daemons
of earth or
middle air,
but by a
blessed troop
of angelic
spirits, sent
down by the
invocation of
the guardian
saint.

But he said nought to me."

"I fear thee, ancient Mariner!"
"Be calm, thou Wedding-Guest!
'Twas not those souls that fled in pain,
Which to their corses came again,
But a troop of spirits blest:

For when it dawned—they dropped their arms,
And clustered round the mast;
Sweet sounds rose slowly through their mouths,
And from their bodies passed.

Around, around, flew each sweet sound,
Then darted to the Sun;
Slowly the sounds came back again,
Now mixed, now one by one.

Sometimes a-dropping from the sky
I heard the sky-lark sing;
Sometimes all little birds that are,
How they seemed to fill the sea and air
With their sweet jargoning!

And now 'twas like all instruments,
Now like a lonely flute;
And now it is an angel's song,
That makes the heavens be mute.

It ceased; yet still the sails made on
A pleasant noise till noon,
A noise like of a hidden brook
In the leafy month of June,
That to the sleeping woods all night
Singeth a quiet tune.

Till noon we quietly sailed on,
Yet never a breeze did breathe:
Slowly and smoothly went the ship,
Moved onward from beneath.

The lonesome Spirit from the south pole carries on the ship as far as the Line, in obedience to the angelic troop, but still requireth vengeance.

Under the keel nine fathom deep,
From the land of mist and snow,
The Spirit slid: and it was he
That made the ship to go.
The sails at noon left off their tune,
And the ship stood still also.

The Sun, right up above the mast,
Had fixed her to the ocean:
But in a minute she 'gan stir,
With a short uneasy motion—
Backwards and forwards half her length
With a short uneasy motion.

Then like a pawing horse let go,
She made a sudden bound:
It flung the blood into my head,
And I fell down in a swound.

The Polar Spirit's fellow-daemons, the invisible inhabitants of the element, take part in his wrong; and two of them relate, one to the other, that penance long and heavy for the ancient Mariner hath been accorded to the Polar Spirit, who returneth southward.

How long in that same fit I lay,
I have not to declare;
But ere my living life returned,
I heard and in my soul discerned
Two voices in the air.

'Is it he?' quoth one, 'Is this the man?
By Him who died on cross,
With his cruel bow he laid full low
The harmless Albatross.

The Spirit who bideth by himself
In the land of mist and snow,
He loved the bird that loved the man
Who shot him with his bow.'

The other was a softer voice,
As soft as honey-dew:
Quoth he, 'The man hath penance done,
And penance more will do.'

PART VI

First Voice

" 'But tell me, tell me! speak again,
Thy soft response renewing—
What makes that ship drive on so fast?
What is the ocean doing?'

Second Voice

'Still as a slave before his lord,
The ocean hath no blast;
His great bright eye most silently
Up to the Moon is cast—

If he may know which way to go;
For she guides him smooth or grim.
See, brother, see! how graciously
She looketh down on him.'

First Voice

The Mariner
hath been
cast into a
trance; for
the angelic
power caus-
eth the vessel
to drive
northward
faster than
human life
could en-
dure.

'But why drives on that ship so fast,
Without or wave or wind?'

Second Voice

'The air is cut away before,
And closes from behind.

Fly, brother, fly! more high, more high!
Or we shall be belated:
For slow and slow that ship will go,
When the Mariner's trance is abated.'

The super-
natural
motion is
retarded;
the Mariner
awakes, and
his penance
begins anew.

I woke, and we were sailing on
As in a gentle weather:
'Twas night, calm night, the Moon was high,
The dead men stood together.

All stood together on the deck,
For a charnel-dungeon fitter:
All fixed on me their stony eyes,
That in the Moon did glitter.

The pang, the curse, with which they died,
Had never passed away:
I could not draw my eyes from theirs,
Nor turn them up to pray.

The curse is finally expiated. And now this spell was snapt: once more
I viewed the ocean green,
And looked far forth, yet little saw
Of what had else been seen—

Like one, that on a lonesome road
Doth walk in fear and dread,
And having once turned round walks on,
And turns no more his head;
Because he knows a frightful fiend
Doth close behind him tread.

But soon there breathed a wind on me,
Nor sound nor motion made:
Its path was not upon the sea,
In ripple or in shade.

It raised my hair, it fanned my cheek
Like a meadow-gale of spring—
It mingled strangely with my fears,
Yet it felt like a welcoming.

Swiftly, swiftly flew the ship,
Yet she sailed softly too:
Sweetly, sweetly blew the breeze—
On me alone it blew.

And the ancient Mariner beholdeth his native country. Oh! dream of joy! is this indeed
The light-house top I see?
Is this the hill? is this the kirk?
Is this mine our countree?

We drifted o'er the harbor-bar,
And I with sobs did pray—
O let me be awake, my God!
Or let me sleep alway.

The harbor-bay was clear as glass,
So smoothly it was strewn!
And on the bay the moonlight lay,
And the shadow of the Moon.

The rock shone bright, the kirk no less,
That stands above the rock:
The moonlight steeped in silentness
The steady weathercock.

And the bay was white with silent light
Till rising from the same,
Full many shapes, that shadows were,
In crimson colors came.

A little distance from the prow
Those crimson shadows were:
I turned my eyes upon the deck—
Oh, Christ, what saw I there!

The angelic
spirits leave
the dead
bodies,

And appear
in their own
forms of light.

Each corse lay flat, lifeless and flat,
And, by the holy rood!
A man all light, a seraph-man,
On every corse there stood.

This seraph-band, each waved his hand;
It was a heavenly sight!
They stood as signals to the land,
Each one a lovely light;

This seraph-band, each waved his hand,
No voice did they impart—
No voice; but oh! the silence sank
Like music on my heart.

But soon I heard the dash of oars,
I heard the Pilot's cheer;
My head was turned perforce away,
And I saw a boat appear.

The Pilot and the Pilot's boy,
I heard them coming fast:
Dear Lord in Heaven! it was a joy
The dead men could not blast.

I saw a third—I heard his voice:
It is the Hermit good!
He singeth loud his godly hymns
That he makes in the wood.
He'll shrieve my soul; he'll wash away
The Albatross's blood.

PART VII

The Hermit
of the Wood. "This Hermit good lives in that wood
Which slopes down to the sea.
How loudly his sweet voice he rears!
He loves to talk with marineres
That come from a far countree.

He kneels at morn, and noon, and eve—
He hath a cushion plump:
It is the moss that wholly hides
The rotted old oak-stump.

The skiff-boat neared: I heard them talk,
'Why, this is strange, I trow!
Where are those lights so many and fair,
That signal made but now?'

Approacheth
the ship with
wonder. 'Strange, by my faith!' the Hermit said—
'And they answered not our cheer!
The planks look warped! and see those sails,
How thin they are and sere!
I never saw aught like to them,
Unless perchance it were

Brown skeletons of leaves that lag
My forest-brook along;
When the ivy-tod is heavy with snow,
And the owlet whoops to the wolf below,
That eats the she-wolf's young.'

'Dear Lord! it hath a fiendish look—
(The Pilot made reply)
I am a-feared'—'Push on, push on!'
Said the Hermit cheerily.

The boat came closer to the ship,
But I nor spake nor stirred;
The boat came close beneath the ship,
And straight a sound was heard.

The ship
suddenly sink-
eth. Under the water it rumbled on,
Still louder and more dread:
It reached the ship, it split the bay;
The ship went down like lead.

The ancient
Mariner is
saved in the
Pilot's boat.
Stunned by that loud and dreadful sound,
Which sky and ocean smote,
Like one that hath been seven days drowned
My body lay afloat;
But swift as dreams, myself I found
Within the Pilot's boat.

Upon the whirl, where sank the ship,
The boat spun round and round;
And all was still, save that the hill
Was telling of the sound.

I moved my lips—the Pilot shrieked
And fell down in a fit;
The holy Hermit raised his eyes,
And prayed where he did sit.

I took the oars: the Pilot's boy,
Who now doth crazy go,
Laughed loud and long, and all the while
His eyes went to and fro.
'Ha! ha!' quoth he, 'full plain I see,
The Devil knows how to row.'

And now, all in my own countree,
I stood on the firm land!
The Hermit stepped forth from the boat,
And scarcely he could stand.

The ancient
Mariner
earnestly en-
treateth the
Hermit to
shrieve him;
and the
penance of
life falls on
him.
'O shrieve me, shrieve me, holy man!'
The Hermit crossed his brow.
'Say quick,' quoth he, 'I bid thee say—
What manner of man art thou?'

Forthwith this frame of mine was wrenched
With a woful agony.
Which forced me to begin my tale;
And then it left me free.

And ever
and anon
throughout
his future life
an agony
constraineth
Since then, at an uncertain hour,
That agony returns:
And till my ghastly tale is told,
This heart within me burns.

him to travel from land to land,

I pass, like night, from land to land;
I have strange power of speech;
That moment that his face I see,
I know the man that must hear me:
To him my tale I teach.

What loud uproar bursts from that door!
The wedding-guests are there:
But in the garden-bower the bride
And bride-maids singing are:
And hark the little vesper bell
Which biddeth me to prayer!

O Wedding-Guest! this soul hath been
Alone on a wide, wide sea;
So lonely 'twas, that God himself
Scarce seemed there to be.

O sweeter than the marriage-feast,
'Tis sweeter far to me,
To walk together to the kirk
With a goodly company!—

To walk together to the kirk,
And all together pray,
While each to his great Father bends,
Old men, and babes, and loving friends,
And youths and maidens gay!

And to teach, by his own example, love and rev-erence to all things that God made and loveth.

Farewell, farewell! but this I tell
To thee, thou Wedding-Guest!
He prayeth well, who loveth well
Both man and bird and beast.

He prayeth best, who loveth best
All things both great and small;
For the dear God who loveth us,
He made and loveth all."

The Mariner, whose eye is bright,
Whose beard with age is hoar,
Is gone: and now the Wedding-Guest
Turned from the Bridegroom's door.

He went like one that hath been stunned,
And is of sense forlorn:
A sadder and a wiser man,
He rose the morrow morn.

More than one biographer has declared sadly that Coleridge suc-
cumbed to fantasy and laudanum. Yet, if the combination produced
a great deal of inane verse, it also made possible some of the strang-
est and most beautiful pictures in English poetry. Although a
man's habits and his creations do not always correspond, the greatest
unfinished dream poem ever written sprang indirectly from Cole-
ridge's reading and directly from his addiction to drugs. Coleridge
himself explains the composition of KUBLA KHAN in a preface writ-
ten in the third person. One afternoon in his twenty-fifth year, he
took an opiate and fell asleep in a chair at the moment he was
reading this sentence in Purchas' PILGRIMAGE: "Here the Khan
Kubla commanded a palace to be built, and a stately garden there-
unto. And thus ten miles of fertile ground were enclosed with a
wall." Coleridge continued for about three hours in a profound
sleep, and during that time he had, so he tells us, "the most vivid
confidence that he could not have composed less than from two to
three hundred lines . . . without any sensation or consciousness of
effort. On awaking he appeared to himself to have a distant recol-
lection of the whole, and taking his pen, ink, and paper, instantly
and eagerly wrote down the lines that are here preserved. At this
moment he was unfortunately called out by a person on business
from Porlock and detained by him above an hour, and on return
to his room found, to his no small surprise and mortification, that
though he still retained some vague recollection of the general pur-
port of the vision, yet with the exception of some eight or ten scat-
tered lines and images, all the rest had passed away."

Lovers of poetry may never be able to forgive the "person from
Porlock," but Coleridge was somehow able to put some of the "still
surviving recollections" to paper and achieve a miraculous frag-
ment. Vivid yet visionary, KUBLA KHAN paints a terrestrial paradise
which, like some Gothic triumph of the imagination, is as wonder-
ful as it is incredible.

Kubla Khan

In Xanadu did Kubla Khan
  A stately pleasure-dome decree:
Where Alph, the sacred river, ran
Through caverns measureless to man
  Down to a sunless sea.
So twice five miles of fertile ground
With walls and towers were girdled round:
And here were gardens bright with sinuous rills,
Where blossomed many an incense-bearing tree,
And here were forests ancient as the hills,
Enfolding sunny spots of greenery.

But oh! that deep romantic chasm which slanted
Down the green hill athwart a cedarn cover!
A savage place; as holy and enchanted
As e'er beneath a waning moon was haunted
By woman wailing for her demon-lover!
And from this chasm, with ceaseless turmoil seething,
As if this earth in fast thick pants were breathing,
A mighty fountain momently was forced,
Amid whose swift half-intermitted burst
Huge fragments vaulted like rebounding hail,
Or chaffy grain beneath the thresher's flail:
And 'mid these dancing rocks at once and ever
It flung up momently the sacred river.
Five miles meandering with a mazy motion
Through wood and dale the sacred river ran,
Then reached the caverns measureless to man,
And sank in tumult to a lifeless ocean:
And 'mid this tumult Kubla heard from far
Ancestral voices prophesying war!

    The shadow of the dome of pleasure
    Floated midway on the waves;
    Where was heard the mingled measure
    From the fountain and the caves.
It was a miracle of rare device,
A sunny pleasure-dome with caves of ice!

    A damsel with a dulcimer
    In a vision once I saw:

It was an Abyssinian maid,
And on her dulcimer she played,
Singing of Mount Abora.
Could I revive within me
Her symphony and song,
To such a deep delight 'twould win me,
That with music loud and long,
I would build that dome in air,
That sunny dome! those caves of ice!
And all who heard should see them there,
And all should cry, Beware! Beware!
His flashing eyes, his floating hair!
Weave a circle round him thrice,
And close your eyes with holy dread,
For he on honey-dew hath fed,
And drunk the milk of Paradise.

Coleridge sank progressively under the spell of opium. He vis-
ited Scotland with the Wordsworths, left his family to voyage in
the Mediterranean, remained in Malta almost a year, and spent
ten months in Naples and Rome. But he could not free himself
from his dependence on the drug, if, indeed, he wanted to; it is
possible that he left home and friends to indulge himself alone
and without reproach. When he returned to England, it was evi-
dent that he desperately needed assistance. Friends helped him to
obtain work and money; in his early forties he was taken care of
by Dr. Gillman, a friendly surgeon whose interests were "other
than medical." For the last eighteen years of his life, years that
were in many ways his happiest, Coleridge rarely left the Gillman
home. He died in his sixty-second year, July 25, 1834.

Coleridge's multiple literary roles have been variously appraised.
As a critic he added originality to erudition; his essays, particularly
those on Shakespeare, fuse the critical and creative functions. As a
thinker, Coleridge let himself drift on the winds of doctrine; he
lacked both direction and integration. His mind was, as Hazlitt
wrote, "tangential. . . . Hardly a speculation has been left on record
from the earliest time, but it is loosely folded up in Mr. Coleridge's
memory, like a rich but somewhat tattered piece of tapestry. But,"
Hazlitt remarked with a malicious nod toward Wordsworth, "Cole-
ridge's discursive reason would not let him trammel himself into
a poet laureate or stamp distributor. . . . He could not realize all he

knew or thought; other stimulants kept up the intoxicating dream, the fever and the madness of his early impressions."

Two of Coleridge's four children, Hartley and Sara, inherited their father's imaginative gifts. Both wrote poetry and essays which brought them reputations not wholly built upon the family name.

ROBERT SOUTHEY
[1774–1843]

ROBERT SOUTHEY's collected verse, together with the superfluously explanatory notes, crowds ten volumes. His prose fills about forty. Never before or since has Pegasus been so hobbled; Southey not only put a bridle upon the fiery creature, but relentlessly drove the winged horse to market.

Son of an unsuccessful merchant, Southey was born August 12, 1774, in Bristol. At fourteen he entered Westminster School and was expelled for writing an article against the common practice of flogging. The humiliation aggravated Southey's spirit of protest. At nineteen he wrote an insurrectionary epic poem, JOAN OF ARC; at twenty he espoused the cause of the French Revolution, became the leader of the "pantisocrats" (see page 665), and almost persuaded Coleridge to migrate to America and found a practical utopia by the side of the poetical Susquehanna.

Twenty years later there was no trace left of the revolutionary youth. Southey had not only his own family to support, but Coleridge's. He became a valued contributor to THE QUARTERLY REVIEW, the most prominent Tory sheet of the period. In his fortieth year, Southey was offered the laureateship upon the death of Henry James Pye, the laureate who, it was said, attained the eminence by rescuing the wig of George III while His Majesty was out hunting. (Byron wrote that Pye was prominently respectable in everything but his poetry.) Sir Walter Scott, who had been proposed for the honor, refused it and recommended Southey, who accepted it. Byron, full of republican ardor, attacked Southey and his principles; the mocking opening of DON JUAN (see page 706) excoriated him in "good, simple, savage verse."

Southey continued to avoid a pressing and often hostile world.

He immured himself in a library of some fifteen thousand volumes; Wordsworth remarked that Southey away from his books seemed out of his element. Honors and troubles descended on him simultaneously. He was recovering from the loss of several children when he suffered a new affliction. "I have been parted from my wife by something worse than death," he wrote at sixty. "Forty years she has been the life of my life, and I have left her this day in a lunatic asylum." Three years later his wife died; two years after her death, Southey remarried. His own mind began to fail. He died in his seventieth year, March 21, 1843, and a bust to his memory was placed in the Poets' Corner of Westminster Abbey.

For all their bulk, Southey's fifty volumes of prose and verse give the impression of something never quite completed. Haste and uncertain standards account for much of the sense of disappointment. Of the prose, the best is in his least literary work, his letters. Of the poetry, little survives except a ballad or two, a little didactic verse—chiefly as the butt of ridicule (see page 950)—and the ironic stanzas on the "famous victory" won at Blenheim in 1704.

The Battle of Blenheim

It was a summer evening,
    Old Kaspar's work was done,
And he before his cottage door
    Was sitting in the sun,
And by him sported on the green
His little grandchild Wilhemine.

She saw her brother Peterkin
    Roll something large and round,
Which he beside the rivulet
    In playing there had found;
He came to ask what he had found,
That was so large, and smooth, and round.

Old Kaspar took it from the boy,
    Who stood expectant by;
And then the old man shook his head,
    And with a natural sigh,
" 'Tis some poor fellow's skull," said he,
"Who fell in the great victory.

"I find them in the garden,
    For there's many here about;
And often when I go to plough,
    The ploughshare turns them out!
For many thousand men," said he,
"Were slain in that great victory."

"Now tell us what 'twas all about,"
    Young Peterkin, he cries;
And little Wilhemine looks up
    With wonder-waiting eyes;
"Now tell us all about the war,
And what they fought each other for."

"It was the English," Kaspar cried,
    "Who put the French to rout;
But what they fought each other for,
    I could not well make out;
But everybody said," quoth he,
"That 'twas a famous victory.

"My father lived at Blenheim then,
    Yon little stream hard by;
They burnt his dwelling to the ground,
    And he was forced to fly;
So with his wife and child he fled,
Nor had he where to rest his head.

"With fire and sword the country round
    Was wasted far and wide,
And many a childing mother then,
    And new-born baby died;
But things like that, you know, must be
At every famous victory.

"They say it was a shocking sight
    After the field was won;
For many thousand bodies here
    Lay rotting in the sun;
But things like that, you know, must be
After a famous victory.

"Great praise the Duke of Marlbro' won,
    And our good Prince Eugene."

"Why 'twas a very wicked thing!"
Said little Wilhemine.
"Nay, nay, my little girl," quoth he,
"It was a famous victory.

"And everybody praised the Duke
Who this great fight did win."
"But what good came of it at last?"
Quoth little Peterkin.
"Why that I cannot tell," said he,
"But 'twas a famous victory." ·

WALTER SAVAGE LANDOR
[1775–1864]

W ALTER SAVAGE LANDOR was perpetually in conflict with the
world and himself. The poet composed some of the most lucid
and restrained poems of the century; the person fulfilled all the im-
plications of his middle name. His almost ninety years were a suc-
cession of petty quarrels and public rages, libels and lawsuits, great
humiliations and ungratifying triumphs. When he was nineteen, an
undergraduate at Trinity College, Oxford, Landor differed politi-
cally with a student who refused to share his suddenly espoused
republican principles; thereupon he fired a gun at his "enemy."
Expelled from college and, later, forgiven, Landor refused to return.
He fought with his father, and when, as eldest son, he received his
inheritance, he sold the ancestral estate and lost his patrimony. At
thirty-three he volunteered in the Spanish army against Napoleon,
but, according to his first biographer, "his troop dispersed or melted
away, and he came back to England in as great a hurry as he had
left." At thirty-six he attended a ball at Bath, and was fascinated by
a girl sixteen years his junior. Although he had had several love
affairs, he determined to marry the young and penniless Julia Thuil-
lier; before the honeymoon was over it was evident that he had
married a little tyrant whose shrewishness was the least of her vices.
Landor became more rampant than ever. He wrote seditious articles
against the government, and had to leave England. He went to Italy,

affronted an official, and was ordered out of Como. It was also in Italy that he threw his cook out of the kitchen window into a flower bed and suddenly shouted, "My God! I forgot about the violets!" Irrepressible and litigious, he had to be prevented from fighting a duel with a neighbor because of the water supply.

Hotheaded in youth, irascible in middle age, Landor was ruined by his temper. At sixty, after twenty-four years of unhappy marriage, he separated from his wife, who impudently housed a lover in the Fiesole villa. He hoped for comfort from his children, whom he had indulged, but they turned against him. He was allowed living expenses only after he had made over his property to the ungrateful family. The friendship of Browning and the admiration of strangers were all that saved him from an embittered old age. He died, within three months of his ninetieth birthday, September 17, 1864.

Landor's work furnishes a proof that a man's art does not parallel his life; nothing could be more dissimilar than Landor's biography and the aesthetics of his craft. There is never anything eccentric or cantankerous in either his balanced verse or the polished prose of his IMAGINARY CONVERSATIONS, a feat of careful reconstruction. The short poems may lack warmth and flexibility, but they are as poised as they are pure. Few English lyrics are more chaste than the poem to Rose Aylmer, daughter of a devoted friend—a brief elegy written when Landor heard the news of her death. Few stanzas are more exquisite than the series of poems to "Ianthe" (Sophia Jane Swift), an early sweetheart who remained the symbol of Landor's unrealized happiness. It is significant that these nostalgic love poems were written between Landor's late fifties and the year before his death. The last of the series was composed in his eighty-eighth year.

Rose Aylmer

Ah, what avails the sceptred race!
Ah, what the form divine!
What every virtue, every grace!
Rose Aylmer, all were thine.
Rose Aylmer, whom these wakeful eyes
May weep, but never see,
A night of memories and sighs
I consecrate to thee.

Ianthe

FROM YOU, IANTHE

From you, Ianthe, little troubles pass
Like little ripples down a sunny river;
Your pleasures spring like daisies in the grass,
Cut down, and up again as blithe as ever.

PAST RUINED ILION

Past ruined Ilion Helen lives;
Alcestis rises from the shades.
Verse calls them forth; 'tis verse that gives
Immortal youth to mortal maids.

Soon shall oblivion's deepening veil
Hide all the peopled hills you see,
The gay, the proud, while lovers hail
These many summers you and me.

AUTUMN

Mild is the parting year, and sweet
The odor of the falling spray;
Life passes on more rudely fleet,
And balmless is its closing day.

I wait its close, I court its gloom,
But mourn that never must there fall
Or on my breast or on my tomb
The tear that would have soothed it all.

WELL I REMEMBER

Well I remember how you smiled
To see me write your name upon
The soft sea-sand. "O! *what a child!*
You think you're writing upon stone!"
I have since written what no tide
Shall ever wash away, what men
Unborn shall read o'er ocean wide
And find Ianthe's name again.

Genially caricatured as the stormy Boythorn in Dickens' BLEAK HOUSE, misread in his day, Landor has been idealized in our own. George Moore and William Butler Yeats hailed him as the embodiment of aesthetic perfection. "The most violent of men," wrote Yeats, "he used his intellect to disengage a visionary image of perfect sanity, seen always in the most serene and classic art imaginable." Never ecstatic, rarely attempting the note of rapture, Landor's voice is low-pitched, cool, almost too well controlled. It is the tone of an old nobility, the marble calm of THE GREEK ANTHOLOGY.

Mother, I Cannot Mind My Wheel

Mother, I cannot mind my wheel;
    My fingers ache, my lips are dry;
O, if you felt the pain I feel!
    But O, who ever felt as I?

No longer could I doubt him true—
    All other men may use deceit.
He always said my eyes were blue,
    And often swore my lips were sweet.

Dirce

Stand close around, ye Stygian set,
    With Dirce in one boat conveyed,
Or Charon, seeing, may forget
    That he is old and she a shade.

Twenty Years Hence

Twenty years hence my eyes may grow
If not quite dim, yet rather so,
Still yours from others they shall know
    Twenty years hence.

Twenty years hence though it may hap
That I be called to take a nap
In a cool cell where thunder-clap
        Was never heard,

There breathe but o'er my arch of grass
A not too sadly sighed *Alas,*
And I shall catch, ere you can pass,
        That wingéd word.

Very True, the Linnets Sing

Very true, the linnets sing
Sweetest in the leaves of spring;
You have found in all these leaves
That which changes and deceives,
And, to pine by sun or star,
Left them, false ones as they are.
But there be who walk beside
Autumn's, till they all have died,
And who lend a patient ear
To low notes from branches sere.

Nowhere is Landor's serenity more evident than in the quatrains written in his old age. The proudest of these is also the most ironically pathetic; "I strove with none, for none was worth my strife," Landor cries with an arrogance that can deceive no one. This quatrain, ON HIS SEVENTY-FIFTH BIRTHDAY, furnishes a curious contrast to Browning's PROSPICE (page 876) and Tennyson's CROSSING THE BAR (page 838). But ON HIS NINTH DECADE combines truth with poetry. Here style and substance are finally united.

On His Seventy-fifth Birthday

I strove with none, for none was worth my strife.
Nature I loved and, next to Nature, Art;
I warmed both hands before the fire of life;
It sinks, and I am ready to depart.

On Death

Death stands above me, whispering low
I know not what into my ear;
Of his strange language all I know
Is, there is not a word of fear.

On His Ninth Decade

To my ninth decade I have tottered on,
And no soft arm bends now my steps to steady;
She who once led me where she would is gone,
So when he calls me, Death shall find me ready.

GEORGE GORDON, LORD BYRON
[1788–1824]

THE term "Byronic" has become a characterization which is also
a criticism, and Byron's biography is not only more romantic
but more readable than his verse. Most of the poems have worn
badly, but the legend has never lost its fascination. Born George
Gordon Byron in London, January 22, 1788, the boy's inheritance
could scarcely have been worse. His father, according to Ernest
Hartley Coleridge, one of Byron's early editors, was a "libertine by
choice and in an eminent degree." His mother, a descendant of
James I of Scotland, was abnormally vain, hysterical, and wholly
incapable of dealing with her difficult child. Her father had com-
mitted suicide, and it was suspected that she had inherited his
neurotic fears.

Lame at birth, Byron was further weakened by infantile paraly-
sis, and his profligacy, the very bravado of his life, was a continued
overcompensation for his feeling of physical inferiority. Born only
remotely to the title, he suddenly became heir-presumptive at the

age of six; the death of his great-uncle brought him the title and the estate in his eleventh year. When Byron entered Cambridge at seventeen, he was already well read in Latin and Greek, and he had fallen deeply in love at least twice. JUVENILE POEMS appeared anonymously when he was an undergraduate of eighteen; a few months later the volume was reissued under his own name as HOURS OF IDLENESS. It was severely criticized by THE EDINBURGH REVIEW, and the article inspired Byron's first characteristically slashing work, a rhymed satire entitled ENGLISH BARDS AND SCOTCH REVIEWERS.

Nervously histrionic, Byron lived in action; he saw to it that events moved rapidly as soon as he came of age. From 1809 to 1811 he traveled in Europe and Asia Minor, swam the Hellespont, made love indiscriminately, contracted malarial fever, and wrote continuously. Upon his return at twenty-three, he took his seat in the House of Lords and published the first two cantos of CHILDE HAROLD'S PILGRIMAGE, an almost undisguised autobiography of the melancholy poet as a distracted pleasure seeker. The work was a success from the very beginning.

Byron literally woke to find himself famous at twenty-four. His first speech in the House of Lords was a passionate defense of work· ers who had wrecked newly installed machinery that threatened their future. Society, aroused from its boredom, lionized him not only as a "poet of passion" but as a brilliant politician. There were those who already referred to him as a statesman, and Byron did nothing to discourage the adulation. He went from one affair to another. In spite of his clubfoot and spindly legs, he was extraordinarily attractive; his features were both delicate and sensual, and his brow had the pallor which women find irresistible in a poet. He was pursued by the wife of the future Lord Melbourne, Lady Caroline Lamb, who masqueraded as a boy in order to visit him in his rooms and who, when he tired of her, tried to stab herself at a ball which was the talk of London. From Lady Caroline he went to Lady Oxford, who was twice his age, and from Lady Oxford to Lady Frances Webster, whom Byron idealized as "Ginevra" and "Medora." Then he met his half-sister Augusta, who had married her cousin, a Colonel Leigh. The mutual attraction was immediate, and Byron took no pains to conceal the nature of their happiness together.

Too brief for our passion, too long for our peace,
Was that hour—Oh, when can its hope, can its memory cease?

He delighted in open avowals; he repeated the theme boldly:

We repent, we abjure, we will break from the chain;
We must part, we must fly—to unite it again.

A few months later Byron married the pretty and capricious Anne Isabella ("Annabella") Milbanke. Within a year, less than a month after the birth of a daughter, his wife returned to her family, charged that Byron was guilty of incest with his half sister, and demanded a separation. Railing at the hypocrisies of society, he thereupon left England, never to return.

In the spring of 1816 Byron joined Shelley, Mary Godwin, and her stepsister Claire Clairmont, who had become Byron's latest mistress and who bore him a daughter, Allegra. But it was impossible for Byron to be faithful to anything but his own wayward impulses. He was, as he assured Thomas Moore, "studious in the day, dissolute in the evening." A list of Byron's inamoratas, besides those already enumerated, would include Marianna Segati, his landlord's wife in Venice; Margarita Cogni, La Fornarina ("the little furnace"), a violent product of the Venetian slums; the twenty-year-old Countess Teresa Guiccioli, who, although married, openly proclaimed herself Byron's mistress and traveled about with him for four years—to say nothing of casual ladies and anonymous chambermaids. "Unnamed and unnumbered," wrote Peter Quennell in BYRON IN ITALY, "his concubines came and went."

Meanwhile Byron's creative faculty was more active than ever. In Europe he composed THE PRISONER OF CHILLON, MANFRED, and MAZEPPA, finished CHILDE HAROLD, and began DON JUAN. The romantic-revolutionary tone of his verse was belittled in England, but on the Continent Byron was hailed as a champion of liberty. An insurrectionary and militant spirit invaded even the love poems; the lyric WE'LL GO NO MORE A-ROVING still surprises us with the second stanza:

For the sword outwears the sheath,
And the soul wears out the breast,
And the heart must pause to breathe,
And Love itself have rest.

But the hater of tyrants was too much an aristocrat to love common humanity. "It is not that I adulate the people," Byron wrote in DON JUAN:

. . . I wish men to be free
As much from mobs as kings . . .

The consequence is, being of no party,
I shall offend all parties:—never mind!
My words, at least, are more sincere and hearty
Than if I sought to sail before the wind.

He satirized the theme in a rough epigram which put a personal
edge to his passion for liberty:

When a Man Hath No Freedom to Fight for at Home

When a man hath no freedom to fight for at home,
  Let him combat for that of his neighbors;
Let him think of the glories of Greece and of Rome,
  And get knocked on the head for his labors.

To do good to Mankind is the chivalrous plan,
  And is always as nobly requited;
Then battle for Freedom wherever you can,
  And, if not shot or hanged, you'll get knighted.

Byron's concern with human emancipation found one of its
noblest expressions in a long poem and a sonnet to a Swiss patriot,
François de Bonnivard, imprisoned for his political opinions. Byron
took several liberties with the facts in THE PRISONER OF CHILLON,
with whom Byron undoubtedly identified himself; but the sonnet
a far finer poem, is unmarred by false dramatization.

Sonnet on Chillon

Eternal Spirit of the chainless Mind!
  Brightest in dungeons, Liberty! thou art,
  For there thy habitation is the heart—
The heart which love of thee alone can bind;
And when thy sons to fetters are consigned—
  To fetters, and the damp vault's dayless gloom,
  Their country conquers with their martyrdom,
And Freedom's fame finds wings on every wind.

Chillon! thy prison is a holy place,
And thy sad floor an altar—for 'twas trod,
Until his very steps have left a trace
Worn, as if thy cold pavement were a sod,
By Bonnivard! May none those marks efface!
For they appeal from tyranny to God.

In 1821 Byron joined an impending revolution in Italy which came to nothing. In 1823 he again attempted to lead a revolt. He learned that numbers of intransigents were attempting a liberation of Greece, and, after offering money and advice, he joined them. Byron was now eager to find "a soldier's grave." But he was denied that final heroic gesture. The climate and his previous excesses proved too much for him. For months he suffered from fits of dizziness and spasms of pain. His illness increased; he was seized with ague, followed by delirium. He died April 19, 1824, three months more than thirty-six years old. His last words were said to be, "Forward! Courage! Don't be afraid! Follow my example!"

Most of Byron's impulses were in opposition to each other. Byron was a genuinely romantic poet, and a melodramatic poseur; a stern ironist, and a sentimentalist who inflated every protestation; an impassioned rebel with an abstract love of justice, and a nineteenth-century Narcissus whose love for himself was one of the great romances of history. This duality was the core of his creativeness; the period of his greatest debauchery was also the period of his greatest achievements.

When We Two Parted

When we two parted
  In silence and tears,
Half broken-hearted
  To sever for years,
Pale grew thy cheek and cold,
  Colder thy kiss;
Truly that hour foretold
  Sorrow to this.

The dew of the morning
  Sunk chill on my brow—
It felt like the warning
  Of what I feel now.

Thy vows are all broken,
    And light is thy fame;
I hear thy name spoken,
    And share in its shame.

They name thee before me,
    A knell to mine ear;
A shudder comes o'er me—
    Why wert thou so dear?
They know not I knew thee,
    Who knew thee too well:—
Long, long shall I rue thee,
    Too deeply to tell.

In secret we met—
    In silence I grieve
That thy heart could forget,
    Thy spirit deceive.
If I should meet thee
    After long years,
How should I greet thee?—
    With silence and tears.

She Walks in Beauty

She walks in beauty, like the night
Of cloudless climes and starry skies,
And all that's best of dark and bright
Meet in her aspect and her eyes;
Thus mellowed to that tender light
Which heaven to gaudy day denies.

One shade the more, one ray the less,
Had half impaired the nameless grace
Which waves in every raven tress
Or softly lightens o'er her face,
Where thoughts serenely sweet express
How pure, how dear their dwelling-place.

And on that cheek and o'er that brow
So soft, so calm, yet eloquent,

The smiles that win, the tints that glow
But tell of days in goodness spent,
A mind at peace with all below,
A heart whose love is innocent.

We'll Go No More A-Roving

So, we'll go no more a-roving
  So late into the night,
Though the heart be still as loving,
  And the moon be still as bright.

For the sword outwears its sheath,
  And the soul wears out the breast,
And the heart must pause to breathe,
  And love itself have rest.

Though the night was made for loving,
  And the day returns too soon,
Yet we'll go no more a-roving
  By the light of the moon.

Stanzas for Music

There be none of Beauty's daughters
  With a magic like thee;
And like music on the waters
  Is thy sweet voice to me:
When, as if its sound were causing
The charmed Ocean's pausing,
The waves lie still and gleaming,
And the lulled winds seem dreaming:

And the midnight moon is weaving
  Her bright chain o'er the deep;
Whose breast is gently heaving,
  As an infant's asleep:
So the spirit bows before thee,
To listen and adore thee;
With a full but soft emotion,
Like the swell of summer's ocean.

Farewell

Farewell! if ever fondest prayer
    For other's weal availed on high,
Mine will not all be lost in air,
    But waft thy name beyond the sky.
'Twere vain to speak, to weep, to sigh:
    Oh! more than tears of blood can tell,
When wrung from guilt's expiring eye,
    Are in that word—Farewell!—Farewell!

These lips are mute, these eyes are dry;
    But in my breast and in my brain,
Awake the pangs that pass not by,
    The thought that ne'er shall sleep again.
My soul nor deigns nor dares complain,
    Though grief and passion there rebel:
I only know we loved in vain;
    I only feel—Farewell!—Farewell!

As a theory, the romantic movement had nothing but good to recommend it. It was based upon the need of quickened perception, continually aroused imagination, and a broad humanitarian impulse. Its triumphs were many and spectacular, but its dangers were great, and its failures inevitable. The imaginative power, too often overprodded, fell into exaggeration. The humanitarian instinct degenerated into undiscriminating sentiment which, unguarded and uncontrolled, indulged itself in orgies of sentimentality. Following Wordsworth and Coleridge, influenced by Shelley, Byron rode the second wave of romanticism with abandon. He was every one of his heroes—the adventurous Harold, the mocking Beppo, the half-remorseful, half-defiant Manfred, the elegantly pensive Lucifer in CAIN, the piratical Conrad in THE CORSAIR, the cynical and self-infatuated Juan. He was a revolutionary and a rake, a creature of the moment and an exiled "pilgrim of eternity."

Waterloo

There was a sound of revelry by night,
And Belgium's capital had gathered then
Her Beauty and her Chivalry, and bright
The lamps shone o'er fair women and brave men;
A thousand hearts beat happily; and when
Music arose with its voluptuous swell,
Soft eyes looked love to eyes which spake again,
And all went merry as a marriage bell;
But hush! hark! a deep sound strikes like a rising knell!

Did ye not hear it?—No; 'twas but the wind,
Or the car rattling o'er the stony street;
On with the dance! let joy be unconfined;
No sleep till morn, when Youth and Pleasure meet
To chase the glowing Hours with flying feet—
But hark!—that heavy sound breaks in once more,
As if the clouds its echo would repeat;
And nearer, clearer, deadlier than before!
Arm! Arm! it is—it is—the cannon's opening roar!

Within a windowed niche of that high hall
Sat Brunswick's fated chieftain; he did hear
That sound the first amidst the festival,
And caught its tone with Death's prophetic ear;
And when they smiled because he deemed it near,
His heart more truly knew that peal too well
Which stretched his father on a bloody bier,
And roused the vengeance blood alone could quell;
He rushed into the field, and, foremost fighting, fell.

Ah! then and there was hurrying to and fro,
And gathering tears, and tremblings of distress,
And cheeks all pale, which but an hour ago
Blushed at the praise of their own loveliness;
And there were sudden partings, such as press
The life from out young hearts, and choking sighs
Which ne'er might be repeated; who could guess
If ever more should meet those mutual eyes,
Since upon night so sweet such awful morn could rise!

And there was mounting in hot haste—the steed,
The mustering squadron, and the clattering car,
Went pouring forward with impetuous speed,
And swiftly forming in the ranks of war—
And the deep thunder peal on peal afar;
And near, the beat of the alarming drum
Roused up the soldier ere the morning star;
While thronged the citizens with terror dumb,
Or whispering, with white lips—"The foe! they come! they come!"

And wild and high the *Cameron's Gathering* rose!
The war-note of Lochiel, which Albyn's hills
Have heard, and heard, too, have her Saxon foes:—
How in the noon of night that pibroch thrills,
Savage and shrill! But with the breath which fills
Their mountain-pipe, so fill the mountaineers
With the fierce native daring which instills
The stirring memory of a thousand years,
And Evan's—Donald's—fame rings in each clansman's ears!

And Ardennes waves above them her green leaves,
Dewy with Nature's tear-drops as they pass,
Grieving, if aught inanimate e'er grieves,
Over the unreturning brave,—alas!
Ere evening to be trodden like the grass
Which now beneath them, but above shall grow
In its next verdure, when this fiery mass
Of living valor, rolling on the foe
And burning with high hope shall molder cold and low.

Last noon beheld them full of lusty life,
Last eve in Beauty's circle proudly gay,
The midnight brought the signal-sound of strife,
The morn the marshaling in arms,—the day
Battle's magnificently stern array!
The thunder-clouds close o'er it, which when rent
The earth is covered thick with other clay,
Which her own clay shall cover, heaped and pent,
Rider and horse,—friend, foe,—in one red burial blent!

from CHILDE HAROLD'S PILGRIMAGE

Ocean

Roll on, thou deep and dark blue Ocean—roll!
Ten thousand fleets sweep over thee in vain;
Man marks the earth with ruin; his control
Stops with the shore; upon the watery plain
The wrecks are all thy deed, nor doth remain
A shadow of man's ravage, save his own,
When for a moment, like a drop of rain,
He sinks into thy depths with bubbling groan,
Without a grave, unknelled, uncoffined and unknown.

His steps are not upon thy paths—thy fields
Are not a spoil for him—thou dost arise
And shake him from thee; the vile strength he wields
For earth's destruction thou dost all despise,
Spurning him from thy bosom to the skies,
And sendst him, shivering in thy playful spray,
And howling, to his Gods, where haply lies
His petty hope in some near port or bay,
And dashest him again to earth—there let him lay.

The armaments which thunderstrike the walls
Of rock-built cities, bidding nations quake,
And monarchs tremble in their capitals,
The oak leviathans, whose huge ribs make
Their clay creator the vain title take
Of lord of thee, and arbiter of war:—
These are thy toys, and, as the snowy flake,
They melt into thy yeast of waves, which mar
Alike the Armada's pride, or spoils of Trafalgar.

Thy shores are empires, changed in all save thee—
Assyria, Greece, Rome, Carthage, what are they?
Thy waters washed them power while they were free,
And many a tyrant since: their shores obey
The stranger, slave or savage; their decay
Has dried up realms to deserts:—not so thou,
Unchangeable save to thy wild waves' play—
Time writes no wrinkle on thine azure brow—
Such as creation's dawn beheld, thou rollest now.

Thou glorious mirror, where the Almighty's form
Glasses itself in tempests: in all time,
Calm or convulsed—in breeze, or gale, or storm,
Icing the pole, or in the torrid clime
Dark-heaving; boundless, endless, and sublime—
The image of Eternity—the throne
Of the Invisible; even from out thy slime
The monsters of the deep are made; each zone
Obeys thee; thou goest forth, dread, fathomless, alone.

from CHILDE HAROLD'S PILGRIMAGE

Southey and Wordsworth

Bob Southey! You're a poet—Poet laureate,
    And representative of all the race;
Although 'tis true that you turned out a Tory at
    Last—yours has lately been a common case;
And now, my Epic Renegade! what are ye at?
    With all the Lakers,[1] in and out of place?
A nest of tuneful persons, to my eye
Like "four and twenty Blackbirds in a pye; [2]

"Which pye being opened they began to sing"
    (This old song and new simile holds good),
"A dainty dish to set before the King,"
    Or Regent, who admires such kind of food;—
And Coleridge, too, has lately taken wing,
    But like a hawk encumbered with his hood—
Explaining metaphysics to the nation—
I wish he would explain his Explanation.

You, Bob! are rather insolent, you know,
    At being disappointed in your wish
To supersede all warblers here below,
    And be the only Blackbird in the dish;
And then you overstrain yourself, or so,
    And tumble downward like the flying fish
Gasping on deck, because you soar too high, Bob,
And fall for lack of moisture quite a-dry, Bob!

[1] *The Lake School of poets, Coleridge, Southey, and Wordsworth, who lived
in the neighborhood of the English lakes.*
[2] *The pun here is directed against Henry James Pye (see page 687), who
became laureate in 1790, and who was the target of contemporary derision.*

And Wordsworth, in a rather long "Excursion"
(I think the quarto holds five hundred pages),
Has given a sample from the vasty version
Of his new system to perplex the sages;
'Tis poetry—at least by his assertion,
And may appear so when the dog-star rages—
And he who understands it would be able
To add a story to the Tower of Babel.

You—Gentlemen! by dint of long seclusion
From better company, have kept your own
At Keswick, and through still continued fusion
Of one another's minds, at last have grown
To deem as a most logical conclusion,
That poesy has wreaths for you alone;
There is a narrowness in such a notion,
Which makes me wish you'd change your lakes for ocean.

I would not imitate the petty thought,
Nor coin my self-love to so base a vice,
For all the glory your conversion brought,
Since gold alone should not have been its price,
You have your salary; was't for that you wrought?
And Wordsworth has his place in the Excise.
You're shabby fellows—true—but poets still,
And duly seated on the Immortal Hill.

from DON JUAN

Evening

O Hesperus! thou bringest all good things—
Home to the weary, to the hungry cheer,
To the young bird the parent's brooding wings,
The welcome stall to the o'erlabored steer:
Whate'er of peace about our hearthstone clings,
Whate'er our household gods protect of dear,
Are gathered round us by thy look of rest;
Thou bring'st the child, too, to the mother's breast.

Soft hour! which wakes the wish and melts the heart
Of those who sail the seas, on the first day
When they from their sweet friends are torn apart;
Or fills with love the pilgrim on his way

As the far bell of vesper makes him start,
Seeming to weep the dying day's decay;
Is this a fancy which our reason scorns?
Ah! surely nothing dies but something mourns.

from DON JUAN

Matthew Arnold summed it up for his contemporaries in ME
MORIAL VERSES:

When Byron's eyes were shut in death
We bowed our head and held our breath.
He taught us little; but our soul
Had *felt* him like the thunder's roll.

Uncritically overproductive, frankly confessional, Byron shocked
and fascinated his generation. The shock has gone out of his work,
but the fascination, mixed and somewhat blurred, remains.

JOHN CLARE
[1793–1864]

JOHN CLARE, who failed to support himself as poet and peasant,
spent the last twenty-seven years of his life in an insane asylum.
As a result most commentators have created legends about him which
are as sensational as they are misleading. It was not until about
sixty years after Clare's death that Edmund Blunden and Alan
Porter re-examined the conflicting evidence, reread his two thou
sand poems, of which more than two thirds have never been pub-
lished, and presented a clear picture of the man and his work.

Son of a farm laborer, John Clare was born July 13, 1793, at
Helpstone, in a cottage melodramatically described as "a narrow
wretched hut, more like a prison than a human dwelling." The
boy was put to work at twelve and got what little schooling he re-
ceived at night. At thirteen, he saw a neighbor thrown from the
top of a hay wagon and break his neck; the sight so affected Clare
that his mind was temporarily unbalanced. At sixteen he fell in
love with Mary Joyce, daughter of a well-to-do farmer, who forbade

their meetings. Clare never quite recovered from this early hurt; the wound grew worse with age. In his imagination he was wedded to Mary; long after she had died and Clare had married Patty Turner, he held long conversations with Mary under the delusion that she was alive and his wife.

From his sixteenth to his twenty-fourth year Clare worked as a gardener, enlisted in the militia, and was employed in a limekiln. At twenty-four he met his wife-to-be, and issued a PROPOSAL FOR PUBLISHING BY SUBSCRIPTION A COLLECTION OF ORIGINAL TRIFLES ON MISCELLANEOUS SUBJECTS IN VERSE. Only seven subscribers responded to the appeal. Worse, Clare was discharged from the limekiln for distributing his prospectus during working hours, and at twenty-five had to ask for parish relief. A bookseller named Drury, who had seen Clare's circular, interested John Taylor, publisher of Keats and Shelley; after an anxious wait of nearly two years, Taylor published Clare's POEMS DESCRIPTIVE OF RURAL LIFE AND SCENERY.

Clare's first volume was an immediate success. Three editions were sold in as many months. The London intelligentsia made Clare the season's fashion much as the Edinburgh coteries had feted Burns. He was hailed as "The Northamptonshire Peasant Poet." Lord Milton entertained him—in the servants' hall—and Lady Milton offered to give him any book that was his favorite, but Clare was confused and could think of nothing. "Lord Fitzwilliam, and Lady Fitzwilliam, too, talked to me and noticed me kindly, and his Lordship gave me some advice which I had done well to have noticed better than I have. He bade me beware of booksellers and warned me not to be fed with promises." Besides the advice, Lord Fitzwilliam presented Clare with seventeen pounds, on the strength of which Clare married Patty Turner shortly before the birth of their first child.

Lord Fitzwilliam's warnings were unhappily justified. Drury, the bookseller, and Taylor, the publisher, saw to it that Clare's royalties were absorbed in "advertising," "commissions," "deductions to agents," and the all-covering "sundries." They suspected that Clare was regarded as a novelty, a bucolic ten days' wonder in the metropolis, and they were right. Although Taylor published THE VILLAGE MINSTREL AND OTHER POEMS in two volumes a year after the publication of Clare's first book, the critics were no longer interested. In 1820 Clare had been trotted from one drawing room to another and had been besieged by visitors eager to drink his health at the tavern. Now he was alone except for a growing family. Continuing to work in the fields, Clare offered to sell his entire output for five years to Taylor for two hundred pounds; but the cautious Taylor rejected the offer with evasive generalities and advised Clare not to be "ambitious but remain in the state in which God had placed him."

Clare began to suffer from overwork and illness. Farmers refused to employ him. He drank to escape his worries, and worried himself into spells of drinking. Two more volumes were published reluctantly and unprofitably, and Clare had premonitions intensified by ominous dreams. He hawked his poems from house to house, dragging a sack of unsold books as much as thirty miles in one day. There were nine people dependent upon him when, in his forty-fourth year, he was placed in a private asylum. A few years later he was committed to the Northampton County Asylum, and it was here that he wrote some of his most lucid verse.

I Am

WRITTEN IN NORTHAMPTON COUNTY ASYLUM

I am: yet what I am none cares or knows,
   My friends forsake me like a memory lost;
I am the self-consumer of my woes,
   They rise and vanish in oblivious host,
Like shades in love and death's oblivion lost;
And yet I am, and live with shadows tost.

Into the nothingness of scorn and noise,
   Into the living sea of waking dreams,
Where there is neither sense of life nor joys,
   But the vast shipwreck of my life's esteems;
And e'en the dearest—that I loved the best—
Are strange—nay, rather stranger than the rest.

I long for scenes where man has never trod;
   A place where woman never smiled or wept;
There to abide with my Creator, God,
   And sleep as I in childhood sweetly slept:
Untroubling and untroubled where I lie;
The grass below—above the vaulted sky.

Clare continued to write to the end, and the words of the "harmless lunatic" were never more precise and expressive than in his last phase. He died quietly May 20, 1864.

Considered as a curiosity by his contemporaries, forgotten for almost a century, Clare has been appreciated only in the last twenty years. He has been compared in some quarters to Blake, and, although the comparison may be excessive, there is no doubt about Clare's fresh vision and clear spontaneity.

Secret Love

I hid my love when young till I
Couldn't bear the buzzing of a fly;
I hid my love to my despite
Till I could not bear to look at light:
I dare not gaze upon her face
But left her memory in each place;
Where'er I saw a wild flower lie
I kissed and bade my love good-bye.

I met her in the greenest dells
Where dewdrops pearl the wood blue-bells
The lost breeze kissed her bright blue eye,
The bee kissed and went singing by,
A sunbeam found a passage there,
A gold chain round her neck so fair;
As secret as the wild bee's song
She lay there all the summer long.

I hid my love in field and town
Till e'en the breeze would knock me down,
The bees seemed singing ballads o'er,
The fly's bass turned a lion's roar;
And even silence found a tongue,
To haunt me all the summer long;
The riddle nature could not prove
Was nothing else but secret love.

The Dying Child

He could not die when trees were green,
For he loved the time too well.
His little hands, when flowers were seen,
Were held for the bluebell,
As he was carried o'er the green.

His eye glanced at the white-nosed bee;
He knew those children of the Spring:
When he was well and on the lea
He held one in his hands to sing,
Which filled his heart with glee.

Infants, the children of the Spring!
How can an infant die
When butterflies are on the wing,
Green grass, and such a sky?
How can they die at Spring?

He held his hands for daisies white,
And then for violets blue,
And took them all to bed at night
That in the green fields grew,
As childhood's sweet delight.

And then he shut his little eyes,
And flowers would notice not;
Birds' nests and eggs caused no surprise,
He now no blossoms got:
They met with plaintive sighs.

When Winter came and blasts did sigh,
And bare were plain and tree,
As he for ease in bed did lie
His soul seemed with the free,
He died so quietly.

Clare's spell is his own. His scenes are familiar, but they are never commonplace; his language is simple but seldom trite. Every detail is recorded as sharply as though it had never before been observed. "There is," wrote Edmund Blunden, "no poet who in his nature poetry so completely subdues self and mood, and deals with the topic for its own sake." If Clare's charm is limited because of its bucolic setting, it is unsurpassed in its purity.

Young Lambs

The spring is coming by a many signs;
The trays are up, the hedges broken down
That fenced the haystack, and the remnant shines
Like some old antique fragment weathered brown.
And where suns peep, in every sheltered place,
The little early buttercups unfold
A glittering star or two—till many trace
The edges of the blackthorn clumps in gold.
And then a little lamb bolts up behind
The hill, and wags his tail to meet the yoe;
And then another, sheltered from the wind,
Lies all his length as dead—and lets me go
Close by, and never stirs, but basking lies,
With legs stretched out as though he could not rise.

Firwood

The fir trees taper into twigs and wear
The rich blue green of summer all the year,
Softening the roughest tempest almost calm
And offering shelter ever still and warm
To the small path that towels underneath,
Where loudest winds—almost as summer's breath—
Scarce fan the weed that lingers green below,
When others out of doors are lost in frost and snow.
And sweet the music trembles on the ear
As the wind suthers through each tiny spear,
Makeshifts for leaves; and yet, so rich they show,
Winter is almost summer where they grow.

Evening Primrose

When once the sun sinks in the west,
And dew-drops pearl the evening's breast,
Almost as pale as moonbeams are,
Or its companionable star,

The evening primrose opes anew
Its delicate blossoms to the dew;
And, shunning-hermit of the light,
Wastes its fair bloom upon the night,
Who, blindfold to its fond caresses,
Knows not the beauty he possesses.
Thus it blooms on till night is by
And day looks out with open eye,
Abashed at the gaze it cannot shun,
It faints and withers, and is done.

Clock-o'-Clay

In the cowslip pips I lie,
Hidden from the buzzing fly,
While green grass beneath me lies,
Pearled with dew like fishes' eyes,
Here I lie, a clock-o'-clay,
Waiting for the time o' day.

While the forest quakes surprise,
And the wild wind sobs and sighs,
My home rocks as like to fall,
On its pillar green and tall;
When the pattering rain drives by
Clock-o'-clay keeps warm and dry.

Day by day and night by night,
All the week I hide from sight;
In the cowslip pips I lie,
In the rain still warm and dry;
Day and night, and night and day,
Red, black-spotted clock-o'-clay.

My home shakes in wind and showers,
Pale green pillar topped with flowers,
Bending at the wild wind's breath,
Till I touch the grass beneath;
Here I live, lone clock-o'-clay,
Watching for the time of day.

PERCY BYSSHE SHELLEY
[1792–1822]

Two beings fought it out in the body of Percy Bysshe Shelley. One was an uncompromising zealot, a passionate seeker after truth. The other was a victim of illusions, "a beautiful and ineffectual angel, beating in the void his luminous wings in vain."

Born at Field Place, near the little Sussex village of Horsham, on August 4, 1792, Percy was the son of Timothy Shelley. The poet's grandfather, Sir Bysshe Shelley, was the son of an emigrant and had been born in Newark, New Jersey. Returning to England, he married successively two heiresses, built up a fortune, and, according to William Michael Rossetti, "lived in sullen and penurious retirement." Even as a child Shelley was brilliant and hypersensitive, resentful of all authority, and, when hurt, quick to become hysterical. These characteristics, together with his physical beauty, made him unpopular among his fellows. His schooling at Eton and Oxford was a long misery. He was cruelly mocked by the younger boys, badgered and bullied by the older students. As a result Shelley became so nonconformist that he refused to accept any form of discipline. When an Eton master found Shelley's room full of blue chemical flames, the young scientist explained, "Sir, I am trying to call up the Devil." Turning away from the brute world to the necromancy of a dream, he heartened himself with Godwin's anarchical POLITICAL JUSTICE, and was dubbed "mad Shelley." At nineteen he was expelled from Oxford for having published, anonymously, THE NECESSITY OF ATHEISM.

Returning home to an angry father, supported by pocket money supplied by his sisters, Shelley met Harriet Westbrook, daughter of a hotelkeeper. Harriet was sixteen, and when Shelley learned that her father insisted on her returning to school, he determined to rescue her from "persecution." Shelley had not yet recovered from a love affair with his cousin Harriet Grove, who was alarmed at his efforts to convert her to his "heresies." But the young crusader, roused with new zeal, ran away with Harriet Westbrook, married her at Edinburgh—although he still objected to the despotic institution of marriage—and spent his honeymoon in Ireland, distributing copies of a pamphlet, DECLARATION OF RIGHTS, by hand, from balloons, and in bottles set adrift.

Upon his return to England Shelley became a father at twenty-one, engaged in a warm but platonic intimacy with Elizabeth Hitchener, a schoolmistress, and published his first important poem, QUEEN MAB, which denounced religion and aggressively criticized the structure of human society. A few months later, Shelley began corresponding with Godwin, met his daughter, Mary Wollstone-craft Godwin, and immediately fell in love with her. She was seventeen, a radical like her father, and, like Shelley, a philosophic anarchist. In July, 1814, the two eloped to Switzerland.

Shelley's life became increasingly complicated with the Godwin family, which was, in itself, a fine study in complication. Mary was Godwin's daughter by his first wife, author of THE RIGHTS OF WOMEN. Before her marriage, the first Mrs. Godwin had borne a daughter to Gilbert Imlay, an American in Paris; this daughter, Fanny, committed suicide in 1816, and it was rumored that her death was due to a hopeless love of Shelley. Godwin's second wife was a Mrs. Clairmont, whose daughter by her first marriage was Clara Mary Jane ("Claire") Clairmont, who became Byron's mistress and bore him a daughter, Allegra. Claire insisted upon accompanying Shelley and Mary to the Continent. When they returned in 1815 Shelley found that he had again become a father—Harriet having given birth to a son—and that he had inherited property worth six thousand pounds a year from his grandfather. Shelley assigned two hundred pounds a year to his wife Harriet and invited her to share his establishment with Mary, an invitation Harriet declined. Shelley and Mary spent the next summer in Switzerland—again accompanied by Claire—and their return to England was followed by the suicides of Fanny and Harriet. Shelley's wife had always threatened self-destruction, but Shelley believed that she had talked herself out of the act; the discovery of her body in the Serpentine was a shock from which he never fully recovered.

Shelley married Miss Godwin in December, 1816, but their peace was shattered by Harriet's father, who demanded the custody of his two grandchildren on the charges that Shelley had deserted his wife and that, because of his antisocial principles, he was morally unfit to bring up the children. Lord Chancellor Eldon affirmed the charges and appointed a Dr. Hume as guardian; whereupon the baffled poet countered with a set of furious verses beginning, "Thy country's curse is on thee!"

Shelley received the Lord Chancellor's verdict as a kind of excommunication and sentence of exile. In 1818, like Byron before him, he left England for Italy, and, like Byron, never returned. Soon after his departure, he wrote a sonnet which, though flawed in form, is a perfect expression of Shelley's feeling for his fatherland, his humiliation and grief, and his ineradicable hope.

England in 1819

An old, mad, blind, despised, and dying king—[1]
Princes, the dregs of their dull race, who flow
Through public scorn—mud from a muddy spring;
Rulers, who neither see, nor feel, nor know,
But leech-like to their fainting country cling,
Till they drop, blind in blood, without a blow;
A people starved and stabbed in the untilled field—
An army, which liberticide and prey
Makes as a two-edged sword to all who wield—
Golden and sanguine laws which tempt and slay—
Religion Christless, Godless—a book sealed;
A Senate—Time's worst statute unrepealed—
Are graves, from which a glorious Phantom may
Burst, to illumine our tempestuous day.

In Italy Byron and Shelley became close companions, and the last phase of Shelley's life was a period of full creativeness as well as the time of his greatest intellectual growth. Besides his attachment for Byron, whom he idolized and influenced, he became infatuated with Emilia Viviani and Mrs. Jane Williams, both of whom inspired some of Shelley's most famous love poems. But he maintained his emotional equilibrium. "I think one is always in love with something or other," he wrote. "The error consists in seeking in a mortal image the likeness of what is perhaps eternal."

Shelley found the "likeness of what is perhaps eternal" not only in "mortal images" but in the immortal imagery of the poems written in his late twenties: THE CENCI, that marvelous poetic drama; PROMETHEUS UNBOUND, the triumphant vision of a perfect future; HELLAS, a glorification of the Greek revolt; EPIPSYCHIDION, a hymn

[1] *George III.*

to abstract beauty and spiritual love inspired by Emilia Viviani; and ADONAIS, that magnificent elegy in which Shelley, vindicating all poets in his defense of Keats, "in another's fate now wept his own."

In the late spring of 1821 the Shelleys moved to a villa on the Gulf of Spezia. Their friend Lieutenant Edward Williams had designed a small boat, which was speedy but none too safe. On July 1, 1822, Shelley and Williams sailed over to Leghorn to greet Byron and Leigh Hunt, who had just arrived in Italy. On July 8 they started to return, but never reached home. Just what happened is unknown. It has never been determined whether the boat capsized, collided with some larger vessel, or was run down by pirates. Two weeks later the two bodies were washed ashore; a volume of Keats was found in Shelley's pocket. Since the Italian laws required complete destruction because of the plague, the bodies were buried in quicklime. But Trelawny and other friends dug them up and burned the corpses on the beach; at the last moment, Trelawny snatched the poet's heart from the pyre. Shelley's ashes were collected and buried in the Protestant Cemetery in Rome, where the body of Keats had already been interred. Had he lived another month, Shelley would have been thirty years old.

"Poets," wrote Shelley at the conclusion of THE DEFENSE OF POETRY, "are the unacknowledged legislators of the world." As a legislator, Shelley would have been a severe and stubborn insurrectionary. Misjudged as a licentious pagan by a self-righteous world, he was essentially a passionate believer in universal goodness, even in human perfectibility. A dedicated poet of protest, he always had, as he wrote in his preface to PROMETHEUS UNBOUND, "a passion for reforming the world."

Two extremes of Shelley's protesting spirit are manifest in the SONG TO THE MEN OF ENGLAND and the Final Chorus from HELLAS. Here condemnation turns to affirmation, and scorn ascends to prophecy.

❧ *Song to the Men of England*

Men of England, wherefore plough
For the lords who lay ye low?
Wherefore weave with toil and care
The rich robes your tyrants wear?

Wherefore feed, and clothe, and save,
From the cradle to the grave,
Those ungrateful drones who would
Drain your sweat—nay, drink your blood!

Wherefore, Bees of England, forge
Many a weapon, chain, and scourge,
That these stingless drones may spoil
The forced produce of your toil?

Have ye leisure, comfort, calm,
Shelter, food, love's gentle balm?
Or what is it ye buy so dear
With your pain and with your fear?

The seed ye sow, another reaps;
The wealth ye find, another keeps;
The robes ye weave, another wears;
The arms ye forge, another bears.

Sow seed—but let no tyrant reap;
Find wealth—let no impostor heap;
Weave robes—let not the idle wear;
Forge arms—in your defence to bear.

Shrink to your cellars, holes, and cells;
In halls ye deck, another dwells.
Why shake the chains ye wrought? Ye see
The steel ye tempered glance on ye.

With plough and spade, and hoe and loom,
Trace your grave, and build your tomb,
And weave your winding-sheet, till fair
England be your sepulchre.

A New World

The world's great age begins anew,
    The golden years return,
The earth doth like a snake renew
    Her winter weeds outworn:
Heaven smiles, and faiths and empires gleam,
Like wrecks of a dissolving dream.

A brighter Hellas rears its mountains
From waves serener far;
A new Peneus rolls his fountains
Against the morning star.
Where fairer Tempes bloom, there sleep
Young Cyclads on a sunnier deep.

A loftier Argo cleaves the main,
Fraught with a later prize;
Another Orpheus sings again,
And loves, and weeps, and dies.
A new Ulysses leaves once more
Calypso for his native shore.

Oh! write no more the tale of Troy,
If earth death's scroll must be!
Nor mix with Laian rage the joy
Which dawns upon the free,
Altho' a subtler Sphinx renew
Riddles of death Thebes never knew.

Another Athens shall arise,
And to remoter time
Bequeath, like sunset to the skies,
The splendor of its prime;
And leave, if naught so bright may live,
All earth can take or heaven can give.

Saturn and Love their long repose
Shall burst, more bright and good
Than all who fell, than One who rose,
Than many unsubdued:
Not gold, not blood, their altar dowers,
But votive tears and symbol flowers.

Oh, cease! must hate and death return?
Cease! must men kill and die?
Cease! drain not to its dregs the urn
Of bitter prophecy.
The world is weary of the past.
Oh, might it die or rest at last!
Final Chorus: HELLAS

Although the idea of revolution burns through Shelley's pages,
it is doubtful that most readers are drawn to the poet because of
his message. It is the music, the ardent imagination, which first

arrest and then hold the reader; it is the power of communicating acute emotion, of intense yearning which is all the more cherished because it cannot be consummated. Shelley may be admired for his insurgent and iconoclastic spirit, but he is loved for his sheer effluence, the overbrimming lyricism, the ever-fertile fancy, the profound hypnotic power.

To a Skylark

Hail to thee, blithe Spirit!
   Bird thou never wert,
That from Heaven, or near it,
   Pourest thy full heart
In profuse strains of unpremeditated art.

   Higher still and higher
   From the earth thou springest
Like a cloud of fire;
   The blue deep thou wingest,
And singing still dost soar, and soaring ever singest.

   In the golden lightning
   Of the sunken sun
O'er which clouds are bright'ning,
   Thou dost float and run,
Like an unbodied joy whose race is just begun.

   The pale purple even
   Melts around thy flight;
Like a star of Heaven
   In the broad daylight
Thou art unseen, but yet I hear thy shrill delight:

   Keen as are the arrows
   Of that silver sphere,
Whose intense lamp narrows
   In the white dawn clear
Until we hardly see—we feel that it is there.

   All the earth and air
   With thy voice is loud,
As, when night is bare,
   From one lonely cloud
The moon rains out her beams, and heaven is overflowed.

What thou art we know not;
  What is most like thee?
From rainbow clouds there flow not
  Drops so bright to see
As from thy presence showers a rain of melody.

Like a poet hidden
  In the light of thought,
Singing hymns unbidden,
  Till the world is wrought
To sympathy with hopes and fears it heeded not:

Like a high-born maiden
  In a palace tower,
Soothing her love-laden
  Soul in secret hour
With music sweet as love, which overflows her bower:

Like a glow-worm golden
  In a dell of dew,
Scattering unbeholden
  Its aerial hue
Among the flowers and grass, which screen it from the view:

Like a rose embowered
  In its own green leaves,
By warm winds deflowered,
  Till the scent it gives
Makes faint with too much sweet these heavy-winged thieves.

Sound of vernal showers
  On the twinkling grass,
Rain-awakened flowers,
  All that ever was
Joyous, and clear, and fresh, thy music doth surpass.

Teach us, sprite or bird,
  What sweet thoughts are thine:
I have never heard
  Praise of love or wine
That panted forth a flood of rapture so divine.

Chorus hymeneal
  Or triumphal chaunt
Matched with thine, would be all
  But an empty vaunt—
A thing wherein we feel there is some hidden want.

What objects are the fountains
Of thy happy strain?
What fields, or waves, or mountains?
What shapes of sky or plain?
What love of thine own kind? what ignorance of pain?

With thy clear keen joyance
Languor cannot be:
Shadow of annoyance
Never came near thee:
Thou lovest, but ne'er knew love's sad satiety.

Waking or asleep,
Thou of death must deem
Things more true and deep
Than we mortals dream,
Or how could thy notes flow in such a crystal stream?

We look before and after,
And pine for what is not:
Our sincerest laughter
With some pain is fraught;
Our sweetest songs are those that tell of saddest thought.

Yet if we could scorn
Hate, and pride, and fear;
If we were things born
Not to shed a tear,
I know not how thy joy we ever should come near.

Better than all measures
Of delightful sound,
Better than all treasures
That in books are found,
Thy skill to poet were, thou scorner of the ground!

Teach me half the gladness
That thy brain must know,
Such harmonious madness
From my lips would flow
The world should listen then, as I am listening now!

To Night

Swiftly walk o'er the western wave,
    Spirit of Night!
Out of the misty eastern cave,
Where, all the long and lone daylight,
Thou wovest dreams of joy and fear,
Which make thee terrible and dear—
    Swift be thy flight!

Wrap thy form in a mantle gray,
    Star-inwrought!
Blind with thine hair the eyes of day;
Kiss her until she be wearied out,
Then wander o'er city, and sea, and land,
Touching all with thine opiate wand—
    Come, long-sought!

When I arose and saw the dawn,
    I sighed for thee;
When light rode high, and the dew was gone,
And noon lay heavy on flower and tree,
And the weary day turned to his rest,
Lingering like an unloved guest,
    I sighed for thee.

Thy brother Death came, and cried,
    Wouldst thou me?
Thy sweet child Sleep, the filmy-eyed,
Murmured like a noontide bee,
Shall I nestle near thy side?
Wouldst thou me?—And I replied,
    No, not thee!

Death will come when thou art dead,
    Soon, too soon—
Sleep will come when thou art fled;
Of neither would I ask the boon
I ask of thee, beloved Night—
Swift be thine approaching flight,
    Come soon, soon!

The Waning Moon

And like a dying lady, lean and pale,
Who totters forth, wrapped in a gauzy veil,
Out of her chamber, led by the insane
And feeble wanderings of her fading brain,
The moon arose up in the murky East,
A white and shapeless mass.

To the Moon

Art thou pale for weariness
Of climbing heaven and gazing on the earth,
Wandering companionless
Among the stars that have a different birth—
And ever changing, like a joyless eye
That finds no object worth its constancy?

Love's Philosophy

The fountains mingle with the river
And the rivers with the Ocean,
The winds of Heaven mix for ever
With a sweet emotion;
Nothing in the world is single;
All things by a law divine
In one spirit meet and mingle.
Why not I with thine?—

See the mountains kiss high Heaven
And the waves clasp one another;
No sister-flower would be forgiven
If it disdained its brother;
And the sunlight clasps the earth
And the moonbeams kiss the sea:
What is all this sweet work worth
If thou kiss not me?

Music, When Soft Voices Die

Music, when soft voices die,
Vibrates in the memory—
Odors, when sweet violets sicken,
Live within the sense they quicken.

Rose leaves, when the rose is dead,
Are heaped for the beloved's bed;
And so thy thoughts, when thou art gone,
Love itself shall slumber on.

To ———[1]

THE DESIRE OF THE MOTH

One word is too often profaned
    For me to profane it,
One feeling too falsely disdained
    For thee to disdain it;
One hope is too like despair
    For prudence to smother,
And pity from thee more dear
    Than that from another.

I can give not what men call love,
    But wilt thou accept not
The worship the heart lifts above
    And the Heavens reject not,—
The desire of the moth for the star,
    Of the night for the morrow,
The devotion to something afar
    From the sphere of our sorrow?

The Indian Serenade

I arise from dreams of thee
In the first sweet sleep of night,
When the winds are breathing low,
And the stars are shining bright

[1] *Jane Williams, see page 717.*

I arise from dreams of thee,
And a spirit in my feet
Hath led me—who knows how?
To thy chamber window, Sweet!

The wandering airs they faint
On the dark, the silent stream—
The champak odors fail
Like sweet thoughts in a dream;
The nightingale's complaint,
It dies upon her heart;
As I must on thine,
Oh, beloved as thou art!

O lift me from the grass!
I die! I faint! I fail!
Let thy love in kisses rain
On my lips and eyelids pale.
My cheek is cold and white, alas!
My heart beats loud and fast;—
Oh! press it to thine own again,
Where it will break at last.

When the Lamp Is Shattered

When the lamp is shattered,
The light in the dust lies dead;
When the cloud is scattered,
The rainbow's glory is shed;
When the lute is broken,
Sweet tones are remembered not;
When the lips have spoken,
Loved accents are soon forgot.

As music and splendor
Survive not the lamp and the lute,
The heart's echoes render
No song when the spirit is mute:—
No song but sad dirges,
Like the wind through a ruined cell,
Or the mournful surges
That ring the dead seaman's knell.

When hearts have once mingled,
Love first leaves the well-built nest;
The weak one is singled
To endure what it once possessed.
O Love! who bewailest
The frailty of all things here,
Why choose you the frailest
For your cradle, your home, and your bier?

Its passions will rock thee,
As the storms rock the ravens on high;
Bright reason will mock thee,
Like the sun from a wintry sky.
From thy nest every rafter
Will rot, and thine eagle home
Leave thee naked to laughter,
When leaves fall and cold winds come.

Song

Rarely, rarely comest thou,
Spirit of Delight!
Wherefore hast thou left me now
Many a day and night?
Many a weary night and day
'Tis since thou art fled away.

How shall ever one like me
Win thee back again?
With the joyous and the free
Thou wilt scoff at pain.
Spirit false! thou hast forgot
All but those who need thee not.

As a lizard with the shade
Of a trembling leaf,
Thou with sorrow art dismayed;
Even the sighs of grief
Reproach thee, that thou art not near,
And reproach thou wilt not hear.

Let me set my mournful ditty
To a merry measure;—

Thou wilt never come for pity,
  Thou wilt come for pleasure;
Pity then will cut away
Those cruel wings, and thou wilt stay.

I love all that thou lovest,
  Spirit of Delight!
The fresh Earth in new leaves dressed,
  And the starry night;
Autumn evening, and the morn
When the golden mists are born.

I love snow and all the forms
  Of the radiant frost;
I love waves, and winds, and storms,
  Everything almost
Which is Nature's, and may be
Untainted by man's misery.

I love tranquil solitude,
  And such society
As is quiet, wise, and good;
  Between thee and me
What difference? but thou dost possess
The things I seek, not love them less.

I love Love—though he has wings,
  And like light can flee,
But above all other things,
  Spirit, I love thee—
Thou art love and life! O come!
Make once more my heart thy home!

  The superb ODE TO THE WEST WIND was conceived and chiefly
written, so Shelley tells us, "in a wood that skirts the Arno, near
Florence, on a day when the tempestuous wind, whose temperature
is at once mild and animating, was collecting the vapors which pour
down the autumnal rains." Apart from the force of the swiftly
changing images, the poem is technically exciting for the way the
rise and fall of the wind is suggested by the long-rolling sentences,
and the manner in which the autumnal music is suspended through
the interlocking *terza rima,* the linked "third rhyme" employed so
differently by Dante.

Ode to the West Wind

I

O wild West Wind, thou breath of Autumn's being,
Thou, from whose unseen presence the leaves dead
Are driven, like ghosts from an enchanter fleeing,

Yellow, and black, and pale, and hectic red,
Pestilence-stricken multitudes: O thou,
Who chariotest to their dark wintry bed

The wingèd seeds, where they lie cold and low,
Each like a corpse within its grave, until
Thine azure sister of the Spring shall blow

Her clarion o'er the dreaming earth, and fill
(Driving sweet buds like flocks to feed in air)
With living hues and odors plain and hill:

Wild Spirit, which art moving everywhere;
Destroyer and preserver; hear, oh, hear!

II

Thou on whose stream, 'mid the steep sky's commotion,
Loose clouds like earth's decaying leaves are shed,
Shook from the tangled boughs of Heaven and Ocean,

Angels of rain and lightning: there are spread
On the blue surface of thine aery surge,
Like the bright hair uplifted from the head

Of some fierce Maenad, even from the dim verge
Of the horizon to the zenith's height,
The locks of the approaching storm. Thou dirge

Of the dying year, to which this closing night
Will be the dome of a vast sepulchre,
Vaulted with all thy congregated might

Of vapors, from whose solid atmosphere
Black rain, and fire, and hail will burst: oh, hear!

III

Thou who didst waken from his summer dreams
The blue Mediterranean, where he lay,
Lulled by the coil of his crystàlline streams,

Beside a pumice isle in Baiae's bay,
And saw in sleep old palaces and towers
Quivering within the wave's intenser day,

All overgrown with azure moss and flowers
So sweet, the sense faints picturing them! Thou
For whose path the Atlantic's level powers

Cleave themselves into chasms, while far below
The sea-blooms and the oozy woods which wear
The sapless foliage of the ocean, know

Thy voice, and suddenly grow gray with fear,
And tremble and despoil themselves: oh, hear!

IV

If I were a dead leaf thou mightest bear;
If I were a swift cloud to fly with thee;
A wave to pant beneath thy power, and share

The impulse of thy strength, only less free
Than thou, O uncontrollable! If even
I were as in my boyhood, and could be

The comrade of thy wanderings over Heaven,
As then, when to outstrip thy skiey speed
Scarce seemed a vision; I would ne'er have striven

As thus with thee in prayer in my sore need.
Oh, lift me as a wave, a leaf, a cloud!
I fall upon the thorns of life! I bleed!

A heavy weight of hours has chained and bowed
One too like thee: tameless, and swift, and proud.

V

Make me thy lyre, even as the forest is:
What if my leaves are falling like its own!
The tumult of thy mighty harmonies

Will take from both a deep, autumnal tone,
Sweet though in sadness. Be thou, Spirit fierce,
My spirit! Be thou me, impetuous one!

Drive my dead thoughts over the universe
Like withered leaves to quicken a new birth!
And, by the incantation of this verse,

Scatter, as from an unextinguished hearth
Ashes and sparks, my words among mankind!
Be through my lips to unawakened earth

The trumpet of a prophecy! O Wind,
If Winter comes, can Spring be far behind?

Although Shelley is ranked among the great ones, his fame was
wholly posthumous. Rarely praised for his work during his life-
time, he felt that the world had refused to consider him as a poet.
It was inevitable that, when he composed ADONAIS, he should iden-
tify himself with Keats, whom he knew only slightly, but who
seemed to Shelley to be another rejected poet, victim of oppression.
ADONAIS, like Milton's LYCIDAS (see page 447), is an elegy in the
antique form of a memorial idyl: the invocation, the personifica-
tion of a grief-stricken Nature, the pastoral procession of mourning
fellow poets, and the concluding consolation. But, although the
classic mold is never broken, the poem is a personal outcry, a
Shelleyan succession of verbal melodies and subtly modulated
images.

Adonais

I weep for Adonais—he is dead!
Oh, weep for Adonais! though our tears
Thaw not the frost which binds so dear a head!
And thou, sad Hour, selected from all years
To mourn our loss, rouse thy obscure compeers,

And teach them thine own sorrow! Say: "With me
Died Adonais; till the Future dares
Forget the Past, his fate and fame shall be
An echo and a light unto eternity."

Where wert thou, mighty Mother, when he lay,
When thy son lay, pierced by the shaft which flies
In darkness? Where was lorn Urania
When Adonais died? With veiled eyes,
'Mid listening Echoes, in her Paradise
She sate, while one, with soft enamored breath,
Rekindled all the fading melodies,
With which, like flowers that mock the corse beneath,
He had adorned and hid the coming bulk of death.

Oh, weep for Adonais—he is dead!
Wake, melancholy Mother, wake and weep!
Yet wherefore? Quench within their burning bed
Thy fiery tears, and let thy loud heart keep,
Like his, a mute and uncomplaining sleep;
For he is gone, where all things wise and fair
Descend—oh, dream not that the amorous Deep
Will yet restore him to the vital air;
Death feeds on his mute voice, and laughs at our despair.

Most musical of mourners, weep again!
Lament anew, Urania!—He [1] died—
Who was the Sire of an immortal strain,
Blind, old, and lonely, when his country's pride,
The priest, the slave, and the liberticide,
Trampled and mocked with many a loathed rite
Of lust and blood; he went, unterrified,
Into the gulf of death; but his clear Sprite
Yet reigns o'er earth—the third among the sons of light.

Most musical of mourners, weep anew!
Not all to that bright station dared to climb;
And happier they their happiness who knew,
Whose tapers yet burn through that night of time
In which suns perished; others more sublime,
Struck by the envious wrath of man or god,
Have sunk, extinct in their refulgent prime;
And some yet live, treading the thorny road,
Which leads, through toil and hate, to Fame's serene abode.

[1] *Milton.*

But now, thy youngest, dearest one has perished,
The nursling of thy widowhood, who grew,
Like a pale flower by some sad maiden cherished,
And fed with true-love tears, instead of dew;
Most musical of mourners, weep anew!
Thy extreme hope, the loveliest and the last,
The bloom, whose petals, nipped before they blew,
Died on the promise of the fruit, is waste;
The broken lily lies—the storm is overpast.

To that high Capital,[2] where kingly Death
Keeps his pale court in beauty and decay,
He came; and bought, with price of purest breath,
A grave among the eternal.—Come away!
Haste, while the vault of blue Italian day
Is yet his fitting charnel-roof! while still
He lies, as if in dewy sleep he lay;
Awake him not! surely he takes his fill
Of deep and liquid rest, forgetful of all ill.

He will awake no more, oh, never more!—
Within the twilight chamber spreads apace
The shadow of white Death, and at the door
Invisible Corruption waits to trace
His extreme way to her dim dwelling-place;
The eternal Hunger sits, but pity and awe
Soothe her pale rage, nor dares she to deface
So fair a prey, till darkness and the law
Of change shall o'er his sleep the mortal curtain draw.

Oh, weep for Adonais!—The quick Dreams,
The passion-winged Ministers of thought,
Who were his flocks, whom near the living streams
Of his young spirit he fed, and whom he taught
The love which was its music, wander not—
Wander no more, from kindling brain to brain,
But droop there, whence they sprung; and mourn their lot
Round the cold heart, where, after their sweet pain,
They ne'er will gather strength, or find a home again.

And one with trembling hands clasps his cold head,
And fans him with her moonlight wings, and cries:
"Our love, our hope, our sorrow, is not dead;
See, on the silken fringe of his faint eyes,

[2] *Rome, where Keats died and was buried.*

Like dew upon a sleeping flower, there lies
A tear some Dream has loosened from his brain."
Lost Angel of a ruined Paradise!
She knew not 'twas her own; as with no stain
She faded, like a cloud which had outwept its rain.

One from a lucid urn of starry dew
Washed his light limbs as if embalming them;
Another clipped her profuse locks, and threw
The wreath upon him, like an anadem,
Which frozen tears instead of pearls begem;
Another in her willful grief would break
Her bow and winged reeds, as if to stem
A greater loss with one which was more weak;
And dull the barbed fire against his frozen cheek.

Another Splendor on his mouth alit,
That mouth, whence it was wont to draw the breath
Which gave it strength to pierce the guarded wit,
And pass into the panting heart beneath
With lightning and with music; the damp death
Quenched its caress upon his icy lips;
And, as a dying meteor stains a wreath
Of moonlight vapor, which the cold night clips,
It flushed through his pale limbs, and passed to its eclipse.

And others came—Desires and Adorations,
Winged Persuasions and veiled Destinies,
Splendors, and Glooms, and glimmering Incarnations
Of hopes and fears, and twilight Phantasies;
And Sorrow, with her family of Sighs,
And Pleasure, blind with tears, led by the gleam
Of her own dying smile instead of eyes,
Came in slow pomp—the moving pomp might seem
Like pageantry of mist on an autumnal stream.

All he had loved, and molded into thought
From shape, and hue, and odor, and sweet sound,
Lamented Adonais. Morning sought
Her eastern watchtower, and her hair unbound,
Wet with the tears which should adorn the ground,
Dimmed the aërial eyes that kindle day;
Afar the melancholy thunder moaned,
Pale Ocean in unquiet slumber lay,
And the wild winds flew round, sobbing in their dismay.

Lost Echo sits amid the voiceless mountains,
And feeds her grief with his remembered lay,
And will no more reply to winds or fountains,
Or amorous birds perched on the young green spray,
Or herdsman's horn, or bell at closing day;
Since she can mimic not his lips, more dear
Than those for whose disdain she pined away
Into a shadow of all sounds—a drear
Murmur, between their songs, is all the woodmen hear.

Grief made the young Spring wild, and she threw down
Her kindling buds, as if she Autumn were,
Or they dead leaves; since her delight is flown,
For whom should she have waked the sullen year?
To Phoebus was not Hyacinth so dear
Nor to himself Narcissus, as to both
Thou, Adonais. Wan they stand and sere
Amid the faint companions of their youth,
With dew all turned to tears; odor, to sighing ruth.

Thy spirit's sister, the lorn nightingale,
Mourns not her mate with such melodious pain;
Not so the eagle, who like thee could scale
Heaven, and could nourish in the sun's domain
Her mighty youth with morning, doth complain,
Soaring and screaming round her empty nest,
As Albion wails for thee. The curse of Cain
Light on his head who pierced thy innocent breast,
And scared the angel soul that was its earthly guest!

Ah, woe is me! Winter is come and gone,
But grief returns with the revolving year;
The airs and streams renew their joyous tone;
The ants, the bees, the swallows reappear;
Fresh leaves and flowers deck the dead Seasons' bier;
The amorous birds now pair in every brake,
And build their mossy homes in field and brere;
And the green lizard, and the golden snake,
Like unimprisoned flames, out of their trance awake.

Through wood and stream and field and hill and ocean
A quickening life from the earth's heart has burst,
As it has ever done, with change and motion,
From the great morning of the world when first
God dawned on Chaos; in its stream immersed,

The lamps of heaven flash with a softer light;
All baser things pant with life's sacred thirst,
Diffuse themselves, and spend in love's delight
The beauty and the joy of their renewèd might.

The leprous corpse, touched by this spirit tender,
Exhales itself in flowers of gentle breath;
Like incarnations of the stars, when splendor
Is changed to fragrance, they illumine death
And mock the merry worm that wakes beneath;
Naught we know, dies. Shall that alone which knows
Be as a sword consumed before the sheath
By sightless lightning?—the intense atom glows
A moment, then is quenched in a most cold repose.

Alas! that all we loved of him should be,
But for our grief, as if it had not been,
And grief itself be mortal! Woe is me!
Whence are we, and why are we? Of what scene
The actors or spectators? Great and mean
Meet massed in death, who lends what life must borrow.
As long as skies are blue, and fields are green,
Evening must usher night, night urge the morrow,
Month follow month with woe, and year wake year to sorrow.

He will awake no more, oh, never more!
"Wake thou," cried Misery, "childless Mother, rise
Out of thy sleep, and slake, in thy heart's core,
A wound more fierce than his with tears and sighs."
And all the Dreams that watched Urania's eyes,
And all the Echoes whom their sister's song
Had held in holy silence, cried: "Arise!"
Swift as a Thought by the snake Memory stung,
From her ambrosial rest the fading Splendor sprung.

She rose like an autumnal Night, that springs
Out of the East, and follows wild and drear
The golden Day, which, on eternal wings,
Even as a ghost abandoning a bier,
Had left the earth a corpse. Sorrow and fear
So struck, so roused, so rapt Urania;
So saddened round her like an atmosphere
Of stormy mist; so swept her on her way
Even to the mournful place where Adonais lay.

Out of her secret Paradise she sped,
Through camps and cities rough with stone, and steel,
And human hearts, which to her aëry tread
Yielding not, wounded the invisible
Palms of her tender feet where'er they fell;
And barbed tongues, and thoughts more sharp than they,
Rent the soft Form they never could repel,
Whose sacred blood, like the young tears of May,
Paved with eternal flowers that undeserving way.

In the death chamber for a moment Death,
Shamed by the presence of that living Might,
Blushed to annihilation, and the breath
Revisited those lips, and life's pale light
Flashed through those limbs, so late her dear delight.
"Leave me not wild and drear and comfortless,
As silent lightning leaves the starless night!
Leave me not!" cried Urania. Her distress
Roused Death; Death rose and smiled, and met her vain caress.

"Stay yet awhile! speak to me once again;
Kiss me, so long but as a kiss may live;
And in my heartless breast and burning brain
That word, that kiss, shall all thoughts else survive,
With food of saddest memory kept alive,
Now thou art dead, as if it were a part
Of thee, my Adonais! I would give
All that I am to be as thou now art!
But I am chained to Time, and cannot thence depart!

"O gentle child, beautiful as thou wert,
Why didst thou leave the trodden paths of men
Too soon, and with weak hands though mighty heart
Dare the unpastured dragon in his den?
Defenseless as thou wert, oh, where was then
Wisdom the mirrored shield, or scorn the spear?
Or hadst thou waited the full cycle, when
Thy spirit should have filled its crescent sphere,
The monsters of life's waste had fled from thee like deer.

"The herded wolves, bold only to pursue;
The obscene ravens, clamorous o'er the dead;
The vultures to the conqueror's banner true,
Who feed where Desolation first has fed,

And whose wings rain contagion—how they fled,
When like Apollo, from his golden bow,
The Pythian of the age,[3] one arrow sped
And smiled!—The spoilers tempt no second blow;
They fawn on the proud feet that spurn them lying low.

"The Sun comes forth, and many reptiles spawn;
He sets, and each ephemeral insect then
Is gathered into death without a dawn,
And the immortal stars awake again;
So is it in the world of living men:
A godlike mind soars forth, in its delight
Making earth bare and veiling heaven, and when
It sinks, the swarms that dimmed or shared its light
Leave to its kindred lamps the spirit's awful night."

Thus ceased she; and the mountain shepherds came,
Their garlands sere, their magic mantles rent;
The Pilgrim of Eternity,[4] whose fame
Over his living head like heaven is bent,
An early but enduring monument,
Came, veiling all the lightnings of his song
In sorrow; from her wilds Ierne [5] sent
The sweetest lyrist of her saddest wrong,[6]
And love taught grief to fall like music from his tongue.

Midst others of less note, came one frail Form,[7]
A phantom among men, companionless
As the last cloud of an expiring storm
Whose thunder is its knell; he, as I guess,
Had gazed on Nature's naked loveliness,
Actaeon-like, and now he fled astray
With feeble steps o'er the world's wilderness,
And his own thoughts, along that rugged way,
Pursued, like raging hounds, their father and their prey.

A pardlike Spirit beautiful and swift—
A Love in desolation masked—a Power
Girt round with weaknesses:—it can scarce uplift
The weight of the superincumbent hour;
It is a dying lamp, a falling shower,

[3] *Byron, who attacked the venomous critics as Apollo attacked the Python.*
[4] *Byron.* [5] *Ireland.* [6] *Thomas Moore.*
[7] *Shelley himself, mixing self-pity with pity for Keats.*

A breaking billow—even whilst we speak
Is it not broken? On the withering flower
The killing sun smiles brightly; on a cheek
The life can burn in blood, even while the heart may break.

His head was bound with pansies overblown,
And faded violets, white, and pied, and blue;
And a light spear topped with a cypress cone,
Round whose rude shaft dark ivy-tresses grew
Yet dripping with the forest's noonday dew,
Vibrated, as the ever-beating heart
Shook the weak hand that grasped it; of that crew
He came the last, neglected and apart;
A herd-abandoned deer, struck by the hunter's dart.

All stood aloof, and at his partial moan
Smiled through their tears; well knew that gentle band
Who in another's fate now wept his own;
As, in the accents of an unknown land,
He sung new sorrow; sad Urania scanned
The Stranger's mien, and murmured, "Who art thou?"
He answered not, but with a sudden hand
Made bare his branded and ensanguined brow,
Which was like Cain's or Christ's—Oh! that it should be so!

What softer voice is hushed over the dead?
Athwart what brow is that dark mantle thrown?
What form leans sadly o'er the white deathbed,
In mockery of monumental stone,
The heavy heart heaving without a moan?
If it be He,[8] who, gentlest of the wise,
Taught, soothed, loved, honored the departed one,
Let me not vex with inharmonious sighs
The silence of that heart's accepted sacrifice.

Our Adonais has drunk poison—oh!
What deaf and viperous murderer could crown
Life's early cup with such a draught of woe?
The nameless worm would now itself disown.
It felt, yet could escape, the magic tone
Whose prelude held all envy, hate, and wrong,
But what was howling in one breast alone,
Silent with expectation of the song,
Whose master's hand is cold, whose silver lyre unstrung.

[8] *Leigh Hunt, close friend of Keats.*

Live thou, whose infamy is not thy fame!
Live! fear no heavier chastisement from me,
Thou noteless blot on a remembered name!
But be thyself, and know thyself to be!
And ever at thy season be thou free
To spill the venom when thy fangs o'erflow.
Remorse and self-contempt shall cling to thee;
Hot shame shall burn upon thy secret brow,
And like a beaten hound tremble thou shalt—as now.

Nor let us weep that our delight is fled
Far from these carrion kites that scream below;
He wakes or sleeps with the enduring dead;
Thou canst not soar where he is sitting now.—
Dust to the dust! but the pure spirit shall flow
Back to the burning fountain whence it came,
A portion of the Eternal, which must glow
Through time and change, unquenchably the same,
Whilst thy cold embers choke the sordid hearth of shame.

Peace, peace! he is not dead, he doth not sleep—
He hath awakened from the dream of life—
'Tis we who, lost in stormy visions, keep
With phantoms an unprofitable strife,
And in mad trance strike with our spirit's knife
Invulnerable nothings.—*We* decay
Like corpses in a charnel; fear and grief
Convulse us and consume us day by day,
And cold hopes swarm like worms within our living clay.

He has outsoared the shadow of our night;
Envy and calumny and hate and pain,
And that unrest which men miscall delight,
Can touch him not and torture not again;
From the contagion of the world's slow stain
He is secure, and now can never mourn
A heart grown cold, a head grown gray in vain;
Nor, when the spirit's self has ceased to burn,
With sparkless ashes load an unlamented urn.

He lives, he wakes—'tis Death is dead, not he;
Mourn not for Adonais.—Thou young Dawn,
Turn all thy dew to splendor, for from thee
The spirit thou lamentest is not gone;

Ye caverns and ye forests, cease to moan!
Cease, ye faint flowers and fountains, and thou Air,
Which like a mourning veil thy scarf hadst thrown
O'er the abandoned Earth, now leave it bare
Even to the joyous stars which smile on its despair!

He is made one with Nature; there is heard
His voice in all her music, from the moan
Of thunder, to the song of night's sweet bird;
He is a presence to be felt and known
In darkness and in light, from herb and stone,
Spreading itself where'er that Power may move
Which has withdrawn his being to its own;
Which wields the world with never-wearied love,
Sustains it from beneath, and kindles it above.

He is a portion of the loveliness
Which once he made more lovely; he doth bear
His part, while the one Spirit's plastic stress
Sweeps through the dull, dense world, compelling there
All new successions to the forms they wear;
Torturing th' unwilling dross that checks its flight
To its own likeness, as each mass may bear;
And bursting in its beauty and its might
From trees and beasts and men into the Heaven's light.

The splendors of the firmament of time
May be eclipsed, but are extinguished not;
Like stars to their appointed height they climb
And death is a low mist which cannot blot
The brightness it may veil. When lofty thought
Lifts a young heart above its mortal lair,
And love and life contend in it for what
Shall be its earthly doom, the dead live there
And move like winds of light on dark and stormy air.

The inheritors of unfulfilled renown
Rose from their thrones, built beyond mortal thought,
Far in the Unapparent. Chatterton
Rose pale; his solemn agony had not
Yet faded from him. Sidney, as he fought
And as he fell and as he lived and loved,
Sublimely mild, a Spirit without spot,
Arose. And Lucan, by his death approved—
Oblivion, as they rose, shrank like a thing reproved.

And many more, whose names on earth are dark
But whose transmitted effluence cannot die
So long as fire outlives the parent spark,
Rose, robed in dazzling immortality.
"Thou art become as one of us," they cry,
"It was for thee yon kingless sphere has long
Swung blind in unascended majesty,
Silent alone amid an Heaven of Song.
Assume thy winged throne, thou Vesper of our throng!"

Who mourns for Adonais? oh, come forth,
Fond wretch! and know thyself and him aright.
Clasp with thy panting soul the pendulous Earth;
As from a center, dart thy spirit's light
Beyond all worlds, until its spacious might
Satiate the void circumference. Then shrink
Even to a point within our day and night;
And keep thy heart light, lest it make thee sink,
When hope has kindled hope, and lured thee to the brink.

Or go to Rome, which is the sepulchre,
Oh, not of him, but of our joy; 'tis naught
That ages, empires, and religions there
Lie buried in the ravage they have wrought;
For such as he can lend—they borrow not
Glory from those who made the world their prey;
And he is gathered to the kings of thought
Who waged contention with their time's decay,
And of the past are all that cannot pass away.

Go thou to Rome—at once the Paradise,
The grave, the city, and the wilderness;
And where its wrecks like shattered mountains rise,
And flowering weeds and fragrant copses dress
The bones of Desolation's nakedness,
Pass, till the Spirit of the spot shall lead
Thy footsteps to a slope of green access
Where, like an infant's smile, over the dead
A light of laughing flowers along the grass is spread.

And gray walls molder round, on which dull Time
Feeds, like slow fire upon a hoary brand;
And one keen pyramid with wedge sublime,
Pavilioning the dust of him who planned

This refuge for his memory, doth stand
Like flame transformed to marble; and beneath,
A field is spread, on which a newer band
Have pitched in Heaven's smile their camp of death,
Welcoming him we lose with scarce extinguished breath.

Here pause. These graves are all too young as yet
To have outgrown the sorrow which consigned
Its charge to each; and if the seal is set,
Here, on one fountain of a mourning mind,
Break it not thou! too surely shalt thou find
Thine own well full, if thou returnest home,
Of tears and gall. From the world's bitter wind
Seek shelter in the shadow of the tomb.
What Adonais is, why fear we to become?

The One [9] remains, the many change and pass;
Heaven's light forever shines, earth's shadows fly;
Life, like a dome of many-colored glass,
Stains the white radiance of Eternity,
Until Death tramples it to fragments.—Die,
If thou wouldst be with that which thou dost seek!
Follow where all is fled!—Rome's azure sky,
Flowers, ruins, statues, music, words, are weak
The glory they transfuse with fitting truth to speak.

Why linger, why turn back, why shrink, my Heart?
Thy hopes are gone before; from all things here
They have departed; thou shouldst now depart!
A light is past from the revolving year,
And man, and woman; and what still is dear
Attracts to crush, repels to make thee wither.
The soft sky smiles—the low wind whispers near;
'Tis Adonais calls! oh, hasten thither,
No more let Life divide what Death can join together.

That Light whose smile kindles the universe,
That Beauty in which all things work and move,
That Benediction which the eclipsing Curse
Of birth can quench not, that sustaining Love
Which, through the web of being blindly wove
By man and beast and earth and air and sea,

---

[9] *Ultimate Reality, "the white radiance of Eternity," unseen until Death shat-
ters the colored dome of life.*

Burns bright or dim, as each are mirrors of
The fire for which all thirst, now beams on me,
Consuming the last clouds of cold mortality.

The breath whose might I have invoked in song
Descends on me; my spirit's bark is driven,
Far from the shore, far from the trembling throng
Whose sails were never to the tempest given;
The massy earth and spheréd skies are riven!
I am borne darkly, fearfully, afar;
Whilst burning through the inmost veil of Heaven,
The soul of Adonais, like a star,
Beacons from the abode where the Eternal are.

The first collected edition of Shelley's poems was not published
until 1839, seventeen years after his death, and the collection was
prefaced by Mrs. Shelley. Many readers were surprised by the pene-
tration of the foreword. They should not have been, for Mary
Wollstonecraft Shelley was the author of some seven or eight vol-
umes, including the celebrated macabre FRANKENSTEIN, which she
had written at the age of twenty-one. Two of Mrs. Shelley's sen-
tences have never been bettered: "No poet was ever warmed by a
more genuine and unforced inspiration. His extreme sensibility
gave the intensity of passion to his intellectual pursuits and ren-
dered his mind keenly alive to every perception of outward objects,
as well as to his internal sensations."

Shelley's failures are those of excess. He erred on the side of
brilliance, of overenergetic compulsion. He was not always able to
give body to his abstractions or to idealize reality. But the best of
his work has not been surpassed by any lyric poet, with the possible
exception of Keats. It is not in a single poem that Shelley's full
greatness may be felt, but, as the poet W. J. Turner wrote, "in the
impression made by his work as a whole—an impression of one of
the most exalted and sublime spirits the world has ever seen."

Ozymandias

I met a traveler from an antique land,
Who said: Two vast and trunkless legs of stone
Stand in the desert. Near them, on the sand,
Half sunk, a shattered visage lies, whose frown,

And wrinkled lip, and sneer of cold command,
Tell that its sculptor well those passions read,
Which yet survive, stamped on these lifeless things,
The hand that mocked them, and the heart that fed:
And on the pedestal these words appear:
"My name is Ozymandias, King of Kings:
Look on my works, ye Mighty, and despair!"
Nothing beside remains. Round the decay
Of that colossal wreck, boundless and bare
The lone and level sands stretch far away.

The Cloud

I bring fresh showers for the thirsting flowers,
    From the seas and the streams;
I bear light shade for the leaves when laid
    In their noonday dreams.
From my wings are shaken the dews that waken
    The sweet buds every one,
When rocked to rest on their mother's breast,
    As she dances about the sun.
I wield the flail of the lashing hail,
    And whiten the green plains under,
And then again I dissolve it in rain,
    And laugh as I pass in thunder.

I sift the snow on the mountains below,
    And their great pines groan aghast;
And all the night 'tis my pillow white,
    While I sleep in the arms of the blast.
Sublime on the towers of my skiey bowers,
    Lightning, my pilot, sits;
In a cavern under is fettered the thunder,
    It struggles and howls at fits;

Over earth and ocean, with gentle motion,
    This pilot is guiding me,
Lured by the love of the genii that move
    In the depths of the purple sea;
Over the rills, and the crags, and the hills,
    Over the lakes and the plains,

Wherever he dream, under mountain or stream,
    The Spirit he loves remains;
And I all the while bask in Heaven's blue smile,
    Whilst he is dissolving in rains.

The sanguine Sunrise, with his meteor eyes,
    And his burning plumes outspread,
Leaps on the back of my sailing rack,
    When the morning star shines dead;
As on the jag of a mountain crag,
    Which an earthquake rocks and swings,
An eagle alit one moment may sit
    In the light of its golden wings.
And when Sunset may breathe, from the lit sea beneath,
    Its ardors of rest and of love,
And the crimson pall of eve may fall
    From the depth of Heaven above,
With wings folded I rest, on mine aery nest,
    As still as a brooding dove.

That orbèd maiden with white fire laden,
    Whom mortals call the Moon,
Glides glimmering o'er my fleece-like floor,
    By the midnight breezes strewn;
And wherever the beat of her unseen feet,
    Which only the angels hear,
May have broken the woof of my tent's thin roof,
    The stars peep behind her and peer;
And I laugh to see them whirl and flee,
    Like a swarm of golden bees,
When I widen the rent in my wind-built tent,
    Till the calm rivers, lakes, and seas,
Like strips of the sky fallen through me on high,
    Are each paved with the moon and these.

I bind the Sun's throne with a burning zone,
    And the Moon's with a girdle of pearl;
The volcanoes are dim, and the stars reel and swim
    When the whirlwinds my banner unfurl.
From cape to cape, with a bridge-like shape,
    Over a torrent sea,
Sunbeam-proof, I hang like a roof,—
    The mountains its columns be.
The triumphal arch through which I march
    With hurricane, fire, and snow,

When the Powers of the air are chained to my chair,
    Is the million-colored bow;
The sphere-fire above its soft colors wove,
    While the moist Earth was laughing below.

I am the daughter of Earth and Water,
    And the nursling of the Sky;
I pass through the pores of the ocean and shores;
    I change, but I cannot die.
For after the rain when with never a stain
    The pavilion of Heaven is bare,
And the winds and sunbeams with their convex gleams
    Build up the blue dome of air,
I silently laugh at my own cenotaph,
    And out of the caverns of rain,
Like a child from the womb, like a ghost from the tomb,
    I arise and unbuild it again.

A Lament

O world! O life! O time!
On whose last steps I climb,
    Trembling at that where I had stood before;
When will return the glory of your prime?
    No more—Oh, never more!

Out of the day and night
A joy has taken flight;
    Fresh spring, and summer, and winter hoar,
Move my faint heart with grief, but with delight
    No more—Oh, never more!

A Dirge

Rough wind, that moanest loud
    Grief too sad for song;
Wild wind, when sullen cloud
    Knells all the night long;
Sad storm, whose tears are vain,
Bare woods, whose branches strain,
Deep caves and dreary main,—
    Wail, for the world's wrong!

Music

Silver key of the fountain of tears,
  Where the spirit drinks till the brain is wild;
Softest grave of a thousand fears,
  Where their mother, Care, like a drowsy child,
    Is laid asleep in flowers.

JOHN KEATS

[1795–1821]

READING some of the titles of Keats's poems—ENDYMION, HYPE-
RION, SONNET TO HOMER, HYMN TO APOLLO, ON SEEING THE
ELGIN MARBLES, ODE ON A GRECIAN URN—the ignorant reader might
conclude that the poet was the product of a special environment, a
cloistered spirit, perhaps the son of an aristocrat or a professor of
Greek. But Keats was not reared in an ivory tower. His father took
care of the horses and cleaned the stalls in his grandfather's livery
stable.

Born in London in 1795—the day is variously given as October 29
and October 31—John Keats was the oldest son of Thomas Keats
and Frances Jennings, daughter of the livery-stable proprietor.
When Keats was ten years old his father was killed by a fall from
a horse; his mother remarried within a year, but was soon separated
from her new husband and returned to her mother's house in Ed-
monton. During his boyhood, Keats alternated between his grand-
mother's home in the country and the school at Enfield, a suburb
of London, for the widow could not afford to send him to Harrow.
Although he was finely built, he was not frail. Instead of the deli-
cate legendary poet, Keats was anything but effeminate; he over-
compensated for inner insecurity by an outer pugnacity. At school
he was well known as a fighter. Cowden Clarke, son of the head-
master at Enfield, remembered his "terrier courage" and wrote that
Keats's passion often grew ungovernable: "His brother George,
being considerably taller and stronger, used frequently to hold him
down by main force."

His mother died of tuberculosis when he was fifteen, and a guardian was appointed for John and his brother—a relationship described with sensitive irony in E. M. Forster's short story MR. AND MRS. ABBEY'S DIFFICULTIES. At sixteen Keats was apprenticed to a surgeon of Edmonton; at nineteen he ran away to London and studied sporadically at hospitals in the metropolis. Before Keats left Edmonton, Cowden Clarke had given him a copy of Spenser's THE FAERIE QUEENE; when Clarke came up to London, the young men found Homer in Chapman's spirited translation. They spent a whole autumn night in excited discovery, reading the rich passages aloud. At ten o'clock the following morning Clarke, who had had little sleep, received a communication from Keats, who had not slept at all. It was the poem ON FIRST LOOKING INTO CHAPMAN'S HOMER, one of the world's most famous sonnets.

On First Looking into Chapman's Homer

Much have I travell'd in the realms of gold,
  And many goodly states and kingdoms seen;
  Round many western islands have I been
Which bards in fealty to Apollo hold.
Oft of one wide expanse had I been told
  That deep-brow'd Homer ruled as his demesne:
  Yet did I never breathe its pure serene
Till I heard Chapman speak out loud and bold.

Then felt I like some watcher of the skies
  When a new planet swims into his ken;
Or like stout Cortez when with eagle eyes
  He stared at the Pacific—and all his men
Look'd at each other with a wild surmise—
  Silent, upon a peak in Darien.

Keats's adventurous mind may have been wandering when, in the magnificent picture of the explorer staring at the Pacific, he wrote "Cortez" instead of "Balboa," but his sensitivity to words was never keener. Two manuscripts of this poem exist; the first, in the Amy Lowell collection, is a remarkable contrast to the second. In the first draft Homer was not "deep-brow'd" but "low-brow'd." The seventh line was originally "Yet could I never judge what men could mean," but Keats's fine ear made him alter the awkward syllables to the highly suggestible and unforgettable "Yet never did I breathe its pure serene." That "pure serene" is the essence of Keats distilled in a phrase.

Although Keats was duly licensed, he never practiced medicine. Unhappy events crowded fast upon him; he withdrew from the contemporary world of difficult experience to live in a world of antique dreams. "Glory and loveliness have passed away," he wrote to Leigh Hunt in the dedication of his first volume. A year later, in a Preface to ENDYMION, he emphasized the sentiment: "I hope I have not in too late a day touched the beautiful mythology of Greece and dulled its brightness." He took to haunting the British Museum, and in particular the rooms which contained the Greek vases, marbles, and ruined portions of the Parthenon. "Poetry must surprise by a fine excess," Keats had declared; and in the British Museum there was a superfluity of beauty to delight the most romantic and sensation-loving spirit. ODE ON A GRECIAN URN unites with "fine excess" the two aspects of reality: beauty and truth—the beauty of the sensual world and the truth of the imagination.

Ode on a Grecian Urn

Thou still unravish'd bride of quietness,
    Thou foster-child of silence and slow time,
Sylvan historian, who canst thus express
    A flowery tale more sweetly than our rhyme:
What leaf-fring'd legend haunts about thy shape
    Of deities or mortals, or of both,
        In Tempe or the dales of Arcady?
What men or gods are these? What maidens loth?
What mad pursuit? What struggle to escape?
    What pipes and timbrels? What wild ecstasy?

Heard melodies are sweet, but those unheard
    Are sweeter; therefore, ye soft pipes, play on;
Not to the sensual ear, but, more endear'd,
    Pipe to the spirit ditties of no tone:
Fair youth, beneath the trees, thou canst not leave
    Thy song, nor ever can those trees be bare;
        Bold Lover, never, never canst thou kiss,
Though winning near the goal—yet, do not grieve;
    She cannot fade, though thou hast not thy bliss,
        For ever wilt thou love, and she be fair!

Ah, happy, happy boughs! that cannot shed
  Your leaves, nor ever bid the Spring adieu;
And, happy melodist, unwearièd,
  For ever piping songs for ever new;
More happy love! more happy, happy love!
  For ever warm and still to be enjoy'd,
    For ever panting, and for ever young;
All breathing human passion far above,
  That leaves a heart high-sorrowful and cloy'd,
    A burning forehead, and a parching tongue.

Who are these coming to the sacrifice?
  To what green altar, O mysterious priest,
Lead'st thou that heifer lowing at the skies,
  And all her silken flanks with garlands drest?
What little town by river or sea shore,
  Or mountain-built with peaceful citadel,
    Is emptied of this folk, this pious morn?
And, little town, thy streets for evermore
  Will silent be; and not a soul to tell
    Why thou art desolate, can e'er return.

O Attic shape! Fair attitude! with brede
  Of marble men and maidens overwrought,
With forest branches and the trodden weed;
  Thou, silent form, dost tease us out of thought
As doth eternity. Cold Pastoral!
  When old age shall this generation waste,
    Thou shalt remain, in midst of other woe
Than ours, a friend to man, to whom thou say'st,
  "Beauty is truth, truth beauty—that is all
    Ye know on earth, and all ye need to know."

The ODE ON A GRECIAN URN was a direct result of Keats's pre-
occupation with Greek myths and the plastic embodiments of it
which he found in the British Museum. It seems improbable that
the ode was a description of any particular urn. It is far more likely
that Keats was reconstructing the design from the Parthenon, re-
calling it through the eye of imagination. The "mad pursuit" and
"wild ecstasy" are no longer part of a sculptured ritual; the "marble
men and maidens" take on warm flesh and leaping blood.

It is a cultural oddity that the passion for Greek legend, which
affected Byron and Shelley no less than Keats, was not given its
first great impetus by a poet but by a political envoy. Had it not

been for Lord Elgin's spoliation of the Parthenon, the famous frieze and pediment of Phidias would have remained in Athens. With the acquisition of the marble pieces, the British Museum became an ally of Greece, and the poets turned to an older romanticism than their immediate predecessors; without quite repudiating Scott and Coleridge they deserted medievalism for Hellenism. Keats acknowledged his debt to Lord Elgin without uncertainty; the twenty-one-year-old poet—already "a sick eagle looking at the sky"— paid his tribute in a sonnet of praise.

On Seeing the Elgin Marbles

My spirit is too weak—mortality
   Weighs heavily on me like unwilling sleep,
   And each imagined pinnacle and steep
Of godlike hardship tells me I must die
Like a sick eagle looking at the sky.
   Yet 'tis a gentle luxury to weep
   That I have not the cloudy winds to keep,
Fresh for the opening of the morning's eye.
Such dim-conceived glories of the brain,
   Bring round the heart an indescribable feud;
So do these wonders a most dizzy pain,
   That mingles Grecian grandeur with the rude
Wasting of old Time—with a billowy main—
   A sun—a shadow of a magnitude.

At twenty-one Keats met his first "sponsor," the poet Leigh Hunt, who was generous in his recognition of younger and better poets. For the first time Keats moved in a wholly literary atmosphere; through Hunt he met Shelley, Coleridge, and Wordsworth. With none of these except Hunt did the acquaintance ripen into real friendship; Shelley esteemed Keats, but objected that he wrote on principles which Shelley opposed, and Wordsworth dampened the young poet's fervor by referring to his HYMN TO PAN as "a pretty piece of paganism." Encouraged by Hunt, Keats published his first volume, POEMS, before he was twenty-one. It was followed in a year by ENDYMION.

Keats had gone to the countryside in the hope of curing a throat trouble which was to develop into the consumption that caused his death three years later. When he returned to London, he found himself viciously attacked by the two leading critical reviews, BLACKWOOD'S MAGAZINE and THE QUARTERLY REVIEW. The articles were not merely critical onslaughts but personal assaults. The reviewers commented harshly on the friendship of Hunt, who had made many enemies, spoke sneeringly of Keats's humble beginnings, and treated the young poet as a vicious example of the "Cockney school." Keats was deeply hurt as well as discouraged by the reviews; he even considered abandoning literature. Several of his friends believed that the brutality of the attacks hastened his end. Byron wrote:

> "Who killed John Keats?"
> "I," said the *Quarterly,*
> So savage and tartarly;
> " 'Twas one of my feats."

But, although depressed by the offending criticisms, Keats was not killed by them. He had other and more personal troubles. The family was breaking up. His brother George had left for America. His brother Tom, whom he had nursed for months, died of tuberculosis. By this time it was obvious to Keats that he himself had inherited the fatal family weakness. To make the situation still more tragic, he fell hopelessly in love with the charming but lightly flirtatious Fanny Brawne.

Keats's passion for Fanny Brawne, complicated by the increasing malignancy of his disease and the uncertainty of his future, was a headlong desperation. Unable to possess her, he became abnormally possessive. He tormented himself and her with frantic talks, letters, and poems. In the sonnet beginning "I cry your mercy—pity," Keats revealed his uncontrollable and jealous love. The poem is not a smoothly molded work of art, but an agonized self-expression. It stammers with the lover's anguish, stumbles on in a wild demand, pauses breathlessly to tantalize the unfortunate dreamer with the "sweet minor zest of love, your kiss," with the beloved's hands and her "warm, white, lucent, million-pleasured breast," and rushes on to its fevered conclusion.

To Fanny

I cry your mercy—pity—love!—aye, love!
  Merciful love that tantalizes not,
One-thoughted, never-wandering, guileless love,
  Unmasked, and being seen—without a blot!
O! let me have thee whole,—all—all—be mine!
  That shape, that fairness, that sweet minor zest
Of love, your kiss,—those hands, those eyes divine,
  That warm, white, lucent, million-pleasured breast,—
Yourself—your soul—in pity give me all,
  Withhold no atom's atom or I die,
Or living on perhaps, your wretched thrall,
  Forget, in the mist of idle misery,
Life's purposes,—the palate of my mind
Losing its gust, and my ambition blind!

It was in the unhappiest period of Keats's life that he wrote the poems by which he is most remembered. In one year, 1819, he created most of the great odes, THE EVE OF ST. AGNES, and the beautifully archaic LA BELLE DAME SANS MERCI. LA BELLE DAME SANS MERCI is a splendid example of Keats's "remaking" power. Written more than three centuries after the ballad of TRUE THOMAS (see page 146), Keats's poem is also about a mortal seduced by an immortal. But in the modern ballad the poet becomes a knight and the Queen of Elfland is a "faery's child." Here also the woman is an enchantress, and magic and doom—the doom of love—establish a kinship between the despairing poet of the nineteenth century and the unknown balladist of the sixteenth.

La Belle Dame Sans Merci

Ah, what can ail thee, wretched wight,
  Alone and palely loitering?
The sedge is withered from the lake,
  And no birds sing.

Ah, what can ail thee, wretched wight,
  So haggard and so woe-begone?
The squirrel's granary is full,
  And the harvest's done.

I see a lily on thy brow
    With anguish moist and fever dew,
And on thy cheek a fading rose
    Fast withereth too.

I met a lady in the meads,
    Full beautiful, a faery's child:
Her hair was long, her foot was light,
    And her eyes were wild.

I set her on my pacing steed,
    And nothing else saw all day long;
For sideways would she lean, and sing
    A faery's song.

I made a garland for her head,
    And bracelets too, and fragrant zone;
She looked at me as she did love,
    And made sweet moan.

She found me roots of relish sweet,
    And honey wild, and manna dew,
And sure in language strange she said,
    "I love thee true!"

She took me to her elfin grot,
    And there she gazed and sighed deep,
And there I shut her wild, sad eyes—
    So kissed to sleep.

And there we slumbered on the moss,
    And there I dreamed, ah! woe betide,
The latest dream I ever dreamed
    On the cold hill side.

I saw pale kings, and princes too,
    Pale warriors, death-pale were they all;
Who cried—"La belle Dame sans merci
    Hath thee in thrall!"

I saw their starved lips in the gloam,
    With horrid warning gaped wide,
And I awoke and found me here,
    On the cold hill side.

> And this is why I sojourn here,
> Alone and palely loitering,
> Though the sedge is withered from the lake,
> And no birds sing.

In 1820 Keats knew that his illness was becoming progressively worse. He tried the English seashore, again to no avail. Fanny Brawne nursed him, but her nearness aggravated his pain. In July his last and best volume was issued, but the cordiality with which it was received could not restore him to health. In September Keats sailed for Italy, and composed his last poem, the sonnet beginning "Bright star, would I were stedfast as thou art," while he was passing down the Channel. Significantly enough, this most moving of Keats's love poems was written in a volume of Shakespeare's, facing A LOVER'S COMPLAINT.

Bright Star, Would I Were Stedfast

Bright star, would I were stedfast as thou art—
Not in lone splendor hung aloft the night,
And watching, with eternal lids apart,
Like nature's patient sleepless Eremite,[1]
The moving waters at their priestlike task
Of pure ablution round earth's human shores,
Or gazing on the new soft fallen mask
Of snow upon the mountains and the moors:
No—yet still stedfast, still unchangeable,
Pillowed upon my fair love's ripening breast
To feel for ever its soft fall and swell,
Awake for ever in a sweet unrest;
Still, still to hear her tender-taken breath,
And so live ever—or else swoon to death.

Keats reached Rome in November. Within a month he had a final relapse. He died February 23, 1821, and was buried in the Protestant Cemetery in Rome. His first published poem had appeared when he was twenty-two; he was dead at twenty-six.

Keats's short life was a flash of painful ecstasy, and the intensity of his nature is everywhere in his poetry. The verse is vivid and definite, lavish with a feeling of textures, with minute felicities of touch and taste, "filling every sense with spiritual sweets." The

[1] *Hermit.*

early poems are almost too profuse, too lush in sensuousness, too
decoratively detailed. But the later work is both more brilliant
and more controlled. The perceptions are delicately exact, the pic-
tures are translucent. No poet has more subtly communicated
complex and luxuriant sensations.

THE EVE OF ST. AGNES is opulent in storytelling and in suggestion,
a tale which is also a painting, an old-world tapestry, and an alle-
gory of young love triumphing over a world of hate. The kaleido-
scope of sensations begins dramatically with the first verse. St.
Agnes' Eve—January 20—is proverbially the coldest of the year, and
the effect of cold is emphasized not only by the "bitter chill" of the
first line, but by the owl hunched miserably in his feathers, the
hare limping and trembling through the frozen grass, the silently
huddled flock, the numb fingers of the Beadsman (literally, a pray-
ing man), and the breath visibly suspended in the freezing air. The
wintry atmosphere is heightened by the hot proclamation of "silver,
snarling trumpets"; fragrant quiet succeeds the boisterous revelry,
and the lovers vanish in "an elfin-storm from faery land."

In this poem three devices reveal Keats's debt to antiquity. He
repeats and elaborates the legend that girls are permitted a vision
of their future husbands on St. Agnes' Eve; the lover awakes his
beloved with "an ancient ditty, long since mute" entitled LA BELLE
DAME SANS MERCI; and the poem itself is written in the stately nine-
line stanza invented by Spenser in the sixteenth century.

The Eve of St. Agnes

St. Agnes' Eve—Ah, bitter chill it was!
The owl, for all his feathers, was a-cold;
The hare limped trembling through the frozen grass,
And silent was the flock in woolly fold:
Numb were the Beadsman's fingers while he told
His rosary, and while his frosted breath,
Like pious incense from a censer old,
Seemed taking flight for heaven, without a death,
Past the sweet Virgin's picture, while his prayer he saith.

His prayer he saith, this patient, holy man;
Then takes his lamp, and riseth from his knees,
And back returneth, meager, barefoot, wan,
Along the chapel aisle by slow degrees:

The sculptured dead, on each side, seem to freeze,
Imprisoned in black, purgatorial rails:
Knights, ladies, praying in dumb orat'ries,
He passeth by, and his weak spirit fails
To think how they may ache in icy hoods and mails.

Northward he turneth through a little door,
And scarce three steps, ere Music's golden tongue
Flattered to tears this aged man and poor;
But no—already had his death-bell rung:
The joys of all his life were said and sung;
His was harsh penance on St. Agnes' Eve:
Another way he went, and soon among
Rough ashes sat he for his soul's reprieve,
And all night kept awake, for sinners' sake to grieve.

That ancient Beadsman heard the prelude soft;
And so it chanced, for many a door was wide,
From hurry to and fro. Soon, up aloft,
The silver, snarling trumpets 'gan to chide:
The level chambers, ready with their pride,
Were glowing to receive a thousand guests.
The carved angels, ever eager-eyed,
Stared, where upon their heads the cornice rests,
With hair blown back, and wings put crosswise on their breasts.

At length burst in the argent revelry,
With plume, tiara, and all rich array,
Numerous as shadows haunting faerily
The brain new-stuffed, in youth, with triumphs gay
Of old romance. These let us wish away,
And turn, sole-thoughted, to one Lady there,
Whose heart had brooded, all that wintry day,
On love, and winged St. Agnes' saintly care,
As she had heard old dames full many times declare.

They told her how, upon St. Agnes' Eve,
Young virgins might have visions of delight,
And soft adorings from their loves receive
Upon the honeyed middle of the night,
If ceremonies due they did aright;
As, supperless to bed they must retire,
And couch supine their beauties, lily white;
Nor look behind, nor sideways, but require
Of Heaven with upward eyes for all that they desire.

Full of this whim was thoughtful Madeline:
The music, yearning like a God in pain,
She scarcely heard: her maiden eyes divine,
Fixed on the floor, saw many a sweeping train
Pass by—she heeded not at all: in vain
Came many a tiptoe, amorous cavalier,
And back retired; not cooled by high disdain,
But she saw not: her heart was otherwhere;
She sighed for Agnes' dreams, the sweetest of the year.

She danced along with vague, regardless eyes,
Anxious her lips, her breathing quick and short:
The hallowed hour was near at hand: she sighs
Amid the timbrels, and the thronged resort
Of whisperers in anger or in sport;
'Mid looks of love, defiance, hate, and scorn,
Hoodwinked with faery fancy; all amort,
Save to St. Agnes and her lambs unshorn,
And all the bliss to be before tomorrow morn.

So, purposing each moment to retire,
She lingered still. Meantime, across the moors,
Had come young Porphyro, with heart on fire
For Madeline. Beside the portal doors,
Buttressed from moonlight, stands he, and implores
All saints to give him sight of Madeline,
But for one moment in the tedious hours,
That he might gaze and worship all unseen;
Perchance speak, kneel, touch, kiss—in sooth such things have been.

He ventures in: let no buzzed whisper tell,
All eyes be muffled, or a hundred swords
Will storm his heart, Love's feverous citadel:
For him, those chambers held barbarian hordes,
Hyena foemen, and hot-blooded lords,
Whose very dogs would execrations howl
Against his lineage; not one breast affords
Him any mercy in that mansion foul,
Save one old beldame, weak in body and in soul.

Ah, happy chance! the aged creature came,
Shuffling along with ivory-headed wand,
To where he stood, hid from the torch's flame,
Behind a broad hall pillar, far beyond

The sound of merriment and chorus bland.
He startled her: but soon she knew his face,
And grasped his fingers in her palsied hand,
Saying, "Mercy, Porphyro! hie thee from this place;
They are all here tonight, the whole bloody-thirsty race!

"Get hence! get hence! there's dwarfish Hildebrand:
He had a fever late, and in the fit
He cursed thee and thine, both house and land:
Then there's that old Lord Maurice, not a whit
More tame for his gray hairs—Alas me! flit!
Flit like a ghost away."—"Ah, Gossip dear,
We're safe enough; here in this arm-chair sit,
And tell me how—" "Good saints! not here, not here!
Follow me, child, or else these stones will be thy bier."

He followed through a lowly arched way,
Brushing the cobwebs with his lofty plume;
And as she muttered "Well-a—well-a-day!"
He found him in a little moonlight room,
Pale, latticed, chill, and silent as a tomb.
"Now tell me where is Madeline," said he,
"O tell me, Angela, by the holy loom
Which none but secret sisterhood may see,
When they St. Agnes' wool are weaving piously."

"St. Agnes! Ah! it is St. Agnes' Eve—
Yet men will murder upon holy days.
Thou must hold water in a witch's sieve,
And be liege-lord of all the Elves and Fays
To venture so: it fills me with amaze
To see thee, Porphyro!—St. Agnes' Eve!
God's help! my lady fair the conjurer plays
This very night: good angels her deceive!
But let me laugh awhile,—I've mickle time to grieve."

Feebly she laugheth in the languid moon,
While Porphyro upon her face doth look,
Like puzzled urchin on an aged crone
Who keepeth closed a wondrous riddle-book,
As spectacled she sits in chimney nook.
But soon his eyes grew brilliant, when she told
His lady's purpose; and he scarce could brook
Tears, at the thought of those enchantments cold,
And Madeline asleep in lap of legends old.

Sudden a thought came like a full-blown rose,
Flushing his brow, and in his pained heart
Made purple riot: then doth he propose
A stratagem, that makes the beldame start:
"A cruel man and impious thou art!
Sweet lady, let her pray, and sleep and dream
Alone with her good angels, far apart
From wicked men like thee. Go, go! I deem
Thou canst not surely be the same that thou didst seem."

"I will not harm her, by all saints I swear!"
Quoth Porphyro: "O may I ne'er find grace
When my weak voice shall whisper its last prayer,
If one of her soft ringlets I displace,
Or look with ruffian passion in her face.
Good Angela, believe me, by these tears;
Or I will, even in a moment's space,
Awake, with horrid shout, my foemen's ears,
And beard them, though they be more fanged than wolves and bears."

"Ah! why wilt thou affright a feeble soul?
A poor, weak, palsy-stricken, churchyard thing,
Whose passing-bell may ere the midnight toll;
Whose prayers for thee, each morn and evening,
Were never missed." Thus plaining, doth she bring
A gentler speech from burning Porphyro;
So woeful, and of such deep sorrowing,
That Angela gives promise she will do
Whatever he shall wish, betide her weal or woe.

Which was, to lead him, in close secrecy,
Even to Madeline's chamber, and there hide
Him in a closet, of such privacy
That he might see her beauty unespied,
And win perhaps that night a peerless bride,
While legioned fairies paced the coverlet,
And pale enchantment held her sleepy-eyed.
Never on such a night have lovers met,
Since Merlin paid his Demon all the monstrous debt.

"It shall be as thou wishest," said the Dame:
"All cates and dainties shall be stored there
Quickly on this feast-night: by the tambour frame
Her own lute thou wilt see: no time to spare,

For I am slow and feeble, and scarce dare
On such a catering trust my dizzy head.
Wait here, my child, with patience; kneel in prayer
The while. Ah! thou must needs the lady wed,
Or may I never leave my grave among the dead."

So saying she hobbled off with busy fear.
The lover's endless minutes slowly passed;
The dame returned, and whispered in his ear
To follow her; with aged eyes aghast
From fright of dim espial. Safe at last
Through many a dusky gallery, they gain
The maiden's chamber, silken, hushed and chaste;
Where Porphyro took covert, pleased amain.
His poor guide hurried back with agues in her brain.

Her faltering hand upon the balustrade,
Old Angela was feeling for the stair,
When Madeline, St. Agnes' charmed maid,
Rose, like a missioned spirit, unaware:
With silver taper's light, and pious care,
She turned, and down the aged gossip led
To a safe level matting. Now prepare,
Young Porphyro, for gazing on that bed;
She comes, she comes again, like ring-dove frayed and fled.

Out went the taper as she hurried in;
Its little smoke, in pallid moonshine, died:
She closed the door, she panted, all akin
To spirits of the air, and visions wide:
No uttered syllable, or, woe betide!
But to her heart, her heart was voluble,
Paining with eloquence her balmy side;
As though a tongueless nightingale should swell
Her throat in vain, and die, heart-stifled, in her dell.

A casement high and triple-arched there was,
All garlanded with carven imageries,
Of fruits, and flowers, and bunches of knot-grass,
And diamonded with panes of quaint device,
Innumerable of stains and splendid dyes,
As are the tiger-moth's deep-damasked wings;
And in the midst, 'mong thousand heraldries,
And twilight saints, and dim emblazonings,
A shielded scutcheon blushed with blood of queens and kings.

Full on this casement shone the wintry moon,
And threw warm gules on Madeline's fair breast,
As down she knelt for Heaven's grace and boon;
Rose-bloom fell on her hands, together prest,
And on her silver cross soft amethyst,
And on her hair a glory, like a saint:
She seemed a splendid angel, newly drest,
Save wings, for heaven:—Porphyro grew faint:
She knelt, so pure a thing, so free from mortal taint.

Anon his heart revives: her vespers done,
Of all its wreathed pearls her hair she frees;
Unclasps her warmed jewels one by one;
Loosens her fragrant bodice; by degrees
Her rich attire creeps rustling to her knees:
Half-hidden, like a mermaid in sea-weed,
Pensive awhile she dreams awake, and sees,
In fancy, fair St. Agnes in her bed,
But dares not look behind, or all the charm is fled.

Soon, trembling in her soft and chilly nest,
In sort of wakeful swoon, perplexed she lay,
Until the poppied warmth of sleep oppressed
Her soothed limbs, and soul fatigued away;
Flown, like a thought, until the morrow-day;
Blissfully havened both from joy and pain;
Clasped like a missal where swart Paynims pray;
Blinded alike from sunshine and from rain,
As though a rose should shut, and be a bud again.

Stolen to this paradise, and so entranced,
Porphyro gazed upon her empty dress,
And listened to her breathing, if it chanced
To wake into a slumberous tenderness;
Which when he heard, that minute did he bless,
And breathed himself: then from the closet crept,
Noiseless as fear in a wide wilderness,
And over the hushed carpet, silent, stept,
And 'tween the curtains peeped, where, lo!—how fast she slept.

Then by the bed-side, where the faded moon
Made a dim, silver twilight, soft he set
A table, and, half anguished, threw thereon
A cloth of woven crimson, gold, and jet:—

O for some drowsy Morphean amulet!
The boisterous, midnight, festive clarion,
The kettle-drum, and far-heard clarinet,
Affray his ears, though but in dying tone:—
The hall-door shuts again, and all the noise is gone.

And still she slept an azure-lidded sleep,
In blanched linen, smooth, and lavendered,
While he from forth the closet brought a heap
Of candied apple, quince, and plum, and gourd;
With jellies soother than the creamy curd,
And lucent syrops, tinct with cinnamon;
Manna and dates, in argosy transferred
From Fez; and spiced dainties, every one,
From silken Samarcand to cedared Lebanon.

These delicates he heaped with glowing hand
On golden dishes and in baskets bright
Of wreathed silver: sumptuous they stand
In the retired quiet of the night,
Filling the chilly room with perfume light.—
"And now, my love, my seraph fair, awake!
Thou art my heaven, and I thine eremite:
Open thine eyes, for meek St. Agnes' sake,
Or I shall drowse beside thee, so my soul doth ache."

Thus whispering, his warm, unnerved arm
Sank in her pillow. Shaded was her dream
By the dusk curtains:—'twas a midnight charm
Impossible to melt as iced stream:
The lustrous salvers in the moonlight gleam;
Broad golden fringe upon the carpet lies:
It seemed he never, never could redeem
From such a stedfast spell his lady's eyes;
So mused awhile, entoiled in woofed phantasies.

Awakening up, he took her hollow lute,—
Tumultuous,—and, in chords that tenderest be,
He played an ancient ditty, long since mute,
In Provence called, "La belle dame sans mercy":
Close to her ear touching the melody;—
Wherewith disturbed, she uttered a soft moan:
He ceased—she panted quick—and suddenly
Her blue affrayed eyes wide open shone:
Upon his knees he sank, pale as smooth-sculptured stone.

Her eyes were open, but she still beheld,
Now wide awake, the vision of her sleep:
There was a painful change, that nigh expelled
The blisses of her dream so pure and deep
At which fair Madeline began to weep,
And moan forth witless words with many a sigh,
While still her gaze on Porphyro would keep;
Who knelt, with joined hands and piteous eye,
Fearing to move or speak, she looked so dreamingly.

"Ah, Porphyro!" said she, "but even now
Thy voice was at sweet tremble in mine ear,
Made tuneable with every sweetest vow;
And those sad eyes were spiritual and clear:
How changed thou art! how pallid, chill, and drear!
Give me that voice again, my Porphyro,
Those looks immortal, those complainings dear!
Oh, leave me not in this eternal woe,
For if thou diest, my Love, I know not where to go."

Beyond a mortal man impassioned far
At these voluptuous accents, he arose,
Ethereal, flushed, and like a throbbing star
Seen 'mid the sapphire heaven's deep repose;
Into her dream he melted, as the rose
Blendeth its odor with the violet,—
Solution sweet: meantime the frost-wind blows
Like Love's alarum, pattering the sharp sleet
Against the window-panes; St. Agnes' moon hath set.

'Tis dark: quick pattereth the flaw-blown sleet.
"This is no dream, my bride, my Madeline!"
'Tis dark: the iced gusts still rave and beat:
"No dream, alas! alas! and woe is mine!
Porphyro will leave me here to fade and pine.
Cruel! what traitor could thee hither bring?
I curse not, for my heart is lost in thine,
Though thou forsakest a deceived thing;—
A dove forlorn and lost with sick unpruned wing."

"My Madeline! sweet dreamer! lovely bride!
Say, may I be for aye thy vassal blest?
Thy beauty's shield, heart-shaped and vermeil-dyed?
Ah, silver shrine, here will I take my rest

After so many hours of toil and quest,
A famished pilgrim,—saved by miracle.
Though I have found, I will not rob thy nest,
Saving of thy sweet self; if thou think'st well
To trust, fair Madeline, to no rude infidel.

"Hark! 'tis an elfin-storm from faery land,
Of haggard seeming, but a boon indeed:
Arise—arise! the morning is at hand;—
The bloated wassailers will never heed;—
Let us away, my love, with happy speed;
There are no ears to hear, or eyes to see,—
Drowned all in Rhenish and the sleepy mead:
Awake! arise! my love, and fearless be,
For o'er the southern moors I have a home for thee."

She hurried at his words, beset with fears,
For there were sleeping dragons all around,
At glaring watch, perhaps, with ready spears—
Down the wide stairs a darkling way they found;
In all the house was heard no human sound.
A chain-drooped lamp was flickering by each door;
The arras, rich with horseman, hawk, and hound,
Fluttered in the besieging wind's uproar;
And the long carpets rose along the gusty floor.

They glide, like phantoms, into the wide hall;
Like phantoms, to the iron porch they glide,
Where lay the Porter, in uneasy sprawl,
With a huge empty flagon by his side:
The wakeful bloodhound rose, and shook his hide,
But his sagacious eye an inmate owns:
By one, and one, the bolts full easy slide:—
The chains lie silent on the footworn stones;
The key turns, and the door upon its hinges groans.

And they are gone: aye, ages long ago
These lovers fled away into the storm.
That night the Baron dreamt of many a woe,
And all his warrior-guests with shade and form
Of witch, and demon, and large coffin-worm,
Were long be-nightmared. Angela the old
Died palsy-twitched, with meager face deform;
The Beadsman, after thousand aves told,
For aye unsought-for slept among his ashes cold.

Sensory richness fills all the great odes of Keats. ODE TO AUTUMN,
seemingly a picture and little more, exudes a "mellow fruitfulness"
and the drowsy "fume of poppies" while small gnats mourn "in a
wailful choir . . . and gathering swallows twitter in the skies." The
ODE ON MELANCHOLY, one of the shortest as well as one of the most
poignant of the odes, achieves solemnity and a sense of heaviness
by the weighted movement of the lines. The ODE TO A NIGHTINGALE,
the most quoted as well as the most carefully elaborated, is magic
throughout. Charles Armitage Brown, with whom Keats stayed in
1819, gave this account of the poem's genesis: "In the spring a
nightingale had built her nest near my house. Keats felt a tranquil
and continual joy in her song; one morning he took his chair from
the breakfast table to the grass plot under a plum tree, where he
sat for two or three hours. When he came into the house, I per-
ceived he had some scraps of paper in his hand, and these he was
quietly thrusting behind the books. On inquiry, I found those
scraps, four or five in number; the writing was not well legible,
and it was difficult to arrange the stanzas. With his assistance I suc-
ceeded, and this was his ODE TO A NIGHTINGALE."

Ode to a Nightingale

My heart aches, and a drowsy numbness pains
    My sense, as though of hemlock I had drunk,
Or emptied some dull opiate to the drains
    One minute past, and Lethe-wards had sunk:
'Tis not through envy of thy happy lot,
    But being too happy in thy happiness,—
      That thou, light-winged Dryad of the trees,
        In some melodious plot
Of beechen green, and shadows numberless,
    Singest of summer in full-throated ease.

O for a draught of vintage, that hath been
    Cooled a long age in the deep-delved earth,
Tasting of Flora and the country green,
    Dance, and Provençal song, and sun-burnt mirth!
O for a beaker full of the warm South,
    Full of the true, the blushful Hippocrene,
      With beaded bubbles winking at the brim,
        And purple-stained mouth;
That I might drink, and leave the world unseen,
    And with thee fade away into the forest dim:

Fade far away, dissolve, and quite forget
  What thou among the leaves hast never known,
The weariness, the fever, and the fret
  Here, where men sit and hear each other groan;
Where palsy shakes a few, sad, last gray hairs,
    Where youth grows pale, and spectre-thin, and dies;
      Where but to think is to be full of sorrow
        And leaden-eyed despairs;
    Where beauty cannot keep her lustrous eyes,
      Or new love pine at them beyond tomorrow.

Away! away! for I will fly to thee,
  Not charioted by Bacchus and his pards,
But on the viewless wings of Poesy,
  Though the dull brain perplexes and retards:
Already with thee! tender is the night,
    And haply the Queen-Moon is on her throne,
      Clustered around by all her starry fays;
        But here there is no light,
    Save what from heaven is with the breezes blown
      Through verdurous glooms and winding mossy ways.

I cannot see what flowers are at my feet,
  Nor what soft incense hangs upon the boughs,
But, in embalmed darkness, guess each sweet
  Wherewith the seasonable month endows
The grass, the thicket, and the fruit-tree wild;
    White hawthorn, and the pastoral eglantine;
      Fast-fading violets covered up in leaves;
        And mid-May's eldest child,
    The coming musk-rose, full of dewy wine,
      The murmurous haunt of flies on summer eves.

Darkling I listen; and for many a time
  I have been half in love with easeful Death,
Called him soft names in many a mused rhyme,
  To take into the air my quiet breath;
Now more than ever seems it rich to die,
    To cease upon the midnight with no pain,
      While thou art pouring forth thy soul abroad
        In such an ecstasy!
    Still wouldst thou sing, and I have ears in vain—
      To thy high requiem become a sod.

Thou wast not born for death, immortal Bird!
　No hungry generations tread thee down;
The voice I hear this passing night was heard
　In ancient days by emperor and clown:
Perhaps the self-same song that found a path
　　Through the sad heart of Ruth, when, sick for home,
　　She stood in tears amid the alien corn;
　　　The same that oft-times hath
　Charmed magic casements, opening on the foam
　Of perilous seas, in faery lands forlorn.

Forlorn! the very word is like a bell
　To toll me back from thee to my sole self!
Adieu! the fancy cannot cheat so well
　As she is famed to do, deceiving elf.
Adieu! adieu! thy plaintive anthem fades
　　Past the near meadows, over the still stream,
　　Up the hill-side; and now 'tis buried deep
　　　In the next valley-glades:
　Was it a vision, or a waking dream?
　Fled is that music:—do I wake or sleep?

Ode to Autumn

Season of mists and mellow fruitfulness,
　Close bosom-friend of the maturing sun;
Conspiring with him how to load and bless
　With fruit the vines that round the thatch-eaves run;
To bend with apples the mossed cottage-trees,
　And fill all fruit with ripeness to the core;
　　To swell the gourd, and plump the hazel shells
　With a sweet kernel; to set budding more,
And still more, later flowers for the bees,
Until they think warm days will never cease,
　　For Summer has o'er-brimmed their clammy cells.

Who hath not seen thee oft amid thy store?
　Sometimes whoever seeks abroad may find
Thee sitting careless on a granary floor,
　Thy hair soft-lifted by the winnowing wind;
Or on a half-reaped furrow sound asleep,
　　Drowsed with the fume of poppies, while thy hook
　　Spares the next swath and all its twined flowers;

And sometimes like a gleaner thou dost keep
   Steady thy laden head across a brook;
   Or by a cider-press, with patient look,
     Thou watchest the last oozings, hours by hours.

Where are the songs of Spring? Ay, where are they?
   Think not of them, thou hast thy music too,—
While barred clouds bloom the soft-dying day,
   And touch the stubble-plains with rosy hue;
Then in a wailful choir, the small gnats mourn
   Among the river sallows, borne aloft
     Or sinking as the light wind lives or dies;
And full-grown lambs loud bleat from hilly bourn;
   Hedge-crickets sing; and now with treble soft
   The redbreast whistles from a garden-croft,
     And gathering swallows twitter in the skies.

Ode on Melancholy

No, no! go not to Lethe, neither twist
   Wolf's-bane, tight-rooted, for its poisonous wine;
Nor suffer thy pale forehead to be kissed
   By nightshade, ruby grape of Proserpine;
Make not your rosary of yew-berries,
   Nor let the beetle nor the death-moth be
     Your mournful Psyche, nor the downy owl
A partner in your sorrow's mysteries;
   For shade to shade will come too drowsily,
     And drown the wakeful anguish of the soul.

But when the melancholy fit shall fall
   Sudden from heaven like a weeping cloud,
That fosters the droop-headed flowers all,
   And hides the green hill in an April shroud;
Then glut thy sorrow on a morning rose,
   Or on the rainbow of the salt sand-wave,
     Or on the wealth of globed peonies;
Or if thy mistress some rich anger shows,
   Emprison her soft hand, and let her rave,
     And feed deep, deep upon her peerless eyes.

She dwells with Beauty—Beauty that must die;
   And Joy, whose hand is ever at his lips

> Bidding adieu; and aching Pleasure nigh,
>   Turning to poison while the bee-mouth sips:
> Ay, in the very temple of delight
>   Veiled Melancholy has her sovran shrine,
>   Though seen of none save him whose strenuous tongue
>   Can burst Joy's grape against his palate fine:
> His soul shall taste the sadness of her might,
>   And be among her cloudy trophies hung.

One of Keats's most charming small poems was an impromptu performance, the result of a challenge. One December day while Hunt and Keats were seated in front of the hearth, listening to the crickets, "the cheerful little grasshoppers of the fireside," Hunt proposed that they should both write competing sonnets ON THE GRASS-HOPPER AND CRICKET. Cowden Clarke, friend of Keats's youth, timed them, and Keats won. Hunt wrote a pretty little tribute to the "sweet and tiny cousins" of the field and hearth, but Keats, who modestly preferred Hunt's treatment to his own, achieved one of his almost perfect effects. The calm finality of the first line is not diminished by Keats's characteristic contrast of hot sun and cool shade. The return of the grasshopper at the end is a particularly happy touch. "This end," wrote Amy Lowell in her comprehensive biography, "is not only beautiful as regards the technical pattern, it is so in regard to the mental pattern as well."

On the Grasshopper and Cricket

> The poetry of earth is never dead:
>   When all the birds are faint with the hot sun,
>   And hide in cooling trees, a voice will run
> From hedge to hedge about the new-mown mead;
> That is the grasshopper's—he takes the lead
>   In summer luxury,—he has never done
>   With his delights, for when tired out with fun
> He rests at ease beneath some pleasant weed.
> The poetry of earth is ceasing never:
>   On a lone winter evening, when the frost
> Has wrought a silence, from the stove there shrills
> The cricket's song, in warmth increasing ever,
>   And seems to one, in drowsiness half-lost,
> The grasshopper's among some grassy hills.

"I am certain of nothing," Keats wrote in one of those letters which eloquently complement his poetry, "but the holiness of the heart's affections and the truth of imagination. . . . What the imagination seizes as beauty must be truth, whether it existed before or not. The imagination may be compared to Adam's dream—he awoke and found it true." The principle of beauty, the concluding "motto" of the ODE ON A GRECIAN URN, was Keats's highest truth, a truth not inconsistent with his cry, "O for a life of sensations rather than of thoughts!"

Like Milton, to whom Keats progressively turned, Keats lived in "poetical luxury." Recent commentators have exalted Keats even beyond Milton. Commenting on his power of "concentrating all the far-reaching resources of language on one point," the late poet laureate, Robert Bridges, wrote: "This is only found in the greatest poets, and is rare even in them. It is no doubt for the possession of this power that Keats has often been likened to Shakespeare, and very justly, for Shakespeare is of all poets the greatest master of it."

A Thing of Beauty

A thing of beauty is a joy for ever:
Its loveliness increases; it will never
Pass into nothingness; but still will keep
A bower quiet for us, and a sleep
Full of sweet dreams, and health, and quiet breathing.
Therefore, on every morrow, are we wreathing
A flowery band to bind us to the earth,
Spite of despondence, of the inhuman dearth
Of noble natures, of the gloomy days,
Of all the unhealthy and o'er-darkened ways
Made for our searching: yes, in spite of all,
Some shape of beauty moves away the pall
From our dark spirits. Such the sun, the moon,
Trees old and young, sprouting a shady boon
For simple sheep; and such are daffodils
With the green world they live in; and clear rills
That for themselves a cooling covert make
'Gainst the hot season; the mid-forest brake,
Rich with a sprinkling of fair musk-rose blooms:
And such too is the grandeur of the dooms

We have imagined for the mighty dead;
All lovely tales that we have heard or read:
An endless fountain of immortal drink,
Pouring unto us from the heaven's brink.
from ENDYMION

To One Who Has Been Long in City Pent

To one who has been long in city pent,
    'Tis very sweet to look into the fair
    And open face of heaven,—to breathe a prayer
Full in the smile of the blue firmament.
Who is more happy, when, with heart's content,
    Fatigued he sinks into some pleasant lair
    Of wavy grass, and reads a debonair
And gentle tale of love and languishment?
Returning home at evening, with an ear
    Catching the notes of Philomel,—an eye
Watching the sailing cloudlet's bright career,
    He mourns that day so soon has glided by,
E'en like the passage of an angel's tear
    That falls through the clear ether silently.

On the Sea

It keeps eternal whisperings around
    Desolate shores, and with its mighty swell
    Gluts twice ten thousand caverns, till the spell
Of Hecate leaves them their old shadowy sound.
Often 'tis in such gentle temper found,
    That scarcely will the very smallest shell
    Be moved for days from where it sometime fell,
When last the winds of heaven were unbound.
Oh ye! who have your eye-balls vexed and tired,
    Feast them upon the wideness of the Sea;
Oh ye! whose ears are dinned with uproar rude,
    Or fed too much with cloying melody,—
Sit ye near some old cavern's mouth, and brood
Until ye start, as if the sea-nymphs quired!

Keats never completed his most ambitious work, HYPERION, an
epic of the overthrow of the elder gods, but the first lines of that

massive fragment are among his greatest accomplishments. "The whole sentiment of gigantic despair," wrote H. Buxton Forman, "reflected around the fallen god of the Titan dynasty, and permeating the landscape, is resumed in the most perfect manner in the incident of the motionless fallen leaf, a line almost as intense and full of the essence of poetry as any line in our language."

Saturn

Deep in the shady sadness of a vale
Far sunken from the healthy breath of morn,
Far from the fiery noon, and eve's one star,
Sat gray-haired Saturn, quiet as a stone,
Still as the silence round about his lair;
Forest on forest hung about his head
Like cloud on cloud. No stir of air was there,
Not so much life as on a summer's day
Robs not one light seed from the feathered grass,
But where the dead leaf fell, there did it rest.
A stream went voiceless by, still deadened more
By reason of his fallen divinity
Spreading a shade: the Naiad 'mid her reeds
Pressed her cold finger closer to her lips.

Along the margin-sand large foot-marks went,
No further than to where his feet had strayed,
And slept there since. Upon the sodden ground
His old right hand lay nerveless, listless, dead,
Unsceptred; and his realmless eyes were closed;
While his bowed head seemed listening to the Earth,
His ancient mother, for some comfort yet.

from HYPERION

When I Have Fears That I May Cease to Be

When I have fears that I may cease to be
Before my pen has gleaned my teeming brain,
Before high-piled books, in charactery,
Hold like rich garners the full ripened grain;
When I behold, upon the night's starred face,
Huge cloudy symbols of a high romance,

And think that I may never live to trace
  Their shadows, with the magic hand of chance;
And when I feel, fair creature of an hour,
  That I shall never look upon thee more,
Never have relish in the faery power
  Of unreflecting love;—then on the shore
Of the wide world I stand alone, and think
Till love and fame to nothingness do sink.

The poetry of Keats may be limited because of its very concentration, its rapt attention to detail and absorption in beauty. But never has poetry been enclosed in an atmosphere of purer enchantment.

XIII

Faith, Doubt, and Democracy

WILLIAM CULLEN BRYANT
[1794–1878]

THANATOPSIS, the first important American poem, was written by a boy of seventeen and, when first published, was considered a hoax. Bryant's father found the manuscript in the family desk, copied it, and sent it to the NORTH AMERICAN REVIEW. Richard Henry Dana, author of TWO YEARS BEFORE THE MAST, told the editor he had been imposed upon. "No one, on this side of the Atlantic," said Dana, "is capable of writing such verses."

Born in a log house at Cummington, Massachusetts, November 3, 1794, William Cullen Bryant was descended from *Mayflower* Pilgrims. He was a frail but scarcely pampered child. His father, a country doctor, attempted to reduce his son's abnormally large head by soaking it every morning in a spring of cold water, and the boy was put to work raising timber frames, helping at the mill, and cutting the twigs for the whipping birch which was "as much a part of the necessary furniture as the crane that hung in the fire place."

Although the boy was kept busy doing countless chores, he was precociously studious. Two months after learning the Greek alphabet, he read the entire New Testament. In 1808 he printed his first book of verse, THE EMBARGO: OR SKETCHES OF THE TIMES, which bore the subtitle "A Satire by a Youth of Thirteen," and which called upon President Thomas Jefferson "to resign because he was incapable of managing the Government." Entering Williams College at sixteen, he left in his sophomore year because of lack of means to continue.

One evening when Bryant was about twenty-two he was going along the road, worried about his prospects. It was December, an overcast twilight. Suddenly the clouds broke, the heavens glowed "with the last steps of day," and a lone bird flew up and vanished into the sunset. The dissolving clouds, the solitary bird, and Bryant's own meditation fused in TO A WATERFOWL, a poem which, frankly didactic, transcends sermonizing.

To a Waterfowl

Whither, 'midst falling dew,
While glow the heavens with the last steps of day,
Far, through their rosy depths, dost thou pursue
    Thy solitary way!

Vainly the fowler's eye
Might mark thy distant flight to do thee wrong,
As, darkly painted on the crimson sky,
    Thy figure floats along.

Seek'st thou the plashy brink
Of weedy lake, or marge of river wide,
Or where the rocking billows rise and sink
    On the chafed ocean side?

There is a power whose care
Teaches thy way along that pathless coast,—
The desert and illimitable air,—
    Lone wandering, but not lost.

All day thy wings have fanned,
At that far height, the cold, thin atmosphere,
Yet stoop not, weary, to the welcome land,
    Though the dark night is near.

And soon that toil shall end;
Soon shalt thou find a summer home, and rest,
And scream among thy fellows; reeds shall bend,
    Soon, o'er thy sheltered nest.

Thou'rt gone, the abyss of heaven
Hath swallowed up thy form; yet, on my heart
Deeply hath sunk the lesson thou hast given,
    And shall not soon depart.

He who, from zone to zone,
Guides through the boundless sky thy certain flight,
In the long way that I must tread alone,
    Will lead my steps aright.

A few months later Bryant studied law, practiced at Great Barrington, Massachusetts, married at twenty-six, and at thirty became one of the editors of the NEW YORK EVENING POST. After two years he was made editor in chief, and held that position for fifty years. He was acclaimed "the first citizen of the Republic," and divided his days between poetry and journalism. In his eighty-fourth year he stood uncovered in the blazing sun while he delivered an address at the dedication of a statue to Mazzini in Central Park, New York. Ascending a flight of stairs a little later, he was overcome by dizziness and fell, suffering a concussion of the brain. He died June 12, 1878.

It has been said that in youth Bryant wrote for old men and in his old age for children. Death is the traditional preoccupation of adolescence, and THANATOPSIS is perhaps the most famous projection of that concern. The poem triumphs over its pompous beginning, and with the line "Yet not to thine eternal resting-place" rises from expansive rhetoric to clear eloquence.

Thanatopsis

To him who in the love of nature holds
Communion with her visible forms, she speaks
A various language; for his gayer hours
She has a voice of gladness, and a smile
And eloquence of beauty; and she glides
Into his darker musings, with a mild
And healing sympathy that steals away
Their sharpness ere he is aware. When thoughts
Of the last bitter hour come like a blight
Over thy spirit, and sad images
Of the stern agony, and shroud, and pall,
And breathless darkness, and the narrow house,

Make thee to shudder, and grow sick at heart;—
Go forth, under the open sky, and list
To Nature's teachings, while from all around—
Earth and her waters, and the depths of air—
Comes a still voice. Yet a few days, and thee
The all-beholding sun shall see no more
In all his course; nor yet in the cold ground,
Where thy pale form was laid, with many tears,
Nor in the embrace of ocean, shall exist
Thy image. Earth, that nourished thee, shall claim
Thy growth, to be resolved to earth again,
And, lost each human trace, surrendering up
Thine individual being, shalt thou go
To mix forever with the elements,
To be a brother to the insensible rock
And to the sluggish clod, which the rude swain
Turns with his share, and treads upon. The oak
Shall send his roots abroad, and pierce thy mold.

    Yet not to thine eternal resting-place
Shalt thou retire alone, nor couldst thou wish
Couch more magnificent. Thou shalt lie down
With patriarchs of the infant world—with kings,
The powerful of the earth—the wise, the good,
Fair forms, and hoary seers of ages past,
All in one mighty sepulchre. The hills
Rock-ribbed and ancient as the sun,—the vales
Stretching in pensive quietness between;
The venerable woods—rivers that move
In majesty, and the complaining brooks
That make the meadows green; and, poured round all,
Old Ocean's gray and melancholy waste,—
Are but the solemn decorations all
Of the great tomb of man. The golden sun,
The planets, all the infinite host of heaven,
Are shining on the sad abodes of death
Through the still lapse of ages. All that tread
The globe are but a handful to the tribes
That slumber in its bosom.—Take the wings
Of morning, pierce the Barcan wilderness,
Or lose thyself in the continuous woods
Where rolls the Oregon, and hears no sound,
Save his own dashings—yet the dead are there:
And millions in those solitudes, since first

The flight of years began, have laid them down
In their last sleep—the dead reign there alone.

So shalt thou rest—and what if thou withdraw
In silence from the living, and no friend
Take note of thy departure? All that breathe
Will share thy destiny. The gay will laugh
When thou art gone, the solemn brood of care
Plod on, and each one as before will chase
His favorite phantom; yet all these shall leave
Their mirth and their employments, and shall come
And make their bed with thee. As the long train
Of ages glides away, the sons of men—
The youth in life's fresh spring, and he who goes
In the full strength of years, matron and maid,
The speechless babe, and the gray-headed man—
Shall one by one be gathered to thy side,
By those, who in their turn shall follow them.

So live, that when thy summons comes to join
The innumerable caravan, which moves
To that mysterious realm, where each shall take
His chamber in the silent halls of death,
Thou go not, like the quarry-slave at night,
Scourged to his dungeon, but, sustained and soothed
By an unfaltering trust, approach thy grave
Like one who wraps the drapery of his couch
About him, and lies down to pleasant dreams.

Bryant's world is neither an exciting nor a romantic one, but it is
a world to which the reader may come, after heat and turbulence,
for reassuring quiet. It is not enchanted ground, but it is a true
haven.

JOHN GREENLEAF WHITTIER
[1807–1892]

THE most militant of the New England poets, John Greenleaf
Whittier, was born December 17, 1807, at Haverhill, Massachu
setts. Unlike his famous contemporaries, Whittier had a background
of little education and practically no money. The first eighteen

years of his life were spent on a farm, and it was not until he had turned nineteen that he was able to attend Haverhill Academy for two terms. He paid for the tuition with his own savings, chiefly from shoemaking, and, according to his first biographer, "calculated every item of expense so closely that he knew before the beginning of the term he would have twenty-five cents to spare at its close."

At eighteen Whittier had seen his first poem printed in a local newspaper, the Newburyport FREE PRESS. The editor was William Lloyd Garrison, and under Garrison's influence Whittier was stirred to a fever of abolitionism. Born a Quaker, Whittier became a crusader, the poet and politician of the antislavery cause. He served in the legislature, and was assailed as a fanatic. He edited a newspaper, and saw his office burned down by a pro-slavery mob. After his fortieth year, he lived in Amesbury, with his sister, in Wordsworthian seclusion. He died at the patriarchal age of eighty-five, September 7, 1892.

A more vehement spirit than his noted compatriots, Whittier was a less skillful craftsman. His homely ballads, however, have never lost their appeal. Such a poem as BARBARA FRIETCHIE continues to be relished partly because of the straightforwardness of the simple couplets, partly because it seems to belong to the folk stuff of a nation. Even if, as historians have insisted, the event is fictitious, it is the sort of gallant incident that should have happened.

Barbara Frietchie

Up from the meadows rich with corn,
Clear in the cool September morn,

The clustered spires of Frederick stand
Green-walled by the hills of Maryland.

Round about them orchards sweep,
Apple and peach tree fruited deep,

Fair as a garden of the Lord,
To the eyes of the famished rebel horde,

On that pleasant morn of the early fall
When Lee marched over the mountain wall—

Over the mountains, winding down,
Horse and foot into Frederick town.

Forty flags with their silver stars,
Forty flags with their crimson bars,

Flapped in the morning wind; the sun
Of noon looked down, and saw not one.

Up rose old Barbara Frietchie then,
Bowed with her fourscore years and ten;

Bravest of all in Frederick town,
She took up the flag the men hauled down;

In her attic-window the staff she set,
To show that one heart was loyal yet.

Up the street came the rebel tread,
Stonewall Jackson riding ahead.

Under his slouch hat left and right
He glanced: the old flag met his sight.

"Halt!"—the dust-brown ranks stood fast;
"Fire!"—out blazed the rifle-blast.

It shivered the window, pane and sash;
It rent the banner with seam and gash.

Quick, as it fell, from the broken staff
Dame Barbara snatched the silken scarf;

She leaned far out on the window-sill,
And shook it forth with a royal will.

"Shoot, if you must, this old gray head,
But spare your country's flag," she said.

A shade of sadness, a blush of shame,
Over the face of the leader came;

The nobler nature within him stirred
To life at that woman's deed and word:

"Who touches a hair of yon gray head
Dies like a dog! March on!" he said.

All day long through Frederick street
Sounded the tread of marching feet;

All day long that free flag tost
Over the heads of the rebel host.

Ever its torn folds rose and fell
On the loyal winds that loved it well;

And through the hill-gaps sunset light
Shone over it with a warm good-night.

Barbara Frietchie's work is o'er,
And the rebel rides on his raids no more.

Honor to her! and let a tear
Fall, for her sake, on Stonewall's bier.

Over Barbara Frietchie's grave,
Flag of freedom and union wave!

Peace and order and beauty draw
Round thy symbol of light and law;

And ever the stars above look down
On thy stars below in Frederick town.

The bucolic elements in his verse have led many readers to think of Whittier as a ruder Wordsworth, a Massachusetts Burns without the Scottish plowman's gift of song. But Whittier's country verse exhales native air. It is American colonial life which is lovingly recorded in SNOW-BOUND, Whittier's highest poetic achievement. Rich in characterization, graphic in interior details, it is an almost perfect genre poem, a small epic in homespun.

Winter Day

The sun that brief December day
Rose cheerless over hills of gray,
And, darkly circled, gave at noon
A sadder light than waning moon.

Slow tracing down the thickening sky
Its mute and ominous prophecy,
A portent seeming less than threat,
It sank from sight before it set.
A chill no coat, however stout,
Of homespun stuff could quite shut out,
A hard, dull bitterness of cold,
That checked, mid-vein, the circling race
Of life-blood in the sharpened face
The coming of the snow-storm told.
The wind blew east; we heard the roar
Of Ocean on his wintry shore,
And felt the strong pulse throbbing there
Beat with low rhythm our inland air.
Meanwhile we did our nightly chores,
Brought in the wood from out of doors,
Littered the stalls, and from the mows
Raked down the herd's-grass for the cows:
Heard the horse whinnying for his corn;
And, sharply clashing horn on horn,
Impatient down the stanchion rows
The cattle shake their walnut bows;
While, peering from his early perch
Upon the scaffold's pole of birch,
The cock his crested helmet bent
And down his querulous challenge sent.

from SNOW-BOUND

Winter Night

As night drew on, and, from the crest
Of wooded knolls that ridged the west,
The sun, a snow-blown traveller, sank
From sight beneath the smothering bank
We piled, with care, our nightly stack
Of wood against the chimney-back,—
The oaken log, green, huge, and thick,
And on its top the stout back-stick;
The knotty forestick laid apart,
And filled between with curious art
The ragged brush; then, hovering near,
We watched the first red blaze appear,
Heard the sharp crackle, caught the gleam

On whitewashed wall and sagging beam,
Until the old, rude-furnished room
Burst, flower-like, into rosy bloom;
While radiant with a mimic flame
Outside the sparkling drift became,
And through the bare-boughed lilac-tree
Our own warm hearth seemed blazing free.
The crane and pendent trammels showed,
The Turks' heads on the andirons glowed;
While childish fancy, prompt to tell
The meaning of the miracle,
Whispered the old rhyme: *"Under the tree,*
When fire outdoors burns merrily,
There the witches are making tea."

The moon above the eastern wood
Shone at its full; the hill-range stood
Transfigured in the silver flood,
Its blown snows flashing cold and keen,
Dead white, save where some sharp ravine
Took shadow, or the sombre green
Of hemlocks turned to pitchy black
Against the whiteness at their back.
For such a world and such a night
Most fitting that unwarming light,
Which only seemed where'er it fell
To make the coldness visible.

from SNOW-BOUND

RALPH WALDO EMERSON

[1803–1882]

BORN May 25, 1803, in Boston, Massachusetts, of ministerial stock,
Ralph Waldo Emerson was destined for the ministry. After
graduating from Harvard College and Harvard Divinity School, he
was ordained in his twenty-sixth year. Three years later he left the
pulpit, unable to believe in the ritual.

At twenty-nine one part of Emerson's life had ended. He had
married Ellen Tucker, and was in a fair way of becoming influen-

tial not only as a chaplain but as an educator. Three years after his marriage, his wife—like Emerson's father and two of his brothers— died of tuberculosis. Emerson journeyed abroad, met Coleridge, formed a warm friendship with Carlyle, recovered his health, and returned to America, where he became a resident of Concord, Massachusetts. He remarried, turned to the lecture platform, and published his first volume, NATURE, a milestone in American letters. "Nature," Emerson contended, "is the incarnation of thought. The world is the mind precipitated." Poems and essays followed with ever-growing strength and conviction. Emerson spoke up for intellectual as well as religious independence; he held that humanity had lost self-rule and self-reliance, that man was dominated by things rather than by thought. As a result of Emerson's attack on the conventions, clergymen assailed his "heresies" and Harvard closed its lecture rooms to him. Thirty years later he received an honorary degree from Harvard and was chosen one of its overseers. At sixty-seven he gave a course in philosophy at Cambridge.

His house had burned down in his seventieth year, and Emerson had been weakened by exposure and disheartened by the loss of his books and furniture. Friends sent him abroad and admirers rebuilt the house to the last detail. Emerson returned as "The Sage of Concord" to spend his days in increasing solitude. But he was still energetic; at seventy-seven he loved to swim naked in Walden Pond. His memory faded. Nevertheless, when he had trouble remembering people and even words, he recalled characteristics. Once, wishing for his umbrella, he said, "I can't tell its name, but I can tell its history. Strangers take it away." At the burial of Longfellow he declared, "That gentleman was a sweet and beautiful soul—but I have forgotten his name." The end was a gradual diminishing, and Emerson died at Concord, April 27, 1882.

Emerson's love of Concord reveals itself in one of his most characteristic although one of his least-quoted poems, TWO RIVERS. The Indian name "Musketaquit" is explained in Thoreau's A WEEK ON THE CONCORD AND MERRIMACK RIVERS:

The Musketaquit, or Grass-ground River, though probably as old as the Nile or Euphrates, did not begin to have a place in civilized history until the fame of its grassy meadows and its fish attracted settlers out of England in 1635, when it received the other but kindred name of Concord from the first plantation on its banks, which appears to have been commenced in a spirit of peace and harmony. It will be Grass-ground River as long as grass grows and water runs here; it will be Concord River only while men lead peaceable lives on its banks.

Two Rivers

Thy summer voice, Musketaquit,
Repeats the music of the rain;
But sweeter rivers pulsing flit
Through thee, as thou through Concord Plain.

Thou in thy narrow banks are pent:
The stream I love unbounded goes
Through flood and sea and firmament;
Through light, through life, it forward flows.

I see the inundation sweet,
I hear the spending of the stream
Through years, through men, through Nature fleet,
Through love and thought, through power and dream.

Musketaquit, a goblin strong,
Of shard and flint makes jewels gay;
They lose their grief who hear his song,
And where he winds is the day of day.

So forth and brighter fares my stream—
Who drink it shall not thirst again;
No darkness stains its equal gleam,
And ages drop in it like rain.

The suavity of Emerson's verse is deceptive. The surface is so limpid, so easily persuasive, that it appears conventional. But the ideas embodied in the poems are energetic and radical ideas; they are, like Emerson himself, not only truth-loving but truth-living. They celebrate the democratic man, but they do not idealize him; they recognize evil as well as good; they regard doubt not as a fixed denial but as "a cry for faith rising from the dust of dead creeds." Even love, which demands every sacrifice, must be free of moral impositions; for "when half-gods go, the gods arrive."

Give All to Love

Give all to love;
Obey thy heart;
Friends, kindred, days,
Estate, good-fame,
Plans, credit, and the Muse—
Nothing refuse.

'Tis a brave master;
Let it have scope:
Follow it utterly,
Hope beyond hope:
High and more high
It dives into noon,
With wing unspent,
Untold intent;
But it is a god,
Knows its own path,
And the outlets of the sky.

It was not for the mean;
It requireth courage stout,
Souls above doubt,
Valor unbending;
Such 'twill reward—
They shall return
More than they were,
And ever ascending.

Leave all for love;
Yet, hear me, yet,
One word more thy heart behoved,
One pulse more of firm endeavor—
Keep thee today,
Tomorrow, forever,
Free as an Arab
Of thy beloved.

Cling with life to the maid;
But when the surprise,
First vague shadow of surmise
Flits across her bosom young

Of a joy apart from thee,
Free be she, fancy-free;
Nor thou detain her vesture's hem,
Nor the palest rose she flung
From her summer diadem.

Though thou loved her as thyself,
As a self of purer clay,
Though her parting dims the day,
Stealing grace from all alive;
Heartily know,
When half-gods go,
The gods arrive.

In a long poem, MERLIN, Emerson tells the poet—and, by infer'
ence, the reader—that he must

. . . . . mount to Paradise
By the stairway of surprise.

Surprise is the element which characterizes Emerson's best poetry,
the pithy suggestiveness which influenced his Amherst disciple,
Emily Dickinson. His meaning has often been questioned. The
pantheistic BRAHMA has been parodied and misunderstood, although
the title should make it plain that the speaker is not meant to be
Emerson but the god of nature. In this poem, accident and design,
life and death, are harmonized in the all-resolving paradox of
existence.

Brahma

If the red slayer think he slays,
    Or if the slain think he is slain,
They know not well the subtle ways
    I keep, and pass, and turn again.

Far or forgot to me is near;
    Shadow and sunlight are the same;
The vanished gods to me appear;
    And one to me are shame and fame.

They reckon ill who leave me out;
    When me they fly, I am the wings;
I am the doubter and the doubt,
    And I the hymn the Brahmin sings.

The strong gods pine for my abode,
    And pine in vain the sacred Seven;
But thou, meek lover of the good!
    Find me, and turn thy back on heaven.

Emerson's range and integrity overcome his occasional lack of melody and structural carelessness. His scope includes the passion of the CONCORD HYMN, the pictorial delicacy of THE SNOWSTORM, and the Thoreaulike sententiousness of THE RHODORA and FORBEARANCE. The value of Emerson's poetry, however, is not in what it teaches but what it confirms. A hint here, a phrase there, a gnomic suggestion taking us breathlessly—we seize him by intuition or not at all.

Concord Hymn

By the rude bridge that arched the flood,
    Their flag to April's breeze unfurled,
Here once the embattled farmers stood,
    And fired the shot heard round the world.

The foe long since in silence slept;
    Alike the conqueror silent sleeps;
And Time the ruined bridge has swept
    Down the dark stream that seaward creeps.

On this green bank, by this soft stream,
    We set to-day a votive stone;
That memory may their deed redeem,
    When, like our sires, our sons are gone.

Spirit, that made those heroes dare
    To die, and leave their children free,
Bid Time and Nature gently spare
    The shaft we raise to them and thee.

The Snowstorm

Announced by all the trumpets of the sky,
Arrives the snow, and, driving o'er the fields,
Seems nowhere to alight: the whited air
Hides hills and woods, the river, and the heaven,
And veils the farmhouse at the garden's end.
The sled and traveler stopped, the courier's feet
Delayed, all friends shut out, the housemates sit
Around the radiant fireplace, inclosed
In a tumultuous privacy of storm.

Come, see the north wind's masonry.
Out of an unseen quarry evermore
Furnished with tile, the fierce artificer
Curves his white bastions with projected roof
Round every windward stake, or tree, or door.
Speeding, the myriad-handed, his wild work
So fanciful, so savage, naught cares he
For number or proportion. Mockingly
On coop or kennel he hangs Parian wreaths;
A swan-like form invests the hidden thorn;
Fills up the farmer's lane from wall to wall,
Maugre the farmer's sighs; and at the gate
A tapering turret overtops the work.
And when his hours are numbered, and the world
Is all his own, retiring, as he were not,
Leaves, when the sun appears, astonished Art
To mimic in slow structures, stone by stone,
Built in an age, the mad wind's night-work,
The frolic architecture of the snow.

Days

Daughters of Time, the hypocritic Days,
Muffled and dumb like barefoot dervishes,
And marching single in an endless file,
Bring diadems and fagots in their hands.
To each they offer gifts after his will,
Bread, kingdoms, stars, and sky that holds them all.

I, in my pleached garden, watched the pomp,
Forgot my morning wishes, hastily
Took a few herbs and apples, and the Day
Turned and departed silent. I, too late,
Under her solemn fillet saw the scorn.

The Rhodora

ON BEING ASKED, WHENCE IS THE FLOWER?

In May, when sea-winds pierced our solitudes,
I found the fresh Rhodora in the woods,
Spreading its leafless blooms in a damp nook,
To please the desert and the sluggish brook.
The purple petals, fallen in the pool,
Made the black water with their beauty gay;
Here might the red-bird come his plumes to cool,
And court the flower that cheapens his array.
Rhodora! if the sages ask thee why
This charm is wasted on the earth and sky,
Tell them, dear, that if eyes were made for seeing,
Then Beauty is its own excuse for being:
Why thou wert there, O rival of the rose!
I never thought to ask, I never knew:
But, in my simple ignorance, suppose
The self-same Power that brought me there brought you.

Forbearance

Hast thou named all the birds without a gun?
Loved the wood-rose, and left it on its stalk?
At rich men's tables eaten bread and pulse?
Unarmed, faced danger with a heart of trust?
And loved so well a high behavior,
In man or maid, that thou from speech refrained,
Nobility more nobly to repay?—
O, be my friend, and teach me to be thine!

THOMAS LOVELL BEDDOES
[1803–1849]

THOMAS LOVELL BEDDOES was a lost anachronism, a bizarre Eliza-
bethan dramatist who happened to live in the nineteenth cen-
tury. Beddoes' father was a famous physician and quasi scientist;
his mother was a sister of Maria Edgeworth, the novelist. At seven-
teen Beddoes entered Pembroke College, Oxford, immersed himself
in the works of the lesser Elizabethan and Jacobean playwrights,
and at nineteen published the violent but fragmentary THE BRIDE'S
TRAGEDY. A fantastic and still more uneven drama, DEATH'S JEST-
BOOK, was begun in Beddoes' twenty-second year, completed in his
twenty-sixth, and continually revised until his death. "I am con-
vinced that the man who is to awaken the drama must be a bold,
trampling fellow," Beddoes wrote to a friend, "no creeper into
wormholes!" But Beddoes was unable to live up to his audacious
program. If he was, as he was sometimes called, "the last of the
Elizabethans," he was not influenced by the greatest of these; "he
imbibed," wrote Saintsbury, "rather from the night-shade of Webster
and Tourneur than from the vine of Shakespeare."

Beddoes himself might have been a character in the most macabre
of his plays. He lived in Europe practically all his life, practiced
medicine in Zurich, and lived with a baker whom he resolved to
turn into a great actor. He hired a theater for one night so that
the baker could play the part of Hotspur; and when the two friends
separated after a quarrel, Beddoes tried to kill himself. At forty-
three he visited England and called upon his relatives, gravely
riding upon a donkey. He tried to set fire to Drury Lane Theater
with a five-pound note as a protest against the English stage. Re-
turning to the Continent, he died in Basel, January 26, 1849; it was
suspected, though never proved, that he committed suicide by tak-
ing poison.

If Beddoes' dramas are spasmodic, his poems are not. The songs
interpolated in the plays are exquisite and almost perfect. Whether
the mood is sensuous, as in lines beginning "If there were dreams
to sell," insinuatingly chill, as in THE PHANTOM WOOER with its
"little snakes of silver throat," or grimly jocular, as in THE CARRION
CROW, the music is as persuasive as it is precise. If the lyrics are

Gothic, preoccupied with death and decay, they are authentic in their fitful genius. If they are fragmentary, they are fragments of gold.

Dream-Pedlary

If there were dreams to sell,
   What would you buy?
Some cost a passing bell;
   Some a light sigh,
That shakes from Life's fresh crown
Only a rose-leaf down.
If there were dreams to sell,
Merry and sad to tell,
And the crier rung the bell,
   What would you buy?

A cottage lone and still,
   With bowers nigh,
Shadowy, my woes to still,
   Until I die.
Such pearl from Life's fresh crown
Fain would I shake me down.
Were dreams to have at will,
This would best heal my ill,
   This would I buy.

If there are ghosts to raise,
   What shall I call,
Out of hell's murky haze,
   Heaven's blue pall?
Raise my loved long-lost boy
To lead me to his joy.
   There are no ghosts to raise;
   Out of death lead no ways;
     Vain is the call.

Know'st thou not ghosts to sue?
   No love thou hast.
Else lie, as I will do,
   And breathe thy last.
So out of Life's fresh crown
Fall like a rose-leaf down.
   Thus are the ghosts to woo;
   Thus are all dreams made true,
     Ever to last!

Stanzas

The mighty thought of an old world
Fans, like a dragon's wing unfurled,
The surface of my yearnings deep;
And solemn shadows then awake,
Like the fish-lizard in the lake,
Troubling a planet's morning sleep.

My waking is a Titan's dream,
Where a strange sun, long set, doth beam
Through Montezuma's cypress bough:
Through the fern wilderness forlorn
Glisten the giant hart's great horn
And serpents vast with helmèd brow.

The measureless from caverns rise
With steps of earthquake, thunderous cries,
And graze upon the lofty wood;
The palmy grove, through which doth gleam
Such antediluvian ocean's stream,
Haunts shadowy my domestic mood.

from THE IVORY GATE

Song

How many times do I love thee, dear?
    Tell me how many thoughts there be
        In the atmosphere
        Of a new-fall'n year,
Whose white and sable hours appear
    The latest flake of Eternity:
So many times do I love thee, dear.

How many times do I love again?
    Tell me how many beads there are
        In a silver chain
        Of evening rain,
Unravelled from the tumbling main,
    And threading the eye of a yellow star:
So many times do I love again.

from TORRISMOND

The Phantom Wooer

A ghost, that loved a lady fair,
Ever in the starry air
   Of midnight at her pillow stood;
And, with a sweetness skies above
The luring words of human love,
   Her soul the phantom wooed.
Sweet and sweet is their poisoned note,
The little snakes of silver throat,
In mossy skulls that nest and lie,
Ever singing 'die, oh! die.'

Young soul put off your flesh, and come
With me into the quiet tomb,
   Our bed is lovely, dark, and sweet;
The earth will swing us, as she goes,
Beneath our coverlid of snows,
   And the warm leaden sheet.
Dear and dear is their poisoned note.
The little snakes of silver throat,
In mossy skulls that nest and lie,
Ever singing 'die, oh! die.'

The Carrion Crow

Old Adam, the carrion crow,
   The old crow of Cairo;
He sat in the shower, and let it flow
   Under his tail and over his crest;
     And through every feather
     Leaked the wet weather;
And the bough swung under his nest;
For his beak it was heavy with marrow.
   Is that the wind dying? O no;
   It's only two devils, that blow
     Through a murderer's bones, to and fro,
     In the ghosts' moonshine.

Ho! Eve, my grey carrion wife,
   When we have supped on kings' marrow,

Where shall we drink and make merry our life?
Our nest it is queen Cleopatra's skull,
   'Tis cloven and cracked,
   And battered and hacked,
But with tears of blue eyes it is full:
Let us drink them, my raven of Cairo.
   Is that the wind dying? O no;
   It's only two devils, that blow
   Through a murderer's bones, to and fro,
   In the ghosts' moonshine.

from DEATH'S JEST-BOOK

ELIZABETH BARRETT BROWNING
[1806–1861]

WHEN Robert Browning stormed into her life, Elizabeth Barrett was a thirty-nine-year-old invalid. Daughter of a jealously dominating father, Elizabeth was born near Durham, March 6, 1806. At twelve she wrote THE BATTLE OF MARATHON, an "epic" of four books, which her father caused to be printed. At fifteen she injured her spine, and confinement in the London house on Wimpole Street ("Newgate prison turned inside out") affected her lungs. The grief caused by the death of a beloved brother by drowning and her father's refusal to allow any of his children to marry made her a recluse. Approaching her forties, she seemed destined for a life of gloom and uneventfulness.

Two events suddenly dispelled the gloom. On May 20, 1845, after a protracted correspondence, Elizabeth Barrett granted Robert Browning's request for a visit. On September 12, 1846, she escaped the possessive vigilance of her father and was secretly married to the poet, who was six years her junior. The couple left immediately for Italy, partly because of the mild climate, partly because of the cost of living; and in Italy they remained until her death.

"I love your verses with all my heart, dear Miss Barrett," Robert Browning began his first letter to the poet, who was, at that time, far more famous than he. Then after a page or two of critical compliments, he added impetuously, "And I love you too." That love was increasingly returned. It was rewarded by countless tributes,

pre-eminently by the SONNETS FROM THE PORTUGUESE. The poems
had been written by stealth, with no thought of publication; even
the title was a slight effort at concealment. But it was obvious that
these sonnets were not translations, and the title was an intimate
acknowledgment of her husband's playful way of calling her "my
little Portuguese" because of her olive skin.

Sonnets from the Portuguese

3

Unlike are we, unlike, O princely Heart!
Unlike our uses and our destinies.
Our ministering two angels look surprise
On one another, as they strike athwart
Their wings in passing. Thou, bethink thee, art
A guest for queens to social pageantries,
With gages from a hundred brighter eyes
Than tears even can make mine, to play thy part
Of chief musician. What hast *thou* to do
With looking from the lattice-lights at me,
A poor, tired, wandering singer, singing through
The dark, and leaning up a cypress-tree?
The chrism is on thine head—on mine, the dew—
And Death must dig the level where these agree.

6

Go from me. Yet I feel that I shall stand
Henceforward in thy shadow. Nevermore
Alone upon the threshold of my door
Of individual life, I shall command
The uses of my soul, nor lift my hand
Serenely in the sunshine as before,
Without the sense of that which I forbore—
Thy touch upon the palm. The widest land
Doom takes to part us, leaves thy heart in mine
With pulses that beat double. What I do
And what I dream include thee, as the wine
Must taste of its own grapes. And when I sue
God for myself, He hears that name of thine,
And sees within my eyes the tears of two.

14

If thou must love me, let it be for naught
Except for love's sake only. Do not say,
"I love her for her smile—her look—her way
Of speaking gently—for a trick of thought
That falls in well with mine, and certes brought
A sense of pleasant ease on such a day"—
For these things in themselves, Belovèd, may
Be changed, or change for thee—and love, so wrought,
May be unwrought so. Neither love me for
Thine own dear pity's wiping my cheeks dry—
A creature might forget to weep, who bore
Thy comfort long, and lose thy love thereby!
But love me for love's sake, that evermore
Thou may'st love on, through love's eternity.

22

When our two souls stand up erect and strong,
Face to face, silent, drawing nigh and nigher,
Until the lengthening wings break into fire
At either curvèd point,—what bitter wrong
Can the earth do to us, that we should not long
Be here contented? Think. In mounting higher,
The angels would press on us and aspire
To drop some golden orb of perfect song
Into our deep, dear silence. Let us stay
Rather on earth, Belovèd,—where the unfit,
Contrarious moods of men recoil away
And isolate pure spirits, and permit
A place to stand and love in for a day,
With darkness and the death-hour rounding it.

43

How do I love thee? Let me count the ways.
I love thee to the depth and breadth and height
My soul can reach, when feeling out of sight
For the ends of Being and ideal Grace.
I love thee to the level of every day's
Most quiet need, by sun and candle-light.
I love thee freely, as men strive for right;

I love thee purely, as they turn from praise.
I love thee with the passion put to use
In my old griefs, and with my childhood's faith.
I love thee with a love I seemed to lose
With my lost saints—I love thee with the breath,
Smiles, tears, of all my life!—and, if God choose,
I shall but love thee better after death.

Mrs. Browning's eminence has declined during the last half century. Her sonnets were once considered "the finest in any language since Shakespeare's"; but a few years ago the late Virginia Woolf cruelly declared that "the only place in the mansion of literature" to which Mrs. Browning could be assigned "is downstairs in the servants' quarters in company with Mrs. Hemans, Eliza Cook, Jean Ingelow . . ." It is true that Mrs. Browning's poetry is too diffuse, too unreservedly "emotional." As G. K. Chesterton recently wrote, "She cannot leave anything alone, she cannot write a line, without a conceit. She gives the reader the impression that she never declined a fancy." Nevertheless, her sincere femininity more than compensates for any sentimentality; the sonnet beginning "How do I love thee" is one of the most eloquent love poems in the language. Her best work, especially where the strict form of the sonnet compels concentration, is her gentlest. If it sometimes fails in control, it never lacks fervor.

Grief

I tell you hopeless grief is passionless,
That only men incredulous of despair,
Half-taught in anguish, through the midnight air
Beat upward to God's throne in loud access
Of shrieking and reproach. Full desertness
In souls, as countries, lieth silent-bare
Under the blanching, vertical eye-glare
Of the absolute heavens. Deep-hearted man, express
Grief for thy dead in silence like to death—
Most like a monumental statue set
In everlasting watch and moveless woe
Till itself crumble to the dust beneath.
Touch it; the marble eyelids are not wet;
If it could weep, it could arise and go.

After he heard that his favorite daughter had dared to defy his authority by a runaway marriage, Mr. Barrett forbade his children ever to mention Elizabeth's name, and melodramatically foretold an early end of the romance. His prophecy was not fulfilled. Mrs. Browning recovered her health sufficiently to bear a son in her forty-fourth year, to enjoy the company of many visitors, and live an idyllic life with her poet-husband in Florence for fifteen years after her escape from Wimpole Street. She died in Browning's arms June 30, 1861.

HENRY WADSWORTH LONGFELLOW
[1807–1882]

O VERPRAISED in his time, underrated in our own, Longfellow seems to be remembered for his worst. He has been misrepresented in textbooks as a prosy preacher in verse; schoolchildren have been forced to memorize his most sententious platitudes. The poet has suffered from unhappy repetitions of:

> Life is real! Life is earnest!
> And the grave is not its goal;
> "Dust thou art, to dust returnest"
> Was not spoken of the soul.

and the moral but meaningless:

> "Oh stay," the maiden said, "and rest
> Thy weary head upon this breast."
> A tear stood in his bright blue eye,
> But still he answered with a sigh,
>   "Excelsior!"

But Longfellow was not only a writer of maxims and wall mottoes. He was a true scholar, a devoted teacher—he held his first class at Bowdoin at six in the morning—and, as a poet, something of a pioneer. Born February 27, 1807, in Portland, Maine, of an old New England family, Longfellow was descended from Priscilla and

John Alden. He entered Bowdoin College at fifteen, traveled abroad at twenty, and, after two years of absorption, returned to bring the romantic tradition to America. He became an expert linguist—Dutch was the only language that resisted him—and steeped himself in German literature. His lyrics are an embodiment of his favorite mood, *Gemütlichkeit,* twilight lengthening into evening, "the children's hour," the genial lamp, the undisturbing book. His study of the Finnish national epic, the KALEVALA, was reflected in an attempt to create an American Indian epic, HIAWATHA. One of the first American poets to employ American themes, Longfellow stressed the charms of legendry rather than the problems of contemporary affairs. His POEMS OF SLAVERY were thin and nostalgic instead of forceful; tales of the past inspired (and prettified) EVANGELINE and THE COURTSHIP OF MILES STANDISH. American history prompted one of his most vigorous ballads, PAUL REVERE'S RIDE, a poem that has never lost its power as a story told in swinging rhyme.

Paul Revere's Ride

Listen, my children, and you shall hear
Of the midnight ride of Paul Revere,
On the eighteenth of April, in Seventy-five;
Hardly a man is now alive
Who remembers that famous day and year.

He said to his friend, "If the British march
By land or sea from the town tonight,
Hang a lantern aloft in the belfry arch
Of the North Church tower as a signal light—
One, if by land, and two, if by sea;
And I on the opposite shore will be,
Ready to ride and spread the alarm
Through every Middlesex village and farm,
For the country folk to be up and to arm."

Then he said, "Good night!" and with muffled oar
Silently rowed to the Charlestown shore,
Just as the moon rose over the bay,
Where swinging wide at her moorings lay
The Somerset, British man-of-war;

A phantom ship, with each mast and spar
Across the moon like a prison bar,
And a huge black hulk, that was magnified
By its own reflection in the tide.

Meanwhile, his friend, through alley and street,
Wanders and watches with eager ears,
Till in the silence around him he hears
The muster of men at the barrack door,
The sound of arms, and the tramp of feet,
And the measured tread of the grenadiers,
Marching down to their boats on the shore.

Then he climbed the tower of the Old North Church
By the wooden stairs, with stealthy tread,
To the belfry-chamber overhead,
And startled the pigeons from their perch
On the somber rafters, that round him made
Masses and moving shapes of shade—
By the trembling ladder, steep and tall,
To the highest window in the wall,
Where he paused to listen and look down
A moment on the roofs of the town,
And the moonlight flowing over all.

Beneath, in the churchyard, lay the dead,
In their night-encampment on the hill,
Wrapped in silence so deep and still
That he could hear, like a sentinel's tread,
The watchful night-wind, as it went
Creeping along from tent to tent,
And seeming to whisper, "All is well!"
A moment only he feels the spell
Of the place and the hour, and the secret dread
Of the lonely belfry and the dead;
For suddenly all his thoughts are bent
On a shadowy something far away,
Where the river widens to meet the bay—
A line of black that bends and floats
On the rising tide, like a bridge of boats.

Meanwhile, impatient to mount and ride,
Booted and spurred, with a heavy stride
On the opposite shore walked Paul Revere.

Now he patted his horse's side,
Now gazed at the landscape far and near,
Then, impetuous, stamped the earth,
And turned and tightened his saddle-girth;
But mostly he watched with eager search
The belfry-tower of the Old North Church,
As it rose above the graves on the hill,
Lonely and spectral and somber and still.
And lo! as he looks, on the belfry's height
A glimmer, and then a gleam of light!
He springs to the saddle, the bridle he turns,
But lingers and gazes, till full on his sight
A second lamp in the belfry burns!

A hurry of hoofs in a village street,
A shape in the moonlight, a bulk in the dark,
And beneath, from the pebbles, in passing, a spark
Struck out by a steed flying fearless and fleet;
That was all! And yet, through the gloom and the light,
The fate of a nation was riding that night;
And the spark struck out by that steed in his flight,
Kindled the land into flame with its heat.

He has left the village and mounted the steep,
And beneath him, tranquil and broad and deep,
Is the Mystic, meeting the ocean tides;
And under the alders that skirt its edge,
Now soft on the sand, now loud on the ledge,
Is heard the tramp of his steed as he rides.

It was twelve by the village clock
When he crossed the bridge into Medford town.
He heard the crowing of the cock,
And the barking of the farmer's dog,
And felt the damp of the river fog,
That rises after the sun goes down.

It was one by the village clock,
When he galloped into Lexington.
He saw the gilded weathercock
Swim in the moonlight as he passed,
And the meeting-house windows, blank and bare,
Gaze at him with a spectral glare,
As if they already stood aghast
At the bloody work they would look upon.

It was two by the village clock,
When he came to the bridge in Concord town.
He heard the bleating of the flock,
And the twitter of birds among the trees,
And felt the breath of the morning breeze
Blowing over the meadows brown.
And one was safe and asleep in his bed
Who at the bridge would be first to fall,
Who that day would be lying dead,
Pierced by a British musket-ball.

You know the rest. In the books you have read,
How the British Regulars fired and fled—
How the farmers gave them ball for ball,
From behind each fence and farmyard wall,
Chasing the redcoats down the lane,
Then crossing the fields to emerge again
Under the trees at the turn of the road,
And only pausing to fire and load.
So through the night rode Paul Revere;
And so through the night went his cry of alarm
To every Middlesex village and farm—
A cry of defiance, and not of fear,
A voice in the darkness, a knock at the door,
And a word that shall echo forevermore!
For, borne on the night-wind of the Past,
Through all our history, to the last,
In the hour of darkness and peril and need,
The people will waken and listen to hear
The hurrying hoofbeats of that steed,
And the midnight message of Paul Revere.

At twenty-four Longfellow married Mary Potter, daughter of a Portland judge. A dozen years after her death in childbed, the poet took a second wife, the lovely Frances Elizabeth Appleton. One afternoon, thirty years later, Mrs. Longfellow was sealing up some envelopes, and the burning wax fell on her flimsy dress, which immediately caught fire. Although Longfellow extinguished the blaze, she was so badly burned that she died the next morning. Longfellow never recovered from the shock. He continued to write and travel, but "the household poet" was no longer at home in the world. He died March 24, 1882, and his death was mourned in Europe as well as America. England set up his marble bust in the Poets' Corner of Westminster Abbey.

While it is true that Longfellow's facility too often betrays him into fatuousness, and his didacticism, as Friedrich Schoenemann says, "turns the poet of the people into a poet for the pedagogues," his serenity is apparent even in his literary poems. Greater poets have penned tributes to Chaucer and Milton; none have written more quietly and sympathetically of "the poet of the dawn" and the "mighty undulations" of England's "sightless bard."

Chaucer

An old man in a lodge within a park;
   The chamber walls depicted all around
   With portraitures of huntsman, hawk, and hound,
   And the hurt deer. He listeneth to the lark,
Whose song comes with the sunshine through the dark
   Of painted glass in leaden lattice bound;
   He listeneth and he laugheth at the sound,
   Then writeth in a book like any clerk.
He is the poet of the dawn, who wrote
   The Canterbury Tales, and his old age
   Made beautiful with song; and as I read
I hear the crowing cock, I hear the note
   Of lark and linnet, and from every page
   Rise odors of ploughed field or flowery mead.

Milton

I pace the sounding sea-beach and behold
   How the voluminous billows roll and run,
   Upheaving and subsiding, while the sun
   Shines through their sheeted emerald far unrolled
And the ninth wave, slow gathering fold by fold
   All its loose-flowing garments into one,
   Plunges upon the shore, and floods the dun
   Pale reach of sands, and changes them to gold.
So in majestic cadence rise and fall
   The mighty undulations of thy song,
   O sightless bard, England's Mæonides!
And ever and anon, high over all
   Uplifted, a ninth wave superb and strong,
   Floods all the soul with its melodious seas.

Although Longfellow has been justly criticized for putting into ambling verse everything he heard, read, and remembered, the best of his poetry is not bookish. If he relies too often on mere naturalness and the quiet *Abendstimmung*, his lines are tender and transparent.

The Day Is Done

The day is done, and the darkness
   Falls from the wings of Night,
As a feather is wafted downward
   From an eagle in his flight.

I see the lights of the village
   Gleam through the rain and the mist,
And a feeling of sadness comes o'er me
   That my soul cannot resist:

A feeling of sadness and longing,
   That is not akin to pain,
And resembles sorrow only
   As the mist resembles the rain.

Come, read to me some poem,
   Some simple and heartfelt lay,
That shall soothe this restless feeling,
   And banish the thoughts of day.

Not from the grand old masters,
   Not from the bards sublime,
Whose distant footsteps echo
   Through the corridors of Time.

For, like strains of martial music,
   Their mighty thoughts suggest
Life's endless toil and endeavor;
   And tonight I long for rest.

Read from some humbler poet,
   Whose songs gushed from his heart,
As showers from the clouds of summer,
   Or tears from the eyelids start;

Who, through long days of labor,
   And nights devoid of ease,
Still heard in his soul the music
   Of wonderful melodies.

Such songs have power to quiet
   The restless pulse of care,
And come like the benediction
   That follows after prayer.

Then read from the treasured volume
   The poem of thy choice,
And lend to the rhyme of the poet
   The beauty of thy voice.

And the night shall be filled with music,
   And the cares, that infest the day,
Shall fold their tents, like the Arabs,
   And as silently steal away.

Nature

As a fond mother, when the day is o'er,
   Leads by the hand her little child to bed,
   Half willing, half reluctant to be led,
   And leave his broken playthings on the floor,
Still gazing at them through the open door,
   Nor wholly reassured and comforted
   By promises of others in their stead,
   Which, though more splendid, may not please him more;
So Nature deals with us, and takes away
   Our playthings one by one, and by the hand
   Leads us to rest so gently, that we go
Scarce knowing if we wish to go or stay,
   Being too full of sleep to understand
   How far the unknown transcends the what we know.

Hymn to the Night

I heard the trailing garments of the Night
   Sweep through her marble halls!
I saw her sable skirts all fringed with light
   From the celestial walls.

I felt her presence, by its spell of might,
   Stoop o'er me from above;
The calm, majestic presence of the Night,
   As of the one I love.

I heard the sounds of sorrow and delight,
   The manifold, soft chimes,
That fill the haunted chambers of the Night,
   Like some old poet's rhymes.

From the cool cisterns of the midnight air
   My spirit drank repose;
The fountain of perpetual peace flows there—
   From those deep cisterns flows.

O holy Night! from thee I learn to bear
   What man has borne before.
Thou layest thy finger on the lips of Care,
   And they complain no more.

Peace! Peace! Orestes-like I breathe this prayer!
   Descend with broad-winged flight,
The welcome, the thrice-prayed for, the most fair,
   The best-beloved Night!

EDGAR ALLAN POE
[1809–1849]

THE stormy, star-crossed life of Edgar Allan Poe was prefigured in his youth. His parents were actors, and he was born, January 19, 1809, in Boston, Massachusetts, during one of their spasmodic peregrinations. Less than a year after his birth, his father disappeared. Two years later his mother died, and the child Edgar was adopted by John Allan, a prosperous merchant of Richmond, Virginia, who gave him a home as well as his middle name.

   Young Poe entered boyhood with every advantage. His foster father sent him to an exclusive school in England and to the University of Virginia, but, by the time he was seventeen, Poe already exhibited the combination of weakness and recklessness which was to plague him the rest of his life. He drank and ran into debt, and was obliged to leave the university before he was eighteen. The period was one of painful confusion. Poe had become engaged to a pretty girl of fifteen; returning to Richmond in disgrace, he learned that his Sarah Elmira was about to be married. He quarreled with his foster father, and ran away from home. He enlisted in the army, and published his first volume, TAMERLANE AND OTHER POEMS, five months after his eighteenth birthday. It is significant that the book was published anonymously "By a Bostonian" and that the motto chosen for the title page was a couplet from Cowper:

> Young heads are giddy, and young hearts are warm,
> And make mistakes for manhood to reform.

As a first step toward "reform" Poe returned South, patched up the quarrel with his foster father, and visited his aunt, Mrs. Maria Clemm, her seven-year-old daughter Virginia, and his brother William Henry, who was dying of drink and consumption. Mr. Allan made it possible for Poe to enter West Point in his twenty-second year. Six months later Poe was dismissed for disobeying orders.

Repudiated by his foster father, Poe was now homeless and penniless. Resolved to earn his living by hack-work, he came to New York and worked as a proofreader. From this time on the outcast fought a losing struggle with poverty, illness, and alcohol. He drove himself to creation; he wrote desperately in every medium and on every subject—short stories, essays, poems, analyses of handwriting, a plagiarized book on conchology. At twenty-four he achieved momentary success when his story MS. FOUND IN A BOTTLE won a prize; the award was fifty dollars. At twenty-six the "weary, wayworn wanderer" married his cousin Virginia, then thirteen years old and tubercular. Poe's next ten years were a succession of brief triumphs and long defeats. He was irregularly engaged as editor and regularly discharged. He disappeared for days and was brought home delirious; he could no longer exist without stimulants. For every friend he made he lost two. He fluttered for a while in literary dovecotes among the "female poets" of the day, a bedraggled raven among the twitterers. The situation became hopeless. In a frantic effort to live on the little money that he had borrowed and Mrs. Clemm had begged, Poe moved the battered family to Fordham, then a little village thirteen miles out of New York. Here Poe was in such need that he could not afford stamps to mail his manuscripts or wood to heat the stove. His old army coat served as a blanket, and Virginia was warmed by a tortoise-shell cat that slept on her bosom. At Fordham Virginia died, and Poe collapsed completely.

Poe was now thirty-eight, obviously neurotic and almost insanely depressed. He turned to various women for platonic friendship and mothering. At thirty-nine he became practically engaged to the widowed Sarah Helen Whitman, who was forty-five; at the same time he wrote passionate letters to Mrs. Richmond ("Annie"), a Massachusetts married woman. He attempted suicide, and was saved because his stomach could not tolerate the overdose. Pursued by hallucinations, Poe disappeared in Baltimore. On October 3, 1849, he was found in a tavern, "his face haggard and unwashed, his hair unkempt, and his whole physique repulsive." On October 7, 1849, he died in a Baltimore hospital.

Although criticism has raged about Poe's character and the final importance of his poetry, his original and intense genius cannot be questioned. The quality of his gift as well as the tragedy of his life is indicated in the words of Sir Francis Bacon which are on the Poe Memorial Gate at West Point: "There is no exquisite beauty without some strangeness in the proportion."

Strangeness is the chief characteristic of Poe's multiform work. It is manifest in the lyric TO HELEN which stems from his youth and which fulfills Poe's attempt to create "pure poetry"—"no mere appreciation of the beauty before us, but a wild effort to reach the beauty above."

TO HELEN was Poe's tribute to Mrs. Jane Stanard, mother of one of his boyhood friends, and sixteen years older than Poe. She died when the poet was fifteen, and he haunted her grave with morbid persistence. So great was Poe's fixation that when he proposed to another woman twenty years later, he compared her to "the friend of my boyhood, the tenderest of this world's most womanly souls, and an angel to my forlorn and darkened nature."

To Helen

Helen, thy beauty is to me
  Like those Nicéan barks of yore,
That gently, o'er a perfumed sea,
  The weary, way-worn wanderer bore
  To his own native shore.

On desperate seas long wont to roam,
Thy hyacinth hair, thy classic face,
Thy Naiad airs have brought me home
To the glory that was Greece,
And the grandeur that was Rome.

Lo! in yon brilliant window-niche
How statue-like I see thee stand,
The agate lamp within thy hand!
Ah, Psyche, from the regions which
Are Holy-Land!

Toward the end of his career Poe's conduct became so erratic
that he seemed to leave reality. Too distracted to make decisions,
he evaded action; unable to choose between security and emotional
fantasy, he hoped, somehow, to achieve both. He could give up
neither the wealthy widow, Mrs. Whitman, nor the fluttering Annie
Richmond, who appears as the unhappy heroine of FOR ANNIE and
the backward-longing ANNABEL LEE. As was inevitable, he lost both.

Annabel Lee

It was many and many a year ago,
　　In a kingdom by the sea,
That a maiden there lived whom you may know
　　By the name of Annabel Lee;—
And this maiden she lived with no other thought
　　Than to love and be loved by me.

She was a child and I was a child,
　　In this kingdom by the sea,
But we loved with a love that was more than love—
　　I and my Annabel Lee—
With a love that the winged seraphs of Heaven
　　Coveted her and me.

And this was the reason that, long ago,
　　In this kingdom by the sea,
A wind blew out of a cloud, by night
　　Chilling my Annabel Lee;
So that her highborn kinsmen came
　　And bore her away from me,
To shut her up in a sepulchre
　　In this kingdom by the sea.

> The angels, not half so happy in Heaven,
>   Went envying her and me:
> Yes! that was the reason (as all men know,
>   In this kingdom by the sea)
> That the wind came out of the cloud, chilling
>   And killing my Annabel Lee.
>
> But our love it was stronger by far than the love
>   Of those who were older than we—
>   Of many far wiser than we—
> And neither the angels in Heaven above
>   Nor the demons down under the sea,
> Can ever dissever my soul from the soul
>   Of the beautiful Annabel Lee:—
>
> For the moon never beams without bringing me dreams
>   Of the beautiful Annabel Lee;
> And the stars never rise but I see the bright eyes
>   Of the beautiful Annabel Lee;
> And so, all the night-tide, I lie down by the side
> Of my darling, my darling, my life and my bride,
>   In her sepulchre there by the sea—
>   In her tomb by the sounding sea.

This indefiniteness affected Poe's work. Recognizing it, he made it part of his program. "A poem, in my opinion," wrote Poe, "is opposed to a work of science by having, for its immediate object, an indefinite instead of a definite pleasure—being a poem only so far as this object is attained." Although Poe's definition is so restricted that it is false, he lived up to it. There are few recognizable emotions and no "messages" in his lines; Poe scarcely ever united penetrating experience with persuasive words. Words were his strength and weakness; words fascinated and betrayed him. With few exceptions, Poe's most often quoted poems are his worst. THE RAVEN is a declamation piece in which the serious idea is made ridiculous by cheap theatricalism, hypnotic rhythm, and a comic rhyme scheme. THE BELLS is a childish piling up of sounds, a wearisome echolalia; as George Barker recently wrote, it "is not a poem, it is a game." Emerson spoke of Poe as the "jingle man," and there is some basis for the characterization. But the best of his poems move with the magic of unreality, with the impossible but inescapable logic of a dream.

To One in Paradise

Thou wast all that to me, love,
  For which my soul did pine—
A green isle in the sea, love,
  A fountain and a shrine,
All wreathed with fairy fruits and flowers,
  And all the flowers were mine.

Ah, dream too bright to last!
  Ah, starry Hope! that didst arise
But to be overcast!
  A voice from out the Future cries,
"On! on!"—but o'er the Past
  (Dim gulf!) my spirit hovering lies
Mute, motionless, aghast!

For, alas! alas! with me
  The light of Life is o'er!
No more—no more—no more—
  (Such language holds the solemn sea
To the sands upon the shore)
  Shall bloom the thunder-blasted tree,
Or the stricken eagle soar!

And all my days are trances,
  And all my nightly dreams
Are where thy gray eye glances,
  And where thy footstep gleams—
In what ethereal dances,
  By what eternal streams.

A Dream Within a Dream

Take this kiss upon thy brow!
And, in parting from you now,
Thus much let me avow—
You are not wrong, to deem
That my days have been a dream;
Yet if Hope has flown away
In a night, or in a day,

In a vision, or in none,
Is it therefore the less *gone?*
All that we see or seem
Is but a dream within a dream.

I stand amid the roar
Of a surf-tormented shore,
And I hold within my hand
Grains of the golden sand—
How few! yet how they creep
Through my fingers to the deep,
While I weep—while I weep!
O God! can I not grasp
Them with a tighter clasp?
O God! can I not save
One from the pitiless wave?
Is *all* that we see or seem
But a dream within a dream?

The Sleeper

At midnight, in the month of June,
I stand beneath the mystic moon.
An opiate vapor, dewy, dim,
Exhales from out her golden rim,
And, softly dropping, drop by drop,
Upon the quiet mountain-top,
Steals drowsily and musically
Into the universal valley.
The rosemary nods upon the grave;
The lily lolls upon the wave;
Wrapping the fog about its breast,
The ruin molders into rest;
Looking like Lethe, see! the lake
A conscious slumber seems to take,
And would not, for the world, awake.
All beauty sleeps!—and lo! where lies
Irene, with her destinies!

O lady bright! can it be right,
This window open to the night?
The wanton airs, from the tree-top,
Laughingly through the lattice drop;

The bodiless airs, a wizard rout,
Flit through thy chamber in and out,
And wave the curtain canopy
So fitfully, so fearfully,
Above the closed and fringéd lid
'Neath which thy slumbering soul lies hid,
That, o'er the floor, and down the wall,
Like ghosts the shadows rise and fall.
O lady dear, hast thou no fear?
Why and what art thou dreaming here?
Sure thou art come o'er far-off seas,
A wonder to these garden trees!
Strange is thy pallor: strange thy dress:
Strange, above all, thy length of tress,
And all this solemn silentness!

The lady sleeps. Oh, may her sleep,
Which is enduring, so be deep!
Heaven have her in its sacred keep!
This chamber changed for one more holy,
This bed for one more melancholy,
I pray to God that she may lie
Forever with unopened eye,
While the pale sheeted ghosts go by.

My love, she sleeps. Oh, may her sleep,
As it is lasting, so be deep!
Soft may the worms about her creep!
Far in the forest, dim and old,
For her may some tall vault unfold:
Some vault that oft hath flung its black
And winged panels fluttering back,
Triumphant, o'er the crested palls
Of her grand family funerals;
Some sepulchre, remote, alone,
Against whose portal she hath thrown,
In childhood, many an idle stone:
Some tomb from out whose sounding door
She ne'er shall force an echo more,
Thrilling to think, poor child of sin,
It was the dead who groaned within!

The Haunted Palace

In the greenest of our valleys
   By good angels tenanted,
Once a fair and stately palace—
   Radiant palace—reared its head.
In the monarch Thought's dominion—
   It stood there!
Never seraph spread a pinion
   Over fabric half so fair!

Banners yellow, glorious, golden,
   On its roof did float and flow,
(This—all this—was in the olden
   Time long ago),
And every gentle air that dallied,
   In that sweet day,
Along the ramparts plumed and pallid,
   A winged odor went away.

Wanderers in that happy valley,
   Through two luminous windows, saw
Spirits moving musically,
   To a lute's well-tuned law,
Round about a throne where, sitting,
   (Porphyrogene!) [1]
In state his glory well befitting,
   The ruler of the realm was seen.

And all with pearl and ruby glowing
   Was the fair palace door,
Through which came flowing, flowing, flowing,
   And sparkling evermore,
A troop of Echoes, whose sweet duty
   Was but to sing,
In voices of surpassing beauty,
   The wit and wisdom of their king.

But evil things, in robes of sorrow,
   Assailed the monarch's high estate.
(Ah, let us mourn!—for never morrow
   Shall dawn upon him, desolate!)

[1] *Of royal blood.*

> And round about his home the glory
> That blushed and bloomed,
> Is but a dim-remembered story
> Of the old time entombed.
>
> And travellers, now, within that valley,
> Through the red-litten windows see
> Vast forms, that move fantastically
> To a discordant melody,
> While, like a ghastly rapid river,
> Through the pale door
> A hideous throng rush out forever
> And laugh—but smile no more.
> *from* THE FALL OF THE HOUSE OF USHER

The future may rate Poe as a poet and author of bizarre tales less highly than as the inventor of the short story whose descendants in fiction are such masters of deduction as Conan Doyle and such experts in pseudo science as Jules Verne and H. G. Wells. It is possible that Poe's lurid history may continue to overshadow his work; it becomes progressively harder to believe in his misty mid-region of dank tarns, dim lakes, and scoriac rivers—especially since his life was so much more terrible than his museum of Gothic horrors. But there can be no doubt about the persistence of his aim, a pure passion of dedication, and the spell of his strange and melancholy music. Poe himself said it in ROMANCE:

> That little time with lyre and rhyme
> To while away—forbidden things!
> My heart would feel to be a crime
> Unless it trembled with the strings.

Too often Poe wallows in ornate banalities, in a gaudy tastelessness. But there are, as in the powerful THE CITY IN THE SEA, the moments of ascending beauty, unearthly radiance. Poe's world is the "ultimate, dim Thule," a realm forsaken and ghost-ridden. But if the landscape is dark, it is enchanted; and, though the outlines are wavering, they are drawn to the last shadowy inlet.

The City in the Sea

Lo! Death has reared himself a throne
In a strange city lying alone
Far down within the dim West,
Where the good and the bad and the worst and the best
Have gone to their eternal rest.
There shrines and palaces and towers
(Time-eaten towers that tremble not!)
Resemble nothing that is ours.
Around, by lifting winds forgot,
Resignedly beneath the sky
The melancholy waters lie.

No rays from the holy heaven come down
On the long night-time of that town;
But light from out the lurid sea
Streams up the turrets silently—
Gleams up the pinnacles far and free—
Up domes—up spires—up kingly halls—
Up fanes—up Babylon-like walls—
Up shadowy long-forgotten bowers
Of sculptured ivy and stone flowers—
Up many and many a marvelous shrine
Whose wreathed friezes intertwine
The viol, the violet, and the vine.

Resignedly beneath the sky
The melancholy waters lie.
So blend the turrets and shadows there
That all seem pendulous in air,
While from a proud tower in the town
Death looks gigantically down.

There open fanes and gaping graves
Yawn level with the luminous waves;
But not the riches there that lie
In each idol's diamond eye—
Not the gaily-jeweled dead
Tempt the waters from their bed;
For no ripples curl, alas!
Along that wilderness of glass—

No swellings tell that winds may be
Upon some far-off happier sea—
No heavings hint that winds have been
On seas less hideously serene.

But lo, a stir is in the air!
The wave—there is a movement there!
As if the towers had thrust aside,
In slightly sinking, the dull tide—
As if their tops had feebly given
A void within the filmy Heaven.
The waves have now a redder glow—
The hours are breathing faint and low—
And when, amid no earthly moans,
Down, down that town shall settle hence,
Hell, rising from a thousand thrones,
Shall do it reverence.

ALFRED TENNYSON

[1809–1892]

UNLIKE most poets, Alfred Tennyson was reared in comfort and died in the peerage. The fourth of twelve children, he was born August 6, 1809, at Somersby, in Lincolnshire, and the placid scenery of his childhood is continually reflected in his work. Precocious as a child, he composed blank verse at the age of eight, wrote hundreds of lines in imitation of Pope at the age of ten, and at twelve made an analysis of Milton's SAMSON AGONISTES. At eighteen, a few months before he entered Trinity College, Cambridge, he collaborated with his brother Charles on his first published volume, POEMS BY TWO BROTHERS.

At Cambridge Tennyson became the center of an admiring group which included Arthur Henry Hallam, who was to be memorialized by the poet, and Edward FitzGerald, who achieved his own immortality. At twenty-one, while still an undergraduate, Tennyson published his POEMS, CHIEFLY LYRICAL. Two years later he presented a larger collection, POEMS, and received his first rude public affront.

The same critic who had attacked Keats in THE QUARTERLY REVIEW castigated the young Tennyson for his voluptuousness, his ornate images, his few metrical innovations and errors in taste. He belittled Tennyson's fecundity and scorned the "self-assured prodigy" as "another star in that galaxy of poetry of which the lamented Keats was the harbinger." The sneer is the more astonishing since this early volume contained some of Tennyson's most accomplished poems, such as THE LADY OF SHALOTT, THE LOTOS EATERS, THE MILLER'S DAUGHTER, and MARIANA.

Mariana

"Mariana in the moated grange."—MEASURE FOR MEASURE

With blackest moss the flower-plots
    Were thickly crusted, one and all:
The rusted nails fell from the knots
    That held the peach to the garden-wall.
The broken sheds look'd sad and strange:
    Unlifted was the clinking latch;
    Weeded and worn the ancient thatch
Upon the lonely moated grange.
        She only said, "My life is dreary,
            He cometh not," she said;
        She said, "I am aweary, aweary,
            I would that I were dead!"

Her tears fell with the dews at even;
    Her tears fell ere the dews were dried;
She could not look on the sweet heaven,
    Either at morn or eventide.
After the flitting of the bats,
    When thickest dark did trance the sky,
    She drew her casement-curtain by,
And glanced athwart the glooming flats.
        She only said, "The night is dreary,
            He cometh not," she said;
        She said, "I am aweary, aweary,
            I would that I were dead!"

Upon the middle of the night,
    Waking she heard the night-fowl crow:

The cock sung out an hour ere light:
    From the dark fen the oxen's low
Came to her: without hope of change,
    In sleep she seem'd to walk forlorn,
    Till cold winds woke the gray-eyed morn
About the lonely moated grange.
        She only said, "The day is dreary,
            He cometh not," she said;
        She said, "I am aweary, aweary,
            I would that I were dead!"

About a stone-cast from the wall
    A sluice with blacken'd waters slept,
And o'er it many, round and small,
    The cluster'd marish-mosses crept.
Hard by a poplar shook alway,
    All silver-green with gnarlèd bark:
    For leagues no other tree did mark
The level waste, the rounding gray.
        She only said, "My life is dreary,
            He cometh not," she said;
        She said, "I am aweary, aweary,
            I would that I were dead!"

And ever when the moon was low,
    And the shrill winds were up and away,
In the white curtain, to and fro,
    She saw the gusty shadow sway.
But when the moon was very low,
    And wild winds bound within their cell,
    The shadow of the poplar fell
Upon her bed, across her brow.
        She only said, "The night is dreary,
            He cometh not," she said;
        She said, "I am aweary, aweary,
            I would that I were dead!"

All day within the dreamy house,
    The doors upon their hinges creak'd;
The blue fly sung in the pane; the mouse
    Behind the mouldering wainscot shriek'd,
Or from the crevice peer'd about.
    Old faces glimmer'd thro' the doors,
    Old footsteps trod the upper floors,

Old voices called her from without.
    She only said, "The day is dreary,
        He cometh not," she said;
    She said, "I am aweary, aweary,
        I would that I were dead!"

The Miller's Daughter

It is the miller's daughter,
    And she is grown so dear, so dear,
That I would be the jewel
    That trembles at her ear:
For hid in ringlets day and night,
I'd touch her neck so warm and white.

And I would be the girdle
    About her dainty, dainty waist,
And her heart would beat against me,
    In sorrow and in rest:
And I should know if it beat right,
I'd clasp it round so close and tight.

And I would be the necklace,
    And all day long to fall and rise
Upon her balmy bosom,
    With her laughter or her sighs:
And I would lie so light, so light,
I scarce should be unclasped at night.

The bond between Tennyson and Hallam was unusually close. It grew firmer when, upon graduation, the two friends volunteered for a few months in the Spanish insurgent army, and was cemented when Hallam became betrothed to Tennyson's sister. It was tragically broken when, three years later, Hallam burst a blood vessel and died before he was twenty-three. Tennyson was so affected that he withdrew from ordinary activities; even his health was impaired. His long IN MEMORIAM A. H. H. is not only a record of his grief but a revelation of Tennyson's philosophy, the conflict of faith and doubt and final affirmation.

FROM

In Memoriam A. H. H.

PROEM

Strong Son of God, immortal Love,
  Whom we, that have not seen thy face,
  By faith, and faith alone, embrace,
Believing where we cannot prove;

Thine are these orbs of light and shade;
  Thou madest Life in man and brute;
  Thou madest Death; and lo, thy foot
Is on the skull which thou hast made.

Thou wilt not leave us in the dust;
  Thou madest man, he knows not why,
  He thinks he was not made to die;
And thou hast made him: thou art just.

Thou seemest human and divine,
  The highest, holiest manhood, thou.
  Our wills are ours, we know not how;
Our wills are ours, to make them thine.

Our little systems have their day;
  They have their day and cease to be;
  They are but broken lights of thee,
And thou, O Lord, art more than they.

We have but faith: we cannot know,
  For knowledge is of things we see;
  And yet we trust it comes from thee,
A beam in darkness: let it grow.

Let knowledge grow from more to more,
  But more of reverence in us dwell;
  That mind and soul, according well,
May make one music as before,

But vaster. We are fools and slight;
  We mock thee when we do not fear:
  But help thy foolish ones to bear;
Help thy vain worlds to bear thy light.

Forgive what seemed my sin in me;
   What seemed my worth since I began;
   For merit lives from man to man,
And not from man, O Lord, to thee.

Forgive my grief for one removed,
   Thy creature, whom I found so fair.
   I trust he lives in thee, and there
I find him worthier to be loved.

Forgive these wild and wandering cries,
   Confusions of a wasted youth;
   Forgive them where they fail in truth,
And in thy wisdom make me wise.

CALM IS THE MORN

Calm is the morn without a sound,
   Calm as to suit a calmer grief,
   And only through the faded leaf
The chestnut pattering to the ground:

Calm and deep peace on this high wold,
   And on these dews that drench the furze,
   And all the silvery gossamers
That twinkle into green and gold:

Calm and still light on yon great plain
   That sweeps with all its autumn bowers,
   And crowded farms and lessening towers,
To mingle with the bounding main:

Calm and deep peace in this wide air,
   These leaves that redden to the fall;
   And in my heart, if calm at all,
If any calm, a calm despair:

Calm on the seas, and silver sleep,
   And waves that sway themselves in rest,
   And dead calm in that noble breast
Which heaves but with the heaving deep.

OH YET WE TRUST

Oh yet we trust that somehow good
  Will be the final goal of ill,
  To pangs of nature, sins of will,
Defects of doubt, and taints of blood;

That nothing walks with aimless feet;
  That not one life shall be destroyed,
  Or cast as rubbish to the void,
When God hath made the pile complete;

That not a worm is cloven in vain;
  That not a moth with vain desire
  Is shriveled in a fruitless fire,
Or but subserves another's gain.

Behold, we know not anything;
  I can but trust that good shall fall
  At last—far off—at last, to all,
And every winter change to spring.

So runs my dream: but what am I?
  An infant crying in the night:
  An infant crying for the light:
And with no language but a cry.

RING OUT, WILD BELLS

Ring out, wild bells, to the wild sky,
  The flying cloud, the frosty light:
  The year is dying in the night;
Ring out, wild bells, and let him die.

Ring out the old, ring in the new,
  Ring, happy bells, across the snow:
  The year is going, let him go;
Ring out the false, ring in the true.

Ring out the grief that saps the mind,
  For those that here we see no more;
  Ring out the feud of rich and poor,
Ring in redress to all mankind.

> Ring out a slowly dying cause,
>   And ancient forms of party strife;
>   Ring in the nobler modes of life,
> With sweeter manners, purer laws.
>
> Ring out the want, the care, the sin,
>   The faithless coldness of the times;
>   Ring out, ring out my mournful rhymes,
> But ring the fuller minstrel in.
>
> Ring out false pride in place and blood,
>   The civic slander and the spite;
>   Ring in the love of truth and right,
> Ring in the common love of good.
>
> Ring out old shapes of foul disease;
>   Ring out the narrowing lust of gold;
>   Ring out the thousand wars of old,
> Ring in the thousand years of peace.
>
> Ring in the valiant man and free,
>   The larger heart, the kindlier hand;
>   Ring out the darkness of the land,
> Ring in the Christ that is to be.

After Hallam's death Tennyson underwent a long and unhappy period of apathy. He shunned society and turned his back upon those in power. He visited the Lake District but was reluctant to intrude upon Wordsworth, who had expressed a desire to meet the young poet. He sold the estate he had inherited, invested the proceeds in a "Patent Decorative Carving Company," and lost all his money. It was ten years before he could be induced to issue another volume.

Suddenly, with the publication of the two-volume edition of his POEMS in 1842, Tennyson became famous. He was acclaimed everywhere. Wordsworth hailed him as "decidedly the first of our living poets," and Sir Robert Peel bestowed upon him a pension of two hundred pounds a year. In 1850, at the age of forty-one, Tennyson was happily married to Emily Sellwood, to whom he had been engaged during fourteen years of poverty—"the peace of God came into my life when I wedded her"—and Queen Victoria appointed him poet laureate. Two years later his first child was born and was christened Hallam.

Fortitude had come back into Tennyson's life. In ULYSSES he firmly expressed the quality of courage. Here is the heroism which has "enjoyed greatly, suffered greatly," the determination to venture "beyond the utmost bound of human thought." It is true that the Victorian poet could not resist moralizing. But his was a moralizing age, and Tennyson lifted the strain to a triumphant persistence:

> To strive, to seek, to find, and not to yield.

Ulysses

It little profits that an idle king,
By this still hearth, among these barren crags,
Matched with an aged wife, I mete and dole
Unequal laws unto a savage race,
That hoard, and sleep, and feed, and know not me.
I cannot rest from travel: I will drink
Life to the lees: all times I have enjoyed
Greatly, have suffered greatly, both with those
That loved me, and alone; on shore, and when
Through scudding drifts the rainy Hyades
Vext the dim sea. I am become a name;
For always roaming with a hungry heart
Much have I seen and known: cities of men
And manners, climates, councils, governments,
Myself not least, but honored of them all,—
And drunk delight of battle with my peers,
Far on the ringing plains of windy Troy.
I am a part of all that I have met;
Yet all experience is an arch wherethrough
Gleams that untraveled world, whose margin fades
For ever and for ever when I move.
How dull it is to pause, to make an end,
To rust unburnished, not to shine in use!
As though to breathe were life. Life piled on life
Were all too little, and of one to me
Little remains: but every hour is saved
From that eternal silence, something more,
A bringer of new things; and vile it were
For some three suns to store and hoard myself,
And this gray spirit yearning in desire
To follow knowledge, like a sinking star,
Beyond the utmost bound of human thought.

This is my son, mine own Telemachus,
To whom I leave the scepter and the isle—
Well-loved of me, discerning to fulfill
This labor, by slow prudence to make mild
A rugged people, and through soft degrees
Subdue them to the useful and the good.
Most blameless is he, centered in the sphere
Of common duties, decent not to fail
In offices of tenderness, and pay
Meet adoration to my household gods,
When I am gone. He works his work, I mine.
    There lies the port: the vessel puffs her sail:
There gloom the dark broad seas. My mariners,
Souls that have toiled, and wrought, and thought with me—
That ever with a frolic welcome took
The thunder and the sunshine, and opposed
Free hearts, free foreheads—you and I are old;
Old age hath yet his honor and his toil;
Death closes all: but something ere the end,
Some work of noble note, may yet be done,
Not unbecoming men that strove with Gods.
The lights begin to twinkle from the rocks:
The long day wanes: the slow moon climbs: the deep
Moans round with many voices. Come, my friends,
'Tis not too late to seek a newer world.
Push off, and sitting well in order smite
The sounding furrows; for my purpose holds
To sail beyond the sunset, and the baths
Of all the western stars, until I die.
It may be that the gulfs will wash us down:
It may be we shall touch the Happy Isles,
And see the great Achilles, whom we knew.
Though much is taken, much abides; and though
We are not now that strength which in old days
Moved earth and heaven, that which we are, we are,—
One equal temper of heroic hearts,
Made weak by time and fate, but strong in will
To strive, to seek, to find, and not to yield.

From his forties until the end of his life, Tennyson's position as
England's most popular poet was unchallenged. He wrote plays and
poems with increasing energy; one of his dramas, BECKET, was suc-
cessfully produced by Sir Henry Irving. He was often invited to
read before Queen Victoria, and it was said that Her Majesty turned

to Tennyson for her poetry as instinctively as she turned to Disraeli for her politics. This was natural enough, for Tennyson, as G. K. Chesterton tartly observed, "held a great many of the same views as Queen Victoria, though he was gifted with a more fortunate literary style."

In his early seventies Tennyson became intimately associated with Gladstone, then Prime Minister, and the two men made a voyage together to Norway and Denmark. Gladstone offered Tennyson a peerage and, after some hesitation, the poet accepted the honor. He was seventy-five years old. Nine years later, while reading Shakespeare's CYMBELINE, he died, October 6, 1892.

Tennyson has suffered from his adulators as well as from his detractors, and it has never been determined whether he merely reflected or helped to establish the smug optimism and sentimentality of his day. Many critics have pictured him as a cross between the people's traditional minstrel and the conventional maiden aunt. He has been attacked for primness; for his transformation of Malory's MORTE D'ARTHUR, that savage pageant of the Middle Ages, into the IDYLLS OF THE KING, that Victorian Sunday-school picnic; for celebrating small ideas rather than great causes. But if Tennyson lacks passion, he does not lack picturesqueness. His craftsmanship redeems his too-perfect niceties; in his hands the devices of poetry become supple and self-concealing. The variety of his music has seldom been surpassed. THE PRINCESS is a veritable anthology of lyrics.

Songs from The Princess

SWEET AND LOW

Sweet and low, sweet and low,
   Wind of the western sea,
Low, low, breathe and blow,
   Wind of the western sea!
Over the rolling waters go,
Come from the dying moon, and blow,
   Blow him again to me;
While my little one, while my pretty one, sleeps.

Sleep and rest, sleep and rest,
   Father will come to thee soon;

Rest, rest, on mother's breast,
　　Father will come to thee soon;
Father will come to his babe in the nest,
Silver sails all out of the west
　　Under the silver moon:
Sleep, my little one, sleep, my pretty one, sleep.

THE SPLENDOR FALLS

The splendor falls on castle walls
　　And snowy summits old in story:
The long light shakes across the lakes,
　　And the wild cataract leaps in glory.
Blow, bugle, blow, set the wild echoes flying,
Blow, bugle; answer, echoes, dying, dying, dying.

O hark, O hear! how thin and clear,
　　And thinner, clearer, farther going!
O sweet and far from cliff and scar
　　The horns of Elfland faintly blowing!
Blow, let us hear the purple glens replying:
Blow, bugle; answer, echoes, dying, dying, dying.

O love, they die in yon rich sky,
　　They faint on hill or field or river:
Our echoes roll from soul to soul,
　　And grow for ever and for ever.
Blow, bugle, blow, set the wild echoes flying,
And answer, echoes, answer, dying, dying, dying.

TEARS, IDLE TEARS

Tears, idle tears, I know not what they mean,
Tears from the depth of some divine despair
Rise in the heart, and gather to the eyes,
In looking on the happy autumn-fields,
And thinking of the days that are no more.

Fresh as the first beam glittering on a sail,
That brings our friends up from the underworld,
Sad as the last which reddens over one
That sinks with all we love below the verge;
So sad, so fresh, the days that are no more.

Ah, sad and strange as in dark summer dawns
The earliest pipe of half-awakened birds
To dying ears, when unto dying eyes
The casement slowly grows a glimmering square;
So sad, so strange, the days that are no more.

Dear as remembered kisses after death,
And sweet as those by hopeless fancy feigned
On lips that are for others; deep as love,
Deep as first love, and wild with all regret;
O Death in Life, the days that are no more!

THY VOICE IS HEARD

Thy voice is heard through rolling drums
    That beat to battle where he stands;
Thy face across his fancy comes,
    And gives the battle to his hands.
A moment, while the trumpets blow,
    He sees his brood about thy knee;
The next, like fire he meets the foe,
    And strikes him dead for thine and thee.

HOME THEY BROUGHT HER WARRIOR

Home they brought her warrior dead:
    She nor swooned, nor uttered cry:
All her maidens, watching, said,
    "She must weep or she will die."

Then they praised him, soft and low,
    Called him worthy to be loved,
Truest friend and noblest foe;
    Yet she neither spoke nor moved.

Stole a maiden from her place,
    Lightly to the warrior stept,
Took the face-cloth from the face;
    Yet she neither moved nor wept.

Rose a nurse of ninety years,
    Set his child upon her knee—
Like summer tempest came her tears—
    "Sweet my child, I live for thee."

ASK ME NO MORE

Ask me no more. The moon may draw the sea;
  The cloud may stoop from heaven and take the shape,
  With fold to fold, of mountain or of cape;
But O too fond, when have I answered thee?
      Ask me no more.

Ask me no more. What answer should I give?
  I love not hollow cheek or faded eye;
  Yet, O my friend, I will not have thee die!
Ask me no more, lest I should bid thee live;
      Ask me no more.

Ask me no more. Thy fate and mine are sealed;
  I strove against the stream and all in vain;
  Let the great river take me to the main.
No more, dear love, for at a touch I yield;
      Ask me no more.

NOW SLEEPS THE CRIMSON PETAL

Now sleeps the crimson petal, now the white;
Nor waves the cypress in the palace walk;
Nor winks the gold fin in the porphyry font.
The firefly wakens. Waken thou with me.

Now droops the milk-white peacock like a ghost,
And like a ghost she glimmers on to me.

Now lies the Earth all Danaë to the stars,
And all thy heart lies open unto me.

Now slides the silent meteor on, and leaves
A shining furrow, as thy thoughts in me.

Now folds the lily all her sweetness up,
And slips into the bosom of the lake;
So fold thyself, my dearest, thou, and slip
Into my bosom and be lost in me.

An Idyl

Come down, O maid, from yonder mountain height.
What pleasure lives in height (the shepherd sang)
In height and cold, the splendor of the hills?
But cease to move so near the heavens, and cease
To glide a sunbeam by the blasted pine,
To sit a star upon the sparkling spire;
And come, for Love is of the valley, come,
For Love is of the valley, come thou down
And find him; by the happy threshold, he,
Or hand in hand with Plenty in the maize,
Or red with spirted purple of the vats,
Or foxlike in the vine; nor cares to walk
With Death and Morning on the silver horns,
Nor wilt thou snare him in the white ravine,
Nor find him dropt upon the firths of ice
That huddling slant in furrow-cloven falls
To roll the torrent out of dusky doors.
But follow; let the torrent dance thee down
To find him in the valley; let the wild
Lean-headed eagles yelp alone, and leave
The monstrous ledges there to slope, and spill
Their thousand wreaths of dangling water-smoke
That like a broken purpose waste in air.
So waste not thou, but come; for all the vales
Await thee; azure pillars of the hearth
Arise to thee; the children call, and I
Thy shepherd pipe, and sweet is every sound,
Sweeter thy voice, but every sound is sweet;
Myriads of rivulets hurrying thro' the lawn,
The moan of doves in immemorial elms,
And murmuring of innumerable bees.

from THE PRINCESS

Although Tennyson did not assume the prophetic mantle of a Nostradamus, some of his poems embody prophecies much less veiled than the cryptic French astrologer's. In LOCKSLEY HALL, which contains the most famous of Tennyson's predictions, the hero prefigured the future long before the days of the airplane, and saw:

. . . the heavens fill with commerce, argosies of magic sails,
Pilots of the purple twilight, dropping down with costly bales;

Heard the heavens fill with shouting, and there rained a ghastly dew
From the nations' airy navies grappling in the central blue;

Far along the world-wide whisper of the southwind rushing warm,
With the standards of the peoples plunging through the thunder-
    storm.

Tennyson, envisioning the materialism of an age "staled by fre-
quence, shrunk by usage," looked beyond international conflicts.
He predicted that humanity would rise above its material and com-
petitive successes to a universal brotherhood.

Till the war-drum throbbed no longer, and the battle-
    flags were furled
In the Parliament of man, the Federation of the world.

It is, however, not in prophecy but in lucidity and music that
Tennyson excels, in what Edmund Gosse terms "his broad undulat-
ing sweetness." It is eminently a power of clear condensation which
distinguishes Tennyson's lyrics, which concentrates the spirit of the
long IN MEMORIAM in the four brief stanzas of BREAK, BREAK, BREAK
and in the valedictory CROSSING THE BAR, which Tennyson requested
to be placed at the end of his poems.

Break, Break, Break

Break, break, break,
    On thy cold gray stones, O Sea!
And I would that my tongue could utter
    The thoughts that arise in me.

O well for the fisherman's boy,
    That he shouts with his sister at play!
O well for the sailor lad,
    That he sings in his boat on the bay!

And the stately ships go on
    To their haven under the hill;
But O for the touch of a vanished hand,
    And the sound of a voice that is still!

Break, break, break,
  At the foot of thy crags, O Sea!
But the tender grace of a day that is dead
  Will never come back to me.

The Eagle

He clasps the crag with crooked hands:
Close to the sun in lonely lands,
Ringed with the azure world, he stands.

The wrinkled sea beneath him crawls;
He watches from his mountain walls,
And like a thunderbolt he falls.

Flower in the Crannied Wall

Flower in the crannied wall,
I pluck you out of the crannies,
I hold you here, root and all, in my hand,
Little flower—but *if* I could understand
What you are, root and all, and all in all,
I should know what God and man is.

In Love, If Love Be Love

In Love, if Love be Love, if Love be ours,
Faith and unfaith can ne'er be equal powers:
Unfaith in aught is want of faith in all.

It is the little rift within the lute,
That by and by will make the music mute,
And ever widening slowly silence all.

The little rift within the lover's lute
Or little pitted speck in garnered fruit,
That rotting inward slowly moulders all.

It is not worth the keeping: let it go:
But shall it? answer, darling, answer, no.
And trust me not at all or all in all.

from IDYLLS OF THE KING

Crossing the Bar

Sunset and evening star,
    And one clear call for me!
And may there be no moaning of the bar,
    When I put out to sea,

But such a tide as moving seems asleep,
    Too full for sound and foam,
When that which drew from out the boundless deep
    Turns again home.

Twilight and evening bell,
    And after that the dark!
And may there be no sadness of farewell,
    When I embark;

For though from out our bourne of Time and Place
    The flood may bear me far,
I hope to see my Pilot face to face
    When I have crossed the bar.

EDWARD FITZGERALD

[1809–1883]

THE name of Edward FitzGerald is so bound up with the name
of Omar Khayyám that (to English readers, at least) the biography of one inevitably involves the other. To establish the odd
relationship, we must go back almost eight centuries to a village
in northeast Persia.

The manufacture of carpets, for which the district of Khorasan
is still noted, was practiced by old Ibráhim, who specialized in
tough woven cloth for tents. So, when his son was born at Naishapur in Khorasan, the child was named Ghiáthuddin Abulfath Omar
bin Ibráhim al-Khayyámi, which signified nothing more portentous
than that Omar was the true son of al-Khayyámi, or the Tentmaker.
The boy seems to have followed his father's trade. But during

youth he frequented the haunts of the dialecticians, the wandering Sufis, whom he enjoyed and distrusted, and the scientists, whom he feared and worshiped. Soon he was dabbling with, and attempting to fuse, mysticism and mathematics. He became known as Persia's outstanding astronomer. He wrote an authoritative text on algebra; he revised the old astronomical tables; he persuaded the Sultan Malik-Shah to reform the calendar.

When he was not consulting the stars and balancing equations, Omar permitted himself the luxury of poetry. His chief indulgence was the celebration of two intoxicants: verse and the vine. Before he died in 1123 he had composed some five hundred epigrams in quatrains, or *rubais,* peculiar in rhyme and pungent in tone. The stanzas were, for the most part, independent; they embodied a tight and self-contained idea. But they were connected, if not unified, by a careless philosophy: a light, free-thinking hedonism, a frank appeal to enjoy the pleasures of life without too much reflection.

The astronomer died; the tables were again revised; and for six centuries Omar's work was unknown to the Western world. It remained for a secluded English country gentleman to establish the Persian poet-mathematician among the glories of literature. Edward FitzGerald was born at Bredfield House on March 31, 1809, into a well-to-do family. Educated at Trinity College, Cambridge, where he became a friend of Thackeray, FitzGerald did the leisurely studying and traveling expected of him, cultivated music and botany, and, even as a young man, was relieved when he was permitted to retire to the Suffolk countryside. There he settled himself snugly, devoted his days to his friends and his flowers, and led a pleasantly unproductive life until his late forties.

In his fiftieth year, FitzGerald printed a little paper-bound pamphlet of translations which he called THE RUBÁIYÁT OF OMAR KHAY-YÁM. The pamphlet was published anonymously; it attracted little attention. A year later, in 1860, the poets Swinburne and Rossetti discovered the poem; but, legend to the contrary, the work did not thereupon leap into immediate popularity. Eight years passed before a second edition was called for.

Suddenly the poem became a favorite. The mocking quatrains of the eleventh-century Persian were used as a challenge by the nineteenth-century undergraduates, repeated by rebellious lovers, and flung out as a credo by restless men and women. There had already been an undercurrent of protest against the rigidity and moral earnestness of the period. The RUBÁIYÁT served as a small but concentrated expression of the revolt against Victorian conventions, the prevailing smugness, the acquiescent prudery. Religion had been defied by science; noble ideals had come into conflict with practical necessity; smoke-belching machinery was threatening to dispel the once pervasive "sweetness and light." The "message" of FitzGerald's RUBÁIYÁT was something of a slogan and something of an escape. It turned away from commercial imperialism toward an idealized paganism. Half defiantly, half desperately, the younger men and women made FitzGerald-Omar a vogue. Perhaps the most-quoted quatrain of the century was the alluring:

> A Book of Verses underneath the Bough
> A Jug of Wine, a Loaf of Bread—and Thou
>   Beside me singing in the Wilderness—
> Oh, Wilderness were Paradise enow!

Here was a panacea, half tonic, half opiate. It was not so much a compromise of values as a combination of desirables: an avoidance of ordinary existence and a participation in a richer, if somewhat unreal, life. This was the opposite of Mrs. Grundy's middle-class taboos; this was a very denial of negations. "Wine, Woman, and Song" were affirmed and glorified in a mounting paean to pleasure. A Persian Ecclesiastes, through the medium of a staid English squire, assured a perplexed generation that all was vanity; that the glories of this world are better than Paradise to come; that it is wise to take the cash and let the credit go; that life is a meaningless game played by helpless pieces; that worldly ambitions turn into ashes; that in the end—an end which comes all too quickly—wine is a more trustworthy friend and a better comforter than all the philosophers.

Thrust into undesired notice by THE RUBÁIYÁT, FitzGerald attempted for a while to live up to his reputation. He published translations of the AGAMEMNON and the two OEDIPUS tragedies of Sophocles; he wrote a biography of Bernard Barton, his father-in-law and friend of Charles Lamb; he made a compilation of the homely verse of George Crabbe. But he was not designed to be an Eminent Victorian. He was, even among retired gentlemen, unusually reticent ("an idle fellow, one whose friendships were more like loves"), and his wit was kept for private communications. It was not until the letters of "Old Fitz" were published that FitzGerald's personal charm was revealed. He sank back into semiobscurity as though it were a comfortable couch, and died, almost a quarter of a century after the publication of his masterpiece, on June 14, 1883. His end was characteristically calm. He slipped from life painlessly, almost imperceptibly.

Appreciation of Omar-FitzGerald continued to grow. Tennyson wrote a reminiscent poem lauding the "golden Eastern lay" of "that large infidel, your Omar." It is said that when Thomas Hardy was dying in his eighty-eighth year, he asked to have his favorite stanza read to him. It was the verse which runs:

> O Thou, who Man of baser Earth didst make,
> And ev'n with Paradise devise the Snake:
>   For all the Sin wherewith the Face of Man
>   Is blackened—Man's forgiveness give—and take!

No longer dependent upon the vagaries of a period or the tricks of fashion, THE RUBÁIYÁT has outlived cults and commentaries. It has had its influences and imitators. Its spirit is reflected in Housman's A SHROPSHIRE LAD (see page 1023) in which fortitude and fatalism are pitted against each other and finally reconciled. Omar might well have applauded the Shropshire lad's cynical conclusion that

> . . . malt does more than Milton can
> To justify God's way to man—

But the philosophy scarcely matters. The cynicism may be persistent; the mood may be (as FitzGerald himself said) "a desperate sort of thing, at the bottom of all thinking men's minds." But the tune is so gay that even the pessimism seems blithe. The quick but melodic turns of the poem "tease us out of thought." We may argue about the meaning, but we are indisputably held by the music.

FitzGerald's first version of THE RUBÁIYÁT contained only seventy-five quatrains; subsequently he enlarged the work and changed the order of the stanzas. It is generally considered that the best arrangement is the fourth edition, which is the one reprinted here.

The Rubáiyát of Omar Khayyám

Wake! for the Sun, who scattered into flight
The Stars before him from the Field of Night,
  Drives Night along with them from Heav'n, and strikes
The Sultán's Turret with a Shaft of Light.

Before the phantom of False morning died,
Methought a Voice within the Tavern cried,
  "When all the Temple is prepared within,
Why nods the drowsy Worshipper outside?"

And, as the cock crew, those who stood before
The Tavern shouted—"Open then the Door!
  You know how little while we have to stay,
And, once departed, may return no more."

Now the New Year reviving old Desires,
The thoughtful Soul to Solitude retires,
  Where the White Hand of Moses on the Bough
Puts out, and Jesus from the Ground suspires.

Iram indeed is gone with all his Rose,
And Jamshyd's Sev'n-ring'd Cup where no one knows;
  But still a Ruby kindles in the Vine,
And many a Garden by the Water blows.

And David's lips are lockt; but in divine
High-piping Pehleví, with "Wine! Wine! Wine!
  Red Wine!"—the Nightingale cries to the Rose
That sallow cheek of hers to incarnadine.

Come, fill the Cup, and in the fire of Spring
Your Winter-garment of Repentance fling:
  The Bird of Time has but a little way
To flutter—and the Bird is on the Wing.

Whether at Naishápúr or Babylon,
Whether the Cup with sweet or bitter run,
  The Wine of Life keeps oozing drop by drop,
The Leaves of Life keep falling one by one.

Each morn a thousand Roses brings, you say;
Yes, but where leaves the Rose of Yesterday?
  And this first Summer month that brings the Rose
Shall take Jamshyd and Kaikobád away.

Well, let it take them! What have we to do
With Kaikobád the Great, or Kaikhosrú?
  Let Zál and Rustum bluster as they will,
Or Hátim call to Supper—heed not you.

With me along the strip of Herbage strown
That just divides the desert from the sown,
    Where name of Slave and Sultán is forgot—
And Peace to Mahmúd on his golden Throne!

A Book of Verses underneath the Bough,
A Jug of Wine, a Loaf of Bread—and Thou
    Beside me singing in the Wilderness—
Oh, Wilderness were Paradise enow!

Some for the Glories of This World; and some
Sigh for the Prophet's Paradise to come;
    Ah, take the Cash, and let the Credit go,
Nor heed the rumble of a distant Drum!

Look to the blowing Rose about us—"Lo,
Laughing," she says, "into the world I blow,
    At once the silken tassel of my Purse
Tear, and its Treasure on the Garden throw."

And those who husbanded the Golden grain,
And those who flung it to the winds like Rain,
    Alike to no such aureate Earth are turned
As, buried once, Men want dug up again.

The Worldly Hope men set their Hearts upon
Turns Ashes—or it prospers; and anon,
    Like Snow upon the Desert's dusty Face,
Lighting a little hour or two—is gone.

Think, in this battered Caravanserai
Whose Portals are alternate Night and Day,
    How Sultán after Sultán with his Pomp
Abode his destined Hour, and went his way.

They say the Lion and the Lizard keep
The Courts where Jamshyd gloried and drank deep:
    And Bahrám, the great Hunter—the Wild Ass
Stamps o'er his Head, but cannot break his Sleep.

I sometimes think that never blows so red
The Rose as where some buried Cæsar bled;
    That every Hyacinth the Garden wears
Dropt in her Lap from some once lovely Head.

And this reviving Herb whose tender Green
Fledges the River-Lip on which we lean—
    Ah, lean upon it lightly! for who knows
From what once lovely Lip it springs unseen!

Ah, my Belovéd, fill the Cup that clears
To-day of past Regret and future Fears:
    To-morrow!—Why, To-morrow I may be
Myself with Yesterday's Sev'n thousand Years.

For some we loved, the loveliest and the best
That from his Vintage rolling Time hath prest,
    Have drunk their Cup a Round or two before,
And one by one crept silently to rest.

And we, that now make merry in the Room
They left, and Summer dresses in new bloom,
    Ourselves must we beneath the Couch of Earth
Descend—ourselves to make a Couch—for whom?

Ah, make the most of what we yet may spend,
Before we too into the Dust descend;
    Dust into Dust, and under Dust, to lie,
Sans Wine, sans Song, sans Singer, and—sans End!

Alike for those who for To-day prepare,
And those that after some To-morrow stare,
    A Muezzín from the Tower of Darkness cries,
"Fools, your Reward is neither Here nor There."

Why, all the Saints and Sages who discussed
Of the Two Worlds so wisely—they are thrust
    Like foolish Prophets forth; their Words to Scorn
Are scattered, and their Mouths are stopt with Dust.

Myself when young did eagerly frequent
Doctor and Saint, and heard great argument
    About it and about: but evermore
Came out by the same Door where in I went.

With them the seed of Wisdom did I sow,
And with mine own hand wrought to make it grow;
    And this was all the Harvest that I reaped—
"I came like Water, and like Wind I go."

Into this Universe, and *Why* not knowing
Nor *Whence*, like Water willy-nilly flowing;
    And out of it, as Wind along the Waste,
I know not *Whither*, willy-nilly blowing.

What, without asking, hither hurried *Whence?*
And, without asking, *Whither* hurried hence!
    Oh, many a Cup of this forbidden Wine
Must drown the memory of that insolence!

Up from Earth's Centre through the Seventh Gate
I rose, and on the Throne of Saturn sate,
    And many a Knot unravelled by the Road;
But not the Master-knot of Human Fate.

There was the Door to which I found no Key;
There was the Veil through which I might not see:
    Some little talk awhile of Me and Thee
There was—and then no more of Thee and Me.

Earth could not answer; nor the Seas that mourn
In flowing Purple, of their Lord forlorn;
    Nor rolling Heaven, with all his Signs revealed
And hidden by the sleeve of Night and Morn.

Then of the Thee in Me who works behind
The Veil, I lifted up my hands to find
    A Lamp amid the Darkness; and I heard,
As from Without—"The Me within Thee blind!"

Then to the Lip of this poor earthen Urn
I leaned, the Secret of my Life to learn:
    And Lip to Lip it murmured—"While you live,
Drink!—for, once dead, you never shall return."

I think the Vessel, that with fugitive
Articulation answered, once did live,
    And drink; and Ah! the passive Lip I kissed,
How many Kisses might it take—and give!

For I remember stopping by the way
To watch a Potter thumping his wet Clay;
    And with its all-obliterated Tongue
It murmured—"Gently, Brother, gently, pray!"

And has not such a Story from of Old
Down Man's successive generations rolled
    Of such a clod of saturated Earth
Cast by the Maker into Human mould?

And not a drop that from our Cups we throw
For Earth to drink of, but may steal below
    To quench the fire of Anguish in some Eye
There hidden—far beneath, and long ago.

As then the Tulip for her morning sup,
Of Heav'nly Vintage from the soil looks up,
    Do you devoutly do the like, till Heav'n
To Earth invert you—like an empty Cup.

Perplext no more with Human or Divine,
To-morrow's tangle to the winds resign,
    And lose your fingers in the tresses of
The Cypress-slender Minister of Wine.

And if the Wine you drink, the Lip you press,
End in what All begins and ends in—Yes;
    Think then you are To-day what Yesterday
You were—To-morrow you shall not be less.

So when the Angel of the darker Drink
At last shall find you by the river-brink,
    And offering his Cup, invite your Soul
Forth to your Lips to quaff—you shall not shrink.

Why, if the Soul can fling the Dust aside,
And naked on the Air of Heaven ride,
    Were't not a Shame—were't not a Shame for him
n this clay carcase crippled to abide?

'Tis but a Tent where takes his one day's rest
A Sultán to the realm of Death addrest;
    The Sultán rises, and the dark Ferrásh
Strikes, and prepares it for another Guest.

And fear not lest Existence closing your
Account, and mine, should know the like no more;
    The Eternal Sákí [1] from that Bowl has poured
Millions of Bubbles like us, and will pour.

[1] *The cupbearer.*

When You and I behind the Veil are past,
Oh, but the long, long while the World shall last,
   Which of our Coming and Departure heeds
As the Sea's self should heed a pebble-cast.

A Moment's Halt—a momentary taste
Of Being from the Well amid the Waste—
   And Lo!—the phantom Caravan has reached
The Nothing it set out from—Oh, make haste!

Would you that spangle of Existence spend
About The Secret—quick about it, Friend!
   A Hair perhaps divides the False and True—
And upon what, prithee, may life depend?

A Hair perhaps divides the False and True—
Yes; and a single Alif were the clue—
   Could you but find it—to the Treasure-house,
And peradventure to The Master too;

Whose secret Presence, through Creation's veins
Running Quicksilver-like, eludes your pains;
   Taking all shapes from Máh to Máhi; and
They change and perish all—but He remains;

A moment guessed—then back behind the Fold
Immerst of Darkness round the Drama rolled
   Which, for the Pastime of Eternity,
He doth himself contrive, enact, behold.

But if in vain, down on the stubborn floor
Of Earth, and up to Heav'n's unopening Door,
   You gaze To-day, while You are You—how then
To-morrow, when You shall be You no more?

Waste not your Hour, nor in the vain pursuit
Of This and That endeavor and dispute;
   Better be jocund with the fruitful Grape
Than sadden after none, or bitter, Fruit.

You know, my Friends, with what a brave Carouse
I made a Second Marriage in my house;
   Divorced old barren Reason from my Bed,
And took the Daughter of the Vine to Spouse.

For "Is" and "Is-not" though with Rule and Line
And "Up-and-down" by Logic I define,
    Of all that one should care to fathom, I
Was never deep in anything but—Wine.

Ah, but my Computations, People say,
Reduced the Year to better reckoning?—Nay,
    'Twas only striking from the Calendar
Unborn To-morrow, and dead Yesterday.

And lately, by the Tavern Door agape,
Came shining through the Dusk an Angel Shape
    Bearing a Vessel on his Shoulder; and
He bid me taste of it; and 'twas—the Grape!

The Grape that can with Logic Absolute
The Two and Seventy jarring Sects confute:
    The sovereign Alchemist that in a trice
Life's leaden metal into Gold transmute:

The mighty Mahmúd, Allah-breathing Lord,
That all the misbelieving and black Horde
    Of fears and Sorrows that infest the Soul
Scatters before him with his whirlwind Sword.

Why, be this Juice the growth of God, who dare
Blaspheme the twisted tendril as a Snare?
    A Blessing, we should use it, should we not?
And if a Curse—why, then, Who set it there?

I must abjure the Balm of Life, I must,
Scared by some After-reckoning ta'en on trust,
    Or lured with Hope of some Diviner Drink,
To fill the Cup—when crumbled into Dust!

O threats of Hell and Hopes of Paradise!
One thing at least is certain—*This* Life flies;
    One thing is certain and the rest is Lies;
The Flower that once has blown for ever dies.

Strange, is it not? that of the myriads who
Before us passed the door of Darkness through,
    Not one returns to tell us of the Road,
Which to discover we must travel too.

The Revelations of Devout and Learned
Who rose before us, and as Prophets burned,
    Are all but Stories, which, awoke from Sleep
They told their comrades, and to Sleep returned.

I sent my soul through the Invisible,
Some letter of that After-life to spell:
    And by and by my Soul returned to me,
And answered "I Myself am Heav'n and Hell:"

Heav'n but the Vision of fulfilled Desire,
And Hell the Shadow from a Soul on fire
    Cast on the Darkness into which Ourselves,
So late emerged from, shall so soon expire.

We are no other than a moving row
Of Magic Shadow-shapes that come and go
    Round with the Sun-illumined Lantern held
In Midnight by the Master of the Show;

But helpless Pieces of the Game He plays
Upon this Chequer-board of Nights and Days;
    Hither and thither moves, and checks, and slays,
And one by one back in the Closet lays.

The Ball no question makes of Ayes and Noes,
But Here or There as strikes the Player goes;
    And He that tossed you down into the Field,
He knows about it all—HE knows—HE knows!

The Moving Finger writes; and, having writ,
Moves on: nor all your Piety nor Wit
    Shall lure it back to cancel half a Line,
Nor all your Tears wash out a Word of it.

And that inverted Bowl they call the Sky,
Whereunder crawling cooped we live and die,
    Lift not your hands to *It* for help—for It
As impotently moves as you or I.

With Earth's first Clay They did the Last Man knead,
And there of the Last Harvest sowed the Seed:
    And the first Morning of Creation wrote
What the Last Dawn of Reckoning shall read.

Yesterday *This* Day's Madness did prepare;
To-morrow's Silence, Triumph, or Despair:
   Drink! for you know not whence you came, nor why:
Drink! for you know not why you go, nor where.

What! from his helpless Creature be repaid
Pure Gold for what he lent him dross-allayed—
   Sue for a Debt we never did contract,
And cannot answer—Oh, the sorry trade!

O Thou, who didst with Pitfall and with Gin
Beset the Road I was to wander in,
   Thou wilt not with Predestined Evil round
Enmesh, and then impute my Fall to Sin!

O Thou, who Man of baser Earth didst make,
And ev'n with Paradise devise the Snake:
   For all the Sin wherewith the Face of Man
Is blackened—Man's forgiveness give—and take!

As under cover of departing Day
Slunk hunger-stricken Ramazán away,
   Once more within the Potter's house alone
I stood, surrounded by the Shapes of Clay.

Shapes of all Sorts and Sizes, great and small,
That stood along the floor and by the wall;
   And some loquacious Vessels were; and some
Listen'd perhaps, but never talked at all.

Said one among them—"Surely not in vain
My substance of the common Earth was ta'en
   And to this Figure moulded, to be broke,
Or trampled back to shapeless Earth again."

Then said a Second—"Ne'er a peevish Boy
Would break the Bowl from which he drank in joy;
   And He that with his hand the Vessel made
Will surely not in after Wrath destroy."

After a momentary silence spake
Some Vessel of a more ungainly Make;
   "They sneer at me for leaning all awry:
What! did the Hand then of the Potter shake?"

Whereat some one of the loquacious Lot—
I think a Súfi pipkin—waxing hot—
   "All this of Pot and Potter—Tell me then,
Who is the Potter, pray, and who the Pot?"

"Why," said another, "Some there are who tell
Of one who threatens he will toss to Hell
   The luckless Pots he marred in making—Pish!
He's a Good Fellow, and 'twill all be well."

"Well," murmured one, "Let whoso make or buy,
My Clay with long Oblivion is gone dry:
   But fill me with the old familiar Juice,
Methinks I might recover by and by."

So while the Vessels one by one were speaking,
The little Moon looked in that all were seeking:
   And then they jogged each other, "Brother! Brother!
Now for the Porter's shoulder-knot a-creaking!"

Ah, with the Grape my fading Life provide,
And wash the Body whence the Life has died,
   And lay me, shrouded in the living Leaf,
By some not unfrequented Garden-side.

That ev'n my buried Ashes such a snare
Of Vintage shall fling up into the Air
   As not a True-believer passing by
But shall be overtaken unaware.

Indeed the Idols I have loved so long
Have done my credit in this World much wrong:
   Have drowned my Glory in a shallow Cup,
And sold my Reputation for a Song.

Indeed, indeed, Repentance oft before
I swore—but was I sober when I swore?
   And then and then came Spring, and Rose-in-hand
My thread-bare Penitence apieces tore.

And much as Wine has played the Infidel,
And robbed me of my Robe of Honor—Well,
   I wonder often what the Vintners buy
One half so precious as the stuff they sell.

Yet Ah, that Spring should vanish with tne Rose!
That Youth's sweet-scented manuscript should close!
   The Nightingale that in the branches sang,
Ah whence, and whither flown again, who knows!

Would but the desert of the Fountain yield
One glimpse—if dimly, yet indeed, revealed,
   To which the fainting Traveller might spring,
As springs the trampled herbage of the field!

Would but some wingéd Angel ere too late
Arrest the yet unfolded Roll of Fate,
   And make the stern Recorder otherwise
Enregister, or quite obliterate!

Ah Love! could you and I with Him conspire
To grasp this sorry Scheme of Things entire,
   Would not we shatter it to bits—and then
Remould it nearer to the Heart's Desire!

Yon rising Moon that looks for us again—
How oft hereafter will she wax and wane;
   How oft hereafter rising look for us
Through this same Garden—and for *one* in vain!

And when like her, O Sákí, you shall pass
Among the Guests Star-scattered on the Grass,
   And in your joyous errand reach the spot
Where I made One—turn down an empty Glass!

EDWARD LEAR

[1812–1888]

EDWARD LEAR never wanted to be known as a great humorist; he
hoped—and tried hard—to be a great painter. Born in London,
May 12, 1812, of Danish ancestry, he was the youngest of twelve
children. Brought up by his sister, who was twenty-one years older
than he, Edward suffered from asthma and epilepsy from the age
of seven onward. Nevertheless, he lived through seventy-six restless

years, and his malady seems to have interfered little with either his work or his play.

At twenty, already a gifted ornithologist, Lear published a set of drawings of the more uncommon parrots, a work which brought favorable comparisons with Audubon. The thirteenth Earl of Derby engaged him to paint his whole menagerie, and the water-colorist became a permanent favorite with the Derby family—it was for the fifteenth Earl of Derby that he designed his BOOK OF NONSENSE. After his success as a delineator of birds, he determined to become a landscape painter. For ten years he lived and studied abroad. But, although he was the most indefatigable of artisans, a draftsman whose accuracy was such that experts could recognize the geology of the country from Lear's sketches, he never became a successful artist.

Seeking new backgrounds for new stimuli, Lear visited Greece, explored unfrequented Calabria, penetrated the wilds of Albania, traveled to Constantinople, wintered on the Nile, and finally built himself a villa at San Remo, on the Italian Riviera, where he died January 30, 1888. He left countless canvases, water colors, and note-books; one of his friends inherited over ten thousand of his designs.

It was in his thirty-fourth year that Lear interrupted his serious pursuits (including drawing lessons to Queen Victoria) to write his comic limericks, for which he provided the weird illustrations, and the fantastic poems which have become classics of their kind. Established for years in the nursery, such poems as THE YONGHY-BONGHY-BO and THE OWL AND THE PUSSY-CAT have been strangely revalued. In our own time T. S. Eliot has commended the purity of Lear's lyrical gift, and Robert Graves has found unsuspected emotional depths in THE DONG WITH A LUMINOUS NOSE, which seems to Mr. Graves "as tragic as the Greek legend of Cadmus seeking his lost Europa." Mr. Graves also believes that the song which Edward Lear lightly called CALICO PIE presents grief in terms of childish invention; to him it is "as poignant as the idea of Hamlet played by Burbage, the actor, as a comic part," and the little birds suggest "the familiar emblem of unrealized love." But one does not have to believe that Lear wore "the pantomime mask over a tear-stained face" to relish the delight of his laughing syllables.

Calico Pie

Calico pie,
The little birds fly
Down to the calico tree:
Their wings were blue,
And they sang "Tilly-loo!"
Till away they flew;
And they never came back to me.
They never came back,
They never came back,
They never came back to me!

Calico ban,
The little Mice ran
To be ready in time for tea;
Flippity flup,
They drank it all up,
And danced in the cup:
But they never came back to me;
They never came back,
They never came back,
They never came back to me.

Calico drum,
The Grasshoppers come,
The Butterfly, Beetle, and Bee,
Over the ground,
Around and round,
With a hop and a bound;
But they never came back to me:
They never came back,
They never came back,
They never came back to me.

Once in a while Lear exchanged sheer drollery for parody. IN-
CIDENTS IN THE LIFE OF MY UNCLE ARLY is a burlesque of Words-
worth's sentimental RESOLUTION AND INDEPENDENCE, also known as
THE LEECH-GATHERER. But it is the sheer pleasure in whimsical and
unmeaning sound which draws the reader. THE OWL AND THE
PUSSY-CAT and a half-dozen other wild whimsicalities have secured
for Lear the affection of the world. He is eternal childhood's madcap
laureate.

Incidents in the Life of My Uncle Arly

O my agéd Uncle Arly!
Sitting on a heap of Barley
    Through the silent hours of night—
Close beside a leafy thicket:—
On his nose there was a Cricket,
In his hat a Railway-Ticket;—
    (But his shoes were far too tight.)

Long ago, in youth, he squandered
All his goods away, and wandered
    To the Tiniskoop-hills afar.
There on golden sunsets blazing,
Every evening found him gazing—
Singing—"Orb! you're quite amazing!
    How I wonder what you are!"

Like the ancient Medes and Persians,
Always by his own exertions
    He subsisted on those hills;
Whiles—by teaching children spelling;
Or at times by merely yelling,
Or at intervals by selling
    "Propter's Nicodemus Pills."

Later, in his morning rambles
He perceived the moving brambles
    Something square and white disclose;
'Twas a First-class Railway-Ticket;
But, on stooping down to pick it
Off the ground, a pea-green Cricket
    Settled on my uncle's Nose.

Never—never more—oh! never
Did that Cricket leave him ever,
    Dawn or evening, day or night;
Clinging as a constant treasure,
Chirping with a cheerious measure,
Wholly to my uncle's pleasure;—
    (Though his shoes were far too tight.)

So for three-and-forty winters,
Till his shoes were worn to splinters,
    All those hills he wandered o'er—
Sometimes silent, sometimes yelling—
Till he came to Borley-Melling,
Near his old ancestral dwelling;—
    (But his shoes were far too tight.)

On a little heap of Barley
Died my agéd Uncle Arly,
    And they buried him one night—
Close beside the leafy thicket;
There—his hat and Railway-Ticket;
There—his ever-faithful Cricket;—
    (But his shoes were far too tight.)

The Owl and the Pussy-cat

The Owl and the Pussy-cat went to sea
    In a beautiful pea-green boat:
They took some honey, and plenty of money
    Wrapped up in a five-pound note.
The Owl looked up to the stars above,
    And sang to a small guitar,
"O lovely Pussy, O Pussy, my love,
    What a beautiful Pussy you are,
        You are,
        You are!
    What a beautiful Pussy you are!"

Pussy said to the Owl, "You elegant fowl,
    How charmingly sweet you sing!
Oh! let us be married; too long we have tarried:
    But what shall we do for a ring?"
They sailed away, for a year and a day,
    To the land where the bong-tree grows;
And there in a wood a Piggy-wig stood,
    With a ring at the end of his nose,
        His nose,
        His nose,
    With a ring at the end of his nose.

"Dear Pig, are you willing to sell for one shilling
    Your ring?" Said the Piggy, "I will."
So they took it away, and were married next day
    By the turkey who lives on the hill.
They dined on mince and slices of quince,
    Which they ate with a runcible spoon;
And hand in hand, on the edge of the sand,
    They danced by the light of the moon.
        The moon,
        The moon,
    They danced by the light of the moon.

ROBERT BROWNING
[1812–1889]

BROWNING and Tennyson spanned the nineteenth century—a
longevity in startling contrast to the brief careers of Keats and
Shelley. Both poets reflected the changing standards of their times:
the economic struggles sharpened by the contradictory claims of
science and religion, the grudging compromises and gradual re,
forms. Tennyson indicated the Victorian values from priggishness
to liberalism; Browning emphasized the shift from abstract morality
to psychological speculation.

Robert Browning, the most erudite of modern poets, never at,
tended a university. Born May 7, 1812, in Camberwell, a suburb of
London, Browning was educated in the cradle. His mother was the
daughter of a German shipowner who had married a Scottish wom-
an in Dundee. His father, a well-to-do official in the Bank of Eng-
land, was unusually cultured: a good draftsman, a competent versi-
fier, and a lover of the classics. He is pictured, in one of Browning's
poems, as illustrating the siege of Troy by piling up chairs and
tables for the beleaguered city; placing the boy on top of the pile
in the role of Priam; calling the family cat Helen because she had
so often been enticed from home; and pointing to the pony as
Achilles sulking in the stable. His father's library of seven thousand
volumes was supplemented by a few tutors, and Browning's literary
career was determined in boyhood. At twelve he completed a collec-
tion of verses, INCONDITA, which he later destroyed. He discovered

Shelley during adolescence, and at twenty-one published his first volume, PAULINE; it is Shelleyan in idea and manner, the only work of Browning which is frankly imitative.

In his early twenties, Browning learned the delights of travel. He journeyed to Russia and the hill towns of Tuscany; he fell in love with Venice. "Italy," he declared, "was my university." He wrote a drama, PARACELSUS, in which the Renaissance physician seeks to save mankind; and Macready, the most influential actor-manager of the day, urged Browning to write or adapt a play for him. Browning took as his next subject the great Earl of Strafford, whose devotion to Charles I was his undoing, and Macready produced the play at Covent Garden in 1837. STRAFFORD was an instantaneous failure. Macready blamed the play; Browning blamed the actors. The poet swore he would never again be tempted to write for the theater, but in less than two years he was at work on new plays.

In his twenty-eighth year Browning published a long narrative poem so compressed in phrase and large in thought that it was dismissed as a piece of willful obscurity. The poem, SORDELLO, became the butt of literary London. Douglas Jerrold, who tried to read the book while recovering from a severe illness, thought he had lost his mind, and was reassured only when his wife confessed her own failure to understand it. Tennyson said that of SORDELLO's 5800 lines there were just two which he could comprehend. They were the first line of the poem:

> Who will may hear Sordello's story told

and the last line:

> Who would has heard Sordello's story told

and both were lies.

Although few could read SORDELLO with pleasure—few, indeed, read it at all—Browning's essential gift of characterization was apparent, if not yet acknowledged. Browning said it took him twenty-five years to recover from the work on the poem and its reception.

The poems which followed were more comprehensible and far more forcible. THE LOST LEADER was written upon Wordsworth's acceptance of the laureateship. Wordsworth was then seventy-three; and Browning, at thirty-one, recoiled from what he considered a reward for political defection and "a regular face-about of his party." Still influenced by Shelley, the young Browning could not forgive the old poet's "apostasy," his abandonment of liberalism.

The Lost Leader

Just for a handful of silver he left us,
  Just for a riband to stick in his coat—
Found the one gift of which fortune bereft us,
  Lost all the others she lets us devote;
They, with the gold to give, doled him out silver,
  So much was theirs who so little allowed:
How all our copper had gone for his service!
  Rags—were they purple, his heart had been proud!
We that had loved him so, followed him, honored him,
  Lived in his mild and magnificent eye,
Learned his great language, caught his clear accents,
  Made him our pattern to live and to die!
Shakespeare was of us, Milton was for us,
  Burns, Shelley, were with us,—they watch from their graves!
He alone breaks from the van and the freemen,
  He alone sinks to the rear and the slaves!

We shall march prospering,—not thro' his presence;
  Songs may inspirit us,—not from his lyre;
Deeds will be done,—while he boasts his quiescence,
  Still bidding crouch whom the rest bade aspire:
Blot out his name, then, record one lost soul more,
  One task more declined, one more footpath untrod,
One more triumph for devils and sorrow for angels,
  One wrong more to man, one more insult to God!
Life's night begins: let him never come back to us!
  There would be doubt, hesitation and pain,
Forced praise on our part—the glimmer of twilight,
  Never glad confident morning again!
Best fight on well, for we taught him,—strike gallantly,
  Menace our heart ere we master his own;
Then let him receive the new knowledge and wait us,
  Pardoned in Heaven, the first by the throne!

It is unlikely that Wordsworth saw THE LOST LEADER or, seeing it, realized that he had been attacked. Browning later regretted the youthful assault. In a mood that was partly disillusioned, partl self-exonerating, Browning wrote a companion piece, THE PATRIOT, a poem which grew out of Browning's sympathy with the revolution. Here a "world-loser and world-forsaker" pits his courage against the fickleness of the crowd, and the pathos of his defeat is heightened by the ironic tone of the poem.

The Patriot

It was roses, roses, all the way,
  With myrtle mixed in my path like mad:
The house-roofs seemed to heave and sway,
  The church-spires flamed, such flags they had,
A year ago on this very day!

The air broke into a mist with bells,
  The old walls rocked with the crowd and cries.
Had I said, "Good folk, mere noise repels—
  But give me your sun from yonder skies!"
They had answered, "And afterward, what else?"

Alack, it was I who leaped at the sun
  To give it my loving friends to keep!
Nought man could do, have I left undone:
  And you see my harvest, what I reap
This very day, now a year is run.

There's nobody on the house-tops now—
  Just a palsied few at the windows set;
For the best of the sight is, all allow,
  At the Shambles' Gate—or, better yet,
By the very scaffold's foot, I trow.

I go in the rain, and, more than needs,
  A rope cuts both my wrists behind;
And I think, by the feel, my forehead bleeds,
  For they fling, whoever has a mind,
Stones at me for my year's misdeeds.

Thus I entered, and thus I go!
  In triumphs, people have dropped down dead.
"Paid by the World,—what dost thou owe
  Me?" God might question: now instead,
'Tis God shall repay. I am safer so.

Browning's life was almost wholly given to his writing; its milestones are his books. His career was uneventful except for one romance, and that romance, as much a part of literature as anything Browning ever wrote, began in his thirty-third year. Elizabeth Barrett, a poet six years his senior and far more popular than he, had praised Browning in one of her poems. Although she was a confirmed invalid, guarded by a father who was a jealous and oppressive God—the very opposite of Browning's sympathetic father—Browning practically forced his way into the gloomy house, courted her passionately, and eloped with her to his rejuvenating Italy. Wordsworth expressed the hope that the two poets might understand each other.

For fifteen years the Brownings enjoyed a rich life in Italy. Theirs was a busy idyl. Mrs. Browning's health improved, and she gave birth to a son; the once hopeless recluse entertained visitors from England and America. Husband and wife grew deeply interested in Italian politics and art, and the new spirit stimulated a warmer poetry than either had previously written.

Song

The year's at the spring
And day's at the morn;
Morning's at seven;
The hill-side's dew-pearled;
The lark's on the wing;
The snail's on the thorn:
God's in his heaven—
All's right with the world!
from PIPPA PASSES

Song

The moth's kiss, first!
Kiss me as if you made believe
You were not sure, this eve,
How my face, your flower, had pursed
Its petals up; so, here and there
You brush it, till I grow aware
Who wants me, and wide open burst.

The bee's kiss, now!
Kiss me as if you entered gay
My heart at some noonday,
A bud that dares not disallow
The claim, so all is rendered up,
And passively its shattered cup
Over your head to sleep I bow.

from IN A GONDOLA

Two in the Campagna

I wonder do you feel today
    As I have felt since, hand in hand,
We sat down on the grass, to stray
    In spirit better through the land,
This morn of Rome and May?

For me, I touched a thought, I know,
    Has tantalized me many times,
(Like turns of thread the spiders throw
    Mocking across our path) for rhymes
To catch at and let go.

Help me to hold it! First it left
    The yellowing fennel, run to seed
There, branching from the brickwork's cleft,
    Some old tomb's ruin; yonder weed
Took up the floating weft,

Where one small orange cup amassed
    Five beetles—blind and green they grope
Among the honey-meal; and last,
    Everywhere on the grassy slope
I traced it. Hold it fast!

The champaign with its endless fleece
    Of feathery grasses everywhere!
Silence and passion, joy and peace,
    An everlasting wash of air—
Rome's ghost since her decease.

Such life here, through such length of hours,
    Such miracles performed in play,

Such primal naked forms of flowers,
    Such letting Nature have her way
While Heaven looks from its towers!

How say you? Let us, O my dove,
    Let us be unashamed of soul,
As earth lies bare to heaven above!
    How is it under our control
To love or not to love?

I would that you were all to me,
    You that are just so much, no more,
Nor yours, nor mine, nor slave nor free!
    Where does the fault lie? What the core
O' the wound, since wound must be?

I would I could adopt your will,
    See with your eyes, and set my heart
Beating by yours, and drink my fill
    At your soul's springs—your part, my part
In life, for good and ill.

No. I yearn upward—touch you close,
    Then stand away. I kiss your cheek,
Catch your soul's warmth,—I pluck the rose
    And love it more than tongue can speak—
Then the good minute goes.

Already how am I so far
    Out of that minute? Must I go
Still like the thistle-ball, no bar,
    Onward, whenever light winds blow,
Fixed by no friendly star?

Just when I seemed about to learn!
    Where is the thread now? Off again!
The old trick! Only I discern
    Infinite passion and the pain
Of finite hearts that yearn.

Home-Thoughts, from Abroad

Oh, to be in England
Now that April's there,
And whoever wakes in England
Sees, some morning, unaware,
That the lowest boughs and the brush-wood sheaf
Round the elm-tree bole are in tiny leaf,
While the chaffinch sings on the orchard bough
In England—now!

And after April, when May follows,
And the whitethroat builds, and all the swallows!
Hark, where my blossomed pear-tree in the hedge
Leans to the field and scatters on the clover
Blossoms and dewdrops—at the bent-spray's edge—
That's the wise thrush; he sings each song twice over,
Lest you should think he never could recapture
The first fine careless rapture!
And though the fields look rough with hoary dew,
All will be gay when noontide wakes anew
The buttercups, the little children's dower,
—Far brighter than this gaudy melon-flower!

Evelyn Hope

Beautiful Evelyn Hope is dead!
   Sit and watch by her side an hour.
That is her book-shelf, this her bed;
   She plucked that piece of geranium-flower,
Beginning to die, too, in the glass.
   Little has yet been changed, I think—
The shutters are shut, no light may pass
   Save two long rays through the hinge's chink.

Sixteen years old when she died!
   Perhaps she had scarcely heard my name;
It was not her time to love: beside,
   Her life had many a hope and aim,
Duties enough and little cares,
   And now was quiet, now astir—
Till God's hand beckoned unawares,
   And the sweet white brow is all of her.

Is it too late then, Evelyn Hope?
    What, your soul was pure and true,
The good stars met in your horoscope,
    Made you of spirit, fire and dew—
And, just because I was thrice as old,
    And our paths in the world diverged so wide
Each was nought to each, must I be told?
    We were fellow mortals, naught beside?

No, indeed! for God above
    Is great to grant, as mighty to make,
And creates the love to reward the love,—
    I claim you still, for my own love's sake!
Delayed it may be for more lives yet,
    Through worlds I shall traverse, not a few;
Much is to learn, much to forget
    Ere the time be come for taking you.

But the time will come,—at last it will,
    When, Evelyn Hope, what meant (I shall say)
In the lower earth, in the years long still,
    That body and soul so pure and gay?
Why your hair was amber, I shall divine,
    And your mouth of your own geranium's red—
And what you would do with me, in fine,
    In the new life come in the old one's stead.

I have lived (I shall say) so much since then,
    Given up myself so many times,
Gained me the gains of various men,
    Ransacked the ages, spoiled the climes;
Yet one thing, one, in my soul's full scope.
    Either I missed or itself missed me—
And I want and find you, Evelyn Hope!
    What is the issue? let us see!

I loved you, Evelyn, all the while!
    My heart seemed full as it could hold;
There was place and to spare for the frank young smile
    And the red young mouth and the hair's young gold.
So, hush—I will give you this leaf to keep—
    See, I shut it inside the sweet cold hand.
There, that is our secret: go to sleep!
    You will wake, and remember, and understand.

Life in a Love

Escape me?
Never—
Beloved!
While I am I, and you are you,
  So long as the world contains us both,
  Me the loving and you the loth,
While the one eludes, must the other pursue.
My life is a fault at last, I fear:
  It seems too much like a fate, indeed
  Though I do my best I shall scarce succeed.
But what if I fail of my purpose here?
It is but to keep the nerves at strain,
  To dry one's eyes and laugh at a fall,
And baffled, get up and begin again,—
  So the chase takes up one's life, that's all.
While, look but once from your farthest bound
  At me so deep in the dust and dark,
No sooner the old hope drops to ground
  Than a new one, straight to the self-same mark,
      I shape me—
      Ever
      Removed!

Meeting at Night

The grey sea and the long black land;
And the yellow half-moon large and low;
And the startled little waves that leap
In fiery ringlets from their sleep,
As I gain the cove with pushing prow,
And quench its speed i' the slushy sand.

Then a mile of warm sea-scented beach;
Three fields to cross till a farm appears;
A tap at the pane, the quick sharp scratch
And blue spurt of a lighted match,
And a voice less loud, through its joys and fears,
Than the two hearts beating each to each!

With MEN AND WOMEN, published in his forty-fourth year, Browning reached the peak of his career. No poet of the period—indeed, no poet of any time, with the exception of Shakespeare—had so successfully embodied in poetry the complex variations of the human spirit. Browning turned ideas into persons. He gave philosophy substance and made thought take on the form of personal experience. A dramatic poet, he was not a dramatist. It was not in his plays but in his tersely packed poems that his dramatic power is manifest. Never since Shakespeare has there been such a pageant of extraordinary figures. The range is indicated even in a few of Browning's most familiar pieces. Here, in MY LAST DUCHESS, is the brutal and egocentric duke, about to marry the daughter of a count, discussing the marriage settlement with the count's legate; and here, unseen, is his victim, the late duchess. Here, in SOLILOQUY OF THE SPANISH CLOISTER, is the narrow-minded, ritual-loving friar with his sustaining hatred of the ascetic Brother Lawrence, and his plans to ruin the gentle monk. Here, in INCIDENT OF THE FRENCH CAMP, a poem founded upon an actual event, is heroic action without ostentation. And here, in A WOMAN'S LAST WORD, is an uncanny capture of the feminine tone, an amazing assumption of character in which the delicate adjustments of marriage are revealed by the wife.

My Last Duchess

SCENE: FERRARA

That's my last Duchess painted on the wall,
Looking as if she were alive. I call
That piece a wonder, now: Frà Pandolf's hands
Worked busily a day, and there she stands.
Will't please you sit and look at her? I said
"Frà Pandolf" by design, for never read
Strangers like you that pictured countenance,
The depth and passion of its earnest glance,
But to myself they turned (since none puts by
The curtain I have drawn for you, but I)
And seemed as they would ask me, if they durst,
How such a glance came there; so, not the first
Are you to turn and ask thus. Sir, 'twas not
Her husband's presence only, called that spot
Of joy into the Duchess' cheek: perhaps

Frà Pandolf chanced to say, "Her mantle laps
Over my Lady's wrist too much," or "Paint
Must never hope to reproduce the faint
Half-flush that dies along her throat"; such stuff
Was courtesy, she thought, and cause enough
For calling up that spot of joy. She had
A heart—how shall I say?—too soon made glad,
Too easily impressed; she liked whate'er
She looked on, and her looks went everywhere.
Sir, 'twas all one! My favor at her breast,
The dropping of the daylight in the West,
The bough of cherries some officious fool
Broke in the orchard for her, the white mule
She rode with round the terrace—all and each
Would draw from her alike the approving speech,
Or blush, at least. She thanked men,—good; but thanked
Somehow—I know not how—as if she ranked
My gift of a nine-hundred-years'-old name
With anybody's gift. Who'd stoop to blame
This sort of trifling? Even had you skill
In speech—(which I have not)—to make your will
Quite clear to such an one, and say, "Just this
Or that in you disgusts me; here you miss,
Or there exceed the mark"—and if she let
Herself be lessoned so, nor plainly set
Her wits to yours, forsooth, and made excuse,
—E'en then would be some stooping, and I choose
Never to stoop. Oh, sir, she smiled, no doubt,
Whene'er I passed her; but who passed without
Much the same smile? This grew; I gave commands;
Then all smiles stopped together. There she stands
As if alive. Will't please you rise? We'll meet
The company below, then. I repeat,
The Count your master's known munificence
Is ample warrant that no just pretence
Of mine for dowry will be disallowed;
Though his fair daughter's self, as I avowed
At starting, is my object. Nay, we'll go
Together down, sir! Notice Neptune, though,
Taming a sea-horse, thought a rarity,
Which Claus of Innsbruck cast in bronze for me!

Soliloquy of the Spanish Cloister

Gr-r-r—there go, my heart's abhorrence!
    Water your damned flower-pots, do!
If hate killed men, Brother Lawrence,
    God's blood, would not mine kill you!
What? your myrtle-bush wants trimming?
    Oh, that rose has prior claims—
Needs its leaden vase filled brimming?
    Hell dry you up with its flames!

At the meal we sit together;
    Salve tibi! I must hear
Wise talk of the kind of weather,
    Sort of season, time of year:
Not a plenteous cork-crop: scarcely
    Dare we hope oak-galls, I doubt:
What's the Latin name for "parsley"?
    What's the Greek name for Swine's Snout?

Whew! We'll have our platter burnished,
    Laid with care on our own shelf!
With a fire-new spoon we're furnished,
    And a goblet for ourself,
Rinsed like something sacrificial
    Ere 'tis fit to touch our chaps—
Marked with L. for our initial!
    (He-he! There his lily snaps!)

Saint, forsooth! While brown Dolores
    Squats outside the Convent bank
With Sanchicha, telling stories,
    Steeping tresses in the tank,
Blue-black, lustrous, thick like horsehairs,
    —Can't I see his dead eye glow,
Bright as 'twere a Barbary corsair's?
    (That is, if he'd let it show!)

When he finishes refection,
    Knife and fork he never lays
Cross-wise, to my recollection,
    As do I, in Jesu's praise.

I, the Trinity illustrate,
    Drinking watered orange-pulp—
In three sips the Arian frustrate;
    While he drains his at one gulp!

Oh, those melons! If he's able
    We're to have a feast; so nice!
One goes to the Abbot's table,
    All of us get each a slice.
How go on your flowers? None double?
    Not one fruit-sort can you spy?
Strange!—And I, too, at such trouble,
    Keep them close-nipped on the sly!

There's a great text in Galatians,
    Once you trip on it, entails
Twenty-nine distinct damnations,
    One sure, if another fails;
If I trip him just a-dying,
    Sure of heaven as sure can be,
Spin him round and send him flying
    Off to hell, a Manichee?

Or, my scrofulous French novel
    On grey paper with blunt type!
Simply glance at it, you grovel
    Hand and foot in Belial's gripe;
If I double down its pages
    At the woeful sixteenth print,
When he gathers his greengages,
    Ope a sieve and slip it in't?

Or, there's Satan!—One might venture
    Pledge one's soul to him, yet leave
Such a flaw in the indenture
    As he'd miss, till, past retrieve,
Blasted lay that rose-acacia
    We're so proud of. *Hy, Zy, Hine* . . .
'St! There's Vespers! *Plena gratiâ*
    Ave, Virgo! Gr-r-r—you swine!

Incident of the French Camp

You know we French stormed Ratisbon:
  A mile or so away,
On a little mound, Napoleon
  Stood on our storming-day;
With neck out-thrust, you fancy how,
  Legs wide, arms locked behind,
As if to balance the prone brow,
  Oppressive with its mind.

Just as perhaps he mused, "My plans
  That soar, to earth may fall,
Let once my army-leader Lannes
  Waver at yonder wall,"—
Out 'twixt the battery-smokes there flew
  A rider, bound on bound
Full galloping; nor bridle drew
  Until he reached the mound.

Then off there flung in smiling joy,
  And held himself erect
By just his horse's mane, a boy;
  You hardly could suspect
(So tight he kept his lips compressed,
  Scarce any blood came through),
You looked twice ere you saw his breast
  Was all but shot in two.

"Well," cried he, "Emperor, by God's grace
  We've got you Ratisbon!
The Marshal's in the market-place,
  And you'll be there anon
To see your flag-bird flap his vans
  Where I, to heart's desire,
Perched him!" The chief's eye flashed; his plans
  Soared up again like fire.

The chief's eye flashed, but presently
  Softened itself, as sheathes
A film the mother eagle's eye
  When her bruised eaglet breathes:

"You're wounded!" "Nay," his soldier's pride
   Touched to the quick, he said,
"I'm killed, sire!" And, his chief beside,
   Smiling, the boy fell dead.

A Woman's Last Word

Let's contend no more, Love,
   Strive nor weep;
All be as before, Love,
   —Only sleep!

What so wild as words are?
   I and thou
In debate, as birds are,
   Hawk on bough!

See the creature stalking
   While we speak!
Hush and hide the talking,
   Cheek on cheek!

What so false as truth is,
   False to thee?
Where the serpent's tooth is
   Shun the tree—

Where the apple reddens
   Never pry—
Lest we lose our Edens,
   Eve and I.

Be a god and hold me
   With a charm!
Be a man and fold me
   With thine arm!

Teach me, only teach, Love!
   As I ought
I will speak thy speech, **Love,**
   Think thy thought—

Meet, if thou require it,
   Both demands,
Laying flesh and spirit
   In thy hands.

That shall be tomorrow
Not tonight:
I must bury sorrow
Out of sight:

—Must a little weep, Love,
(Foolish me!)
And so fall asleep, Love,
Loved by thee.

To his MEN AND WOMEN Browning added a significant poem dedicated to his wife. It was entitled ONE WORD MORE and it began:

There they are, my fifty men and women
Naming me the fifty poems finished!
Take them, Love, the book and me together:
Where the heart lies, let the brain lie also.

Six years after its publication Mrs. Browning died, and Browning left Florence for England. He never returned to the city which had been the center of their common life. Fame, long delayed, came to him in his fifties with DRAMATIS PERSONAE and THE RING AND THE BOOK, a long narrative poem based on a Roman murder trial, in which the story is presented from a dozen points of view with the exactness of a court record.

The last twenty years of Browning's life brought increasing honors. He wrote constantly and with an ever-growing variety of subject and style. ASOLANDO, a volume prepared at Ásolo, was published on the very day of Browning's death, December 12, 1889, at Venice. He was buried in Westminster Abbey the last day of the year.

The Epilogue to ASOLANDO may well stand as Browning's epitaph. Speaking of it shortly before his death, Browning commented, "It almost looks like bragging to say this, and as if I ought to cancel it. But it's the simple truth; and as it's true, I shall let it stand." Walter Savage Landor, whom the Brownings had befriended during his most trying days, confirmed the poet's estimate. Landor wrote:

. . . Since Chaucer was alive and hale,
No man hath walked along our roads with step
So active, so inquiring eye, or tongue
So varied in discourse.

Epilogue

to ASOLANDO

At the midnight in the silence of the sleep-time,
    When you set your fancies free,
Will they pass to where—by death, fools think, imprisoned—
Low he lies who once so loved you, whom you loved so,
        —Pity me?

Oh to love so, be so loved, yet so mistaken!
    What had I on earth to do
With the slothful, with the mawkish, the unmanly?
Like the aimless, helpless, hopeless, did I drivel
        —Being—who?

One who never turned his back but marched breast forward,
    Never doubted clouds would break,
Never dreamed, though right were worsted, wrong would triumph,
Held we fall to rise, are baffled to fight better,
        Sleep to wake.

No, at noonday in the bustle of man's work-time
    Greet the unseen with a cheer!
Bid him forward, breast and back as either should be,
"Strive and thrive!" cry "Speed,—fight on, fare ever
        There as here!"

Much has been made of Browning's morality and his obscurity.
The obscurity, when it occurs, happens because Browning some-
times uses a subtle and elliptical mode of speech. It does not arise,
as some have charged, from a desire to impress the reader with the
author's erudition. It is not vanity but modesty that takes the in-
telligence of the reader for granted and assumes (perhaps unwar-
rantably) a background of many associations.

Browning's moralizing, once quoted like Scripture by Browning
Societies, is obvious enough; but it is less religious than ethical.
His was a philosophy of imperfection. As the poet wrote in ABT
VOGLER:

The evil is null, is nought, is silence implying sound. . .
On the earth the broken arcs; in the heaven, the perfect round.

It was the striving toward perfection rather than the attainment that mattered most; the onward-going rather than the goal itself. Browning's determined cheerfulness wells up like a dependable geyser. It is the spring of the robust if overlong RABBI BEN EZRA:

> Grow old along with me!
> The best is yet to be,
> The last of life, for which the first was made:
> Our times are in his hand
> Who saith: "A whole I planned,
> Youth shows but half; trust God, see all, nor be afraid."

Accompanying Browning's hopefulness is a devotion to the ideal of service. This high regard echoes Herbert's THE ELIXIR (see page 418), especially the lines:

> A servant with this clause
> Makes drudgery divine;
> Who sweeps a room, as for thy laws,
> Makes that and the action fine.

The sentiment finds its fulfillment in an inconspicuous but significant lyric from PIPPA PASSES:

Service

> All service ranks the same with God.
> If now, as formerly He trod
> Paradise, His presence fills
> Our earth, each only as God wills
> Can work—God's puppets, best and worst,
> Are we; there is no last nor first.
>
> Say not "a small event!" Why "small?"
> Costs it more pain than this, ye call
> A "great event," should come to pass,
> Than that? Untwine me from the mass
> Of deeds which make up life, one deed
> Power shall fall short in, or exceed!
>
> *from* PIPPA PASSES

Browning's other preoccupation was with human aspirations, with the upward struggle of the human soul, with the very failures that test the nobility of man.

> Ah, but a man's reach should exceed his grasp,
> Or what's a heaven for?

Heartiness is perhaps overstressed, and optimism is too unrelievedly buoyant in Browning. It is not easy to "welcome each rebuff that turns earth's smoothness rough," nor, in a bitter age, to concede that "the best is yet to be." But it is impossible to deny the value of Browning's affirmation, the blind faith in perfectibility, even in imperfection. It is the high courage rising from such a poem as PROSPICE ("Look Forward") that endears the yea-saying singer to those who love a poet who is "ever a fighter."

Prospice

Fear death?—to feel the fog in my throat,
       The mist in my face,
When the snows begin, and the blasts denote
       I am nearing the place,
The power of the night, the press of the storm,
       The post of the foe;
Where he stands, the Arch Fear in a visible form,
       Yet the strong man must go:
For the journey is done and the summit attained,
       And the barriers fall,
Though a battle's to fight ere the guerdon be gained,
       The reward of it all.
I was ever a fighter, so—one fight more,
       The best and the last!
I would hate that death bandaged my eyes, and forbore,
       And bade me creep past.
No! let me taste the whole of it, fare like my peers
       The heroes of old,
Bear the brunt, in a minute pay glad life's arrears
       Of pain, darkness and cold.
For sudden the worse turns the best to the brave,
       The black minute's at end,
And the elements' rage, the fiend-voices that rave,
       Shall dwindle, shall blend,

Shall change, shall become first a peace out of pain,
Then a light, then thy breast,
O thou soul of my soul! I shall clasp thee again,
And with God be the rest!

Today Browning is honored less as a teacher and more as a pioneer in a difficult art, the art of psychological portraiture in verse. His soliloquies and narratives hold us with their dramatic tension rather than with their philosophy. He spoke often of the ultimate goal, but it was the urgency, the human adventure, the "one fight more, the best and the last," with which he was most deeply concerned.

After

Take the cloak from his face, and at first
Let the corpse do its worst.

How he lies in his rights of a man!
Death has done all death can.
And, absorbed in the new life he leads,
He recks not, he heeds
Nor his wrong nor my vengeance—both strike
On his senses alike,
And are lost in the solemn and strange
Surprise of the change.

Ha, what avails death to erase
His offence, my disgrace?
I would we were boys as of old
In the field, by the fold—
His outrage, God's patience, man's scorn
Were so easily borne!

I stand here now, he lies in his place—
Cover the face.

Porphyria's Lover

The rain set early in tonight,
The sullen wind was soon awake,
It tore the elm-tops down for spite,
And did its worst to vex the lake:
I listened with heart fit to break.

When glided in Porphyria; straight
   She shut the cold out and the storm,
And kneeled and made the cheerless grate
   Blaze up, and all the cottage warm;
   Which done, she rose, and from her form
Withdrew the dripping cloak and shawl,
   And laid her soiled gloves by, untied
Her hat and let the damp hair fall,
   And, last, she sat down by my side
   And called me. When no voice replied,
She put my arm about her waist,
   And made her smooth white shoulder bare
And all her yellow hair displaced,
   And, stooping, made my cheek lie there,
   And spread, o'er all, her yellow hair,
Murmuring how she loved me—she
   Too weak, for all her heart's endeavor,
To set its struggling passion free
   From pride, and vainer ties dissever,
   And give herself to me for ever.
But passion sometimes would prevail,
   Nor could tonight's gay feast restrain
A sudden thought of one so pale
   For love of her, and all in vain:
   So, she was come through wind and rain.
Be sure I looked up at her eyes
   Happy and proud; at last I knew
Porphyria worshiped me; surprise
   Made my heart swell, and still it grew
   While I debated what to do.
That moment she was mine, mine, fair,
   Perfectly pure and good: I found
A thing to do, and all her hair
   In one long yellow string I wound
   Three times her little throat around,
And strangled her. No pain felt she;
   I am quite sure she felt no pain.
As a shut bud that holds a bee,
   I warily oped her lids: again
   Laughed the blue eyes without a stain.
And I untightened next the tress
   About her neck; her cheek once more
Blushed bright beneath my burning kiss:
   I propped her head up as before,
   Only, this time my shoulder bore

Her head, which droops upon it still:
  The smiling rosy little head,
So glad it has its utmost will,
  That all it scorned at once is fled,
  And I, its love, am gained instead!
Porphyria's love: she guessed not how
  Her darling one wish would be heard.
And thus we sit together now,
  And all night long we have not stirred,
  And yet God has not said a word!

Song

Nay, but you, who do not love her,
  Is she not pure gold, my mistress?
Holds earth aught—speak truth—above her?
  Aught like this tress, see, and this tress,
And this last fairest tress of all,
So fair, see, ere I let it fall?

Because, you spend your lives in praising;
  To praise, you search the wide world over;
Then, why not witness, calmly gazing,
  If earth holds aught—speak truth—above her?
Above this tress, and this I touch
But cannot praise, I love so much!

My Star

All that I know
  Of a certain star
Is, it can throw
  (Like the angled spar)
Now a dart of red,
  Now a dart of blue;
Till my friends have said
  They would fain see, too,
My star that dartles the red and the blue!
Then it stops like a bird; like a flower, hangs furled:
  They must solace themselves with the Saturn above it.
What matter to me if their star is a world?
  Mine has opened its soul to me; therefore I love it.

Browning's rugged individuality is mirrored in the unprecedented range of his work. If it is sometimes too energetic, it is always exciting; if it is overloaded, it expresses the complete man. Browning was never satisfied with easy victories. He had determined, as G. K. Chesterton wrote, "to leave no spot of the cosmos unadorned by his poetry," and he almost succeeded.

EMILY BRONTË

[1818–1848]

IT IS hard to separate the Brontës; they were not only a closely knit family but a group of collaborators. So great a literature of biography and speculation has grown up about them that the individuals have been obscured by the tradition.

The father of the family was Patrick Prunty, an Irishman, who changed his name to Brontë when he came to England, accepted a curacy, and married Maria, daughter of Thomas Branwell, a Penzance merchant. Nine years after the marriage Mrs. Brontë died, leaving six children, two of whom died before they reached the age of twelve. The others were gifted to an extraordinary degree. The one son, Branwell, was educated to be a genius, but his precocity vanished in youth; he failed at everything he attempted, and drank himself to death at thirty-one. The surviving sisters were equally at home in prose and verse. Anne, the mildest of the three, died at twenty-nine, author of two novels, AGNES GREY and THE TENANT OF WILDFELL HALL. Charlotte, author of THE PROFESSOR, VILLETTE, and JANE EYRE, was the only one of the sisters to marry, but her wedded life lasted less than twelve months; she died as a consequence of childbirth in her fortieth year. Emily, the most self-revealing as well as the most stoic of the sisters, surpassed them—as she surpassed all women in literature—in creative intensity. Sent to the school at Roe Head, the institution unforgettably described by Charlotte in JANE EYRE, she suffered from bad food, brutal discipline, and continual homesickness. "Every morning when she awoke," Charlotte wrote in her diary concerning Emily's failure to remain in school, "the vision of home and the moors rushed on her, and darkened and saddened the day that lay before her." Emily ventured into the world only at rare intervals. She taught briefly at a seminary for girls and, with Charlotte, attended a girls' school in Brussels. But she longed for the bleak moors of Haworth:

> Where the grey fox in ferny glens are feeding,
>   Where the wild wind blows on the mountain side.

A tendency toward tuberculosis marked the entire Brontë family. Standing at her brother's grave in a sharp wind, Emily took cold. She was in great pain and sank rapidly. "Stronger than a man," Charlotte wrote, "simpler than a child, her nature stood alone. I have seen nothing like it; but, indeed, I have never seen her parallel in anything." Emily knew she was dying, but she insisted on getting out of bed and dressing herself before she permitted a doctor to attend her. Stoical to the end, she died at thirty, December 19, 1848.

Last Lines

No coward soul is mine,
No trembler in the world's storm-troubled sphere:
  I see Heaven's glories shine,
And faith shines equal, arming me from fear.

O God within my breast,
Almighty, ever-present Deity!
  Life—that in me hast rest,
As I, undying Life, have power in thee!

Vain are the thousand creeds
That move men's hearts, unalterably vain;
  Worthless as withered weeds,
Or idlest froth amid the boundless main,

To waken doubt in one
Holding so fast by thine infinity;
  So surely anchored on
The steadfast rock of immortality.

With wide-embracing love
Thy spirit animates eternal years,
  Pervades and broods above,
Changes, sustains, dissolves, creates, and rears.

> Though earth and moon were gone,
> And suns and universes ceased to be,
> And Thou wert left alone,
> Every existence would exist in Thee.
>
> There is not room for Death,
> Nor atom that his might could render void:
> Thou—Thou art Being and Breath,
> And what Thou art may never be destroyed.

Only one volume of poems was published during the Brontës' lifetime, and that was carefully disguised. The three girls assumed names that were "positively masculine," using the initials of their first names in choosing pseudonyms. Since no publisher would assume the commercial risk, the girls at their own expense brought out POEMS BY CURRER, ELLIS, AND ACTON BELL. Exactly two copies were sold; most of the edition was used to line trunks.

Until recently it was impossible to determine how much of Emily Brontë's poetry was concealed autobiography and how much was unconcealed fantasy. The mystery was cleared up in 1941 by Fanny Elizabeth Ratchford's THE BRONTËS' WEB OF CHILDHOOD. More clearly than any of her predecessors in research, and at odds with most, Miss Ratchford showed that it was futile to base a biography on a subjective interpretation of Emily Brontë's poems. In a remarkable piece of scholarly detective work Miss Ratchford revealed that as children the Brontës escaped from the unhappy Haworth parsonage into a world of shining make-believe. But they did not merely dream of an imaginary country; they created one, called it Gondal, made maps of this fancied island in the Pacific, composed countless poems and legends of its past, and designed a complete if miniature epic. The poems, continued into maturity, were not written, according to Miss Ratchford, "as progressive plot incidents, but were merely the poetic expression of scenes, dramas, and emotions long familiar to her [Emily's] inner vision, carried over, no doubt, from her prose creations." Many students have sought to find Emily's "lover" in the intense and seemingly personal REMEMBRANCE. But the poem is part of the Gondalian cycle, and is uttered by the grieving Rosina of Alcona upon the death of Julius Brenzaida, two leading characters in the Gondal saga.

Remembrance

Cold in the earth, and the deep snow piled above thee!
Far, far removed, cold in the dreary grave!
Have I forgot, my only Love, to love thee,
Severed at last by Time's all-wearing wave?

Now, when alone, do my thoughts no longer hover
Over the mountains, on Angora's shore,
Resting their wings where heath and fern-leaves cover
That noble heart for ever, ever more?

Cold in the earth, and fifteen wild Decembers
From those brown hills, have melted into spring:
Faithful, indeed, is the spirit that remembers
After such years of change and suffering!

Sweet Love of youth, forgive, if I forget thee,
While the world's tide is bearing me along;
Sterner desires and darker hopes beset me,
Hopes which obscure, but cannot do thee wrong.

No other sun has lightened up my heaven,
No other star has ever shone for me;
All my life's bliss from thy dear life was given,
All my life's bliss is in the grave with thee.

But, when the days of golden dreams had perished,
And even Despair was powerless to destroy;
Then did I learn how existence could be cherished,
Strengthened, and fed without the aid of joy.

Then did I check the tears of useless passion,
Weaned my young soul from yearning after thine;
Sternly denied its burning wish to hasten
Down to that tomb already more than mine.

And, even yet, I dare not let it languish,
Dare not indulge in memory's rapturous pain;
Once drinking deep of that divinest anguish,
How could I seek the empty world again?

So many of Emily Brontë's poems had been carelessly copied and incorrectly printed that no authoritative edition was in existence until 1941, when C. W. Hatfield masterfully edited THE COMPLETE POEMS OF EMILY JANE BRONTË from the scattered manuscripts. New treasures were unearthed and long-cherished poems were given their original luster. In a little-known and strongly subjective poem, which Miss Ratchford calls "the noblest apology for genius in the language," Emily Brontë acknowledged her dependence on the "phantom thing" which was her slave yet ruled her imagination. If she steadfastly shunned "the paths that others run" and "cast the world away," it was not Reason but the God of Visions who spoke for her.

God of Visions

Oh, thy bright eyes must answer now,
When Reason, with a scornful brow,
Is mocking at my overthrow;
Oh, thy sweet tongue must plead for me
And tell why I have chosen thee!

Stern Reason is to judgment come,
Arrayed in all her forms of gloom:
Wilt thou, my advocate, be dumb?
No, radiant angel, speak and say
Why I did cast the world away.

Why I have persevered to shun
The common paths that others run;
And on a strange road journeyed on,
Heedless alike of wealth and power—
Of glory's wreath and pleasure's flower.

These, once, indeed, seemed Beings divine;
And they, perchance, heard vows of mine,
And saw my offerings on their shrine;
But careless gifts are seldom prized,
And mine were worthily despised.

So, with a ready heart, I swore
To seek their altar-stone no more;

And gave my spirit to adore
Thee, ever-present, phantom thing—
My slave, my comrade, and my king.

A slave, because I rule thee still;
Incline thee to my changeful will,
And make thy influence good or ill:
A comrade, for by day and night
Thou art my intimate delight—

My darling pain that wounds and sears,
And wrings a blessing out from tears
By deadening me to real cares;
And yet, a king, though prudence well
Have taught thy subject to rebel.

And am I wrong to worship where
Faith cannot doubt, nor hope despair,
Since my own soul can grant my prayer?
Speak, God of visions, plead for me,
And tell why I have chosen thee!

"My sister Emily loved the moors," Charlotte Brontë wrote.
"Flowers brighter than the rose bloomed in the blackest of the
heath for her; out of a sullen hollow in a livid hillside her mind
could make an Eden. She found in the bleak solitude many and
dear delights, and the best loved was—liberty." This wildness, this
love of bleakness and freedom, strengthens the poems and makes
WUTHERING HEIGHTS the greatest novel ever achieved by a woman.
With singular melancholy and concentered passion Emily Brontë
created a dream world, and made it more real than reality.

Fall, Leaves, Fall

Fall, leaves, fall; die, flowers, away;
Lengthen night and shorten day;
Every leaf speaks bliss to me
Fluttering from the autumn tree.

I shall smile when wreaths of snow
Blossom where the rose should grow;
I shall sing when night's decay
Ushers in a drearier day.

The Old Stoic

Riches I hold in light esteem,
And love I laugh to scorn;
And lust of fame was but a dream
That vanished with the morn:

And if I pray, the only prayer
That moves my lips for me
Is, "Leave the heart that now I bear,
And give me liberty!"

Yes, as my swift days near their goal,
'Tis all that I implore—
Through life and death a chainless soul,
With courage to endure.

ARTHUR HUGH CLOUGH
[1819–1861]

BORN on the first day of 1819, son of a prosperous cotton merchant in Liverpool, Arthur Hugh Clough was taken to Charleston, South Carolina, at the age of four. He remained there during his childhood and returned to England to enter Rugby, where he became a favorite of the noted headmaster, Dr. Thomas Arnold. In his early thirties, encouraged by Emerson, he came to the United States to lecture and teach. It was an unsuccessful venture, although Clough considered America "beyond all question the happiest country going."

Back in England, Clough was appointed secretary to a Commission of Report on military education, and his official duties took him abroad. At forty-one his health, never robust, failed; a year later he succumbed to malarial fever. Upon his death Matthew Arnold (see page 921), son of Dr. Thomas Arnold, wrote a commemorating poem, THYRSIS, which some critics have ranked among the great English elegies.

Clough's life was greater in promise than in performance. It is thought that his religious doubts cost him a career. It is certain that intellectual unrest disturbs most of his poetry, and even his "austere love of truth" does not lift his verse above dogged honesty. F. T. Palgrave, the famous Victorian anthologist, said that Clough "lived rather than wrote his poems." But there is one poem which contains Clough's whole spiritual conviction and which has a timeless power. Its long echoes continue to be heard in plays and poems. In April, 1941, it was quoted with great effect by Winston Churchill, Prime Minister of England, as a culmination of one of his most stirring speeches.

Say Not the Struggle Naught Availeth

Say not the struggle naught availeth,
    The labor and the wounds are vain,
The enemy faints not, nor faileth,
    And as things have been they remain.

If hopes were dupes, fears may be liars;
    It may be, in yon smoke conceal'd,
Your comrades chase e'en now the fliers,
    And, but for you, possess the field.

For while the tired waves, vainly breaking,
    Seem here no painful inch to gain,
Far back, through creeks and inlets making,
    Comes silent, flooding in, the main.

And not by eastern windows only,
    When daylight comes, comes in the light;
In front the sun climbs slow, how slowly.
    But westward, look, the land is bright!

XIV

Challenge to Tradition

WALT WHITMAN
[1819–1892]

"LITERATURE, strictly considered, has never recognized the people, and whatever may be said, does not today. It seems as if, so far, there were some natural repugnance between a literary and professional life, and the rude rank spirit of the democracies. . . . I know nothing more rare, even in this country, than a fit scientific estimate and reverent application of the People—of their measureless wealth of latent worth and capacity, their vast artistic contrasts of lights and shades." Thus, in DEMOCRATIC VISTAS, wrote Walt Whitman, in whom the people, with their conflicting expressions of faith, doubt, and democracy, found a confident voice.

He was born Walter Whitman, May 31, 1819, at West Hills, near Huntington, Long Island, of a family of workers. His mother's people were Dutch Quakers, and his maternal grandfather had been a horse breeder. His paternal ancestors had been farmers, but his father turned carpenter and moved his family to Brooklyn, New York. Here the country child became a town boy. He roamed about the docks, explored the alleys, loved the sharp wood smell of his father's shop and the exciting noises of the streets. There were no uneventful days. One Fourth of July, when a library cornerstone was being laid, he was singled out and embraced by Lafayette.

At eleven the young Whitman went to work as an errand boy. At twelve he learned to set type, and at fourteen he was in the composing room of THE LONG ISLAND STAR. For the next twenty years he earned a living as a printer-journalist, reporter, and intermittent teacher. He wrote short and sentimental pieces, innocuous verses, and undistinguished editorials for forgotten newspapers. In his twenty-third year he published FRANKLIN EVANS, OR THE INEBRIATE, a temperance tract disguised as a novel, and which he admitted, with some embarrassment, was written for seventy-five dollars "cash down." In his thirtieth year Whitman left New York to become a special writer on the staff of the New Orleans CRESCENT.

Much has been made of Whitman's sojourn in New Orleans. Certain biographers, worried by passages in his poems which suggest homosexuality, have been quick to supply an orthodox clandestine and unhappy romance. They have furnished various inamoratas to explain not only Whitman's failure to marry, but also his avoidance of women; one of his most recent biographers convinced herself that Whitman's secret love was a young octoroon. Later in life, in order to offset suspicions of sexual abnormality, Whitman boasted that he was the father of six illegitimate children. At another time he implied that he had signed a contract with his father-in-law never to see his wife or children again. Yet Whitman had specifically said he was never married. No child ever came forth to claim him as a father. Although his executors examined everything with microscopic care, no "incriminating" letters were ever unearthed. Until documentary evidence is forthcoming, it is impossible to believe in Whitman's illicit affairs; the New Orleans mistress disappears, and the six children are nothing more than a patriarchal wish-fulfillment.

At thirty-one Walter Whitman, the itinerant journalist, vanished, and the Walt Whitman of tradition emerged. He ceased to write polite sketches and began to fashion a rough and capacious poetry. He exchanged his well-tailored suit for the clothes of a workman and consorted with ferrymen, bus drivers, and other "powerful, uneducated persons." It is related that once when a driver, with whom Walt had often ridden, was sick, Whitman drove the omnibus down Broadway for him and sent the proceeds to his family.

At thirty-one Whitman discovered the American language. Later he planned something between a lecture and a book to be called AN AMERICAN PRIMER, but even now he was in love with muscular sounds, place names, tavern words, words with native brawn. "A perfect user of words uses things," he wrote. "They exude in power and beauty from him—miracles from his hands, miracles from his mouth . . . Monongahela—it rolls with venison richness upon the palate. Mississippi—the word winds with chutes; it rolls a stream three thousand miles long." He continued prophetically, "The appetite of the people of These States is for unhemmed latitude, coarseness, directness, live epithets, expletives, words of opprobrium, resistance."

Prophet and poet spoke together in LEAVES OF GRASS, first published in Whitman's thirty-seventh year. Here were force and flexibility. Here the poet dispensed with "delicate lady-words" and "gloved gentleman-words" in a fierce and limber speech, an idiom like nothing else ever framed. In a quasi-autobiographical set of poems, Whitman identified word and flesh: "Who touches this book touches a man." But LEAVES OF GRASS was not only devoted to a man; its theme was mankind. It dedicated itself to brave, cowardly, chaste, lewd, spiritual and sweating humanity. Whittier literally threw the book into the flames; but Emerson wrote to Whitman, "I give you joy for your free and brave thought. . . . I find the courage of treatment which so delights us, and which large perception only can inspire. I greet you at the beginning of a great career."

Emerson's prediction was not to be fulfilled in Whitman's own time. The "great career" was wholly posthumous; LEAVES OF GRASS was so neglected that Whitman had to write his own inflated reviews in the hope of provoking a controversy. As late as 1900, Barrett Wendell, in his LITERARY HISTORY OF AMERICA, spoke of Whitman's "eccentric insolence of phrase and temper" and concluded that "he was an exotic member of that sterile brotherhood which eagerly greeted him abroad." The critics were revolted not only by Whitman's use of the vernacular, but by his egotism. They failed to realize that Whitman's "I" was a symbol representing the common man and that, when he seemed to celebrate himself, he was celebrating all men.

FROM

Song of Myself

1

I celebrate myself, and sing myself,
And what I assume you shall assume,
For every atom belonging to me as good belongs to you.

I loafe and invite my soul,
I lean and loafe at my ease observing a spear of summer grass.

My tongue, every atom of my blood, form'd from this soil, this air,
Born here of parents born here from parents the same, and their
      parents the same,
I, now thirty-seven years old in perfect health begin,
Hoping to cease not till death.
Creeds and schools in abeyance,
Retiring back a while sufficed at what they are, but never forgotten,
I harbor for good or bad, I permit to speak at every hazard,
Nature without check with original energy.

2

Houses and rooms are full of perfumes, the shelves are crowded
      with perfumes,
I breathe the fragrance myself and know it and like it,
The distillation would intoxicate me also, but I shall not let it.

The atmosphere is not a perfume, it has no taste of the distillation,
      it is odorless,
It is for my mouth forever, I am in love with it,
I will go to the bank by the wood and become undisguised and
      naked,
I am mad for it to be in contact with me.

The smoke of my own breath,
Echoes, ripples, buzz'd whispers, love-root, silk-thread, crotch and
      vine,
My respiration and inspiration, the beating of my heart, the passing
      of blood and air through my lungs,
The sniff of green leaves and dry leaves, and of the shore and dark-
      color'd sea-rocks, and of hay in the barn,
The sound of the belch'd words of my voice loos'd to the eddies of
      the wind,
A few light kisses, a few embraces, a reaching around of arms,
The play of shine and shade on the trees as the supple boughs wag,
The delight alone or in the rush of the streets, or along the fields
      and hill-sides,
The feeling of health, the full-noon trill, the song of me rising
      from bed and meeting the sun.

Have you reckon'd a thousand acres much? have you reckon'd the
    earth much?
Have you practic'd so long to learn to read?
Have you felt so proud to get at the meaning of poems?

Stop this day and night with me and you shall possess the origin of
    all poems,
You shall possess the good of the earth and sun, (there are millions
    of suns left,)
You shall no longer take things at second or third hand, nor look
    through the eyes of the dead, nor feed on the specters in books,
You shall not look through my eyes either, nor take things from me,
You shall listen to all sides and filter them from your self.

6

A child said, *What is the grass?* fetching it to me with full hands;
How could I answer the child? I do not know what it is any more
    than he.

I guess it must be the flag of my disposition, out of hopeful green
    stuff woven.
Or I guess it is the handkerchief of the Lord,
A scented gift and remembrancer designedly dropt,
Bearing the owner's name someway in the corner, that we may see
    and remark, and say *Whose?*

Or I guess the grass is itself a child, the produced babe of the vegeta-
    tion.
Or I guess it is a uniform hieroglyphic,
And it means, Sprouting alike in broad zones and narrow zones,
Growing among black folks as among white,
Kanuck, Tuckahoe, Congressman, Cuff, I give them the same, I re-
    ceive them the same.

And now it seems to me the beautiful uncut hair of graves,

Tenderly will I use you curling grass,
It may be you transpire from the breasts of young men,
It may be if I had known them I would have loved them,
It may be you are from old people, or from offspring taken soon out
    of their mothers' laps,
And here you are the mothers' laps.

This grass is very dark to be from the white heads of old mothers,
Darker than the colorless beards of old men,
Dark to come from under the faint red roofs of mouths.
O I perceive after all so many uttering tongues,
And I perceive they do not come from the roofs of mouths for
    nothing.
I wish I could translate the hints about the dead young men and
    women,
And the hints about old men and mothers, and the offspring taken
    soon out of their laps.

What do you think has become of the young and old men?
And what do you think has become of the women and children?

They are alive and well somewhere,
The smallest sprout shows there is really no death,
And if ever there was it led forward life, and does not wait at the
    end to arrest it,
And ceas'd the moment life appear'd.

All goes onward and outward, nothing collapses,
And to die is different from what anyone supposed, and luckier.

8

The little one sleeps in its cradle,
I lift the gauze and look a long time, and silently brush away
    flies with my hand.

The youngster and the red-faced girl turn aside up the bushy hill,
I peeringly view them from the top.

The suicide sprawls on the bloody floor of the bedroom,
I witness the corpse with its dabbled hair, I note where the pistol
    has fallen.

The blab of the pave, tires of carts, sluff of boot-soles, talk of the
    promenaders,
The heavy omnibus, the driver with his interrogating thumb, the
    clank of the shod horses on the granite floor,
The snow-sleighs, clinking, shouted jokes, pelts of snow-balls,
The hurrahs for popular favorites, the fury of rous'd mobs,
The flap of the curtain'd litter, a sick man inside borne to the hos-
    pital,

The meeting of enemies, the sudden oath, the blows and fall,
The excited crowd, the policeman with his star quickly working
 his passage to the center of the crowd,
The impassive stones that receive and return so many echoes,
What groans of over-fed or half-starv'd who fall sunstruck or in fits,
What exclamations of women taken suddenly who hurry home and
 give birth to babes,
What living and buried speech is always vibrating here, what howls
 restrain'd by decorum,
Arrests of criminals, slights, adulterous offers made, acceptances, re-
 jections with convex lips,
I mind them or the show or resonance of them—I come and I de-
 part.

18

With music strong I come, with my cornets and my drums,
I play not marches for accepted victors only, I play marches for
 conquer'd and slain persons.

Have you heard that it was good to gain the day?
I also say it is good to fall, battles are lost in the same spirit in
 which they are won.

I beat and pound for the dead,
I blow through my embouchures my loudest and gayest for them.

Vivas to those who have fail'd!
And to those whose war-vessels sank in the sea!
And to those themselves who sank in the sea!
And to all generals that lost engagements, and all overcome heroes!
And the numberless unknown heroes equal to the greatest heroes
 known!

20

Who goes there? hankering, gross, mystical, nude;
How is it I extract strength from the beef I eat?

What is a man anyhow? what am I? what are you?

All I mark as my own you shall offset it with your own,
Else it were time lost listening to me.

I do not snivel that snivel the world over,
That months are vacuums and the ground but wallow and filth.

Whimpering and truckling fold with powders for invalids, con-
      formity goes to the fourth-remov'd,
I wear my hat as I please indoors or out.

Why should I pray? why should I venerate and be ceremonious?

Having pried through the strata, analyzed to a hair, counsel'd with
      doctors and calculated close,
I find no sweeter fat than sticks to my own bones.

In all people I see myself, none more and not one a barleycorn less,
And the good or bad I say of myself I say of them.
I know I am solid and sound,
To me the converging objects of the universe perpetually flow,
All are written to me, and I must get what the writing means.

I know I am deathless,
I know this orbit of mine cannot be swept by a carpenter's compass,
I know I shall not pass like a child's carlacue cut with a burnt stick
      at night.

I know I am august,
I do not trouble my spirit to vindicate itself or be understood,
I see that the elementary laws never apologize,
(I reckon I behave no prouder than the level I plant my house by
      after all.)

I exist as I am, that is enough,
If no other in the world be aware I sit content,
And if each and all be aware I sit content.

One world is aware and by far the largest to me, and that is myself,
And whether I come to my own today or in ten thousand or ten
      million years,
I can cheerfully take it now, or with equal cheerfulness I can wait.

My foothold is tenon'd and mortis'd in granite,
I laugh at what you call dissolution,
And I know the amplitude of time.

21

I am the poet of the Body and I am the poet of the Soul,
The pleasures of heaven are with me and the pains of hell are
    with me,
The first I graft and increase upon myself, the latter I translate into
    a new tongue.

I am the poet of the woman the same as the man,
And I say it is as great to be a woman as to be a man,
And I say there is nothing greater than the mother of men.

I chant the chant of dilation or pride,
We have had ducking and deprecating about enough,
I show that size is only development.

Have you outstript the rest? are you the President?
It is a trifle, they will more than arrive there every one, and still
    pass on.

I am he that walks with the tender and growing night,
I call to the earth and sea half-held by the night.

Press close bare-bosom'd night—press close magnetic nourishing
    night!
Night of south winds—night of the large few stars!
Still nodding night—mad naked summer night.

Smile O voluptuous cool-breath'd earth!
Earth of the slumbering and liquid trees!
Earth of departed sunset—earth of the mountains misty-topt!
Earth of the vitreous pour of the full moon just tinged with blue!
Earth of shine and dark mottling the tide of the river!
Earth of the limpid gray of clouds brighter and clearer for my sake!
Far-swooping elbow'd earth—rich apple-blossom'd earth!
Smile, for your lover comes.

Prodigal, you have given me love—therefore I to you give love!
O unspeakable passionate love.

31

I believe a leaf of grass is no less than the journeywork of the stars,
And the pismire is equally perfect, and a grain of sand, and the egg
    of the wren,

And the tree-toad is a chef-d'œuvre for the highest,
And the running blackberry would adorn the parlors of heaven,
And the narrowest hinge in my hand puts to scorn all machinery,
And the cow crunching with depress'd head surpasses any statue,
And a mouse is miracle enough to stagger sextillions of infidels.

I find I incorporate gneiss, coal, long-threaded moss, fruits, grains,
    esculent roots,
And am stucco'd with quadrupeds and birds all over,
And have distanced what is behind me for good reasons,
But call any thing back again when I desire it.

In vain the speeding or shyness,
In vain the plutonic rocks send their old heat against my approach,
In vain the mastodon retreats beneath its own powder'd bones,
In vain objects stand leagues off and assume manifold shapes,
In vain the ocean settling in hollows and the great monsters lying
    low,
In vain the buzzard houses herself with the sky,
In vain the snake slides through the creepers and logs,
In vain the elk takes to the inner passes of the woods,
In vain the razor-bill'd auk sails far north to Labrador,
I follow quickly, I ascend to the nest in the fissure of the cliff.

32

I think I could turn and live with animals, they are so placid and
    self-contain'd,
I stand and look at them long and long.

They do not sweat and whine about their condition,
They do not lie awake in the dark and weep for their sins,
They do not make me sick discussing their duty to God,
Not one is dissatisfied, not one is demented with the mania of own-
    ing things,
Not one kneels to another, nor to his kind that lived thousands of
    years ago,
Not one is respectable or unhappy over the whole earth.

So they show their relations to me and I accept them,
They bring me tokens of myself, they evince them plainly in their
    possession.

I wonder where they get those tokens,
Did I pass that way huge times ago and negligently drop them?
Myself moving forward then and now and forever,
Gathering and showing more always and with velocity,
Infinite and omnigenous, and the like of these among them,
Not too exclusive toward the reachers of my remembrancers,
Picking out here one that I love, and now go with him on brotherly
    terms.

A gigantic beauty of a stallion, fresh and responsive to my caresses,
Head high in the forehead, wide between the ears,
Limbs glossy and supple, tail dusting the ground,
Eyes full of sparkling wickedness, ears finely cut, flexibly moving.
His nostrils dilate as my heels embrace him,
His well-built limbs tremble with pleasure as we race around and
    return.

I but use you a minute, then I resign you, stallion,
Why do I need your paces when I myself out-gallop them?
Even as I stand or sit passing faster than you.

35

Would you hear of an old-time sea-fight?
Would you learn who won by the light of the moon and stars?
List to the yarn, as my grandmother's father the sailor told it to me.

Our foe was no skulk in his ship I tell you, (said he,)
His was the surly English pluck, and there is no tougher or truer,
    and never was, and never will be;
Along the lower'd eve he came horribly raking us.

We closed with him, the yards entangled, the cannon touch'd,
My captain lash'd fast with his own hands.

We had receiv'd some eighteen pound shots under the water,
On our lower-gun-deck two large pieces had burst at the first fire,
    killing all around and blowing up overhead.

Fighting at sun-down, fighting at dark,
Ten o'clock at night, the full moon well up, our leaks on the gain,
    and five feet of water reported,
The master-at-arms loosing the prisoners confined in the afterhold
    to give them a chance for themselves.

The transit to and from the magazine is now stopt by the sentinels,
They see so many strange faces they do not know whom to trust.

Our frigate takes fire,
The other asks if we demand quarter?
If our colors are struck and the fighting done?

Now I laugh content, for I hear the voice of my little captain,
We have not struck, he composedly cries, *we have just begun our
    part of the fighting.*

Only three guns are in use,
One is directed by the captain himself against the enemy's main-
    mast,
Two well-serv'd with grape and canister silence his musketry and
    clear his decks.
The tops alone second the fire of this little battery, especially the
    main-top,
They hold out bravely during the whole of the action.

Not a moment's cease.
The leaks gain fast on the pumps, the fire eats toward the powder-
    magazine.

One of the pumps has been shot away, it is generally thought we
    are sinking.

Serene stands the little captain,
He is not hurried, his voice is neither high nor low,
His eyes give more light to us than our battle-lanterns.

Toward twelve there in the beams of the moon they surrender to us.

                                    40

Flaunt of the sunshine I need not your bask—lie over!
You light surfaces only, I force surfaces and depths also.

Earth! you seem to look for something at my hands,
Say, old top-knot, what do you want?

Behold, I do not give lectures or a little charity,
When I give I give myself.

You there, impotent, loose in the knees,
Open your scarf'd chops till I blow grit within you,
Spread your palms and lift the flaps of your pockets,
I am not to be denied, I compel, I have stores plenty and to spare,
And any thing I have I bestow.

I do not ask who you are, that is not important to me,
You can do nothing and be nothing but what I will infold you.

To cotton-field drudge or cleaner of privies I lean,
On his right cheek I put the family kiss,
And in my soul I swear I never will deny him.

To anyone dying, thither I speed and twist the knob of the door,
Turn the bed-clothes toward the foot of the bed,
Let the physician and the priest go home.

I seize the descending man and raise him with resistless will,
O despairer, here is my neck,
By God, you shall not go down! hang your whole weight upon me.

48

I have said that the soul is not more than the body,
And I have said that the body is not more than the soul,
And nothing, not God, is greater to one than one's self is,
And whoever walks a furlong without sympathy walks to his own
    funeral drest in his shroud,
And I or you pocketless of a dime may purchase the pick of the
    earth,
And to glance with an eye or show a bean in its pod confounds the
    learning of all times,
And there is no trade or employment but the young man following
    it may become a hero,
And there is no object so soft but it makes a hub for the wheel'd
    universe,
And I say to any man or woman, Let your soul stand cool and com-
    posed before a million universes.

And I say to mankind, Be not curious about God,
For I who am curious about each am not curious about God,
(No array of terms can say how much I am at peace about God and
    about death.)

I hear and behold God in every object, yet understand God not in
    the least,
Nor do I understand who there can be more wonderful than myself.

Why should I wish to see God better than this day?
I see something of God each hour of the twenty-four, and each mo-
    ment then,
In the faces of men and women I see God, and in my own face in
    the glass,
I find letters from God dropt in the street, and every one is sign'd
    by God's name,
And I leave them where they are, for I know that wheresoe'er I go,
Others will punctually come for ever and ever.

52

The spotted hawk swoops by and accuses me, he complains of my
    gab and my loitering.

I too am not a bit tamed, I too am untranslatable,
I sound my barbaric yawp over the roofs of the world.

The last scud of day holds back for me,
It flings my likeness after the rest and true as any on the shadow'd
    wilds,
It coaxes me to the vapor and the dusk.

I depart as air, I shake my white locks at the runaway sun,
I effuse my flesh in eddies, and drift it in lacy jags.

I bequeath myself to the dirt to grow from the grass I love,
If you want me again look for me under your boot-soles.

You will hardly know who I am or what I mean,
But I shall be good health to you nevertheless,
And filter and fiber your blood.

Failing to fetch me at first keep encouraged,
Missing me one place search another,
I stop somewhere waiting for you.

    Nothing was mean, nothing was rejected. A leaf of grass was a
miracle as great as the galaxy; the running roadside blackberry was
"fit to adorn the parlors of heaven." In a dream of a new world

Whitman precipitated the American spirit. He implored the Muse to migrate from Greece, to turn away from the past:

Cross out please those immensely overpaid accounts,
That matter of Troy and Achilles' wrath, and Aeneas', Odysseus' wanderings,
Placard "Removed" and "To Let" on the rocks of your snowy Parnassus . . .

And the Muse responded. She made herself at home among "the divine average"; she was not dismayed by the thud of machinery, "not a bit by drainpipe and artificial fertilizers." The "glory of the commonplace" touched new and democratic vistas.

I Hear America Singing

I hear America singing, the varied carols I hear,
Those of mechanics, each one singing his as it should be blithe and strong,
The carpenter singing his as he measures his plank or beam,
The mason singing his as he makes ready for work, or leaves off work,
The boatman singing what belongs to him in his boat, the deckhand singing on the steamboat deck,
The shoemaker singing as he sits on his bench, the hatter singing as he stands,
The wood-cutter's song, the plowboy's on his way in the morning, or at noon intermission or at sundown,
The delicious singing of the mother, or of the young wife at work, or of the girl sewing or washing,
Each singing what belongs to him or her and to none else,
The day what belongs to the day—at night the party of young fellows, robust, friendly,
Singing with open mouths their strong melodious songs.

For You, O Democracy

Come, I will make the continent indissoluble,
I will make the most splendid race the sun ever shone upon,
I will make divine magnetic lands,
With the love of comrades,
With the life-long love of comrades.

I will plant companionship thick as trees along all the rivers of
    America, and along the shores of the great lakes, and all over
    the prairies,
I will make inseparable cities with their arms about each other's
    necks,
            By the love of comrades,
            By the manly love of comrades.

For you these from me, O Democracy, to serve you, ma femme!
For you, for you I am trilling these songs.

Whitman's challenge to tradition did not go unpunished. It af-
fected his private life as well as his public career. After serving as
a wound dresser during the Civil War, he was given a minor clerk-
ship in the Department of the Interior. His chief, who had been a
Methodist preacher, discovered evidences of "immorality" in CHIL-
DREN OF ADAM, and Whitman was summarily dismissed. William
Douglas O'Connor, an abolitionist author, wrote a pamphlet in de-
fense of Whitman and coined the phrase "the Good Gray Poet."
Whitman's phrase about Abraham Lincoln is less well-known, but
it is equally apt: "a Hoosier Michael Angelo."

Lincoln was assassinated while Whitman was still in the Depart-
ment of the Interior. In the fourth edition of LEAVES OF GRASS, a
volume which was steadily growing in size and strength, Whitman
included a series of DRUM TAPS which reflected the Civil War and its
consequences. Among the war poems were four MEMORIES OF PRESI-
DENT LINCOLN. One in rhyme soon became popular; another, WHEN
LILACS LAST IN THE DOORYARD BLOOM'D, had to wait almost half a
century before it was recognized as one of the greatest poems, and
certainly the greatest elegy, ever written in America.

O Captain! My Captain!

O Captain! my Captain! our fearful trip is done,
The ship has weathered every rack, the prize we sought is won,
The port is near, the bells I hear, the people all exulting,
While follow eyes the steady keel, the vessel grim and daring;
            But O heart! heart! heart!
            O the bleeding drops of red,
            Where on the deck my Captain lies,
            Fallen cold and dead.

O Captain! my Captain! rise up and hear the bells;
Rise up—for you the flag is flung—for you the bugle trills,
For you bouquets and ribboned wreaths—for you the shores a-crowd-
    ing,
For you they call, the swaying mass, their eager faces turning;
        Here Captain! dear father!
          This arm beneath your head!
            It is some dream that on the deck,
              You've fallen cold and dead.

My Captain does not answer, his lips are pale and still,
My father does not feel my arm, he has no pulse nor will,
The ship is anchored safe and sound, its voyage closed and done,
From fearful trip the victor ship comes in with object won;
        Exult, O shores, and ring, O bells!
          But I with mournful tread,
            Walk the deck my Captain lies,
              Fallen cold and dead.

When Lilacs Last in the Dooryard Bloom'd

1

When lilacs last in the dooryard bloom'd,
And the great star early droop'd in the western sky in the night,
I mourn'd, and yet shall mourn with ever-returning spring.

Ever-returning spring, trinity sure to me you bring,
Lilac blooming perennial and drooping star in the west,
And thought of him I love.

2

O powerful western fallen star!
O shades of night—O moody, tearful night!
O great star disappear'd—O the black murk that hides the star!
O cruel hands that hold me powerless—O helpless soul of me!
O harsh surrounding cloud that will not free my soul.

3

In the dooryard fronting an old farm-house near the whitewash'd
    palings,
Stands the lilac-bush tall-growing with heart-shaped leaves of rich
    green,

With many a pointed blossom rising delicate, with the perfume
    strong I love,
With every leaf a miracle—and from this bush in the dooryard,
With delicate-color'd blossoms and heart-shaped leaves of rich green,
A sprig with its flower I break.

4

In the swamp in secluded recesses,
A shy and hidden bird is warbling a song.

Solitary the thrush,
The hermit withdrawn to himself, avoiding the settlements,
Sings by himself a song.

Song of the bleeding throat,
Death's outlet song of life, (for well dear brother I know,
If thou wast not granted to sing thou would'st surely die.)

5

Over the breast of the spring, the land, amid cities,
Amid lanes and through old woods, where lately the violets peep'd
    from the ground, spotting the gray débris,
Amid the grass in the fields each side of the lanes, passing the end-
    less grass,
Passing the yellow-spear'd wheat, every grain from its shroud in the
    dark-brown fields uprisen,
Passing the apple-tree blows of white and pink in the orchards,
Carrying a corpse to where it shall rest in the grave,
Night and day journeys a coffin.

6

Coffin that passes through lanes and streets,
Through day and night with the great cloud darkening the land,
With the pomp of the inloop'd flags with the cities draped in black,
With the show of the States themselves as of crape-veil'd women
    standing,
With processions long and winding and the flambeaus of the night,
With the countless torches lit, with the silent sea of faces and the
    unbared heads,

With the waiting depot, the arriving coffin, and the somber faces,
With dirges through the night, with the thousand voices rising
    strong and solemn,
With all the mournful voices of the dirges pour'd around the coffin,
The dim-lit churches and the shuddering organs—where amid these
    you journey,
With the tolling tolling bells' perpetual clang,
Here, coffin that slowly passes,
I give you my sprig of lilac.

7

(Nor for you, for one alone,
Blossoms and branches green to coffins all I bring,
For fresh as the morning, thus would I chant a song for you O sane
    and sacred death.

All over bouquets of roses,
O death, I cover you over with roses and early lilies,
But mostly and now the lilac that blooms the first,
Copious I break, I break the sprigs from the bushes,
With loaded arms I come, pouring for you,
For you and the coffins all of you O death.)

8

O western orb sailing the heaven,
Now I know what you must have meant as a month since I walk'd,
As I walk'd in silence the transparent shadowy night,
As I saw you had something to tell as you bent to me night after
    night,
As you droop'd from the sky low down as if to my side, (while the
    other stars all look'd on,)
As we wander'd together the solemn night, (for something I know
    not what kept me from sleep,)
As the night advanced, and I saw on the rim of the west how full
    you were of woe,
As I stood on the rising ground in the breeze in the cool transparent
    night,
As I watch'd where you pass'd and was lost in the netherward black
    of the night,
As my soul in its trouble dissatisfied sank, as where you sad orb,
Concluded, dropt in the night, and was gone.

9

Sing on there in the swamp,
O singer bashful and tender, I hear your notes, I hear your call,
I hear, I come presently, I understand you,
But a moment I linger, for the lustrous star has detain'd me,
The star my departing comrade holds and detains me.

10

O how shall I warble myself for the dead one there I loved?
And how shall I deck my song for the large sweet soul that has
     gone?
And what shall my perfume be for the grave of him I love?

Sea-winds blown from east and west,
Blown from the Eastern sea and blown from the Western sea, till
     there on the prairies meeting,
These and with these and the breath of my chant,
I'll perfume the grave of him I love.

11

O what shall I hang on the chamber walls?
And what shall the pictures be that I hang on the walls,
To adorn the burial-house of him I love?
Pictures of growing spring and farms and homes,
With the Fourth-month eve at sundown, and the gray smoke lucid
     and bright,
With floods of the yellow gold of the gorgeous, indolent, sinking
     sun, burning, expanding the air,
With the fresh sweet herbage under foot, and the pale green leaves
     of the trees prolific,
In the distance the flowing glaze, the breast of the river, with a
     wind-dapple here and there,
With ranging hills on the banks, with many a line against the sky,
     and shadows,
And the city at hand, with dwellings so dense, and stacks of chim-
     neys,
And all the scenes of life and the workshops, and the workmen
     homeward returning.

12

Lo, body and soul—this land,
My own Manhattan with spires, and the sparkling and hurrying
   tides, and the ships,
The varied and ample land, the South and the North in the light,
   Ohio's shores and flashing Missouri,
And ever the far-spreading prairies cover'd with grass and corn.

Lo, the most excellent sun so calm and haughty,
The violet and purple morn with just-felt breezes,
The gentle soft-born measureless light,
The miracle spreading bathing all, the fulfill'd noon,
The coming eve delicious, the welcome night and the stars,
Over my cities shining all, enveloping man and land.

13

Sing on, sing on you gray-brown bird,
Sing from the swamps, the recesses, pour your chant from the
   bushes,
Limitless out of the dusk, out of the cedars and pines.
Sing on dearest brother, warble your reedy song,
Loud human song, with voice of uttermost woe.

O liquid and free and tender!
O wild and loose to my soul—O wondrous singer!
You only I hear—yet the star holds me, (but will soon depart,)
Yet the lilac with mastering odor holds me.

14

Now while I sat in the day and look'd forth,
In the close of the day with its light and the fields of spring, and
   the farmers preparing their crops,
In the large unconscious scenery of my land with its lakes and
   forests,
In the heavenly aerial beauty, (after the perturb'd winds and the
   storms,)
Under the arching heavens of the afternoon swift passing, and the
   voices of children and women,
The many-moving sea-tides, and I saw the ships how they sail'd,

And the summer approaching with richness, and the fields all busy
    with labor,
And the infinite separate houses, how they all went on, each with
    its meals and minutia of daily usages,
And the streets how their throbbings throbb'd, and the cities pent
    —lo, then and there,
Falling upon them all and among them all, enveloping me with
    the rest,
Appear'd the cloud, appear'd the long black trail,
And I knew death, its thought, and the sacred knowledge of death.

Then with the knowledge of death as walking one side of me,
And the thought of death close-walking the other side of me,
And I in the middle as with companions, and as holding the hands
    of companions,
I fled forth to the hiding receiving night that talks not,
Down to the shores of the water, the path by the swamp in the
    dimness,
To the solemn shadowy cedars and ghostly pines so still.

And the singer so shy to the rest receiv'd me,
The gray-brown bird I know receiv'd us comrades three,
And he sang the carol of death, and a verse for him I love.

From deep secluded recesses,
From the fragrant cedars and the ghostly pines so still,
Came the carol of the bird.

And the charm of the carol rapt me
As I held as if by their hands my comrades in the night,
And the voice of my spirit tallied the song of the bird.

Come lovely and soothing death,
Undulate round the world, serenely arriving, arriving,
In the day, in the night, to all, to each,
Sooner or later delicate death.

Prais'd be the fathomless universe,
For life and joy, and for objects and knowledge curious,
And for love, sweet love—but praise! praise! praise!
For the sure-enwinding arms of cool-enfolding death.

Dark mother always gliding near with soft feet,
Have none chanted for thee a chant of fullest welcome?

Then I chant it for thee, I glorify thee above all,
I bring thee a song that when thou must indeed come, come un-
falteringly.

Approach strong deliveress,
When it is so, when thou hast taken them I joyously sing the dead,
Lost in the loving floating ocean of thee,
Laved in the flood of thy bliss O death.

From me to thee glad serenades,
Dances for thee I propose saluting thee, adornments and feastings
for thee,
And the sights of the open landscape and the high-spread sky are
fitting,
And life and the fields, and the huge and thoughtful night.

The night in silence under many a star,
The ocean shore and the husky whispering wave whose voice I
know,
And the soul turning to thee O vast and well-veil'd death,
And the body gratefully nestling close to thee.

Over the tree-tops I float thee a song,
Over the rising and sinking waves, over the myriad fields and the
prairies wide,
Over the dense-pack'd cities all and the teeming wharves and ways,
I float this carol with joy, with joy to thee O death.

15

To the tally of my soul,
Loud and strong kept up the gray-brown bird,
With pure deliberate notes spreading filling the night.

Loud in the pines and cedars dim,
Clear in the freshness moist and the swamp-perfume,
And I with my comrades there in the night.

While my sight that was bound in my eyes unclosed,
As to long panoramas of visions.

And I saw askant the armies,
I saw as in noiseless dreams hundreds of battle-flags,
Borne through the smoke of the battles and pierc'd with missiles
I saw them,
And carried hither **and yon** through the smoke, and torn and
bloody.

And at last but a few shreds left on the staffs, (and all in silence,)
And the staffs all splinter'd and broken.

I saw battle-corpses, myriads of them,
And the white skeletons of young men, I saw them,
I saw the débris and débris of all the slain soldiers of the war,
But I saw they were not as was thought,
They themselves were fully at rest, they suffer'd not,
The living remain'd and suffer'd, the mother suffer'd,
And the wife and the child and the musing comrade suffer'd,
And the armies that remain'd suffer'd.

16

Passing the visions, passing the night,
Passing, unloosing the hold of my comrades' hands,
Passing the song of the hermit bird and the tallying song of my soul,
Victorious song, death's outlet song, yet varying ever-altering song,
As low and wailing, yet clear the notes, rising and falling, flooding
the night,
Sadly sinking and fainting, as warning and warning, and yet again
bursting with joy,
Covering the earth and filling the spread of the heaven,
As that powerful psalm in the night I heard from recesses,
Passing, I leave thee lilac with heart-shaped leaves,
I leave thee there in the dooryard, blooming, returning with spring.

I cease from my song for thee,
From my gaze on thee in the west, fronting the west, communing
with thee,
O comrade lustrous with silver face in the night.

Yet each to keep and all, retrievements out of the night,
The song, the wondrous chant of the gray-brown bird,
And the tallying chant, the echo arous'd in my soul,
With the lustrous and drooping star with the countenance full of
woe,
With the holders holding my hand nearing the call of the bird,
Comrades mine and I in the midst, and their memory ever to keep,
for the dead I loved so well,
For the sweetest, wisest soul of all my days and lands—and this for
his dear sake,
Lilac and star and bird twined with the chant of my soul,
There in the fragrant pines and the cedars dusk and dim.

In his fifty-fourth year Whitman was struck by paralysis. Three months later his mother died, and he seems never to have recovered from the effect of her death. Years later he wrote that he was "still enveloped in thoughts of my dear mother, the most perfect and magnetic character, the rarest combination of practical, moral, and spiritual of all and any I have ever known—and by me O so much the most deeply loved."

Whitman spent the last years of his life in Camden, New Jersey, where his mother had died. Confined by paralysis and poverty-stricken, he was helped by a few friends. In 1891 he prepared the final "deathbed edition" of LEAVES OF GRASS, which had grown from thirty-two poems to approximately three hundred, and pictured himself "much like some hard-cased dilapidated grim ancient shell-fish or time-banged conch—no legs, utterly nonlocomotive—cast up high and dry on the shore sands." He died at Camden, in his seventy-third year, March 26, 1892.

The Last Invocation

At the last, tenderly,
From the walls of the powerful fortress'd house,
From the clasp of the knitted locks, from the keep of the well-closed
    doors,
Let me be wafted.

Let me glide noiselessly forth;
With the key of softness unlock the locks—with a whisper,
Set ope the doors O soul.

Tenderly—be not impatient,
(Strong is your hold O mortal flesh.
Strong is your hold O love.)

Poets to Come

Poets to come! orators, singers, musicians to come!
Not to-day is to justify me and answer what I am for,
But you, a new brood, native, athletic, continental, greater than
    before known,

Arouse! for you must justify me.
I myself but write one or two indicative words for the future,
I but advance a moment only to wheel and hurry back in the
      darkness.

I am a man who, sauntering along without fully stopping, turns a
      casual look upon you and then averts his face,
Leaving it to you to prove and define it,
Expecting the main things from you.

When I Heard the Learn'd Astronomer

When I heard the learn'd astronomer,
When the proofs, the figures, were ranged in columns before me,
When I was shown the charts and diagrams, to add, divide, and
      measure them,
When I sitting heard the astronomer where he lectured with much
      applause in the lecture-room,
How soon unaccountable I became tired and sick,
Till rising and gliding out I wander'd off by myself,
In the mystical moist night-air, and from time to time,
Look'd up in perfect silence at the stars.

The Commonplace

The commonplace I sing;
How cheap is health! how cheap nobility!
Abstinence, no falsehood, no gluttony, lust;
The open air I sing, freedom, toleration,
(Take here the mainest lesson—less from books—less from the
      schools,)
The common day and night—the common earth and waters,
Your farm—your work, trade, occupation,
The democratic wisdom underneath, like solid ground for all.

A Noiseless Patient Spider

A noiseless patient spider,
I mark'd where on a little promontory it stood isolated,
Mark'd how to explore the vacant vast surrounding,
It launch'd forth filament, filament, filament, out of itself.
Ever unreeling them, ever tirelessly speeding them.

And you O my soul where you stand,
Surrounded, detached, in measureless oceans of space,
Ceaselessly musing, venturing, throwing, seeking the spheres to
　　connect them.
Till the bridge you will need be form'd, till the ductile anchor hold,
Till the gossamer thread you fling catch somewhere, O my soul.

Reconciliation

Word over all, beautiful as the sky,
Beautiful that war and all its deeds of carnage must in time be
　　utterly lost,
That the hands of the sisters Death and Night incessantly softly
　　wash again, and ever again, this soil'd world;
For my enemy is dead, a man divine as myself is dead,
I look where he lies white-faced and still in the coffin—I draw near,
Bend down and touch lightly with my lips the white face in the
　　coffin.

Darest Thou Now, O Soul

Darest thou now, O soul,
Walk out with me toward the unknown region,
Where neither ground is for the feet nor any path to follow?

No map there, nor guide,
Nor voice sounding, nor touch of human hand,
Nor face with blooming flesh, nor lips, nor eyes, are in that land.

I know it not, O soul,
Nor dost thou; all is a blank before us;
All waits undreamed of in that region, that inaccessible land.

Till when the ties loosen,
All but the ties eternal, Time and Space,
Nor darkness, gravitation, sense, nor any bounds bounding us.

Then we burst forth, we float,
In Time and Space, O soul, prepared for them,
Equal, equipped at last (O joy! O fruit of all!) them to fulfill, O soul.

"What I assume you shall assume," wrote Whitman in an all-embracing exaltation of the democratic character. "In all people I see myself." Buoyed up by tremendous expectations and unrestrained by the gathering threats to his idealism, Whitman was guilty of overinclusiveness. He tried to force the reader to a comprehension of a vast world by a catalogue of its details. To overemphasis he added overconfidence. Kenneth Allott, in (of all places!) a biography of Jules Verne, speaks of "Whitman's exuber-ant Rousseau-Rotarian voice," and there is justice as well as wit in the incongruous epigram. Whitman's unflagging optimism and high hopes were dashed by events he could not foresee. In THE BEGINNINGS OF CRITICAL REALISM IN AMERICA, V. L. Parrington remarks that Whitman was "a great figure, the greatest assuredly in our literature—yet perhaps only a great child."

Whitman was "a great child" in the sense that he was both a realist and a mystic. A single, separate person, he sang of all existence, of "Life immense in passion, pulse, and power." A visionary, he beheld a future greater than all the past, a land of "inseparable cities" teeming with "the lifelong love of comrades." Prophet for a possible millennium, he was also an indomitable pioneer; exploring new roads, he was swept by tidal rhythms. Biographer of democracy, he contained a continent.

HERMAN MELVILLE
[1819–1891]

LIKE Whitman, Herman Melville fought a losing battle with fate. A pioneer in American giantism, writing novels that were extended poems in prose, scorned by the critics and neglected by the public, he died in obscurity.

Melville's beginnings were auspicious enough. He was born in New York City, August 1, 1819, in a well-to-do family. When Melville was twelve, his father died, leaving a wife with eight children to be taken care of by her relatives near Albany, New York. Orphaned and half educated, young Melville attempted to teach school. Failing as a teacher, he became a clerk. A failure again, he ran away to sea and shipped as a common sailor. After a disillusioning experience abroad, he returned to America and hoped to settle in the little town of Lansingburgh, New York. But the sea was in his veins; at twenty-one he began pursuing the great whale which, to him, was not only an adventure and an education, but a symbol. He wrote: "If, at my death my executors (or more properly, my creditors) find any precious manuscripts in my desk, then I prospectively ascribe all the honor and glory to whaling; for a whaleship was my Yale and Harvard." Twice Melville jumped ship, lived among South Sea cannibals, and made a dusky Eden in Tahiti. The need of medical attention to an infected leg forced him to return reluctantly to what he termed "snivelization."

At twenty-six Melville entered the literary world with TYPEE, and on the promise of its reception he married the daughter of Judge Shaw, a Boston Brahmin. TYPEE was an adventure story in which the criticism of contemporary society was present but submerged; it was his one popular success. The volumes which followed questioned current standards; for fifteen years Melville dared to create works which challenged values and assailed the political-moral structure of his day. It took years to produce his masterpiece, MOBY-DICK, and Melville emerged from the work with energy drained and health impaired. Few readers recognized the overpowering force of the book, a book which has since been recognized as a prose epic and a poetic allegory; "one of the first great mythologies to be created in the modern world," wrote Lewis Mumford, "created out of the stuff of that world, its science, its exploration, its terrestrial daring." Most of the critics appraised MOBY-DICK as a fair yarn ruined by the author's perverse symbolism. One of them termed Melville's style "mad as a March hare; gibbering, screaming, like an incurable Bedlamite, reckless of keeper or strait jacket." It is true that the narration sprawls and that the pattern is sometimes twisted. But a prodigious current runs through the book; it impels Ahab's Shakespearean soliloquies as well as the lyrical digressions. The power of the sea is in MOBY-DICK as the power of the earth is in LEAVES OF GRASS.

The Whale

The ribs and terrors in the whale,
   Arched over me a dismal gloom,
While all God's sun-lit waves rolled by,
   And left me deepening down to doom.

I saw the opening maw of hell,
  With endless pains and sorrows there;
Which none but they that feel can tell—
  Oh, I was plunging to despair.

In black distress, I called my God,
  When I could scarce believe Him mine,
He bowed His ear to my complaints—
  No more the whale did me confine.

With speed He flew to my relief,
  As on a radiant dolphin borne;
Awful, yet bright, as lightning shone
  The face of my Deliverer God.

My song for ever shall record
  That terrible, that joyful hour;
I give the glory to my God,
  His all the mercy and the power.

from MOBY-DICK

Melville's last forty years were unhappy spasms of creation and ill-health. He had ceased to be a popular novelist. At fifty he turned to poetry; his last book was a collection of verse. "All Fame is patronage," Melville once wrote. "Let me be infamous." He died September 28, 1891, a foundered ship, sinking (in Raymond Weaver's phrase) "without a ripple of renown."

MOBY-DICK is not an isolated peak. Melville's verses, and particularly his BATTLE PIECES, are eminences illumined by lightning strokes. Much of the poetry has been lost, much of it is out of print. But the living flame burns in the fragments. The young sailor, buried for years, comes to life; the adventurer who had withdrawn from the world, refusing to share its slavery, re-enters it with a dream of freedom.

The Martyr

*Indicative of the passion of the people on the
15th of April, 1865, after the assassination of Lincoln*

Good Friday was the day
  Of the prodigy and crime,
When they killed him in his pity,
  When they killed him in his prime

Of clemency and calm—
When with yearning he was filled
To redeem the evil-willed,
And, though conqueror, be kind;
But they killed him in his kindness,
In their madness and their blindness,
And they killed him from behind.

There is sobbing of the strong,
And a pall upon the land;
But the People in their weeping
Bare the iron hand;
Beware the People weeping
When they bare the iron hand.

He lieth in his blood—
The father in his face;
They have killed him, the Forgiver—
The Avenger takes his place,
The Avenger wisely stern,
Who in righteousness shall do
What the heavens call him to,
And the parricides remand;
For they killed him in his kindness,
In their madness and their blindness,
And his blood is on their hand.

There is sobbing of the strong,
And a pall upon the land;
But the People in their weeping
Bare the iron hand;
Beware the People weeping
When they bare the iron hand.

The March into Virginia

JULY, 1861

Did all the lets and bars appear
To every just or larger end,
Whence should come the trust and cheer?
Youth must its ignorant impulse lend—
Age finds place in the rear.
All wars are boyish, and are fought by boys,

The champions and enthusiasts of the state:
  Turbid ardors and vain joys
    Not barrenly abate—
  Stimulants to the power mature,
    Preparatives of fate.

Who here forecasteth the event?
What heart but spurns at precedent
And warnings of the wise,
Contemned foreclosures of surprise?
The banners play, the bugles call,
The air is blue and prodigal.
  No berrying party, pleasure-wooed,
No picnic party in the May,
Ever went less loth than they
  Into that leafy neighborhood.
In Bacchic glee they file toward Fate,
Moloch's uninitiate;
Expectancy, and glad surmise
Of battle's unknown mysteries.
All they feel is this: 'tis glory,
A rapture sharp, though transitory,
Yet lasting in belaureled story.
So they gaily go to fight,
Chatting left and laughing right.

But some who this blithe mood present,
  As on in lightsome files they fare,
Shall die experienced ere three days are spent—
  Perish, enlightened by the volleyed glare;
Or shame survive, and like to adamant,
  The throe of Second Manassas share.

In strength and amplitude Melville has only two equals in America: Emerson and Whitman, both of whom, being children of light, are alien to his dark grandeur. Against their positive yea-saying, Melville pits his challenging No. He is their disturbing opponent, and he measures up to them.

MATTHEW ARNOLD
[1822–1888]

MATTHEW ARNOLD was destined to be a poet who preached wistfully to the world. His blend of skepticism and faith expressed the spirit of two generations, and, until recently, his prim canons of poetry dominated English criticism.

Son of Thomas Arnold, the famous headmaster of Rugby, Matthew Arnold was born near Staines, December 24, 1822. At eighteen his first publication, ALARIC AT ROME, won a prize at Rugby; at twenty-one, his poem CROMWELL won the important Newdigate Prize at Oxford. For four years after graduation he earned a small living as private secretary, but marriage at the age of twenty-nine compelled him to seek an increased income. He accepted an appointment as inspector of schools, a position which was more conducive to criticism than creation and which he held for thirty-five years. Toward the end of his life he came to the United States to lecture. He died of heart failure at Liverpool in his sixty-sixth year.

It has been said that Arnold's much-anthologized verse is respected but no longer loved, that his social criticism is infrequently read, and that he is quoted only for a few phrases, such as "sweetness and light" and his definition of poetry as "a criticism of life." His poetic activity lasted less than ten years, yet Arnold did not underestimate his verse. "My poems," he wrote, "represent, on the whole, the main movement of mind of the last quarter of a century, and thus they will probably have their day as people become conscious of what that movement of mind is, and interested in the literary productions which reflect it. It might fairly be urged that I have less poetical sentiment than Tennyson, and less intellectual vigor and abundance than Browning; yet, because I have perhaps more of a fusion of the two than either of them, I am likely enough to have my turn, as they have had theirs."

Whether or not Arnold's estimate of his own poetry was accurate, his verse unquestionably justifies his definition. It is distinctly "a criticism of life." It is ethical, earnest, and melancholy in tone. What was once considered to be its great virtue now seems to be its chief defect: its purposeful "high seriousness" is muted by the low emotional pitch. But poetry is not all song; and here, for the most part, instead of singing, it searches.

Dover Beach

The sea is calm tonight,
The tide is full, the moon lies fair
Upon the straits;—on the French coast the light
Gleams and is gone; the cliffs of England stand,
Glimmering and vast, out in the tranquil bay.
Come to the window, sweet is the night-air!

Only, from the long line of spray
Where the sea meets the moon-blanched land,
Listen! you hear the grating roar
Of pebbles which the waves draw back, and fling,
At their return, up the high strand,
Begin, and cease, and then again begin,
With tremulous cadence slow, and bring
The eternal note of sadness in.

Sophocles long ago
Heard it on the Aegean, and it brought
Into his mind the turbid ebb and flow
Of human misery; we
Find also in the sound a thought,
Hearing it by this distant northern sea.

The Sea of Faith
Was once, too, at the full, and round earth's shore
Lay like the folds of a bright girdle furled.
But now I only hear
Its melancholy, long, withdrawing roar,
Retreating, to the breath
Of the night-wind, down the vast edges drear
And naked shingles of the world.

Ah, love, let us be true
To one another! for the world, which seems
To lie before us like a land of dreams,
So various, so beautiful, so new,
Hath really neither joy, nor love, nor light.

Nor certitude, nor peace, nor help for pain;
And we are here as on a darkling plain
Swept with confused alarms of struggle and flight,
Where ignorant armies clash by night.

Quiet Work

One lesson, Nature, let me learn of thee,
One lesson which in every wind is blown,
One lesson of two duties kept at one
Though the loud world proclaim their enmity—
Of toil unsevered from tranquillity,
Of labor, that in lasting fruit outgrows
Far noisier schemes, accomplished in repose,
Too great for haste, too high for rivalry!

Yes, while on earth a thousand discords ring,
Man's fitful uproar mingling with his toil,
Still do thy sleepless ministers move on,
Their glorious tasks in silence perfecting;
Still working, blaming still our vain turmoil,
Laborers that shall not fail, when man is gone.

Shakespeare

Others abide our question. Thou art free.
We ask and ask. Thou smilest, and art still,
Out-topping knowledge. For the loftiest hill,
Who to the stars uncrowns his majesty,
Planting his steadfast footsteps in the sea,
Making the heaven of heavens his dwelling-place,
Spares but the cloudy border of his base
To the foiled searching of mortality;
And thou, who didst the stars and sunbeams know,
Self-schooled, self-scanned, self-honored, self-secure,
Didst tread on earth unguessed at.—Better so!
All pains the immortal spirit must endure,
All weakness which impairs, all griefs which bow,
Find their sole speech in that victorious brow.

Requiescat

Strew on her roses, roses,
    And never a spray of yew:
In quiet she reposes;
    Ah, would that I did too!

Her mirth the world required;
    She bathed it in smiles of glee.
But her heart was tired, tired,
    And now they let her be.

Her life was turning, turning,
    In mazes of heat and sound.
But for peace her soul was yearning,
    And now peace laps her round.

Her cabined, ample spirit,
    It fluttered and failed for breath;
Tonight it doth inherit
    The vasty hall of death.

The Last Word

Creep into thy narrow bed,
Creep, and let no more be said!
Vain thy onset! all stands fast.
Thou thyself must break at last.

Let the long contention cease!
Geese are swans, and swans are geese.
Let them have it how they will!
Thou art tired; best be still.

They out-talked thee, hissed thee, tore thee?
Better men fared thus before thee;
Fired their ringing shot and passed,
Hotly charged—and sank at last.

Charge once more, then, and be dumb!
Let the victors, when they come,
When the forts of folly fall,
Find thy body by the wall!

COVENTRY PATMORE
[1823–1896]

BORN July 23, 1823, in Epping Forest, Coventry Kersey Dighton Patmore was almost crippled by his name. His father was an ambitious if commonplace author, and the Patmores expected great things of their offspring. It was planned that Coventry should become a painter; he joined the Pre-Raphaelite group and contributed to its organ THE GERM. His gift as an artist being negligible, he turned to literature, and Thackeray hailed him as a coming genius. Unfortunately, POEMS, published in Patmore's twenty-first year, was thin and mawkish, and, although Dante Gabriel Rossetti befriended the book, the critics condemned it. At twenty-four, Patmore became an assistant librarian in the British Museum, married happily, and devoted most of his life to a celebration of domesticity.

THE ANGEL IN THE HOUSE, a collection of some one hundred and fifty poems in praise of married love, is characterized by its sentimental title. Yet Ruskin spoke of the verses as "sparkling humilities," and if they are not passionate, they are gently persuasive.

A Farewell

With all my will, but much against my heart,
We two now part.
My Very Dear,
Our solace is, the sad road lies so clear.
It needs no art,
With faint, averted feet
And many a tear,
In our opposéd paths to persevere.
Go thou to East, I West.
We will not say
There's any hope, it is so far away.
But, O my Best,
When the one darling of our widowhead,
The nursling Grief,
Is dead.

And no dews blur our eyes
To see the peach-bloom come in evening skies,
Perchance we may,
Where now this night is day,
And even through faith of still averted feet,
Making full circle of our banishment,
Amazéd meet;
The bitter journey to the bourne so sweet
Seasoning the termless feast of our content
With tears of recognition never dry.

After fifteen years of uneventful felicity, Mrs. Patmore died. Three years later Patmore married a recent convert to Catholicism and became a Catholic himself. His second wife was a woman of means, and Patmore was able to give up his post in the British Museum and purchase a large place in Ashdown Forest. He was so proud of his status as country squire that he wrote and published HOW I MANAGED MY ESTATE. His second wife died in 1880, and, within a year, Patmore married again. He died in his seventy-fourth year, November 26, 1896.

After his death Alice Meynell wrote, "Essentially he had but one subject: human love as a mystery; and but one character: an impassioned spirituality." Today Patmore's verse seems more intimate than impassioned. There is no doubt about its warmth, its true simplicity. As Patmore himself wrote in one of the shortest but one of his most profound poems:

For want of me the world's course will not fail;
When all its work is done the lie shall rot.
The truth is great, and shall prevail,
When none cares whether it prevail or not.

The Toys

My little son, who looked from thoughtful eyes
And moved and spoke in quiet grown-up wise,
Having my law the seventh time disobeyed,
I struck him, and dismissed
With hard words and unkissed,
—His mother, who was patient, being dead.
Then, fearing lest his grief should hinder sleep,
I visited his bed,

But found him slumbering deep,
With darkened eyelids, and their lashes yet
From his late sobbing wet.
And I, with moan,
Kissing away his tears, left others of my own;
For, on a table drawn beside his head,
He had put, within his reach,
A box of counters and a red-veined stone,
A piece of glass abraded by the beach,
And six or seven shells,
A bottle with bluebells,
And two French copper coins, ranged there with careful art,
To comfort his sad heart.
So when that night I prayed
To God, I wept, and said:
"Ah, when at last we lie with trancéd breath,
Not vexing Thee in death,
And Thou rememberest of what toys
We made our joys,
How weakly understood
Thy great commanded good,
Then, fatherly not less
Than I whom Thou hast molded from the clay,
Thou'lt leave Thy wrath, and say,
'I will be sorry for their childishness.' "

The Married Lover

Why, having won her, do I woo?
   Because her spirit's vestal grace
Provokes me always to pursue,
   But, spirit-like, eludes embrace. . . .

Because, although in act and word
   As lowly as a wife can be,
Her manners, when they call me lord,
   Remind me 'tis by courtesy.

Because her gay and lofty brows,
   When all is won which hope can ask,
Reflect a light of hopeless snows
   That bright in virgin ether bask;

Because, tho' free of the outer court
I am, this Temple keeps its shrine
Sacred to Heaven; because, in short,
She's not and never can be mine.

Truth

Here, in this little bay,
Full of tumultous life and great repose,
Where, twice a day,
The purposeless, glad ocean comes and goes,
Under high cliffs, and far from the huge town,
I sit me down.
For want of me the world's course will not fail;
When all its work is done, the lie shall rot.
The truth is great, and shall prevail,
When none cares whether it prevail or not.

GEORGE MEREDITH

[1828–1909]

ONE of the few novelists whose poetry excelled their prose,
George Meredith was born in Portsmouth, in Hampshire,
February 12, 1828. His father was a tailor and outfitter at the naval
station, but the family affairs deteriorated after the death of Mere-
dith's mother. The boy's education was fitful; he was taught pri-
vately at home and at a Moravian school in Germany. At sixteen
he began to study law and entered a London solicitor's office. Hav-
ing neither inclination nor talent for the legal profession, he at-
tempted journalism, for which he was scarcely better fitted. At
twenty-one he married the daughter of the novelist Thomas Love
Peacock, a widow eight years older than he. The marriage was not
a success. Meredith himself recognized it as a blunder, and his wife
deserted him and their young son some years later. When his wife
died, Meredith remarried at thirty-six, and his second wife was his
devoted companion until her death in 1885. The discordant ending

of Meredith's first marriage ("the union of this ever-diverse pair") is reflected in the sequence of semisonnets—actually, poems of four united quatrains—which Meredith ironically entitled MODERN LOVE.

FROM

Modern Love

Thus piteously Love closed what he begat:
The union of this ever-diverse pair!
These two were rapid falcons in a snare,
Condemned to do the flitting of the bat.
Lovers beneath the singing sky of May,
They wandered once, clear as the dew on flowers,
But they fed not on the advancing hours:
Their hearts held cravings for the buried day.
Then each applied to each that fatal knife,
Deep questioning, which probes to endless dole.
Ah, what a dusty answer gets the soul
When hot for certainties in this our life!
In tragic hints here see what evermore
Moves dark as yonder midnight ocean's force,
Thundering like ramping hosts of warrior horse,
To throw that faint thin line upon the shore!

Meanwhile, Meredith had acted as war correspondent in Italy (a period reflected in several of his novels) and had become editorial adviser. Thomas Hardy, the other Victorian who became equally famous as poet and novelist, was one of Meredith's discoveries. Although he wrote continually and energetically—one edition of his works ran to thirty-nine volumes—Meredith's vogue did not begin until forty years after the publication of his first books. In his seventy-seventh year he received the Order of Merit, rarely bestowed upon men of letters. He died at eighty-one, May 18, 1909.

Meredith's prose style has been a stumbling block for many. It is mannered and involved, devoted to pretentious characters and preposterous conversations. His novels have a way of elaborating and dissecting the smallest nuance of meaning; praised for their subtlety, many of them seem to be nothing more than tremendous trifles.

Meredith's poems, liberated from tortuous narration, are free of

his prose mannerisms. They are thoughtful and vigorous, and some-
times (as in LUCIFER IN STARLIGHT) richly imaginative. Tennyson
declared that he could never get the music of LOVE IN THE VALLEY
out of his mind.

Lucifer in Starlight

On a starred night Prince Lucifer uprose.
Tired of his dark dominion swung the fiend
Above the rolling ball in cloud part screened,
Where sinners hugged their spectre of repose.
Poor prey to his hot fit of pride were those.
And now upon his western wing he leaned,
Now his huge bulk o'er Afric's sands careened,
Now the black planet shadowed Arctic snows.
Soaring through wider zones that pricked his scars
With memory of the old revolt from Awe,
He reached a middle height, and at the stars,
Which are the brain of heaven, he looked, and sank.
Around the ancient track marched, rank on rank,
The army of unalterable law.

FROM

Love in the Valley

Under yonder beech-tree single on the greensward,
    Couched with her arms behind her golden head,
Knees and tresses folded to slip and ripple idly,
    Lies my young love sleeping in the shade.
Had I the heart to slide an arm beneath her,
    Press her parting lips as her waist I gather slow,
Waking in amazement she could not but embrace me:
    Then would she hold me and never let me go?

Shy as the squirrel and wayward as the swallow,
    Swift as the swallow along the river's light
Circleting the surface to meet his mirrored winglets,
    Fleeter she seems in her stay than in her flight.
Shy as the squirrel that leaps among the pine-tops,
    Wayward as the swallow overhead at set of sun,
She whom I love is hard to catch and conquer;
    Hard. but O the glory of the winning were she won!

When her mother tends her before the laughing mirror,
  Tying up her laces, looping up her hair,
Often she thinks, were this wild thing wedded,
  More love should I have, and much less care.
When her mother tends her before the lighted mirror,
  Loosening her laces, combing down her curls,
Often she thinks, were this wild thing wedded,
  I should miss but one for many boys and girls.

Heartless she is as the shadow in the meadows
  Flying to the hills on a blue and breezy noon.
No, she is athirst and drinking up her wonder:
  Earth to her is young as the slip of the new moon.
Deals she an unkindness, 'tis but her rapid measure,
  Even as in a dance; and her smile can heal no less:
Like the swinging May-cloud that pelts the flowers with hailstones
  Off a sunny border, she was made to bruise and bless.

Lovely are the curves of the white owl sweeping
  Wavy in the dusk lit by one large star.
Lone on the fir-branch, his rattle-note unvaried,
  Brooding o'er the gloom, spins the brown eve-jar.
Darker grows the valley, more and more forgetting:
  So were it with me if forgetting could be willed.
Tell the grassy hollow that holds the bubbling well-spring,
  Tell it to forget the source that keeps it filled.

Stepping down the hill with her fair companions,
  Arm in arm, all against the raying West,
Boldly she sings, to the merry tune she marches,
  Brave in her shape, and sweeter unpossessed.
Sweeter, for she is what my heart first awaking
  Whispered the world was; morning light is she.
Love that so desires would fain keep her changeless;
  Fain would fling the net, and fain have her free.

DANTE GABRIEL ROSSETTI
[1828–1882]

THE alien Rossettis were a queer family to have made so deep an impression on English art and literature. The father was an Italian poet, a political refugee who became a professor at King's College; the mother was half Italian. There were four children born within a year of each other. The oldest, Maria Francesca Rossetti, became a nun. The elder son, Dante Gabriel Rossetti, soon established himself as a painter, poet, and head of a furiously controversial group. The second son, William Michael, was an art critic and man of letters, editor of THE GERM. Christina Georgina Rossetti, youngest of the children, became a devout and purely lyrical poet.

Born in London, May 12, 1828, Dante Gabriel Rossetti grew up in the "strange society of Italian exiles and English eccentrics which his father had gathered about him." He wrote and illustrated his own poems even as a child. At twenty, ambitious to design great allegories, he became a pupil of the artist Ford Madox Brown; Brown made him draw pickle jars. But Rossetti was impatient for public notice. A few months later, he gathered about him a group of students and organized the Pre-Raphaelite Brotherhood as a revolt from current academic standards and a protest against an accelerated industrialism. The name, intimating that the art of painting had declined with Raphael, began as a slogan and became a trade-mark.

Rossetti's paintings set the standard for the group. They were realistic in detail yet vaguely symbolic in effect, full of odd "off" colors and a sexless sensuality. The matching poetry was equally sultry and languid. The Brotherhood was violently attacked, even by Charles Dickens, as "ugly," "impertinent," "sacrilegious." But Rossetti was undisturbed; he was seeking not only "perfect fidelity" but the perfect model. He found the latter in Elizabeth Siddall. She was seventeen, a milliner's assistant, tall, with gray-green eyes and hair "like dazzling copper," delicately built and slightly tubercular. She became Rossetti's mistress and the Brotherhood's favorite model. It was presumed that Rossetti and Elizabeth Siddall were engaged, but Rossetti waited ten years before he married her. Her health became steadily worse and her husband more difficult. She took laudanum in ever-increasing quantities. Two years after the marriage Rossetti came home and found his wife dying of an overdose of the drug. It was never known whether her death was accidental or suicidal. Overcome with grief, and possibly remorse, Rossetti put all his love poems in the casket. Nine years later, in order to bring out a collection of his poems, the coffin was dug up and the manuscript exhumed.

FROM

The House of Life

LOVE-SIGHT

When do I see thee most, beloved one?
When in the light the spirits of mine eyes
Before thy face, their altar, solemnize
The worship of that Love through thee made known?
Or when, in the dusk hours (we two alone),
Close-kissed and eloquent of still replies
Thy twilight-hidden glimmering visage lies,
And my soul only sees thy soul its own?

O love, my love! if I no more should see
Thyself, nor on the earth the shadow of thee,
Nor image of thine eyes in any spring,—
How then should sound upon Life's darkening slope
The ground-whirl of the perished leaves of Hope,
The wind of Death's imperishable wing?

SILENT NOON

Your hands lie open in the long fresh grass,
The finger-points look through like rosy blooms;
Your eyes smile peace. The pasture gleams and glooms
'Neath billowing skies that scatter and amass.
All round our nest, far as the eye can pass,
Are golden kingcup-fields with silver edge
Where the cow-parsley skirts the hawthorn-hedge.
'Tis visible silence, still as the hour-glass.

Deep in the sun-searched growths the dragon-fly
Hangs like a blue thread loosened from the sky:—
So this winged hour is dropt to us from above.
Oh! clasp we to our hearts, for deathless dower,
This close-companioned inarticulate hour
When twofold silence was the song of love.

BODY'S BEAUTY

Of Adam's first wife, Lilith, it is told
(The witch he loved before the gift of Eve,)
That, ere the snake's, her sweet tongue could deceive,
And her enchanted hair was the first gold.
And still she sits, young while the earth is old,
And, subtly of herself contemplative,
Draws men to watch the bright net she can weave,
Till heart and body and life are in its hold.

The rose and poppy are her flowers; for where
Is he not found, O Lilith, whom shed scent
And soft-shed kisses and soft sleep shall snare?
Lo! as that youth's eyes burned at thine, so went
Thy spell through him, and left his straight neck bent,
And round his heart one strangling golden hair.

Sudden Light

I have been here before,
　　But when or how I cannot tell:
I know the grass beyond the door,
　　The sweet keen smell,
The sighing sound, the lights around the shore.

You have been mine before,—
　　How long ago I may not know:
But just when at that swallow's soar
　　Your neck turned so,
Some veil did fall,—I knew it all of yore.

Has this been thus before?
　　And shall not thus time's eddying flight
Still with our lives our loves restore
　　In death's despite,
And day and night yield one delight once more?

After his wife's death Rossetti continued to work in many mediums. Besides mingling the arts of writing and painting, he made designs for stained glass and murals. His reputation mounted, his income rose to three thousand pounds a year, but he grew more and more depressed. Gloomy and suspicious, he drew near the edge of insanity; he lived on fantasy and narcotics. Shunning people, he cultivated the society of beasts. Deluding himself that his wife's spirit was reincarnated in some animal, his home became a menagerie. At various times he housed woodchucks, owls, an Irish deerhound, a raven (in homage of Poe), an Australian opossum that slept in a centerpiece on the table, a white peacock that died under a sofa, a zebu, and (without humorous intent) a laughing jackass. A raccoon lived in a bureau drawer, and an armadillo gnawed its way out through a neighbor's kitchen. A prey to insomnia, Rossetti found a new drug, chloral, which made him still more melancholy and accelerated his end. He died April 9, 1882, while his best book, BALLADS AND SONNETS, was being printed.

Rossetti is not only a poet's poet, but a painter's poet. His verse is composed as though for a canvas—rich, and sometimes stiff, with color. Instead of being "fleshly," as was once charged, it is disembodied, unearthly, and hypnotic. Its supernatural overtones recall Poe, and Rossetti was not unaware of the influence. THE BLESSED DAMOZEL, Rossetti's most famous poem, was written as a complement to THE RAVEN. "I saw at once," Rossetti said, "that Poe had done the utmost it was possible to do with the grief of the lover on earth; I determined to reverse the conditions, and give utterance to the yearning of the loved one in heaven." Rossetti thereupon created not only a more mystical poem than his model, but a far more beautiful one.

The Blessed Damozel

The blessed damozel leaned out
  From the gold bar of Heaven;
Her eyes were deeper than the depth
  Of waters stilled at even;
She had three lilies in her hand,
  And the stars in her hair were seven.

Her robe, ungirt from clasp to hem,
  No wrought flowers did adorn,

But a white rose of Mary's gift,
    For service meetly worn;
Her hair that lay along her back
    Was yellow like ripe corn.

Herseemed she scarce had been a day
    One of God's choristers;
The wonder was not yet quite gone
    From that still look of hers;
Albeit, to them she left, her day
    Had counted as ten years.

(To one, it is ten years of years.
    . . . Yet now, and in this place,
Surely she leaned o'er me—her hair
    Fell all about my face. . . .
Nothing: the autumn fall of leaves.
    The whole year sets apace.)

It was the rampart of God's house
    That she was standing on;
By God built over the sheer depth
    The which is Space begun;
So high, that looking downward thence
    She scarce could see the sun.

It lies in Heaven, across the flood
    Of ether, as a bridge.
Beneath the tides of day and night
    With flame and darkness ridge
The void, as low as where this earth
    Spins like a fretful midge.

Around her, lovers, newly met
    'Mid deathless love's acclaims,
Spoke evermore among themselves
    Their heart-remembered names;
And the souls mounting up to God
    Went by her like thin flames.

And still she bowed herself and stooped
    Out of the circling charm;
Until her bosom must have made
    The bar she leaned on warm,
And the lilies lay as if asleep
    Along her bended arm.

From the fixed place of Heaven she saw
   Time like a pulse shake fierce
Through all the worlds. Her gaze still strove
   Within the gulf to pierce
Its path; and now she spoke as when
   The stars sang in their spheres.

The sun was gone now; the curled moon
   Was like a little feather
Fluttering far down the gulf; and now
   She spoke through the still weather.
Her voice was like the voice the stars
   Had when they sang together.

(Ah sweet! Even now, in that bird's song,
   Strove not her accents there,
Fain to be hearkened? When those bells
   Possessed the mid-day air,
Strove not her steps to reach my side
   Down all the echoing stair?)

"I wish that he were come to me,
   For he will come," she said.
"Have I not prayed in Heaven?—on earth,
   Lord, Lord, has he not prayed?
Are not two prayers a perfect strength?
   And shall I feel afraid?

"When round his head the aureole clings,
   And he is clothed in white,
I'll take his hand and go with him
   To the deep wells of light;
As unto a stream we will step down,
   And bathe there in God's sight.

"We two will stand beside that shrine,
   Occult, withheld, untrod,
Whose lamps are stirred continually
   With prayer sent up to God;
And see our old prayers, granted, melt
   Each like a little cloud.

"We two will lie i' the shadow of
   That living mystic tree
Within whose secret growth the Dove
   Is sometimes felt to be.

While every leaf that His plumes touch
  Saith His Name audibly.

"And I myself will teach to him,
  I myself, lying so,
The songs I sing here; which his voice
  Shall pause in, hushed and slow,
And find some knowledge at each pause,
  Or some new thing to know."

(Alas! We two, we two, thou say'st!
  Yea, one wast thou with me
That once of old. But shall God lift
  To endless unity
The soul whose likeness with thy soul
  Was but its love for thee?)

"We two," she said, "will seek the groves
  Where the lady Mary is,
With her five handmaidens, whose names
  Are five sweet symphonies,
Cecily, Gertrude, Magdalen,
  Margaret and Rosalys.

"Circlewise sit they, with bound locks
  And foreheads garlanded;
Into the fine cloth white like flame
  Weaving the golden thread,
To fashion the birth-robes for them
  Who are just born, being dead.

"He shall fear, haply, and be dumb:
  Then will I lay my cheek
To his, and tell about our love,
  Not once abashed or weak:
And the dear Mother will approve
  My pride, and let me speak.

"Herself shall bring us, hand in hand,
  To Him round whom all souls
Kneel, the clear-ranged unnumbered heads
  Bowed with their aureoles:
And angels meeting us shall sing
  To their citherns and citoles.

"There will I ask of Christ the Lord
   Thus much for him and me:—
Only to live as once on earth
   With Love, only to be,
As then awhile, for ever now
   Together, I and he."

She gazed and listened and then said,
   Less sad of speech than mild:—
"All this is when he comes." She ceased.
   The light thrilled towards her, filled
With angels in strong level flight.
   Her eyes prayed, and she smiled.

(I saw her smile.) But soon their path
   Was vague in distant spheres:
And then she cast her arms along
   The golden barriers,
And laid her face between her hands,
   And wept. (I heard her tears.)

CHRISTINA ROSSETTI
[1830–1894]

CHRISTINA GEORGINA, youngest of the Rossettis, was born December 5, 1830, in London. Although her mother was half English, her father was wholly Italian, a famous scholar in exile, and the Rossetti household was crowded with literary refugees, "good-natured Neapolitans, keen Tuscans, and emphatic Romans." The melodic Italian speech must have inspired Christina Rossetti's musical verse, for at twelve she was writing English lyrics of singular fluency. Unpretentious and devoted, neither she nor her work was happy. Differing from her Bohemian brother, Dante Gabriel, and more like her older sister, who became a nun, she found the world evil. She repudiated pleasure: "I cannot possibly use the word 'happy' without meaning something beyond this present life."

UPHILL, one of her most famous poems, expresses her prevailing attitude with dignity and pathos. The lines owe their appeal, as Viola Meynell wrote, "to the simplicity which could reduce the

whole struggle of man to that single day's faring along a road, with
an inn and its open door at the end."

Uphill

Does the road wind uphill all the way?
   Yes, to the very end.
Will the day's journey take the whole long day?
   From morn to night, my friend.

But is there for the night a resting-place?
   A roof for when the slow dark hours begin.
May not the darkness hide it from my face?
   You cannot miss that inn.

Shall I meet other wayfarers at night?
   Those who have gone before.
Then must I knock, or call when just in sight?
   They will not keep you standing at that door.

Shall I find comfort, travel-sore and weak?
   Of labor you shall find the sum.
Will there be beds for me and all who seek?
   Yea, beds for all who come.

Twice she refused to marry because of religious scruples. Baptized
in the Church of England, she dismissed James Collinson, a minor
Pre-Raphaelite, because he was a Catholic convert. Later, in love
with Charles Cayley, a scholar of her own faith, she feared marriage
with one who did not seem to be "religious enough." Spiritually
committed to the Heavenly Bridegroom, she could not surrender
to any earthly lover. Confident neither of self nor of salvation, she
became a recluse; for fifteen years she rarely spent a night away
from her mother.

Suffering from a chronic weakness of heart most of her life,
Christina Rossetti never ceased ministering to the poor. In her
early sixties she was operated on for cancer, but the inevitable end
was only postponed. She died, literally in the act of prayer, De-
cember 29, 1894.

Christina Rossetti's spirit persists in her poetry. The verse, limited
in range, is exquisite in phrase, flexible in music. Slight in form,

transparent in texture, it defies analysis. One of the most reticent spirits, she was also one of the few women whose lyrics and sonnets will survive.

A Birthday

My heart is like a singing bird
    Whose nest is in a watered shoot;
My heart is like an apple-tree
    Whose boughs are bent with thick-set fruit;
My heart is like a rainbow shell
    That paddles in a halcyon sea;
My heart is gladder than all these
    Because my love is come to me.

Raise me a dais of silk and down;
    Hang it with vair and purple dyes;
Carve it in doves and pomegranates,
    And peacocks with a hundred eyes;
Work it in gold and silver grapes,
    In leaves and silver fleur-de-lys;
Because the birthday of my life
    Is come, my love is come to me.

When I Am Dead, My Dearest

When I am dead, my dearest,
Sing no sad songs for me;
Plant thou no roses at my head,
Nor shady cypress-tree:
Be the green grass above me
With showers and dewdrops wet;
And if thou wilt, remember,
And if thou wilt, forget.

I shall not see the shadows,
I shall not feel the rain;
I shall not hear the nightingale
Sing on, as if in pain:
And dreaming through the twilight
That doth not rise nor set,
Haply I may remember,
And haply may forget.

Aloof

The irresponsive silence of the land,
The irresponsive sounding of the sea,
Speak both one message of one sense to me:—
"Aloof, aloof, we stand aloof; so stand
Thou too aloof bound with the flawless band
Of inner solitude; we bind not thee.
But who from thy self-chain shall set thee free?
What heart shall touch thy heart? what hand thy hand?"

And I am sometimes proud and sometimes meek,
And sometimes I remember days of old
When fellowship seemed not so far to seek
And all the world and I seemed much less cold,
And at the rainbow's foot lay surely gold,
And hope felt strong and life itself not weak.

Remember

Remember me when I am gone away,
Gone far away into the silent land;
When you can no more hold me by the hand,
Nor I half turn to go, yet turning stay.
Remember me when no more, day by day,
You tell me of our future that you planned;
Only remember me; you understand
It will be late to counsel then or pray.

Yet if you should forget me for a while
And afterwards remember, do not grieve;
For if the darkness and corruption leave
A vestige of the thoughts that once I had,
Better by far you should forget and smile
Than that you should remember and be sad.

Rest

O Earth, lie heavily upon her eyes;
Seal her sweet eyes weary of watching, Earth;
Lie close around her: leave no room for mirth
With its harsh laughter, nor for sound of sighs.

She hath no questions, she hath no replies,
Hushed in and curtained with a blessèd dearth
Of all that irked her from the hour of birth;
With stillness that is almost Paradise.

Darkness more clear than noonday holdeth her,
Silence more musical than any song;
Even her very heart has ceased to stir.
Until the morning of Eternity
Her rest shall not begin nor end, but be;
And when she wakes she will not think it long.

SLEEPING AT LAST is as characteristic as it is appropriately named.
The poem, Christina Rossetti's last, was written shortly before her
death.

Sleeping at Last

Sleeping at last, the struggle and horror past,
Sleeping at last, the trouble and tumult over,
Cold and white, out of sight of friend and of lover,
Sleeping at last.

No more a tired heart downcast or overcast,
No more pangs that wring or shifting fears that hover,
Sleeping at last in a dreamless sleep locked fast.

Fast asleep. Singing birds in their leafy cover
Cannot wake her, nor shake her the gusty blast.
Under the purple thyme and the purple clover
Sleeping at last.

EMILY DICKINSON
[1830–1886]

THE two greatest women poets of the century were strangely
paired. Born in the same year, the English Christina Rossetti
and the American Emily Dickinson matched each other and were
each other's integral opposite. Their outer lives were strikingly simi-

lar: both women were abnormally reticent; both loved deeply but remained unmarried; both secluded themselves from the world. But the mingling of frustration and resignation was wholly different in their expressions. Christina Rossetti wrote as a devout Anglican who abased herself before God; Emily Dickinson disclosed herself as a protesting Puritan who challenged the Deity. Christina Rossetti's tone is melancholy, a sadness that affects the soul but never probes the intellect; Emily Dickinson's note is sharp and impertinent, yet searchingly introspective. In technique the differences are even more marked. The Englishwoman's verse is formal, traditional in pattern and phrase. The American woman's poetry is experimental, reckless in rhyme and audacious in idiom.

Emily Dickinson's biography is brief and almost bare of events. She was born December 10, 1830, in Amherst, Massachusetts, and at Amherst she lived, except for a few excursions, all her fifty-six years. At seventeen she entered South Hadley Female Seminary a few miles from town, disliked it at once, and, a determined rebel, returned home. At twenty-three she spent a few weeks in Washington with her father, whom she adored, and visited in Philadelphia. After her return to Amherst, she became a recluse. She rarely crossed her threshold; even in the house, visitors saw her only as a figure vanishing down a corridor. Little was known of her except that she was an indefatigable letter writer but made others address her envelopes, that she always wore white but refused to be fitted for her clothes, and that her gifts of cookies and garden flowers were usually accompanied by a few cryptic lines of verse. She became the village oddity, and died of Bright's disease, May 15, 1886, in the house in which she was born.

Three biographers published mutually contradictory accounts of the event which made Emily Dickinson a hermit. Two of the stories were sensational; only one, guardedly related by her niece, Martha Dickinson Bianchi, was plausible. Further research by George F. Whicher made it plain that, in Philadelphia, Emily Dickinson fell in love with the Reverend Charles Wadsworth, who was married, and only three or four meetings took place. "So we must keep apart," she wrote at the end of one of her secret poems:

> With just the door ajar
> That oceans are,
> And prayer,
> And that pale sustenance,
> Despair.

There was no love affair in the ordinary sense, but the poet felt herself dedicated to the man's spirit, if not to the man. It is possible that the pastor was unconscious of the profound emotion he had awakened; it is also possible that the poet was dramatizing her abnegation and grief. But the love poems are there, greater than the experience, poignant, transfigured, among the finest poems ever written by a woman.

The Soul Selects

The soul selects her own society,
Then shuts the door;
On her divine majority
Obtrude no more.

Unmoved, she notes the chariots pausing
At her low gate;
Unmoved, an emperor is kneeling
Upon her mat.

I've known her from an ample nation
Choose one;
Then close the valves of her attention
Like stone.

My Life Closed Twice

My life closed twice before its close;
It yet remains to see
If Immortality unveil
A third event to me,

So huge, so hopeless to conceive,
As these that twice befell.
Parting is all we know of heaven,
And all we need of hell.

Of All the Souls That Stand Create

Of all the souls that stand create
I have elected one.
When sense from spirit files away,
And subterfuge is done;

When that which is and that which was
Apart, intrinsic, stand,
And this brief tragedy of flesh
Is shifted like a sand;

When figures show their royal front
And mists are carved away—
Behold the atom I preferred
To all the lists of clay!

Although love was a preoccupation, it was not Emily Dickinson's single, or even dominating, theme. Alone and disdainful of notice, she ranged the universe. During her life only four of her poems appeared in print, and these were published "by stealth," without her knowledge. After her death more than one thousand poems were unearthed, most of them hidden in boxes and bureau drawers; many are still unpublished. Six volumes appeared posthumously, the first in 1890, the most recent as late as 1935. Originally her editors divided the poems, none of which bore a title, into four categories: Life, Love, Nature, Time and Eternity. In each of the groups the paradoxical poet is supreme, a mystic and a madcap. She announces whimsically:

To make a prairie it takes a clover and one bee—
And revery.
The revery alone will do
If bees are few.

Her profundities are always achieved with nimble delicacy. Lightnings "skip like mice" and intuitions flash from her pages casually, almost inconsequentially.

The Mountains Grow Unnoticed

The mountains grow unnoticed,
Their purple figures rise
Without attempt, exhaustion,
Assistance or applause.

In their eternal faces
The sun with broad delight
Looks long—and last—and golden,
For fellowship at night.

Nowhere in poetry is there a style more precise and unpredictable. Exact observation heightened by accurate fancy reveals the hummingbird as "a resonance of emerald," the wind "tapping like a tired man," a dog's "belated" feet like "intermittent plush," a gentlewoman's "dimity convictions," frost as "the blond assassin," Indian summer repeating "the old, old sophistries of June." Everywhere there is an appropriateness which is both discriminating and startling.

I Never Saw a Moor

I never saw a moor,
I never saw the sea;
Yet know I how the heather looks,
And what a wave must be.

I never spoke with God,
Nor visited in Heaven;
Yet certain am I of the spot
As if the chart were given.

Apparently With No Surprise

Apparently with no surprise
To any happy flower,
The frost beheads it at its play
In accidental power.

The blond assassin passes on;
The sun proceeds unmoved
To measure off another day
For an approving God.

The Heart Asks Pleasure First

The heart asks pleasure first;
And then, excuse from pain;
And then, those little anodynes
That deaden suffering;

And then, to go to sleep;
And then, if it should be
The will of its Inquisitor,
The liberty to die.

There Is No Frigate Like a Book

There is no frigate like a book
To take us lands away,
Nor any courser like a page
Of prancing poetry.

This traverse may the poorest take
Without oppress of toll;
How frugal is the chariot
That bears a human soul!

Although her experiences were few, Emily Dickinson ventured further than most of her contemporaries in the uncharted territory of the mind. She dared the darkness with a light but confident foot, an explorer whose compass was divination.

LEWIS CARROLL
[1832–1898]

THE two greatest English masters of nonsense were also masters in arts and sciences which were anything but nonsensical. The maddest verbal music in the language was perfected by Edward Lear, a topographical landscape painter. His successor in inspired nonsense was Lewis Carroll, a university lecturer, a noted mathematician, and a deacon in holy orders.

Lewis Carroll was born Charles Lutwidge Dodgson in Cheshire, January 27, 1832. He entered Christ Church College at nineteen, became a deacon at twenty-nine, and lectured on mathematics at Oxford for twenty-six years. He published many treatises under such alluring titles as THE FORMULAE OF PLANE TRIGONOMETRY and A SYLLABUS of ALGEBRAICAL GEOMETRY. It is said that when Queen Victoria discovered that Dodgson was the author of ALICE'S ADVENTURES IN WONDERLAND, she made it known that more of the author's work would be acceptable to the royal eye. Dodgson thereupon presented the Queen with AN ELEMENTARY TREATISE ON DETERMINANTS.

Fond of children, and particularly attached to young Alice Liddell, Dodgson, using the pseudonym of "Lewis Carroll," wrote a series of books which are appreciated far more by sophisticated maturity than by the children to whom they were addressed. This is understandable, for Lewis Carroll's nonsense is not only logical but symbolical. THROUGH THE LOOKING-GLASS is an elaborately disguised game of chess, and the whimsical rhymes which appear through Carroll's volumes for uncritical youngsters are, for the most part, critical parodies of the didactic poems of the period. THE CROCODILE, from ALICE'S ADVENTURES IN WONDERLAND, is a burlesque of Isaac Watts's moral stanzas AGAINST IDLENESS AND MISCHIEF beginning:

> How doth the little busy bee
> Improve each shining hour,
> And gather honey all the day
> From every opening flower!

The Crocodile

How doth the little crocodile
  Improve his shining tail,
And pour the waters of the Nile
  On every shining scale!

How cheerfully he seems to grin,
  How neatly spreads his claws,
And welcomes little fishes in
  With gently smiling jaws!

Carroll's lines beginning "Twinkle, twinkle, little bat" is a joke on Jane Taylor, author of ORIGINAL POEMS FOR INFANT MINDS. The captivating FATHER WILLIAM, a seemingly irresponsible set of rhymes, is actually a satire. It is a brilliant if cruel caricature of Robert Southey's THE OLD MAN'S COMFORTS, AND HOW HE GAINED THEM, which begins:

"You are old, Father William," the young man cried,
  "The few locks which are left you are gray;
You are hale, Father William, a hearty old man,
  Now tell me the reason, I pray."

"In the days of my youth," Father William replied,
  "I remembered that youth would fly fast,
And abused not my health, and my vigor at first,
  That I never might need them at last."

Carroll's "hearty old man" is anything but the sanctimonious babbler of Southey's poem. His logic is even more startling than his vigor.

Father William

"You are old, Father William," the young man said,
  "And your hair has become very white;
And yet you incessantly stand on your head—
  Do you think, at your age, it is right?"

"In my youth," Father William replied to his son,
 "I feared it might injure the brain;
But, now that I'm perfectly sure I have none,
 Why, I do it again and again."

"You are old," said the youth, "as I mentioned before,
 And have grown most uncommonly fat;
Yet you turned a back-somersault in at the door—
 Pray, what is the reason of that?"

"In my youth," said the sage, as he shook his gray locks,
 "I kept all my limbs very supple
By the use of this ointment—one shilling the box—
 Allow me to sell you a couple?"

"You are old," said the youth, "and your jaws are too weak
 For anything tougher than suet;
Yet you finished the goose, with the bones and the beak—
 Pray, how did you manage to do it?"

"In my youth," said his father, "I took to the law,
 And argued each case with my wife;
And the muscular strength which it gave to my jaw
 Has lasted the rest of my life."

"You are old," said the youth, "one would hardly suppose
 That your eye was as steady as ever;
Yet you balanced an eel on the end of your nose—
 What made you so awfully clever?"

"I have answered three questions, and that is enough,"
 Said his father. "Don't give yourself airs!
Do you think I can listen all day to such stuff?
 Be off, or I'll kick you down-stairs!"

Even JABBERWOCKY, from THROUGH THE LOOKING-GLASS, is logical
in its puzzling language. Carroll furnished a glossary of the in-
vented words, paraphrasing the proverb about pence and pounds:
"Take care of the sounds and the sense will take care of itself."
Some of the words have ceased to be nonsense—"chortle" and
"burble" for example—and have become part of our vocabulary.
Carroll declared that many of the adjectives were "portmanteau
words"—two meanings packed into one word, such as *slithy: lithe*
and *slimy,* and *frumious,* a combination of *fuming* and *furious.*

Jabberwocky

'Twas brillig, and the slithy toves
    Did gyre and gimble in the wabe:
All mimsy were the borogoves,
    And the mome raths outgrabe.

"Beware the Jabberwock, my son!
    The jaws that bite, the claws that catch!
Beware the Jubjub bird, and shun
    The frumious Bandersnatch!"

He took his vorpal sword in hand;
    Long time the manxome foe he sought—
So rested he by the Tumtum tree,
    And stood awhile in thought.

And, as in uffish thought he stood,
    The Jabberwock, with eyes of flame,
Came whiffling through the tulgey wood,
    And burbled as it came!

One, two! One, two! And through and through
    The vorpal blade went snicker-snack!
He left it dead, and with its head
    He went galumphing back.

"And hast thou slain the Jabberwock?
    Come to my arms, my beamish boy!
O frabjous day! Callooh, Callay!"
    He chortled in his joy.

'Twas brillig, and the slithy toves
    Did gyre and gimble in the wabe:
All mimsy were the borogoves,
    And the mome raths outgrabe.

Dodgson always kept himself apart from Carroll. To the last he refused to be identified with his pseudonym. Nevertheless, he continued to invent a kind of nonsense which was mathematically precise, to design ingenious games, problems, and memory systems, as though, wrote Eleanor Farjeon, "most of the affairs of life could

be conducted delightfully through a series of games and tricks."
He died at Guildford, January 14, 1898.

W. S. GILBERT
[1836–1911]

THE names of Gilbert and Sullivan suggest a union as close as
the Siamese Twins or, since they were separable, an attachment
no less traditional than Beaumont and Fletcher. Yet the two
friends had divergent aims, quarreled about careers, and parted
over a triviality.

William Schwenck Gilbert, the librettist of the partnership, was
born November 18, 1836, in London. He was educated at King's
College, became a militia officer, a clerk in the Privy Council office,
and a practicing lawyer. In his twenty-fifth year he began writing
for the magazine FUN, making his own drawings. His combination
of verses and drawings, later christened THE BAB BALLADS, reminded
some critics of Edward Lear, but Gilbert owed nothing to any
model. "For THE BAB BALLADS," Deems Taylor wrote recently, "Gil-
bert invented a new race of people, creatures who were not so much
caricatures of existing humans as a strange, autochthonous goblin
species that was like nothing on land or sea. . . . In insane reasona-
bleness THE BAB BALLADS are surpassed only by the two ALICE books."
One of the best, and possibly the most famous of THE BAB BALLADS,
was rejected by PUNCH on the ground that it was "too cannibalistic
for its readers' tastes." It was THE YARN OF THE "NANCY BELL."

The Yarn of the "Nancy Bell"

'T was on the shores that round our coast
   From Deal to Ramsgate span,
That I found alone on a piece of stone
   An elderly naval man.

His hair was weedy, his beard was long,
   And weedy and long was he,
And I heard this wight on the shore recite,
   In a singular minor key:

"Oh, I am a cook and the captain bold,
    And the mate of the *Nancy* brig,
And a bo'sun tight, and a midshipmite,
    And the crew of the captain's gig."

And he shook his fists and he tore his hair,
    Till I really felt afraid,
For I couldn't help thinking the man had been drinking,
    And so I simply said:

"Oh, elderly man, it's little I know
    Of the duties of men of the sea,
And I'll eat my hand if I understand
    How you can possibly be

"At once a cook, and a captain bold,
    And the mate of the *Nancy* brig,
And a bo'sun tight, and midshipmite,
    And the crew of the captain's gig."

Then he gave a hitch to his trousers, which
    Is a trick all seamen larn,
And having got rid of a thumping quid,
    He spun this painful yarn:

" 'T was in the good ship *Nancy Bell*
    That we sailed to the Indian Sea,
And there on a reef we come to grief,
    Which has often occurred to me.

"And pretty nigh all the crew was drowned
    (There was seventy-seven o' soul),
And only ten of the *Nancy's* men
    Said 'Here!' to the muster-roll.

"There was me and the cook and the captain bold,
    And the mate of the *Nancy* brig,
And the bo'sun tight, and a midshipmite,
    And the crew of the captain's gig.

"For a month we'd neither wittles nor drink,
    Till a-hungry we did feel,
So we drawed a lot, and accordin' shot
    The captain for our meal.

"The next lot fell to the *Nancy's* mate,
 And a delicate dish he made;
Then our appetite with the midshipmite
 We seven survivors stayed.

"And then we murdered the bo'sun tight,
 And he much resembled pig;
Then we wittled free, did the cook and me,
 On the crew of the captain's gig.

"Then only the cook and me was left,
 And the delicate question, 'Which
Of us two goes to the kettle?' arose,
 And we argued it out as sich.

"For I loved that cook as a brother, I did,
 And the cook he worshipped me;
But we'd both be blowed if we'd either be stowed
 In the other chap's hold, you see.

" 'I'll be eat if you dines off me,' says Tom.
 'Yes, that,' says I, 'you'll be,—
I'm boiled if I die, my friend,' quoth I.
 And 'Exactly so,' quoth he.

"Says he, 'Dear James, to murder me
 Were a foolish thing to do,
For don't you see that you can't cook *me*,
 While I can—and will—cook *you!*'

"So he boils the water, and takes the salt
 And the pepper in portions true
(Which he never forgot), and some chopped **shalot**,
 And some sage and parsley too.

" 'Come here,' says he, with a proper pride,
 Which his smiling features tell,
' 'T will soothing be if I let you see
 How extremely nice you'll smell.'

"And he stirred it round and round and **round**,
 And he sniffed at the foaming froth;
When I ups with his heels, and smothers his **squeals**
 In the scum of the boiling broth.

"And I eat that cook in a week or less,
   And—as I eating be
The last of his chops, why, I almost drops,
   For a vessel in sight I see.

.   .   .   .   .   .

"And I never larf, and I never smile,
   And I never lark nor play,
But sit and croak, and a single joke
   I have—which is to say:

"Oh, I am a cook and a captain bold,
   And the mate of the *Nancy* brig,
And a bo'sun tight, and midshipmite,
   And the crew of the captain's gig!"

In his thirty-first year, Gilbert turned to the stage and wrote pantomimes, melodramas, burlesques, and sentimental pieces. Ten years later he met the ideal partner, Arthur Sullivan, and the two men collaborated on the most brilliant series of light operas ever composed. Many of the plots were taken from THE BAB BALLADS, enlarged, and pointed at the foibles of the day. The Gilbert and Sullivan operas were hilariously received and enjoyed no less because of their social criticism. PINAFORE is still a sardonic commentary on political officeholders. PATIENCE ridicules the pretentions of every aesthetic "school." IOLANTHE mocks blue blood in general and stuffy, somnolent peers in particular.

The House of Lords

When Britain *really* ruled the waves
   (In good Queen Bess's time)
The House of Peers made no pretence
To intellectual eminence
   Or scholarship sublime;
Yet Britain won her proudest bays
In good Queen Bess's glorious days.

When Wellington thrashed Bonaparte,
   As every child can tell,
The House of Peers throughout the war
Did nothing in particular

And did it very well;
Yet Britain set the world ablaze
In good King George's glorious days.

And while the House of Peers withholds
  Its legislative hand,
And noble statesmen do not itch
To interfere with matters which
  They do not understand,
As bright will shine Great Britain's rays
As in King George's glorious days.

from IOLANTHE

A Policeman's Lot

When a felon's not engaged in his employment,
  Or maturing his felonious little plans,
His capacity for innocent enjoyment
  Is just as great as any honest man's.
Our feelings we with difficulty smother
  When constabulary duty's to be done;
Ah, take one consideration with another,
  A policeman's lot is not a happy one.

When the enterprising burglar's not a-burgling,
  When the cut-throat isn't occupied in crime,
He loves to hear the little brook a-gurgling,
  And listen to the merry village chime.
When the coster's finished jumping on his mother,
  He loves to lie a-basking in the sun;
Ah, take one consideration with another,
  A policeman's lot is not a happy one.

from THE PIRATES OF PENZANCE

Unusually dexterous in technique, Gilbert's light verse has been the delight and despair of a hundred imitators. His rhymes are as astounding as they are fresh; his meters are tricky but exact; the ideas nonchalantly mingle absurdity and satire. A librettist by profession, Gilbert was a writer of true lyrics by instinct.

To the Terrestrial Globe

BY A MISERABLE WRETCH

Roll on, thou ball, roll on!
Through pathless realms of Space
    Roll on!
What though I'm in a sorry case?
What though I cannot meet my bills?
What though I suffer toothache's ills?
What though I swallow countless pills?
    Never *you* mind!
    Roll on!

Roll on, thou ball, roll on!
Through seas of inky air
    Roll on!
It's true I've got no shirts to wear;
It's true my butcher's bill is due;
It's true my prospects all look blue—
But don't let that unsettle you!
    Never *you* mind!
    Roll on!
             [It rolls on.]

In 1911 Gilbert was entertaining two young ladies near his home. They went swimming; one of the young women found herself out of her depth and cried for help. Although Gilbert was over seventy-four, he plunged in and attempted to rescue her. The exertion was too much for him. He died of heart failure May 29, 1911.

ALGERNON CHARLES SWINBURNE
[1837–1909]

ALGERNON CHARLES SWINBURNE has been more variously described than any other poet of his century. Edmund Gosse pictured him, with his thin body, waving red hair, and birdlike head, as a brilliant but ridiculous flamingo. T. Earle Welby likened him to a pagan apparition at a Victorian tea party, "leaping onto the sleek lawn to stamp its goat foot in challenge, to deride with its screech of laughter the admirable decorum of the conversation."

The personality who, according to Edgell Rickword, "shattered the virginal reticence of Victoria's serenest years with a book of poems," was born in London April 5, 1837. His forebears were distinguished aristocrats. His father was an admiral, descendant of an old Northumbrian family; his grandfather was Sir John Edward Swinburne; his mother was the daughter of the third Earl of Ashburnham. Spoiled and precocious, Swinburne attended Eton and Oxford without being graduated from either. He fell in love with medievalism and its interpretation by the Pre-Raphaelites. In his early twenties he attempted to outdo the excesses of the young Bohemians, and was successful, although at great cost to his physique and character. His unusually frail hands and delicate features gave him an elfin look, which was belied by his appetite for alcohol. He was, however, not a robust drinker, and soon passed into a state of unconsciousness. It is said that Rossetti always pinned his address to his coat collar so that Swinburne would be sure of being delivered to his own home.

At twenty-three Swinburne published his first volume, two poetic dramas dedicated to Rossetti. The blank verse was fluent, and the interspersed lyrics were graceful, but the critics were not impressed. Five years later there appeared his ATALANTA IN CALYDON, and the critics squandered their superlatives. In ATALANTA IN CALYDON Swinburne attempted to "reproduce for English readers the likeness of a Greek tragedy with something of its true poetic life and charm." But the exuberance was anything but Greek, and the mounting syllables carried a sumptuous and orchestral music new to English ears. The spirit was rebellious, a defiance of the creeds by which men live, but it was the melodiousness which made the young men of the period shout the choruses to each other. The pure extravagance, the happy (if too insistent) alliteration—the "lisp of leaves and ripple of rain," the "leaf to flower and flower to fruit" —and the unflagging verve created an effect of magic to which we are not yet immune.

When the Hounds of Spring

When the hounds of spring are on winter's traces,
    The mother of months in meadow or plain
Fills the shadows and windy places
    With lisp of leaves and ripple of rain;
And the brown bright nightingale amorous
Is half assuaged for Itylus,
For the Thracian ships and the foreign faces,
    The tongueless vigil, and all the pain.

Come with bows bent and with emptying of quivers,
    Maiden most perfect, lady of light,
With a noise of winds and many rivers,
    With a clamor of waters, and with might;
Bind on thy sandals, O thou most fleet,
Over the splendor and speed of thy feet;
For the faint east quickens, the wan west shivers,
    Round the feet of the day and the feet of the night.

Where shall we find her, how shall we sing to her,
    Fold our hands round her knees, and cling?
O that man's heart were as fire and could spring to her,
    Fire, or the strength of the streams that spring!
For the stars and the winds are unto her
As raiment, as songs of the harp-player;
For the risen stars and the fallen cling to her,
    And the southwest-wind and the west-wind sing.

For winter's rains and ruins are over,
    And all the season of snows and sins;
The days dividing lover and lover,
    The light that loses, the night that wins;
And time remembered is grief forgotten,
And frosts are slain and flowers begotten,
And in green underwood and cover
    Blossom by blossom the spring begins.

The full streams feed on flower of rushes,
    Ripe grasses trammel a traveling foot,
The faint fresh flame of the young year flushes
    From leaf to flower and flower to fruit;

And fruit and leaf are as gold and fire,
And the oat is heard above the lyre,
And the hoofed heel of a satyr crushes
    The chestnut-husk at the chestnut-root.

And Pan by noon and Bacchus by night,
    Fleeter of foot than the fleet-foot kid,
Follows with dancing and fills with delight
    The Maenad and the Bassarid;
And soft as lips that laugh and hide
The laughing leaves of the trees divide,
And screen from seeing and leave in sight
    The god pursuing, the maiden hid.

The ivy falls with the Bacchanal's hair
    Over her eyebrows hiding her eyes;
The wild vine slipping down leaves bare
    Her bright breast shortening into sighs;
The wild vine slips with the weight of its leaves,
But the berried ivy catches and cleaves
To the limbs that glitter, the feet that scare
    The wolf that follows, the fawn that flies.

from ATALANTA IN CALYDON

Man

Before the beginning of years,
    There came to the making of man
Time, with a gift of tears;
    Grief, with a glass that ran;
Pleasure, with pain for leaven;
    Summer, with flowers that fell;
Remembrance fallen from heaven,
    And madness risen from hell;
Strength without hands to smite;
    Love that endures for a breath;
Night, the shadow of light,
    And life, the shadow of death.

And the high gods took in hand
    Fire, and the falling of tears,
And a measure of sliding sand
    From under the feet of the years;

And froth and drift of the sea;
  And dust of the laboring earth;
And bodies of things to be
  In the houses of death and of birth;
And wrought with weeping and laughter,
  And fashioned with loathing and love,
With life before and after
  And death beneath and above,
For a day and a night and a morrow,
  That his strength might endure for a span
With travail and heavy sorrow,
  The holy spirit of man.

From the winds of the north and the south
  They gathered as unto strife;
They breathed upon his mouth,
  They filled his body with life;
Eyesight and speech they wrought
  For the veils of the soul therein,
A time for labor and thought,
  A time to serve and to sin;
They gave him light in his ways,
  And love, and a space for delight,
And beauty and length of days,
  And night, and sleep in the night.
His speech is a burning fire;
  With his lips he travaileth;
In his heart is a blind desire,
  In his eyes foreknowledge of death;
He weaves, and is clothed with derision;
  Sows, and he shall not reap;
His life is a watch or a vision
  Between a sleep and a sleep.
from ATALANTA IN CALYDON

Swinburne's star continued to rise. His POEMS AND BALLADS, pub-
lished a year after ATALANTA IN CALYDON, took the literary world by
storm. At thirty Swinburne was a sensation; he was not only a poet,
but a controversy. His verses spoke vaguely of liberty and rebellion,
but the vagueness was concealed by a superabundant imagery and
a verbal furiousness. The moralists were quick to use such words
as "vicious" and "libidinous"; they were alarmed to find the limp
lilies of the Pre-Raphaelites grafted on the evil flowers of Baude-

laire. But Swinburne's celebration of "the roses and raptures of vice" is a poetic naughtiness rather than actual depravity; it is, as Edward Thomas pointed out, "from the lips outward. In the spirit of gay and amateur perversity he flatters sin with appellations of virtue, as George Herbert gave his religious poetry the unction of love."

Nowhere are Swinburne's paganism and pantheism more effectively presented than in THE GARDEN OF PROSERPINE. Here, in a tribute to the queen of the lower world, Swinburne speaks not only as the beauty-intoxicated Englishman, but as a pagan Roman. Here, more than in most poems, his archaic speech is not perverse but richly appropriate.

The Garden of Proserpine

Here, where the world is quiet;
    Here, where all trouble seems
Dead winds' and spent waves' riot
    In doubtful dreams of dreams;
I watch the green field growing
For reaping folk and sowing,
For harvest-time and mowing,
    A sleepy world of streams.

I am tired of tears and laughter,
    And men that laugh and weep;
Of what may come hereafter
    For men that sow to reap:
I am weary of days and hours,
Blown buds of barren flowers,
Desires and dreams and powers
    And everything but sleep.

Here life has death for neighbor,
    And far from eye or ear
Wan waves and wet winds labor,
    Weak ships and spirits steer;
They drive adrift, and whither
They wot not who make thither;
But no such winds blow hither,
    And no such things grow here.

No growth of moor or coppice,
  No heather-flower or vine,
But bloomless buds of poppies,
  Green grapes of Proserpine,
Pale beds of blowing rushes,
Where no leaf blooms or blushes
Save this whereout she crushes
  For dead men deadly wine.

Pale, without name or number,
  In fruitless fields of corn,
They bow themselves and slumber
  All night till light is born;
And like a soul belated,
In hell and heaven unmated,
By cloud and mist abated
  Comes out of darkness morn.

Though one were strong as seven,
  He too with death shall dwell,
Nor wake with wings in heaven,
  Nor weep for pains in hell;
Though one were fair as roses,
His beauty clouds and closes;
And well though love reposes,
  In the end it is not well.

Pale, beyond porch and portal,
  Crowned with calm leaves, she stands
Who gathers all things mortal
  With cold immortal hands;
Her languid lips are sweeter
Than love's who fears to greet her,
To men that mix and meet her
  From many times and lands.

She waits for each and other,
  She waits for all men born;
Forgets the earth her mother,
  The life of fruits and corn;
And spring and seed and swallow
Take wing for her and follow
Where summer song rings hollow
  And flowers are put to scorn.

There go the loves that wither,
  The old loves with wearier wings;
And all dead years draw thither,
  And all disastrous things;
Dead dreams of days forsaken,
Blind buds that snows have shaken,
Wild leaves that winds have taken,
  Red strays of ruined springs.

We are not sure of sorrow;
  And joy was never sure;
Today will die tomorrow;
  Time stoops to no man's lure;
And love, grown faint and fretful,
With lips but half regretful
Sighs, and with eyes forgetful
  Weeps that no loves endure.

From too much love of living,
  From hope and fear set free,
We thank with brief thanksgiving
  Whatever gods may be
That no life lives for ever;
That dead men rise up never;
That even the weariest river
  Winds somewhere safe to sea.

Then star nor sun shall waken,
  Nor any change of light:
Nor sound of waters shaken,
  Nor any sound or sight:
Nor wintry leaves nor vernal,
Nor days nor things diurnal;
Only the sleep eternal
  In an eternal night.

In his thirties, Swinburne began a series of dramas in imitation
of the Elizabethans. CHASTELARD, the first of a trilogy of plays cen-
tering about the tragedy of Queen Mary, was written at twenty-
eight; the concluding MARY STUART was not published until sixteen
years later. Swinburne's debt to the Elizabethans was acknowledged
not only by his plays but by the sonnets he wrote in praise of
Shakespeare, Marlowe, Webster, and other playwrights of the pe-
riod.

William Shakespeare

Not if men's tongues and angels' all in one
Spake, might the word be said that might speak Thee.
Streams, winds, woods, flowers, fields, mountains, yea, the sea,
What power is in them all to praise the sun?
His praise is this,—he can be praised of none.
Man, woman, child, praise God for him; but he
Exults not to be worshipped, but to be.

He is; and, being, beholds his work well done.
All joy, all glory, all sorrow, all strength, all mirth,
Are his: without him, day were night on earth.
Time knows not his from time's own period.
All lutes, all harps, all viols, all flutes, all lyres,
Fall dumb before him ere one string suspires.
All stars are angels; but the sun is God.

Christopher Marlowe

Crowned, girdled, garbed, and shod with light and fire,
Son first-born of the morning, sovereign star!
Soul nearest ours of all, that wert most far,
Most far off in the abysm of time, thy lyre
Hung highest above the dawn-enkindled quire
Where all ye sang together, all that are,
And all the starry songs behind thy car
Rang sequence, all our souls acclaim thee sire.

"If all the pens that ever poets held
Had fed the feeling of their masters' thoughts,"
And as with rush of hurtling chariots
The flight of all their spirits were impelled
Toward one great end, thy glory—nay, not then,
Not yet might'st thou be praised enough of men.

In SONGS BEFORE SUNRISE Swinburne hailed the Italian patriot,
Mazzini, and announced another revolt, a protest against political
restraint rather than moral conventions. POEMS AND BALLADS: SECOND
SERIES continued "the noble pleasure of praising" and glorified
Victor Hugo. But in his early forties it was evident that Swin-

burne's ambitions and dissipations were too much for him. His friend Theodore Watts-Dunton came to the rescue and took charge of him the last thirty years of his life. Max Beerbohm's NO 2. THE PINES is a brilliant if irreverent account of Swinburne's declining days. The poet softened into a mild little country gentleman; he grew deaf; he adored babies. But he continued to write with never-abating energy. The old fire was gone, but not the gift of phrase and the mastery of sound. He died, after an attack of pneumonia, at the home of Watts-Dunton, April 10, 1909.

Song

Love laid his sleepless head
On a thorny rosy bed;
And his eyes with tears were red,
And pale his lips as the dead.

And fear and sorrow and scorn
Kept watch by his head forlorn,
Till the night was overworn,
And the world was merry with morn.

And Joy came up with the day,
And kissed Love's lips as he lay,
And the watchers ghostly and gray
Sped from his pillow away.

And his eyes as the dawn grew bright,
And his lips waxed ruddy as light:
Sorrow may reign for a night,
But day shall bring back delight.

The Sea

I will go back to the great sweet mother,
    Mother and lover of men, the sea.
I will go down to her, I and none other,
    Close with her, kiss her and mix her with me;
Cling to her, strive with her, hold her fast.
O fair white mother, in days long past
Born without sister, born without brother,
    Set free my soul as thy soul is free.

O fair green-girdled mother of mine,
   Sea, that art clothed with the sun and the rain,
Thy sweet hard kisses are strong like wine,
   Thy large embraces are keen like pain.
Save me and hide me with all thy waves,
Find me one grave of thy thousand graves,
Those pure cold populous graves of thine,
   Wrought without hand in a world without stain.

I shall sleep, and move with the moving ships,
   Change as the winds change, veer in the tide;
My lips will feast on the foam of thy lips,
   I shall rise with thy rising, with thee subside;
Sleep, and not know if she be, if she were,
Filled full with life to the eyes and hair,
As a rose is fulfilled to the roseleaf tips
   With splendid summer and perfume and pride.

This woven raiment of nights and days,
   Were it once cast off and unwound from me,
Naked and glad would I walk in thy ways,
   Alive and aware of thy ways and thee;
Clear of the whole world, hidden at home,
Clothed with the green and crowned with the foam,
A pulse of the life of thy straits and bays,
   A vein in the heart of the streams of the sea.

from THE TRIUMPH OF TIME

It is fitting that some of Swinburne's best poetry should be about the sea, for his is a rise and fall of crashing sounds which first stimulate and then engulf the reader. Swinburne delighted in sensations rather than passion, in shocks and hurrying waves of excitement. Too often the reader, swept by Swinburne's echoing vowels and consonants, is swept away from the subject. This is not surprising, for, in spite of his imposing erudition, Swinburne was not a thinker. His mind, as Max Beerbohm wittily concluded, "rose ever away from reason to rhapsody. Neither was he human. . . . He was a singing bird that could build no nest. He was a youth who could not afford to age."

THOMAS HARDY
[1840–1928]

A SUCCESSFUL novelist, Thomas Hardy wrote nothing but poetry after his fifty-seventh year, and continued to publish verse until the day of his death, thirty years later. He was born June 2, 1840, in Dorsetshire; the Wessex landscape was the beloved background of his work. His father was a stonemason, and the boy was apprenticed to an architect; at twenty-three he won a prize offered by the Royal Institute of British Architects. But Hardy, doubtful of sermons in stones, saw no future for himself in the profession. He had already written some poetry, for which he had found no publisher. Engaged to be married, and encouraged by Meredith, he turned to the more profitable trade of storytelling and wrote his first novel, DESPERATE REMEDIES, at the age of thirty. During the next twenty-five years Hardy published a dozen challenging novels of character and environment. Readers were fascinated by his dispassionate naturalism, but the more conservative critics were suspicious of his rough honesty. In 1895 JUDE THE OBSCURE was attacked as "immoral," and Hardy was so deeply offended that, as he said, "it cured him of all interest in novel-writing."

Hardy had often deplored the necessity that made him write the novels, which he referred to as "pot-boilers." Now he considered himself free to return to poetry, his first love and his last. After his fifty-eighth year, nine volumes of poems were published, including THE DYNASTS, a huge epic-drama of the Napoleonic Wars in one hundred and thirty scenes, which has been called "the biggest and most consistent exhibition of fatalism in literature."

Fatalism was the keynote of Hardy's work. It was his answer to the pastoral idealism of Wordsworth, the indomitable optimism of Browning, and the unthinking pantheism of Swinburne. Hardy knew nature too intimately to believe that it was benign. He saw the grim warfare of the farmer, the tragedies of drought and disease, the continual struggle and inevitable defeat of plant and man. If the universe was governed at all, it was governed by accident. God, maintained Hardy, had ceased to be concerned with man; if He thought of this world at all, He thought of it as one of His failures.

It was neither cruelty nor kindness that ruled, but chance. "Crass Casualty obstructs the sun and rain," Hardy concluded grimly in the poem significantly entitled HAP.

But Hardy could not regard a pitiless universe without pity. Dubious about human values, he was stirred by the strivings of humanity. Man was noblest in defeat, and in nobility there was hope. On the darkest of days, Hardy heard that hope in a storm-tossed thrush, "frail, gaunt and small," who had chosen to fling his song and his soul through unrelieved gloom.

The Darkling Thrush

I leaned upon a coppice gate
    When frost was specter-gray,
And winter's dregs made desolate
    The weakening eye of day.
The tangled bine-stems scored the sky
    Like strings from broken lyres,
And all mankind that haunted nigh
    Had sought their household fires.

The land's sharp features seemed to be
    The Century's corpse outleant;
His crypt the cloudy canopy,
    The wind his death-lament.
The ancient pulse of germ and birth
    Was shrunken hard and dry,
And every spirit upon earth
    Seemed fervorless as I.

At once a voice burst forth among
    The bleak twigs overhead
In a full-hearted evensong
    Of joy unlimited;
An aged thrush, frail, gaunt and small,
    In blast-beruffled plume,
Had chosen thus to fling his soul
    Upon the growing gloom.

So little cause for carolings
    Of such ecstatic sound
Was written on terrestrial things
    Afar or nigh around,

> That I could think there trembled through
> His happy good-night air
> Some blessed hope, whereof he knew
> And I was unaware.

Hardy wrote with objective power in every form and on almost every subject. His was an ungainly force, a dogged and appealing clumsiness. Only a few of his poems are autobiographical. One of the best of these, AFTERWARDS, was written during the latter part of his life and reveals his close scrutiny of little things. THE IMPER-CIPIENT, a much earlier poem, is a scarcely less veiled disclosure of his philosophy.

Afterwards

When the Present has latched its postern behind my tremulous stay,
   And the May month flaps its glad green leaves like wings,
Delicate-filmed as new-spun silk, will the neighbors say,
   "He was a man who used to notice such things"?

If it be in the dusk when, like an eyelid's soundless blink,
   The dewfall-hawk comes crossing the shades to alight
Upon the wind-warped upland thorn, a gazer may think,
   "To him this must have been a familiar sight."

If I pass during some nocturnal blackness, mothy and warm,
   When the hedgehog travels furtively over the lawn,
One may say, "He strove that such innocent creatures should come
     to no harm,
   But he could do little for them; and now he is gone."

If, when hearing that I have been stilled at last, they stand at the
     door,
   Watching the full-starred heavens that winter sees,
Will this thought rise on those who will meet my face no more,
   "He was one who had an eye for such mysteries"?

And will any say when my bell of quittance is heard in the gloom,
   And a crossing breeze cuts a pause in its outrollings,
Till they rise again, as they were a new bell's boom,
   "He hears it not now, but used to notice such things"?

The Impercipient

AT A CATHEDRAL SERVICE

That with this bright believing band
   I have no claim to be,
That faiths by which my comrades stand
   Seem fantasies to me,
And mirage-mists their Shining Land,
   Is a strange destiny.

Why thus my soul should be consigned
   To infelicity,
Why always I must feel as blind
   To sights my brethren see,
Why joys they've found I cannot find,
   Abides a mystery.

Since heart of mine knows not that ease
   Which they know; since it be
That He who breathes All's Well to these
   Breathes no All's-Well to me,
My lack might move their sympathies
   And Christian charity!

I am like a gazer who should mark
   An inland company
Standing upfingered, with, "Hark! hark!
   The glorious distant sea!"
And feel, "Alas, 'tis but yon dark
   And wind-swept pine to me!"

Yet I would bear my shortcomings
   With meet tranquillity,
But for the charge that blessed things
   I'd liefer not have be.
O, doth a bird deprived of wings
   Go earth-bound wilfully!

   .   .   .   .   .

Enough. As yet disquiet clings
   About us. Rest shall we.

Hardy was twice married. His domestic life was amusingly but cruelly lampooned by W. Somerset Maugham in CAKES AND ALE, OR THE SKELETON IN THE CUPBOARD. In 1910 he was given the Order of Merit, but his pleasure in that honor did not lessen his pride in being asked to preside at little ceremonies in his own village. He died in his eighty-eighth year, January 11, 1928. His ashes were placed in Westminster Abbey. But his heart, as requested in his will, was buried in the Wessex countryside he loved so well.

WILFRID SCAWEN BLUNT

[1840–1922]

IF WILFRID SCAWEN BLUNT was not the great poet some of his contemporaries thought him, he was a success in more than a literary way. T. Earle Welby puts the case for Blunt nicely if incompletely: "To have married Byron's granddaughter, bred Arab horses, and been admired by Henley is to have made a great deal of life."

Blunt was born to be a rebellious and even romantic figure. His father was a famous soldier, and the son entered the diplomatic service at eighteen. After a career which took him from Athens to Madrid, and from Lisbon to South America, Blunt married the daughter of the Earl of Lovelace and retired from the service. He was then thirty. Two years later he inherited Crabbet Park, a handsome estate in Sussex, and established a stable for the breeding of Arab horses. This interest took him to Arabia, where he became a passionate sympathizer with the Mohammedan cause. He devoted much time to the Islamic movement, in direct opposition to British policy. He identified himself with all minorities. He spoke up for the Egyptians and condemned the war against the Boers.

At forty-seven Blunt was arrested for helping the Irish insurgents and was sentenced to prison for two months. The experience is recorded in a series of protesting sonnets entitled IN VINCULIS.

The Deeds That Might Have Been

There are wrongs done in the fair face of heaven
Which cry aloud for vengeance, and shall cry;
Loves beautiful in strength whose wit has striven
Vainly with loss and man's inconstancy;
Dead children's faces watched by souls that die;
Pure streams defiled; fair forests idly riven;
A nation suppliant in its agony
Calling on justice, and no help is given.

All these are pitiful. Yet, after tears,
Come rest and sleep and calm forgetfulness,
And God's good providence consoles the years.
Only the coward heart which did not guess,
The dreamer of brave deeds that might have been,
Shall cureless ache with wounds forever green.

from IN VINCULIS

At eighty Blunt published MY DIARIES, a work so candid, so criti-
cal of British diplomacy, that the publisher withdrew it. Blunt had
already brought out three volumes of poetry; to the fourth edition
of one of them he added this note: "No life is perfect that has not
been lived—youth in feeling—manhood in battle—old age in medi-
tation." Having experienced all, he died content in his eighty-third
year, September 11, 1922.

Blunt's verse is more emotional than classical. But his sonnets—
particularly the sequences ESTHER: A YOUNG MAN'S TRAGEDY and THE
LOVE SONNETS OF PROTEUS—are as effectively simple as they are sin-
cere. The ESTHER poems have the moving force of a personal outcry.

FROM

Esther

He who has once been happy is for aye
Out of destruction's reach. His fortune then
Holds nothing secret; and Eternity,
Which is a mystery to other men,

Has like a woman given him its joy.
 Time is his conquest. Life, if it should fret,
Has paid him tribute. He can bear to die,
 He who has once been happy! When I set
The world before me and survey its range,
 Its mean ambitions, its scant fantasies,
The shreds of pleasure which for lack of change
 Men wrap around them and call happiness,
The poor delights which are the tale and sum
Of the world's courage in its martyrdom;

When I hear laughter from a tavern door,
 When I see crowds agape and in the rain
Watching on tiptoe and with stifled roar
 To see a rocket fired or a bull slain,
When misers handle gold, when orators
 Touch strong men's hearts with glory till they weep,
When cities deck their streets for barren wars
 Which have laid waste their youth, and when I keep
Calmly the count of my own life and see
 On what poor stuff my manhood's dreams were fed
Till I too learned what dole of vanity
 Will serve a human soul for daily bread,
—Then I remember that I once was young
And lived with Esther the world's gods among.

The sonnets to Juliet in the PROTEUS volume are only a little less impassioned than those to Esther. At least one of them, a late nineteenth-century echo of Drayton's lines beginning "Since there's no help, come, let us kiss and part" (see page 250), is worthy to stand beside its famous sixteenth-century model.

Farewell

Juliet, farewell. I would not be forgiven
Even if I forgave. These words must be
The last between us two in Earth or Heaven,
The last and bitterest. You are henceforth free
For ever from my bitter words and me.
You shall not at my hand be further vexed
With either love, reproach or jealousy
(So help me Heaven), in this world or the next.

Our souls are single for all time to come
And for eternity, and this farewell
Is as the trumpet note, the crack of doom,
Which heralds an eternal silence. Hell
Has no more fixed and absolute decree.
And Heaven and Hell may meet,—yet never we.
                    from THE LOVE SONNETS OF PROTEUS

ARTHUR O'SHAUGHNESSY
[1844–1881]

ARTHUR O'SHAUGHNESSY is known for a single famous poem, and that one is never quoted in the form in which it was written. The "singer of one song" was born in London, March 14, 1844, and was employed in various clerical capacities by the British Museum; he ended up in its zoological department, where he specialized in icthyology. O'Shaughnessy was, for a while, one of Rossetti's undistinguished disciples. Frail in health, he rarely left his native city, had no experiences outside of books, and died of influenza in his thirty-seventh year.

Most of O'Shaughnessy's poetry is facile, the kind of verse which is easier to write than to read. Even the continually reprinted ODE was once a garrulous string of verses. The anthologist F. T. Palgrave deserves at least part of the credit for the fame of the lines, Palgrave having cut down an overwritten poem of nine stanzas to an almost perfect three. It is Palgrave's condensed version that is quoted, one of the most musical and most imaginative poems about poetry ever written.

Ode

We are the music-makers,
　　And we are the dreamers of dreams,
Wandering by lone sea-breakers,
　　And sitting by desolate streams;
World-losers and world-forsakers,
　　On whom the pale moon gleams:
Yet we are the movers and shakers
　　Of the world for ever, it seems.

With wonderful deathless ditties
We build up the world's great cities,
   And out of a fabulous story
   We fashion an empire's glory:
One man with a dream, at pleasure,
   Shall go forth and conquer a crown;
And three with a new song's measure
   Can trample an empire down.

We, in the ages lying
   In the buried past of the earth,
Built Nineveh with our sighing,
   And Babel itself with our mirth;
And o'erthrew them with prophesying
   To the old of the new world's worth;
For each age is a dream that is dying,
   Or one that is coming to birth.

GERARD MANLEY HOPKINS
[1844–1889]

GERARD MANLEY HOPKINS, perhaps the most difficult and cer-
tainly one of the most original poets of the century, was born
at Stratford, Essex, June 11, 1844. He was educated at Balliol Col-
lege, Oxford, where his writing was commended and where he was
strongly influenced by Walter Pater and Pater's highly colored
style. In his twenty-third year Hopkins became a Roman Catholic
and burned his early verses. Eleven years later he was ordained to
the priesthood. After serving as a missionary in Liverpool, he was
given a church in Oxford. A Jesuit, he taught Rhetoric and Greek
at University College in Dublin. There he spent the last five years
of his life.

Although Hopkins wrote a great deal of spiritual-sensual poetry,
none of his poems appeared during his lifetime. His manuscripts
were left to his friend Robert Bridges, later poet laureate, and it
was not until thirty years after Hopkins' death that his extraordi-
nary verse was published. A second edition, including some addi-
tional poems, appeared in 1931, and Hopkins was belatedly discov-
ered. He was attacked as an eccentric and hailed as an originator.

The younger men admired, and many of them imitated, his metrical experiments, his breathless pace in which grammar was sacrificed for the sake of speed, his way of telescoping ideas by cutting off every nonessential word. Hopkins luxuriated in extravagance; to him the world was not only colorful but prodigal, overflowing with a divine largess. He delighted in "couple-colored" oddities, the rose-moles along the sides of trout, freckles and finches' wings, all things contrary, "counter, original, spare, strange," all the entrancing superfluities of creation.

Pied Beauty

Glory be to God for dappled things—
   For skies of couple-color as a brinded cow;
     For rose-moles all in stipple upon trout that swim;
Fresh-firecoal chestnut-falls; finches' wings;
   Landscape plotted and pieced—fold, fallow, and plow;
     And all trades, their gear and tackle and trim.

All things counter, original, spare, strange;
   Whatever is fickle, freckled (who knows how?)
     With swift, slow; sweet, sour; adazzle, dim;
He fathers-forth whose beauty is past change:
     Praise Him.

Hopkins saw the whole world "barbarous in beauty." Even the inanimate "azurous hung hills" expressed the "brute beauty and valor" of existence and woke "Man's mounting spirit in his bonehouse." Hopkins spoke of Swinburne's "delirium-tremendous imagination," but Hopkins' imagination was far more reckless and opulent. To him everything was "charged with the grandeur of God."

God's Grandeur

The world is charged with the grandeur of God.
   It will flame out, like shining from shook foil;
   It gathers to a greatness, like the ooze of oil
Crushed. Why do men then now not reck his rod?

Generations have trod, have trod, have trod;
  And all is seared with trade; bleared, smeared with toil;
  And wears man's smudge and shares man's smell: the soil
Is bare now, nor can foot feel, being shod.

And for all this, nature is never spent;
  There lives the dearest freshness deep down things;
And though the last lights off the black West went
  Oh, morning, at the brown brink eastward, springs—
Because the Holy Ghost over the bent
  World broods with warm breast and with ah! bright wings.

It was not an erratic wildness in Hopkins but a daring purpose which broke down the traditional poetic idiom and reformed it into a new speech. Hopkins crowded metaphors with almost more associations than they could bear; he leaped, with the agility of lightning, from one image to another. Readers often have difficulty following the extraordinary rush of language, in which sounds, sights, textures, and ideas seem thrown pell-mell. But there is order in Hopkins' speed, a definite if seemingly kaleidoscopic design in the swiftness of his "terrible sincerity."

Hopkins' passionate devoutness was an answer not only to Hardy's atheism, but to the skeptical spirit of an age floundering between a religion it had discarded and a science it feared to accept. Unhampered by the confusion about him, unconcerned with publication, Hopkins composed the finest religious poems written since the seventeenth century.

Heaven : Haven

A NUN TAKES THE VEIL

I have desired to go
  Where springs not fail,
To fields where flies no sharp and sided hail,
  And a few lilies blow.

And I have asked to be
  Where no storms come,
Where the green swell is in the havens dumb,
  And out of the swing of the sea.

The Habit of Perfection

Elected Silence, sing to me
And beat upon my whorléd ear,
Pipe me to pastures still, and be
The music that I care to hear.

Shape nothing, lips; be lovely-dumb;
It is the shut, the curfew sent
From there where all surrenders come
Which only makes you eloquent.

Be shelléd, eyes, with double dark
And find the uncreated light:
This ruck and reel which you remark
Coils, keeps, and teases simple sight.

Palate, the hatch of tasty lust,
Desire not to be rinsed with wine:
The can must be so sweet, the crust
So fresh that come in fasts divine!

Nostrils, your careless breath that spend
Upon the stir and keep of pride,
What relish shall the censers send
Along the sanctuary side!

O feel-of-primrose hands, O feet
That want the yield of plushy sward,
But you shall walk the golden street
And you unhouse and house the Lord.

And, Poverty, be thou the bride
And now the marriage feast begun,
And lily-colored clothes provide
Your spouse not labored-at nor spun.

Unlike such equally affirmative spirits as Wordsworth and Whitman, Hopkins can never be a popular poet. He cannot be a companion to the ordinary individual, for he shows no appreciation of the struggles of the average man. But within the scope of his vision and the range of his genius, he is magnificent.

ROBERT BRIDGES
[1844–1930]

THE sixteenth poet laureate of England, Robert Bridges, was a noted surgeon who abandoned his practice at thirty-six, and a lyric poet who published a long philosophical poem, by some considered his most important work, at the age of eighty-five. He was born at Walmer, October 23, 1844, was educated at Corpus Christi College, Oxford, and became a general practitioner in London. Almost at the same time he joined the staff at St. Bartholomew's Hospital, from which he retired, after a serious illness in 1881, to devote himself entirely to literature.

Although Bridges published eight plays and many small volumes of verse, all of them had a small circulation. The poet was almost unknown to the public until the appearance of his POETICAL WORKS, at which time he was sixty-eight. The following year, he was appointed poet laureate, succeeding the innocuous Alfred Austin.

Bridges' failure to achieve popularity is easy enough to understand. His ideas were direct and his emotions simple, but his preoccupation with meters made him construct lines that were too subtle for wide enjoyment. Even a poem on a dead child was forced into an involved metrical pattern.

> So I lay thee there, thy sunken eyelids closing—
> Go lie thou there in the coffin, thy last little bed!—
> Propping thy wise, sad head,
> Thy firm, pale hands across thy chest disposing.

Most readers considered Bridges a cold classicist; they respected him, but they could not love him. Nevertheless, under the archaic diction and technical experiments there is a persistently sweet strain of music.

> I love all beauteous things,
> I seek and adore them;
> God hath no better praise,
> And man in his hasty days
> Is honored for them.

Serenity and fastidiousness mark his work, a quiet if somewhat severe contemplation of beauty. Praising Bridges' delight in beauty, Charles Williams adds, "It is a delight which may require a certain similarity of temperament or a certain prolonged discipline before it can be accepted, especially from a reader used to more violent effects." But no discipline is needed to enjoy the dexterously muted melodies.

Nightingales

Beautiful must be the mountains whence ye come,
And bright in the fruitful valleys the streams wherefrom
      Ye learn your song:
Where are those starry woods? O might I wander there,
  Among the flowers, which in that heavenly air
      Bloom the year long!

Nay, barren are those mountains and spent the streams:
Our song is the voice of desire, that haunts our dreams,
      A throe of the heart,
Whose pining visions dim, forbidden hopes profound,
  No dying cadence nor long sigh can sound,
      For all our art.

Alone, aloud in the raptured ear of men
We pour our dark nocturnal secret; and then,
      As night is withdrawn
From these sweet-springing meads and bursting boughs of May,
  Dream, while the innumerable choir of day
      Welcome the dawn.

London Snow

When men were all asleep the snow came flying,
In large white flakes falling on the city brown,
Stealthily and perpetually settling and loosely lying,
  Hushing the latest traffic of the drowsy town;
Deadening, muffling, stifling its murmurs failing;
Lazily and incessantly floating down and down;
  Silently sifting and veiling road, roof and railing;
Hiding difference, making unevenness even,
  Into angles and crevices softly drifting and sailing.

All night it fell, and when full inches seven
It lay in the depth of its uncompacted lightness,
The clouds blew off from a high and frosty heaven;
And all woke earlier for the unaccustomed brightness
Of the winter dawning, the strange unheavenly glare:
The eye marveled—marveled at the dazzling whiteness;
The ear hearkened to the stillness of the solemn air;
No sound of wheel rumbling nor of foot falling,
And the busy morning cries came thin and spare.
Then boys I heard, as they went to school, calling;
They gathered up the crystal manna to freeze
Their tongues with tasting, their hands with snow-balling;
Or rioted in a drift, plunging up to the knees;
Or peering up from under the white-mossed wonder,
"O look at the trees!" they cried. "O look at the trees!"
With lessened load, a few carts creak and blunder,
Following along the white deserted way,
A country company long dispersed asunder:
When now already the sun, in pale display
Standing by Paul's high dome, spread forth below
His sparkling beams, and awoke the stir of the day.
For now doors open, and war is waged with the snow;
And trains of somber men, past tale of number,
Tread long brown paths, as toward their toil they go:
But even for them awhile no cares encumber
Their minds diverted; the daily word is unspoken,
The daily thoughts of labor and sorrow slumber
At the sight of the beauty that greets them, for the charm they
    have broken.

At seventy-four Bridges edited the poems of Gerard Manley Hopkins (see page 977), poems which were the very opposite of Bridges' restrained consciousness and deliberate harmonies. At eighty-five he published THE TESTAMENT OF BEAUTY, a work which was compared to Wordsworth's PRELUDE, and which, wrote Robert Hillyer, "combines with the philosopher's learning and reasoning the persuasion of beauty itself." A year after the publication of his impressive and possibly major work, Bridges died, following a short illness, April 21, 1930.

W. E. HENLEY

[1849–1903]

N O ONE ever sang more courageously of life than William Ernest
Henley, who was a cripple for more than forty years. At the
age of twelve in Gloucester, where he was born, it was discovered
that the boy was suffering from a tubercular disease of the bone.
One leg was amputated, and some years later the doctors advised
the amputation of the other. Henley, who was then twenty-four,
went to the Edinburgh Infirmary, was treated by Lister, the founder
of antiseptic surgery, and, after twenty months, the disease was
checked and the foot saved.

One of Henley's most constant visitors at the hospital was Robert
Louis Stevenson. A year his junior and, later, his best friend, Steven-
son is clearly pictured in APPARITION, one of the sketches and son-
nets entitled IN HOSPITAL.

Apparition

Thin-legged, thin-chested, slight unspeakably,
Neat-footed and weak-fingered; in his face—
Lean, large-boned, curved of beak and touched with race,
Bold-lipped, rich-tinted, mutable as the sea,
The brown eyes radiant with vivacity—
There shines a brilliant and romantic grace,
A spirit intense and rare, with trace on trace
Of passion, impudence and energy.
Valiant in velvet, light in ragged luck,
Most vain, most generous, sternly critical,
Buffoon and poet, lover and sensualist;
A deal of Ariel, just a streak of Puck,
Much Antony, of Hamlet most of all,
And something of the Shorter-Catechist.

It was in the Edinburgh hospital that Henley wrote many of his
best-known verses. The "bludgeonings of chance"—a Hardyesque
phrase—could not defeat his tough spirit. He said it by implica-

tion in a score of lyrics, explicitly in INVICTUS (literally "Uncon-
quered") that grim defiance from the black Pit of Hell.

Invictus

Out of the night that covers me,
  Black as the Pit from pole to pole,
I thank whatever gods may be
  For my unconquerable soul.

In the fell clutch of circumstance
  I have not winced nor cried aloud.
Under the bludgeonings of chance
  My head is bloody, but unbowed.

Beyond this place of wrath and tears
  Looms but the horror of the shade,
And yet the menace of the years
  Finds, and shall find me, unafraid.

It matters not how strait the gate,
  How charged with punishments the scroll,
I am the master of my fate:
  I am the captain of my soul.

Two years after leaving the hospital Henley went to London and
became an editor on a magazine. He made many gratifying dis-
coveries among the younger writers, but drove himself ruthlessly.
Editorial work kept him from expressing himself more fully in
verse. "After spending the better part of my life in the pursuit of
poetry," he wrote in self-exculpation, "I found myself so utterly
unmarketable that I had to own myself beaten in art, and to addict
myself to journalism." Later, however, the impulse to write poetry
was still strong, and Henley found that, "after all, the lyrical in-
stinct had slept, not died."

The lyrical instinct triumphed. The early gusto was succeeded by
a delicate music and, as in MARGARITAE SORORI (a poem written in
memory of his wife's sister Margaret), a grave and dignified un-
rhymed measure.

The Blackbird

The nightingale has a lyre of gold,
  The lark's is a clarion call,
And the blackbird plays but a boxwood flute,
  But I love him best of all.

For his song is all of the joy of life,
  And we in the mad, spring weather,
We two have listened till he sang
  Our hearts and lips together.

Madam Life

Madam Life's a piece in bloom
  Death goes dogging everywhere:
She's the tenant of the room,
  He's the ruffian on the stair.

You shall see her as a friend,
  You shall bilk him once and twice;
But he'll trap you in the end,
  And he'll stick you for her price.

With his kneebones at your chest,
  And his knuckles in your throat,
You would reason—plead—protest!
  Clutching at her petticoat.

But she's heard it all before,
  Well she knows you've had your **fun**,
Gingerly she gains the door,
  And your little job is done.

Margaritae Sorori

A late lark twitters from the quiet skies;
And from the west,
Where the sun, his day's work ended,
Lingers as in content,

There falls on the old, gray city
An influence luminous and serene,
A shining peace.

The smoke ascends
In a rosy-and-golden haze. The spires
Shine, and are changed. In the valley
Shadows rise. The lark sings on. The sun,
Closing his benediction,
Sinks, and the darkening air
Thrills with a sense of the triumphing night—
Night with her train of stars
And her great gift of sleep.

So be my passing!
My task accomplished and the long day done,
My wages taken, and in my heart
Some late lark singing,
Let me be gathered to the quiet west,
The sundown splendid and serene,
Death.

Henley continued busy and belligerent until forty-five, when the
death of his five-year-old daughter broke his heart. He wrote for
several years more, but the spirit had gone out of him. He was at
work on a preface for the Tudor Bible when he died, July 12, 1903.

ROBERT LOUIS STEVENSON
[1850–1894]

H ENLEY's etching of the "thin-legged, thin-chested" Robert Louis
Stevenson portrayed the youth with diagnostic accuracy, for
Stevenson was a consumptive. His life was a pitiful attempt to find
a climate in which he could survive.

The man whom Henley pictured as a combination of lover and
sensualist, a happy Ariel and a melancholy Hamlet, a mischievous
Puck and a Calvinist preacher, was born November 13, 1850, in
Edinburgh. An only child, frail from birth, he received little regu-
lar schooling. It was hoped that he would become a lighthouse

engineer, following the family profession, but poor health made this impossible. The ancestral love of the sea was in him. He studied law dutifully and went so far as to be called to the bar in his twenty-sixth year, but he never practiced. Instead, he began to write, enjoying himself in rhyme and training himself as narrator and essayist by sedulously studying the masters of prose. When it was apparent that his disease was crippling him, Stevenson gladly responded to the sea call and went abroad for warmth and sunshine.

In France Stevenson met Mrs. Fanny Osbourne, an American widow, followed her to California, and, after almost succumbing to the rigors of the journey, married her in his thirtieth year. The couple were poor; they lived in a shabby mining camp. But Stevenson made the place bright with "bird-song at morning and starshine at night."

Romance

I will make you brooches and toys for your delight
Of bird-song at morning and star-shine at night.
I will make a palace fit for you and me,
Of green days in forests and blue days at sea.

I will make my kitchen, and you shall keep your room,
Where white flows the river and bright blows the broom,
And you shall wash your linen and keep your body white
In rainfall at morning and dewfall at night.

And this shall be for music when no one else is near,
The fine song for singing, the rare song to hear!
That only I remember, that only you admire,
Of the broad road that stretches and the roadside fire.

Although Stevenson had written tales and travel books which had been well received, it was not until the publication of TREASURE ISLAND in 1883 that he became popular. Three years later his fame was definitely established with THE STRANGE CASE OF DR. JEKYLL AND MR. HYDE. At thirty-five he published A CHILD'S GARDEN OF VERSES with some misgiving; but the collection Stevenson hesitated to offer to the public has grown to be a universal favorite, second only to Mother Goose in its appeal to every generation.

Escape at Bedtime

The lights from the parlor and kitchen shone out
    Through the blinds and the windows and bars;
And high overhead and all moving about,
    There were thousands of millions of stars.
There ne'er were such thousands of leaves on a tree,
    Nor of people in church or the park,
As the crowds of the stars that looked down upon me,
    And that glittered and winked in the dark.

The Dog, and the Plough, and the Hunter, and all,
    And the star of the sailor, and Mars,
These shone in the sky, and the pail by the wall
    Would be half full of water and stars.
They saw me at last, and they chased me with cries,
    And they soon had me packed into bed;
But the glory kept shining and bright in my eyes,
    And the stars going round in my head.

Stevenson's serious poetry is unpretentious, but its quiet romanticism has a warm and heartening glow. Lucid without being brilliant, precise without being stiff, it retains its old charm.

Bright Is the Ring of Words

Bright is the ring of words
    When the right man rings them,
Fair is the fall of songs
    When the singer sings them.
Still they are caroled and said—
    On wings they are carried—
After the singer is dead
    And the maker buried.

Low as the singer lies
    In the field of heather,
Songs of his fashion bring
    The swains together.

And when the west is red
With the sunset embers,
The lover lingers and sings
And the maid remembers.

Ditty

TO AN AIR FROM BACH

The cock shall crow
In the morning grey,
The bugles blow
At the break of day:
The cock shall sing and the merry bugles ring,
And all the little brown birds sing upon the spray.

The thorn shall blow
In the month of May,
And my love shall go
In her holiday array:
But I shall lie in the kirkyard nigh
While all the little brown birds sing upon the spray.

The Celestial Surgeon

If I have faltered more or less
In my great task of happiness;
If I have moved among my race
And shown no glorious morning face;
If beams from happy human eyes
Have moved me not; if morning skies,
Books, and my food, and summer rain
Knocked on my sullen heart in vain:—
Lord, Thy most pointed pleasure take
And stab my spirit broad awake;
Or, Lord, if too obdurate I,
Choose Thou, before that spirit die,
A piercing pain, a killing sin,
And to my dead heart run them in!

Fighting his ever-progressing disease, Stevenson traveled through America. A winter at Saranac Lake in the Adirondack Mountains gave him a respite, but the following year he grew worse and craved the sea again. He left San Francisco for a voyage among the islands of the South Sea, and what was intended to be an excursion became a voluntary exile. Death found him in Samoa, December 3, 1894. Sixty natives carried him to a peak on the Pacific, and there a tablet was placed carved with the lines from his REQUIEM which Stevenson always intended as his epitaph.

Requiem

Under the wide and starry sky,
Dig the grave and let me lie.
Glad did I live and gladly die,
    And I laid me down with a will.

This be the verse you grave for me:
Here he lies where he longed to be;
Home is the sailor, home from sea,
    And the hunter home from the hill.

EDWIN MARKHAM
[1852–1940]

O NE of the most indignant poems of social protest was written by a quiet teacher, Edwin Markham, born in Oregon City, Oregon, April 23, 1852. Markham grew up in California, worked on a cattle ranch, entered the State Normal School at San José, and became a superintendent of schools. Social consciousness was awakening. The world of aristocracy was at war with the world of wealth; in the conflict the worker was the victim. Seeing Millet's painting of a bowed, broken toiler, Markham made the French peasant a symbol of all workers, and wrote THE MAN WITH THE HOE. The poem was immediately successful upon its appearance in the San Francisco EXAMINER the last year of the nineteenth century. It

was copied in every part of the world. It caught up the passion for
social justice that was waiting to be expressed and was hailed as
"the battle cry of the next thousand years." Not in protest against
toil but against the exploitation of labor, Markham saw the well-to-
do farmer as the Yeoman; but here in the Millet picture, he wrote,
"is his opposite: the Hoeman, the landless workman of the world."

The Man With the Hoe

Bowed by the weight of centuries he leans
Upon his hoe and gazes on the ground,
The emptiness of ages in his face,
And on his back the burden of the world.
Who made him dead to rapture and despair,
A thing that grieves not and that never hopes,
Stolid and stunned, a brother to the ox?
Who loosened and let down this brutal jaw?
Whose was the hand that slanted back this brow?
Whose breath blew out the light within this brain?

Is this the Thing the Lord God made and gave
To have dominion over sea and land;
To trace the stars and search the heavens for power;
To feel the passion of Eternity?
Is this the dream He dreamed who shaped the suns
And marked their ways upon the ancient deep?
Down all the caverns of Hell to their last gulf
There is no shape more terrible than this—
More tongued with censure of the world's blind greed—
More filled with signs and portents for the soul—
More packt with danger to the universe.

What gulfs between him and the seraphim!
Slave of the wheel of labor, what to him
Are Plato and the swing of Pleiades?
What the long reaches of the peaks of song,
The rift of dawn, the reddening of the rose?
Through this dread shape the suffering ages look;
Time's tragedy is in that aching stoop;
Through this dread shape humanity betrayed,
Plundered, profaned, and disinherited,
Cries protest to the Judges of the World,
A protest that is also prophecy.

O masters, lords and rulers in all lands,
Is this the handiwork you give to God,
This monstrous thing distorted and soul-quenched?
How will you ever straighten up this shape;
Touch it again with immortality;
Give back the upward looking and the light;
Rebuild in it the music and the dream;
Make right the immemorial infamies,
Perfidious wrongs, immedicable woes?

O masters, lords and rulers in all lands,
How will the Future reckon with this man?
How answer his brute question in that hour
When whirlwinds of rebellion shake all shores?
How will it be with kingdoms and with kings—
With those who shaped him to the thing he is—
When this dumb terror shall rise to judge the world,
After the silence of the centuries?

Once established as a writer, Markham produced a great quantity
of verse; but it was unoriginal in subject, undistinguished in style.
Readers had come to the regretful conclusion that Markham was
the poet of a single poem, when suddenly the author of THE MAN
WITH THE HOE published LINCOLN, THE MAN OF THE PEOPLE. Less
magniloquent than its predecessor, the Lincoln poem is more com-
pact in thought, more restrained in utterance. The central image
is powerful and the concluding figure is as appropriate as it is
eloquent, a truly noble climax.

The poem, selected from more than two hundred tributes to the
martyr-President, was read at the dedication ceremonies of the Lin-
coln Memorial at Washington, D. C., May 30, 1922.

Lincoln, the Man of the People

When the Norn Mother saw the Whirlwind Hour
Greatening and darkening as it hurried on,
She left the Heaven of Heroes and came down
To make a man to meet the mortal need.
She took the tried clay of the common road—
Clay warm yet with the genial heat of earth,
Dasht through it all a strain of prophecy;
Tempered the heap with thrill of human tears;

Then mixt a laughter with the serious stuff.
Into the shape she breathed a flame to light
That tender, tragic, ever-changing face;
And laid on him a sense of the Mystic Powers,
Moving—all husht—behind the mortal veil.
Here was a man to hold against the world,
A man to match the mountains and the sea.

The color of the ground was in him, the red earth;
The smack and tang of elemental things:
The rectitude and patience of the cliff;
The good-will of the rain that loves all leaves;
The friendly welcome of the wayside well;
The courage of the bird that dares the sea;
The gladness of the wind that shakes the corn;
The pity of the snow that hides all scars;
The secrecy of streams that make their way
Under the mountain to the rifted rock;
The tolerance and equity of light
That gives as freely to the shrinking flower
As to the great oak flaring to the wind—
To the grave's low hill as to the Matterhorn
That shoulders out the sky. Sprung from the West,
He drank the valorous youth of a new world.
The strength of virgin forests braced his mind,
The hush of spacious prairies stilled his soul.
His words were oaks in acorns; and his thoughts
Were roots that firmly gript the granite truth.

Up from log cabin to the Capitol,
One fire was on his spirit, one resolve—
To send the keen ax to the root of wrong,
Clearing a free way for the feet of God,
The eyes of conscience testing every stroke,
To make his deed the measure of a man.
He built the rail-pile as he built the State,
Pouring his splendid strength through every blow:
The grip that swung the ax in Illinois
Was on the pen that set a people free.

So came the Captain with the mighty heart.
And when the judgment thunders split the house,
Wrenching the rafters from their ancient rest,
He held the ridgepole up, and spiked again
The rafters of the Home. He held his place—

Held the long purpose like a growing tree—
Held on through blame and faltered not at praise.
And when he fell in whirlwind, he went down
As when a lordly cedar, green with boughs,
Goes down with a great shout upon the hills,
And leaves a lonesome place against the sky.

In his late forties Markham came East and made his home on
Staten Island. Rugged and patriarchal, he overcame criticism and
illness. He grew more beautiful with age; someone said that Mark-
ham in his seventies looked like a composite picture of all the New
England poets. A more cautious admirer observed him as "a deity
dispossessed and declining on a suburban Olympus." His life
spanned the continent. Born near one ocean, Markham died facing
the other, at eighty-eight, March 7, 1940.

OSCAR WILDE

[1856–1900]

CULTIVATED affectation and whispered scandal increased Wilde's
renown as a playwright and poet; a criminal trial ruined it.
He was a notoriously spoiled child of society until his fortieth year;
at forty-three he was an almost unrecognizable derelict. Son of a
distinguished but profligate Irish surgeon and a highly affected
mother, Oscar Fingal O'Flahertie Wills Wilde was born October
16, 1856, in Dublin, Ireland. He was educated at Trinity College,
Dublin, and at Magdalen College, Oxford, where he won the New-
digate Prize at twenty-one for his poem RAVENNA. Even as an under-
graduate he had become celebrated as an "artist in attitudes." He
wore a languishing look and long hair; his clothes were oddly cut
and carefully cobwebby, "with a tender bloom like cold gravy"; he
said he despaired of living up to his blue china. By the time he had
left Oxford he had become the recognized leader of the Aesthetic
Movement. PUNCH, England's most famous humorous weekly, never
tired of caricaturing him and his velveteen breeches. A few years
later his bizarre cult was immortally burlesqued in W. S. Gilbert's
PATIENCE.

At twenty-six Wilde made a spectacular lecture tour through the

United States. The Americans refused to take his dandyism seriously, but they enjoyed quoting his statement to the customs authorities that he had "nothing to declare except his genius" and that he was disappointed by the Atlantic Ocean.

At twenty-eight Wilde married and, for a while, seemed to adjust himself to normal domesticity. But he remarked that "women spoil every romance by trying to make it last forever," and, after a short period of virtue, Wilde began dallying with "the raptures and roses of vice." He wrote a great deal of rococo prose, a few glittering period plays in which banter takes the place of ideas, several charming if overwritten fairy tales, and a novel, THE PICTURE OF DORIAN GRAY, which is a cross between an allegory and a leer, a work which may well be described as satyrical.

As a poet, Wilde sinks beneath the burden of his baroque manner. The language of his verse is tinsel, the thinking is tawdry. One of his earliest poems is among his best. REQUIESCAT ("May she rest in peace") was written in memory of Wilde's sister who died in childhood. It is interesting to compare the lines with Matthew Arnold's poem by the same name, on page 924.

Requiescat

Tread lightly, she is near
    Under the snow,
Speak gently, she can hear
    The daisies grow.

All her bright golden hair
    Tarnished with rust,
She that was young and fair
    Fallen to dust.

Lily-like, white as snow,
    She hardly knew
She was a woman, so
    Sweetly she grew.

Coffin-board, heavy stone
    Lie on her breast;
I vex my heart alone,
    She is at rest.

       Peace, peace; she cannot hear
         Lyre or sonnet;
       All my life's buried here.
         Heap earth upon it.

Wilde was in his fortieth year when the Marquis of Queensberry accused him of undue intimacy with the latter's son, Lord Alfred Douglas. Wilde was unwisely advised to bring suit for libel against the Marquis, lost the suit, was faced with arrest, and was tried for statutory offenses under the criminal law. Found guilty, he was sentenced to two years at hard labor. His prison experiences are recorded in the prose of DE PROFUNDIS, a defense which is also a confession, and THE BALLAD OF READING GAOL, in many ways his most sincere work.

FROM

The Ballad of Reading Gaol

Yet each man kills the thing he loves,
   By each let this be heard,
Some do it with a bitter look,
   Some with a flattering word,
The coward does it with a kiss,
   The brave man with a sword!

Some kill their love when they are young,
   And some when they are old;
Some strangle with the hands of Lust,
   Some with the hands of Gold:
The kindest use a knife, because
   The dead so soon grow cold.

Some love too little, some too long,
   Some sell, and others buy;
Some do the deed with many tears,
   And some without a sigh:
For each man kills the thing he loves,
   Yet each man does not die.

He does not die a death of shame
   On a day of dark disgrace,

Nor have a noose about his neck,
    Nor a cloth upon his face,
Nor drop feet foremost through the floor
    Into an empty space.

He did not wring his hands nor weep,
    Nor did he peak or pine,
But he drank the air as though it held
    Some healthful anodyne;
With open mouth he drank the sun
    As though it had been wine!

And I and all the souls in pain,
    Who tramped the other ring,
Forgot if we ourselves had done
    A great or little thing,
And watched with gaze of dull amaze
    The man who had to swing.

And strange it was to see him pass
    With a step so light and gay,
And strange it was to see him look
    So wistfully at the day,
And strange it was to think that he
    Had such a debt to pay.

.   .   .   .   .   °

For oak and elm have pleasant leaves
    That in the spring-time shoot:
But grim to see is the gallows-tree,
    With its adder-bitten root,
And, green or dry, a man must die
    Before it bears its fruit!

The loftiest place is that seat of grace
    For which all worldlings try:
But who would stand in hempen band
    Upon a scaffold high,
And through a murderer's collar take
    His last look at the sky?

It is sweet to dance to violins
    When Love and Life are fair:
To dance to flutes, to dance to lutes
    Is delicate and rare:
But it is not sweet with nimble feet
    To dance upon the air!

So with curious eyes and sick surmise
　　We watched him day by day,
And wondered if each one of us
　　Would end the self-same way,
For none can tell to what red Hell
　　His sightless soul may stray.

At last the dead man walked no more
　　Amongst the Trial Men,
And I knew that he was standing up
　　In the black dock's dreadful pen,
And that never would I see his face
　　In God's sweet world again.

Like two doomed ships that pass in storm
　　We had crossed each other's way:
But we made no sign, we said no word,
　　We had no word to say;
For we did not meet in the holy night,
　　But in the shameful day.

A prison wall was round us both,
　　Two outcast men we were:
The world had thrust us from its heart,
　　And God from out His care:
And the iron gin that waits for Sin
　　Had caught us in its snare.

After his release from prison, Wilde changed his name, moved to the Continent, and drank himself to death. He died of cerebral meningitis, November 30, 1900. He was buried according to the rites of the Roman Catholic Church, in the cemetery of Bagneux, on the outskirts of Paris. Lord Alfred Douglas was chief mourner.

SIR WILLIAM WATSON

[1858–1935]

AUTHOR of odes that were once considered Wordsworthian and elegies that were favorably compared to Tennyson's IN MEMORIAM, William Watson is remembered for only a few epigrams and one short lyric. He was born in Yorkshire, August 2,

1858, and began writing in his childhood. After several volumes had appeared, it became the custom to refer to Watson's poetry as "lofty" and "dignified"; few critics had the bad grace to say that it was derivative and rather dull. Queen Victoria voiced her admiration for LACRYMAE MUSARUM, Watson's elegy on Tennyson; Gladstone suggested that the author be made poet laureate. Watson, together with Rudyard Kipling and the "impossible" Swinburne, was seriously considered for the laureateship; but the authorities, unable to come to an agreement, awarded the honor to the unknown Alfred Austin, an ultraconservative journalist.

After a too-promising start, Watson's career ended abruptly. He was snubbed by a prime minister for some tactless verses; his contemporaries were embarrassed by the poet's garrulous rhymes; the younger men were either scornful or silent. At sixty he was almost forgotten. At seventy he was so desperately in need that a committee had to raise funds for him. He died in obscurity August 13, 1935.

Miscast in the role of prophet, Watson was one of the last of the Royal Purple tradition. Never careless, he was often too pompous, too intent upon wrapping himself in the oversize mantles of Milton, Wordsworth, and Tennyson. The shorter poems, and particularly the EPIGRAMS, are more certainly his own.

Two Epigrams

LOVE

Love, like a bird, hath perched upon a spray
   For thee and me to hearken what he sings.
Contented, he forgets to fly away;
   But hush! Remind not Eros of his wings.

THE POET

The Poet gathers fruit from every tree,
Yea, grapes from thorns and figs from thistles he.
Plucked by his hand, the basest weed that grows
Towers to a lily, reddens to a rose.

Watson's ambitious WORDSWORTH'S GRAVE and THE PRINCE'S QUEST are seldom read; his many volumes are no longer printed. But the lighthearted song beginning "April, April" continues to be uncritically quoted.

Song

April, April,
Laugh thy girlish laughter;
Then, the moment after,
Weep thy girlish tears,
April, that mine ears
Like a lover greetest,
If I tell thee, sweetest,
All my hopes and fear.
April, April,
Laugh thy golden laughter,
But, the moment after,
Weep thy golden tears!

FRANCIS THOMPSON
[1859–1907]

A SEVENTEENTH-CENTURY mystic thrust into the embattled commercialism of the late nineteenth century, Francis Thompson withdrew from a world in which he could not compete into a world of religious fantasy where he was comforted if not secure. He was born December 18, 1859, in Lancashire. Son of a doctor, he was educated to succeed his father. But, after making vague declarations that he hoped to be a priest, and after failing three times to pass his medical examinations, it was apparent that he was not interested in medicine. The family was outraged, and Thompson, at twenty-five, cut himself adrift and went to London. No one was less capable of supporting himself in the crowded metropolis. For at least four years he sold matches at street corners, ran errands, called cabs, and sank to an incredible level of poverty. His father sent him a few shillings a week in care of the reading room at the British Museum, but Thompson became so shabby that he was refused admittance. Literally starving, he was rescued by a prostitute who took him to her room, fed him, and gave him shelter.

Thompson now began to write; his first poem was penned on blue paper used to wrap sugar. He submitted an article and some verse to Wilfrid Meynell, editor of MERRY ENGLAND, but Meynell's letter of acceptance failed to locate Thompson. When Thompson was finally found and urged to come to the editorial office, he looked like a wild and hounded thing. His shoes were broken; there was no shirt under his closely buttoned ragged coat. Finally, according to Francis Meynell, Wilfrid Meynell's son, "he was persuaded, though with difficulty, to come off the streets; and even to give up for many years the laudanum he had been taking. For the remaining nineteen years of his life he had an existence at any rate three-quarters protected from the physical tragedies of his starved and homeless young manhood."

Meynell induced Thompson to spend two years at Stonington Priory to cure him of the effects of the drug; it was while he was living with the Franciscan monks that Thompson wrote the ecstatic essay on Shelley and the even more rhapsodic THE HOUND OF HEAVEN. The title was probably derived from Shelley, who in PROMETHEUS UNBOUND speaks of "Heaven's wingéd hound." In a turbulent vision, Thompson saw man as the human quarry, the frightened spirit running to hide in nature, and God as the divine hunter, pursuer and rescuer. Thompson employed every device to heighten the effect of the extraordinary pursuit: a riotous pace and an elaborately ornamented speech, archaic phrases and new words—some of them coined by Thompson—and a headlong extravagance of style.

The Hound of Heaven

I fled Him, down the nights and down the days;
   I fled Him, down the arches of the years;
I fled Him, down the labyrinthine ways
   Of my own mind; and in the mist of tears
I hid from Him, and under running laughter.
        Up vistaed hopes I sped;
        And shot, precipitated,
Adown Titanic glooms of chasmed fears,
   From those strong Feet that followed, followed after.
       But with unhurrying chase,
       And unperturbéd pace,
   Deliberate speed, majestic instancy,
       They beat—and a Voice beat
       More instant than the Feet—
"All things betray thee, who betrayest Me."

I pleaded, outlaw-wise,
By many a hearted casement, curtained red,
  Trellised with intertwining charities
(For, though I knew His love Who followéd,
      Yet was I sore adread
Lest, having Him, I must have naught beside);
But, if one little casement parted wide,
  The gust of His approach would clash it to:
  Fear wist not to evade, as Love wist to pursue
Across the margent of the world I fled,
  And troubled the gold gateways of the stars,
  Smiting for shelter on their clangèd bars;
      Fretted to dulcet jars
And silvern chatter the pale ports o' the moon.
I said to Dawn: Be sudden—to Eve: Be soon;
  With thy young skiey blossoms heap me over
      From this tremendous Lover—
Float thy vague veil about me, lest He see!
  I tempted all His servitors, but to find
My own betrayal in their constancy,
In faith to Him their fickleness to me,
  Their traitorous trueness, and their loyal deceit.
To all swift things for swiftness did I sue;
  Clung to the whistling mane of every wind.
      But whether they swept, smoothly fleet,
    The long savannahs of the blue;
      Or whether, Thunder-driven,
      They clanged his chariot 'thwart a heaven,
Plashy with flying lightnings round the spurn o' their feet:—
  Fear wist not to evade as Love wist to pursue.
      Still with unhurrying chase,
      And unperturbéd pace,
    Deliberate speed, majestic instancy,
      Came on the following Feet,
      And a Voice above their beat—
    "Naught shelters thee, who wilt not shelter Me."

I sought no more that after which I strayed
      In face of man or maid;
But still within the little children's eyes
      Seems something, something that replies,
They at least are for me, surely for me!
I turned me to them very wistfully;
But just as their young eyes grew sudden fair
      With dawning answers there,

Their angel plucked them from me by the hair.
"Come then, ye other children, Nature's—share
With me" (said I) "your delicate fellowship;
    Let me greet you lip to lip,
    Let me twine with you caresses,
      Wantoning
    With our Lady-Mother's vagrant tresses,
      Banqueting
    With her in her wind-walled palace,
    Underneath her azured daïs,
    Quaffing, as your taintless way is,
      From a chalice
Lucent-weeping out of the dayspring."
      So it was done:
I in their delicate fellowship was one—
Drew the bolt of Nature's secrecies.
    I knew all the swift importings
    On the willful face of skies;
    I knew how the clouds arise
    Spumed of the wild sea-snortings;
      All that's born or dies
    Rose and drooped with; made them shapers
Of mine own moods, or wailful or divine;
    With them joyed and was bereaven.
    I was heavy with the even,
    When she lit her glimmering tapers
    Round the day's dead sanctities.
    I laughed in the morning's eyes.
I triumphed and I saddened with all weather,
    Heaven and I wept together,
And its sweet tears were salt with mortal mine;

Against the red throb of its sunset-heart
    I laid my own to beat,
    And share commingling heat;
But not by that, by that, was eased my human smart.
In vain my tears were wet on Heaven's gray cheek.
For ah! we know not what each other says,
    These things and I; in sound *I* speak—
Their sound is but their stir, they speak by silences.
Nature, poor stepdame, cannot slake my drouth;
    Let her, if she would owe me,
Drop yon blue bosom-veil of sky, and show me
    The breasts o' her tenderness:

Never did any milk of hers once bless
    My thirsting mouth.
    Nigh and nigh draws the chase,
    With unperturbéd pace,
  Deliberate speed, majestic instancy;
    And past those noiséd Feet
    A Voice comes yet more fleet—
  "Lo! naught contents thee, who content'st not Me."

Naked I wait Thy love's uplifted stroke!
My harness piece by piece Thou hast hewn from me,
    And smitten me to my knee;
    I am defenseless utterly.
    I slept, methinks, and woke,
And, slowly gazing, find me stripped in sleep.
In the rash lustihead of my young powers,
    I shook the pillaring hours
And pulled my life upon me; grimed with smears,
I stand amid the dust o' the mounded years—
My mangled youth lies dead beneath the heap.
My days have crackled and gone up in smoke,
Have puffed and burst as sun-starts on a stream.
    Yea, faileth now even dream
The dreamer, and the lute the lutanist;
Even the linked fantasies, in whose blossomy twist
I swung the earth a trinket at my wrist,
Are yielding; cords of all too weak account
For earth with heavy griefs so overplused.
    Ah! is Thy love indeed
A weed, albeit an amaranthine weed,
Suffering no flowers except its own to mount?
    Ah! must—
    Designer infinite!—
Ah! must Thou char the wood ere Thou canst limn with it?
My freshness spent its wavering shower i' the dust;
And now my heart is as a broken fount,
Wherein tear-drippings stagnate, spilt down ever
    From the dank thoughts that shiver
Upon the sighful branches of my mind.
    Such is; what is to be?
The pulp so bitter, how shall taste the rind?
I dimly guess what Time in mists confounds;
Yet ever and anon a trumpet sounds
From the hid battlements of Eternity;
Those shaken mists a space unsettle, then

Round the half-glimpsed turrets slowly wash again.
But not ere him who summoneth
I first have seen, enwound
With glooming robes purpureal, cypress-crowned;
His name I know, and what his trumpet saith.
Whether man's heart or life it be which yields
Thee harvest, must Thy harvest-fields
Be dunged with rotten death?

Now of that long pursuit
Comes on at hand the bruit;
That Voice is round me like a bursting sea:
"And is thy earth so marred,
Shattered in shard on shard?
Lo, all things fly thee, for thou fliest Me!
Strange, piteous, futile thing!
Wherefore should any set thee love apart?
Seeing none but I makes much of naught" (He said),
"And human love needs human meriting:
How hast thou merited—
Of all man's clotted clay the dingiest clot?
Alack, thou knowest not
How little worthy of any love thou art!
Whom wilt thou find to love ignoble thee
Save Me, save only Me?
All which I took from thee I did but take,
Not for thy harms,
But just that thou might'st seek it in My arms.
All which thy child's mistake
Fancies as lost, I have stored for thee at home:
Rise, clasp My hand, and come!"

Halts by me that footfall:
Is my gloom, after all,
Shade of His hand, outstretched caressingly?
"Ah, fondest, blindest, weakest,
I am He Whom thou seekest!
Thou dravest love from thee, who dravest Me."

"To be the poet of the return to Nature is somewhat," wrote
Thompson. "But I would be the poet of the return to God." That
desire was not fulfilled without difficulty, and it accounts for the
obstacles readers may find in Thompson's poetry. He was obviously

indebted to Crashaw (see page 466) and Crashaw's metaphysical involvements. Thompson often confused glitter with gold, sometimes achieving a baroque magnificence, sometimes falling from the grand manner into the grand-opera manner. But the best of his work is clear enough; it glows with a "honey of wild flame."

To a Snowflake

What heart could have thought you?
Past our devisal
(O filigree petal!)
Fashioned so purely,
Fragilely, surely,
From what Paradisal
Imagineless metal,
Too costly for cost?
Who hammered you, wrought you,
From argentine vapor?—
"God was my shaper.
Passing surmisal,
He hammered, He wrought me,
From curled silver vapor,
To lust of his mind:—
Thou couldst not have thought me!
So purely, so palely,
Tinily, surely,
Mightily, frailly,
Insculped and embossed,
With His hammer of wind,
And His graver of frost."

A posthumous poem contains Thompson's most moving lines. It is a reminiscence of the time Thompson slept on benches and saw from the depths "the traffic of Jacob's ladder pitched between Heaven and Charing Cross." Wilfrid Meynell, who found the poem among Thompson's papers, spoke of "these triumphing stanzas" in which we see "in retrospect, as did he, those days and nights of human dereliction he spent beside London's River, and in the shadow—but all radiance to him—of Charing Cross."

In No Strange Land

"THE KINGDOM OF GOD IS WITHIN YOU"

O world invisible, we view thee,
O world intangible, we touch thee,
O world unknowable, we know thee,
Inapprehensible, we clutch thee!

Does the fish soar to find the ocean,
The eagle plunge to find the air—
That we ask of the stars in motion
If they have rumor of thee there?

Not where the wheeling systems darken,
And our benumbed conceiving soars!—
The drift of pinions, would we hearken,
Beats at our own clay-shuttered doors.

The angels keep their ancient places;—
Turn but a stone, and start a wing!
'Tis ye, 'tis your estranged faces,
That miss the many-splendored thing.

But (when so sad thou canst not sadder)
Cry—and upon thy so sore loss
Shall shine the traffic of Jacob's ladder
Pitched betwixt Heaven and Charing Cross.

Yea, in the night, my Soul, my daughter,
Cry—clinging Heaven by the hems;
And lo, Christ walking on the water
Not of Gennesareth, but Thames!

In his mid-forties Thompson's health, never robust, failed him. He contracted tuberculosis and died in London, November 13, 1907.

FIVE AMERICAN FOLK SONGS

Most American folk songs are importations. Brought over by the settlers, influenced by a new environment, changed to reflect another scene and setting, they still show their origins. Under different titles, and celebrating another set of characters, the story songs of Vermont and the hillbilly tunes of the Appalachians are largely adaptations of such English and Scottish border ballads as BARBARA ALLEN, THE HANGMAN'S SONG, THE TWO SISTERS, and LORD RANDAL.

But a few—and perhaps the best—of American ballads are genuinely native, as original in theme as they are racy in idiom. Beginning as reports of local events or current beliefs or merely play songs, they have become part of the national life. The five most vivid are also the most popular: DIXIE, MY OLD KENTUCKY HOME, FRANKIE AND JOHNNY, CASEY JONES, and JOHN HENRY. Unlike most folk songs, the authorship of at least two of them is known.

DIXIE, the battle cry of the South, was not written for a marching song but for a minstrel show. To complete the irony, its author was not a Southern patriot, but a professional entertainer from Ohio.

Daniel Decatur Emmett was born in 1815, in Mt. Vernon, Ohio. His father was a blacksmith, and the boy's character was hammered out, Emmett liked to say, on the anvil. From thirteen to seventeen he worked on small-town newspapers; at eighteen he got into the army as a fife player; at nineteen he traveled with circus bands. In his mid-thirties, he organized the first colored minstrel troop, after consulting a dictionary to satisfy himself that the word "minstrel" was not too inappropriate. His organization was immediately successful and widely imitated, and Emmett was soon prosperous enough to afford a manager and talk of retiring.

One morning—it was September 18, 1859—Emmett told his wife that the show needed a new "walk-around" with a lively melody and words that could be picked up easily. Emmett started improvising on his violin, kept it up all day, and finally had the tune with most of the words. His wife liked it. So did the rest of the nation.

Dixie

I wish I was in de land ob cotton,
Old times dar am not forgotten;
  Look away! Look away! Look away! Dixie land!
In Dixie land whar I was born in,
Early on one frosty mornin'
  Look away! Look away! Look away! Dixie land!

Missus married Will de weaber;
William was a gay deceaber;
When he put his arm around 'er,
He looked as fierce as a forty-pounder.

While missus libbed, she libbed in clover,
When she died, she died all over;
So here's a health to de nex' ole missus,
An' all de gals dat want to kiss us.

Now ef you want to drive 'way sorrow,
Come an' hear dis song tomorrow;
Den hoe it down an' scratch your grabble—
To Dixie's land I'm boun' to trabble.

Chorus

Den I wish I was in Dixie. Hooray! Hooray!
In Dixie land I'll take my stand, an' lib an' die in Dixie.
Away! Away! Away down south in Dixie!
Away! Away! Away down south in Dixie!

Some of the simplest American songs are also the most melancholy—and most of them were written and composed by Stephen Collins Foster. Foster was born, patriotically enough, on July 4, 1826. Son of a prosperous Pittsburgh merchant related by marriage to President Buchanan, the child was a natural musician. At twelve he played on several instruments; at thirteen he composed a song which was widely circulated. At seventeen he went into business with his brother in Cincinnati, Ohio, and became more prolific than ever. His melodies were highly singable, his words were easily remembered; they were repeated and parodied until they became the most popular songs of the period. There was something of the primitive singer in Foster, but the simplicity was often spoiled by Foster's canny knowledge of the nostalgic demands of the public. He was an uncultured Schubert, a commercialized Burns. He mixed pathos with bathos, and let himself slip from true sentiment into bald sentimentality. But the best of his songs combine picturesqueness and genuine emotion.

Although Foster wrote more than one hundred and thirty ballads and innumerable dance tunes, his last days were spent in abject poverty. He was only thirty-eight when he died in the charity ward of Bellevue, New York City, January 13, 1864.

Seventy-seven years after his death, Foster was established as a national classic. MY OLD KENTUCKY HOME was enthusiastically sung at the annual Kentucky Derby. A postage stamp was issued in Foster's honor. The radio blared forth his melodies in determined repetition and distorted tempi. A bronze portrait bust was unveiled in the Hall of Fame for Great Americans. The man who had been regarded as an intemperate tunesmith had become the acknowledged singer of the people.

My Old Kentucky Home

The sun shines bright in the old Kentucky home;
    'Tis summer, the darkeys are gay;
The corn-top's ripe, and the meadow's in the bloom,
    While the birds make music all the day.
The young folks roll on the little cabin floor,
    All merry, all happy and bright;
By-'n'-by hard times comes a-knocking at the door:—
    Then my old Kentucky home, good-night!

    Weep no more, my lady,
    O, weep no more to-day!
We will sing one song for the old Kentucky home,
    For the old Kentucky home, far away.

They hunt no more for the 'possum and the coon,
    On the meadow, the hill, and the shore;
They sing no more by the glimmer of the moon,
    On the bench by the old cabin door.

The day goes by like a shadow o'er the heart,
  With sorrow, where all was delight;
The time has come when the darkeys have to part:—
  Then my old Kentucky home, good-night!

The head must bow, and the back will have to bend,
  Wherever the darkey may go;
A few more days, and the trouble all will end,
  In the field where the sugar-canes grow.
A few more days for to tote the weary load—
  No matter, 'twill never be light;
A few more days till we totter on the road:—
  Then my old Kentucky home, good-night!

    Weep no more, my lady,
    O, weep no more to-day!
We will sing one song for the old Kentucky home,
  For the old Kentucky home, far away.

Although it is impossible to ascertain the authorship of FRANKIE AND JOHNNY, the date can be approximated. Some researchers maintain that the song dates back to 1850 and that the scene of the sordid tragedy was Natchez-under-the-Hill. But John Huston has shown, if he has not conclusively proved, that the time was 1899, the locale St. Louis, and the heroine an actual Frankie Baker who shot her "mack," or *maquereau,* in a jealous brawl.

By 1935 the song had taken so firm a hold on the popular imagination that two dramas, a moving picture, and a ballet had been built about the tale, and more than twenty versions were in existence, some melodramatic, some ribald, and several unprintable.

Frankie and Johnny

Frankie and Johnny were lovers, O Lordy, how they could love!
Swore to be true to each other, true as the stars above.
  He was her man, but he done her wrong.

Frankie she was a good woman, just like everyone knows.
She spent a hundred dollars for a suit of Johnny's clothes.
  He was her man, but he done her wrong.

Frankie and Johnny went walking, Johnny in a brand new suit.
"Oh, good Lord," says Frankie, "don't my Johnny look cute?"
    He was her man, but he done her wrong.

Frankie went down to Memphis, she went on the evening train.
She paid one hundred dollars for Johnny a watch and chain.
    He was her man, but he done her wrong.

Frankie lived in the crib-house, crib-house had only two doors;
Gave all her money to Johnny, he spent it on those parlor whores.
    He was her man, but he done her wrong.

Frankie went down to the corner to buy a glass of beer,
Says to the fat bartender, "Has my lovingest man been here?
    He was my man, but he's doing me wrong."

"Ain't going to tell you no story; ain't going to tell you no lie,
I seen your man 'bout an hour ago with a girl named Nellie Bly.
    If he's your man, he's doing you wrong."

Frankie went down to the pawnshop, she didn't go there for fun;
She hocked all of her jewelry, bought a pearl-handled forty-four gun
    For to get her man who was doing her wrong.

Frankie went down to the hotel, she rang that hotel bell.
"Stand back, all you chippies, or I'll blow you all to hell.
    I want my man, who's doing me wrong."

Frankie threw back her kimono, she took out her forty-four,
Root-a-toot-toot three times she shot right through that hotel door
    She was after her man who was doing her wrong.

Johnny grabbed off his Stetson, "Oh, good Lord, Frankie, don't
    shoot!"
But Frankie pulled the trigger and the gun went root-a-toot-toot.
    He was her man, but she shot him down.

"Roll me over easy; roll me over slow;
Roll me over on my left side, for the bullet is hurting me so.
    I was her man, but I done her wrong."

Oh, bring on your rubber-tired hearses; bring on your rubber-tired
    hacks;
They're taking Johnny to the cemetery, and they ain't a-bringing
    him back.
    He was her man, but he done her wrong.

Now it was not murder in the second degree, it was not murder in
    the third.
The woman simply dropped her man, like a hunter drops his bird.
    He was her man and he done her wrong.

"Oh, put me in that dungeon. Oh, put me in that cell.
Put me where the northeast wind blows from the southwest corner
    of hell.
    I shot my man 'cause he done me wrong."

Frankie walked up the scaffold, as calm as a girl can be,
And turning her eyes to heaven she said, "Good Lord, I'm coming
    to thee.
    He was my man, and I done him wrong."

This story has got no moral, this story has got no end.
This story only goes to show that there ain't no good in men.
    He was her man, but he done her wrong.

    The American heritage of folk heroes includes not only the tram-
pling giants of tall stories, but hard-living, loud-laughing pioneers.
These heroes have grown larger with time: Dan'l Boone, Davy
Crockett, Jean Lafitte, Buffalo Bill, and Johnny Appleseed, as well
as such mythical workers as Paul Bunyan, Mike Fink, Casey Jones,
and John Henry. Since these characters live in an atmosphere of
free braggadocio, it is natural that their songs are full of swagger-
ing and artless robustiousness. The ballad of CASEY JONES is typical
in its casual beginning, its tragic denouement, and unexpectedly
rowdy end.

    The fabled brave engineer was a real person, John Luther Jones,
of Cayce (pronounced Casey), Kentucky, and the much-sung colli-
sion actually happened, April 30, 1900. A tablet erected to Jones's
memory at Cayce states: "While running the Illinois Central Fast
Mail, and by no fault of his, his engine bolted through three
freight cars. . . . Casey died with his hand clenched to the brake
helve, and his was the only life lost." Contrary to the song, however,
Mrs. Jones's children did not have "another papa on the Salt Lake
Line."

Casey Jones[1]

Come all you rounders if you want to hear
The story of a brave engineer;
Casey Jones was the rounder's name,
On a six-eight wheeler, boys, he won his fame.

Caller called Casey at half-past four,
He kissed his wife at the station door,
Mounted to the cabin with orders in his hand,
And took his farewell trip to the Promised Land.

    Casey Jones, mounted to the cabin,
    Casey Jones, with his orders in his hand!
    Casey Jones, mounted to the cabin,
    Took his farewell trip into the Promised Land.

Put in your water and shovel in your coal,
Put your head out the window, watch them drivers roll,
I'll run her till she leaves the rail,
'Cause we're eight hours late with the western mail!

He looked at his watch and his watch was slow,
Looked at the water and the water was low,
Turned to his fireboy and then he said,
"We're goin' to reach 'Frisco, but we'll all be dead!"

Casey pulled up that Reno Hill,
Tooted for the crossing with an awful shrill,
The switchman knew by the engine's moans
That the man at the throttle was Casey Jones.

He pulled up short two miles from the place,
Number Four stared him right in the face,
Turned to his fireboy, said, "You'd better jump,
'Cause there's two locomotives that's a-goin' to bump!"

Casey said, just before he died,
"There's two more roads I'd like to ride."
Fireboy said, "What could they be?"
"The Southern Pacific and the Santa Fe."

---

[1] *The original version, copyright 1909 by Newton & Seibert; copyright renewed 1936; Shapiro, Bernstein & Company, proprietors.*

Mrs. Jones sat on her bed a-sighin',
Got a message that Casey was dyin',
Said, "Go to bed, children, and hush your cryin',
'Cause you got another papa on the Salt Lake Line."

Casey Jones! Got another papa!
Casey Jones, on the Salt Lake Line!
Casey Jones! Got another papa!
You got another papa on the Salt Lake Line!

Among the heroes of extravagant exploits, none is greater than
John Henry. This steel-driving Negro who pitted his strength
against the modern steam-drill and "died with his hammer in his
hand" is a mythical American of the machine age. Many parts of
the country have claimed John Henry. There are records of his
prowess in a dozen states; one account in West Virginia specifically
pictures him as six feet two, two hundred and thirty pounds,
straight as an arrow, and "black as a kittle in hell."

John Henry

John Henry was a little baby,
    Setting on his mammy's knee,
Said "The Big Bend Tunnel on the C. & O. Road
    Is gonna be the death of me,
        Lawd, gonna be the death of me."

One day his captain told him,
    How he had bet a man
That John Henry could beat his steam drill down,
    Cause John Henry was the best in the land,
        John Henry was the best in the land.

John Henry walked in the tunnel,
    His captain by his side;
The mountain so tall, John Henry so small,
    He laid down his hammer and he cried,
        Laid down his hammer and he cried.

John Henry kissed his hammer;
    White man turned on the steam;
Shaker held John Henry's steel;
    Was the biggest race the world had ever seen,
        Lawd, biggest race the world ever seen.

John Henry on the right side
  The steam drill on the left,
"Before I'll let your steam drill beat me down,
  I'll hammer my fool self to death,
    Hammer my fool self to death."

Captain heard a mighty rumbling,
  Said, "The mountain must be caving in."
John Henry said to the captain,
  "It's my hammer sucking de wind,
    My hammer sucking de wind."

John Henry said to his captain,
  "A man ain't nothin' but a man,
But before I'll let dat steam drill beat me down,
  I'll die wid my hammer in my hand,
    Lawd, die wid my hammer in my hand."

John Henry hammering on the mountain,
  The whistle blew for half-past two,
The last words his captain heard him say,
  "I've done hammered my insides in two,
    Lawd, I've hammered my insides in two."

The hammer that John Henry swung
  It weighed over twelve pound,
He broke a rib in his left-hand side
  And his intrels fell on the ground,
    Lawd, his intrels fell on the ground.

They took John Henry to the river,
  And buried him in the sand,
And every locomotive come a-roaring by,
  Says, "There lies that steel-drivin' man,
    Lawd, there lies that steel-drivin' man!"

A folk song is made by the blurring changes rung by its singers, whether they are craft-conscious musicians or unself-conscious slaves, cowboys, lumberjacks, and guttersnipes. The future of the folk song is, therefore, unlimited. The spread of mechanized music may temporarily discourage folk singing; but the pleasure of personal performance is one that cannot be satisfied by vicarious mediums. It is possible that the radio may well encourage further variations and spread the range of words and ideas. Its very scope and diffusion may create a new tradition and make national what is now regional.

Meanwhile, the folk songs grow in number and vigor, around the hearth and in the backwoods with brusque camaraderie.

FOUR NEGRO SPIRITUALS

THE Negro spirituals, which many musicians consider America's purest melodies, are a blend of savagely rhythmic chants and placid Christian hymns. The stirring combination, first heard in the 1820's, was like nothing previously created in the new world. To the Negroes, the Bible seemed a replica of their own tragic history. The sufferings of the Israelites in Egypt were their own; the punishment of the wealthy masters was identified with their half-hopeless hopes. They sang of Jordan and Jericho, but it was their own walls that were to come tumbling down; it was a black Moses who was to say to the Pharaohs of the Southland, "Let my people go."

It was not until after the Civil War that the songs began to be written down. Today there are more than a hundred collections of the "black and unknown bards of long ago," as James Weldon Johnson called them, and new versions are constantly being discovered. They are of varying literary merit. But the best of them express not only a deep emotional sincerity but a robust poetic quality as well. Some of the happiest effects in the spirituals are the sudden shifts in mood, the childlike responses that make the imagery at once homely and daring. Thus the railroad—an apocalyptic wonder to the plantation slaves—becomes the iron steed on which King Jesus rides, the modern Elijah's chariot on which all the congregation, the "little chillun," are urged to get on board. To the barefoot blacks, a pair of shoes was as precious as the spotless robe which, in some free hereafter, they would wear to walk all over God's heaven.

Joshua Fit de Battle of Jericho

Joshua fit de battle of Jericho,
Jericho, Jericho,
Joshua fit de battle of Jericho,
And de walls come tumbling down.

You may talk about yo' king of Gideon
Talk about yo' man of Saul,
Dere's none like good old Joshua
At de battle of Jericho.

Up to de walls of Jericho,
He marched with spear in hand;
"Go blow dem ram horns," Joshua cried,
"Kase de battle am in my hand."

Den de lamb ram sheep-horns begin to blow,
Trumpets begin to sound,
Joshua commanded de chillun to shout,
And de walls come tumbling down.

Dat morning,
Joshua fit de battle of Jericho,
Jericho, Jericho,
Joshua fit de battle of Jericho,
And de walls come tumbling down.

Steal Away

Steal away, steal away, steal away to Jesus.
Steal away, steal away home,
I ain't got long to stay here.

My Lord, He calls me,
He calls me by the thunder,
The trumpet sounds within-a my soul;
I ain't got long to stay here.

Steal away, steal away, steal away to Jesus,
Steal away, steal away home,
I ain't got long to stay here.

Green trees a-bending,
Po' sinner stands a-trembling
The trumpet sounds within-a my soul;
I ain't got long to stay here.

Steal away, steal away, steal away to Jesus.
Steal away, steal away home,
I ain't got long to stay here.

The Crucifixion

They crucified my Lord,
    And He never said a mumbaling word.
They crucified my Lord,
    And He never said a mumbaling word.
Not a word—not a word—not a word.

They nailed Him to the tree,
    And He never said a mumbaling word.
They nailed Him to the tree,
    And He never said a mumbaling word.
Not a word—not a word—not a word.

They pierced Him in the side,
    And He never said a mumbaling word.
They pierced Him in the side,
    And He never said a mumbaling word.
Not a word—not a word—not a word.

The blood came twinkaling down,
    And He never said a mumbaling word.
The blood came twinkaling down,
    And He never said a mumbaling word.
Not a word—not a word—not a word.

He bowed His head and died,
    And He never said a mumbaling word.
He bowed His head and died,
    And He never said a mumbaling word.
Not a word—not a word—not a word.

Strictly speaking, WATER-BOY is not a spiritual, but a work song. It is said to have originated toward the end of the nineteenth century, and it has been credited to a Negro convict in Georgia. Working in the chain gang under the pitiless sun, he calls for the boy who carries the water. As the boy delays coming and the convict continues to break stone, the singer reviews his life, particularly his devotion to gambling which has brought him to the present pass. The convict's boasting of his strength with the hammer seems to be an unconscious echo of JOHN HENRY.

Water-Boy

Water-Boy, where are yo' hidin'?
If yo' don't-a come, I'm gwineter tell-a yo' Mammy.

Dere ain't no hammer dat's on-a dis mountain,
Dat ring-a like mine, boys, dat ring-a like mine.
Done bus' dis rock, boys, f'om hyah to Macon,
All de way to de jail, boys, yes, back to de jail.

Yo' Jack-o'-Di'monds, yo' Jack-o'-Di'monds,
I know yo' of old, boys, yas, I know yo' of old.
Yo' robbed ma pocket, yas, robba ma pocket,
Done robba ma pocket of silver an' gold.

Water-Boy, where are yo' hidin'?
If yo' don't-a come, I'm gwineter tell-a yo' Mammy.
Oh, Water-Boy!

XV

The World of the Twentieth Century

A. E. HOUSMAN
[1859–1936]

A PESSIMISM darker than Omar-FitzGerald's and even more intense than Hardy's was voiced by a cloistered scholar, a professor of Latin, who wrote blithely about murder and suicide, personal betrayal and cosmic injustice.

Alfred Edward Housman was born in a village in Worcestershire, near Shropshire, the county which became the scene of his poetry. Educated at St. John's College, Oxford, he failed in an important examination. The setback destroyed his hope of an immediate scholastic appointment at a large university and forced him to accept the work of a civil servant (actually a kind of clerkship) in the Patent Office. He worked ten years in this uncongenial position.

Early in youth Housman was drawn toward paganism. He was, he said, a deist at thirteen and an atheist before he was twenty-one. During his ten years' clerkship, he devoted every spare hour to a study of the classics, and in 1892 he was made professor of Latin at University College, London. He remained there twenty years. In 1911 he went to Cambridge University and taught and lectured there almost until the day of his death, April 30, 1936.

Housman's withdrawal from the world had become proverbial. His brother, Laurence Housman, explains what seemed to be an antisocial feeling. In MY BROTHER, A. E. HOUSMAN, Laurence Housman quotes a passage from T. E. Lawrence's SEVEN PILLARS OF WISDOM:

> There was my craving to be liked—so strong and nervous that never could I open myself friendly to another. The terror of failure in an effort so important made me shrink from trying. . . . There was a craving to be famous, and a horror of being known to like being known. Contempt for my passion for distinction made me refuse every offered honor.

Laurence Housman tells us that his brother wrote in the margin against this passage: "This is me."

Housman's inverted "passion for distinction" made him disguise his work as well as himself. He originally intended to call A SHROPSHIRE LAD, his first and most famous book, POEMS BY TERENCE HEARSAY. The rejected title explains the personal reference in the often-quoted EPILOGUE, which sums up Housman's central philosophy.

Epilogue

"Terence, this is stupid stuff;
You eat your victuals fast enough;
There can't be much amiss, 'tis clear,
To see the rate you drink your beer.
But oh, good Lord, the verse you make,
It gives a chap the belly-ache.
The cow, the old cow, she is dead;
It sleeps well, the horned head:
We poor lads, 'tis our turn now
To hear such tunes as killed the cow.
Pretty friendship 'tis to rhyme
Your friends to death before their time
Moping melancholy mad:
Come, pipe a tune to dance to, lad."

Why, if 'tis dancing you would be,
There's brisker pipes than poetry.
Say, for what were hop-yards meant,
Or why was Burton built on Trent?
Oh, many a peer of England brews
Livelier liquor than the Muse,

And malt does more than Milton can
To justify God's ways to man.
Ale, man, ale's the stuff to drink
For fellows whom it hurts to think:
Look into the pewter pot
To see the world as the world's not.
And faith, 'tis pleasant till 'tis past:
The mischief is that 'twill not last.
Oh, I have been to Ludlow fair
And left my necktie God knows where,
And carried half way home, or near,
Pints and quarts of Ludlow beer:
Then the world seemed none so bad,
And I myself a sterling lad;
And down in lovely muck I've lain,
Happy till I woke again.
Then I saw the morning sky:
Heigho, the tale was all a lie;
The world, it was the old world yet,
I was I, my things were wet,
And nothing now remained to do
But begin the game anew.

Therefore, since the world has still
Much good, but much less good than ill,
And while the sun and moon endure
Luck's a chance, but trouble's sure,
I'd face it as a wise man would,
And train for ill and not for good.
'Tis true, the stuff I bring for sale
Is not so brisk a brew as ale:
Out of a stem that scored the hand
I wrung it in a weary land.
But take it: if the smack is sour,
The better for the embittered hour;
It should do good to heart and head
When your soul is in my soul's stead;
And I will friend you, if I may,
In the dark and cloudy day.

There was a king reigned in the East:
There, when kings will sit to feast,
They get their fill before they think
With poisoned meat and poisoned drink.
He gathered all that springs to birth

From the many-venomed earth;
First a little, thence to more,
He sampled all her killing store;
And easy, smiling, seasoned sound,
Sat the king when healths went round.
They put arsenic in his meat
And stared aghast to watch him eat;
They poured strychnine in his cup
And shook to see him drink it up:
They shook, they stared as white's their shirt:
Them it was their poison hurt.
—I tell the tale that I heard told.
Mithridates, he died old.

After A SHROPSHIRE LAD became popular, Housman was surprised
when critics referred to his poetry as having a "classical" origin. He
insisted that, although he may have been unconsciously influenced
by the Greeks and Latins, the chief sources of the book were Scot-
tish Border ballads, Shakespeare's songs, and Heine's lyrics. The
combination is apparent in everything Housman published, even
in the posthumous work. It explains Housman's deceptive simplic-
ity and sparsely decorated verse, a verse whose sweetness is strength-
ened by its severity.

With Rue My Heart Is Laden

With rue my heart is laden
    For golden friends I had,
For many a rose-lipt maiden
    And many a lightfoot lad.

By brooks too broad for leaping
    The lightfoot boys are laid;
The rose-lipt girls are sleeping
    In fields where roses fade.

Loveliest of Trees

Loveliest of trees, the cherry now
Is hung with bloom along the bough,
And stands about the woodland ride
Wearing white for Eastertide.

Now, of my threescore years and ten,
Twenty will not come again,
And take from seventy springs a score,
It only leaves me fifty more.

And since to look at things in bloom
Fifty springs are little room,
About the woodlands I will go
To see the cherry hung with snow.

When I Was One-and-Twenty

When I was one-and-twenty
    I heard a wise man say,
"Give crowns and pounds and guineas
    But not your heart away;
Give pearls away and rubies
    But keep your fancy free."
But I was one-and-twenty,
    No use to talk to me.

When I was one-and-twenty
    I heard him say again,
"The heart out of the bosom
    Was never given in vain;
'Tis paid with sighs a-plenty
    And sold for endless rue."
And I am two-and-twenty,
    And oh, 'tis true, 'tis true.

Is My Team Ploughing

"Is my team ploughing,
    That I was used to drive
And hear the harness jingle
    When I was man alive?"

Aye, the horses trample,
    The harness jingles now;
No change though you lie under
    The land you used to plough.

"Is football playing
  Along the river shore,
With lads to chase the leather,
  Now I stand up no more?"

Aye, the ball is flying,
  The lads play heart and soul;
The goal stands up, the keeper
  Stands up to keep the goal.

"Is my girl happy,
  That I thought hard to leave,
And has she tired of weeping
  As she lies down at eve?"

Aye, she lies down lightly,
  She lies not down to weep:
Your girl is well contented.
  Be still, my lad, and sleep.

"Is my friend hearty,
  Now I am thin and pine;
And has he found to sleep in
  A better bed than mine?"

Aye, lad, I lie easy,
  I lie as lads would choose;
I cheer a dead man's sweetheart.
  Never ask me whose.

I Hoed and Trenched and Weeded

I hoed and trenched and weeded,
  And took the flowers to fair:
I brought them home unheeded;
  The hue was not the wear.

So up and down I sow them
  For lads like me to find,
When I shall lie below them,
  A dead man out of mind.

Some seeds the birds devour,
And some the season mars,
But here and there will flower
The solitary stars,

And fields will yearly bear them
As light-leaved spring comes on,
And luckless lads will wear them
When I am dead and gone.

In a world of infidelity and unreason, Housman insists, only death
has dignity. The heart out of the bosom is given in vain; lightfoot
lads drink and die, and there is small joy in their brief athleticism.
It is a merry-mournful tune that Housman sings, but it is the more
memorable for its undiluted acid sharpness.

To an Athlete Dying Young

The time you won your town the race
We chaired you through the market-place;
Man and boy stood cheering by,
And home we brought you shoulder-high.

Today, the road all runners come,
Shoulder-high we bring you home,
And set you at your threshold down.
Townsman of a stiller town.

Smart lad, to slip betimes away
From fields where glory does not stay,
And early though the laurel grows
It withers quicker than the rose.

Eyes the shady night has shut
Cannot see the record cut,
And silence sounds no worse than cheers
After earth has stopped the ears:

Now you will not swell the rout
Of lads that wore their honors out,
Runners whom renown outran
And the name died before the man.

So set, before its echoes fade,
The fleet foot on the sill of shade,
And hold to the low lintel up
The still-defended challenge-cup.

And round that early-laureled head
Will flock to gaze the strengthless dead,
And find unwithered on its curls
The garland briefer than a girl's.

Echoing Hardy, and opposed to Wordsworth, Housman has no illusions about the goodness of existence. Nature is evil, he tells us; the countryside riots in haphazard cruelty. Man is "a stranger and afraid in a world he never made." The sensible person trains for ill and not for good. Injustice is a constant, and there is no hope from heaven: "High heaven and earth ail from the prime foundation."

The troubles of our proud and angry dust
Are from eternity, and shall not fail.

Yet Housman adds a note of stoicism, a reply to the overwhelming iniquities.

Bear them we can, and if we can we must.
Shoulder the sky, my lad, and drink your ale.

Be Still, My Soul, Be Still

Be still, my soul, be still; the arms you bear are brittle,
    Earth and high heaven are fixt of old and founded strong.
Think rather,—call to thought, if now you grieve a little,
    The days when we had rest, O soul, for they were long.

Men loved unkindness then, but lightless in the quarry
    I slept and saw not; tears fell down, I did not mourn;
Sweat ran and blood sprang out and I was never sorry:
    Then it was well with me, in days ere I was born.

Now, and I muse for why and never find the reason,
    I pace the earth, and drink the air, and feel the sun.
Be still, be still, my soul; it is but for a season:
    Let us endure an hour and see injustice done.

Ay, look: high heaven and earth ail from the prime foundation;
  All thoughts to rive the heart are here, and all are vain:
Horror and scorn and hate and fear and indignation—
  Oh, why did I awake? When shall I sleep again?

When I Watch the Living Meet

When I watch the living meet,
  And the moving pageant file
Warm and breathing through the street
  Where I lodge a little while,

If the heats of hate and lust
  In the house of flesh are strong,
Let me mind the house of dust
  Where my sojourn shall be long.

In the nation that is not
  Nothing stands that stood before;
There revenges are forgot,
  And the hater hates no more;

Lovers lying two and two
  Ask not whom they sleep beside,
And the bridegroom all night through
  Never turns him to the bride.

Fortitude can be learned, Housman assures us grimly. "Luck's a chance, but trouble's sure," he repeats, like a cheerful prophet of doom. The pessimism would be unbearable but for Housman's brisk measures and his unfailing artistry. The reader is diverted from a pervading hopelessness by the poet's brief but graphic revelations of the English countryside, by the quick play of his irony, and by the exquisite lyricism which frames it all.

The scrupulous craftsmanship may be gathered from the fact that twenty-six years passed between Housman's first book and his second, significantly if inaccurately entitled LAST POEMS. (A third volume, MORE POEMS, was published the year of his death.) Housman's notebooks show how carefully he worked for the exact word. Laurence Housman discloses that, in the superb description of the clock striking the quarters in EIGHT O'CLOCK, the word "tossed" was arrived at only after Housman had tried and rejected "loosed," "spilt," "cast," "told," "dealt," and "pitched."

Eight o'Clock

He stood, and heard the steeple
  Sprinkle the quarters on the morning town.
One, two, three, four, to market-place and people
  It tossed them down.

Strapped, noosed, nighing his hour,
  He stood and counted them and cursed his luck;
And then the clock collected in the tower
  Its strength, and struck.

Housman's criticisms were chiefly confined to controversies about literature and, in particular, the process of creation. Contemptuous of careless work, he wrote occasional prose that is full of the same edged phrasing which distinguishes his poetry. He epitomized Swinburne's verbosity by declaring, "Swinburne has now said not only all he has to say about everything, but all he has to say about nothing." His chief scorn was directed against pretentious scholarship, and one of his victims drew this devastating sentence: "Nature, not content with denying to Mr. X the faculty of thinking, has endowed him with the faculty of writing."

It has been said that, because of his severely disciplined tone and his epigrammatic line, Housman may well be considered the greatest Latin poet who ever wrote in English.

GEORGE SANTAYANA
[1863–1952]

SUPERFICIALLY George Santayana seems to have little in common with A. E. Housman, but, unknown to each other, they shared the same classical point of view if not the same ironic skepticism. "My own moral philosophy," wrote Santayana, "may not seem very robust or joyous. The owl hooting from his wintry bough cannot be chanticleer crowing in the barnyard, yet he is sacred to Minerva."

A Spaniard by birth (Madrid, December 16, 1863), son of Spanish parents, Santayana was taken to Boston at the age of nine. Educated at the Boston Latin School and Harvard, he began teaching philosophy at Harvard in his mid-twenties. In the 1900's his students—among whom were T. S. Eliot, Conrad Aiken, and Felix Frankfurter—considered him an inspired teacher, but Santayana actively disliked the academic tradition. Shortly before his fiftieth birthday he received an inheritance, resigned his professorship, and went abroad. He lived for a while in Oxford and Paris and finally settled in Rome.

Santayana's work, as befits a philosopher, is concerned with moral values. Writing chiefly on aesthetics and religious philosophy, Santayana remained a writer for the few until the appearance of THE LAST PURITAN, published in his seventy-second year. THE LAST PURITAN is a novel which, widely discussed, anticipated John P. Marquand's caustic examinations of the New England spirit. It was Santayana's one popular success, but readers were by no means united in their approval. Robert Hillyer spoke of the author

> . . . who alone
> Among philosophers still seeks their Stone;
> Whose irony, in golden prose alloyed
> With doubt, yet yields not to the acid Freud;
> Who, after years of rightful fame defrauded,
> Wrote one bad book at last—and all applauded.

Santayana has apologized for his poetry by saying that English was not his native language and that he was, at best, an apprentice in a great school. "I never drank in in childhood the homely cadences and ditties which in pure spontaneous poetry set the essential key. . . . Moreover, I am city-bred, and that companionship with nature, those rural notes which for English poets are almost inseparable from poetic feeling, fail me altogether. . . . My approach to language is literary, my images are only metaphors, and sometimes it seems to me that I resemble my countryman Don Quixote, when in his airy flights he was merely perched on a high horse and a wooden Pegasus."

Santayana's modesty is becoming but misleading. His verse is not, as he insists, "thin in texture," but richly woven. His sonnets are particularly warm in phrase and deep in feeling. More affirmative than most of his writing they are among the finest contemporary examples of the form.

O World

O world, thou choosest not the better part!
It is not wisdom to be only wise,
And on the inward vision close the eyes,
But it is wisdom to believe the heart.
Columbus found a world, and had no chart,
Save one that faith deciphered in the skies;
To trust the soul's invincible surmise
Was all his science and his only art.
Our knowledge is a torch of smoky pine
That lights the pathway but one step ahead
Across a void of mystery and dread.
Bid, then, the tender light of faith to shine
By which alone the mortal heart is led
Unto the thinking of the thought divine.

Deem Not, Because You See Me

Deem not, because you see me in the press
Of this world's children run my fated race,
That I blaspheme against a proffered grace,
Or leave unlearned the love of holiness.
I honor not that sanctity the less
Whose aureole illumines not my face,
But dare not tread the secret, holy place
To which the priest and prophet have access.
For some are born to be beatified
By anguish, and by grievous penance done;
And some, to furnish forth the age's pride,
And to be praised of men beneath the sun;
And some are born to stand perplexed aside
From so much sorrow—of whom I am one.

With You a Part of Me

With you a part of me hath passed away;
For in the peopled forest of my mind
A tree made leafless by this wintry wind
Shall never don again its green array.

Chapel and fireside, country road and bay,
Have something of their friendliness resigned;
Another, if I would, I could not find,
And I am grown much older in a day.
But yet I treasure in my memory
Your gift of charity, and young heart's ease,
And the dear honor of your amity;
For these once mine, my life is rich with these.
And I scarce know which part may greater be—
What I keep of you, or you rob from me.

What Riches Have You?

What riches have you that you deem me poor,
Or what large comfort that you call me sad?
Tell me what makes you so exceeding glad:
Is your earth happy or your heaven sure?
I hope for heaven, since the stars endure
And bring such tidings as our fathers had.
I know no deeper doubt to make me mad,
I need no brighter love to keep me pure.
To me the faiths of old are daily bread;
I bless their hope, I bless their will to save,
And my deep heart still meaneth what they said.
It makes me happy that the soul is brave,
And, being so much kinsman to the dead,
I walk contented to the peopled grave.

WILLIAM BUTLER YEATS

[1865–1939]

SHELLEY's remark that "poets are the unacknowledged legislators
of the world" is usually regarded as a flight of youthful rhetoric.
Yet, besides being a poet and playwright, William Butler Yeats was
a senator and served the Irish Free State from 1922 to 1928.

Yeats was born June 13, 1865, at Sandymount, near Dublin. His
family was distinguished in the arts; his father was a well-known
painter, and Yeats studied at the Royal Dublin Society. But, when

he began contributing to the Irish periodicals, it was apparent that his medium was not the brush but the pen. In his early twenties Yeats went to London, joined the Rhymers' Club, which specialized in the latest aestheticism, and imitated the Pre-Raphaelites. But the affectations of the moment could not hold him. His devotion to Ireland was so intense that he returned to the varying aspects of its counties, to integrate himself with the problems of his own land, and express a life that had never been given full expression. With the collaboration of a few others, Yeats was responsible for the renascence of culture in Ireland; he helped to establish not only the Gaelic League but also the Irish Literary Theater. It was to be a communal adventure based upon native material. In his late twenties Yeats wrote enthusiastically: "I would have Ireland re-create the ancient arts, the arts as they were understood in Judea, in India, in Scandinavia, in Greece and Rome, in every ancient land as they were understood when they moved a whole people, and not a few people who have grown up in a leisure class and made this understanding their business."

To further this aim Yeats wrote dramas and lyrics centering about Irish legendry. He re-created folklore, published eloquent essays, and perfected a poetry of vague music and delicate nostalgia.

The Lake Isle of Innisfree

I will arise and go now, and go to Innisfree,
And a small cabin build there, of clay and wattles made;
Nine bean rows will I have there, a hive for the honey bee,
    And live alone in the bee-loud glade.

And I shall have some peace there, for peace comes dropping slow,
Dropping from the veils of the morning to where the cricket sings;
There midnight's all a glimmer, and noon a purple glow,
    And evening full of the linnet's wings.

I will arise and go now, for always night and day
I hear lake water lapping with low sounds by the shore;
While I stand on the roadway, or on the pavements gray,
    I hear it in the deep heart's core.

To his admirers it seemed that Yeats had found himself in a set of charming abstractions and lovely, though rather facile, symbols.

But at fifty Yeats turned against his own idiom. Freeing himself from shadowy waters and a wavering music, he dealt with actualities; his lines became subtler and, at the same time, more precise. Even when he employed mythological themes, he changed them from remote fantasies into the semblance of an immediate experience. In complete contrast to his early Pre-Raphaelite leanings, when he "hid his face amid a crowd of stars," he began to express his delight "in the whole man—blood, imagination, intellect, running together."

Leda and the Swan

A sudden blow: the great wings beating still
Above the staggering girl, her thighs caressed
By the dark webs, her nape caught in his bill,
He holds her helpless breast upon his breast.

How can those terrified vague fingers push
The feathered glory from her loosening thighs?
And how can body, laid in that white rush,
But feel the strange heart beating where it lies?

A shudder in the loins engenders there
The broken wall, the burning roof and tower
And Agamemnon dead.
               Being so caught up,
So mastered by the brute blood of the air,
Did she put on his knowledge with his power
Before the indifferent beak could let her drop?

Yeats continued to pursue that delight "in the whole man" and express it in some of the richest poetry of the period. He who had loved "symbols, popular beliefs, and old scraps of verse that made Ireland romantic to herself" declared that "the new Ireland, overwhelmed by responsibility, begins to long for psychological truths." His intellectual power increased. In A DIALOGUE OF SELF AND SOUL he wrote:

I am content to follow to its source,
Every event in action or in thought;
Measure the lot; forgive myself the lot!
When such as I cast out remorse

So great a sweetness flows into the breast
We must laugh and we must sing,
We are blest by everything,
Everything we look upon is blest.

The language became more and more straightforward. Quietly but fiercely it probed for "psychological truth." It faced personal disappointment and national despair.

An Irish Airman Foresees His Death

I know that I shall meet my fate
Somewhere among the clouds above;
Those that I fight I do not hate,
Those that I guard I do not love;
My country is Kiltartan Cross,
My countrymen Kiltartan's poor,
No likely end could bring them loss
Or leave them happier than before.
Nor law, nor duty bade me fight,
Nor public men, nor cheering crowds,
A lonely impulse of delight
Drove to this tumult in the clouds;
I balanced all, brought all to mind,
The years to come seemed waste of breath,
A waste of breath the years behind
In balance with this life, this death.

AMONG SCHOOL CHILDREN is an integration and a summary. In this candid yet complex poem, so different from the early musical verse, the "sixty-year-old smiling public man" remembers his own youth and the woman he loved in young manhood, the magnificent and unattainable Maud Gonne. In a blend of disillusion and self-mockery he questions the certainty of all philosophies—"Old clothes upon old sticks to scare a bird"—and the figure reminds him of himself in age, "a comfortable kind of scarecrow."

Among School Children

I

I walk through the long schoolroom questioning;
A kind old nun in a white hood replies;
The children learn to cipher and to sing,
To study reading-books and history,
To cut and sew, be neat in everything
In the best modern way—the children's eyes
In momentary wonder stare upon
A sixty-year-old smiling public man.

II

I dream of a Ledaean body, bent
Above a sinking fire, a tale that she
Told of a harsh reproof, or trivial event
That changed some childish day to tragedy—
Told, and it seemed that our two natures blent
Into a sphere from youthful sympathy,
Or else, to alter Plato's parable,
Into the yolk and the white of one shell.

III

And thinking of that fit of grief or rage
I look upon one child or t'other there
And wonder if she stood so at that age—
For even daughters of the swan can share
Something of every paddler's heritage—
And had that color upon cheek or hair,
And thereupon my heart is driven wild:
She stands before me as a living child.

IV

Her present image floats into the mind—
Did Quattrocento finger fashion it
Hollow of cheek as though it drank the wind
And took a mess of shadows for its meat?

And I though never of Ledaean kind
Had pretty plumage once—enough of that,
Better to smile on all that smile, and show
There is a comfortable kind of scarecrow.

V

What youthful mother, a shape upon her lap
Honey of generation had betrayed,
And that must sleep, shriek, struggle to escape
As recollection or the drug decide,
Would think her son, did she but see that shape
With sixty or more winters on its head,
A compensation for the pang of his birth,
Or the uncertainty of his setting forth?

VI

Plato thought nature but a spume that plays
Upon a ghostly paradigm of things;
Solider Aristotle played the taws
Upon the bottom of a king of kings;
World-famous golden-thighed Pythagoras
Fingered upon a fiddle-stick or strings
What a star sang and careless Muses heard:
Old clothes upon old sticks to scare a bird.

VII

Both nuns and mothers worship images,
But those the candles light are not as those
That animate a mother's reveries,
But keep a marble or a bronze repose.
And yet they too break hearts—O Presences
That passion, piety or affection knows,
And that all heavenly glory symbolize—
O self-born mockers of man's enterprise;

VIII

Labor is blossoming or dancing where
The body is not bruised to pleasure soul,
Nor beauty born out of its own despair,
Nor blear-eyed wisdom out of midnight oil.

> O chestnut tree, great rooted blossomer,
> Are you the leaf, the blossom or the bole?
> O body swayed to music, O brightening glance,
> How can we know the dancer from the dance?

In old age Yeats lost faith in the average man whom he had once championed. He revolted against the middle classes who "fumble in the greasy till, and add the half-pence to the pence." Long ago he had given up his dream of a culturally awakened Ireland—

> Romantic Ireland's dead and gone,
> It's with O'Leary in the grave.

Yeats yearned for "an aristocratic order" and inveighed against "the vulgarity and the materialism whereon England has founded her worst life and the whole life she sends us." His poetry began to express anger and impotence. In his seventies, lashed by the chaotic forces that threatened from without and frustrated by the loss of power within, he offered this quatrain as a "final apology":

> You think it horrible that Lust and Rage
> Should dance attendance upon my old age;
> They were not such a plague when I was young.
> What else have I to spur me into song?

Yeats spent much of his time during his last years in southern Europe. He died, after a brief illness, at Roquebrune, near Nice, January 28, 1939. He had already written his own epitaph:

> Cast a cold eye
> On life, on death.
> Horseman, pass by.

Tributes to Yeats's living power increased after his death. Books of interpretation and dozens of critical essays reappraised his varying work. The most rounded poem was written by W. H. Auden, IN MEMORY OF W. B. YEATS (see page 1204), a poem which ends:

> Follow, poet, follow right
> To the bottom of the night,
> With your unconstraining voice
> Still persuade us to rejoice . . .

> In the deserts of the heart
> Let the healing fountain start,
> In the prison of his days
> Teach the free man how to praise.

RUDYARD KIPLING
[1865–1936]

COMING out of India, Rudyard Kipling swept into English litera-
ture like a salt sea gale. He burst through doors that had been
tightly sealed by the Victorians and threw open the preciously dec-
orated Pre-Raphaelite windows. Challenging the vogue of the senti-
mentally archaic, Kipling exalted the world of prosaic things. An
uncrowned laureate of machinery, he sang of the grimy by-products
of science and of all those who did the work of the world: engineers,
road builders, explorers, stokers, sailors, and soldiers.

Born December 30, 1865, at Bombay, India, of English parents,
Kipling was taken to England at the age of six. He attended the
United Service College at Westward Ho!, in North Devon, a place
that is pictured in STALKY & CO., a book which many readers find
highly amusing, but which Edmund Wilson considers "a hair-
raising picture of the sadism of the English public school."

When Kipling returned to India, he became sub-editor of the
LAHORE CIVIL AND MILITARY GAZETTE. At twenty-one he published
his first volume, a collection of verse; at twenty-two he produced
his first narrative, PLAIN TALES FROM THE HILLS. According to Wil-
son, Kipling took the part of the natives and the Tommies because
they were victimized, and he, too, had been a victim of cruelty.
Whether or not the theory is tenable, Kipling added a new prov-
ince to English literature. As Somerset Maugham wrote: "Rudyard
Kipling was the first to blaze the trail through new-found country,
and no one has invested it with more glamor, no one has made it
more exciting. . . . He not only created characters, he created men."

Fuzzy-Wuzzy

We've fought with many men acrost the seas,
  An' some of 'em was brave an' some was not:
The Paythan an' the Zulu an' Burmese;
  But the Fuzzy was the finest o' the lot.
We never got a ha'porth's change of 'im:
  'E squatted in the scrub an' 'ocked our 'orses,
'E cut our sentries up at Sua*kim*,
  An' 'e played the cat an' banjo with our forces.
    So 'ere's *to* you, Fuzzy-Wuzzy, at your 'ome in the Sowdan;
    You're a pore benighted 'eathen but a first-class fightin' man;
    We gives you your certifikit, an' if you want it signed
    We'll come an' 'ave a romp with you whenever you're inclined.

We took our chanst among the Kyber 'ills,
  The Boers knocked us silly at a mile,
The Burman guv us Irriwaddy chills,
  An' a Zulu *impi* dished us up in style:
But all we ever got from such as they
  Was pop to what the Fuzzy made us swaller;
We 'eld our bloomin' own, the papers say,
  But man for man the Fuzzy knocked us 'oller.
    Then 'ere's *to* you, Fuzzy-Wuzzy, an' the missis and the kid;
    Our orders was to break you, an' of course we went an' did.
    We sloshed you with Martinis, an' it wasn't 'ardly fair;
    But for all the odds agin you, Fuzzy-Wuz, you bruk the
      square.

'E 'asn't got no papers, of 'is own,
  'E 'asn't got no medals nor rewards,
So we must certify the skill 'e's shown
  In usin' of 'is long two-'anded swords;
When 'e's 'oppin' in an' out among the bush
  With 'is coffin-'eaded shield an' shovel-spear,
A 'appy day with Fuzzy on the rush
  Will last a 'ealthy Tommy for a year.
    So 'ere's *to* you, Fuzzy-Wuzzy, an' your friends which are no
      more,
    If we 'adn't lost some messmates we would 'elp you to
      deplore;
    But give an' take's the gospel, an' we'll call the bargain fair,
    For if you 'ave lost more than us, you crumpled up the
      square!

'E rushes at the smoke when we let drive,
  An', before we know, 'e's 'ackin' at our 'ead;
'E's all 'ot sand an' ginger when alive,
  An' 'e's generally shammin' when 'e's dead.
'E's a daisy, 'e's a ducky, 'e's a lamb!
'E's a injia-rubber idiot on the spree,
'E's the on'y thing that doesn't care a damn
  For the Regiment o' British Infantree.
   So 'ere's *to* you, Fuzzy-Wuzzy, at your 'ome in the Sowdan;
   You're a pore benighted 'eathen but a first-class fightin' man;
   An 'ere's *to* you, Fuzzy-Wuzzy, with your 'ayrick 'ead of 'air—
   You big black boundin' beggar—for you bruk a British square.

Danny Deever

"What are the bugles blowin' for?" said Files-on-Parade.
"To turn you out, to turn you out," the Color-Sergeant said.
"What makes you look so white, so white?" said Files-on-Parade.
"I'm dreadin' what I've got to watch," the Color-Sergeant said.
   For they're hangin' Danny Deever, you can 'ear the Dead March
     play,
   The regiment's in 'ollow square—they're hangin' him today;
   They've taken of his buttons off an' cut his stripes away,
   An' they're hangin' Danny Deever in the mornin'.

"What makes the rear-rank breathe so 'ard?" said Files-on-Parade.
"It's bitter cold, it's bitter cold," the Color-Sergeant said.
"What makes that front-rank man fall down?" says Files-on-Parade.
"A touch of sun, a touch of sun," the Color-Sergeant said.
   They are hangin' Danny Deever, they are marchin' of 'im round.
   They 'ave 'alted Danny Deever by 'is coffin on the ground:
   An 'e'll swing in 'arf a minute for a sneakin' shootin' hound—
   O they're hangin' Danny Deever in the mornin'!

" 'Is cot was right-'and cot to mine," said Files-on-Parade.
" 'E's sleepin' out an' far tonight," the Color-Sergeant said.
"I've drunk 'is beer a score o' times," said Files-on-Parade.
" 'E's drinkin' bitter beer alone," the Color-Sergeant said.
   They are hangin' Danny Deever, you must mark 'im to 'is place,
   For 'e shot a comrade sleepin'—you must look 'im in the face;
   Nine 'undred of 'is county an' the regiment's disgrace,
   While they're hangin' Danny Deever in the mornin'.

"What's that so black agin the sun?" said Files-on-Parade.
"It's Danny fightin' 'ard for life," the Color-Sergeant said.
"What's that that whimpers over'ead?" said Files-on-Parade.
"It's Danny's soul that's passin' now," the Color-Sergeant said.
    For they're done with Danny Deever, you can 'ear the quickstep
      play,
    The regiment's in column, an' they're marchin' us away;
    Ho! the young recruits are shakin', an' they'll want their beer
      today,
    After hangin' Danny Deever in the mornin'.

Mandalay

By the old Moulmein Pagoda, lookin' eastward to the sea,
There's a Burma girl a-settin', an' I know she thinks o' me;
For the wind is in the palm-trees, an' the temple bells they say:
"Come you back, you British soldier; come you back to Mandalay!"
    Come you back to Mandalay,
    Where the old Flotilla lay:
    Can't you 'ear their paddles chunkin' from Rangoon to
      Mandalay?
    On the road to Mandalay,
    Where the flyin'-fishes play,
    An' the dawn comes up like thunder outer China 'crost the
      Bay!

'Er petticut was yaller an' 'er little cap was green,
An' 'er name was Supi-yaw-let—jes' the same as Theebaw's Queen,
An' I seed her fust a-smokin' of a whackin' white cheroot,
An' a-wastin' Christian kisses on an 'eathen idol's foot:
    Bloomin' idol made o' mud—
    What they called the Great Gawd Budd—
    Plucky lot she cared for idols when I kissed 'er where she stud!
    On the road to Mandalay—

When the mist was on the rice-fields an' the sun was droppin' slow,
She'd git 'er little banjo an' she'd sing *"Kulla-lo-lo!"*
With 'er arm upon my shoulder an' her cheek agin my cheek
We useter watch the steamers an' the *hathis* pilin' teak.
    Elephints a-pilin' teak
    In the sludgy, squdgy creek,
    Where the silence 'ung that 'eavy you was 'arf afraid to speak!
    On the road to Mandalay—

But that's all shove be'ind me—long ago an' fur away,
An' there ain't no 'busses runnin' from the Bank to Mandalay;
An' I'm learnin' 'ere in London what the ten-year sodger tells:
"If you've 'eard the East a-callin', why, you won't 'eed nothin' else."
      No! you won't 'eed nothin' else
      But them spicy garlic smells
      An' the sunshine an' the palm-trees an' the tinkly temple-bells!
      On the road to Mandalay—

I am sick o' wastin' leather on these gritty pavin'-stones,
An' the blasted Henglish drizzle wakes the fever in my bones;
'Tho' I walks with fifty 'ousemaids outer Chelsea to the Strand,
An' they talks a lot o' lovin', but wot do they understand?
      Beefy face an' grubby 'and—
      Law! wot *do* they understand?
      I've a neater, sweeter maiden in a cleaner, greener land!
      On the road to Mandalay—

Ship me somewheres east of Suez where the best is like the worst,
Where there aren't no Ten Commandments, an' a man can raise a
            thirst:
For the temple-bells are callin', an' it's there that I would be—
By the old Moulmein Pagoda, lookin' lazy at the sea—
      On the road to Mandalay,
      Where the old Flotilla lay,
      With our sick beneath the awnings when we went to Manda-
      lay!
      Oh, the road to Mandalay,
      Where the flyin'-fishes play,
      An' the dawn comes up like thunder outer China 'crost the
      Bay!

Famous at twenty-seven, Kipling traveled around the world. He
married an American, Caroline Balestier, and lived for a few years
in Brattleboro, Vermont. It is probable that Kipling would have
remained in America, where he wrote several of his most popular
works, if a quarrel with his brother-in-law had not driven him back
to England. Suspicious and apprehensive, he became antisocial.
His daughter had died, and the loss of a son during the First World
War embittered him. He secluded himself in the Sussex village of
Burwash.

In his later work Kipling identified himself with the lords and
masters, governors of Empire. His heartiness became exaggerated,

his imperialism brazenly militant. Yet RECESSIONAL, Kipling's most famous poem, was a daring rebuke. Written at the time of Queen Victoria's Diamond Jubilee, Kipling reminded the British Empire of man's impermanent grandeur: "Lo, all our pomp of yesterday is one with Nineveh and Tyre!" The very title, indicating the hymn sung at the close of a service, was a warning and a prophecy.

Recessional

God of our fathers, known of old,
    Lord of our far-flung battle-line,
Beneath whose awful hand we hold
    Dominion over palm and pine—
Lord God of Hosts, be with us yet,
Lest we forget—lest we forget!

The tumult and the shouting dies;
    The captains and the kings depart:
Still stands Thine ancient sacrifice,
    An humble and a contrite heart.
Lord God of Hosts, be with us yet,
Lest we forget—lest we forget!

Far-called, our navies melt away;
    On dune and headland sinks the fire:
Lo, all our pomp of yesterday
    Is one with Nineveh and Tyre!
Judge of the Nations, spare us yet,
Lest we forget—lest we forget!

If, drunk with sight of power, we loose
    Wild tongues that have not Thee in awe,
Such boastings as the Gentiles use,
    Or lesser breeds without the Law—
Lord God of Hosts, be with us yet,
Lest we forget—lest we forget!

For heathen heart that puts her trust
    In reeking tube and iron shard,
All valiant dust that builds on dust,
    And, guarding, calls not Thee to guard,
For frantic boast and foolish word—
Thy Mercy on Thy People, Lord!

In his forty-second year Kipling received the Nobel Prize for
literature. A few years later it became the fashion to belittle Kip-
ling's work. It was implied that he, like one of his own titles, was
"The Light That Failed"; in 1935 a deprecating editorial referred
to him as "the forgotten man of English literature." He died Janu-
ary 18, 1936, a few weeks after his seventieth birthday.

Although it is conceded that Kipling was a master of the modern
short story, his poetry has been variously judged. His verse has
suffered from its very ease as well as from the extremes of praise and
disapproval. A new generation is beginning to re-estimate his pecul-
iar combination of pounding rhythms and delicate accents, of
exuberance and nostalgia. It is significant that A CHOICE OF KIPLING'S
VERSE was unexpectedly and enthusiastically compiled by T. S. Eliot
in 1941.

L'Envoi

What is the moral? Who rides may read.
When the night is thick and the tracks are blind
A friend at a pinch is a friend indeed,
But a fool to wait for the laggard behind.
Down to Gehenna or up to the Throne,
He travels the fastest who travels alone.

White hands cling to the tightened rein,
Slipping the spur from the booted heel,
Tenderest voices cry "Turn again!"
Red lips tarnish the scabbarded steel.
High hopes faint on a warm hearth stone—
He travels the fastest who travels alone.

One may fall but he falls by himself—
Falls by himself with himself to blame.
One may attain and to him is pelf—
Loot of the city in Gold or Fame.
Plunder of earth shall be all his own
Who travels the fastest and travels alone.

Wherefore the more ye be holpen and stayed,
Stayed by a friend in the hour of toil,
Sing the heretical song I have made—
His be the labor and yours be the spoil.
Win by his aid and the aid disown—
He travels the fastest who travels alone!

In spite of a critical minority, it seems likely that Kipling will outlive most of his generation as a people's poet; he will be redis- covered again and again. The best of his lines are refreshingly out- spoken, brimming with vitality. His story poems have the natural force which characterizes true narrative verse. Kipling may well have written the popular measures of one age and the remembered ballads of another.

ERNEST DOWSON
[1867–1900]

D EAD at thirty-two, Dowson's life was as luckless as his career was frail. It was a brief career of wine and roses—roses flung riotously but unhappily—as though in a disordered dream. He wrote his own autobiography in the eight lines entitled VITAE SUMMA BREVIS SPEM NOS VETAT INCOHARE LONGAM, a quotation from Horace's first book of ODES: "The shortness of life prevents us from entertaining far-off hopes."

Vitae Summa Brevis Spem Nos Vetat Incohare Longam

They are not long, the weeping and the laughter,
    Love and desire and hate;
I think they have no portion in us after
        We pass the gate.

They are not long, the days of wine and roses:
    Out of a misty dream
Our path emerges for a while, then closes
        Within a dream.

Dowson was born at Belmont Hill, in Kent, August 2, 1867. His family was an eminent one; his great-uncle was Prime Minister of New Zealand. Although Dowson attended Queen's College, Oxford, he left without finishing his studies, went to London, and joined the Rhymers' Club. Alternating between fits of religion and dissipation, he lived recklessly. He fell idealistically in love with a waitress, daughter of a restaurant keeper, but she understood neither his verse nor his reticence. She was his "Cynara," and it was to her that he wrote his universally known poem with a Latin title that she found even more inexplicable than the man who adored her with such virginal devotion. The title was from Dowson's favorite Horace, from the beginning of the fourth book of ODES: "I am not what I was under the reign of the lovely Cynara."

Non Sum Qualis Eram Bonae Sub Regno Cynarae

Last night, ah, yesternight, betwixt her lips and mine
There fell thy shadow, Cynara! thy breath was shed
Upon my soul between the kisses and the wine;
And I was desolate and sick of an old passion,
    Yea, I was desolate and bowed my head:
I have been faithful to thee, Cynara! in my fashion.

All night upon mine heart I felt her warm heart beat,
Night-long within mine arms in love and sleep she lay;
Surely the kisses of her bought red mouth were sweet;
But I was desolate and sick of an old passion,
    When I awoke and found the dawn was gray:
I have been faithful to thee, Cynara! in my fashion.

I have forgot much, Cynara! gone with the wind,
Flung roses, roses riotously with the throng,
Dancing, to put thy pale, lost lilies out of mind;
But I was desolate and sick of an old passion,
    Yea, all the time, because the dance was long:
I have been faithful to thee, Cynara! in my fashion.

I cried for madder music and for stronger wine,
But when the feast is finished and the lamps expire,
Then falls thy shadow, Cynara! the night is thine;
And I am desolate and sick of an old passion,
    Yea, hungry for the lips of my desire:
I have been faithful to thee, Cynara! in my fashion.

The puzzled and finally impatient "Cynara" ran away and married a waiter. Dowson, feeling that his life was ruined, became irresponsible. Instead of drinking haphazardly, he drank deliberately. His father had left him an old dock, and Dowson hid there, in cabmen's shelters, living in utmost squalor. "He drifted about in whatever company came his way," wrote Arthur Symons; "he let heedlessness develop into a curious disregard of personal tidiness."

Dowson tried to forget his misery in France. But, though he made friends with innkeepers, he got into fights with the fishermen who came in to drink. It was too late to toughen his fragile spirit by contact with rough animal life. His VILLANELLE OF THE POET'S ROAD is not only an exquisite use of an old French form, but also a confession of Dowson's frustrated desire.

Villanelle of the Poet's Road

Wine and woman and song,
   Three things garnish our way:
Yet is day over long.

Lest we do our youth wrong,
   Gather them while we may:
Wine and woman and song.

Three things render us strong,
   Vine leaves, kisses and bay:
Yet is day over long.

Unto us they belong,
   Us the bitter and gay,
Wine and woman and song.

We, as we pass along,
   Are sad that they will not stay;
Yet is day over long.

Fruits and flowers among,
   What is better than they:
Wine and woman and song?
Yet is day over long.

Venus had rejected his garlands. Now, toward the end of his life, Dowson lit a candle to the Virgin. He died, a convert to the Roman Catholic Church, February 23, 1900.

Much of the literature of the 1890's seems written on plush; but Dowson's intensity rose above decadence. Limited by his temperament, defeated by life, Dowson left a few unique things. "In a subdued way," wrote Donald Davidson in BRITISH POETRY OF THE EIGHTEEN-NINETIES, "he was an English Poe, half angel, half Bohemian—a saint of the gutter, a Catullus lost in the wilderness of English respectability."

EDWIN ARLINGTON ROBINSON
[1869–1935]

A FTER Whitman had celebrated "the divine average," poetry in America became more concerned with the common man. Edwin Arlington Robinson went further; he devoted himself not only to the ordinary individual, but also to the misfits and the outcasts, those who were unable to maintain themselves in a world of ruthless efficiency. Robinson protested against acquisitiveness and success at any cost; he almost made a fetish of failure. This was perhaps inevitable, for Robinson's own life was, except for a few short intervals, a dignified and losing battle.

Robinson was born December 22, 1869, in the village of Head Tide, Maine, and, while still a child, moved to the near-by town of Gardiner. At twenty-one he entered Harvard College and left it two years later. At twenty-seven he issued a privately printed collection of verse. But he feared to market himself as a poet, and there seemed little future for him as a breadwinner. "This itch for authorship," he wrote, "is worse than the devil and spoils a man for anything else." He went to New York, tried to earn a living as an inspector in the New York subway, and almost starved. At thirty-five he was rescued from poverty by President Theodore Roosevelt, who gave him a clerkship in the New York Custom House. But if Robinson was relieved, he was not elated. He remained sympathetic to the cheated dreamers, the bewildered mediocrities. He created an entire gallery of American figures like Richard Cory, who, hiding his despair, "glittered when he walked," and Miniver Cheevy, the incompetent "child of scorn," with his futile dream of escape.

Richard Cory

Whenever Richard Cory went down town,
   We people on the pavement looked at him:
He was a gentleman from sole to crown,
   Clean favored, and imperially slim.

And he was always quietly arrayed,
   And he was always human when he talked;
But still he fluttered pulses when he said,
   "Good-morning," and he glittered when he walked.

And he was rich—yes, richer than a king—
   And admirably schooled in every grace:
In fine, we thought that he was everything
   To make us wish that we were in his place.

So on we worked, and waited for the light,
   And went without the meat, and cursed the bread;
And Richard Cory, one calm summer night,
   Went home and put a bullet through his head.

Miniver Cheevy

Miniver Cheevy, child of scorn,
   Grew lean while he assailed the seasons;
He wept that he was ever born,
   And he had reasons.

Miniver loved the days of old
   When swords were bright and steeds were prancing;
The vision of a warrior bold
   Would set him dancing.

Miniver sighed for what was not,
   And dreamed, and rested from his labors;
He dreamed of Thebes and Camelot,
   And Priam's neighbors.

Miniver mourned the ripe renown
   That made so many a name so fragrant;
He mourned Romance, now on the town,
   And Art, a vagrant.

Miniver loved the Medici,
   Albeit he had never seen one;
He would have sinned incessantly
   Could he have been one.

Miniver cursed the commonplace
   And eyed a khaki suit with loathing;
He missed the medieval grace
   Of iron clothing.

Miniver scorned the gold he sought,
   But sore annoyed was he without it;
Miniver thought, and thought, and thought,
   And thought about it.

Miniver Cheevy, born too late,
   Scratched his head and kept on thinking;
Miniver coughed, and called it fate,
   And kept on drinking.

Reuben Bright

Because he was a butcher and thereby
Did earn an honest living (and did right)
I would not have you think that Reuben Bright
Was any more a brute than you or I;
For when they told him that his wife must die,
He stared at them and shook with grief and fright,
And cried like a great baby half that night,
And made the women cry to see him cry.

And after she was dead, and he had paid
The singers and the sexton and the rest,
He packed a lot of things that she had made
Most mournfully away in an old chest
Of hers, and put some chopped-up cedar boughs
In with them, and tore down the slaughter-house.

Success came late to Robinson. Until his late fifties he had been a poet admired only by the few. TRISTRAM, published in his fifty-eighth year, made him famous. Strangely enough, the romantic mysticism of this book-length poem—part of an Arthurian cycle—was far less characteristic of the author than the earthy New England portraits. The unexpected, and even unlooked-for, triumph was actually harmful. Robinson began to fear the future, to feel that everything he wrote would be pitted against TRISTRAM. For seven years he drove himself to write an annual volume in a vain effort to live up to the standard set for him. Three times he was awarded the Pulitzer Prize. Nevertheless, he refused to be feted; he doomed himself to solitude. Distrusting most men and fearing almost all women, he became a laconic, lonely man, a man obsessed by defeat and in love with death.

Robinson had schooled himself so severely that he could express the depths of isolation even in so restricted, and usually artificial, a form as the villanelle—witness THE HOUSE ON THE HILL.

The House on the Hill

They are all gone away,
  The House is shut and still,
There is nothing more to say.

Through broken walls and gray
  The winds blow bleak and shrill;
They are all gone away.

Nor is there one today
  To speak them good or ill:
There is nothing more to say.

Why is it then we stray
  Around that sunken sill?
They are all gone away,

And our poor fancy-play
  For them is wasted skill:
There is nothing more to say.

There is ruin and decay
  In the House on the Hill:
They are all gone away,
There is nothing more to say.

Robinson lived most of his summers at the MacDowell colony, in Peterboro, New Hampshire, where he was the center of adulation. He divided his winters between Boston and New York. Except for occasional evenings of conviviality, he withdrew from an oppressive world. In his mid-sixties he became seriously ill. When he was finally taken to the New York Hospital, it was impossible to operate successfully. He died April 6, 1935.

Although much was made of Robinson's pessimism, even the darkest of his monologues are enlivened by the sparkle of imagination and the flicker of wit. The compact lyrics read like extended epigrams; the longer poems are lit with shrewd humor. Sometimes the humor is unaffectedly tender, as in MR. FLOOD'S PARTY, that touching picture of a battered derelict nursing his companionable jug and putting it down with trembling care, "knowing that most things break."

Mr. Flood's Party

Old Eben Flood, climbing alone one night
Over the hill between the town below
And the forsaken upland hermitage
That held as much as he should ever know
On earth again of home, paused warily.
The road was his with not a native near;
And Eben, having leisure, said aloud,
For no man else in Tilbury Town to hear:

"Well, Mr. Flood, we have the harvest moon
Again, and we may not have many more;
The bird is on the wing, the poet says,
And you and I have said it here before.
Drink to the bird." He raised up to the light
The jug that he had gone so far to fill,
And answered huskily: "Well, Mr. Flood,
Since you propose it, I believe I will."

Alone, as if enduring to the end
A valiant armor of scarred hopes outworn,
He stood there in the middle of the road
Like Roland's ghost winding a silent horn.

Below him, in the town among the trees,
Where friends of other days had honored him,
A phantom salutation of the dead
Rang thinly till old Eben's eyes were dim.

Then, as a mother lays her sleeping child
Down tenderly, fearing it may awake,
He set the jug down slowly at his feet
With trembling care, knowing that most things break;
And only when assured that on firm earth
It stood, as the uncertain lives of men
Assuredly did not, he paced away,
And with his hand extended paused again:

"Well, Mr. Flood, we have not met like this
In a long time; and many a change has come
To both of us, I fear, since last it was
We had a drop together. Welcome home!"
Convivially returning with himself,
Again he raised the jug up to the light;
And with an acquiescent quaver said:
"Well, Mr. Flood, if you insist, I might.

"Only a very little, Mr. Flood—
For auld lang syne. No more, sir; that will do."
So, for the time, apparently it did,
And Eben evidently thought so too;
For soon amid the silver loneliness
Of night he lifted up his voice and sang,
Secure, with only two moons listening,
Until the whole harmonious landscape rang—

'For auld lang syne." The weary throat gave out,
The last word wavered; and the song being done,
He raised again the jug regretfully
And shook his head, and was again alone.
There was not much that was ahead of him,
And there was nothing in the town below—
Where strangers would have shut the many doors
That many friends had opened long ago.

Robinson's letters have been published, but they reveal little of
the man. His spiritual autobiography as well as his philosophy is
in RICHARD CORY, in MINIVER CHEEVY, even—and perhaps especially—
in MR. FLOOD'S PARTY.

EDGAR LEE MASTERS
[1869–1950]

AFTER three books of innocuous verse, two of which were published
under pseudonyms, and seven plays, all of which were failures,
Edgar Lee Masters seemed defeated as a writer and devoted himself
to the practice of law. A few years later, at forty-five, he wrote
SPOON RIVER ANTHOLOGY, a landmark in contemporary literature.

Born August 23, 1869, in Garnett, Kansas, Edgar Lee Masters
was taken to Illinois as a child. His father, a man of "dark pug-
nacity," lost money, and the boy's schooling was haphazard; at six-
teen he had to do odd jobs for a living. He worked as printer's
devil, harvest hand, and clerk in a drugstore, and spent his savings
on books. He attended Knox College, thought of being a teacher,
but entered his father's law office. In his twenty-second year he was
admitted to the bar.

Masters had published verse since youth; by the time he was
twenty-four he had written some four hundred poems. His work
showed little besides promise, energy, and a confused worship of
Poe, Whitman, Shelley, Milton, and Swinburne. Suddenly the poet
emerged in a new and surprising manner. Employing the loose, un-
rhymed line of Whitman and the concise summaries of THE GREEK
ANTHOLOGY, Masters presented a collection of free-verse biographies,
some of them imaginary, but many based upon people he knew in
Illinois. He called it SPOON RIVER ANTHOLOGY, and even those who
were repelled by its brute realism had to acknowledge its honesty.
A critical examination of village life, the book was a forerunner of
Sinclair Lewis' MAIN STREET and the ensuing fiction which chal-
lenged smugness and complacent hypocrisy.

In SPOON RIVER ANTHOLOGY the intrigues as well as the monotony
of small-town life are synthesized; but, although hatred and disgust
dominate the mood, pity is not lacking. The prologue begins in a
key of regret, a tender parody of Villon's lines beginning "Where
are the snows of yesteryear?"

Where are Elmer, Herman, Bert, Tom and Charley,
The weak of will, the strong of arm, the clown, the boozer, the
    fighter?
All, all, are sleeping on the hill.

One of the most affecting pages in SPOON RIVER ANTHOLOGY vivifies the tragedy of Abraham Lincoln's requited but unfulfilled love for Ann Rutledge, the New Salem tavernkeeper's daughter. Lincoln was twenty-five; she was a little more than twenty. "The earth was their footstool," wrote Carl Sandburg in ABRAHAM LINCOLN: THE PRAIRIE YEARS, "the sky was a sheaf of blue dreams; the rise of the blood-gold rim of a full moon in the evening was almost too much to live, see, and remember." But before they could be married she died of fever, and Lincoln carried the scars of that burning throughout his life. "He was a changed man keeping to himself the gray mystery of that change."

Ann Rutledge

Out of me unworthy and unknown
The vibrations of deathless music:
"With malice toward none, with charity for all."
Out of me the forgiveness of millions toward millions,
And the beneficent face of a nation
Shining with justice and truth.
I am Ann Rutledge who sleep beneath these weeds,
Beloved in life of Abraham Lincoln,
Wedded to him, not through union,
But through separation.
Bloom forever, O Republic,
From the dust of my bosom!

SPOON RIVER ANTHOLOGY is primarily not a book of verse but a book of characters; as such it has been relished by people who do not usually read poetry. It is full of forthright strength and angry energy; even its tenderness is rugged, never soft and not too sympathetic. But a hunger for beauty struggles through the desperation and cruelty.

Fiddler Jones

The earth keeps some vibration going
There in your heart, and that is you.
And if the people find you can fiddle,
Why, fiddle you must, for all your life.
What do you see, a harvest of clover?

Or a meadow to walk through to the river?
The wind's in the corn; you rub your hands
For beeves hereafter ready for market;
Or else you hear the rustle of skirts
Like the girls when dancing at Little Grove.
To Cooney Potter a pillar of dust
Or whirling leaves meant ruinous drouth;
They looked to me like Red-Head Sammy
Stepping it off, to "Toor-a-Loor."
How could I till my forty acres
Not to speak of getting more,
With a medley of horns, bassoons and piccolos
Stirred in my brain by crows and robins
And the creak of a wind-mill—only these?
And I never started to plow in my life
That some one did not stop in the road
And take me away to a dance or picnic.
I ended up with forty acres;
I ended up with a broken fiddle—
And a broken laugh, and a thousand memories,
And not a single regret.

SPOON RIVER ANTHOLOGY is Masters' lonely eminence. The many volumes written before and after that work are a disheartening array, heavily rhetorical, platitudinous, verbose. The industry is unflagging; between his sixty-sixth and sixty-ninth years Masters published nine volumes—a long autobiography, a novel, three biographies, and four collections of poems. Of his fifty books, only one seems likely to survive. That one remains not so much for its poetry as for its authentic portrait of a man and his bitter times. Its cumulative epitaphs compose a living American document, harsh, unhappy, but desperately honest. Self-doomed to unhappiness, Masters died after a long illness in 1950.

CHARLOTTE MEW

[1869–1928]

ALMOST unknown to the world of men, and little known even in the world of letters, Charlotte Mew wrote two small volumes of firm and distinguished poetry. She was born November 15, 1869, daughter of an architect who died when she was an infant. The struggle with poverty began in childhood; she and her sister Anne never had quite enough funds for comfort. She was happiest in the countryside, but, unable to live there, she was forced to seek a meager living in London. One of her happiest excursions was a week end in Wessex where she was the guest of Thomas Hardy, who said: "She is the least pretentious but undoubtedly the best woman poet of our day." In her late fifties, through the joint efforts of Hardy, Masefield, and others, she was granted a civil-list pension. But, though this kept her alive, her spirit sank beneath the weight of personal maladjustments and private griefs. She never married. The death of her mother made her more of a recluse than ever. After the death of her sister, there was no one to whom she could turn. A severe illness sent her to a nursing home in her sixtieth year. Feeling there was nothing to live for, she committed suicide at the hospital, March 24, 1928.

In an obituary note, Sidney Cockerell wrote, "Charlotte and Anne Mew had more than a little in them of what made another Charlotte and Anne, and their sister Emily, what they were. They were indeed like two Brontë sisters reincarnate." It will never be known how much of her work Charlotte Mew destroyed in a critical passion for perfection. Her published pieces number no more than sixty. Yet these are not only the intensification but the distillation of emotion. The few long poems are probingly meditative; even the lyrics are grave and sonorous.

Sea Love

Tide be runnin' the great world over:
  'Twas only last June month I mind that we
Was thinkin' the toss and the call in the breast of the lover
  So everlastin' as the sea.

Here's the same little fishes that sputter and swim,
  Wi' the moon's old glim on the gray, wet sand;
An' him no more to me nor me to him
  Than the wind goin' over my hand.

I Have Been Through the Gates

His heart, to me, was a place of palaces and pinnacles and shining
    towers;
I saw it then as we see things in dreams,—I do not remember how
    long I slept;
I remember the trees, and the high, white walls, and how the sun
    was always on the towers;
The walls are standing today, and the gates: I have been through
    the gates, I have groped, I have crept
Back, back. There is dust in the streets, and blood; they are empty;
    darkness is over them;
His heart is a place with the lights gone out, forsaken by great
    winds and the heavenly rain, unclean and unswept,
Like the heart of the holy city, old, blind, beautiful Jerusalem,
Over which Christ wept.

Charlotte Mew had a gift for making her personal outcry impersonal. BESIDE THE BED is a human experience, but the transformation into verse gives it an unearthly solemnity. It is one of the shortest but one of the most beautiful of dirges.

Beside the Bed

Someone has shut the shining eyes, straightened and folded
    The wandering hands quietly covering the unquiet breast:
So, smoothed and silenced you lie, like a child, not again to be
    questioned or scolded:
    But, for you, not one of us believes that this is rest.

Not so to close the windows down can cloud and deaden
    The blue beyond: or to screen the wavering flame subdue its
    breath:
Why, if I lay my cheek to your cheek, your gray lips, like dawn,
    would quiver and redden,
    Breaking into the old, odd smile at this fraud of death.

Because all night you have not turned to us or spoken
    It is time for you to wake; your dreams were never very deep:
I, for one, have seen the thin bright, twisted threads of them
    dimmed suddenly and broken.
    This is only a most piteous pretense of sleep!

THE FARMER'S BRIDE, the title poem of Charlotte Mew's first book, is half lyric, half narrative. It is a little masterpiece, of which Harold Monro wrote: "The outline of THE FARMER'S BRIDE would have resolved itself in the mind of Mrs. Browning into a poem of at least two thousand lines; Browning might have worked it up to six thousand . . . Charlotte Mew tells the whole touching story in forty-six lines."

The Farmer's Bride

Three Summers since I chose a maid,
Too young maybe—but more's to do
At harvest-time than bide and woo.
  When us was wed she turned afraid
Of love and me and all things human;
Like the shut of a winter's day.
Her smile went out, and 'twasn't a woman—
  More like a little frightened fay.
    One night, in the Fall, she runned away.

"Out 'mong the sheep, her be," they said,
'Should properly have been abed;
But sure enough she wasn't there
Lying awake with her wide brown stare.
So over seven-acre field and up-along across the down
We chased her, flying like a hare
Before our lanterns. To Church-Town
  All in a shiver and a scare
We caught her, fetched her home at last
  And turned the key upon her, fast.

She does the work about the house
As well as most, but like a mouse:
  Happy enough to chat and play
  With birds and rabbits and such as they,
  So long as men-folk keep away.
"Not near, not near!" her eyes beseech
When one of us comes within reach.
  The women say that beasts in stall
  Look round like children at her call.
  I've hardly heard her speak at all.

Shy as a leveret, swift as he,
Straight and slight as a young larch tree,

Sweet as the first wild violets, she
To her wild self. But what to me?

The short days shorten and the oaks are brown,
  The blue smoke rises to the low gray sky,
One leaf in the still air falls slowly down,
  A magpie's spotted feathers lie
On the black earth spread white with rime,
The berries redden up to Christmas-time.
  What's Christmas-time without there be
Some other in the house than we!

She sleeps up in the attic there
  Alone, poor maid. 'Tis but a stair
Betwixt us. Oh! my God! the down,
The soft young down of her, the brown,
The brown of her—her eyes, her hair, her hair . . .

W. H. DAVIES

[1870–1940]

"A GENUINE innocent, writing odds and ends of verse about odds and ends of things," is the way Bernard Shaw described W. H. Davies in his preface to THE AUTOBIOGRAPHY OF A SUPER-TRAMP. William Henry Davies lived up to the characterization. He was born in a public house, incongruously called Church House, in Monmouthshire, April 20, 1870. His parents were Welsh countrymen, and the boy educated himself. He became a cattleman, a berry picker, and, as the title of his autobiography indicates, a panhandler. He came to the United States, remained there six years, rode the rails, and had his right foot cut off by a train in Canada. Returning to England in his early thirties, he supported himself by peddling and, when necessary, begging.

It was not until his thirty-fifth year that Davies decided to be a poet, and had his book set up in a printer's shop with money he had, somehow, saved. As a poet, he was as fecund as he was determined. Between 1906 and the year of his death, Davies issued twenty-three volumes—five of autobiography, eighteen of verse—

and more than six hundred poems. His birdlike simplicities and almost mindless fluency made it difficult for the critics to separate what was good, bad, and indifferent in his blithe verse. He was called "a Welsh Herrick," and many of his lines justified the appellation. Davies sang ingenuously and tirelessly of a fair world, of happy mornings and evenings full of pleasant reverie.

> Sing out, my Soul, thy songs of joy;
>   Such as a happy bird will sing
> Beneath a rainbow's lovely arch
>   In early spring.

Davies regarded with an air of continual surprise the objects which everyone takes for granted. His sense of wonder was unfailing. Glowworms and lovely ladies, staring sheep and the moon "with her white fleet of stars," were observed as rapturously as though no one had noticed them before. A butterfly on a stone, or the juxtaposition of a rainbow and a cuckoo, was all Davies needed for a full life.

Leisure

> What is this life if, full of care,
> We have no time to stand and stare.
>
> No time to stand beneath the boughs
> And stare as long as sheep or cows.
>
> No time to see, when woods we pass,
> Where squirrels hide their nuts in grass.
>
> No time to see, in broad daylight,
> Streams full of stars, like skies at night.
>
> No time to turn at Beauty's glance,
> And watch her feet, how they can dance.
>
> No time to wait till her mouth can
> Enrich that smile her eyes began.
>
> A poor life this if, full of care,
> We have no time to stand and stare.

The Example

Here's an example from
  A Butterfly;
That on a rough, hard rock
  Happy can lie;
Friendless and all alone
On this unsweetened stone.

Now let my bed be hard,
  No care take I;
I'll make my joy like this
  Small Butterfly,
Whose happy heart has power
To make a stone a flower.

Davies had superintended four constantly enlarging editions of his COLLECTED POEMS and was planning another assembly when he died at seventy, September 26, 1940.

Although Davies, more than any poet of the twentieth century, recalls Herrick, he was indebted to other forerunners, mostly Elizabethan. Another influence, less obvious but more integral, was that of Blake; many of Davies' shorter lyrics are echoes, perhaps unconscious, of SONGS OF INNOCENCE. Even more direct though far less deep than his inspired source, Davies remained a charming rather than a great poet. He could not frame burning images and prophetic visions. He was content with quiet pictures and miniature panoramas, a Blake in words of one syllable.

Ambition

I had Ambition, by which sin
  The angels fell;
I climbed and, step by step, O Lord,
  Ascended into Hell.

Returning now to peace and quiet,
  And made more wise,
Let my descent and fall, O Lord,
  Be into Paradise.

RALPH HODGSON
[1872–1962]

Born in Yorkshire in 1872, Ralph Hodgson was a contradiction in his own terms. He was so reticent that he refused to be interviewed or to prepare the shortest statement for works of reference; yet he waged a violent campaign to end the custom of docking dogs' tails and clipping their ears. Known to a small circle as a person of few words and a writer of a few poems, he was celebrated in a larger sphere, the sporting world, as a breeder and judge of bull terriers. In youth he worked as a pressman in London and was employed as draftsman on an evening paper. In his early thirties, with the artist Claud Lovat Fraser, he founded The Sign of Flying Fame for the publication of pamphlets, broadsides, and chapbooks.

At fifty-three Hodgson went to Japan as lecturer on English literature at Sendai University, about two hundred miles from Tokyo. He remained there several years, but in 1939, with his American wife, he came to the United States. After trying various retreats, he bought a place—half farm, half bird sanctuary—near Canton, Ohio, and revived the project of a small press, which he called Packington's Pound; late "Flying Fame," London. This time he furnished and hand-colored his own illustrations.

Hodgson's poetry adheres to the tradition in form, but its spirit has its own singularity. One or two of the longer poems, particularly THE SONG OF HONOR, may carry overtones of Christopher Smart's A SONG TO DAVID. The lyrics, however, are altogether Hodgson's, fresh without freakishness, original without straining for originality. EVE takes one of the oldest symbols in literature, the mother of mankind, and translates it into a new world in terms of a young English girl. TIME, YOU OLD GYPSY MAN employs another familiar symbol to create one of the most haunting of modern lyrics.

Eve

Eve, with her basket, was
Deep in the bells and grass,
Wading in bells and grass
Up to her knees

Picking a dish of sweet
Berries and plums to eat,
Down in the bells and grass
Under the trees.

Mute as a mouse in a
Corner the cobra lay,
Curled round a bough of the
Cinnamon tall. . . .
Now to get even and
Humble proud heaven and
Now was the moment or
Never at all.

"Eva!" Each syllable
Light as a flower fell,
"Eva!" he whispered the
Wondering maid,
Soft as a bubble sung
Out of a linnet's lung,
Soft and most silverly
"Eva!" he said.

Picture that orchard sprite;
Eve, with her body white,
Supple and smooth to her
Slim finger tips;
Wondering, listening,
Listening, wondering,
Eve with a berry
Half-way to her lips.

Oh, had our simple Eve
Seen through the make-believe!
Had she but known the
Pretender he was!
Out of the boughs he came,
Whispering still her name,
Tumbling in twenty rings
Into the grass.

Here was the strangest pair
In the world anywhere,
Eve in the bells and grass
Kneeling, and he

Telling his story low. . . .
Singing birds saw them go
Down the dark path to
The Blasphemous Tree.

Oh, what a clatter when
Titmouse and Jenny Wren
Saw him successful and
Taking his leave!
How the birds rated him,
How they all hated him!
How they all pitied
Poor motherless Eve!

Picture her crying
Outside in the lane,
Eve, with no dish of sweet
Berries and plums to eat,
Haunting the gate of the
Orchard in vain. . . .
Picture the lewd delight
Under the hill tonight—
"Eva!" the toast goes round,
"Eva!" again.

Time, You Old Gypsy Man

Time, you old gypsy man,
    Will you not stay,
Put up your caravan
    Just for one day?

All things I'll give you
Will you be my guest,
Bells for your jennet
Of silver the best,
Goldsmiths shall beat you
A great golden ring,
Peacocks shall bow to you,
Little boys sing,
Oh, and sweet girls will
Festoon you with may.

Time, you old gypsy,
Why hasten away?

Last week in Babylon,
Last night in Rome,
Morning, and in the crush
Under Paul's dome;
Under Paul's dial
You tighten your rein—
Only a moment,
And off once again;
Off to some city
Now blind in the womb,
Off to another
Ere that's in the tomb.

Time, you old gypsy man,
  Will you not stay,
Put up your caravan
  Just for one day?

Silver Wedding

In the middle of the night
He started up
At a cry from his sleeping Bride—
A bat from some ruin
In a heart he'd never searched,
Nay, hardly seen inside:

"Want me and take me
For the woman that I am
And not for her that died,
The lovely chit nineteen
I one time was,
And am no more," she cried

WALTER DE LA MARE
[1873–1956]

IT HAS BEEN said that Walter de la Mare wrote more for antiquity than for posterity, and it is true that he dwelt in an enchanted past rather than in a disturbing present. His is the domain of vanished childhood, of impossible dreams, of lovely ghosts from a romantic and forgotten world. His poetry is conceived in the mood of memory. Sadly it recalls the little truants, "the children magic hath stolen away," silver reeds in a silver stream, a bird sliding through the frosty air, a beautiful lady of the West Country.

> But beauty vanishes; beauty passes;
> However rare—rare it be.
> And when I crumble, who will remember
> This lady of the West Country?

The sense of loss runs through de la Mare's verse like a persistent refrain. The word "gone" beats through his bell-like lines; he loves all that is irrecoverable, "all that's past," he says in one of his most poignant lyrics.

All That's Past

Very old are the woods;
   And the buds that break
Out of the briar's boughs,
   When March winds wake,
So old with their beauty are—
   Oh, no man knows
Through what wild centuries
   Roves back the rose.

Very old are the brooks;
   And the rills that rise
Where snows sleep cold beneath
   The azure skies

    Sing such a history
      Of come and gone,
    Their every drop is as wise
      As Solomon.

    Very old are we men;
      Our dreams are tales
    Told in dim Eden
      By Eve's nightingales;
    We wake and whisper awhile,
      But, the day gone by,
    Silence and sleep like fields
      Of amaranth lie.

Walter de la Mare was born at Charlton in Kent, April 25, 1873, descended from a Huguenot family, and related to Browning. Educated at St. Paul's School in London, he was unable to attend college. At eighteen he went into business, remaining in the English branch of the Standard Oil Company for twenty years. His first volume, SONGS OF CHILDHOOD, was not published until he was almost thirty, and it appeared under the anagrammatic pseudonym of "Walter Ramal." Since that publication de la Mare has composed and edited more than forty volumes—novels, short stories, and anthologies, as well as books of poems—most of which explore a strange limbo, a veiled borderland, half juvenile, half supernatural.

The Song of Shadows

    Sweep thy faint strings, Musician,
      With thy long lean hand;
    Downward the starry tapers burn,
      Sinks soft the waning sand;
    The old hound whimpers couched in sleep,
      The embers smolder low;
    Across the walls the shadows
      Come, and go.

    Sweep softly thy strings, Musician,
      The minutes mount to hours;
    Frost on the windless casement weaves
      A labyrinth of flowers;

Ghosts linger in the darkening air,
  Hearken at the open door;
Music hath called them, dreaming,
  Home once more.

"Nature itself," wrote de la Mare, "resembles a veil over some further reality of which the imagination in its visionary moments seems to achieve a more direct evidence." It is in the "visionary moments" that de la Mare triumphs; the area just beyond realism is his true home. Nowhere is this better exemplified than in THE LISTENERS. In this poem the traditional adventure story takes on new significance. It can be interpreted in many ways, as the record of an actual quest or as a symbol, as a fable of man's eternal attempt to answer life's riddle or as a courageous challenge to terror. But no contemporary poem is more provocative, more purely a work of the imagination, a work that does not explain but never fails to illumine.

The Listeners

"Is there anybody there?" said the Traveler,
  Knocking on the moonlit door;
And his horse in the silence champed the grasses
  Of the forest's ferny floor.
And a bird flew up out of the turret,
  Above the Traveler's head:
And he smote upon the door again a second time;
  "Is there anybody there?" he said.
But no one descended to the Traveler;
  No head from the leaf-fringed sill
Leaned over and looked into his gray eyes,
  Where he stood perplexed and still.
But only a host of phantom listeners
  That dwelt in the lone house then
Stood listening in the quiet of the moonlight
  To that voice from the world of men:
Stood thronging the faint moonbeams on the dark stair
  That goes down to the empty hall,
Hearkening in an air stirred and shaken
  By the lonely Traveler's call.
And he felt in his heart their strangeness,
  Their stillness answering his cry,

While his horse moved, cropping the dark turf,
'Neath the starred and leafy sky;
For he suddenly smote on the door, even
Louder, and lifted his head:—
"Tell them I came, and no one answered,
That I kept my word," he said.
Never the least stir made the listeners,
Though every word he spake
Fell echoing through the shadowiness of the still house
From the one man left awake:
Aye, they heard his foot upon the stirrup,
And the sound of iron on stone,
And how the silence surged softly backward,
When the plunging hoofs were gone.

TRUMBULL STICKNEY
[1874–1904]

Born June 20, 1874, in Geneva, Switzerland, of New England parents, Trumbull Stickney was something of a prodigy in childhood. Entering Harvard at seventeen, he was graduated with high classical honors, went abroad, and studied at the Sorbonne. The University of Paris awarded him a degree never before conferred on an American. At twenty-nine he returned to the United States as instructor of Greek at Harvard. A year later, barely thirty, he died of a tumor on the brain.

The early published verse as well as the posthumous poems indicate what Stickney might have accomplished with fuller life and experience. Unknown to all but a few, Stickney's lines are proud, stoical with "wise denials," and stern peace. Only a sonnet or two survives, still sonorous with the music of a vanished day.

Live Blindly and Upon the Hour

Live blindly and upon the hour. The Lord,
Who was the Future, died full long ago.
Knowledge which is the Past is folly. Go,
Poor child, and be not to thyself abhorred.

Around thine earth sun-wingéd winds do blow
And planets roll; a meteor draws his sword;
The rainbow breaks his seven-colored chord
And the long strips of river-silver flow:
Awake! Give thyself to the lovely hours.
Drinking their lips, catch thou the dream in flight
About their fragile hairs' aërial gold.
Thou art divine, thou livest—as of old
Apollo springing naked to the light,
And all his island shivered into flowers.

Mount Lykaion

Alone on Lykaion since man hath been
Stand on the height two columns, where at rest
Two eagles hewn of gold sit looking East
Forever; and the sun goes up between.
Far down around the mountain's oval green
An order keeps the falling stones abreast.
Below within the chaos last and least
A river like a curl of light is seen.
Beyond the river lies the even sea,
Beyond the sea another ghost of sky—
O God, support the sickness of my eye
Lest the far space and long antiquity
Suck out my heart, and on this awful ground
The great wind kill my little shell with sound.

from SONNETS FROM GREECE

G. K. CHESTERTON

[1874–1936]

IT WAS Chesterton's misfortune that, as a poet, he was considered
a master of paradox. His gift for brilliant contradiction was his
undoing. He exploited it from the beginning and allowed it to
dictate a philosophy of words rather than ideas, a rational irration-
alism. Objecting with impartial violence to both capitalism and

socialism, he championed a fictitious medievalism and advocated a New Order which was nothing more than an old disorder.

Born in London, May 29, 1874, educated at St. Paul's School and the Slade School of Art, Gilbert Keith Chesterton was a journalist most of his life. Nothing bored him; everything bothered him, profitably. By the time he was sixty-two—he died June 14, 1936—he had written fantastic novels and serious plays, narrative poems and detective stories combining murder with sermonizing, solid biographies and whimsical essays that changed into parables, art criticisms and faintly disguised religious tracts; a total of more than one hundred works. The titles often furnished the clue: THE POET AND THE LUNATICS, THE SCANDAL OF FATHER BROWN, THE MAN WHO WAS THURSDAY, THE CLUB OF QUEER TRADES, and, most characteristically, TREMENDOUS TRIFLES.

The poetry sometimes escapes into quieter territory than the topsy-turvy land which Chesterton cultivated with such gusto. In verse the epigrams do not turn upon themselves so tirelessly and so tiresomely; the twist of thought is natural, witty and graceful. Hearing the phrase "vile dust," Chesterton imagines the earth in protest, the dead stones speaking, and the body of man remembering the day of Creation:

> When God to all his paladins
>   By his own splendor swore
> To make a fairer face than heaven,
>   Of dust and nothing more.

Chesterton delighted to beat the strong gongs of rhyme, notably in the long and booming LEPANTO. But his finest lines are in such restrained lyrics as A PRAYER IN DARKNESS and the tersely ironic ELEGY IN A COUNTRY CHURCHYARD, with its grim reply to Gray's resigned poem, on page 555.

A Prayer in Darkness

> This much, O heaven—if I should brood or rave,
>   Pity me not; but let the world be fed,
>   Yea, in my madness if I strike me dead,
> Heed you the grass that grows upon my grave.

If I dare snarl between this sun and sod,
  Whimper and clamor, give me grace to own,
  In sun and rain and fruit in season shown,
The shining silence of the scorn of God.

Thank God the stars are set beyond my power,
  If I must travail in a night of wrath;
  Thank God my tears will never vex a moth,
Nor any curse of mine cut down a flower.

Men say the sun was darkened: yet I had
  Thought it beat brightly, even on—Calvary:
  And He that hung upon the Torturing Tree
Heard all the crickets singing, and was glad.

Elegy in a Country Churchyard

The men that worked for England
They have their graves at home;
And bees and birds of England
About the cross can roam.

But they that fought for England,
Following a falling star,
Alas, alas, for England
They have their graves afar.

And they that rule in England
In stately conclave met,
Alas, alas, for England
They have no graves as yet.

AMY LOWELL

[1874–1925]

EXTRAORDINARILY prolific, Amy Lowell the poet was always breathlessly in the rear of Amy Lowell the propagandist. She flourished in controversy and lived on attack.

She was born February 9, 1874, in Brookline, Massachusetts.

There were famous pioneers, traders, and teachers in her family. James Russell Lowell, the New England poet, was her grandfather's cousin; her brother Percival was the astronomer who mapped out the much-disputed canals on Mars; another brother, Abbott Lawrence, was president of Harvard University. She had nursed vague hopes for the stage; but a glandular defect which made her seem even larger than she was precluded such a career—"I'm nothing but a disease," she complained with wry jocularity.

At twenty-eight she determined to be a poet, and for nine years she studied the classics and the works of her contemporaries; she experimented in every form. Her first book, published in her thirty-eighth year, was obviously imitative; she was still learning her craft.

At the beginning of the First World War, Amy Lowell went to London and "captured" the Imagist movement from Ezra Pound— Pound subsequently referred to the members as "Amygists." She reorganized the group, made it a fighting word, and stormed up and down the country on a crusade of furious emancipation. Smoking her famous cigars, she tyrannized over editors and brought every kind of influence into play—wealth, charm, family background, good fellowship, cajolery, and dictatorial commands—to carry forward her powerful offensive. The air seethed with loud efforts to "free" poetry from the shackles of rhyme, regular rhythm, and other traditional assets. But Amy Lowell could not be held by strictures—not even her own; she tried every poetic device and brilliantly violated the Imagist "manifesto." Her own poetry extended beyond the artificial tenets of the *vers libre* school, and her most colorful poem, PATTERNS, is a proof of her practice rather than her theories.

Patterns

I walk down the garden-paths,
And all the daffodils
Are blowing, and the bright blue squills.
I walk down the patterned garden-paths
In my stiff, brocaded gown.
With my powdered hair and jeweled fan,
I too am a rare
Pattern. As I wander down
The garden-paths.

My dress is richly figured,
And the train
Makes a pink and silver stain
On the gravel, and the thrift
Of the borders.
Just a plate of current fashion,
Tripping by in high-heeled, ribboned shoes.
Not a softness anywhere about me,
Only whalebone and brocade.
And I sink on a seat in the shade
Of a lime-tree. For my passion
Wars against the stiff brocade.
The daffodils and squills
Flutter in the breeze
As they please.
And I weep;
For the lime-tree is in blossom
And one small flower has dropped upon my bosom.

And the plashing of waterdrops
In the marble fountain
Comes down the garden-paths.
The dripping never stops.
Underneath my stiffened gown
Is the softness of a woman bathing in a marble basin,
A basin in the midst of hedges grown
So thick, she cannot see her lover hiding,
But she guesses he is near,
And the sliding of the water
Seems the stroking of a dear
Hand upon her.
What is Summer in a fine brocaded gown!
I should like to see it lying in a heap upon the ground.
All the pink and silver crumpled up on the ground.

I would be the pink and silver as I ran along the paths,
And he would stumble after,
Bewildered by my laughter.
I should see the sun flashing from his sword-hilt and the buckles
    on his shoes.
I would choose
To lead him in a maze along the patterned paths,
A bright and laughing maze for my heavy-booted lover.
Till he caught me in the shade,
And the buttons of his waistcoat bruised my body as he clasped me,

Aching, melting, unafraid.
With the shadows of the leaves and the sundrops,
And the plopping of the waterdrops,
All about us in the open afternoon—
I am very like to swoon
With the weight of this brocade,
For the sun sifts through the shade.

Underneath the fallen blossom
In my bosom
Is a letter I have hid.
It was brought to me this morning by a rider from the Duke.
"Madam, we regret to inform you that Lord Hartwell
Died in action Thursday sen'night."
As I read it in the white, morning sunlight,
The letters squirmed like snakes.
"Any answer, Madam?" said my footman.
"No," I told him.
"See that the messenger takes some refreshment.
"No, no answer."
And I walked into the garden,
Up and down the patterned paths,
In my stiff, correct brocade.
The blue and yellow flowers stood up proudly in the sun,
Each one.
I stood upright too,
Held rigid to the pattern
By the stiffness of my gown;
Up and down I walked,
Up and down.

In a month he would have been my husband.
In a month, here, underneath this lime,
We would have broke the pattern;
He for me, and I for him,
He as Colonel, I as Lady,
On this shady seat.
He had a whim
That sunlight carried blessing.
And I answered, "It shall be as you have said."
Now he is dead.

In Summer and in Winter I shall walk
Up and down
The patterned garden-paths

In my stiff, brocaded gown.
The squills and daffodils
Will give place to pillared roses, and to asters, and to snow.
I shall go
Up and down
In my gown.
Gorgeously arrayed,
Boned and stayed.
And the softness of my body will be guarded from embrace
By each button, hook, and lace.
For the man who should loose me is dead,
Fighting with the Duke in Flanders,
In a pattern called a war.
Christ! What are patterns for?

A sick woman, Amy Lowell worked relentlessly. The labor on the two-volume biography of Keats may not have killed her, but it hastened her end. In her late forties she ruptured the small blood vessels of her eyes and suffered irremediable pains in the head and groin. After having been unsuccessfully operated upon more than once, she died of a paralytic stroke May 12, 1925. The following year her WHAT'S O'CLOCK was posthumously awarded the Pulitzer Prize.

Her ten volumes of poems, once so challenging a part of every "advanced" library, now look prim. The storm of controversy seems a tempest about technique in a shopworn teapot. But if Amy Lowell's poetry suffered because she had "everything except genius," if her "school," like most schools, is dated and academic, her spirit is not dead.

ROBERT FROST
[1875–1963]

THE most penetrating interpreter of modern New England, author of books whose areas seemed defined by their titles—NORTH OF BOSTON, MOUNTAIN INTERVAL, NEW HAMPSHIRE—Robert Frost was born in the Far West, in San Francisco, March 26, 1875. Both his parents had been schoolteachers, and both had been born in the East, where his forefathers had lived for eight generations.

His father died when Frost was ten, and his mother brought her children back to their paternal grandfather in Lawrence, Massachusetts. Here young Frost went to school and became a bobbin boy in one of the mills. At seventeen he entered Dartmouth, but remained there only a few months. He married at twenty, went to Harvard, and, after wrestling with the curriculum, left it within two years. He said he had stopped learning and might as well teach. Never a pedagogue but an "awakener," Frost taught in country schools and academies. He also made shoes, edited a weekly paper, and wrote poetry. In 1900 he began to farm at Derry, New Hampshire.

Eleven years later, confessing himself beaten as a farmer, Frost sold his acres and, with wife and four children, sailed for England. In England Frost encountered, for the first time, the world of writers and publishers. He did not like it, although his first two books were published in England. In 1915 Frost returned to America. He was now in his fortieth year, unknown and without funds.

Suddenly, with the American publication of NORTH OF BOSTON, Frost was famous. Critics of every school united to praise these stern bucolics, so different from the traditional English pastorals. Here was the very blood and sinew of a country, an embodiment of New England which transcended boundaries. This was poetic realism, but it was as teasing-tender as it was severe. The very opening lines were a racy invitation:

> I'm going out to clean the pasture spring;
> I'll only stop to rake the leaves away
> (And wait to watch the water clear, I may):
> I sha'n't be gone long.—You come too.

This was unquestionably a poetry of personal experience, but it was, nevertheless, full of symbols. The symbolic element was no less significant for being taken from the business of everyday life and for being conveyed by innuendo and understatement.

> Something there is that doesn't love a wall

says Frost, and the reader is free to accept the statement as a literal fact or as an implied protest against barriers. Philosophy and understatement continually play through Frost's talk-flavored blank verse. Even his most dramatic monologues are illuminated by the humor of reservation, of philosophic banter. BIRCHES begins with pure observation:

observation gives way to imagination; and the poem develops into something which is both a fantasy and a philosophy. THE DEATH OF THE HIRED MAN almost conceals its pathos in asides about self-respect and the way to build a load of hay, in unforgettable differences as to the definition of "home," in the sheer fancy of a moon falling down the west, "dragging the whole sky with it to the hills."

Birches

When I see birches bend to left and right
Across the line of straighter darker trees,
I like to think some boy's been swinging them.
But swinging doesn't bend them down to stay.
Ice-storms do that. Often you must have seen them
Loaded with ice a sunny winter morning
After a rain. They click upon themselves
As the breeze rises, and turn many-colored
As the stir cracks and crazes their enamel.
Soon the sun's warmth makes them shed crystal shells
Shattering and avalanching on the snow-crust—
Such heaps of broken glass to sweep away
You'd think the inner dome of heaven had fallen.
They are dragged to the withered bracken by the load,
And they seem not to break; though once they are bowed
So low for long, they never right themselves:
You may see their trunks arching in the woods
Years afterwards, trailing their leaves on the ground
Like girls on hands and knees that throw their hair
Before them over their heads to dry in the sun.
But I was going to say when Truth broke in
With all her matter-of-fact about the ice-storm
I should prefer to have some boy bend them
As he went out and in to fetch the cows—
Some boy too far from town to learn baseball,
Whose only play was what he found himself,
Summer or winter, and could play alone.
One by one he subdued his father's trees
By riding them down over and over again
Until he took the stiffness out of them,
And not one but hung limp, not one was left
For him to conquer. He learned all there was
To learn about not launching out too soon
And so not carrying the tree away

Clear to the ground. He always kept his poise
To the top branches, climbing carefully
With the same pains you use to fill a cup
Up to the brim, and even above the brim.
Then he flung outward, feet first, with a swish,
Kicking his way down through the air to the ground.

So was I once myself a swinger of birches;
And so I dream of going back to be.
It's when I'm weary of considerations,
And life is too much like a pathless wood
Where your face burns and tickles with the cobwebs
Broken across it, and one eye is weeping
From a twig's having lashed across it open.
I'd like to get away from earth awhile
And then come back to it and begin over.
May no fate willfully misunderstand me
And half grant what I wish and snatch me away
Not to return. Earth's the right place for love:
I don't know where it's likely to go better.
I'd like to go by climbing a birch tree,
And climb black branches up a snow-white trunk
Toward heaven, till the tree could bear no more,
But dipped its top and set me down again.
That would be good both going and coming back.
One could do worse than be a swinger of birches.

The Death of the Hired Man

Mary sat musing on the lamp-flame at the table
Waiting for Warren. When she heard his step,
She ran on tip-toe down the darkened passage
To meet him in the doorway with the news
And put him on his guard. "Silas is back."
She pushed him outward with her through the door
And shut it after her. "Be kind," she said.
She took the market things from Warren's arms
And set them on the porch, then drew him down
To sit beside her on the wooden steps.

"When was I ever anything but kind to him?
But I'll not have the fellow back," he said.
"I told him so last haying, didn't I?

'If he left then,' I said, 'that ended it.'
What good is he? Who else will harbor him
At his age for the little he can do?
What help he is there's no depending on.
Off he goes always when I need him most.
'He thinks he ought to earn a little pay,
Enough at least to buy tobacco with,
So he won't have to beg and be beholden.'
'All right,' I say, 'I can't afford to pay
Any fixed wages, though I wish I could.'
'Someone else can.' 'Then someone else will have to.'
I shouldn't mind his bettering himself
If that was what it was. You can be certain,
When he begins like that, there's someone at him
Trying to coax him off with pocket-money,—
In haying time, when any help is scarce.
In winter he comes back to us. I'm done."

"Sh! not so loud: he'll hear you," Mary said.

"I want him to: he'll have to soon or late."

"He's worn out. He's asleep beside the stove.
When I came up from Rowe's I found him here,
Huddled against the barn-door fast asleep,
A miserable sight, and frightening, too—
You needn't smile—I didn't recognize him—
I wasn't looking for him—and he's changed.
Wait till you see."

        "Where did you say he'd been?"

"He didn't say. I dragged him to the house,
And gave him tea and tried to make him smoke.
I tried to make him talk about his travels,
Nothing would do: he just kept nodding off."

"What did he say? Did he say anything?"

"But little."

        "Anything? Mary, confess
He said he'd come to ditch the meadow for me."

"Warren!"

        "But did he? I just want to know."

"Of course he did. What would you have him say?
Surely you wouldn't grudge the poor old man
Some humble way to save his self-respect.
He added, if you really care to know,
He meant to clear the upper pasture, too.
That sounds like something you have heard before?
Warren, I wish you could have heard the way
He jumbled everything. I stopped to look
Two or three times—he made me feel so queer—
To see if he was talking in his sleep.
He ran on Harold Wilson—you remember—
The boy you had in haying four years since.
He's finished school, and teaching in his college.
Silas declares you'll have to get him back.
He says they two will make a team for work:
Between them they will lay this farm as smooth!
The way he mixed that in with other things.
He thinks young Wilson a likely lad, though daft
On education—you know how they fought
All through July under the blazing sun,
Silas up on the cart to build the load,
Harold along beside to pitch it on."

"Yes, I took care to keep well out of earshot."

"Well, those days trouble Silas like a dream.
You wouldn't think they would. How some things linger!
Harold's young college boy's assurance piqued him.
After so many years he still keeps finding
Good arguments he sees he might have used.
I sympathize. I know just how it feels
To think of the right thing to say too late.
Harold's associated in his mind with Latin.
He asked me what I thought of Harold's saying
He studied Latin like the violin
Because he liked it—that an argument!
He said he couldn't make the boy believe
He could find water with a hazel prong—
Which showed how much good school had ever done him.
He wanted to go over that. But most of all
He thinks if he could have another chance
To teach him how to build a load of hay—"

"I know, that's Silas' one accomplishment.
He bundles every forkful in its place,

And tags and numbers it for future reference,
So he can find and easily dislodge it
In the unloading. Silas does that well.
He takes it out in bunches like birds' nests.
You never see him standing on the hay
He s trying to lift, straining to lift himself."

"He thinks if he could teach him that, he'd be
Some good perhaps to someone in the world.
He hates to see a boy the fool of books.
Poor Silas, so concerned for other folk,
And nothing to look backward to with pride,
And nothing to look forward to with hope,
So now and never any different."

Part of a moon was falling down the west,
Dragging the whole sky with it to the hills.
Its light poured softly in her lap. She saw
And spread her apron to it. She put out her hand
Among the harp-like morning-glory strings,
Taut with the dew from garden bed to eaves,
As if she played unheard the tenderness
That wrought on him beside her in the night.
"Warren," she said, "he has come home to die:
You needn't be afraid he'll leave you this time."

"Home," he mocked gently.

                              "Yes, what else but home?
It all depends on what you mean by home.
Of course he's nothing to us, any more
Than was the hound that came a stranger to us
Out of the woods, worn out upon the trail."

"Home is the place where, when you have to go there,
They have to take you in."

                              "I should have called it
Something you somehow haven't to deserve."

Warren leaned out and took a step or two,
Picked up a little stick, and brought it back
And broke it in his hand and tossed it by.
"Silas has better claim on us, you think,
Than on his brother? Thirteen little miles

As the road winds would bring him to his door.
Silas has walked that far no doubt today.
Why didn't he go there? His brother's rich,
A somebody—director in the bank."

"He never told us that."

                    "We know it though."

"I think his brother ought to help, of course.
I'll see to that if there is need. He ought of right
To take him in, and might be willing to—
He may be better than appearances.
But have some pity on Silas. Do you think
If he'd had any pride in claiming kin
Or anything he looked for from his brother,
He'd keep so still about him all this time?"

"I wonder what's between them."

                                    "I can tell you.
Silas is what he is—we wouldn't mind him—
But just the kind that kinsfolk can't abide.
He never did a thing so very bad.
He don't know why he isn't quite as good
As anyone. He won't be made ashamed
To please his brother, worthless though he is."

"I can't think Si ever hurt anyone."

"No, but he hurt my heart the way he lay
And rolled his old head on that sharp-edged chair-back
He wouldn't let me put him on the lounge.
You must go in and see what you can do.
I made the bed up for him there tonight.
You'll be surprised at him—how much he's broken.
His working days are done; I'm sure of it."

"I'd not be in a hurry to say that."

"I haven't been. Go, look, see for yourself.
But, Warren, please remember how it is:
He's come to help you ditch the meadow.
He has a plan. You mustn't laugh at him.
He may not speak of it, and then he may.
I'll sit and see if that small sailing cloud
Will hit or miss the moon."

                                        It hit the moon.
                Then there were three there, making a dim row,
                The moon, the little silver cloud, and she.

                Warren returned—too soon, it seemed to her,
                Slipped to her side, caught up her hand and waited.

                "Warren?" she questioned.

                                        "Dead," was all he answered.

After returning to America Frost went back to the hills of his
ancestors. But he was no longer allowed to farm in privacy, and,
once again, he found himself teaching. He managed to avoid the
classroom and act as a "poetic radiator" on lecture platforms and
as "poet in residence" at the University of Michigan, Amherst, Har-
vard, and Dartmouth. He received the Pulitzer Prize in 1924, 1931,
1937, and 1942, the only American author to win that coveted
award four times.

NORTH OF BOSTON had established the author as a dramatic poet;
his power as a lyric poet came as a surprise, only a few critics
remembering that Frost's first book, A BOY'S WILL, was a collection
of lyrics. Like the monologues, the later lyrics are distinguished by
inner seriousness and outer humor. They dispense with irrelevant
ornaments; many of them are as spare as the New England moun-
tains against which they are placed—"a further range" in every
sense. Saying less than they imply, they stir the mind and lift the
heart. Never have experience and intuition been more sensitively
combined.

Fire and Ice

                Some say the world will end in fire,
                Some say in ice.
                From what I've tasted of desire
                I hold with those who favor fire.
                But if it had to perish twice,
                I think I know enough of hate
                To say that for destruction ice
                Is also great
                And would suffice.

Tree at My Window

Tree at my window, window tree,
My sash is lowered when night comes on;
But let there never be curtain drawn
Between you and me.

Vague dream-head lifted out of the ground,
And thing next most diffuse to cloud,
Not all your light tongues talking aloud
Could be profound.

But, tree, I have seen you taken and tossed,
And if you have seen me when I slept,
You have seen me when I was taken and swept
And all but lost.

That day she put our heads together,
Fate had her imagination about her,
Your head so much concerned with outer,
Mine with inner, weather.

Stopping by Woods on a Snowy Evening

Whose woods these are I think I know.
His house is in the village though;
He will not see me stopping here
To watch his woods fill up with snow.

My little horse must think it queer
To stop without a farmhouse near
Between the woods and frozen lake
The darkest evening of the year.

He gives his harness bells a shake
To ask if there is some mistake.
The only other sound's the sweep
Of easy wind and downy flake.

The woods are lovely, dark and deep,
But I have promises to keep,
And miles to go before I sleep,
And miles to go before I sleep.

Frost's style, appealing to readers of every class, unites opposites. It is colloquial yet elevated, simple yet elusive. The fact has a way of turning into a fancy, and the playfulness sets off the profundities. Such a poem as TWO TRAMPS IN MUD-TIME turns a small autobiographical experience into a complete philosophy of life. The language is the language of everyday; the scene is an ordinary one; the images are familiar and exact without being commonplace. But it is the tone—part earnestness, part raillery—which is not only persuasive but immediately convincing.

Two Tramps in Mud-Time

Out of the mud two strangers came
And caught me splitting wood in the yard.
And one of them put me off my aim
By hailing cheerily "Hit them hard!"
I knew pretty well why he dropped behind
And let the other go on a way.
I knew pretty well what he had in mind:
He wanted to take my job for pay.

Good blocks of beech it was I split,
As large around as the chopping-block;
And every piece I squarely hit
Fell splinterless as a cloven rock.
The blows that a life of self-control
Spares to strike for the common good
That day, giving a loose to my soul,
I spent on the unimportant wood.

The sun was warm but the wind was chill.
You know how it is with an April day:
When the sun is out and the wind is still,
You're one month on in the middle of May.
But if you so much as dare to speak,
A cloud comes over the sunlit arch,
A wind comes off a frozen peak,
And you're two months back in the middle of March.

A bluebird comes tenderly up to alight
And fronts the wind to unruffle a plume,
His song so pitched as not to excite
A single flower as yet to bloom.

It is snowing a flake: and he half knew
Winter was only playing possum.
Except in color he isn't blue,
But he wouldn't advise a thing to blossom.

The water for which we may have to look
In summertime with a witching-wand,
In every wheelrut's now a brook,
In every print of a hoof a pond.
Be glad of water, but don't forget
The lurking frost in the earth beneath
That will steal forth after the sun is set
And show on the water its crystal teeth.

The time when most I loved my task
These two must make me love it more
By coming with what they came to ask.
You'd think I never had felt before
The weight of an ax-head poised aloft,
The grip on earth of outspread feet,
The life of muscles rocking soft
And smooth and moist in vernal heat.

Out of the woods two hulking tramps
(From sleeping God knows where last night
But not long since in the lumber camps).
They thought all chopping was theirs of right.
Men of the woods and lumber-jacks,
They judged me by their appropriate tool.
Except as a fellow handled an ax,
They had no way of knowing a fool.

Nothing on either side was said.
They knew they had but to stay their stay
And all their logic would fill my head:
As that I had no right to play
With what was another man's work for gain.
My right might be love but theirs was need.
And where the two exist in twain
Theirs was the better right—agreed.

But yield who will to their separation,
My object in life is to unite
My avocation and my vocation
As my two eyes make one in sight.

Only where love and need are one,
And the work is play for mortal stakes,
Is the deed ever really done
For Heaven and the future's sakes.

At sixty-seven Frost published A WITNESS TREE, a further proof
that with the years his gifts had not declined, but had grown in
firmness, clarity, and wisdom. Never had the poet written more suc-
cinctly, especially in the philosophic lyrics, laconic but loving. The
new poems bore Frost's characteristic tone with surprising vigor: a
reflective intensity, seasoned in experience, fresh in emotion.

Come In

As I came to the edge of the woods,
Thrush music—hark!
Now if it was dusk outside,
Inside it was dark.

Too dark in the woods for a bird
By sleight of wing
To better its perch for the night,
Though it still could sing.

The last of the light of the sun
That had died in the west
Still lived for one song more
In a thrush's breast.

Far in the pillared dark
Thrush music went—
Almost like a call to come in
To the dark and lament.

But no, I was out for stars:
I would not come in.
I meant not even if asked,
And I hadn't been.

"A poem," wrote Frost in a foreword to his COLLECTED POEMS,
"begins in delight and ends in wisdom. The figure is the same as
for love." Later, considering the quality of surprise in poetry, he

added: "For me the initial delight is in the surprise of remember-
ing something I didn't know I knew." The sentence may well
explain Frost's hold upon his readers. They have not only learned
something new; they have recalled, with a new significance, some-
thing old. They have remembered something they had forgotten
they knew—and loved.

CARL SANDBURG
[1878–1967]

M ORE ambitiously than any poet since Whitman, Carl Sandburg
ranged over America. He celebrated steel mills and corn-
fields; he rhapsodized Chicago, "Hog Butcher for the World," and
wrote nocturnes in a deserted brickyard. Born Charles August Sand-
burg, January 6, 1878, at Galesburg, Illinois, he was entitled to be
known as the laureate of industrial America, for his was a life of
many labors. At thirteen he went to work delivering milk. Before
he was twenty he had earned a living as porter in a barbershop,
sceneshifter, truck handler, dishwasher, turner's apprentice, and
harvest hand. At twenty-one he enlisted in the Sixth Illinois Volun-
teers and was in Puerto Rico during the Spanish-American War.
On his return to the United States, Sandburg entered Lombard
College in his native Galesburg, became editor of the college paper,
captain of the basketball team, and janitor of the gymnasium.
After leaving college he was a salesman, advertising manager, and,
for many years, a journalist.

Unknown as a poet until his thirty-ninth year, Sandburg
startled the literary world with CHICAGO POEMS. It was alternately
attacked and praised for its revolutionary ardor, its loosely vigorous
language, and its unflinching realism. It was soon apparent, how-
ever, that Sandburg was using the common American speech, even
slang, with surety, and that he was fulfilling Whitman's demand
for "limber, lasting, fierce words." It also became evident that his
fermenting violence was an overcompensation for a streak of mys-
ticism, and that his toughness usually broke down into unashamed
tenderness.

Cool Tombs

When Abraham Lincoln was shoveled into the tombs, he forgot the
    copperheads and the assassin . . . in the dust, in the cool tombs.

And Ulysses Grant lost all thought of con men and Wall Street,
    cash and collateral turned ashes . . . in the dust, in the cool
    tombs.

Pocahontas' body, lovely as a poplar, sweet as a red haw in Novem-
    ber or a pawpaw in May, did she wonder? does she remember?
    . . . in the dust, in the cool tombs?

Take any streetful of people buying clothes and groceries, cheering
    a hero or throwing confetti and blowing tin horns . . . tell me
    if the lovers are losers . . . tell me if any get more than the
    lovers . . . in the dust . . . in the cool tombs.

Grass

Pile the bodies high at Austerlitz and Waterloo.
Shovel them under and let me work—
          I am the grass; I cover all.

And pile them high at Gettysburg
And pile them high at Ypres and Verdun.
Shovel them under and let me work.
Two years, ten years, and passengers ask the conductor:
          What place is this?
          Where are we now?

          I am the grass.
          Let me work.

"Poetry," declared Sandburg, in one of his thirty-eight tentative
definitions of poetry, "is a series of explanations of life, fading off
into horizons too swift for explanation." And again, "Poetry is the
opening and closing of a door, leaving those who look through to
guess about what is seen during a moment." Sandburg lived up to

his definitions. Even the most straightforward of his poems are allusive and somewhat enigmatic. Combining satire and sentiment, they leave the reader "to guess about what is seen during a moment."

Losers

If I should pass the tomb of Jonah
I would stop there and sit for a while;
Because I was swallowed one time deep in the dark
And came out alive after all.

If I pass the burial spot of Nero
I shall say to the wind, "Well, well!"—
I who have fiddled in a world on fire,
I who have done so many stunts not worth the doing.

I am looking for the grave of Sinbad too.
I want to shake his ghost-hand and say,
"Neither of us died very early, did we?"

And the last sleeping-place of Nebuchadnezzar—
When I arrive there I shall tell the wind:
"You ate grass; I have eaten crow—
Who is better off now or next year?"

Jack Cade, John Brown, Jesse James,
There too I could sit down and stop for a while.
I think I could tell their headstones:
"God, let me remember all good losers."

I could ask people to throw ashes on their heads
In the name of that sergeant at Belleau Woods.
Walking into the drumfires, calling his men,
"Come on, you . . . Do you want to live forever?"

After his early forties Sandburg spent most of his time traveling about the United States, examining folkways and assembling documents for his monumental work on Lincoln. In his fiftieth year he published THE AMERICAN SONGBAG, a collection of two hundred and eighty songs and ballads gathered from convicts and cowboys, work gangs and "play-parties," and from all people who sing "because they must." About one hundred of the songs had never been printed before. Six volumes were necessary to complete the ABRAHAM LINCOLN biography. The first two volumes, THE PRAIRIE YEARS, were printed in 1926; the last four volumes, THE WAR YEARS, appeared thirteen years later. His autobiographical ALWAYS THE YOUNG STRANGERS was published in 1953.

Sandburg's affirmations grew stronger with age. His passionate advocacy of the common man reaches its height in THE PEOPLE, YES. Written in his fifty-eighth year, the work is not only a combination of homely glories, "a synthesis of hyacinths and biscuits," but an omnibus of history and tall tales, gossip and prophecy. Here are the people, cheated and misled, but, beneath their skepticism, as wise as they are strong.

The People Will Live On

The people will live on.
The learning and blundering people will live on.
They will be tricked and sold and again sold
And go back to the nourishing earth for rootholds,
The people so peculiar in renewal and comeback,
You can't laugh off their capacity to take it.
The mammoth rests between his cyclonic dramas.

The people so often sleepy, weary, enigmatic,
is a vast huddle with many units saying:
"I earn my living.
I make enough to get by
and it takes all my time.
If I had more time
I could do more for myself
and maybe for others.
I could read and study
and talk things over
and find out about things.
It takes time.
I wish I had the time."

The people is a tragic and comic two-face:
hero and hoodlum: phantom and gorilla twist-
ing to moan with a gargoyle mouth: "They
buy me and sell me . . . it's a game . . .
sometime I'll break loose . . ."

Once having marched
Over the margins of animal necessity,
Over the grim line of sheer subsistence
    Then man came
To the deeper rituals of his bones,
To the lights lighter than any bones,
To the time for thinking things over,
To the dance, the song, the story,
Or the hours given over to dreaming,
    Once having so marched.

Between the finite limitations of the five senses
and the endless yearnings of man for the beyond
the people hold to the humdrum bidding of work and food
while reaching out when it comes their way
for lights beyond the prison of the five senses,
for keepsakes lasting beyond any hunger or death.
    This reaching is alive.
The panderers and liars have violated and smutted it.
    Yet this reaching is alive yet
    for lights and keepsakes.

        The people know the salt of the sea
        and the strength of the winds
        lashing the corners of the earth.
        The people take the earth
        as a tomb of rest and a cradle of hope.
        Who else speaks for the Family of Man?
        They are in tune and step
        with constellations of universal law.

The people is a polychrome,
a spectrum and a prism
held in a moving monolith,
a console organ of changing themes,
a clavilux of color poems
wherein the sea offers fog
and the fog moves off in rain
and the labrador sunset shortens
to a nocturne of clear stars
serene over the shot spray
of northern lights.

The steel mill sky is alive.
The fire breaks white and zigzag
shot on a gun-metal gloaming.

Man is a long time coming.
Man will yet win.
Brother may yet line up with brother:

This old anvil laughs at many broken hammers.
There are men who can't be bought.
The fireborn are at home in fire.
The stars make no noise.
You can't hinder the wind from blowing.
Time is a great teacher.
Who can live without hope?

In the darkness with a great bundle of grief
the people march.
In the night, and overhead a shovel of stars for
keeps, the people march:

> "Where to? what next?"
> *from* THE PEOPLE, YES

JOHN MASEFIELD
[1878–1967]

EXCEPT during one short period Masefield wrote in a mood of reminiscence. Although his rhymed narratives were considered "ultrarealistic" and shocked many of his compatriots, Masefield was a traditionalist in love with the past and devoted to the spirit of romance, especially on the high seas. He was born June 1, 1878, in Herefordshire, son of a lawyer, but the growing boy refused to remain at a desk. At fourteen he shipped on a merchantman and became a wanderer for ten years. His ventures took him to America, where he worked in a Yonkers carpet factory (as recounted forty years later in IN THE MILL) and in a Greenwich Village saloon. He discovered Chaucer, and the robust humanity of the fourteenth-century poet inspired him to put his own way of life into verse. His sympathies were naturally not with "the princes and prelates and periwigged charioteers," but with:

The men of the tattered battalion which fights till it dies,
Dazed with the dust of the battle, the din and the cries,
The men with the broken heads and the blood running in their
eyes . . .

The sailor, the stoker of steamers, the man with the clout,
The chantyman bent at the halliards putting a tune to
    the shout,
The drowsy man at the wheel and the tired look-out.

SALT WATER BALLADS is a collection of lyrics which are sometimes raffish, sometimes sentimental, written in the sailor's speech, and, considering that it was published in the poet's mid-twenties, curiously nostalgic.

Sea-Fever

I must go down to the seas again, to the lonely sea and the sky,
And all I ask is a tall ship and a star to steer her by,
And the wheel's kick and the wind's song and the white sail's
    shaking,
And a gray mist on the sea's face and a gray dawn breaking.

I must go down to the seas again, for the call of the running tide
Is a wild call and a clear call that may not be denied;
And all I ask is a windy day with the white clouds flying,
And the flung spray and the blown spume, and the sea-gulls crying.

I must go down to the seas again to the vagrant gypsy life.
To the gull's way and the whale's way where the wind's like a
    whetted knife;
And all I ask is a merry yarn from a laughing fellow-rover,
And quiet sleep and a sweet dream when the long trick's over.

In his thirties Masefield excited readers with a series of narrative poems or rhymed yarns about "common characters" who suffered violently, sinned and reformed, and mixed profanity with ecstasy. They were followed by REYNARD THE FOX, a poem about hunting by a man who did not hunt—the sympathy being with the fox—a poem that became a transcription of the spirit of rural England. It is said that this poem convinced the authorities that Masefield was en- titled to the laureateship; succeeding Robert Bridges, he received the honor in 1930.

After becoming poet laureate, Masefield wrote with increasing determination and lessening power. Before he was sixty he had published more than seventy-five books of poems, plays, novels, essays, adaptations, studies of Shakespeare, public addresses, and stories for boys. The later verse is prolix and undistinguished, but the tediousness is forgotten in the stimulation of the early high-spirited and courageous syllables.

Tomorrow

Oh yesterday the cutting edge drank thirstily and deep,
The upland outlaws ringed us in and herded us as sheep,
They drove us from the stricken field and bayed us into keep;
    But tomorrow,
    By the living God, we'll try the game again!

Oh yesterday our little troop was ridden through and through,
Our swaying, tattered pennons fled, a broken, beaten few,
And all a summer afternoon they hunted us and slew;
    But tomorrow,
    By the living God, we'll try the game again!

And here upon the turret-top the bale-fire glowers red,
The wake-lights burn and drip about our hacked, disfigured dead,
And many a broken heart is here and many a broken head;
    But tomorrow,
    By the living God, we'll try the game again!

VACHEL LINDSAY

[1879–1931]

A MISSIONARY who preached the Gospel through a saxophone, an evangelist who spoke in terms of sheer fantasy, a patriot who saw America as a perpetual county fair, "every soul resident in the earth's one circus tent"—this was Vachel Lindsay, disciple of beauty and ballyhoo.

He was born November 10, 1879, in Springfield, Illinois, a city whose possibilities suggested a visionary future for the United States, a place that would restore lost Atlantis and rebuild Jeru-salem on its green and pleasant soil.

Art was to be Lindsay's career; he studied drawing at the Art Institute of Chicago and the New York School of Art. But, after imitating Blake and Beardsley, he devoted himself to crusades. He lectured for the Anti-Saloon League, preached a "Gospel of Beauty" in the South, and tramped through the Middle West, exchanging a pamphlet of poems, RHYMES TO BE TRADED FOR BREAD, for food and a night's lodging. Restlessness was his demon, so he made it into a religion. He was Saint Francis and Johnny Appleseed in one.

In his first book, GENERAL WILLIAM BOOTH ENTERS INTO HEAVEN, Lindsay announced a new fusion. Uniting the old Greek chant with what he termed the "Higher Vaudeville," he combined religion and ragtime. He brought over into verse the blare of street-corner Salvationists, the syncopation of dance bands, the noise and nervous energy of whole communities. It was a new thing in American poetry, semibarbaric but deeply emotional, brilliantly colored, richly musical, and tremendously effective.

General William Booth Enters into Heaven

(TO BE SUNG TO THE TUNE OF "THE BLOOD OF THE LAMB"
WITH INDICATED INSTRUMENTS)

I

(*Bass drum beaten loudly.*)
Booth led boldly with his big bass drum—
(Are you washed in the blood of the Lamb?)
The Saints smiled gravely and they said: "He's come."
(Are you washed in the blood of the Lamb?)
Walking lepers followed, rank on rank,
Lurching bravos from the ditches dank,
Drabs from the alleyways and drug fiends pale—
Minds still passion-ridden, soul-powers frail:—
Vermin-eaten saints with moldy breath,
Unwashed legions with the ways of Death—
(Are you washed in the blood of the Lamb?)

(*Banjos.*)
Every slum had sent its half-a-score
The round world over. (Booth had groaned for more.)
Every banner that the wide world flies
Bloomed with glory and transcendent dyes.

Big-voiced lasses made their banjos bang,
Tranced, fanatical they shrieked and sang:—
"Are you washed in the blood of the Lamb?"
Hallelujah! it was queer to see
Bull-necked convicts with that land make free.
Loons with trumpets blowed a blare, blare, blare
On, on upward thro' the golden air!
(Are you washed in the blood of the Lamb?)

II

(Bass drum slower and softer.)
Booth died blind and still by faith he trod,
Eyes still dazzled by the ways of God.
Booth led boldly, and he looked the chief,
Eagle countenance in sharp relief,
Beard a-flying, air of high command
Unabated in that holy land.

(Sweet flute music.)
Jesus came from out the court-house door,
Stretched his hands above the passing poor.
Booth saw not, but led his queer ones there
Round and round the mighty court-house square.
Yet in an instant all that blear review
Marched on spotless, clad in raiment new.
The lame were straightened, withered limbs uncurled
And blind eyes opened on a new, sweet world.

(Bass drum louder.)
Drabs and vixens in a flash made whole!
Gone was the weasel-head, the snout, the jowl!
Sages and sibyls now, and athletes clean,
Rulers of empires, and of forests green!

*(Grand chorus of all instruments. Tambourines to the fore-
    ground.)*
The hosts were sandaled, and their wings were fire!
(Are you washed in the blood of the Lamb?)
But their noise played havoc with the angel-choir.
(Are you washed in the blood of the Lamb?)
Oh, shout Salvation! it was good to see
Kings and Princes by the Lamb set free.
The banjos rattled and the tambourines
Jing-jing-jingled in the hands of Queens.

(Reverently sung, no instruments.)
And when Booth halted by the curb for prayer
He saw his Master thro' the flag-filled air.
Christ came gently with a robe and crown
For Booth the soldier, while the throng knelt down.
He saw King Jesus. They were face to face,
And he knelt a-weeping in that holy place.
Are you washed in the blood of the Lamb?

His reputation established with his first volume, Lindsay quickened the tempo and broadened his effects. He exploited his own dynamic personality and depended largely on exaggeration. His vision of America became a motley Nirvana, a congregation of pioneers and baseball players, Presidents and "movie queens," a country where such incongruous figures as William Jennings Bryan and John L. Sullivan, Andrew Jackson and P. T. Barnum, were enshrined not merely as symbols but as demigods.

Lindsay's comedy was only partly planned. The half-conscious humor made THE CONGO both grandiose and absurd; it turned THE KALLYOPE YELL from a college cheer into a rhapsody, and lifted THE DANIEL JAZZ into a grotesque extravaganza.

The Daniel Jazz

Darius the Mede was a king and a wonder.   *Beginning*
His eye was proud, and his voice was thunder.   *with a strain*
He kept bad lions in a monstrous den.   *of "Dixie."*
He fed up the lions on Christian men.

Daniel was the chief hired man of the land.   *With a touch*
He stirred up the jazz in the palace band.   *of "Alexan-*
He whitewashed the cellar. He shovelled in the coal.   *der's Ragtime*
And Daniel kept a-praying:—"Lord save my soul."   *Band."*
Daniel kept a-praying "Lord save my soul."
Daniel kept a-praying "Lord save my soul."

Daniel was the butler, swagger and swell.
He ran up stairs. He answered the bell.
And he would let in whoever came a-calling:—
Saints so holy, scamps so appalling.
"Old man Ahab leaves his card.
Elisha and the bears are a-waiting in the yard.
Here comes Pharaoh and his snakes a-calling.

Here comes Cain and his wife a-calling.
Shadrach, Meshach and Abednego for tea.
Here comes Jonah and the whale,
And the Sea!
Here comes St. Peter and his fishing pole.
Here comes Judas and his silver a-calling.
Here comes old Beelzebub a-calling."
And Daniel kept a-praying:—"Lord save my soul."
Daniel kept a-praying:—"Lord save my soul."
Daniel kept a-praying:—"Lord save my soul."

His sweetheart and his mother were Christian and meek.
They washed and ironed for Darius every week.
One Thursday he met them at the door:—
Paid them as usual, but acted sore.

He said:—"Your Daniel is a dead little pigeon.
He's a good hard worker, but he talks religion."
And he showed them Daniel in the lions' cage.
Daniel standing quietly, the lions in a rage.
His good old mother cried:—
"Lord save him."
And Daniel's tender sweetheart cried:—
"Lord save him."

And she was a golden lily in the dew.
And she was as sweet as an apple on the tree
And she was as fine as a melon in the corn-field,
Gliding and lovely as a ship on the sea,
Gliding and lovely as a ship on the sea.

And she prayed to the Lord:—
"Send Gabriel. Send Gabriel."

King Darius said to the lions:—
"Bite Daniel. Bite Daniel.
Bite him. Bite him. Bite him!"

Thus roared the lions:—
"We want Daniel, Daniel, Daniel,
We want Daniel, Daniel, Daniel.
Grrrrrrrrrrrrrrrrrrrrrrrrrrrrrrrrrrrrrrrrrrrrrrrrrrrrr   *Here the au-*
                                                          dience roars.
Grrrrrrrrrrrrrrrrrrrrrrrrrrrrrrrrrrrrrrrrrrrrrrrrrrrrr"

And Daniel did not frown,
Daniel did not cry.

He kept on looking at the sky.
And the Lord said to Gabriel:—
"Go chain the lions down,   *The audience*
Go chain the lions down.   *sings this with*
                                  the leader, to
Go chain the lions down."   *the old negro*
                                  tune.

And *Gabriel* chained the lions,
And *Gabriel* chained the lions,
And *Gabriel* chained the lions,
And Daniel got out of the den,
And Daniel got out of the den,
And Daniel got out of the den.
And Darius said:—"You're a Christian child,"
Darius said:—"You're a Christian child,"
Darius said:—"You're a Christian child,"
And gave him his job again,
And gave him his job again,
And gave him his job again.

The golden dream could not be carried over into reality; it broke
into bits of leaden memories. Lindsay began to grow ashamed of
his "roaring, epic, ragtime tune"; he suddenly became sentimental
and resuscitated the coy lace-valentine rhymes of his youth. He
distrusted his hearers when they applauded, and despised them
when he felt they were being entertained without being uplifted.

Baffled at fifty, desperately tired, Lindsay tried to retreat. He had
traded too long upon fantasy. His creative strength was gone; he
had exhausted himself and his audiences. At fifty-two the most
demanded poet-performer of his day was no longer in demand. His
faith shaken, his following lost, he considered himself a failure. On
the night of December 5, 1931, he drank a bottle of Lysol, and died
in the house in which he was born.

HAROLD MONRO

[1879–1932]

I T is not easy to be charming and bizarre at the same time, but
Harold Monro accomplished this remarkable fusion. His life
was a mixture of fantasy and practicality, and his work reflected
his life.

Born in Brussels of Scottish parents in 1879, Monro was taken to England as a child. Educated at Radley and Caius College, Cambridge, he became an author, editor, and publisher. In his thirty-third year, with the help of Alida Klemantaski, whom he later married, he founded the Poetry Bookshop, which became a center for the younger men and was responsible for the publication of the biennial GEORGIAN POETRY. Fashions changed, but Monro remained an influence until his death, March 16, 1932.

"The test of intellect is more important than tests of prosody or tradition," wrote Monro. "The passing event and its effect on the mind is everything." He endeavored to arrest the passing event, to capture the most trivial aspects of ordinary life, the creak of a door, the kettle puffing "a tentacle of breath," a piece of paper in the wastebasket shoving another piece, the "independent" pencil breaking its own point, the "ruminating" clock stirring its slow body, the minutes "pricking" their ears and running about. Making the inanimate not only animate but articulate, Monro shaped an odd verse that is both whimsical and metaphysical.

Solitude

When you have tidied all things for the night,
And while your thoughts are fading to their sleep,
You'll pause a moment in the late firelight,
Too sorrowful to weep.

The large and gentle furniture has stood
In sympathetic silence all the day
With that old kindness of domestic wood;
Nevertheless the haunted room will say:
"Someone must be away."

The little dog rolls over half awake,
Stretches his paws, yawns, looking up at you,
Wags his tail very slightly for your sake,
That you may feel he is unhappy too.

A distant engine whistles, or the floor
Creaks, or the wandering night-wind bangs a door.

Silence is scattered like a broken glass.
The minutes prick their ears and run about,

Then one by one subside again and pass
Sedately in, monotonously out.

You bend your head and wipe away a tear.
Solitude walks one heavy step more near.

WALLACE STEVENS
[1879–1955]

WALLACE STEVENS has been placed in more categories than any
other contemporary poet. He has been called a symbolist, an
unrealist, a platonist, an impressionist, an abstractionist whose po-
etry is "beyond good and evil, beyond hope and despair, beyond
thought of any kind." The poet himself might not object to the
comparison with the abstract painters, for one of his recent volumes
was entitled THE MAN WITH THE BLUE GUITAR and was, by implica-
tion, a kind of homage to Picasso.

Stevens was born October 2, 1879, in Reading, Pennsylvania, of
Dutch and German descent. Educated at Harvard, he was admitted
to the bar in his twenty-fifth year, and practiced law in New York.
Twelve years later he moved to Connecticut, specialized in in-
surance law, and, in 1934, became vice-president of the Hartford
Accident and Indemnity Company.

"Wallace Stevens is a rhetorician," wrote Howard Baker, poet
and teacher, "a persuasive artificer of the poetic line. . . . His poetry
gets part of its loftiness from brilliant epithets and daring images."
Stevens himself asks:

> Is the function of the poet here mere sound,
> Subtler than the ornatest prophecy
> To stuff the ear?

There are no explicit answers in Stevens. Everything is implied;
if anything is stated, it is stated in terms of something else. All the
arts are wittily confused in a luxuriance which Stevens once called
"the essential gaudiness of poetry." Thus, one of his most fanciful
and delicately rounded poems, PETER QUINCE AT THE CLAVIER, ap-
peals to all the senses. Sight and sound, taste and touch, contribute

to make a comparison (always implied) between love and music, innocence and sensuality, the body's death and beauty's deathlessness. The four contrasting sections suggest the four movements of a symphony: the stately presentation of the main theme, the meditative slow movement, the mischievous scherzo, and the grave recapitulation of the finale.

Peter Quince at the Clavier

I

Just as my fingers on these keys
Make music, so the self-same sounds
On my spirit make a music, too.

Music is feeling, then, not sound;
And thus it is that what I feel,
Here in this room, desiring you,

Thinking of your blue-shadowed silk,
Is music. It is like the strain
Waked in the elders by Susanna:

Of a green evening, clear and warm,
She bathed in her still garden, while
The red-eyed elders, watching, felt

The basses of their beings throb
In witching chords, and their thin blood
Pulse pizzicati of Hosanna.

II

In the green water, clear and warm,
Susanna lay,
She searched
The touch of springs,
And found
Concealed imaginings.
She sighed,
For so much melody.

Upon the bank, she stood
In the cool
Of spent emotions.
She felt, among the leaves,
The dew
Of old devotions.

She walked upon the grass,
Still quavering.
The winds were like her maids
On timid feet,
Fetching her woven scarves,
Yet wavering.

A breath upon her hand
Muted the night.
She turned—
A cymbal crashed,
And roaring horns.

III

Soon, with a noise like tambourines,
Came her attendant Byzantines.

They wondered why Susanna cried
Against the elders by her side;

And as they whispered, the refrain
Was like a willow swept by rain.

Anon, their lamps' uplifted flame
Revealed Susanna and her shame.

And then, the simpering Byzantines
Fled, with a noise like tambourines.

IV

Beauty is momentary in the mind—
The fitful tracing of a portal;
But in the flesh it is immortal.

The body dies; the body's beauty lives.
So evenings die, in their green going,
A wave, interminably flowing.
So gardens die, their meek breath scenting
The cowl of Winter, done repenting.
So maidens die, to the auroral
Celebration of a maiden's choral.

Susanna's music touched the bawdy strings
Of those white elders; but, escaping,
Left only Death's ironic scraping.
Now, in its immortality, it plays
On the clear viol of her memory,
And makes a constant sacrament of praise.

Stevens' seventy-fifth birthday was marked by the publication of his COLLECTED POEMS, a book of more than five hundred pages. His explorations of the relation between the world of reality and the world of the imagination had always been appreciated, but his admirers were a small and rather exclusive group. By 1954, however, his scrupulously studied but evocative style had won a generation of readers, as well as honors, and had established a poetry of peculiar authority, "not ideas about the thing but the thing itself."

The Poems of Our Climate

I

Clear water in a brilliant bowl,
Pink and white carnations. The light
In the room more like a snowy air,
Reflecting snow. A newly-fallen snow
At the end of winter when afternoons return.
Pink and white carnations—one desires
So much more than that. The day itself
Is simplified: a bowl of white,
Cold, a cold porcelain, low and round,
With nothing more than the carnations there.

II

Say even that this complete simplicity
Stripped one of all one's torments, concealed
The evilly compounded, vital I
And made it fresh in a world of white,

A world of clear water, brilliant-edged,
Still one would want more, one would need more,
More than a world of white and snowy scents.

III

There would still remain the never-resting mind,
So that one would want to escape, come back
To what had been so long composed.
The imperfect is our paradise.
Note that, in this bitterness, delight,
Since the imperfect is so hot in us,
Lies in flawed words and stubborn sounds.

JAMES STEPHENS
[1882–1950]

JAMES STEPHENS' most characteristic poetry sounds as though it were dictated by a wise old elf interrupted by an irresponsible gamin. Actually, Stephens is a man who, playing with light diablerie in youth, is concerned in maturity with nothing less than essential truths. He was born in 1882 in Dublin. Too poor to receive a formal education, he wandered over Ireland and was "discovered" by the poet and economist George Russell ("Æ"). Stephens' INSURRECTIONS, published in his twenty-seventh year, received immediate praise for its mixture of anger and sensitivity. The inherent impishness grew more dominating in subsequent volumes. Like a grown-up child, the poet delighted to contemplate a world peopled with romantic pirates and dancing centaurs, a heaven with God's beard swinging "far out of sight behind the world's curve." His universe sometimes was overcast, as a lonely God roamed to "the fringes of the infinite," hoping to hide from the very thought of Space. But it was usually brisk with merriment, with madcap angels sowing poppy seeds, and an old reprobate squirming with laughter on God's throne for a moment, then tumbling down—

> Scraping old moons, and twisting, heels and head,
> A chuckle in the void.

Stephens' later philosophy is the expression of an Irish seer. It is universal—and debatable. But there is no arguing with the early "chuckle in the void." The poet died December 26, 1950.

What Thomas an Buile Said in a Pub

I saw God. Do you doubt it?
    Do you dare to doubt it?
I saw the Almighty Man. His hand
Was resting on a mountain, and
He looked upon the World and all about it:
I saw Him plainer than you see me now,
    You mustn't doubt it.

He was not satisfied;
    His look was all dissatisfied.
His beard swung on a wind far out of sight
Behind the world's curve, and there was light
Most fearful from His forehead, and He sighed,
"That star went always wrong, and from the start
    I was dissatisfied."

He lifted up His hand—
    I say He heaved a dreadful hand
Over the spinning Earth. Then I said, "Stay,
You must not strike it, God; I'm in the way;
And I will never move from where I stand."
He said, "Dear child, I feared that you were dead,"
    And stayed His hand.

WILLIAM CARLOS WILLIAMS
[1883–1963]

I T IS probable that the impartial exactness which has marked the
medical career of Dr. William Carlos Williams has had its effect
upon his poetry. He was born September 17, 1883, in Rutherford,
New Jersey, where he has always lived and practiced. Educated in
New York, Switzerland, and the University of Pennsylvania, he was
graduated in medicine in his twenty-fourth year. At twenty-six he
published his first volume, and he has pursued the dual career of
poet and doctor ever since.

When his COMPLETE COLLECTED POEMS appeared, it was evident

that at fifty-five Williams had progressed from an early preciosity to a full acceptance of the American idiom and the emotion "which clusters about common things." Williams regarded the objects of his scrutiny with such impartial affection that it was said no one could love anything as much as Williams loved everything. But there was no denying a power which gains impressiveness with further reading. In a lean colloquial speech Williams depicts the everyday world in small but vivid details. He cuts away ornate decoration and stresses not only the significance of the object but the emotion behind the object.

Tract

I will teach you my townspeople
how to perform a funeral—
for you have it over a troop
of artists—
unless one should scour the world—
you have the ground sense necessary.

See! the hearse leads.
I begin with a design for a hearse.
For Christ's sake not black—
nor white either—and not polished!
Let it be weathered—like a farm wagon—
with gilt wheels (this could be
applied fresh at small expense)
or no wheels at all:
a rough dray to drag over the ground.

Knock the glass out!
My God—glass, my townspeople!
For what purpose? Is it for the dead
to look out or for us to see
how well he is housed or to see
the flowers or the lack of them—
or what?

To keep the rain and snow from him?
He will have a heavier rain soon:
pebbles and dirt and what not.
Let there be no glass—

and no upholstery! phew!
and no little brass rollers
and small easy wheels on the bottom—
my townspeople what are you thinking of!

A rough plain hearse then
with gilt wheels and no top at all.
On this the coffin lies
by its own weight.

No wreaths please—
especially no hot-house flowers!
Some common memento is better,
something he prized and is known by:
his old clothes—a few books perhaps—
God knows what! You realize
how we are about these things,
my townspeople—
something will be found—anything—
even flowers if he had come to that.
So much for the hearse.

For heaven's sake though see to the driver!
Take off the silk hat! In fact
that's no place at all for him
up there unceremoniously
dragging our friend out to his own dignity!
Bring him down—bring him down!
Low and inconspicuous! I'd not have him ride
on the wagon at all—damn him—
the undertaker's understrapper!
Let him hold the reins
and walk at the side
and inconspicuously too!

Then briefly as to yourselves:
Walk behind—as they do in France,
seventh class, or, if you ride,
Hell take curtains! Go with some show
of inconvenience; sit openly—
to the weather as to grief.
Or do you think you can shut grief in?

What—from us? We who have perhaps
nothing to lose? Share with us
share with us—it will be money
in your pockets.

       Go now
I think you are ready.

The Hounded Lovers

Where shall we go?
Where shall we go
  who are in love?

Juliet went
to Friar Laurence's cell,
  but we have no rest.

Rain water lies
on the hard-packed ground,
  reflecting
  the morning sky,

But where shall we go?
We cannot resolve ourselves
  into a dew

Or sink into the earth.
Shall we postpone it
  to Eternity?

The dry heads
of the goldenrod,
  turned to stiff ghosts,

Jerk at their dead
stalks, signalling hieroglyphs
  of grave warning.

Where shall we go?
The movement of benediction
  does not turn back
  the cold wind.

SARA TEASDALE

[1884–1933]

A FRANK and unhappy refrain ran through Sara Teasdale's verse. "Why am I unsatisfied?" she asked herself and the world, and replied with another question:

> O beauty, are you not enough?
> Why am I crying after love?

Her life was a sad and finally tragic pursuit of the answer. The physical facts are few. Sara Teasdale was born August 8, 1884, in St. Louis, Missouri. She traveled sporadically in Europe, meanwhile longing for America; but, once back, was restless at home. The poet Vachel Lindsay fell in love with her, but, though she was more than half in love with him, his exuberance frightened her even more than his eccentricities. At thirty she married a businessman, Ernst Filsinger, a devotee who should have been the perfect husband. But her health was never robust, and her temperament was too nervous. Unable to share her life with anyone, she retreated into a spinsterlike privacy. She did not resent the man; she resented marriage.

> My heart has grown rich with the passing of years,
>   I have less need now than when I was young
> To share myself with every comer,
>   Or shape my thoughts into words with my tongue.

The natural opposite of Anna Wickham, Sara Teasdale voiced no revolt. She was content to be a solitary. One day, fifteen years after her marriage, without a word to her most intimate friends, she went to Reno and obtained a divorce. In her mid-forties she was more alone than she had ever been, more alone than she wanted to be. She was not, as she had assured herself, "self-complete as a flower or a stone." Her poems grew more and more autumnal. Unlike the facile early stanzas, once so popular, the later lyrics are serene in their confession of love and loss.

> That what we never have, remains;
>   It is the things we have that go.

The poetry began to sound premonitions of the end. The nostalgic strain of her youth was echoed in a somber key, the music more and more restrained.

Let It Be Forgotten

Let it be forgotten, as a flower is forgotten,
    Forgotten as a fire that once was singing gold,
Let it be forgotten for ever and ever,
    Time is a kind friend, he will make us old.

If anyone asks, say it was forgotten
    Long and long ago,
As a flower, as a fire, as a hushed footfall
    In a long-forgotten snow.

The death of Vachel Lindsay increased her sense of loss. Weakened by an attack of pneumonia, she suffered a nervous breakdown. A year and a month after Lindsay's suicide, she took an overdose of sleeping tablets and died January 28, 1933.

Until the last six years of her life Sara Teasdale wrote too easily and too much. The best of her poetry is characterized by the title of her ripest book, FLAME AND SHADOW. "The poet," she wrote to a friend, "should try to give his poem the quiet swiftness of flame, so that the reader will feel and not think while he is reading. But the thinking will come afterwards." There is no new trick of utterance, little surprise, and seemingly little thought in Sara Teasdale's melodious lines. The thinking comes afterwards.

I Shall Not Care

When I am dead and over me bright April
    Shakes out her rain-drenched hair,
Though you should lean above me broken-hearted,
    I shall not care.

I shall have peace, as leafy trees are peaceful
    When rain bends down the bough;
And I shall be more silent and cold-hearted
    Than you are now.

D. H. LAWRENCE
[1885–1930]

NO MAN ever tried to run away from himself more desperately than David Herbert Lawrence. "I wish I were going to Thibet," he wrote to a friend on the eve of one of his travels, "or Kamschatka—or Tahiti—to the ultima, ultima Thule . . . I feel sometimes I shall go mad because there is nowhere to go, no 'new world.' One of these days I shall be departing in some rash fashion to some foolish place."

Lawrence was born September 11, 1885, in Eastwood, a colliery town in Nottinghamshire. His father was a miner who drank himself into beating his wife and bullying David, the youngest of three sons. As a result Lawrence's affections were fixed upon his mother, an almost crippling attachment which is disclosed in Lawrence's best novel, the autobiographical SONS AND LOVERS. In youth he was a clerk, a teacher in a country school, and, in his twenty-sixth year, a novelist. At twenty-six, shortly after the death of his mother, which shook the foundations of his health, he fell in love with a married woman. She was Frieda von Richtofen, sister of a famous German flier, seven years his senior, mother of three children. They eloped, lived abroad, and, two years later, were married. But there was little peace for them in England. The First World War had started; the Lawrences, victims of spy-hunting fever, were hounded from place to place.

Lawrence's long pilgrimage began. He denounced the "artificial complexities of civilization" and left England, never to live there again. He became Poe's own "weary, wayworn wanderer," but for him there was no mothering "native shore." He tried living in Florence, Sicily, France, Ceylon, Australia, Tahiti, Mexico, New Mexico, back to Florence—always "departing in some rash fashion to some foolish place," always seeking the lost security, "the ultima, ultima Thule." He hated groups and colonies, but he was always trying to start a colony of his own; the pagan in him was opposed by the fanatical Puritan with an itch to reform.

An exhibition of his paintings was raided; three of his novels were censored and suppressed. Tubercular and self-tormented, Lawrence fought to the end. He died at forty-five on the French Riviera, March 2, 1930.

Sex and society were Lawrence's demonic preoccupations. Obsessed with the evils of civilization, he yearned for a primitive way of life, agitated for a state that, somehow, joined anarchy with dictatorship, and worshiped the unconscious. He made a fetish of instinct; he wrote of self-division and sex renewal as though his throat were "choked in its own crimson." Never before has there been such an exaltation and terror of passion, such a dependence on "the hot blood's blindfold art."

Love on the Farm

What large, dark hands are those at the window
Grasping in the golden light
Which weaves its way through the evening wind
    At my heart's delight?

Ah, only the leaves! But in the west
I see a redness suddenly come
Into the evening's anxious breast—
    'Tis the wound of love goes home!

The woodbine creeps abroad
Calling low to her lover:
    The sunlit flirt who all the day
    Has poised above her lips in play
    And stolen kisses, shallow and gay
    Of pollen, now has gone away—
        She woos the moth with her sweet, low word,
And when above her his moth-wings hover
Then her bright breast she will uncover
And yield her honey-drop to her lover.

Into the yellow, evening glow
Saunters a man from the farm below;
Leans, and looks in at the low-built shed
Where the swallow has hung her marriage bed.
    The bird lies warm against the wall.
    She glances quick her startled eyes
    Towards him, then she turns away
    Her small head, making warm display
    Of red upon the throat. Her terrors sway

Her out of the nest's warm, busy ball,
Whose plaintive cry is heard as she flies
In one blue stoop from out the sties
Into the twilight's empty hall.

Oh, water-hen, beside the rushes,
Hide your quaintly scarlet blushes,
Still your quick tail, lie still as dead,
Till the distance folds over his ominous tread!
The rabbit presses back her ears,
Turns back her liquid, anguished eyes
And crouches low; then with wild spring
Spurts from the terror of his oncoming;
To be choked back, the wire ring
Her frantic effort throttling:
Piteous brown ball of quivering fears!
Ah, soon in his large, hard hands she dies,
And swings all loose from the swing of his walk!
Yet calm and kindly are his eyes
And ready to open in brown surprise
Should I not answer to his talk
Or should he my tears surmise.

I hear his hand on the latch, and rise from my chair
Watching the door open; he flashes bare
His strong teeth in a smile, and flashes his eyes
In a smile like triumph upon me; then careless-wise
He flings the rabbit soft on the table board
And comes toward me: ah! the uplifted sword
Of his hand against my bosom! and oh, the broad
Blade of his glance that asks me to applaud
His coming! With his hand he turns my face to him
And caresses me with his fingers that still smell grim
Of rabbit's fur! God, I am caught in a snare!
I know not what fine wire is round my throat;
I only know I let him finger there
My pulse of life, and let him nose like a stoat
Who sniffs with joy before he drinks the blood.

And down his mouth comes to my mouth! and down
His bright dark eyes come over me, like a hood
Upon my mind! his lips meet mine, and a flood
Of sweet fire sweeps across me, so I drown
Against him, die, and find death good.

During his lifetime Lawrence published thirty-seven books; about
ten more appeared posthumously—a body of strangely powerful work
and a long record of suffering, anger, and ecstasy. In furious but
eloquent prose and verse he lashed out against the stupidity of the
intelligence; he extolled a fluid "vitalism," a sex-fearful, sex-driven
mindlessness. Lawrence had an uncanny way of creating tension in
a casual scene and precipitating a crisis with the turn of a dramatic
phrase. His early impassioned, curiously feminine lyrics achieve as
much intensity as the later tortured prose.

A Youth Mowing

There are four men mowing down by the Isar;
I can hear the swish of the scythe-strokes, four
Sharp breaths taken; yea, and I
Am sorry for what's in store.

The first man out of the four that's mowing
Is mine, I claim him once and for all;
Though it's sorry I am, on his young feet, knowing
None of the trouble he's led to stall.

As he sees me bringing the dinner, he lifts
His head as proud as a deer that looks
Shoulder-deep out of the corn; and wipes
His scythe-blade bright, unhooks

The scythe-stone and over the stubble to me.
Lad, thou hast gotten a child in me,
Laddie, a man thou'lt ha'e to be,
Yea, though I'm sorry for thee.

Somewhat disguised portraits of Lawrence appear in Kay Boyle's
REST CURE, Aldous Huxley's POINT COUNTER POINT, in which Law-
rence is "Mark Rampion," and Osbert Sitwell's MIRACLE ON SINAI.
In the ten years following his death more than ten volumes of remi-
niscence, biography, and analysis of Lawrence were published. Harry
T. Moore's more recent THE LIFE AND WORKS OF D. H. LAWRENCE is a
comprehensive as well as an authoritative résumé.

EZRA POUND
[1885–1972]

A N ANGRY expatriate who, in his twenties, began scolding his mother country from the vantage point of Europe, Ezra Pound was born in Hailey, Idaho, October 30, 1885. At fifteen he entered the University of Pennsylvania and was graduated at twenty from Hamilton College. After a brief pedagogical career as "instructor with professorial functions," Pound simultaneously left the academic life and America. He lived in London, Paris, and various towns in Italy; except for a short and bellicose visit in 1939 he never returned to the United States. At forty he established himself on the Italian Riviera; at fifty-six he delivered broadsides over the official Fascist radio.

In May, 1945, when he was sixty, he was taken prisoner and indicted for treason. Brought to Washington, Pound escaped trial when four psychiatrists testified that the poet was of unsound mind. In 1946 he was committed to St. Elizabeth's Hospital as an insane person. His CANTOS, over which much good ink and bad blood had been spilled, remained unfinished. Pound had written seventy-one of the contemplated one hundred, one group (*The Pisan Cantos*) had been awarded the Bollingen Prize. The award roused a storm of protests, for it had been conferred by the Fellows of the Library of Congress and was assumed to have semiofficial approval. As a result, Pound became more of a controversial figure than ever.

Pound's work had several metamorphoses. It influenced many; its stress upon the exact word as opposed to a decorative generality was responsible for the Imagists. Yeats acknowledged that his change from a rhetorical to a colloquial speech was largely due to Pound, even though later in life Yeats declared that Pound had "more style than form . . . a style constantly interrupted, broken, twisted into nervous obsession, nightmare, stammering confusion," and that he wrote like "a brilliant improvisator translating at sight from an unknown Greek masterpiece."

But, though Pound changed his manner with his point of view, the poetry survives. Even the early verse is interesting; it blends the old poetic diction with a fiercely living speech.

Ballad of the Goodly Fere[1]

SIMON ZELOTES SPEAKETH IT SOMEWHILE AFTER THE CRUCIFIXION

Ha' we lost the goodliest fere o' all
For the priests and the gallows tree?
Aye, lover he was of brawny men,
O' ships and the open sea.

When they came wi' a host to take Our Man
His smile was good to see,
"First let these go!" quo' our Goodly Fere,
"Or I'll see ye damned," says he.

Aye, he sent us out through the crossed high spears,
And the scorn of his laugh rang free,
"Why took ye not me when I walked about
Alone in the town?" says he.

Oh we drank his "Hale" in the good red wine
When we last made company,
No capon priest was the Goodly Fere
But a man o' men was he.

I ha' seen him drive a hundred men
Wi' a bundle o' cords swung free,
When they took the high and holy house
For their pawn and treasury.

They'll no get him a' in a book I think
Though they write it cunningly;
No mouse of the scrolls was the Goodly Fere
But aye loved the open sea.

If they think they ha' snared our Goodly Fere
They are fools to the last degree.
"I'll go to the feast," quo' our Goodly Fere,
"Though I go to the gallows tree."

"Ye ha' seen me heal the lame and the blind,
And wake the dead," says he,
"Ye shall see one thing to master all:
'Tis how a brave man dies on the tree."

1 *Mate, companion.*

A son of God was the Goodly Fere
That bade us his brothers be.
I ha' seen him cow a thousand men.
I ha' seen him upon the tree.

He cried no cry when they drave the nails
And the blood gushed hot and free,
The hounds of the crimson sky gave tongue
But never a cry cried he.

I ha' seen him cow a thousand men
On the hills o' Galilee,
They whined as he walked out calm between,
Wi' his eyes like the gray o' the sea.

Like the sea that brooks no voyaging
With the winds unleashed and free,
Like the sea that he cowed at Gennesaret
Wi' twey words spoke' suddenly.

A master of men was the Goodly Fere,
A mate of the wind and sea,
If they think they ha' slain our Goodly Fere

They are fools eternally.
I ha' seen him eat o' the honey-comb
Sin' they nailed him to the tree.

At one time Pound let it be known that, when the CANTOS were completed, the work would have a monumental structure "like that of a Bach fugue"; at another time readers were told that it was a huge COMMEDIA, Pound having yet to construct the PARADISO which was to follow his INFERNO and PURGATORIO. In the CANTOS everything is derived and juxtaposed with a kind of inverted pedantry: Chinese ideograms and dialectics about Social Credit, magnificent seascapes and sniggering jokes, Greek myths and elliptical attacks on usury. No poem of the period succeeded so completely in splitting the critics far apart from each other. "The CANTOS form an unparalleled history of a world seen from the shores which are the home of our civilization," wrote Ford Madox Ford. "About the poems," demurred Edward Fitzgerald, "there hangs a dismal mist of unresolved confusion."

Canto I

And then went down to the ship,
Set keel to breakers, forth on the godly sea, and
We set up mast and sail on that swart ship,
Bore sheep aboard her, and our bodies also
Heavy with weeping, and winds from sternward
Bore us out onward with bellying canvas,
Circe's this craft, the trim-coifed goddess.
Then sat we amidships, wind jamming the tiller,
Thus with stretched sail, we went over sea till day's end.
Sun to his slumber, shadows o'er all the ocean,
Came we then to the bounds of deepest water,
To the Kimmerian lands, and peopled cities
Covered with close-webbed mist, unpierced ever
With glitter of sun-ray
Nor with stars stretched, nor looking back from heaven
Swartest night stretched over wretched men there.
The ocean flowing backward, came we then to the place
Aforesaid by Circe.
Here did they rites, Perimedes and Eurylochus,
And drawing sword from my hip
I dug the ell-square pitkin;
Poured we libations unto each the dead,
First mead and then sweet wine, water mixed with white flour.
Then prayed I many a prayer to the sickly death's-heads;
As set in Ithaca, sterile bulls of the best
For sacrifice, heaping the pyre with goods,
A sheep to Tiresias only, black and a bell-sheep.
Dark blood flowed in the fosse,
Souls out of Erebus, cadaverous dead, of brides
Of youths and of the old who had borne much;
Souls stained with recent tears, girls tender,
Men many, mauled with bronze lance heads,
Battle spoil, bearing yet dreory [1] arms,
These many crowded about me; with shouting,
Pallor upon me, cried to my men for more beasts;
Slaughtered the herds, sheep slain of bronze;
Poured ointment, cried to the gods,
To Pluto the strong, and praised Proserpine;
Unsheathed the narrow sword.

---

[1] Dreory: Anglo-Saxon for "bloody."

I sat to keep off the impetuous impotent dead,
Till I should hear Tiresias.
But first Elpenor came, our friend Elpenor,
Unburied, cast on the wide earth,
Limbs that we left in the house of Circe,
Unwept, unwrapped in sepulchre, since toils urged other.
Pitiful spirit. And I cried in hurried speech:
"Elpenor, how art thou come to this dark coast?
"Cam'st thou afoot, outstripping seamen?"
        And he in heavy speech:
"Ill fate and abundant wine. I slept in Circe's ingle.
"Going down the long ladder unguarded,
"I fell against the buttress,
"Shattered the nape-nerve, the soul sought Avernus.
"But thou, O King, I bid remember me, unwept, unburied,
"Heap up mine arms, be tomb by sea-board, and inscribed:
" 'A man of no fortune and with a name to come.'
"And set my oar up, that I swung mid fellows."

And Anticlea came, whom I beat off, and then Tiresias Theban,
Holding his golden wand, knew me, and spoke first:
"A second time? why? man of ill star,
"Facing the sunless dead and this joyless region?
"Stand from the fosse, leave me my bloody bever
"For soothsay."
        And I stepped back,
And he strong with the blood, said then: "Odysseus
"Shalt return through spiteful Neptune, over dark seas,
"Lose all companions." And then Anticlea came.
Lie quiet Divus. I mean that is Andreas Divus,
In officina Wecheli, 1538, out of Homer.
And he sailed, by Sirens and thence outward and away
And unto Circe.
        Venerandam,
In the Cretan's phrase, with the golden crown, Aphrodite,
Cypri munimenta sortita est, mirthful, oricalchi, with golden
Girdles and breast bands, thou with dark eyelids
Bearing the golden bough of Argicida.

ELINOR WYLIE

[1885–1928]

ELINOR WYLIE characterized herself in her love of patrician delicacies, fine filigree, mother-of-pearl, exquisite lacquers, silver trickery, a hummingbird's wing in hammered gold. Her quality, her very features, were depicted when she made a catalogue of what she considered beautiful people:

> A tall throat, round as a column;
> A mournful mouth, small and solemn,
> Having, to confound the mourner,
> Irony in either corner . . .
>
> The eyes large and wide apart.
> They carry a dagger in the heart
> So keen and clean it never rankles . . .
> They wear small bones in wrists and ankles.

Thomas Browne, she announced, was her spiritual brother and Shelley her *alter ego*. Beauty for her was innocent and ruthless; neither good nor evil, it had "the hard heart of a child." She studied herself in the carefully polished mirror of her verse. Sometimes the results of the scrutiny were disguised; sometimes they were purposely revealing, as in the last poem from the sequence WILD PEACHES, which, with her permission, was renamed PURITAN SONNET.

Puritan Sonnet

> Down to the Puritan marrow of my bones
> There's something in this richness that 1 hate.
> I love the look, austere, immaculate,
> Of landscapes drawn in pearly monotones.
> There's something in my very blood that owns
> Bare hills, cold silver on a sky of slate,
> A thread of water, churned to milky spate
> Streaming through slanted pastures fenced with stones.

I love those skies, thin blue or snowy gray,
Those fields sparse-planted, rendering meager sheaves;
That spring, briefer than apple-blossom's breath,
Summer, so much too beautiful to stay,
Swift autumn, like a bonfire of leaves,
And sleepy winter, like the sleep of death.

She was born Elinor Hoyt September 7, 1885, in Somerville, New Jersey, of, as she liked to say, "pure Pennsylvania stock." Her grandfather was Governor of Pennsylvania, and her father became Solicitor General during the administration of Theodore Roosevelt. At twenty she married Philip Hichborn, son of a rear admiral, and had a child; three years later she eloped with Horace Wylie. The couple lived in England until Wylie obtained his divorce; the outbreak of the First World War forced them back to America. In 1923 she divorced her second husband and married the poet William Rose Benét.

A small volume of poems, chiefly juvenilia, had been privately printed in England in 1912, but Elinor Wylie was thirty-six before NETS TO CATCH THE WIND, her first representative book of poems, appeared. The verse was delicate but firm; it had the clarity as well as the coldness of crystal. It was, like the woman herself, fastidious and subtle. Technically it was seldom less than brilliant; never has the texture of a winter day, the very silence of snow, been so skillfully communicated as in VELVET SHOES.

Velvet Shoes

Let us walk in the white snow
    In a soundless space;
With footsteps quiet and slow,
    At a tranquil pace,
    Under veils of white lace.

I shall go shod in silk,
    And you in wool,
White as a white cow's milk,
    More beautiful
    Than the breast of a gull.

We shall walk through the still town
  In a windless peace;
We shall step upon white down,
  Upon silver fleece,
  Upon softer than these.

We shall walk in velvet shoes:
  Wherever we go
Silence will fall like dews
  On white silence below.
  We shall walk in the snow.

Each successive volume increased Elinor Wylie's dexterity; the
increase in depth was not evident until the last. In her forty-first
year she went alone to England for an extended period of rest and
novel writing. Two years later she suffered an almost fatal accident.
Slightly paralyzed, she recovered sufficiently to return to America
for the Christmas holiday and prepare the manuscript of ANGELS AND
EARTHLY CREATURES for the press. On December 15, 1928, she made
the final arrangement of her book. The following day she was dead.

Let No Charitable Hope

Now let no charitable hope
Confuse my mind with images
Of eagle and of antelope;
I am in nature none of these.

I was, being human, born alone;
I am, being woman, hard beset;
I live by squeezing from a stone
The little nourishment I get.

In masks outrageous and austere
The years go by in single file;
But none has merited my fear,
And none has quite escaped my smile.

Toward the last Elinor Wylie recognized the dangers of her own
technique. She studied to disdain

The frail, the overfine
That tapers to a line
Knotted about the brain.

She endeavored to unite the elegance of the Elizabethans and the intellectual passion of the metaphysicians. It is significant that the title of her first book was a quotation from Webster and the last was from Donne.

WILLIAM ROSE BENÉT

[1886–1950]

ALL the Benéts were poets at heart, and most of them were poets in practice. Of Spanish origin, the family had come to Florida in the eighteenth century. The grandfather was an army man; the father followed the same career, but in him "burned a reverence for the word." He read verse to his children, and they—William Rose, Stephen Vincent, and Laura—published no less than thirty volumes of poetry.

William Rose Benét was born February 2, 1886, at Fort Hamilton in New York Harbor. He was expected to enter West Point and follow the career of his father and grandfather, but he attended the Sheffield Scientific School at Yale and was graduated in his twenty-second year. It was as a poet, however, not as a scientist, that he made his way. He was assistant editor of THE CENTURY MAGAZINE and helped found THE SATURDAY REVIEW OF LITERATURE. He was four times married, the second time to Elinor Wylie, the dedicatee of his most representative poems, MAN POSSESSED.

Although Benét has written voluminously, he is most himself in narrative verse. His early poetry is rich and exotic, but somewhat too highly spiced. The later work controls its wayward fantasy and restrains its cantering rhymes. The native scene emerges distinctly, and American myths from Harlem to the Wild West take on new vigor. The saga of JESSE JAMES, for example, is condensed in verse which is something like an old-fashioned dime novel and something like the Robin Hood story translated by Hollywood.

Jesse James

A DESIGN IN RED AND YELLOW FOR A NICKEL LIBRARY

Jesse James was a two-gun man,
  (Roll on, Missouri!)
Strong-arm chief of an outlaw clan,
  (From Kansas to Illinois!)
He twirled an old Colt forty-five;
  (Roll on, Missouri!)
They never took Jesse James alive.
  (Roll, Missouri, roll!)

Jesse James was King of the Wes';
  (Cataracts in the Missouri!)
He'd a di'mon' heart in his lef' breas';
  (Brown Missouri rolls!)
He'd a fire in his heart no hurt could stifle;
  (Thunder, Missouri!)
Lion eyes an' a Winchester rifle.
  (Missouri, roll down!)

Jesse James rode a pinto hawse;
Come at night to a water-cawse;
Tetched with the rowel that pinto's flank;
She sprung the torrent from bank to bank.

Jesse rode through a sleepin' town;
Looked the moonlit street both up an' down;
Crack-crack-crack, the street ran flames
An' a great voice cried, "I'm Jesse James!"

Hawse an' afoot they're after Jess!
  (Roll on, Missouri!)
Spurrin' an' spurrin'—but he's gone Wes'.
  (Brown Missouri rolls!)
He was ten foot tall when he stood in his boots;
  (Lightnin' like the Missouri!)
More'n a match fer sich galoots.
  (Roll, Missouri, roll!)

Jesse James rode outa the sage;
Roun' the rocks come the swayin' stage;
Straddlin' the road a giant stan's
An' a great voice bellers, "Throw up yer han's!"

Jesse raked in the di'mon' rings,
The big gold watches an' the yuther things;
Jesse divvied 'em then an' thar
With a cryin' child had lost her mar.

. . . .

They're creepin'; they're crawlin'; they're stalkin' Jess;
    (Roll on, Missouri!)
They's a rumor he's gone much further Wes';
    (Roll, Missouri, roll!)
They's word of a cayuse hitched to the bars
    (Ruddy clouds on Missouri!)
Of a golden sunset that busts into stars.
    (Missouri, roll down!)

Jesse James rode hell fer leather;
He was a hawse an' a man together;
In a cave in a mountain high up in air
He lived with a rattlesnake, a wolf, an' a bear.

Jesse's heart was as sof' as a woman;
Fer guts an' stren'th he was sooper-human;
He could put six shots through a woodpecker's eye
And take in one swaller a gallon o' rye.

They sought him here an' they sought him there,
    (Roll on, Missouri!)
But he strides by night through the ways of the air;
    (Brown Missouri rolls!)
They say he was took an' they say he is dead,
    (Thunder, Missouri!)
But he ain't—he's a sunset overhead!
    (Missouri down to the sea!)

Jesse James was a Hercules.
When he went through the woods he tore up the trees.
When he went on the plains he smoked the groun'
An' the hull lan' shuddered fer miles aroun'.

Jesse James wore a red bandanner
That waved on the breeze like the Star Spangled Banner;
In seven states he cut up dadoes.
He's gone with the buffler an' the desperadoes.

Yes, Jesse James was a two-gun man
    (Roll on, Missouri!)
The same as when this song began;
    (From Kansas to Illinois!)
An' when you see a sunset bust into flames
    (Lightnin' light the Missouri!)
Or a thunderstorm blaze—that's Jesse James!
    (Hear that Missouri roll!)

At fifty-five Benét published THE DUST WHICH IS GOD, a semi-autobiographical poem of 559 pages, a book which, offered as a novel, is a personal revelation and a picture of a period. It was awarded the Pulitzer Prize for the best book of poetry published in 1941. A few years later Benét suffered his first heart attack. He survived, however, and published two more collections of his vigorous verse before his death May 4, 1950.

HILDA DOOLITTLE
[1886–1961]

H. D. MAY not have been "the perfect Imagist," but she was the only one of the group who consistently put into practice the theory of pure imagery. Born Hilda Doolittle in Bethlehem, Pennsylvania, September 10, 1886, she entered Bryn Mawr in 1904, but was forced to leave after two years because of poor health. In her twenties she went abroad, met Ezra Pound, and, with him, helped to establish the Imagist movement. She married Richard Aldington, one of the members of the group, but separated from her husband at the end of the First World War and subsequently divorced him. She lived in England and Switzerland; except for a short visit, she never returned to the United States. To Amy Lowell's disappointment, she refused to be dragged into the *vers libre* controversy; she preferred to remain semianonymous, and signed her work only with her initials.

H. D.'s early poetry was so definitely sculptured that it arrested emotion at the source. The language was exact but chill; beauty seemed fixed in a frozen gesture. In HYMEN, however, and in the succeeding volumes H. D. added sensuousness to precision. As her work grew more formal it became more flexible in music, warmer in emotion. She wrote almost entirely of the classical world, but her insight brought ancient figures to life and made the remote immediate.

Never More Will the Wind

Never more will the wind
Cherish you again,
Never more will the rain.

Never more
Shall we find you bright
In the snow and wind.

The snow is melted,
The snow is gone,
And you are flown:

Like a bird out of our hand,
Like a light out of our heart,
You are gone.
from HYMEN

Lethe

Nor skin nor hide nor fleece
Shall cover you,
Nor curtain of crimson nor fine
Shelter of cedar-wood be over you,
Nor the fir-tree
Nor the pine.

Nor sight of whin nor gorse
Nor river-yew,
Nor fragrance of flowering bush,

Nor wailing of reed-bird to waken you.
Nor of linnet
Nor of thrush.

Nor word nor touch nor sight
Of lover, you
Shall long through the night but for this:
The roll of the full tide to cover you
Without question,
Without kiss.

RUPERT BROOKE

[1887–1915]

R UPERT BROOKE's beauty, exquisite but masculine, was a legend
even in his own day. He stood six feet tall, athletically built,
his finely modeled head topped with a crown of shining hair. "A
golden young Apollo," said Edward Thomas; "to look at, he was
part of the youth of the world."

Son of an assistant master at Rugby, Rupert Brooke was born at
the famous school for boys August 3, 1887. Educated at Rugby and
King's College, Cambridge, he published his first book at twenty-
four, a book of influences but radiant with Brooke's own pleasure
in the senses. He was never halfhearted, never blasé. His intellectual
appetite was enormous, his physical enthusiasm inexhaustible. "I
want to walk a thousand miles," he wrote to a friend, "and write
one thousand plays, and sing one thousand poems, and drink one
thousand pots of beer, and kiss one thousand girls." He delighted,
said Walter de la Mare, "in things for themselves, not merely for
their beauty. . . . The theme of his poetry is the life of the mind, the
senses, the feelings—life here and now." He was, in the most inclu·
sive sense, the great lover.

The Great Lover

I have been so great a lover: filled my days
So proudly with the splendor of Love's praise,
The pain, the calm, and the astonishment,
Desire illimitable, and still content,

And all dear names men use, to cheat despair,
For the perplexed and viewless streams that bear
Our hearts at random down the dark of life.
Now, ere the unthinking silence on that strife
Steals down, I would cheat drowsy Death so far,
My night shall be remembered for a star
That outshone all the suns of all men's days.
Shall I not crown them with immortal praise
Whom I have loved, who have given me, dared with me
High secrets, and in darkness knelt to see
The inenarrable godhead of delight?
Love is a flame:—we have beaconed the world's night.
A city:—and we have built it, these and I.
An emperor:—we have taught the world to die.
So, for their sakes I loved, ere I go hence,
And the high cause of Love's magnificence,
And to keep loyalties young, I'll write those names
Golden for ever, eagles, crying flames,
And set them as a banner, that men may know,
To dare the generations, burn, and blow
Out on the wind of Time, shining and streaming. . . .

These I have loved:
       White plates and cups, clean-gleaming,
Ringed with blue lines; and feathery, faëry dust;
Wet roofs, beneath the lamp-light; the strong crust
Of friendly bread; and many-tasting food;
Rainbows; and the blue bitter smoke of wood;
And radiant raindrops couching in cool flowers;
And flowers themselves, that sway through sunny hours,
Dreaming of moths that drink them under the moon;
Then, the cool kindliness of sheets, that soon
Smooth away trouble; and the rough male kiss
Of blankets; grainy wood; live hair that is
Shining and free; blue-massing clouds; the keen
Unpassioned beauty of a great machine;
The benison of hot water; furs to touch;
The good smell of old clothes; and other such—
The comfortable smell of friendly fingers,
Hair's fragrance, and the musty reek that lingers
About dead leaves and last year's ferns. . . .
                     Dear names,
And thousand others throng to me! Royal flames;
Sweet water's dimpling laugh from tap or spring;

Holes in the ground; and voices that do sing:
Voices in laughter, too; and body's pain,
Soon turned to peace; and the deep-panting train;
Firm sands; the little dulling edge of foam
That browns and dwindles as the wave goes home;
And washen stones, gay for an hour; the cold
Graveness of iron; moist black earthen mold;
Sleep; and high places; footprints in the dew;
And oaks; and brown horse-chestnuts, glossy-new;
And new-peeled sticks; and shining pools on grass;—
All these have been my loves. And these shall pass,
Whatever passes not, in the great hour,
Nor all my passion, all my prayers, have power
To hold them with me through the gate of Death.
They'll play deserter, turn with the traitor breath,
Break the high bond we made, and sell Love's trust
And sacramental covenant to the dust.
—Oh, never a doubt but, somewhere, I shall wake,
And give what's left of love again, and make
New friends now strangers. . . .
                   But the best I've known
Stays here, and changes, breaks, grows old, is blown
About the winds of the world, and fades from brains
Of living men, and dies.
                   Nothing remains.

O dear my loves, O faithless, once again
This one last gift I give: that after men
Shall know, and later lovers, far-removed
Praise you, "All these were lovely"; say, "He loved."

Shortly after the outbreak of the First World War Brooke entered the Royal Naval Division and took part in the unsuccessful defense of Antwerp. A few months later, on his way to the Dardanelles, he contracted blood poison and died April 23, 1915. He was buried on the island of Skyros, in his twenty-eighth year.

Ardor intensified the least of Brooke's activities. "He flung himself into the world," wrote Walter de la Mare, "as a wasp pounces into a cake shop, Hotspur into the fighting." As a soldier he was no less fervent than as a poet. In the sonnet which begins "If I should die, think only this of me," Brooke expressed a patriotism which lifts itself above nationalism, "all evil shed away, a pulse in the eternal mind."

The Soldier

If I should die, think only this of me;
  That there's some corner of a foreign field
That is for ever England. There shall be
  In that rich earth a richer dust concealed;
A dust whom England bore, shaped, made aware,
  Gave, once, her flowers to love, her ways to roam,
A body of England's breathing English air,
  Washed by the rivers, blest by suns of home.

And think, this heart, all evil shed away,
  A pulse in the eternal mind, no less
    Gives somewhere back the thoughts by England given;
Her sights and sounds; dreams happy as her day;
  And laughter, learnt of friends; and gentleness,
    In hearts at peace, under an English heaven.

DAME EDITH SITWELL
[1887–1964]

THE Sitwells precipitated themselves upon a postwar England with eruptive satires, impudent burlesques, and megaphonic challenges. There were three of them—Osbert, Sacheverell, and Edith, the most gifted of the family—and they throve upon their well-advertised eccentricities. In prose and verse, as well as personal performances, they ridiculed the ingenuousness of the Georgians and mocked the nostalgia of their more wistful contemporaries. Gibing at the outworn patterns of class and the bankruptcy of an aristocratic culture, they purposely distorted statement and suggestion, cause and effect. For a literature of rhetoric they substituted a literature of nerves.

Descended from a line of Norman chiefs who reputedly accompanied William the Conqueror, Edith Sitwell was born at Scarborough, Yorkshire, in 1887. Her grandfather was the Earl of Londesborough, and her father was the fourth baronet of his line. Oldest of the three living Sitwell coadjutors, she was privately educated, traveled extensively, and left the imposing six-hundred-year-old estate to live in London. She wrote fluently: strange verse, orthodox biographies, criticisms of modern verse and appreciation of eighteenth-century styles.

Most of Miss Sitwell's poetry achieves its extraordinary effect by mixed syncopated rhythms, ironic overtones, and a skillful confusion of visual and tactile images. An AUBADE—or morning song—begins:

> Jane, Jane,
> Tall as a crane,
> The morning light creaks down again.
>
> Comb your cockscomb-ragged hair;
> Jane, Jane, come down the stair.
>
> Each dull blunt wooden stalactite
> Of rain creaks, hardened by the light,
>
> Sounding like an overtone
> From some lonely world unknown . .
>
> The light would show (if it could harden)
> Eternities of kitchen-garden,
>
> Cockscomb flowers that none will pluck,
> And wooden flowers that 'gin to cluck.

Thus Miss Sitwell, seeing the early-morning world through the eyes of the kitchenmaid, pictures the overhanging rain hardening into a "dull blunt wooden stalactite," the "eternities" of kitchen garden always in need of weeding, and flowers that "cluck," since most of them are lorded over by the proud cockscombs. Character as well as scene is established by such a method, extreme but logical, just as a kind of adult nonsense is achieved by the jazz rhythms of a jingle which clangs its way into the mind:

> When
> Sir
> Beelzebub called for his syllabub in the hotel in Hell
> Where Proserpine fell,
> Blue as the gendarmerie were the waves of the sea,
> (Rocking and shocking the bar-maid.)
> Nobody comes to give him his rum but the
> Rim of the sky hippopotamus-glum . . .

Miss Sitwell's later work seldom depends on startling shifts of tone and kaleidoscopic images in surrealist nursery rhymes. The human drama becomes her concern, and she considers it with deep understanding and in simple terms. One of her most recent poems is her most forceful. Using toward the climax two lines from the end of Marlowe's DOCTOR FAUSTUS (see page 328), she dramatically combines the world of legend with the world of frightful actuality, and brings Gethsemane to bombed London.

Still Falls the Rain

(THE RAIDS, 1940: NIGHT AND DAWN)

Still falls the Rain—
Dark as the world of man, black as our loss—
Blind as the nineteen hundred and forty nails upon the Cross

Still falls the Rain
With a sound like the pulse of the heart that is changed to the
    hammer beat
In the Potter's Field, and the sound of the impious feet

On the Tomb:
        Still falls the Rain
In the Field of Blood where the small hopes breed and the human
    brain
Nurtures its greed, that worm with the brow of Cain.

Still falls the Rain
At the feet of the Starved Man hung upon the Cross,
Christ that each day, each night, nails there, have mercy on us—
On Dives and on Lazarus:
Under the Rain the sore and the gold are as one.

Still falls the Rain—
Still falls the Blood from the Starved Man's wounded Side:
He bears in His Heart all wounds,—those of the light that died,
The last faint spark
In the self-murdered heart, the wounds of the sad uncomprehending
    dark,
The wounds of the baited bear,—
The blind and weeping bear whom the keepers beat
On his helpless flesh . . . the tears of the hunted hare.

Still falls the Rain—
Then—"O Ile leape up to my God! Who pulles me doune?—
See, see where Christ's blood streames in the firmament."
It flows from the Brow we nailed upon the tree
Deep to the dying, to the thirsting heart
That holds the fires of the world,—dark-smirched with pain
As Caesar's laurel crown.

Then sounds the voice of One who, like the heart of man,
Was once a child who among beasts has lain—
"Still do I love, still shed my innocent light, my Blood, for thee."

ROBINSON JEFFERS
[1887–1962]

To ROBINSON JEFFERS the earth was hopelessly prostrate; people were "all compelled, all unhappy, all helpless"; human nature was "ignoble in its quiet times, mean in its pleasures, slavish in the mass"; civilization was a transient sickness, and consciousness a walking disease. There was only the alleviation of a "divinely superfluous beauty," of moments when a tragic deed might "shine terribly against the dark magnificence of things," and there was always death, the beautiful though capricious savior, "the gay child with the gypsy eyes." God is cruel; but Jeffers, like a pessimistic Francis Thompson, acknowledges there is no escaping him.

The world's God is treacherous and full of unreason; a torturer,
    but also
The only foundation and the only fountain.
Who fights him eats his own flesh and perishes of hunger.

In lines of uncompromising negation but indubitable force, Jeffers praises stoical defeat and desperate energy; he regards an unnecessary, and almost irrelevant, humanity with pity if not with active sympathy.

Unmeasured power, incredible passion, enormous craft: no thought
    apparent but burns darkly

Smothered with its own smoke in the human brain-vault: no thought
    outside: a certain measure in phenomena:
The fountains of the boiling stars, the flowers on the foreland, the
    ever-returning roses of dawn.

Robinson Jeffers was born January 10, 1887, in Pittsburgh, Penn-
sylvania. Son of a theologian and a mother twenty-three years younger
than the father, Jeffers was brought up on the classics. His father
took him through Europe on walking trips, and the boy attended
schools in Switzerland and Germany for three years. His academic
education was completed at Southern California in medicine and at
the University of Washington in forestry.

A legacy left by a cousin made it possible for Jeffers to give all his
time to writing; his first and most uncharacteristic volume, FLAGONS
AND APPLES, was published at his own expense. At twenty-six he
married Una Call Kuster and planned to go to England. But the
news of the war turned them back to California, and when they
reached Carmel, Jeffers said that "it was evident that we had come
without knowing it to our inevitable place." There Jeffers remained.
Years later, with his own hands and with the help of his twin sons,
he built a house not of ivory but of headland boulders. Neverthe-
less, it was a tower in which he could immure himself and escape
the world.

Since 1912 Jeffers has published twenty volumes of verse which
announce a powerful if somewhat monotonous pessimism, a fearful
hatred of life and an obsession with "self-destructive" love. "The
calm to look for is the calm at the whirlwind's heart," he assures a
war-torn world in BE ANGRY AT THE SUN. But all of his poems are not
complacent preludes to Doomsday. Again and again Jeffers praises
a violent individualism, and writes melodramatically about the
tragic struggle toward self-realization, bitter recognition, and the
ennobling power of pain.

Post Mortem

Happy people die whole, they are all dissolved in a moment, they
    have had what they wanted,
No hard gifts; the unhappy
Linger a space, but pain is a thing that is glad to be forgotten; but
    one who has given

His heart to a cause or a country,
His ghost may spaniel it a while, disconsolate to watch it. I was won-
    dering how long the spirit
That sheds this verse will remain
When the nostrils are nipped, when the brain rots in its vault or
    bubbles in the violence of fire
To be ash in metal. I was thinking
Some stalks of the wood whose roots I married to the earth of this
    place will stand five centuries;
I held the roots in my hand,
The stems of the trees between two fingers; how many remote gen-
    erations of women
Will drink joy from men's loins,
And dragged from between the thighs of what mothers will giggle
    at my ghost when it curses the axmen,
Gray impotent voice on the sea-wind,
When the last trunk falls? The women's abundance will have built
    roofs over all this foreland;
Will have buried the rock foundations
I laid here: the women's exuberance will canker and fail in its time
    and like clouds the houses
Unframe, the granite of the prime
Stand from the heaps: come storm and wash clean: the plaster is all
    run to the sea and the steel
All rusted; the foreland resumes
The form we loved when we saw it. Though one at the end of the
    age and far off from this place
Should meet my presence in a poem,
The ghost would not care but be here, long sunset shadow in the
    seams of the granite, and forgotten
The flesh, a spirit for the stone.

If most values are inconsequential in a universe which flees "the
contagion of consciousness," the protesting mortal may learn hardi-
hood from the rocks; he can draw courage, though no comfort, from
the merciless air. There still is "the leopard-footed evening," and,
for pure contemplation, the wings of hawks, the storm dances of
gulls, the heartbreaking beauty which remains when there is no
heart to break for it. And, sometimes, there is a brief joy of the writ-
ten word, the "honey of peace in old poems."

To the Stone-Cutters

Stone-cutters fighting time with marble, you foredefeated
Challengers of oblivion,
Eat cynical earnings, knowing rock splits, records fall down,
The square-limbed Roman letters
Scale in the thaws, wear in the rain. The poet as well
Builds his monument mockingly;
For man will be blotted out, the blithe earth die, the brave sun
Die blind and blacken to the heart:
Yet stones have stood for a thousand years, and pained thoughts
found
The honey of peace in old poems.

MARIANNE MOORE
[1887–1972]

ALTHOUGH Marianne Moore was born in St. Louis, Missouri, November 15, 1887, most of her life was spent in the eastern section of the United States. She received her B.A. from Bryn Mawr in 1909; taught stenography at the Indian School at Carlisle, Pennsylvania, from 1911 to 1915; and, after that, supported herself as a librarian, editor, and poet. As a poet she was daring but exceptionally modest; a few of her friends had to "pirate" some of her poems in order to have her first volume published in 1921. Three years later she received the Dial Award of two thousand dollars for "distinguished service for American Letters."

From that time on Miss Moore never lacked honors. Her SELECTED POEMS (1935) carried an introductory tribute by T. S. Eliot. WHAT ARE YEARS? (1941) received salvos of critical praise because of Miss Moore's fastidious discriminations, her odd but precious images, her extraordinarily skillful interweaving of curious quotations, obscure data, and fascinating references—a highly dexterous kind of poetic montage.

COLLECTED POEMS (1951) again proved that no poet owed more to more sources than Miss Moore, yet no contemporary author was more original. The book won all three of the most coveted awards:

the National Book Award, the Bollingen Prize, and the Pulitzer Prize. Among pages of brilliantly bizarre and queerly patterned verse, the volume contained "What Are Years?" and "In Distrust of Merits," which was ranked by many as the most eloquent poem of the Second World War. In the face of this national acclaim Miss Moore, consistently modest, declared: "I can see no reason for calling my work poetry except that there is no other category in which to put it. Anyone could do what I do, and I am, therefore, the more grateful that those whose judgment I trust should regard it as poetry."

What Are Years?

What is our innocence,
what is our guilt? All are
   naked, none is safe. And whence
is courage: the unanswered question,
the resolute doubt—
dumbly calling, deadly listening—that
in misfortune, even death,
     encourages others
     and in its defeat, stirs

   the soul to be strong? He
sees deep and is glad, who
   accedes to mortality
and in his imprisonment, rises
upon himself as
the sea in a chasm, struggling to be
free and unable to be,
     in its surrounding
     finds its continuing.

   So he who strongly feels,
behaves. The very bird,
   grown taller as he sings, steels
his form straight up. Though he is captive,
his mighty singing
says, satisfaction is a lowly
thing, how pure a thing is joy.
     This is mortality,
     this is eternity.

In Distrust of Merits

Strengthened to live, strengthened to die for
   medals and positioned victories?
They're fighting, fighting, fighting the blind
   man who thinks he sees,—
who cannot see that the enslaver is
enslaved; the hater, harmed. O shining O
     firm star, O tumultuous
      ocean lashed till small things go
     as they will, the mountainous
      wave makes us who look, know

depth. Lost at sea before they fought! O
   star of David, star of Bethlehem,
O black imperial lion
   of the Lord—emblem
of a risen world—be joined at last, be
joined. There is hate's crown beneath which all is
     death; there's love's without which none
      is king; the blessed deeds bless
     the halo. As contagion
      of sickness makes sickness,

contagion of trust can make trust. They're
   fighting in deserts and caves, one by
one, in battalions and squadrons;
   they're fighting that I
may yet recover from the disease, *my*
self; some have it lightly, some will die. "Man's
     wolf to man?" And we devour
      ourselves? The enemy could not
     have made a greater breach in our
      defenses. One pilot-

ing a blind man can escape him, but
   Job disheartened by false comfort knew,
that nothing is so defeating
   as a blind man who
can see. O alive who are dead, who are
proud not to see, O small dust of the earth

that walks so arrogantly,
    trust begets power and faith is
an affectionate thing. We
    vow, we make this promise

to the fighting—it's a promise—"We'll
    never hate black, white, red, yellow, Jew,
Gentile, Untouchable." We are
    not competent to
make our vows. With set jaw they are fighting,
fighting, fighting,—some we love whom we know,
    some we love but know not—that
        hearts may feel and not be numb.
    It cures me; or am I what
        I can't believe in? Some

in snow, some on crags, some in quicksands,
    little by little, much by much, they
are fighting fighting fighting that where
    there was death there may
be life. "When a man is prey to anger,
he is moved by outside things; when he holds
    his ground in patience patience
        patience, that is action or
    beauty," the soldier's defense
        and hardest armor for

the fight. The world's an orphan's home. Shall
    we never have peace without sorrow?
without pleas of the dying for
    help that won't come? O
quiet form upon the dust, I cannot
look and yet I must. If these great patient
    dyings—all these agonies
        and woundbearings and blood shed—
    can teach us how to live, these
        dyings were not wasted.

Hate-hardened heart, O heart of iron,
    iron is iron till it is rust.
There never was a war that was
    not inward; I must
fight till I have conquered in myself what
causes war, but I would not believe it.

> I inwardly did nothing,
> O Iscariotlike crime!
> Beauty is everlasting
> and dust is for a time.

T. S. ELIOT
[1888–1965]

MORE than any other contemporary, Thomas Stearns Eliot influenced poetry on both sides of the Atlantic. A naturalized Englishman, he came of Puritan New England stock and was born in St. Louis, Missouri, September 26, 1888. He was educated at Harvard, of which a distant relative, Charles W. Eliot, was president, and concluded his studies at the Sorbonne and Oxford. In his mid-twenties he settled in London, taught at a boys' school, worked in a bank, became an assistant editor, and, in his infrequent leisure periods, wrote poetry and critical essays. His first collection created a small sensation. PRUFROCK, published in 1917, was immediately hailed as a new manner in English literature and belittled as an echo of Laforgue and the French symbolists to whom Eliot was indebted. The subject matter was strange; the technique was puzzling; the style—alternately sonorous and discordant, elaborately obscure and conversationally simple—was harshly criticized and widely imitated. The unprepared reader may have been shocked, but he was shocked awake.

The title poem, THE LOVE SONG OF J. ALFRED PRUFROCK, was written while Eliot was still an undergraduate at Harvard. One of his first, and still one of his most famous poems, it is a highly allusive picture of decadence against the background of a sterile society. Concentrating upon moments of intensity, omitting all but the most vital commentary, Eliot portrays a tired world through the eyes of an ultrafastidious and futile dilettante. The title sets the mood for the poem with its contrast between the alluring LOVE SONG and the unromantic business signature of J. ALFRED PRUFROCK. The irony is stressed by the quotation from Dante: "If I thought my answer were to one who could possibly return to this world, then this flame would shake no more. But since, if what I hear is true, that none ever did return alive from these depths, I answer you without fear of misrepresentation." The discord suggested by the title is continued in the opening stanza with its inviting promise:

Let us go then, you and I,
When the evening is spread out against the sky—

And then the shock, the reminder of the world's desperate illness:

Like a patient etherized upon a table.

The poem proceeds on this double level. The startling but logical images, the bizarre but suggestive epithets, carry on the contrary movement and emphasize the ambivalence of the central character. An inhibited, culture-ridden, prematurely old young man ("grown slightly bald"), Prufrock loses himself between intensities and trivialities, between great emotions and the futility of days spent in small talk—"In the room the women come and go, talking of Michelangelo"—and a life "measured out with coffee spoons." He is aware of passion everywhere about him, but he cannot rouse himself to it.

Do I dare
Disturb the universe?

.   .   .   .   .   .

I know the voices dying with a dying fall
Beneath the music from a farther room.
So how should I presume?

Prufrock can live only in terms of art, images of the past, escapes from responsible action. He procrastinates and isolates himself, a modern Hamlet. But he does not flatter himself even here.

No! I am not Prince Hamlet, nor was meant to be;
Am an attendant lord, one that will do
To swell a progress, start a scene or two . . .
Full of high sentence, but a bit obtuse;
At times, indeed, almost ridiculous—
Almost, at times, the Fool.

The mockery of the prefatory quotation from Dante is now fully revealed as each verse presents the defeat of the irresolute Prufrock, too priggish for pathos, too sunk in his depths ever to "return alive" to this world.

The Love Song of J. Alfred Prufrock

S'io credesse che mia risposta fosse
A persona che mai tornasse al mondo,
Questa fiamma staria senza piu scosse.
Ma perciocche giammai di questo fondo
Non torno vivo alcun, s'i'odo il vero,
Senza tema d'infamia ti rispondo.

Let us go then, you and I,
When the evening is spread out against the sky
Like a patient etherized upon a table;
Let us go, through certain half-deserted streets,
The muttering retreats
Of restless nights in one-night cheap hotels
And sawdust restaurants with oyster-shells:
Streets that follow like a tedious argument
Of insidious intent
To lead you to an overwhelming question. . . .
Oh, do not ask, "What is it?"
Let us go and make our visit.

In the room the women come and go
Talking of Michelangelo.

The yellow fog that rubs its back upon the window-panes,
The yellow smoke that rubs its muzzle on the window-panes,
Licked its tongue into the corners of the evening,
Lingered upon the pools that stand in drains,
Let fall upon its back the soot that falls from chimneys,
Slipped by the terrace, made a sudden leap,
And seeing that it was a soft October night,
Curled once about the house, and fell asleep.

And indeed there will be time
For the yellow smoke that slides along the street,
Rubbing its back upon the window-panes;
There will be time, there will be time
To prepare a face to meet the faces that you meet;
There will be time to murder and create,
And time for all the works and days of hands
That lift and drop a question on your plate;

Time for you and time for me,
And time yet for a hundred indecisions,
And for a hundred visions and revisions,
Before the taking of a toast and tea.

In the room the women come and go
Talking of Michelangelo.

And indeed there will be time
To wonder, "Do I dare?" and, "Do I dare?"
Time to turn back and descend the stair,
With a bald spot in the middle of my hair—
(They will say: "How his hair is growing thin!")
My morning coat, my collar mounting firmly to the chin,
My necktie rich and modest, but asserted by a simple pin—
(They will say: "But how his arms and legs are thin!")
Do I dare
Disturb the universe?
In a minute there is time
For decisions and revisions which a minute will reverse.

For I have known them all already, known them all:
Have known the evenings, mornings, afternoons,
I have measured out my life with coffee spoons;
I know the voices dying with a dying fall
Beneath the music from a farther room.
         So how should I presume?

And I have known the eyes already, known them all—
The eyes that fix you in a formulated phrase,
And when I am formulated, sprawling on a pin,
When I am pinned and wriggling on the wall,
Then how should I begin
To spit out all the butt-ends of my days and ways?
         And how should I presume?

And I have known the arms already, known them all—
Arms that are braceleted and white and bare
(But in the lamplight, downed with light brown hair!)
Is it perfume from a dress
That makes me so digress?
Arms that lie along a table, or wrap about a shawl,
         And should I then presume?
         And how should I begin?

                    .   .   .   .

Shall I say, I have gone at dusk through narrow streets
And watched the smoke that rises from the pipes
Of lonely men in shirt-sleeves, leaning out of windows? . . .

I should have been a pair of ragged claws
Scuttling across the floors of silent seas.

      .   .   .   .

And the afternoon, the evening, sleeps so peacefully!
Smoothed by long fingers,
Asleep . . . tired . . . or it malingers,
Stretched on the floor, here beside you and me.
Should I, after tea and cakes and ices,
Have the strength to force the moment to its crisis?
But though I have wept and fasted, wept and prayed,
Though I have seen my head (grown slightly bald) brought in upon
    a platter,
I am no prophet—and here's no great matter;
I have seen the moment of my greatness flicker,
And I have seen the eternal Footman hold my coat, and snicker,
And in short, I was afraid.

And would it have been worth it, after all,
After the cups, the marmalade, the tea,
Among the porcelain, among some talk of you and me,
Would it have been worth while,
To have bitten off the matter with a smile,
To have squeezed the universe into a ball
To roll it toward some overwhelming question,
To say: "I am Lazarus, come from the dead,
Come back to tell you all, I shall tell you all"—
If one, settling a pillow by her head,
    Should say: "That is not what I meant at all;
    That is not it, at all."

And would it have been worth it, after all,
Would it have been worth while,
After the sunsets and the dooryards and the sprinkled streets,
After the novels, after the teacups, after the skirts that trail along
    the floor—
And this, and so much more?—
It is impossible to say just what I mean!
But as if a magic lantern threw the nerves in patterns on a screen:
Would it have been worth while
If one, settling a pillow or throwing off a shawl,

And turning toward the window, should say:
    "That is not it at all,
    That is not what I meant, at all."

                    .   .   .   .

No! I am not Prince Hamlet, nor was meant to be;
Am an attendant lord, one that will do
To swell a progress, start a scene or two,
Advise the prince; no doubt, an easy tool,
Deferential, glad to be of use,
Politic, cautious, and meticulous;
Full of high sentence, but a bit obtuse;
At times, indeed, almost ridiculous—
Almost, at times, the Fool.

I grow old. . . . I grow old. . . .
I shall wear the bottoms of my trousers rolled.

Shall I part my hair behind? Do I dare to eat a peach?
I shall wear white flannel trousers, and walk upon the beach.
I have heard the mermaids singing, each to each.

I do not think that they will sing to me.

I have seen them riding seaward on the waves
Combing the white hair of the waves blown back
When the wind blows the water white and black.
We have lingered in the chambers of the sea
By sea-girls wreathed with seaweed red and brown
Till human voices wake us, and we drown.

Most of Eliot's predecessors were divided between an allegiance
to the past and a loyalty to the present scene. Eliot superimposed
the past upon the present—usually an idealized past against a vulgar
present—and interpreted modernity by quoting Donne, Webster,
Wagner, without supplying quotation marks. His colleagues were
searching for security in the midst of roaring industry, reclaimed
farms, teeming prairies, sky-searching cities. Eliot uncovered death-
in-life everywhere. He explored a land of drought, of vacant lots
cluttered with old newspapers, of musty parlors and filthy alleys, of
cheap boardinghouses and rivers sweating oil. The result of his ex-
ploration was THE WASTE LAND, which, with its extension of the
death wish, characterized a whole period. THE HOLLOW MEN pic-
tured a still more hopeless state of desolation. In bitter but precise

phrases, here, as David Daiches wrote, "is an impressive symbolic picture of an age without belief, without value, without meaning." It is an exhausted world in which men gather on stony soil in a valley of dying stars, a world of "shape without form, gesture without motion," a world that ends:

> Not with a bang but a whimper.

Eliot had reached an impasse. Having found the limits of emptiness, he groped back to an established faith. In his fortieth year he became an English citizen and declared himself a "classicist in literature, royalist in politics, and Anglo-Catholic in religion." The turning point is seen at its best in JOURNEY OF THE MAGI. Here Eliot turns away from ignominy to a contemplation of glory. After the hope of a new birth, it is impossible to remain at ease in disbelief or half-faith, "in the old dispensation." Salvation is glimpsed in a miraculous vision of the past, but the terms are the terms of the present.

Journey of the Magi

"A cold coming we had of it,
Just the worst time of the year
For a journey, and such a long journey:
The ways deep and the weather sharp,
The very dead of winter."
And the camels galled, sore-footed, refractory,
Lying down in the melting snow.
There were times we regretted
The summer palaces on slopes, the terraces,
And the silken girls bringing sherbet.
Then the camel men cursing and grumbling
And running away, and wanting their liquor and women,
And the night-fires going out, and the lack of shelters,
And the cities hostile and the towns unfriendly
And the villages dirty and charging high prices:
A hard time we had of it.
At the end we preferred to travel all night,
Sleeping in snatches,
With the voices singing in our ears, saying
That this was all folly.

Then at dawn we came down to a temperate valley,
Wet, below the snow line, smelling of vegetation;
With a running stream and a water-mill beating the darkness,
And three trees on the low sky,
And an old white horse galloped away in the meadow.
Then we came to a tavern with vine-leaves over the lintel,
Six hands at an open door dicing for pieces of silver,
And feet kicking the empty wine-skins.
But there was no information, and so we continued
And arriving at evening, not a moment too soon
Finding the place; it was (you may say) satisfactory.

All this was a long time ago, I remember,
And I would do it again, but set down
This set down
This: were we led all that way for
Birth or Death? There was a Birth, certainly,
We had evidence and no doubt. I had seen birth and death,
But had thought they were different; this Birth was
Hard and bitter agony for us, like Death, our death.
We returned to our places, these Kingdoms,
But no longer at ease here, in the old dispensation,
With an alien people clutching their gods.
I should be glad of another death.

Eliot's mother had written a poetic drama, SAVONAROLA; at forty-six Eliot wrote a poetic play about another martyr, Thomas Becket, and entitled it MURDER IN THE CATHEDRAL. Its pious affirmation was accentuated by ASH WEDNESDAY, considered by many to be one of the best of modern religious poems. The religious note was extended and intensified in FOUR QUARTETS (1943) which ranged in tone from the flatly colloquial to the raptly mystical and revolved about the conflicts between time and timelessness. Five years later Eliot was awarded the Nobel Prize for his work "as a trail-blazing pioneer of modern poetry." His play, THE COCKTAIL PARTY, produced in New York in 1950, received a somewhat puzzled but generally enthusiastic press. It was followed three years later by THE CONFIDENTIAL CLERK, an intellectual farce, part Euripedes and part Gilbert and Sullivan, packed with nimble repartee. Even those who were confused by the ambiguities, acknowledged the playwright's extraordinary compressions and allusiveness. In his sixties Eliot was the most discussed as well as the most widely quoted poet of his day.

JOHN CROWE RANSOM
[1888–1974]

INFLUENCED by T. S. Eliot but retaining his own Southern inflection, John Crowe Ransom fashioned a verse that was both bland and tart. Its characteristic tone, a grave gaiety, is heard even when the poet announces a death:

> Here lies a lady of beauty and high degree.
> Of chills and fever she died, of fever and chills,
> The delight of her husband, her aunts, an infant of three,
> And of medicos marveling sweetly on her ills.

Such mock seriousness identifies Ransom's idiom. Sometimes it grows so broadly pedantic that it approaches parody, but it is customarily balanced between philosophic irony and whimsical fantasy.

Lady Lost

This morning, there flew up the lane
A timid lady-bird to our bird-bath
And eyed her image dolefully as death;
This afternoon, knocked on our windowpane
To be let in from the rain.

And when I caught her eye
She looked aside, but at the clapping thunder
And sight of the whole earth blazing up like tinder
Looked in on us again most miserably,
Indeed as if she would cry.

So I will go out into the park and say,
"Who has lost a delicate brown-eyed lady
In the West End Section? Or has anybody
Injured some fine woman in some dark way,
Last night or yesterday?

"Let the owner come and claim possession,
No questions will be asked. But stroke her gently

> With loving words, and she will evidently
> Resume her full soft-haired white-breasted fashion,
> And her right home and her right passion."

A minister's son, John Crowe Ransom was born April 30, 1888, in Pulaski, Tennessee. Educated at Vanderbilt University, he was a Rhodes scholar at Oxford, and returned to Tennessee to teach. He remained on the faculty of Vanderbilt University for more than twenty years, headed a group of controversial writers, and established THE FUGITIVE, a magazine of regional experiment. In his fiftieth year, he went to Kenyon College, Ohio, where he founded THE KENYON REVIEW.

A patrician agrarian, Ransom sweetens the soil and plows old ground for new crops. He localizes subjects as old as poetry itself. PIAZZA PIECE is typical. The setting is native; one can almost detect a Southern accent in the dialogue of the elderly suitor and the young charmer in her bower of roses. But the dying roses suggest the transiency of beauty, the "spectral" singing reminds us that the moon is a dead body—and the gray man in a dustcoat and the young belle become two figures in one of the oldest allegories: *Tod und das Mädchen,* Death and the Lady.

Piazza Piece

—I am a gentleman in a dustcoat trying
To make you hear. Your ears are soft and small
And listen to an old man not at all;
They want the young men's whispering and sighing.
But see the roses on your trellis dying
And hear the spectral singing of the moon—
For I must have my lovely lady soon.
I am a gentleman in a dustcoat trying.

—I am a lady young in beauty waiting
Until my truelove comes, and then we kiss.
But what gray man among the vines is this
Whose words are dry and faint as in a dream?
Back from my trellis, sir, before I scream!
I am a lady young in beauty waiting.

CONRAD AIKEN
[1889–1973]

CONRAD AIKEN's poetry is a long hymn to chaos, but it is a softly cushioned chaos set in a charmingly iridescent void. His tone poems (miscalled "symphonies") are heavy with blurred harmonies and a somewhat too cultivated vagueness. All the rough edges of reality are smoothed down through subtly diminished cadences in a kind of whispered incantation. It is a sweet mellifluousness, a little like Chopin's languid nocturnes and more than a little like the subaqueous, wavering melodies of Debussy:

> The profound gloom of bells among still trees,
> Like a rolling of huge boulders beneath seas.

Conrad Potter Aiken was born August 5, 1889, in Savannah, Georgia, of New England parents. Taken north as a child after the tragic deaths of his mother and father, he studied at Middlesex School in Massachusetts, and, at eighteen, entered Harvard, where he became class poet and close friend of T. S. Eliot. His studies had been interrupted by a trip abroad and, after graduating with the class of 1912, Aiken, with an independent income, was able to travel freely. In his early thirties he determined to live in England and made his home in the Sussex coast town of Rye. A few years later he returned to America as tutor in English at Harvard. For the next ten years Aiken alternated between both sides of the Atlantic. In his early fifties he apparently decided to settle down with his third wife on the Massachusetts shore, "the proud possessor of an eight-acre plantation of poison ivy in the midmost jungle of Cape Cod."

Aiken's passion for music is exceeded only by his preoccupation with psychoanalysis. The attempted fusion of the two has made his poetry distinctive but undisciplined. Too ready to respond to every twitch of the unconscious, Aiken's verse is nebular in structure, atmospheric, indefinite.

> There is a fountain in a wood
> Where wavering lies a moon:
> It plays to the slowly falling leaves
> A sleepy tune.

But indefiniteness is part of the charm of Aiken's verse. Few modern lyrics can match the hypnotic movement of THIS IS THE SHAPE OF THE LEAF. The poet takes a set of detached images and gives them a resonance which is abstract and yet poignant.

This Is the Shape of the Leaf

This is the shape of the leaf, and this of the flower,
And this the pale bole of the tree
Which watches its bough in a pool of unwavering water
In a land we never shall see.

The thrush on the bough is silent, the dew falls softly,
In the evening is hardly a sound. . . .
And the three beautiful pilgrims who come here together
Touch lightly the dust of the ground.

Touch it with feet that trouble the dust but as wings do,
Come shyly together, are still,
Like dancers who wait in a pause of the music, for music
The exquisite silence to fill . . .

This is the thought of the first, and this of the second,
And this the grave thought of the third:
"Linger we thus for a moment, palely expectant,
And silence will end, and the bird

"Sing the pure phrase, sweet phrase, clear phrase in the twilight
To fill the blue bell of the world;
And we, who on music so leaflike have drifted together,
Leaflike apart shall be whirled

"Into what but the beauty of silence, silence forever? . . ."
. . . This is the shape of the tree,
And the flower, and the leaf, and the three pale beautiful pilgrims:
This is what you are to me.

from PRIAPUS AND THE POOL

For many years Aiken continued to explore the dim reaches of self-analysis, particularly "the process of vicarious wish fulfillment by which civilized man enriches his circumscribed life." Nowhere were his investigations better rewarded than in SENLIN: A BIOGRAPHY, best of all in the section generally known as MORNING SONG. Here the poet dispenses with muffled chords and cloudy minors to evoke the immensities beneath the overfamiliar and just beyond the casual fact.

Morning Song

It is morning, Senlin says, and in the morning
When the light drips through the shutters like the dew,
I arise, I face the sunrise,
And do the things my fathers learned to do.
Stars in the purple dusk above the rooftops
Pale in a saffron mist and seem to die,
And I myself on a swiftly tilting planet
Stand before a glass and tie my tie.

Vine-leaves tap my window,
Dew-drops sing to the garden stones,
The robin chirps in the chinaberry tree
Repeating three clear tones.

It is morning. I stand by the mirror
And tie my tie once more.
While waves far off in a pale rose twilight
Crash on a white sand shore.
I stand by a mirror and comb my hair:
How small and white my face!—
The green earth tilts through a sphere of air
And bathes in a flame of space.
There are houses hanging above the stars
And stars hung under a sea . . .
And a sun far off in a shell of silence
Dapples my walls for me. . . .

It is morning, Senlin says, and in the morning
Should I not pause in the light to remember God?
Upright and firm I stand on a star unstable,
He is immense and lonely as a cloud.
I will dedicate this moment before my mirror
To him alone, for him I will comb my hair.
Accept these humble offerings, clouds of silence!
I will think of you as I descend the stair.

Vine-leaves tap my window,
The snail-track shines on the stones;
Dew-drops flash from the chinaberry tree
Repeating two clear tones.

It is morning, I awake from a bed of silence,
Shining I rise from the starless waters of sleep.
The walls are about me still as in the evening,
I am the same, and the same name still I keep.
The earth revolves with me, yet makes no motion,
The stars pale silently in a coral sky.
In a whistling void I stand before my mirror,
Unconcerned, and tie my tie.

There are horses neighing on far-off hills
Tossing their long white manes,
And mountains flash in the rose-white dusk,
Their shoulders black with rains. . . .
It is morning, I stand by the mirror
And surprise my soul once more;
The blue air rushes above my ceiling,
There are suns beneath my floor. . . .

. . . It is morning, Senlin says, I ascend from darkness
And depart on the winds of space for I know not where;
My watch is wound, a key is in my pocket,
And the sky is darkened as I descend the stair.
There are shadows across the windows, clouds in heaven,
And a god among the stars; and I will go
Thinking of him as I might think of daybreak
And humming a tune I know. . . .

Vine-leaves tap at the window,
Dew-drops sing to the garden stones,
The robin chirps in the chinaberry tree
Repeating three clear tones.
                    from SENLIN: A BIOGRAPHY

By the time he was fifty-two Aiken had published four novels, four collections of short stories, two books of criticism, and eighteen volumes of poetry. His SELECTED POEMS received the Pulitzer Prize award for 1930. A rapturous study of his work by Houston Peterson was aptly entitled THE MELODY OF CHAOS. His dreamlike autobiography, punningly entitled USHANT, appeared in 1952.

W. J. TURNER
[1889–1947]

ALMOST unknown in America, and read in England chiefly as a music critic, W. J. Turner has appeared in anthologies of modern verse because of one small lyric. It is a lyric of escape, of incantation; the spell is worked not only by the faraway associations but by the very sounding of exotic syllables: Chimborazo, Cotopaxi, Popocatepetl.

Romance

When I was but thirteen or so
    I went into a golden land,
Chimborazo, Cotopaxi
    Took me by the hand.

My father died, my brother too,
    They passed like fleeting dreams,
I stood where Popocatepetl
    In the sunlight gleams.

I dimly heard the master's voice
    And boys far-off at play—
Chimborazo, Cotopaxi
    Had stolen me away.

I walked in a great golden dream
    To and fro from school—
Shining Popocatepetl
    The dusty streets did rule.

I walked home with a gold dark boy
    And never a word I'd say;
Chimborazo, Cotopaxi
    Had taken my speech away.

I gazed entranced upon his face
    Fairer than any flower—
O shining Popocatepetl,
    It was thy magic hour.

> The houses, people, traffic seemed
> Thin fading dreams by day;
> Chimborazo, Cotopaxi,
> They had stolen my soul away!

Walter James Turner was born in 1889 in Melbourne, Australia, where his father was organist in St. Paul's Pro-Cathedral. Educated at Scotch College, Melbourne, Turner went to Europe at seventeen, studied in Germany, and traveled for almost five years through the Continent and South Africa. At twenty-seven he became music critic of THE NEW STATESMAN; at thirty he wrote dramatic criticism for THE LONDON MERCURY; at thirty-two he was literary editor of THE DAILY HERALD. Before he was fifty, Turner had published two plays, a fantastic novel, seven volumes of essays, fifteen books of verse, and the best critical biographies of Berlioz and Mozart. He was planning still larger works when he died in his fifty-eighth year.

EDNA ST. VINCENT MILLAY
[1892–1950]

AT NINETEEN Edna St. Vincent Millay, born February 22, 1892, in Rockland, Maine, wrote an extraordinary poem of more than two hundred lines. Entitled RENASCENCE, it began as nonchalantly, and almost as aimlessly, as a child's rhyme:

> All I could see from where I stood
> Was three long mountains and a wood;
> I turned and looked another way,
> And saw three islands in a bay.

Imperceptible, with scarcely a change in tone, the poem reached a climax of exaltation:

> God, I can push the grass apart
> And lay my finger on Thy heart!

Nothing Miss Millay wrote subsequently recaptured that ecstasy; only the later sonnets compensated with a sad wisdom for the dazzled innocence. The sonnets, scattered through ten books and gathered in one volume in Miss Millay's fiftieth year, range from Elizabethan rhetoric to contemporary plain speaking. Even the thinnest of them are craftsmanlike exercises, and the best of them are superb uses of the form.

Pity Me Not

Pity me not because the light of day
At close of day no longer walks the sky;
Pity me not for beauties passed away
From field and thicket as the year goes by;
Pity me not the waning of the moon,
Nor that the ebbing tide goes out to sea,
Nor that a man's desire is hushed so soon,
And you no longer look with love on me.

This have I known always: love is no more
Than the wide blossom which the wind assails,
Than the great tide that treads the shifting shore,
Strewing fresh wreckage gathered in the gales.
Pity me that the heart is slow to learn
What the swift mind beholds at every turn.

Miss Millay attended Vassar and, after her graduation in 1917, supported herself by writing short stories under pseudonyms and by acting with the Provincetown Players. Her Greenwich Village days are reflected in the arch cleverness and flippant protests of A FEW FIGS FROM THISTLES. The serious poet triumphs in SECOND APRIL, published in Miss Millay's twenty-ninth year. Disillusion takes the place of banter; the fears of age and death—Miss Millay's foreboding leitmotifs—sound their warnings. In 1923 she was awarded the Pulitzer Prize and, in the same year, married Eugen Jan Boissevain and moved to the Berkshires. There she became a recluse and something of a legend; she died there October 19, 1950.

Her critics often accused her of forcing her emotion and simulating passion "at the pitch of romantic extravagance." But, for the most part, the artistry is admirable. At its best, real feeling dominates, more than verbally inspired; delight and despair sometimes combine in an effortless nobility. The lapses in taste, the seemingly fatal blemishes, are forgotten in her triumphs.

On Hearing a Symphony of Beethoven

Sweet sounds, oh, beautiful music, do not cease!
Reject me not into the world again.
With you alone is excellence and peace,
Mankind made plausible, his purpose plain.
Enchanted in your air benign and shrewd,
With limbs a-sprawl and empty faces pale,
The spiteful and the stingy and the rude
Sleep like the scullions in the fairy-tale.
This moment is the best the world can give:
The tranquil blossom on the tortured stem.
Reject me not, sweet sounds! oh, let me live,
Till Doom espy my towers and scatter them,
A city spell-bound under the aging sun.
Music my rampart, and my only one.

Many of the sonnets are lyrical in effect, and many of the early lyrics are as direct and unaffected as a girl singing to please herself. The later work is quite different. Experience brings no happiness to the mature poet. A crepuscular light throws long shadows over the landscape. The key is the key of loss. "Gone, gone again is summer, the lovely." "Now goes under, and I watch it go under, the sun that will not rise again." "When evening darkens the water and the stream is dull."

Autumn is no less on me that a rose
Hugs the brown bough and sighs before it goes.

The music darkens with unhappy knowledge, with the mutations of love and the permanence of death.

Dirge Without Music

I am not resigned to the shutting away of loving hearts in the hard
    ground.
So it is, and so it will be, for so it has been, time out of mind:
Into the darkness they go, the wise and the lovely. Crowned
With lilies and with laurel they go; but I am not resigned.

Lovers and thinkers, into the earth with you.
Be one with the dull, the indiscriminate dust.
A fragment of what you felt, of what you knew,
A formula, a phrase remains,—but the best is lost.

The answers quick and keen, the honest look, the laughter, the love,—
They are gone. They have gone to feed the roses. Elegant and curled
Is the blossom. Fragrant is the blossom. I know. But I do not approve.
More precious was the light in your eyes than all the roses in the
　　world.

Down, down, down into the darkness of the grave
Gently they go, the beautiful, the tender, the kind;
Quietly they go, the intelligent, the witty, the brave.
I know. But I do not approve. And I am not resigned.

Although this poet's work has been liberally, and at times hysterically, applauded, one sonnet has been insufficiently praised. To JESUS ON HIS BIRTHDAY is the utterance of a frustrated idealist. Discarding the note of personal romanticism, she speaks with a bitterness and broken pride, a human cry against disappointing humanity. It is a declaration which has the ring of timelessness.

To Jesus on His Birthday

For this your mother sweated in the cold,
For this you bled upon the bitter tree:
A yard of tinsel ribbon bought and sold;
A paper wreath; a day at home for me.
The merry bells ring out, the people kneel;
Up goes the man of God before the crowd;
With voice of honey and with eyes of steel
He drones your humble gospel to the proud.
Nobody listens. Less than the wind that blows
Are all your words to us you died to save.
O Prince of Peace! O Sharon's dewy Rose!
How mute you lie within your vaulted grave.
The stone the angel rolled away with tears
Is back upon your mouth these thousand years.

ARCHIBALD MACLEISH
[1892–1982]

THE last thing that Archibald MacLeish would have predicted was that he would become executive librarian of the Library of Congress and a recognized, though often anonymous, voice of government. A champion of the advance guard in literature, he admired originality wherever he found it. Before he achieved his own idiom, he experimented with every modern device and never grudged to pay tribute to his predecessors.

Archibald MacLeish, lawyer, teacher, soldier, editor, and always a poet, was born May 7, 1892, at Glencoe, Illinois. His father, "a cold, tall rigorous man of beautiful speech," was a Chicago merchant born in Scotland; his mother, who had taught at Vassar and was his father's third wife, came from a Connecticut seafaring family. MacLeish attended Hotchkiss School, hated it, and went to Yale, where he distinguished himself in athletics. His prowess on the football and swimming teams did not prevent him from winning a Phi Beta Kappa key. Being graduated at twenty-three, he entered the Harvard Law School and, in the second year, led his class. At twenty-four he married. At twenty-five he joined a hospital unit, went to France, was transferred to the field artillery, and had the rank of captain when the First World War ended.

Upon his return to the United States after the armistice, MacLeish taught for a year in the Harvard Law School, entered a Boston attorney's office, and practiced for three years. Suddenly, in 1923, he closed his desk and, armed with an independent income, went abroad with his wife and two children. For five years he traveled about Europe, visited Persia, and spent a summer in Normandy. In early 1929 he went to Mexico, following the route of Cortez from the coast inland. The result of his journey (plus the reading of Bernal Díaz del Castillo's TRUE HISTORY OF THE CONQUEST OF NEW SPAIN) was CONQUISTADOR, which won the Pulitzer Prize for 1933.

The chief characteristic of MacLeish's poetry is its employment of old devices for new ends. Alliteration and assonance take on fresh values in his vivid lines; brusque phrases alternating with long suspended sentences create a surprising tension. No modern poet has used repetition—that dangerous contrivance—with such effectiveness.

Even the formal sonnet has a new sound and dramatic power, as in the imaginative THE END OF THE WORLD.

The End of the World

Quite unexpectedly as Vasserot
The armless ambidextrian was lighting
A match between his great and second toe
And Ralph the lion was engaged in biting
The neck of Madame Sossman while the drum
Pointed, and Teeny was about to cough
In waltz-time swinging Jocko by the thumb—
Quite unexpectedly the top blew off.

And there, there overhead, there, there, hung over
Those thousands of white faces, those dazed eyes,
There in the starless dark, the poise, the hover,
There with vast wings across the canceled skies,
There in the sudden blackness, the black pall
Of nothing, nothing, nothing—nothing at all.

Suspense and imagination emphasize MacLeish's later work, from THE POT OF EARTH, written at thirty-one, to THE LAND OF THE FREE, a "sound track" published in his forty-sixth year. A poem should not only state and suggest, it should act, says MacLeish:

A poem should not mean
But be.

Such poems as EPISTLE TO BE LEFT IN THE EARTH and IMMORTAL AUTUMN have lives of their own. They transcend commentary; they have implications that look forward and backward in time.

Epistle to Be Left in the Earth

. . . It is colder now
             there are many stars
                        we are drifting
North by the Great Bear
             the leaves are falling

The water is stone in the scooped rocks
                              to southward
Red sun gray air
                    the crows are
Slow on their crooked wings
                              the jays have left us
Long since we passed the flares of Orion
Each man believes in his heart he will die
Many have written last thoughts and last letters
None know if our deaths are now or forever
None know if this wandering earth will be found

We lie down and the snow covers our garments
I pray you
            you (if any open this writing)
Make in your mouths the words that were our names
I will tell you all we have learned
                              I will tell you everything
The earth is round
                    there are springs under the orchards
The loam cuts with a blunt knife
                              beware of
Elms in thunder
                    the lights in the sky are stars
We think they do not see
                              we think also
The trees do not know nor the leaves of the grasses
                                                hear us
The birds too are ignorant
                    Do not listen
Do not stand at dark in the open windows
We before you have heard this
                              they are voices
They are not words at all but the wind rising
Also none among us has seen God
(. . . We have thought often
The flaws of sun in the late and driving weather
Pointed to one tree but it was not so)
As for the nights I warn you the nights are dangerous
The wind changes at night and the dreams come

It is very cold
                    there are strange stars near Arcturus

Voices are crying an unknown name in the sky

Immortal Autumn

I speak this poem now with grave and level voice
In praise of autumn of the far-horn-winding fall
I praise the flower-barren fields the clouds the tall
Unanswering branches where the wind makes sullen noise

I praise the fall it is the human season now
No more the foreign sun does meddle at our earth
Enforce the green and thaw the frozen soil to birth
Nor winter yet weigh all with silence the pine bough

But now in autumn with the black and outcast crows
Share we the spacious world the whispering year is gone
There is more room to live now the once secret dawn
Comes late by daylight and the dark unguarded goes

Between the mutinous brave burning of the leaves
And winter's covering of our hearts with his deep snow
We are alone there are no evening birds we know
The naked moon the tame stars circle at our eaves

It is the human season on this sterile air
Do words outcarry breath the sound goes on and on
I hear a dead man's cry from autumn long since gone

I cry to you beyond this bitter air.

PUBLIC SPEECH, issued in MacLeish's forty-fourth year, marked a turning point. The poet determinedly faced the material of his day and the problems of the American scene. A few years later he wrote the first, and still the most important, verse play for radio, THE FALL OF THE CITY, and followed it, in 1938, with the equally impressive anti-Fascist AIR RAID. In 1939 he was appointed librarian of the Library of Congress. In 1941, continuing to serve as librarian, he became director of the Office of Facts and Figures. After World War II, MacLeish taught at Harvard; his COLLECTED POEMS received the Pulitzer Prize award in 1953.

It was charged that, having discovered the power of suggestion, poets were forcing it beyond the limits of intelligibility. MacLeish kept his symbols under control; even the private allusions were always part of a communication. Some critics found YOU, ANDREW MARVELL puzzling in purpose and willfully obscure in title. But the intention is as clear as the poem itself, one of the most beautiful of contemporary lyrics. A lyric of gradual cadences and slow tension, the suspense is achieved by the varying pictures of night's ominous approach and the colorful associations of exotic places; it is heightened by the lack of punctuation, sustained by the cumulative intensity of the one long sentence. And the title? The poet gently reminds us that another poet, Andrew Marvell (see page 480), warned his "coy mistress" of the "always rising of the night" and "the deserts of vast eternity"—

> But at my back I always hear
> Time's winged chariot hurrying near.

The "shadow of the night comes on . . ." And the deeper sense is suggested by the persistent echo in time.

You, Andrew Marvell

And here face down beneath the sun
And here upon earth's noonward height
To feel the always coming on
The always rising of the night

To feel creep up the curving east
The earthly chill of dusk and slow
Upon those under lands the vast
And ever-climbing shadow grow

And strange at Ecbatan the trees
Take leaf by leaf the evening strange
The flooding dark about their knees
The mountains over Persia change

And now at Kermanshah the gate
Dark empty and the withered grass
And through the twilight now the late
Few travelers in the westward pass

And Baghdad darken and the bridge
Across the silent river gone
And through Arabia the edge
Of evening widen and steal on

And deepen on Palmyra's street
The wheel rut in the ruined stone
And Lebanon fade out and Crete
High through the clouds and overblown

And over Sicily the air
Still flashing with the landward gulls
And loom and slowly disappear
The sails above the shadowy hulls

And Spain go under and the shore
Of Africa the gilded sand
And evening vanish and no more
The low pale light across that land

Nor now the long light on the sea—

And here face downward in the sun
To feel how swift how secretly
The shadow of the night comes on. . . .

MacLeish is not only a poet but an interpreter of the spirit which animates poetry. This is attested by his prose, in particular by an excerpt from a recent essay: "In that great unfinished definition of poetry in which Aristotle distinguished poetry from history he said: History draws things which have happened, but poetry things which may possibly happen. . . . The possibility of which Aristotle speaks is human possibility. In this time in which everything is possible except the spirit to desire and the love to choose, poetry becomes again the one deliverer of the people."

WILFRED OWEN
[1893–1918]

DEAD at twenty-five, Wilfred Owen left a few lyrics and sonnets that must be reckoned among the most moving poems produced by any war. Born March 18, 1893, at Oswestry, England, Owen was educated at Birkenhead Institute and London University, and spent some time in France as a private tutor. At the outbreak of the war he joined a rifle corps and, although his health had been impaired since childhood, fought steadily for two years until he was invalided home. A year later he returned to the front, and was awarded the Military Cross for gallantry. A month after receiving the honor, and a week before the armistice, Owen was killed in action, November 4, 1918. His one book was not published until nearly two years after his death.

Unknown at the time of his death, Owen influenced poets that followed him twenty years later. His peculiar suspensions, consonances and dissonances, were adopted by such postwar poets as W. H. Auden and Stephen Spender. Owen's efforts to find substitutes for rhyme—substitutes which, because of their unexpectedness, would enrich the verse—are best illustrated in STRANGE MEETING, perhaps the most powerfully projected of all war poems.

Strange Meeting

It seemed that out of the battle I escaped
Down some profound dull tunnel, long since scooped
Through granites which Titanic wars had groined.
Yet also there encumbered sleepers groaned,
Too fast in thought or death to be bestirred.
Then, as I probed them, one sprang up, and stared
With piteous recognition in fixed eyes,
Lifting distressful hands as if to bless.
And by his smile, I knew that sullen hall;
By his dead smile I knew I stood in Hell.
With a thousand pains that vision's face was grained;
Yet no blood reached there from the upper ground,
And no guns thumped, or down the flues made moan.
"Strange, friend," I said, "here is no cause to mourn."
"None," said the other, "save the undone years,
The hopelessness. Whatever hope is yours,
Was my life also; I went hunting wild
After the wildest beauty in the world,
Which lies not calm in eyes, or braided hair,
But mocks the steady running of the hour,
And if it grieves, grieves richlier than here.
For by my glee might many men have laughed,
And of my weeping something has been left,
Which must die now. I mean the truth untold,
The pity of war, the pity war distilled.

Now men will go content with what we spoiled,
Or, discontent, boil bloody, and be spilled.
They will be swift with swiftness of the tigress,
None will break ranks, though nations trek from progress
Courage was mine, and I had mystery,
Wisdom was mine, and I had mastery;
To miss the march of this retreating world
Into vain citadels that are not walled.
Then when much blood had clogged their chariot-wheels
I would go up and wash them from sweet wells,
Even with truths that lie too deep for taint.
I would have poured my spirit without stint
But not through wounds; not on the cess of war.
Foreheads of men have bled where no wounds were.
I am the enemy you killed, my friend.
I knew you in this death; for so you frowned
Yesterday through me as you jabbed and killed.
I parried; but my hands were loath and cold.
Let us sleep now. . . ."

While Owen was recuperating at an English hospital in 1917, he
met Siegfried Sassoon. With characteristic modesty Owen considered
himself "not worthy to light Sassoon's pipe," but he surpassed his
fellow soldier-poet in the ability to project the feeling of shock and
dark emptiness. It was Sassoon who, having discovered Owen, said
in his introduction to the posthumous POEMS: "He never wrote his
poems (as so many war poets did) to make the effect of a personal
gesture. He pitied others; he did not pity himself."

Anthem for Doomed Youth

What passing-bells for these who die as cattle?
Only the monstrous anger of the guns.
Only the stuttering rifles' rapid rattle
Can patter out their hasty orisons.
No mockeries for them; no prayers nor bells,
Nor any voice of mourning save the choirs,—
The shrill, demented choirs of wailing shells;
And bugles calling for them from sad shires.

What candles may be held to speed them all?
Not in the hands of boys, but in their eyes
Shall shine the holy glimmers of good-bys.
The pallor of girls' brows shall be their pall;
Their flowers the tenderness of patient minds,
And each slow dusk a drawing-down of blinds.

"It is impossible," wrote Edmund Blunden in the enlarged edition of Owen's POEMS published in 1931, "to become deeply acquainted with Owen's work and not be haunted by comparisons between his genius and his premature death and the wonder and tragedy of his admired Keats." Keats had been Owen's idol in youth. At eighteen he made a pilgrimage to Keats's house at Teignmouth, and spoke of the sea which seemed to share his grief for one "whose name was writ in water." But Owen's full poetic power was not manifest until the last year of his life. The poems written in the shadow of his death survive him, Sassoon wrote, "as his true and splendid testament." The poem FUTILITY is his own unplanned tragic epitaph.

Futility

Move him into the sun—
Gently its touch awoke him once,
At home, whispering of fields unsown.
Always it woke him, even in France.
Until this morning and this snow.
If anything might rouse him now
The kind old sun will know.

Think how it wakes the seeds—
Woke, once, the clay of a cold star.
Are limbs, so dear-achieved, are sides
Full-nerved,—still warm,—too hard to stir?
Was it for this the clay grew tall?
—Oh, what made fatuous sunbeams toil
To break earth's sleep at all?

MARK VON DOREN
[1894–1972]

ONE of a country doctor's five sons, Mark Van Doren was born
July 13, 1894, in Hope, Illinois. Graduating at twenty from
the University of Illinois, he went to New York and undertook ad-
vanced work at Columbia. After the First World War, in which he
served in the infantry, he received his doctor's degree and began
teaching at Columbia. He was literary editor of THE NATION from
1924 to 1928.

Although Van Doren has distinguished himself as a critic, his
chief concern has been the writing of poetry. Six volumes of his verse
appeared before the Pulitzer Prize was awarded to his COLLECTED
POEMS: 1922–1938 in 1940. In the same year Van Doren began to
preside over the radio program INVITATION TO LEARNING.

Van Doren's influences are strictly native. The early verse owes
something to Robert Frost; the later A WINTER DIARY brings Whittier
to the present scene. But Van Doren's accent, quiet and cool, is his
own. His persuasive individuality is communicated in a tone which
is alternately straightforward and semimystical.

Proper Clay

Their little room grew light with cries;
He woke and heard them thread the dark,
He woke and felt them like the rays
Of some unlawful dawn at work:

Some random sunrise, lost and small,
That found the room's heart, vein by vein.
But she was whispering to the wall,
And he must see what she had seen.

He asked her gently, and she wept.
"Oh, I have dreamed the ancient dream.
My time was on me, and I slept;
And I grew greater than I am;

"And lay like dead; but when I lived,
Three wingéd midwives wrapped the child.
It was a god that I had loved,
It was a hero I had held.

"Stretch out your mortal hands, I beg.
Say common sentences to me.
Lie cold and still, that I may brag
How close I am to proper clay.

"Let this within me hear the truth.
Speak loud to it." He stopped her lips.
He smoothed the covers over both.
It was a dream perhaps, perhaps . . .

Yet why this radiance round the room?
And why this trembling at her waist?
And then he smiled. It was the same
Undoubted flesh that he had kissed;

She lay unchanged from what she was,
She cried as ever woman cried.
Yet why this light along his brows?
And whence the music no one made?

E. E. CUMMINGS
[1894–1962]

A NOSE-THUMBING satirist and a lyrical sentimentalist, irresponsible
clown and angry critic, Edward Estlin Cummings delighted in
being the Peck's Bad Boy of American poetry.

He was born October 14, 1894, in Cambridge, Massachusetts, where
his father taught English at Harvard and later became minister of
Old South Church in Boston. Educated at Harvard, Cummings
served in the ambulance corps during the First World War and, be-
cause of a censor's error, spent three months in a detention camp, an
experience recorded in THE ENORMOUS ROOM. He was almost thirty
upon the appearance of his first volume of poems, TULIPS AND CHIM-
NEYS, a book that was original to the point of eccentricity. Perhaps
the chief surprise was the incongruous mixture of archaic diction

and contemporary slang, of soft affectations and a violently disrupted typography. Taking a cue from the advertiser's layout, Cummings confronted the eye with broken lines of verse, often by words broken up by irrelevant punctuation. Sometimes these displays arrested the attention of the reader; sometimes they merely annoyed him.

At his best Cummings does not rely upon typographical oddities. His subject matter is traditional; the beauty of spring, the redness of roses, the pleasure of love, the pain of death.

> since feeling is first
> who pays any attention
> to the syntax of things
> will never wholly kiss you;
>
> wholly to be a fool
> while Spring is in the world
> my blood approves.

Cummings' work is seemingly a set of nondescript, and sometimes obscene, variations on familiar, even banal, themes. Once past the barrier of his singular style, the reader will discover a surprisingly old-fashioned sensual romanticist.

O Sweet Spontaneous Earth

> O sweet spontaneous
> earth how often have
> the
> doting
>   fingers of
> prurient philosophers pinched
> and
> poked
> thee
> , has the naughty thumb
> of science prodded
> thy
>   beauty   , how
> often have religions taken
> thee upon their scraggy knees
> squeezing and

buffeting thee that thou mightest conceive
gods
    (but
true
to the incomparable
couch of death thy
rhythmic
lover

    thou answerest

them only with
      spring)

The emphasis on visual effects may be explained by the fact that
Cummings is a painter as well as a writer. One of his volumes was
entitled CIOPW, indicating that its contents consisted of drawings and
paintings in Charcoal, Ink, Oil, Pencil, and Watercolor. Cummings
has also published plays and a ballet, TOM. But it is as a lyrical poet,
not as a draftsman or a thinker, that he will arouse—and probably
hold—an audience.

Somewhere I Have Never Travelled

somewhere i have never travelled, gladly beyond
any experience, your eyes have their silence:
in your most frail gesture are things which enclose me,
or which i cannot touch because they are too near

your slightest look easily will unclose me
though i have closed myself as fingers,
you open always petal by petal myself as Spring opens
(touching skilfully, mysteriously) her first rose

or if your wish be to close me, i and
my life will shut very beautifully, suddenly,
as when the heart of this flower imagines
the snow carefully everywhere descending;

nothing which we are to perceive in this world equals
the power of your intense fragility: whose texture
compels me with the color of its countries,
rendering death and forever with each breathing

(i do not know what it is about you that closes
and opens; only something in me understands
the voice of your eyes is deeper than all roses)
nobody, not even the rain, has such small hands

At sixty Cummings collected some six hundred of his odd, impudent, ingenious and sometimes inspired pieces in an imposing volume, POEMS: 1923–1954. Although the uncritical poet still relied heavily on rhetoric and roses, he gave the standard platitudes about love, spring, and death new verbal twists. The tone continued to alternate between tender-minded stock sentiments and tough-talking arrogance, but the soft romanticisms were offset by a hard integrity and many moments of sudden magic.

STEPHEN VINCENT BENÉT
[1898–1943]

GENERAL STEPHEN VINCENT BENÉT, chief of ordnance of the United States Army, wrote a TREATISE ON MILITARY LAW which became a standard authority. Two generations later his grandson, bearing his grandfather's name, wrote JOHN BROWN'S BODY, an epic of the Civil War.

Stephen Vincent Benét was born July 22, 1898, in Bethlehem, Pennsylvania, and spent his boyhood in California and Georgia, where his father was stationed at various government arsenals. He entered Yale at seventeen and in the same year published his first volume, a book of dramatic portraits in verse entitled FIVE MEN AND POMPEY. After getting his degree, he engaged briefly in the advertising business, but soon began to support himself by writing. Dissatisfied with the imitativeness of his early work Benét started to explore American backgrounds. One of the first of his attempts in the new manner, THE BALLAD OF WILLIAM SYCAMORE, begins:

My father, he was a mountaineer,
His fist was a knotty hammer;
He was quick on his feet as a running deer,
And he spoke with a Yankee stammer.

Resolutely indigenous, the poem ends:

> Go play with the towns you have built of blocks
> The towns where you would have bound me!
> I sleep in my earth like a tired fox,
> And my buffalo have found me.

THE MOUNTAIN WHIPPOORWILL is an extension of the native ballad, vigorous and harshly resonant. Best of Benét's story poems, this fantasy, roughened with the tang of earth, is not confined to the Georgia which furnishes the setting.

The Mountain Whippoorwill

OR, HOW HILL-BILLY JIM WON THE GREAT FIDDLERS' PRIZE

Up in the mountains, it's lonesome all the time,
(Sof' win' slewin' thu' the sweet-potato vine.)

Up in the mountains, it's lonesome for a child,
(Whippoorwills a-callin' when the sap runs wild.)

Up in the mountains, mountains in the fog,
Everythin's as lazy as an old houn' dog.

Born in the mountains, never raised a pet,
Don't want nuthin' an' never got it yet.

Born in the mountains, lonesome-born,
Raised runnin' ragged thu' the cockleburrs and corn.

Never knew my pappy, mebbe never should.
Think he was a fiddle made of mountain laurel-wood.

Never had a mammy to teach me pretty-please.
Think she was a whippoorwill, a-skitin' thu' the trees.

Never had a brother ner a whole pair of pants,
But when I start to fiddle, why, yuh got to start to dance!

Listen to my fiddle—Kingdom Come—Kingdom Come!
Hear the frogs a-chunkin' "Jug o' rum, Jug o' rum!"
Hear that mountain whippoorwill be lonesome in the air,
An' I'll tell yuh how I travelled to the Essex County Fair.

Essex County has a mighty pretty fair,
All the smarty fiddlers from the South come there.

Elbows flyin' as they rosin up the bow
For the First Prize Contest in the Georgia Fiddlers' Show.

Old Dan Wheeling, with his whiskers in his ears,
King-pin fiddler for nearly twenty years.

Big Tom Sargent, with his blue wall-eye,
An' Little Jimmy Weezer that can make a fiddle cry.

All sittin' roun', spittin' high an' struttin' proud,
(Listen, little whippoorwill, yuh better bug yore eyes!)
Tun-a-tun-a-tunin' while the jedges told the crowd
Them that got the mostest claps 'd win the bestest prize.

Everybody waitin' for the first tweedle-dee,
When in comes a-stumblin'—hill-billy me!

Bowed right pretty to the jedges an' the rest,
Took a silver dollar from a hole inside my vest,

Plunked it on the table an' said, "There's my callin' card!
An' anyone that licks me—well, he's got to fiddle hard!"

Old Dan Wheeling, he was laughin' fit to holler,
Little Jimmy Weezer said, "There's one dead dollar!"

Big Tom Sargent had a yaller-toothy grin,
But I tucked my little whippoorwill spang underneath my chin,
An' petted it an' tuned it till the jedges said, "Begin!"

Big Tom Sargent was the first in line;
He could fiddle all the bugs off a sweet-potato vine.

He could fiddle down a possum from a mile-high tree,
He could fiddle up a whale from the bottom of the sea.

Yuh could hear hands spankin' till they spanked each other raw,
When he finished variations on "Turkey in the Straw."

Little Jimmy Weezer was the next to play;
He could fiddle all night, he could fiddle all day.

He could fiddle chills, he could fiddle fever,
He could make a fiddle rustle like a lowland river.

He could make a fiddle croon like a lovin' woman.
An' they clapped like thunder when he'd finished strummin'.

Then came the ruck of the bob-tailed fiddlers,
The let's-go-easies, the fair-to-middlers.

They got their claps an' they lost their bicker,
An' they all settled back for some more corn-licker.

An' the crowd was tired of their no-count squealing,
When out in the center steps Old Dan Wheeling.

He fiddled high and he fiddled low,
(Listen, little whippoorwill, yuh got to spread yore wings!)
He fiddled and fiddled with a cherrywood bow,
(Old Dan Wheeling's got bee-honey in his strings).

He fiddled the wind by the lonesome moon,
He fiddled a most almighty tune.

He started fiddling like a ghost.
He ended fiddling like a host.

He fiddled north an' he fiddled south,
He fiddled the heart right out of yore mouth.

He fiddled here an' he fiddled there.
He fiddled salvation everywhere.

When he was finished, the crowd cut loose,
(Whippoorwill, they's rain on yore breast.)
An' I sat there wonderin' "What's the use?"
(Whippoorwill, fly home to yore nest.)

But I stood up pert an' I took my bow,
An' my fiddle went to my shoulder, so.

An'—they wasn't no crowd to get me fazed—
But I was alone where I was raised.

Up in the mountains, so still it makes yuh skeered
Where God lies sleepin' in his big white beard.

An' I heard the sound of the squirrel in the pine,
An' I heard the earth a-breathin' thu' the long night-time.

They've fiddled the rose, and they've fiddled the thorn,
But they haven't fiddled the mountain-corn.

They've fiddled sinful an' fiddled moral,
But they haven't fiddled the breshwood-laurel.

They've fiddled loud, and they've fiddled still,
But they haven't fiddled the whippoorwill.

I started off with a *dump-diddle-dump,*
(Oh, hell's broke loose in Georgia!)
Skunk-cabbage growin' by the bee-gum stump.
(Whippoorwill, yo're singin' now!)

My mother was a whippoorwill pert,
My father, he was lazy,
But I'm hell broke loose in a new store shirt
To fiddle all Georgia crazy.

Swing yore partners—up an' down the middle!
Sashay now—oh, listen to that fiddle!
Flapjacks flippin' on a red-hot griddle,
An' hell's broke loose,
Hell's broke loose,
Fire on the mountains—snakes in the grass.
Satan's here a-bilin'—oh, Lordy, let him pass!
Go down Moses, set my people free;
Pop goes the weasel thu' the old Red Sea!
Jonah sittin' on a hickory-bough,
Up jumps a whale—an' where's yore prophet now?
Rabbit in the pea-patch, possum in the pot,
Try an' stop my fiddle, now my fiddle's gettin' hot!

Whippoorwill, singin' thu' the mountain hush,
Whippoorwill, shoutin' from the burnin' bush,
Whippoorwill, cryin' in the stable-door,
Sing tonight as yuh never sang before!
Hell's broke loose like a stompin' mountain-shoat,
Sing till yuh bust the gold in yore throat!
Hell's broke loose for forty miles aroun'
Bound to stop yore music if yuh don't sing it **down.**
Sing on the mountains, little whippoorwill,
Sing to the valleys, an' slap 'em with a hill,
For I'm struttin' high as an eagle's quill,
An' hell's broke loose,
Hell's broke loose,
Hell's broke loose in Georgia!

They wasn't a sound when I stopped bowin',
(Whippoorwill, yuh can sing no more.)
But, somewhere or other, the dawn was growin',
(Oh, mountain whippoorwill!)

An' I thought, "I've fiddled all night an' lost,
Yo're a good hill-billy, but yuh've been bossed."

So I went to congratulate old man Dan,
—But he put his fiddle into my han'—
An' then the noise of the crowd began!

A Guggenheim fellowship gave Benét the leisure necessary to complete his chief work, JOHN BROWN'S BODY, which revealed the impact of the Civil War on a set of diverse characters. The book, which Hervey Allen said was "exhaustingly alive," received the Pulitzer Prize award for 1929.

As versatile in poetry as his brother, William Rose Benét (see page 1131), Stephen Vincent Benét had a more pronounced gift for fiction. Before he was forty, he was the author of five novels and three collections of short stories. One of his tall tales, THE DEVIL AND DANIEL WEBSTER, attained the eminence of a contemporary classic; it was made into a play, an opera, and a moving picture. He died, at the very peak of his career of a heart attack, in his forty-fifth year.

HART CRANE

[1899–1932]

THE experimenter risks the apathy of the public and the dialectics of the professional critic. Modern poetry has been the target for attack because it has seemed overcomplicated and has been made still more difficult by a confusion of theories. But the poets faced a confused and increasingly complicated world, and it was not always possible to express in simple terms the welter of their experiences.

One of the most daring attempts to summarize the fluctuating aspects of the modern scene was made by Hart Crane, who did not live to complete the synthesis. Crane was born July 21, 1899, in Garrettsville, Ohio, and published his first poem at sixteen. He was unhappy in childhood, self-driven in youth, and self-doomed in manhood. In the year that his parents permanently separated, Crane left high school and found work in a print shop. The rest of his life was a succession of jobs—candy packer, shipyard riveter, reporter, advertising copy writer, manager of a tearoom—and between jobs he drank recklessly. His fits of drunkenness were accompanied by sexual irregularities; he suffered from the extremes of self-glory and guilt. Escaping to Europe and Mexico, sharpening his sensibilities and blunting his faculties, he grew more and more unstable. In his thirty-third year he resolved to return to America and responsibilities. But he never fulfilled his resolution. On April 26, 1932, he jumped from a northbound steamer in the Gulf of Mexico.

Because of the difficulties of his language, it is not always easy to enjoy Crane's work. The difficulties do not arise from a lack of ideas, but, on the contrary, from an overcrowding of them, from a piling up of emotional and pictorial effects. Crane's images are bewildering because he departed from the usual method of image making. He discarded the logical progress of an idea, and substituted a set of wide-ranging associations. Instead of being single, the ideas came in clusters; instead of being closely related and quickly recognizable, they divided themselves with strange variety. One figure set off another until an entire chain of metaphors was ignited. Thus Crane's poetry is one in which the thought progresses in wild leaps over sudden gaps. It is expansive and, at the same time, explosive.

The early poems are particularly obscure because of the mixture of metaphors, oblique references, and broken syntax. The theme, as Allen Tate pointed out in his foreword to Crane's WHITE BUILDINGS, "never appears in explicit statement. . . . The logical meaning can never be derived, but the poetical meaning is a direct intuition."

Crane was seeking a centralizing theme. In THE BRIDGE, finished in his thirty-first year, he almost found it. THE BRIDGE attempts to express the "Myth of America" by uniting national figures, history, early legends, and modern inventions. Crane's symbols for a gigantically expansive America are the Brooklyn Bridge, the airplane, the subway train. "Unless poetry can absorb the machine," he wrote, "acclimatize it as naturally and casually as trees, cattle, galleons, castles, and all other human associations of the past, then poetry has failed of its full contemporary function."

Writing about THE RIVER, one section of THE BRIDGE, Crane declared that the subway was "a figurative, psychological vehicle for transporting the reader to the Middle West." THE RIVER begins with "an intentional burlesque on the cultural confusion of the present —a great conglomeration of noises analogous to the strident impression of a fast express rushing by":

> Stick your patent name on a signboard
> brother—all over—going west—young man
> Tintex—Japalac—Certain-teed Overalls ads
> and land sakes! under the new playbill ripped
> in the guaranteed corner—see Bert Williams—what?
> Minstrels when you steal a chicken just
> save me the wing, for it isn't
> Erie it ain't for miles around a
> Mazda—and the telegraphic night coming on . . .

But soon the jazz tempo slackens, the noises blend into a quiet flow of sound, the rhythm settles down to "a steady pedestrian gait," and the reader is carried into interior after interior, "all of it funneled by the Mississippi." The river of steel develops into the "Father of Waters."

The River

> Down, down—born pioneers in time's despite,
> Grimed tributaries to an ancient flow—
> They win no frontier by their wayward plight,
> But drift in stillness, as from Jordan's brow.

You will not hear it as the sea; even stone
Is not more hushed by gravity . . . But slow,
As loth to take more tribute—sliding prone
Like one whose eyes were buried long ago

The River, spreading, flows—and spends your dream
What are you, lost within this tideless spell?
You are your father's father, and the stream—
A liquid theme that floating niggers swell.

Damp tonnage and alluvial march of days—
Nights turbid, vascular with silted shale
And roots surrendered down of moraine clays:
The Mississippi drinks the farthest dale.

O quarrying passion, undertowed sunlight!
The basalt surface drags a jungle grace
Ochreous and lynx-barred in lengthening might;
Patience! and you shall reach the biding place!

Over De Soto's bones the freighted floors
Throb past the City storied of three thrones.
Down two more turns the Mississippi pours
(Anon tall ironsides up from salt lagoons)

And flows within itself, heaps itself free.
All fades but one thin skyline 'round . . . Ahead
No embrace opens but the stinging sea;
The River lifts itself from its long bed,

Poised wholly on its dream, a mustard glow,
Tortured with history, its one will—flow!
—The Passion spreads in wide tongues, choked and slow
Meeting the Gulf, hosannas silently below.

                                    from THE BRIDGE

The Broken Tower

The bell-rope that gathers God at dawn
Dispatches me as though I dropped down the knell
Of a spent day—to wander the cathedral lawn
From pit to crucifix, feet chill on steps from hell.

Have you not heard, have you not seen that corps
Of shadows in the tower, whose shoulders sway
Antiphonal carillons launched before
The stars are caught and hived in the sun's ray?

The bells, I say, the bells break down their tower;
And swing I know not where. Their tongues engrave
Membrane through marrow, my long-scattered score
Of broken intervals. . . . And I, their sexton slave!

Oval encyclicals in canyons heaping
The impasse high with choir. Banked voices slain!
Pagodas, campaniles with reveilles outleaping—
O terraced echoes prostrate on the plain! . . .

And so it was I entered the broken world
To trace the visionary company of love, its voice
An instant in the wind (I know not whither hurled)
But not for long to hold each desperate choice.

My word I poured. But was it cognate, scored
Of that tribunal monarch of the air
Whose thigh embronzes earth, strikes crystal Word
In wounds pledged once to hope—cleft to despair?

The steep encroachments of my blood left me
No answer (could blood hold such a lofty tower
As flings the question true?)—or is it she
Whose sweet mortality stirs latent power?—

And through whose pulse I hear, counting the strokes
My veins recall and add, revived and sure
The angelus of wars my chest evokes:
What I hold healed, original now, and pure . . .

And builds, within, a tower that is not stone
(Not stone can jacket heaven)—but slip
Of pebbles—visible wings of silence sown
In azure circles, widening as they dip

The matrix of the heart, lift down the eye
That shrines the quiet lake and swells a tower . . .
The commodious, tall decorum of that sky
Unseals her earth, and lifts love in its shower.

Designed as an epic, THE BRIDGE is actually a series of loosely connected lyrics. Crane's last work tended toward a simplification and a clearer structure. At the time of his death he was preparing for publication a volume to be called KEY WEST. ROYAL PALM, richly figurative yet controlled, indicates the order which the poet was attempting to make out of inner chaos.

Royal Palm

Green rustlings, more-than-regal charities
Drift coolly from that tower of whispered light.
Amid the noontide's blazed asperities
I watched the sun's most gracious anchorite

Climb up as by communings, year on year
Uneaten of the earth or aught earth holds,
And the gray trunk, that's elephantine, rear
Its frondings sighing in aethereal folds.

Forever fruitless, and beyond that yield
Of sweat the jungle presses with hot love
And tendril till our deathward breath is sealed—
It grazes the horizons, launched above

Mortality—ascending emerald-bright,
A fountain at salute, a crown in view—
Unshackled, casual of its azured height,
As though it soared suchwise through heaven too.

LÉONIE ADAMS
[1899–1988]

AT NINETEEN Léonie Adams announced her faith in the imaginative vision. In APRIL MORTALITY, her first published poem, she wrote:

With all the drifting race of men
Thou also art begot to mourn
That she is crucified again,
The lonely Beauty yet unborn.

And if thou dreamest to have won
Some touch of her in permanence,
'Tis the old cheating of the sun,
The intricate lovely play of sense.

That vision sustained her; it strengthened one of the least spectacular but finest sensitivities of the period.

Léonie Adams was born December 9, 1899, in Brooklyn, New York, and was raised with unusual strictness. She had not been allowed to travel on the subway until she went to Barnard, and then, although she was eighteen, her father accompanied her. After getting her degree from Barnard, Miss Adams received a Guggenheim Fellowship, lived abroad for two years, and returned to teach at New York University and later at Sarah Lawrence College. She married the critic, William Troy, and, after teaching at Bennington, returned to New York.

Although there are few surface changes in Miss Adams' verse, her poetry shows the growth of a shy wonder into an intense and semi-devotional lyricism. It is suggested even in her early stanzas:

I watched the hills drink the last color of light,
All shapes grow bright and wane on the pale air,
Till down the traitorous east there came the night,
And swept the circle of my seeing bare.

Descriptions that seem most candid take on uncommon emphasis in Miss Adams' lyrics. A rarefied atmosphere surrounds her delicate perceptions; even the richly detailed picture of a country scene is uplifted by a spirit that transcends personality.

Country Summer

Now the rich cherry whose sleek wood
And top with silver petals traced,
Like a strict box its gems encased,
Has spilt from out that cunning lid,
All in an innocent green round,
Those melting rubies which it hid;
With moss ripe-strawberry-encrusted,
So birds get half, and minds lapse merry
To taste that deep-red, lark's-bite berry,
And blackcap-bloom is yellow-dusted.

The wren that thieved it in the eaves
A trailer of the rose could catch
To her poor droopy sloven thatch,
And side by side with the wren's brood—
O lovely time of beggars' luck—
Opens the quaint and hairy bud;
And full and golden is the yield
Of cows that never have to house,
But all night nibble under boughs,
Or cool their sides in the moist field.

Into the rooms flow meadow airs,
The warm farm-baking smell blows round;
Inside and out, and sky and ground
Are much the same; the wishing star,
Hesperus, kind and early-born,
Is risen only finger-far.
All stars stand close in summer air,
And tremble, and look mild as amber;
When wicks are lighted in the chamber
You might say stars were settling there.

Now straightening from the flowery hay,
Down the still light the mowers look;
Or turn, because their dreaming shook,
And they waked half to other days,
When left alone in yellow-stubble
The rusty-coated mare would graze.
Yet thick the lazy dreams are born,
Another thought can come to mind,
But like the shivering of the wind,
Morning and evening in the corn.

Without being imitative, Léonie Adams suggests Vaughan (see page 487) and the seventeenth-century metaphysical poets. She records with almost religious ecstasy the changing shapes of earth, the fluid seasons, the twilit revelations of a "blue which sucks whole planets in." The mood is mystical in which all matter is "sanctified, dipped in a gold stain."

Sundown

This is the time lean woods shall spend
A steeped-up twilight, and the pale evening drink,
And the perilous roe, the leaper to the west brink,
Trembling and bright, to the caverned cloud descend.

Now shall you see pent oak gone gusty and frantic,
Stooped with dry weeping, ruinously unloosing
The sparse disheveled leaf, or reared and tossing
A dreary scarecrow bough in funeral antic.

Aye, tatter you and rend,
Oak heart, to your profession mourning; not obscure
The outcome, not crepuscular; on the deep floor,
Sable and gold match lusters and contend.

And rags of shrouding will not muffle the slain.
This is the immortal extinction, the priceless wound
Not to be staunched. The live gold leaks beyond,
And matter's sanctified, dipped in a gold stain.

The best of her previous work, together with hitherto uncollected
pieces, appeared in POEMS: A SELECTION in 1954. It was a small
volume but penetrating in its intensity. Delicate in texture and
quiet in tone, it contained some of the finest lyrics of the period.

OGDEN NASH
[1902–1971]

IT SEEMS incredible that a new form of light verse should have
been invented, perfected, and ruined by one man as late as the
first third of the twentieth century, but that feat was accomplished
by Ogden Nash. Nash's haphazard measures, impossible rhymes, and
slightly lunatic manner delighted his readers and deceived his imi-
tators, who attempted to achieve, without success, Nash's dizzy blend
of sense and nonsense. No one but Nash was able to put such point
into such seemingly pointless off-rhymes as:

> He who is ridden by a conscience
> Worries about a lot of nonscience.

and:

Poor girls with nothing to their names but a compromising letter
   or two can get rich and joyous
From a brief trip to their loyous.

and:

> Many an infant that screams like a calliope
> Could be soothed by a little attention to its diope.

and:

> The wasp and all his numerous family
> I look upon as a major calamily.
> He throws open his nest with prodigality,
> But I distrust his waspitality.

It is little wonder that when the brightest jewels from Nash's six
volumes were assembled in THE FACE IS FAMILIAR, the collection be-
came known as THE GOLDEN TRASHERY OF OGDEN NASHERY.

Very Like a Whale

One thing that literature would be greatly the better for
Would be a more restricted employment by authors of simile and
   metaphor.
Authors of all races, be they Greeks, Romans, Teutons or Celts,
Can't seem just to say that anything is the thing it is but have to go
   out of their way to say that it is like something else.
What does it mean when we are told
That the Assyrian came down like a wolf on the fold?
In the first place, George Gordon Byron had had enough experience
To know that it probably wasn't just one Assyrian, it was a *lot* of
   Assyrians.
However, as too many arguments are apt to induce apoplexy and
   thus hinder longevity,
We'll let it pass as one Assyrian for the sake of brevity.

Now then, this particular Assyrian, the one whose cohorts were
  gleaming in purple and gold,
Just what does the poet mean when he says he came down like a
  wolf on the fold?
In heaven and earth more than is dreamed of in our philosophy
  there are a great many things,
But I don't imagine that among them there is a wolf with purple
  and gold cohorts or purple and gold anythings.
No, no, Lord Byron, before I'll believe that this Assyrian was actu-
  ally like a wolf I must have some kind of proof;
Did he run on all fours and did he have a hairy tail and a big red
  mouth and big white teeth and did he say Woof woof woof?
Frankly I think it very unlikely, and all you were entitled to say, at
  the very most,
Was that the Assyrian cohorts came down like a lot of Assyrian
  cohorts about to destroy the Hebrew host.
But that wasn't fancy enough for Lord Byron, oh dear me, no, he
  had to invent a lot of figures of speech and then interpolate
  them,
With the result that whenever you mention Old Testament soldiers
  to people they say Oh yes, they're the ones that a lot of wolves
  dressed up in gold and purple ate them.
That's the kind of thing that's being done all the time by poets,
  from Homer to Tennyson;
They're always comparing ladies to lilies and veal to venison,
And they always say things like that the snow is a white blanket
  after a winter storm.
Oh it is, is it, all right then, you sleep under a six-inch blanket of
  snow and I'll sleep under a half-inch blanket of unpoetical
  blanket material and we'll see which one keeps warm,
And after that maybe you'll begin to comprehend dimly
What I mean by too much metaphor and simile.

Ogden Nash was born August 6, 1903, in Rye, New York. His
schooling was fitful. At eighteen he entered Harvard, but left after
a year. He spent another year at St. George's School in Rhode Island
where, he says, he wrecked his nervous system carving lamb for
fourteen-year-olds. He became a bond salesman, and sold one bond
—to his grandmother; he wrote slogans for cards and advertising
matter for publishers. He joined the staff of THE NEW YORKER, left it
for free lancing and Hollywood, and published his first book, not
perceived that a new tempo as well as a new manner had been added
inaccurately entitled HARD LINES, at twenty-seven. It was immediately

to "social verse," and that no one since W. S. Gilbert had tossed pun, rhyme, and reason about with such brilliance. A trickster, Nash was also an innovator.

Kind of an Ode to Duty

O Duty,
Why hast thou not the visage of a sweetie or a cutie?
Why glitter thy spectacles so ominously?
Why art thou clad so abominously?
Why art thou so different from Venus
And why do thou and I have so few interests mutually in common
    between us?
Why art thou fifty per cent martyr
And fifty-one per cent Tartar?

Why is it thy unfortunate wont
To try to attract people by calling on them either to leave undone
    the deeds they like, or to do the deeds they don't?
Why art thou so like an April post-mortem
Or something that died in the ortumn?
Above all, why dost thou continue to hound me?
Why art thou always albatrossly hanging around me?

Thou so ubiquitous,
And I so iniquitous.
I seem to be the one person in the world thou art perpetually
    preaching at who or to who;
Whatever looks like fun, there art thou standing between me and it,
    calling you-hoo.
O Duty, Duty!
How noble a man should I be hadst thou the visage of a sweetie or
    a cutie!
But as it is thou art so much forbiddinger than a Wodehouse hero's
    forbiddingest aunt
That in the words of the poet, When Duty whispers low, Thou must,
    this erstwhile youth replies, I just can't.

Seemingly irresponsible, Nash's verse is often as purposeful as it is original. Beneath the wild mispronunciations, there are witty pronouncements on a variety of topics; Nash's soft questions do not turn away wrath, and his nonsense has a way of turning into criticism.

MERRILL MOORE
[1903–1957]

A PSYCHIATRIST, authority on alcoholism, author of some twenty-five medical papers, including the idyllic SYPHILIS AND SASSAFRAS, Merrill Moore published eight volumes and several pamphlets of sonnets before his fiftieth year. At twenty-four he had written about nine thousand sonnets; at thirty-five he published a volume starkly entitled M, accurately indicating that the book contained one thousand pages of sonnets. Moore himself does not know exactly how many sonnets he has composed during a busy life, but a rough estimate accounts for a total between sixty and seventy thousand—more sonnets than had been produced by all the leading sonneteers who ever wrote in English.

If Moore's sonnets intimidate the reader with sheer bulk, they charm with their unpredictability, their superb casualness. In rapid-fire succession they present a genre picture, an abnormal case history, a reasoned meditation, a mad dream, a compact drama, and chaos in fourteen lines.

Warning to One

Death is the strongest of all living things,
And when it happens do not look in the eyes
For a dead fire or a lack-luster there;
But listen for the words that fall from lips
Or do not fall. Silence is not death;
It merely means that one who is conserving breath
Is not concerned with tattle and small quips.

Watch the quick fingers and the way they move
During unguarded moments—words of love
And love's caresses may be cold as ice,
And cold the glitter of engagement rings.
Death is the sword that hangs on a single hair;
And that thin tenuous hair is no more than love,
And yours is the silly head it hangs above.

Born September 11, 1903, in Columbia, Tennessee, Merrill Moore was educated at Nashville. He attended Vanderbilt University, where he was one of the youngest members of the group known as The Fugitives, and was graduated at twenty-one. He supported himself by teaching in night school and at a Negro university. At twenty-five he received his M.D. degree, interned in Nashville, moved to Boston, where he joined the Harvard Medical School, became neurologist at the Boston City Hospital, and built up a large practice as specialist in nervous and mental diseases. The titles of his later volumes have a certain significance: CLINICAL SONNETS, ILLEGITIMATE SONNETS, and CASE RECORD FROM A SONNETORIUM.

Moore has never been able to give his work that finish which means final perfection; it is easier for him to write a new poem than revise an old one. He has been known to improvise a sonnet and dictate it to a soundscriber, which he carries in his car, during a change of traffic lights. Moore's sonnets range the world for their themes, from the clinic to a contemplation of the farthest nebula, from the fantasies of the unconscious to love poems which mingle passion and raillery.

The Noise That Time Makes

That noise that Time makes in passing by
Is very slight but even you can hear it
Having not necessarily to be near it,
Needing only the slightest will to try!

Hold the receiver of a telephone
To your ear when no one is talking on the line
And what may at first sound to you like the whine
Of wind over distant wires is Time's own
Garments brushing against a windy cloud.

That same noise again but not so well
Can be heard by taking a large cockle shell
From the sand and holding it against your head;
Then you can hear Time's footsteps as they pass
Over the earth brushing the eternal grass.

W. H. AUDEN
[1907–1973]

Aᴛᴛᴇʀ the First World War, poetry in England suffered a sudden decrease in vitality. During the conflict many of the brilliant young men—Rupert Brooke, Wilfred Owen, Edward Thomas, Charles Hamilton Sorley, Isaac Rosenberg, among others—were killed before they achieved their full utterance. Those who returned could not take up their work where they had left it. Some of them suffered physically from shell shock; others were psychologically shocked out of their former heartiness and confident way of life.

Seeking reassurance as well as refuge, many of the English poets turned to the consoling countryside. But another generation, faced with another war, repudiated the tradition-loving Georgians. They could not be comforted by bucolics in a falsely pastoral setting. Unlike their immediate predecessors, the young men of the 1930s were willing to confront the darker side of life, the exhausted soil and exploited labor, the spiritual emptiness and economic bankruptcy. The "postwar poets," led by W. H. Auden and Stephen Spender, sounded a call to action. They turned away from nostalgic thoughts of an idealized past to grapple with the difficult present; they sought to bring poetry out of a world of shadows into the full light of general life. Their impact might be compared to that of Wordsworth and Coleridge. They, too, restored vitality to English poetry; they recovered ground lost by their immediate predecessors. They reestablished the former activity of language; they went farther, extending the poetic vocabulary along new scientific and intellectual frontiers.

Wystan Hugh Auden, the most brilliant of the "postwar" group, expressed more fully than his contemporaries a sick world. "What do you think about England, this country of ours where nobody is well?" he asked in 1932 at the beginning of ᴛʜᴇ ᴏʀᴀᴛᴏʀs, and the note was maintained to reflect a time of agonized insecurity and isolation. Born February 21, 1907, in York, England, Auden was educated at Christ Church, Oxford, and became a teacher. For five years he taught in a boys' school at Malvern. In his late twenties he joined a film unit; at thirty-one he came to America and took out citizenship papers. In the United States he alternated between various universities and Hollywood.

Auden's early poetry is restlessly experimental, influenced by the echnique of T. S. Eliot (see page 1149), Wilfred Owen (see page 1173), and Gerard Manley Hopkins (see page 977). Hopkins' breathless tempo, his blend of alliteration and concealed rhyme, his very accents, are heard in such lines as:

> Which of you waking early and watching daybreak
> Will not hasten in heart, handsome, aware of wonder
> At light unleashed, advancing, a leader of movement,
> Breaking like surf on turf on road and roof . . .

Many of Auden's brilliant early effects are both gained and obscured by his easy virtuosity, by a continual play of private references and remote allusions. At thirty, Auden suddenly clarified his style without sacrificing emotional intensity. Still protesting against a world sick of old standards, distrustful of new values, and in love with death, Auden emphasized a new lyricism, a romantic reaction against conventional romanticism. The note is heard in:

> Lay your sleeping head, my love,
> Human on my faithless arm;

and, more extensively, in the quietly poignant LOOK, STRANGER.

Look, Stranger

> Look, stranger, at this island now
> The leaping light for your delight discovers,
> Stand stable here
> And silent be,
> That through the channels of the ear
> May wander like a river
> The swaying sound of the sea.
>
> Here at the small field's ending pause
> Where the chalk wall falls to the foam, and its tall ledges
> Oppose the pluck
> And knock of the tide,
> And the shingle scrambles after the suck-
> ing surf, and the gull lodges
> A moment on its sheer side.

Far off like floating seeds the ships
Diverge on urgent voluntary errands;
And the full view
Indeed may enter
And move in memory as now these clouds do,
That pass the harbor mirror
And all the summer through the water saunter.

The most unpredictable as well as the most provocative writer
of his generation, Auden at thirty-four had written two travel books,
five volumes of verse—one of them, THE DOUBLE MAN, a seventeen-
hundred-line chain of couplets as epigrammatic as Pope's—compiled
two anthologies, and collaborated on two plays. More than most of
his fellows, Auden speaks as the multiple man. LAW, SAY THE GAR-
DENERS, IS THE SUN, a triumph over impertinence, unites the dexter-
ous craftsman and the smiling iconoclast, the sensitive lover and the
supple wit.

Law, Say the Gardeners, Is the Sun

Law, say the gardeners, is the sun,
Law is the one
All gardeners obey
Tomorrow, yesterday, today.

Law is the wisdom of the old
The impotent grandfathers shrilly scold;
The grandchildren put out a treble tongue,
Law is the senses of the young.

Law, says the priest with a priestly look,
Expounding to an unpriestly people,
Law is the words in my priestly book,
Law is my pulpit and my steeple.

Law, says the judge as he looks down his nose,
Speaking clearly and most severely,
Law is as I've told you before,
Law is as you know I suppose,
Law is but let me explain it once more,
Law is The Law.

Yet law-abiding scholars write;
Law is neither wrong nor right,
Law is only crimes
Punished by places and by times,
Law is the clothes men wear
Anytime, anywhere,
Law is Good-morning and Good-night.

Others say, Law is our Fate;
Others say, Law is our State;
Others say, others say
Law is no more,
Law is gone away.

And always the loud angry crowd
Very angry and very loud
Law is We,
And always the soft idiot softly **Me**.

If we, dear, know we know no more
Than they about the law,
If I no more than you
Know what we should and should **not do**
Except that all agree
Gladly or miserably
That the law is
And that all know this,
If therefore thinking it absurd
To identify Law with some other word,
Unlike so many men
I cannot say Law is again,
No more than they can we suppress
The universal wish to guess
Or slip out of our own position
Into an unconcerned condition.

Although I can at least confine
Your vanity and mine
To stating timidly
A timid similarity,
We shall boast anyway:
Like love I say.

Like love we dont know where or why
Like love we cant compel or fly
Like love we often weep
Like love we seldom keep.

Although Auden often alternates between a confused symbolism
and a hard-bitten, hard-biting plain speech, the best of his poetry
proceeds neither from the coterie nor the music-hall mind which
prompted the trifling "popular" rhymes in competition with light-
verse writers and singers of "blues." Auden is most distinguished
when he is most divided; his work is all the more affecting because
it is a record of ambivalence. His hesitations between tradition and
revolution communicate not only a sense of painful bewilderment
but also of estrangement. Yet Auden moves toward affirmation. He
progresses from the strange torment of the early LETTER TO A WOUND
to the hope of brotherhood ("We must love one another or die")
and understanding companionship ("Teach the free man how to
praise"). It is a hope that culminates in the obituary poem written
shortly after the death of Yeats (see page 1035), a poem that is an
estimate and a prayer as well as an elegy.

In Memory of W. B. Yeats

1

He disappeared in the dead of winter:
The brooks were frozen, the airports almost deserted,
And snow disfigured the public statues;
The mercury sank in the mouth of the dying day.
O all the instruments agree
The day of his death was a dark cold day.

Far from his illness
The wolves ran on through the evergreen forests,
The peasant river was untempted by the fashionable quays;
By mourning tongues
The death of the poet was kept from his poems.

But for him it was his last afternoon as himself,
An afternoon of nurses and rumors;
The provinces of his body revolted,

The squares of his mind were empty,
Silence invaded the suburbs,
The current of his feeling failed: he became his admirers.

Now he is scattered among a hundred cities
And wholly given over to unfamiliar affections;
To find his happiness in another kind of wood
And be punished under a foreign code of conscience.
The words of a dead man
Are modified in the guts of the living.

But in the importance and noise of tomorrow
When the brokers are roaring like beasts on the floor of the Bourse,
And the poor have the sufferings to which they are fairly accus-
    tomed,
And each in the cell of himself is almost convinced of his freedom;
A few thousand will think of this day
As one thinks of a day when one did something slightly unusual.

O all the instruments agree
The day of his death was a dark cold day.

2

You were silly like us: your gift survived it all;
The parish of rich women, physical decay,
Yourself; mad Ireland hurt you into poetry.
Now Ireland has her madness and her weather still,
For poetry makes nothing happen: it survives
In the valley of its saying where executives
Would never want to tamper; it flows south
From ranches of isolation and the busy griefs,
Raw towns that we believe and die in; it survives,
A way of happening, a mouth.

3

Earth, receive an honored guest;
William Yeats is laid to rest:
Let the Irish vessel lie
Emptied of its poetry.

Time that is intolerant
Of the brave and innocent,
And indifferent in a week
To a beautiful physique,

Worships language and forgives
Everyone by whom it lives;
Pardons cowardice, conceit,
Lays its honors at their feet.

Time that with this strange excuse
Pardoned Kipling and his views,
And will pardon Paul Claudel,
Pardons him for writing well.

In the nightmare of the dark
All the dogs of Europe bark,
And the living nations wait,
Each sequestered in its hate;

Intellectual disgrace
Stares from every human face,
And the seas of pity lie
Locked and frozen in each eye.

Follow, poet, follow right
To the bottom of the night,
With your unconstraining voice
Still persuade us to rejoice;

With the farming of a verse
Make a vineyard of the curse,
Sing of human unsuccess
In a rapture of distress;

In the deserts of the heart
Let the healing fountain start,
In the prison of his days
Teach the free man how to praise.

Auden's later work exhibits a human warmth and a humility
barely suggested by the dazzle of his early cerebrations. Many of the
images in his COLLECTED POEMS and in some of the poems in NONES
may seem chill and even ominous, full of a "menacing mutter," but
they show new depths of feeling. Auden's erudition and inventive-
ness have joined to display a sense of rich reserve and an intensified
communication.

Musée des Beaux Arts

About suffering they were never wrong,
The Old Masters: how well they understood
Its human position; how it takes place
While someone else is eating or opening a window or just walking
    dully along;
How, when the aged are reverently, passionately waiting
For the miraculous birth, there always must be
Children who did not specially want it to happen, skating
On a pond at the edge of the wood:
They never forgot
That even the dreadful martyrdom must run its course
Anyhow in a corner, some untidy spot
Where the dogs go on with their doggy life and the torturer's horse
Scratches its innocent behind on a tree.

In Brueghel's *Icarus,* for instance: how everything turns away
Quite leisurely from the disaster; the ploughman may
Have heard the splash, the forsaken cry,
But for him it was not an important failure; the sun shone
As it had to on the white legs disappearing into the green
Water; and the expensive delicate ship that must have seen
Something amazing, a boy falling out of the sky,
Had somewhere to get to and sailed calmly on.

THEODORE ROETHKE
[1908–1963]

A SUBTLE artisan whom Dylan Thomas considered the most original of the younger poets, Theodore Roethke was born May 25, 1908, in Saginaw, Michigan. Educated in his native state and at Harvard, Roethke became a teacher; his connection with various colleges brought him from one extreme of the country to the other, from Lafayette College, Penn State, and Bennington to the University of Washington.

Roethke was slow to publish. His first volume, OPEN HOUSE, did not appear until he was thirty-three. By the time he had reached his mid-forties, he was the author of four distinguished volumes, one of which, THE WAKING, had been awarded the Pulitzer Prize in 1953. He also wrote stories and satires, as well as poems for children, under the pseudonym of Winterset Rethberg.

His poetry underwent a gradual but pronounced series of changes, developing from forthright lyrics of recognizable people and places through loose autobiographical reminiscences to surrealist, or supra-rational, explorations. Much of Roethke's poetry accomplishes a release of the unconscious mind, stressing odd but illuminating figments of memory and imagination. While the surface is often puzzling, the melodic line is as simple as a nursery rhyme, composed of a child's words remembered and heightened in maturity. The half-mocking, half-mournful humor suggests the music of Prokofiev and the drawings of Paul Klee. Referring to the first part of THE LOST SON, Roethke wrote: " 'The Flight' is just what it says it is: a terrified running away—with alternate periods of hallucinatory waiting (the voices, etcetera); the protagonist so geared-up, so over-alive, that he is hunting, like a primitive, for some animistic suggestion, some clue to existence from the sub-human. These he sees and yet does not see; they are almost tail-flicks from another world, seen out of the corner of the eye. In a sense he goes in and out of rationality: he hangs in the balance between the human and the animal."

The Flight

At Woodlawn I heard the dead cry:
I was lulled by the slamming of iron,
A slow drip over stones,
Toads brooding in wells.
All the leaves stuck out their tongues;
I shook the softening chalk of my bones,
Saying,
Snail, snail, glister me forward,
Bird, soft-sigh me home,
Worm, be with me.
This is my hard time.

Fished in an old wound,
The soft pond of repose;
Nothing nibbled my line,
Not even the minnows came.

Sat in an empty house
Watching shadows crawl,
Scratching.
There was one fly.

Voice, come out of the silence.
Say something.
Appear in the form of a spider
Or a moth beating the curtain.

  Tell me:
  Which is the way I take;
  Out of what door do I go,
  Where and to whom?

    Dark hollows said, lee to the wind,
    The moon said, back of an eel,
    The salt said, look by the sea,
    Your tears are not enough praise,
    You will find no comfort here,
    In the kingdom of bang and blab.

  Running lightly over spongy ground,
  Past the pasture of flat stones,
  The three elms,
  The sheep strewn on a field,
  Over a rickety bridge
  Toward the quick-water, wrinkling and rippling.

  Hunting along the rivers,
  Down among the rubbish, the bug-riddled foliage,
  By the muddy pond-edge, by the bog-holes,
  By the shrunken lake, hunting, in the heat of summer.

The shape of a rat?
    It's bigger than that.
    It's less than a leg
    And more than a nose,
    Just under the water
    It usually goes.

Is it soft like a mouse?
Can it wrinkle its nose?
Could it come in the house
On the tips of its toes?

Take the skin of a cat
And the back of an eel,
Then roll them in grease,—
That's the way it would feel.

It's sleek as an otter
With wide webby toes
Just under the water
It usually goes.

from THE LOST SON

Roethke's later poems are less backward-seeking but fully as intuitional as the earlier verse. Semi-obscurity gives way to connotative clarity, and eerie sensibilities are disciplined without losing their boldness. The love poems combine light play and sensuousness; they radiate ecstasy as their physical exultations blend with spiritual exaltation.

Poem

I knew a woman, lovely in her bones,
When small birds sighed, she would sigh back at them;
Ah, when she moved, she moved more ways than one.
The shapes a bright container can contain!
Of her choice virtues only gods should speak,
Or English poets who grew up on Greek
(I'd have them sing in chorus, cheek to cheek.)

How well her wishes went! She stroked my chin,
She taught me Turn, and Counter-turn, and Stand;
She taught me Touch, that undulant white skin:
I nibbled meekly from her proffered hand;
She was the sickle; I, poor I, the rake,
Coming behind her for her pretty sake
(But what prodigious mowing we did make.)

Love likes a gander, and adores a goose:
Her full lips pursed, the errant note to seize;
She played it quick, she played it light and loose;
My eyes, they dazzled at her flowing knees;
Her several parts could keep a pure repose,
Or one hip quiver with a mobile nose
(She moved in circles, and those circles moved.)

Let seed be grass, and grass turn into hay:
I'm martyr to a motion not my own;
What's freedom for? To know eternity.
I swear she cast a shadow white as stone.
But who would count eternity in days?
These old bones live to learn her wanton ways:
(I measure time by how a body sways.)

STEPHEN SPENDER
[1909–   ]

AT TWENTY-NINE, just before the outbreak of the Second World
War, Stephen Spender wrote: "The violence of the times we
are living in, the necessity of sweeping and general and immediate
action, tend to dwarf the experience of the individual." Before that
he had written: "Surely the point at which modern poetry becomes
revolutionary is the point where it tries to define truths which are
related to the world around us: to politics and economics. It is revo-
lutionary because it has retired altogether from the attempt to find
satisfaction in the 'possible worlds' of mythology: it is back in the
world which surrounds us."

Stephen Spender was nine years old when the First World War
ended and thirty when the Second World War began. Born Febru-
ary 28, 1909, near London, he spent his youth in the nervous uncer-
tainties of a false peace, in the long tension between two wars. But
Spender, unlike many of his fellows, did not fear his times. He
refused to retreat, to isolate himself in a hermetically sealed art. He
was particularly insistent that poetry should reaffirm its power and
responsibility, accept the world of the airplane and the radio, speak
to living men about the living age. "Drink from here energy,"
Spender insisted, pointing to a world of violent action, "as from the
electric charge of a battery." And with energy Spender called for
compassion. How could we ever doubt the common heart of human-
ity he asked, how could it be

. . . That works, money, interest, building could ever hide
The palpable and obvious love of man!

Less obscure, more certain of his symbols than Auden, Spender
writes with a passion emphasized by quietness. His technique is

assured without being exciting, but his tone is moving. His vein of "lyrical speculation," wrote the critic David Daiches, "produces poetry which can hold its own with anything produced in the century." AN ELEMENTARY SCHOOL CLASSROOM IN A SLUM is not an attempt to escape hard actuality and "find satisfaction in the 'possible worlds' of mythology." Rather it is a contrast between the "possible worlds" of poetry, as exemplified by Shakespeare, and beauty, symbolized by pictures of travel, and the grim world of politics and economics "which surrounds us."

An Elementary School Classroom in a Slum

Far far from gusty waves, these children's faces.
Like rootless weeds the torn hair round their paleness.
The tall girl with her weighed-down head. The paper-
seeming boy with rat's eyes. The stunted unlucky heir
Of twisted bones, reciting a father's gnarled disease,
His lesson from his desk. At back of the dim class,
One unnoted, sweet and young: his eyes live in a dream
Of squirrels' game, in tree room, other than this.

On sour cream walls, donations. Shakespeare's head
Cloudless at dawn, civilized dome riding all cities.
Belled, flowery, Tyrolese valley. Open-handed map
Awarding the world its world. And yet, for these
Children, these windows, not this world, are world,
Where all their future's painted with a fog,
A narrow street sealed in with a lead sky,
Far, far from rivers, capes, and stars of words.

Surely Shakespeare is wicked, the map a bad example
With ships and sun and love tempting them to steal—
For lives that slyly turn in their cramped holes
From fog to endless night? On their slag heap, these children
Wear skins peeped through by bones and spectacles of steel
With mended glass, like bottle bits on stones.
All of their time and space and foggy slum
So blot their maps with slums as big as doom.

Unless, governor, teacher, inspector, visitor,
This map becomes their window and these windows
That open on their lives like crouching tombs
Break, O break open, till they break the town

And show the children to the fields and all their world
Azure on their sands, to let their tongues
Run naked into books, the white and green leaves open
The history theirs whose language is the sun.

Without being didactic Spender is essentially an interpreter of baffled but onward-struggling men; with all its modern imagery his is a poetry prompted by a moral sense. The depths of his moral convictions are sounded in the lines beginning "I think continually of those who were truly great." In one of the noblest rhapsodies of the period, Spender praises the pioneers, the unsung fighters, firebringers, children of the sun. In a lyrical ODE (see page 976) O'Shaughnessy celebrated the poets who built up the world's great cities:

> One man with a dream, at pleasure,
>   Shall go forth and conquer a crown;
> And three with a new song's measure
>   Can trample an empire down.

Spender extends the implication. He exalts "those who in their lives fought for life, who," he says in a triumphant coda:

> ... wore at their hearts the fire's center.
> Born of the sun they traveled a short while towards the sun,
> And left the vivid air signed with their honor.

Such lines have an almost Shakespearean eloquence. They are authoritative; most of all, they are noble.

I Think Continually of Those

I think continually of those who were truly great.
Who, from the womb, remembered the soul's history
Through corridors of light where the hours are suns,
Endless and singing. Whose lovely ambition
Was that their lips, still touched with fire,
Should tell of the spirit clothed from head to foot in song.
And who hoarded from the spring branches
The desires falling across their bodies like blossoms.

What is precious is never to forget
The essential delight of the blood drawn from ageless springs
Breaking through rocks in worlds before our earth.
Never to deny its pleasure in the simple morning light
Nor its grave evening demand for love.
Never to allow gradually the traffic to smother
With noise and fog the flowering of the spirit.

Near the snow, near the sun, in the highest fields
See how these names are fêted by the waving grass,
And by the streamers of white cloud,
And whispers of wind in the listening sky;
The names of those who in their lives fought for life,
Who wore at their hearts the fire's center.
Born of the sun they traveled a short while towards the sun,
And left the vivid air signed with their honor.

In a time of darkness and confusion, poetry again expresses the
flowering of the spirit of a greater humanity, of dreamers and work-
ers, the yea sayers stubbornly "bringing light to life," leaving "the
vivid air signed with their honor."

ELIZABETH BISHOP
[1911–1979]

Pressed for a statement of writing principles embodying her the-
ory of poetry, Elizabeth Bishop replied: "No matter what the-
ories one may have, I doubt very much that they are in one's mind
at the moment of writing a poem or that there is even a physical
possibility that they could be. Theories can only be based on inter-
pretations of other poets' poems, or one's own in retrospect, or wish-
ful thinking." Elizabeth Bishop's poetry has challenged and with-
stood analysis because of its peculiar fusion of free whimsicality and
intellectual control.

She was born February 8, 1911, in Worcester, Massachusetts, was
graduated from Vassar College, and traveled widely. After she re-
ceived a Fellowship for her volume, NORTH AND SOUTH, she was, for
a while, Consultant in Poetry to the Library of Congress. Her origin
and long sojourns in the South may account for the distinctive color

of her images which combine tropical floridity with New England
severity. "The Fish," a miniature Moby Dick, is an excellent ex-
ample of her sharp scrutiny and soaring imagination.

The Fish

I caught a tremendous fish
and held him beside the boat
half out of water, with my hook
fast in a corner of his mouth.
He didn't fight.
He hadn't fought at all.
He hung a grunting weight,
battered and venerable
and homely. Here and there
his brown skin hung in strips
like ancient wall-paper,
and its pattern of darker brown
was like wall-paper:
shapes like full-blown roses
stained and lost through age.
He was speckled with barnacles,
fine rosettes of lime,
and infested
with tiny white sea-lice,
and underneath two or three
rags of green weed hung down.
While his gills were breathing in
the terrible oxygen
—the frightening gills
fresh and crisp with blood,
that can cut so badly—
I thought of the coarse white flesh
packed in like feathers,
the big bones and the little bones,
the dramatic reds and blacks
of his shiny entrails,
and the pink swim-bladder
like a big peony.
I looked into his eyes
which were far larger than mine
but shallower, and yellowed,

the irises backed and packed
with tarnished tinfoil
seen through the lenses
of old scratched isinglass.
They shifted a little, but not
to return my stare.
—It was more like the tipping
of an object toward the light.
I admired his sullen face,
the mechanism of his jaw,
and then I saw
that from his lower lip
—if you could call it a lip—
grim, wet, and weapon-like,
hung five old pieces of fish-line,
or four and a wire leader
with the swivel still attached,
with all their five big hooks
grown firmly in his mouth.
A green line, frayed at the end
where he broke it, two heavier lines,
and a fine black thread
still crimped from the strain and snap
when it broke and he got away.
Like medals with their ribbons
frayed and wavering,
a five-haired beard of wisdom
trailing from his aching jaw.
I stared and stared
and victory filled up
the little rented boat,
from the pool of bilge
where oil had spread a rainbow
around the rusted engine
to the bailer rusted orange,
the sun-cracked thwarts,
the oarlocks on their strings,
the gunnels—until everything
was rainbow, rainbow, rainbow!
And I let the fish go.

KARL SHAPIRO
[1913–   ]

A POET deeply disturbed by the dilemmas of his day but who re-
garded them with unfailing wit, Karl Shapiro was born Novem-
ber 10, 1913, in Baltimore, Maryland. He attended the University of
Virginia and Johns Hopkins University, was inducted into the Army
and, during the Second World War, was sent overseas as a sergeant.
For three years (1942–1945) he served in the South Pacific, and it
was there that his first three books were put together. One of them,
V-LETTER, won the Pulitzer Prize in 1945; another, ESSAY ON RHYME,
was a remarkable feat of erudition, written by a soldier thousands
of miles from any library. After the war he acted as Consultant in
Poetry at the Library of Congress, was editor of the magazine POETRY,
and taught creative writing.

The early poems vibrate with hatred of injustice and resentment
against the stereotyped sentiments which Shapiro felt had misled
his generation. "Certainly our contemporary man should feel di-
vested of the stock attitudes of the last generation, the stance of the
political intellectual, the proletarian, the expert, the salesman, the
world-traveler, the pundit-poet." But, for all his indignation, Sha-
piro is neither a pessimist nor an evangelist. His irony is bitter but
compassionate; he can regard pain with a kind of wounded whimsi-
cality.

The Leg

Among the iodoform, in twilight-sleep,
What have I lost? he first inquires,
Peers in the middle distance where a pain,
Ghost of a nurse, hazily moves, and day,
Her blinding presence pressing in his eyes
And now his ears. They are handling him
With rubber hands. He wants to get up.

One day beside some flowers near his nose
He will be thinking, *When will I look at it?*
And pain, still in the middle distance, will reply

At what? and he will know it's gone,
O where! and begin to tremble and cry.
He will begin to cry as a child cries
Whose puppy is mangled under a screaming wheel.

Later, as if deliberately, his fingers
Begin to explore the stump. He learns a shape
That is comfortable and tucked in like a sock.
This has a sense of humor, this can despise
The finest surgical limb, the dignity of limping,
The nonsense of wheel-chairs. Now he smiles to the wall:
The amputation becomes an acquisition.

For the leg is wondering where he is (all is not lost)
And surely he has a duty to the leg;
He is its injury, the leg is his orphan,
He must cultivate the mind of the leg,
Pray for the part that is missing, pray for peace
In the image of man, pray, pray for its safety,
And after a little it will die quietly.

The body, what is it, Father, but a sign
To love the force that grows us, to give back
What in Thy palm is senselessness and mud?
Knead, knead the substance of our understanding
Which must be beautiful in flesh to walk,
That if Thou take me angrily in hand
And hurl me to the shark, I shall not die!

COLLECTED POEMS, published when Shapiro was forty, shows a con-
siderable advance in range and persuasion. The idiom is simpler,
the tone sharper, the emotion more frankly personal. "Buick" is
typical of the poet's happier mood, an example of how the mechani-
cal material of the modern world is lifted until it attains the pitch
of ecstasy.

Buick

As a sloop with a sweep of immaculate wing on her delicate spine
And a keel as steel as a root that holds in the sea as she leans,
Leaning and laughing, my warm-hearted beauty, you ride, you ride,
You tack on the curves with parabola speed and a kiss of goodbye,
Like a thoroughbred sloop, my new high-spirited spirit, my kiss.

As my foot suggests that you leap in the air with your hips of a girl,
My finger that praises your wheel and announces your voices of song,
Flouncing your skirts, you blueness of joy, you flirt of politeness,
You leap, you intelligence, essence of wheelness with silvery nose,
And your platinum clocks of excitement stir like the hairs of a fern.

But how alien you are from the booming belts of your birth and the
 smoke
Where you turned on the stinging lathes of Detroit and Lansing at
 night
And shrieked at the torch in your secret parts and the amorous tests,
But now with your eyes that enter the future of roads you forget;
You are all instinct with your phosphorous glow and your streaking
 hair.

And now when we stop it is not as the bird from the shell that I
 leave
Of the leathery pilot who steps from his bird with a sneer of delight,
And not as the ignorant beast do you squat and watch me depart,
But with exquisite breathing you smile, with satisfaction of love,
And I touch you again as you tick in the silence and settle in sleep.

MURIEL RUKEYSER
[1913–1980]

MURIEL RUKEYSER is one of the younger poets who uses the material of modern life without self-consciousness. For her a truck rumbling along in the dark before dawn is a more natural prelude to sunrise than the lark at heaven's gate; the airplane is a more rousing if more ominous symbol of man's longing for freedom than the traditional flight of released doves. Her images rise from the tension and terror of the contemporary scene.

Born December 15, 1913, in New York City, Muriel Rukeyser attended Vassar and Columbia, became a statistician, and worked her way through a ground-course at Roosevelt Aviation School. The varied experiences were embodied in her first book, THEORY OF FLIGHT, published when she was twenty-two. By her mid-thirties she was the author of six more volumes of poetry, the most notable being BEAST IN VIEW and ORPHEUS, as well as a biography of the scientist Willard Gibbs.

Complex but rarely obscure, Muriel Rukeyser's poems are characterized by their abrupt change of mood and action, by their interpenetration of music and meaning, most of all by their rousing and sometimes runaway fervor. It is difficult to tell where the unconscious propulsion ends and the conscious artist begins. "My own experience," she wrote, "is that the work on a poem 'surfaces' several times, with new submergence after each rising. The 'idea' for a poem may come as an image thrown against memory, as a sound of words that sets off a traveling of sound and meaning, as a curve of emotion (a form) plotted by certain crises of events or image or sound, or as a title which evokes a sense of inner relations." Whatever the genesis of her work, the result is a poetry which is introspective but socially conscious, highly individualized and passionately affirmative.

Effort at Speech Between Two People

Speak to me.   Take my hand.   What are you now?
I will tell you all.   I will conceal nothing.
When I was three, a little child read a story about a rabbit
who died, in the story, and I crawled under a chair:
a pink rabbit: it was my birthday, and a candle
burnt a sore spot on my finger, and I was told to be happy.

Oh, grow to know me.   I am not happy.   I will be open:
Now I am thinking of white sails against a sky like music,
like glad horns blowing, and birds tilting, and an arm about me.
There was one I loved, who wanted to live, sailing.

Speak to me.   Take my hand.   What are you now?
When I was nine, I was fruitily sentimental,
fluid: and my widowed aunt played Chopin,
and I bent my head on the painted woodwork, and wept.
I want now to be close to you.   I would
link the minutes of my days close, somehow, to your days.

I am not happy.   I will be open.
I have liked lamps in evening corners, and quiet poems.
There has been fear in my life.   Sometimes I speculate
On what a tragedy his life was, really.

Take my hand.   Fist my mind in your hand.   What are you
  now?
When I was fourteen, I had dreams of suicide,
and I stood at a steep window, at sunset, hoping toward death:
if the light had not melted clouds and plains to beauty,
if light had not transformed that day, I would have leapt.
I am unhappy.   I am lonely.   Speak to me.

I will be open.   I think he never loved me:
he loved the bright beaches, the little lips of foam
that ride small waves, he loved the veer of gulls:
he said with a gay mouth: I love you.   Grow to know me.

What are you now?   If we could touch one another,
if these our separate entities could come to grips,
clenched like a Chinese puzzle . . . yesterday
I stood in a crowded street that was live with people,
and no one spoke a word, and the morning shone.
Everyone silent, moving. . . . Take my hand.   Speak to me.

HENRY REED

[1914–1986]

MAKING the routine event seem remarkable and giving classic
legends contemporary significance, Henry Reed fashioned an
idiom, alternately playful and poignant, out of incongruities. He
was born in 1914 in Birmingham, England, and was educated at the
University there. During World War II he was in the Army and
conscribed out of it into the Foreign Office. After the armistice he
spent much of his time broadcasting on books and films, writing
radio scripts on extended themes—his five-part "Ishmael" is a set of
lyrical variations on Melville's MOBY DICK—as well as a study of
Thomas Hardy.

Reed established himself as another poet who marked a return
to lucidity. The return was not, however, merely a reaction. Reed
did not hark back to the standard stereotypes of the Georgians and
the glib rhetoric of the Edwardians. He learned from Eliot and
Auden without imitating them. In "Lessons of the War," for ex-
ample, Reed juxtaposes the matter-of-fact instructions of the man-
ual of arms and the indescribable beauty of spring with delicacy and
sardonic humor.

Lessons of the War

NAMING OF PARTS

Today we have naming of parts. Yesterday,
We had daily cleaning. And tomorrow morning,
We shall have what to do after firing. But today,
Today we have naming of parts. Japonica
Glistens like coral in all of the neighbouring gardens,
        And today we have naming of parts.

This is the lower sling swivel. And this
Is the upper sling swivel, whose use you will see,
When you are given your slings. And this is the piling swivel,
Which in your case you have not got. The branches
Hold in the gardens their silent, eloquent gestures,
        Which in our case we have not got.

This is the safety-catch, which is always released
With an easy flick of the thumb. And please do not let me
See anyone using his finger. You can do it quite easy
If you have any strength in your thumb. The blossoms
Are fragile and motionless, never letting anyone see
        Any of them using their finger.

And this you can see is the bolt. The purpose of this
Is to open the breech, as you see. We can slide it
Rapidly backwards and forwards: we call this
Easing the spring. And rapidly backwards and forwards
The early bees are assaulting and fumbling the flowers:
        They call it easing the Spring.

They call it easing the Spring: it is perfectly easy
If you have any strength in your thumb: like the bolt,
And the breech, and the cocking-piece, and the point of
        balance,
Which in our case we have not got; and the almond-blossom
Silent in all of the gardens and the bees going backwards and
        forwards,
        For today we have naming of parts.

DYLAN THOMAS
[1914–1953]

THE most spectacularly effusive poet of the period, Dylan Thomas, was born in Carmarthenshire, Wales, October 27, 1914. After a catch-as-can education, he tried journalism, gave it up, and earned a living by writing film scripts and reading poetry. PORTRAIT OF THE ARTIST AS A YOUNG DOG was a slightly disguised autobiography written at twenty-five. His first book, however, was put together at twenty and was entitled 18 POEMS, which, with subsequent poems and short stories, was published in America in 1939 as THE WORLD I BREATHE. A later collection, IN COUNTRY SLEEP, appeared in 1952. A comprehensive COLLECTED POEMS was issued in 1953.

Thomas's vocabulary is both sensuous and violent. His lines leap and shout and all but leave the printed page in an excess of abandon. The words often bewildered those unaccustomed to such onrushing syllables and seemingly inchoate images. But the imagery establishes a logic of its own; interlocking phrases, echoing sounds, and balanced repetitions reveal designs which are not only intricate but fascinating. Strong emotion is always evinced; the words have the power of incantation and evoke an indefinite but individual magic. Thomas identifies himself with the elemental forces of nature—"the force that through the green fuse drives the flower drives my green age; that blasts the root is my destroyer." Although Thomas's poetry is intuitive rather than deliberate, its passion is so genuine, its spirit so persuasive, that few readers can resist it.

The Hand That Signed the Paper Felled a City

The hand that signed the paper felled a city;
Five sovereign fingers taxed the breath,
Doubled the globe of dead and halved a country;
These five kings did a king to death.

The mighty hand leads to a sloping shoulder,
The finger joints are cramped with chalk;
A goose's quill has put an end to murder
That put an end to talk.

> The hand that signed the treaty bred a fever,
> And famine grew, and locusts came;
> Great is the hand that holds dominion over
> Man by a scribbled name.
>
> The five kings count the dead but do not soften
> The crusted wound nor pat the brow;
> A hand rules pity as a hand rules heaven;
> Hands have no tears to flow.

At thirty-five Thomas described himself as "old, small, dark, intelligent, and daring-doting-dotting eyed . . . balding and toothlessing." During his third visit to the United States, where he attracted large audiences with his resonant and almost incantatory readings, he expected to confer with Igor Stravinsky concerning plans for an opera similar to his pageant-play UNDER MILK WOOD. Parties given for him in New York were particularly convivial—Thomas was a large and steady drinker—but the festivities were followed by a sudden collapse. He died of a virulent brain disease on November 9, 1953, a few days after his thirty-ninth birthday.

Much of Thomas's work was autobiographical to an unusual degree. "Fern Hill," a joyful picture of summer on the boy's Welsh farm, is not only nostalgic but spontaneous with a blithe love for all earthy luxuriance. The air Thomas breathed was taut with wonder; he took part in the tumult of living with a child's rich and irresponsible enjoyment.

Fern Hill

Now as I was young and easy under the apple boughs
About the lilting house and happy as the grass was green,
     The night above the dingle starry,
       Time let me hail and climb
     Golden in the heydays of his eyes,
And honored among wagons I was prince of the apple towns
And once below a time I lordly had the trees and leaves
       Trail with daisies and barley
     Down the rivers of the windfall light.

And as I was green and carefree, famous among the barns
About the happy yard and singing as the farm was home,

In the sun that is young once only,
　　Time let me play and be
　　Golden in the mercy of his means,
And green and golden I was huntsman and herdsman, the
　　　　calves
Sang to my horn, the foxes on the hills barked clear and cold,
　　And the sabbath rang slowly
　　In the pebbles of the holy streams.

All the sun long it was running, it was lovely, the hay-
Fields high as the house, the tunes from the chimneys, it was air
　　And playing, lovely and watery
　　　　And fire green as grass.
　　And nightly under the simple stars
As I rode to sleep the owls were bearing the farm away,
All the moon long I heard, blessed among stables, the nightjars
　　Flying with the ricks, and horses
　　　　Flashing into the dark.

And then to awake, and the farm, like a wanderer white
With the dew, come back, the cock on his shoulder: it was all
　　Shining, it was Adam and maiden,
　　　　The sky gathered again
　　And the sun grew round that very day.
So it must have been after the birth of the simple light
In the first, spinning place, the spellbound horses walking warm
　　Out of the whinnying green stable
　　　　On to the fields of praise.

And honored among foxes and pheasants by the gay house
Under the new-made clouds and happy as the heart was long
　　In the sun born over and over,
　　　　I ran my heedless ways,
　　My wishes raced through the house-high hay
And nothing I cared, at my sky blue trades, that time allows
In all his tuneful turning so few and such morning songs
　　Before the children green and golden
　　　　Follow him out of grace.

Nothing I cared, in the lamb white days, that time would take
　　　　me
Up to the swallow-thronged loft by the shadow of my hand,
　　In the moon that is always rising,
　　　　Nor that riding to sleep
　　I should hear him fly with the high fields

And wake to the farm forever fled from the childless land.
Oh as I was young and easy in the mercy of his means,
    Time held me green and dying
    Though I sang in my chains like the sea.

ROBERT LOWELL
[1917–1977]

ACCLAIMED by his colleagues as the most provocative and power-
ful poet who had appeared in America for years, Robert Traill
Spence Lowell was a Puritan Lowell in revolt. He was born March
1, 1917, in Boston, Massachusetts, attended Harvard and Kenyon
College, where he taught briefly, and Louisiana State University.
Although he attempted to enlist in the Army in 1943, he was re-
jected; when he was drafted, he refused to serve on the grounds
that the bombing of civilians was unprincipled murder. As a con-
scientious objector, he served five months in a Federal prison.

Like James Russell Lowell, his great-grandfather's brother, and
Amy Lowell, a distant cousin, Robert Lowell was a nonconformer.
LORD WEARY'S CASTLE, which won the Pulitzer Prize in 1946, is full
of an impassioned exasperation. His hatred of what New England
had become is intensified by his concept of what it was and what it
could be. The poetry develops into a muffled, tortured outcry
against the corruption of the times, the voicing of a need to find
some faith in a world torn between frivolity and failure. "The
poems understand the world as a conflict of opposites," wrote
Randall Jarrell in *The Nation*. "In this struggle one opposite is
. . . the inertia of the complacent self, the satisfied persistence in
evil that is damnation. Into this realm of necessity, the poems push
everything that is closed, turned inward, that blinds or binds: the
Old Law, imperialism, militarism, capitalism, Calvinism, Authority,
the Father, the 'proper Bostonians,' the rich who will 'do every-
thing for the poor except get off their backs.' But struggling within
this like leaven, is everything that is free or open, that grows or is
willing to change: here is the generosity or willingness or openness
that is itself salvation. . . . This is the realm of freedom, of the
Grace that has replaced the Law, of the perfect liberator whom
the poet calls Christ."

Where the Rainbow Ends

I saw the sky descending, black and white,
Not blue, on Boston where the winters wore
The skulls to jack-o'-lanterns on the slates,
And Hunger's skin-and-bone retrievers tore
The chickadee and shrike. The thorn tree waits
Its victim and tonight
The worms will eat the deadwood to the foot
Of Ararat: the scythers, Time and Death,
Helmed locusts, move upon the tree of breath;
The wild ingrafted olive and the root

Are withered, and a winter drifts to where
The Pepperpot, ironic rainbow, spans
Charles River and its scales of scorched-earth miles
I saw my city in the Scales, the pans
Of judgment rising and descending. Piles
Of dead leaves char the air—
And I am a red arrow on this graph
Of Revelations. Every dove is sold.
The Chapel's sharp-shinned eagle shifts its hold
On serpent-Time, the rainbow's epitaph.

In Boston serpents whistle at the cold.
The victim climbs the altar steps and sings:
"Hosannah to the lion, lamb, and beast
Who fans the furnace-face of IS with wings:
I breathe the ether of my marriage feast."
At the high altar, gold
And a fair cloth. I kneel and the wings beat
My cheek. What can the dove of Jesus give
You now but wisdom, exile? Stand and live,
The dove has brought an olive branch to eat.

As a Plane Tree by the Water

Darkness has called to darkness, and disgrace
Elbows about our windows in this planned
Babel of Boston where our money talks
And multiplies the darkness of a land

Of preparation where the Virgin walks
And roses spiral her enamelled face
Or fall to splinters on unwatered streets.
Our Lady of Babylon, go by, go by,
I was once the apple of your eye;
Flies, flies are on the plane tree, on the streets.

The flies, the flies, the flies of Babylon
Buzz in my ear-drums while the devil's long
Dirge of the people detonates the hour
For floating cities where his golden tongue
Enchants the masons of the Babel Tower
To raise tomorrow's city to the sun
That never sets upon these hell-fire streets
Of Boston, where the sunlight is a sword
Striking at the withholder of the Lord:
Flies, flies are on the plane tree, on the streets.

Flies strike the miraculous waters of the iced
Atlantic and the eyes of Bernadette
Who saw Our Lady standing in the cave
At Massabielle, saw her so squarely that
Her vision put out reason's eyes. The grave
Is open-mouthed and swallowed up in Christ.
O walls of Jericho! And all the streets
To our Atlantic wall are singing: "Sing,
Sing for the resurrection of the King."
Flies, flies are on the plane tree, on the streets.

MAY SWENSON
[1919–1989]

IN THE 1940s another generation of poets reacted against emotional expansiveness and devoted itself to intellectual austerities. Many of the younger writers seemed to regard a poem not only as an act of self-analysis but, since most of them were critics and teachers, as a verbal expression created mainly to be dissected. Scorning popularity, they sought for singularity; distrusting the romantic attitude, they found a dry, flat utterance which turned personal experience into an erudite, brilliant, but depersonalized reportage.

Within a decade the pendulum had swung back toward a poetry which had warmth, ardor, and even passion as its motivating force. Among the poets whose work proceeded from physical delight and spiritual stress was May Swenson. She was born May 28, 1919, in Logan, Utah, of Mormon parents. The first of ten children, she was educated at Utah State Agricultural College, where her father taught Mechanical Engineering. After finishing college, she came to New York, worked as a trade-journal writer, author's assistant, secretary, and dictaphone operator. She followed the policy of saving part of her salary until she had enough for a few months away from work. Her first collection, ANOTHER ANIMAL, was published as part of a series entitled POETS OF TODAY.

Strange without being strained, May Swenson's work is completely itself; it stems from no other poet. Its images are odd but exact—she speaks of a sky "cobbled with clouds," of a bird's eyes as "seeds in a quartered apple," of a lion's head "heavy with heraldic curls," of the "knuckled fist of the heart," of love as "a rain of diamonds in the mind," of the sea "champing" upon small stones "like Demosthenes' mouth, whose many stumblings make him suave." The idiom is strictly contemporary in its blending of intelligence and intuition; if comparisons are demanded, one might say that this is the kind of poetry Emily Dickinson might have written had she read D. H. Lawrence.

Evolution

the stone
would like to be
Alive like me

the rooted tree
longs to be Free

the mute beast
envies my fate
Articulate

on this ball
half dark
half light
i walk Upright
i lie Prone
within the night

beautiful each Shape
to see
wonderful each Thing
to name
here a stone
there a tree
here a river
there a Flame

marvelous to Stroke
the patient beasts
within their yoke

how i Yearn
for the lion
in his den
though he spurn
the touch of men

the longing
that i know
is in the Stone also
it must be

the same that rises
in the Tree
the longing
in the Lion's call
speaks for all

o to Endure
like the stone
sufficient
to itself alone

or Reincarnate
like the tree
be born each spring
to greenery

or like the lion
without law
to roam the Wild
on velvet paw

but if walking i meet
a Creature like me
on the street
two-legged
with human face
to recognize
is to embrace

wonders pale
beauties dim
during my delight
with Him

an Evolution
strange
two tongues Touch
exchange
a Feast unknown
to stone
or tree or beast

At first sight some of the poems seem a set of descriptive and typographical distortions. But the lines are arranged so that they are read more slowly, with due regard for weight and emphasis, while the unusual descriptions transform the actual world into a world of magic. "Poetry," wrote May Swenson, "must do more than interpret the particulars of experience of the poet's own generation and environment. It must also speak to and for every age, past and future. Its material should be such that a savage would have found it familiar, and such that Neo-Man a thousand years from now may say, 'Yes, I have felt this too.' . . . The fact that our present civilization seems sealed and smothered in synthetic wrappings makes it only the more imperative for poetry to insist with all its strength on uttering the elemental." The poetry lives up to the program. Here are intensities of observation and heightened sensitivities which flare into images of pure vision.

Feel Like a Bird

feel like A Bird
understand
he has no hand

instead A Wing
close-lapped
mysterious thing

in sleeveless coat
he halves The Air
skipping there
like water-licked boat

lands on star-toes
finger-beak in
feather-pocket
finds no coin

in neat head like
seeds in A Quartered
Apple eyes join
sniping at opposites
stereoscope The Scene
Before

close to floor giddy
no arms to fling
A Third Sail
spreads for calm
his tail

hand better
than A Wing?
to gather A Heap
to count
to clasp A Mate?

or leap
lone-free and mount
on muffled shoulders
to span A Fate?

RICHARD WILBUR
[1921–   ]

ONE of the most intellectual yet one of the most persuasive
poets of his generation, Richard Wilbur was born March 1,
1921, in New York City. He was educated at Amherst College and
Harvard University, leaving to serve overseas two years in Italy,
France, and Germany. He returned to teach, first at Wellesley, later
at Harvard. At thirty-two he was awarded the Prix de Rome. Mean-
while, he had published two volumes, THE BEAUTIFUL CHANGES and
CEREMONY AND OTHER POEMS.

Wilbur's outstanding quality is his dexterous use of form and
depth of feeling, complex in matter and straightforward in emo-
tion. Challenging and, at the same time, charming, his lines are
strengthened by a half-concealed force; he accomplishes difficult
effects with a minimum of strain and a maximum of precision.
Wilbur can take the most commonplace subject matter—a potato,
a washline, the daily newspaper—and make the reader see with
wonder, as though for the first time, the objects of the poet's con-
templation. Without being a perfectionist, Wilbur's lines attain an
almost perfect organization. Commenting on the limitations of
strict poetic forms, Wilbur wrote: "Subtle variation is unrecog-

nizable without the pre-existence of a norm. . . . Form, in slowing
and complicating the writing process, calls out the poet's full talents,
and thereby insures a greater care and cleverness in the choice and
disposition of words. In general, I would say that limitation makes
for power: the strength of the genie comes of his being confined
in a bottle."

Potato

An underground grower, blind and a common brown;
Got a misshapen look, it's nudged where it could;
Simple as soil yet crowded as earth with all.

Cut open raw, it looses a cool clean stench,
Mineral acid seeping from pores of prest meal;
It is like breaching a strangely refreshing tomb:

Therein the taste of first stones, the hands of dead slaves,
Waters men drank in the earliest frightful woods,
Flint chips, and peat, and the cinders of buried camps.

Scrubbed under faucet water the planet skin
Polishes yellow, but tears to the plain insides;
Parching, the white's blue-hearted like hungry hands.

All of the cold dark kitchens, and war-frozen gray
Evening at window; I remember so many
Peeling potatoes quietly into chipt pails.

"It was potatoes saved us, they kept us alive."
Then they had something to say akin to praise
For the mean earth-apples, too common to cherish or steal.

Times being hard, the Sikh and the Senegalese,
Hobo and Okie, the body of Jesus the Jew,
Vestigial virtues, are eaten; we shall survive.

After the Last Bulletins

After the last bulletins the windows darken
And the whole city founders easily and deep,
Sliding on all its pillows
To the thronged Atlantis of personal sleep,

And the wind rises. The wind rises and bowls
The day's litter of news in the alleys. Trash
Tears itself on the railings,
Soars and falls with a soft crash,

Tumbles and soars again. In empty lots
Our journals spiral in a fierce noyade
Of all we thought to think,
Or caught in corners cramp and wad

And twist our words. And some from gutters flail
Their tatters at the tired patrolman's feet
Like all that fisted snow
That cried beside his long retreat

Damn you! damn you! to the emperor's horses' heels.
Oh none too soon through the air white and dry
Will the clear announcer's voice
Beat like a dove, and you and I

From the heart's anarch and responsible town
Rise by the subway-mouth to life again,
Bearing the morning papers,
And cross the park where saintlike men,

White and absorbed, with stick and bag remove
The litter of the night, and footsteps rouse
With confident morning sound
The songbirds in the public boughs.

The poems written since the publication of Wilbur's first two
books have an increasing wit, a freshness of language and vitality
of thought. He accomplishes, said Louise Bogan, "an ease of pace,
a seemingly effortless advance to a resolute conclusion. . . . Wilbur's
gift of fitting the poetic pattern to the material involves all sorts
of delicate adjustments of the outward senses to the inner ear."
Proof of such commendation can be found in many instances,
notably in a poem written in Rome in 1954, "Love Calls Us to the
Things of This World," which takes its title from St. Augustine.

Love Calls Us to the Things of This World

The eyes open to a cry of pulleys,
And spirited from sleep, the astounded soul
Hangs for a moment bodiless and simple
As false dawn.
                  Outside the open window
The morning air is all awash with angels.

Some are in bed-sheets, some are in blouses,
Some are in smocks: but truly there they are.
Now they are rising together in calm swells
Of halcyon feeling, filling whatever they wear
With the deep joy of their impersonal breathing;

Now they are flying in place, conveying
The terrible speed of their omnipresence, moving
And staying like white water; and now of a sudden
They swoon down into so rapt a quiet
That nobody seems to be there.
                         The soul shrinks

From all that it is about to remember,
From the punctual rape of every blessed day,
And cries,
           "Oh, let there be nothing on earth but laundry,
Nothing but rosy hands in the rising steam
And clear dances done in the sight of heaven."

Yet, as the sun acknowledges
With a warm look the world's hunks and colors,
The soul descends once more in bitter love
To accept the waking body, saying now
In a changed voice as the man yawns and rises,

"Bring them down from their ruddy gallows;
Let there be clean linen for the backs of thieves;
Let lovers go fresh and sweet to be undone,
And the heaviest nuns walk in a pure floating
Of dark habits,
               keeping their difficult balance."

ACKNOWLEDGMENTS

Botteghe Oscure. For LOVE CALLS US TO THE THINGS OF THIS WORLD by Richard Wilbur.

Brandt and Brandt, Inc. For THE MOUNTAIN WHIPPOORWILL from BALLADS AND POEMS, published by Farrar & Rinehart, Inc., copyright, 1925, by Stephen Vincent Benét; O SWEET SPONTANEOUS EARTH and SOMEWHERE I HAVE NEVER TRAVELLED from COLLECTED POEMS OF E. E. CUMMINGS, published by Harcourt, Brace and Company, copyright, 1923, 1925, 1931, 1935, 1938, by E. E. Cummings, copyright, 1926, by Boni & Liveright; PITY ME NOT from THE HARP WEAVER AND OTHER POEMS, published by Harper & Brothers, copyright, 1920, 1921, 1922, 1923, by Edna St. Vincent Millay; DIRGE WITHOUT MUSIC from SECOND APRIL, published by Harper & Brothers, copyright, 1921, by Edna St. Vincent Millay; ON HEARING A SYMPHONY OF BEETHOVEN and TO JESUS ON HIS BIRTHDAY from THE BUCK IN THE SNOW, published by Harper & Brothers, copyright, 1928, by Edna St. Vincent Millay.

The Clarendon Press (Oxford). For the selections from THE SHORTER POEMS OF ROBERT BRIDGES.

The John Day Company, Inc. For the selections from HIGH FALCON AND OTHER POEMS by Léonie Adams.

Dodd, Mead & Company, Inc. For JESSE JAMES from GOLDEN FLEECE by William Rose Benét, copyright, 1935, by Dodd, Mead & Company, Inc.; THE GREAT LOVER and THE SOLDIER from COLLECTED POEMS OF RUPERT BROOKE, copyright, 1915, by Dodd, Mead & Company, Inc.; A PRAYER IN DARKNESS and ELEGY IN A COUNTRY CHURCHYARD from COLLECTED POEMS OF G. K. CHESTERTON, copyright by Dodd, Mead & Company, Inc.

Doubleday & Company, Inc. For "The Flight" from THE LOST SON AND OTHER POEMS by Theodore Roethke. Copyright 1947 by The University of the South, reprinted by permission of Doubleday & Company, Inc.

Harcourt, Brace and Company. For THE LOVE SONG OF J. ALFRED PRUFROCK and JOURNEY OF THE MAGI from COLLECTED POEMS OF T. S.

ELIOT, copyright, 1936, by Harcourt, Brace and Company, Inc.; LOSERS from SMOKE AND STEEL by Carl Sandburg, copyright, 1920, by Harcourt, Brace and Company, Inc.; THE PEOPLE WILL LIVE ON from THE PEOPLE, YES by Carl Sandburg, copyright, 1936, by Harcourt, Brace and Company, Inc.; LESSONS OF THE WAR from A MAP OF VERONA AND OTHER POEMS by Henry Reed, copyright 1947 by Henry Reed, reprinted by permission of Harcourt, Brace and Company, Inc.; WHERE THE RAINBOW ENDS and AS A PLANE TREE BY THE WATER from LORD WEARY'S CASTLE by Robert Lowell, copyright 1944, 1946 by Robert Lowell, reprinted by permission of Harcourt, Brace and Company, Inc.; POTATO by Richard Wilbur from THE BEAUTIFUL CHANGES AND OTHER POEMS by Richard Wilbur, copyright 1947 by Richard Wilbur, reprinted by permission of Harcourt, Brace and Company, Inc.

Ralph Hodgson. For the selections from POEMS and SILVER WEDDING AND OTHER POEMS, printed at Packington's Pound and copyright, 1941, by Ralph Hodgson.

Henry Holt and Company, Inc. For the selections from, and as the authorized publishers of, A SHROPSHIRE LAD by A. E. Housman, LAST POEMS by A. E. Housman; PEACOCK PIE by Walter De la Mare and COLLECTED POEMS by Walter De la Mare; CORNHUSKERS by Carl Sandburg; from the COLLECTED POEMS OF ROBERT FROST, and A WITNESS TREE by Robert Frost; and COLLECTED POEMS: 1922–1938 by Mark Van Doren.

Houghton Mifflin Company. For the selections from POEMS 1924–1933 by Archibald MacLeish; MEN, WOMEN AND GHOSTS by Amy Lowell; THE COMPLETE POEMS OF JOHN GREENLEAF WHITTIER, THE COMPLETE POEMS OF HENRY WADSWORTH LONGFELLOW, THE COMPLETE POEMS OF RALPH WALDO EMERSON, "The Fish" from NORTH AND SOUTH by Elizabeth Bishop, all of which are used by permission of, and by arrangement with the publishers, Houghton Mifflin Company.

B. W. Huebsch. For the selection from the American edition of POEMS by Wilfred Owen.

Alfred A. Knopf, Inc. For TWO GENTLEMEN IN BONDS by John Crowe Ransom, HARMONIUM by Wallace Stevens, THE COLLECTED POEMS OF WALLACE STEVENS, copyright 1942, 1954, and THE COLLECTED POEMS OF ELINOR WYLIE.

Little, Brown and Company. For the selections from the POEMS OF EMILY DICKINSON, edited by Martha Dickinson Bianchi and Alfred Leete Hampson, and from THE FACE IS FAMILIAR by Ogden

Nash, all of which are reprinted by special permission of Little, Brown and Company.

Liveright Publishing Corporation. For the selections from THE COLLECTED POEMS OF HART CRANE, copyright 1933, Liveright Inc., THE COLLECTED POEMS OF H. D., and PERSONAE OF EZRA POUND.

Longmans, Green & Company, Inc. For Frank Ernest Hill's translation of THE NUN'S PRIEST'S TALE from THE CANTERBURY TALES by Geoffrey Chaucer.

The Macmillan Company. For the selections from THE COLLECTED POEMS OF THOMAS HARDY, POEMS by Ralph Hodgson, THE COLLECTED POEMS OF VACHEL LINDSAY, THE COLLECTED POEMS OF JOHN MASEFIELD, SATURDAY MARKET by Charlotte Mew, THE COLLECTED POEMS OF E. A. ROBINSON, THE COLLECTED POEMS OF SARA TEASDALE, THE COLLECTED POEMS OF JAMES STEPHENS, COLLECTED POEMS OF MARIANNE MOORE, and THE COLLECTED POEMS OF WILLIAM BUTLER YEATS, all of which are used by special permission of The Macmillan Company, publishers.

Virgil Markham. For THE MAN WITH THE HOE and LINCOLN, THE MAN OF THE PEOPLE by his father, copyright by Edwin Markham.

Edgar Lee Masters. For the selections from SPOON RIVER ANTHOLOGY, published by The Macmillan Company, copyright by Edgar Lee Masters, and used with his consent.

New Directions. For "The Hand that Signed the Paper Felled a City" from THE WORLD I BREATHE by Dylan Thomas, copyright 1946, by New Directions, "Fern Hill" from COLLECTED POEMS by Dylan Thomas, copyright 1953 and published by New Directions, and "Canto I" from CANTOS OF EZRA POUND, copyright 1949 by Ezra Pound and published by New Directions.

Oxford University Press. For the selections from THE COLLECTED POEMS OF W. H. DAVIES and THE POEMS OF GERARD MANLEY HOPKINS, reprinted by permission of the publishers and the poet's family.

Laurence Pollinger, of Pearn Pollinger and Higham, Ltd. London. For Edith Sitwell's STILL FALLS THE RAIN.

Random House, Inc. For the selections from ON THIS ISLAND by W. H. Auden, ANOTHER TIME by W. H. Auden, THE SELECTED POETRY OF ROBINSON JEFFERS, POEMS by Stephen Spender, and RUINS AND VISIONS by Stephen Spender, "The Leg" from V-LETTER AND OTHER POEMS by Karl Shapiro, copyright 1944 by Karl Shapiro, "Buick" from PERSON, PLACE AND THING by Karl Shapiro, copyright 1941 by

Karl Shapiro, all of which are reprinted by permission of Random House, Inc.

Theodore Roethke. For "Poem," originally published in THE LONDON TIMES LITERARY SUPPLEMENT.

Muriel Rukeyser. For "Effort at Speech Between Two People" from THEORY OF FLIGHT, published by Yale University Press.

Charles Scribner's Sons. For the selections from THE SELECTED POEMS OF CONRAD AIKEN, THE CHILDREN OF THE NIGHT by Edwin Arlington Robinson, THE TOWN DOWN THE RIVER by Edwin Arlington Robinson, POEMS by George Santayana, the translation of Chaucer's BALLADE OF GOOD COUNSEL from THE MAN BEHIND THE BOOK by Henry Van Dyke, "Feel Like a Bird" and "Evolution," copyright 1949, 1954, by May Swenson; reprinted from POETS OF TODAY and used by permission of the publishers, Charles Scribner's Sons.

Shapiro, Bernstein & Company. For the original version of CASEY JONES.

Henry A. Stickney and **William W. Mathewson.** For the selection from THE POEMS OF TRUMBELL STICKNEY.

The Viking Press, Inc. and **B. W. Huebsch, Inc.** For the selections from LOOK! WE HAVE COME THROUGH! by D. H. Lawrence and THE COLLECTED POEMS OF D. H. LAWRENCE, copyright, 1929, by Jonathan Cape and Harrison Smith, Inc. By permission of The Viking Press, Inc.

Richard Wilbur. For "After the Last Bulletins," originally published in *The New Yorker,* and "Love Calls Us to the Things of This World," copyright, 1955, by Richard Wilbur.

L. U.

SOURCES OF REFERENCE

Besides the standard biographies and the works specifically mentioned in the commentaries, constant use has been made of THE DICTIONARY OF NATIONAL BIOGRAPHY and THE ENCYCLOPAEDIA BRITANNICA. Together with these obvious sources of reference, the poetry has been reread in the light of old records and new evidence. The most rewarding volumes of reappraisal are listed below not only as an acknowledgment but as a lure for further reading.

WORD-HOARD. Translated and arranged by Margaret Williams. Sheed & Ward.

THE BEGINNINGS OF ENGLISH LITERATURE. By W. L. Renwick and Harold Orton. Robert M. McBride and Company.

THE ENGLISH RENAISSANCE. By V. De Sola Pinto and Bruce Pattison. Robert M. McBride and Company.

POETRY OF THE ENGLISH RENAISSANCE: 1509–1660. By J. William Hebel and Hoyt H. Hudson. F. S. Crofts & Company.

CHRISTOPHER MARLOWE: THE MAN IN HIS TIME. By John Bakeless. William Morrow and Company.

THE METAPHYSICAL POETS: A STUDY IN RELIGIOUS EXPERIENCE. By Helen C. White. The Macmillan Company.

RARE POEMS OF THE SEVENTEENTH CENTURY. Chosen and edited by L. Birkett Marshall. Cambridge University Press.

A REVOLUTION IN EUROPEAN POETRY: 1660–1900. By Emery Neff. Columbia University Press.

TRADITION AND ROMANTICISM. By B. Ifor Evans. Longmans, Green and Company.

THE JOURNALS OF DOROTHY WORDSWORTH. Edited by Ernest de Selincourt. The Macmillan Company.

DOROTHY WORDSWORTH. By Catherine MacDonald MacLean. The Viking Press, Inc.

WORDSWORTH IN A NEW LIGHT. By Emile Legouis. Harvard University Press.

REASON AND BEAUTY IN THE POETIC MIND. By Charles Williams. Oxford University Press.

AN EIGHTEENTH CENTURY MISCELLANY. Edited by Louis Kronenberger. G. P. Putnam's Sons.

MINOR POETS OF THE EIGHTEENTH CENTURY. By Hugh I'Anson Fausset. E. P. Dutton & Co.

GREAT NAMES. Edited by W. J. Turner. The Dial Press.

ANNALS OF THE POETS. By Chard Powers Smith. Charles Scribner's Sons.

MILTON'S BLINDNESS. By Eleanor Gertrude Brown. Columbia University Press.

THE BRONTËS' WEB OF CHILDHOOD. By Fannie Elizabeth Ratchford. Columbia University Press.

EMERSON AND OTHERS. By Van Wyck Brooks. E. P. Dutton & Co.

YOUNG LONGFELLOW. By Lawrance Thompson. The Macmillan Company.

ISRAFEL: THE LIFE AND TIMES OF EDGAR ALLAN POE. By Hervey Allen. Doubleday, Doran & Company, Inc.

BYRON IN ITALY. By Peter Quennell. The Viking Press, Inc.

HART CRANE: THE LIFE OF AN AMERICAN POET. By Philip Horton. W. W. Norton & Company.

THE WORLD'S BODY. By John Crowe Ransom. Charles Scribner's Sons.

POETRY AND THE MODERN WORLD. By David Daiches. University of Chicago Press.

MODERN POETRY AND THE TRADITION. By Cleanth Brooks. University of North Carolina Press.

PRACTICAL CRITICISM: A STUDY OF LITERARY JUDGMENT. By I. A. Richards. Harcourt, Brace and Company.

THE POETIC MIND. By Frederick Clarke Prescott. The Macmillan Company.

THE POET AS CITIZEN. By Arthur Quiller-Couch. The Macmillan Company.

AXEL'S CASTLE: A STUDY IN THE IMAGINATIVE LITERATURE OF 1870 TO 1930. By Edmund Wilson. Charles Scribner's Sons.

THE WOUND AND THE BOW. By Edmund Wilson. Houghton Mifflin Company.

INDEX

[NOTE: Small capitals are used for titles of literary works. Large capitals are used for quoted authors. Roman type indicates persons mentioned in passing. All italic numerals refer to actual quotation, roman numerals to passing mention.]

INDEX OF FIRST LINES